THE AMERICAN CRIMINAL

THE NATIVE WHITE CRIMINAL OF NATIVE PARENTAGE

———————

STATISTICAL LABORATORY OF THE DIVISION OF ANTHROPOLOGY
HARVARD UNIVERSITY

FIELD WORKERS

ARTHUR R. KELLY	*Anthropometrist*
WILLIAM V. MACKAYE	*Anthropometrist*
HENRY LAPPIN	*Assistant Anthropometrist*
HAROLD WOLFF	*Assistant Anthropometrist*

LABORATORY STAFF

PEARL B. HURWITZ	*Editor and Statistician*
DOROTHY M. JOHNSON	*Statistician*
SARAH R. COTTON	*Hollerith Operator*
CHARITY A. MASON	*Proof Reader*
CARL C. SELTZER	*Consulting Statistician*

THE AMERICAN CRIMINAL

AN ANTHROPOLOGICAL STUDY

By EARNEST ALBERT HOOTON

WITH THE COLLABORATION OF

THE STATISTICAL LABORATORY OF THE DIVISION OF ANTHROPOLOGY
HARVARD UNIVERSITY

THE NATIVE WHITE CRIMINAL OF NATIVE PARENTAGE

GREENWOOD PRESS, PUBLISHERS
WESTPORT, CONNECTICUT

The Library of Congress cataloged this book as follows:

Hooton, Earnest Albert, 1887–1954.
　　The American criminal; an anthropological study. [1]
The native white criminal of native parentage. With the
collaboration of the Statistical Laboratory of the Division
of Anthropology, Harvard University. New York, Greenwood Press [1969, °1939]

　　1 v. (various pagings) illus. 27 cm.

　　Bibliographical footnotes.

　　1. Criminal anthropology. 2. Crime and criminals — U. S.
i. Harvard University. Dept. of Anthropology. ii. Title.

HV6035.H65　1969　　　　364.3　　　　　　　　69–13935
　　　　　　　　　　　　　　　　　　　　　　　　　MARC

Library of Congress　　　　　　[5]

Reprinted in 1969 by Greenwood Press, Inc.,
51 Riverside Avenue, Westport, CT 06880

Library of Congress catalog card number 69-13935
ISBN 0-8371-0481-5

Printed in the United States of America

10　9　8　7　6　5　4　3　2

To

SHELDON GLUECK
INSTIGATOR OF THIS SURVEY

AND

WINFRED OVERHOLSER
SPONSOR AND COLLABORATOR

PREFACE

CERTAIN difficulties appertain to the writing of a preface to an allegedly scientific monograph. In the first place, the preface is supposed to be read, if at all, before the ingenuous purchaser, the cautious borrower, or the cynical reviewer commits his mind to the deep of the work. A preface should therefore be in the nature of an *apéritif* which will stimulate the mental palate of the prospective reader — which will whet his appetite for the ensuing banquet. Unfortunately, the preface to a scientific work is necessarily written after the volume has been completed, if it is to be a statement of facts rather than a record of aspirations. Consequently, the jaded author approaches this final task in a state of satiety, if not of complete disillusion. He is, so to speak, "fed up." The meal may have been a good one, but he has had enough. The present writer, like a dyspeptic head-waiter, is more disposed to warn off banqueters than to lure them on. This is a desperately dull statistical work upon a depressing subject and with positive but discouraging results. It is enlivened by no succulent anecdotes about criminals and no titivating "case histories." It offers no panacea for criminal redemption. The object of the present investigation is to ascertain whether criminals differ physically from law-abiding citizens of the same race, nationality, and economic status, and if so, why. The reader may add, "And if so, what of it?" The unpalatable fact of the matter is that it is a relatively futile procedure to tinker with the machinery of criminal justice, to strengthen and wash the hands of the police, to reason with the criminal or to pray over him, if the germ plasm which produces that criminal is scum. There are possibly too many human beings in the world; there are certainly too many criminals; there are probably too many criminologists. If criminals as a group should be demonstrated to be biological inferiors, no sociological palliative will ameliorate the reign of terror which organized malefactors have instituted in this country. The number of silk purses which can be made from sows' ears is altogether incommensurate with the effort and expense involved in attempting the transformation.

There are perhaps some earnest students of criminology who are still optimistic enough to believe that improved methods of penology may bring about the rehabilitation of a majority of adult incarcerated criminals. There are certainly many who have confidence that preventive measures applied to the early environment of the criminal-to-be may inhibit the development of his antisocial tendencies and even eradicate them entirely. I suppose that no socially-minded person would put a stop to the losing battle which educators, social reformers, criminologists, jurists, and the clergy are fighting against the overwhelming forces of crime. However, it begins to be distressingly apparent that we shall have to fight the devil with fire rather than with holy water. There should be no abatement of efforts to purge the criminalistic environment of its toxic factors, to inculcate adequate standards of honesty and morality into every individual child, to work patiently toward the redemption of reclaimable juvenile delinquents, and even to reform the adult criminal. Let us no longer delude ourselves, however, with the fond hope that a social cancer can be cured with sugar pills and hospitalization. It demands the knife.

It may be rash for an anthropologist who makes no pretension of an expert knowledge of the multiple ramifications of criminological problems, to give vent to an opinion upon methods of crime prevention. Certainly his personal conclusions as to the solution of the difficulty should be divorced completely from the objective results of the investigation itself. The facts point unequivocally to the necessity of delving below the sociological top-soil into the biological substratum in which the root of the matter is embedded. But no suggestions or speculations on the part of the writer concerning practical measures should prejudice the examination by the reader of the data hereinafter discussed. It is for this reason that I judge it expedient to defer the presentation of my ideas upon the subject of the elimination and prevention of crime until all of the factual matter of this survey has been set forth and analyzed. If the reader has sufficient patience to follow me through the maze of statistics which is absolutely essential for the demonstration of the facts of the case, he will be in a position to appraise the validity of my findings. Then he may or may not think it worth while to proceed further and ascertain what I think ought to be done about the criminal.

The acknowledgment of help and encouragement received during the long years of field work and analysis involved in a survey of considerable magnitude would be a pleasure, if one were certain that the results of the investigation reflect credit upon its backers. It sometimes happens that individuals thanked in a preface regard the printing of their names in the nature of a betrayal of misplaced confidence. They feel themselves in the unpleasant position of liability occupied by the directors of a liquidating bank. It therefore is incumbent upon the author to absolve from all responsibility for the methods and results of this investigation the generous and optimistic friends who have supported this survey. Some of these lent their assistance by reason of a sincere belief in the usefulness of the project, others because of a possibly ingenuous trust in the capability of the investigator, still others because of a willingness to take a sporting chance, or through sheer amiability. If this work is to be the target of a bristling array of hostile spears, the author, like Arnold von Winkelried, would gather them all to his own breast. If, on the other hand, there is to be any distribution of laurels, the following heads are highly eligible.

Foremost among the instigators and abettors of this conspiracy against orthodox criminology were Professor Sheldon Glueck of the Harvard Law School and Dr. Winfred Overholser, formerly Commissioner, Massachusetts Department of Mental Diseases. Professor Glueck, an adventurous and liberal leader in the field of criminology, was, so to speak, the cow which kicked over Mrs. O'Leary's lantern. He started the conflagration by suggesting that a survey of criminal anthropology might be initiated under the aegis of the sociological and psychiatric investigation which was being conducted by the Division of the Examination of Prisoners, Massachusetts State Department of Mental Diseases. He introduced the author to Dr. Winfred Overholser, director of that survey, and one of the most resourceful and competent collaborators and scientific promoters with whom a mere anthropologist has ever been privileged to work. Dr. Overholser carried the anthropometric budget on his own broad shoulders, or those of his Division, for more than a year. His authority and his genial and persuasive personality opened the doors of the prisons to our anthropometric investigators, not only in Massachusetts, but also in nearly all of the other states investigated. He cooperated actively, efficiently, and delightfully. He advised often and wisely.

In a subsequent effort to ensure the extension and completion of the survey by persuading various bodies possessed of research funds to grant their subsidization, the author is immeasurably indebted to a number of colleagues in Harvard University and in other institutions. First and foremost he wishes to acknowledge the Herculean labors of Professor Edwin F. Gay, to whose indomitable assaults upon the Social Science Research Council and the Milton Fund he owes the preservation of his orphan project. To Professor Roland B. Dixon, his late regretted colleague, and to George Grafton Wilson he is indebted for similar and equally timely assistance. Among the friends of this project are also to be enumerated Professors Felix Frankfurter, Sam Bass Warner, Harlow Shapley, and William Yandell Elliot of Harvard University, President Comstock and Dean Bernice Brown Cronkhite of Radcliffe College, Professor Raymond Moley of Columbia University, Professor John Lewis Gillin of the University of Wisconsin, Professor T. Wingate Todd of Western Reserve University, Eleanor T. Glueck.

The author is grateful to the following givers of funds which made possible the carrying out of the research: Massachusetts State Department of Mental Diseases, Bureau of International Research of Harvard University and Radcliffe College, Milton Fund of Harvard University, Social Science Research Council, American Academy of Arts and Sciences, Division of Social Sciences of the Rockefeller Foundation, Mr. Donald Scott of the Peabody Museum.

Facilities for anthropometric work upon inmates of institutions or upon civilian groups were obtained through the cooperation of the following individuals:

Massachusetts. The late Dr. George Kline, formerly Commissioner, Massachusetts Department of Mental Diseases, and Dr. Winfred Overholser, formerly Chief, Division of the Examination of Prisoners; Hon. Sanford Bates, formerly Massachusetts Commissioner of Correction; Dr. James H. Means, Massachusetts General Hospital; Dr. Charles F. Wilinsky, Beth Israel Hospital; Mr. Sidney Bergman, Beth Israel Hospital; Dr. Ralph M. Chambers, Superintendent, Taunton State Hospital; Mr. William Hendry, Warden, State Prison, Charlestown; Mr. Charles T. Judge, Superintendent, Massachusetts Reformatory, Concord; Mr. Henry J. Strann, Superintendent and Treasurer, State Farm, Bridgewater; Mr. William T. Hanson, Medical Director, State Farm, Bridgewater; the late Col. Frank P. Williams, State Surgeon, Massachusetts National Guard; Mr. Irving L. Rosenthal, Sheriff, Barnstable County; Mr. John Nicholson, Sheriff, Berkshire County; Mr. Isaac E. Willetts, Sheriff, Bristol County; Mr. Arthur G. Wells, Sheriff, Essex County; Mr. James B. Bridges, Sheriff, Franklin County; Mr. Fred W. Doane, Master of House of Correction, Franklin County; Mr. Embury P. Clark, Sheriff, Hampden County; Mr. Albert G. Beckmann, Sheriff, Hampshire County; Mr. John R. Fairbairn, Sheriff, Middlesex County; Mr. Samuel H. Capen, Sheriff, Norfolk County; Mr. Earl P. Blake, Sheriff, Plymouth County; Mr. John A. Keliher, Sheriff, Suffolk County; Mr. George F. A. Mulcahy, Master of House of Correction; Mr. Albert F. Richardson, Sheriff, Worcester County.

Tennessee. Captain Richard H. Lyle, Commissioner, State of Tennessee Department of Institutions; Mr. A. A. McCorkle, Warden, Tennessee State Penitentiary; Professor G. W. Dyer, Vanderbilt University; Dr. Walker, Meharry Medical School; President Thomas E. Jones, Fisk University; Professor Paul Radin, Fisk University, Mr. Paul Gordon, Fisk University.

Kentucky. Mr. M. F. Conley, Commissioner, Kentucky State Prisons, and Mr. Lynn Rouser, both of Frankfort; Superintendent H. M. Beard, Kentucky State Reformatory, Frankfort; Rev. Mr. Stucker, Kentucky State Reformatory, Frankfort; Superintendent Chilton, State Penitentiary, Eddyville.

Texas. Professor J. E. Pearce, Department of Anthropology, University of Texas, Austin; Mr. R. H. Baker, Chairman, Texas Prison Board, Houston; Mrs. Elizabeth Speer, Secretary, Texas Prison Board, Houston; Mr. W. H. Mead, General Manager, Texas Prison System, Huntsville; Mr. R. J. Flanagan, Manager, Imperial State Farm, Sugarland; Captain Spear, Manager, Huntsville; Captain H. J. Jackson, Manager, Ramsey Farm, Ottey; Captain J. H. Rozzell, Manager, Blue Ridge State Farm, Hobby; Captain Hickman, Manager, Clemmons Farm, Terry Landing.

North Carolina. Professor Howard W. Odum, Institute for Research in Social Sciences, University of North Carolina, Chapel Hill; Superintendent George Ross Pou, State Prison, Raleigh; Dr. James E. Shepard, North Carolina College for Negroes, Durham.

Wisconsin. Mr. Oscar Lee, Warden, Wisconsin State Prison, Waupun.

Arizona. Mr. Scott White, Superintendent, Arizona State Prison, Florence; Mr. Thomas A. French, Assistant Superintendent, Arizona State Prison, Florence; Mr. William Delbridge, Secretary, Arizona State Prison, Florence.

Colorado. Professor E. B. Renaud, University of Denver, Denver; Mr. Charles J. Moynohan, President, State Board of Corrections, Canon City; Dr. Holmes, Canon City; Mr. Eugene Crawford, Warden, Colorado State Penitentiary, Canon City; Mr. C. C. Horn, Colorado State Penitentiary, Canon City; Mr. William Curtis, Deputy Warden, Buena Vista Reformatory; Mr. Heenan, Chief Clerk, Buena Vista Reformatory.

New Mexico. Superintendent P. J. Dugan, State's Prison, Santa Fe.

Missouri. Professor A. F. Kuhlman, University of Missouri, Columbia; Mr. T. S. Mosby, Commissioner of Pardons and Paroles, State of Missouri Department of Penal Institutions, Jefferson City; Mr. A. H. Harrison, Director, Missouri State Penitentiary, Jefferson City; Mr. Leslie Rudolph, Warden, Missouri State Penitentiary, Jefferson City.

District of Columbia. Mr. Leon E. Truesdell, Chief Statistician for Population, Department of Commerce, Bureau of Census, Washington, D. C.

The successful prosecution of the anthropometric field work which furnishes the material of this survey is principally due to the energy, tact, and initiative of Dr. Arthur R. Kelly and Mr. William V. MacKaye, the chief anthropometrists. Valuable contributions to the field work were also made by Mr. Harold Wolff, Dr. Henry Lappin, and Mr. Percy Hodges.

In the early stages of reduction of the data, excellent services were rendered by

Ruth MacDuffie MacKaye, Rowena Kelly, Margaret B. Grady, Dr. Alfred Hurwitz, and Mr. William R. Lessa, as well as by the anthropometric field staff. The greater part of the task of sorting and tabulating has been carried out by the Laboratory's skillful Hollerith operator, Sarah R. Cotton, who has also participated in the statistical reduction of the data. Others who assisted efficiently in the statistical analysis are Constance Tyler Woodbury, Dr. Carl C. Seltzer, and Mr. David Band.

However, the lion's share of whatever of credit may accrue from this work belongs without question to the two chief statisticians of the Harvard Anthropometric Laboratory: Pearl B. Hurwitz and Dorothy M. Johnson. These brilliant and indefatigable young women have accomplished between them most of the gigantic task of statistical analysis involved in this research. Nor has their contribution been limited to mere mathematical calculation and the compilation of tables. Each has enhanced the value of the work by astute and penetrating criticism of the methods of analysis employed and of the deductions drawn from the data. Many lapses of the author in accuracy of statement and in logic have been detected and corrected by these alert and intelligent collaborators. They have striven valiantly to clarify his turgid style and to moderate his masculine extravagance of thought and expression by persistent interposition of the literal-minded feminine viewpoint. They have borne the heat and burden of the day; whereas the actual writer of these words has merely toiled fitfully and intermittently, with considerable intervals of lolling in the shade.

Since people have to go on living their lives, even while portentous manuscripts gather dust awaiting publication, the absorption into domestic life of my two invaluable assistants, Mrs. Hurwitz and Mrs. Johnson, has necessitated the entrusting of the actual proof-reading and final editorial work of this volume to a new laboratory generation. The principal burden of this task has been carried most efficiently by Miss Charity Mason. The admirably typed tables are the work of Miss Elizabeth Warren.

No one who is perpetually afflicted by the necessity of reading and criticizing the scientific manuscripts of successive generations of his students and former students, is likely to be willing to request similar service and sacrifice with respect to his own work. So then, it is with a particularly lively sense of gratitude that the author acknowledges his indebtedness to Dr. Carl C. Seltzer, who volunteered to read the manuscript of this work and contributed much excellent criticism and many helpful suggestions.

The present volume deals with the results of a study of 4212 native White prisoners of native parentage in prisons and reformatories, and of a comparable civilian check sample. A second volume will be concerned with the material relating to native Whites of foreign parentage by nationalities, foreign Whites, and criminal and civil insane. The final volume will be devoted to the study of County Jail prisoners, Negroes, Negroids, and Mexicans.

It seems improbable that any reader, however hardy and enthusiastic, will be able to endure a complete page-by-page perusal of this book. Every reader is advised to attempt the Introduction and the Conclusions. The credulous and the casual may confine themselves to these chapters. The supporting data in the body of the work may be consulted by those readers who are more ambitious or more critical.

Peabody Museum of Harvard University   EARNEST A. HOOTON
July 16, 1938

CONTENTS

THE NATIVE WHITE CRIMINAL OF NATIVE PARENTAGE

Chapter I

INTRODUCTION

THE PROBLEM

THE relationship between man's anatomy and his behavior has been the subject of endless speculation, infinite argument, and infinitesimal scientific research. Chiromancy, physiognomy, and phrenology have been the playing fields for cranks and charlatans so long that self-respecting students cannot embark upon the most cautious investigation of the dependence of mind upon body without exposing themselves to the charge of quackery. The reaction against the facile assumptions of Gall, Lavater, and other sincere but misguided seekers of anatomical short-cuts through the maze of human conduct, has been so violent that a flat denial of the smallest correlations between body, mind, and behavior has become almost axiomatic, not only among social scientists, but also in the medical profession and in anthropology.

A species of moral sanction has been lent to the disavowals of psycho-physical interdependence by the democratic doctrine of human equality — too frequently torn from its justifiable political context and indiscriminately applied to bio-sociological phenomena. In the field of serious racial studies any suggestion that the physical features which constitute the outward signs of a common inheritance, are accompanied by, or indicative of, psychological or sociological tendencies, is treated as a sin against the Holy Ghost of Science — unforgivable, inexpiable, and utterly damning.

For this universal and apparently ineradicable prejudice we have to thank principally the propagandists who have used alleged evidence of racial inequality as an excuse for their schemes of political domination. Such malicious attempts to create nationalistic solidarity by arousing racial antagonisms merit the most severe condemnation. As a result of this abuse of the term "race," students of anthropology have been forced to lean backward in their denunciations of spurious implications as to its cultural and psychological implications. This attitude has been exaggerated often on account of a sympathy for, or participation in, the sufferings of peoples who have been victimized by racial antagonisms.

The general result of these influences has been to restrict racial studies to mere anatomical and biometric description and to concentrate the attention of most physical anthropologists upon the safer problems of growth, and the supposed environmental modifications of human types due to climate, diet, functional adaptation, or what not. If the combinations of hereditary physical features which constitute racial types have no correlates in the psychological processes and the behavior of those types, there can be no sociological profit in racial studies. Certainly the investigation of physical types *in vacuo* can have slight significance except for the feeble aesthete. Science cares little or nothing for the best in the sense of "the most beautiful," but is deeply concerned in ascertaining those variations in the human organism which affect its physiological and psychological functioning. I suppose that no scientifically qualified person would venture to deny that the physiological well-being of the human organism is not exclusively dependent upon its state of nutrition, its lack of exposure to and infection by micro-organisms, its habitus, and other more or less exclusively environmental factors. He would insist also upon the importance of the quality of the organism itself — the stability and harmony of its multitudinous component parts — in short, the individual constitutional endowment. Since the aim of the physician is still primarily curative rather than preventive, he naturally devotes his efforts to the amelioration of the environment of the organism, striving to aid it to realize its optimum functioning. He can do little or nothing to correct its hereditary defects, although he recognizes the limitations of healthful functioning set up by them. He tries to make the best of the hereditary material at his disposal. The psychiatrist is in precisely the same position. He is forced to confine his efforts, for the most part, to corrective measures directed toward mental habits and the general environment of the organism, since he cannot change its hereditary endowment.

Sociologists and social workers are primarily and almost exclusively concerned with the effect of the interplay of environmental forces upon the individual and upon society. The complexity of these forces is so great that they find it convenient to assume that the human material upon which the environmental factors operate is completely homogeneous in its hereditary make-up, or, at any rate, that the hereditarily variable factors are insignificant in the final resultant of the action of environmental forces upon the organism. The social anthropologist is likely to take a similar point of view.

To the eugenist has been left the ungrateful task of emphasizing the impossibility of making good bricks without straw, and it must be admitted with regret that eugenics has drawn unto itself the same ilk of vicious propagandist which has prostituted the study of racial differences to the service of national and class prejudice. What is known of human heredity really amounts to exceedingly little, and it is extremely easy to expose the abysmal ignorance of amateur eugenists, who have initiated a program of hereditary reform without the firm basis of scientific knowledge, which, as yet, is almost completely lacking. Reflections upon his ancestry and hereditary physical and mental make-up are the hardest of all for the individual to bear, since nothing can be done about it. You may criticize his habits with some impunity and strive to improve his environment without arousing his animosity, but you cannot depreciate his heredity without inviting an immediate and violent retaliation.

All of this makes it comfortable, safe, and practicable for the student of human behavior to neglect the hereditary basis, which it is almost impossible to isolate, totally impossible to change, and exceedingly inexpedient to stress.

However, neither biological ignorance nor the diplomatic exigencies of social work can justify the categorical denials of hereditary influences in crime which are commonly emitted by sociologists. For many of these humanitarian practitioners resent even the suggestion that the biological status of the criminal may repay investigation. One can only infer that they regard an anthropological interest in the criminal as a species of wanton trespass upon their professional preserves.

Now it is far from my intention to belittle the efforts of the sincere, intelligent, and conscientious workers who have poured out so much blood and treasure upon the investigation of the causes of crime, and the devising of methods for preventing delinquency and reclaiming the criminal. Prison reform, probation, the juvenile court, the searching out of the familial and neighborhood cess-pools which breed criminality — all of these are substantial achievements which no fair-minded person should decry. Yet it cannot be claimed that the sociologists have succeeded where the juries and the police have failed. They have not reached a solution of the crime problem. The sociological approach may have been near enough to grapple with it, but it is not sufficiently potent to put it down.

Psychologists and psychiatrists have busied themselves with the study of criminals for many years and there is little doubt that the psychiatric approach, when joined with skilled sociological cooperation, has shed a great deal of light upon the causation of crime and has enjoyed a certain measure of success in the field of crime prevention and the reclamation of delinquents. There are, however, certain difficulties inherent in this method of approach which have not as yet been resolved and seem to be well-nigh incapable of solution. The first and knottiest of these is the essential intangibility and impalpability of psychological processes. If one could put his finger upon a mental defect — as upon a wart — or could measure a subnormal mentality with a clinical thermometer as the physician determines a subnormal temperature, the task of the psychiatrist would be at least simplified. The diagnosis of mental disease and the determination of mental defect remain, however, somewhat speculative and highly subject to the personal equation of the investigator. It has been remarked with some justice that in the field of criminology psychologists and psychiatrists have often based their diagnoses of mental defect and disease upon the very same antisocial behavior which they attribute to the aforesaid psychopathic or mentally defective states. There is no logical validity in a judgment that a man is crazy because he has committed a murder and that he has committed the murder because he is crazy. It is again the abstract quality of psychological processes which has led to the further difficulty confronting the psychiatrist — the absence of norms for mental states. Possibly the greatest merit of the psychiatric approach is that it concerns itself primarily with the organism of the criminal rather than more or less exclusively with his environment. At the same time it does not or should not neglect the influence of environmental factors upon that organism.

It is no part of this discussion to examine the extent to which the criminal's behavior is determined by his mental deficiency or sufficiency, or by the state of his mental health. Nor is it incumbent upon us to attempt to ascertain to what precise degree the career of the delinquent is an effect of his social environment. Our task is to study the physical characteristics of criminals with the purpose of discovering whether or not these are wholly irrelevant to their antisocial conduct.

We may first examine the *a priori* basis for an assumption that the behavioristic tendencies of man may be related in some fashion to his physical characteristics. It can scarcely be denied that, in a general way, the behavior of different kinds of animals is an expression or function of their several organisms. Thus the behavior of chimpanzees, though individually varying, is in general chimpanzee behavior and arises from the morphology, physiology, and psychology of that particular animal genus. We cannot assert that the chimpanzee behavior pattern is caused by the chimpanzee type of ear, of dentition, of prehensile foot, or even of cerebral convolutions, but we do maintain that an animal whose details of structure are those of a chimpanzee will inevitably conduct himself in a manner befitting that ape. While as yet there is insufficient experimental basis for a clear distinction between chimpanzee behavior and gorilla behavior, the evidence thus far collected by psycho-biologists indicates that there is fully as much difference between these two animals in this respect as in bodily characteristics. Since then the behavior of an animal arises from its general bodily organization, or, at any rate, is characteristic of the latter, it would appear that the physical characteristics of any animal should afford some clue to the type and quality of his mental and emotional responses, always allowing for individual variation and differentiating environmental influences. But this of course does not imply that any particular morphological variation of a bodily part, or any combination of such variations, is causally related to the generic, specific, or individual behavior of that animal. They are merely bound together in an indissoluble organic association of such a nature that one may be to some extent predicted from the other.

Human mental processes and human behavior are, of course, sharply distinct from those of anthropoid apes, and the differences are inherent in the organisms of the families, and not merely the effects of divergent environmental forces. These differences are, moreover, qualitative as well as quantitative, just as are their respective physical differences. Within the human species (if we wish to adhere to the dogma of the specific unity of all modern men) there are well defined physical differences which demarcate mankind into distinct physical types which we call races. The combinations of physical features which constitute racial types are due to characters inherited in each race from its individual ancestral stock. The differences, like those which distinguish man from any ape, are both qualitative and quantitative, although by no means so great as those subsisting between the human family as a whole and the anthropoid ape family. It is therefore reasonable to suppose that different physical racial types of man will exhibit mental and emotional qualities diverging one from another, in conformity to their respective peculiarities of physical organization which are of hereditary origin. Even if one is so wrong-headed as to deny the hereditary origin of these physical variations and to ascribe them all to environmental molding, it nevertheless follows that the mental and emotional processes and ultimately the behavior of the animal will be modified in correlation with the change in its physical attributes.

This is very far from an insistence upon the direct causal relationship between the physical minutiae of an animal and his psychological processes — much less his behavior. All of these are varied expressions of the organism bound up together in their common heredity and modified in their several directions by the common environment.

Thus it would appear that racial physical differences should naturally be associated with racial psychological differences and that the behavior of distinct racial stocks should vary in accordance with their physical and psychological divergences. Yet it may be stated without fear of refutation that hitherto no racial psychological differences have been demonstrated in any adequately scientific manner, to say nothing of racial differences in behavior. The lack of such demonstrated racial differences in psychology need not, however, be attributed to a *de facto* absence of such differences.

On the contrary it may be ascribed with certainty to the crudity and general inadequacy not only of methods hitherto devised for the measurement of psychological
differences, but also of the anthropological technique employed for isolation and determination of racial physical types. It should be completely obvious that racial psychological differences cannot be examined until we are able to select for such psychological investigation racial physical types. Before you pick fleas off a dog you must
catch your dog. To some extent the slipshod thinking, faulty technique, and meager
achievement of the physical anthropologist in the definition, classification, and study
of racial types are responsible for the failure of the psychologist. But the latter has
too often rushed in where the former fears to tread and has attempted to ascertain
racial psychological differences, without knowing or caring anything about the basic
physical racial elements involved in his experimental material. It is impossible to
discover racial psychological differences from series selected solely on the basis of
nationality, geographic area, linguistic stock, or on any other fallacious assumption
as to the nature of race. When we add to the virtual impossibility of getting any clear
results of this nature from heterogeneous and hybridized human material, the complicating factors of variable and divergent environmental influences upon the individual
and the group, the problem is hopeless.

It should be the duty of the physical anthropologist to provide an accurate classification of physical human types, both racial and individual, based upon the exhaustive
analysis of abundant metric and morphological data. This would enable the psychiatrist, the psychologist, and the sociologist to proceed to the study of mental processes
and social conduct in groups and individuals without having the additional complicating factors of racial, physical heterogeneity to confuse his psychological and sociological issues. Such preliminary anthropological work would, in a measure, eliminate from
the problem of determining the causality of human behavior the dubious, disturbing,
and ever present element of physical hereditary influences. Whether these are negligible or not, such a procedure would enormously simplify the task of the social
scientist.

The relation of social behavior to the physical characteristics of the organism, both
in the individual and in the group, can be studied perhaps most advantageously in
criminals. This statement may be challenged and requires amplification and explanation. A criminal, for our present purpose, is a person who is under sentence in a
penal institution, having been convicted for an antisocial act punishable by commitment to such an institution. There is here no presupposition that the criminal is a
biologically or psychologically abnormal being or that he is a victim of a malign environment. There is no assumption as to the nature of crime, except that it is any
kind of an act which in the society under observation is punishable by commitment to
a penal institution. Crimes are obviously infractions of more or less arbitrary social
rules, and whether an act is or is not accounted a crime, depends not only upon the
nature of that act, but also upon the attitude of society toward it, which may differ
radically from time to time and in diversely constituted political, social, and ethnic
groups.

There is, however, one constant element in all conceptions of crime — one im-
mutable feature in a Protean form — the criminal act is always an offense against
society sufficiently heinous to actuate a large proportion of the society to demand

its punishment through processes of law and to secure such legislation and some measure of its enforcement. Therefore the criminal is a person distinguished by the commission of an overt act against society and he exemplifies for us an extreme of human conduct, thus making himself an excellent subject for the investigation of the relation of physique to behavior.

The identification and apprehension of an individual who has committed a crime is most frequently accomplished by a description of his personal appearance, his anatomical peculiarities, his combination of metric bodily variations, or the unique individual variations of his fingerprint patterns. The use of such methods merely helps to ascertain what particular individual is responsible for a given act. It simply distinguishes him from the rest of mankind who are innocent of that one offense. It does not imply that the physical features which define and identify him are causally related to his antisocial conduct. Similarly, it may be worth while to examine the physical characteristics of large groups of criminals to discover whether they are in any sense physically homogeneous, and if so whether they are distinguishable from noncriminals. Here again there is no necessary implication of causality — at least in the sense of a direct relationship between the physical characteristics of criminals and their antisocial conduct. If, however, it were demonstrated that criminals do indeed differ physically in a significant degree and in a constant direction from law-abiding citizens, the question would be raised as to the meaning of such differences. It is conceivable that the linkage of bodily features with mental processes may be such that the former may be taken as a basis of prediction of the latter. Whether the association of physical and psychological characters is due to hereditary influences or environmental influences, or to the combined influences of both, it is none the less important if in reality it exists. There is certainly no scientific validity in denying on a priori grounds or from sheer prejudice the possibility of such an association, which if discovered might be of some practical diagnostic utility.

Again, since different types of criminal acts are obviously the result of diverse motives and widely different psychological states, it is clear that any physical or mental differentiation of the criminal should manifest itself in as great or greater degree amongst criminals classified according to their types of offense, as between criminals as a group and non-criminals. None of these ideas are novel, but they must be re-stated here, because they have never been demonstrated to be true nor have they been finally refuted by any adequate body of scientific evidence, in spite of current assumptions on the part of sociologists, penologists, and others who are interested in crime either professionally or in any less serious way.

The criminal is classified as such exclusively on the basis of his behavior exemplified by an antisocial act of which he has been convicted. It is quite as legitimate and logical to investigate the bodily and mental correlates of such behavior as to study the environment within which the behavior occurs. We may perhaps compare the individual criminal with an embryo floating in the amniotic fluid which is its environment. The palpable organic portion of the criminal is the foetal body which also includes its nervous system and the rudiment of its mind. The behavior of the individual — in the case of the foetus, its movements — is the result of bodily and possibly psychic stimuli on the one hand and of the environment on the other. The environment influences simultaneously the body, the mind, and the behavior of the individual. All of these are intimately and functionally related and we cannot disregard any of these interrelationships without jeopardizing our comprehension of the complete situation.

It has been the fashion among certain competent psychiatrists and sociologists who have been laboring in the field of criminological investigation to insist upon dealing with the "individual delinquent" on the ground that the nexus of hereditary and environmental influences in each case is so different that any profitable analysis of groups of delinquents is impossible and that generalizations drawn from massed data are invalid. Certainly the behavior of any individual is an individual problem, and corrective and preventive measures must be suited to the individual case. However, it is unfortunately true that society has not the time to concern itself with the details of the heredity, the environment, and the intricate web of circumstances which result in the individual criminal offense. To go at the problem in this way, admirable as the results may be, is too costly and too time-consuming, when the vast numbers of potential and actual delinquents are taken into consideration.

> "If seven maids with seven mops swept it for half a year,
> Do you suppose," the Walrus said, "that they could get it clear?"
> "I doubt it," said the Carpenter, and shed a bitter tear.

Just as the experimental zoologist requires the preliminary work of the taxonomist in order that he may keep his genera, species, and varieties distinct in his genetic or physiological studies, so must the criminologist discriminate between the different races and nationalities involved in his investigation so that he will not further complicate an already sufficiently involved problem by the organic heterogeneity of his experimental material. No one supposes that the work of the classificationist adequately accounts for all of the individual variations within any stated zoological group. But his processes of grouping and pigeon-holing related animals by morphological features afford the necessary preliminary step for the intensive examination of the organism and its functioning within that group. Similarly the description and analysis of the various races of the United States, with especial reference to their antisocial behavior, do not presuppose that their differences in criminal propensities, if there are any, are directly related to their physical racial characteristics. Such processes merely clear the ground for a more accurate study of the causes of crime within each racial group, the complicating racial factor having been eliminated by dealing with each racial group separately. In exactly the same manner, one would make sure of the homogeneity of breed of one's laboratory animals before subjecting them to experiments involving the effects of diet, heat, light, et cetera. The same considerations apply to the study of offenders by nationalities.

It is essential at this point to discuss briefly the anthropological significance of nationality in relation to crime, as contrasted with the criminological implication of race. Races are physical groupings of mankind established on the basis of heritable morphological and metric features. A nation is a large body of people under a central government, usually inhabiting a geographical area with defined boundaries, and further possessing certain cultural traits in common, such as customs, historical traditions, and often language. While nationality does not connote race, it is by no means devoid of biological significance. For nations are, almost invariably, great inbred groups, and as such present certain recurrent physical types which are the result of the hereditary perpetuation of specific racial blends. These national physical types are often as easily recognizable as the so-called racial types and exhibit more definite patterns of behavior. Such a state of affairs is readily understandable, since persons of the same nationality often not only participate in a common physical inheritance, but also in a common fund of tradition and mores. They exhibit not only a restricted range of physical characters, but also some degree of social and psychological solidarity. United by heredity, nativity, education, and existence within the same state, nationals are likely to manifest also similar criminal propensities. For example, Italians may be criminologically more homogeneous than a group of persons selected as members of the Mediterranean race on the basis of identity of inherited physical features, but derived from several different nationalities. When groups of diverse nationality immigrate into the United States, they retain respectively their national physical characteristics and in some measure their national traditions and mores.

Hence in an anthropological study of the criminal it is essential to deal with each nationality separately, because each has in some degree its own physical and cultural individuality. When the relation of crime to physique within a specified nationality has been ascertained, we may proceed further to pool the different nationalities and to attempt studies of the relation of racial physical types to crime within our combined international series. Or again, quite irrespective of national or racial considerations, we may select combinations of physical characters, such as body build, and investigate their criminological significance in a series which is racially and nationally heterogeneous. But in order to achieve any putatively correct interpretation of the significance of race or bodily constitution in relation to crime, it is necessary first to isolate the criminological resultants of the combination of hereditary and environmental forces comprised under nationality.

It is rather surprising that this simple but important consideration of race and nationality has been almost completely neglected in all work in criminal anthropology and criminal psychopathology hitherto done, but less surprising that it is frequently disregarded in criminological studies approached from the sociological point of view. We are not primarily concerned with these latter, except to explain and in some measure to answer the violent objections frequently opposed by sociologists to any investigator who dares to enter the field of criminology from the anthropological angle. But we are very intimately concerned with the methods and results of previous anthropological investigations of the criminal and it will be necessary to review and to appraise the results derived from them.

Before entering into such a historical summary and criticism of the earlier work in criminal anthropology, it is necessary to digress briefly in order to comment upon one stupid objection that is perennially advanced by those who wish to deny any measure of utility to investigations of criminals. This is a statement to the effect that it is useless to study incarcerated criminals because they represent only the failures of those habitually and purposefully engaged in antisocial pursuits. The further implication is that any physical, mental, or sociological qualities — especially of inferiority — which are displayed by convicted prisoners are probably not shared by the more clever criminals who escape arrest and conviction. Of course this argument, pushed to a logical extreme, applies not only to physical studies of the convicted criminal, but also to psychological and sociological studies.

In the first place, anyone with the slightest knowledge of criminal statistics should be aware that a great number of criminals (probably more than half) are recidivists, and that those who are first offenders are more than likely to be re-convicted and re-sentenced after they have been released. In other words, a very large, but indeterminate proportion of the crimes to be committed in this country or in any other country within the next few years will be committed by persons now in penal institutions subsequent to their release therefrom. Thus the study of convicted criminals is by no means an investigation of those whose criminal career is finished. Many, if not most of them, will try again, and probably a considerable proportion will escape future convictions for one or more criminal acts actually committed. Again, the presumption that successful criminals are rarely or never convicted, even in this notoriously lax country, may well be incorrect. I doubt very much that any considerable proportion of the crimes committed in the United States is perpetrated by persons who steadily pursue antisocial careers without ever falling into the clutches of the law. Even if there are such persons they must be in the minority, and to give up in despair the study of the vast majority because we cannot identify a few hypothetical successful eluders of punishment, would be a ridiculous and pusillanimous procedure. This nonsensical idea implies that the majority of criminals are at large in the supposedly law-abiding population, and that the hundreds of thousands convicted and incarcerated represent merely the equivalent of the bankrupts among business men. It hints that most men commit crimes and that only the stupid ones get caught. Even if this were the case (and I do not think that any intelligent person will accept such a notion), it would be no more sensible to neglect the study of convicted criminals because some escape conviction, than to give up studying the hospitalized victims of infantile paralysis because the majority of children exposed to this disease escape it, or having contracted it, do not come into the hospital clinics where their disease may be treated and where preventive measures for the non-infected are being sought.

HISTORICAL SUMMARY OF CRIMINAL ANTHROPOLOGY

LOMBROSO

The theories and researches of Cesare Lombroso have been summarized and criticized so often that it seems unnecessary to recapitulate them in detail here. The crucial Lombrosian idea was that criminals are distinguished from law-abiding citizens by the manifestation of multiple physical anomalies which are of atavistic or degenerative origin. The theory of atavism postulates a reversion to a primitive or subhuman type of man, characterized physically by a variety of inferior morphological features reminiscent of apes and lower primates, occurring in the more simian fossil men, and to some extent preserved in modern savages. There is a further implication that the mentality of such atavistic individuals is also that of the primitive man or the savage, and that consequently the behavior of these "throw-backs" is contrary to the rules of modern civilized society. The degenerative theory is at the opposite pole from the atavistic and is almost incompatible with the latter. Degeneration implies pathology. The degenerate is the product of diseased ancestral stocks which have ceased to evolve progressively and are well along in the process of devolution — simulating frequently in their pathological offspring the rudimentary physical and mental attributes of the primitive man.

Both of these theories, held successively or simultaneously by Lombroso and his followers, emphasize the hereditary basis of antisocial conduct and stress the organism of the criminal to the exclusion of his environment. Underlying these conceptions is the conviction that the criminal is a biological anomaly and that crime is also, to some extent, an abnormal biological phenomenon.

I am not interested here in criticizing the logic of Lombroso's deductions, which is frequently very faulty, nor in deriding his somewhat unsuccessful endeavor simultaneously to run with the atavistic hare and to hunt with the degenerative hounds. My only purpose is to examine the contention of Lombroso and his school that criminals are physically differentiated from law-abiding persons and to discuss the reasons for their success or failure in establishing this thesis.

The first line of attack was by means of the study of craniology. Lombroso maintained that the skulls of criminals are characterized by a larger percentage of pathological and primitive features than are those of the non-criminal population. His results were confirmed by some craniologists and denied by others. Without entering into the details of the literature, which I have studied very closely, I propose to state my conclusions upon this phase of Lombroso's work, although they are not particularly relevant to the present investigation.

After dismissing a considerable number of metric and morphological features of the criminal skull, in which various investigators have shown that criminals do not differ significantly from the law-abiding population, one is left with a large residue of abnormalities and anomalies, which, on the face value of the evidence presented by those who have conducted the researches, are far more common in criminals than in civilians. The most important and convincing evidences of criminal deviation are in cranial capacity and in cranial and facial asymmetry. In cranial capacity the bulk of the evidence seems to indicate an abnormal distribution among criminals rather than a consistent size inferiority. Criminals seem to show unduly large frequencies both of the sub-average or sub-normal capacities and of the unusually large cranial cubes. Unfortunately, however, the technique of measuring cranial capacity yields such different results in the hands of different observers that no physical anthropologist is willing to place much reliance upon deviations in means, unless he is able to convince himself that the methods and results of the various observers are comparable. No one who has perused the body of evidence relating to the cranial capacity of criminals can avoid the conclusion that the entire mass of material must be re-studied according to a uniform and satisfactory technique before any definitive results are obtainable. In spite of this fact the bulk of the evidence indicates the probability that Lombroso was correct in his contention that criminals are excessively variable in this measurement. In the absence, however, of conclusive results with regard to the cranial capacity of the criminal, it would be a waste of time to discuss the possible significance of criminal variation in this feature.

In the case of cranial and facial asymmetry, another kind of difficulty is involved. Lombroso and subsequent investigators have, almost without exception, contented themselves with a mere subjective description of the presence or absence, and the degree of, such asymmetry, and have not developed any quantitative method of appraising it. Such a procedure is perfectly comprehensible to the craniologist, who knows very well by experience that asymmetries are easy of observation, but extremely difficult to measure satisfactorily (since they present themselves in all three dimensions) without developing a very complicated and laborious technique. Consequently, the validity of Lombroso's conclusions as to the prevalence of cranial and facial asymmetry in the criminal skull is impaired by the possibility that his enthusiasm for his theory may have led him unconsciously to exaggerate the frequency and degree of this anomaly. Anyone who has attempted to master the method of grading non-mensurable morphological development is well aware of the great personal equation which affects such estimates, even of a skilled observer who is not obsessed by a theory. This same type of objection applies equally to all qualitative judgments of cranial and other anatomical features. It is for this reason that the physical anthropologist should endeavor, wherever possible, to secure some metric expression of qualitative differences, or, at any rate, to establish the validity of his differences in qualitatively observed characters by showing that they are supported by metric differences. Making due allowance, however, for the *a priori* bias of the hobby-riding criminologist, the testimony of observed cranial features seems to establish at least a probability that Lombroso was in the main justified in his assertion that pronounced asymmetries together with all sorts of anomalies are more frequent in the criminal than in the civilian skull.

To my mind, however, the most serious objections which can be raised against the evidence of criminal craniology are the numerical inadequacy of the criminal and civilian samples studied, the ethnic and racial heterogeneity of the material, and the lack of any scientific statistical analysis of the data assembled by the various students. Since these criticisms apply equally to the anthropometric observations made by Lombroso and the other criminologists on living subjects, we may defer a fuller discussion of them to a later phase of this exposition.

The actual status of the entire subject of criminal craniology may be summed up as follows: The claims of Lombroso with respect to the profusion of metric deviations and morphological anomalies of the criminal skull have never been scientifically refuted by a satisfactory demonstration that the crania of criminals are not significantly different from those of civilians. On the other hand, the Lombrosian presentation of data is so faulty in method and so partisan in spirit, that his alleged results are easily demolished by the exposure of his weakness of technique and the citation of contradictory conclusions arrived at by his equally biased opponents. No impartial and accurate investigator has taken the trouble to go into the whole question with sufficient thoroughness either to refute or to confirm Lombroso's claims. The entire problem has been settled by argument and destructive criticism of Lombrosian technique and logic, rather than by examination of the facts of the case. Consequently, the question has never been settled at all and is in exactly the same state of uncertainty as when Lombroso first advanced his claims and his opponents denied them. A completely new survey of all documented criminal crania, carefully distinguished as to race and nationality, and compared with adequate samples of the crania of civilians of the same ethnic and racial origin, will furnish the only solution of this problem. Such a survey will necessitate the use of statistical and biometric methods which were unknown to Lombroso. Whether or not there is available for such a survey an adequate amount of criminal and civilian craniological material which is properly documented, I am unable to say. Certainly no such cranial series are available in the United States, but it is wholly possible that the task might be essayed in European museums.

In the previous discussion I have anticipated the most serious objections which must be raised against the acceptance of Lombroso's evidence of criminal anomaly in living delinquents. These are: inadequacy of the samples studied; the mixing up of diverse ethnic and racial strains in the material investigated; and the lack of a scientific method of statistical analysis. All of these require further elaboration and explanation.

Any anthropometric sample consisting of a hundred persons or less is very unlikely to show either the full range of variation or a representative distribution of physical characters found in the population from which it is drawn. Small samples are usually gathered from one place or, at any rate, from a restricted geographical area, and are likely to be weighted unduly by local types or by the chance inclusion of unrepresentative individuals. Unless there is available some adequate statistical method of appraising the amount of perfectly fortuitous divergence in comparing the characteristics of two or more small samples, no valid conclusions may be drawn from such differences. Even when the significance of differences is estimated according to modern statistical methods in terms of the probable errors, the influence of personal equations of the observer and of local conditions affecting the nature of the sample is such as to cast doubt upon the reliability of such differences. Small samples of criminals may indeed show marked deviations from similar samples of civilians, which would be confirmed in studies of larger groups, but one can never be certain that the differences are not due to chance or to personal equation or to some complicating geographical or sociological factor, unless the numbers of observations involved are big enough to insure a fair representation of the populations considered. It should be noted, however, that mere magnitude of a sample does not in itself guarantee its representative character. The latter is dependent also upon a method of sampling which involves a careful selection of adequate numbers from every class and division of the population to be studied.

When sampling is purely random, increase in the size of a series is an insurance against errors of chance. With selected samples the same holds true within the limitations of validity imposed by the methods of selection utilized.

In studies of criminal anthropology, adequate numbers of observations upon criminals have been made in some cases, but rarely have these been compared with a sufficient sample of the civilian population. The following table, compiled from Havelock Ellis'[1] compendium of the results secured by the students of the Lombrosian school, illustrates the usual size of civilian and criminal samples employed by these criminal anthropologists.

From this table, I have omitted, for the most part, the instances in which statistics regarding criminals are given without any comparison of a civil check sample, and, in every case, the numerous examples in which percentages are quoted without any reference to the numbers of cases upon which they are based. There are only three or four of the investigations enumerated above in which an adequate number of observations upon criminals has been checked against a sufficient group of the same observations made upon civilians. Of course these examples are merely taken as they occur in

[1] H. Ellis, *The Criminal* (5th edition, 1920), pp. 53–133.

successive pages of Ellis' summary of criminal anthropology. Other larger and more adequately checked criminal investigations have been made by the Lombrosian school, but I think that the samples here listed are typical. It is, of course, difficult to carry on detailed studies of large groups, and it is more difficult to obtain civilian samples for comparative purposes than to secure access to criminal material. In a good many cases the differences between such small samples might be evaluated by the use of the probable error, but this constant was not in use at the time these researches were carried out. It should be noted that when a large number of subjects are included in the

TABLE I–1

NUMBERS OF OBSERVATIONS EMPLOYED BY CRIMINAL ANTHROPOLOGISTS

Character	Number of Criminals	Number of Civilians	Investigator
Cranial anomalies	100 (paralytics)	80	Näcke
Brain weights	137	—	Bischoff
Brain weights	130	—	Tenchini
Brain weights	30	—	Mingazzini
Brains	9	80	Mondio
Wisdom teeth	400	57	Carrara
Ears	600	200	Ottolenghi
Hair color	1,720	900	Marro, Ottolenghi
General anthropometry	4,500	10,000	Marty
Muscular system	18	12	Guerra
Vertebrae and ribs	41	39	Tenchini
Handedness	91	81	Marro
Tactile sensibility	103	27	Ramlot
Eyesight	190	100	Bono
Color blindness	321	32,000	Holmgren
Hearing	110	69	Gradenigo
Olfactory acuteness	80	50	Ottolenghi
Taste	80	110	Ottolenghi
Sensory acuteness	150	50	Tarnowsky

sample of the Italian school, the characters investigated are either single features or, at best, a very few measurements and observations.

Even more serious than the inadequate size of the criminal and civilian samples studied by the Italian school, is its complete disregard of the racial heterogeneity of the material examined. The Lombrosians seem habitually to assume that criminals are more or less of the same type the world over, irrespective of race and nationality, and that the characteristics demonstrated in the case, for example, of Italian criminals, will be found to occur with equal frequency in German or French offenders. The same assumption seems to hold for civilians. The conception that there are but two types of men — normal and criminal — and that these types transcend the physical differences which distinguish the various races of man, is almost too fantastic for serious consideration. It should be apparent to every layman, as well as to every anthropologist, that the hereditary physical differences which distinguish the great groups of man one from another are far larger than the differences between "normal" and "abnormal" individuals within the same racial group. A Negro criminal may differ from a law-abiding Negro, but he will differ much more markedly from any criminal belonging to one of the so-called White races. If one is disposed to admit that criminals do indeed differ from "normal" persons, they must diverge from their own particular racial pattern. But it is hardly conceivable that such divergence is always in the same direction and of such an extent as to make one unified criminal type irrespective of race. Then if there are "criminal types," there must be a multiplicity of them, just as there are numerous racial types. Consequently it is utterly futile to investigate the difference between criminals and civilians without first making sure that both belong to the same racial group and are thus physically comparable.

Every civilized state today has a racially heterogeneous and mixed population. It is quite obvious therefore that physical differences found to obtain between criminals and civilians of any given nationality may quite well depend upon a different representation of the various racial strains and mixed types in the criminals and civilians respectively. In a country like Italy, where it is well known that various racial groups are predominant in different sections, one must not overlook the complicating ethnic factor in the comparison of criminals from different districts with civilians. The criminologists of the Italian school are, however, by no means the only offenders in their disregard of complicating racial factors. Virtually all European students of criminology have fallen into this error, including even Charles Goring, the acclaimed destroyer of Lombrosian theories.

Certainly no blame can be attached to the Lombrosian criminologists for not utilizing in their studies the methods of statistical analysis which have been developed by Karl Pearson and the biometricians, since these tools had not yet been invented at the time when most of the work in criminal anthropology was being carried on. I have already referred to the value of the probable error [2] in appraising the validity of means and other constants and the significance of differences between means. The standard deviation is an invaluable measure of dispersion; the coefficient of variation facilitates the comparison of the variabilities of measurements of disparate ranges and means; the coefficient of correlation measures the extent to which one of a pair of variables changes its value when the other is altered by any amount; the coefficient of mean square contingency measures on a scale from zero to unity the intensity of the association of pairs of attributes over and above chance expectation. These and other statistical devices, unknown to Lombroso and his contemporaries, make it possible to analyze biometric data with sufficient precision to secure results reliable enough to clear away the cloud of uncertainty and suspicion which hangs so heavily over the raw material and dubious findings of the early criminal anthropologists. It is, nevertheless, possible to use modern statistical methods as a sort of camouflage, under the cover of which facts may be perverted in a much more subtle and dangerous way than if they are merely subjected to the naïve and crude arithmetic of the old-fashioned physical anthropologist.

One of the greatest defects of Lombrosian presentation of criminal anthropological data is the sensational anecdotal method which is utilized to clinch arguments. Individual case descriptions are still copiously spread over the pages of most works on criminology. Although these are absolutely essential as the primary sources from which general deductions may be drawn, they are quite useless and misleading when intro-

[2] Cf. p. 14.

duced singly into discussions, since it is perfectly evident that they are not random selections or illustrations, but rather special cases chosen to bolster up some particular argument. Generalization from a single case, which is often encouraged by the use of such anecdotes, is wholly unscientific.

It is only fair to the Lombrosian school to refute here the charge against it laid by Goring and repeated by many secondary source writers on criminology — to wit that Lombroso's theory of the criminal type drew its inspiration from Gall and Lavater, and the pseudo-sciences of phrenology and physiognomy. Nothing in the writings of the criminal anthropologists indicates that they were influenced in the slightest by the erroneous brain localizations of the phrenologists, and the anatomical points which they emphasize have nothing whatever to do with the cranial bumps aggrandized by Gall. The craniological and somatological features studied are all of definitely racial, pathological, degenerative, or primatoid significance. Some of them were undoubtedly overemphasized and exaggerated, but all are within the legitimate scope of rational scientific investigation. It must be admitted however that the impressionistic descriptions of the countenances and appearances of various types of criminals do smack of physiognomy. The present writer in his youth, spent two summers as a civilian employee in the contract labor shops of one of our state penitentiaries, and fell into the habit of associating certain types of offenses with the facial expressions of those who committed them. Such physiognomic impressions are very common among those who have dealt with large numbers of criminals. Since, however, they cannot be reduced to any scientific method of description and analysis, they should be omitted from any serious attempt to investigate the physical and mental characteristics of criminals. Impressions of physiognomic type may indeed have some measure of validity, but they are so entirely subject to the personal equation of the observer, and so totally incapable of verification, that they should not be introduced to the detriment of quantitative scientific technique.

My general conclusions upon the work of Lombroso may be summarized briefly. The central thesis that the criminal deviates psychologically and anatomically from the normal law-abiding citizen was not conclusively proved by Lombroso and the criminal anthropologists, but it has never been refuted. The same is true of the conception of distinct physical types of criminals differentiated by the nature of their offenses. Neither Lombroso nor any of his followers could have established their cases on the basis of the amount and type of data and the methods of statistical analysis employed during their period of research activity. Such conceptions as that of the born or instinctive criminal, of the moral imbecile, and the epileptoid criminal, may be left by the physical anthropologist for consideration by the psychiatrists after the question of the anatomical distinctiveness of the criminal, or his lack of such differentiation, has been settled. The psychological characteristics and the etiology of hypothetical physical types of criminals must await the demonstrations of such types. Questions of ultimate causation cannot be settled on grounds of inherent probability or improbability.

Cesare Lombroso was a great pioneer in the study of the relation of physique to conduct. He threw off many brilliant suggestions together with not a few which were logically impossible. The state of anthropological and psychological knowledge of his age did not permit a scientific proof of his contentions. What the work of the Italian school did demonstrate conclusively was that the relation of physique to mentality and through mentality to social behavior requires further investigation by improved methods, and that the problem is by no means so simple as conceived by the criminal anthropologists who invoked mere heredity, nor so hopelessly complex as represented by the sociologists who lose themselves in an inextricable maze of environmental complications.

GORING

Criticism of Methods

The work of Charles Goring entitled *The English Convict*, published in 1913, has been generally regarded as the final refutation of Lombroso's theories pertaining to "criminal types." Charles Goring was a deputy medical officer in the English prison service, who fell heir to a project for the anthropometric study of English criminals initiated by another prison physician, Dr. Griffiths, in 1901. This project called for measurements upon a large sample of criminals and comparison of these with the civilian population in order to ascertain whether or not there were any significant physical differences. The observations were at first carried on by a number of prison medical officers, but ultimately Dr. Goring did more than half of the work of gathering data, supervised the printing of the tables of raw measurements, and undertook the analysis of the results. The statistical analysis of the material was carried on in the Biometric Laboratory of University College under the guidance of Professor Karl Pearson. Dr. Goring was a victim of pneumonia in 1919.

No one who has made a thorough study of Goring's great work, *The English Convict*, can fail to recognize the statistical genius of this man. In the opinion of the present writer Goring's volume represents a more substantial contribution to methods of anthropometric analysis than anyone had made previously. The majority of the statistical devices utilized are the inventions of Professor Karl Pearson, to whom Anthropology is so greatly indebted, but the masterly application of these methods was the achievement of Goring. It is, nevertheless, unavoidable that certain adverse and even harsh criticism of Goring's great work be expressed here. Despite these criticisms, the present writer entertains a profound admiration for the work of that undoubted genius.

The most serious charge which must be brought against Goring is that he allowed his work to be influenced and in many details to be vitiated by a violent prejudice against Lombroso and all of his theories. Goring is perfectly frank in admitting this bias — indeed, he states as the objects of his work:[3]

(I) To clear from the ground the remains of the old criminology, based upon conjecture, prejudice, and questionable observation;

(II) to found a new knowledge of the criminal, upon facts scientifically acquired, and upon inferences scientifically verified: such facts and inferences yielding, by virtue of their own established accuracy, unimpeachable conclusions.

And again:[4]

As a result of this attitude of mind, of its haphazard methods of investigation, of its desire to adjust fact to theory, rather than to formulate theory by observation of fact — as a result of all this, we have that modern criminology we have described: an organized system of self-evident confusion

[3] C. Goring, *The English Convict* (London, 1913), p. 18.
[4] Goring, 1913, p. 15.

whose parallel is only to be found in the astrology, alchemy, and other credulities of the Middle Ages. And, just as alchemy was a superstitious study, based upon a preconceived belief in the philosopher's stone; just as astrology was a superstitious study based upon the preconceived belief in the influence of the heavenly bodies on terrestrial affairs: so has criminology been a superstitious study, based upon a preconceived notion of the criminality of criminals as found in prison.

These quotations, which might be multiplied, show clearly enough the spirit in which Goring embarked upon his studies of criminal anthropology. I will not assert that many of these strictures upon "the superstition of criminology" are undeserved. On the contrary, I must admit a sympathy for Goring's moral indignation upon this subject. These expressions, however, give little promise of a cold-blooded scientific impartiality in the analysis of facts. Goring approaches the problem rather with a "previous conviction" — of quite a different nature than the previous convictions which will be frequently discussed in the body of the present work.

Here again is the plain statement of Goring's bias:[5]

This, then, is our contention: admitting that the criminal does possess all the characters that have been attributed to him; admitting, even, that he is marked by a "dome-shaped" head, and by a face like a "bird of prey"; admitting that he is drunken, impulsive, obstinate, dirty, and without control — despite all this, we maintain that he is not an abnormal man. He may represent a selected class of normal man; many of his qualities may present extreme degrees from the normal average: yet the fact remains that, in the pattern of his mind and body, in his feelings, thoughts, desires, and recognition of right and wrong, and in his behaviour, however outrageous it may be, he exists by the same nature, and is moved by the same springs of action, that affect the conduct, and constitute the quality, of normal human beings.

However much one may admire the emotional humanitarianism of this dictum, it can scarcely be claimed that such an attitude is consistent with the objective examination of facts which is indispensable to the scientific method. Nevertheless, there could be no valid objection to Goring's assumption, had he divorced his emotional conviction from his statistical treatment of the data collected and even from his method of collecting such data.

Unfortunately, it must be asserted here that Goring persistently, although probably unconsciously, used his statistical genius to twist the results of his investigation so that they would conform to his bias.

The principal methods of distorting evidence employed by this brilliant statistician must be enumerated and discussed. They are five in number. (1) He makes unjustifiable use of predictions based upon the coefficient of correlation: i.e. he "corrects for" the influence of irrelevant sociological or physical features upon the particular feature of a criminal offense group or his criminal series as a whole, thereby speciously reducing to alleged insignificance actually existing differences between classes of criminals or between criminals and non-criminals.

(2) He makes a practice of impugning the validity of his original data when differences between criminal classes or between criminals and civilians are irreducible by statistical correction. In such cases Goring either depreciates the value of the data or, frequently, resorts to a re-measuring of a smaller sample — the results of the new sample usually conforming to his bias. He then discards the original data

(3) He uses comparative data which are not legitimately comparable, having been

[5] Goring, 1913, p. 24.

derived from different populations, measured by different techniques, and being totally unrepresentative of the general population from which the English convicts are drawn.

(4) He selects anthropometric measurements and observations many of which have never figured as criminologically important, and excludes from his research a considerable number of the physical features which have been generally regarded by criminal anthropologists as the most significant in differentiation of criminal types.

(5) He disregards completely the possibility of the racial heterogeneity of his criminal series and gives very little consideration to the question of nationality. Goring's tables of raw data include not only English, Scotch, and Welsh, but also a considerable proportion of Irish, and a smattering of other nationalities and races, including Italians, Jews, Hindus, and even Negroes. However there is reason for believing that he was careful to exclude from most of his calculations all but the British. It is not clear whether the Scotch and Welsh were removed from the British series, thus making the sample analyzed purely English.

Goring's Use of Statistical Predictions

If a subgroup of murderers, for example, shows a mean head length which differs significantly (in terms of probable errors) from the mean value of head length of the entire criminal series, Goring employs a statistical prediction to allow for differences in age, stature, et cetera between the murderers and the total criminals, since the difference in head length may depend upon these complicating factors. The object of such a prediction is to ascertain what residual difference, if any, obtains between murderers and total criminals, apart from those due to stature, age, et cetera. There are two methods of dealing with such a problem.

The simpler method involves the selection of samples of murderers and other criminals which are virtually identical in stature and age, thus eliminating the complicating factors. This method, occasionally employed by the present writer, is by far the safer, but a huge series must be available in order to permit the sorting out for analysis of samples which are homogeneous and at the same time of adequate size. Goring never employs this straightforward method, which is the only certainly valid means of eliminating the influence of disturbing factors. However it should be noted that Goring had no access to electric sorting and tabulating devices which perform these laborious operations mechanically.

The alternative method is to use a statistical correction based upon a coefficient of correlation. If head length increases with age, the general relationship between the two variables may be expressed on a scale of zero to unity, by the product moment correlation coefficient "r." This coefficient enables us to say that generally the change in the mean value of one variable will be "r" times any assigned change in the other. Therefore, if murderers are younger than criminals at large and head length is correlated with age, the difference in head length between the murderers and the total group to be expected as a result of the age deviation is "r" times the differences of the means of the ages expressed in terms of the standard deviation units. If this figure then be deducted from the mean of the murderers' head length, we have arrived at a theoretical prediction of the mean of murderers' head lengths, if the said murderers were of the same age as the total criminal group. Then if the difference between this, the predicted mean of murderers, and the actual mean of the total criminal series is reduced to a negligible amount, the conclusion is that, apart from age influence, there is no difference between the head length of murderers and that of all other criminals. If there exists also a correlation between head length and stature, the crude differences between the murderers and the total criminals can be reduced still further by deducting a similar correction based upon the coefficient of correlation of head length with stature. The limit of such corrections, introduced to diminish crude differences between groups, is determined only by the number of corrections based upon correlation coefficients which the statistician employs.

This method in itself is valuable when employed legitimately. But Goring misuses it. It must be understood that the value of a coefficient of correlation for purposes of prediction depends upon its size and upon its probable error (due to accidents of the sampling process). The coefficient ranges from zero to unity. A coefficient equalling .5 on this scale is very important: a perfect correlation would be 1. A perfect correlation would imply that a change in the value of one or two variables would be accompanied by a proportional change in the other. Any correlation coefficient less than .25 obviously indicates a very slight relationship between two variables in question and one which is practically useless for purposes of prediction, since the two variables are so feebly related. Goring habitually uses low and insignificant coefficients of correlation as a basis of prediction, since in spite of their lack of meaning they reduce to his satisfaction the unwanted differences between types of criminals which he frequently encounters in his raw data. Examples of the use of small or insignificant coefficients of correlation for such prediction follow:[6]

Head length with age, .153 ± .014
Head breadth with age, .152 ± .014; head breadth with stature, .153 ± .014
Head index with age, .014 ± .014; head index with stature −.080 ± .014
Head circumference with age, .173 ± .014
Head height with age, .027 ± .014; head height with stature, .189 ± .013
Facial length with age, −.025 ± .014
Facial index with stature, −.114 ± .014
Auricular-nasal radius with age, .085 ± .014
Auricular-alveolar radius with stature, .052 ± .014
Gnathic index with age, −.083 ± .014; gnathic index with stature, −.042 ± .014

One can peruse Goring page by page and find in almost every statistical prediction the use of coefficients of correlation which are so low as to be of no value. Sometimes he employs coefficients which are even insignificant in terms of their own probable errors, and, consequently, are statistically absolutely *nil*. The reason for such illegitimate use is not far to seek. However low and insignificant a correlation may be, the use of it in a prediction helps to diminish the difference between groups which Goring wishes to explain away. The use of three or four insignificant correlations in a prediction will eat away any difference between one group of criminals and another, or between criminals and civilians, thus proving Goring's contention that no such difference exists. But these predictions based upon low and insignificant correlations mean precisely nothing, and their employment for this purpose is, to say the least, disingenuous.

[6] Goring, 1913, pp. 54–72.

Quite apart from the question of the size and statistical significance of coefficients of correlation used for prediction is that of the type of relationship for which correction legitimately can be made in appraising physical differences between criminal groups or between criminals and non-criminals. In examining, for instance, the difference between the occipital projections of murderers and all other criminals, it may be justifiable to attempt to reduce them to a common basis of age and stature (if these are correlated with occipital projection) in order to find out what differences may obtain between the occipital projection of murderers and other criminals, apart from the differences which are affected by age and stature. But is it not the primary object of any investigation of this nature to ascertain whether classes of criminals do indeed differ physically from each other and from the civilian population, rather than to attempt to reduce the different classes of criminals to a purely hypothetical basis of identity in all physical characters save one, and then to find out whether they would be different in this one character, if they were alike in the others (which they are not)? It seems to me that Goring succeeds in disembodying his criminal material completely and reducing his actual data to mathematical abstractions which represent nothing real. Actually, the coefficient of correlation does not necessarily indicate a causal relationship between the two variables involved. Thus if stature is correlated with head length positively, it increases as head length increases, but there is no implication that the increase of stature causes the increase of head length or *vice versa*. It may be, and probably is, some third force which influences them both simultaneously. Then if two groups of criminals differing in head length also differ in stature, there is no real justification for assuming that their difference in head length is due to the difference in stature, and hence applying a correction for stature to their differences in head length. In other words, the entire method of the use of statistical prediction in allowing for the influence of associated characters is of little or no value, except in raising some highly abstract and altogether theoretical possibilities of causation.

If one really wishes to eliminate the complicating influences of correlated features in contrasting two groups, that elimination must be carried out by the sorting and selection of real groups and not by juggling with mathematical equations. There is, however, a certain measure of somewhat abstract value to this procedure when it is properly employed. Quite apart from the use of insignificant coefficients of correlation as a basis of prediction, it ought to be clear that the only complicating factors for which correction can be made in studies of the physical features of a population are measurable physical characters. Goring, however, frequently introduces a correction for "intelligence," whereby he attempts to predict what the head length of a given sample would be, were this sample of the same mean intelligence as the total series.

In the first place we may inquire by what method Goring measured intelligence. He did not utilize any of the standard tests, such as the Binet-Simon, probably because the period of his investigation antedates the general use of such methods. He depended rather upon general estimates of the intelligence of individuals, formed apparently from a sort of consensus of opinion of the prison officials:[7]

According to estimates of their general intelligence, our criminal subjects have been distributed within five categories called intelligent, fairly intelligent, unintelligent, weak-minded, and imbecile, respectively. Regarding this classification, we may say that it consists chiefly and originally of a two-

[7] Goring, 1913, p. 247.

fold division of criminals into weak-minded or imbecile, and non-weak-minded — a simple separation, based upon broad estimates of mental capacity, which we may safely state to be entirely free from the personal equation of any one observer. The conditions, in fact, determining the official description of a prisoner as weak-minded, are so manifold and stereotyped, and include the exercise of, and the agreement between, the judgments of so many individuals, that the actual relative weak-mindedness of the officially designated "weak-minded" prisoner may be regarded as an established fact, subject to no greater amount of error than attaches to any general consensus of verdict between men whose *métier* it is to express opinions upon technical subjects of the kind we are considering.

It seems to me probable that these crude judgments as to the intelligence of criminals may be, on the whole, valid, but Goring then proceeds to assume that these mental qualities follow a normal law of distribution, and employs Sheppard's tables of the ordinates of the normal curve to determine the means and standard deviations of each intelligence group. This gives him a basis for calculating a product moment coefficient of correlation of intelligence with any other measurable variable. We then find him introducing into his predictions of the means of physical characters a correction for intelligence. For example, in occipital projection, he employs to reduce his material to a standard basis of intelligence a correlation of occipital projection with intelligence which is $-.036 \pm .021$.[8] Perhaps a few more instances of the use of the correlation coefficients of physical features with intelligence may be instructive:[9]

Chin projection with intelligence, $.090 \pm .021$
Length of right ear with intelligence, $.103 \pm .021$
Distance between eyes with intelligence, $.057 \pm .030$
Concurrency of eyebrows with intelligence, $.047 \pm .021$
"Good" eyesight with intelligence, $.034 \pm .021$
Hearing with intelligence, $.101 \pm .021$
Nose inclination with intelligence, $-.048 \pm .021$
Texture of hair with intelligence, $.028 \pm .030$

In fairness it must be stated that some of these insignificant correlations are not used for purposes of correction or prediction, but they are used by Goring whenever he finds any important differences in the offense types of his criminals which he wishes to explain away. An even more serious error is Goring's attempt to reduce groups of human beings to a standard basis of intelligence and to predict what their physical characteristics would be if they were all equally imbecile, weak-minded, fairly intelligent, or intelligent. Of what use is a statement that the correlation ratio of occipital projection with crime, for constant age, stature, and intelligence, is $.052$? What we wish to learn is whether criminals committing one type of offense are physically different from other classes of offenders and not the result of a dubious mathematical calculation of the status of these physical differences if all the criminals are assumed to be equally intelligent.

The entire work of Goring bristles with such logical fallacies and such statistical sophistries, all devoted to his purpose of proving that criminals are not different from non-criminals, and that, if they are, they would not be if they were of the same age, the same stature, and the same intelligence — in short a triumphant demonstration of the obvious fact that if due allowance be made for all of the physical and mental differences

[8] Goring, 1913, p. 73.
[9] Goring, 1913, pp. 77–98.

between criminals and non-criminals, the former are not different from the latter. Since this work is not primarily a *critique* of Goring, space forbids a further discussion of his use of statistical methods which are equally dubious in many processes other than those described above. None of his results or conclusions in statistical matters can be accepted without a careful scrutiny of the processes he employs, and such a scrutiny frequently reveals that the basic facts are radically different from the end product of his statistical treatment.

Goring's Practice of Allowing for Personal Equation

In certain morphological observations collected by a number of observers Goring finds it necessary to allow for a personal equation. He does this by repeating the observation in question using fewer data and but one observer. This would seem to be an unobjectionable procedure, were it not for the fact that he utilizes it principally in cases where his larger body of data shows significant offense group differentiations in the feature under examination, and that the repetition of the observation by one observer (probably Goring himself) usually results in reducing to insignificance the correlation ratio or other coefficient denoting physical differentiation. A few examples may be cited:[10]

Occipital projection, 2341 observations, correlation ratio with crime, .129 ± .014
Occipital projection, 997 observations, correlation ratio with crime, .052 ± .02
Chin projection, 2339 observations, correlation ratio with crime, .147 ± .014
Chin projection, 997 observations, correlation ratio with crime, .074 ± .021

In two instances only the regathering of data by one observer yields correlation ratios as high as or higher than the original large series. These are length of right and left ear.[11] In these cases the data show that in the smaller remeasured groups the correlation ratios are as high as in the original large series gathered by several observers, and that the ultimate reduction of this coefficient to what Goring considers insignificance is not entirely effected by reducing the personal equation, but by adding a correction for intelligence not introduced into the large series. Yet he says:[12]

An examination of the figures in these tables will make it sufficiently clear that, when reduced to a standardized basis of age, stature, and intelligence, and when the influence of personal equation upon the measurements has been, as far as possible, eliminated, there is no appreciable relation between ear length and criminal proclivity; that is to say, the amount of relation is inappreciable in so far as differences in the nature of crime are in any way a measure of difference in such proclivity.

The viciousness of accepting original data when the results are in accordance with a preconceived notion and of rejecting the same data and gathering new to disprove them when the results run contrary to the author's bias, is patent. But even if we overlook this methodological defect, we can scarcely condemn too strongly the introduction of additional correctional factors to make the new data conform and the referring of such complaisant results to the elimination of the personal equation.

When all other devices fail, Goring is frequently found to depreciate the value of significant relations between crime and physical features by impugning his own data.

[10] Goring, 1913, pp. 73–77.
[11] Goring, 1913, pp. 78–80.
[12] Goring, 1913, p. 78.

Thus we find a correlation ratio [13] of grayness with crime amounting to .251. After correcting for age (legitimately in my opinion) the correlation ratio is reduced to .184. He then corrects for "intelligence" reducing it further to .125. He finally explains away a significant deficiency of grayness in sexual offenders by suggesting that "our rough method for detecting the presence of grayness, would inevitably give rise to some amount of error in the statistics, by allowing smaller degrees of this character to be overlooked."

A slightly different example of Goring's method of dealing with unpalatable results is seen in his treatment of the Lombrosian stigma of tattooing. He finds a crude correlation ratio of .327 ± .027 with nature of crime. He applies corrections for age, intelligence, and service in the army and navy. But the coefficient is reduced thereby only to .321 ± .029. He then suggests that urban or rural residence is probably at the bottom of this correlation, but does not apply a correction *in toto*, apparently because he fears that it will be unsatisfactory. He nevertheless concludes:[14]

> We.do not pretend to have analyzed the matter exhaustively; but the statistical evidence before us is sufficient for an interim conclusion that although criminals, like the law-abiding public, differ considerably in the extent to which they are tattooed, these differences have no special relation to criminal proclivity; and that they tend to disappear when differences are allowed for in other conditions associated with tattooing, of which age, intelligence, service in the army or navy, and urban or rural residence, are the principal ones.

Similarly, a correlation [15] of shade of hair with nature of crime amounting to .228 is referred to a difference in social class, without any effort to demonstrate the statistical validity of such a conclusion.

A careful study of Goring's observational data on Lombrosian stigmata will show that many of them actually confirm the findings of Lombroso rather than refute them. But his methods of evading such a conclusion and of distorting the results lead him always to a denial of any association between type of offense and physical features, however patent that association may be in his raw data.

Goring's Use of the Correlation Ratio

It is necessary to comment also upon Goring's use of the correlation ratio. This constant, like the product moment coefficient of correlation, varies from zero to unity. It is, according to Goring, the ratio of the deviation (from the general mean of the total group) of the means of the subgroups, to the standard deviation of the total group of criminals. It measures the degree of differentiation of the several offense subgroups from the total criminal series.[16]

[13] Goring, 1913, pp. 99–101.
[14] Goring, 1913, p. 104.
[15] Goring, 1913, p. 97.
[16] Dr. C. C. Seltzer, a very keen student of the application of statistical methods to physical anthropology, questions the validity of such use of the correlation ratio as Goring habitually makes. In his opinion the correlation ratio can be used properly only in relating variables and ought not to be employed for measuring the intensity of association between "nature of crime" as defined by offense subgroups and such variables as head length and stature. He says (in a personal communication):

"The correlation ratio is perfectly valid when used for two graduated variables representing a bivariate normal surface or one approximating it. But in my opinion, it has dubious validity when used (as Goring uses it) to measure the intensity of the association of an ungraduated attribute such as 'nature of crime' broken down into offense subgroups (forgery and fraud, sexual offenses, damage to property, etc.) and a

Goring, in commenting upon the low values of such correlation ratios and coefficients of correlation found (partly by the use of multiple corrections) states:[17]

It is clear, for instance, that the coefficient of .1 represents a degree of association too microscopic to be revealed by unaided observations; that coefficients of .3, and over, represent a strength of association whose existence, more or less roughly apprehended, would be patent to everyday observation; that amounts of association measured by coefficients of .5 and .6, respectively, would hardly be differentiated by ordinary observational experience, and that no degree of association equivalent to a coefficient of less than .6 is of much practical service for individual prediction — it is clear that these coefficients would be of no greater service, in fact, than would be the knowledge of an individual's baldness in the predicting of his age. The fatuity of Lombroso's pretensions, and predictings of criminality from the presence or absence of physical stigmata — the associations of physical characters with crime, if existent at all, being hardly any of them greater than .1 — is manifest from these considerations.

---

normal variate such as stature or head length. These crime categories cannot be reasonably considered as graduated functions of the criminal diathesis but are strictly ungraduated attributes in the Yule sense.

"There are several reasons for reaching this conclusion. In the first place there appear certain limitations with respect to the absolute values of the correlation ratio. The use of ungraduated crime subgroups in the place of one variate when there are only five subgroups makes it impossible to obtain very high values in the nature of .8 or .9 owing in part to the grouping process. For like the contingency table the correlation ratio tends to the higher values or magnitudes as the intervals become finer and finer. Secondly, a correlation ratio of unity could only be obtained when the variability of every individual from his crime subgroup would be zero, and when the deviations of the means of the crime subgroups are equal to the standard deviation of the entire series. But in this type of material these prerequisites cannot be satisfied. It is impossible when dealing with the anthropometrics of *homo sapiens* to obtain a condition where there would be no variation in a group of individuals for a particular measure, no matter on what basis this group is divided. Normal or nearly normal variation in man with respect to anthropometric measures is a cardinal attribute. The condition of homoscedasticy could be easily fulfilled in normal bivariate frequency distributions, but for five subgroups this would still lead to a correlation ratio considerably less than one.

"With respect to the interpretation of values of the correlation ratio obtained on this type of material, the following comments seem to me quite apposite. Values of the correlation ratio for this type of material should not be interpreted on a progressive scale of 0 to 1, but on a relative scale with other values within its own sphere. By this I mean that a correlation ratio of .15 between crime subgroups and, let us say, stature does not signify by itself that there is a very low degree (within the sampling error) of association between crime and stature. This may or may not be true depending on the nature of the universe of crime and constitution. One can say that a correlation ratio of .15 between crime subgroups and stature shows a higher degree of association than crime subgroups and head length with a correlation ratio of only .05. In other words, within its own sphere, correlation ratios may be compared one against the other depending on its absolute value, but not interpreted alone on a zero to one scale in terms of degrees of association. In addition, since the limit of the value of the correlation ratio when used for crime subgroups is in part dependent on the number of subgroups used, then it is quite apparent that in the interpretation of such values certain ones less than unity may in reality indicate perfect association.

"Attention should be called to the fact that such material may possess a considerable degree of attenuation owing to the relative inaccuracy of the measurements and subgroup classifications. The presence of this condition plays a considerable rôle in the accuracy of the interpretation of the correlation values. And finally, the values of the correlation ratio are *a priori* determined by the nature of the material itself. In dealing with crime and constitution it is ridiculous to try to predict a person's crime from his head length or stature, but it may well be true that murderers have longer heads than sexual offenders, and in turn sexual offenders may have longer heads than burglars. Accordingly, in this type of material low correlations in the order of .2 or .15 or .1 or even less do not necessarily mean that there is an extremely low or virtually no association between crime and anthropometric characters. On the contrary they may well signify (within the sampling error(?)) that there is a distinct and significant association."

I myself am inclined to think that Dr. Seltzer's criticism is partially, if not completely justifiable. However, I must confess that my statistical knowledge is too limited to enable me to pronounce judgment in the matter. At various stages of this survey I have made a limited use, after the manner of Goring, of the correlation ratio. However, no important finding of this investigation is based upon its utilization, since the relationship between any single anthropometric variable and nature of offense is not only small, but, in my opinion, unimportant.

[17] Goring, 1913, p. 02.

But the reader should understand a peculiarity of correlation ratios which renders high values almost impossible in any random selection of criminals classified by type of offense. The correlation ratio depends for its value upon the amount of deviation of subgroups from the total series. Now in all criminal series selected at random, the burglary and larceny group is far larger than any other. In Goring's series this group usually exceeds 50 per cent of the total criminals. Consequently, the standard deviation and mean of the entire series are unduly weighted by this great offense group, and unless the smaller offense subgroups deviate strongly from this preponderant subgroup, a large value of the correlation ratio cannot be produced. In other words, correlation ratios upon subgroups which include one of such excessive size that it overbalances all the others, are almost inevitably small.[18]

Goring's strictures upon the evaluation of correlation ratios and coefficients of correlation on the basis of their position in a scale ranging from zero to unity are misleading in his own examples. In the case of the correlation ratio a small value may be significant on account of the almost inevitable reduction of the ratio effected by the preponderance of one very large subgroup. Again, in both coefficients of correlation and correlation ratios, low values which are obtained after making allowance for the complicating effect of characters known to be correlated with the variables whose relation is being studied must be interpreted on a scale different from that applied to crude, uncorrected coefficients and ratios. A residual or corrected coefficient of correlation of .1, obtained after the correction of a crude coefficient for one or more factors, may really indicate considerable intensity of correlation.

Finally, the real meaning of correlations and associations of anthropometric and sociological data is not revealed by the mathematical processes which yield coefficients of different values. In fact the calculation of such measures is as likely to confuse the student who is attempting to determine causation as to clarify the relationships under examination.

Goring's Use of Comparative Data

In order to find out whether or not criminals are physically differentiated from the non-criminal population, one must ascertain the physical status of an adequate sample of the general population. Further, the same measurements should be taken upon the general population sample as upon the criminals, by the same technique, and, if possible, by the same observers. These conditions are very difficult to realize, principally because access to the general population for anthropometric purposes is by no means easy. Further, when samples of the general population are measured, they are inevitably selected samples and they may not be representative of that section of the general population from which criminals are drawn. It is, in fact, well nigh impossible to secure a civilian check sample which is not open to objection on grounds of its selective nature. Consequently, the fact that Goring failed to secure any civilian check series upon which to take all the measurements and observations which had been carried out in his criminal series, is understandable, and even pardonable. The lack of such comparative

[18] Dr. Seltzer's comment upon this point is that the whole difficulty arises from the fact that crime in this sense is not a variable and that the subgroups are too few to work with. The difficulty of the preponderant subgroups would never arise in a correlation ratio based upon two real variables, since a larger number of arrays or columns would be involved.

data forced him to depend upon whatever series he could gather from literature which he judged to be more or less comparable with his own criminal material. Unfortunately none of these series included more than a few of the measurements or indices which he had taken, with the result that except in a few measurements Goring did not compare his civilians with criminals at all. How then can he claim that criminals are no different from civilians? The comparative series actually employed include 3000 measurements of other criminals by Macdonell, measurements of 1000 Cambridge undergraduates quoted by Macdonell, measurements of 959 Oxford students by E. Shuster, measurements of 118 officers and men of the Royal Engineers, measurements of Scotch insane by Tocher, of Scotch school boys by the same investigator, with other scattering data. In no case do we find more than a few measurements of criminals compared with a few corresponding measurements of socially and ethnically diverse groups of the general population.

In the few comparisons of criminals with civilians actually made by Goring, we encounter the same sophistries in analysis that characterize his studies of criminals by offense groups. For example, he compares Cambridge undergraduates with criminals and finds that, after making due allowance for stature and age, the criminals have a deficiency in head breadth of $2.89 \pm .13$ millimeters. He explains this by recalling that the criminals have closely cropped heads and suggests that this fact would tend to diminish unduly the transverse diameter of the skull.[19] But any anthropologist knows that cranial calipers, when properly used, push through the hair to the scalp and are wholly unaffected by length of head hair. He invokes the same factor of cropped heads to explain criminal deficiencies not only in breadth, but also in length and height when compared with Oxford undergraduates, and begs the whole question by attempting to show that the universities differ more from each other in head measurements than either do from criminals.[20]

Goring's conception of a triumphant demonstration that criminals are not differentiated from civilians is to list a set of measurements in which criminals resemble this, that, or the other civilian group — stressing the fortuitous coincidences in different groups and suppressing the differences:[21]

In mean head-length, there is no difference between criminals and Cambridge students; in mean head-breadth, there is only 1 mm. difference, and in head-height, there is no difference between convicts and the University College staff; in mean head-index, Oxford students, as well as the University staff, are almost identical with criminals; and in mean circumference of head, criminals and Scottish students correspond in a similarly close degree. In fact, from a knowledge only of an undergraduate's cephalic measurements, a better judgment could be given as to whether he were studying at an English or Scottish University than a prediction could be made as to whether he would eventually become a University professor or a convicted felon.

In this statement he suppresses the fact that Cambridge students have much broader heads and higher indices than criminals; that criminals have much shorter, narrower, lower heads than Oxford students, and much smaller head circumferences; that University College staff members have much broader and longer heads than the convicts; and that Scottish students have significantly longer, broader, and lower heads. In fact he emphasizes only such facts as agree with his prejudice and disregards all others. It

[19] Goring, 1913, p. 143.
[20] Goring, 1913, p. 144.
[21] Goring, 1913, p. 145.

would be equally possible to pick out a few measurements in which Whites are not different from Negroes, others in which they are not different from Australians, and still others in which they are not different from Mongolians, and to conclude therefrom that Whites do not differ significantly from other races. In brief, Goring's use of comparative data is a complete misuse, since he has no properly comparable data and from the data which are available stresses only such comparisons as tend to prove his case.

Goring's Selection of Measurements

Goring actually did not study many of the criminological features emphasized by the Lombrosian School, but based his conclusions upon a majority of features not considered of criminological importance by the earlier students. He completely neglected cranial asymmetry (except mean contours), shape of the ears, development of the lower jaw, malar projection, teeth, wrinkles, forehead, brow ridges. He dealt with size of head, facial asymmetry, prognathism, hairiness (in part), shape and deflection of nose, tattooing, and palates, but in most of these cases he had no comparative material from the general population. He emphasized particularly the length-breadth or cephalic index, which is of primarily racial significance, and also the raw dimensions of the head and face. Many of the indices and measurements which he studied have not been made the basis of criminal diagnosis by anthropologists. Nevertheless, the list of features examined by Goring is defensible on the ground that he selected those which seemed to him most suitable for exact measurements and observations, neglecting those which might be expected to yield results too largely affected by personal bias. While it is quite evident that Goring possessed only a slight knowledge of the principles and technique of physical anthropology, it seems to me that defects in his list of measurements and observations are of altogether minor importance.

Ethnic and Racial Heterogeneity of Goring's Sample of Criminals

In Goring's tables of measurements and observations upon individual convicts are included the anthropometric records of considerable numbers of persons who are not English. In Tables I–2 and I–3 we have attempted to tabulate nationality and nativity of Goring's material from his raw data. The object of this tabulation was to determine from the totals whether or not Goring excluded from his tables of measurements of "English convicts" the sundry Irish, Jews, Germans, Hindus, and Negroes whose anthropometric records occur in that publication. The results of this tabulation seem to show that our suspicion that Goring mixed up different races and nationalities in his study of English convicts was unfounded, except in cases of stature and weight. The population of Great Britain is, of course, racially heterogeneous. It would have been possible to divide the Goring sample of English convicts into a number of different physical types of probably diverse racial origins and to study the criminological differences of these types. Such a procedure has been omitted so often in purely anthropological studies of populations that it would be unfair to stress unduly its neglect in an investigation conducted by a medical officer whose sole interest in the problem was criminological. Nevertheless, the lack of racial discrimination leaves many of the physical issues in confusion.

Goring's failure to study the inmates of English prisons by nationality is less excusable. His material was sufficient to furnish sizeable samples of Welsh, Irish, and Scotch, in addition to his great group of English convicts. It is quite clear, however, that he had no real comprehension of the importance of nationality either in respect of physical or of criminological differentiation. His only attempt to relate nationality to crime [22] is a correlation ratio based upon only 297 individuals, in which English,

TABLE I–2

NATIONALITY OF GORING'S ENGLISH CONVICTS; SERIAL NUMBERS I–1000; 1801–2000; 2501–3000

Nationality	Number	Per Cent
English	1344	79.06
Irish	123	7.24
Welsh	48	2.82
Scotch	30	1.76
Canadian	2	.12
American	16	.94
Swedish	0	0.00
Norwegian	2	.12
German	42	2.47
Swiss	2	.12
French	9	.53
Spanish	6	.35
Portuguese	1	.06
South American	1	.06
Italian	13	.76
Austrian	1	.06
Russian	27	1.59
Greek	3	.18
Negro	2	.12
Afghan Hindu	1	.06
East Indian	1	.06
Egyptian	1	.06
Hungarian	1	.06
Mixed	24	1.41
Total	1700	

TABLE I–3

BIRTHPLACE OF GORING'S ENGLISH CONVICTS; SERIAL NUMBERS I001–1800; 2001–2200; 2351–2500

Birthplace	Number	Per Cent
England	1008	90.16
Ireland	33	2.95
Wales	11	.98
Scotland	13	1.16
Germany	8	.72
United States	15	1.34
Switzerland	3	.27
France	3	.27
Spain	2	.18
Italy	2	.18
Austria	2	.18
Australia	5	.45
New Zealand	4	.36
India	1	.09
Holland	2	.18
Malay Peninsula	1	.09
Channel Islands	1	.09
Poland	1	.09
Ceylon	1	.09
Bavaria	1	.09
Tasmania	1	.09
Total	1118	

Welsh, and Scotch are combined in a subgroup comprising 244 persons. No significant correlation could result from such a grouping.

Conclusions on Goring

There are many portions of Goring's work which are of great value. His notable contributions are in the study of criminal physique (which he finds definitely inferior, thus confirming the conclusions of Lombroso), in the influence of age upon crime, in the vital statistics of the criminal, in the mental differentiation of the criminal (which again agrees with Lombrosian ideas), and in his investigations of "force of circumstances," fertility, and heredity. He cannot be denied great credit for his painstaking investigation of these important aspects of crime. He also deserves abundant praise for

[22] Goring, 1913, p. 421.

the variety of delicate and ingenious statistical devices he employs, although his method of using them is frequently culpable.

In his efforts to disprove physical differentiation of the criminal Goring displays most of the faults which he charges to Lombroso, and others of which Lombroso was never guilty. In an early stage of Goring's work, Professor Karl Pearson asked him this question:[23]

"And what if Lombroso's theory be established by your analysis?" —

"I shall accept it as the foundation of criminology, but shall none the less condemn Lombroso as a traitor to science."

Professor Pearson quotes this reply with apparent approbation, but it seems to the present writer to epitomize the lack of an objective viewpoint and the prejudice which inevitably vitiate the work of the scientist who approaches his task with an emotional preconception of its issue.

Actually Goring left the problem of the relation of the criminal's physique to his offense unsolved. Mathematical formulae and verbal sophistries may befuddle lay readers, but no one who reads and understands Goring's *English Convict* can accept his conclusions, unless he shares the prejudice of that author.

History and Material of the Present Survey

In 1916, as an instructor in Harvard University, the writer initiated a half-course entitled "Criminal Anthropology and Race Mixture." The portion devoted to Criminal Anthropology included a review of the theories of Lombroso and his school, and an extended study and critique of the then recently published work of Charles Goring. All this led to the general conclusion that the physique of the criminal, his anthropological differentiation, or lack of it, and the racial and ethnic variation in criminal propensity were subjects which had to be reopened and investigated thoroughly in the light of modern anthropological method and scientific impartiality. Among the graduate students who took this course, at some time or other, were several who have since distinguished themselves in various scientific fields. Of these perhaps the most brilliant and the most interested was a young sociologist and graduate in law named Sheldon Glueck. Dr. Glueck's continued interest in this subject as a branch of Criminology was directly responsible for the inauguration of the present survey. The writer made several abortive efforts to organize some sort of project for the anthropological study of criminals, but nothing came of them until the spring of 1926. At this time Dr. Glueck introduced him to Dr. Winfred A. Overholser, then Director of the Division of the Examination of Prisoners, Massachusetts State Department of Mental Diseases. Dr. Overholser was directing a sociological and psychiatric study of some thousands of prisoners in the Massachusetts county jails. He and the late Dr. G. M. Kline, Commissioner of Mental Diseases, very kindly offered the cooperation of the Department in an anthropometric study of county jail prisoners, the results of which were to be correlated with the sociological and psychiatric data of their investigation. Consequently, two graduate students were trained to undertake the measurement and observation of the prisoners. These were William V. Mackaye and Henry Lappin. Throughout the summer these men worked in the jails, being maintained by the State

[23] Goring, Abridged Edition, 1919, p. xii.

Department of Mental Diseases. In the autumn Arthur R. Kelly, another graduate student, replaced Lappin in the field work. At the end of 1926 a sample of 2000 observations upon county jail prisoners had been gathered, and it was then decided to embark upon the larger project of studying the major offenders in the prisons and reformatories. This work was accomplished in Massachusetts under the aegis of the State Department of Mental Diseases. Civil and criminal insane inmates of state institutions were measured and observed in the same fashion. In order to make the survey of national scope, it was necessary to seek financial assistance which was secured — not without great difficulty — through the generosity of the persons and agencies to whom acknowledgment has been made in the preface of this work.

The choice of states in which the work was to be carried on was governed partially by the possibility of securing permission to work in the penal institutions, and partially by the necessity of getting samples which would represent adequately, so far as possible, the different ethnic and racial elements in the population of the United States. In securing the requisite permits for work, Dr. Winfred Overholser and the State Department of Mental Diseases again furnished invaluable assistance.

The large sample studied in Massachusetts was thought to afford a good representation of most of the foreign stocks domiciled in the country. In order to obtain, if possible, a sample of the Scandinavian and German peoples residing in the Middle West, the state of Wisconsin was selected and the inmates of the penitentiary at Waupun were measured and observed. In Missouri a similarly complete study was planned, but only the Negro prisoners were actually observed and measured.

It seemed very desirable to examine thoroughly large series of the Old American mountain stocks of the South and to secure at the same time sufficient series of Negro and Negroid offenders. By permission of the authorities, the institutions of the states of North Carolina, Tennessee, and Kentucky were visited and their inmates measured. The problem of the criminality of the Mexican immigrant was approached by studying the states of Texas, New Mexico, Arizona, and Colorado.

Altogether ten states were investigated, and it is felt that no section of the country has been neglected, save only the states of the Pacific seaboard which contain no ethnic elements unrepresented in the states of our sample, excepting larger proportions of Japanese and Chinese. Since the total of Chinese and Japanese prisoners of both sexes present in prisons, reformatories, jails, and workhouses of the United States on January 1, 1923 was only 368, it appears that the omission of the states in which these peoples are principally domiciled is not serious.

The acquisition of a check sample of the civil population, with which to compare the criminals, was an extremely difficult task. The two field investigators had little time to pursue in the various states the long course of diplomatic negotiations which would enable them to secure access to civilians for anthropometric purposes. At no time was it thought feasible to attempt to measure civilians in every one of the states in which the criminals were studied. Our effort was rather to provide a numerically adequate sample of every race and nationality represented in the criminal population. In Massachusetts the criminal insane data secured at Bridgewater were matched by an equivalent study of the civil insane at the Taunton hospital. Civil insane Negroes were studied at the hospital in Goldsboro, North Carolina, and both Whites and other stocks in the hospital for the insane at Pueblo, Colorado.

Check samples of the law-abiding and presumably normal population were gathered in Massachusetts, Tennessee, and North Carolina. In Massachusetts, through the kind offices of the State Department of Mental Diseases and by the permission of the Adjutant General, an effort was made to measure the personnel of the militia in the armories on their drill nights. This plan resulted in less than two hundred measurements, since the militia officers were uncooperative. The experiment of setting up a measuring booth in the bathing house of the public resort at Revere Beach was not particularly successful and yielded only a few subjects. However, through the kindness of the authorities of the Massachusetts General Hospital, permission was secured to measure the out-patients of its dispensary, and a large and satisfactory sample was secured — most of the measurements being taken by Mr. Harold A. Wolff, who was also attached to the criminal survey as a statistical assistant. A similar permission was granted by the officials of the Beth Israel Hospital, who gave every facility for the study of their out-patients.

In Tennessee the anthropometric observer managed to secure permission to measure 146 Nashville firemen. Although they represent a physically and occupationally selected group, these firemen, when dispersed among the other persons of the check sample of similar origin, do not weight unduly the total group.

In Tennessee and North Carolina also the field observers were able to secure considerable series of Negro and Negroid adults — some college students and others of less educated status. Thus the complete check sample of civilians includes approximately 909 White civilians and 1067 Negro or Negroid civilians, apart from the civil insane who have been kept separate. In addition to these series there are available for purposes of comparison a number of large groups measured and observed by workers of the Harvard Laboratory in connection with other projects. Since, for the most part, the same technique and virtually the same measurements and observations have been used, these additional series are closely comparable with the data of the survey. Tables I–4 and I–5 [24] indicate the number and provenience of the subjects studied. The question of the nature of the check samples requires some further discussion. Prisoners and insane are, of course, selected groups drawn, for the most part, from more poorly educated and economically depressed classes. With whom should these selected groups be compared? It seems obvious that the criminal insane of a given race and nationality should be compared with the civil insane of the same ethnic and racial origin, and this has been done. In the case of criminals and civilians the problem is much more complicated. In our particular situation the simplest comparative material would have been Harvard College students, of whom a large anthropometric sample could have been obtained without much difficulty. It seemed however unfair to utilize such material for comparison, since these students, for the most part, come from the class which is most favored economically and represent a diametrically opposite selection to the criminals. The same would be more or less true of any college group, and, in the case of the Negro samples, many of which are college students, the latter were accepted only because of the extreme difficulty of securing any material at all, and have been kept rigidly separate from the non-college Negroes in the various comparisons instituted.

The Massachusetts militia seemed, on the whole, to be fairly suitable material for comparison with the criminals of Massachusetts, subject to certain reservations. The

[24] Pages 34 and 35.

militiamen are selected to some extent by their physical qualifications, by their age, and by their urban residence. In as much as enlistment in the militia is contingent upon the passing of a physical examination, it may be assumed that its members are, on the whole, of superior physique to the criminals. This difficulty was obviated, in our opinion, by distributing the militiamen among the other groups in our civilian

TABLE I–4

NUMBER OF SUBJECTS

Statistically analyzed	17,076	
Measured but not analyzed		
Massachusetts County Jail	108	(Negroes, Negroids, Indians, et cetera in too small groups)
Massachusetts Bridgewater Criminal Insane	153	(Negroes, Unknown race, Foreign parentage groups too small for seriation — as 2 Italians, 5 Scandinavians)
All States Prison and Reformatory	166	(Unknown Parentage, Indians, et cetera)
Massachusetts Taunton Civil Insane . .	45	(Indians, Unknown, and Parentage groups too small for seriation)
Colorado Civil Insane	23	(Indians, Negroes, Unknown, and Parentage groups too small for seriation)
White Civil Samples	94	(Small Parentage groups in Hospital, Firemen, and Militia groups)
	589	

check samples. Allowance can be made for age differences by sorting out comparable groups, or, when the samples are too small, by utilizing predictions based upon correlation coefficients, if the coefficients in question are of sufficient importance to necessitate such corrections. The possible difficulty involved in the more largely urban character of the check samples, as compared with the prisoners, cannot be resolved in any simple manner. Upon this difference in residence depends, to a certain extent, occupational and educational deviations between the criminals and the civilians. The criminals will show a much higher proportion of agriculturists and of those who have not received the advantages of the superior facilities for education afforded by the cities. It is possible only to bear in mind these differentiating factors and to make some allowance for them in estimating the value of the results of the comparison.

The social and economic classes from which the rank and file of the militia are drawn are quite diversified and probably fairly comparable with those from which criminals are recruited, although doubtless the militiamen are somewhat more prosperous. Several of the individuals measured in the militia drill-halls had been previously measured in one or other of the county jails.

The Massachusetts General Hospital out-patients seem to constitute socially and economically an even more suitable group for comparison with the prisoners. The out-patients are not physically inferior, in the sense of being chronic invalids or bedridden, but include, in the majority of instances, persons who have come to the clinics for the treatment of some ailment which may be very slight, or merely temporary — frequently an injury due to an accident. The same considerations apply to the out-patients measured in the Beth Israel Hospital.

In the spring of 1928 the two principal anthropometric field workers had finished the collecting of data from the ten states included in the survey. Since, however, the

TABLE I-5

NUMBER AND STATE OF SUBJECTS STUDIED

	Mass.	Tenn.	Ken.	Texas	N. C.	Wis.	Southwest	Missouri	Totals
County Jail = 2,004									
Native White	376	..	..	..	..	..	..	..	376
Native of foreign parentage	840	..	..	..	..	..	..	..	840
Foreign of foreign parentage	687	..	..	..	..	..	..	..	687
Negro	12	..	..	..	..	..	..	..	12
Negroid	89	..	..	..	..	..	..	..	89
Prison and Reformatory = 10,953									
Native White	338	423	1,187	915	448	297	604	..	4,212
Native of foreign parentage	649	30	32	241	15	236	350	..	1,553
Foreign of foreign parentage	387	4	9	257	2	162	276	..	1,097
Negro	17	158	156	194	83	16	22	120	766
Negroid	91	430	703	889	279	27	105	801	3,325
Criminal Insane = 743									
Native White	170	..	..	..	..	..	..	..	170
Native of foreign parentage	209	..	..	..	..	..	..	..	209
Foreign of foreign parentage	325	..	..	..	..	..	..	..	325
Negroid	39	..	..	..	..	..	..	..	39
Defective Delinquents = 173									
Native White	58	..	..	..	..	..	..	..	58
Native of foreign parentage	94	..	..	..	..	..	..	..	94
Foreign of foreign parentage	21	..	..	..	..	..	..	..	21
Civil Check Samples = 3,203									
Sane = 1,976									
Native White	167	146	..	..	..	..	..	..	313
Native of foreign parentage	289	..	..	..	..	..	..	..	289
Foreign of foreign parentage	307	..	..	..	..	..	..	..	307
College Negro	..	31	..	..	47	..	..	..	78
College Negroid	..	153	..	..	398	..	..	..	551
Non-college Negro	42	186	..	..	..	..	..	..	228
Non-college Negroid	41	169	..	..	..	..	..	..	210
Insane = 1,227									
Native White	134	..	..	..	..	..	166	..	300
Native of foreign parentage	138	..	..	..	..	..	91	..	229
Foreign of foreign parentage	165	..	..	..	..	..	135	..	300
Negro	..	..	..	..	73	..	..	..	73
Negroid	..	..	..	..	325	..	..	..	325
Totals by States	5,685	1,730	2,087	2,496	1,670	738	1,749	921	17,076

writer was not satisfied with the size of the check sample, the summer of 1929 was devoted to the gathering of the additional material from the Massachusetts General Hospital and the Beth Israel Hospital.

The summer of 1928 was spent in the calculation of indices by the laboratory staff, enlarged temporarily to about 25 members by the inclusion of the graduates of a statistical course at Simmons College. In the space of three months 13 indices were calculated and recalculated (by way of check) for every one of approximately 17,000 records. The next nine months witnessed the "precoding" of the raw data. A code was devised whereby the information on each recorded sheet was translated into numbers, ranging from 1 to 12, each fact being recorded in one of 80 appropriately numbered columns, corresponding with the numbered holes to be punched in the Hollerith sorting and tabulating cards. This process was enormously time-consuming. Then followed the punching and verifying of the actual cards. For each individual record a card was punched on a Hollerith key-punch machine. The card was then verified, either mechanically by punching a second card and superimposing the two, or by checking the card against the code numbers on the precoding sheet.

In the fall of 1929 most of the data were ready for the actual process of sorting, tabulating, and subsequent statistical reduction. The next three years carried through this prodigious labor, virtually to its conclusion — thanks to the skill, industry, and devotion of the statistical staff.

TECHNIQUE AND METHODS OF THE PRESENT SURVEY

ANTHROPOMETRIC TECHNIQUE

Training of Observers

All of the observers were graduate students who had specialized in Physical Anthropology, having taken lecture and laboratory courses under the writer. Before beginning the work they were given further instruction and practice in the taking of measurements and observations. The technique of measuring was demonstrated upon subjects and each observer practised until the results of his measurements were in agreement with those of the writer. For the first year the observers worked together in the same institutions, frequently comparing techniques and checking measurements to assure themselves of the comparability of their methods. After this they separated and worked in different states for nearly two years. This separation ultimately led to a divergence between the two principal observers in the technique of ear measurement, mentioned below,[25] and in the development of certain personal equations in morphological observation which are discussed hereafter.

The training in morphological observation consisted in the detailed observation of a number of subjects by the writer in the presence of the prospective field workers, followed by independent observations by the students and a checking, comparison, and discussion of details of difference and questionable points. The observers did not take the field until the writer was assured of the proper standardization of their observational technique and their fundamental agreement upon all points. However, morphological observations are extremely difficult, since the observer has to keep in mind an

[25] Page 61.

ideal standard of judgment, based upon his conception of the average or modal development of each feature in the adult male Northwestern European. Such an average adult male Northwestern European is conceived as of rather tall stature (172 centimeters or more), medium build, head neither pronouncedly dolichocephalic nor brachycephalic, face neither very long and thin, nor very short and broad — in fact all features developed in such a degree as to be inconspicuous and "ordinary" to the eye of the trained observer.

Instruments

Each observer was provided with the instruments listed below. All instruments were checked and rechecked on a standardized gauge provided by Dr. Aleš Hrdlička, United States National Museum, Washington, D. C.

1. Anthropometer. The standard, metrically calibrated anthropometers manufactured by P. Hermann, Rickenbach and Son, and by Alig and Baumgärtel were used. They were overhauled and rechecked at intervals, and when the joints were sprung, the points bent, or the butts worn, they were replaced.
2. Sliding caliper. Hermann, and Alig and Baumgärtel
3. Spreading caliper. Hermann, and Alig and Baumgärtel
4. Steel metric tape. Starret and Co.
5. Head spanners: (a) The Western Reserve head spanner. Manufactured in the Anatomical Laboratory of Western Reserve University by Professor T. Wingate Todd. This instrument has rubber-tipped rods which are inserted into the auditory meatus of the subject. An infra-orbital gauge permits the adjustment to the Frankfort plane. (Used by Observer A throughout and by Observers B and C in county jail series and civilian check sample.) (b) G. D. Williams head spanner. In this instrument the ends of steel rods are adjusted to the tragion notch and the head height is measured from the intertragia diameters. An infra-orbital gauge provides for the adjustment to the Frankfort plane. (Used by Observer B in his prison, criminal insane, and civil insane series.)
6. Scales. Standard beam scales were provided by the various institutions.

CLASSIFICATION OF DATA

Measurements

Some twenty odd measurements were taken on each subject.

1. Weight. (Standard beam scale.) The subjects were measured without hat, coat, shoes, or waistcoat, but otherwise with ordinary clothing. Allowances for clothing are discussed under the subject of weight.[26] The deduction which must be made is on the average 3 pounds. In analysis the grouping interval is 10 pounds. (In the case of the Massachusetts militia and the Tennessee firemen and Nashville Negroes most recent weights given by subjects were recorded. Since the grouping interval is 10 pounds the error due to this factor is probably negligible.)
2. Stature. (Anthropometer.) Height from vertex. The subject stands with heels together, arms hanging at side, shoulders erect, eyes directed horizontally, the head

[26] Chapter XI, pp. 202–203.

being in the eye-ear plane. The anthropometer is held directly in front of the subject, the butt upon the floor and the axis vertical. One hand manipulates the sliding sleeve of the anthropometer arm and the other guides the end of the arm into contact with the vertex. The reading is in centimeters and millimeters.[27] In analysis the grouping interval is 3 centimeters.

3. Biacromial diameter. (Anthropometer used as sliding caliper.) Breadth between acromion processes. The subject stands as in measurement 2. The observer places one hand on each of the arms of the anthropometer, finds the acromia by palpation and guides the points of the arms with index fingers to acromia.[28] In analysis the grouping interval is 3 centimeters.

4. Chest depth. (Anthropometer used as sliding caliper.) Antero-posterior diameter, at nipple level. This measurement is taken from the left side with the left arm of the subject hanging by his side, and the anthropometer (sliding caliper) between the subject's arm and the body wall. The fixed arm of the sliding caliper is held at the nipple level and the sliding arm is applied to the spinous processes of the thoracic vertebrae at a somewhat lower level, so that the diameter is perpendicular to the plane of the front wall of the chest. The point of application of sliding arms to vertebral spines is approximately at the level of the inferior angles of the scapulae. In analysis the grouping interval is 2 centimeters.

5. Chest breadth. (Anthropometer used as sliding caliper.) Breadth of the chest at nipple level. The subject stands as in measurement 2. The observer places the flat side of the sliding caliper against the chest at nipple level, standing in front of the subject and directing the sides of the anthropometric arms to contact with the lateral chest walls. The measurement is taken with the chest at rest, between inspiration and expiration, a mean being observed. The caliper arms are directed somewhat downward, being perpendicular to the front wall of the chest which slopes downward and forward.[29] In analysis the grouping interval used is 3 centimeters.

6. Sitting height. (Anthropometer.) Height from vertex to level of the plane upon which the subject is sitting in the most erect position possible. The subject sits upon a flat box or upon a table. The thighs are horizontal and the legs vertical. The observer feels the lumbar region to be sure that the lumbar curve is not relaxed and that the spine is held as nearly as possible in the erect standing position. The gluteal and extensor muscles of the thigh are relaxed, the subject resting on the ischial tuberosities. The head is in the eye-ear plane. The anthropometer is held vertical and the measurement taken from the rear.[30] In analysis the grouping interval is 3 centimeters.

7. Head length. (Spreading caliper.) Maximum glabello-occipital length in the median sagittal plane. The observer places the point of the fixed caliper arm on glabella, standing on the left of the subject and holding the caliper point between the thumb and first finger of his left hand. With his right hand he moves the left caliper up and down the median occipital line, watching the scale until a maximum reading is obtained. The left caliper point is fixed on glabella and no pressure is exerted.[31] In analysis the grouping interval is 3 millimeters.

[27] R. Martin, *Lehrbuch der Anthropologie* (2nd edition, Jena, 1928), I, 150.
[28] Martin, 1928, I, 159.
[20] Martin, 1928, I, 160.
[30] Martin, 1928, I, 156.   [31] Martin, 1928, I, 180.

8. Head breadth. (Spreading caliper.) Maximum breadth of the head perpendicular to the median sagittal plane. The observer holds the arms of the calipers just above their points, standing behind the subject. The points are applied lightly to the head, being kept in the same horizontal and lateral vertical plane. The points are moved forward and backward and up and down until a maximum reading is obtained, the observer watching the caliper scale. The horizontal arm of the caliper scale facilitates the keeping of the caliper points in the proper planes.[32] In analysis the grouping interval is 3 millimeters.

9. Head height. (Western Reserve and Williams head spanners.) Distance from vertex to middle of line connecting the centers of the auditory meatus (Western Reserve head spanner) or to the line connecting the tragia (Williams head spanner), in both cases the head in the eye-ear plane. The observer holds the spanner in the left hand, adjusts it to the subject with the right hand and manipulates the vertical sliding scale so that it comes in contact with the subject's vertex. In analysis the grouping interval is 3 millimeters.

10. Head circumference. (Steel metric tape.) Maximum head circumference above the brow ridges. The observer holds the free end of the tape in his left hand with his forefinger nail on the zero mark. This portion of the tape is held on the right temporal crest just above the brow ridge. With the right hand the tape is carried around the occiput at its most projecting point, crosses the temporal crest on the left side in a position corresponding to the fixed end of the right side, extends across the frontal and overlaps the zero point on the right temporal crest. Several readings are made in order to secure the maximum diameter. The observer pulls the tape tight so as to eliminate, as far as possible, differences due to thickness of hair. This measurement does not include the brow ridges.[33] The grouping interval is 12 millimeters.

11. Minimum frontal diameter. (Spreading caliper.) Smallest distance between the temporal crests on the frontal bone above the brow ridges. One arm of the spreading caliper, near the extremity, is held in each hand of the observer. With his forefingers he determines the points of nearest approximation of the temporal crests and applies the tips of the calipers to these points, recording the diameter between them. This measurement was correctly taken in the county jail series, but the rather high means of the prison-reformatory series and of the check sample indicate that both observers developed the habit of permitting the caliper points to slip back on the temporal muscles, thus adding from 2 millimeters to 4 millimeters to the true minimum frontal diameter. Consequently, this measurement, as recorded in the majority of the series, is in reality the breadth of the frontal bone between the postorbital constrictions. In analysis the grouping interval is 4 millimeters.

12. Bizygomatic diameter. (Spreading caliper.) Maximum diameter between the zygomatic arches. The observer holds the caliper arms near the extremities in his right and left hands between thumbs and second fingers and with his forefingers palpates to make sure that the points of the calipers are on the zygomatic arches. The instrument is moved forward and backward until a maximum reading is obtained, care being taken that the caliper points are kept in the same horizontal and lateral vertical plane.[34] The grouping interval is 5 millimeters.

[32] Martin, 1928, I, 182.
[33] Martin, 1928, I, 194.

[34] Martin, 1928, I, 183.

13. Total face height. (Sliding caliper.) Distance from nasion (midpoint of the naso-frontal suture) to gnathion (midpoint on the lower border of the mandibular symphysis). Nasion is located by running the thumb nail of the right hand up the bridge of the nose (the surface of the nail against the nose) until the edge of the thumb nail finds the groove which marks the naso-frontal suture. The nail is then pressed into the flesh so as to leave an indentation, marking the site of the suture. The upper, or fixed arm of the sliding caliper, is held in the left hand between the thumb and the first finger, the little finger and the ulnar side of the palm resting against the forehead of the subject to hold the caliper steady. The point of the fixed caliper arm is now applied to nasion and held there with the left hand resting against the forehead. The right hand manipulates the moving arm of the caliper and applies the point of it to the middle of the under surface of the mandible. Care is taken that the mouth of the subject is closed and the teeth in occlusion.[35] The grouping interval is 5 millimeters.

14. Upper face height. (Sliding caliper.) Height from nasion to alveolar point. The caliper is manipulated as in the total face height except that the lower landmark is the point on the gums of the subject between the upper median incisor teeth. The upper lip of the subject is lifted by the lower and sliding arm of the caliper, but the point of the caliper does not come into actual contact with teeth or gum. The caliper is cleansed after this measurement in a sterilizing solution. Another method of reaching the point without touching the caliper to the lips is to have the subject retract the upper lip. This, however, is likely to move the skin in the nasion region, thus displacing the nail indentation which marks the naso-frontal suture.[36] The grouping interval is 5 millimeters.

15. Nose height. (Sliding caliper.) Height from nasion to subnasale. The caliper is manipulated as in the two preceding measurements except that the lower landmark is the juncture of the nasal septum with the lip.[37] The grouping interval is 4 millimeters.

16. Nose breadth. (Sliding caliper.) Maximum breadth between the most lateral points of the nasal alae. This is a contact measurement and no compression of the alae is effected by the caliper arms.[38] The grouping interval is 3 millimeters.

17. Bigonial diameter. (Sliding caliper.) Diameter between the gonia (hinder inferior angles of the mandible). The spreading caliper arms are held in the hands and the index fingers locate the most laterally projecting angles of the mandible at the junction of the ascending rami with the horizontal rami.[39] In analysis the grouping interval is 4 millimeters.

18. Ear length. (Sliding caliper.) Distance from the uppermost point on the helix to the lowest point on the lobe. The left hand holds the upper fixed arm of the caliper with the measuring scale parallel with the long axis of the ear. The right hand brings the sliding arm into contact with the lowest point of the ear. The left ear is measured.[40] In analysis the grouping interval is 4 millimeters.

19. Ear breadth. (Sliding caliper.) (a) Observer B. Distance from the most posterior point on the helix to the line marking the insertion of the ear. The caliper is held horizontally with the measuring scale above the ear and the fixed arm (flat end) tangent to the insertion of the ear and parallel to its long axis. With the right hand the

[35] Martin, 1928, I, 187.
[36] Martin, 1928, I, 187.
[37] Martin, 1928, I, 188.

[38] Martin, 1928, I, 185.
[39] Martin, 1928, I, 183.
[40] Martin, 1928, I, 190.

sliding arm of the caliper is brought into contact with the most posterior point on the border of the helix.[41]

(b) Observer A. Observer A deviated from the technique described above. He held the caliper horizontally above the ear and measured from the upper point of ear insertion to the posterior point on the edge of the helix. This measurement yields means 2–3 millimeters more than the standard technique, and for this reason, the data of Observer A and of Observer B have been separated in analysis.

20. Other measurements taken, but not included in the analysis:

       a. Height of acromion (Anthropometer)

       b. Height of dactylion (Anthropometer)

       c. Total hand length (Sliding caliper)

       d. Palm length (Sliding caliper)

       e. Palm breadth (Sliding caliper). Hand measurements were taken on relatively few subjects.

Indices

The following indices were calculated from the data:

1.	Relative shoulder breadth.	Biacromial diameter × 100 / stature
2.	Relative sitting height.	Sitting height × 100 / stature
3.	Cephalic index.	Head breadth × 100 / head length
4.	Cephalo-facial index.	Bizygomatic diameter × 100 / head breadth
5.	Length-height index.[42]	Head height × 100 / head length
6.	Breadth-height index.[42]	Head height × 100 / head breadth
7.	Facial index.	Total face height × 100 / bizygomatic diameter
8.	Upper facial index.	Upper face height × 100 / bizygomatic diameter
9.	Nasal index.	Nose breadth × 100 / nose height
10.	Ear index.[42]	Ear breadth × 100 / ear length
11.	Zygo-frontal index.	Minimum frontal diameter × 100 / bizygomatic diameter
12.	Fronto-parietal index.	Minimum frontal diameter × 100 / head breadth
13.	Zygo-gonial index.	Bigonial diameter × 100 / bizygomatic diameter

Sociological Observations

The sociological observations included in the survey were, for the most part, confined to such elementary facts as could be gathered from the prison records, since the resources of the project did not permit the employment of independent sociological investigators. In the case of a selected sample of the county jail prisoners, both sociological and psychological data were gathered by expert field workers of the Massachusetts State Department of Mental Diseases. Most of the sociological facts were

[41] Martin, 1928, I, 190.
[42] Data of each observer calculated separately.

copied directly from the prison and reformatory records, but in some few instances it was necessary to supplement the information so acquired by personal interrogation of the prisoners. Such questions were reduced to the indispensable minimum on account of the possibility of subjects furnishing false information. None of the sociological information could be checked, but there is little doubt that it is, in the main, accurate. It has not, however, the absolute validity which characterizes the measurements and observations made directly upon the persons of the prisoners.

At the outset of the investigation the writer had ambitions to send into the field psychological and sociological investigators as well as anthropologists, but it very soon became evident that all of his energies would be necessary to finance, even inadequately, the two anthropometric observers who were actually the principal collectors of the data. In many of the institutions visited the field workers copied out extensive excerpts from the prison and hospital records, including social and medical histories. Only a limited use of these had been made in analysis on account of the vast bulk of data. In the following pages the nature of the sociological and genealogical data will be explained and discussed. The information gathered is as follows:

1. Name. Recorded, but not utilized in analysis.

2. Age. This was recorded as the age at the last birthday. It was checked from the prison records. In analysis the grouping interval is 5 years.

3. Sex. All of the individuals studied were adult males, with the exception of a small group of adult females from the State Reformatory at Sherborn, Massachusetts. This group has been omitted from the analysis.

4. Occupation. This information was secured from the records. The writer has entertained a considerable skepticism as to the reality of many of the occupations assigned — largely because of the considerable number of prisoners who are really professional criminals or persons of no occupation. However, this skepticism has been diminished considerably in the course of detailed analysis of the data, because of the high correlations displayed between occupation and various sociological and physical characters. It is also perfectly obvious to anyone who has dealt extensively with prisoners that the degree of imaginativeness necessary for the invention of many of the occupations listed is quite outside of the range of average criminal possibilities. Few criminals are gifted — even in mendacity. The details of occupation have been tabulated, but are not published here. For purposes of this investigation, occupations have been classified according to a scheme devised by Dr. Winfred Overholser, which is a modification of the classification utilized by the United States Census. Since the investigation was originally undertaken to provide comparative data for the sociological and psychiatric survey of county jail prisoners in Massachusetts carried on by the Massachusetts Department of Mental Diseases, we have naturally adopted insofar as practicable, the sociological classifications utilized in that survey. The classification follows:

a. Extractive. Agriculture, forestry, animal husbandry, fishing, mining

b. Laborers. Unskilled, odd jobs, and not otherwise specified

c. Semi-skilled laborers and factory operatives. Laundry workers, machinists, mechanics, stationary engineers, structural iron-workers, firemen, blacksmiths, factory workers in general

   d. Transportation. Teamsters, chauffeurs, truckmen, expressmen, railroad and
       street-railway employees, sailors (except Navy)
   e. Skilled trades. Building trades, electricians, paper hangers, painters
   f. Trade. Storekeepers, clerks in stores, commercial travellers, real estate,
       insurance
   g. Public service. Policemen, mail carriers, firemen, soldiers, Navy sailors
   h. Semi-professional. Draftsmen, photographers, musicians, actors, under-
       takers, telegraphers
   i. Professional. Doctors, lawyers, ministers, teachers
   j. Personal service. Restaurant workers, barbers, elevator men, janitors, por-
       ters, practical nurses, attendants in hospitals, cleaners
   k. Clerical. Clerks, book-keepers, accountants
   l. All others, none, or not observed

5. Religion. The religious affiliations of the subjects were recorded.

6. Offense. The offense of the subject was copied from the prison records. In
analysis the offenses of prison and reformatory inmates were classified according to the
following scheme:

   a. First degree murder
   b. Second degree murder and other lesser homicide
   c. Assault and all other personal violence (except rape)
   d. Robbery
   e. Burglary (breaking and entering), larceny, receiving stolen goods
   f. Forgery, fraud
   g. Rape
   h. Other sex offenses
   i. Offenses against public welfare (health and safety), including carrying con-
       cealed weapons, traffic in narcotics, illegal practice of profession, violating
       liquor laws, violating automobile laws
   j. Arson and all other offenses

In the county jail group a more elaborate classification was adopted in dealing with
the sample the data of which were to be correlated with the sociological and psychiatric
facts gained by the survey of the State Department of Mental Diseases.

Naturally there are defects in this offense classification, which is in the nature of a
compromise. Under larceny, for example, there are doubtless included many offenses
which are really fraudulent and should properly fall into the class of forgery and fraud.
Our data do not permit us to investigate the nature of the offense. We must accept the
mere statement of the record. On account of the many subgroups into which our material had to be divided on the basis of race and nationality, it was imperative that the
offense classification be kept as simple as possible, in order that the groups finally selected for analysis should be of sufficient size to furnish representative samples.

7. Previous convictions, length of sentence. Previous convictions were noted, when
they appeared upon the prison records. In analysis this material was divided into
three categories — "Yes," "No," and "Unknown or not observed." Undoubtedly the
number of individuals with previous convictions is in reality much greater than the
prison records show. The data on length of sentence were not analyzed.

8. Education. The following categories were adopted from Dr. Overholser's scheme for the analysis of educational qualifications:

a. Illiterate
b. Read and write (no schooling)
c. 1st–5th grade
d. 6th grade
e. 7th grade
f. 8th grade
g. High school or business college, 1st–2nd
h. High school or business college, 3rd–4th
i. College, 1–4
j. Professional school
k. Not observed or unknown

9. Race, parentage. The primary racial and parentage classification was as follows:

a. White, native born of native parentage
b. White, native born of foreign or mixed parentage
c. White, foreign born
d. Negro
e. Negroid (mixed Negro and White)
f. Indian (pure or mixed)
g. Other
h. Unknown
i. Not observed

The birthplaces of each subject and of his father and mother and the nationality of each were recorded. In native born of native parentage the ethnic elements known to exist in the ancestry were reported under the headings "Extraction of Father," "Extraction of Mother." On the basis of these data the subjects were divided into groups: native White of native parentage, native White of foreign or mixed parentage subdivided by nationality of parents, and foreign White — again subdivided according to nationality. Since the present volume deals only with native Whites of native parentage, the classification and grouping of nationalities adopted for the native Whites of foreign parentage and for the native Whites of foreign birth will not be discussed here. These groups will be analyzed in the second volume of the results of the study, together with the civil and criminal insane — native White of native parentage, native White of foreign parentage, and foreign born White. The data relating to the birthplace of subjects and their extraction, in the case of native Whites of native parentage, have been tabulated, but no group sortings by extraction or place of birth have been made.

10. Marital State, offspring. Marital status was recorded in the following categories:

a. Single
b. Married
c. Divorced or separated
d. Widower
e. Unknown
f. Not observed

The number and sex of offspring of the prisoner were noted on the raw data blanks, but this information has not been tabulated.

Psychological Data

The mental classification of subjects and the grouping of intelligence quotients were adopted from the scheme devised by Dr. Winfred Overholser for the survey conducted by the Massachusetts State Department of Mental Diseases. Unfortunately the data secured were scanty, since we were obliged to confine ourselves to the copying of such records as were available in the various institutions, except in the limited sample of Massachusetts county jail prisoners studied by Dr. Overholser. The following categories were utilized:

1. Mental Classification
   a. Alcoholism
   b. Drug addiction
   c. Epilepsy
   d. Low normal or borderline intelligence
   e. Mental deficiency
   f. Psychopathic personality
   g. Dementia praecox, manic depressive psychosis
   h. Alcoholic psychosis
   i. Traumatic, senile, or arteriosclerotic psychosis
   j. General paresis
   k. Other psychosis or neurosis
   l. None

2. Intelligence Quotient
   a. 45 or under
   b. 46–55
   c. 56–65
   d. 66–75
   e. 76–85
   f. 86–95
   g. 96–105
   h. 106 or over
   i. Not observed
   j. Estimated feeble-minded
   k. Estimated low normal or borderline intelligence
   l. Estimated average intelligence

Morphological Observations

Each character is graded, when present, on a five-fold scale: very small, submedium, medium, large, and very large.[43] The grade "medium" does not represent a mean or mode on a frequency curve, but rather such an area and position in the curve as is delimited by a line on each side of the mean at a distance of 1 sigma from the mean. Thus the "medium" category should include rather more than half of a normally constituted series. Of course such a conception is purely theoretical, but it is translated into practice in the observations by remembering that the "medium" class includes a fairly wide range of variation and that the extreme categories should be reserved for extreme cases — that when in doubt, classification should be "medium."

The following morphological observations were taken:[44]

1. Moles, tattooing, freckles
2. Hair quantity
   a. Head
   b. Beard
   c. Body
3. Skin color. Red white, pale white, ruddy, olive, light yellow-brown, light brown, medium yellow-brown, medium red-brown, copper, dark brown, black
4. Hair form. Straight, low waves, deep waves, curly, frizzly, woolly
5. Hair texture. Coarse, medium, fine
6. Hair color. Black, dark brown, reddish brown, light brown, ash-blond, golden, red, gray

[43] In analysis some of the five-fold grades have been reduced to three.
[44] Categories have been listed for those observations which cannot be graded.

7. Eye color. Black, dark brown, light brown, blue-brown, gray-brown, green-brown, blue, gray
8. Sclera. Clear, speckled, yellow
9. Iris. Homogeneous, rayed, zoned, speckled, diffuse
10. Eye folds. Epicanthus, median, external
11. Palpebral opening
   a. Height
   b. Obliquity up or down
12. Eyebrows
   a. Thickness
   b. Concurrency
   c. Lateral extension
13. Brow ridges
   a. Size
   b. Form. Median, continuous
   c. Glabella
14. Forehead
   a. Height
   b. Breadth
   c. Slope
15. Nose
   a. Nasion depression
   b. Nasal root. Height, breadth
   c. Nasal bridge. Height, breadth
   d. Nasal profile. Concave, straight, convex, concavo-convex
   e. Nasal tip. Thickness; elevation or depression
   f. Nasal wings. Compressed, medium, flaring
   g. Nasal septum. Straight, concave, convex; inclination up or down; deflection right or left
   h. Fracture
   i. Acne
16. Lips
   a. Integumental thickness
   b. Membranous thickness
   c. Seam
17. Prognathism
   a. Alveolar
   b. Facial
18. Chin
   a. Prominence
   b. Form. Median, bilateral
19. Malars prominence
20. Cheeks fullness
21. Gonial angles
22. Wrinkling

23. Teeth
    a. Eruption. Complete, unerupted
    b. Wear
    c. Caries
    d. Lost
    e. Shovel incisors
24. Bite. Under, edge-to-edge, slight over, marked over
25. Palate
    a. Height
    b. Breadth
26. Mouth breather
27. Ears
    a. Lobes. Development; form: attached or free, notched, divided
    b. Roll of helix
    c. Darwin's point
    d. Antihelix
    e. Protrusion
28. Temporal fullness
29. Occipital protrusion
30. Lambdoid flattening
31. Facial asymmetry
32. Neck
    a. Length
    b. Thickness
33. Shoulders slope

Pathology

Since our anthropometric survey did not include a medical examination, pathological data were confined to those copied from the records. Except in a few of the Massachusetts institutions and in the sample of county jail prisoners studied by Dr. Overholser, these records were so scanty as to be of little value. The results have been tabulated, but are not worthy of publication.

ANALYSIS OF DATA

Preliminary Statistical and Clerical Work

The individual record blanks sent in by the field workers were in excess of 17,100. These were filed according to states and institutions. Thirteen indices were calculated for each subject and were rechecked by a second calculation. The indices within the range of Furst's *Index-Tabellen* [45] were taken from that work. The others were divided out on Marchant and Monroe electric calculating machines. Upon each individual record sheet was stamped a serial combination of numbers indicating its classification as to state, institution, race, and parentage.

It was now necessary to devise a code whereby the metric, morphological, and sociological data pertaining to each individual could be transferred to a Hollerith punch

[45] C. M. Furst, *Index-Tabellen zum Anthropometrischen Gebrauche* (Jena, 1902).

card. This having been done, the required data for each individual were stamped on a special precoding sheet, which was virtually an enlarged copy of the standard Hollerith punch card, especially divided with column headings to suit the arrangement of the code for the investigation. On each precoding sheet the serial number of the subject was stamped. The precoding sheets were used by the key punch operators as guides for the punching of the Hollerith tabulating cards.

Electric Sorting and Tabulating Apparatus

Although the use of mechanical and electrical sorting and tabulating apparatus is well known in the commercial and statistical world, the application of these devices to anthropometric research has been limited and, consequently, the machines, the method of their employment, and the possibilities of analysis which they afford may be described briefly here.[46]

The basic unit of the electric tabulating method is the tabulating card, which is designed to contain all data pertinent to a given subject. Holes punched in the card at various points represent the information which is to be handled. The cards are available in capacities ranging from 34 to 80 columns of digits, each column provided with spaces for the punching of holes numbered from o to 11. In this survey an 80-column card was used. The columns are divided into groups or "fields," each of which is headed with a descriptive caption. The groups or fields are arranged according to the requirements of the data. The cards come in various colors, so that different colors may be used for various classes of material.

Raw information is recorded on the cards by a key punch, the keys of which are operated like those of a typewriter. The machine has twelve punching keys, each of which governs the punching of one of a vertical line of digits on the card. The zero key punches in the zero position on the card, the 1 key in the 1 position, et cetera. Thus if "black" hair is represented in the code by hole 1 of column 54, the operator, upon reaching that column, presses key 1.

Punched card production ranges from a few hundred to 5000 per eight-hour day, according to the quantity of information to be recorded and the skill of the operator. In the present survey, a skilled operator recording some 125 items of information concerning each subject on a single card, can produce 300–400 cards in a seven-hour day.

The verifier is used to prove mechanically the accuracy of the punching. It is operated similarly to the key punch. The original data are used as the source of information and when the key action coincides with the previously punched holes the machine feeds the cards to the left. When a key cannot be depressed, the passage of the card is stopped, signifying that an error has been made. The unverified part of the card is invisible to the operator, so that no suggestion of the previous punching can influence the operator. When the data to be put upon the card are very complex, involving the subdivision of many columns (double, triple or quadruple punching), the most effective method of verification is the punching of a second card. This is superimposed upon the original card and errors are revealed by failures of the holes in the

[46] All of the apparatus employed in the sorting and tabulating of the data of this survey has been furnished by the Tabulating Machine Company Division of the International Business Machines Corporation. The description of the machines and their utilization has been adapted from the descriptive material provided by that organization.

HOLLERITH ELECTRIC CARD PUNCHER

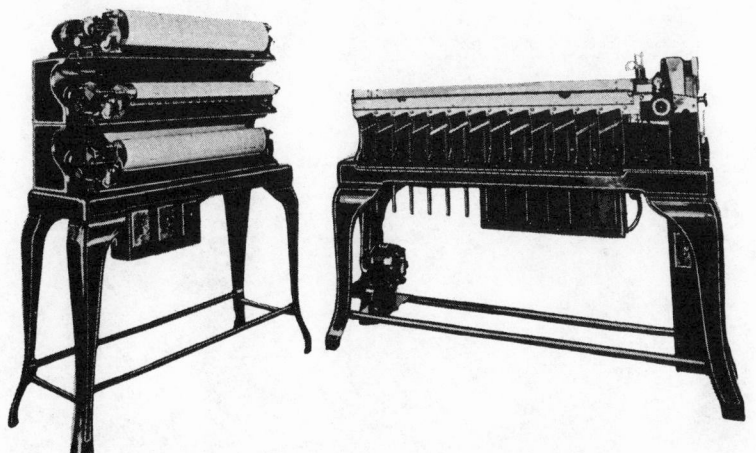

THREE BANK PRINTING
CARD COUNTER

HOLLERITH ELECTRIC
CARD SORTER

(Courtesy of the International Business Machines Corporation)

two cards to coincide. Both methods of verification were employed in this survey, but the last named has now entirely superseded the use of the mechanical verifier, which checks only the first hole punched in any single column and is consequently inefficient in double punched cards. The electric duplicating key punch is used to duplicate automatically cards already punched which have become worn, or of which copies are desired. With this machine, also, it is necessary to use the keys to punch subdivided columns, since it operates automatically only upon the first hole punched in any single column.

The data on the punched cards are tabulated by the electric card-counting, printing sorter. The cards are fed into the sorter which distributes them at the rate of 400 per minute into twelve pockets, each of the latter corresponding to one of the numbered holes in a single column on the tabulating card. The sorter may be set to sort upon any one of the 80 columns of the card. The printing card-counter operates simultaneously with the sorter. This device totals the count for each position punched in any particular column of digits on the cards and prints these totals. The two machines, operating in unison, sort on one column and simultaneously total the count in that and two additional columns. Thus, if a miscellaneous group of the cards representing individual subjects of the survey, is fed into the sorter, the latter, sorting on column 1, divides these cards into racial subgroups, prints the totals of each of these racial subgroups, at the same time counting and printing the numbers in each parentage classification (columns 2 and 3).

By the use of this Hollerith sorting and counting apparatus the seriations of the frequencies of any measurement or observation are produced in an incredibly short time, correlation tables are built up, and individual types characterized by any given combination of physical and sociological features are distinguished and enumerated. This apparatus enlarges almost infinitely the possibilities of statistical anthropological analysis of anthropometric data. In a few minutes it carries through and prints the results of sorting and counting processes which would require whole days and perhaps weeks of labor by a large clerical staff, if the operations were done by hand.

The system also provides for the totalizing of punched tabulating cards by means of the tabulating machine which adds the digits in each column, but this accounting machine is not utilized in the analysis of the class of data represented in this survey, since the numbered holes on the punch cards do not correspond to digits of numerical significance but are code numbers which represent grouped frequencies or observational characters. When the actual raw measurements are punched into the cards, utilizing the corresponding numbers of the holes in one or more columns, the tabulating machine carries through most of the adding processes necessary for the computation of such constants as the coefficient of correlation.

After the data are sorted and counted, the frequencies and totals are copied on special printed summary sheets which reproduce the code numbers and categories of the various measurements, indices, and observations; provide spaces for the insertion of frequencies and for the recording of the means, standard deviations, coefficients of variation, probable errors, and percentages. Special coordinate paper is used for correlation and contingency tables.

The computations are done on Marchant and Monroe electric calculating machines which perform addition, subtraction, multiplication, and division automatically. Each statistical constant is calculated by one computer and checked by a second. The final stage of the reduction of data consists in the compilation of tables.

Statistical Methods

The methods of statistical analysis employed in this survey are, in general, those commonly used by biometricians, with some modification and simplification. In detail of plan, the treatment corresponds roughly to that of Goring's "English Convict," although there are certain radical divergences of viewpoint and usage, most of which have been discussed above. The statistical constants most frequently employed are the arithmetic mean, the standard deviation, the coefficient of variation, the product moment coefficient of correlation, the correlation ratio, the coefficient of mean square contingency, and the probable errors of these constants. A brief discussion of these statistical devices follows.

The Frequency Distribution. Measurements are applied only to quantities which can present more than one numerical value. Such variables must be noted down, not arbitrarily as they happen to occur, but in some regular ranking or classification, in order that the mind may grasp the significance of the record. The intervals of the classes of measurements should be equidistant and may correspond to a single unit of measurement, such as a millimeter, or to any specified and convenient number of such units. The manner in which the observations are distributed over successive equal intervals of a scale is called the frequency distribution. The first step in the arrangement of metric data is to classify the observations according to their frequencies in each successive division of the frequency scale. This classification is called a seriation. Such a seriation of a group of observations of stature will give the number of individuals in each stature group from the lowest to the highest. The groups or class intervals may be single centimeters or greater. As soon as a seriation has been prepared, we can see at a glance the range (maximum and minimum of the series), and the classes which contain the greatest and least number of frequencies. We begin to comprehend the composition, dispersion, and central trend of the seriation.

When frequencies are plotted on squared paper, with the horizontal base line indicating the values of the class intervals on a scale (the abscissa) and the vertical lines representing by their heights the numbers of observations or frequencies (the ordinates), the points representing the frequencies at the intersections of the vertical and horizontal lines may be joined together by straight lines. The diagram thus completed is called a frequency polygon. If the class intervals are made smaller and smaller and the numbers of observations proportionately increased the frequency polygon will approach more and more closely to a smooth curve. This is termed a frequency curve. The most usual curve in anthropometric measurements is the symmetrical distribution. This type of distribution is found in most, if not all anthropological measurements. In this distribution the class frequencies decrease to zero symmetrically on either side of a central maximum. Moderately asymmetrical distributions may occur, in which the class frequencies decrease with greater rapidity on one side of the maximum than on the other. Such an asymmetrical frequency is found often in observations of weight.

The properties of the frequency distribution must be analyzed in any study and comparison of series of anthropometric measurements. The most important properties to be studied are the averages or maximum points of the distributions, their dispersions or spreads, and their relative dispersions or variabilities. These involve the determination of the arithmetic mean, the standard deviation, and the coefficient of variation.

The Arithmetic Mean. The arithmetic mean of a series is the quotient of the sum of the values of the variable divided by their number. It is often designated by the simple word "mean" or "average." In this survey the arithmetic mean is approximated by forming a frequency table and treating all the values in each class as if they were identical with the mid-value of the class interval. The class interval is treated throughout as the unit of measurement and the difference between the mean and the mid-value of some arbitrarily chosen class interval is computed instead of the value of the mean.[47]

The Standard Deviation. This is the square root of the arithmetic mean of the squares of all deviations measured from the arithmetic mean of the series of observations. If the standard deviation be denoted by σ, and the deviation from the arithmetic mean by x, the sum of values by Σ, and the number of observations by N, then $\sigma^2 = \dfrac{1}{N}\Sigma(x^2)$. The squaring of the deviations from the mean is for the purpose of eliminating differences in signs of the deviations, since the simple sum of the plus and minus deviations from the mean is necessarily zero. The standard deviation is a measure of the dispersion of a series. It measures roughly the average degree to which each individual event in a series may be expected to deviate from the mean of the series. Since the comparison of anthropometric series is based upon the dispersion or variability of the series, as well as the position of the mean, this constant is of great importance. The range also expresses the spread or dispersion, but it is likely to be dependent upon the size of the series and is in no way so valuable as the standard deviation.

In a grouped frequency distribution, the formula for the calculation of the standard deviation is $\sigma = \sqrt{\dfrac{\Sigma(f\xi^2)}{N}}$, if Σ be the sum of all values, ξ the deviations from the mean in terms of class frequencies, f the frequencies in any class interval, N the number of observations, and σ the standard deviation.[48]

The Coefficient of Variation. This is the ratio of the absolute measure of dispersion to the mean from which the deviations were measured. It is in fact the percentage ratio of the standard deviation to the arithmetic mean. The formula is $v = 100 \cdot \dfrac{\sigma}{M}$, where v represents the coefficient of variation, σ the standard deviation, and M the arithmetic mean. Since its magnitude is independent of the units of measurement employed it may be used conveniently as means of comparing the variabilities of measurements of different magnitudes, as for example the length of the head and the breadth of the nose.[49]

The Coefficient of Correlation. When two variables are related to each other in such a way that an alteration in the value of one is accompanied by an alteration of

---

[47] G. Udney Yule, *An Introduction to the Theory of Statistics* (8th edition, London, 1927), pp. 108–116. (Most of the explanations of statistical constants in this section are adapted from this standard work.)

[48] Yule, 1927, p. 134 ff.

[49] Yule, 1927, p. 149.

value in the other, they are said to be correlated. If alteration in the value of one of a pair of variables is unaccompanied by any change of value in the other, they are uncorrelated. It is often of great importance in anthropometric analysis to secure some means of measuring the correlation between two variables — as, for example, the height of the nose and the breadth of the nose. A perfect correlation implies that any given change of the value of one of the two variables is accompanied by a regular change in the value of the other — that, infallibly, an increment of a certain amount to head length is accompanied by an increment of a proportionate, although not necessarily equal amount, to head breadth. When the increase of a value of one of a pair of variables is accompanied by an increase in the other, the correlation is said to be positive; when an increase in one variable is accompanied by a decrease in the other, the correlation is negative.

Professor Karl Pearson has devised a method for measuring such a relationship between two variables and has called it the product moment coefficient of correlation. It measures on a scale from zero to unity the extent to which the value of one of a pair of variables is affected by an alteration in the value of the other. Thus a correlation coefficient of less than .25 indicates that on the whole the relationship between the two variables, although appreciable, is small. A coefficient of .50 indicates that the relationship is important, and one of .75 that it is very close indeed. It should be noted, however, that a high correlation does not necessarily imply that the change in one of the two variables actually causes the change in the other. Both may be effected by a common force which acts upon them equally and simultaneously, so that they are not interdependent, although their values alter in association.

There are a number of important uses of such a coefficient of correlation in anthropological analysis. For example it enables the student to ascertain to what extent bodily proportions remain constant when body size is altered. High correlations between many pairs of bodily measurements indicate that a certain homogeneity of body type is preserved through various alterations of body size. In some instances there is a causal implication in a correlation, as when it is shown that stature is positively correlated with age up to the period of maturity, although, even here, it can scarcely be argued that the increase of stature is caused by age, since it is in reality due to growth factors which are operative during certain ages and which cause a cumulative increase of body height.

Under certain conditions, the so-called regression equations, which are derived from the coefficient of correlation, may be used to predict the value of one of two correlated variables for any assigned value of the other. Charles Goring's use of such predictions has been discussed previously (pp. 20–21).

The derivation of the formula for the calculation of the product moment coefficient of correlation and the various arithmetical steps of the process are described in all standard works on biometric statistics and need not be repeated here. The formula is usually expressed thus: $r = \Sigma(xy)/N \cdot \sigma_x\ \sigma_y$, if r is the coefficient of correlation, $\Sigma\ (xy)$ the sum of the cross products of the deviations of the pairs of variables from their respective means, N the total number of observations, and σ_x, σ_y the standard deviations of the two variables, respectively X and Y.

The correlation ratio is a measure used to obtain a general expression of the extent to which the means of subgroups or arrays deviate from the mean of the series comprising all of the observations of the arrays. The deviations are to be interpreted in this sense as root mean square deviations of the subgroups, each weighted by the number of individuals in the subgroup. The formula is

$$\eta = \sqrt{[\,\{\,n_1(m_1 - M) + n_2(m_2 - M) + \ldots\,\}\,/N\,]}\,\big/\,\sigma_M$$

when n_1, n_2, n_3, et cetera represent the number of individuals in the respective subgroups, m_1, m_2, m_3, et cetera, the means of the respective subgroups, M the mean of the total group, N the total number of individuals, and σ_M the standard deviation of the entire series. This correlation ratio varies from zero to unity, as does the product moment coefficient of correlation, but it should be noted that it measures only the average extent to which the means of the subgroup differ from that of the entire series. If one of the subgroups is very large, and the others comparatively small, since the deviations are weighted by the number of individuals in each subgroup, the value of the correlation ratio will be necessarily low, unless the mean of the preponderant subgroup differs markedly from that of the entire series of which it may constitute the largest proportion. Thus in all criminals classified according to offense groups, the larceny group far exceeds any other offense group in numbers and is likely to constitute some 40–50 per cent of the total series. Accordingly, correlation ratios are inevitably low, since the deviation of the preponderant subgroup from the total mean to which it contributes the majority of individual observations is necessarily small. Hence small correlation ratios are often of much greater significance than their value on a scale from zero to unity would appear, upon first glance, to indicate.[50]

The Coefficient of Mean Square Contingency. When we deal with the presence or absence of some attribute, as opposed to the metric values of some variable, the product moment coefficient of correlation and the correlation ratio are not generally applicable and cannot be used, save upon certain assumptions which need not be entertained here. Professor Karl Pearson's coefficient of mean square contingency permits the measurement on a scale from zero to unity of the degree of association of pairs of attributes, without any assumption as to their continuous distribution in a scale of variation and irrespective of the order in which these pairs of attributes occur. Thus, if it is desired to measure the association between hair color and eye color, or between type of offense and hair color, such a coefficient is most useful. What the coefficient of mean square contingency actually measures is the degree to which the various combinations of pairs of attributes depart from a purely chance distribution or from independence. According to the law of probability if the frequency of A_m's be denoted by (A_m) and the frequency of B_n's by (B_n), and the frequency of objects or individuals possessing both characters by $(A_m B_n)$, then if A's and B's be completely independent in the universe at large, $(A_m B_n) = \dfrac{(A_m)(B_n)}{N} = (A_m B_n)_0$. In other words the expected

frequency of combination of pairs of attributes is equal to the product of the total number of frequencies of attribute A in the series and the total number of frequencies of attribute B in the series divided by N (the total number of observations of the series). $(A_m B_n)_0$ may be called the independence frequency. The coefficient of mean square contingency is based upon the difference between the expected or independence

---

[50] Cf. pp. 25–27 for a discussion of this constant.

frequencies and the actual frequencies. However, since some of the differences are minus and some are plus, a mere addition might cancel them out. Therefore in order to obviate the difficulty the differences are squared and expressed as a ratio of the expected frequencies. Thus we have

$$\sum \left(\frac{[(A_m B_n) - (A_m B_n)_0]^2}{(A_m B_n)_0} \right)$$ and by reduction, since the sum of both the $(A\ B)$'s

and the $(A\ B)_0$'s is equal to the total number of observations, N :

$$\sum \left\{ \frac{(A_m B_n)^2}{(A_m B_n)_0} \right\} - N.$$

The expression in brackets is then the sum of the squares of the actual frequencies of pairs of attributes divided by their expected (independence) frequencies. If this expression be denoted by S, we have for C, the coefficient of mean square contingency,

$$C = \sqrt{\frac{S - N}{S}}.$$[51] This coefficient expresses on a scale between zero and unity the

extent to which pairs of attributes in their actual combinations depart from chance expectation.

The coefficient of mean square contingency can be zero only when there is no deviation from the independent frequency in any compartment of the table. Such a condition cannot be realized in limited samples and consequently the coefficient is more than zero in any case. In other words, some part of the value of the coefficient is attributable to the sampling process. A correction for this may be introduced,[52] but this is hardly necessary if the coefficient is interpreted with caution. In any event, the coefficient indicates nothing more than the extent to which the associations of the two attributes depart from independence. The actual nature of the relationship between the attributes can be ascertained only by consulting the contingency tables in which the associations of the attributes are listed. From such a table it is quite easy to determine whether the value of the coefficient is due to erratic and random distribution of the frequencies of paired attributes, or on the other hand whether it is due to a consistent association of attributes, which in their graded categories correspond to increasing or decreasing values of actual variables.

In this work the coefficient of mean square contingency is used as a general measure of association between non-measurable, qualitative attributes, but no significance is attached to moderate or high values of the coefficient unless a consistent regression is exhibited in the compartments of the contingency table.

The Normal Curve and the Probable Error. It is generally admitted that the majority of anthropometric measurements when plotted in a frequency curve approximate what is known as a normal distribution. The characteristics of such a distribution are that the curve is symmetrical about its mean, which coincides with the summit, and that it falls away rapidly and symmetrically from each side of the mean by a definite law of diminution until it nearly reaches the base line, when it continues indefinitely in both directions. Such a curve can be built up by tossing a number of coins simultaneously a great many times, and recording the number of heads in each throw. If ten coins are

[51] Yule, 1927, pp. 64–65.
[52] Cf. Goring, 1913, p. 107, footnote.

tossed together some 2000 times, a symmetrical or approximately symmetrical frequency curve will be built up with the peak or mean of the curve at 5 heads. This indicates that the distribution in question is in the nature of a chance distribution. It is not altogether clear why anthropometric measurements should generally approximate such a chance distribution, and, in point of fact, they only approximate it and rarely realize it. A possible explanation is that every anthropometric variable is so composite in its nature that in an indefinitely large sample of the population its distribution is regulated by the law of independent probability, since the elements of the variable are relatively independent of each other. It may be that the heterogeneity of modern populations from a racial and hereditary standpoint contributes to a general or random distribution of metric and morphological physical characters which would not occur in a racially homogeneous group. However that may be, the important fact for present purposes is that anthropometric characters seem to conform to this symmetrical type of distribution, sufficiently to enable us to utilize the known mathematical properties of an ideal normal curve in the analysis of human measurements, without troubling, in every individual case, to fit a curve to the distribution of the sample to be studied.

The proportions of the area of a normal curve cut off by an ordinate (perpendicular to the base line) at any given distance from the mean (in terms of the standard deviation) have been worked out once and for all, and are available in statistical tables. Thus an ordinate drawn at a distance from the mean equal to the standard deviation cuts off some 16 per cent of the whole area of the curve on one side, and about 68 per cent of the entire distribution will be included between ordinates at $\pm \sigma$. An ordinate at twice the standard deviation cuts off only 2.3 per cent of the area of the curve, and consequently, an ordinate at $\pm 2 \sigma$ contains some 95.4 per cent of the distribution. Since an ordinate at 3 times the standard deviation cuts off a fraction of the area of the curve equal to only 135 parts in 100,000, it is evident that 99.7 per cent of the area is included within a range of $\pm 3 \sigma$. Thus in a normal distribution a range of 6 times the standard deviation will include the great bulk of the observations.

The distribution of a series becomes approximately normal only when the number of observations is large, and the use of the properties of the normal curve must be restricted to the distributions which are known to approximate the normal. Small samples are likely to be unrepresentative because the random selection of a few individuals is almost sure to include a disproportionate number of observations in this or that frequency class of the distribution. For example one hundred observations of stature in a population of large size may yield a range of stature which is too small, and a mean of stature which is either too high or too low, adequately to represent the true distribution of the population. The probable error is a constant which enables us to estimate the amount of error which is likely to arise in samples, owing to their numerical inadequacy and their failure to realize the approximately normal distribution which would be found in the frequencies of the entire universe from which the sample is drawn. The probable error is a quantity such that greater and less errors of simple sampling may be expected with about equal frequency, providing that the distribution of errors is normal. It is usually written after an observed constant with the $\pm$ sign before it, and indicates that the odds are even that the true value of the constant lies somewhere within a range of that amount either above or below the observed value. Thus the mean of stature of a sample may be written 171.90 $\pm$ .07, which implies that the observed mean of stature is 171.90 centimeters and that the odds are even that the true mean of an indefinitely large sample would lie somewhere between a range of .07 centimeters above or below this value. Granting the applicability of the properties of the normal curve to the study of anthropometric samples, the probable error is a most useful device in anthropometric analysis, since it enables us to appraise the amount to which our observations are likely to deviate from the true mean because of the small size of the samples studied. It should be noted that the probable error in no way takes into account errors of observation or errors resulting from a personal equation between two observers: it concerns only the errors that are involved in the sampling process.

It is evident that an error or deviation which is equal to, or a little more than, the probable error is as likely as not to be merely the result of sampling or the random selection of a small group of observations. A deviation which exceeds twice the probable error in either direction is likely to occur as the result of sampling alone about 18 times in 100 trials — or the odds are about 4.6 to 1 against its occurring at any one trial. A deviation exceeding 3 times the probable error may be expected to occur only about 4 times in 100 trials and one exceeding 4 times the probable error only 7 times in 1000 trials. The odds against the occurrence of deviations equal to 3 times the probable error, as a result of simple sampling, are about 22 to 1, and, in the case of 4 times the probable error, 142 to 1. It is evident, then, that the probable error enables one to gauge not only the accuracy of his observed results, so far as they are affected by the random sampling process (including the size of the sample), but also the validity of differences between corresponding observations made upon two different samples.

The probable error of the mean is calculated by the following formula:

$$p.e._M = .6745 \ \frac{\sigma}{\sqrt{N}} .$$

The probable error of the standard deviation: $p.e._\sigma = .6745 \ \dfrac{\sigma}{\sqrt{2N}} .$

The probable error of the coefficient of correlation: $p.e._r = .6745 \ \dfrac{1-r^2}{\sqrt{N}}$ and of the

coefficient of variation: $p.e._v = .6745 \ \dfrac{v}{\sqrt{2N}} .$

The probable error of a sum or difference of constants of two samples, assumed to have been drawn from different universes, is $p.e._{12} = \sqrt{p.e._1{}^2 + p.e._2{}^2}$, if $p.e._1$ and $p.e._2$ are the probable errors of the constants of the two samples under consideration.

When we compare the means or other constants of two anthropometric samples, we wish to discover whether the differences between the constants arise merely from the fluctuations incident to the sampling processes, or whether, on the basis of probability, these differences are actually due to some factor or factors other than chance and inherent in the series themselves. Consequently we appraise the differences in means or other constants in terms of their probable errors. That is, we divide the difference by its probable error. Such a difference in terms of its probable error is usually written in this work under the caption "x p.e." which means "number of times the probable error."

If the "x p.e." is less than 2, the difference is certainly insignificant, since the chances are almost even that it has arisen from the conditions of sampling. If the difference in terms of its probable error is 2 to 3, the chances are that it is insignificant, since such differences may arise from simple sampling in 18 per cent of cases. If the "x $p.e.$" is 3 to 4, it is probably significant, since such differences may be expected to arise from sampling in only 4 per cent of cases. If the difference is four or more times its probable error, its significance is virtually a certainty since the odds against its occurrence as an accident of sampling are 142 to 1. Hence differences must equal or exceed three times their probable error before any confidence may be placed in their validity.

It is not, however, by any single significant difference between the constants of two series that their statistical identity or diversity is determined. It is rather by the array of the differences of all of their constants, each difference being appraised in terms of its probable error. Virtually what we do when we compare the statistical constants of two series is to superimpose their arrays of means or other constants and judge of their distinctness by the distribution of differences, much as if these differences were a distribution curve. From the tables of deviates of the ideal frequency curve we can determine how many deviations of a given magnitude in terms of their probable errors are to be expected in any given number of observations taken from two random samples. The expected percentages of deviations of varying values are listed below.

TABLE I–6

NUMBER OF TIMES AMOUNT OF DEVIATION IN MEAN MEASURE MAY BE EXPECTED IF GROUPS ARE REPLACED BY RANDOM SAMPLES

	x–1	1–2	2–3	3–4	4–5	5–6	6–7
Per cent	50.00	32.27	13.43	3.60	0.62	0.07	0.002

If we compare the actual deviations with the expected percentage of deviations of given values we can easily ascertain whether the two samples differ from each other only to the extent which may be reasonably attributed to the chances of the sampling process, or whether they are so different as to make it certain that they are drawn from different universes.[53]

[53] I am indebted to Dr. C. C. Seltzer for calling my attention to the necessity of explaining that such a table as I–6, recording the amount of deviation in mean measure to be expected in random samples, is only very roughly applicable to the comparisons of anthropometric samples, since the samples are not entirely independent. Simple sampling involves the assumption that the following conditions are fulfilled: (a) that all of the samples and the individual contributions to each sample are taken precisely under the same conditions, and (b) that the individual events or appearances of a character are quite independent (Yule, 1927, p. 261). Now it is quite obvious that these conditions cannot ordinarily be fulfilled in anthropometry. The various samples are collected at different times and in different places, often by different observers, varying perhaps somewhat in their techniques. Again the events recorded are not entirely independent of each other. For example fair hair and blue eyes are positively associated; the occurrence of the one is not independent of the occurrence of the other. Similarly, in the case of anthropometric variables, the recorded values of a single dimension such as head length are not always independent of the values of another dimension such as head breadth. As a matter of fact, head length is usually correlated with head breadth, i.e. a change in the value of the one dimension is associated with some degree of change in the other. Consequently, the samples are not strictly speaking "random." They are not completely independent.

These considerations and qualifications do not, however, entirely destroy the utility of the use of amounts of deviation to be expected in random samples, as a gauge for testing the significance of differences in the arrays of means or in the frequency of attributes observed in different anthropometric samples. They only

It is upon this broad basis of differences appraised individually and collectively with respect to their statistical significance that the problem of the diversity or identity of criminal offense groups when compared amongst themselves, or of criminals as a group when compared with civilians, has been attacked.

The most rigid test of the separateness or differentiation of a subgroup, such as an offense group of criminals, is not to compare it with any other subgroup, but to compare it with the total series of criminals — the universe of which it is a part. The method utilized for the examination of the anthropological differentiation of offense subgroups in this work is one devised by Goring. Each subgroup is compared with a random sample of the total series, numerically equal to the subgroup. Such a sample has the mean and standard deviation of the entire series, but the same number of observations as the subgroup with which it is compared. The differences between means or other constants are appraised on the basis of their probable errors, as if the two samples were drawn from different universes. The decision as to the identity of the subgroup with a random sample of the entire group or series is based, as before, on the number and magnitude of significant differences.

The errors of proportions or percentages of morphological observations in subgroups, when compared with the proportions in total series of which the subgroups form component parts, are tested by the use of probable error given by the following

formula: $p.e._{01}{}^2 = .6745 \dfrac{p_0 q_0}{n_1 + n_2} \cdot \dfrac{n_2}{n_1}$ when p_0 represents the ouserved proportion

of the attribute in the total series, q_o the proportion of the series in which the attribute is lacking, n_1, the number of observations in the sample to be tested, n_2 the total of observations of the series minus the number in the subgroup.[54]

When two samples drawn from different materials or universes are to be compared, the formula utilized for testing the significance of difference is

$$p.e._{12}{}^2 = .6745 \, \frac{p_1 q_1}{n_1} + \frac{p_2, q_2}{n_2}.{}^{55}$$

Personal Equations and Differences in Technique

Measurements. In order to appraise the personal equations developed in measuring by the two principal observers in the course of three years of field work, two comparable series of their data were seriated and the statistical constants calculated. Both of these series were native Whites of native parentage. A similar comparison was made

---

make it necessary to scrutinize very carefully apparently "significant" differences before accepting them as such. In other words differences between anthropometric samples, which are seemingly valid, in terms of measures of their probable errors and expectation in random samples, may really be due to personal equation of the observer, to the correlation of events, or to some other lack of fulfillment of the conditions of simple sampling.

[54] The derivation of this formula is given in Yule, 1927, p. 271.

[55] Yule, 1927, p. 269, formula (6).

In a few instances Yule's formula (5) has been utilized. This is

$$p.e._{12}{}^2 \ .6745 \ p_0 q_0 \ \left(\frac{1}{n_1} + \frac{1}{n_2} \right) \ \ldots$$

between all of the native Whites of native parentage grouped together in the respective series of Observers A and B.

The individual ranges, means, standard deviations, coefficients of variation and their probable errors were carefully scrutinized and compared. The individual ranges were found to be virtually identical. On the whole, Observer B tended to present series with slightly higher standard deviations than those of Observer A, but the differences were usually insignificant, and may have been caused in some measure by the much smaller size of the series measured by Observer B.

In order to test the differences still further, each of the observers' series was subdivided into the ten offense categories and the statistical constants were calculated for these subgroups. Thus for every measurement and observation, the means and other constants of ten subgroups and of the total were contrasted for the two observers. Since these offense groups differ considerably in their physical characteristics, it was thought that consistent differences in technique would be shown up by the uniformity of the deviations of means of one observer from that of the other. This proved to be the case. A certain margin of error for the actual differences of one group from another, owing to diversity of ethnic strains and the formation of local types, had to be taken into account. Many of the means of the total series of the two observers were significantly different, but these differences were, for the most part, such as might well be attributed to factors making for diversity, as mentioned above. Usually the deviations in the subgroups were inconsistent, indicating that these were not caused by the personal equations of the observers in taking the measurements.

In two measurements only the comparison of constants indicated serious differences of technique between the two observers. The first of these was head height in which Observer A used the Western Reserve head spanner throughout, whereas Observer B used the Williams head spanner in the greater part of his series. Although the former instrument measures head height from the auditory meatus and the latter from the tragion points, identical values may be obtained by the use of both instruments, provided that the observer inserts the ear rods of the Western Reserve spanner far enough into the auditory meatus and lifts the entire instrument so as to take the weight off the rods. Since, however, this procedure is invariably very painful for the subject and really impracticable for field technique where the good-will of the subjects is indispensable for the success of the work, the rods are not usually thrust home nor the instrument pulled upward. Consequently this instrument, in common with others based upon the insertion of rods into the meatus, usually yields measurements from 5 millimeters to 10 millimeters higher than those taken from the tragion point which is exactly on the level with porion — the point on the upper border of the tympanic ring.

Table I–7 shows the difference in means between subjects measured by Observer B with one instrument and comparable groups measured with the other instrument — also the differences in mean head heights between the entire series of Observer A (Western Reserve spanner) and Observer B (Williams spanner). It would be simple enough to introduce a correction which would reduce the measurements made by one technique to that made by the other. However, upon mature consideration, it was decided to keep the two sets of measurements separate — since they are really different measurements — and to use them to compare one with the other as additional means of testing deviations of head height in the various offense groups and check samples. If both observers, using different instruments and different techniques, agree, for example, in finding that arson offenders are deficient in head height when compared with other criminals, the case for differentiation is much better supported than if the results of one were reduced to comparability and pooled with those of the other by some artificial coefficient of correction.

In Table I-7 it should be noted that between Observer B's measurements of the head height of criminal and civil insane, using different instruments, there is a weighted

TABLE I-7

DIFFERENCES OF MEANS OF HEAD HEIGHT IN COMPARABLE GROUPS MEASURED WITH WESTERN RESERVE AND WILLIAMS HEAD SPANNERS RESPECTIVELY

| | Western Reserve Spanner — Observer B (Bridgewater, Mass., Criminal Insane) | | Williams Spanner — Observer B (Taunton, Mass., and Colorado Civil Insane) | | Difference of means (mm.) |
	Number	Mean	Number	Mean	
Native Whites, Native Parentage	170	133.68	300	127.29	6.39
Native Whites, Foreign Parentage					
England, Wales	49	132.78	78	127.32	5.46
Ireland	136	133.05	76	129.27	3.78
French (Canada) ..	24	134.64	20	132.30	2.34
Foreign Whites					
England, Wales	38	133.59	56	127.65	5.94
Ireland	74	132.12	30	127.71	4.41
Italy	78	131.31	13	118.62	12.69
Central Europe	57	131.88	53	125.61	6.27
Balkans	78	132.45	36	125.91	6.54

Weighted mean of differences of means, 1366 observations   6.01 mm.

| | Observer A — Western Reserve Spanner (Prison, Reformatory) | | Observer B — Williams Spanner (Prison, Reformatory) | | Difference of means (mm.) |
	Number	Mean	Number	Mean	
Native Whites, Native Parentage ..	2857	132.66 ± 1.07	1347	$121.26 \pm .11$	11.40 mm.

mean difference of 6.01 millimeters, whereas between the measurements of Observer A and Observer B, both on native White criminals of native parentage, the mean difference amounts to the staggering figure of 11.40. It is evident, therefore, that the differences in technique brought about by the employment of different head spanners are exaggerated by a personal equation. The very high probable error of the mean of Observer A's measurements of head height with the Western Reserve spanner is significant, when one notes the great size of his series and recalls that the probable error of the mean is .6745 times the standard deviation divided by the square root of the number of observations. These facts are ample justification for our decision to keep the series of the two observers separate, although it cannot be ascertained how much of the difference is referable to technique and personal equation, and how much represents an actual difference between the series measured.

The other measurements in which a serious personal equation was manifested are the length and breadth of the ear. Here are the differences:

| | Ear Length | | Ear Breadth | |
	Number	Mean	Number	Mean
Observer A	2854	61.66 ± .06	2854	37.77 ± .04
Observer B	1349	58.30 ± .08	1348	36.03 ± .05
Difference		3.36 mm.		1.74 mm.

The difference in ear breadths is sufficiently explicable by Observer A's known deviation in technique, and by the probable actual group differences. The difference in ear length can be explained satisfactorily only by the supposition that Observer B must have compressed the ear to some extent in this measurement. Here again a corrective factor might be introduced, but it seems the better method to deal separately with the series of the two observers.

Observations. The principal method of appraising the personal equations of observers which developed in the course of their field work was the same in the case of observations as in measurements. The percentages of frequencies for each variation of any observed character were carefully compared in every offense subgroup and in the combined total of native Whites of native parentage studied by the respective observers. Since both series were of approximately the same ethnic composition, the distributions ought to be similar in each character, apart from a certain margin of leeway which must be allowed for the sampling process and for real divergences in local types. Any radical difference in observational judgment should manifest itself by a consistent excess of one observer or other, both in subgroups and in the total series. Space forbids the printing of the numerous and detailed tables on the basis of which the observations were graded with respect to the importance of the personal equation, but extracts from these tables and typical examples of various degrees of agreement and disagreement will be given. Ultimately the observations were divided into four grades or categories as follows:

a. Excellent agreement (evidently no personal equation)
b. Fair agreement (personal equation probably very small)
c. Considerable discrepancy (personal equation probably large)
d. Radical difference (personal equation certainly so large that the observation must be discarded or only one observer's data employed)

In some cases it was possible to arrive at a method of eliminating the personal equation of one observer by going over all of his material and correcting the observations by the use of the accompanying photographs. This was done by the other observer, after the matter had been thoroughly examined by the writer and both assistants, and the correctness of the standard of one or the other observer had been

TABLE I–8

Examples of Agreement and Disagreement in Observations by Observers A and B
(total series only)

	Observer A		Observer B	
	Number	Per Cent	Number	Per Cent
Class A Observations				
Hair color				
Black	164	5.82	53	3.94
Dark brown	934	33.12	496	36.85
Reddish brown	586	20.78	247	18.35
Light brown	698	24.75	375	27.86
Ash-blond	82	2.91	14	1.04
Golden	96	3.40	49	3.64
Red	132	4.68	29	2.15
Gray, white	128	4.54	83	6.17
Iris				
Homogeneous	220	7.72	104	7.72
Rayed	733	25.73	401	29.75
Zoned	895	31.41	404	29.97
Speckled	717	25.17	362	26.85
Diffused	284	9.97	77	5.71
Eye folds				
Epicanthus	156	5.47	29	2.15
Median	362	12.69	178	13.20
External	263	9.22	113	8.38
Absent	2071	72.62	1028	76.26
Forehead slope				
Absent, submedium	216	7.55	127	9.41
Medium	1655	57.83	759	56.26
Pronounced	991	34.63	463	34.32
Nasal root height				
Submedium	78	2.72	26	1.93
Medium	2308	80.62	1111	82.36
Pronounced	477	16.66	212	15.72
Class B Observations				
Eye color				
Dark brown	83	2.91	56	4.15
Light brown	47	1.65	82	6.08
Blue-brown	604	21.18	249	18.46
Gray-brown	712	24.97	18	1.33
Green-brown	642	22.52	495	36.69
Blue	613	21.50	189	14.01
Blue-gray	150	5.26	260	19.27
Forehead height				
Submedium	341	11.92	191	14.16
Medium	1918	67.04	730	54.11
Pronounced	602	21.04	428	31.73
Nasal root breadth				
Submedium	68	2.38	183	13.57
Medium	2562	89.55	1016	75.32
Pronounced	231	8.07	150	11.12
Nasal tip thickness				
Submedium	224	7.85	207	15.34
Medium	2021	70.81	878	65.08
Pronounced	609	21.34	264	19.57

TABLE I–8 *(continued)*

EXAMPLES OF AGREEMENT AND DISAGREEMENT IN OBSERVATIONS BY OBSERVERS A AND B
(TOTAL SERIES ONLY)

	Observer A		Observer B	
	Number	Per Cent	Number	Per Cent
Lips integumental thickness				
Submedium	468	16.41	72	5.34
Medium	2274	79.73	1150	85.25
Pronounced	110	3.86	127	9.41
Class C Observations				
Hair quantity, head				
Small	332	11.58	134	9.95
Medium	1834	64.15	1127	83.67
Large	694	24.27	86	6.38
Skin color				
Red white	1131	39.50	200	14.84
Pale white	1679	58.64	935	69.36
Ruddy	20	0.70	12	0.89
Olive	32	1.12	91	6.75
Light yellow brown	1	0.04	2	0.15
Light brown	0	0	108	8.01
Lips membranous thickness				
Submedium	335	11.73	366	27.13
Medium	2129	74.52	728	53.97
Upper submedium,				
Lower pronounced	290	10.15	237	17.57
Pronounced	103	3.60	18	1.33
Alveolar prognathism				
Absent	2193	76.65	1276	94.59
Submedium	503	17.58	47	3.48
Medium	152	5.31	21	1.56
Pronounced	13	0.45	5	0.37
Malar prominence				
Submedium	153	5.39	103	7.64
Medium	1825	64.26	1067	79.10
Pronounced	862	30.35	179	13.27
Class D Observations				
Hair texture				
Coarse	1532	54.10	242	18.02
Medium	576	20.34	968	72.08
Fine	724	25.56	133	9.90
Palpebral opening height				
Submedium	177	6.19	307	22.76
Medium	1870	65.43	928	68.79
Pronounced	811	28.38	114	8.45
Eyebrow concurrency				
Absent	1725	60.34	460	34.12
Submedium	494	17.28	580	43.03
Medium	442	15.46	284	21.07
Pronounced	198	6.92	24	1.78
Forehead breadth				
Submedium	47	1.64	159	11.79
Medium	1659	58.01	887	65.75
Pronounced	1154	40.35	303	22.46

confirmed. Such cases were comparatively few, and arose, usually, from some misunderstanding of the observation in question which the erring observer had developed. In most cases, however, the writer preferred to discard the observations of one or the other, and, usually, of both. In a few observations the data yielded ample evidence that one observer had neglected the observation — presumably because he considered it unimportant. In these cases the observation blanks were not filled out in the majority of the series by that observer.

In the Class A observations the agreement in percentages of the two observers in the various categories of observations is extremely close — in fact almost miraculously close. The observations in this class demonstrate by this agreement not only that there is no personal equation between the observers, but also that the entire series is homogeneous with respect to these observations and consequently that the two series may be combined and treated as one without any doubt as to the legitimacy of this procedure.

In the Class B observations the aggregates of percental differences — which theoretically might amount to 200 per cent — are much higher, and there are indications here and there of personal equations. Nevertheless the agreements are sufficiently close to make it probable that discrepancies between the results of the two observers are largely referable to the heterogeneity of their respective series rather than to their personal equations. Take as a specific instance eye color. A perusal of the table will show that the two observers are in close agreement with respect to dark brown, light brown, and blue-brown eyes, but diverge strongly in their percentages of gray-brown and blue-gray. Here I suspect a decided personal equation, but only in the appraisal of two or three categories of eye color. In another case in the same table — thickness of nasal tip — it seems probable that a slight difference of opinion between the observers arose as to the boundary between submedium or thin and medium. However, it is wholly possible that the differences were actually in their material rather than in their judgments. These Class B observations have been combined into one series, on the supposition that the total series strikes a mean between the divergent opinions of the two observers and probably represents a better judgment than would either of their separate series. In analysis, however, B observations are used reservedly.

The Class C observations show still larger discrepancies in the series of the two observers, as may be seen from the table. While a considerable share of the differences may be attributable to the actual constitution of the series, yet there is little doubt of the existence of a serious personal equation. Again the series have been combined, on the assumption that they represent a fairer estimate together than taken singly, but Class C observations are utilized in the final results of this study only with the very greatest caution.

In Class D observations the differences, are so great as to necessitate the discarding of the results of one or both observers. In some cases it was discovered that one or other observer had actually made a mistake in the observation which necessitated the throwing away of his material. With one exception (tattooing) Class D observations have been dismissed from all consideration in the analysis. Tattooing has been analyzed separately and differences in this feature have not been counted in the tabulation of statistically significant divergences.

The combination of the series of the two observers into one total series depends for its validity, in the case of the existence of some personal equation, upon the approximate parity of each observer's representation in the various offense subgroups of the series. It is quite clear that if Observer A and Observer B have personal equations in a certain observation, an irregular distribution of their percentage representations in various offense groups will weight the offense groups with the personal equations of one or the other observer. However, the following table indicates that the proportional contributions of each observer to the total series are so similar in several offense groups that the possibility of this disturbing factor is nearly eliminated.

Table I–9 shows that Observers A and B are represented in four of ten offense groups in practically the same proportions as they are in the total combined series. These offense groups are: robbery, burglary and larceny, forgery and fraud, arson and all others. In three groups Observer A is excessively represented to the extent of 10 to 12 per cent. These are: first degree murder, second degree murder, versus public welfare. In the three remaining groups Observer B is unduly represented: assault (excess 25.54 per cent), rape (excess 10.61 per cent), other sex (excess 13.67 per cent).

TABLE I–9

PERCENTAL CONTRIBUTIONS OF OBSERVERS A AND B TO PRISON AND REFORMATORY SERIES OF NATIVE WHITES OF NATIVE PARENTAGE

	Observer A			Observer B			
	Number Observed	Per Cent Observed	Per Cent of Total	Number Observed	Per Cent Observed	Per Cent of Total	Total
First degree murder	247	8.63	79.17	65	4.82	20.83	312
Second degree murder ..	481	16.80	77.70	138	10.23	22.30	619
Assault	34	1.19	42.43	46	3.41	57.57	80
Robbery	276	9.64	66.67	138	10.23	33.33	414
Burglary and larceny ..	1044	36.46	64.76	568	42.10	35.24	1612
Forgery and fraud	314	10.97	67.24	153	11.34	32.76	467
Rape	113	3.95	57.36	84	6.23	42.64	197
Other sex	82	2.86	54.30	69	5.12	45.70	151
Vs. public welfare	202	7.06	78.60	55	4.08	21.40	257
Arson and all other	70	2.44	67.96	33	2.45	32.04	103
Total	2863		67.97	1349		32.03	4212

Every offense subgroup in the series is compared in this study with the total of criminals, comprising all of the offense subgroups. Evidently, robbery, burglary and larceny, forgery and fraud, and arson and all others may be so compared without fear of weighting by undue representation of either observer. In the two murder offense groups and in versus public welfare, care must be taken to provide against the undue influence of Observer A, amounting to 10 to 12 per cent. In assault, rape, and other sex we must be on our guard against Observer B. Actually, this observer preponderates only in the assault group, which is by far the smallest of the series (only 80 individuals) and which is, in any case, so unimportant that very little attention is paid to its deviations in the analysis of offense subgroup differences. In all cases of Class A observations, personal equations of the observers may be disregarded safely, whatever the constitution of the offense subgroup.

Actually the writer is now convinced that he has done some injustice to the observers by overestimating their personal equations. The original comparison of the data of the two observers was made upon the basis of their respective results in North Carolina and in Kentucky, on the one hand, and of their total series of native White prisoners of native parentage, on the other. This comparison was based upon the assumption that the old American stocks of these near-by states and of the various other states were sufficiently homogeneous, ethnically and racially, to justify their combination. At a rather advanced stage of the analysis a lurking suspicion that the state groups constituted differentiated local physical types grew to a horrible certainty. It then became necessary to compare each observer's data for each state with his own data for other states and with the entire series, and to determine the degree of state differentiation. The result (cf. Chapters III and IV) was a clear demonstration that the same observer working in different states exhibited quite different observational results and quite different measurement means. In fact one observer working in two states would show quite as much difference between his own state series as one of his state series would display when compared with a state series studied by the other observer. Since, presumably, neither observer altered his personal equation in moving from one state to another, it is clear that a much greater proportion of the differences in observations between the observers is attributable to actual state differentiation than was considered possible in the appraisal made above. Nevertheless, the writer adheres to his classification of observations and to his resolution to give little or no weight to observations in which there is a radical difference between the total series of the two observers, since he considers this to be the soundest method.

The following list gives the various observations classified according to the agreement of the two observers and our consequent estimate of their validity.

Class A (close agreement)	*Class B* (fair agreement)
Hair form	Eye color
Hair color	Sclera
Iris	Eyebrow thickness
Eye folds	Forehead height
Forehead slope	Nasal root breadth
Nasal root height	Nasal bridge breadth
Nasal bridge height	Nasal tip thickness
Nasal septum inclination	Nasal septum deflection
Chin form	Lips integumental thickness
Cheeks wrinkling	Lip seam
Teeth wear	Facial prognathism
Teeth lost	Gonial angles
Bite	Facial asymmetry
Ear lobes	
Ear lobes attachment	
Roll of helix	
Ear protrusion	
Neck	
Shoulder slope	

Class C
  (wide discrepancy)

Hair quantity, head, beard, body
Skin color
Nasion depression
Nasal profile
Lips membranous thickness
Alveolar prognathism
Malars prominence
Cheeks fullness
Caries
Darwin's point
Antihelix prominence
Temporal fullness
Lambdoid flattening

Class D
  (radical difference)

Moles
Tattooing
Freckles
Hair texture
Palpebral opening height
Palpebral opening obliquity
Eyebrow concurrency
Eyebrows lateral extension
Brow ridges
Glabella
Forehead breadth
Nasal tip elevation or depression
Nasal wings
Nasal septum
Nose fracture
Acne
Chin prominence
Teeth eruption
Shovel incisors
Palate
Mouth breather
Occipital protrusion

Class A		*Class B*		*Class C*		*Class D*		
Number	Per Cent	Number	Per Cent	Number	Per Cent	Number	Per Cent	Total
19	27.14	13	18.57	16	22.86	22	31.43	70

Correction for State Sampling and for Observational Equation

The extraordinary and extensive differences between the native born criminals of native parentage in the several states, when considered according to the state of their incarceration, will be demonstrated. These differences are no doubt due in large measure to the formation of locally inbred types in the Old American stocks of isolated areas. They are certainly enhanced to some degree by the observational equations of the two observers — not only between Observer A and Observer B, but also between the data of the same observer gathered at different times in different states. We must devise some method of eliminating the influences both of state type and of observational equation. For it is obvious that the distinctive characteristics of first degree murderers, if the offense group is overloaded with Kentuckians, may reflect the local type of that state and the idiosyncrasies of the anthropologist who collected the data, rather than any physical peculiarities of broad criminological significance.

By the following very simple method, a prediction of the average metric features of any offense group or its proportional distribution of any observed feature may be based upon its state composition. Let us first consider the state prediction of any metrical character in an offense group. If n_1, n_2, n_3 . . . equal the numbers of individuals in any offense group contributed respectively by the several states represented; m_1, m_2, m_3 . . . the means of the character observed in each total state series respectively; and N the number of the individuals in the total offense group, then the state prediction of any offense group may be represented by the following equation:

$$\text{State prediction of any mean of an offense group} = \frac{n_1(m_1) + n_2(m_2) + n_3(m_3) + \cdots}{N}$$

Similarly, in morphological or sociological observations, if the same notation is used for the numbers contributed to the offense group by the respective states, and if the proportions or percentages of the character observed in each of the respective total state series be designated by p_1, p_2, p_3, et cetera, then

$$\text{State prediction of percentage of any observed character of an offense group} = \frac{n_1(p_1) + n_2(p_2) + n_3(p_3) + \cdots}{N}$$

These equations represent, then, the mean or the percentage of any feature in a given offense group, predicted from the numerical contributions of the several states to that particular offense group and the mean values or percentage occurrences of features observed in each respective total state series.

Now let d_1 = the difference between the observed mean of a measurement or index in any offense group and the observed mean of the entire series, or the difference between the percentage of an attribute or character observed in an offense group and the percentage of that same attribute or character found in the total series. Also, let d_2 = the difference between the actually observed mean (or percentage of an attribute) in any given offense group and the mean (or percentage) predicted for the offense group, on the basis of state composition, by the use of the above formulae. Then if $d_2 = d_1$ and the signs of both differences are the same, d_1 — the difference between the observed quantity in the offense group and the observed quantity in the total series — is independent of state sampling. For the quantity observed in the offense subgroup exceeds (or falls below) the amount predicted on the basis of state composition to the same extent as the offense group observation exceeds (or falls below) the amount observed in the total series. Thus, if the offense group difference from the total series is, for example, an excess of 10 per cent of red hair, and if the offense group also shows 10 per cent more of red hair than would be expected from the state prediction, quite obviously this excess of offense group over total series cannot be due to state sampling.

But if the signs of d_1 and d_2 are opposite, d_1 — the difference between the observed quantity in the offense group and the quantity in the total series — may be attributed wholly to state sampling, since that difference is only the amount, or less than the amount, which might be expected to occur on the basis of the proportional representation of the several states in the offense group and the differences in the character which obtain between entire state series. Thus, if the offense group shows 10 per cent more of red hair than the total series but 10 per cent less of red hair than would be expected to occur in the offense group, on the basis of the proportions of red-haired men in the several state series, weighted by numbers which each state contributes to that particular offense group, d_1 is invalid because of state sampling. For in this case an even greater difference between the offense group and the total series than is actually observed would be expected from the state composition of the former.

Again, if d_1 is greater than d_2 and the signs of both differences are like, all of the difference which can be regarded as independent of state sampling is that amount represented by d_2 — the difference between the observed mean or percentage in the offense group and the amount predicted from state composition. The residue of d_1 is the excess to be expected from state composition. In such a case d_2 — the independent difference — can be appraised in terms of the probable error of d_1 — the total difference between offense group and total series. This follows from the fact that the number of the subgroup and the number of the total series are the same, whether the probable error of the difference is applied to the total difference (d_1) or a residual difference independent of state sampling (d_2). For the probable errors of differences between means of a subgroup and of a total series are not based upon the values of the respective means, but upon the numbers of observations in subgroup and total group, respectively. In the case of attributes, a similar use of the probable error of the difference between the offense group and the total series (d_1) may be used for the scaled down independent difference (d_2), since the probable error of difference between subgroup and series is not based upon the amount or proportion of the character observed in the subgroup, but only upon the numbers of the subgroup and total series, respectively, and the proportions of the character found in the total combined series.[56]

The predictions made on the basis of state composition of offense subgroups are used in this work only for establishing the independence of actually observed differences between the subgroups and the total series and for correcting by reduction such differences as may be due in part or wholly to state composition. The predictions are not employed artificially to enhance observed differences. Thus if the percentage of black hair in the total series is, let us say, 10, and the percentage of black hair in a certain offense group, first degree murderers, for example, is 7, then $d_1 = -3.00$ per cent. But let us suppose that the percentage of first degree murderers with black hair, predicted from the state composition of that offense group, is 15 per cent. Then $d_2 = -8.00$ per cent. But only the value of d_1 (-3.00) is used as the measure of differentiation between first degree murderers and the total series, because that is all of the difference which has actually been observed. The additional amount of difference expected from state prediction has not been realized and it is quite contrary to the policy of this research to exaggerate observed differences by substituting for them the differences between prediction and realization.

In this way state predictions and corrections operate only to validate or to decrease observed differences, never to increase them. Such a one-sided application of state corrections loads the dice against organic differentiation. I have employed it in this manner only because I wish to avoid the slightest suspicion of bolstering the hypothesis of a relation between the organism and its behavior by a theoretical inflation of dif-

---

[56] Cf. 58. In calculating the state predictions a single table of dispersion of offenses by states has been used for the percentage contribution of each state to the combined offense subgroup, in the cases of all measurements, indices, and observations. Thus slight differences in the percental contributions of the respective states in this or that table, due to the fact that a few individual measurements may have been omitted, have been disregarded. It is believed that, in such a large series, deviations due to such casual omissions are very unlikely to have any appreciable effect upon the value of the state prediction, which is, in any event, a rough approximation.

ferences. I am willing to use state predictions to explain away differences, wholly or in part, but never to exaggerate them. I feel extremely virtuous in so doing, because I am using statistical devices of correction exclusively to minimize and to reduce the positive results of criminological differentiation which I am attempting to establish. If I am to be accused of any bias in favor of the biological or organic basis of crime (and I do not expect to escape such accusations), I can at any rate point out that I have scrupulously applied every legitimate statistical means of reducing and explaining criminological differences which might be utilized by an honest anti-Lombrosian.

Chapter II

SOCIOLOGY

General Distribution of Prison and Reformatory Series

Parentage of Total Series

OUR prison and reformatory series consists of 10,953 males from ten states. These states are Massachusetts, Wisconsin, Missouri, North Carolina, Kentucky, Tennessee, Texas, Colorado, New Mexico, and Arizona. Prisoners in state prisons and reformatories, including both sexes, numbered on January 1, 1927, 91,188 persons, and on January 1, 1928, 101,624 persons.[1] There is no information available concerning the numbers of each sex for the total prison population present in 1927 and 1928, but of the number of prisoners received in these institutions during 1928, 92.56 per cent were males, and of the total prisoners present in all institutions on January 1, 1923, 95.2 per cent were males. Our prison and reformatory series constitutes 10.78 per cent of the numbers of prisoners present on January 1, 1928, irrespective of sex, and probably between 11 and 12 per cent of the male prisoners. It may be considered, therefore, an adequately large sample of the prison and reformatory population.

There are no data available concerning the race and nativity of the prisoners present on January 1, 1928. On January 1, 1923, 55.3 per cent of the male prisoners present in prisons and reformatories were native Whites. In our series 52.64 per cent conform to this classification. Foreign born Whites constituted 12.4 per cent of the prison male population of January 1, 1923, and 10.02 per cent of our sample of 1927–28.

Negroes in 1923 were 31 per cent of the prison and reformatory male population. They constitute 37.35 per cent of our sample (including Negroes and Negroids). Judging then from the 1923 prison population, it would appear that our series represents fairly well the racial and nativity distribution of the male prison and reformatory population of 1927–28, but is probably slightly high in Negroes and Negroids.

Table II–1 gives the distribution of all prison subjects according to racial origin and offense category. In the present volume we have to consider only the native Whites of native parentage, who constitute 38.46 per cent of our entire prison series. The percentages indicate the proportion of each offense group which is found in each racial group and of each racial group in each offense group.

A rough idea of the differentiation of the racial groups by type of offense may be gained from the ranking table on the following page.

Such a crude ranking, however, has little or no validity, because it weights all cate-

[1] *Prisoners in State and Federal Prisons and Reformatories*, 1928, U. S. Department of Commerce, Bureau of the Census, Washington, D. C., p. 5.

gories of offense equally and disregards the actual amount and significance of the excesses for each crime in the various racial groups. Ultimate consideration of racial differences in offense must be reserved for a later volume.

TABLE II-2

RANKING OF RACIAL GROUPS OF TOTAL PRISON AND REFORMATORY SERIES BY OFFENSE

	Native Whites of Native Parentage	Native Whites of Foreign Parentage	Foreign Whites	Negroids	Negroes
First degree murder	3	5	4	2	1
Second degree murder	4	5	3	1	2
Assault	4	2	1	3	5
Robbery	4	1	5	2	3
Burglary and larceny	4	2	5	3	1
Forgery and fraud	1	2	4	3	5
Rape	3	2	1	4	5
Other sex	2	3	1	4	5
Vs. public welfare	1	4	2	3	5
Arson and all other	3	1	2	5	4
Mean	2.9	2.7	2.8	3.0	3.6
Rank	3	1	2	4	5

STATE DISTRIBUTION OF NATIVE WHITES OF NATIVE PARENTAGE

The 4212 native White criminals of native parentage were measured and observed in the prisons and reformatories of nine states, namely: Massachusetts, Tennessee, Kentucky, Texas, North Carolina, Wisconsin, Arizona, Colorado, and New Mexico. The particular group which is the subject of this volume is heavily weighted by the inclusion therein of 28.18 per cent of Kentuckians and 21.72 per cent of Texans. The states of Kentucky and Tennessee were selected for study partly because of a desire to include in the series a large sample of the Old American mountain stock. The southern states were also chosen in part because of the necessity of securing in the criminal survey a representative group of Negroes; and the southwestern states came into the picture because of the advisability of studying the Mexican criminal element.

Thus it happens that this particular sample of native born White criminals of native parentage consists largely of southerners. Massachusetts and Wisconsin, the only two northern states included, furnish only 15 per cent of the series. But no reasonable objection can be raised against the provenience of these native Whites, since we have naturally included them in whatever state we have found them, and the predominance of southerners among them is a natural effect of the concentration of Old American stocks in these states.

More individuals from Massachusetts have been studied in the general survey than from any other state, and if the sample of the old native White population in penal institutions of Massachusetts is small, it is probably because of the high proportion of first generation native Whites and of the foreign born.

Rather more serious than the sectional distribution as a whole is the disproportionate contribution of various states to this or that offense group. This is due in part to differences in the criminal laws of the various states. States which have capital punishment naturally contribute few or no members of the first degree murder group.

In Table II–3 are recorded the numbers of each crime category supplied by the various states and the totals for each state. The percentages show the proportion of each offense in the total series, the proportion of the criminals of each state in each offense group, and the proportion which each state contributes to the total of each offense group.

Thus the percentages of the first row show that Massachusetts has contributed 8.02 per cent of the entire series, but only .64 per cent of the first degree murderers. Similarly, this state has provided more than its quota of assault, robbery, larceny, rape, other sex, and arson and all other offenders, but less than its quota of both murder groups, of the forgery and fraud group, and of the versus public welfare group.

The numbers of prisoners from Arizona and New Mexico are so small that they scarcely affect the series and the proportions from these states in the various crime categories cannot be taken as safely representative of the criminal propensities of the states in question.

Colorado is high in assault, robbery, forgery, rape, other sex, and versus public welfare, and low in second degree murder, larceny, and arson and all other offenses. But, since the total contribution of Colorado to the series is but 11.32 per cent, its disproportionate contributions to various offense groups are not sufficient to weight any group.

Texas contributes 21.72 per cent of the entire series. It yields an unduly great number of forgery and fraud criminals — no less than 37.04 per cent of the entire series — and very seriously weights the versus public welfare group, to which it contributes the enormous proportion of 57.98 per cent. In all other offenses save robbery, Texas falls below its expected quota.

Wisconsin yields only 7.05 per cent of the entire series. But this state provides 22.34 per cent of the rape group and 18.75 per cent of the assault group.

Kentucky is the state from which the greatest percentage of this series is drawn (28.18). It contributes an enormously disproportionate percentage of first degree murderers (53.53 per cent) and of second degree murderers (44.91). Evidently the homicide groups are badly overloaded with Kentuckians.

Tennessee contributes a most excessive proportion, relative to its total numbers, to the second degree murder group (17.61 per cent of the offense group as against 10.04 per cent of the series). North Carolina also provides an undue number of second degree murderers, and likewise of assault, larceny, and other sex offenders.

On the whole, however, the most important overweighting of individual offense groups, of which we must take cognizance, and which we must consider in appraising the physical characters of these offense groups are the following: (1) forgery and fraud (overloaded with Texans), (2) versus public welfare (overloaded with Texans), (3) rape (overloaded with Wisconsin criminals), (4) first degree murder (overloaded with Kentuckians), (5) second degree murder (overloaded by Kentucky, Tennessee, and North Carolina).

If the native Whites of native parentage were physically homogeneous, irrespective of their states of origin or imprisonment, the disproportionate contributions of the several states to the various offense groups could be disregarded. Since, however, marked state differentiation in physical type exists, it has been necessary to correct for irregularities of state sampling.[2]

EXTRACTION

In all the series of native born Whites of native parentage, the nationalities of fathers' and mothers' stocks were recorded if known. Table II–4 lists these extractions when they are recorded as other than straight "American." Of the prison and reformatory series of native Whites, 1,552 individuals, or 36.85 per cent of the series, are recorded as having extractions other than merely American. The table shows also the total percentages of extractions listed in the several states. These are extremely low in Kentucky (4.21 per cent) and in Tennessee (8.75 per cent), and very high in Wisconsin (83.50 per cent), North Carolina (75.22 per cent), Massachusetts (68.64 per cent), and Colorado (46.54 per cent). It seems fair to assume that those states in which the smallest reports of foreign extraction are found are those in which the inhabitants are of such old American lineage that they have lost knowledge of their original ethnic ancestry, whereas those who report large percentages of foreign extraction contain higher proportions of the more recent immigrants who still retain some recollection of the national origins of their families. Under such circumstances the high percentages of foreign extractions reported in Massachusetts, Wisconsin, and Colorado are easily referable to their large proportions of comparatively recent immigrants — groups which have been in this country long enough for the second native born generation to grow up and get into jail. Such an explanation can scarcely be valid in the state of North Carolina,[3] which in 1930 had a population of only 8,788 foreign born Whites, 7,919 native Whites of foreign parentage, and 9,678 native Whites of mixed parentage, out of a total population of 2,226,160. In fact, of all the states studied, North Carolina has the largest proportion of native born Whites of native parentage. The more complete record of the extraction of native born White prisoners of native parentage in North Carolina cannot then imply that these prisoners are the offspring of comparatively recent European immigration, but merely indicates that our information, for one reason or other, is more complete for this state than for most others where old American stocks are largely domiciled. This exception casts considerable doubt upon our initial assumption that reports of extraction indicate relatively short American ancestry.

Table II–5 on page 75 gives the ranking of the more important foreign elements in the native White prisoners of native parentage in the several states.

It is obvious from the tables that Irish strains are far the most common in the ancestry of all reporting groups of prisoners. In the prison and reformatory series the Irish strains rank first in every state except North Carolina. No less than 36 per cent of all of the reported extractions are Irish, not including the Scotch-Irish, and other Irish mixtures. English descent ranks first in North Carolina and second or third in most of the other states. In the total prison and reformatory series English strains take second place in the non-American extractions reported and comprise 20.68 per cent of the total extractions. German strains rank second in Wisconsin, Kentucky, Arizona, and New Mexico and in total series take third place with 11.66 per cent.

---

[2] Cf. Ch. I, pp. 67–70.
[3] Census Reports, Department of Commerce, Washington, D. C., 1930.

This stock is most poorly represented in Massachusetts and North Carolina prisoners. Scotch-Irish strains are strongest in Texas and in North Carolina, where they rank respectively second and third. In the total series the Scotch-Irish extractions are fourth with 9.08 per cent. French strains, presumably French Canadian, occupy fifth

TABLE II–5

RANKING OF LEADING FOREIGN ELEMENTS IN NATIVE WHITE PRISONERS OF NATIVE PARENTAGE
BY STATES

	Mass.	Tenn.	Ky.	Texas	N. C.	Wis.	Ariz.	Col.	N. Mex.	Rank in Total Series
Irish-American	1	1	1	1	2	1	1	1	1	1
English-American	2	5	3	4	1	3	3	2	3	2
German-American	5	3	2	3	4	2	2	3	2	3
Scotch-Irish	7	.	5	2	3	6	5	6	5	4
French-American	3	2	5	7	7	4	4	7	5	5
Scotch-American	4	4	5	5	5	5	6	4	4	6

place in the total rankings with 6.77 per cent. The French are third in Massachusetts, second in Tennessee, and fourth in Wisconsin. The Tennessee ranking is probably insignificant. The Scotch are in sixth place in the total ranking with 6.44 per cent. In no state do Scotch extractions rank higher than fourth. The total of Dutch extraction is 56, or 3.61 per cent of the total series.

All of the other extractions reported are insignificant in number, including even the Italian, which is reported in but 11 cases of the 1552 records in the prison and reformatory series.

It is clear that our criminal series is principally of Old American stock and that the ethnic strains represented are, in the great majority of cases, Irish, English, Scotch, and German. Racially one would expect a predominance of Nordic and Mediterranean strains, with some admixture of Alpine, probably brought in, for the most part, by the Germans and the French Canadians, although doubtless present in a minor degree in the stocks from the British Isles.

The civilian check sample consists of 167 men from Massachusetts and 146 from Tennessee. In the Massachusetts sample presumably Old American extractions comprise 23.95 per cent, but in the Tennessee sample 58.90 per cent (Text Tables XI–a, XI–b). For the rest, English extractions lead in the Massachusetts civil sample with 36.53 per cent, and Irish follow with 26.95 per cent. In the Tennessee civilians, the Irish are second to the Old Americans with 16.44 per cent, and the English third with 14.38 per cent. Minor strains in the civilian check samples are: Scotch — Massachusetts 4.19, Tennessee 6.16; German — Massachusetts 2.40, Tennessee 3.42; French — Massachusetts 2.99, Tennessee 0.

RELIGIOUS AFFILIATIONS

The religious affiliations of native born criminals of native parentage were recorded but have not been subjected to any intensive analysis, because they are of comparatively small importance. However, they have been tabulated by ethnic extraction in the various states, particularly in the hope that the division between Catholics and Protestants may give some indication as to the proportions of North Irish, or Scotch-Irish, and of South Irish in the large group of Irish extraction.

Table II–6 contains the general religious data for Massachusetts. In this state series Catholics comprise 57.07 per cent and Protestants 39.20 per cent. Very few profess no religious affiliation. Catholics are proportionately most numerous among the Irish-Americans, followed by the French Canadians and the French-Americans (excluding groups represented by only one individual). Protestants are in the majority among English, German, Old American, and Scotch extractions. Table II–7 separates the Massachusetts religious data into Charlestown Prison and Concord Reformatory groups. The object of this subdivision is to discover whether the younger offenders differ from the older prison group in religious profession and particularly to get some clue as to whether or not the reformatory inmates of Irish extraction are predominantly the offspring of recent South Irish Catholic immigrant families or, possibly, of older Scotch-Irish Protestant immigrants. Actually the table throws no light upon this subject since virtually all of Irish descent, whether in prison or reformatory, are Catholic. Probably, then, most of them come from the south of Ireland.

Tennessee is peculiar in this matter of religious affiliations because no less than 65.18 per cent report none whatsoever, as against, for example, only 3.72 per cent in Massachusetts. Under these circumstances the data are of little use. It may be noted however that 10 of 33 persons of Irish descent in this state report themselves Catholics, as against 4, or 12.12 per cent of Protestants. The other 19 have no religious affiliation.

In Kentucky the irreligious amount to 14.73 per cent. Catholicism predominates in no extraction group. Of the Irish 18 or 50 per cent are Protestant and 15 or 41.67 per cent are Catholic.

Texas includes 45.75 per cent with no religious affiliation. In all of the larger extraction groups the Protestants are more numerous than the Catholics. Of the persons of Irish descent 46, or 43.81 per cent, are Protestant and 11, or 10.48 per cent, are Catholic. It is possible that Ulstermen predominate among the Irish of this state.

Wisconsin, like Massachusetts, reveals but a small percentage of persons stating that they have no religion. In every one of the larger groups Protestants are in the majority. The Irish have 27 Protestants, or 64.29 per cent, and 13 Catholics, or 30.95 per cent. This probably indicates a large proportion of North Irish, but the total returns from Wisconsin are very small.

In the Southwest all of the major groups are predominantly Protestant (total 76.85 per cent), with the exception of Mexican-Americans (81.25 per cent Catholics). Only 3.94 per cent report no religion.

Of the total criminals of Irish extraction 40.67 per cent are Protestants and 42.56 per cent are Catholics. Nearly all of the Massachusetts Irish-Americans are Catholic and probably come from the south of Ireland. In Tennessee Irish Catholics are more numerous than Irish Protestants, but there are very few of either category. More Irish-Americans of this state report no religion at all. In all of the rest of the states there are more Protestants than Catholics among the native born criminals of native parentage, but of Irish extraction. There is then some reason for supposing that the

Massachusetts Irish-Americans belong predominantly to the more recent Southern Irish strains and the Irish of the other states include more from the Ulster provinces.

Of 164 persons of German extraction 68.90 per cent are Protestant. The Catholic Germans are likely to come from the south of Germany and to include more Alpine racial elements than those from the north.

Of course these data take no account of changes of faith and can only provide the roughest sort of an estimate as to ethnic origins, if they are worth anything at all in this connection.

The high percentage in Tennessee reporting no religious affiliation is very puzzling, considering the fundamentalist reputation of that state. It may be nothing more than a coincidence that Tennessee most closely approximates the general criminal type of this series, that it provides more extra-state inmates than any other state considered, and that it has by far the highest proportion of criminals asserting themselves to have no religious belief.

Table II–13 gives the complete data on religious affiliation by ethnic extraction. The totals show 60.36 per cent of Protestants, 14.67 per cent of Catholics, and 24.97 per cent without any religious affiliation at all. Table II–14 records the rankings of the various categories of religion in the different extractions. Of the ethnic groups of any considerable size the Welsh rank highest in Protestant affiliation with 92.31 per cent, the English second with 82.94 per cent, the Germans next with 68.90 per cent. The leading Catholic groups are Mexican-American with 82.50 per cent and French Canadian with 80 per cent. The highest ranking group with no religious affiliation is Old American with 31.66 per cent.

The outstanding facts of this tabulation are the low percentage of Catholicism and the high percentage of no religious affiliation among the Old Americans, the almost equal division of Irish between Catholicism and Protestantism indicating probably a somewhat similar division between South Irish and North Irish. The very large percentage of total extractions professing no religion at all is of great interest. Tennessee and Texas are notable for their high proportions of the irreligious, while Kentucky, Massachusetts, Wisconsin, and the Southwest show very small percentages in this category. There are some indications that the longer a criminal's ancestors have been residents of this country, the less likely is that criminal to have any religious affiliation.

NATIVE STATES OF EXTRA-STATE INMATES

Table II–15 records the birthplace by states of inmates of institutions in states other than their native states. Of the total prison and reformatory series 1286 individuals or 30.53 per cent are incarcerated outside of their native states. The percentages for each state are given in the table. They are at a minimum in Kentucky with 13.56 per cent and at a maximum in Arizona with 72.34 per cent. The extra-state prisoners in Massachusetts are principally from New York and the states of New England. Similarly the extra-state inmates measured in Kentucky are nearly all natives of adjacent states, with natives of Tennessee constituting more than one third of the extra-state total. In North Carolina the native born prisoners of native parentage who are not natives of North Carolina are usually natives of South Carolina or Tennessee, with a fair proportion from Virginia and other near-by southern states. In Tennessee the natives of Kentucky are most numerous, with Mississippi and Missouri coming next in rank. Evidently in Massachusetts and the South Atlantic and East South Central states, as here represented, native White prisoners of native parentage, when they are not natives of the state in which they are imprisoned, are, for the most part, from near-by states.

The extra-state inmates of the Wisconsin penitentiary (native Whites of native parentage) are natives of 28 other states, with New York and Michigan dividing first place. Less than half of these extra-state inmates come from the near-by middle western states. The extra-state inmates of Texas prisons are natives of 33 different states. The most important native state of these Texan prisoners is Tennessee, which contributes almost twice as many natives as any other state. Other important states are Oklahoma, Missouri, Kentucky, Alabama, Arkansas, Mississippi, Louisiana, and Illinois. Clearly the native White prisoners of native parentage incarcerated in Texas, but not born there, have, for the most part, drifted in from other southern states farther to the east. The same is true in New Mexico and Arizona. In the former the largest contributor to the native White prisoners of native parentage is Texas, with almost one third of the total extra-state inmates. Colorado yields native White prisoners of native parentage born in 37 states other than Colorado. Easily leading in its contributions is Missouri, followed by Kansas, Illinois, Iowa, and Texas. On the whole Colorado is by far the most cosmopolitan of the states in the nativities of its native born White prisoners of native parentage. Each state seems to present a majority of its own natives with the exceptions of Colorado, Arizona, and New Mexico.

Table II–16 compares the proportions of native born Whites living within or outside of the state of their birth with the proportions of native White prisoners of native parentage in our series correspondingly domiciled. It also records for each of these categories, the extra-state residents by states of their nativity in order of magnitude of contribution. The object of this tabulation is to discover whether or not our prison and reformatory series of native Whites of native parentage represents a fair sample of the native population in the various states with respect to their nativity and states of origin. Naturally in most states the percentage of prisoners coming from other states is greater than the percentage of extra-state residents in the general population, because prisoners are adult males and the general population includes large proportions of children and women who are less mobile than men.

The closest fit of the prison population to the nativity composition of the general population of a state is in Kentucky, where the difference is only 2.2 per cent excess of extra-state natives in the prison series. The contributing states are the same, and in virtually the same order. Next comes North Carolina which has no less than 90 per cent of native residents, but only 79.2 per cent of the native White prisoners of native parentage of North Carolinian birth. The states which are the most important contributors to the North Carolina prison population are the same as in the general population, with one exception. Tennessee obtrudes itself into the prison situation in North Carolina by furnishing the quota of delinquents which should come from Georgia on the basis of the composition of the general population.

Massachusetts has a slightly larger excess of extra-state born prisoners than North Carolina, but they come from the same states which figure in the composition of the general population of Massachusetts. Wisconsin comes next with 28.3 per cent of extra-state born prisoners. Curiously New York and Indiana take the place of Iowa in being important contributors to the prisoners in contrast with the general population composition of Wisconsin. In Tennessee still more of the prisoners come from other states, but Georgia and Alabama, which are important in the general population, yield to Missouri in the prison contributions.

The most notable fact with respect to the Texas statistics of state nativity is that Tennessee leads the states contributing to the criminal population, whereas it is fourth in contributions to the general population. Kentucky also obtrudes itself into the prison population, while Louisiana and Mississippi are left out.

The other states of the Southwest show a similar nativity in the criminal population to that of the civil population, except that in each instance the extra-state inmates of the penal institutions are proportionately much higher than in the older states.

This comparison seems to show that the native White prisoners of native parentage in the states considered form a fairly representative sample of the elements of such origin in those states, so far as nativity is concerned. These White criminals, native born of native parentage, seem to be nearly as much a product of the states of their incarceration as is the general population born and brought up in the same states. There is little indication that this group of criminals is in any sense a migratory and cosmopolitan band of professionals. It consists rather of the element in the local population of each state which for some reason or other is selected for delinquency. If the Old American stock has differentiated into state types in any of the older and less industrialized states, these types should be reproduced in the native born criminals of native parentage from the several states.

PREVIOUS CONVICTIONS

Table II–17 gives the raw data on previous convictions which were copied from the prison and reformatory records. Information is available in the cases of 3655 prisoners out of a total of 4212. Undoubtedly this information is defective and shows a lower total of previous convictions than in reality exists. Thirty-nine per cent of our series have records of previous convictions, while the United States Census report of prisoners committed in 1928 shows that 56.6 per cent of the male offenders who were reported as to previous commitment were recidivists.[4]

It is quite useless to attempt to discuss the raw differences in recidivism of the offense groups without first taking into consideration the differences which may be due to state sampling. For it is clear that the records in the various states are of different degrees of completeness. What we really desire to know is the difference in recidivism among various types of offenders apart from any effect which may be exerted by the characters of the records and the laxity or rigidity of law enforcement in the several states.

Table II–18 gives the data on previous convictions in the various states. The records are very unsatisfactory in many of the states. From North Carolina we have nothing at all. Massachusetts and Wisconsin show the highest percentage of recidivists, but this probably reflects the superior character of the records in the penal institutions of those states rather than the incorrigibility of the inmates of those institutions.

[4] *Prisoners*, Bureau of the Census, Department of Commerce, Washington, D. C., 1928.

Table II–19 not only gives the significance in terms of probable errors of the crude deviations of offense groups from the total series, but also takes into consideration the question of state sampling and finally summarizes the significant offense group differences which survive the state sampling correction. Let us consider this summary. We are left with very marked deficiencies in the percentage of recidivists in first and second degree murderers, in rapists and other sex offenders, and in versus public welfare offenders, and with large excesses of persons previously convicted in the burglary and larceny group. It is not surprising that murderers are commonly first offenders, and that burglars and thieves are frequently habitual criminals, but it is astonishing to observe that versus public welfare criminals, who are usually bootleggers, have the lowest record of all in previous convictions. This may be due to the fact that the bootleggers in this series are native Whites of native parentage, mostly from rural districts, where "moonshining" is a traditional private avocation rather than the business of criminal organizations. Metropolitan bootlegging may be rather in the hands of foreign born persons, or native born of foreign parentage.

MARITAL STATUS

Table II–20 gives the crude percentages and numbers of individuals in each marital status for each offense group. On the face value of the figures it seems that the robbery and burglary and larceny groups are notable for their high proportions of single men, that other sex, versus public welfare, and arson and all others are the most frequently married offenders, and that divorce, separation, and widowhood are especially common in first degree murderers and in the two classes of sex offenders. However, before these apparent differences can be accepted we must take into consideration and make allowance for the possible complications of disproportionate state representation in the offense groups and age differences. We may first clear away the effects of state sampling.

Table II–21 gives the numbers and crude percentages of marital status for the several states studied. A glance at this table reveals the fact that the various state samples differ quite remarkably in marital status. Outstanding are the large proportions of single men in the Massachusetts and Southwestern samples, the high percentage of married Texans, and the great proportion of divorced or separated men and widowers from Wisconsin.

Table II–22 predicts for each offense group the percentage of men of each status to be expected on the basis of state composition, indicates the difference between actual and predicted percentages, compares those differences with those actually observed between the offense subgroups and the total series, and finally summarizes the significant differences in marital status which are independent of state sampling. We need discuss only the summary. It is quite evident that most of the differences are independent of state sampling. The only difference which seems at first blush significant and proves to be due to state overloading is the excess of divorced persons among rapists. This turns out to be an effect of the Wisconsin predominance in that offense group. Otherwise we are left with the differences which attract attention in the crude tables.

However, it is quite clear that age of the offenders is very important in affecting their marital status. The older the offense group the larger proportion of married, widowed, and divorced men it is likely to include. Therefore we must make a prediction as to the marital status of each group based upon its age composition and compare that with the actual frequencies. Only the differences which supervene ordinary age effects upon marital status can be of any particular criminological importance in distinguishing the offense groups.

Table II–23 enumerates the numbers and percentages of individuals in each marital category for the entire series of native White criminals of native parentage classified by age groups of five years each. A brief consideration of this table will be instructive. The percentages of single men diminish very rapidly up to the age of 35 years, and thereafter slowly to the age of 55 years. In the last three age groups they increase slightly, but this increase is probably insignificant because of the small numbers of individuals in these groups. Similarly, the percentages of married men increase very rapidly up to the age of 35 years and thereafter slowly up to 55 years. The last three age groups also show a slight falling of the marriage rate. The divorced and separated men are comparatively few. The percentages increase slowly up to the age of 30 years and then remain more or less stationary up to the age of 50 years. Thereafter the percentages are very irregular, but, in general, decline up to the final, small 65–69 year group, which shows a sharp increase. The percentages of widowers are quite irregular throughout, doubtless because of the small numbers and the large sampling error. On the whole, they are very much higher in the last four age groups — from fifty years upward — averaging in these groups more than 10 per cent of all individuals. It is quite apparent from this table that marital state is very closely associated with age and that no deductions as to the marital condition of criminals can be valid unless age factors are considered.

Table II–24 corrects marital state for age in offense groups which have previously shown deviations from the total series which remain significant after correction for state sampling, and Table II–25 summarizes the differences as to their significance and independence of the age factor. Only this latter table requires comment. The deficiency in single men and the excess of married men among first degree murderers are seen to be largely dependent upon their advanced ages. They do, however, show a significant excess of widowers, even when due allowance has been made for their age. The only possible explanation which I can offer is that the undue proportion of widowers may reflect the extent to which first degree murderers are imprisoned for killing their wives. Goring came to a similar conclusion with regard to the excess of marriages among his "violence against the person" group of criminals.[5] In our case, as in his, the explanation must be regarded as a suggestion, rather than a demonstration, since our data do not permit us to examine the identities of the victims of these criminals.

Second degree murderers show deficiencies of single men and excesses of married men, independent of age, but no excess of widowers. Obviously we cannot invoke the same explanation as in the case of first degree murderers, but again we must agree with Goring that marriage seems positively correlated with crimes of violence. The assault group is also excessively married, but the excesses do not survive the correction for age, probably because of the very small size of this offense group and the consequently large values of its probable errors.

Both robbers, and burglars and thieves show deficiencies of married men and ex-

[5] Goring, 1913, p. 326.

cesses of single men over and beyond the allowances which must be made for their low mean ages. The tendency of these classes of offenders to remain unmarried perhaps relates to their economic status, which is low. Recidivism is by far the most frequent in these groups and it is certain that repeated imprisonments would be a deterrent to marriage.

Forgers and fraudulent criminals do not differ significantly in their marital status from the total series of criminals. An excess of married men and widowers among rapists is reduced to probable insignificance when age is taken into consideration. Other sex offenders show a deficiency of single men which is independent of age, but excesses of married men and widowers are not certainly valid when allowance is made for age. On the whole it appears that the single state is unduly rare in all classes of sex offenders.

Versus public welfare criminals and arson and all other offenders also show great excess of married men and deficiency of celibates. The high marriage rates of bootleggers and incendiaries which compose the majority of these two classes are interesting, but puzzling. The economic pressure of married life may be somewhat of an incentive toward the commission of crimes of these natures.

Our final conclusion is that robbers, burglars, and thieves are excessively unmarried when compared with total criminals; that murderers of both classes and probably all violence against the person offenders are on the contrary distinguished by their high marriage rates; that in general sex offenders, offenders against public welfare, and arson criminals likewise tend to be married to a far larger extent than would be expected from consideration of their ages only. The coefficient of mean square contingency of marriage with offense is .28 and it quite obviously indicates a real relationship between these sociological states in criminals.

OCCUPATION

Table II–26 gives the crude data for occupations by offense groups. Of the nine states from which the criminal sample has been drawn, Massachusetts alone can be described as a primarily industrial area. The other states are principally agricultural, although Colorado, New Mexico, and Arizona may perhaps be designated as ranching and mining areas. It is evidently of little profit to consider the occupational distributions without taking into account state distribution. The crude data show, for example, that 31.63 per cent of all of the native White criminals of native parentage belong to extractive occupations, which include agriculture, mining, stock raising, lumbering, forestry, and fishing. There are only 16.72 per cent of unskilled laborers and 17.40 per cent of factory workers. Of course these figures are strongly influenced by the rural character of most of the states studied.

Table II–27 gives the occupational distribution by states and brings out the marked contrast between Massachusetts and the other states studied. The very high percentage of laborers listed in North Carolina may be due to the recording of farm laborers as laborers unspecified. Occupational classifications are usually ambiguous in the matter of classifying "laborers," since these are sometimes distributed among the various categories and sometimes separated out as a distinct class.

Table II–28 simplifies the crude relationship of offense and occupation by giving the rank of each occupation in each offense group, its general ranking by offense groups, and its total series ranking based upon percentages of individuals in the entire series. The extractive occupations rank first in every offense except robbery, in which they fall to third place. Their general offense ranking is first and their total series ranking also. Laborers are second in all offenses except forgery and fraud and versus public welfare in which they drop to third place. Laborers are second in general offense ranking and third in individual series ranking. Factory workers rank second or third in most offenses, but first in robbery and fourth in assault. Their general offense ranking is third and total series ranking second. Skilled trades are generally in fourth place, but rise to third place in assault and drop to fifth place in second degree murder and in arson and all others. Transportation is notable only in its high rank in second degree murder (fourth) and its low rank in forgery and fraud (seventh). Trade is notable for its high rank in versus public welfare (probably bootlegging), in other sex offenses, and in forgery and fraud. Personal service ranks high in arson and low in forgery and fraud. Clerical takes a high place in forgery and fraud (fifth) and is low in rape (tenth). The last three occupational categories show no remarkable deviations in spe-

TABLE II–28

RANKING OF OCCUPATION BY OFFENSES

Occupation	First Degree Murder	Second Degree Murder	Assault	Robbery	Burglary Larceny	Forgery Fraud	Rape	Other Sex	Versus Public Welfare	Arson and All Others	General Offense Ranking	Total Series Ranking
Extractive	1	1	1	3	1	1	1	1	1	1	1	1
Laborer	2	2	2	2	2	3	2	2	3	2	2	3
Factory	3	3	4	1	3	2	3	3	2	2	3	2
Skilled trades	4	5	3	4	4	4	4	4	4	5	4	4
Transportation	5	4	5	6	6	7	5	7	6	6	5	5
Trade	6	6	7	7	7	5	7	4	4	7	6	7
Personal service	7	7	6	5	5	8	6	6	7	4	7	6
Clerical	8	9	9	8	9	5	10	7	8	9	8	8
Semi-professional	10	11	8	9	8	9	8	11	9	9	9	9
Public service	10	8	10	11	10	10	8	10	9	11	10	11
Professional	9	10	10	10	11	11	11	9	9	8	11	10

TABLE II–29

RANKING OF OCCUPATION BY STATES

Occupation	Mass.	Tenn.	Ky.	Texas	N. C.	Wis.	Ariz. Col. N. Mex.	General State Ranking	Total Series Ranking
Factory	1	2	3	2	2	4	2	1	2
Extractive	9	1	1	1	3	2	1	2	1
Laborer	3	3	2	5	1	1	3	2	3
Skilled trades	4	4	4	3	4	5	6	4	4
Transportation	2	5	5	6	8	6	5	5	5
Personal service	6	7	7	4	6	3	4	5	6
Trade	5	6	6	7	5	8	7	7	7
Clerical	7	8	8	8	7	7	8	8	8
Semi-professional	8	9	10	9	11	9	9	9	9
Public service	10	10	9	11	10	10	11	10	11
Professional	11	11	11	10	9	11	10	11	10

cific offense rankings. It is perhaps surprising, however, to note that the professional class is last in forgery and fraud and ranks relatively high in arson and all others.

Table II–29 similarly ranks the occupations by states. Factory workers rank first only in Massachusetts, but attain first place in mean general state ranking. They drop to fourth place only in Wisconsin. In the individual ranking of the total series factory workers are second. Extractive occupations are first in most states, but drop to third in North Carolina and to ninth in Massachusetts. Their general state ranking is second, and individual series ranking first. Laborers tie for second place in general state ranking. They drop to fifth place in Texas. Skilled trades are notable for their high ranking in Texas and low ranking in Arizona, Colorado, and New Mexico. Transportation rises to second place in Massachusetts and drops to eighth place in North Carolina. Its general ranking is fifth. Personal service is unaccountably high (third place) in Wisconsin. Trade is very low in Wisconsin. The clerical occupations are consistently in seventh or eighth place in every state. Their general rank is eighth. Semi-professional, public service, and professional show no marked state deviations.

We are especially concerned in this study with such occupational differentiation among the criminals as may be both statistically significant and independent of state sampling. We are not interested in the preponderance of extractive occupations among murderers if that fact merely reflects the primarily agricultural character of the states from which our sample originates. Therefore we may at once proceed to Table II–30 which gives not only the differences between offense groups and the total series in occupational categories, but also predicts the expected occupations on the basis of state composition, gives the differences between predicted and actual occurrence, and finally summarizes those occupations which show significant and independent differentiations in the offense groups.

The extractive category of occupations is characterized by marked independent excesses of both classes of murderers and of offenders versus public welfare. It is strongly deficient in robbers and in persons convicted of burglary and larceny, and of forgery and fraud. The laborer class shows a small excess of burglars and thieves and a small deficiency of fraudulent criminals. Factory workers exhibit a strong excess of robbers and a small excess of burglars and thieves. This occupational class is deficient in second degree murder. Skilled trades are remarkable for their excess of assault offenders. They are also slightly deficient in second degree murder. The trade class is significantly high in forgery and fraud, but slightly deficient in burglary and larceny. In the latter category of offenses the semi-professional class shows a slight but significant independent difference. The professional class is curiously high in other sex offenses, and exhibits also an excess of forgery and fraud. It is deficient in thieves and burglars. Personal service workers are slightly high in burglary and larceny and deficient in second degree murder. The clerical occupational category has an excess of forgery and fraud offenders and a deficiency of second degree murderers.

There are a few independent excesses of occupational representations in the offense groups which merit comment. The first of these is the unduly large number of murderers who belong to the extractive occupations — presumably farmers, for the most part. Is agricultural life conducive to homicide, or are the men who choose to till the soil so constituted as to incline toward deeds of violence against the person? The isolation of farm life may tend to develop psychoses in persons of psychopathic predisposition, and constant contact with a limited number of human associates may tend to animosities which lead to killings. Of course in the mountain districts of Kentucky and Tennessee feudal killings are a part of the social tradition, but ample allowance for this local factor has been made in the corrections for state sampling. The marked deficiency of burglary and larceny in the extractive class is doubtless due to the limited opportunities for breaking and entering and theft which are afforded by farm life. The fewness of convictions for robbery may be attributed also to the rural conditions of extractive life.

The excess of assault in skilled trades is inexplicable. The great number of persons of extractive occupation who fall under the versus public welfare offense grouping is perhaps connected with "moonshining" in Kentucky and Tennessee and smuggling of liquor across the border in Texas. Almost 58 per cent of these offenders are from the latter state.

Educational and physical differentiation of occupational groups is discussed in Chapter VIII.

Table II–31 gives the distribution of occupations by age groups. Extractive occupations increase with comparative regularity from the younger to the older groups. This circumstance reflects to some extent the tendency of farmers to be imprisoned for serious offenses carrying long sentences — such as murder and rape. It may imply also some disinclination on the part of the younger generation to engage in extractive occupations. Factory workers are commonest between the ages of 20 and 29 years and decrease gradually thereafter. This fact is possibly attributable to the rigorous physical demands made upon such workers. Skilled tradesmen are most frequent between the ages of 30 and 54 years. Persons engaged in trade and in the professions become gradually more numerous in successive age groups. Most of the other occupational groups seem to show little or no regression upon age.

With the exception of the extractive categories, the age distribution of occupation seems to correspond roughly to the physical vigor and strength required in each category and to the amount of training and experience which are prerequisites for learning the occupation.

EDUCATION

The educational attainments of our native White prisoners of native parentage are of considerable interest in their relation to type of offense and state of origin. We shall consider first the educational status of the total series and of the subgroups irrespective of the complicating effect of state sampling. We shall then make the proper corrections for state sampling in order to determine whether the offense groups are differentiated in scholastic attainments apart from the varying opportunities of education offered by the different states.

Table II–32 gives the numbers and percentages of the total series and of the offense subgroups for each educational category. The series contains 10.16 per cent of illiterates and 4.21 per cent of persons who can read and write but who have had no formal education. Of the total number of native White prisoners in 1910 reporting as to literacy, 4.5 per cent were designated as illiterate. In the same year there were 3.2 per cent of illiterates in the general population of males 15 years or over. Our 1927–28 native White criminals of native parentage thus compare very unfavorably with native

White prisoners committed in 1910 and with the general population of that period. However, a better comparison is that of the prisoners of our series by states with the native White prisoners committed in 1910 from the census areas in which those states are included. The lack of later census figures on the literacy of prisoners distinguished by nativity compels us to utilize the somewhat antiquated data of 1910.

It is obvious that the comparisons in Table II–33 must be interpreted with great caution, since the subjects included in the census material are native Whites while our series consists of native Whites of native parentage. Furthermore, the dates are different and states are compared with census districts. Massachusetts native Whites of native parentage seem more literate than the native Whites of New England committed in 1910, and our series from Texas, Wisconsin, and the Southwest also show less illiteracy than the 1910 material with which they are compared. In Kentucky, Tennessee, and North Carolina no such diminution of illiteracy seems to have taken place.

At this point we may consider a portion of Table II–34 which lists the educational qualifications by states. The appalling proportion of illiterates from the states just mentioned springs to the eye. Evidently the educational status of the offense groups is likely to be affected markedly by the states from which the prisoners are drawn.

In every educational category up to the seventh grade first degree murderers are in excess of the percentage of the entire criminal series in that category. In the higher educational classes first degree murderers are consistently deficient. Second degree murderers are in excess up to the sixth grade and thereafter deficient. Assault criminals do not deviate strongly from the general series in the distribution of their educational attainments. Robbers are deficient in their percentages up to the seventh grade and in excess in subsequent higher categories. Burglary and larceny follows closely the series distribution, showing however a slight deficiency of illiterates and a slight excess of high school attendants. Forgery and fraud is notably deficient in categories up to the seventh grade and strongly in excess in the higher categories, whereas in rape the deficiencies and excesses are reversed. Other sex offenses show an irregular distribution. Versus public welfare displays a heaping up of frequencies in the grammar school grades.

In Table II–35 the offense groups are ranked by comparing the combined percentages of illiterates and "read and write only" with the combined percentages of those who have reached the third year of high school or some higher educational status, and by expressing the latter (B) as a ratio of the former (A). This ranking shows the educational preeminence of the forgery and fraud group, the comparatively good showing of the robbery group, and the tremendous decline terminating in the abysmal ignorance of the murderers.

Table II–36 shows the ranking of states by the same method and demonstrates clearly the educational superiority of the Massachusetts criminals and the low status of Tennessee, North Carolina, and Kentucky. The Massachusetts ranking is probably elevated by the inclusion in the series of a reformatory group of comparatively young prisoners.

Table II–37 gives all of the details whereby the independence of, or dependence upon, state composition is demonstrated for each offense group in each educational category. The summary lists the educational dfferentiation of the offense groups over and beyond the influence of state origin. We may epitomize these findings by offense groups.

The illiteracy of first degree murder is more than would be expected from state composition, but not significantly more. The excess of this offense group in the "read and write only" category is significant and independent of state sampling. The deficiencies of first degree murder in first and second years of high school and in college

TABLE II–35

EDUCATIONAL RANKING BY OFFENSES

	A Illiterates, Read and Write Per Cent	B 3rd–4th Year High, College, Professional Per Cent	Ratio of B to A	Rank
Forgery and fraud	8.41	19.40	2.31	I
Robbery	5.35	10.70	2.00	2
Burglary and larceny	11.20	7.26	0.65	3
Assault	11.25	6.25	0.56	4
Other sex	21.47	10.07	0.47	5
Arson and all other	13.86	5.94	0.43	6
Versus public welfare	14.90	5.49	0.37	7
Rape	16.32	4.08	0.25	8
Second degree murder ...	25.89	2.75	0.11	9
First degree murder	24.67	2.60	0.10	10
Total series	14.37	7.72	0.54	..

TABLE II–36

EDUCATIONAL RANKING BY STATES

	A Illiterates, Read and Write Per Cent	B 3rd–4th Year High, College, Professional Per Cent	Ratio of B to A	Rank
Massachusetts	1.20	14.29	11.91	I
Wisconsin	4.76	11.56	2.43	2
Southwest	4.38	9.44	2.16	3
Texas	11.63	11.74	1.01	4
Tennessee	16.12	7.35	0.46	5
North Carolina	17.38	5.20	0.30	6
Kentucky	25.93	2.04	0.08	7
Total series	14.37	7.72	0.54	..

are also independent and significant. All in all, first degree murderers are more ignorant than total criminals, over and above any allowance which can be made for their state derivation.

Second degree murder is even more markedly differentiated by a consistently greater ignorance than is to be expected from state composition. Its deviations are largely independent of state sampling.

The assault group shows no educational deviations which are not complicated by state sampling.

The robbery group is almost unaffected by state sampling in its deficiencies of poorly educated persons and excesses of well-educated persons.

Burglary and larceny is independent of state sampling in its deficiencies of illiterates and readers and writers only; it is also independent in its excesses of persons who have reached the seventh grade and the first two years of high school.

The high educational attainments of the forgery and fraud group are not dependent upon state composition.

The rape group shows deficiencies of persons who have reached the first two years of high school and who have attended college, which are independent of state sampling.

The other sex, versus public welfare, and arson and all other groups show no educational differentiation which is not complicated and nullified by chance and state sampling.

In conclusion it may be stated that both classes of murderers are definitely stigmatized by excessive illiteracy and poor educational attainments and that rapists are to a lesser degree distinguished by deficiencies of well-educated persons. Equally outstanding is the educational preeminence of the forgery and fraud and robbery groups. Burglars and thieves occupy an intermediate position. The general educational rankings of various offense groups of prisoners are practically unaffected by the varying and disproportionate contributions of advanced and benighted states to these offense groups.

One expects the proportions of illiterates to increase in the successively older age groups, and they do. This increase is also noted in the "read and write only" group, but it is not so marked. There is no clear regression upon age among criminals who have reached the first seven grades of primary school. Attainment of eighth grade and the first two years of high school decreases with advancing age. The highest educational attainments seem independent of age except in the extreme age groups. On the whole there is no consistent relationship of the age of criminals to their degree of educational attainment.

Summary of Sociological Observations

In Tables II–39 to II–48 the sociological differences of the several offense groups have been listed according to their statistical significance and the dependence upon, or independence of, state sampling. The sociological features included in this summary are: previous convictions, marital state, occupation, and education. These four offer together 26 categories in which each offense group may differ from the total series. Some of these categories are more or less complementary (e.g., single and married), so that a significant deviation in one is likely to carry with it an opposite deviation in the other. In some of these sociological features it has been necessary to take into account the influence of age, as well as that of state sampling, but in no case does this question of age seem to require statistical correction except in the matter of marital state.

After each offense group has been considered in detail we may appraise the total degree of statistical differentiation of the series in comparison expectation in random samples.

First Degree Murder. In this offense group deviations which are significant and independent of state sampling total 9 of 26 or 34.62 per cent. Six more crude differences which were significant are reduced to unreliability by the effects of state composition.

The significant and independent differences in marital state include excess of married men and deficiency of single men. These two differences, however, have been shown to be involved in the high mean age of the group and must not be considered criminologically important. An excess of widowers is, however, independent both of age and of state sampling.

Occupationally the first degree murderers are characterized by an excess of the extractive category (mostly farmers). This is independent of state composition. Deficiencies in laborers and factory operatives are invalidated by state sampling. Deficiencies in almost every other occupational category occur, but the values of the differences do not equal three times their probable errors and the deviations may therefore be considered as possibly insignificant.

Educationally, first degree murderers are distinguished by excesses of persons who can read and write, but have not attended school, and by deficiencies of persons who have reached the first two years of high school, or have attended college. Many other educational categories show excesses or deficiencies, but all of these fail to attain significance when state sampling is taken into consideration.

First degree murderers show the smallest percentage of persons with recorded previous convictions — a deficiency which remains valid when allowance has been made for state sampling.

This offense is particularly characteristic of Kentucky, among the states studied. This state contributes 53.53 per cent of all first degree murderers, although its general contribution to the total prison series is only 28.18 per cent. Furthermore, although in the total series only 7.41 per cent of criminals are first degree murderers, 14.07 per cent of Kentuckians belong to this offense group. In this connection it is of interest to note that the Kentucky prisoners include fewer extra-state born inmates than any other state series.

We may conclude that, apart from inequalities of state distribution, first degree murderers are sociologically distinct from the criminals at large in the following respects:

(1) In their greater lack of educational attainments, since they are the most poorly educated of all criminal groups.

(2) In the high percentage of widowers found among them.

(3) In the disproportionately large number of persons belonging to extractive occupations.

(4) In the infrequency of their recorded previous convictions.

Second Degree Murder. Second degree murderers exhibit significant differences independent of state sampling in 14 features, or 53.85 per cent of those included in the listing. The deviations are very similar to those of the first degree murderers, but are more numerous, probably because of the larger size of the sample and the consequently smaller value of the probable errors of percentages. Second degree murderers include an excess of persons with no recorded previous convictions.

In marital status there is the same deficiency of unmarried and excess of married men, but it is independent of state sampling and of age. There is however no excess of widowers, although a possibly valid excess of divorced and separated men.

Again in this group we find a great excess of extractive occupations and deficiencies of most other categories — independent of state sampling in the cases of skilled trades, factory, personal service, and clerical.

This group is also very ignorant, showing independent excesses of illiterates, of persons who have attended the first five grades of schools, and deficiencies in the higher educational categories. Second degree murderers show a low percentage of previous convictions, but the deficiency is invalidated by state sampling.

Tennessee, Kentucky, and North Carolina are the largest contributors to this offense group. Its distinctive features when compared with the series at large are then:

(1) Excess of married men, deficiency of single men.
(2) Excess of persons engaged in extractive occupations.
(3) Excess of illiterates and poorly educated persons.
(4) Excess of persons with no previous convictions.

Assault. This offense group is distinguished in only 3 sociological categories or 11.54 per cent. It shows an independent excess of married men and deficiency of single men. It has a very remarkable occupational excess in skilled trades which I cannot explain. It is not distinguished in education from the total criminal series. The assault criminals are scattered in the various state groups and constitute the smallest offense group studied.

Robbery. This group shows deviations significant and independent of state sampling in 10 sociological features or 38.46 per cent. It has an excess of unmarried men which is also independent of age. It is drawn to a disproportionately large extent from the factory class and is deficient in the extractive category. An excess in the clerical category is possibly insignificant (2.98 p.e.) when corrected for state sampling.

Educationally the robbers are deficient in all the lowest grades of scholastic attainment and in excess in the eighth grade and high school categories, after due allowance has been made for state sampling. The group is not distinguished in previous convictions. It is derived from all of the states, with Texas and Kentucky leading in their contributions.

Its main sociological features may be summarized as follows:

(1) Excess of single men.
(2) Excess of factory workers and deficiency of extractives.
(3) Excess of eighth grade and high school attendants, dearth of illiterates and primary school attendants.

Burglary and Larceny. The Burglary and Larceny group shows significant excesses in 16 sociological categories or 61.54 per cent. Its many differences may be due in part to its very large size and the consequent smallness of probable errors of percentages. This group shows, firstly, an excess of persons with previous convictions.

Its marked deficiency of married men is independent both of state sampling and of age, but a deficiency of widowers is due to the young mean age of the group. Occupationally this group shows excesses of laborers, factory operatives, semi-professional and personal service workers, and is deficient in the extractive, trade, and professional categories. All of these differences are independent of state sampling.

The educational attainments of these burglars and thieves are neither exceptionally poor (deficiencies of illiterates and read and write) nor very good (independent excesses of seventh grade and first two years of high school, deficiency of college attendants). Most of the states studied contribute about their just quotas to this group.

The summary of sociological differentiae is:

(1) Excess of single men.

(2) Excess of laborers, factory operatives, personal service.

(3) Deficiency of illiterates and very poorly educated persons, excess of moderately educated persons.

(4) Highest proportion of recidivists.

Forgery and Fraud. The deviations of the forgery and fraud group which are significant and independent of state sampling are 10 in number, or 38.46 per cent. The group displays no marital differentiation from the series at large. In occupation, as might be expected, it shows significant and independent excesses of the clerical, trade, and professional categories, with deficiencies of laborers and extractives. Its educational peculiarities include excesses in high school and college and deficiencies of illiterates and primary school attendants. It is undifferentiated in previous convictions and is unduly loaded with criminals from Texas.

Rape. This group shows 7 sociological features or 26.92 per cent of deviations which are significant and independent of state sampling. However in marital state its deficiency of single men and its excesses of married men and widowers are complicated by age effects and cannot be considered of certain value. The rape group shows no certainly significant occupational differences. Its only educational deviations which are significant and independent of state sampling are deficiencies of the first two high school years and of college. On the whole the group is poorly educated. It shows a marked deficiency of previous convictions which is independent of state sampling. This group has received a disproportionately large contribution from the Wisconsin series.

Other Sex Offenses. The other sex offenders are significantly distinguished in 5 features or 19.23 per cent. Their deficiency of single men is independent of age complications, but the excess of married men and of widowers is partially due to their advanced mean age. The only other sociological feature of this group which shows differentiation that is significant and independent of state sampling is its excess in the professional occupational category. A deficiency of recidivists is invalidated by state sampling, but an excess of persons with no previous convictions is valid. The state derivation of the group is not remarkable.

Versus Public Welfare. This group displays only 5 features which are significantly differentiated independently of state sampling. It is characterized by a deficiency of recidivists. Its great excess of married men and deficiency of single men is independent, in large measure, of age composition. The group is also notable for its unduly high proportion of extractives. Educationally it shows no certainly significant differences, although its scholastic attainments are, in general, inferior.

Arson and All Other Offenses. This residual group is least differentiated sociologically, since it shows only 2 differences which are significant and independent of state sampling. These are an excess of married men and a deficiency of single men, both of which are beyond age expectations.

GENERAL STATISTICAL DIFFERENTIATION

Table II–49 presents the numbers and percentages of sociological differences according to their significance and dependence upon, or independence of, state sampling. The most markedly differentiated group is burglary and larceny, and the least is arson and all others. The high differentiation of the burglars and thieves is probably due only in part to the large size of the group. Professional criminals are undoubtedly numerous in this offense class. The small differentiation of the arson and all other group is perhaps effected by the miscellaneous and residual character of the offenses included in it. It should be noted that murderers show the highest percentages of significant differences which are invaliated by state sampling. This is caused by the great excess of Kentucky criminals in these two offense groups.

Table II–50 records the differentiation of total sociological characters, namely: previous convictions, marital state, occupation and education. Any total sociological character is regarded as differentiated when one or more of its subcategories shows a difference between the offense group and the total which is significant and independent of state sampling. Since each of the four total sociological characters is tested in ten offense subgroups, the total of sociological characters is 40. Of these 29, or 72.50 per cent, are significantly differentiated. The only offense subgroup which is not certainly differentiated over and beyond expectation in random samples is arson and all other offenses, which has but one of the four characters in which it differs from the total group significantly and beyond what is attributable to state sampling. Actually, expectation in random samples would call for less than 4 of 100 characters to show significant differentiation through chance alone.

No student of sociology will be surprised at the results of this investigation in the cruder elements of the sociology of delinquents. Their broad significance lies in the fact that state sampling, and when necessary, age differences, have been eliminated as complicating factors. There is no implication of causality in this demonstration of the sociological differences evinced by criminals of the various offense groups. But if we should find that the sociological peculiarities are unaccompanied by physical differentiation, it might be assumed with some reason that environment is more potent than heredity in crime causation.

Chapter III

METRIC AND INDICIAL DIFFERENTIATION
BY STATES

MEASUREMENTS AND INDICES

AGE. Table III–1 [1] shows the considerable disparity in age composition between the criminals observed in the various states. All of the state groups except Tennessee and the combined Southwestern series (Colorado, Arizona, New Mexico) are significantly different in mean age from the total series of native born criminals of native parentage. The youngest mean age is found in the Massachusetts group which is 3.20 years lower than the average of the total series. This is doubtless due in part to the inclusion of inmates of the Concord Reformatory. The group from Wisconsin is the oldest, with a mean age of 34.95 years — 4.25 years in excess of the series average. Texas criminals are also significantly older than the total group. The maximum difference in mean ages (7.45 years) occurs between the criminals of Massachusetts and Wisconsin. These age differences must be taken into account in the appraisal of other state deviations from the total series.

Weight. Three of the state groups deviate significantly from the total series in mean weight. These are Massachusetts (−5.00 pounds, 6.76 p.e.), Wisconsin (−3.60 pounds, 4.56 p.e.), and Texas (3.60 pounds, 7.83 p.e.). These differences cannot depend primarily upon age, since Massachusetts, which is the youngest group, and Wisconsin, the oldest, both deviate significantly from the total group by way of deficiency.

Table III–3 presents the mean weights of states in descending order together with their mean ages. There seems to be little significant group correlation. Individually the product moment coefficient of correlation of weight with age is only .13 ± .01 for the total series.

Height. All of the state groups except Tennessee and North Carolina differ signifi-

---

[1] The grouping interval for age is 5 years, and the youngest age class in all tables appears as 15–19. Actually, however, the series contains but 4 individuals of the age of 15 years. For all practical purposes the lowermost age limit, including enough frequencies to influence the series, is 18 years. The frequencies and percentages of observations in the 15–19 year age group are as follows:

Age	Number	Per Cent
15	4	.71
16	13	2.29
17	47	8.23
18	123	21.69
19	380	67.07
Total	567	99.99

cantly from the stature mean of the whole series. The minus deviations are Wisconsin (−2.43 cm., 9.72 p.e.), Massachusetts (−2.13 cm., 8.88 p.e.), and the Southwest (−.96 cm., 5.33 p.e.). Kentucky has an excess of .39 cm., 3.00 p.e., and Texas one of 1.23 cm., 8.79 p.e. The shortest groups are Wisconsin, the oldest, and Massachusetts, the youngest. The general independence of stature and age is shown by the co-

TABLE III–3

COMPARISON OF MEAN WEIGHTS AND MEAN AGES BY STATES

	Mean Weight	Mean Age
Texas	154.50	33.45
North Carolina	152.70	28.40
Southwest	150.80	30.60
Tennessee	150.60	29.80
Kentucky	149.80	29.65
Wisconsin	147.30	34.95
Massachusetts	145.90	27.50
Total	150.90	30.70

efficient of correlation (−.03 ± .01). On the other hand stature and weight are closely related (r = .48 ± .01).

Biacromial Diameter. States showing significant deviations from the total series in biacromial diameter are Massachusetts (−.24 cm., 3.00 p.e.), Kentucky (−.21 cm. 5.25 p.e.), Southwest (.18 cm., 3.00 p.e.), and Texas (.21 cm., 4.20 p.e.). These deviations are uncorrelated with age (r = −.02 ± .01), but significantly correlated with weight (r = .41 ± .01) and with stature (r = .30 ± .01).

Chest Depth. In chest depth the following states show significant deviations from the mean of the total series: North Carolina (−.82 cm., 13.67 p.e.), Wisconsin (−.32 cm., 4.57 p.e.), Kentucky (.20 cm., 6.67 p.e.), and Texas (.26 cm., 6.50 p.e.). These differences are strongly correlated with weight (r = .55 ± .01) and less markedly with stature (r = .21 ± .01).

Chest Breadth. The Massachusetts group is the only state series with a marked deficiency in mean chest breadth (−.81 cm., 11.57 p.e.), while Texas (.12 cm., 3.00 p.e.), Kentucky (.15 cm., 3.75 p.e.), and Tennessee (.21 cm., 3.50 p.e.) show slight but significant mean excesses. These are markedly correlated with weight (r = .57 ± .01) and less so with stature (r = .28 ± .01).

Sitting Height. All of the state groups except the Southwestern deviate significantly from the total mean in sitting height. These deviations are: Massachusetts (−1.2 cm., 9.46 p.e.), Tennessee (−.66 cm., 6.00 p.e.), Kentucky (−.27 cm., 3.86 p.e.) Wisconsin (.42 cm., 3.00 p.e.), Texas (.63 cm., 7.88 p.e.), and North Carolina (.6 cm., 6.27 p.e.). The difference of Wisconsin is rather unexpected because this state is the shortest stature group and would be expected to show a deficiency in sitting height rather than an excess. The correlations are age (r = −.04 ± .01), weight (r = .45 ± .01), and stature (r = .70 ± .01).

Head Length. All of the states except Wisconsin have significant deviations from the mean of head length in the total series. These are as follows: Tennessee (−1.8

mm., 9.00 p.e.), Massachusetts (−1.41 mm., 5.88 p.e.), Texas (−.87 mm., 6.21 p.e.), Southwest (.72 mm., 4.00 p.e.), Kentucky (.78 mm., 6.00 p.e.), and North Carolina (.81 mm., 3.86 p.e.). The correlations involved are: age (r = .03 ± .01), weight (r = .34 ± .01), and stature (r = .26 ± .01). The differences are then dependent upon size and bulk rather than upon age.

Head Breadth. Head breadth shows fewer deviations from the total mean than does head length. The significant differences are: North Carolina (−.54 mm., 3.18 p.e.), Kentucky (−.51 mm., 4.64 p.e.), Wisconsin (1.62 mm., 7.71 p.e.). The relevant correlations are age (r = .08 ± .01), weight (r = .31 ± .01), and stature (r = .15 ± .01). Of these the only significant one is with weight and it is notable that Wisconsin, the second shortest and second lightest state group, has the largest mean head breadth. This implies a difference in racial extraction for the Middle Western state.

Head Height. In this measurement the state groups studied by the two observers must be kept distinct and compared with their respective totals, since the instruments and techniques employed were different. All of Observer A's states differ significantly from his total mean. The deviations are: Kentucky (−.78 mm., 7.09 p.e.), Texas (.45 mm., 3.75 p.e.), Massachusetts (.72 mm., 3.60 p.e.), and Tennessee (.72 mm., 4.00 p.e.). In the case of Observer B the deviations are even greater and are equally all-inclusive. They are: North Carolina (−2.58 mm., 13.58 p.e.), Southwest (1.05 mm., 6.18 p.e.), and Wisconsin (1.80 mm., 7.50 p.e.). The correlations involved are: age (Observer A, r = −.04 ± .01; Observer B, r = −.01 ± .02), weight (Observer A, r = .22 ± .01; Observer B, r = .21 ± .02), and stature (Observer A, r = .24 ± .01; Observer B, r = .15 ± .02). Evidently here again the correlations of importance are with stature and weight, but beyond this there are probably undiscovered differences in racial extraction.

Head Circumference. The state differences are universal and great. They are: North Carolina (−6.60 mm., 12.94 p.e.), Southwest (−6.00 mm., 13.64 p.e.), Wisconsin (−4.80 mm., 6.49 p.e.), Massachusetts (−2.40 mm., 4.07 p.e.), Kentucky (3.00 mm., 9.38 p.e.), Texas (4.32 mm., 12.00 p.e.), Tennessee (4.56 mm., 5.77 p.e.). The correlations involved are weight (r = .41 ± .01) and stature (r = .31 ± .01). Apart from these it seems probable that a heterogeneity in racial extraction may contribute to the diversity in this measurement.

Minimum Frontal Diameter. All of the states except Wisconsin again show significant deviations. The deficiencies are: Kentucky (−2.28 mm., 22.80 p.e.), Massachusetts (−1.16 mm., 6.44 p.e.). The excesses are: Southwest (.64 mm., 4.92 p.e.), North Carolina (1.16 mm., 7.25 p.e.), Tennessee (1.48 mm., 9.25 p.e.), and Texas (1.56 mm., 14.18 p.e.). The correlation of minimum frontal diameter with stature is .20 ± .01. The correlation with weight has not been calculated but it is probably as large, if not larger than that with stature.

Bizygomatic Diameter. The significant deviations in means of states over the total series are as follows: Massachusetts (−1.30 mm., 6.50 p.e.), Kentucky (−.60 mm., 6.00 p.e.), Texas (.90 mm., 7.50 p.e.), Wisconsin (.95 mm., 4.52 p.e.). Relevant correlations are: age (r = .10 ± .01), weight (r = .47 ± .01), stature (r = .25 ± .01). In spite of these relationships, Wisconsin, the second shortest and second lightest of all of the state groups, has absolutely the highest mean of bizygomatic diameter.

Total Face Height. The mean of total face height is greatest in Massachusetts, the shortest and youngest group, and smallest in North Carolina, which is one of the taller groups but ranks low also in mean age. Significant deviations are as follows: North Carolina (−.90 mm., 4.29 p.e.), Texas (−.50 mm., 3.57 p.e.), Southwest (.70 mm., 3.89 p.e.), and Massachusetts (1.30 mm., 5.42 p.e.). The correlations involved are: age ($r = .02 \pm .01$), weight ($r = .22 \pm .01$), and stature ($r = .24 \pm .01$). Since Massachusetts ranks lowest in weight and height, its high mean of the measurement runs contrary to the correlation trend.

Upper Face Height. Upper face height shows more marked state variations than total face height and these are not wholly in accordance with the differences exhibited in the larger measurement, probably because of variations in the height of the mandibular symphysis. The significant deviations are: Texas (−1.00 mm., 10.00 p.e.), Tennessee (−.75 mm., 5.00 p.e.), Massachusetts (−.60 mm., 3.53 p.e.), Kentucky (−.40 mm., 4.44 p.e.), North Carolina (.80 mm., 5.71 p.e.), Wisconsin (1.30 mm., 7.22 p.e.), and Southwest (1.85 mm., 15.42 p.e.). The correlation with age ($r = −.01 \pm .01$) is nil.

Nose Height. Significant state deviations in this measurement are: North Carolina (−1.28 mm., 10.67 p.e.), Kentucky (−.44 mm., 5.50 p.e.), Southwest (1.24 mm., 11.27 p.e.), and Wisconsin (1.52 mm., 10.13 p.e.). In this case the correlation with age is important ($r = .26 \pm .01$) and the differences may well be due in large measure to this factor. The mean ages of the various state groups agree in general with this supposition. Wisconsin, the oldest group, has the longest average nose, and the younger groups fall without exception below the mean nasal height of the series.

Nose Breadth. In this measurement the following significant deviations occur: North Carolina (−.84 mm., 9.33 p.e.), Massachusetts (−.75 mm., 7.50 p.e.), Kentucky (−.36 mm., 6.00 p.e.), Southwest (.42 mm., 5.25 p.e.), Tennessee (.54 mm., 6.00 p.e.), and Texas (.69 mm., 11.50 p.e.). Relevant correlations are: age ($r = .18 \pm .01$) and weight ($r = .28 \pm .01$).

Bigonial Diameter. In this measurement (hinder breadth of jaws) the following states are differentiated from the total criminal group: Massachusetts (−1.72 mm., 8.19 p.e.), North Carolina (−1.36 mm., 7.56 p.e.), Southwest (−.48 mm., 3.00 p.e.), and Texas (1.40 mm., 10.77 p.e.). The correlation with weight is high ($r = .37 \pm .01$).

Table III–21 shows that there is by no means a perfect group correlation between bigonial diameter and weight.

Ear Length. In the ear dimensions the state groups of the two observers have been kept separate, on account of differences in their techniques of taking these measurements. Observer A's four state groups show the following significant deviations: Kentucky (−1.32 mm., 13.20 p.e.), Texas (1.84 mm., 16.73 p.e.). In Observer B's series the deviations are: Southwest (−.44 mm., 3.67 p.e.), Wisconsin (.68 mm., 3.78 p.e.). The correlations of age with ear length have not been calculated, because it is well known that they are significantly high and must be taken into consideration. The correlations with height are: Observer A ($r = .24 \pm .01$), Observer B ($r = .24 \pm .02$). The correlations of height and age may well be responsible for the magnitude of these state differences. In both observers' series the oldest state groups have the longest ears, irrespective of stature, but the youngest groups do not show the minimum values. There must be, therefore, factors other than stature and age which are involved in the state differences.

Ear Breadth. All of Observer A's states are distinctive in means of this measurement. The deviations are: Massachusetts (−1.05 mm., 10.50 p.e.), Kentucky (−.30 mm., 5.00 p.e.), Texas (.45 mm., 7.50 p.e.), and Tennessee (.75 mm., 8.33 p.e.). In Observer B's series the deviations are: North Carolina (−.68 mm., 7.56 p.e.), Southwest (.25 mm., 3.12 p.e.), and Wisconsin (.73 mm., 6.64 p.e.). The correlation involved is: age (Observer A, r = .21 ± .01; Observer B, r = .25 ± .02). In both observers' series the youngest groups have the narrowest ears, and in the series of B the oldest group has the broadest ears, although it is the shortest. In the series of A, the Tennessee group has the broadest ears, although it ranks fourth in age, third in stature, and fourth in weight.

TABLE III–21

COMPARISON OF MEAN WEIGHTS AND MEAN BIGONIAL DIAMETERS

	Mean Bigonial	Mean Weight
Texas	109.18	154.50
Tennessee	108.30	150.60
Kentucky	107.78	149.80
Wisconsin	107.78	147.30
Southwest	107.30	150.80
North Carolina	106.42	152.70
Massachusetts	106.06	145.90
Total Series	107.78	150.90

Relative Shoulder Breadth. The following are the significant deviations of state groups in relative shoulder breadth: Tennessee (−.36, 9.00 p.e.), North Carolina (−.16, 4.00 p.e.), Kentucky (−.14, 4.67 p.e.), Southwest (.24, 6.00 p.e.), Massachusetts (.44, 8.80 p.e.), and Wisconsin (.54, 10.80 p.e.). These deviations though statistically significant are quite small. The correlation with weight (r = .09 ± .01) is insignificant. It is notable that the shortest groups, Massachusetts and Wisconsin, have the highest relative shoulder breadths.

Relative Sitting Height. The deviations by states are: Tennessee (−.58, 11.60 p.e.), Kentucky (−.22, 7.33 p.e.), North Carolina (.22, 4.40 p.e.), Southwest (.26, 6.50 p.e.), and Wisconsin (.98, 16.33 p.e.). The correlations involved are age (r = .01 ± .01), and weight (r = −.01 ± .01). The state differences are evidently due to neither of these, nor to stature, since the shortest group, Wisconsin, has the highest relative sitting height, whereas Massachusetts, which is scarcely greater in mean stature, is slightly below the mean in relative sitting height.

Cephalic Index. The deviations of state means of cephalic indices are absolutely very small, although they are statistically significant in all groups save one. A range of 1.41 index units separates the extremes of the state means. The deviations are North Carolina (−.66, 6.60 p.e.), Kentucky (−.56, 9.33 p.e.), Massachusetts (.45, 3.75 p.e.), Texas (.45, 6.43 p.e.), Wisconsin (.72, 5.54 p.e.), and Tennessee (.75, 6.82 p.e.). The correlations involved are: age (r = .04 ± .01), weight (r = −.04 ± .01), and stature (r = −.09 ± .01). These amount to nothing. The variabilities of the states are quite similar, as are also the ranges. All of these groups are mesocephalic and include all varieties of length-breadth index.

Cephalo-facial Index. In this index Massachusetts is strongly divergent, because of its low mean bizygomatic diameter. The deviations are: Massachusetts (−.96, 8.73 p.e.), Texas (.27, 3.86 p.e.), and North Carolina (.36, 3.60 p.e.). On the whole, the states are only slightly differentiated in this index.

Length-Height Index. The data of the two observers have been kept separate on account of differences of instruments and technique. The deviations are: Observer A — Kentucky (−.84, 14.00 p.e.), Texas (.42, 6.00 p.e.), Massachusetts (.75, 6.25 p.e.), and Tennessee (.93, 9.30 p.e.); Observer B — North Carolina (−1.41, 12.82 p.e.), Southwest (.51, 5.67 p.e.), and Wisconsin (1.05, 8.08 p.e.). Tennessee and Wisconsin, the most brachycephalic states, show the strongest tendency toward hypsicephaly. The correlations of this index with stature are: Observer A (r = .03 ± .01), Observer B (r = −.03 ± .02).

Breadth-Height Index. Observer A's series include two significant deviations: Kentucky (−.30, 3.75 p.e.) and Massachusetts (.60, 4.29 p.e.). Observer B's series are more strongly differentiated: North Carolina (−1.32, 11.00 p.e.), Wisconsin (.60, 4.00 p.e.), and Southwest (.66, 6.00 p.e.). The correlation with stature, calculated for Observer A only, is .12 ± .01.

Facial Index. The most strongly deviating state group in the facial index is Massachusetts (1.96, 10.32 p.e.). Other significant deviations are: Texas (−.92, 7.67 p.e.) and North Carolina (−.68, 4.00 p.e.). Correlations involved are: age (r = −.10 ± .01), weight (r = −.10 ± .01), and stature (r = .05 ± .01). All of the groups show ranges from extreme euryprosopy to marked leptoprosopy.

Upper Facial Index. The significant state deviations in this index are: Texas (−1.02, 12.75 p.e.), Tennessee (−.54, 4.50 p.e.), North Carolina (.57, 5.18 p.e.), Wisconsin (.63, 4.50 p.e.), and Southwest (1.23, 12.30 p.e.). The correlation with age is (r = −.07 ± .01). A notable feature is the failure of Massachusetts, which is the most leptoprosopic group, to exhibit a significant excess in the upper facial index, and the marked excess in this index shown by the combined groups of New Mexico, Arizona, and Colorado.

Nasal Index. The deviations of this index are: Wisconsin (−1.60, 5.93 p.e.), Massachusetts (−1.16, 4.64 p.e.), Southwest (−.92, 4.84 p.e.), Texas (1.12, 7.47 p.e.), and Tennessee (1.60, 7.27 p.e.). The correlations are: age (r = −.03 ± .01), weight (r = .11 ± .01), and stature (r = −.03 ± .01). None of these is sufficiently marked to influence the deviations listed above. The most leptorrhine groups — Wisconsin and Massachusetts — are the shortest and lightest, but respectively the youngest and oldest.

Ear Index. These indices have been kept separate in the series of the two observers. Observer A's deviations are: Massachusetts (−1.04, 6.12 p.e.), Texas (−.84, 8.40 p.e.), and Kentucky (.76, 8.44 p.e.). The deviations of the states studied by Observer B are: North Carolina (−1.60, 10.00 p.e.) and Southwest (.88, 6.29 p.e.). The correlations are: age (Observer A: r = −.15 ± .01, Observer B: r = −.12 ± .02); and stature (Observer A: r = −.06 ± .01, Observer B: r = −.07 ± .02). These correlations are insufficient to account for the state differences.

Zygo-frontal Index. In this index Kentucky and Tennessee seem to present the extremes of contrast. The deviations are: Kentucky (−1.28, 21.33 p.e.), Southwest (.44, 4.89 p.e.), Texas (.56, 8.00 p.e.), North Carolina (.72, 7.20 p.e.), and Tennessee

(1.04, 10.40 p.e.). The differences are due to variations in the minimum frontal diameter, more than to differences in the bizygomatic diameter. Since the minimum frontal diameter seems to have been affected by an error of technique in measurement into which both observers seem to have fallen in the later stages of their work, I am not disposed to stress these differences.

Fronto-parietal Index. The state deviations of this index are: Kentucky (−1.20, 20.00 p.e.), Massachusetts (−.57, 4.75 p.e.), Wisconsin (−.48, 4.00 p.e.), Southwest (.36, 4.00 p.e.), Texas (.84, 12.00 p.e.), Tennessee (.87, 8.70 p.e.), and North Carolina (.99, 9.90 p.e.).

Zygo-gonial Index. The state deviations are as follows: North Carolina (−1.05, 8.75 p.e.), Wisconsin (−.60, 4.29 p.e.), Southwest (−.42, 4.20 p.e.), Kentucky (.33, 4.71 p.e.), and Texas (.51, 6.38 p.e.).

SUMMARY OF METRICAL AND INDICIAL DIFFERENCES

Massachusetts. The Massachusetts group of native born criminals of native parentage shows significant differences from the mean of all native criminals of native parentage in no less than 25 of 33 measurements and indices. It is, then, strongly differentiated as a group. It is the second youngest and shortest, lightest, narrowest in the shoulder and chest, smallest in sitting height, and in bizygomatic diameter of all of the state groups. It has relatively the longest and narrowest facial proportions of any state group studied, and also has the narrowest jaws. The details of differences and their value in terms of their probable errors are shown in Table III–42. The Massachusetts series is metrically closest to that from Kentucky. In spite of a great disparity in age, the Massachusetts group seems to resemble the Wisconsin group more nearly than it does the series from any other state, except Kentucky.

Tennessee. Tennessee is the least markedly differentiated from the total series of any of the state groups. Nevertheless it differs significantly in 17 of 33 measurements and indices and is metrically distinct. It has the shortest head length of any state group, but, curiously, the largest circumference. This seems to be related to a rather large minimum frontal diameter, which is exceeded only in Texas. The Tennessee group exceeds all others in the nasal index, apparently because the upper face and nose are short, and the latter is broader than the general mean. The zygo-frontal index in this group is at a maximum, on account of the large value of the minimum frontal diameter.

Kentucky. Although the Kentucky series is the largest from any state and comprises more than one quarter of the whole prison series of native Whites of native parentage, it diverges significantly in 26 of 33 metric and indicial characters. In many instances these divergences owe their significance to the small values of the probable errors rather than to their magnitudes. Specifically, the Kentucky group is a year below mean age, a little more than a pound below mean weight, but slightly above mean height and significantly narrow-shouldered. It is especially deficient in minimum frontal diameter and in ear length. Indicially it is distinguished by its low mean values of the zygo-frontal and fronto-parietal indices, both of which are related to its extremely low minimum frontal average.

Texas. Texas is differentiated in 28 of 33 characters. It is above the mean in weight and height and is the heaviest of all of the state groups. In minimum frontal diameter it exceeds all other groups, and it likewise exhibits the maximum averages for nose breadth and jaw breadth (bigonial). It has the lowest values of both total and upper facial indices, indicating that the prisoners from this state have relatively the shortest and broadest faces.

North Carolina. North Carolina differs from the mean of the whole series in 26 of 33 measurements and indices. This state group is 2.30 years below mean age, 1.80 pounds above mean weight, and slightly above mean height. It has the longest mean head length, the smallest mean head breadth, and the most dolichocephalic index. The nose in this group is shortest on the average of any of the state groups. The jaws are also very narrow. The fronto-parietal index is the maximum of the series. This group has the smallest cranial circumference of any in the series.

Wisconsin. Wisconsin is differentiated in 22 of 33 metric characters. It is the oldest group, the shortest, and the second lightest. It has the greatest mean head breadth of any group. The upper face height is great and the nose height (possibly because of age) is the greatest in any group. The nasal index is the most leptorrhine, or lowest. Relative sitting height is higher in this group than in any other.

Southwest (Colorado, Arizona, New Mexico). This group is differentiated in 23 of 33 metric features. The most important of these is an excessive upper facial height, which involves also great length of nose and the maximum value of the upper facial index.

Conclusions on State Differentiation in Metric and Indicial Features

Table III–43 presents a summary of the number and significance of deviations of measurements and indices of the state groups from the total series of native White criminals of native parentage. These deviations are expressed in terms of their probable errors and are compared with the number of deviations of corresponding magnitudes to be expected in a random sample drawn from the same population. If the state deviations were similarly distributed to those of the random sample and of lesser or equal magnitudes, we should be able to conclude that, apart from accidents inherent in the sampling process, the native White criminals of native parentage are undifferentiated from the total series in the several states. Quite the contrary is the case. The number and degree of the deviations in each state are so great as to indicate that the state groups represent samples drawn from radically different populations than the one which comprises the total criminal series.

Table III–44 gives the ranking of the various states in significant deviations of measurements and indices. Texas is the most strongly deviating state and Tennessee is nearest to a random sample of the entire series.

Information as to the states of birth of native Whites of native parentage permits us to compile Table III–45, showing the contributions of native sons of each state studied to the prison population of the other states. Tennessee's leading rôle is most suggestive, in view of the fact that Tennessee criminals depart least in metric features from a random sample of the entire criminal series of native Whites of native parentage. However there are not enough Tennessee natives in the prisons of other states to sway the means of those state series toward Tennessee values. Almost all of the Tennessee natives found in other prisons occur in Texas, North Carolina, and Kentucky —

which states lead in their metrical divergences from the total criminal series. Furthermore, Texas and Kentucky tie for second place in their contributions of natives to the prisons of other states.

TABLE III–44

RANKING OF STATES IN METRIC AND INDICIAL DIFFERENTIATION

	Significant Deviations in Measurements		Significant Deviations in Indices		Combined Features	
	Number	Rank	Number	Rank	Number	Rank
Texas	18	1	10	2	28	1
North Carolina	14	4	12	1	26	2
Kentucky	17	2	9	4	26	2
Massachusetts	16	3	9	4	25	4
Southwest	13	5	10	2	23	5
Wisconsin	13	5	9	4	22	6
Tennessee	9	7	8	7	17	7

TABLE III–45

CONTRIBUTIONS OF STATES STUDIED TO EXTRA-STATE INMATES OF PRISONS IN REMAINING STATES

	Natives in Other State Prisons		
	Number	Per Cent	Rank
Tennessee	138	10.73	1
Texas	59	4.59	2
Kentucky	59	4.59	2
Southwest	16	1.25	4
North Carolina	12	0.93	5
Massachusetts	6	0.47	6
Wisconsin	3	0.23	7
Total	293	22.79	

Probably the geographically central position of Tennessee with respect to the other states investigated has most to do with its major contributions to their prison populations and with its minimum divergence from the generalized metric means of the total series.

We must defer final consideration of the causes and significance of state differences in the physique of criminals until all of the evidence — sociological, metric, and morphological — has been fully analyzed.

Chapter IV

MORPHOLOGICAL DIFFERENTIATION
BY STATES

Distribution and Excesses of Observed Graded Characters

TATTOOING (Observer A only). Table IV–1 shows the differences between four states in frequency of tattoo marks on criminals. Evidently this practice is commonest among Massachusetts and Texas criminals, and least common in Tennessee, but the differences are not large enough to warrant much investigation. Massachusetts and Texas criminals are much more frequently urban residents than the criminals from Tennessee and Kentucky, and the first two states are also on the seaboard and probably include more sailors in the criminal population. These facts may partially explain the difference in proportions of criminals tattooed.

TABLE IV–1

TATTOOING BY STATES (OBSERVER A)

| | None | | Some | | Extensive | | |
	Number	Per Cent	Number	Per Cent	Number	Per Cent	Total
Massachusetts	279	82.79	49	14.54	9	2.67	337
Tennessee	378	90.00	34	8.10	8	1.90	420
Kentucky	1029	86.84	135	11.39	21	1.77	1185
Texas	739	80.76	136	14.86	40	4.37	915
Total	2425	84.88	354	12.39	78	2.73	2857

The fact that these criminals were measured and observed stripped only to the waist makes the data on tattooing of little value. Observer B's records of tattooing were so obviously defective that they were discarded entirely.

Hair Quantity. Estimates of hair quantity are subject to an observational equation which is enhanced by variations in the closeness of haircut and shave. Hair quantity also is largely dependent upon age. Young people are likely to have thick head hair and scanty beard and body hair, while in elderly persons an opposite combination is prevalent. The states differ widely in distribution of hair quantity. Often the observations of the same worker vary greatly in different states.

Table IV–2 gives the distribution of hair quantity by categories for the different states and different regions of the body. Table IV–3 details the significance of the differences in the extreme categories.

Thick head hair is excessively present in Texas and Kentucky, and significantly deficient in Wisconsin, Massachusetts, North Carolina, and the Southwest. In the last two state groups thin hair is also deficient, while it is present in excess in Texas.

Thick beards are in excess in Wisconsin, Texas, Massachusetts, and the Southwest. They are deficient in Kentucky, Tennessee, and North Carolina. Thin beards are notably common in North Carolina, Tennessee, and the Southwest. They are deficient in Massachusetts, Kentucky, and Texas.

Excesses of thick body hair are found in Texas and Kentucky, in which states also sparse body hair is deficient. Massachusetts is peculiar in showing great excesses of medium body hair and deficiencies of both small and large. Tennessee, North Carolina, the Southwest, and Wisconsin all show excess of sparse hair.

Table IV-4 gives rankings of states in various categories of hair quantities. These rankings are made in each category by assigning first place to the lowest percentage of submedium or small amount of hair and first place to the largest percentage of large

TABLE IV-4

RANKINGS OF STATES IN HAIR QUANTITY AND MEAN AGES

	Mean Age	Head Hair Rank	Beard Rank	Body Hair Rank	Beard and Body Mean Rank
Southwest	30.60	1	5	4	5
North Carolina	28.40	1	7	7	7
Tennessee	29.80	3	6	6	6
Kentucky	29.65	3	4	1	3
Texas	33.45	5	2	1	1
Massachusetts	27.50	6	1	3	2
Wisconsin	34.95	7	2	4	4

or abundant hair and then determining the general ranking from the combined scores. The results are crude, but give some idea of the comparative status of the different state samples.

Thus it is apparent that those groups in which head hair is thickest are thinnest in beard and body hair. North Carolina, for example, ranks first in quantity of head hair and last in beard and body hair. On the contrary, Texas, which is fifth in thickness of head hair, is first in mean ranking of beard and body hair. In Table IV-4 the state groups are arranged in order of thickness of head hair and the mean age of each group is also recorded. The correlation with age is by no means perfect. Massachusetts is particularly anomalous in being the youngest group, yet occupying only sixth place in thickness of head hair.

Since the above rankings entirely neglect the medium category of hair quantity we may well consider Table IV-5 in which the states are grouped by similarities of excesses.

Tennessee, North Carolina, and the Southwest are alike in showing excesses of medium head hair, and of sparse beard and body hair, although the Southwest also shows a small excess of thick beards. None of the other states particularly resembles any group in its distribution of hair quantity.

It is probable that apart from age complications a considerable personal equation on the part of the observers has tended to confuse the results. It would be unwise, under the circumstances, to give great weight to this observation.

Skin Color. A perusal of Table IV–6 clearly demonstrates that the observations of skin color in Whites are of no great value. This is partly because of lack of a proper scale of measurement. (The Von Luschan scale was used by Observer B, and a descrip-

TABLE IV–5

GROUPINGS OF STATES BY EXCESSES OF HAIR QUANTITY

	Head	Beard	Body
Southwest	Excess of medium	Excess of small and large	Excess of small
Tennessee	Excess of medium	Excess of small	Excess of small
North Carolina	Excess of medium	Excess of small	Excess of small
Massachusetts	Excess of medium	Excess of medium and large	Excess of medium
Wisconsin	Excess of medium	Excess of large	Excess of small
Texas	Excess of large and small	Excess of large	Excess of large
Kentucky	Excess of large	Excess of medium	Excess of medium and large

tive scale by Observer A.) The situation was made worse by the fact that Observer B in certain states observed skin color upon the forehead alone and not also upon an unexposed part. Consequently his observations are complicated by tanning in those states which he visited during the summertime when a considerable proportion of prisoners were working out-of-doors. This accounts for the high percentage of olive and yellow-brown in North Carolina prisoners and for the huge excesses of pale white skins in the Southwest and in Wisconsin. Under these circumstances state differences in skin color seem quite unreliable and need not be discussed further.

Hair Form. All of the states show a vast predominance of straight hair (Table IV–7). This is probably exaggerated to some extent by prison hair crops. Probable errors of excesses have been calculated only for straight and low wave categories. Texas and Massachusetts both show deficiencies of straight hair and more curved hair than occurs in the other states. Texas shows a significant excess of low waves, whereas in Massachusetts the excesses occur in the deep-waved and curly types. Wisconsin shows a very large excess of straight hair and a deficiency of all curved varieties. The Southwest also shows a significant excess of straight hair. The state differences in hair quantity seem to be supported by the differences in distribution of hair form.

The two observers are at such great variance in estimates of hair texture that this observation has been discarded. Observations subject to a marked personal equation may be utilized only when corrections for state sampling are made. This correction also takes care of observational equation.

Hair Color. Differences in hair color are manifold and significant (Tables IV–9, 10). The Southwestern states are markedly deficient in black hair, whereas Texas has a significant excess. North Carolina, Kentucky, and Wisconsin have unduly large proportions of dark brown hair, while Tennessee, Texas, and the Southwest are deficient in this shade. Massachusetts, the Southwest, and Texas show excesses of reddish brown hair, which is deficient in Tennessee and North Carolina. On the other hand light brown hair is significantly in excess in the Tennessee and Southwestern series and deficient in Massachusetts, Texas, and Wisconsin. Ash-blond hair is common in Kentucky and rare in North Carolina. Golden hair is in excess in the Southwest, but

TABLE IV–11

RANKING OF STATES IN LIGHTNESS OF HAIR AND MEAN AGES

	Dark (black, dark brown)		Medium (reddish brown, light brown)		Light (ash-blond, golden, red)		Rank in Lightness	Age	Gray, White	
	Per Cent	Rank	Per Cent	Rank	Per Cent	Rank			Per Cent	Rank
Southwest	28.45	1	56.91	1	9.48	5	1	30.60	5.16	4
Tennessee	33.25	2	51.09	2	10.13	3	1	29.80	5.54	3
Texas	37.39	3	43.97	4	12.50	1	3	33.45	6.14	2
Massachusetts	37.72	4	50.00	3	10.77	2	4	27.50	1.50	7
Kentucky	42.47	5	43.91	5	9.78	4	5	29.65	3.83	5
North Carolina	52.01	7	39.96	6	5.35	6	6	28.40	2.68	6
Wisconsin	48.82	6	34.00	7	3.70	7	7	34.95	13.47	1
Total	39.54		45.88		9.52			30.70	5.06	

deficient in Wisconsin. Red hair is most frequent in Texas and uncommon in Wisconsin and North Carolina. Gray and white hair are uncommon in the Massachusetts, North Carolina, and Kentucky series, but very common in the Wisconsin criminals. The first three series named have the youngest mean ages, whereas the Wisconsin group is the oldest.

In Table IV–11 a ranking in lightness of hair color has been achieved by adding the percentages of black and dark brown and scoring first rank for the minimum, adding reddish brown and light brown and scoring first rank for the maximum, adding ash-blond, golden and red, and scoring first place for the maximum, and then combining all of these three ratings and giving first rank in lightness for minimum score. In the same table rankings for gray and white hair are recorded together with mean ages of the several states.

The Southwest and Tennessee tie for first rank in lightness of hair. The Southwest has slightly less dark hair than Tennessee, and more medium hair, but less of the light shades. Texas has absolutely the most light hair, but achieves only third place in ranking for lightness on account of its larger percentage of dark hair. Massachusetts follows very closely upon Texas and its lower place in the ranking for lightness may be an effect of its small percentage of gray and white hair. This is, of course, associated with its very young mean age. North Carolina and Wisconsin are the darkest states, principally because of their high percentage of dark hair and low percentage of light hair. Wisconsin, however, has by far the highest proportion of gray and white hair, since it is the oldest group by several years. This excessive grayness may affect its ranking in lightness.

Rank in grayness of hair accords closely with mean age. Slight variations are probably attributable to accidents of sampling.

Eye Color. Excesses of dark brown eyes are found in Wisconsin and Massachusetts and a deficiency of this shade in Tennessee (Table IV–13). Light brown eyes are greatly in excess in the Southwest and significantly rare in Kentucky, Massachusetts, and Texas. Blue-brown eyes are extraordinarily prevalent in Tennessee and somewhat deficient in the Southwest, Texas, and Kentucky. Gray-brown eyes are found in high proportions of the series of Observer A, except Massachusetts, and are almost absent from Observer B's series. Here a personal equation almost certainly exists. In Texas gray-brown eyes reach the enormous percentage of 41.68. They are also in excess in Kentucky, but deficient in every other state. Green-brown eyes are excessively represented in North Carolina, the Southwest, and Massachusetts, but deficient in Texas and Tennessee. Blue eyes are significantly in excess in Kentucky, but deficient in Tennessee, North Carolina, and the Southwest. Blue-gray eyes are at a maximum in Wisconsin and significantly in excess in North Carolina, the Southwest, and Massachusetts. They are markedly deficient in all other states.

It may be seen that eye color is very irregularly distributed in our series and there is little doubt that the data are complicated by personal equations in the appraisal of the mixed forms and in distinctions between blue and blue-gray.

Table IV–14 ranks the several states in lightness of eye pigmentation by assigning first rank to the minimum of dark eyes, first to the maximum of medium or mixed eyes,

TABLE IV–14

RANKING OF STATES IN LIGHTNESS OF EYES

	Dark (dark brown, light brown)		Medium (blue-brown, gray-brown, green-brown)		Light (blue, blue-gray)		Mean Rank in Lightness
	Per Cent	Rank	Per Cent	Rank	Per Cent	Rank	
Kentucky	3.90	1	65.59	3	30.50	5	1
Texas	4.49	2	70.24	2	25.28	6	2
Tennessee	4.75	3	80.52	1	14.73	7	3
North Carolina	5.13	4	62.72	4	32.14	3	3
Massachusetts.	6.85	5	60.41	5	32.74	2	5
Wisconsin	9.77	6	51.52	7	38.72	1	6
Southwest	14.24	7	54.30	6	31.46	4	7
Total	6.38		64.76		28.86		

and first to the maximum of light eyes. The general ranking represents the mean score of each state. Tennessee is anomalous in its very high percentage of mixed eyes and low percentage of light eyes. Wisconsin is also remarkable for its high rank in light eyes and also in dark eyes. North Carolina and Massachusetts resemble each other most closely in combinations of eye shades. They also come nearest to the general series distribution.

If we compare rankings of lightness of hair with those of lightness of eyes we have the following table:

This table (IV–15) brings out a number of curious facts. The Southwest, which ties for first place in lightness of hair, has the darkest eyes. Kentucky and North Carolina — states which have a good deal of dark hair — rank high in lightness of eyes. Tennessee and Texas are consistent in having high ranking in both lightness of hair and lightness of eyes, Massachusetts in its median position, and Wisconsin in having both dark hair and dark eyes. The entire series shows much more dark hair than light hair and many more light eyes than dark eyes.

Naturally these rankings and percentages do not imply individual correlations, but they do indicate the great mixture of types which occurs in this criminal series and the

TABLE IV–15

CONTRASTED RANKINGS OF STATES IN LIGHTNESS OF HAIR AND EYES

	Hair Rank	Eyes Rank
Southwest	I	7
Tennessee	I	3
Texas	3	2
Massachusetts	4	5
Kentucky	5	I
North Carolina	6	3
Wisconsin	7	6

probable inequality of individual pigmentation. They also show how necessary it is to make corrections for state sampling, not only on account of local differences, but also to take care of the personal equation of the observers, which certainly is in evidence.

Sclera. This observation is of little value, since there is present a decided personal equation on the part of the observers (Tables IV–16, 17). Observer B finds almost no cases of speckled or yellow sclerae. Observer A finds speckled sclerae in a high percentage of Massachusetts criminals, but very rare elsewhere.

Iris. Massachusetts has an excess of rayed irides, a deficiency of diffused and speckled irides (Table IV–18, 19). Tennessee has a deficiency of rayed irides, and excesses of speckled and diffused irides. Kentucky has a significant deficiency of zoned irides and significant excesses of the homogeneous, rayed, and diffused categories. Texas has a large excess of zoned irides, an excess of diffused irides, and deficiencies of rayed and speckled irides. North Carolina has a deficiency of homogeneous and zoned irides and an excess of speckled irides. Wisconsin has a great excess of zoned irides, an insignificant excess of homogeneous irides, and deficiencies in the other categories. The Southwest presents an excess of rayed irides and a deficiency of zoned irides. No state conforms to the distribution of the series as a whole.

Eye Folds. Wisconsin and Tennessee are outstanding by reason of the rarity of any kind of eye fold among the prison samples (Tables IV–20, 21). Massachusetts is distinguished by very large excesses of median and external folds. Kentucky far outstrips the other states in frequency of internal epicanthic folds. North Carolina of all states is nearest the combined series in distribution of eye folds.

Eyebrow Thickness. Tennessee shows a great heaping up of observations in the medium category (Tables IV–22, 23). Kentucky has an excess of submedium eyebrows; North Carolina and the Southwest exceed in pronounced eyebrows. Texas adheres almost exactly to proportions of the total series. The states of Observer B show a much greater consistency in the various gradations than do those of Observer A.

Forehead Height. A pronounced excess of low forehead heights, at the expense of the medium category, occurs in North Carolina (Tables IV–24, 25). Kentucky shows a much smaller excess in this grade. Wisconsin is very deficient in submedium heights and greatly in excess in the pronounced category. The Southwest shows an even larger excess in the pronounced category, but wholly at the expense of the medium proportion. Texas and Tennessee both show disproportionately large medium percentages at the expense of both extremes. Massachusetts is close to the distribution of the total series.

Forehead Slope. Texas and Massachusetts alike exhibit excess of medium forehead slope and marked deficiencies in the extreme categories (Tables IV–26, 27). Tennessee has by far the largest representation of persons with absent or submedium forehead slope and is significantly deficient in proportion of pronounced slope. Kentucky shows the greatest excess of sloping foreheads. North Carolina has excesses both of foreheads with little or no slope, and those with pronounced slope.

Nasion Depression. This is another observation which seems subject to a marked personal equation (Table IV–28). No probable errors have been calculated. Wisconsin, Tennessee, and the Southwest show observations heaped up in the medium category and very small proportions in the extremes. North Carolina has a great excess of submedium observations. Massachusetts observations are heavily weighted in the pronounced class, and Kentucky in both pronounced and submedium categories. No single state approximates the proportions found in the combined series.

Nasal Root Height. State differences in nasal root height are principally in the medium and pronounced categories (Tables IV–29, 30). Tennessee, Texas, Wisconsin, and the Southwest show excesses in the medium category and deficiencies in pronounced. North Carolina and Massachusetts show excesses in pronounced and deficiencies in medium. Kentucky is close to the proportions of the combined series, although this state shows a significant excess of low nasal roots.

Nasal Root Breadth. This observation is most erratic in state distribution (Tables IV–31, 32). Tennessee prisoners are practically all in the medium category. Massachusetts shows a tremendous excess of pronounced nasal root breadth and Wisconsin an almost equally great excess of submedium. North Carolina shows an excess of submedium and the Southwest, on the contrary, an excess of pronounced. Kentucky and Texas, like Tennessee, are very high in the medium category and low in the extremes.

Nasal Bridge Height. The state differentiations in observed height of nasal bridge are in the categories of medium and pronounced height (Tables IV–33, 34). Excesses of medium height, and consequent deficiencies of pronounced height, occur in Wisconsin, Tennessee, and Texas. Excesses of pronounced height and deficiencies in medium height are found in North Carolina, Kentucky, and Massachusetts. The states of the Southwest approximate the proportions of the entire series most closely, but show a perceptible excess of the medium category. These state differences cannot have been brought about by the personal equations of the two observers, since their respective state series are inconsistent in regard to the direction of their excesses. The insignificance of the percentages with submedium nasal bridge height is striking.

Nasal Bridge Breadth. Massachusetts and the Southwest are alike in showing deficiencies of submedium and medium bridge breadths and great excesses of pronounced breadths (Tables IV–35, 36). Tennessee, Kentucky, and Texas are very high in the medium category and significantly low in the extremes. North Carolina is near to the otal series distribution. Wisconsin alone displays a huge excess of submedium nasal breadths. The state differentiation is very marked.

Nasal Profile. Observations of the nasal profile (Tables IV–37, 38) are undoubtedly complicated and to some extent vitiated by certain personal equations manifested by the two observers, and particularly by Observer B. The latter seems to have felt a distinct reluctance to employ the category straight. Consequently all of his state series are markedly deficient in that category. On the other hand, the same observer manifested a strong proclivity for classifying nasal profiles as convex, whereas Observer A seems to have had a preference for concavo-convex. As a matter of fact it is extremely difficult to distinguish between these several categories.

The two observers apparently agree in their definition of the category concave. Wisconsin, Massachusetts, and North Carolina show excesses of this classification, while Kentucky and Texas are notably deficient.

Within Observer A's series Massachusetts is notable for its excesses of concave noses and deficiencies of convex noses. Kentucky and Texas stand out because of their relative deficiency in concave noses. Kentucky is strongly in excess in concavo-convex noses and Texas in straight noses.

The only practicable method of equating the data of the two observers is to combine straight with concave and convex with concavo-convex. This gives the following table:

TABLE IV–39

COMBINED CATEGORIES OF NASAL PROFILE BY STATES

	Concave, Straight		Convex, Concavo-convex		
	Number	Per Cent	Number	Per Cent	Total Number
Southwest	165	27.32	439	72.68	604
Kentucky	366	30.92	818	69.09	1184
North Carolina	149	33.26	299	66.74	448
Tennessee	147	34.75	276	65.25	423
Wisconsin	106	35.69	191	64.31	297
Texas	340	37.24	573	62.76	913
Massachusetts	137	41.02	197	58.99	334
Total	1410	33.55	2793	66.45	4203

On this basis it is apparent that the Southwest states and Kentucky are differentiated by excess of convex and concavo-convex noses and deficiency of straight and concave noses; that Massachusetts and Texas are distinguished by excesses of straight and concave noses and deficiencies of convex and concavo-convex noses, and that the other states do not differ markedly from the proportions found in the entire series.

Nasal Tip Thickness. Tennessee shows an excess of medium tips and deficiencies in both of the extreme categories (Tables IV–40, 41). Massachusetts, the Southwest, and Texas have excesses of thick tips. North Carolina and Wisconsin show excesses of thin tips and deficiencies of thick tips. Kentucky has an excess of submedium tips. All of the excesses mentioned are statistically significant.

Nasal Septum Inclination. North Carolina and Wisconsin have very marked excesses of upward inclinations and Kentucky a smaller but significant excess (Tables

IV–42, 43). Tennessee and Texas are disproportionately high in the down category. Massachusetts and the Southwest approximate the distribution of the combined series.

Septum Deflection. Tennessee and Texas show by far the smallest percentages of deflected nasal septa, while North Carolina has the unenviable distinction of the maximum incidence of this defect (Tables IV–44, 45). Kentucky and Wisconsin occupy intermediate positions with very similar frequencies. No state approximates the total series distribution. Deflections to the right are more than twice as common as those to the left.

Lips — Integumental Thickness. Tennessee, Wisconsin, North Carolina, and Texas show great excesses of medium lips and deficiencies in the extreme categories (Tables IV–46, 47). Massachusetts has a great excess of submedium or thin lips. The Southwest is distinguished by a high percentage of pronounced or thick integumental lips, while Kentucky has a marked excess of thin lips and a small but significant excess also of thick lips.

Lips — Membranous Thickness. Tennessee shows a huge excess of lips of medium thickness with all other categories deficiently represented (Tables IV–48, 49). North Carolina and Wisconsin display large excesses of thin or submedium lips, with excess also in the upper submedium, lower pronounced category. In this latter grade Massachusetts is disproportionately high, and both Tennessee and Kentucky markedly deficient. The Southwest approaches nearest to the combined series distribution. Kentucky is the only state which shows a significant excess of thick lips.

Lip Seam. Wisconsin has a high percentage of medium development of this feature with deficiencies in the extremes (Tables IV–50, 51). Massachusetts and the Southwest are also high in the medium category, and the former is low in proportion of those with submedium or absent lip seams. Texas has a very large excess of persons in whom the lip seam is absent or submedium. Tennessee and North Carolina are close to the distribution of the total series. Kentucky is the only state with a significant excess of pronounced lip seams.

Alveolar Prognathism. Some personal equation in this observation is indicated by the consistently smaller proportions of this feature observed by Observer B when contrasted with the states worked by Observer A (Tables IV–52, 53). Thus we find North Carolina, Wisconsin, and the Southwest show a very small incidence of alveolar prognathism. Observer A's states vary widely. Massachusetts shows a huge excess of alveolar prognathism, Kentucky and Texas smaller excesses. Tennessee is nearest of all states to the distribution of the combined series.

Facial Prognathism. Personal equation is again suggested by the fact that Observer B's series show consistently smaller percentages of facial prognathism of all grades than are exhibited in the series from the states studied by Observer A (Tables IV–54, 55). The differences are not, however, great. In Massachusetts a much higher proportion of persons with prognathism is recorded than in any other state. At the other extreme is the Southwest with less than 4 per cent reported as showing any prognathism at all.

Chin Form. All states show larger or smaller majorities of median chins (Tables IV–56, 57). Wisconsin, Tennessee, and Massachusetts, in the order named, have the largest excess of this chin form. North Carolina, Texas, and the Southwest show the highest proportions of bilateral chins. Kentucky approaches closest to the total series distribution.

Malars — Prominence. The outstanding state differences include a vast excess of pronounced malars in Texas and a tremendous overweighting of the Wisconsin material in the medium category at the expense of both extremes (Tables IV–58, 59). North Carolina includes a far higher percentage of persons with submedium malar prominence than any other state. A smaller excess of submedium malars occurs in Kentucky. The distributions in Massachusetts, Tennessee, and the Southwest are generally similar. No state approximates the total series distribution.

Cheek Fullness. Personal equation is probably operative in this observation (Tables IV–60, 61). North Carolina, Wisconsin, and the Southwest (Observer B's series) all show excesses of submedium cheek fullness and deficiencies in the pronounced category. Texas is outstanding because of the great prevalence of persons with full cheeks. Tennessee is remarkable for the heaping of frequencies in the medium category. The observations show that Observer B obtained quite consistent results in his several states, whereas the series of Observer A fluctuate greatly. I am not disposed to put great faith in this observation.

Gonial Angles. Texas again, as in cheek fullness, is notable for its great excess of pronounced or outstanding gonial angles (Tables IV–62, 63). Tennessee, on the contrary, is distinguished by an excess of submedium angles. Wisconsin displays a great excess in the medium category. Kentucky adheres closely to the proportions of the combined series.

Cheeks — Wrinkling. This observation depends to some extent upon the age composition of the several state series (Table IV–64). Massachusetts with the youngest mean age has the highest percentage of persons who are unwrinkled or slightly so. But Wisconsin, the oldest group, is next in order. The Southwest and Kentucky show the proportions which approach nearest to the total series distribution. Tennessee and Texas both have very high proportions of wrinkles. Texas is the second oldest group, but Tennessee is below the mean age of the total series. It is obvious, therefore, that recorded degrees of wrinkling depend not alone upon age, but, in a probably greater degree, upon other factors — possibly individual variation, state type variation, or observational equation.

Teeth Wear. Tennessee (curiously enough) is the only state in which is recorded a considerable percentage of subjects whose teeth show no wear (Table IV–65), and at the same time it displays the highest proportion of criminals with teeth pronouncedly worn. Otherwise the state groups show no important differentiation, despite deviations in mean age.

Teeth Caries. Here again a careful perusal of the tables indicates or suggests a complicating personal equation (Tables IV–66, 67). Observer B finds practically no cases in which caries are totally absent and comparatively small percentages in which they are numerous. Observer A finds high percentages of individuals with many caries. North Carolina is especially high in the few category, as contrasted with the none and many extremes. Wisconsin and the Southwest (the other states of Observer B) are also unduly high in the middle category. Massachusetts, Texas, and Tennessee all show very high percentages of persons with many caries. No state approximates the distribution of the total series.

Teeth Lost. Wisconsin, the oldest group, shows by far the highest percentage of persons with many teeth lost and is low in proportion of those who have lost none (Tables IV–68, 69). However, Massachusetts, the youngest group, has the smallest proportion of persons who have lost no teeth. North Carolina prisoners have significantly better teeth than those of any other state, according to these data. Tennessee and Kentucky approximate the proportions found in the entire criminal series.

Bite. Underbites are extraordinarily frequent in the Southwest, rather common in Massachusetts, and very rare in Texas and North Carolina (Tables IV–70, 71). Edge-to-edge bites reach a maximum frequency in Tennessee and are also unduly common in Kentucky and North Carolina. They are markedly infrequent in Texas and Massachusetts. The slight overbite which is normal is most frequent in North Carolina and Wisconsin. Marked overbites are notably in excess in Texas and deficient in Tennessee, North Carolina, the Southwest, and possibly in Wisconsin.

Ear Lobes — Development. Massachusetts shows a great excess of small ear lobes together with a deficiency of medium and pronounced lobes (Tables IV–72, 73). The Southwest states show also an excess of small lobes, and a deficiency of medium lobes, but are not distinguished in proportion of large lobes. Kentucky shows excesses of both small and large lobes, with a deficiency in the category of medium development. Tennessee, Wisconsin, and North Carolina show excess of medium development and deficiencies in the extreme categories. Texas is distinguished by a high percentage of large lobes. These differences are probably conditioned largely by the age composition of the various state series.

Ear Lobes — Attachment. Massachusetts is strongly differentiated by its excessive proportion of attached ear lobes (Tables IV–74, 75). North Carolina shows a possibly significant excess of this feature. Attached lobes are significantly deficient in Kentucky.

Roll of Helix. Kentucky is notable for its excess of submedium rolled helices and a corresponding deficiency in the combined medium and pronounced category (Tables IV–76, 77). Wisconsin is markedly differentiated in the opposite direction.

Darwin's Point. This observation appears to be complicated by a personal equation (Tables IV–78, 79). Observer B's estimates of the frequency of pronounced Darwin's points fall far below those of Observer A. Against this supposition must be weighed the fact that both observers find the minimum frequency of pronounced Darwin's points where the proportions of submedium rolled helices are smallest. Texas and Kentucky are outstanding for their high frequencies of pronounced Darwinian points, North Carolina and Wisconsin for the rarity of this feature. All states are differentiated from the series total with the exception of Tennessee.

Antihelix Prominence. Tennessee has an enormous excess of observations in the medium category and is markedly deficient in both extremes (Tables IV–81, 82). Kentucky and Texas are also very high in medium observations, but are low only in pronounced developments. North Carolina, Wisconsin, and the Southwest (all Observer B's states) are markedly in excess in the pronounced category. Massachusetts and Texas both have excess of submedium developments, but the former has also an excess of prominent antihelices. Some personal equation is suspected in this observation.

Ears — Protrusion. The following state series are characterized by excessive proportions of pronounced ear protrusion: Kentucky, Southwest, and North Carolina (Tables

IV–82, 83). Kentucky also shows an excess of submedium ear protrusion. Wisconsin, Tennessee, and Massachusetts are notable for their excesses in the medium category. Wisconsin and Texas also exhibit deficiencies in submedium protrusion. No state conforms to the proportions found in the combined series.

Temporal Fullness. This observation has a very irregular state distribution, perhaps enhanced by some observational equation (Tables IV–84, 85). Massachusetts and Wisconsin have nearly all of the observed frequencies in the medium class. The Southwest also shows a great excess in this category. Tennessee, Kentucky, and Texas have great excesses in the submedium category, and Kentucky also shows an excess of pronounced temporal regions. North Carolina shows a large excess of pronounced temporal regions and a deficiency of submedium.

Lambdoid Flattening. Observer B consistently finds much higher percentages of lambdoid flattening than does Observer A (Table IV–86). But the latter shows radically different proportions in his different states. The tabulated results do not inspire confidence. As they stand they indicate that lambdoid flattening is very rare in the Texas and Tennessee series, slightly more common in Massachusetts, present in 40 to 50 per cent of the prisoners from Kentucky, Wisconsin, and North Carolina, and reaches the staggering proportion of 72.71 per cent in the Southwest.

Facial Asymmetry. Wisconsin and the Southwest states show marked excesses of the proportions of subjects which have no facial asymmetry (Tables IV–87, 88). Texas adheres closely to the proportions of the combined series in all categories of the observation. North Carolina, Kentucky, and Massachusetts display excesses of asymmetries to the right, whereas Tennessee shows a marked excess of left asymmetries.

Neck. Wisconsin is most distinguished by an excessive prevalence of necks of medium length and breadth (Tables IV–89, 90). To a lesser extent this is true of Massachusetts. Long, thin necks are disproportionately frequent in North Carolina and Tennessee. Short, thick necks are uncommon in all states but seem to be unduly frequent in Kentucky.

Shoulder Slope. Massachusetts and Wisconsin are alike in showing very high proportions of medium slope and marked deficiencies in the pronounced category (Tables IV–91, 92). Kentucky and North Carolina both show large percentages with pronounced shoulder slope. Tennessee and the Southwest adhere fairly closely to the proportions found in the combined series. Texas shows a heaping up in the medium category which is considerably less marked than the trends in Massachusetts and Wisconsin, but is nevertheless significant. Texas alone is significantly deficient in slight or submedium shoulder slope.

SUMMARY OF EXCESSES BY STATES

In Table IV–93 the numbers and percentages of significant deviations in the state groups are listed for both metric and morphological features; rankings for extent of deviations from the total series are given to each, and a general rank is also assigned to each on the basis of the combined percentage of significant deviations in metric and morphological features. A state is tabulated as showing a significant excess in its deviations in any measurement or any grade of an observation when the difference between the state mean or percentage and that of the total series equals or exceeds three times the probable error of the difference.

We may first consider the deviations and rankings in subcategories of morphological features. These range from 74.76 per cent of significant deviations in Wisconsin to 62.14 per cent in Tennessee. Tennessee is easily the least deviating group. The mean deviation of all of the groups is 69.90 per cent of the observation subgrades. The entire series shows 72.29 per cent of metric and and indicial deviations. Thus the gross deviations in observations are practically identical in quantity with those derived from caliper measurements.

TABLE IV–93

RANKING OF STATES ACCORDING TO METRIC AND MORPHOLOGICAL DIFFERENTIATION
IN TERMS OF THE PROBABLE ERROR

	Significant Deviations in Measurements and Indices (out of 33)			Significant Deviations in Observations (out of 103)			Combined Features (136)		
	Number	Per Cent	Rank	Number	Per Cent	Rank	Number	Per Cent	Rank
Texas	28	84.85	1	75	72.82	3	103	75.74	1
North Carolina ...	26	78.79	2	76	73.79	2	102	75.00	2
Kentucky	26	78.79	2	75	72.82	3	101	74.26	3
Wisconsin	22	66.67	6	77	74.76	1	99	72.79	4
Massachusetts	25	75.76	4	69	66.99	5	94	69.12	5
Southwest	23	69.70	5	68	66.02	6	91	66.91	6
Tennessee	17	51.52	7	64	62.14	7	81	59.56	7
Total	167	72.29		504	69.90		671	70.48	

A comparison of the percentages and rankings for each state in metric and observational features respectively indicates the consistency of the groups in their combined physical deviations. Thus Texas which has the highest rank in metric deviations is third in observational subcategory deviations, with 12.03 per cent fewer of the latter. North Carolina is second in both rankings with 5.00 per cent less of observational than of metric deviations. Kentucky is second in metric ranking and third in observational ranking with 5.97 difference between percentages of significant deviations in the two categories. Massachusetts is fourth in metric features and fifth in morphological features, with 8.77 per cent more of the former. We then come to the one inconsistent state — Wisconsin. It is sixth in metric deviations with 66.67 per cent, but first in morphological deviations with 74.76 per cent — a difference, however, of only 8.09 per cent. How may this be explained? One point to be considered is the mean age of the Wisconsin group. This exceeds the total series mean by 4.25 years and the mean of the next oldest group (Texas) by 1.50 years. A number of extreme deviations might be expected from this circumstance. Again Wisconsin is the shortest group and the second lightest group — conditions which may be correlated with morphological deviations from the mean. There remains a residuum of differences which must be referred to the peculiarity of the state type.

The high rank in metric deviations of Texas is due to the superior size of the criminals from this state and the large size of its series. The comparatively low position in deviations in the three states of the Southwest may possibly be attributed to the fact that here are combined three state subgroups which include a preponderant proportion of persons born in other states (70 per cent). This heterogeneity would tend to make the Southwest group approximate a sample of the entire series.

The position of Tennessee as the least deviating group in both metric and morphological features corresponds with its most central geographical position, relative to the other states, and with the fact that there are more natives of Tennessee imprisoned in the other states than of any single state studied.

Massachusetts and Wisconsin are the only northern states studied and neither of their series includes an appreciable proportion of natives of the other states which make up our total prison and reformatory sample of native Whites of native parentage. It is interesting to note that the greatest disparity in mean age exists between these two groups and yet they are the shortest, lightest, and most leptorrhine of the state series. The low mean value of the nasal index in these states recalls the theory that the comparative width of the nose is lower in the colder climates. These two states resemble each other in elements of foreign extraction in that they alone of our series include a considerable proportion of French strains. These are much more numerous in Massachusetts than in Wisconsin. The latter state has by far the highest percentages of persons of Scandinavian and German origin found in our series.

It would be of great anthropological interest to investigate in detail the inter-state resemblances and differences with reference to environmental and ethnic factors. However, this study is not primarily an inquiry into state differences between criminals. Consequently we can afford to deal with this problem only so far as it affects the broader question of the general physical differentiation of the delinquent.

Tables IV–94 to IV–100 list for each state the significant and insignificant differences of the various morphological features, as well as the status of those observations in which the probable errors of differences from the total series have not been calculated.

Table IV–101 finally lists for each state the number and percentage of complete morphological characters which differ significantly in one or more of their subcategories from the total series. In this table a complete morphological character is counted but once, irrespective of the number of its differentiated subcategories, providing, of course, that at least one subcategory of the character shows significant difference. There are 47 complete morphological characters considered and we should expect random samples of the series to show, on the average, 2.02 of the 47 characters displaying differences from the total series in excess of three times their probable error, as a result of chance. Actually the number of differentiated complete morphological observations ranges from 32 in Tennessee to 41 in Texas. Thus each state series is overwhelmingly differentiated from a random sample of the total series in morphological characters. While it is certain that these state differentiations are somewhat exaggerated by the operation of the personal equations of the two observers, it must be concluded, none the less, that the bulk of these deviations are due to the formation of local state types, presumably the result of inbreeding, variation, and selection.

Chapter V

ANTHROPOMETRIC AND INDICIAL DIFFERENTIATION BY OFFENSE GROUPS

CORRELATION OF METRIC AND INDICIAL FEATURES

COEFFICIENTS of correlation are commonly used in physical anthropology for the purpose of showing the interdependence or dependence of pairs of bodily measurements, indices, or measurements and indices. It has been pointed out in the Introduction (page 52) that a close correlation between two variables does not necessarily mean that the change in the value of one actually causes the value of the other to change. In fact, there is absolutely no implication of any such causal relationship between the two variables.

Nevertheless, there are certain correlations in which the presumption of a causal relationship between the two variables may be justified. One of these is the correlation between age and weight in young and middle-aged adults. An advance in chronological age does not in itself imply an increase in weight, but there are undoubtedly certain factors in the aging organism which tend to bring about increase in weight and various alterations in bodily dimensions. Similarly age and stature are highly correlated in infants, children, and adolescents. This does not mean that increase in years actually causes increase in stature, but that certain growth factors are continuously operative during these ages and effect cumulative changes in stature. In the case of bodily dimensions or features which are subject to age changes of this kind, it seems legitimate either to equalize the ages of groups before comparing the measurements or morphological features affected by age, or to make corrections for age based upon predictions utilizing the coefficient of correlation. The number of anthropometric correlations in which such predictions are justifiable is, however, very limited.

In the present investigation a considerable number of coefficients of correlation have been calculated, but very few of them are utilizable for purposes of prediction. Most of them merely show the lack of any close relationship between the dimensions of bodily parts in our series.

These coefficients of correlation will be presented in tabular form by groups and will be discussed briefly.

Age Correlations. Table V–1 presents a number of correlations of measurements and indices with age, the entire series of native White criminals of native parentage being utilized in the correlations. The total number varies slightly, but in general approximates 4200 individuals.

A glance at this table shows that the relationship between age and most of these variables is negligible. In 13 of 24 cases the coefficient of correlation, which may range from zero to unity, is less than .10. Since the value of a prediction depends upon the intensity of the correlation, in order to be utilizable for purposes of prediction a coefficient of correlation should hardly be less than .25. Even for such values the relationship between the two variables is so small that a prediction based upon it can have little accuracy. However, I have stretched my conscience and made predictions from some lower correlations, merely because I wish to escape the accusation that I am hanging on to crude differences by quibbling over statistical correction. The only conceivably utilizable coefficients in this table are those with weight (.13 ± .01), nose height (.26 ± .01), nose breadth (.18 ± .01), ear length (A, .35 ± .01; B, .28 ± .02), ear breadth (A, .21 ± .01; B, .25 ± .02), and ear index (A, −.15 ± .01; B, −.12 ± .02). In the section contrasting offense groups by means of measurements and indices with the total means of the criminal series, these correlations have been used for predictions in order to eliminate age differences — albeit with doubts and misgivings. It is, however, extremely important to eliminate from the anthropological differences which distinguish various types of offenders such as may be markedly affected by age factors. Prediction by means of the coefficient of correlation is the simplest method of allowing for age differences, although by no means the most valid.

Weight Correlations. Table V–2 lists the coefficients of correlation of weight with various metric and indicial features. Weight is significantly correlated with all of the measurements, but the correlations with age and with indices are very low. All of the correlations with body measurements are sufficiently high so that they could be used, if necessary, as the basis of predictions. The question then arises as to the desirability of making a correction for weight in appraising the significance of offense group deviations from the total series in these measurements.

Both weight and bodily diameters are expressions of size. As the size of an animal increases, weight and bodily dimensions in general increase. It can scarcely be maintained that it is the weight which affects the dimensions. It might be argued with more plausibility that the bodily dimensions control the weight. There can be no utility in attempting to predict what the dimensions of an offense group might be if it were of the same mean weight as another offense group of different dimensions. Whatever results such a prediction might give, they would prove nothing, except that hypothetical alterations of body size affect both weight and gross dimensions. If versus public welfare offenders are taller and heavier than criminals in general, it can serve no useful purpose to attempt by mathematical formulae to estimate whether their superior height would be maintained if their weight were reduced to the general series mean. Age does carry with it a complex of bodily changes which makes legitimate, or at least pardonable, the utilization of predictions and corrections for age differences. Such a procedure does not seem logical or justifiable in the case of intercorrelated bodily features.

An interesting anthropological fact which arises from these correlations of weight with other features is that, so far as this series can be taken as representative, predictions of almost any body dimension could be made more accurately from weight than from any other single measurement.

Height Correlations. Height shows moderate correlations with most bodily dimensions, because, all things being equal, as stature increases other dimensions of the body increase. But it is not increased stature which brings about the increase in other dimensions. General growth factors regulate both.

The highest correlation with stature is sitting height (.70 ± .01). This is a spurious correlation, however, since sitting height, or trunk length, is a component of stature. The correlation of weight with height is second in order of magnitude (.48 ± .01). None of the head or face indices is significantly correlated with stature.

Other Correlations. Tables V–4 through V–8 list a number of other coefficients of correlation calculated on the total series of native White criminals of native parentage. None of them has been used for predictions or corrections and no further comment upon them is necessary.

MEASUREMENTS AND INDICES

In the following sections dealing with the differences between offense groups and the total series in measurements and indices, the reader may first scrutinize the tables of means and other constants, next the differences between state prediction and offense group observations and between offense group observation and the total series, each difference with its proper sign and the latter with its probable error and value in terms of the probable error (*x* p.e.). Finally, at the end of each table the summary gives differences which are significant and independent of state sampling with their values in terms of their probable errors, and differences which are crudely significant but invalidated by the correction for state sampling, together with the amount and value of the residual independent differences, if any, in terms of their probable errors. These tables require little or no commentary in the text, since each offense group is subsequently discussed according to the number and character of the significant and independent difference which it manifests when compared with the total series. It is the sum total of distinctive features in each offense group which is important, rather than the offense group differences of individual features or measurements.

Age. The average age of 4188 native born criminals of native parentage is 30.70 years. Evidently then, the bulk of this sample is made up of young men. The range in age class intervals of five years is from 15 years to 79 years. That the sample is not homogeneous as to age is indicated by the high standard deviation (11.4 years). The standard deviations of the offense groups hover about that of the total series with the exception of the robbery and larceny groups, which are much more homogeneous, and consist apparently of an overwhelming majority of youthful criminals.

An inspection of the means of the offense groups clearly shows that the younger criminals are concentrated in the two offense groups just named. This fact cannot be due entirely to the shorter terms imposed for minor crimes, since robbery often carries a heavy sentence. One might expect the oldest offense group to be that of first degree murder, since that crime usually carries with it a life sentence. Such is not the case. The oldest offense group is versus public welfare, which includes a miscellaneous category of crimes such as carrying concealed weapons and peddling drugs. No less than 80.33 per cent of this offense group are violators of the liquor laws. Presumably the high mean age of these offenders is not a result of the long terms of imprisonment which they incur. The average age of rapists is also high (36.1 years), but this is probably conditioned by their long sentences. On the other hand, the group called other sex shows a still higher mean, although the difference is probably not statistically significant. It seems probable that this group is affected in age composition by factors having to do with family life (adultery, bigamy, incest), and with abnormal tendencies which occasionally manifest themselves in aging individuals.

The correlation ratio between age and offense (.40 ± .01) is high. It seems probable, however, that length of sentence for crimes of varying seriousness affects this ratio more than any real correlation between age of the offender and his criminal proclivity. Exceptions to this generalization are probably robbery, larceny, offenses versus public welfare, and possibly other sex offenses.

All offense groups, with the exception of forgery and fraud, differ significantly in mean age from the mean of the total series, even after due allowance has been made for state sampling.

Weight. The mean weight of the total series (subjects without coat, vest, and shoes) is 150.90 pounds. The standard deviation (20.20 pounds) is high. Table V–11 gives the mean weights of the offense groups and shows considerable deviations from the total series mean. Before we can arrive at any conclusion concerning the importance of the offense group variations we must make allowance not only for chance variations due to the sampling process, but also for two other complicating factors. The first of these is age difference and the second is difference due to state composition.

Weight is generally assumed to increase with age. Consequently older offense groups may be expected to show greater mean weights than the younger groups. The method used in allowing for weight is that employed by Goring and based upon the coefficient of correlation between weight and age.[1] Since the coefficient in this series is only .13 ± .01 it is hardly large enough to give any valid prediction of weight, and might be dismissed as insignificant. However, in order to forestall any possible charge of disregarding age effects in appraising our results, we shall utilize the method, albeit with reservations as to its validity.

The prediction formula whereby allowance is made for one associated character is as follows:

$$\frac{y - \bar{y}}{\sigma_y} = \frac{x - \bar{x}}{\sigma_x} r_{xy},$$

where $(\bar{y})$ = mean for the total series, (y) = mean for the offense group, and (σ_y) = the standard deviation of the predicted character (i.e. weight); and $(\bar{x})$ = the mean of the total series, (x) = the mean of the offense group, and (σ_x) = the standard deviation of the associated character to be allowed for (i.e. age); and (r_{xy}) the correlation coefficient between the two associated characters (x and y); and $(\frac{y - \bar{y}}{\sigma_y})$ = the difference, with regard to the predicted character, between the mean of an offense group and the mean of the total series, expressed in terms of the standard deviation of this character; and $(\frac{x - \bar{x}}{\sigma_x})$ = a corresponding difference, with regard to the character allowed for, between the average of the total series and of the offense group respectively, expressed in terms of the standard deviation of that character.[2]

Table V–12 gives the mean ages, the weights predicted from those ages, with the probable errors of the predictions, the observed weights, the differences between the ob-

---

[1] Goring, 1913, p. 36 f.
[2] Goring, 1913, p. 37. For a full demonstration of the method, see this author.

served weights and predicted weights and the value of those differences in terms of probable errors of the predictions. We can be sure that a difference is significant only if it exceeds three times the probable error of the prediction. An inspection of this table reveals several important differences. First degree murderers and forgers are

TABLE V–12

AGE CORRECTION FOR WEIGHT

	Mean Age	Predicted Weight Mean	Observed Weight Mean	Difference	x p.e.
First degree murder ..	37.80	152.53 ± .81	155.50	2.97	3.67
Second degree murder	34.05	151.67 ± .56	152.10	.43	.77
Assault	34.00	151.66 ± 1.59	151.70	.04	.03
Robbery	26.75	149.99 ± .69	149.40	−.59	.86
Burglary and larceny..	26.50	149.93 ± .35	148.90	−1.03	2.94
Forgery and fraud	30.25	150.80 ± .65	153.20	2.40	3.69
Rape	36.10	152.14 ± 1.00	149.20	−2.94	2.94
Other sex	37.10	152.37 ± 1.13	152.70	.33	.29
Versus public welfare	38.25	152.64 ± .88	154.30	1.66	1.89
Arson and all other ..	33.05	151.44 ± 1.38	148.20	−3.24	2.35

significantly heavier than would be expected from the predictions based upon their ages. These differences in weight are not then dependent upon age.

Burglary and larceny and rape fall below the mean weights predicted from their ages, but in each case the value of the difference in terms of the probable error falls just below the limit of significance and is therefore not altogether reliable. Arson and all other offenses also shows a marked deficiency which is not certainly valid.

However, we have still to take into consideration and make allowance for the effects of state sampling. We shall next consider this complication, disregarding the question of age.

When the difference between the actual mean of an offense group and the mean predicted on the basis of state composition is as great as, or greater than, the difference between the actually observed mean of that offense group and the mean of the total series, the effect of state sampling and personal equation of the observer as expressed in the state series is nil. Thus, Table V–13 shows that so far as state sampling is concerned, the significant differences of the offense groups are valid, with the exception of forgery and fraud and versus public welfare. In some of the other offense groups the differences between state predictions and actual observations are slightly smaller than between offense group and total series, but in no case are the discrepancies large enough to invalidate the significance of the group difference in terms of its probable error. In the case of rape, the difference between prediction and observation is only −.58 whereas the difference between actual observation of the offense group and mean of the series is −1.70 ± 1.01. Since this difference is only 1.68 times its probable error it is, in any event, insignificant.

However, in the case of forgery and fraud the difference between state prediction and actual observation is 1.60, whereas the difference between the observed mean of the subgroup and the total series mean is 2.30. Evidently the independent difference between the offense group and the total series is merely the amount by which the actual mean of the offense group exceeds the mean predicted from state composition, and in the same direction as the difference between offense group and total series. This is 1.60. If, then, it is expressed in terms of the probable error of the difference between the mean of the offense group and the random sample of the total series, since the probable error is ± .66, the difference is reduced to 2.42 times its probable error and is possibly insignificant. Hence the excess of weight in the forgery and fraud group may be due to state composition in large part. Similarly the independent difference between state prediction and offense mean in versus public welfare is 1.62 whereas the difference between the offense group mean and total series is 3.40 ± .89. Writing the independent difference 1.62 ± .89 we find it to be only 1.82 times its probable error. Therefore, this difference is rendered statistically insignificant by state sampling.

Thus we have found that first degree murderers and forgers and fraudulent offenders are heavier than would be expected from their ages and that burglary and larceny and arson criminals are probably lighter. Considerable deviations in weight of the rapists are not certainly independent of age differences (Table V–12). But Table V–13 shows that the actual deviation of the rapists is probably an effect of the sampling process, and that the deviations of the forgery and fraud and versus public welfare groups are complicated by the matter of state representation.

We, therefore, conclude that the only weight difference in our series which has a general criminological validity (i.e. is free from accidents of sampling and effects of age and state composition) is the excess weight of first degree murderers. It seems probable, however, that the weight deficiency of the burglary and larceny group is also of real importance, since it is not caused by state sampling and falls below age expectation to an extent of 2.94 times the probable error. It is, therefore, almost unaffected by age.

Nose Height. The correlation of nose height with age is .26 ± .01. Since this is an appreciable relationship it becomes advisable to make a prediction correcting nose height for age. Table V–41 gives the data on this subject. None of the offense groups are differentiated significantly apart from age.

Table V–42 corrects for state composition. While several offense groups show differences independent of state sampling, these are all dependent upon age and, consequently, of no criminological importance.

Nose Breadth. The correlation of nose breadth with age is .18 ± .01. This is scarcely of a value to warrant the use of predictions. However, if predictions are made, the results appear as in Table V–44. On this basis the only groups which deviate significantly in nose breadth apart from age are robbery and versus public welfare, both of which show small excesses. Table V–45, however, shows that the only groups in which differences are independent of state sampling are burglary and larceny and versus public welfare. The last named is then the sole group which shows a significant excess which is both independent of state sampling and of age.

SUMMARY OF CORRELATION RATIOS OF OFFENSE WITH METRIC AND INDICIAL FEATURES

Table V–78 recapitulates the correlation ratios of offense with metrical and indicial characters. The first group of correlation ratios deals with 20 characters, 3 of which show separate ratios for each observer's data.[3] No correlation ratio below .10 can be

[3] For discussion of correlation ratios, cf. p. 25.

considered of any general importance. Eleven of the 20 characters exhibit correlation ratios equal or in excess of that figure. We may consider their significance.

By far the highest correlation ratio of any measurement with offense is that of age —.40 ± .01. But this correlation ratio does not reflect the relation of type of offense to age, because it does not deal with the ages of the criminals at the time of commitment, but rather with their ages when measured. Consequently, it depends very considerably upon the gravity of the offense, or rather the length of the sentence. The higher mean ages of first degree murder, rape, et cetera, are probably due in part to the long sentences imposed for these crimes. Hence this correlation ratio has no broad criminological significance.

The correlation ratio of weight with offense, .11 ± .01, is affected to some extent by the age differentiation of the group, since the coefficient of correlation of age with weight is .13 ± .01. Weight is even more closely connected with stature, the coefficient of correlation being .48 ± .01. It, therefore, seems probable that the correlation ratio of weight with offense depends largely upon these two complicating factors. Chest depth and chest breadth are also closely correlated with weight and stature and their ratios with offense cannot be considered apart from these associated factors. Head height shows a moderate correlation with weight, and this must affect the correlation ratio of offense with head height. Similarly, cranial circumference is strongly correlated both with weight and height and its correlation ratio with offense is dependent to some extent upon these variables. Nose height is also strongly correlated with age, and bigonial diameter with weight. Similar complicating relationships apply to ear length and ear breadth.

Correlation ratios which are so strongly affected by age that their significance with offense seems small are nose height, nose breadth, ear breadth, and ear length. We are left with weight, height, chest depth and breadth, head height, head circumference, and bigonial diameter, as features which seem to have some interrelated influence upon type of offense, apart from considerations of age. None of these correlation ratios is high enough to be of any individual diagnostic value as a criminal type criterion. Nor should anyone expect that any single measurement would be thus significant in distinguishing one kind of offender from another.

None of the correlation ratios of offense with various indices is high enough to warrant a protracted discussion. One or two groups may deviate significantly from the mean of the whole series in this or that index, but there is no indication of an important relationship between offense and any specific bodily index.

No anthropologist would expect that any single bodily index or any single bodily dimension would be valuable as a criminological criterion when taken by itself. Indeed, no such anthropometric criterion can stand alone, even as a means of racial classification. If criminals are differentiated by physical type, according to the offense they commit, multiple criteria must be employed, since by combinations of features only can types be established. One measurement or index may in its range of variation or in the direction of its variation constitute a peculiarity of some given type or offense group, but it cannot be distinctive for each and every offense group or criminal type.

Our problem in this section is to ascertain whether each of the offense groups of native White criminals of native birth differs in a statistically significant degree from a random sample of the entire combined offense groups, such a random sample being of a size equal to the subgroup with which it is compared. We must discover whether or not the deviations of the offense group means are due to chance alone, and whether significant deviations are sufficiently numerous in each group to establish its physical distinctiveness.

Differences of less than twice the probable error of the difference between the means of the subgroup and that of a random sample of the whole group are obviously of no importance, since they may be expected to occur in no less than 82 per cent of the features studied, through chance alone. Differences of more than twice the probable error may be expected to occur in no more than 18 per cent of the measurements, if chance alone is responsible for the deviations. Differences of more than three times the probable error of the differences between the mean of the offense group and the random sample may be expected to occur through chance alone not oftener than four times in a hundred samples.

We shall then consider each subgroup first of all to ascertain whether it is anthropometrically distinct through other causes than the chances of random sampling.

If we do find such groups distinct — any or all of them — we must inquire further into the causes of their distinctiveness. But here we are primarily concerned with the question of how they differ, rather than the question of why they differ. We especially desire to find out what a murderer displays in distinctive physical features, rather than the ultimate cause of his physical separateness. Consequently we need not concern ourselves very deeply with difficult questions as to the interdependence of one physical difference upon another. If murderers have larger heads because they are taller, they none the less have larger heads and are so distinguished. We may speculate upon the questions of ultimate causation, but we can hardly hope to answer them.

First Degree Murder. Table V–79 lists the deviations in measurements and indices of the first degree murderers. We need consider only those which are significant and independent of state sampling and we must be assured that none of them is due primarily to age differences. First of all we note that these murderers are more than 7 years older in mean age than the average of the criminal series. This difference is undoubtedly due rather to the length of sentence than to the actual age of the criminals at the time their offenses were committed. First degree murderers are significantly heavier than other criminals. While the crude difference is somewhat reduced when age is taken into consideration, the excess remains significant. These offenders are also significantly above the mean in stature, chest depth, and chest breadth. These excesses are, of course, correlated with their overweight, but are none the less important. The next significant difference which is independent of state sampling is an excess of nose height. This, however, disappears when due allowance is made for age, and it has no ultimate criminological importance. There is no reason for believing that bigonial diameter is particularly affected by age and so we may accept the next difference which is an excess of this measurement. For ear length and breadth we have two sets of measurements made by the two observers. One finds an excess in ear length and the other in ear breadth. We know that both of these measurements are correlated with age — since the ears grow during middle life and old age. Again the two observers are not in agreement in their excesses. Consequently we are probably justified in dismissing these ear deviations as of dubious value. There remain significant deficiencies in relative shoulder breadth, relative sitting height, and zygo-frontal index, and an excess in zygo-gonial index.

Therefore when all complicating factors of state sampling, personal equation, and age differences have been cleared away, we conclude the first degree murderers are differentiated from their fellow criminals at large — the total series in which they themselves are included — by their greater age, greater weight, greater height, greater chest depth and chest breadth, broader jaws, smaller shoulder breadth relative to stature, inferior relative sitting height, narrower foreheads relative to their facial breadth, and broader jaws relative to their facial breadth.

In a total of 39 measurements and indices first degree murderers deviate significantly in 10 or 25.64 per cent (when deviations of three measurements are excluded because affected by age or by observational equation). These differences are vastly greater and more numerous than would be expected to occur in random samples.

Second Degree Murder. The significant differences of second degree murder which are independent of state sampling include: an excess of 3.35 years in age, an excess of chest depth, a deficiency of head height, and of the length-height and breadth-height indices. The last three named differences are all in the data of Observer A. In head height, however, Observer B also finds a significant deficiency in second degree murder, but in his material the deficiency does not retain significance when allowance has been made for state sampling. Precisely the same obtains in the case of the length-height index in the material of Observer B. The latter further agrees in finding a deficiency in the breadth-height index, but it is only 1.64 p.e. On the whole, then, the agreement of the two observers seems to indicate that the deficiency in head height and in the height indices should be accepted as valid.

Of 39 measurements and indices 5 or 12.82 per cent display significant deviations, apart from effects of age and state sampling. These are sufficient and more than sufficient to distinguish the second degree murder group from a random sample of the total series.

Assault. The assault criminals show an age excess of 3.09 years, a significant excess in biacromial (shoulder breadth), and a deficiency of the breadth-height index confined to the data of Observer A. Both observers agree in finding deficiencies of head height, and of both height indices, but they attain significance only in this one instance. Almost none of the differences of the assault group attain the prescribed measure of significance (3 p.e.). This is probably because of the very small size of the group (only 80 individuals) which makes the probable error of means very high. If we discard the breadth-height index deficiency which is attested by one observer only, we are left with only 2 of 39 measurements and indices which show significant differences independent of state sampling. This percentage of excesses (5.13) is greater than would be expected in a random sample, but is nevertheless trifling. Evidently the group is too small for a satisfactory examination of its physical differentiation.

Robbery. The robbers are 3.95 years below mean age, deficient in chest depth, in excess in head height (Observer A), in bizygomatic diameter, deficient in ear length (Observer B only), and in excess in nasal index. The head height excess of Observer A may be accepted since it is paralleled by a similar excess of Observer B which is invalidated by state sampling. The ear length deficiency of Observer B is not supported by a significant deviation in the same direction on the part of Observer A, and in any case it is probably due to age. Therefore it may be disregarded.

Altogether then we have 5 of 39 measurements and indices which deviate significantly in this group, apart from allowances made for age and for state sampling. This excess of 12.82 per cent of features is much more than would be expected in random samples.

Burglary and Larceny. The burglary and larceny group is overwhelmingly differentiated from a random sample of the total series. The number of differentiated features is to some extent increased by the great size of this offense group (1612 individuals) which reduces the probable error of means. In reality burglars and thieves may be no more strongly differentiated from total criminals than are assault convicts, but the latter are insufficiently represented, whereas the former constitute no less than 39.17 per cent of the entire series. On the other hand it should be noted that this large offense group is compared with the total series (which includes its own members) and therefore the criteria of statistical significance are very severe — much more so than if the offense group were compared with all other criminals excluding its own members.

The first significant deviation is a deficiency in mean age amounting to 4.02 years. The burglars and thieves are also deficient in weight to the extent of 1.93 pounds. This measurement is affected by age, but the deficiency remains significant, even when age correction has been made. Other significant deficiencies of this group include chest depth and chest breadth, head length, head circumference, bizygomatic diameter, nose height, nose breadth, bigonial diameter, ear length, and ear breadth. Nose height and nose breadth are affected by age, and when due allowance is made for the age deficiency of the burglars and thieves, the differences of this group are reduced to insignificance. No attempt has been made to introduce an age correction for ear length and breadth, but it may be assumed that these differences also are largely dependent upon the age factor. The only significantly deviating index is the zygo-frontal in which the group shows an excess.

If we eliminate the differences in nose and ear dimensions we are left with the following significant deviations which are independent of age, personal equation, and state sampling: deficiencies in age, weight, chest diameter, head length, head circumference, bizygomatic diameter, bigonial diameter, and excess of breadth of forehead relative to jaw breadth (zygo-gonial index). Thus we have 9 of 39 measurements and indices or 23.08 per cent which show significant differentiation.

It is worthy of note that the physical differentiation of this group of criminals consists almost entirely of size deficiency manifested in some degree in almost every measurement, although frequently the deficiencies do not attain statistical significance.

Forgery and Fraud. This group does not differ significantly in mean age from the total series. It exhibits only 4 differentiated features which are free from the effects of state sampling. These are excesses in sitting height and head length, in head circumference and in total face height. None of these are subject to any marked age effect.

The total of differentiated features is 4 of 39 or 10.26 per cent — a considerably larger portion than would be expected in random samples.

The forgery and fraud group presents a number of significant excesses which are invalidated by state sampling. These include increased height and weight and several other dimensional means which are superior to the general average. The large proportion in this group of Texans, who are big men, accounts for the invalidation of many of the crude differences.

Rape. This group presents an excess of 4.84 years in mean age, a deficiency in stature and in sitting height, an excess in chest depth and in relative shoulder breadth. These deviations are independent of state sampling and presumably unaffected by age. Four other deviations are invalidated by state sampling, which in this case represents the disproportionately large contribution of the state of Wisconsin to the offense group.

The total of differentiated features is 5 of 39 or 12.82 per cent.

Other Sex Offenses. This group is differentiated only by an excess of age (6.40 years) and of nose height, and a deficiency in the ear index attested by one observer. Since the excess in nose height is insignificant apart from the age difference, and since the ear difference, if valid, is probably dependent upon age factors, we may conclude that the other sex group differs from the total series only in age, and is anthropometrically indistinguishable.

Versus Public Welfare. Since this group is overloaded again with Texans many crudely significant differences are invalidated by state sampling. Those which remain are an age excess of 6.27 years, an excess of chest depth, bizygomatic diameter, nose breadth, bigonial diameter, ear length (Observer A), cephalo-facial index and a deficiency of ear index (Observer A). The excessive nose breadth remains significant when an age correction has been carried out. The ear differences may be dismissed as due to age or personal equation. There remain 6 of 39 features which are undeniably differentiated, or 15.38 per cent.

Arson and All Other Offenses. This group shows an excess of 2.35 years in age, an excess of chest breadth, and a deficiency of minimum frontal diameter, as well as an excess of ear length attested by Observer B only. This latter may be dismissed, leaving us with only 3 differentiated characters or 7.69 per cent. Although this is more than expectation, it seems to be of no great importance.

Summary of Metric and Indicial Differentiation of Offense Groups

Table V–89 compares the distributions of metrical and indicial deviations of the offense groups, in terms of their probable errors, with the distributions to be expected of deviations of random samples of like size. In the case of measurements every single offense group shows numerous deviations of such magnitudes as to be entirely outside of the range of the sampling process. In the case of the indices the significant deviations are fewer and of smaller values, but nevertheless far transcend the limits of chance. The deviations listed are those which are independent of state sampling, but elimination of those complicated by age changes has not been made in the table.

Table V–90 summarizes the measurements and indices according to number and percentages of various categories of significance and insignificance. Finally Table V–91 not only lists the numbers and percentages of significant metric and indicial devi ations which are independent of state sampling, but also tabulates those which are affected by age and subtracts them from the crudely independent differences, thus giving totals and subtotals of the features which may be considered to show differentiation of general criminological significance, after due allowance has been made for all complicating factors. The deductions are based upon correlations of affected features with age in the case of nose height (Table V–41), nose breadth (Table V–46), and weight (Table V–12). In the cases of ear length, ear breadth, and ear indices the withdrawal of these features from the independently significant list is due in part to a known personal equation between the two observers, but also due in some degree to the certainty of their high correlations with age — correlations which, however, have not been worked out in the series.

Thus we note in the third column of the table that residual significant differences in measurements range from 8, or 34.78 per cent, to 1, or 4.35 per cent, in different subgroups. The total of differentiated measurements is 40 or 17.39 per cent. We should expect in random samples less than 4 per cent of such differences. Every offense group is certainly differentiated in measurements with the exception of other sex and assault. In these two cases we may consider that the number of divergent measurements is too small to be of anthropological importance, especially since age is counted as one of the characters. The most strongly differentiated groups are, in order: burglary and larceny, first degree murder, and versus public welfare.

Indicial differentiation is far less marked. It is entirely lacking in assault, forgery and fraud, other sex, and arson and all other offenses. It is marked only in first degree murder, which has 4 of 16, or 25 per cent, of deviations which are independent of age and state sampling. Second degree murder has two deviating indices and the other offense groups one or none. However, not even one such deviation would be expected in random samples of similar size. The total percentage of deviating indices is 6.25, which is more than can be attributed to chance.

The final column of the table pools the numbers and percentages of differentiated measurements and indices. It is apparent that without any question all of the subgroups except other sex and assault are anthropometrically distinct from random samples of the total prison series.

A general consideration of the meaning of this anthropometric differentiation must await the result of a similar inquiry into the differences in morphological observations manifested by the several offense groups. Here it may be stated only that a rigid examination of the anthropometric features of these criminals classified by offense groups, shows unmistakably that the different classes of offenders show distinctive excesses of means of measurements and indices.

Chapter VI

MORPHOLOGICAL DIFFERENTIATION BY OFFENSE GROUPS

W E have seen that eight of ten offense groups are metrically or indicially distinguished from the total prison series in that they exhibit a sufficient number of excesses, independent of state composition and of age effects, to make it wholly improbable that they represent random samples deviating in physical features through chance alone. It is now necessary to proceed to the examination of the differentiation of the offense groups in morphological characters, graded quantitatively or qualitatively by the observers. The problem presented is much more difficult than that attacked in the preceding chapter, because of the greater personal equations of the observers and because of the mathematically unwieldy character of attributes as contrasted with variables. The procedure is, however, virtually identical with that adopted in the case of measurements and indices. The various observations are tabulated singly by numbers and percentages for each offense group and for the total series. The differences of offense groups from the total series are appraised in terms of their probable errors and their dependence upon, or independence of, state composition. Comments upon the individual tables, are, for the most part, omitted, since each tabular summary tells its own story. The various morphological differences are then accumulated by offense groups and the morphological differentiations of the offense groups are discussed. Physical features affected by age changes are then examined and a residual count of the number and significance of offense group deviations completes the chapter. These ultimate differences are, presumably, free from the effects of sampling, state composition, and age differences. They are supposedly of criminological importance.

Tattooing. A brief reference to tattooing is necessary here, since our data relating to this feature have not been included in the listing of morphological deviations. This is a stock Lombrosian observation, of the D grade, with Observer B's data omitted because he obviously neglected to record this feature. About 15 per cent of 2857 prisoners in the data of Observer A were tattooed. The most marked excess in tattooing is found in the robbery group which has 8.46 per cent less of untattooed persons than the series at large (6.13 p.e.). At the opposite extreme are the murderers. The first degree murder group shows an excess of untattooed persons amounting to 6.93 per cent (4.68 p.e.) and the second degree murder group, an excess of 6.72 per cent (6.72 p.e.). Burglars and thieves seem to show a slight deficiency of untattooed individuals (-3.30 per cent, 5.59 p.e.) and the versus public welfare group, an excess.

The table also shows that the robbery group is not only oftenest tattooed but is also one of the two most extensively tattooed offense classes. The interesting degree of differentiation in this feature is reflected by the appreciable contingency coefficient (.14).

The value of this observation is impaired not only by the necessity of discarding the data of Observer B, but also by the fact that the subjects were not examined naked, but only stripped to the waist. Hence a good many tattoo marks inevitably escaped the record.

SUMMARY OF CONTINGENCIES OF OFFENSE WITH MORPHOLOGICAL FEATURES

Table VI–92 lists the coefficients of mean square contingency of various observations upon type of offense. These coefficients are arranged in three classes A, B, and C, according to the absence of personal equation between the two observers, the presence of a slight personal equation, or the presence of a marked personal equation. (Cf. Introduction, p. 61.)

These coefficients express the extent to which the various offense groups are differentiated in morphological observations. They do not specify the nature of such differentiations. The coefficients range from .06 (eyebrow thickness) to .26 (cheeks wrinkling) on a scale of which the theoretical limits are zero and unity. The modal value of the coefficient of mean square contingency in this list is .10 — which expresses a very feeble degree of differentiation. Only 4 of 40 coefficients, or 10 per cent, reach a value of .20 or more. Three of these — wrinkling, teeth wear, teeth lost — depend principally upon the age differences of the several offense groups and consequently have no broad criminological significance. The other — hair color — also includes an important age factor.

These tables illustrate again the fact brought out in connection with the correlation ratios of offense with metric features — namely that no single anthropological feature has any general diagnostic value for the distinguishing of every different type of offender.

A metric or morphological feature may be significantly in excess in this or that offense group, and may be for some particular class of crime useful as one element in a distinctive combination of physical features. But no offense group manifests exclusively any single gradation of a morphological character; far less are all of the offense groups characterized by the exhibition of mutually exclusive morphological gradations. Excesses of one or another morphological peculiarity are all that can be expected to define an offense group, and it is clear that we can hardly look for such excesses in more than one or two of the ten offense groups when we are considering the distribution of a single morphological character. Hence the low value of these coefficients of mean square contingency. If we were to discover that all murderers have straight hair, all thieves wavy hair, and all sex offenders curly hair, we should have stumbled upon an anthropological miracle, and, at the same time, we should be impaled upon the horns of a sociological dilemma, inasmuch as we should have upon our hands several other types of offense and no exclusive variations of hair form which they could show.

SUMMARY OF DIFFERENTIATION BY COMBINATIONS OF MORPHOLOGICAL FEATURES ON BASIS OF STATE COMPOSITION

Tables VI–93 through VI–102 list the characters, their divergences in percentages, and the values of the divergences in terms of their probable errors, for each offense group. In these tables may be noted those characters in which each offense group differs only insignificantly from a random sample of the entire series, those in which the differences are crudely significant but have been rendered invalid by taking into account the influence of state sampling, and finally those which persist in remaining significant in spite of allowances for the effects of state sampling.

However, before even the significant differences which are independent of state sampling can be adjudged criminologically significant, we must take account of the differences in morphological features which may be the result of the varying ages of the individuals and groups. It is quite obvious, for example, that gray hair is an old age phenomenon, and that if any offense group is distinguished by an excess of gray hair, the chances are that this feature is a manifestation of the advanced mean age of the group rather than a symptom of the type of its criminality. This investigation into the effect of age upon morphological features involves the tabulation of the distribution of each feature by age groups, the predictions of the distribution of each character in each group according to its age composition, the difference between observation and prediction and its value in terms of the probable error. Only after these further processes shall we be able to list and finally to appraise the residual group differences which are significant after all allowances have been made, not only for state sampling and personal equation, but also for the different age composition of the offense groups.

GENERAL STATISTICAL DIFFERENTIATION OF OBSERVATIONS ON BASIS OF STATE COMPOSITION

Table VI–103 gives the numbers and percentages of subcategories of observations in the various offense groups classified according to their significance and their dependence upon, or independence of, state sampling. Significant differences independent of state sampling are those which equal or exceed three times the probable error of the difference between the subgroup considered as a random sample of the entire series and the percentage in the total series after deductions have been made for the effect of state sampling. These are the only differences which are of assured criminological significance. If the subcategories of each observation were independent and uncorrelated, we should expect no more than four per cent of them to exhibit significant differences in random samples. However these subcategories are obviously not independent, since, for example, the proportion of a group observed to have thin head hair affects the proportions of the group with medium or thick head hair. Thus, although Table VI–103 gives the percentages of differentiated and undifferentiated subcategories and shows that eight of the ten offense subgroups display significant differences independent of state sampling in more than four per cent of cases, a safe appraisal of total morphological independence of the offense subgroup cannot be deduced from it. Reservations must be made for the fact that the correlated subcategories of single observations tend to influence each other in the piling up of significant differences. In order to avoid these difficulties and to be absolutely safe in drawing conclusions on the subject of significant morphological differentiation, Table VI–104 has been drawn up. In this table are calculated the numbers of total morphological characters observed to be significantly differentiated as against the number of total characters expected to show significant differentiation in random samples. Each morphological character consists of several subcategories, but the total character is counted but once, irrespective of the fact that it may show more than one differentiated subcategory, or only one. One may assume that the total characters are feebly intercorrelated, as contrasted with the obvious interdependence of their sub-categories, so that the criterion of independence of total characters approximately holds true and we are enabled to test the significance of differences against hypothetical random and totally uncorrelated samples.

The expectation of chance differentiation in random samples is 2.02 of 47 total morphological characters. It should be noted that all of the ten offense groups except assault and arson and all other offenses greatly exceed in their number of independently differentiated characters the number to be expected in random samples. Assault includes but one total morphological character which is independently differentiated, and arson and all other offenses exhibits 3 differentiated characters. The other offense subgroups show a range of differentiated characters from 6 in forgery and fraud to 23 in burglary and larceny.

In the case of assault we are dealing with a group numerically so small (80 individuals) that the probable errors of percentages are very large. Consequently no morphological feature of this group can be statistically differentiated to a significant degree unless it displays a divergence from the group total which is absolutely very large — much larger than is anthropologically probable in samples drawn from a series of approximately the same ethnic and racial composition. The raw magnitudes and numbers of morphological divergences displayed by this small assault group furnish abundant indications that, were the group of adequate size, it would be significantly differentiated. Nevertheless, the fact remains that it cannot be demonstrated to be morphologically distinct on the basis of the sample included in the present series.

In the case of the arson and all other group the lack of strong differentiation may be due in part to its being a residual group including a miscellany of offenses, although the arson criminals are by far the most common in the group. Moreover, this group is also very small — containing in fact only 102 persons — and the size of its probable errors militates against statistical differentiation.

With the exceptions of the two offense groups noted, it may be seen that these criminals, classified by nature of offense, are overwhelmingly differentiated — each offense group from a random sample of the total series.

RELATION OF MORPHOLOGICAL OBSERVATIONS TO AGE GROUPING

PERCENTILE DISTRIBUTION BY AGE GROUPING

Since many important physical features are subject to marked age changes, it is clear that we cannot appraise the value of their excessive manifestation in this or that criminal offense group unless we take into consideration the age composition of that group. For example a statement that murderers have thin hair and robbers have thin beards has no value whatsoever unless allowance has been made for the difference in ages of the two groups. If we know the distribution of each grade of a physical feature in each successive age group, we are enabled by this knowledge to make a prediction as to the expected frequency of any age-affected character in an offense group, by utilizing the number of individuals of various ages in that offense group together with the total series percentages of occurrences of any specified grade of the character in the respective age groups.

The tables VI–105–149 list the distribution of observed characters by age groups and will serve as the basis for eliminating age effects. These tables also merit some brief discussion because of the rarity of such age-graded observational data. A brief examination of each table will demonstrate the dependence upon, or independence of, age in the case of the morphological feature tabulated.

Hair Quantity — Head. Sparse hair (quantity "small") increases rapidly up to the age of 55 years and is irregularly distributed in the last three small age groups. Medium thickness of hair decreases similarly but shows a curious and possibly insignificant increase in the last three age groups. Thick hair ("large") diminishes with fair regularity from age group to age group.

Hair Quantity — Beard. Sparse beards seem to decrease up to the age of 45 years and thereafter to increase irregularly. Medium beards increase to a maximum at 30–34 years and then diminish slowly, and in the last three age groups, very irregularly. Thick beards increase with age and reach a maximum at 45–49 years. Thereafter they diminish. Clearly the regression of beard thickness upon age is not so pronounced as that of head hair.

Hair Quantity — Body. Small quantity of body hair diminishes up to the 45–49 year age group and thereafter seems to increase irregularly. Medium quantity increases up to 55 years and then diminishes. Large quantity increases up to 45 years and then falls off. These tables on hair quantity suggest that in old age beard and body hair become somewhat more sparse than in middle life, and that head hair, if retained through middle age, is likely to remain fairly thick in later years.

Skin Color. There is a very slight tendency for red white skin color to increase up to the 55–59 year age group and thereafter to decrease. This is accompanied by a gradual decrease in pale white skin up to the 60–64 year age group, after which it increases again, slightly and possibly significantly. Dark skins are irregularly distributed throughout.

Hair Form. Straight hair increases slightly with age; low waves show a very slight decrease; deep waves decrease markedly but irregularly, and there is also some diminution of the proportion of curly hair with advancing age.

Hair Color. Black hair increases up to the 55–59 year age group and then decreases. Dark brown hair increases up to 45 years and then decreases. Red brown hair decreases definitely in the 50–54 year age group and thereafter. Light brown hair shows a gradual and fairly regular diminution in succeeding age groups. Ash blond hair becomes very uncommon after the age of 30 years, and golden hair after 44 years. Red hair diminishes gradually through the age groups. Gray and white hair increase slowly up to the 45–49 year age group and very rapidly in subsequent groups.

Eye Color. The regression of eye color upon age is uncertain. Dark brown eyes seem to be rare in the groups from 45 years old upward. Light brown eyes are irregular in their distribution. Blue-brown eyes seem to increase in the age groups 50 years and over; gray-brown eyes are irregular. Green-brown eyes definitely decrease with advancing years. Blue eyes decrease up to the 55 year age group and then take a sudden upward jump in the last three small groups. This old age increase may be due to sampling. Blue-gray eyes remain fairly constant up to the age of 45 years and then increase irregularly.

Sclera. Clear sclerae seem to diminish slightly and speckled sclerae to increase in the 50–54 year age group and subsequent groups.

Iris. Homogeneous irides show no regression upon age. Rayed, zoned, and speckled irides maintain similar proportions through the age groups. Diffused irides show some decrease in the age groups 55 years and above.

Eye Folds. Epicanthic folds are at a maximum in the 15–19 year age group and are rare after 50 years. Median folds decrease with age and external folds increase, reaching a maximum in the 50–54 year age group.

Eyebrow Thickness. Medium eyebrows seem to diminish in frequency, and pronounced or thick eyebrows to increase, with advancing age. There is also an indication of a slight increase of submedium or thin eyebrows after the age of 34 years.

Eyebrow Concurrency. Eyebrow concurrency, contrary to expectation, seems to diminish with age. The regression in the several categories is marked. This observation has not been utilized to any great extent in the analysis of data, because of a suspicion that it is complicated by a marked personal equation on the part of the two observers. It may be that the thickening of eyebrows in middle and advanced years tends to cause observers to underestimate the degree of concurrency.

Forehead Height. Foreheads of medium height decrease, and those in the pronounced category increase, with advancing age. The data raise the question as to the effect of receding hair and baldness upon the judgment of the observers as to height of forehead.

Forehead Breadth. Forehead breadth exhibits no regression upon age.

Forehead Slope. The only perceptible relation of forehead slope to age is the higher percentage of absent and submedium slopes in the 15–19 year age group.

Nasal Root Height. No age change is apparent in nasal root height.

Nasal Root Breadth. Nasal root breadth shows excesses of the pronounced grade in the age groups between 40 and 55 years. This may be due to middle age obesity, but is quite possibly an effect of sampling.

Nasal Bridge Height. The middle-aged and elderly groups show slight excesses of pronounced bridge height.

Nasal Bridge Breadth. Medium breadths of the nasal bridge decrease in middle age and later years; pronounced breadths increase. This is probably an effect of obesity.

Nasal Profile. Concave profiles diminish with advancing years. Straight noses remain nearly constant. Convex noses increase with fair regularity; concavo-convex profiles are irregularly distributed.

Nasal Tip Thickness. Thin tips seem most frequent between the ages of 30 and 45, but this may be due to sampling. Medium tips decrease, and thick or pronounced tips increase in succeeding age groups.

Nasal Wings. Medium wings decrease with age. Flaring wings increase.

Nasal Septum. The shape of the septum shows no clear relationship to age.

Nasal Septum Inclination. Inclinations upward decrease with age; downward inclinations increase.

Nasal Septum Deflection. Deflection of the nasal septum seems unrelated to age.

Lips — Integumental Thickness. There is no apparent regression of the integumental thickness of the lips upon age.

Lips — Membranous Thickness. Submedium thickness of the membranous lips increases with age; medium thickness decreases; pronounced thickness decreases.

Lip Seam. Pronounced and medium lip seams decrease with age; absent and submedium lip seams increase. The regression is quite regular except that pronounced seams appear to reach a maximum in early adult years and then to diminish.

Alveolar Prognathism. Alveolar prognathism diminishes slightly in the oldest age groups; doubtless because of loss of teeth and alveolar absorption.

Facial Prognathism. Facial prognathism seems to be little affected by age, if at all.

Chin Form. Chin form is unrelated to age.

Malars — Prominence. Pronounced malar projection is least common in the 15–19 and 65–69 age classes. Otherwise the age groups appear to vary irregularly.

Cheeks — Fullness. Submedium cheek fullness increases regularly with advancing age. Medium fullness decreases. Pronounced fullness is commonest between 40 and 55 years of age.

Gonial Angles. In gonial angles there is a marked tendency for submedium and medium prominence to be least between the ages of 30 and 50 years and for prominent angles to be most common. This is probably due to middle age fleshiness. In the young and old age groups flaring gonial angles are less common.

Cheeks — Wrinkling. Wrinkling of the cheeks, as would be expected, shows a very regular regression upon age — the most consistent of any heretofore considered.

Teeth Wear. Slight or medium degrees of wear of the teeth decrease regularly with age; pronounced wear increases.

Teeth Caries. Individuals with few caries decrease; those with many increase in successive age groups.

Teeth Lost. The number of teeth lost increases rapidly in successive age groups.

Bite. Underbites are very rare and seem to occur almost exclusively in the younger age groups. Edge-to-edge bites increase regularly with advancing years. Slight overbites decrease irregularly in the successive groups. Marked overbites apparently remain relatively constant in distribution.

Ear Lobes. On the whole, submedium and medium ear lobes decrease with advancing years, while pronounced ear lobes increase. However, the regression is by no means so regular and so steep as might be expected in this feature.

Ear Lobes — Attachment. Free ear lobes become commoner in middle and old age and attached ear lobes are less frequent. The regression is not pronounced and the distributions are irregular.

Roll of Helix. No clear relationship of roll of the helix to age is perceptible.

Darwin's Point. Darwin's point seems to be absent with increasing frequency in the middle-aged and elderly groups.

Ear Protrusion. No relationship of ear protrusion to age is distinguishable in the table.

Asymmetry. Both left and right asymmetries appear to increase with advancing years.

Neck. There is no regression of neck proportions upon age.

Shoulder Slope. The distributions of shoulder slope are irregular and seem to bear no relationship to age.

PREDICTIONS AND DIFFERENCES ON BASIS OF AGE GROUPING

It is obviously unnecessary to make age corrections in the case of features which show offense group differentiation which is either insignificant or invalidated by state sampling. But those differences which still exceed three times their probable errors when due allowance has been made for state sampling, must be examined and corrected for age grouping if we are to arrive at conclusions which have any general validity. Even in the case of features which seem to exhibit little regression upon age, it seems a better method to make the test of age prediction, for we must not lay ourselves open to the charge of Lombrosianism, even if we regard with marked disapproval the bias against criminological positivism which inspired Goring to utilize every possible statistical device for reducing the crude offense differences which his data exhibit.

In the following tables, then, whatever independent and significant differences have survived the tests of statistical sampling and random sampling are subjected to age predictions. These predictions are made by the same method as that utilized in correcting for state sampling. The predicted proportion of a subcategory of an observation in any offense subgroup is obtained by multiplying the percentage of that subcategory which occurs in the total series for any age group by the number of persons in that age group which are found in the offense subgroup, and dividing the sum of these products by the total number of individuals in that offense group. It is, in short, the mean of the proportions of the subcategory in the respective age groups, weighted by the numbers of persons in the total offense group which fall in each age group. Only those which prove to show excesses which are still significant when age has been taken into consideration can be accepted as ultimately valid.

In each table is listed the predicted percentage on the basis of age grouping, the difference between observed and predicted percentages, the difference of subgroup and total series and its value in terms of the probable error, and finally the difference between the age prediction and the subgroup observation and its value in terms of the probable error of the subgroup. It is this last which determines the validity of the difference.

We may consider these tables briefly, for they are extremely instructive. In Table VI–150 we observe that of 5 excesses in head hair quantity, which were found to be significant and independent of state sampling, only one survives the age correction. This is an excess of small head hair quantity in forgery and fraud.

In beard quantity a deficiency of small in robbery is unaffected by age correction; a similar one in forgery and fraud persists after a deduction for age; and an excess of small in burglary and larceny is reduced to possible insignificance.

In body hair quantity a deficiency of small in first degree murder and an excess of small in burglary and larceny survive age correction.

In hair form, which is presumably little affected by age, a deficiency of straight in robbery and an excess of low waves, and the reverse of these differences in other sex offenders, remain valid.

A large number of significant differences in hair color are obliterated by the age correction. The only ones which persist are an excess of ash blond in arson and all other and an excess of golden in burglary and larceny.

In eye color the two significant differences which are independent of state sampling — an excess of light brown in burglary and larceny and of blue-gray in rape — retain their validity. This is true also of an excess of diffused irides in the robbery group. Rape shows an excess of speckled sclerae which is independent of age.

The differentiations of eyefolds which are independent of state sampling and significant successfully resist age correction. These are an excess of epicanthus in arson and of median folds in robbery.

The one independent and significant difference in forehead slope — a deficiency of pronounced in burglary and larceny — becomes insignificant when age correction is applied. On the other hand, the differentiations of nasal root height, with one exception, are unaffected by age. These include an excess of submedium in assault and in the same group a deficiency of medium and an excess of pronounced, and in burglary and larceny an excess of medium and a deficiency of pronounced. A deficiency of medium in first degree murder is invalidated by age correction.

In nasal bridge height two differences in the robbery group are eliminated by age correction, while an excess of medium and a deficiency of pronounced in forgery and fraud, and an excess of pronounced in second degree murder, remain valid.

The one independent and significant difference of nasal bridge breadth — a deficiency of submedium in first degree murder — is unaffected by age correction. However, only one of five differences in nasal profile — an excess of concave in burglary and larceny — survives the age correction.

All of the differentiations in nasal tip thickness and nasal septum inclination are invalidated by age. On the other hand the two differences in deflection of the septum — both pertaining to the rape group — are independent of age.

Deficiencies of submedium integumental lip thickness in forgery and fraud and versus public welfare, a deficiency in submedium membranous lip thickness in forgery and fraud, and an excess in other sex offenses are the only lip features which escape age invalidation.

The only groups independently characterized by prognathism are arson and all other offenses, which shows a marked excess of a submedium degree of this feature, and rape, which has a small excess of pronounced alveolar prognathism.

Variations in chin form are unaffected by age correction. These include excess of median chin and deficiency of bilateral chin in first degree murder and deviations in the opposite direction in second degree murder.

In lateral prominence of malars 3 of 4 significant differences survive age correction. These are an excess of submedium in first degree murder, and deficiencies of medium and excess of pronounced in versus public welfare.

One of 4 differences remains significant after age correction in the case of fullness of cheeks. This is an excess of submedium in other sex.

The one independent difference in projection of gonial angles — a deficiency of submedium — is unaffected by age correction.

Most of the independent differences in wrinkling of cheeks naturally succumb to age corrections. Four of 17 differences, however, survive. These are a deficiency of absent in second degree murder, an excess of absent in robbery, an excess of slight or medium in second degree murder, and a deficiency of the same category in robbery. An excess of pronounced wrinkles in second degree murder just misses significance.

Wear of the teeth is also markedly affected by age. Actually 3 of 14 differences survive age correction, and 3 others attain possible but not certain significance. Second degree murder is definitely characterized by a deficiency of slight and medium wear and probably by an excess of pronounced. Forgery and fraud is characterized both by an excess of slight or medium and a deficiency of pronounced. Robbery shows a possibly significant excess of slight and medium and a possibly significant deficiency of pronounced.

Caries of the teeth show but one certain difference which supervenes age correction. This is an excess of none among second degree murderers. A deficiency of few caries and an excess of many in the case of versus public welfare attain possible significance.

Not a single difference in number of teeth lost reaches the value of three times its probable error when deductions have been made for age differences.

Bite seems less affected by age than other dental features. Three of 8 differences remain significant after age correction. These are: an excess of underbites in burglary and larceny and a deficiency of edge-to-edge bite, a deficiency of edge-to-edge in robbery, and a possibly insignificant excess of slight overbite in the same group.

Ear lobes are generally considered to show considerable growth in middle and old age. Nevertheless, the independent and significant differences display considerable resistance against obliteration by age correction. Two out of three differences maintain their significance and the other remains possibly significant. Versus public welfare shows a deficiency of submedium lobes and first degree murder an excess of pronounced lobes. A deficiency of pronounced lobes in burglary and larceny is reduced to possible insignificance.

The two independent differences in attachment of ear lobes are but slightly reduced by age correction and retain their validity. These are a deficiency of attached lobes and an excess of free lobes in versus public welfare.

The only independent excesses in roll of helix and Darwin's point — one for each — are neutralized by age correction. A deficiency of submedium antihelix prominence in first degree murder is unaffected by age correction, as are an excess of medium protrusion of the ear and a deficiency of pronounced protrusion in robbery.

Excesses of right facial asymmetries in rape and other sex offenses supervene age correction, but 3 other differences are obliterated. A deficiency of none in first degree murder may be significant, since it amounts to 2.69 p.e. after correction has been made for age difference.

The one excess in neck proportions disappears with age correction, but the excess of slight shoulder slope in first degree murder remains valid.

DIFFERENTIATION BY COMBINATIONS OF MORPHOLOGICAL FEATURES ON BASIS OF STATE AND AGE COMPOSITION

First Degree Murder. Of 164 tabulated subcategories of observations in this offense group, 24 or 14.63 per cent showed significant differences from a random sample of the total series after corrections had been made for state sampling. When these differences are further corrected for age sampling no less than 16 or 67.50 per cent of them are invalidated. There remain significant and independent of state and age sampling 8 differences, or 4.88 per cent of the total subcategories of observations. These comprise differentiations of 7 of 47 complete morphological characters, or 14.89 per cent of those studied. The group then shows indisputable morphological differentiation. That is to say — apart from peculiarities of the first degree murder group which may be attributed to its distinctive blend of state physical types, and apart from the fact that the generally advanced ages of the individuals of this group result in senile physical manifestations, first degree murderers are characterized by more observational differentiae than would be expected in a like number of criminals chosen at random from our total series.

These ultimately significant features are: a deficiency of men with scanty body hair, a deficiency of submedium nasal bridge breadths, an excess of median chins and a deficiency of bilateral chins, an excess of submedium malar prominence, an excess of large or pronounced ear lobes, a deficiency of submedium prominence of the antihelix of the ear, and an excess of slight shoulder slopes.

These features in which first degree murderers display excesses are indeed few and seemingly trivial. They are not impressive at first blush. However, if the reader considers the extensive process of sifting and paring and eliminating which has left us with this small residue, the remarkable fact is that a criminal offense group should show any differences at all which are independent of age and state sampling and which are of such a magnitude in relation to their probable errors that they may be expected to occur but 4 times in one hundred samples.

Second Degree Murder. Second degree murderers show 21 of 164 morphological subcategories, or 12.80 per cent, which differentiate them from a random sample of the total criminals after due allowance has been made for state sampling. Fourteen of these 21 differences are reduced to the margin of possible insignificance by age corrections. This leaves only 7 characters, or 4.27 per cent of the total subcategories of observations, which are certainly of ultimate significance. Of the 14 differences which are rendered possibly insignificant by age correction, 8 retain values in excess of twice their probable errors and may be significant. The number of total morphological characters differentiated is 5, or 10.64 per cent of the 47 studied. Thus second degree murder exceeds slightly the number of significantly differentiated subcategories which would be expected in a random sample (if these subcategories were mutually independent) and very greatly exceeds the expected number of significantly differentiated total morphological characters (which *are* virtually independent of each other). Morphologically, then, second degree murderers are sufficiently distinct from total criminals.

The subcategories of observations in this group which are significant when allowance has been made for state and age sampling are: an excess of pronounced nasal bridge heights, a deficiency of median chins and an excess of bilateral chins, a deficiency of absence of cheek wrinkles, an excess of slight or medium wrinkling (and probably an excess of pronounced wrinkling), a deficiency of teeth with slight or medium wear (and a probable excess of pronounced wear), and a deficiency of teeth with no caries.

Assault. The small assault group offers only 3 features, or 1.83 per cent of the total subcategories of observations, which are significant and independent of state sampling. These 3 observations are found to be independent of age, but all of them pertain to variations of the same morphological character — nasal root height. Hence but one of 47 independent morphological characters shows distinction and it cannot be said that the assault group is certainly differentiated from a random sample of the entire series. Nevertheless, the number of subcategories of features which show differences between two and three times their own probable errors is 25, whereas in random samples of the same size (if the subcategories of total observations were independent) only 17 differ ences of such magnitude would be expected. The small size of this group and its consequently large probable errors have been frequently mentioned. It seems altogether probable that an adequate sample of assault criminals would show morphological distinctiveness.

The three residual excesses in the assault group are: excesses of pronounced nasal root height and of submedium nasal root height and a deficiency of medium height. These few and contradictory differentiae are insufficient to define a morphological group.

Robbery. In the robbery group 25 of 164 subcategories of observations, or 15.24 per cent of the total, are significant when allowance has been made for state sampling. After age correction 10 of these differences, or 6.10 per cent of total subcategories, survive. These independent differences distinguish 7 complete morphological observations or 14.89 per cent of the total. Since not more than 2 of the 47 studied would be expected to show such differentiation through accidents of sampling, it is clear that the robbery group is morphologically distinct from the total criminal series.

The morphological differentiae of robbery, independent of state sampling and of age, are: in hair quantity — deficiency of sparse beards; in hair form — deficiency of straight and excess of low waves; in iris pattern — excess of diffused irides; also in wrinkling — deficiency of slight and medium cheek wrinkles and excess of none; in dental occlusion — deficiency of edge-to-edge bite; in ear protrusion — excess of medium and deficiency of pronounced.

Burglary and Larceny. This group displays no less than 38 of 164 subcategories of observations, or 20.73 per cent, which are significant and independent of state sampling. However, the number is reduced to 8 when allowance has been made for age differences. Hence only 4.88 per cent of subcategories, or hardly more than would be expected in a random sample if the subcategories were mutually independent, are ultimately significant. Yet the number of total morphological characters differentiated is 6, or 12.77 per cent of those studied. It therefore is certain that the offense group is morphologically differentiated from the total series of native White criminals of native parentage.

The differentiated characters and their independently distinguished subcategories are: body hair quantity — excess of submedium; hair color — excess of golden; eye color — excess of light brown; nasal root height — excess of medium and deficiency of pronounced; nasal profile — excess of concave; dental occlusion — excess of underbite and deficiency of edge-to-edge bite.

Forgery and Fraud. In this group there are 8 subcategories of observations, or 4.88 per cent, which are significantly differentiated and independent of state sampling. Since the mean age of the group is that of the total series, none of the observations is invalidated by age correction. The offense group is statistically differentiated from a random sample of the entire series by distinctive features found in 6 of 47 total morphological characters, or 12.77 per cent.

The total characters and their distinctive subcategories by which this forgery and fraud group is morphologically differentiated are: head hair quantity — excess of small; beard hair quantity — deficiency of submedium; nasal bridge height — excess of medium and deficiency of pronounced: integumental lip thickness — deficiency of submedium; membranous lip thickness — deficiencies of submedium; wear of teeth — excess of slight or medium and deficiency of pronounced.

Rape. The rape group shows 16 of 164 subcategories of observations, or 9.75 per cent, which are significant and independent of state sampling. However, since this group is considerably above the mean age of the series, all but 6 of these differences are rendered insignificant by age correction. Thus there remain but 3.66 per cent of all subcategory differences which are certainly significant and independent of age sampling. These would be insufficient to differentiate the group statistically, were it not for the fact that they are distributed among 5 complete and independent morphological observations, or 10.64 per cent of the total. This proportion of differentiated total features is about two-and-one-half times expectation in random samples. Hence we may regard the rape group as morphologically differentiated from the total series, even when allowances for state sampling and for age have been made.

The significantly differing total characters and their distinctive subcategories are: eye color — excess of blue-gray; sclera — excess of speckled; nasal septum deflection — excess of right deflections and deficiency of no deflection; alveolar prognathism — excess of pronounced; facial asymmetry — excess of right asymmetry.

Other Sex Offenses. The other sex offenses group of criminals manifests 16 of 164 subcategories of observations, or 9.75 per cent, which differ significantly and independently of state composition from a random sample of the entire series. However, 11 of these differences are obliterated by age correction, leaving only 5, or 3.66 per cent of all subcategory differences, which are ultimately important. This amount is no more than would be expected in a random sample if all of the subcategories of observations were independent. However, these subcategory differences distinguish 4 of 47 complete morphological characters, or 8.51 per cent — more than twice expectation in random samples. On the whole, then, it may be stated that other sex offenders are morphologically differentiated from a random sample of the total series, when due allowance has been made for state sampling and for age.

The morphological features and their distinguishing subcategories in the other sex offense group are: hair form — excess of straight and deficiency of low waves; membranous lip thickness — excess of submedium; cheek fullness — excess of submedium; facial asymmetry — excess of asymmetries to the right.

Versus Public Welfare. This group displays 18 of 164 differences in subcategories of observations (10.97 per cent) which are significant and independent of state sampling. This number is reduced to 7, or 4.27 per cent, when age corrections have been applied. The number of complete morphological observations or total morphological categories differentiated is 5 or 10.64 per cent — far more than enough to justify the conclusion that this offense group is morphologically distinct.

The differentiated observations and their subcategories for the versus public welfare group are: integumental lip thickness — deficiency of submedium; malar prominence — deficiency of submedium and excess of pronounced; gonial angles — deficiency of submedium; size of ear lobes — deficiency of submedium; attachment of ear lobes — deficiency of attached and excess of free.

Arson and All Other Offenses. This miscellaneous group shows only 3 of 164 subcategories of observations, or 1.83 per cent of the total, which are significant and independent of state sampling. None of them is invalidated by age correction. Since each of these 3 differentiated subcategories belongs to a different complete morphological observation, the total of differentiated morphological characters is 3 of 47, or 6.38 per cent. This exceeds slightly the amount to be expected in random samples.

In spite of the fewness of differentiated characters in the arson and all other offenses group, those which are distinctive are of considerable interest. They are: hair color — excess of ash blond; eyefolds — excess of internal (epicanthic) folds; alveolar prognathism — excess of slight or submedium. This group is barely distinguishable morphologically from a random sample of the total series after state and age corrections have been applied.

GENERAL STATISTICAL DIFFERENTIATION OF MORPHOLOGICAL OBSERVATIONS ON BASIS OF STATE AND AGE COMPOSITION

Table VI–196 summarizes the numbers and percentages of subcategories of morphological observations in the different offense groups, classified according to their significance. By age and state corrections the percentage of criminologically important deviations in the combined offense groups has been reduced from an initial 15.55 per cent of subcategories to a residual 5.04 per cent. If all of these 164 subcategories of morphological observations were uncorrelated and mutually independent, we should expect about 4 per cent of statistically significant differences of subcategories to occur as a result of the sampling process. Under these circumstances 4 of the 10 offense groups would fail to exceed in their significant deviations (after state and age correction) the amount to be expected as a result of chance in random samples drawn from the entire series. However, since the subcategories of a single observation (e.g. head hair quantity — small, medium, large) are obviously interdependent, the random sampling expectation cannot be applied strictly to the mere count of subcategory deviations. On the other hand, it may be assumed that the complete morphological characters (each of which has two or more subcategories according to size, development, quality, etc.) do approximately fulfill the conditions required for testing expectation by comparison with random samples. These complete categories are not dependent upon each other, although they may be, to some extent, intercorrelated. Therefore, the appraisal of independence and of morphological difference is based upon the number and percentage of complete morphological observations which show differences significant over and beyond the corrections for state and age sampling. A complete morphological character is regarded as differentiated if one of its subcategories shows an independent difference. If all of its categories show significant differences, it is still counted as but one differentiated morphological observation.

Thus we have in Table VI–197 the numbers and percentages of differentiated complete morphological observations, for each offense group and for the total of the offense groups. Not more than two of the total of 47 morphological categories would be expected to show significant differences merely through the chances of the sampling process. Table VI–197 shows that 9 of the 10 offense groups show morphological differences considerably in excess of the expected 4 per cent. Definitely, assault with only one differentiated category (2.13 per cent) cannot be distinguished morphologically from a random sample of the total series. The only other group which is not strongly differentiated is the miscellaneous arson and all other offenses class.

Thus the sociological differentiation of the offense groups first demonstrated, and the indicial and anthropometric differentiation subsequently shown, are accompanied by a differentiation in observed morphological features. In short, native White criminals of native parentage, classified according to the nature of their crimes, are both sociologically and anthropologically distinct from random samples of the series of which they form parts, even when all differences are obliterated which may be ascribed to age changes, to chance, to state composition of the offense groups, and to personal equation. This is a conclusion of great criminological importance. It indicates that crime is not exclusively a sociological phenomenon, but also a biological phenomenon.

Chapter VII

PHYSICAL DIFFERENTIATION BY PREVIOUS CONVICTIONS

IF criminals as a physical group are differentiated from civilians of similar ethnic origin, it is possible that habitual criminals will be physically differentiated from first offenders. As yet the differences between criminals and civilians have not been demonstrated, but overwhelming proof of such differentiation will be offered in later chapters of this volume. Here we may forestall such a demonstration by making a brief examination into the question of physical differences between criminals with known previous convictions and those whose previous criminal careers are unrecorded or non-existent. There is not the slightest doubt that a much higher proportion of our criminals have previously served jail or prison sentences than our records show. Massachusetts and Wisconsin are the only states of our series in which the records of previous convictions command confidence. In these two states the percentage of recidivism is much higher than in the south and the southwest. Consequently we are faced by two difficulties in investigating differences between recidivists and first offenders: (a) the certainty that many in our series classified as lacking previous convictions have, in fact, been incarcerated before, (b) the disproportionate contributions of the various states to the previously convicted subgroup owing to variations in the accuracy of their criminal records. The first difficulty cannot be eradicated. Nevertheless, if we actually find significant differences between recidivists and supposed first offenders it can be assumed that these differences would be greatly enhanced if the records were more accurate. The disproportionate contributions of the several states can be equalized by using a prediction for state composition as in our other studies.

If we are comparing the differences of means of two subgroups drawn from a total series, and wish to take into consideration the effect of variation in state composition upon the means of the respective subgroups, the application of the principle of correction differs from the cases previously considered (subgroup versus total series). For we now have the comparison of differences in means both of which are affected by state sampling, instead of but one subgroup to be compared with a total series of which the state composition does not vary.

First of all, it is necessary to make predictions for the values of each of the means of the subgroups utilizing the weighted means of the characters observed in total state series. Let us call these predicted means m_1 and m_2, and the observed mean of the respective subgroups M_1 and M_2. The $m_1 - m_2 = a$ the difference of the predicted means of the subgroups, which is equivalent to the amount of difference which would be expected to arise as a result of state sampling. Also $M_1 - M_2 = b$ the observed difference between means of subgroups, uncorrected for state sampling. The $b - a =$ the crude

observed differences of means minus the differences expected on the basis of variation
in state composition. These are then the differences independent of state sampling. If
the signs of b and a are similar and b is greater than a the residuum or difference is independent of state sampling. If $b = a$ and the signs are similar, then b is entirely dependent on state sampling, since it is only the amount of difference to be expected from
state composition, and in the same direction. If the signs of b and a are opposite, then
the difference expressed by b is independent of state sampling, since it is in the opposite
direction from what would be predicted on the basis of state composition. Therefore
the independent differences are in the first case $b - a$, in the second case o, and in the
third case b and not $b + a$, since we use predictions only for scaling down differences
and never for enhancing them. In either case the independent difference is divided by
the probable error of b in order to test its significance.

We may now proceed to the discussion of the actual results obtained by comparing
recidivists with non-recidivists. The crude differentiation of the recidivists from those
not previously convicted amounts to 15 of 33 measurements and indices (counting but
once the measurements and derived indices in which the results of the two observers
have been kept separate). This differentiation of 45.4 per cent is, of course, overwhelming. Most of the gross measurements show inferior size on the part of the recidivists.
When, however, the corrections for state sampling are made, nearly all of the differences are invalidated. They are due, in considerable degree, to the overweighting of
the recidivists with criminals from Massachusetts and Wisconsin, who are much smaller
than those from the other states. There remain significant only three differences: a deficiency of weight on the part of the recidivists, one of chest breadth, and a deficiency of
ear index found only in the series of Observer A and in contradiction to an insignificant
excess found by Observer B. These results are tabulated in Table VII–4. Neglecting
this last unconfirmed difference we have a residuum of two significant deviations from
a total of 33 or 6.06 per cent. Such a proportion of significant difference is more than
would be expected in two random samples drawn from the same population. It leaves
us in some uncertainty as to the actual validity of recidivist difference from the non-
recidivist series.

In order to pursue this question a little further, the differences between the two
subgroups in hair color, hair form, and eye color were also examined (Tables IV–5–10).
Here all of the very few crudely significant differences are rendered insignificant by
state sampling.

Another factor which might complicate crude differences between the previously
convicted and those not so recorded is the proportion of each class offender in the respective subgroups. Since the offense groups are physically differentiated, it follows
that an excess of this or that type of offender in the previously convicted group might
result in differences between recidivists and non-recidivists which are contingent upon
the series composition in the matter of offense representation. This question was investigated by taking the burglary and larceny subgroups only and comparing recidivists
with non-recidivists. The size inferiority of the recidivists was quite as marked in the
burglary and larceny group as in the total subseries, but here again the matter of
state composition indicated that the results were specious, since the burglary and larceny recidivists are badly overloaded with the small men from Massachusetts and
Wisconsin — the states which have the best records of recidivism. For this reason it

seems superfluous to publish the statistics of the burglary and larceny comparisons.

It is evident that the only really satisfactory way of ascertaining the differences between recidivists and non-recidivists would be to compare them, each subdivided into crime categories, within the total series of the same state. Such a procedure would leave us with very small samples for comparison in the case of Massachusetts and Wisconsin, and in the other states would be unprofitable, because of our lack of faith in the completeness of their records of previous convictions.

Since the question of size inferiority of recidivists is of very great importance, it is necessary to go beyond the mere enumeration of those residually independent differences which remain significant after corrections for state sampling. We must consider the number and direction of residual differences, irrespective of their fulfilling, or failing to fulfill our stated measure of validity, three times the probable error. There are 20 separate measurements including age. Head height, ear length, and ear breadth are separated into the respective materials of the two observers, so that these may be counted as 3 measurements instead of 6. Now in 10 of these 17 measurements the actually observed means of the recidivists fall below those of the non-recidivists to a degree greater than the predicted means of the recidivists fall short of the predicted means of the non-recidivists. In other words the recidivists in these 10 measurements show size deficiency over and beyond what can be attributed to state sampling. In one measurement, head length, the actual difference observed between recidivists and total series is an excess rather than a deficiency, but this excess considerably exceeds the corresponding excess of the predicted difference. In two measurements, head breadth and head circumference, the observed differences between recidivists and non-recidivists are in the direction opposite from what would be expected on the basis of the predictions for state sampling. Thus out of a total of 17 measurements we have 10 in which size inferiority of recidivists supervenes state predictions, and three in which the recidivists are bigger than the non-recidivists.

There are also 13 indices to be considered (counting but once the length-height, breadth-height, and ear indices separated according to the data of the two observers). In three of these indices (cephalic, cephalo-facial, and zygo-gonial) the actual means of the recidivists fall below those of the non-recidivists to a greater extent than would be expected from the corresponding state predictions. We can then assert that in 58.82 per cent of measurements recidivists are (significantly or insignificantly) inferior in size to non-recidivists over and beyond the amounts which are attributable to state sampling, and that in 17.65 per cent of measurements they exceed in size the non-recidivists to a degree, or in a direction, contrary to state expectation. Similar excess deviations occur in 3 of 13 indices or 23.08 per cent.

Now to my mind a decided trend of insignificant differences in the same direction quite supervenes the matter of the statistical validity of those differences. In other words, I am convinced that recidivists are in fact smaller than non-recidivists, over and beyond the complicating influence of state sampling, because there is in one-third of cases an excess of inferiority in the recidivists over what can be predicted from state composition. Nor am I particularly perturbed by the fact that size inferiority of recidivists may be due to their overweighting by members of the offense groups which are inferior in body size, since that inferiority of body size is inextricably connected with recidivism. "Things equal to the same thing are equal to each other."

Chapter VIII

DIFFERENTIATION BY OCCUPATION

THE SIGNIFICANCE OF PHYSICAL DIFFERENTIATION BY OCCUPATION

IF criminals of similar racial and ethnic origin are physically differentiated according to the types of offense which they have committed, one would expect them also to show some physical differentiation according to occupational classes. The reasons for this are clear. Firstly, the same physical qualifications which may tend to select a man for a certain type of occupation may also influence the type of his antisocial acts. For example, small and puny men are likely to be selected for the occupations which do not require great physical strength, such as personal service and clerical; although laborers include all sorts of physical types unqualified by education, intelligence, or experience for any skilled pursuit. Again these physically inferior types are less likely to commit crimes of violence against the person than those which are more robust.

The diversification of antisocial opportunities in its dependence upon occupational class is probably more important than the selection caused by physical qualifications. Thus in the clerical class the opportunities for forgery, fraud, larceny, and other gainful offenses are much more abundant than in the extractive and laborer categories. The urban environment of the factory operative is peculiarly conducive to such offenses as robbery and burglary. The isolation of farm life, on the other hand, provides few opportunities for forgery, burglary, and robbery, but is extremely productive of offenses against the person, such as murder and rape.

Much more important than the physical qualifications of occupations or the criminal opportunities which they afford, are the mental and educational status of the individual. Mental capacity and educational status cannot be separated in most of our material, because of the absence of reliable psychological tests or other data for mental classification. Nevertheless, it is obvious that defective or inferior mentality limits the educational attainments of the individual and to a considerable extent determines his occupational status. Stupidity and ignorance also seem to be directly or indirectly responsible for many crimes against the person which are in no way gainful.

Another element which must be taken into account is the racial and ethnic factor. Although all of the offenders of this series are, supposedly, native born of native parentage, they undoubtedly represent a considerable diversity of national and racial origins. This diversity carries with it not only differences in physical type but also occupational tendencies. Certain immigrant stocks tend to settle in cities and to take up urban occupations. Examples of such stocks are the Irish and the Italians. Our native born criminals of native parentage certainly include a considerable proportion of the descendants of Irish immigrants who have adhered to this urban environment and to the occupations of city life. On the other hand, many of the second generation of Germans, Scandinavians, and other nationalities have continued to pursue the traditional agricultural occupations of their immigrant grandparents.

Finally, we must take into consideration the actual physical modifications in the individual which may be brought about by his occupation. Manual labor produces a muscular development which may be contrasted with the flabbiness resulting from sedentary occupations. It is difficult and virtually impossible to isolate the various factors which are conducive to physical differentiation of occupational classes, and to appraise their respective importances, but together they should result in groups which are in many features distinct.

A serious obstacle to the differentiation of occupational physical types in criminals is, however, the fact that many of these criminals, if not most of them, may never have engaged seriously in the occupations to which they lay claim. Thus the Gluecks have ascertained that inmates of the Concord Reformatory have, as a rule, very poor industrial records both prior to commitment and subsequent to their paroles. These young men held jobs, for the most part, for very short periods and frequently abandoned them upon the slightest provocation.[1] In a good many cases the occupations of criminals are probably fictitious, or, at any rate, followed so intermittently, practised so half-heartedly, and changed so frequently that the degree of physical differentiation by occupation, which might result from the various factors mentioned above, would be much slighter than in the law-abiding industrial population.

Under these circumstances, it has not seemed worth while to pursue the question of occupational differences through all of the many measurements, indices, and morphological observations which are recorded for each individual of the criminal series. Only a few of the more significant metric and observational criteria have been selected for examination.

OCCUPATIONAL CLASSIFICATION

The occupational categories here recognized were adopted from the classification utilized by the survey carried on under the auspices of the Massachusetts Department of Mental Diseases, Division of the Examination of Prisoners. Since the present study was inaugurated in order to supplement the sociological and psychiatric data of that survey with anthropometric information, it was essential that the sociological classifications of both researches be identical. The assignment of all recorded occupations to the eleven categories here recognized raised many difficulties. This work fell to the lot of the clerical force in the Harvard Anthropometric and Statistical Laboratory.

Table VIII–1 lists the details of occupational assignment under each category. It will be apparent to the reader who examines this table carefully that some of the classifications are dubious, and a few of them plainly erroneous. Thus, to the element of doubt as to the reality of recorded occupations, there is added an additional disturbing factor — questionable and erroneous classification.

The extractive category includes agriculture, mining, animal husbandry, fishing, and forestry. The details of occupations listed in the table include none which does not properly belong to the extractive category. In the next category — laborer — a considerable number of dubious assignments may be noted. The large majority of the class (81.02 per cent) are day laborers, but 5.99 per cent are textile workers and 2.93 per

[1] Sheldon and Eleanor T. Glueck, *500 Criminal Careers* (New York, 1930), pp. 169 ff.

cent shoe workers. These may have been unskilled laborers, but, on the other hand, it seems probable that many or most of them might well have been classified under factory operatives. There is also in this category a miscellaneous group comprising 10.06 per cent of the total. Here there are several incorrect classifications — usually involving but one single individual. A timekeeper, for example, should be put in the clerical category. A crane operator and a stonecutter ought to be assigned to skilled trades. Chair makers and weavers properly belong to the factory class. It seems probable that at least 10 per cent of the individuals in the laborer category claim occupations which are somewhat above the requirements of unskilled labor.

In the factory category there is only a small minority (4.51 per cent) of persons whose occupations are listed simply as factory workers. No less than 60.51 per cent are mechanics or machinists. Here also a few individuals in the miscellaneous group may have been mistakenly classified. However, the large majority of this group are clearly persons who claim to have earned their living by operating machinery of one sort or other in manufacturing plants.

The transportation category offers no difficulty. The skilled trades include mostly the building trades. Again in the miscellaneous group (16.97 per cent) certain individual classifications are clearly due to mistakes in judgment or to clerical errors. An interior decorator ought to be put in the semi-professional class. An excavator should be classified as a laborer, unless he happens to be an archaeologist. A chemist should fall into the professional category. In the trade list the appearance of warehouse man and freight caller may be seriously questioned.

This table of occupational details with its considerable number of dubious classifications has been included and discussed in order to emphasize the fact that an appreciable error is introduced not only by the somewhat arbitrary and vague nature of the classification by categories, but also by mistakes in judgment on the part of the clerical force which coded the raw data sheets. On the whole, however, it seems probable that the vast majority of occupations has been correctly classified and that the few individuals misplaced would be insufficient to influence the physical composition of the several categories. A possible exception is the laborer group, which certainly includes a considerable percentage of persons who should have been assigned either to factory or to other categories.

A few comments upon the general composition of the occupational categories may be apposite. The extractive class is overwhelmingly agricultural (four-fifths) with a residue consisting mostly of miners (one-sixth). Over 80 per cent of the laborers are unskilled day laborers. The remainder consists, for the most part, of persons who are trade helpers, or factory laborers. The factory group consists largely of machinists and mechanics, with a considerable sprinkling of engineers and firemen. The transportation group has been recruited principally from chauffeurs, railroad men, and truckmen. It includes very few sailors. The skilled trades category is composed almost exclusively of persons belonging to the building trades. Painters lead, and carpenters, electricians, and plumbers follow in order of representation.

The trade group is made up principally of salesmen and sales clerks. Printers and musicians are the most important contributors to the semi-professional category. Cooks and barbers predominate in the personal service group. Bookkeepers and accountants lead the clerical category.

If, in spite of the blurring of occupational class outlines, which results from mendacious records and errors in classification, there should be demonstrated any distinctiveness of physical type according to assigned occupation, it could be deduced that a careful study of the physical features of properly authenticated occupational groups would yield much more definite results. Habitual criminals are not habitually engaged in honest occupations.

EDUCATION

Table VIII–2 shows the expected high relationship between education and occupation. The coefficient of mean square contingency is .57. The most illiterate occupational categories are extractive and laborer. The best educated are professional, clerical, semi-professional, and trade, in the order named.

The extractive occupations include the largest percentage of both illiterates and poorly educated persons. No less than 19.09 per cent are illiterate. Excesses are shown by this occupational category in every educational class up to the sixth grade, and thereafter deficiencies which increase in magnitude as the educational qualifications increase. Only 3, or .23 per cent, of 1294 criminals in the extractive category have attended college.

The laborer class, although in general very poorly educated, is distinctly superior to the extractive category in this regard. The former shows excesses in most of the lower educational groupings up to the eighth grade and thereafter exhibits deficiencies. A higher proportion of the laborers is presumably of urban residence, and, consequently, they have had better educational opportunities than the persons belonging to the extractive occupations.

The professional class, here limited to physicians and surgeons, teachers, lawyers, and clergymen, includes only 27 criminals in this series. None of these discontinued his education before reaching high school, and 74.07 per cent had college educations. Professional schools were attended by 4, or 14.81 per cent.

The clerical occupational class includes no illiterates and exhibits proportional deficiencies in all educational groupings up to the first two years of high school. In this grouping and thereafter it shows great excesses. Of the clerical criminals 28.21 per cent have attended college.

The semi-professional class shows marked deficiencies in the lower educational groupings, but begins to manifest excesses in the eighth grade and continues to show them thereafter. The trade group also is deficient in the lower educational classes and similarly begins to show excesses in the 1st–2nd year high school grouping. Its deficiencies in the lower classifications are smaller, and its excesses in the highest groupings are also smaller than those of the semi-professional class.

The public service class contains only 27 criminals and is so irregularly distributed in the educational groupings that no definite conclusions can be drawn as to its educational attainments, except that they are, in general, low.

If the educational attainments be summarized by combining those who are illiterate, those who read and write but have had no formal schooling, and those who have reached the first five grades into a lower class; the sixth, seventh, and eighth grades into a middle class; and higher education in an upper class, the array of percentages furnishes a convenient method of ranking the occupation groups according to their de-

TABLE VIII–4

SUMMARY OF EDUCATION BY OCCUPATION GROUPING

	Illiterate, Read and Write, 1st–5th Grade	6th–8th Grade	High School, College, Professional School	Educational Rank
	Per Cent	Per Cent	Per Cent	
Professional	0	0	100.00	1
Clerical	2.56	22.22	75.21	2
Semi-professional	7.25	39.14	53.62	3
Trade	18.00	30.33	51.65	4
Personal service	20.71	47.50	31.79	5
Skilled trades	24.53	50.40	25.05	6
Factory	28.07	42.74	29.20	7
Transportation	28.32	47.67	24.00	8
Public service	40.73	40.74	18.52	9
Laborer	50.90	38.69	10.41	10
Extractive	60.43	32.23	7.34	11

gree of education. Table VIII–4 gives this data. It clearly shows that public service criminals belong in ninth place, transportation in eighth place, factory, seventh, skilled trades, sixth, and personal service, fifth.

PIGMENTATION

Hair Color. Occupational differentiation in hair color is slight. Black hair seems to be most frequent among the professional and semi-professional classes, but the samples in these classes are too small to command confidence. Dark brown hair is excessively represented in the public service group, but again the numbers included are too few to be reliable. (The excess is equal to only 2.75 times its probable error.) Red-brown hair is commonest in the transportation class (excess equalling 3.15 p.e.) and light brown hair is excessively present in the semi-professional and clerical classes (excesses equalling 2.30 and 2.71 p.e.). Ash-blond and golden hair are also most frequent in the clerical class, but the excesses are not statistically significant.

In order to reduce the elaborate hair color scheme of Table VIII–5 to more digestible dimensions, Table VIII–7 has been compiled, which classifies hair color in three categories, and omits the small and variable percentage of gray and white. This table gives combined percentages from which the offense groups may be ranked in order of blondness.[2] On this basis the blondest occupational group is the clerical, followed by the professional and transportation groups. The darkest group is the public service group, followed by the trade and laborer groups. But the table also shows that the differentiation of occupational groups by hair color is of no great importance.

Eye Color. Table VIII–8 gives the distribution of the occupational groups by eye colors. The table is intricate and confusing because of the numerous shades and the small size of some of the occupational groups — notably the public service, professional, and semi-professional. A few comments on individual shades may, however, be apposite.

[2] The method of ranking employed involves the combined scoring of the three main categories when first rank is assigned to the least dark hair, the most medium colored hair, and the most light hair.

TABLE VIII-7

SUMMARY OF HAIR COLOR BY OCCUPATION GROUPING

	Dark (black and dark brown)	Medium (reddish brown and light brown)	Light (ash-blond, golden, red)	Order of Blondness
Clerical	35.65	46.95	11.31	1
Professional	37.04	48.15	11.11	2
Transportation	34.67	50.67	8.33	3
Factory	38.03	49.16	10.14	4
Semi-professional	39.70	51.47	7.35	5
Skilled trades	40.43	42.32	10.24	6
Extractive	40.22	44.74	9.05	6
Personal service	40.72	41.43	10.71	8
Laborer	41.94	45.46	8.80	9
Trade	43.54	42.10	7.65	10
Public service	55.55	37.04	0	11

Dark brown eyes are rare in all groups, but commonest in the laborer (4.26 p.e.) and personal service groups (1.33 p.e.). Light brown eyes are almost as rare, but show unexpectedly large percentages in professional, semi-professional (excess 4.12 p.e.), public service (excess 1.99 p.e.), and clerical occupations (excess 3.64 p.e.). However, all of these occupational groups are small. The mixed eyes are blue-brown, gray-brown, and green-brown. It would be unprofitable to emphasize differences in the distribution of these shades, since I believe them to be subject to a marked personal equation on the part of the observers. Blue eyes show their maximum frequency in the extractive class (excess 7.61 p.e.), followed closely by public service, trade, and transportation (in which, however, the excesses are statistically insignificant). Significant deficiencies of blue eyes are found in laborers and personal service.

Some order may be introduced into the chaos by combining eye shades into light, mixed, and dark (Table VIII-10). Then a rank in lightness may be assigned arbitrarily by grading the occupational groups once for each combined category of eye color — assigning the number 1 to the group having the smallest percentage of dark eyes, similarly in the mixed eyes and light eyes assigning the number 1 to the group having the largest percentage of such shades, and finally arriving at a ranking by adding for each group the scores of the three categories of eye color, and assigning final rank on the basis of sum totals, the minimum sum conferring the highest rank for lightness, and so on, in order. This method, however, has the disadvantage of counting mixed eyes for lightness.

On this basis, the lightest-eyed group is transportation, followed by skilled trades, and extractive. Clerical, professional, and semi-professional have the darkest eyes, in the order named.

It is quite apparent, however, that the occupational differentiation by eye color is very slight. An excess or deficiency of five per cent in this or that category of eye color cannot be of any practical importance.

General Conclusions on Pigmentation. Medium shades of brown hair and medium or mixed eyes predominate in every occupational group except the public service group, which includes only 27 individuals. Dark hair is much more common in all classes than dark eyes, whereas light eyes are far more prevalent than light hair. In general, the lightest-pigmented group is the transportation class. It owes its position to its low rank in occurrence of dark eyes and dark hair. The public service class, which is unreliably small, is peculiar in that it is absolutely devoid of blond hair, but has the high-

TABLE VIII–10

SUMMARY OF EYE COLOR BY OCCUPATION GROUPING

	Dark (dark brown, light brown)	Mixed (gray-brown, green-brown, blue-brown)	Light (blue, blue-gray)	Rank (in lightness)
	Per Cent	Per Cent	Per Cent	
Transportation	4.62	63.69	31.68	1
Skilled trades	4.82	66.75	28.42	2
Extractive	5.30	63.70	31.00	3
Trade	5.19	67.92	26.88	4
Factory	6.16	65.83	28.01	5
Public service	7.41	55.55	37.03	6
Personal service	8.52	68.79	22.70	7
Laborer	8.34	62.87	28.80	8
Semi-professional	10.15	68.12	21.74	9
Professional	11.11	59.25	29.63	10
Clerical	10.26	63.25	26.50	11

est percentage of blue eyes. One suspects here the presence of a large proportion of individuals with the Keltic combination of dark hair and blue eyes.

It would be even less possible to distinguish the occupations of these criminals by their complexions than so to distinguish their offenses.

METRIC AND INDICIAL FEATURES

Age. The means of ages in the various occupational groups are shown in Table VIII–11. The youngest is the factory group (difference 6.38 p.e.), which averages 28.90 years old, and the oldest is the very small professional group with a mean of 42.40 years (difference 7.61 p.e.). The latter is more than eight years older than any other group. If data were available it probably could be shown that criminals who belong to a profession commit their offenses later in life than those in other occupations, for the simple reason that a man is usually at least twenty-five years old before he is ready to enter a profession and criminal offenses committed before he has finished his preparation are almost certain to prevent his embarking upon a professional career.

I suppose that the young mean ages of the laborer and factory groups are connected in some degree both with the tendency for delinquency to express itself at an early age in urban residents, and with the inability of habitual delinquents to hold jobs requiring a high degree of skill. To some extent, occupations which require longer years of preparation seem to yield delinquents of greater mean age, since a law-abiding youth and an extensive education are prerequisites of their practice.

Weight. Weight depends upon gross stature and bodily size, age, state of nutrition, constitutional type, and other factors. By far the heaviest occupational group is the small professional group, which averages 170.80 pounds — more than 17 pounds greater han any other group, and nearly 20 pounds above the mean of the series (a difference qualling 6.26 p.e.). This is partly due to the superiority in age of the members of this ery small group, and due also in part to the exclusion of any very light individuals. Apart from these considerations it must be remembered that professional men lead sedntary lives. Succeeding measurements will tend to show that this wholly inadequate ccupational sample seems to conform to a distinct body type.

Persons belonging to the clerical class also lead sedentary lives, but they are the ightest of all the occupational groups, though by no means the youngest. Since the clerks re also among the shortest of the occupational groups, it may be that small stature nd slight body build are factors which tend to select individuals for such occupaions. The fact that the personal service class, whose members are also relatively sedntary and presumably do no hard physical labor, are also light in weight and rather hort in stature, may lend some credibility to such a supposition. But laborers, who ertainly perform hard physical work, are only a little taller and heavier than the cleri-al and personal service groups. Laborers, however, are below average in age, and it nust be emphasized that they do not represent a class selected by any physical require-nents, but rather a residual occupational class which includes all sorts of persons in-eriorly qualified both in physique and in mentality.

On the whole, the occupational differentiation in weight is greater than one would xpect and is not easily explained on the basis of selection. Two of eleven classes are ignificantly differentiated from the mean weight of the entire series: laborers by a de-ciency, and the professional class by an excess. Deficiencies in personal service and erical classes approach the margin of significance.

Height. Three of the occupational classes are certainly differentiated in height rom the total series. These are laborers (deficiency −0.87 cm., 5.12 p.e.), personal ervice (−1.17 cm., 4.50 p.e.), and clerical (−1.23 cm., 3.08 p.e.). The semi-profes-ional class is below average height, but the deficiency is not certainly significant on ccount of the small size of this class. The extractive group is tallest, but it exceeds the otal mean by only .21 cm. On the whole, occupational groups seem to be fairly strongly ifferentiated in stature since presumably significant deviations from the mean of the otal series occur in 27.27 per cent.

Sitting Height. No occupational group diverges significantly from the entire series a sitting height.

Head Length. Although the occupational groups show slight variations in the mean f head length, none of these is of certain significance. The largest deviation is that of he professional class (2.04 mm., 2.40 p.e.). The excess shown by this class may be alid, since it is supported by a considerable number of other metric divergences from he means of the total group. However, the class is composed of so few individuals (27), hat the probable errors of means are very large, and, consequently, deviations which re of appreciable magnitude are statistically insignificant.

Head Breadth. This measurement shows significant deviations from the mean of the ntire sample in five of eleven occupational groups. These are: extractive (−.33 mm., .30 p.e.), laborer (−.45 mm., 3.21 p.e.), factory (.54 mm., 3.86 p.e.), trade (.90 mm., .69 p.e.), clerical (1.53 mm., 4.64 p.e.). Divergences in other groups are as great or reater, but cannot be considered significant because of the small size of the occupa-onal groups in question and the consequent magnitude of the probable errors of their means. Judging from raw means it seems probable that the broadest heads are found in the professional, clerical, and semi-professional classes in descending order, and tha the narrowest heads occur in the public service, laborer, personal service, and extrac tive occupations. In spite of the statistical insignificance of many of the deviations, the array of means seems to support the supposition that the better educated criminals in higher economic occupations have somewhat broader heads than the more ignorant in unskilled occupations.

Head Circumference. The single deviation in head circumference is that of the laborer group which shows a deficiency of 3.24 mm., 7.53 p.e. The maximum value i reached in the professional class, but the excess fails to attain reliability (6.00 mm. 2.76 p.e.), probably because of the small size of the subgroup.

Minimum Frontal Diameter. This measurement shows significant deviations in fou groups. These are extractive ($-.40$ mm., 4.44 p.e.), factory (.56 mm., 4.67 p.e.), semi professional (1.28 mm., 3.28 p.e.), and professional (3.08 mm., 4.81 p.e.). Another im portant difference which does not attain the measure of certain significance, probably because of the small size of the occupational group in question, is: public servic (-1.36 mm., 2.16 p.e.). Here again one is left with the impression that a more ade quate representation of some of the smaller occupational groups would establish a gen eral relationship between breadth of forehead and occupation, the higher occupation showing the greater diameters.

Bizygomatic Diameter. The only significantly deviating group in this dimension i the professional with an excess of 3.75 mm., 5.43 p.e.

Cephalic Index. Although this index shows slight deviations from the total mean i many groups, the only significant differences are found in the laborer group ($-.3$ units, 3.67 p.e.), the factory group (.33 units, 4.12 p.e.), and the semi-professiona (1.77 units, 6.56 p.e.). The array of means, however, seems to indicate that the bette educated occupations show slightly higher mean cephalic indices.

Facial Index. None of the occupational groups differs significantly from the tota series in the mean of the facial index.

Nasal Index. The lowest mean nasal index is found in the clerical group (deficienc -2.08 units, 4.84 p.e.). The highest mean value occurs in the professional group (ex cess 2.60 units, 2.95 p.e.) but it is not certainly significant. On the other hand the per sonal service group exhibits a smaller but significant excess (2.00 units, 7.41 p.e.).

SUMMARY OF OCCUPATIONAL DIFFERENCES

Extractive. This group, consisting mostly of farmers, but including also stock breeders, miners, and fishermen, is notable because of its high percentage of illiterac and generally low educational attainment. It is the most ignorant of all occupationa groups and ranks highest in murder.

In hair color the extractive group is not differentiated from the criminal series a large. It is peculiar, however, in its excess of blue eyes, in proportions of which it out ranks all other occupational groups.

The extractive class exhibits significant differences (equal to or in excess of thre times the probable error) in 3 of 12 measurements and indices here considered, includ ing age. This group is older than the mean of the total series, and has a smaller mea head breadth and a narrower forehead. An excess in head circumference is possibly significant.

The amount of physical differentiation displayed by this occupational class is in excess of what would be expected were this class merely a random sample of the entire group. Although all body builds are represented in this class, it should be noted that the short types and the tall-heavy type are deficient, and that an excess of tall-medium weight men occurs. (Cf. Chap. IX, p. 167.)

Laborers. Laborers are also distinguished by their illiteracy and lack of good educations. They show no peculiarities of hair color, although tending to rank among the darker-haired occupational groups. In eye color they show a significant excess of the dark brown shade, a significant deficiency of blue eyes, and an excess of blue-gray eyes.

Laborers deviate significantly in 6 of 12 metric characters considered, including age. They are younger than the average, lighter in weight, shorter, narrower in head breadth, smaller in head circumference, more dolichocephalic than the mean. They show in addition an elevation of the mean nasal index which is possibly significant.

On the basis of the few characters studied, the laborer class is statistically distinct in anthropometric features from the total series. This class includes all body types, but the short-medium weight type is strongly in excess, whereas short-slender, tall-slender, and tall-heavy types are somewhat deficient. (Chap. IX, p. 167.)

Factory. Educationally the factory group is not outstanding. It ranks seventh in scholastic attainment. It ranks fourth in lightness of hair color, but includes no significant excess of any hair shade. In eye color it is equally undistinguished, ranking fifth in lightness.

Four of 12 metric and indicial features in the factory group show valid deviations from the total mean. The most notable of these is a deficiency in age. The other important differences are excesses of head breadth, forehead breadth, and cephalic index. Evidently there are more brachycephals in this group than in the series at large.

This group shows a larger number of significant deviations from total means than would be expected in a random sample. It is evidently differentiated, although not very markedly, from the total series of native born criminals of native parentage.

Tall-heavy and tall-slender types are disproportionately represented in this occupational category, whereas short-medium weight and tall-medium weight types are somewhat deficient. All types do occur. (Chap. IX, p. 167.)

Transportation. The transportation group ranks eighth in education among the eleven occupational classes. In hair color it is distinguished by its high percentage of red-brown shades and by a deficiency in dark brown. It ranks third in lightness of hair. In eye color this group is not significantly differentiated in any one shade, but as a whole ranks first in lightness of eyes.

In age the transportation group falls well below the total mean. It is not certainly differentiated in any measurement or index, although an excess of weight (1.90 lbs., .32 p.e.) may possibly be valid. In general the transportation group cannot be said to be anthropometrically distinct from the criminal series at large.

The body build type which is disproportionately represented in this group is short-heavy, but as in almost all other occupational categories, the medium height-medium weight type is in the majority. (Chap. IX, p. 167.)

Skilled Trades. The criminals who claim to belong to skilled trades are indifferently educated, ranking sixth as a group in this respect. In pigmentation of hair and eyes this class is undistinguished. Moreover, it does not differ significantly from the mean of the total criminal series in any metric character, and, so far as can be judged from the characters studied, it is indistinguishable from a random sample of all native born criminals of native parentage.

Trade. The trade group is better educated than the average, ranking fourth. In hair color and eye color it is not outstanding. Its significant metric divergences are an excess in mean age and in head breadth. It has a mean weight slightly above the average of the total series, but the deviation is equal to only 2.27 times the probable error and is of uncertain validity. An excess of head circumference is also dubious. In physical features this group shows more marked deviations from the mean of the series than would be expected to occur in a random sample.

Public Service. This is a very small group, consisting of only 27 individuals. Hence its deviations cannot be statistically significant unless they are very large. It is poorly educated, ranking ninth. In hair color it is the darkest of the occupational groups, being entirely devoid of blond and red hair. It, nevertheless, ranks as the median class (sixth) in lightness of eyes. It is older than the average of the series and heavier, but these deviations are not certainly significant. Deficiencies in head breadth, forehead breadth, and cephalic index, and excesses in facial and nasal index are of doubtful significance. It must be concluded that the public service group is not statistically differentiated in anthropometric characters, but the magnitude of its metrical divergence leaves one with the impression that a larger sample would show that this occupational type is physically distinct.

Semi-professional. The semi-professional group includes only 69 individuals. It is well educated, ranking third in scholastic attainment. It ranks high in light brown eyes and light brown hair, although its general position in the pigment scale of hair and eye is not extreme. The metric excesses of certain significance include the cephalic index with a mean of 80.34 which marks the group as the most brachycephalic of the series and also an elevation of the minimum frontal diameter. An excess approaching significance (1.26 mm., 2.86 p.e.) also occurs in head breadth. These deviations are associated with a height deficiency of 1.47 cm., which is only 2.77 times its probable error but stamps this group as the shortest of the occupational classes. With two of twelve metric and indicial features significantly differentiated and with two others approaching the margin of significant differentiation there can be little doubt of the anthropometric distinctiveness of this specialized occupational group.

Professional. This group, although it includes only 27 persons, is most clearly and emphatically divergent from the series' average in its characteristics. In education it outranks all other groups. In hair color it ranks second in scale of lightness, although in eye color it ranks tenth. But these pigment features are of uncertain validity, owing to the small number in the group and the large number of shades of hair color and eye color used in classification.

Metrically this group is significantly divergent in 4 of 12 features, including age. It is the oldest and heaviest group. It has great and significant excesses in minimum frontal diameter and bizygomatic diameter. It shows large, but statistically uncertain excesses in head length, head breadth, and nasal index. It is insignificantly below average height and somewhat rounder-headed than the average. There is no question of its anthropological distinctiveness.

In proportion to its numbers the short-heavy type is significantly in excess in this group, and to a lesser extent the tall-heavy and medium-heavy types.

Personal Service. The personal service group ranks fifth in educational attainments. The hair color is somewhat darker than in the series at large and there is a significant deficiency of blue eyes. This group shows significant deviations in 2 of 12 metric features considered. It is deficient in height and has a higher mean nasal index than that of the total series. It is underweight by an amount which barely misses statistical significance. It can scarcely be considered a random physical sample of the entire series since its deviations from the means of the entire series are more numerous and of greater magnitude than would be expected to occur in such a random sample. Short-medium weight and short-slender types are in excess in this group, while medium height-heavy and tall-heavy types are deficient.

Clerical. The clerical group is comparatively small, containing only 117 persons. The members of the group are very well educated, ranking second in this respect. This occupational class ranks first in lightness of hair color, although it is not distinguished by significant excesses of any particular shade. It contains a notable excess of persons with light brown eyes and is deficient in the lighter eyes. It thus stands in the peculiar position of having the highest rank in lightness of hair and the lowest in lightness of eyes. The mean age of this group is 1.40 years above that of the series at large, but this difference is only 2.00 times its probable error. The clerical group also falls markedly below the series mean in weight and in height. The deficiency in weight (3.50 pounds, 2.65 p.e.) is not certainly significant, but that in stature (-1.23 cm., 3.08 p.e.) is probably reliable. A significant excess (1.53 mm., 4.64 p.e.) occurs in head breadth, and a marked deficiency (-2.08 units, 4.84 p.e.) in the nasal index. The group is thus the most leptorrhine of all the occupational classes. The metric deviations are sufficiently numerous and of such magnitude as to establish the physical distinctiveness of the clerical group.

Short-slender types are disproportionately well represented in this group, and also, to a lesser extent, short-heavy types.

Conclusions

In general the relationship between education and occupation in this criminal group is very close. It is so close that the educational attainments of the individual criminals seem to substantiate, to a considerable degree, their claims to the various occupations with their differing academic requirements. One could predict the occupation of the criminal from his education much more accurately than he could predict his offense. Eight of the 11 occupational groups of criminals (extractive, laborer, factory, trade, semi-professional, professional, personal service, and clerical) are significantly differentiated from the total criminal series in the metric physical traits studied. Only two of the groups — transportation and skilled trades — seem to show little or no tendency toward physical distinctiveness. A third, public service, seems to owe its lack of differentiation to its numerical insufficiency. Of all the groups, the furthest removed from the series as a whole is the professional class, which in education, age, and almost all physical characteristics, is remote from the ruck of criminals.

The degree of occupational differentiation in physical characters is, however, moderate, and in no wise comparable with the differentiation which occurs between the offense groups, or between the prisoners classified according to the states in which they are convicted. It is extremely improbable that physical differences dependent upon occupation are sufficient in number and importance to complicate the question of differences in the offense groups. On the contrary it seems reasonable to suppose that the same factors which select physical types for specific occupations are operative in the determination of the nature of the offenses which are committed.

The fact that a moderate degree of physical differentiation by occupational types has been demonstrated is the strongest evidence for the validity of the occupational claims made by the criminals.

Pigmentation factors, here, as in all other sociological or geographical classifications of this analysis, seem of little or no importance. There are, however, indistinct implications of some racial or ethnic proclivities in the occupations of the criminals, which are perhaps more important in establishing the occupational types than are the mere constitutional factors of size and strength. Our data with regard to the ancestry and ethnic origins of these native born criminals of native parentage are not sufficiently precise to enable us to isolate these racial factors. It would appear that the long-headed races are unduly represented in the extractive, laborer, public service, and personal service classes, whereas the factory, trade, semi-professional, professional, and clerical classes include more round-heads. One can perhaps go a little further and suggest that tall, dolichocephalic, light-pigmented racial elements are at a maximum in the extractive class; that shorter, brunet, dolichocephalic strains are particularly noticeable in the laborer and personal service groups; that brunet, round-headed, and short stocks are most amply represented in the semi-professional group, and perhaps in the factory group, whereas the professional and clerical classes seem to include more blond brachycephals, or, at any rate, more blondism in association with brachycephaly, and stout types in the former group as contrasted with slender and shorter types in the latter.

Chapter IX

DIFFERENTIATION BY BODY BUILD TYPES

METHOD OF SORTING

THE relation of body build or constitutional type to delinquency is worthy of investigation. There are many indices employed for the expression of body build. Obviously the most important factors concerned are height and weight. In the present study the following process of sorting was adopted to distinguish several types. The entire series of native White criminals of native parentage was divided into three groups — short, medium, and tall. The division into these groups was not made upon any arbitrary basis, but was determined by the mean and standard deviation of stature in the entire series. The medium stature class was fixed to include all individuals within a range of 1 σ on either side of the mean, or as nearly 1 σ as the grouping intervals permitted. Thus the medium group included statures between 164 centimeters and 179 centimeters, the short group all statures up to and including 163 centimeters, and the tall group, all individuals 179 centimeters and more in height.

The next step was to subdivide the stature classes according to weight. For this purpose, the mean and standard deviation of weight were calculated for each of the stature groups — short, medium, and tall. Then in each group the medium class was delimited exactly in the same way as previously — by including in it all individuals within a range of 1 σ on either side of the mean. The slender and heavy classes were thus composed of individuals outside of a range of 1 σ on either side of the mean. The result of this process of twofold sorting was to establish nine classes with respect to height and weight: short-slender, short-medium weight, short-heavy, medium height-slender, medium height-medium weight, medium height-heavy, tall-slender, tall-medium weight, tall-heavy. Obviously these designations and the class subdivisions themselves are entirely relative to the height and weight of the total series and have not been established by any hypothetical and arbitrary "universal" criteria.

Since an ordinate drawn at ± 1 σ from the mean cuts off 16 per cent of the area of a normal curve, we should expect our middle stature class to include some 68 per cent of the entire series of criminals, if the distribution were normal. Actually the medium class as to height includes 3002 criminals or 76.78 per cent of the 3910 included in the sorting. The short class includes only 335 individuals, or 8.57 per cent, the tall class 573 individuals or 14.65 per cent.

It is important to note here that the exact division of the series into stature groups based upon the standard deviation, and weight groups based upon the standard deviation of weight in the stature subgroups, could not be carried out exactly on account of the grouping of weight and stature units in the seriations and in the punching of individual record cards. The class interval in stature was 3 centimeters and in weight ten pounds. In selecting as the middle group or medium group an area in the curve between ordinates drawn at 1 σ on either side of the mean, it was only possible to choose the class intervals which would most nearly satisfy these requirements. The actual effect of selecting the medium class within these approximations dictated by class intervals in the seriations was to enlarge unduly the medium category of stature at the expense of the extremes. Dr. Seltzer has calculated the overloading of the medium stature group, on account of this exigency, at about 350 individuals, largely at the expense of the short group. On the other hand, the arrangement of the weight class intervals, together with the skewing of the weight curve toward the heavy side, resulted in a piling up of an excess over normal distribution in the heavy group of almost 300 individuals, with the slender class about 100 individuals short, and the medium class about 200 individuals short.

Under these circumstances our stature weight groups are only crude approximations to the ideal divisions which might have been secured by cutting the distribution curves of ungrouped seriations accurately to 1 σ on either side of the mean, if both stature and weight distributions were approximately normal. From these considerations it follows that many of the clear regressions of stature and weight, taken singly, upon various sociological characters are inevitably fogged and obscured, not only by the taking of stature and weight in combination, but also by the necessarily inaccurate application of the principle of class division.

Of course the separate regressions of stature and weight upon offense and upon various other sociological characteristics have been dealt with in other sections of this work. In this section the important findings are those new associations which appear when stature and weight categories are taken in combination in individuals, whenever those associations are not predictable from the separate regressions of stature and weight upon sociological characters. Almost as important criminologically are the breakdowns of the separate associations to be expected from the regressions of stature and weight taken singly, when these are taken in combination, as in the present special study. However, the breakdown of expected regressions may in any case be attributable in part, or even wholly, to the inaccuracies of class partitioning, as discussed above.

The short-medium weight subclass includes 217 persons or 64.78 per cent of the shorts. The medium height-medium weight subclass includes 1925 persons, or 64.12 per cent of the medium height classes. The tall-medium weight subclass includes 56.72 of all the talls.

The short-slender subclass includes only 64 persons, or 19.10 per cent of all shorts, the short-heavy group 54 persons, or 16.12 per cent of all shorts. The medium height-slender subgroup includes 348 individuals, or 11.59 per cent of all medium heights, the medium height-heavy subgroup 729 individuals, or 24.28 per cent of all medium heights. The tall-slender subgroup consists of 114 individuals, 19.90 per cent of all talls; the tall-heavy group, 134 persons, 23.39 per cent.

Thus we have nine body build subgroups. It is our task firstly, to ascertain whether these subgroups bear any relation to type of offense, and if that proves to be the case, to continue to investigate their physical and sociological characteristics.

STATE DISTRIBUTION OF BODY BUILD GROUPS

Table IX–1 shows the state distribution of body build groups, while the excesses together with their values in terms of probable errors are found in Table IX–2. From these data it may be gathered that the short-slender group and the short-medium group are both in excess in Massachusetts, Wisconsin, and the Southwest, but significantly deficient in Texas, and probably deficient in Tennessee, Kentucky, and North Carolina. The short-heavy group is almost certainly in excess in Wisconsin and deficient in Tennessee. Statistical excesses of this group in Massachusetts, Texas, and North Carolina do not attain significance, nor do deficiencies in Kentucky and the Southwest. The medium height-slender group is deficient in Texas and North Carolina, and possibly in excess in Kentucky. Men of medium height and medium weight are in excess in the Massachusetts and Tennessee prisoners and deficient in Wisconsin and possibly in Texas. Medium height-heavy men are unduly few in Massachusetts and probably in excess in the Southwest. Tall-slender men show no statistically significant state deviations, but are apparently commoner in Tennessee and Texas than in the other states. Tall men of medium weight are deficient in Massachusetts and in marked excess in Texas. The same is true of tall-heavy men.

Tables IX–3 and IX–4 show the associations of the states' samples with stature and weight separately. Obviously, short statures occur particularly in Massachusetts, Wisconsin, and Southwestern prisoners, while tall men occur especially in Texas. Medium statures are found proportionately in most of the state samples. Slender men again are in excess in Wisconsin, Massachusetts, and Kentucky, whereas Texas has an excess of heavy weights.

At this point it seems essential to explain why, in this section, no predictions and corrections have been employed in order to eliminate from the conclusions upon body build types the complicating influences which may result from the state sampling process. In the examination of physical differentiation of criminals by offense groups, the purpose was to ascertain whether individuals convicted of a certain type of crime could be distinguished anthropologically, as a group, from the aggregate of all criminals. Under these circumstances it was desirable to establish broad criminological differentiations which would not be distorted by the over-representation of this or that state physical type in any offense group.

The orientation of the present discussion is different. Our assumption is that all nine of our body build types occur in each of the nine states (which is indeed the case) and we wish to discover the sociological differentiation of these types irrespective of their state of origin. Tall, thin men may be commoner in one state than in another, but we have no reason for assuming that it is residence in this or that state which makes them tall and thin. If each of our nine body build types was confined to one of the nine states represented in our series, we should still be justified in studying their social differentiation by body build types and in deducing that such social differentiation arose from body build type and not from state of residence. Only if the physical environment in each state were absolutely distinct from that of every other state, and if each state contained an exclusive physical type and that alone, and an invariable and exclusive cultural pattern appertaining to that type, could we reasonably attribute physical type and cultural pattern to state environment.

Admitting that a tall slender man is moᵣe likely to be illiterate if he lives in Tennessee than if he lives in Massachusetts, because there are more illiterates in the former state than in the latter, we are nevertheless, for present purposes only, proceeding upon the assumption that the organism creates its culture, rather than that the culture creates the organism. If short, fat men lead in rape, and if short, fat men are commonest in Texas, I see no reason whatsoever for worrying about the question as to whether it is residence in Texas which makes men short and fat and makes them prone to rape. For in any event short, fat men are rapists. Here we are concerned with the crude associations of body build, among other things with crime. It would be interesting, of course, to apply corrections for state sampling to this study of body build, in order to ascertain whether the various differentiae of social characteristics would survive this theoretical elimination of the effects of local blends and state social environment. This task must be left for other hands than mine.

Sociological Characteristics

OFFENSE

Tables IX–5 and IX–6 show the numbers and percentages of each body build in the offense groups and the positive, negative, or indifferent association of each body build with the various offenses. Let us first consider the short-slender type. The percentage of first degree murder in this type is not significantly different from that of first degree murderers in the total series. There is a slight, but insignificant excess of second degree murder and a similarly insignificant lack of assault. Robbers are slightly, but not significantly fewer. Persons committed for larceny and burglary are strongly in excess, but the excess is not statistically significant. All the other offense groups show small and probable insignificant deviations from the percentages of the specific offenses making up the total series. We may then conclude that the short-slender type may be distinguished by its high proportion of thieves and burglars, but the excess cannot be relied upon, on account of the small size of the group and the consequent magnitude of probable errors of percentages.

The short-medium weight type is definitely deficient in both classes of murderers but the deficiency is significant only in first degree murder. It also has an insignificant excess of persons committed for burglary and larceny (2.06 p.e.) but it is particularly notable for its high percentage of rapists.

The short-heavy type is notably deficient in murderers, falling far beₗow any other group in the sum of the proportions of the two murder groups. Nevertheless, on account of the small size of the series, the differences are of uncertain validity. It is high in assault, but not significantly so. It shows a slight excess of forgers, but its really great excess is in rape and other sex offenses, in both of which it far surpasses any other group, containing twice as many of these sex offenders in proportion to its numbers. Here again the differences, although great, equal only 2.41 p.e. and 2.18 p.e. respectively.

The medium height-slender group is slightly deficient in murderers, insignificantly high in thieves and burglars, and otherwise is not distinguished.

The great medium height-medium weight type is definitely low in first degree murder, somewhat high in robbers, thieves, and burglars, low in forgers and versus public welfare offenders, and high in arson and all other offenses. Most of its deviations are statistically significant, not because of their magnitude, but because of the small probable errors.

When we reach the medium height-heavy type, we find it beginning to show unreliable excesses in both murder groups, a marked deficiency in burglary and larceny, slight excesses in forgery and in other sex offenses, and a very great excess of persons convicted for offenses against public welfare (mostly bootleggers), in which it exceeds all other body types.

The most outstanding group in its differentiation, is, however, the tall-slender group. It stands at the top of the list in second degree murder and second in first degree murder, although neither of these excesses is statistically significant. It has no assault criminals whatsoever. It shows the highest percentage of robbers, by far, and the smallest of thieves and burglars. It is high in forgery and includes almost no sex offenders. It is high in offenses versus public welfare.

The tall-medium weight type is slightly high in first degree murder and slightly low in burglary and larceny. It exceeds all other classes in forgery and is low in sex offenses.

The tall-heavy class is highest in first degree murder (3.38 p.e.), high in assault, low in robbery, very low in burglary and larceny, high in forgery, low in rape, but high in other sex offenses, and shows an excess also in versus public welfare. Most of the excesses are not, however, equal to twice their probable errors.

Many of the peculiarities of the body types with reference to offense might seem trivial and fortuitous were it not for the clear regression which is exhibited when one considers the groups in order, beginning with the three short groups. These regressions supervene the statistical insignificance of the majority of the differences.

In first degree murder it is apparent that the three short groups are in general lowest, the three medium groups are intermediate, and the three tall groups are highest. The same general regression is seen in second degree murder, although it is not so clear. Within each of the short, medium, and tall divisions, there is a regression in the subgroups, depending apparently upon weight. Thus in the short groups, both types of murder are most frequent in the short-slender subgroup and much less frequent in the medium and heavy subgroups.

In the medium height groups murder of both types seems to increase, in general, from the slender to the heavy weights.

If we reverse the classification and consider weight first, we find that in the slender groups murders are least frequent in the medium heights and most frequent in the talls. In the medium weight groups, murder of both kinds increases regularly from shorts to talls. In the heavy weights, first degree murder similarly increases from shorts to talls. The correlation ratios of stature with offense and of weight with offense in the total series, are, respectively, .11 ± .01, and .16 ± .01. Neither of these is especially high. When combined in body build they yield a contingency coefficient of .17, which again is not high, but is nevertheless significant.

The assault criminals are so few in the aggregate that it is difficult to draw any conclusions from their build distribution. It may be merely a coincidence that no assault criminals occur in the short-slender and tall-slender groups, whereas the short-heavy group, which is numerically the smallest of all groups, contains two such persons convicted of assault, and thus yields the highest percentage of all groups in this offense (3.70 per cent).

Robbery is an offense certainly less common among the short groups than among those of medium stature or tall. Among the slender groups it increases abruptly with stature, from the minimum percentage, 6.25, in the short-slender group, to 9.20 in the medium height-slender group, and 15.79, the maximum, in the tall-slender group. In both the medium weight and the heavy weight groups it is at a minimum among the shorts, and reaches its maximum among those of medium height.

Burglary and larceny are evidently positively associated with shortness and slender or medium weight, taken in combination. They are negatively associated with tallness and heavy weight. In the short classes these offenses are at the series maximum in the short-slender group and decline through the medium weight and heavy weight classes. The same regression manifests itself in the medium height groups — i.e. the offense proportion decreases with weight. In the tall groups, however, the minimum proportion of burglars and thieves occurs in the slender subgroup and the maximum in the medium weight subgroup. Considering this type of offense by weight groups, we find a regular decrease in the slender groups with increasing stature, the same phenomenon in the medium weight groups, and in the heavy groups the maximum in the short class and much smaller but approximately equal proportions in the medium stature and tall groups.

Forgery increases with weight in the short groups, and is at a maximum in subgroups of great stature.

Rape shows a very strong association with the build groups. In general it is more frequent in the short groups than in the medium or tall groups, and increases with weight in the height groups. Specifically in the short groups it increases with weight and reaches its series maximum among the short-heavy group. Similarly, but in less marked fashion, in the medium height group it rises from its minimum in slender to its maximum in heavy. In the tall groups its minimum is again in the slender class, but the maximum is in the medium weight class. Other sex offenses behave in much the same way as rape — being commonest in each stature class in the heavy groups and declining in frequency from shorts to talls.

Versus public welfare offenses show a gradual increase in successively higher stature groups, and seem to show also some increase with additions of weight.

In general there is from the standpoint of criminology, a surprising and peculiar relationship between offense and body build, which seems at times to depend principally upon stature, and again to be correlated rather with weight. Table IX–7 associates stature with offense; Table IX–8, weight with offense. Murder, robbery, forgery and fraud, and versus public welfare offenses increase with statural increments; assault, burglary and larceny, sex offenses, and arson and all others decrease. Murder, forgery and fraud, and versus public welfare offenses increase with weight, as do probably sex offenses. Robbery and burglary and larceny diminish with increasing weight. The extremes of contrast may be emphasized by a comparison of the two opposite build groups — short-heavy and tall-slender. (Table IX–9.)

First degree murder is more than three times as common in the tall-slender type as in the short-heavy type, and second degree murder more than twice as common. The total percentage of murderers in the short-heavy type is 12.96, whereas 30.70 per cent of the tall-slender type have been convicted of homicide. Again the percentage of assault criminals in the short-heavy type (3.70) is the maximum for the entire criminal series, whereas there are none at all in the tall-slender type. Robbery is more than twice as common in the latter type as in the former. On the other hand, thieves and burglars are in excess among the short-heavy men to the extent of 9.94 per cent. There is little difference between the two types in forgery, but in rape the short-heavy men top the series, while the tall-slender men are at the bottom. Similarly, in other sex offenses the short-heavy men rank first, whereas none of the tall-slender type have been incarcerated for such crimes. Total sex offenses are more than nine times as common among the short-heavy men as among the tall-slender. The latter type is also higher in offenses versus public welfare.

If we compare the other two extreme types — short-slender and tall-heavy (Table IX–10), the contrasts in distribution of offenses are far less marked. The tall-heavy type is higher in first degree murder, but lower in second degree murder. The outstanding difference between the two groups lies in the great excess of burglary and larceny in the short-slender group, amounting to 14.04 per cent. In the tall-heavy group forgery and offenses versus public welfare are considerably more common.

Somewhat stronger contrasts exist between the short-medium weight and the tall-heavy types (Table IX–11). These include excesses of murder, forgery and fraud, and versus public welfare in the tall-heavy type, and of sex offenses in the short-medium weight type.

The differences between the short-slender and the tall-slender type (Table IX–12) are again great, and very similar to those existing between the short-heavy and tall-slender types. The former is much lower in murder, robbery, forgery and fraud, and versus public welfare offenses, and a great deal higher in burglary and larceny and in all sorts of sex offenses.

The short-heavy and tall-heavy types (Table IX–13) are much closer together in offense distribution, but the former has less than half as much murder and more than twice as many sex offenses.

If the medium height classes be compared with the talls or the shorts less marked differences appear. Table IX–14 shows the comparison of medium height-medium weight with tall-medium weight. The differences are small. Without laboring through comparisons of every body type with every other it is clear that the differences in offense which are associated with body build are numerous and important, and particularly so when the body-builds of extremely contrasting types are considered.

PREVIOUS CONVICTIONS

The maximum percentage of previous convictions (48.33) occurs in the short-slender group, and the minimum (29.06) in the tall-heavy group. Thus these extremes of build differentiation manifest the greatest difference in proportion of recidivism. However, the most striking feature of Table IX–15 is the regular decrease of recidivism in each stature class from the slender to the heavy types. In other words, slender men have had the most previous convictions, men of medium weight are intermediate, and heavy men include the smallest proportion of recidivists. Slightly less marked is the decrease of recidivism with increasing stature classes. This regression is manifested in each group except the heavy group, which shows maximum recidivism in the medium height class, and minimum recidivism in the tall class. The conclusion that recidivism is related to body build is unescapable.

MARITAL STATE

Marital state is closely related to age and its association with body build is complicated by this circumstance. The highest percentage of single men (58.91) is found in the medium height-slender group, and the lowest (30.60) in the tall-heavy group. The former group has a mean age of 30.05 years and the latter 33.55 years. The difference of three and one-half years is probably insufficient to account for the discrepancy in the marital proportions.

Actually it may be seen that in each stature class the percentage of single men declines from slender to heavy. This is probably related to the increase of weight with age and the increase of the proportion married, with age. There seems to be very little relationship between stature and marriage except that, in general, the proportion of single men declines from the shorter to the taller groups.

TABLE IX–17

AGE AND MARITAL STATE IN BODY BUILD TYPES

	Single	Married	Mean Age
	Per Cent	Per Cent	
Tall-heavy	30.60	55.97	33.55
Medium height-heavy	38.14	54.23	33.70
Short-heavy	47.17	35.85	36.70
Tall-medium weight	48.60	47.04	29.90
Medium height-medium weight	51.08	43.10	29.25
Short-medium weight	51.39	42.59	29.90
Tall-slender	51.79	46.43	29.15
Short-slender	57.14	38.10	31.50
Medium height-slender	58.91	35.06	30.05

Table IX–17 arranges the body build groups in ascending order of proportions of single individuals, and also gives the percentage married in each group and the mean age of the group.

It shows very clearly that the percentage of single men increases regularly from the heavy through the medium to the slender groups. In each group also the tall men are least frequently single, and in two of the three cases the short men include the highest proportion of bachelors. The mean ages of the groups do not afford much support for the supposition that marital status and weight are greatly dependent upon the age factor. The heavy groups are those which contain the lowest proportions of single men, and they are above the mean age of the series, but there is no marked regression upon age in the other classes. The oldest group does not contain the smallest proportion of single men, nor the youngest, the highest.

In Table IX–16 the column indicating percentages of divorced men in the several build groups shows an identical regression upon weight. In each class the percentage of divorced men rises from the slender through the medium weight to the heavy. There seems to be no direct relationship to stature. Widowers also increase in proportions from the slender minimum to the heavy maximum.

The general result of the foregoing tabulations of marital status and body build is to reveal a very striking tendency for proportions of married men to increase from the slender to the heavy builds and a less marked but definite indication that the percentage of married criminals increases from shorts to talls.

OCCUPATION

In discussing the relation of body build to occupation we may first consider the various occupations in their regression upon body types and then the distribution of body types among the several occupational categories. The data for this discussion are presented in Tables IX–18 and IX–19.

The extractive occupations are most poorly represented in the short-slender type and most abundantly in the tall-medium weight type, both differences being statistically valid. The most marked regression is upon height, since the proportion of extractive persons increases steadily from the short to the tall classes.

In the laborer class the only fact of interest is the great excess in the short-medium weight type (4.24 p.e.). In the factory category pronounced but statistically insignificant excesses are found in the tall-heavy, and tall-slender body types. Transportation shows a large excess in the short-heavy type which is statistically insignificant. Skilled trades are rather evenly distributed among the build groups. Trade shows a dubious excess in the short-slender group, but is otherwise undifferentiated. Public service shows a significant excess in the tall-heavy group. Semi-professional occupations are disproportionately represented in the short-slender class. The professional occupations are clearly related to weight in that they are not usually represented in the slender classes and increase in frequency from medium weights to heavy weights. Personal service is clearly more common among the short types, but seems not to be connected with weight. Clerical occupations are greatly in excess in the short-slender type.

Turning to a consideration of the distribution of occupations in each body type, we find that the short-slender type is notable for its high proportions of trade, semi-professional, and clerical occupations. It is markedly deficient in extractive and laborer representatives.

The short-medium weight type is overloaded with laborers, and has a small excess of personal service. In most other occupational categories it shows slight proportional deficiencies.

The short-heavy type is outstanding by reason of greater or smaller excesses in the transportation, professional, personal service, and clerical occupations. It is low in other occupational representation.

The medium-height slender type is distributed about in the proportions of the entire series.

The medium height-medium weight class is occupationally undifferentiated.

The medium height-heavy type is somewhat high in extractive occupations, in trade, and in semi-professional pursuits, but is not significantly differentiated, except by its deficiency in personal service.

The tall-slender body build is high in extractive, factory, and transportation pursuits. It also shows an excess in trade. However none of its deviations are statistically reliable. The tall-medium weight build is especially notable for its great excess in extractive occupations.

The tall-heavy type shows a notable excess in factory occupations, and a perceptible superiority in transportation and public service, but is low in extractive, laborer, and personal service categories.

In general it is noticeable that the greatest occupational differentiation occurs in the extreme types of body build, especially the short-slender, short-heavy, and tall-slender types. Undoubtedly to some extent the physical build of these criminals has influenced their choice of occupation. This is particularly marked in the dearth of short-slender men in occupations involving hard manual labor.

The total significant differentiation amounts to 8 of 99 categories or 8.08 per cent, which is roughly twice the amount which might be expected as a result of chance. However, on the whole, it cannot be said that this series shows a very close relationship of body build to occupation. The coefficient of mean square contingency is only .17.

EDUCATION

The tabulation (Table IX–20) of body build in relation to educational status reveals no clear association.

Illiterates are at a minimum in the short-slender type and reach a maximum in the tall-slender body build. There seems to be no regression of illiteracy upon either height or weight.

TABLE IX–21

RATIO OF COMBINED 3RD AND 4TH HIGH SCHOOL, COLLEGE, AND PROFESSIONAL SCHOOL ATTENDANTS TO COMBINED ILLITERATES AND READ AND WRITE, BY BODY BUILD TYPES

	A Illiterate, Read and Write	B 3rd–4th High, College, Professional School	Ratio of B to A
Short-slender	7.81	12.50	1.60
Tall-heavy	14.18	14.93	1.05
Medium height-slender	9.82	9.25	0.94
Tall-slender	14.91	13.16	0.88
Short-heavy	11.11	9.25	0.83
Medium height-heavy	15.33	8.16	0.53
Tall-medium weight	14.51	6.48	0.45
Medium height-medium weight	15.23	6.48	0.43
Short-medium weight	16.28	4.66	0.29

Table IX–21 gives the percentage for each build type of (A) illiterates and those who can read and write but have had no formal education, and (B) those who reached the third year of high school or more advanced educational stages. It also gives the ratios of the well-educated class (B) to the very poorly educated (A) for each body type. Taking these ratios as a measure of educational rank, it may be observed that the short-slender class is the best educated and the short-medium weight class the most deficient in this respect. There is no regression upon the stature of the body-build types and very little upon the weight. Nevertheless, the coefficient of mean square con tingency, .20, is higher than those with offense and occupation, a fact which illustrates the extreme caution which must be observed in interpreting this coefficient. Casual and irrelevant irregularities may elevate it to an apparently significant figure, while again small but significant differences which have a real regressional value may yield a low and apparently unimportant coefficient.

PHYSICAL CHARACTERISTICS

AGE

The regression of age upon body build should be interesting. *A priori* one should expect that age would increase from the slender groups through the medium groups to the heavy groups, since weight increases to some extent with age. To a lesser extent one should expect age to decrease from the short groups to the tall groups, not only because there is a slight loss of stature after middle age (which is probably largely offset by lack of full growth in the younger groups), but principally because there is overwhelming evidence that stature in the United States is increasing in the younger generations.

The data presented in Table IX–22 enable us to test these expectations. The tall-slender group is lowest in mean age (29.15 years) and the short-heavy group is oldest (36.70 years). The three heavy groups are all above the mean age of the series, but the short-slender group is comparatively old (31.50 years) and the tall-medium weight is comparatively young (29.90 years) — the latter having the same mean age as the short-medium weight group. It is apparent, therefore, that whereas age has some relation to body build, the correlation is by no means complete, and there are other factors involved which are quite independent of age.

WEIGHT AND HEIGHT

Weight and height may be discussed together profitably because the build sortings were made upon the basis of these combined criteria. Tables IX–23 and IX–24 present the data for this discussion. In each height group, mean statures tend to increase slightly, but fairly regularly, as one progresses from the slender to the heavy types. The increase of weight in the weight groups as one passes from short to tall types is much more marked. The latter is to be expected, and possibly the former also.

It remains only to point out the sharp distinctions in body type which are effected by making these stature and weight sortings. The short-slender group averages 158.01 centimeters in stature (62.21 inches) and 111.40 pounds in weight. The short-medium weight group is slightly taller (159.99 centimeters or 62.99 inches) and averages 133.40 pounds. The short-heavy type is 159.96 centimeters (62.98 inches) and averages 162.90 pounds. The medium height-slender type averages 169.29 centimeters (66.65 inches) and 122.70 pounds. The medium height-medium weight type has a mean stature of 171.36 centimeters (67.46 inches) and an average weight of 145.50 pounds. The medium height-heavy group has means of 172.95 centimeters (68.09 inches) and 174 pounds respectively. The tall-slender type is 181.38 centimeters (71.41 inches) tall, and 141.70 pounds in weight. The tall-medium weight type is 181.92 centimeters (71.62 inches) and averages 163.90 pounds in weight. Finally the tall-heavy class is no less than 182.70 centimeters (71.93 inches) in height and on the average 196.90 pounds in weight.

It is obvious then that our body build types are very strongly differentiated, each from every other, and they range from very small men indeed to near-giants. A glance at the standard deviations and coefficients of variability of weight and height shows that all groups fall considerably below the values for the total series in these constants — as indeed they should from the method by which they were sorted out. In every subgroup the standard deviations of weight rise consistently from the slender to the heavy types, thus indicating a greater variability on the part of the latter. This regression is not observed in the case of stature.

The larger numbers in the tall groups as compared with the short groups indicate that the whole distribution is skewed toward heights above the mean. A part of this skewness is attributable, however, to inaccuracy of application of the class division method rendered necessary by the exigencies of grouping.

OTHER PHYSICAL CHARACTERISTICS

Cephalic Index. The build types are not strongly differentiated in the means of the cephalic (length-breadth) index. However Table IX–25 shows very clearly that the short groups have the highest mean indices, that the groups of medium stature have intermediate indices, and that the tall groups are most nearly dolichocephalic. Within the stature groups there seems to be no regression upon weight — heavy men, medium and slender men all having substantially the same mean cephalic indices.

Facial Index. Table IX–26 gives the means of the facial index for the body build types. None of these differs very markedly from the mean of the total series, but certain regressions are apparent, even when the differences between the means may not be statistically significant. The most marked relationship is with weight. In every stature group, the heavy subgroup has the lowest mean facial index — i.e. the face is shorter relative to its breadth. This is probably because heavy men usually have fat faces. The short men present slightly lower means of this index than the men of medium stature, and the tall groups, taken together, have slightly higher means than the groups of medium height. The difference is not so marked as in the case of the cephalic index, but the two indices agree in showing the tendency for taller men to have relatively narrower heads and faces than the shorter types. In the case of the facial index there is present a relation to weight which is much more clear and important than the relation to stature, whereas in the cephalic index the reverse is true.

Nasal Index. The body build types are more strongly differentiated in nasal index than in the cephalic or facial indices. In each stature group the index increases regularly from the slender to the heavy types, but the array of means indicates also that there is a general decrease in the value of the nasal index as stature increases. However, the lowest mean is found in the medium height-slender group, although it probably does not differ significantly from the slightly higher means of the short-slender and tall-slender types. The regressions upon stature are mostly clearly seen in the heavy and medium weight types: short-heavy 69.42; medium height-heavy 68.22; tall-heavy 67.58. The corresponding values in the medium weight types are: short-medium weight 67.50; medium height-medium weight 66.58; tall-medium weight 65.74.

Hair Color. Tables IX–28 and IX–29 give the distribution of hair colors among the body types. It is extremely irregular and shows no regression either upon height or upon weight. The build types are quite inconsistent within themselves in the proportions of various hair shades which they contain. For example, the short-slender type has no black-haired individuals at all, but is also very low in the lighter shades of hair. Some of these irregularities are caused, no doubt, by the very small size of several of the extreme groups.

In order to clarify the situation and to give some rough idea of the grading of these body types in hair color, Table IX–30 has been prepared, in which the percentages of black and dark brown have been lumped together under "dark," red-brown and light brown under "medium," and ash-blond, golden, and red under "light." In each body type gray and white hair have been excluded and percentages of the other shades recalculated. However, the use of the percentages in Table IX–28 would not affect the rankings. The latter have been made in the manner heretofore described — i.e., by assigning the rank 1 to the lowest percentage of dark hair, rank 1 to the highest percentage of medium hair, rank 1 to the highest percentage of light hair, and then determining the final rank from the sum of the rankings of the three combined categories.

TABLE IX–30

SUMMARY OF HAIR COLOR IN BODY BUILD TYPES

	Dark (black and dark brown)	Medium (red brown and light brown)	Light (ash-blond, golden, and red)	Rank in Lightness
	Per Cent	Per Cent	Per Cent	
Medium height-slender	38.37	49.24	12.39	1
Tall-medium weight	39.31	50.31	10.38	2
Short-slender	37.50	55.36	7.14	3
Medium height-medium weight	40.76	49.81	9.43	4
Short-medium weight	43.00	45.89	11.11	5
Medium height-heavy	44.04	45.87	10.09	6
Tall-slender	49.55	38.74	11.71	7
Tall-heavy	44.72	47.97	7.32	8
Short-heavy	51.02	40.82	8.16	9
Total	41.60	48.46	9.94	

In this manner a rough gradation has been obtained. The lightest hair is found in the medium height-slender class, and the darkest in the short-heavy class. It is quite evident, however, that there is little or no correlation of hair color with these body types. A few characteristics are perhaps worthy of mention. The short-slender type is highest in medium shades of hair, lowest in dark hair, and has very few light-haired individuals. The tall-slender type is very high in both dark hair and light hair and low in the medium shades. None of the heavy types is high in blondism, and two of them are high in proportions of dark hair. Medium and slender builds seem on the whole to go with the lighter shades of hair. It should be emphasized, however, that the results of the attempt to relate hair color to body type are largely negative.

Eye Color. As in hair color, so in eye color there is little relationship to body build type. The data presented in Table IX–31 and IX–32 show how small are the differences between the types. In Table IX–33 the observations are condensed and summarized and a rough ranking in scale of lightness has been assigned to each group. This is far from agreeing with the similar ranking on the basis of hair color. Indeed, the short-heavy type ranks first in lightness of eyes and last in lightness of hair. When the body type groups are arranged in order of lightness a distinct difference is discernible be-

TABLE IX–33

SUMMARY OF EYE COLOR IN BODY BUILD TYPES

	Dark (dark brown, light brown)	Medium (blue-brown, gray-brown, green-brown)	Light (blue, blue-gray)	Rank in Lightness
	Per Cent	Per Cent	Per Cent	
Short-heavy	3.70	68.52	27.78	I
Medium-heavy	4.00	67.31	28.69	I
Tall-slender	4.55	66.36	29.09	3
Tall-medium	5.23	65.23	29.53	4
Medium-slender	6.59	63.61	29.80	5
Medium-medium	6.46	65.13	28.42	6
Short-slender	9.38	65.63	25.00	7
Tall-heavy	9.70	65.67	24.63	8
Short-medium	10.14	65.44	24.43	9
Total	6.18	65.52	28.30	

tween the lightest and the darkest, but a redistribution of about 7 per cent of eye shades would equalize even the extremes.

Hair Color and Eye Color. In the total series there are 5.06 per cent of black hair and 6.18 per cent of dark eyes (dark brown and light brown). There are 9.43 per cent of light hair and 28.30 per cent of light eyes. Undoubtedly the majority of persons with dark brown hair, who constitute 34.39 per cent of the entire series, have mixed eyes, and many of those with light brown hair (25.66 per cent of the series) have blue or blue-gray eyes. Also a fair proportion of the dark-haired population must possess the combination of dark hair and light eyes, common in the so-called Keltic type. On the whole then, the pigment data are of virtually no value in connection with the body types here distinguished.

SUMMARY OF BODY BUILD TYPES

SHORT-SLENDER

Physical Characteristics. The short-slender type consists of 64 persons. It has a mean stature of 158.01 centimeters and a mean weight of 111.40 pounds. The cephalic index averages 79.35, which is the highest of any body build group. The range of individual cephalic indices is from 74 to 91. This body build type includes a higher percentage of brachycephals than any other group, although the other short groups are virtually equal to it in mean cephalic index. All sorts of faces — from short and broad to relatively long and narrow — are included in this type, but the average facial index (87.86) is moderate. The nasal index, which averages 65.02, indicates a prevalent leptorrhiny — slightly more pronounced than in most other body build types. Hair color is more predominantly of the medium shades than in any other group. Black hair is entirely absent and light hair is also at the series minimum. Dark eyes are, however, much more frequent than in the total series, and light eyes less frequent. On the basis of the few physical criteria investigated we cannot be sure that this body build group is an unified, distinct type, except in stature and weight.

Sociological Characteristics. The short-slender type is notable in its offense composition because it is first in burglary and larceny, but last in robbery, forgery, and in arson and all other offenses. It is second in second degree murder, but very low in rape and in offenses versus public welfare. It ranks first in percentage of those recorded as having had previous convictions. This group contains the second highest percentage of single men, although it has a higher mean age than four of the other build groups. In occupations it is interesting because of its first ranking in clerical, semi-professional, and trade categories. It is also high in personal service, but contains the fewest laborers and members of extractive occupations found in any build group. The short-slender group is, on the whole, the best educated group, since it contains the lowest percentage of illiterates and persons who can barely read and write, and is very high in its proportion of those who have reached the last two years of high school or have attended college.

Altogether this short-slender group is the smallest, lightest in weight, most round-headed, most often convicted, most addicted to burglary and larceny, and least to forgery and robbery. It is among the least married, is the best educated, and the most frequently engaged in clerical and other sedentary occupations.

SHORT-MEDIUM

Physical Characteristics. The short-medium weight group consists of 217 men with a mean age of 29.90 years, an average stature of 159.99 centimeters, and an average weight of 133.40 pounds. It has a high mesocephalic index (mean 79.08), a mesoprosopic facial index (mean 87.38), and a leptorrhine nasal index (mean 67.50), which is, however, substantially higher than that of the short-slender type. This group includes more dark-haired individuals than the short-slender group and also more with blond and red hair. Being somewhat younger than the latter type it includes fewer men with gray and white hair. The short-medium type is exactly in the middle of the group of body build types in regard to lightness of hair. In eye color, however, it is at the bottom of the group, having the largest percentage of dark eyes and the smallest percentage of light eyes. It is, however, by no means homogeneous in eye pigmentation, nor yet in that of hair.

Sociological Characteristics. The short-medium weight type shares with the short-heavy type the honor of ranking lowest in murder. It is also lowest in offenses versus public welfare, and below the median in robbery, forgery, and other sex offenses. It ranks first in arson and all other offenses, but this, of course, is a small and miscellaneous offense group. In previous convictions this group occupies second rank, pressing closely upon the short-slender type. In percentage of unmarried men it comes fourth. In occupation this class ranks far above all others in proportion of laborers, and also leads the list in personal service. It is low in most other occupations, and has the smallest percentage of factory workers found in any group. The short-medium group is the most poorly educated of all the body build types, having the smallest ratio of well-educated men to illiterates and those who can read and write only.

We may then summarize this group by describing it as a type of short stature and medium build, rather young in mean age, with all shades of hair and more dark eyes than any other build type, mesocephalic, mesoprosopic and leptorrhine. It ranks first only in arson and all other offenses and is creditably next to the last in homicide. It contains more laborers and personal servants than any other group and is the most ignorant.

SHORT-HEAVY

Physical Characteristics. The short-heavy group is the smallest since it includes only 54 individuals. It is also the oldest, having a mean age of 36.70 years. The members of this type may be described as short fat men, because their average stature is only 159.96 centimeters, but their mean weight is 162.90 pounds. The weights run up as high as 230 pounds in individual cases. The short-heavy men have the second highest percentage of brachycephals with relatively the shortest and broadest faces of all the body build types. They also have the relatively broadest noses, but are, nevertheless, leptorrhine (69.42). These oldish men have the darkest pigmented hair of the body build types, combining a low proportion of light hair with a low proportion of medium shades and a high percentage of dark brown and black hair. In contradistinction, they have a high proportion of light eyes and the lowest proportion of dark eyes — the combination (including the highest percentage of mixed eyes) giving them first rank in lightness of eyes. It is evident, therefore, that they are far from homogeneous in pigmentation and probably include many with light eyes and dark hair.

Sociological Characteristics. The short-heavy type is one of the most clearly cut in its sociological characteristics. In offenses it ranks first in rape, first in other sex offenses, and first in assault. But it is last in murder, and next to the bottom in robbery. It is eighth in percentage of previous convictions. It shows, in spite of its age, a rather high percentage of unmarried men, but ranks first in divorcés and widowers. This type includes the highest percentage of professional men and of those engaged in transportation, and is also high in clerical workers. It is in the middle of the groups as regards educational attainments.

We may then picture a small group of short, fat men, with roundish heads and faces and relatively broad noses who are rather light in pigmentation of eyes, but dark as to hair (although, of course, all combinations occur). These middle-aged corpulent criminals seem to be decidedly lecherous, being preeminent in sex offenses. But they rarely commit homicide.

MEDIUM HEIGHT-SLENDER

Physical Characteristics. The medium height-slender group of 348 men averages 30.05 years in age, 169.29 centimeters in stature, and 122.70 pounds in weight. Its average cephalic index is 78.27, and its mean facial index 88.90. It is the most leptoprosopic type of those here delimited. Similarly the nasal index (mean 64.70) is the lowest or most leptorrhine. Although having the relatively narrowest faces and noses the heads of this type are on the average mesocephalic. The medium-height slender type has also the highest proportion of light hair, and ranks first in lightness of hair pigment. Nevertheless it includes persons of all hair shades. In eye color this type occupies the middle of the series.

Sociological Characteristics. The medium height-slender group is not outstanding in differentiation of offenses. It occupies third place in robbery, burglary and larceny, and is low in most other offenses. It is third in proportion of previous convictions. It has the highest proportion of unmarried men. Occupationally it is also undistinguished, except in having the highest percentage of skilled trades and ranking second in laborers. It is third in educational ranking.

Altogether, this type, although the most blond in hair color, with the narrowest noses and the narrowest faces, has little sociological distinction.

MEDIUM HEIGHT-MEDIUM WEIGHT

Physical Characteristics. This type, medium in respect to stature and body build, is by far the largest of the series, since it includes 1925 persons. Its mean age (29.25 years) is slightly below that of the total series, making it second youngest of the body build types. The means for stature and weight are 171.36 centimeters, and 145.50 pounds respectively. In both of these measurements the type falls somewhat below the mean of the total series. In cephalic index it is almost exactly at the series mean, averaging 78.60. It occupies a similar position in nasal index and in facial index, being mesoprosopic and moderately leptorrhine. In pigmentation of hair and eyes it is equally undistinguished. In fact, physically this type might represent a random sample of the entire series. It is the average native born American criminal of native parentage. This statement does not imply, however, that the type is homogeneous. In spite of its great size, its coefficients of variability for the different measurements and indices are not specially low, but occupy, like the type itself, a medium position.

Sociological Characteristics. In offenses the medium height-medium weight type is undistinguished. It is second in robbery and second in arson and all other offenses. Both of these are small offense categories. It is fourth in rank in previous convictions. It is in the middle of the series as regards marital status. Occupationally it is rather an inferior type, being high in laborers and factory workers, and low in the professional, semi-professional, and clerical classes. In conformity with its submedium occupational status, it is next to the bottom in educational rating, having the second largest percentage of illiterates and near-illiterates, and the next to the last position in percentage of well-educated persons.

MEDIUM HEIGHT-HEAVY

Physical Characteristics. The medium height-heavy type consists of 729 men, with mean age of 33.70 years, a mean stature of 172.95 centimeters, and a mean weight of 174 pounds. Its cephalic index (78.75) is higher than that of any of the other groups of medium stature, as is also its mean nasal index (68.22). The facial index is lower, implying the presence of a large proportion of men with relatively short and broad faces. It ranks sixth in lightness of hair, being somewhat deficient in the medium shades. In contradiction to its hair pigmentation eye color is somewhat lighter than the mean. In fact this group is second in lightness of eyes.

Sociological Characteristics. The medium height-heavy type ranks first in offenses versus public welfare, and contains, presumably, the highest percentage of bootleggers. It ranks second in combined sex offenses, and is well up in murder. It is, however, next to the bottom in burglary and larceny and apparently quite low in assault. It has the unenviable position of standing first in mean rating in all crimes. Nevertheless, it is in seventh place in proportions of previous convictions. It is eighth in proportions of unmarried men. This class is not individual in occupational distribution, although it is rather high in the extractive category, and in semi-professional pursuits. It has a high percentage of college men, but ranks only sixth in education.

TALL-SLENDER

Physical Characteristics. The tall-slender group consists of only 114 men, and is the youngest of the build types (mean age 29.15 years). The average stature is 181.38 centimeters (71.41 inches). The mean weight is only 141.70 pounds. The mean cephalic index (78.00) indicates a large proportion of dolichocephals. The facial index (87.74) is nearly at the mean of the total series. The nasal index, however, is low (65.46). In hair pigmentation this type is very inconsistent since it has the second highest proportion of black and dark brown hair, and the second highest proportion of light hair. Its variability is further marked by the fact that it ranks third in lightness of eye color.

Sociological Characteristics. The tall-slender group is as well defined in offense as in body build. It is second in first degree murder and first in second degree murder and ranks first in combined classes of murder. It ranks first in robbery, last in burglary and larceny, and in both categories of sex offenses. It is second in versus public welfare third in forgery, but eighth in assault. In previous convictions it is the median group. It is third in percentage of unmarried men and includes the smallest proportion of divorced men and widowers. In occupations this group is notably high in the extractive category and in factory operatives, in both of which it ranks second. It is slightly high in transportation and in trade, and low in most other classifications. Educationally it is much mixed having the highest proportion of illiterates of any build group, and at the same time ranking second in proportion of well-educated men.

Evidently these very tall and thin men include a considerable element of the ignorant agricultural feudists of the Tennessee and Kentucky mountains. The urban representation is probably responsible for most of the robbery, forgery, larceny, et cetera. The rather high proportion of versus public welfare may reflect the moonshining avocations of the Southern mountaineers.

TALL-MEDIUM WEIGHT

Physical Characteristics. This group of 325 men is also rather young (average 29.90 years). It has a mean stature of 181.92 centimeters and a mean weight of 163.90 pounds. The mean cephalic index (78.15) is not especially distinctive, although below the average of the total series. The facial index (88.54) is second highest in the entire group, and the nasal index (65.74) is below the mean of the total series (66.70). This group ranks second in lightness of hair, principally because of its preeminence in red-headed men and its high proportion of blonds. It has a large percentage of blue eyes, but ranks only fourth in general lightness of eye pigmentation.

Sociological Characteristics. The tall-medium weight group is first in forgery, ties in ranking with the short-slender and tall-heavy for second place in combined murders and is otherwise undistinguished. It is sixth in percentage of previous convictions and in percentage of unmarried men. In occupations it is notable as leading the list of the body types in proportions of extractive. It is slightly high in personal service and clerical, and slightly low in factory, laborer, and skilled trades. It is a badly educated group, ranking seventh in scholastic attainment.

Here again one suspects the rural men of this type to be responsible for the murder and the urban members for the high forgery rate. This class is comparatively low in burglary and larceny.

TALL-HEAVY

Physical Characteristics. The tall-heavy type includes 134 men, averaging 33.55 years in age, 182.70 centimeters in stature (71.93 inches), and weighing on the average 196.90 pounds. The mean cephalic index (77.91) is the lowest of all body types, but the facial index (87.54) is moderate, and the average nasal index (67.58) is above the mean of the series. These two indices are undoubtedly influenced by the corpulency of the group. This group is second darkest in hair color, and ranks first in percentage of black hair. It is very low in blondism and rufosity. It has more dark brown eyes than any other group and ranks next to the darkest in general eye pigmentation.

Sociological Characteristics. The tall-heavy group ranks first in first degree murder, and ties for second in general murder ranking. It is second in assault, second in forgery, and second in other sex offenses. It is seventh in burglary and larceny, and eighth in rape. It has the fewest previous convictions (proportionally) of any body build group. Although not the oldest, it contains the smallest proportion of unmarried men. It is first in percentage of factory operatives, first in public service, second in transportation, and low in most other occupations. This group is second in educational ranking, having the highest percentage of college men (8.21).

DISCUSSION OF RESULTS

Our body build types, established solely upon the basis of individual combinations of weight and height, have been shown to display certain differences in their sociological characteristics — offense, marital status, previous convictions, occupation, and education. We must attempt firstly to synthesize these relationships and then to interpret them. Further we must inquire into the nature of these body build types — whether they represent constitutional somatic variants, racial or ethnic types, local environmental varieties, or merely age groups.

Table IX–34 will help us to envisage as a whole the sociological differentiations of these body build groups. It consists merely of rankings for each group, based upon arrays of percentages. These rankings have been made up from raw percentages so that differences between one rank and another may, in some cases, be statistically insignificant. Yet they do show trends of the body build groups.

We may consider first the different kinds of offenses. Table IX–34 shows that the tall-heavy, tall-slender, and tall-medium builds occupy the first three rankings in first degree murder, and that short-medium, and short-heavy types occupy the two last places. The medium height-heavy class ranks fourth. Thus the four tallest types commit the most first degree murder, and two of the three short classes are very low in this offense. Second degree murder is not so regularly distributed, since the tall-heavy class drops to sixth and the short-slender class rises to second. But the short-medium and short-heavy retain their low rankings. It is noticeable that the tall-heavy type, which ranks first in first degree murder, is last in percentage of previous convictions, last in percentage of unmarried men, second in education, low in extractive occupations and

TABLE IX–34

RANKINGS IN BODY BUILD TYPES

	Short Slender	Short Medium	Short Heavy	Medium Slender	Medium Medium	Medium Heavy	Tall Slender	Tall Medium	Tall Heavy
Offense									
First degree murder	5	9	8	6	7	4	2	3	1
Second degree murder	2	7	9	8	5	3	1	4	6
Assault	8	3	1	5	6	7	8	4	2
Robbery	9	8	7	3	2	4	1	5	6
Burglary and larceny	1	2	5	3	4	8	9	6	7
Forgery and fraud	9	6	4	7	8	5	3	1	2
Rape	7	2	1	5	4	3	9	6	8
Other sex	4	6	1	5	7	3	9	8	2
Versus public welfare	8	9	5	6	7	1	2	4	3
Arson and all other	9	1	3	5	2	4	7	6	8
All offenses	9	7	2	7	6	1	5	4	3
Previous convictions — yes	1	2	8	3	4	7	5	6	9
Age	4	6	1	5	8	2	9	6	3
Marital state — single	2	4	7	1	5	8	3	6	9
Education ratio	1	9	5	3	8	6	4	7	2
Occupation									
Extractive	9	6	8	5	4	3	2	1	7
Laborer	9	1	5	2	3	4	8	6	7
Factory	4	9	6	5	3	7	2	8	1
Professional, semi-professional, and clerical	1	4	2	6	9	5	8	7	3

first in factory. But if we take into consideration the sociological characteristics of the tall-medium and tall-slender classes, which rank third and second respectively in first degree murder, we find that the sociological facts do not agree in all respects with those noted in the case of the ranking tall-heavy type. It is true that these types and also the medium-heavy type, which ranks fourth, are all low in previous convictions, but they vary greatly in age ranking, in educational ranking, and in occupational ranking.

Again if we consider the short-medium, short-heavy, and medium-medium types which are the lowest three in first degree murder, it is evident that they are quite dissimilar in other sociological characters and even in age. In other words, this offense is more clearly related to body type than to sociological characteristics, as far as these data are valid.

Second degree murder follows a rank pattern very similar to that of first degree, except that the short-slender type rises to second place, and the tall-heavy type, which is first in first degree murder drops to sixth rank. The most consistent behavior in combined murder rankings is that of the tall-slender type which is either first or second, and of the short-medium and short-heavy types which are either last, or last but one, in both of these crimes. The tall-medium weight and the medium-heavy group retain rather high rankings in this category of homicide.

We are driven then to the conclusion that tallness is especially associated with murder in this series, and that short men of medium weight or, especially, of heavy weight, are the least inclined to this form of crime. We may defer discussion of the causality of this phenomenon to a later stage when the significance of the body build types will be examined.

Assault is a crime so poorly represented in this series that conclusions upon its relation to the body build types must be quite tentative. The ranking group in this offense is the short-heavy, but this may be an accident of sampling. The tall-heavy group ranks next, and the short-medium third. The tall-heavy and short-heavy types have the darkest hair pigmentation of all the body types. Since the actual number of assault criminals in the short-heavy type is but two, and in the tall-heavy type, only four, it is hardly worth while to emphasize rankings in this offense. Both of these groups leading in assault, however, are near the bottom of the list in percentage of previous convictions, in the percentage of unmarried men, in the percentage of extractive occupation. They are both high in the professional, semi-professional, and clerical classes, and above the mean in age. The low rating of the short-slender type in this offense is probably related directly to the inferior body size and strength in this group. The tall-slender type is also at the bottom as regards this crime, but it again is a numerically small class, and we must consider the possibility of the complete absence of assault criminals in these two build types being merely the effect of chance in the case of an infrequent offense and small samples. The expectation of assault criminals in the short-slender group is 1.21 and in the tall-slender group 2.16. On the other hand one would expect to find in the short-heavy group 1.02 assault criminals, whereas there are two (Table IX–5). The expectation is $\dfrac{n_1\, n_a}{N}$ when n_1 = total of offense group, n_a = total of body build group, N = total individuals in series. Since we cannot reasonably expect criminals to occur in fractional parts, it is obvious that too much weight should not be placed upon excesses of one or two persons in these small groups, when the offense in question is so rare.

Robbery is a comparatively frequent offense, constituting 9.69 per cent of the convictions here represented. Table IX–34 shows that the tall-slender type ranks first in this crime, and Table IX–5 indicates that it is substantially in the lead in this offense. The three medium height types take the next three places and the three short types occupy the last rankings. The sociological rankings suggest no general relationship to previous convictions, age, marital state, or occupation. There is, however, a very clear indication that the short men avoid this crime.

Burglary and larceny constitute 38.85 per cent of all the crimes. We can depend upon these rankings. The first, second, and third places in this offense category are held by the short-slender, short-medium, and medium-slender types. It is a striking and significant fact that the first three rankings in previous convictions are held by the same three types in the same order. One may fairly conclude that burglars and thieves are most likely to be recidivists and that they tend to be short men of slight or medium build and medium-statured men of slight build more frequently than any other body build types. They are far less likely to be tall men or medium men of heavy build. The types which lead in these offenses are all at or below the mean age of the series, although not the youngest. The ranking type, short-slender, is first in education, but the second type, short-medium, is last. Again the short-slender type which ranks first is ninth in percentage of laborers, while the short-medium class which ranks second is first in this occupational category, and the medium-slender type, third in larceny, is second also in percentage of laborers. In marital status there is a better agreement since all of these three groups are high in percentages of single men. These then are the general relationships which seem to emerge from a survey of the ranking of body types with respect to burglary and larceny and associated sociological facts: (1) Short men of slender or medium build and medium height men of slender build are unduly selected for these offenses, which are at a minimum in the tall and heavy groups. (2) The men convicted of these offenses are also highest in percentage of previous convictions recorded. (3) They tend to be close to the average age of the criminal series as a whole and to include higher proportions of single men. (4) The body build types ranking highest in this offense category are quite heterogeneous in educational qualifications and in percentages of occupations represented. (5) Body build and previous convictions are more closely related to burglary and larceny than any other features or conditions here examined.

Forgery constitutes 10.92 per cent of the offenses represented in this series. Tall-medium, tall-heavy, and tall-slender men occupy the first three rankings in this offense. These classes all rank low in percentage of previous convictions and in the percentage of laborers included. No consistent relation with age, marital status, or education is manifest. It is notable that the short-slender, short-medium, and medium-slender types, which rank first in burglary and larceny, are ninth, sixth, and seventh in forgery, whereas the tall-slender, tall-medium, and tall-heavy types, occupy respectively, ninth, sixth, and seventh places in burglary and larceny. Consequently it may be concluded that a marked propensity for the one type of offense is compensated by a disinclination toward the other in these contrasted statural types. The lack of a positive and significant association of education and occupation with forgery is unexpected.

Of the 3910 criminals included in this body build series 181, or 4.63 per cent, have been convicted of rape. The short-heavy and short-medium types far outrank the others in this offense. The medium height-heavy type is third, and the tall-heavy and tall-slender types occupy the last two rankings. The two body types highest in this offense present no important agreement in other sociological rankings, except that they are both rather high in laborers and in the professional, semi-professional, and clerical classes, and low in the extractive occupations. Since, however, the percentages of rapists in these body build types reach only 9.26 and 8.30 per cent, it can hardly be expected that their general sociological status will conform to their similar rankings in this offense. All of the tall types present low rankings in rape, but the short-slender type is also very low in this offense, ranking seventh. The most complete contrast exists between the short-heavy and tall-slender types which rank respectively first and last in this offense. This contrast extends to nearly all of their sociological and physical characteristics, but since it is equally marked in a number of other offenses — notably first degree and second degree murder — it can scarcely be invoked to explain the build type difference in such a relatively infrequent crime as rape. This offense, however, does seem to show a stronger relationship to the body builds than to any single socio-logical factor.

Other sex offenses constitute 3.68 per cent of the convictions of the series. The rankings in rape and other sex offenses agree more closely than do those for any other pair of offenses. Thus the short-heavy type ranks first in both, the medium-heavy third in both, the medium-slender fifth, and the tall-slender ninth. Such an agreement is, perhaps, to be expected. However, there are several striking inconsistencies in in-dividual groups. For instance, the tall-heavy type is eighth in rape but second in other sex offenses, while the short-medium type is second in rape and sixth in other sex of-fenses. Perhaps we may arrive at a more accurate evaluation of the physical and socio-logical contingencies upon sex offenses by considering the combined rankings of those types which occupy the same places in each sex offense category and by comparing the sociological characteristics of these types only. The short-heavy class ranks first in both categories and first in the combined sex offenses; the medium-heavy class ranks third in both and second in the combined categories; the medium-slender class ranks fifth in both and ties for fourth place in the combination; the tall-slender type ranks ninth or last in both. The two leading classes in combined sex offenses rank re-spectively eighth and seventh in previous convictions. The intermediate medium-slender class is third and the tall-slender class is fifth. The perceptible tendency is for build types high in sex offenders to have been convicted less frequently of prior offenses than those which are low in sex offenses. In age the short-heavy type is first, the medium height-heavy second, the medium height-slender fifth and the tall-slender ninth. The types in which sex offenses are most frequent are then among the highest in mean age, and the smallest proportion of sex offenses occurs in the youngest of the build types. There is, of course, no perfect correlation. The two high ranking types are also very low in percentage of unmarried men. The short-heavy type, which heads the list in sex crimes, has considerably the largest proportion of divorced and widowed men. The medium height-heavy group is somewhat above the mean in this proportion, but not greatly so. The tall-heavy type, which is inconsistent in sex offenses, ranking eighth in rape and second in other sex offenses, is also outstanding by reason of high propor-tions of divorced men and widowers. These marital conditions are to some extent re-lated to age, but, apart from this consideration, it seems clear that sex crimes are more frequently committed by married men than by single men, and that sex offenders include a large proportion of widowed and divorced men. The heavy body build of these of-fenders is probably related to some extent also to their high average age.

There is no apparent relationship between educational rank and rank in combined sex offenses in the body build types. Any clear relationship to occupation is equally lacking.

Offenses versus public welfare are, in the vast majority of cases, violations of liquor laws. They comprise 6.01 of the convictions in this series. The high rankings in this offense are in the following types and order: medium-heavy, tall-slender, tall-heavy, tall-medium. Apart from a generally low ranking in previous convictions, these types seem to display no particular sociological homogeneity. The short-slender and short-medium classes occupy the last places in this offense. This offense group is heav-ly overloaded with Texans (57.98 per cent) and it is inadvisable to draw any sweep-ng inferences from the data in hand. The rankings in arson and all other offenses are of negligible importance, since this miscellaneous category includes only 2.38 per cent of the body build series.

Table IX–34 presents finally the ranking of each build type for all offenses. The short-slender type ranks last in all offenses, but first in burglary and larceny. This means of course that burglary and larceny is to such an extent the predominant offense in this group that the proportions convicted for other crimes are relatively and absolutely very low. The sole exception is second degree murder in which the short-slender type ranks second. The short-medium type is seventh in all offenses, but second in burglary and larceny, which is again the predominant offense category. However, this body type is second in rape. The short-heavy type is second in all offenses, and owes this high position principally to its primacy in assault and in both classes of sex offense. The medium height-slender type is seventh — a place which it shares with the short-medium weight type. The medium height-heavy type ranks first in all offenses, although it actually takes primacy in one offense category only — versus public welfare. This is in spite of the fact that it ranks eighth in burglary and larceny. This high ranking in general is due largely to the comparatively small number who are thieves and burglars, since the residue is so distributed among the other crimes as to rank the type above the median class in most other offenses. The tall-slender group ranks fifth — the median type — in all offenses and is the most variable of all the build types in its rankings, occupying first rank in two offenses and last rank in three. The tall-heavy type is third in all offenses. The most interesting feature of these mean rankings is that the types which rank high in burglary and larceny are low in general offense ranking and *vice versa*. This is, of course, because an excess or deficiency of any size in this predominant category of offense (38.85 of all crimes in the series) naturally results in high or low rankings in most or all of the nine other smaller classes of offense.

We have now to consider the anthropological significance of the body build types which have been sorted out. Are these racial types? The criminals in this particular series are all supposedly native born Whites of native parentage. This means that the majority of them are of British extraction (English, Welsh, Irish, and Scotch).[1] The only other element which is likely to be strongly represented in this sample is German. Doubtless a small proportion of these criminals are of Scandinavian descent, and a still smaller fraction of French Canadian, or other European stock. The Wisconsin and Massachusetts quotas may well contain persons of such extraction. In general, however, it seems clear that the vast majority of these criminals are of Northwestern European descent, coming from areas in which the so-called Nordic race is most strongly represented.

The peoples who migrated to the United States from the British Isles and elsewhere in Europe were already racially mixed. They included, perhaps, a majority of dolichocephals and mesocephals, but also brachycephals and a range of pigment from the fairest blonds to swarthy brunets. Interbreeding of the various types has brought about mixture of hereditary physical traits so that the original racial combinations of features rarely are found, and when they do occur they are most likely to be the result of recombinations. Taken then as a group, any body of Old Americans is likely to represent a considerable variety of mixed racial types, with some few individuals ap-

[1] Cf. data on Extraction, Chapter II, pages 74–75.

proximating original racial types, largely through the chance recombinations of cross-breeding.

The stature of Old Americans is on the average tall when the entire range of human stature is taken into consideration. This is probably due primarily to the fact that the racial elements which originally composed the settlers of the United States, and which are still predominant, were considerably above average stature. Other factors, however, such as heterosis resulting from mixture of allied stocks, favorable environment, et cetera, may be to some extent responsible for this superiority in bodily height. Although the native White criminals of native parentage are inferior in body height to civilians of similar origin, they are still tall, presumably because of their racial heritage.

Since the entire series of native White American criminals of native parentage must be adjudged racially mixed or heterogeneous, it remains to determine whether or not in selecting body build types we have merely isolated groups of different combinations of height and weight which are racially as mixed as the total series, or whether, inadvertently, the build types selected have tended to represent individually predominant strains of this or that racial type which has contributed to the mixture of the entire population. If the latter is the case, the build types ought to present individually more homogeneity and less statistical variability in the indices and pigmentation data than are shown by the entire series. We must then examine these data with this point in mind.

The data on height and weight are of no use for this purpose since the groups were arbitrarily selected on the basis of these measurements. Table IX–25 gives the statistical constants for means of the cephalic index. The standard deviation of the entire group in this measurement is 3.30. The standard deviations of the body type subgroups range from 3.06 to 3.45. None of them are significantly different from the standard deviation of the entire series, so that it is clear that all are equally heterogeneous. There is, however, a slight decrease in the mean index as one progresses from the short to the tall groups. Table IX–35 gives the percentage of each division of the cephalic index in the several body types and in the entire series. It shows very clearly that the proportion of dolichocephals increases from the short to the tall groups, and that, conversely, the brachycephals decrease. It is equally apparent, however, that all types of head form are found in each body build class. Table V–36 yields a correlation ratio of cephalic index with nature of offense for the entire series of native born White criminals of native parentage amounting to .06 ± .01. This correlation ratio is low but it does not necessarily indicate a lack of relationship. As indicated on pages 25 and 26, Dr. Seltzer's recent critical examination of the correlation ratio indicates that this statistical device, when used to express the relationship between a variable and a set of sociological attributes, is misleading and unsatisfactory. A high value of the correlation ratio thus used is virtually out of the question, and a perfect correlation ratio of unity would be attainable only if each sociological category of individuals were characterized by an exclusive and invariable value of the cephalic index. Sociological categories are not variables in a statistical sense and they should not be forced into the Procrustean bed of the correlation ratio, which is a second-rate device for measuring the relations of variables.

Head form is a racial criterion of importance. It is probably fair to conclude that the short types contain more Alpine, East Baltic, Dinaric, and other brachycephalic strains than do the tall classes. Yet the evidence of racial diversification in the body build types is hardly strong enough to warrant the conclusion that the offense and other sociological differentiations are caused primarily by facial factors.

The standard deviation of the facial index in the entire series is 5.20 and in the subgroups ranges from 4.72 to 5.64. None of the build types differs significantly from the total series in the variability of this index. Table IX–36 shows, however, that long narrow faces increase as one progresses from the short to the tall groups and that they decrease from the slender to the heavy groups. The reverse is true in the case of short broad faces. Such a general conformity of face with body build and with head shape is natural enough and may have some racial significance as well as an importance which is derived from its general somatic correlation.

The standard deviation of the nasal index in the total series is 6.84 and in the build types ranges from 6.08 to 7.52. .Again none of the types show significantly less or more variability than does the entire series. The series is, as a whole, leptorrhine. Nevertheless, Table IX–37 shows that the body types exhibit considerable variation in the nasal index in conformity with their builds. The heavy and medium weight types show higher proportions of narrow noses as height increases. The slender types tend to show decreases. Slender men, in general, have the highest proportion of narrow noses and heavy men the lowest. This again furnishes confirmation of our suspicion that the body types recognized carry with them more than mere arbitrary relations of weight and height. But it is easy to see that none of the types are homogeneous in nasal index, although they approach closer to this condition than in the cephalic and facial indices. Again it is possible that this differentiation of the types in nasal index may, to some extent, reflect differences in racial constitution, but there is no certain means of determining whether such be the case.

There are eight shades of hair color listed in Table IX–28 and the body build types show, in general, distributions of the hair shades which are similar to the distributions in the entire series. There are, indeed, inequalities — some of them greater than would be expected to result from chance alone. None of the types is, however, in any sense homogeneous in hair color and none appears to be less variable than the entire series, with the possible exception of the short-slender type. The total series contains 39.45 per cent of individuals with dark hair; the subgroups range from 33.87 per cent to 49.11 per cent of such individuals. The entire series has 45.97 per cent of medium hair shades and the body types range from 37.04 per cent to 50 per cent. In the entire series 9.43 per cent have light hair and the percentages in the subgroups vary from 6.45 to 11.89 per cent. It is evident, therefore, that none of these groups can be considered as a unit in regard to hair pigment in the sense that an ideal racial type should be unified — in the restricted range of its variability. It is, however, obvious that the different groups may vary in the proportions of different racial phenotypes which they include, so far as pigment is a criterion of race.

The situation in eye color is precisely the same, except that the subgroups or body types differ individually from the total series in their distributions by even lesser amounts than in hair color.

The conclusion must be that the types here delimited are body build types in persons of mixed racial antecedents, and that, whereas in one or another type, this or that racial strain may be in the ascendancy, none of them can be said to be racially unified, or even to represent preponderantly a single racial phenotype. What then do these ypes signify? Are they "constitutional types"? No attempt has been made to divide up this criminal series into any of the numerous constitutional type classifications, some of which are based merely upon subjective observations and others upon highly artificial and complex indices of build. Our body build types are merely combinations of weight and stature and apart from those combinations it is doubtful whether they merit the designation "types." Nevertheless, there must be some temperamental or constitutional significance to these body build groups; otherwise they would not exhibit the very marked regression upon offense and upon certain other sociological characteristics which they have been demonstrated to show.

The short-slender type we may assume to be characterized by inferiority in body size and weight. Its preeminence in burglary and larceny may be due in part to the fact that small, light men are likely to be agile and unobtrusive and to some extent are fitted in their body build for becoming sneak thieves, cat-burglars, pickpockets, and for other surreptitious methods of acquiring property. Such puny men may lack the physical courage which is essential to robbery, but it is hard to see why they rank last in forgery, especially since they rank first in education and first in the clerical, semi-professional, and trade categories. One can only suppose that the low rating of the short-slender type in forgery is a mere accident of sampling. The fact that this type ranks first in previous convictions may again be related to its general physical inferiority, since the weaker and less vigorous criminals are likely to be easiest and oftenest apprehended. This is an argument which may be offered as a partial explanation of the general inferiority of size in criminals as compared with civilians, but it certainly does not fully explain it.

The low ranking (ninth place) in extractive and laborer categories, which is a feature of the short-slender type, is again attributable, at least in part, to the inferior physique of the type. Apart from the physical limitations of this group, there may be certain temperamental characteristics which tend to restrict its antisocial activities. What they are, however, and whether or not any racial factors are involved, do not appear from the evidence in hand.

The short-medium weight type is quite similar to the short-slender type in its offense distribution, ranking second in burglary and larceny. But this type with the short-heavy is at the very bottom of the list in murder. It is also second in previous convictions. But this class is an ignorant one which ranks last in education and first in proportion of laborers. It is also high in rape. Its high ranking in arson and all other offenses may indicate inferior mentality. I cannot ascribe to this class any other reason for its recidivism, addiction to burglary and thieving, and low rank in murder, liquor offenses, et cetera, than that it seems to be physically, mentally, and economically, almost the lowest of our criminal build types, and is singularly averse from crimes of violence against the person.

I am equally at a loss to explain the low murder ranking, the excessive tendency to sex crimes, and the high assault rating of the short, fat, dark-haired and roundish-headed men who are the oldest of all our build types. Can it be that no one loves a fat man and that he must seek his sexual satisfaction in felonious assaults? Or are these the brutish Alpines and sensual East Baltics of which the Nordic propagandists rave? Certainly the latter question may be answered negatively.

Again the tall men, who are also longer-headed, seem to show striking propensities

for murder, and each group is differentiated according to weight. Are these constitutional tendencies racial proclivities, or the complicated resultants of a large number o
environmental forces?

We can, of course, invoke the well-known homicidal mores of the Kentucky an
Tennessee mountaineers to explain some of the excesses in murder; and the absence
in those regions, of much that is worth stealing may serve as a deterrent from breakin
and entering and stealing. But it would be almost equally sensible to adduce the lack o
charm of the mountain women as the explanation of the low rank in sex crimes. In vie
of the heterogeneity of social characteristics which these various build types exhibit, i
view of the racial heterogeneity which each seems to present, the only conclusion whic
can be reached at this point is that in some inexplicable way, these body builds ar
bound up with different patterns of behavior, both social and antisocial. The possibi
ity of racial influences being at work here is one which will be investigated fully in th
second volume of this work in which racial sortings will be made in an attempt to iso
late these factors. Here it can only be said in advance that these sortings do show un
deniable racial differences in criminal proclivities, but that they are insufficient t
explain the striking differences in offenses exhibited by the body build types.

The whole series, of course, is overloaded with men from Kentucky and Texas, wh
comprise 51.38 per cent of the total which is derived from nine states. Kentucky, how
ever, with the largest single contribution to the series (28.85 per cent) does not fur
nish a significantly disproportionate quota to any body build type. Texas is signif
cantly low in short-slender, short-medium weight, and medium height-slender group
and high in tall-medium weight, and tall-heavy. Massachusetts and Wisconsin ove
load the short-slender and short-medium weight groups, and the former state is ver
deficient in tall-medium weight and tall-heavy types. These are the most importar
state inequalities and doubtless they affect the strong sociological differentiation of th
extreme types. Since the general cultural and environmental conditions which obtai
in the several states are quite diverse, and since the physical types in these states ar
also diverse, it may be argued that body build differentiation, as here discussed, is a re
sultant of the combination of local state physical types with state cultural pattern
But this merely re-impales us upon the horns of the old dilemma. Does the culture ar
the environment of the state select or create the body build type, or is it the other wa
round?

Frankly, I do not think that many of the sociological differentiae of the body bui
types would survive corrections for state sampling, because the application of such co
rections would iron out not only the general sociological differences which may be a
tributable to physical environment, but would also obliterate the sociological differenc
which may have arisen from the specific ethnic and racial blends which predominate
the several states. Thus if we eliminate state sociological differences, we tend to equa
ize not only physical environments, but also, to some extent, hereditary compositio
We should then be dealing with a discussion of body build *in vacuo*.

The relation of rank in mean age to the nine body build groups and the sum of dev
ations of age rank from offense rank in ten offenses are shown in Table IX–38.

This table shows that the heavy groups are the oldest groups, but that there is litt
regression of weight upon age in the short and slender groups. It further shows th
age tends to decrease as one proceeds from short through medium to tall statures. No

f a median ranking in age goes with a median ranking in offenses, the deviations of age anking from offense ranking ought to be at a minimum in the medium-slender group vhich is fifth in age rank of the nine groups. This proves to be the case, since Table X–38 shows these deviations to be 11 in units of rank. They ought to reach their

TABLE IX–38

RANKING OF BODY BUILD GROUPS IN MEAN AGE AND SUM OF AGE RANK DEVIATIONS FROM
TEN OFFENSE RANKINGS

Body Build	Age Rank	Sum of Deviations of Age Rank from Ten Offense Rankings
Short-heavy	1	34
Medium-heavy	2	24
Tall-heavy	3	25
Short-slender	4	32
Medium-slender	5	11
Tall-medium weight	6	17
Short-medium weight	6	25
Medium-medium weight	8	28
Tall-slender	9	39

naxima in the oldest and youngest age groups and decrease from each of these extremes oward the median age group. The youngest age group (tall-slender, age rank 9) shows ross deviations of 39 units and the oldest (short-heavy, age rank 1) has gross deviaions amounting to 34 units. But it will be seen that there is little consistency in the .eviations of the body build groups which in age fall between the extremes and he median body build group. Thus two body build groups (tall-medium and short-nedium) tie for sixth rank in age, but the former has a total of 17 deviations and the atter a total of 25 deviations.

It is suggested then that age affects both body build and offense diversification in so ar as median age carries with it minimal deviation in offense ranking, and that maximal nd minimal age are associated with the strongest extremes of deviation in body build roup and the maximum divergences between age ranking and offense ranking.

On the whole it seems that our body build groups are not essentially age groups, nor et, racial groups, occupational groups, educational groups, nor groups whose sociologi-al differentiations are determined by any one single factor. They are not even state ypes, since only two of the nine types draw as many of their members as one-third rom any one state. I should conclude, tentatively, that they are constitutional types vith which are linked, quite inexplicably in our present state of knowledge, behavioral ariations.

Chapter X

MORPHOLOGICAL OFFENSE TYPES

THEORETICAL POSSIBILITY OF DISTINGUISHING NATURE OF OFFENSE BY COMBINATIONS OF MORPHOLOGICAL FEATURES

IT has been demonstrated in the preceding sections that most of the offense groups of native White American criminals of native parentage differ significantly from the means of the total criminal series of such origin in a sufficient number of measurements and indices as to warrant the conclusion that the offense groups are anthropometrically distinct from the series as a whole. It has also been shown that in a considerable number of graded morphological observations the several offense groups show individually in this or that character, significant excesses of certain variations which mark them out as different from the series at large. For instance, second degree murderers as a group are characterized by excesses of pronounced nasal bridge height, septum inclination downward, submedium lip thickness, bilateral chins, wrinkling, tooth wear, and edge-to-edge bite. In all of these features they markedly exceed the proportion of such variations found in the total series of native born White criminals of native parentage.

There is, however, no implication that excesses of morphological observations thus singly observed are combined into individual types characterizing each separate offense group. We cannot assume that a second degree murderer will present a combination of all the peculiarities which distinguish the group. The combination of morphological or metric variations in the individual is the only basis of what is commonly called a "type." A type is literally something which is struck out by a die or pattern, or cast from a mould. A physical type is ordinarily recognized by the observer's visual impression of a combination of morphological features. Similar combinations in different individuals create an impression of likeness or identity and we adjudge such individuals to belong to a "type." The lay observer and often the trained anthropologist recognize physical types, usually without analyzing their component morphological variations and without even being conscious of them. They depend merely upon the impression of likeness. This visual recognition of a type is the easiest and most valid method of type differentiation. Unless, however, such visual type identifications are tabulated and confirmed by a statistical demonstration that the persons classified within a type do in reality present similar combinations of morphological features and are actually distinct from other types, they have no scientific validity.

To attempt to distinguish a type empirically by taking the morphological variations of separate features, singly tabulated, and to discover the manner in which these variations are combined in individuals is an almost impossible task. The reason for this is the appalling number of combinations which are mathematically possible when any con siderable number of features and gradations of features are involved in the attempted type combination. Mathematically the number of possible combinations is represented by X^n, if X = the number of gradations or variations of a character recognized, and n = the number of characters considered. Thus, if there are 4 gradations of each character and 5 characters involved, the possible combinations are equal to 4^5 or 1024. Consequently, in order to secure one example of every type combination theoretically possible in 5 characters with 4 gradations to each, it would be necessary to have a sample of 1024 individuals. Clearly, unless there is some sort of linkage in character gradations as morphologically observed, or, in other words, unless certain combinations recur much more frequently than they would on a purely chance basis, there is virtually no mathematical possibility of dividing up small samples into a few types of any degree of morphological complexity.

If the 7 differentiating morphological features in second degree murderers are classified in 3 gradations each, the possible combinations are 2187 and there are only 619 second degree murderers in the series. Unless, then, each offense group is characterized by the possession of a number of morphological variations, each exclusively its own, and each found in an overwhelming majority of the individuals in that offense group, it is perfectly obvious that there is almost no chance of establishing detailed and exclusive offense physical types, whereby a prognosis of the criminal's offense may be made from his physique. Now it may be stated once and for all that practically every morphological and metric variation found in the series occurs in each and every offense group, saving only those offense groups which contain so few individuals that they could not reasonably be expected to include all the range of variation. In other words there is no single morphological feature peculiar to any one offense group — far less any exclusive array of peculiarities for each group. All that we have is an excess in some particular group of this or that feature found in all of the groups, or a number of such excesses. Again, any morphological feature, some specific variation of which characterizes the majority of a group, is almost certain to be such a feature as occurs in the majority of the members of every other offense group. A really distinctive feature is likely to occur in only a few members of the group to which it is more or less peculiar. All of these considerations afford little hope of distinguishing morphological criminal types, characterized by combinations found in the majority of individuals of the several offense groups.

Before we proceed to a demonstration of the futility of such attempts, it is advisable to consider the significance of excesses of separate variations and deviations of individual means in any anthropometric sample drawn from a large series of observations.

Almost all racial classifications hitherto made have been based upon means of metric characters and modes of morphological variations separately observed in samples of the population grouped together on the basis of geographical distribution, language, nationality, or by physical impressions of type similarity unconfirmed by statistical analysis. Thus it is assumed that a group which is characterized by a dolichocephalic mean index, a leptorrhine mean index, a modal occurrence of blond hair, blue eyes, and fair skin, is actually composed of individuals the majority of whom exhibit these features in combination. This assumption is likely to be wholly fallacious when put to the test of actually sorting by combinations. It is of little or no use for the purpose of individual racial diagnosis. Nevertheless, the method of distinguishing groups by differences in separate means and modes is useful in creating a sort of hypothetical group type, which, although not necessarily realized in the majority of individuals, serves to define its *average* deviations from other diverse physical groups, or rather its mean position in respect to a number of important metric and morphological features. Similarly, the generalization that criminals are smaller and lighter than civilians of the same ethnic origin does not mean that every criminal is both smaller and lighter than every civilian; many criminals may be larger and heavier than many civilians and some may be shorter and heavier than some civilians. Such a generalization merely establishes the fact that in samples of civilians and criminals equal in number there are likely to be more short individuals and more light individuals in the latter than in the former. It defines group tendencies which are based upon numbers of individuals and are realized singly perhaps in the majority, and in combination probably in a minority, of cases. The fact that there are many more illiterates among first degree murderers than in criminals at large does not enable one to distinguish a first degree murderer on the sole criterion of illiteracy, but it, nevertheless, gives important information upon the educational status of this type of offender.

Bearing these facts in mind, we must not be too greatly disappointed if we find that group differences in separate characters do not permit us to establish individual type combinations which occur in sufficient numbers and with such exclusiveness in the offense groups as to enable them to be employed for practical purposes of diagnosis.

Methods and Examples of Sorting for Offense Type

For the purpose of testing the combinations of morphological variations in individual offense types in this series, two methods have been devised. The first of these is sorting by excesses. This method consists of arranging the significant excesses of morphological features which occur in any offense groups in order of their gross percentages in the groups and successively sorting for the presence of each of these excess features. Thus in the robbery group we have the following excesses (without corrections for state sampling):

		Robbery	Total Series
		Per Cent	Per Cent
1.	Asymmetry — none	77.33 [1]	73.16
2.	Ear protrusion — medium	64.01	57.07
3.	Ear lobes — attached	44.07	38.80
4.	Hair color — light brown	30.51	25.76
5.	Eye folds — median	18.25	12.86
6.	Hair form — low, deep waves	17.32	12.36
7.	Beard quantity — large	16.50	13.46
8.	Darwin's point — pronounced	14.32	12.98
9.	Iris — diffused	11.74	8.60

[1] These percentages are taken from the original table on Asymmetry by Offense. The present sorting has slightly different totals. (Cf. Table X–4.)

Certain excesses have been omitted from the sortings since they are obviously dependent upon age. The procedure is to take the entire series of criminals and carry out the successive sortings, keeping the robbery group separate from the rest. Each successive sorting leaves only the individuals which possess the feature sorted and all previous features for which sortings have been made. Thus upon the ninth sorting all remaining individuals would exhibit all of the nine morphological peculiarities and would constitute a sorting type. Then if the features sorted are found excessively in the robbery type, each succeeding sorting ought to increase the percentage of robbers among individuals possessing the required characteristics. Eventually one ought to arrive at such an intricate combination as would be found only among robbers and not at all in other offense groups — if indeed the peculiarities are distinctive in combination. Table X–1 gives the result of these sortings. The first sorting — asymmetry none — yields 10.28 per cent of robbers and 89.72 per cent of other criminals. In the fourth sorting, the percentage of robbers with the four characters has risen to 19.65 per cent of all criminals exhibiting this fourfold combination. The fifth sorting carries the percentage of robbers to 88.89 and the sixth sorting consists of 100 per cent robbers. In other words we have secured a combination which in this series of 4212 criminals is found only in robbers. But it should be noticed that successive sortings have depleted our samples until in the sixth sorting which contains 100 per cent of robbers there is one individual only. In other words, we have secured an exclusive physical combination only by excluding all but one person of 4212. This, evidently, is not a very useful procedure since it identifies only one robber of a total 414.

It is depressingly apparent that the predicted futility of looking for exclusive individual morphological combinations which characterize any considerable number of persons in an offense group, is realized by actual trial. In other words sorting by significant excesses of morphological characters is useless, because no exclusive characters are sufficiently widespread in any group and the various excess peculiarities do not occur in combination in enough individuals.

However, it should be noted that the order of sorting greatly affects the number of discards and it is theoretically possible that a large number of individuals in any offense group, thrown out on the first sorting because they lack the character on which the sorting is based, may well show most if not all of the features on which subsequent selections are made.

This possibility can be demonstrated by a second sorting method — that of examining every possible combination of the morphological variations statistically characteristic of a given offense group of criminals.

In order to investigate fully the occurrence of the nine distinctive morphological variations in one subgroup of 414 robbers, every possible combination was sorted out on the Hollerith apparatus. Even in so small a group the sortings and tabulations required the full time of one operator for a period of more than six weeks. Table X–2 gives the raw data resulting from this operation. This table shows how many times and in what percentage of cases each observed variation occurs. It also gives the total of individuals in the robbery subgroup showing combinations of these characters from zero to 9 and the percentage of the group in each category. Thus it may be seen that there were 6 individuals, or 1.45 per cent of the group, in which none of the distinctive characters were present, 131 individuals who showed various combinations of three characters, et cetera. It should be noted that but one individual of the group shows seven of the distinctive characters and none shows eight or nine characters. The commonest number of the characters occurring in the group is three. This number is found in

31.64 per cent of the robber series. The next most frequent number of characters is two, which occurs in 27.05 per cent. Four characters are found in 20.29 per cent.

Table X–3 lists the theoretically posssible numbers of different combinations of characters from zero to 9, the total of which is 512. It also shows the number of different or distinct combinations observed in each category, and the percentage of the possible distinct combinations which actually occur in that category. Thus it may be seen that 69.44 per cent of the possible combinations of two characters actually are found in the group, but only 2.78 per cent of the possible combinations of seven characters. Since there are 414 persons in the group and 127 distinct combinations of nine or fewer characters are shown, we should expect the same combination to occur on the average in 3.26 individuals. The data show that, on the average, 3.34 individuals repeat combinations.

Of the 512 theoretically possible combinations of nine or less characters 127 or 24.8 per cent are actually found in our group of 414 persons. Since, however, 414 is the largest possible number of different combinations which could occur in a group of this size, the percentage of possible combinations realized is 30.67. This agrees fairly well with the average percentage distribution of single characters within the group which is 31.91.

A reference to Table X–4 which shows the occurrence of the nine significant characters by single characters explains clearly enough the reason why combinations of the majority of the characters occur so rarely in individuals. The highest occurrence of any single character of the nine is 73.67 per cent; the lowest occurrence is only 11.84 per cent, and the average occurrence is 31.91 per cent. Theoretically the group would show 3726 individual occurrences of the characters if each of the 414 persons in the group showed all of the nine characters. Actually only 1189 characters or 31.91 per cent of the possible total are displayed by the entire group. The average occurrence is 2.87 characters per individual.

Table X–5 summarizes the most frequently recurring combinations of the nine morphological characters. The two-character combination — asymmetry none, ear protrusion medium — is by far the most common. It includes 34 individuals or 8.21 per cent of the group. These are singly the most widely distributed variations in the group, and are obviously of little diagnostic value. The other common combinations are scarcely more useful for type identification.

Table X–6 analyzes the occurrence of each character singly and in combination with one to six of the other characters, and gives the percentages of the various single and multiple character combinations in each character group. It should be noted that most of the characters show their modal occurrence in combinations with two other characters. The exceptions to this rule are: hair form, low or deep waves; and iris diffused, which occur oftenest in combination with three other characters, and eye folds median, which is found with equal frequency in combination with either two or three other characters. For some reason or other these two characters show the strongest tendencies to occur in multiple combinations. Presumably the reason is that the more characters included in the combination, the more of the infrequent variations are required to make up the combination. But the inclusion of a relatively infrequent variation in a multiple combination weights the percental distribution of that infrequent variation more heavily than the distributions of the common variations are weighted. Hence the tendency of the rarer characters to occur in multiple combinations in a higher proportion of their totals.

Table X–7 analyzes the occurrence of each character singly and in multiple combinations and gives in each case the percentage of the entire robbery group included in each category. Thus the maximum frequency is found in the occurrence of asymmetry none with two other characters. This category includes 104 individuals or 25.12 per cent of the group.

The impression gained from the foregoing analysis is that, within the robbery group, the nine distinctive variations in which it significantly exceeds other offense groups are distributed in completely fortuitous combinations. They can hardly be combined in individuals in any genetic linkage.

As a rough test of comparative frequency of combinations of the morphological variations, supposedly characteristic of robbers, in other crime groups, nine fourfold combinations have been selected in such a manner that each of the 9 distinctive characters is represented in 4 separate combinations. Thus the characters or variations which appear with relative infrequence in the robbery group are as well represented in this selection of nine combinations as are those which are found in the majority of the robbers.

Table X–8 presents the results of these sortings. The first and commonest of the four-character combinations is: asymmetry none, ear protrusion medium, ear lobe attached, hair color light brown. This occurs in 138 persons of the criminal series exclusive of robbers, or 3.28 per cent. It is found in 34 robbers or 8.21 per cent of that offense group. Thus it is more than twice as common in robbers as in other offenders in general. The tabulation also shows the percental occurrence in other offense groups. None of these reaches the proportion found in the robbery group, the closest approximation being 5.82 in arson and all other offenses. If we were to select a sample of 100 criminals out of 4200 we should expect only ten of these to be robbers, but if we selected a sample of the same size with the foregoing character combination, at least 24 of the 100 would be robbers.

The second four-character combination sorted out in the criminals other than robbers is ear protrusion medium, ear lobe attached, hair color light brown, eye fold median. This occurs in only 29 of the non-robbers or .76 per cent, but in 8 of the robbery group, or 1.93 per cent. It is therefore 2.5 times as common in robbers as in other criminals. However, it is so rare in both robbers and non-robbers as to be of no practical importance for purposes of diagnosis.

The next four-character combination — ear lobe attached, hair color light brown, eye folds median, hair form low and deep waves occurs in but 4 of the non-robbers or .10 per cent. It is found in one robber or .24 per cent.

The next four-character combination does not occur at all, either in robbers or in non-robbers. The following two combinations are found each in 2 non-robbers or .05 per cent, but not in any of the robbers.

The seventh four-character combination is found in 8 non-robbers or .19 per cent, and in one robber or .24 per cent. But a glance at the occurrence in the offense subgroups shows that it is found in .43 per cent of forgers and in .37 per cent of burglars and thieves. Therefore if we were to select criminals on the basis of this uncommon combination, we should be more likely to draw burglars, thieves, or forgers, than robbers.

The eighth combination is again very rare. It occurs in .38 per cent of all non-robbers and in .24 per cent of robbers. In every offense group where it is found it is commoner than in the robbery group.

The last combination is found in 1.14 per cent of non-robbers and in 1.69 per cent of robbers. It is commoner among thieves and burglars than among robbers.

Evidently what has been accomplished (and all that has been accomplished) by sorting for combinations of variations which are found significantly in excess in the robbery group is to reduce the odds against any selected criminal being a robber. It seems probable that by selecting four-character combinations of variations which not only occur in a significant excess of robbers as compared with non-robbers, but which also are to be found in 50 per cent or more of robbers, we can reduce the odds against a criminal being a robber from about 9 to 1 to about 4 to 1. But only 29.21 per cent of all robbers have four or more of these significant variations in any sort of a combination. Hence in reducing the odds against robbers in this manner we have lost nearly 71 per cent of our robbers. By getting more and more intricate combinations of distinctive features we can eventually arrive at exclusively robber combinations; but the odds against finding any individual at all with such a combination, be he robber or non-robber, increase so rapidly that the proportion of robber physical combinations in the universe of robbers is evidently negligible. In other words, we find that by successive sortings we have emptied out the baby with the bath.

Apart from the fundamental question of the existence or non-existence of individual criminal types, there are two main sets of difficulties involved in distinguishing physical types in individuals by combinations of morphological variations. The first of these is the almost infinite variety of theoretically possible combinations. This difficulty has been discussed and demonstrated. The second is the personal equation involved in the necessarily subjective grading of morphological variations by different observers. We have no guarantee that two observers will invariably agree that the same individual has a medium ear protrusion, as contrasted with a pronounced ear protrusion. In fact we know that such agreements can be expected, at best, only in a majority of cases. Furthermore the same observer will not invariably pronounce the same judgment upon the same feature in repeated observations. This matter of personal equation in itself might easily be enough to obscure the presence of individual morphological types, if they do in fact exist.

Actually I am convinced that satisfactory typing can be accomplished in but one way — quite a different method of procedure from that adopted in this survey. In order to distinguish individual morphological and metric types, the observer must make his type assignments when he has finished the measurement and observation of each individual. The type cannot be created arbitrarily from the analysis of massed data. The type assignment should rest upon the observer's total morphological impression of physical similarity and not upon any selected criteria. In order to effect such a typing it would be necessary for the observer to look over his series very carefully in advance of any individual studies. If he were a sufficiently skilled anthropologist he would then be able to formulate conceptions or impressions of a number of distinct physical types existent in the group to be studied. He would fix in his mind the range of types and assign to each some name. The types might be designated by racial appellations or by any names chosen at random. For example, in Tennessee one might distinguish a type called Hill-Billy A, and in England a type called Cockney, and another called John Bull. The designation would be merely for labelling purposes and to fix chirographically the observer's sum total conception of morphological identity. Thus each individual would be assigned to a type morphologically determined and arbitrarily named. The validity of these types would be determined by the statistical analysis of the measurements, indices, and observations made upon the individuals composing a type group. If a type is real and not imaginary it will show in the assemblage of its physical features a homogeneity and a restricted range of variation which will distinguish it from other types. Such a valid type should differ significantly in a statistical sense from a random sample of the entire series, and even more markedly from a second type similarly demarcated. If it exists it is capable of statistical validation.

After such physical types are established and validated one may proceed to the investigation of their sociological correlations — to the inquiry, for example, as to their distribution in offense groups of criminals.

Successful morphological typing of this kind is not imaginary. It is on the basis of such typing that every layman every day distinguishes a Chinese from an European, and recognizes that persons are twins. The writer has used this method of morphological typing in craniometric and craniological studies with considerable success and his pupils are applying it to the study of living peoples. Of course competent morphological typing requires a great deal of judgment and experience. It is no task for a beginner. Field typing was not carried out by the observers in the present anthropological survey of criminals for a number of reasons. The first of these (and the most important) was that at the time of the beginning of this survey I had not yet reached a full realization of the importance of this method, although I had already employed it successfully with skulls. I was therefore content to employ the older methods and to investigate stock racial combinations and categories of criminals distinguished according to the offenses for which they were committed. The second reason for neglecting subject typing in the field was the doubt in my mind as to the ability of the field workers to employ this method successfully, because of their comparative lack of experience.

The young men who did the field work were carefully trained in each observation and were painstaking and intelligent, but they had not sufficient experience, in my opinion, to develop clear concepts of morphological type. Since 1927 when the work began, certain of my anthropometric methods have been developed far beyond their pre-depression status, and I am now convinced that the neglect of this typing technique has lost whatever chance there may have been of distinguishing individual offense types of criminals as contrasted with group offense differentiation by physical characteristics — which is not typing at all.

As a matter of fact the demonstration that criminals, crudely classified by offense, actually do show significant physical variation, one group from another, raises very strongly the presumption that there may be individual criminal offense types, although they cannot be established adequately by the hit-or-miss process of trying out various arbitrary combinations. But such types cannot be exclusively allotted to any single offense group; they must be distributed among all of the offense groups, but in such a way that the persons committing one or another kind of offense are disproportionately selected from one or more physical types. There can be no physical type, for example, exclusively devoted to arson, and monopolizing that offense. What this all amounts to is that different physical types of men show diverse criminal tendencies, and that fact is implicit in all of our data and our results, in spite of the absence of satisfactory "stigmata" and the rarity of characteristic individual combinations which can be pieced together from arrays of single measurements, indices, and morphological observations.

Chapter XI

METRIC AND INDICIAL DIFFERENTIATION
BETWEEN CRIMINALS AND CIVILIANS
OF SIMILAR PARENTAGE

COMPARISON OF TOTAL PRISON SERIES AND STATE SUBGROUPS WITH THEIR RESPECTIVE CIVILIAN SAMPLES

SINCE it was impracticable to secure check samples of the civilian population in any of the states studied save Massachusetts and Tennessee, we are forced to compare the criminals of nine states with civilians gathered from these two alone. All the comparisons, criminal and civilian, are of native Whites of native parentage. The discovery, at a relatively late stage of the analysis, that the criminals were strongly differentiated into local (state) types, considerably complicates the comparison.

It is obviously necessary to find out what differences obtain between Massachusetts criminals and civilians of the same state and also those between criminals and civilians both native of Tennessee, in order correctly to interpret the differences between all criminals from nine states and the limited civilian check sample.

Table XI–4 details the metric and indicial differences between total criminals and total civilians, between Massachusetts criminals and civilians, and between Tennessee criminals and civilians, respectively. We must first call attention to the correspondence in direction and significance of deviations between the criminals and civilians of Massachusetts and of Tennessee. These are summarized in the right hand column of Table XI–5. Of the 33 measurements and indices considered, the differences are tabulated in 6 classes according to direction and significance. Important agreements are found in 9 features in which both Massachusetts and Tennessee criminals deviate from their respective civilian check samples significantly and in the same direction (Class 2). The important disagreements in which the deviations are in opposite directions, but significant, are found in only 4 features (Class 4). These are: minimum frontal diameter, bigonial diameter, relative shoulder breadth, and zygogonial index. There are only 4 of the 33 characters in which neither of the state criminal groups deviates significantly from the corresponding civilian group (Classes 1 and 3). In 7 features both state criminal groups deviate in the same direction from the civilians, but in one state the deviation is insignificant and the other is significant (Class 5). Deviations in opposite directions, one significant and the other insignificant, occur in 9 cases. In general, the nature and significance of deviations in the two states agree excellently. Important disagreements (Class 4) occur in only 4 of 33 features or 12.12 per cent.

We must next consider the deviations of all criminals from the combined civilian check sample in terms of the classification of state deviations. These are summarized in the first and second columns of Table XI-5. It may be noted that one of the deviations which in the two state samples was classified as "insignificant and in the same direction" is transferred in the total series to a significant deviation. Of the 9 deviations which in the state samples are classified as significant and in the same direction, 7 remain significant in the comparison of the total criminal series with the restricted civilian check sample. Both of the deviations which in the state samples are "insignificant but in different directions" are transferred to the significant column in the total series comparison. Of the 4 important and significant disagreements between the Massachusetts and Tennessee series, none attains significance in the total series comparison. This is as it should be. Five of the 7 deviations in the same direction, of which one only is significant in the state samples, become significant in the total series comparison. Four of 9 deviations in different directions — one significant, the other insignificant — are valid in the total series.

It is evident that the total series comparison with the total check sample agrees excellently with the individual state comparisons. There are, however, a number of differences which are insignificant in the state samples which attain significance in the larger combined series comparison. It would seem a fair assumption that differences between all criminals and all civilians which are substantiated by corresponding differences between the state samples of criminals and civilians of corresponding state origin are valid (cf. Table XI-6). A few additional observations concerning the metric and indicial comparisons of Massachusetts and Tennessee samples are apposite.

In appraising the respective comparisons of Massachusetts and Tennessee state prison samples with their civilian check series, it is important to reach a decision as to which civilian check sample and which state criminal sample best represents the entire series of civilians and criminals. Again, since each state prison sample must be compared with its own check civilian group, it is desirable to inquire whether, on the whole, the Massachusetts or the Tennessee comparison is more reliable as a gauge against which to set the total series comparison of criminals and non-criminals.

At first examination it seemed probable that the Massachusetts comparison was better, because the disparity in mean age between the two samples was only three years, as against nine years in the Tennessee comparison; because the Tennessee criminals were far inferior to their civilian check sample in body weight, since the latter consisted entirely of a single occupational class — Nashville firemen — who of course represent a physical selection. The corpulence of these firemen seemed to make them a less closely comparable check sample for the Tennessee prison series, than the Massachusetts militiamen and Boston hospital out-patients would be for the Massachusetts criminal series. However, Dr. Carl Seltzer, in appraising the results of the two sets of comparisons, detected certain divergences in the Massachusetts comparison from the total series comparison, which he suspected to be due to a difference in racial extraction between Massachusetts criminals and Massachusetts civilians. Consequently we have tabulated the ethnic extractions of the two series of state comparisons, the data of which are presented in Table XI-a.

In the Tennessee comparison the criminals have nearly 90 per cent of Old American extractions, not otherwise specified. On the other hand, the Nashville firemen

nclude only 59 per cent of Old Americans. However, the rest of their group are de-
ived mainly from Irish and English strains, with six per cent of Scotch and a small
lash of German. Since these are, in fact, the very ethnic strains which are also rep-
esented in the Old American criminals, the racial composition of the two Tennessee
amples may be assumed to be virtually identical, or at any rate very closely similar.

When we turn to the Massachusetts comparisons we find much smaller but ap-
roximately equal percentages of each sample described as Old American. The per-
ons of Scotch descent are substantially equal, but the prison series contains 16.80
er cent fewer of English extraction, 6.83 per cent more of Irish, and 10.72 per cent
nore of French or partially French descent. It is this introduction of a strong French
r French Canadian element which disturbs the Massachusetts comparison, in as
nuch as French Canadians carry much heavier Alpine strains than do the inhabitants
f the British isles. The French are much more inclined to brachycephaly, short broad
aces, and other concomitant features of the head and face. On the whole, then, it

TABLE XI–A
MASSACHUSETTS: CIVIL AND CRIMINAL EXTRACTION

	Civil		Criminal	
	Number	Per Cent	Number	Per Cent
Old American	40	23.95	67	22.41
English	42	36.53	55	19.73
German English	2	..	..	..
Indian English	1	..	..	..
Scotch English	6	..	2	..
Irish English	7	..	1	..
Scotch Irish English	2	..	..	..
Dutch English	..	..	1	..
Scotch English German	1	..	..	..
Irish	37	26.95	99	33.78
Irish German	1	..	..	..
Scotch Irish	2	..	2	..
Irish Italian	2	..	..	..
Dutch Irish	1	..	..	..
French Scotch Irish	1	..	..	..
German Irish	1	..	..	..
Scotch	7	4.19	13	4.35
French	1	2.99	41	13.71
French German	2	..	..	..
French Canadian	1	..	..	..
Spanish French	1	..	..	..
German	4	2.40	10	3.34
Swedish	2	1.20	1	.33
Canadian	1	.60	..	..
Spanish	..	..	1	.33
Portuguese	..	..	1	.33
Italian	1	.60	3	1.00
Polish	..	..	1	.33
Jewish	..	..	1	.33
Russian Jew	1	.60	..	..
	167		299	

seems that Dr. Seltzer's suspicions have been confirmed and that the Tennessee comparison is the more reliable, because it does not involve any marked ethnic and racial discrepancy between the criminals and civilians of the same state.

TABLE XI–B

TENNESSEE: CIVIL AND CRIMINAL EXTRACTION

	Civil		Criminal	
	Number	Per Cent	Number	Per Cent
Old American	86	58.90	332	89.97
English	12	14.38	1	.27
English Irish	6	. .	. .	. .
English Scotch Swiss	1	. .	. .	. .
English Scotch Irish	1	. .	. .	. .
Dutch English	1	. .	. .	. .
Irish	15	16.44	18	4.88
Scotch Irish	5	. .	. .	. .
Dutch Irish	3	. .	. .	. .
Irish German	1	. .	. .	. .
Scotch	8	6.16	3	.81
Scotch Welsh	1	. .	. .	. .
French	. .	. .	6	1.63
German	4	3.42	5	1.36
Swiss German	1	. .	. .	. .
Dutch	. .	. .	1	.27
Portuguese	. .	. .	1	.27
Italian	. .	. .	1	.27
Jewish	. .	. .	1	.27
Turkish	1	.68	. .	. .
	146		369	

It is remarkable that both Massachusetts and Tennessee comparisons exhibit the same number of significant deviations — 21 of 33 measurements and indices. However, 9 of the Massachusetts differences which are significant are indicial, as against 4 in the Tennessee comparison. The criminals of the latter state deviate much more strongly from the civilians in gross measurements. It may be noted that both of these state comparisons are taken from the series of Observer A, who was principally responsible also for the data of the check samples.

When we extend our comparison to the total criminal group, we must appraise in each case the deviations of the check samples from the criminals of similar state origin with the purpose of ascertaining how they agree with the total series result.

The total prison group of native Whites of native parentage differs from the check sample of similar origin in 19 of 33 measurements and indices, or 57.58 per cent. In 14 of these metric features the differences exceed four times the probable error; in they exceed three times the probable error. In 14 measurements and indices the differences are less than twice the probable error and hence cannot be considered valid.

The mean difference of the 19 divergent metrical features, in terms of their probable errors, is 6.48.

Out of the 19 significant deviations in the total comparison, 13 state comparison

;ree in direction of deviation; 7 are also significant in the states. In 3 other devia-
ons out of the 19, one state agrees in significance and direction, the other disagrees.
. is interesting to note that when the one state deviation is significant and the other
significant in opposite direction, in only one case is the state deviation significant in
direction opposed to a significant total deviation. (Relative sitting height, cf. Table
I–6.)

AGE

The criminals of our series have a mean age of 30.70 years as against the mean
;e of 34.50 years in the check sample of civilians. The total series and the Mas-
.chusetts and Tennessee comparisons all agree in showing significant deviations in
e same direction. Table XI–7 gives the age groups of the two series by percentages
id by numbers for each five year interval. It will be observed that in the immature
·oup of 15–19 year old individuals there is a slightly higher proportion of criminals
– an excess of only 2.04 per cent. The percentages in the second age group are sub-
antially identical. If we consider persons between the ages of 20 years and 34 years
clusive, young adults, we find that there are 45.05 per cent of such individuals in
ie civil series and 57.07 per cent in the criminals. Taking the ages 35 years to 54
·ars inclusive as the limits of middle age, there are 32.26 per cent in the civil series
id 24.86 per cent in the criminal series. If persons above the age of 54 years be clas-
fied as old, the civil check sample contains 11.18 per cent of old men and the crim-
al series only 4.54 per cent.

On the whole, the disparity of ages between the groups is small, consisting of a
o4 per cent excess of criminal sub-adults, an excess of young adults in the criminals
nounting to 12.02 per cent, an excess of middle-aged among the civilians, amount-
g to 7.40 per cent, an excess of the aged among the civilians, totalling 6.64 per cent.
. all there are 14.04 per cent more of middle-aged and old men in the civil group. As
fecting measurements, the age differences in composition are most important in the
imature and the old, since certain measurements are smaller in both of these groups.
owever, the incompleted growth of the excess of sub-adult criminals is more or less
fset by the shrinkage of age in the larger proportion of elderly persons in the civil
ieck sample. Nevertheless, measurements and observations which are strongly affected
· age factors must be carefully analyzed before differences in them between the civil
id criminal series can be accepted as valid.

Table XI–8 gives the age distribution of our series of native White criminals of
itive parentage observed in 1927–1928; of prisoners irrespective of sex or parent-
·e or nativity present in penal or reformatory institutions of the United States on
.nuary 1, 1923; of all male prisoners received in penal or reformatory institutions
the United States in 1928; of the civilian native White males of native parentage
cluded in our check sample; of the native White males of native parentage in the
·pulation of that origin 15 years or more of age, and finally the percentage of the
.tire population of native White males of native parentage in each age group. The
st two groups of data are excerpts from the preliminary reports of the United States
·nsus of 1930.

First of all, it should be noted that the age distribution of our native White crim-
al series of native parentage corresponds closely to that of all prisoners present in

1923, except that our series includes an excess of criminals in the 15–19 year grou amounting to 5.1 per cent and a deficiency in the 20–24 year group of 3.4 per cent.

The prisoners received in 1928 also agree closely with our group, but include a co siderable excess in the two younger age groups and corresponding deficiencies in t older groups. This is presumably because of the fact that many young criminals r ceive short sentences and thus the mean age of the prisoners committed in any year likely to be less than that of the whole prison population.

The age distribution of our small civilian check sample has already been compar with that of our criminal series. The table includes a comparison of the percenta of native White males of native parentage in the population of 1930, 15 years a more in age, in order to appraise the representative character of the former. The tir check sample agrees fairly well in its distribution by ages with the corresponding pe centages, although, like the criminal series, it shows an excess of individuals in t 20–24 year old group. In fact this check sample is more closely comparable with t criminal series than is the distribution of native Whites of native parentage in the ge eral population.

When our criminal series (or any of the prison statistics) is compared either wi the civilian check sample or with the general population of native White males of n tive parentage, it is at once apparent that the 15–19 year age group furnishes abo its proper quota of criminals and that the 20–24 year group, the 25–29 year grou and the 30–34 year group all yield excesses of criminals, these excesses diminishing the order of the age groups. Beginning with the 35–39 year group, the criminals sho deficiencies in each succeeding age class. Criminal tendencies seem then to rise to maximum and to decline between the ages of 15 and 35 years.

WEIGHT

The average weight of our criminal series is 11.70 pounds less than that of t check sample of civilians. The Massachusetts and Tennessee comparisons agree wi the total series. This deficiency in weight might be argued to depend to some exte upon the younger mean age of the criminals, since weight increases up to middle ag It would be possible to make a prediction of the mean weight of criminals of the san average age as that of the check sample, by utilizing the coefficient of correlation b tween age and weight and the regression formulae derived from that coefficient. Ho ever, it seems to me that such a method involves one in mathematical speculatio which are little better than sheer guesses, especially when the coefficient of correlati utilized is low, as in this case ($r = .13 \pm .01$). A much safer procedure is to sele from the criminal group a sample of the same age as that of the check series and th eliminate the age disparity by actual selection rather than by mathematical jugglin I have therefore selected a subgroup consisting of all criminals between the ages 35 and 39 years, and have compared this subgroup with the weight of the civili check sample, which is in reality slightly lower in mean age. Then to make assuran doubly sure, I have had the constants of weight calculated for all criminals 35 yea of age or older and have again compared the mean with that of the check samp Table XI–9 gives the result of these comparisons. Criminals between the ages of and 39 years are 7.90 pounds lighter than the mean of the check sample of slight younger age — a difference which amounts to 6.08 times its probable error. Similarly, if we take all criminals above the age of 35 years, we still find them averaging 7.40 pounds lighter than the check sample, a difference equal to 6.44 times its probable error. These elder criminal groups are about 4 pounds heavier than the total criminal series, but are still significantly lighter than the check sample, although they ought to be heavier, being older.

It is evident then that the inferiority of weight of the total criminal group when compared with that of the check sample is not due primarily to the younger mean age of the former. The difference is real.

All of the subjects of this survey, criminal and civil, were measured without hat, shoes, coat, or vest, but with other ordinary clothing. In order to reduce these weights to nude weights it is necessary to subtract, on the average, 3 pounds. This leaves us with a mean weight of 147.90 pounds for our total series of 3919 native White criminals of native parentage at a mean age of 30.70 years. The following comparative data from Hrdlička's studies of Old Americans [1] (whose ancestors on each side for two generations were born in the United States) are apposite.

TABLE XI–10

WEIGHT (NUDE) OF CRIMINAL SERIES COMPARED WITH WEIGHT (NUDE) OF CIVILIAN GROUPS OF SIMILAR ORIGIN

	Authority	Number	Age	Weight
Criminals	This study	3919	30.70	147.90
Criminals (by age groups)				
(1)	This study	374	35–39	151.7
(2)	This study	1104	above 35	152.20
Civilians	This study	312	34.50	159.60
Old Americans (Laboratory series)	Hrdlička	232	37.2	150.3
Old Americans (by age groups)				
(1)	Hrdlička	83	24–29	146.6
(2)	Hrdlička	62	30–39	158.6
(3)	Hrdlička	42	40–49	156.5
(4)	Hrdlička	32	50–59	159.8
(5)	Hrdlička	10	above 59	169.6

Such a comparison brings out very clearly the inferiority in weight of our series of native born criminals of native parentage when compared with the civil check sample of similar origin and with Hrdlička's series of Old Americans. Our civilian check sample is heavier than Hrdlička's series, and is possibly unrepresentatively heavy, because of the inclusion therein of some 140 Nashville, Tennessee, firemen. Firemen are likely to be stout. On the other hand, the check sample also includes 85 persons who were out-patients at the Massachusetts General Hospital in Boston, some of whom may have been underweight on account of ill-health.

I think that there is no escaping the conclusion that this series of criminals is inferior in weight, when compared with samples of similar ethnic origin and of approximately the same age composition, drawn from the civil population.

[1] A. Hrdlička, *Old Americans*, Baltimore, 1925, p. 102.

STATURE

The stature or bodily height of the total criminal series of native Whites of native parentage falls below that of the check sample by 1.02 centimeters, a difference equal to 4.25 times its probable error, and of certain significance. All three comparisons — total series, Massachusetts, and Tennessee — agree in direction of deviations from the civilian sample, but the Tennessee deviation is not statistically significant. The correlation of stature with age in this series is insignificant ($r = -.03 \pm .01$) and consequently no attempt has been made to introduce any correction for age. As a matter of fact, the more youthful composition of the criminal series, as compared with the check sample, should militate in favor of an increased stature of the criminals, since it is well known that the stature of the younger generations in this country is increasing. Other comparative data may be adduced to reinforce the conclusion that criminals are inferior to civilians in stature, so far as this particular series, classified by nativity and parentage, is concerned. (Table XI–11.)

For this purpose the data of Hrdlička[2] pertaining to Old Americans have been utilized, and also certain statistics relating to White soldiers of the Civil War.[3] The anthropometric material collected during the World War[4] unfortunately mixes up Negroes and Whites from the various sections and also gives little or no indication of nativity. However, the material from the mountainous area of Kentucky contains 96.4 per cent of native Whites of native parentage, and only 2.5 per cent of Negroes and may be utilized with caution.

OTHER MEASUREMENTS AND INDICES

Biacromial Diameter. The biacromial diameter or shoulder breadth of the present criminal series falls below that of the civilian check sample by .45 centimeters or 5.00 times the probable error of the difference. All three comparisons agree in the direction of their deviations, but the Massachusetts divergence is insignificant. Since this measurement may be assumed to increase somewhat during maturity, on account of added weight, two subgroups of the criminals have been reseriated and the constants recalculated. The results are shown in Table XI–12. The group of individuals in the criminal series between the ages of 35 and 39 years, within which or very close to which falls the mean age of the check sample, shows a deficiency of .33 centimeters in this dimension as compared with the check sample. Since this difference is only 2.75 times the probable error, it may not be significant. However, when all of the criminals at the age of 35 years or more are included in a second regrouping, their average biacromial diameter falls .51 centimeters below that of the check sample. This difference is 5.10 times the probable error and in its absolute value and significance in terms of the probable error is essentially the same as that shown when the whole series is compared with the check sample. There is then no reason for attributing the narrow shoulders of our criminal group to the inclusion therein of a large number of young males. As a matter of fact the correlation of age with biacromial diameter ($r = -.02 \pm .01$) is insignificant.

---

[2] Hrdlička, 1925, pp. 77, 80.

[3] B. A. Gould, *Investigations in the Military and Anthropological Statistics of American Soldiers*, New York, 1869, p. 123.

[4] C. B. Davenport and A. G. Love, *Army Anthropology*, Washington, 1921, p. 101.

Chest Depth. The chest depth of the total criminal series of native Whites of native parentage is .66 centimeters less than that of the check sample (8.25 p.e.). All three comparisons agree in the direction of their deviation, but the Massachusetts difference is again insignificant. Since it may be argued that this general deficiency is due to the younger mean age of the criminals, the same procedure has been adopted as in other measurements presumably affected by age. The 35–39 year old group, consisting of 403 persons, falls below the mean of he check sample by only 30 centimeters (Table XI–13), a difference which is still significant. However, the criminals of 35 years of age and upward, 1237 in number, actually exceed by .10 centimeters the mean of the check sample. Hence we cannot be sure that the difference between the entire series and that of the check sample is anything more than an effect of age composition. However, if age were the decisive factor, we might expect the criminals of 35 years and upward actually significantly to exceed the mean of the chest depth of the civil sample. This is not the case, since the excess of our older group of criminals is only 1.11 times the probable error. Here we may perhaps reach a decision by having recourse to comparative data outside of the present study.

TABLE XI–14

CHEST DEPTH OF CRIMINAL SERIES COMPARED WITH CHEST DEPTH OF CIVILIAN GROUPS OF SIMILAR ORIGIN

	Authority	Number	Age	Mean
Criminals	This study	4,185	30.70	21.04
Civilians	This study	313	34.50	21.70
Old Americans: laboratory series	Hrdlička	246	37.2 (?)	21.70
Youngest	Hrdlička	25	. . .	20.61
Oldest	Hrdlička	25	. . .	23.03
World War soldiers (native Whites of native parentage)	Davenport and Love	96,583	24.89(?)	21.58

In the above table it may be noted that Hrdlička's [5] entire series of Old Americans, although somewhat older than our civilian check sample, has the same mean chest depth. The youngest 25 of that series have smaller mean chest depth than that of our criminal series, and the 25 oldest have a larger mean. The great group of White soldiers of the World War, irrespective of parentage, have an antero-posterior chest diameter which averages more than .50 centimeters greater than our criminal group.[6] It seems probable that the deficiency in this diameter displayed by our criminals is not due to age, especially when we consider that a significant inferiority still shown by the group which, since it includes persons from 35 to 39 years of age, slightly exceeds in mean age the sample of civilians.

Chest Breadth. The criminals are inferior to the civil check sample mean by .69 centimeters, which is 7.67 times the probable error and therefore significant. All three comparisons agree in direction and significance. Using the method of eliminating age differences previously employed, we find (Table XI–15) that the 35–39

[5] Hrdlička, 1925, p. 307.
[6] Davenport and Love, 1921, p. 514.

year group of criminals, 402 in number, shows a deficiency of .48 centimeters (4.3
p.e.) and the 35–69 group (1235 in number) presents exactly the same deficiency
which in this case equals 4.80 times the probable error. Therefore, apart from age
the chest breadth of the criminals is inferior to that of the civilians.

Hrdlička's [7] series of Old Americans, 246 in number, yields an average lateral di
ameter of 29.76 centimeters, which considerably exceeds both that of our crimina
group (27.48 centimeters) and that of our civil group (28.17 centimeters). Th
mean transverse diameter of chest of 96,583 World War veterans at demobilizatio
was 29.02 centimeters.[8] These large excesses probably indicate some difference i
technique of measurement.

Sitting Height. The sitting height of the total criminal series is insignificantly les
than that of the total civilian check sample (deficiency, −.21 centimeters, 1.50 p.e.)
Yet the Massachusetts and Tennessee criminals are both significantly inferior in thi
measurement to the civilians of their own states (Massachusetts deficiency, −1.3
centimeters, 6.14 p.e.; Tennessee deficiency, −.99 centimeters, 4.95 p.e.). It is pos
sible then that an inclusion in the check sample of adequate proportions of civilian
from the states not represented and which are represented in the criminal serie
might show a general and significant deficiency in this measurement also, on the par
of criminals. Sitting heights of criminals from the states not represented in the chec
sample are evidently greater than those of criminals in Massachusetts and Tennesse

Head Length. This measurement also shows an insignificant deficiency of the tota
criminals from the total check sample (−.42 millimeters, 1.62 p.e.) but again bot
of the state comparisons reveal large and significant deviations on the part of the crim
inals when compared with their own state check samples (Massachusetts: deficienc
−2.22, 5.04 p.e.; Tennessee, deficiency −1.83 millimeters, 4.58 p.e.). Evidently th
Massachusetts and Tennessee deficiencies are compensated by the larger head length
of criminals from the other states. Again the question arises as to the difference
which might obtain between our total criminal series and an adequately distribute
check sample.

Head Breadth. The mean head breadth of the criminal series falls below that c
the check sample by .81 millimeters or 4.05 times the probable error of the difference
The Massachusetts and Tennessee comparisons are not in accord. Tennessee agree
with the total series comparison in showing a significant deficiency on the part of th
criminals (−2.08 millimeters, 6.18 p.e.). Massachusetts criminals show an insignif
cant excess over their state civilians, probably because of the higher percentage c
French elements in the criminal series.

The correlation of head breadth with age is .08 ± .01, which is insignifican
Nevertheless, the head breadths have been recalculated for the 35–39 year old grou
of criminals, and also for all criminals 35 years of age or above. Table XI–1
shows the results of this process. In the 35–39 year old group the deficiency is onl
.15 millimeters and in the 35–69 group it is .24 millimeters. Thus, while the olde
criminals still show smaller head breadth than the check sample, the differences ar
very small and are insignificant when viewed in terms of their probable errors. W
must conclude, then, that the deficiency in head breadth displayed by our crimina

[7] Hrdlička, 1925, p. 307.
[8] Davenport and Love, 1921, p. 514.

is attributable to the age composition of the group, which contains a larger percentage of younger individuals than does the check sample.

However, the following comparative data indicate that both our criminal series and our civil check sample fall below Hrdlička's series of Old American males, so far as the Laboratory and Virginia series are concerned. But Hrdlička's Tennessee Highlanders are inferior in head breadth, both to our criminals and to our civilians. Hrdlička very tentatively suggests that their inferior head breadth may be connected with "their backwardness in that part of the brain and head development which is due to modern education and stresses." [9]

TABLE XI–17

HEAD BREADTH OF CRIMINAL SERIES COMPARED WITH HEAD BREADTH OF CIVILIAN GROUPS OF
SIMILAR ORIGIN

	Authority	Number	Age	Mean
Criminals	This study	4208	15–79	152.14
Civilians	This study	313	15–74	152.95
Old Americans				
Laboratory and Virginia	Hrdlička	594	22–	154.5
Eastern Tennessee	Hrdlička	133	20–39	151.0

Head Height. The mean head height of the civilian check sample of 312 persons, measured with a Western Reserve head-spanner, is 133.50. The head height of 2857 native born American criminals of native parentage, measured by the same technique, is 132.66. The difference .84 is equal to 3.50 times its probable error and is therefore significant. Here there is no necessity of correcting for age differences ($r = -.04 \pm .01$). But neither the Massachusetts nor the Tennessee comparison shows a significant deviation from its check sample. Therefore the deficiency is one of the balance of the criminal series compared with the bi-state check sample.

Head height is such an unreliable measurement and differs so greatly according to the technique used and the personal equation of the observer, that I do not consider it worth while to adduce any comparative data outside of the present survey. Our results seem to justify nothing more than the conclusion that Wisconsin, North Carolina, Kentucky, Texas and other Southwestern criminals have lower heads than civilians drawn from Massachusetts and Tennessee.

Head Circumference. In this dimension our criminals average 6.60 millimeters less than the mean of the civilians, a difference equal to 9.17 times the probable error. All three comparisons agree in the direction and significance of the deviations. Applying the usual method of age correction, by calculating the means for the two older age groups (Table XI–18), we find that the 35–39 year group still falls below the mean of the check sample by 5.40 millimeters (5.93 p.e.) and the 35–69 group is deficient to the extent of 5.76 millimeters (7.38 p.e.). The criminals' inferior head circumference cannot then be ascribed to their more tender age.

Hrdlička does not deal with this measurement in his study of Old Americans.

Minimum Frontal Diameter. The total criminals show an insignificantly larger

[9] Hrdlička, 1925, p. 141.

mean than the civilians of the check sample (excess .28 millimeters, 1.22 p.e.). The two state comparisons are in complete and significant disagreement, since the Massachusetts criminals exceed their civilian check sample by 2.28 millimeters (7.35 p.e.) and the Tennessee criminals fall below the firemen by 1.88 millimeters (5.88 p.e.). I am inclined to attribute the excess of minimum frontal diameter of the Massachusetts criminals over the Massachusetts civilians to the overbalancing effect of brachycephalic French Canadians in the former group. This is one of four significant disagreements between the state comparisons and it leads to an insignificant total series deviation. The measurement was one in which both observers seemed to fall into an error (Chapter I, page 39). The Tennessee firemen show an unduly high mean (114.94 ± .27). I think that we must dismiss the measurement as of dubious reliability.

Bizygomatic Diameter. The total criminals do not differ significantly from the check sample (deficiency −.50 millimeters, 2.08 p.e.). Massachusetts criminals show a slight excess (.05 millimeters, .14 p.e.) and Tennessee criminals a significant deficiency (−2.35 millimeters, 7.12 p.e.). On the one hand we have a possible excess of stockily built French Canadians in the Massachusetts criminal sample, not found in the civilian check series. On the other hand the Tennessee firemen are perhaps broader in the face than an unselected civilian group would be.

Total Face Height. In total face height (nasion-menton) the criminal group falls below the civil group to the extent of 1.50 millimeters (5.56 p.e.). No attempt has been made to introduce any correction for age disparity. Face height increases up to maturity and after maturity decreases. Since the check sample has about the same proportion of very young adults and immature individuals as the criminal series, and a considerably higher proportion of individuals who have passed middle age, any age difference ought to make for a slight inferiority of facial height in the civilians. However, the reverse is the case. The deficiency of the criminals in facial height is not attributable to age.

Both the Tennessee and the Massachusetts comparisons agree in the direction of their deviations with the total series. But in neither of the comparisons does the deficiency reach significance. The deficiency in the total series is greater than in either of the state comparisons and significant. This means that the extra states represented in the criminal series depress the total facial height and make significant deficiencies which are too small to be reliable in the strictly state comparisons. It leaves us with a probability but not a certainty that native White criminals of native parentage have shorter faces than civilians of similar origin.

A comparison of our groups with Hrdlička's [10] Old Americans indicates a superiority of facial height in both our criminal and civilian series over his total series. However, two of his subgroups, consisting of drafted "Engineers," show means somewhat exceeding those of our check sample. The facial heights of the "Laboratory" group seem inordinately small.

Upper Face Height. The upper facial height (nasion-prosthion) of criminals falls below that of the civilian check sample by .70 millimeters, a difference in the means which is equal to 3.68 times its probable error, and is therefore significant. This difference is in agreement with that found in the case of total facial height, although

---

[10] Hrdlička, 1925, pp. 201, 205.

less marked. To some extent this deficiency might be attributed to the younger mean age of the criminals. However, since the excess of age in the check sample is largely found in the middle and old age group, in which reduction of facial height is likely to occur through wear and loss of teeth, it is probable that the younger mean age of the

TABLE XI–19

TOTAL FACE HEIGHT OF CRIMINAL SERIES COMPARED WITH TOTAL FACE HEIGHT
OF CIVILIAN GROUPS OF SIMILAR ORIGIN

	Authority	Number	Age	Mean
Criminals	This study	4209	15–79	121.60
Civilians	This study	313	15–74	123.10
Old Americans				
Total series	Hrdlička	726	. . .	121.15
Laboratory series	Hrdlička	247	. . .	119.25
Drafted "Engineers," southern states	Hrdlička	256	. . .	123.9
Drafted "Engineers," other states	Hrdlička	91	. . .	123.6
Tennessee Highlanders	Hrdlička	132	. . .	120.4

criminals makes, on the average, for increased, rather than decreased, total facial and upper facial height.

Both Massachusetts and Tennessee comparisons agree with the total series in direction of deviation and in significance. Curiously both show even larger and more clearly significant deficiencies (Massachusetts − 1.50 millimeters, 5.00 p.e.; Tennessee − 1.15 millimeters, 4.11 p.e.). Under these circumstances the total series deviation seems valid and the results of upper facial height confirm the shaky conclusions as to the inferiority of the criminals in total facial height.

Nose Height. In the mean of this measurement the criminals are deficient to the extent of 1.84 millimeters when compared with the civil check sample. The difference equals 9.20 times the probable error. Both state comparisons agree with the total series and show even larger deficiencies. Since this measurement increases with age and is correlated with it ($r = .26 \pm .01$), it is necessary to select from the total criminal series subgroups comparable in age with, or older than the civilian sample. The results appear in Table XI–20. In the 35–39 year group of criminals, 407 in number, nose height is still deficient to the extent of .88 millimeters or 4.19 p.e. In the residual group, including all criminals above 35 years of age, the deficiency is .75 millimeters or 4.17 p.e. Hence, apart from age, the criminals have shorter noses than the civilians.

The mean of nasal height in our total series of native White criminals of native parentage is 52.26 millimeters, whereas that of the check sample of civilians is 54.10 millimeters. Hrdlička's [11] Laboratory series of 247 Old Americans has a mean nasal height of 53.5 millimeters. The deficiency of our criminals in this measurement is again exemplified by comparison with the material of Old American Ancestry.

Nose Breadth. The mean of criminal nose breadth is exactly the same as that of the civilian sample. Massachusetts criminals have insignificantly broader noses than civilians (.45 millimeters, 2.65 p.e.) but Tennessee criminals have significantly nar-

[11] Hrdlička, 1925, p. 259.

rower noses than the plump and sedentary fire-fighters (deficiency −.84 millimeters, 6.00 p.e.). Since the firemen have a mean of 36.14 millimeters ±.12, as against 33.56 millimeters ±.15 in Massachusetts civilians, one may suspect that the stalemate is due to the unrepresentatively high mean of the firemen, and that criminals may in fact have wider noses than civilians of similar origin. However, we must not rely upon such suspicions.

Bigonial Diameter. The total prison series shows virtually no difference from the mean of the check sample (−.04 millimeters, .15 p.e.). Actually this deadlock is due to a radical disagreement between the state comparisons, since the Massachusetts felons significantly exceed the citizens of that state (excess 1.40 millimeters, 4.00 p.e.), whereas the Tennessee criminals are far below the big-jowled firemen (deficiency −3.16 millimeters, 8.54 p.e.). The latter public servants present the astounding bigonial mean of 111.46 millimeters ±.32, as compared with the modest figure of 104.66 millimeters ±.28 in the case of the Massachusetts civilians. They unduly elevate the mean of the check sample. On the other hand, it is almost certain that the Massachusetts criminal mean is also unrepresentatively enhanced by the broad faces of the delinquent French Canadians, an element deficient in the civilian check sample. I am inclined therefore to conjecture that a general criminal deficiency in this measurement as compared with civilian means might be demonstrated if the total criminal and civilian series were not weighted by the disparate factors of the two state comparisons.

Ear Length. Observer A's data show a deficiency in ear length of the criminal group when compared to the civilians, amounting to 2.40 millimeters or 12.63 p.e., Massachusetts and Tennessee agreeing. Since this measurement increases largely with age, the usual process of re-seriating selected age groups of the criminals has been carried out (Table XI–21). The 35–39 year old criminal group, 272 in number, shows a deficiency of 1.60 millimeters or 6.15 p.e. Thus the most comparable criminal age group still exhibits a significantly lower mean of ear length than is found in the civilians. The 35 year and upward age group shows only .24 millimeters deficiency or 1.14 p.e. However, this group is, on the average, far older than the civil check sample and cannot be expected to maintain the significant deficiency of the more comparable age groups.

Hrdlička's [12] Laboratory series of Old Americans, 247 in number, shows a mean left ear length of 66.9 millimeters, as compared with 64.06 in our civil sample and 61.66 in Observer A's criminal series of 2854 subjects. However, the mean age of the Laboratory subjects measured by Hrdlička is 42.5 years, as against 34.5 years in our civil sample and 30.7 years in our criminal sample. But a group of Tennessee Highlanders, 100 in number, measured by Hrdlička, and averaging 25.1 years, shows a mean left ear length of 64.2 millimeters. But these Highlanders are much taller than either of our groups, as are also the Laboratory series. Altogether it seems certain that our criminals have unusually short ears when compared with civilians, if due allowance is made for age and statural differences. Hrdlička found that length of the ear increases steadily with years and 12 individuals above 59 years of age average 71.3 millimeters.

Ear Breadth. This measurement increases also in middle life and old age. In Ob-

[12] Hrdlička, 1925, p. 290.

server A's series the criminals fall below the mean of the check sample by 0.39 millimeters, but the difference is only 2.79 times the probable error. Tennessee criminals have a significantly lower mean than Tennessee civilians, but Massachusetts criminals insignificantly exceed their check sample.

When the 35–39 year old group is considered by itself, it is found that the deficiency amounts to only .21 millimeters or 1.24 times the probable error. When all of the criminals 35 years old or more are considered as a group they exceed the mean ear breadth of the check sample by .27 millimeters or 1.93 times the probable error of the difference. While this excess is not statistically significant, it would seem to lead to the conclusion that the deficiency in ear breadth in our criminal series is due to the younger mean age of the criminal group, when compared with the check sample, rather than to any criminological factors.

In the above discussion the ear breadths of Observer A only have been considered, owing to the fact that the two observers varied slightly in their technique of taking ear breadth. Since the greater part of the check sample was measured by Observer A, it seemed necessary to consider his results primarily in the comparison. The differences in technique are explained on pages 40 and 41. As a matter of fact, Observer B's technique is preferable. His mean of ear breadth falls below that of Observer A by 1.74 millimeters. In the following comparative table, the results of both observers are compared with the Old American material gathered by Hrdlička.[13]

TABLE XI–23

EAR BREADTH OF CRIMINAL SERIES COMPARED WITH EAR BREADTH OF CIVILIAN GROUPS OF SIMILAR ORIGIN

	Authority	Number	Age	Mean
Criminals (Observer A)	This study	2854	30.70	37.77
Criminals (Observer A), by age group	This study	274	35–39	37.95
Criminals (Observer B)	This study	1348	30.70	36.02
Civilians	This study	310	34.50	38.16
Old Americans				
Laboratory series	Hrdlička	247	42.5	37.9
Laboratory series, by age group	Hrdlička	63	30–39	37.9
Tennessee Highlanders	Hrdlička	100	25.1	36.5

Relative Shoulder Breadth. The criminals in Massachusetts significantly exceed their civilian check sample (excess .52, 5.20 p.e.), but the Tennessee criminals are equally deficient when compared with the firemen (deficiency −.54, 5.40 p.e.). This disagreement is reflected in the total series which shows no significant difference between criminals and civilians.

Relative Sitting Height. Relative sitting height is an expression of sitting height as a percentage of stature. This index tends to be higher in shorter peoples, all other things being equal. Our criminals exceed the civilian population as represented by our sample by .22 index units on the average (3.67 p.e.). This is a significant, but rather small difference. The Massachusetts comparison agrees with the total series,

[13] Hrdlička, 1925, pp. 291–95.

although in the state groups the excess is insignificant. The Tennessee criminals, however, are significantly lower than their civilian check sample of Nashville firemen. Hrdlička's researches on Old Americans tend to show that relative sitting height decreases with stature and increases with age. Since our criminals are somewhat shorter and somewhat younger than the civilian population, one may suppose that their lower stature would tend to give them a slight superiority in sitting height relative to stature and their lower average age would tend to make their relative sitting height somewhat less than that of the civilians. Perhaps these differences offset each other. In any event, I am not disposed to attribute any very great significance to the slight difference here demonstrated in the means.

It is to be noted, further, that corpulence increases sitting height relative to stature, since the fat person when sitting has a thicker pad of flesh and integument between his ischial tuberosities and the seat. In view of the excess weight of the Tennessee firemen, it is possible that Tennessee inferiority in the criminals is partially attributable to this cause.

TABLE XI–24

RELATIVE SITTING HEIGHT OF CRIMINAL SERIES COMPARED WITH RELATIVE SITTING HEIGHT OF CIVILIAN GROUPS OF SIMILAR ORIGIN

	Authority	Number	Age	Mean
Criminals	This study	4,174	30.75	52.52
Civilians	This study	311	34.50	52.30
Old Americans				
Laboratory series	Hrdlička [a]	247	42.5	52.94
Tennessee series	Hrdlička [a]	133	25.1	52.97
Army Camp, Virginia	Hrdlička and Bean [b]	347	. . .	52.30
World War soldiers	Bean [b]	2,066	. . .	52.4
World War soldiers	Davenport and Love [c]	96,239	. . .	52.56

[a] Hrdlička, 1925, p. 118.
[b] Quoted from Hrdlička, 1925, p. 118.
[c] Davenport and Love, 1921, p. 193.

It is clear from the comparative data cited that the small difference in this index between our civil and criminal groups is of no great importance. Both fall well within the range of other American series.

Cephalic Index. The total criminal series presents an insignificant minus deviation from the total civilians, Tennessee conforming. However, the Massachusetts convicts are significantly rounder-headed than their civilian check series (excess 1.02, 4.64 p.e.) Thus again the cephalic index — that hoary-headed anthropological fraud — belies its ancient reputation for reliability. Of course, in Tennessee, prisoners of largely rural origin are compared with city firemen, whereas in Massachusetts both series are mainly urban. Since the rounder heads of the Massachusetts criminals are probably attributable to their excess of French Canadians, the general criminal deviation toward long-headedness, shown in the total series, and in Tennessee, is the more reliable.

Cephalo-facial Index. This index shows insignificant deviations of criminals from civilians in all of the comparisons.

Length-Height Index. The Massachusetts criminals significantly exceed the Massachusetts civilians in this index (excess .93, 4.23 p.e.) and the Tennessee criminals insignificantly exceed the firemen (excess .57, 2.85 p.e.). However, the total series comparison shows a small deficiency of the total criminals (−.09, .69 p.e.).

Breadth-Height Index. All three comparisons agree in direction, but only the Tennessee excess is significant (.78, 3.54 p.e.).

Facial Index. The facial index of the criminals is lower than that of the civilians by .76 index units. This difference is principally due to states other than Massachusetts and Tennessee, since the criminals of those states do not deviate significantly from their check samples. The total series reflects the extent to which the faces of criminals are shorter relative to their breadth than are the faces of the combined civilian series. The difference amounts to 3.45 times the probable error. This difference is principally due to the shortening of the criminal face. The bizygomatic diameter of the criminal face is only .50 millimeters less than that of civilians, and this difference may be due to the sampling process since it amounts to only 2.08 times the probable error.

The drafted Engineers of Hrdlička's [14] Old American series agree well with our civilian sample and similarly exceed the mean of our criminal group (Table XI–25). His Laboratory series, however, partly on account of greater mean age, but also irrespective of age, shows a lower mean than our criminal sample, because of the quite extraordinarily short facial heights. It is clear that, in spite of their falling below the mean of the civilian check sample, our criminals are by no means outside of the range of the means of other American groups.

In order to test the possible dependence upon age of the differences in facial index apparently disclosed between the criminal group and the check sample, the means of the former have been recalculated by age groups consisting of a subadult group 15–19 years of age, a young adult group 20–34 years of age, and a middle-aged and old-adult group aged between 35 and 69 years. The results are shown in Table XI–26. The index rises from subadult years to young manhood by a mean increment of .44 index units and drops off again in the oldest group by .92 units. Evidently the change due to old age shortening of the face is greater than that brought about by the lengthening of the face from subadult years to maturity. All of these criminal groups fall below the mean of the facial index of the civilian sample, but the 20–34 year old group averages only .44 index units below the civilian mean. However, since the average age of the civilians is 34.5 years and the civilian series includes 43.44 per cent of persons aged more than 35 years, as against 29.40 per cent of such persons in the criminal sample, it is abundantly evident that the age differences in the series ought to make for a higher index in the criminals, whereas the reverse is actually the case. Therefore the inferiority in facial index in the criminals is not due to disparity in age.

Upper Facial Index. The Massachusetts criminals show a significant deficiency (−1.08, 4.15 p.e.). The Tennessee comparison shows an insignificant excess (.09, 0.43 p.e.). In the total series, the criminals display a deficiency which fails to be significant.

Table XI–27 shows the regression of the upper facial index upon age.

Nasal Index. The mean of the nasal index in the criminal series exceeds that of

[14] Hrdlička, 1925, p. 211.

the civil group by 1.96 units, or 7.26 times the probable error of the difference. All three comparisons agree in the direction of their deviations, but the Tennessee difference is insignificant. This higher nasal index on the part of the criminals is due to their shorter noses, as there is no difference in nasal breadths between the two groups. Since it has already been demonstrated that the shortness of the criminal nose cannot be attributed to age, it is clear that this indicial difference is independent also of age influences. Generally speaking we regard a high nasal index or a tendency toward platyrrhiny as a more primitive condition than the narrow-nosed or leptorrhine state.

The mean nasal index of 4199 native White criminals of native parentage is 66.62; that of 313 civilians of similar antecedents is 64.66. Hrdlička's [15] series of 610 Old Americans has a mean nasal index of 65.6. There is considerable variation in his subgroups, the Laboratory group of 247 individuals averaging 67.45, as against 64.40 in a series of 347 Southern "Engineers." This difference may be partially due to age, since the nasal index tends to increase slightly with old age. Other factors entering into the matter are stature and face height. In the case of our criminals, their younger mean age as compared with the check sample should possibly militate in favor of a lower nasal index, but it does not.

Ear Index. The ear index of Observer A's data is most closely comparable to that of the check sample of civilians. It exceeds the latter by 1.88 index units, a difference which is 8.95 times its probable error. It seems clear that our criminals have relatively shorter and broader ears than the comparable civilians. The Massachusetts comparison agrees with the total series, but the Tennessee criminals do not differ significantly from their check sample.

Since ears become longer in middle and old age, the ear index might be expected to decrease with years and the differences between our civil and criminal groups might be attributed to the older mean age of civilians. Table XI–28 re-seriates the ear index of Observer A, dividing the data into three age groups. Observer A's material shows a slight decrease of the index with age. All of the criminal age groups show higher mean indices than that of the civil check sample. The difference in the ear index between civilians and criminals is then not attributable to their disparity in age.

Zygo-frontal Index. This index expresses the breadth of the forehead relative to that of the face, measured across the zygomatic arches. Now a relatively broad forehead in respect to face and jaws may mean nothing more than inferior facial and masticatory development. In other words, it may suggest arrest of facial growth or degeneration. I have no idea why criminals should have absolutely broader foreheads than civilians, unless their superiority is due to wider separation of the temporal muscle crests in persons with feeble temporal musculature. There is, of course, the possibility of a specious difference due to personal equation. Our criminals exceed the civilians by .48 index units which is 3.43 times the probable error. The difference is due both to a greater frontal breadth of the criminals and a diminished bizygomatic diameter.

In this index the Massachusetts comparison agrees in direction and significance with the total series, but the Tennessee criminals do not differ from their civilian check sample.

Fronto-parietal Index. The fronto-parietal index in the criminal series exceeds that of the civilian check sample by .69 index units, or 5.31 times the probable error

[15] Hrdlička, 1925, p. 254.

of the difference. Massachusetts agrees with the total series and exaggerates the difference, but Tennessee deviates insignificantly in the opposite direction. This means that the breadth of the forehead in criminals relative to the maximum breadth of the head across the parietal bones is greater in the delinquents. Specifically this excess in the criminals is due to an insignificantly broader minimum frontal diameter, and a significantly narrower maximum breadth of head.

As I have stated above (p. 39), our field observers, in taking the minimum frontal diameter, slipped into the common error of allowing the points of the spreading calipers to rest in the hollows of the temples slightly lateral to, and posterior to, the points of closest approximation of the temporal crests. Consequently they included in this measurement the thickness of the temporal muscle at these points and the dimensions are too high. Our minimum frontal diameters are not minimum diameters, but merely frontal breadths posterior to, and at the level of, the closest approximation of the temporal crests. This vitiates the fronto-parietal index for any purpose except a comparison between the civil and criminal groups, since the dimension as given here is about 5 millimeters too great. Nevertheless, the difference between the civil and the criminal groups remains to be explained.

This difference might be attributed to the disparity in ages between the groups, since there is a very slight increase of head breadth with age ($r = .08 \pm .01$). Table XI–29 divides the criminals into three age groups and gives the means and other constants of fronto-parietal index for each group. There is a slight decrease of the index with age, but every age group, even the oldest, exceeds the mean of the civilian sample. Hence the differences are not due to the inclusion of more elderly individuals in the check sample, since the 35–69 year old criminal age group which must average nearly 44 years of age, as against 34.5, the mean age of the check sample, still exceeds the mean fronto-parietal index of the civilians.

Zygo-gonial Index. In this index Massachusetts shows a significant excess over its civilian check sample (.90, 3.75 p.e.) and Tennessee a significant deficiency (−.99, 4.12 p.e.). In the total series the difference between criminals and civilians is nil. Taking into consideration the general inferiority of criminal development when compared with ethnically similar civilians, it might be expected that the former would fall below the latter in breadth of jaws relative to breadth of face. In the Tennessee comparison that expectation is realized. In Massachusetts, however, the brachycephalic French element in the criminal sample, almost lacking in the civilian series, is responsible, probably, for the criminal excess of zygo-gonial index. This conclusion would follow from the fact that round heads usually have relatively shorter and broader faces and higher zygo-gonial indices.

SUMMARY OF MEASUREMENTS AND INDICES

The criminals average 3.80 years younger than the check sample of civilians, the disparity occurring principally in the young adult group where there is an excess of criminals, and in the middle-aged and old adult groups which contain excesses of civilians. The difference in ages is not the result of the sampling process, but is rather an expression of the fact that antisocial tendencies manifest themselves most pronouncedly in adolescent and early adult years. Whether the smaller proportion of middle-aged and old men among criminals is due to a decrease of criminal proclivity with age or to a shortened life span among criminals cannot be inferred from our data. The age differences between our criminals and civilians necessitate a careful scrutinizing of physical differences which may depend upon such disparity.

Criminals are markedly below the civilians in body weight, even when due allowance is made for age differences. They are similarly inferior in weight to Old Americans. The deficiency cannot reasonably be attributed to prison diet and hygiene, since these conditions are in all probability superior to those enjoyed by persons of the same prevailingly low economic and social status in the civilian population. The stature of criminals is also inferior to that of civilian native Whites of native parentage and to that of Old Americans. In this case the younger average age of criminals should effect a superiority in their mean stature, since stature is steadily increasing in the younger generations of Americans.

In biacromial breadth (shoulder breadth), chest depth, and chest breadth, the criminals are significantly inferior to the civilians, even when due allowance is made for differences of age between the two samples.

A deficiency in head breadth of the criminals when compared with the civilians is probably due to the larger number of young men in the former series, but a similar deficiency in head circumference is independent of age differences. The total facial height of the criminals is significantly lower than that of the civilian check sample, but both criminals and civilians of our study exceed the mean of the Old Americans measured by Hrdlička. One of the most notable deficiencies of the criminal group is in nose height, and it is displayed in all of the age groups. In this measurement the criminals fall below both our civilian check sample and Hrdlička's Old Americans. Our criminals also have shorter ears than the civilians, irrespective of the differences due to age. The breadth of the nose in criminals, relative to its height, is decidedly greater than in the comparable civilians, and their ears are broader relative to their length. In the fronto-parietal index (breadth of forehead expressed as a percentage of maximum head breadth), the criminals diverge in having means significantly superior to those of civilians. This difference seems to be independent of age.

Head height, upper facial height, and facial index are also lower in the criminals than in the civilians. The last implies faces shorter relative to their breadth. However, Hrdlička's Old Americans fall within the range of our criminal group in this index. Sitting height relative to stature is somewhat greater in the criminals than in the civilians. The difference, although statistically significant, is not great. Finally in the zygo-frontal index (breadth of forehead relative to facial breadth), the criminals exceed the civilians.

In the comparisons of Massachusetts criminals with Massachusetts civilians and of Tennessee criminals with Tennessee firemen, it seems probable that the Tennessee series affords the more reliable results in spite of the highly selected character of the Nashville firemen. For the Massachusetts criminal series includes a brachycephalic French element almost absent from the civilian series, thus creating an ethnic disparity which skews differences in the Massachusetts comparison in a direction opposite to that generally prevalent in the total series comparisons. This Massachusetts distortion especially affects head and face indices, although it is also evident in some of the bodily proportions such as relative shoulder breadth.

Each state has 21 significant deviations — but not of the same measurements in each case. But each of the state comparisons agrees with the total series comparison of civilians with criminals in the direction of the deviations of 18 of 33 measurements and indices.

COMPARISON OF PRISON SERIES BY OFFENSE GROUPS WITH TOTAL CIVIL CHECK SAMPLE

First Degree Murder. First degree murderers are significantly different from the civilian check sample in 18 of 33 measurements and indices listed. They exceed the civilians in mean age by 3.30 years, but are 7.10 pounds lighter, although insignificantly taller. These first degree murderers (312 in number) have narrower shoulders and chests than the civilians, although they do not fall significantly below the latter in chest depth. The head breadths, head heights, and head circumferences are all markedly inferior to those of the civilians, although their head lengths are not. The criminals also show a possibly significant inferiority in forehead breadth ($-.56$ millimeters, 2.00 p.e.) and certainly significant deficiency in total face height (-1.15 millimeters, 3.29 p.e.). Nose height is significantly less than that of the civilians and nasal breadth insignificantly greater. Ear length of first degree murderers is significantly less than that of the check sample, and ear breadth is significantly greater.

In shoulder breadth relative to stature the murderers are well below the civilians. The cephalic index is also significantly lower in the murderers, as is the length-height index. Thus this class of offenders seems to show relatively narrower and lower heads than the civilians. There is also a possibly significant lowering of the facial index in this group ($-.72$, 2.48 p.e.). On the other hand the nasal index of the murderers is markedly higher than that of the civilians, as are also the ear index and the zygogonial index.

In general the divergences of the first degree murderers from the civil check sample are similar to those of the entire criminal group, but of lesser magnitude. However, the first degree murderers show certain divergences which are not characteristic of the criminals as a whole. They are older than the civilians, are not inferior to them in stature, have broader jaw angles — absolutely and relatively to their facial breadths — relatively longer and narrower heads, and heads which are lower relative to their length.

None of the differences between first degree murderers and civilians are of such a nature that the older age of the criminal group in any way affects them.

Second Degree Murder. The second degree murderers, 619 in number, show 17 significant differences from the civil check sample in the 33 measurements and indices listed. In age they are practically identical with the check sample, but are far below the civilians in weight. These murderers are also slightly shorter (.78 centimeters) but the difference is only 2.69 times its probable error and of uncertain significance. They are definitely and markedly inferior to the civilians in biacromial diameter, chest breadth, chest depth, head breadth, head height, head circumference, total and upper face height, nose height, ear length and ear breadth. In the indices the second degree murderers show significantly lower length-breadth (cephalic), length-height, and facial means. They exceed the civilians in nasal index and ear index.

The second degree murderers manifest differences from the civil check sample which diverge from the general differences of the criminal group in that they are relatively longer-headed and relatively lower-headed. In these points they agree with the first degree murderers. None of the differences are attributable to age.

Assault. This is the smallest of offense groups, since it contains only 80 persons. Consequently the probable errors are high and differences to be of certain significance must be of unusual magnitude. As a matter of fact there are only 6 such differences (equal to or exceeding three times the probable error) in the array of 33 measurements and indices. That is a larger number, however, than would be expected to occur in random samples drawn from the same population. The assault criminals are insignificantly younger than the check sample (difference −.50 years), but significantly lighter (10.90 pounds). Their deficiency in height is greater than that of the total criminal series, but still doubtfully significant (−1.26 centimeters, 2.33 p.e.) on account of the small size of this offense group. Differences from the civil check sample which the group shows, but which are not displayed by the criminal series as a whole, are a greater relative shoulder breadth, and (apparently) a lower breadth-height index (difference −1.51, 2.74 p.e.). The significantly broader shoulders relative to height are due to an absolute superiority in shoulder breadth (.18 centimeters, .90 p.e.), which is statistically insignificant, combined with a greater and probably significant deficiency in stature.

Apart from the small size of the group, which conditions the significance of differences, it is, nevertheless, true that this offense group approaches the civilians in general more closely than other offense groups heretofore considered.

Robbery. The robbers (414 in number) diverge significantly from the civil check sample in 18 measurements and indices. They are, on the average, 7.75 years younger and 13.20 pounds lighter than the civilians. In stature they are .90 centimeters shorter, which is, however, only 2.90 times the probable error of the difference. Chest and shoulder diameters are much smaller in the robbers, as is also head circumference. Facial and nasal heights are also much diminished in these criminals, as are the ear diameters.

In indices the robbers surpass the civilians in relative sitting height, nasal, ear, zygo-frontal, and fronto-parietal means, and fall below them significantly in the relation of facial height (both upper and total) to bizygomatic diameter. Some of these differences are possibly increased to some extent by disparity in age, but age corrections would probably efface none of them, since they are by no means primarily due to this factor. The forehead breadth of robbers is .76 millimeters more than that of civilians, a difference equal to 2.92 times its probable error and possibly significant.

Generally speaking, the differences between the robbers and the civilians are in the same measurements and indices and in the same direction as the divergences from the civil check sample manifested by the entire criminal group.

Burglary and Larceny. The larceny group, comprising 1612 individuals, is by far the largest offense group. It diverges from the civil check sample in 21 of 33 measurements and indices. In every dimension except minimum frontal diameter it is inferior to the civilians. The mean age of this offense group is 8 years less than the civilians and the mean weight is 13.70 pounds less. A significant inferiority in this group is in facial breadth, which is below that of all other groups and .95 millimeters below that of the check sample. This group is also the only one in which nose breadth is percep tibly lower than in the check sample. The difference is only .21 millimeters, however, which is but 1.75 times its probable error and therefore may be due to the sampling process.

Indicial differences of the larceny group from the check sample include higher relative sitting height, nasal index, ear index, zygo-frontal index, and fronto-parietal index. Inferiority of the facial index is probable, but the difference does not quite equal three times its probable error.

Forgery and Fraud. The forgery and fraud criminals differ significantly from the civilians in 13 of 33 measurements and indices. This offense group consists of 467 individuals, whose mean age is 4.25 years less than the check sample, and whose mean weight is 9.40 pounds less. The difference in this latter case is still significant, but this is the heaviest of the offense groups. These fraudulent criminals diverge from the civilians in the same direction and, for the most part, in the same measurements and indices as the entire criminal series, but the divergences are fewer and of lesser magnitude. Nevertheless, they are sufficient in number to demarcate clearly this group from the civilians. It is unnecessary to reiterate these differences, details of which can be seen in Table XI-30.

Rape. This group consists of 197 individuals who are insignificantly older (1.60 years) than the check sample. It exhibits 11 certainly significant differences from the civilians, and 7 others which may be significant. In stature this is the shortest of all the offense groups and falls farthest below the civilians. It is also inferior to the civilians in every other measurement, except minimum frontal diameter. A point of interest, although of doubtful significance, is that this group alone of all the offense groups exceeds the civilians in cephalic (length-breadth) index, although indeed the difference is small (.24, 1.14 p.e.). A difference, significant in this group, which is not certainly significant in any other offense group when compared with civilians, is a deficiency in sitting height (−.78 centimeters, 3.54 p.e.). In general the divergences of this group from the civilians are in the same direction and in the same measurements and indices as those of the whole group, but are greater in stature, sitting height, and shoulder breadth, and the indices derived therefrom, and less in most others. It should be noted that these rapists show a lower zygo-gonial index than does the check sample, but the difference (−.48, 2.09 p.e.) may be spurious.

Other Sex Offenses. This group of 151 offenders is 2.60 years older than the check sample mean, 9.90 pounds lighter, and 1.92 centimeters shorter. There are 8 certainly significant differences and 4 more which may be valid. All of the measurements of these criminals are smaller than those of the civilians, with the exception of nose breadth which is insignificantly greater. In most of the measured features the other sex offenders are closer to the civilians than are the criminals at large, stature and sitting height being notable exceptions. Yet the group is statistically differentiated from the civilians, with whom it is wholly comparable in the matter of age.

Versus Public Welfare. This group of 257 persons is 3.75 years older than the civilian check sample, 8.30 pounds lighter, and of the same mean height. It exhibits 15 certainly significant differences from that sample. Distinctive of this group, and hence worthy of mention, are the following: an excessive minimum frontal diameter (1.28 millimeters, 4.27 p.e.), an excessive nose breadth (.78 millimeters, 4.88 p.e.), an excessive bigonial diameter (1.60 millimeters, 4.57 p.e.), an excessive cephalo-facial index (.75, 4.17 p.e.). This is the only group in which ear measurements and indices do not diverge significantly from the means of the civil check sample.

Arson and All Other Offenses. This small residual group, consisting of 103 persons (of whom 33 were convicted of arson and the rest of miscellaneous crimes) is insignificantly younger than the check sample (1.45 years), but significantly lighter (14.40 pounds). It presents 8 certain divergences from the civilians, including that of weight. Most of the metric deviations are on the minus side. Notable, however, is very short stature, an excess in chest breadth (.33 centimeters, 1.83 p.e.), in relative shoulder breadth (.24, 3.00 p.e.) and a possibly significant deficiency in minimum frontal diameter (−.88 millimeters, 2.15 p.e.).

Table XI–31 offers a comparison of the number of significant and insignificant differences between criminals and civilians in offense groups, in the totals of offense groups, in the total series, and in the separate interstate comparisons of Massachusetts and Tennessee. The smaller percentage of significant deviations in the totals of the offense groups as compared with the total combined series is due in part to the small size of the offense groups and their consequently larger probable errors which tend to render a certain number of differences statistically insignificant. It is of considerable interest to note that Massachusetts and Tennessee criminals differ from their respective civilian check samples more markedly than do total criminals. This raises the supposition that a completely adequate check sample drawn from every state represented in the criminal series would differ from that series even more markedly than does the present check sample derived from but two of the nine states.

Tables XI–32–41 list in detail all significant metrical and indicial differences between criminals and civilians for the total series and for the separate offense groups

Chapter XII

SOCIOLOGICAL AND MORPHOLOGICAL DIFFEREN-
TIATION BETWEEN CRIMINALS AND CIVILIANS
OF SIMILAR PARENTAGE

Sociological Comparison of Total Prison Series and State Subgroups with Their Respective Check Samples

TABLE XII–2 summarizes the nature and number of sociological agreements and disagreements between Massachusetts criminals and Massachusetts civilians and Tennessee criminals and Tennessee civilians, respectively, both in state totals and in respect to the deviations of all criminals from the total check sample. The right hand column shows the state deviations from their respective civilian samples. In 25 sociological categories there are only 4 significant deviations of the two sets of criminals from their respective check samples which are in the same direction, and there are an equal number in the opposite direction. The other deviations are both insignificant, or one of the pair is insignificant.

When the deviations of the total criminal series from the total check sample are expressed in terms of nature of the same deviations in the state samples, the first and second columns of the table are produced. The total of the second column shows that 20 of 25 sociological observations display significant differences between the total criminals and the check sample as against 4 of the 25 which deviate significantly and in the same direction in both state comparisons. One of the significant deviations of the state sample which is in the same direction is reduced to insignificance in the total series comparison, and 3 of the significant disagreements appear significant in the total series comparison. The other significant deviations of the total series from the check sample are derived from deviations which are either insignificant in the state comparisons or significant in only one of the two state comparisons. Thus the agreement between total series comparison and between state comparisons is not close. There follows the necessity of examining the disagreements between the two state comparisons. Table XII–1 shows the raw details of the two state comparisons, and Table XII–3 lists various items by classes according to direction and significance of divergence in the total series comparison and in the two state comparisons.

MARITAL STATE

Table XII–4 gives the excesses of the criminal group over the check sample in marital status. It is noted that a significant deficiency of married men, amounting to 12.89 per cent, occurs among the criminals. This is doubtless due in some measure to the lower mean age of the criminals (−3.75 years), but the excess of single criminals is only 6.61 per cent, and the remainder of the deficiency in married criminals is accounted for by an excess of divorced or separated men amounting to 4.23 per cent, and of widowers amounting to 2.05 per cent. All of these differences are significant, in view of their probable errors. Undoubtedly the excess of divorced and separated men reflects the unsatisfactory character of criminals as husbands. It may to some extent express the tendency of wives married to criminals to divorce their husbands. In general, it must be also an expression of the unhappy marital relations which these unfortunates have had, or their slight regard for the marriage tie. But, according to our records, none of the persons included in the civilian check sample were either divorced or separated. This seems either miraculous or mendacious. Our data in regard to marital status of civilians were secured by personal inquiry, rather than by consulting any records, and it is possible that certain divorced men suppressed the fact.

No such allowance need be made for the excess of widowers among the criminals. No one wishes to suppress the fact that he is a widower. The highest percentage of widowers (7.12) occurs in first degree murderers, and I have suggested, without any desire to be facetious, that this may represent, to some extent, the tendency of this class of criminals to murder their wives. However, this cannot apply to the criminal group at large. It is undeniable that persons in jail would have less chance to remarry when their wives died, than would widowers at large.

When all is said and done, it is apparent that criminals are less married, less often happily married, and more often widowed than a roughly comparable sample of civilians, such as we have available. Criminals are not family men.

The comparison of criminals and civilians from the same states — Massachusetts and Tennessee — reveals the fact that in both states, the criminals, as in the total series, are less often married and more often divorced or widowed, than the civilians. However, the excess of single men is found in Tennessee and not in Massachusetts. Indeed Massachusetts criminals are slightly deficient in single men, when compared with their check sample. The large excess of single men in the Tennessee criminal is no doubt referable to the advanced age and highly married status of the firemen with whom they are compared. The comparison of the total criminal series with the entire check sample apparently gives a better picture of the total situation than do the state comparisons.

Table XII-5 adduces comparative data on the marital status of prisoners and males of the general population 15 years or over, for the years 1910, 1920, 1923, and 1930. The prisoners committed in 1910, irrespective of race, nationality, and parentage, were single in 68.6 per cent of cases reported — in 1923, in 53.9 per cent. Of the native Whites committed in this period 54.9 per cent were single. Of our native White of native parentage only 48.63 per cent were single. If our sample is representative of prison and reformatory group incarcerated in 1927–28, it would appear that there are more married criminals of this description than formerly, unless native Whites of native parentage are more frequently married than other criminals. It should be noted however, that the prisoners committed in any year are likely to be younger, and consequently less often married, than the prison population of that year. In 1910, 39.9 per cent of civilian males 15 years or over in the general population were reported as single

gle; in 1920, 35.2 per cent; in our check sample 42.02 per cent. Thus it would appear that the marriage rate for males 15 years or over increased between 1910 and 1923, but the civilian check sample of this study shows a considerable excess of single men, when compared with the census reports of earlier dates. The sample is, of course, very small.

The proportion of divorced men in our criminals is larger than in any of the civil or criminal groups adduced for comparison. The figures indicate an increase in the pro-

TABLE XII–5

MARITAL STATE OF CRIMINAL SERIES COMPARED WITH MARITAL STATE OF CIVILIANS OF SIMILAR ORIGIN

	Date	Number	Single Per Cent	Married Per Cent	Divorced Per Cent	Widowed Per Cent
Criminals (this study)	1927–28	4,160	48.63	44.76	4.23	2.38
Prisoners (all ages)[a]	1910	433,460	68.6	25.3	1.0	4.2
Native white prisoners [b]	1923	11,118	54.9	38.5	3.4	3.2
Total prisoners [b]	1923	17,882	53.9	39.8	2.7	3.5
Civilians (this study)	1928	307	42.02	57.65	0	0.33
Total population (15 and above)[a] ..	1910		38.9	56.1	0.5	4.6
Total population (15 and above)[b] ..	1920	36,920,663	35.2	59.4	0.6	4.8
Total population (15 and above)[b] ..	1930	43,881,021	34.1	60.0	1.1	4.6

[a] *Prisoners and Juvenile Delinquents in the United States,* Bureau of the Census, Washington, D.C., 1910, p. 139.
[b] *Prisoners,* 1923, pp. 82, 84. Committed Jan. 1–June 30, 1923.

portions of divorced men between 1910 and 1930. None of the statistics quoted here is strictly comparable with our civilian and criminal series, since none of the groups is composed exclusively of native Whites of native parentage.

Our civilian check sample, even when the much-married Tennessee firemen are included, shows a somewhat higher percentage of single individuals than is found in the total population of males 15 years and over in the censuses of 1910 and 1920. Therefore it seems fair to conclude that the excesses in marital categories displayed by our total criminal series over the total civilian check sample are valid, and are not due to the presence of the firemen in the check sample or to the unrepresentative character of the latter.

OCCUPATION

Since our check sample of native Whites of native parentage is exclusively urban in origin, the occupational comparison with the criminals is almost worthless. Not only is the check sample practically devoid of persons belonging to the extractive occupations, but it is also heavily loaded with public service workers, on account of the inclusion in it of the large group of Tennessee firemen. For this reason it seems advisable to concentrate our attention upon the comparison of Massachusetts criminals with Massachusetts civilians, since the overweighting of occupations does not affect this comparison. In Massachusetts criminals the proportion of persons of extractive occupation does not significantly exceed that found in the civilian sample, while in Tennessee there is a huge excess of extractive criminals (Table XII–6). Massachusetts shows its largest criminal excess in the unskilled laborers, and a somewhat smaller, but still significant excess of laborers occurs in the Tennessee comparison. Both comparisons show excess of factory operatives among criminals, but this is not significant in Massachusetts, and in Tennessee is wholly misleading. Other significant differences in Massachusetts are: an excess of transportation and personal service, and a deficiency of professional, clerical, and student. In general the Massachusetts comparison shows that criminals are in excess in the lower occupational categories and proportionately deficient in those occupations requiring good educations.

Table XII–7 is an attempt to render the occupational data concerning our native White criminals of native parentage and the civilian check sample comparable with those of the general population derived from the census of 1920 and 1930. The main difficulty in this effort is the laborer class, which in our material is separate, but in the census reports is distributed among the extractive, manufacturing and mechanical industries, and transportation and communication categories. Thus in our criminal series and in our civilian check sample, we have, respectively, 16.72 per cent and 1.98 per cent which must be assigned to other categories in order to correspond with the census. The extractive category of our criminals is already in excess of the 1930 proportion in the general population, and if we add any proportion of the laborers to this class the excess becomes more pronounced. But our civilian check sample has not its due representation in this class. In both of our series the manufacturing and mechanical industries are deficient when compared with the percentages in the general population, but it is probable that this deficiency would disappear, and possibly be replaced by an excess, if the due quota of laborers were added.

The same is true of the transportation and communication class. Trade is disproportionately low in the criminal series, as are public service, professional service, and clerical groupings. Domestic and personal service are represented by an unduly high proportion of criminals.

The check series does not offer a representative sample of the general population since it is too low in extractive, personal service, and mechanical industries classes, and too high in public service and clerical.

It seems safe to conclude that among the criminals, the extractive and domestic and personal service classes are represented by disproportionately large numbers. This is probably true also of unspecified laborers. Trade, professional service, and clerical occupations are probably low among these criminals.

EDUCATION

An impressive sociological difference between our civilian check sample and the criminal series is manifested by the comparison of their educational attainments (Table XII–8). Beginning with the illiterate group and counting through the sixth grade we find significant excess percentages of criminals in every one of these lower educational categories. In the seventh grade group the criminals reach approximate parity with the civilians. In every successively higher educational category thereafter the criminals show significant deficiencies. The greatest excess of criminals is in the lumped class including the first to the fifth grades, and the greatest deficiency, that comprising the third and fourth years of high school.

The poor showing of the criminals in educational attainment, when compared with the civilian check sample, should be discounted to some extent because of the inclusion in the criminal series of a larger percentage of persons from the rural districts of southern states where educational facilities are extremely poor. On the other hand, the civil check sample includes 53.35 per cent of persons measured in Massachusetts, where the opportunities for education are excellent. There can hardly be any valid method of equalizing the factors of educational opportunity in the criminal series and the check sample. In any event, the inferior school advantages enjoyed or utilized by the

TABLE XII–9

ILLITERACY OF CRIMINAL SERIES COMPARED WITH ILLITERACY OF CIVILIAN GROUPS
OF SIMILAR ORIGIN

| | Criminals Illiterates (this series) | | General Population Illiterates | |
	Number	Per Cent	1930 Per Cent	1920 Per Cent
Massachusetts	2	0.60	0.40	0.40
Tennessee	57	13.51	5.40	7.30
Kentucky	234	19.83	5.70	7.00
Texas	35	3.84	1.40	3.00
North Carolina	71	16.03	5.60	8.20
Wisconsin	8	2.72	0.60	0.70
Arizona	..	...	0.50	2.10
Colorado	18	3.03	0.80	1.50
New Mexico	..	...	7.70 [a]	11.60 [a]

[a] Probably includes a large percentage of persons of Mexican parentage.

criminals do not necessarily imply a causal relationship between lack of education and crime. We cannot infer that, if these delinquents had been better educated, fewer of them would have become inmates of penal institutions.

In order to obviate the difficulty of comparing the education of civilians and criminals of different states with varying educational opportunities, the Massachusetts civilians have been compared with the Massachusetts criminals, and the Tennessee civilians with the Tennessee criminals in Table XII–8. The Massachusetts civilians are vastly better educated than the criminals. The results in Tennessee are not so clear cut. The Tennessee criminals show a high proportion of illiterates and persons who can barely read and write, but they include also higher proportions of high school and college attendants than do the civilians. This is again because of the limited occupational status of the Tennessee check sample which is composed of firemen who are, on the whole, poorly educated. Massachusetts criminals are better educated than Nashville, Tennessee, firemen.

Table XII–9 compares the percentage of illiterates among our native White criminals of native parentage by states with the percentages of illiterate native Whites in the general population as recorded in the censuses of 1920 and 1930. It clearly shows the higher illiteracy in the criminals. In our data the states of Arizona, Colorado, and New Mexico are combined, owing to the small number of native Whites of native parentage. All Mexicans and children of Mexican parentage have been removed from our native Whites of native parentage, but probably not from the census data. The latter fact probably accounts for the high illiteracy reported for the native White population of New Mexico, although the census of 1930 does not classify Mexicans as Whites.

Morphological Comparison of Total Prison Series and State Subgroups with Their Respective Check Samples

Table XII–11, like the two similar preceding tables, appraises the deviations of all criminals from all civilians in terms of the agreements, disagreements, directions of deviations, and significance in the comparisons between criminals and civilians of the same two states. The percentage of significant differences in the total series comparison is 63.63 which is slightly higher than the proportion of significant deviations in measurements and indices (57.58 per cent). However, in the case of the morphological observations, the agreements of the two states in deviations which are significant and in the same direction are proportionately much fewer than in measurements and indices. There are only 11.04 per cent of such agreements as against 27.27 per cent in measurements and indices. Significant deviations in opposite directions occur in 16.88 per cent of the state series. Of these 10.39 per cent survive in the total series comparison as significant differences.

The relatively poor agreement between the Massachusetts and Tennessee comparisons may be due in large part to the fact that the Massachusetts criminals include a considerable number of individuals of French-Canadian extraction, whereas this stock is poorly represented in the civilian Massachusetts check sample. The putative result of this ethnic disparity is to give the Massachusetts criminal sample an excess of about 10 per cent of, broadly speaking, Alpine racial traits, which tend in many instances to make it diverge from its check sample in a direction opposite to that shown by the criminals in the Tennessee comparison. Another factor in producing some of these contradictions is the personal equation of Observer C in the Massachusetts check sample of civilians. Finally it is possible that, within the respective state physical types of Massachusetts and Tennessee, criminals may differ from civilians in diverse morphological variations.

It is evident that the analysis of differences between the total criminal series and the check sample will involve the necessity of a careful scrutiny of corresponding differences in the state comparisons, and the matter of the Tennessee-Massachusetts agreement or disagreement will have to be taken into account in each character. On the whole, only total series deviations which agree in direction with those of both of the states can be accepted as valid without examination. These include 30 of 154 observations, or 19.48 per cent. In the case of a disagreement between the Massachusetts and Tennessee comparisons, it seems proper to give more weight to the Tennessee result, since in that comparison we are both more fully assured of the ethnic comparability of civilian and criminal series, and further, we have not to make any allowance for another disturbing factor in the Massachusetts comparison — the injection of Observer C's personal equation into the situation. This third observer was responsible for 50.89 per cent of the Massachusetts check sample.

Tattooing. The classical Lombrosian criminal is excessively tattooed, or at any rate is much more likely to be tattooed than a law-abiding person. Our criminal series show a significantly smaller percentage untattooed, and a significantly larger percentage of

persons having tattoo marks, than the civilian sample (Table XII–13). The total civilian percentage of tattooed persons is only 6.84 and of criminals 15.09. Consequently,
in spite of the excess among delinquents, tattooing cannot be said to be a common habit
in this criminal group. Goring found 43 per cent of his habitual criminals tattooed,
and went to great pains to explain away the excess over occurrence in the civilian
population, by invoking factors of army and navy service, urban residence, et cetera.[1]
His results, nevertheless, confirmed the findings of Lombroso, as do ours, insofar as
his practice is demonstrated to be more common in criminals than in non-criminals.

The state comparisons show that Massachusetts criminals are excessively and significantly more tattooed than Massachusetts civilians, but that Tennessee criminals display only slight and insignificant excesses of tattooing when compared with Nashville
firemen. More tattooing is to be expected in a seaboard and an urban state than in an
inland and rural state. The comparison in Tennessee is hardly valid since the civilian
check sample is exclusively urban. The total series comparison certainly reflects, to
some extent, the more rural and inland character of the criminal samples as compared
with the civilian samples. If these factors could be equalized there would remain, un-
questionably, some excess of tattooing among criminals. I am not inclined, however, to
stress unduly the importance of such an excess.

Hair Quantity: Head, Beard, Body. The criminal series shows marked and significant differences from the civil sample in hair quantity. These differences consist
of deficiencies of persons with small amount of head hair, and excess of persons with
large amount of head hair; excess of persons with sparse beards and deficiencies of
those with medium and large amounts of beard hair; deficiencies of persons with medium or abundant body hair, and excesses of those with a small amount of body hair.
Most of these differences are significant when they are considered in terms of their
probable errors (Table XII–14). The most notable excess is in the percentage of criminals with scanty beards, which is no less than 25.31 per cent or 13.61 times its probable error. Superficially these findings agree with the classic assertions of Lombroso
and his school. However, we must take into consideration the discrepancy in age between the criminal and civil samples. The criminals are on the average 3.80 years
younger than the civilians and there are 12 per cent more of young adult males between the ages of 20 and 35 years in the criminal series than in the civil check sample. Beard and body hair keep on increasing throughout middle age and head hair
becomes more sparse. Consequently we cannot accept these differences at their face
value. Moreover, our observers show such large personal equations in these observations (Class D) that I cannot place great reliance upon differences between the combined criminal series and the civilians.

The divergences between the Massachusetts and Tennessee comparisons in the matter of hair quantity are somewhat puzzling and merit discussion. In the matter of
head hair both comparisons agree with the total series in showing criminals to have
deficiencies of small head hair quantity. The corresponding significant excess on the
part of the criminals occurs, in the case of the Tennessee comparison, in the medium
category. In the Massachusetts and total comparison the excess of criminal hair
quantity is shifted into the large category. This discrepancy may be due, in part, to
a really greater thickness of head hair in Massachusetts criminals than in Tennessee

[1] Goring, 1913, pp. 101–104.

criminals, because of the inclusion in the former group of an excess of men of French Canadian extraction, less well represented in the Massachusetts civilian check sample. I believe that it is influenced also, in considerable measure, by a reluctance on the part of Observer C to record hair quantity as "large." This bias would affect both the total series comparison and the Massachusetts comparison, but not the Tennessee comparison. The latter is therefore the more valid. In any case both series agree with the total in showing, on the whole, heavier head hair in the criminals.

In the matter of beard quantity, the same possibilities are present. All three comparisons show excesses of criminals with small amounts of beard. These excesses are balanced by significant deficiencies in the medium and large categories in the case of Tennessee and total series, but not in Massachusetts. Here again we must consider that the Massachusetts discrepancy is caused either by the excess of Massachusetts criminals of French Canadian extraction, or by the personal equation of Observer C, or by both in combination. In any case, it is clear that all three comparisons agree in indicating a relative sparsity of beard in the criminals.

Finally, in body hair Tennessee and total series agree in showing excesses of small amount in criminals and deficiencies of medium and large. But the Massachusetts comparison shows a deficiency of small amounts in the criminals, a significant excess of medium, and an insignificant excess of large. This discrepancy is definitely attributable to a strangely small number of individuals in the Massachusetts check sample recorded as having thick body hair. The tendency of lumping observations of hair amount in the medium category, so strongly shown in the Massachusetts check sample (Table XII–10), cannot be due entirely to Observer C, since the latter contributed only half of the observations. The other half was observed by Observer A. Yet Massachusetts civilians show less than a quarter of the amount of thick body hair recorded in A's Tennessee firemen. So it would appear that there is a real difference between the civilian check samples in this respect. On the other hand, it is completely certain that the Massachusetts criminals have much higher percentages of thick body hair than criminals of the total series. This may be attributable to the French Canadian element previously remarked. In any event, the data suggest strongly that the Massachusetts comparison is out of line, and that, on the whole, the criminals in general have less body hair than the civilians. If, then, we accept these interpretations, we are left with the general conclusions that head hair is thicker in the criminals, and beard and body hair thinner, than in civilians. This may be, to some extent, an age conditioned difference, since the civilians are generally older than the criminals.

Skin Color. Skin color observations upon Whites are of comparatively little value, in the absence of any satisfactory color scale or means of measuring skin color quantitatively. It is a Class C observation. In this survey skin color was observed upon an unexposed part of the body — usually the chest. I do not attach much importance to the differences between criminals and civilians shown in Table XII–15 because I know that they are complicated by the personal equations of three observers. Excesses of dark skin colors in the total series are due to the large number of these skin shades recorded by Observer B. Excess of red white skin color and deficiencies of pale white are attributable to the recording of Observer A.

Of the three comparisons there is little doubt that the Tennessee is the most reliable. All of the individuals in both series of this comparison were recorded by the same anthropologist, and the civilian and criminal series are of closely comparable ethnic extraction. In this series the criminals show less red white skin than the civilians, more pale white skin, and significantly less of olive skin. This finding agrees with the expectation that incarcerated persons would be more pallid than those of the same stock living a more or less outdoor life.

Hair Form. This is a Class A observation and of considerable importance. The criminals show an excess of straight-haired individuals amounting to 10.19 per cent, and deficiencies of all varieties of curved hair (Table XII–16). No less than 85.35 per cent of the criminal series and 75.16 per cent of the check sample of native Whites of native parentage have straight hair, or are so recorded. This result agrees with the statement of Hrdlička that Old Americans generally have straight hair or nearly so.[2] The question arises whether the excess of straight hair among the criminals may be due to short prison hair-cuts. Slightly wavy hair or even more curved varieties are likely to be recorded as straight when the hair is closely cropped. I do not think, however, that the difference is due entirely to this fact. The habit of cutting prisoners' hair very short is no longer prevalent in most prisons.

The Massachusetts and Tennessee comparisons are in accordance with the total series comparison in exhibiting excess of straight hair, and deficiencies of low waves and deep waves. The first two named differences are significant in all three comparisons. Deficiencies in deep waves do not attain significance in either state comparison, but reach it in the total series. Curly and frizzly hair are so rare as to be of no importance in any of the series here considered.

Hair Color. The principal differences in hair color between the criminal series and the civilian sample lie in an excess of red-brown hair among the criminals amounting to 9 per cent (5.81 p.e.) and a deficiency of gray or white-haired criminals of 8.21 per cent (9.12 p.e.) (Table XII–17). Since hair color is a Class A observation, in which the observers show excellent agreement, there is no reason for attributing the differences to personal equation. However, the excess of gray and white hair among the civilians is undoubtedly due in part to the inclusion in that series of more middle-aged and old men. In the civilian series there are 7.46 per cent more of males between the ages of 35 and 54 years and 6.64 per cent more of men 55 years or older. Since the deficiency in gray-haired and white-haired criminals is only 8.21 per cent it is obvious that the age discrepancy is more than enough to account for the difference.

Owing to differences in the categories of hair color recognized, the material of this survey cannot be compared in detail with Hrdlička's observations on Old Americans. However it is obvious that both our criminal and our civilian series show somewhat higher proportions of black and dark brown hair and also of the blonds and reds than do the Old Americans.

On the whole, it appears that there is nothing distinctive about the hair color of criminals, and, although our criminal sample differs in distribution of hair color from the civil check sample in that it shows more red-brown, this excess is probably or possibly attributable to the younger age of the criminals and is compensated by the excess of grays and whites in the civilians. Red-brown hair shows a marked tendency to become gray or white in middle life, and a few more years added to our criminals'

[2] Hrdlička, 1925, p. 55.

ages might well transfer the excess of red-brown to the gray category, thus equalizing the two series.

The state comparisons reveal that Massachusetts criminals are high in red-brown hair and low in light brown, whereas the opposite is the case in Tennessee. With respect to their civilian samples the two sets of criminals differ significantly in opposite directions. The same observer functioned in both state comparisons. Unless his personal equation shifted radically, the factor involved must be a state difference. The Massachusetts and Tennessee comparisons differ throughout, except that both exhibit deficiencies of dark brown hair (insignificant) and deficiencies of gray or white hair (significant). An excess of 2.38 per cent (2.05 p.e.) of black hair in the Massachusetts criminals and another huge excess of 28.40 per cent of red-brown hair (10.21 p.e.) in the Massachusetts criminal series, as contrasted with its civilian check sample, may well be due to the larger number of criminals of French Canadian extraction in the former series. On the other hand, the Tennessee criminal series, as contrasted with its check sample, shows a marked deficiency of red-brown and a very large excess of light brown (24.30 per cent, 7.64 p.e.). There seems to be no doubt that the Tennessee criminals, on the whole, have lighter hair than their civilian check sample, but that the Massachusetts criminals have darker hair than their comparable civilian group. For reasons previously stated, it is suggested that more weight be given to the Tennessee comparison. Both series show criminal deficiency in gray and white hair.

Eye Color. Eye color is a Class B observation, which is liable to some personal equation, especially in distinguishing the various categories of mixed eyes: blue-brown, gray-brown, and green-brown. Nevertheless, certain significant differences between the civilian sample and the criminal series are valid (Table XII–18). The first of these is a deficiency of dark brown eyes in the criminal series amounting to 3.08 per cent (4.22 p.e.). This is substantiated by a small and insignificant deficiency of light brown eyes among the criminals. Evidently pure dark eyes are less common than in the check sample. On the other hand the mixed eyes, including blue-brown, gray-brown, and green-brown, comprise 64.61 per cent of the criminal series and only 55.27 per cent of the civilian check sample. This difference is certainly of importance. In details of mixed eyes, the criminals are deficient in blue-brown eyes when compared with the check sample, very high in gray-brown, and also in excess in green-browns, although not significantly so. I am not inclined to stress these differences because of the fact that one observer seemed to favor one category in the mixed eye classification, and the other, another.

There is, however, a very important deficiency in blue eyes among the criminals and a less important, though significant excess of gray eyes. In short our criminals are low in pure darks and pure lights, when compared with the civilians, and high in mixed eyes.

The Massachusetts and Tennessee comparisons agree in the direction of their deviations in every category of eye color except green-brown, in which they show insignificant deviations in opposite directions. They both agree with the entire series comparison in presenting deficiencies of dark brown, insignificant deficiencies of light brown, excess of gray-brown, deficiencies of blue, and excesses of blue-gray. They both disagree with the total series comparison in showing excesses of blue-brown, intead of a significant deficiency. Except in one category of mixed eyes, the differ-nces between criminals and civilians seem in general valid.

Table XII–19 is an attempt to extend the comparison of eye color of our criminal nd civil series to other American data. Hrdlička's material dealing with Old Ameri-ans is closely comparable in method of classification and in results obtained, when ll mixed eyes are thrown together. The Old Americans are closer to the civilian heck sample than to the criminals in their high proportion of blue and total light yes, in the lower proportion of mixed eyes, and the larger proportion of darks. Irdlička's series contains more dark eyes proportionately than either our criminal or ivilian check series. On the whole his material substantiates our conclusion that the riminal series is deficient in both light and dark eyes, and high in mixed eyes.

Sclera. Speckled and yellow sclerae or whites of the eyes are significantly less com-non among the criminals than in the civilian check sample (Table XII–20). This ondition is correlated with the smaller number of dark eyes among the criminals. ince pigmented sclerae are found in only 12.78 per cent of the civilians and in 5.05 er cent of the criminals, the absence of such a feature in the majority of criminals is ot distinctive. The Massachusetts criminals are squarely and significantly opposed o the Tennessee and total series comparisons. The contradiction is due partly to the act that Observer A recorded high proportions of speckled and yellow sclerae, while)bservers B and C recorded very small percentages. The Massachusetts comparison s out of line with the total series and the Tennessee comparison because of Observer ''s equation in the Massachusetts check sample. In the total series C is balanced by 3. Hence it comes out the same as the Tennessee comparison in which, according to xpectation, the lighter eyed criminals have less sclerotic pigment.

Iris. The color of the iris is usually homogeneous only in dark brown eyes and in ome blue eyes. Since dark brown and blue eyes are both deficient in the criminal eries, a marked and significant inferiority in the percentage of homogeneous irides is) be expected and does occur (Table XII–21). The deficiency amounts to 16.88 per ent or 15.07 times the probable error. Mixed eyes are most commonly rayed (i.e. the igment radiates out from the pupil); less often the pigment is arranged in a concen-ric zone about the pupil, or the entire iris is irregularly speckled with brown pigment, r diffusely stained in blotches. The criminal series exhibits unexpected excesses of oned and speckled eyes over rayed eyes when compared with the civil sample. This is pparently not due to the personal equation of observers since the observation is Class .. The difference is not, however, of great importance.

Both state comparisons agree with the total series comparison in exhibiting de-ciencies of homogeneous and diffused irides and excesses of zoned and speckled ides. However, Tennessee criminals, when compared with their state civilians, show significant deficiency of rayed irides, whereas Massachusetts criminals show n insignificant excess. In the total series comparison there is an insignificant defi-iency. On the whole, the state comparisons attest the validity of the total series omparison.

Eye Folds. Eye folds of one kind or another occur in 26.21 per cent of criminals nd in 20.19 per cent of the civilian population as represented by our sample. The dif-erence is significant, although not great. In detail, it consists of insignificant excesses f median and external folds in criminals and of a larger and more certainly valid excess of inner epicanthic or so-called Mongoloid folds (Table XII–22). Since the latter folds occur in only 4.40 per cent of our criminals, the distinction is of no great importance. It may be due, partially, to the larger percentage of subadults in our criminal sample, since the internal epicanthus is a feature which tends to disappear with increasing elevation of the nasal bridge during the later stages of growth.

In order to eliminate the age differences which may obscure the comparison of the criminal series with the check sample in the occurrence of eye folds, the former series has been subdivided into age groups (Table XII–23). The epicanthus or inner (Mongoloid) fold decreases from 8.45 per cent in the 15–19 year group to 1.56 per cent in the 35–69 year group. The 20–34 year old group is closest in age composition to the check sample and exhibits 4.69 per cent of such folds as against 1.28 per cent in the total check sample. The oldest group of criminals still shows a slight superiority in percentage of epicanthic folds over the total check sample. Presumably the four epicanthic folds which occur in the check sample are found in the younger men also. On the whole, it appears that the excess of inner epicanthic folds in the criminals is real, and is not an effect of the larger proportions of younger men to be found in that series.

The occurrence of median folds in the criminals decreases from the youngest to the oldest age subgroup. However, there is no difference between the criminals and the civilians in the total occurrence of this feature.

A slight excess of external folds (2.54 per cent, 2.29 p.e.) is not certainly significant in view of its relation to the probable error of the difference. However, Table XII–23 shows that in the criminals the proportion of this feature increases in each successive age group. Since the civilians include higher proportions of individuals in these groups, we should expect that the check sample would display a higher frequency of external folds. The reverse is the case, and the excess in criminals, though statistically dubious, is logically significant.

The conclusion is that the criminals show a higher percentage of inner epicanthic and external epicanthic folds than the civilians, and that these differences are not due to disparity in the age composition of the two groups.

Massachusetts agrees with the total series in the direction of its deviations of eye folds. Tennessee shows insignificant deviations for the most part in the opposite direction. But both states agree in showing slight excesses of epicanthic folds, which in the total series become significant. The disagreement of the Tennessee differences with the general civilian-criminal difference is probably due to the greater age of the Tennessee civilians. This seniority would involve an increased proportion of external folds, in which the Tennessee criminals are below the check sample, contrary to the condition prevailing in Massachusetts and in the series at large.

Eyebrow Thickness. There is an unexpected excess of criminals with thick eyebrows when the civil check sample is brought into comparison (Table XII–24). It amounts to 10.16 per cent or 5.55 times the probable error. The total percentage of criminals with thick eyebrows is 32.28, as against 22.12 in civilians. This is surprising because the criminals include more young men and subadults than does the civilian check sample. Hair quantity observations are generally somewhat unreliable, since the observers showed clear personal equations. In this particular observation, however, the agreement between the observers was fair (Class B). Nevertheless, I d not feel that the observed excess of criminals with thick eyebrows is important or wholly dependable.

Table XII–25, in which the criminals are seriated by three age groups, shows a slight increase in proportions of persons with pronounced eyebrow thickness in successive age grades. Each age group of the criminals shows an excess of pronounced eyebrows and a deficiency of medium eyebrows when compared with the total civilian sample. The difference is, therefore, real, and not due to age inequalities.

The state comparisons of eyebrow thickness between criminals and civilians show that the Massachusetts criminals exhibit a great excess of thick eyebrows as compared with civilians from the same state. This result agrees with the total series comparison. But the Tennessee criminal group shows an excess of medium eyebrows and a deficiency of very thick eyebrows. This condition is possibly due in part to the fact that the Tennessee civilian sample is much older than the criminal sample, the excess in favor of the Tennessee firemen over the Tennessee criminals being far greater than the age superiority of the Massachusetts civilians over the Massachusetts criminals. But the thickening of eyebrows with age is not sufficient to account for the contradiction between the result of the Tennessee comparison and the observations in Massachusetts and in the combined series. A careful examination of the eyebrow thickness data presented separately in the records of the three observers indicates that Observer B tended to record eyebrow thickness as pronounced in almost twice as many cases as did Observer A. Observers A and C did not differ in their appraisal of this feature. Consequently the resulting disagreements are clarified. The excess of thick eyebrows among the criminals of the total comparison is probably due to the influence of B in the total criminal series as contrasted with those of A and C in the check sample. In the Massachusetts comparison we have to consider only A and C. But in the Massachusetts criminals there is an excess of men of French Canadian extraction who have thick eyebrows. It therefore seems that again the Tennessee comparison is more dependable than the total series or Massachusetts comparisons, and that in all probability the criminals tend to have thinner eyebrows than civilians.

Forehead Height. The criminals show an excess of low or submedium foreheads which is statistically significant (Table XII–26). The Massachusetts and Tennessee comparisons agree with the total series. In the medium and pronounced categories of forehead height Tennessee disagrees with the Massachusetts and total comparisons, and the probably higher foreheads of the French Canadian element in the Massachusetts criminals may skew the comparison in that state. But the proportion of high foreheads in the Tennessee civil sample is unusually large. Forehead height is a Class B observation.

Forehead Slope. The total criminal series and the Massachusetts state comparison show that criminals have significant deficiencies of absent, submedium, and medium forehead slopes and excess of pronounced slopes (Table XII–27). The Tennessee comparison presents insignificant differences in the opposite direction. The total series and Massachusetts differences are somewhat enhanced by the observations of Anthropologist C in the check sample. The disagreement of the Tennessee series indicates that no generalization can be made with safety.

Nasion Depression. The total criminal series differs significantly from the civilian check sample in displaying a small excess of persons with submedium nasion depressions, a large deficiency of those with medium depressions, and a large excess of individuals in which the depression is pronounced (Table XII–28). The Massachusetts comparison differs from the total criminal comparison in that it exhibits a deficiency of criminals with submedium nasion depression. The Tennessee comparison agrees with the total series comparison in the direction of its deviations, but none of them is statistically significant. The tentative conclusion from the data is that criminals are likely to show more of the extreme variations of this feature than do civilians, and, especially, that deep nasion depressions occur more frequently in the delinquents. I have little confidence in such a conclusion, because an examination of the various criminal and civilian samples of the three observers shows a strong predilection of Observer A for pronounced depressions, of Observer B for submedium depressions and of Observer C (operating in about 50 per cent of the Massachusetts and 27 per cent of the total check sample) for medium depressions. These equations in combination might easily bring about the above differences. Of course the differences may really exist in the several samples. But in any event the results are dubious.

Nasal Root Height. The external nose changes markedly with advancing years. In childhood and adolescence the bridge and the root are relatively low and broad, but the nasal skeleton becomes more elevated with the onset of maturity, and the breadth of the root and bridge is relatively, if not absolutely, increased. Our criminals have markedly shorter noses than the civilians, and it is surprising to find that nasal root height (a Class A observation) indicates a significant excess of criminals with pronounced development of this feature, when compared with the civilians (Table XII–29). There is a corresponding deficiency of nasal roots of medium height among the delinquents. The Tennessee and Massachusetts comparisons agree with the total series, although in the former the deviations are not statistically significant.

The division of the criminals series into age groups (Table XII–30) unexpectedly shows practically no regression of root height upon age. We are then forced to accept the differences at their face value and to conclude that the usual generalization concerning the increase of nasal root height with age does not apply to our material.

Nasal Root Breadth. In nasal root breadth (a Class B observation) there is a statistically significant excess of criminals with pronounced breadths, a corresponding deficiency of criminals with medium breadths, and a small but valid excess of criminals with submedium breadths (Table XII–31). Massachusetts heaps up an enormous excess of pronounced root breadths in its criminals, but the Tennessee comparison shows no significant difference between criminals and civilians.

A division of the criminal data into age groups indicates almost no regression of root breadth upon age (Table XII–32). Again deficiencies of the medium category and excess of the extreme variations seem to characterize the criminals as opposed to the civilians. In this observation, however, it should be noted that a tendency of Observer A to favor the pronounced category, a preference of B for the submedium category, and a marked predilection of C (in the check sample) for medium, may combine to influence the results found in the total series and Massachusetts comparisons. Possibly then, the criminal tendency toward the extremes is somewhat exaggerated by personal equations.

Nasal Bridge Height. In this Class A observation the criminals again display a great excess of pronounced heights over that shown by the check sample (Table XII–33). Massachusetts exaggerates the trend of the total series, but the Tennessee criminal do not diverge significantly from their check sample. The seriation of nasal bridge height by age groups (Table XII–34) shows the expected increase of pronounced bridge height with advancing age. However in each age group the criminals exceed the civilians in proportions of high roots, and if age were a causal factor in the difference between criminals and civilians, we should expect the former to show larger proportions of medium and submedium bridge heights.

Nasal Bridge Breadth. Again the total criminals show excesses in the extreme categories over the total civilians, and especially so in the pronounced breadths (Table XII–35). Massachusetts criminals greatly surpass their civilian check sample in percentage of broad nasal bridges. Tennessee criminals do not differ significantly from their civilian brothers. The excesses of submedium breadths occur in Observer B's data.

Nasal Profile. The total series comparison shows a probably insignificant excess of criminals with concave noses, certainly significant deficiencies of straight and convex noses among the criminals and a very great excess of concavo-convex noses among the felons (Table XII–36). Both state comparisons agree in the direction of their deviations. Massachusetts exaggerates the deviations of the total series.

Nasal Tip Thickness. Nasal tip thickness (Class B) shows the same excesses of extreme categories on the part of the criminals (Table XII–37). The Massachusetts comparison heaps up a huge excess of pronouncedly thick tips, the Tennessee comparison a moderate excess of thin tips. The disagreement in direction of deviations between Tennessee and Massachusetts may be referred, probably, in part, to the corpulence of the Tennessee firemen, and again, in part, to the broad-nosed French Canadian element in the Massachusetts criminal series.

Nasal Septum Inclination. The inclination of the nasal septum shows a great excess of the up category in the criminals as contrasted with the civilians (Table XII–38). This is a Class A observation. Since the nasal tip tends to drop with advancing years, the criminals have been seriated by age groups. Table XII–39 shows the expected decrease of up inclinations and increase of down inclinations in the successive age groups. In both the 15–19 years and the 20–34 years age groups of criminals the up inclinations are vastly in excess of those displayed by the civilians. But in the 35–69 years criminal group there is 3.13 per cent less of up inclinations than in the civilian sample. However, the mean age of the civilians is 34.50 years and that of the 35–69 years criminal group is 45.20 years. It, therefore, appears that the excess of upward inclinations of the septum in criminals is somewhat greater than would be expected from the age disparity between civilians and criminals. The Massachusetts comparison diverges from the Tennessee and total series comparisons in the direction of its deviations, but insignificantly. This disagreement is not serious, but it nevertheless weakens the total series result. It is due to a very high proportion of upward inclined septa recorded in the Massachusetts civilian sample. The excess of downward inclined septa in the Tennessee firemen is largely responsible for the difference between the criminals and the civilian check sample.

Nasal Septum Deflection. Deflections of the nasal septum in criminals are much more frequent than in the civilian check sample (Table XII–40). The excess is large and significant only in the case of deflections to the right. Both state comparisons show excess of this deflection (insignificant in Tennessee), and both show deficiencies of left deflections which are converted into an insignificant excess in the total series comparison. This is a Class B observation, but the excess of right deflections in the criminals and the deficiency of absent are probably valid.

Nose. Conclusions. The criminals of this series differ markedly from the civilians of the check sample in the distribution of nasal features. The criminals have much shorter noses, which are relatively broader. They include much larger proportions of noses with high and broad roots. The nasal bridge is oftener high and varies more extremely in breadth in criminals than in civilians. The profile of the criminal nose is much more frequently concave, humped, or undulating in prisoners than in civilians at large; it is less often straight. Criminals are more likely than civilians to show very thin or very thick nasal tips, to have septa inclined upward, and to suffer from deflections of the septum to the right.

The observations upon noses are well supported by the measurements. However, it is clear that no particular form of nose is peculiar to, or generally characteristic of, criminals.

Hrdlička's observations upon the noses of Old Americans are not very closely comparable with ours, probably because of slight differences in technique. He finds only 8.7 per cent of his Old American males with concave bridges, as against 18.51 per cent of our civil sample and 22.27 per cent of criminals.[3] Convex noses are recorded in 42 per cent of Old American males, in 29.87 per cent of the civilians of our check sample, and in 20.84 per cent of criminals. Straight noses occur in 22 per cent of Old Americans, in 17.86 per cent of civilians, and in 11.28 per cent of criminals. It is noticeable that our civilians are, in every case, intermediate between our criminals and Hrdlička's Old Americans.

Evidently an observational difference, due to personal equations, obscures the comparison of inclination of the nasal septum in our series with that of Hrdlička. The latter records 56.3 per cent of Old American males with septa "horizontal or nearly so."[4] Our observers find no civilians with horizontal septa and only .43 per cent of criminals. Hrdlička has 32 per cent with septa inclined upward, as against 56.49 per cent in our civilians and 68.14 per cent in our criminals. The Old Americans include 11.7 per cent with downward inclination, whereas the figures in our survey are for civilians 43.50 per cent, and for criminals 31.42 per cent. Clearly our observers differentiated slighter degrees of inclination, thus virtually eliminating the approximately horizontal class. If we resolve Hrdlička's horizontal class, assigning half of it to upward inclination and half to downward, the following comparison results:

TABLE XII–41

SEPTUM INCLINATION OF CRIMINALS COMPARED WITH SEPTUM INCLINATION OF CIVILIANS OF SIMILAR ORIGIN

	Authority	Number	Mean Age	Elevated (Plus ½ Horizontal)	Depressed
Criminals	This study	2858	30.70	68.35	31.64
Civilians	This study	308	34.50	56.49	43.50
Old Americans	Hrdlička	130?	?	60.15	39.85

[3] Hrdlička, 1925, p. 245.
[4] Hrdlička, 1925, p. 246.

This comparison is, of course, of doubtful validity, and the more so since Hrdlička's Laboratory series of Old Americans has a much higher mean age than either of our samples, and thus should exhibit more downward inclined septa. Since Hrdlička does not state the identity of his series, nor its mean age, no certain conclusion can be drawn. However, the comparison indicates that the Old Americans may lie between our civilians and criminals and certainly resemble the civilians in this feature more closely than the delinquents.

Lips — Integumental Thickness. The integumental lips are those areas which in males may be covered by moustache and goatee. Thickness of the tissues in this portion of the face is associated with pronounced development of the *orbicularis oris* muscle, and is characteristic of Negroes and other prognathous races. This Class B observation shows a significant excess of submedium thickness in total criminals when compared with total civilians, and a corresponding deficiency of medium in the criminals (Table XII–42). There is also a probably significant deficiency of the pronounced category in the criminals. The Massachusetts comparison exaggerates the trend of the total series comparison, but the Tennessee group of criminals shows a significant excess of medium lips over the civilians from that state. Here perhaps we may accept the total series result, since it is substantiated in Massachusetts.

Lips — Membranous Thickness. Excesses of submedium membranous lips are also found in the total series and in the Massachusetts comparison (Table XII–43). Tennessee criminals diverge in the opposite direction. The differences are so complicated by personal equations that they seem quite unreliable.

Lip Seam. Finally the total series and Massachusetts comparisons both show excesses of slight or absent lip seams in the criminals, while Tennessee displays no significant deviation from its check sample (Table XII–44). This result is due principally to the equation of Observer C in the check sample. On the whole it seems probable that thin integumental and membranous lips and slightly developed lip seams occur more frequently in criminals than in civilians, but the data are rather conflicting and do not inspire much confidence in any generalization.

Alveolar Prognathism. The total series comparison shows an excess of criminals with slight alveolar prognathism and a deficiency of criminals with medium alveolar prognathism (Table XII–45). The Tennessee criminals do not differ from their check sample. The Massachusetts criminals show a tremendous excess of slight degrees of alveolar prognathism, possibly due to their strong element of French Canadian extraction. There is evidently no consistent difference between criminals and civilians. The observation is Class B.

Facial Prognathism. The total series of criminals shows no significant difference from the check sample. Massachusetts criminals have significantly more prognathism than Massachusetts civilians, but there is no reliable difference between the samples from Tennessee (Table XII–46). On the whole, we must conclude that neither alveolar prognathism nor facial prognathism has any significance in its degree of development in criminals as contrasted with civilians. Such differences as have been recorded could easily have arisen from the effects of the varying personal equations of observers.

Chin Form. No significant difference in chin form between the total criminals and total civilians is evinced (Table XII–47). This lack of differentiation is evidently the result, in part, of the disagreement of the Massachusetts and the Tennessee comparisons, since the latter exhibits an excess of criminals with bilateral chins, and the former a great excess of criminals with median chins.

Malar Prominence. An excess of submedium malar prominence is displayed by the total criminal series over the total civilian check sample (Table XII–48). This evidently has nothing to do with Massachusetts and Tennessee criminals, neither of which groups diverges significantly from its check sample. The Massachusetts criminals show a significant excess of pronounced malars and the Tennessee criminals a significant deficiency. Obviously state differences in opposite directions render the total criminal comparison colorless.

Cheeks — Fullness. The total series comparison shows an excess of submedium cheek fullness in criminals (Table XII–49). This is substantiated in both state comparisons. The Massachusetts criminals show an excess of pronounced cheek fullness and the Tennessee criminals a deficiency. These divergent differences cancel each other and are largely instrumental in bringing about the insignificance of the difference in the total series comparison in the pronounced fullness category.

Gonial Angles. The prominence of the gonial (hinder mandibular) angles is a Class B observation. The total criminal series shows an excess of individuals with submedium prominence, and a deficiency of those with pronounced angles (Table XII–50). The Massachusetts and Tennessee comparisons agree with the total series comparison in regard to the excess of submedium angles among the criminals. This difference appears to be valid. But the Massachusetts criminals show a deficiency of medium gonial angles and an excess of pronounced angles, whereas the Tennessee criminals differ from their check sample in the opposite direction and to a significant degree. The Tennessee result is undoubtedly an effect of the great excess of pronounced gonial angles in the Nashville firemen who compose the check sample. The total series and Massachusetts comparisons are influenced by the equation in the civilian check sample of Observer C whose observations are disproportionately high in the medium category. Therefore the deficiency of pronounced angles in the criminals of the total comparison is unreliable.

The seriation of the criminals by age groups shows an increase in prominence of the gonial angles with advancing years (Table XII–51). Since the civilians are older than the criminals, a deficiency of pronounced angles in the latter group is to be expected. But every criminal age group shows an excess of submedium angles and a deficiency of pronounced angles when compared with the civilians. Therefore the differences between criminals and civilians seem to exceed those which would be attributable to the older mean age of the latter group.

Hrdlička, in his "Old Americans," reports 29.3 per cent of males with submedium gonial angles,[5] as against 12.16 per cent in our criminals, and only 4.15 per cent of our civilian check sample. Again he records 13.4 per cent of Old Americans with angles "slightly to moderately above medium and prominent," whereas 17.41 per cent of our criminals and 22.04 per cent of the check sample are included in this category. Apart from the possibility of this difference being due in some measure to personal equations, Hrdlička's text makes it clear that his Old American Laboratory group is decidedly below average development in this feature: "Bulging angles, such as not infrequently seen among male immigrants, were wholly absent." [6] It may be noted that our crim-

[5] Hrdlička, 1925, p. 282.
[6] Hrdlička, 1925, p. 281.

nals and civil subjects are not "Old Americans" — defined as those whose ancestors on both sides for two generations have been born in the United States — but are merely native Whites of native parentage. However, it is probable that the subjects of our survey are, in a majority of cases, "Old Americans," since 48.86 per cent come from Kentucky, Tennessee, and North Carolina, where Old American stock vastly predominates; 21.72 per cent from Texas, where, apart from Mexicans and Negroes, the population contains a very strong Old American element, and the rest from Massachusetts, Wisconsin, Colorado, New Mexico, and Arizona, where at least a fair proportion of the subjects measured are undoubtedly Old Americans.

At any rate it seems that the Old Americans studied by Hrdlička are nearer to our criminals in this feature than to our civilians, possibly because our check sample includes more persons who are not "Old Americans," than does the criminal series.

Cheeks — Wrinkling. Wrinkling is a Class A observation, but obviously conditioned by age. Hence a great deficiency of criminals with pronounced wrinkling (−11.81 per cent, 8.20 p.e.) cannot be accepted without age correction (Table XII–52). Pronounced wrinkling cannot be expected to manifest itself before the age of 35 years in most male individuals. There is in the civil check sample an excess of 14.04 per cent of individuals 35 years or more in age, when compared with the criminals (cf. Table XI–7). The total deficiency in pronounced wrinkling in criminals amounts to 11.81 per cent when compared with the civilians. Table XII–53 re-seriates wrinkling in the criminals by age groups. It shows very clearly the relation of this feature to advancing age. The excess of criminals below the age of 35 is 14.06 per cent and the excess of unwrinkled criminals is 15.88 per cent. We must conclude, therefore, that apart from age differences, our data afford no evidence of a differentiation between criminals and civilians in wrinkling.

Massachusetts and Tennessee both follow the total series in the direction of their deviations, but in Tennessee only are the deviations of such magnitude as to be statistically significant.

Teeth. In the wear of teeth the criminals show a significant excess of persons with slight or medium wear and an approximately equal deficiency in those with pronounced wear (Table XII–54). This finding is, of course, partially due to age disparity in the groups. The excess of criminals below the age of 35 years is 14.06 per cent, and the excess of criminals with slight or medium tooth wear is 12.30 per cent. Similarly the deficiency of old criminals (35 and more years in age) is 14.04 per cent, and the deficiency in criminals with pronounced tooth wear is 12.68 per cent. It would therefore appear that, apart from age, there is little difference in tooth wear between criminals and civilians. If anything, the criminals show slightly more wear for their years. Table XII–55 re-seriates the criminals by three age groups. The oldest age group of criminals shows much more pronounced wear than the civilian series as a whole, and the other two much less wear.

There is no agreement between the three comparisons in the appraisal of the number of carious teeth (Table XII–56). Massachusetts criminals display, in general, more decayed teeth than their civilian check sample, and Tennessee criminals fewer. The total series shows fewer criminals with no caries and fewer with many caries than is found in the check sample.

The number of teeth lost presents an exactly similar problem (Table XII–57). The criminals show excesses of the none and few categories, amounting to a total of 11.36 per cent, and deficiencies of the many category amounting to the same percentage. This corresponds fairly well with the 14.04 excess of criminals below the age of 35 years. Table XII–58 seriates the criminals by three age groups. On the whole, the prisoners show a lesser excess of persons with little tooth wear and few or no teeth lost than would be expected in view of the proportional excess of younger males in the criminal series. However, the approximately 3 per cent of residual deficiency in number of criminals showing little or no tooth loss may be due in part to the personal equation of observers.

Bite shows a statistically valid difference between the criminals and the civilians in that the criminals have a 10.18 per cent excess of slight overbites, and an equal deficiency of marked overbites (Table XII–59). This difference is not affected by age, so far as I am aware. It would appear that more criminals than civilians possess normal bites.

Tennessee and Massachusetts show significant divergences in percentage of edge-to-edge bite. These become insignificant in the total series comparison. In excesses of slight overbites and deficiencies of marked overbites both state comparisons agree with the total series.

The inconsistency of the state and total comparisons indicate that there are virtually no general differences between the criminals and the civilians in condition of teeth. The slight superiority of criminal dentition over civilian dentition which is apparent in the total comparisons is almost certainly attributable to the younger mean age of the criminals.

Ear Lobes — Size. There are no consistent differences between total criminals and total civilians in size of ear lobes (Table XII–60). Massachusetts criminals have more small ear lobes and more large ear lobes than their check sample, and Tennessee criminals are deficient in both of these extreme variations.

Ear Lobes — Attachment. Here again there is no total series difference (Table XII–61). Tennessee criminals show a significant excess of attached ear lobes.

Roll of Helix. All three comparisons agree in showing great deficiencies of criminals with medium or pronounced roll of the helices (Table XII–62). The age seriation shows that roll of the helix decreases with age (Table XII–63). Since the civilians are much older than the criminals we should expect the former to show higher proportions of helices with submedium roll. The reverse is the case and the difference is general and valid.

Darwin's Point. Darwin's point, the vestige of the free tip of the ear, is more frequently present in the criminals than in the civilians. The state comparisons substantiate the differences of the total series (Table XII–64).

Antihelix Prominence. The total series and the Massachusetts comparisons show excesses of criminals with pronounced development of the antihelix (Table XII–65). The Tennessee criminals do not differ from their check sample.

Ear Protrusion. Both submedium and pronounced protrusion of the ear are in excess in the total criminals when compared with the total civilians (Table XII–66). The Massachusetts comparison agrees with the total series. Tennessee diverges in showing an insignificant deficiency of pronounced ear protrusion on the part of the criminals.

Conclusions on Ears. Criminals do not differ from civilians in the development and attachment of ear lobes, but the criminal ear has a helix less rolled, with a more frequent development of Darwin's point and a greater frequency of pronounced antihelix. Ears of pronounced and submedium projection are more common in criminals than in civilians. Anomalous and deformed ears are not common in our criminal records.

Temporal Fullness. The total series shows an excess of criminals with submedium or pronounced temporal fullness when compared with the check sample (Table XII–67). However, an inspection of the state comparisons reveals such divergences in the deviations as to force the conclusion that the total result is without any significance.

Lambdoid Flattening. An excess of lambdoid flattening in the total prisoners is deprived of any general significance when we note that the two state comparisons show differences in opposite directions (Table XII–68).

Facial Asymmetry. Facial asymmetry (Class B) is not significantly different in the criminals from that in the check sample (Table XII–69). Indeed the civilians show insignificant excesses of both right and left asymmetries when compared with the criminals. Thus a classical criminal stigma fails to manifest itself in this investigation.

Neck. In observed proportions of the neck (Class A) the criminals show a great excess of long, thin necks, and compensating deficiencies in the medium length and breadth, and short, thick categories (Table XII–70). Both states agree with the total series in the direction of their deviations. It is a matter of common observation, however, that the neck thickens in middle life, and is likely to appear shorter and thicker in adults of mature years than in young people. Consequently the criminals have been re-seriated in three age groups (Table XII–71). This table shows that in successive age groups the proportion of criminals with medium necks decreases slightly, the short, thick category becomes perceptibly greater, and the long, thin variety remains constant in its proportions. In every age subgroup the criminals display a marked excess of long thin necks, and a smaller, but significant deficiency of short, thick necks, and of medium necks. We must then conclude that, apart from age, these criminals are distinguished from the civil check sample by the excessive proportion having long, thin necks.

Shoulder Slope. Shoulder slope (Class A) manifests a distinction between criminals and civilians in that the former are characterized by a great excess of pronouncedly sloping shoulders (Table XII–72). Both states agree with the total series, but the Massachusetts deviations are insignificant. Here again, a possible age influence must be considered. A re-seriation of the criminals by age groups shows that slightly sloping shoulders increase in successive age groups, but are never common either among the criminals or among the civilians (Table XII–73). The shoulders of medium slope and of pronounced slope vary irregularly in the age groups, but, on the whole, pronounced shoulder slopes are commonest in the youngest group. Thus, while some age effect may accentuate the difference between the two series, it is wholly insufficient to account for the great disparity. A personal equation may enter in here, but it is not perceptible in the comparison of the records of the two main observers. The only conclusion which can be drawn is that criminals in this series differ from the civilians here brought into comparison in that the former have a larger proportion of individuals with sloping shoulders, as contrasted with an overwhelming predominance of moderate shoulder slopes in the civilians.

SOCIOLOGICAL COMPARISON OF PRISON SERIES BY OFFENSE GROUPS
WITH TOTAL CIVIL CHECK SAMPLE

Marital State. The differentiation of the offense groups with respect to proportions of single men seems principally dependent upon age (Tables XII–74, 75). The younger groups show excesses and the older groups deficiencies. The only group which shows a significant excess of married men is versus public welfare, which is one of the oldest offense groups. Excesses of widowers occur in every group except arson, but these are significant only in the older offense groups.

Occupation. The occupational comparisons are distorted by the large number of firemen in the check sample. Huge excesses of extractive workers and laborers are found in every offense group (Table XII–76). Significant residua would probably remain even if the civilian check sample were not skewed by the preponderance of public service. A few group differentiations are of certain importance. These are the excess of factory workers in robbery and burglary and larceny, of assault criminals in skilled trades; and the deficiencies of second degree murder, burglary and larceny, and rape in trade, of second degree murder in semi-professional, or burglary and larceny in professional. Every offense group except second degree murder shows a significant excess in personal service, and except assault a deficiency in students, and every one except forgery a deficiency (significant or insignificant) in clerical.

Education. Significant excesses of illiterates appear in every offense group (Table XII–77). Persons who can read and write only are also in excess in every offense group, but these excesses are not significant in assault, robbery, and burglary and larceny. In general the excesses of offense groups over civilians are constant through the sixth grade. In the seventh grade the more ignorant offense groups (especially first degree murder) begin to show deficiencies. In the eighth grade all offense groups except robbery show lower proportions than occur in the check sample. In the last two years of high school every offense group shows a significant deficiency. The only offense group which shows an excess of college men over the civilian check sample is forgery and fraud. The excess is not statistically significant.

MORPHOLOGICAL COMPARISON OF PRISON SERIES BY OFFENSE GROUP
WITH TOTAL CIVIL CHECK SAMPLE

Hair Quantity, Head. The excesses of large amounts of head hair among the criminals cannot be attributed exclusively to the younger mean age of the prisoners as compared with the civilians, since the oldest offense group, versus public welfare, shows a marked excess of abundant head hair, although exceeding the mean age of the civilian check sample by nearly four years (Tables XII–74, 78).

Hair Quantity, Beard. Since all offense groups, irrespective of age, show excesses of small amounts of beard hair (Table XII–79), the deficiency of criminals in this respect cannot be due to the low mean age of the prison series (Table XII–74).

Hair Quantity, Body. A perusal of Table XII–80 seems to indicate that differences of the offense groups from the civilians in amounts of body hair may be due almost entirely to age factors.

Skin Color. Excesses of olive skin color among the different offense groups of prisoners are probably due to personal equations of the observers. In general, skin color observations are unreliable and differences should not be stressed (Table XII–81).

Hair Form. The unanimity which the offense groups manifest in showing excesses of straight hair over the proportions observed in the civilian check sample raises anew the question of the possible influence of prison hair cutting upon observations of hair form (Table XII–82). Even if we make a substantial allowance for wavy hair judged to be straight because of close crops in the prisoners, the deficiencies of curly and frizzly hair indicate that curved varieties of hair are indeed less common in criminals than in civilians as represented by the check sample.

Hair Color. The consistency of the deviations in hair color of the different offense groups is remarkable (Table XII–83). Most remarkable is the excess of red-brown hair among the criminals, irrespective of age or offense. Almost equally notable is the deficiency in gray and white hair which occurs in every offense group, irrespective of its age. Note however that these deficiencies do not attain significance in any of the older offense groups.

Eye Color. The agreement of the offense groups in the directions of their eye color deviations from the check sample is again astounding (Table XII–84). Since both Massachusetts and Tennessee comparisons agree absolutely in the direction of their deviations with the total comparison, the differences cannot be attributed to state factors nor to the exclusion of Observer B and the inclusion of Observer C in the observation of the check sample. There is no single significant divergence of an offense group from the trend of the total prison series.

Sclera. The comments upon eye color are equally applicable to the pigmentation of the sclera (Table XII–85). However one exceptional fact must be noted. The Massachusetts comparison disagrees radically with that of the Tennessee and total series comparisons. In the former state more speckled and yellow sclerae are found among criminals than among civilians. Yet the excess of clear sclerae in the total prison group overrides the total civilian sample with its majority of clear eyed Massachusetts subjects. This may mean only that the Tennessee firemen show an unrepresentatively large proportion of pigmented sclerae.

Iris. Every offense group agrees with the total series trend in the distribution of pigment of the iris (Table XII–86). Since both state comparisons agree with that of the total series, the deviations must be accepted as of general criminological significance in native Whites of native parentage.

Eye Folds. Assault, robbery, and burglary and larceny show more median eye folds than the check sample (Table XII–87). Otherwise all the offense groups agree in exhibiting more epicanthic (internal folds), more external folds, fewer median folds and fewer cases of no folds, than are found in the civilians. External folds are commonest in the older offense groups, but epicanthic folds are also at a maximum in two of the oldest groups (first degree murder, other sex offenses). It seems clear that inner (epicanthic) and outer eye folds occur much more frequently in criminals than in civilians.

Eyebrow Thickness. Pronounced eyebrow thickness is commoner in every offense group than in the civilian check sample, in spite of the fact that the high mean age of the Tennessee firemen brings up the average of thick eyebrows for the check sample and that the latter considerably exceeds in average age the criminal series (Table

XII–88). Thin eyebrows are deficient (although insignificantly) only in the two youngest offense groups. This finding is very strange, since we expect eyebrow thickness to increase with age. The difference may be due in part to the equation of Observer C who records a very high percentage (87.36) of eyebrows of medium thickness in his share of the check sample. Of course the observations of this anthropologist may be absolutely correct, but the discrepancy might occur in the way indicated.

Forehead Height. Every offense group shows a significant excess of submedium forehead heights over the civilian check sample (Table XII–89). This excess of low foreheads occurs in both Massachusetts and Tennessee comparisons. However, these comparisons disagree with respect to pronounced forehead heights. In this category the criminals show more excesses over the civilians than deficiencies, but none of the differences attain statistical significance. Observer C's data disagree with those of Observer A in the pronounced and medium categories, thus influencing the total series result.

Forehead Slope. Pronounced forehead slopes are greatly in excess among the criminals, and slight or absent slopes pronouncedly deficient. Again every criminal offense group deviates in the same direction from the civilian check sample (Table XII–90). In the state comparisons Massachusetts supports the total series, while the Tennessee criminals and civilians show no significant differences.

Nasion Depression. Every criminal offense group shows an excess of pronounced nasion depression (Table XII–91). Both state comparisons agree with the total series in this category, but disagree in the submedium category, in which most of the offense groups record excesses also. The results are unreliable on account of personal equation.

Nasal Root Height. All criminal groups show excesses of pronounced nasal root heights (Table XII–92). Both state comparisons support the total series trend. The differences are valid.

Nasal Root Breadth. Nearly every criminal group shows excesses in the extreme categories of nasal breadth (Table XII–93). The Tennessee comparison shows no significant difference in these features between criminals and civilians.

Nasal Bridge Height. Significant excesses of nasal bridge height are recorded in every offense group (Table XII–94). Tennessee criminals do not diverge from their civilian check sample.

Nasal Bridge Breadth. Submedium and pronounced nasal bridge breadths are in excess among criminals, and, more notably, the pronounced breadths. All of the offense groups show deviations in the same direction (Table XII–95). Tennessee criminals as a group again fail to differ significantly from the civilians of that state.

Nasal Profile. There are no deviations of the offense groups which differ significantly from the total series trend in the form of nasal profile, with the exception of an excess of concave noses in the young burglary and larceny group (Table XII–96). Otherwise all offense groups agree in displaying deficiencies of straight and convex noses and excesses of concavo-convex profiles. Both state comparisons agree with the total series result.

Nasal Tip Thickness. All of the offense groups agree in displaying excesses in the extreme categories of nasal tip thickness (Table XII–97). The state comparisons disagree with the total series result.

Nasal Septum Inclination. All criminal offense groups show excesses of upwardly inclined septa (Table XII–98). The Massachusetts comparison disagrees with the total series result, which is affected largely by the excesses of downward inclination among the Tennessee firemen.

Nasal Septum Deflection. Septum deflections to the right are significantly more common in every offense group (Table XII–99). Absence of deflection is more rare in every criminal group than in the civilian check sample. All of the data are in agreement.

Lips — Integumental Thickness. The offense groups are slightly better differentiated in integumental lip thickness than in most other observations (Table XII–100). All but versus public welfare show excess of submedium thickness. This group shows an insignificant excess of medium. A significant deficiency of pronounced thickness is found only in burglary and larceny. The Tennessee comparison is in disagreement with the results in Massachusetts and in the total series.

Lips — Membranous Thickness. Every offense group shows a significant excess of submedium membranous lip thickness, at the expense of medium (Table XII–101). The two state comparisons radically disagree, Tennessee criminals diverging from their civilian check sample in directions opposite to those of the differences in the Massachusetts and total series comparisons. A combination of personal equations is probably responsible for the total and subgroup differences.

Lip Seam. The deviations of lip seam categories of criminals from the proportions shown in the check sample are rather more numerous than in most observations (Table XII–102). Yet no offense group disagrees significantly with the total series comparison. The absence of a lip seam is generally more frequent in the criminals than in the civilians. The state comparisons are inconsistent, except in the criminal excess of lack of the feature. The subgroups showing significant absence of lip seam are, in general, above the mean age of the series.

Alveolar Prognathism. All offense groups show excesses of submedium prognathism and deficiencies of medium prognathism in the alveolar region (Table XII–103). Nearly all of the deviations are statistically valid. The Tennessee comparison shows no significant differentiation between criminals and civilians.

Facial Prognathism. While all of the offense groups tend to follow the total series trend in facial prognathism, no single group shows a deviation of certain significance from the check sample (Table XII–104). There are uncertain indications that sex offenders display more facial prognathism than other criminals and than civilians. In the Massachusetts comparison there is a very definite excess of criminal prognathism. This is not confirmed in the Tennessee comparison nor in that of the total series.

Chin Form. Differences in chin form in the offense groups are insignificant (Table XII–105).

Malar Prominence. In prominence of malars there are some definite offense group differences in deviations from the civilians (Table XII–106). Versus public welfare criminals are remarkable for their malar prominence. (Here there is a state sampling factor to be considered, inasmuch as this offense group is overloaded with Texans.) First and second degree murder and burglary and larceny show significant excesses of submedium malar prominence. The state comparisons are in disagreement.

Cheeks — Fullness. Every offense group shows an excess of submedium cheek fullness and a deficiency of medium fullness (Table XII–107). The versus public welfare group alone shows a significant excess of full cheeks. The state comparisons agree only in exhibiting a criminal excess of thin cheeks.

Gonial Angles. All offense groups save versus public welfare and arson and all other offenses show excesses of submedium prominence of the jaw angles (Table XII–108). The excesses of submedium are significant in both murder groups, in robbery, burglary and larceny, forgery and fraud, and other sex offenses. All of the offense groups except versus public welfare show deficiencies of pronounced gonial angles. These are significant only in robbery, in burglary and larceny, and in arson. The state comparisons disagree in the medium and pronounced categories.

Cheeks — Wrinkling. All offense groups show excesses of persons in which wrinkling is absent (Table XII–109). These excesses are insignificant in the two murder groups and in rape, which have high mean ages. Pronounced wrinkling is deficient in assault, robbery, burglary and larceny, forgery and fraud, and arson and all other offenses. The offense group differences are not wholly consistent with age differences in the several groups. Wrinkling seems to be less common in criminals than in civilians, irrespective of age. The state results are inconsistent.

Teeth Wear. All offense groups show excesses of slight or medium tooth wear and deficiencies of pronounced wear, but these are significant only in the offense groups of low mean age (Table XII–110). The state comparisons disagree in the category of no wear, Massachusetts criminals showing fewer in this grade than occur in the civilian check sample, and Tennessee criminals more.

Teeth Caries. Every offense group shows deficiencies of no caries, excesses of few and deficiencies of many (Table XII–111). The state comparisons are in complete disagreement. No general conclusion can be drawn from the data.

Teeth Lost. The offense group differences in number of teeth lost are not wholly consistent with age variations (Table XII–112). Two of the older offense groups, second degree murder and versus public welfare, seem to show fewer teeth lost than would be expected. The state comparisons disagree, probably because of age differences.

Bite. Normal bites or slight overbites are more common in all criminal groups than in the civilians, and marked overbites are deficient among the criminals (Table XII–113). Edge-to-edge bites are more common in the older offense groups.

Ear Lobes — Development. Offense group differences in development of the ear lobes when compared with the civilians seem to be due largely to age variation (Table XII–114).

Ear Lobes — Attachment. The only significantly deviating offense group is versus public welfare, which shows an excess of free ear lobes (Table XII–115).

Roll of Helix. All of the offense groups agree in deviating from the civilians by excesses of submediumly rolled helices (Table XII–116). The state comparisons support the total series result.

Darwin's Point. In Darwin's point the various offense groups agree closely in their deviations from the civilian check sample (Table XII–117). This feature is more common among the criminals. Assault and other sex offenses are the only groups which fail to show significant deviations — probably because of their small numbers. The state comparisons support the total series result.

Antihelix Prominence. Marked antihelix prominence is more common in every criminal group than among the civilians (Table XII–118). The Tennessee state comparison shows no significant differences.

Ear Protrusion. Every offense group shows a significant excess of pronounced ear protrusion. Most of them also show small excesses of submedium protrusions (Table XII–119). The state comparisons agree.

Temporal Fullness. Excesses of submedium fullness and deficiencies of pronounced fullness in the temporal region occur in every offense group (Table XII–120). But personal equations vitiate the result.

Lambdoid Flattening. Every criminal group except versus public welfare shows a significant excess of lambdoid flattening (Table XII–121). The Massachusetts and Tennessee comparisons disagree, with Tennessee conforming to the series trend.

Asymmetry. In asymmetry there is no certainly significant deviation of any offense group from the civilian check sample (Table XII–122).

Neck. Every offense group shows a significant excess of long thin necks, and a corresponding deficiency of short, thick necks (Table XII–123). The state comparisons agree.

Shoulder Slope. Pronounced shoulder slopes are in excess in every criminal offense group (Table XII–124). First degree murder alone shows also an excess of slight shoulder slope. The state comparisons agree.

SUMMARY OF OBSERVATIONS

The sociological differences between criminals and civilians, as revealed by the materials of this study, are numerous and important (cf. summary Tables XII–126 and XII–138). However, it is extremely difficult, and in many cases impossible, to distinguish the differences which have a general criminological validity from those which are due to the inevitable selectional factors of state sampling, occupational sampling, and other inequalities of the criminal and civil series.

Criminals include a much higher proportion of single persons than is found in the civil population of comparable age, and a considerably higher percentage of divorced or separated men. Apparently fewer criminals than civilians are widowers, presumably because of the low marriage rate of the delinquents.

The most remarkable difference in occupation between our criminals and our civilians is the great excess of persons engaged in extractive occupations (farming, stock-breeding, forestry, fishing, mining) among the delinquents. Some of this excess is referable to the rural provenience of the native White Americans of native parentage in our criminal series, as contrasted with the exclusively urban character of the check sample. When we add to this disturbing factor the presence of nearly 45 per cent of Nashville firemen in the check sample, it becomes apparent that the utility of our civilian series for occupational comparison is practically nil.

Criminals include far more illiterates and poorly educated persons than do comparable samples of the law-abiding population. The delinquents have lower percentages of their numbers in all of the higher educational classes. To some extent the inferior education of these criminals must be discounted because of the fact that a very large proportion of them come from backward states where educational opportunities are very poor. Nevertheless, there is no doubt that native White criminals of

native parentage are far inferior to civilians of the same origin in educational attain
ment. This is far from implying, however, that poor educational opportunities create
criminals.

Tattooing, a practice of ignorant and stupid persons, is commoner among criminals
than among civilians, but in this group of criminals it occurs infrequently — in about
one of seven prisoners. In this country it certainly has very little if any criminological
significance.

Probably criminals have less beard and body hair and more head hair than civil
ians, but the data on these points are not altogether satisfactory.

It is quite certain that criminals include a larger percentage of straight-haired men
as compared with wavy-haired, curly-haired, and frizzly-haired individuals, than is
found in the civilian population of similar origin. But prison hair crops may account
for some portion of the excess of straight-haired criminals, since the wave in head hair
is not perceptible if the latter is cut very short.

The principal difference in hair color between criminals and civilians is in the greater
proportion of red-brown hair and the lesser proportion of gray or white hair in the pris
oners. The latter is due to the younger mean age of the criminals as compared with our
civilian check sample. The excess of red-brown hair in criminals may also be partially
attributable to the same cause, especially if, as I suspect, red-brown hair tends to turn
gray earlier than other shades.

Criminals are deficient in the very light and very dark shades of eye color (blues
and brown) and include an unduly large proportion of men with mixed eyes. Among
criminals homogeneous irides are comparatively rare. Speckled and zoned irides are
present in excessive numbers. Such irides are frequent in mixed eyes, but the charac
teristic pigment distribution of such eyes is rayed, and this is the prevailing arrange
ment among civilians.

There are larger proportions of eye folds among criminals than among our civil
ians, especially inner epicanthic folds, but the excesses are not large. The differences
are not due, however, to age disparity between the samples.

Our data substantiate the findings of the Italian School in that our criminals more
frequently display low foreheads and sloping foreheads than do the civilians of the
check sample, but the personal equations of observers cast some doubt upon this re
sult. The nose is higher in the root, higher in the bridge, and more often undulating
or concavo-convex, in criminals than in our civilians. The septum is prevailingly in
clined upward and the tip is commonly thin or thick rather than medium. The nasal
septum is more frequently deflected than in the check sample. The nose is short and
relatively broad in the average criminal. This series of offenders shows a larger pro
portion of thin-lipped individuals than the comparable non-criminal group. The hinder
angles of the jaws (gonial angles) are more frequently compressed and less often pro
jecting in the delinquents.

Apart from age differences, the criminals show no pronounced divergence from
the civilians in wear of teeth or number of teeth lost, but they display a significantly
small percentage of marked overbites.

The ears of our criminals are smaller and relatively broader than those of the ci
vilians, even when due allowance is made for age difference. The helix or rim of the
ear is more frequently very slightly rolled in the criminals. Darwin's point is oftener

present and well developed. Extremely degenerate or malformed ears are uncommon in this series of prisoners.

This series of native born American criminals of native parentage is particularly distinguished also from the civilian check sample by the inclusion in it of many more individuals with long thin necks and sloping shoulders.

Thus the composite picture of the contrast between the criminal of native birth and native parentage and the civilian, emphasizes the smaller size of the criminal, his inferior weight and poorer body build, his smaller head and face, his straighter hair, and his shorter, relatively broader face, with more prominent but shorter and broader nose, usually snubbed, and frequently deflected. The criminal's jaws are not unduly developed and his ears are somewhat primitive in conformation, but small in size.

It must be emphasized that the differences here presented do not distinguish every native born American criminal of native parentage from the law-abiding persons of similar stock. They are average or composite differences, and cannot be relied upon for purposes of individual diagnosis. At an earlier stage in this investigation we have tested the validity of combinations of "criminal features" in the individual, but it must be re-stated plainly and emphatically here, that there is no single physical feature or morphological variation which is, in any sense, peculiar to criminals. Differences between criminals and non-criminals are in relative frequency of the occurrence of certain variations in groups.

Again, the reader must not lose sight of the fact that the comparison of this large criminal group with a rather small check sample and the elucidation of the differences between the two groups, does not necessarily imply that such differences are universal and would obtain between any two groups of criminals and civilians similarly compared. Especially they must not be taken to apply to any other ethnic or racial groups than the one here discussed. The characteristics of criminals and civilians of different racial and ethnic origin will be considered in another volume.

The interpretation of differences between criminals and civilians must be reserved for the concluding chapters of this book.

SUMMARY OF SOCIOLOGICAL DEVIATIONS OF OFFENSE GROUPS AND OF TOTAL PRISON SERIES FROM CIVILIAN CHECK SAMPLE

Table XII–125 shows the number and percentage of significant and insignificant deviations from the check sample of civilians for each offense group, for the total criminal series, and for the individual state comparisons. Each category of a sociological observation is counted as a separate deviation. The total series shows 80.77 per cent of significant sociological deviations out of a total of 26 sociological categories. In the state comparisons the significant deviations are reduced sharply — to 50 per cent in Massachusetts and to 61.54 per cent in Tennessee. It therefore appears that the sociological differences in the total series comparison are exaggerated by inequalities incident to state sampling which cannot be corrected statistically. These are specifically due to the fact that the check sample is derived from two states only and that the Tennessee check sample consists exclusively of Nashville firemen.

Judging from the Massachusetts comparison the valid residuum of sociological differences unaffected by state sampling would amount to at least 50 per cent of all sociological categories.

The offense group differences from the check sample afford some idea of the degree to which different classes of criminals are sociologically distinguished from civilians of similar parentage. Burglary and larceny and offenses versus public welfare show the strongest differentiation — 69.23 per cent of all categories in each case. First degree murder, second degree murder, and rape comprise the second class in order of sociological differentiation from civilians with 57.7 per cent to 65.4 per cent of significant sociological deviations from the check sample. The smallest percentage of significant sociological deviations occurs in two offense groups — assault, and forgery and fraud. Doubtless the small percentage in the former case is due to the numerical insignificance of the offense group. It seems clear that forgery and fraud is the group least different sociologically from the check sample of civilians. Other groups with comparatively few deviations are robbery, other sex offenses, and arson.

Since we should expect not more than 4 per cent of significant deviations in any offense group which could be attributed to size of samples, it is clear that by offense groups and as a whole our criminals are overwhelmingly different from the civilian check sample. That these differences are not primarily the effect of the sociologically and geographically unrepresentative character of the check sample is indicated not only by the Massachusetts comparison, which is impeccable, but also by the supporting data concerning marital status, education, and occupation, which are derived from census statistics relating to the population of the United States as a whole.

SUMMARY OF MORPHOLOGICAL DEVIATIONS OF OFFENSE GROUPS AND OF TOTAL PRISON SERIES FROM CIVILIAN CHECK SAMPLE

Table XII–137 shows the percentage of significant deviations from the civilian check sample of each offense group, of the total series, and of the state series, for the total categories of each morphological observation.

It may be noted first of all that the total series differs from the total check sample in 61.73 per cent of morphological categories. This difference is reduced to 59.2 per cent in the Massachusetts comparison and to 43.83 per cent in the Tennessee comparison. Evidently the check sample of civilians by its geographical and sociologic selection does not present such great difficulties in the way of a justifiable physic comparison with criminals as in sociological features. The percentage of significant deviations is reduced by 30.77 per cent from the total series figure in Massachusetts sociological categories and by only 2.47 per cent in Massachusetts morphological categories. The Tennessee sociological deviations are 19.23 per cent fewer than those the total series, and the morphological deviations 17.90 per cent fewer. Massachusetts criminals are more strongly differentiated from their check sample of civilians in morphological features than in sociological observations. In Tennessee the reverse obtains. Total criminals are more strongly differentiated from total civilians in sociological than in morphological features, but the difference is possibly referable to the fact that inequalities of sampling tend to enhance sociological differences more than physical differences.

Burglary and larceny lead in percentage of significant morphological deviations ɔm the check sample. This ranking may be affected in some measure by the preponɔrant size of this offense group which reduces its probable errors and renders statisɔally valid numerically smaller deviations than can attain significance in any other ɔense group. Similarly the least deviating group — assault — occupies the correspondɔ position in the sociological ranking. This is again referable, in all probability, to ɔ very small size of the group which makes its probable errors large.

In the various offense groups percentages of significant morphological deviations ɔnge from 36.42 to 62.35, as against a range of 38.46 to 69.23 in the case of sociologɔl phenomena.

The high proportions of deviations in burglary and larceny, and in robbery, are ɔssibly attributable in some degree to the very young mean ages of these offense ɔups when compared with other groups and with the civilian check sample.

In general the offense groups display morphological deviations which are greatly in ɔcess of what might be expected to occur in random samples. These must be radically ɔluced if we consider the exaggerating effects of state sampling and of personal equaɔn, but they cannot be eliminated by such considerations.

Chapter XIII

GENERAL SUMMARY AND CONCLUSIONS

The Problem

STUDIES of the relationship of man's bodily characters to his behavior have fall into scientific disrepute and consequent neglect. This state of affairs is easily e plicable. In the first place this field is the traditional stamping-ground of quac who exploit the credulous public by spurious diagnoses of character and ability fro bodily traits. Again, the association of different grades of mental ability and vario degrees of worldly success with inherited bodily features is revolting to peoples wl cherish democratic ideals. Further, although scientifically competent persons witho exception admit the importance of the organism as a determiner of its own behavic it is expedient and practicable for them to stress rather the contribution of enviro ment to that behavior. This is because the heredity of an existing individual cann be altered, however great its responsibility for the quality and behavior of that inc vidual may have been. The existing organism can be improved only by ameliorati its environment.

It is natural that sociological and psychiatric practitioners confine their trea ment of delinquents to individual environmental remedies. It is quite irrational f them to take the attitude that the physical and mental heredity of the criminal wholly unrelated to his delinquency simply because nothing can be done about a *fa accompli.*

Obviously the different behavior of different classes of animals arises in large pa from the differences in their organisms. A chimpanzee behaves like a chimpanze largely because he is a chimpanzee. Even if one denies this statement, he must adm that the behavior of an animal is to some extent predictable from the structure of th animal. Within the human species it is reasonable to suppose that hereditary, racial, other physical differences may be associated with mental and behavioristic variations. is unnecessary to assume that such associations may be of a causal nature. Raci psychological differences have never been demonstrated scientifically. It seems pro able that failures in this endeavor have been due to the faulty techniques of anthr pologists and psychologists. As long as we are unable either to distinguish physic races or to measure psychological characteristics we can certainly accomplish little the field of racial psychology.

The present investigation is an effort to ascertain whether or not the physical cha acteristics of criminals are in any sense relevant to their crimes. Criminals are sociological category of men. For purposes of this study they are individuals underg ing imprisonment as a result of conviction for some offense punishable by commitme

a penal institution. They are merely persons who have committed offenses against
society which are considered (at least for the time being) of a sufficiently grave character as to justify the temporary or permanent incarceration of the offender. Since
criminals are of all groups sociologically the most clearly stigmatized, they ought to
present a favorable opportunity for an inquiry into the association of physical characteristics with patterns of behavior.

If there are any differences in the behavioristic tendencies of different human races,
they ought to manifest themselves in criminal acts. If there are any physical differences between criminals, classified according to the nature of their offenses, the possibly complicating influence of race can be eliminated only by studies of criminals in
racial groups. It should be emphasized that a possible discovery that some class of offender possesses distinguishing group characteristics of a physical nature, implies little
or nothing as to the nature of the relationship between the bodily features and the
type of behavior manifested.

SUMMARY OF CRIMINAL ANTHROPOLOGY

LOMBROSO

The Italian pioneer, Cesare Lombroso, attempted to demonstrate that criminals are
physically stigmatized by a complex of features of atavistic or degenerative origin. He
stressed the conceptions of the "born" criminal, the epileptic criminal, and the moral
imbecile. Many of his ideas fail to survive the test of critical examination and the evidence offered by him and by his school has failed to convince the majority of students
of criminology. The logic of the Lombrosian School need not be discussed in this work.
The data presented have been appraised briefly. Craniological studies have yielded
conflicting results when conducted by protagonists and antagonists of Lombrosian theories. Out of the welter of contradictory evidence there seems to emerge the probability
that criminal crania do indeed show more anomalies than those of law-abiding citizens.
But this is a probability and nothing more.

However, the chief defects of the Lombrosian School are in the numerical inadequacy of the series studied, in their racial and ethnic heterogeneity, and in the lack of
scientific method of statistical analysis. The differences between criminals and civilians presented by the Italian criminologists are usually unconvincing because the
samples studied are so small that they may be unrepresentative and are certainly untrust-
worthy. All sorts of racial and ethnic types are mixed up in the criminal and civil populations studied, and there is no attempt to distinguish differences which may be of
criminological importance from those which may be due to unequal representation of
various racial strains. The statistical methods whereby biometricians are enabled to
make exact appraisals of the significance of group differences were not in use during
the time of Lombroso. Consequently the entire subject requires a re-examination involving the utilization of numerically adequate samples, the necessary isolation of racial
and ethnic types, and the employment of a satisfactory statistical technique.

GORING

Charles Goring published in 1913 an analysis of the anthropometric examinations
3000 English convicts. From a statistical standpoint this volume is a work of genius

and as a demonstration of the application of biometric methods to anthropologica analysis it is of great and permanent value. Unfortunately the work of Goring was per meated with a violent antagonism to the theories of Lombroso and his school, and thi gifted scientist allowed his prejudice to distort his results. The principal objections t Goring's study have been fully discussed in the introduction to this work. He mad an unjustifiable use of statistical predictions based upon coefficients of correlation i order to "correct" for the sociological or physical factors which complicate the com parisons of different classes of criminals and of criminals with civilians. When the re sults of his data were contrary to his bias he rejected them, or discarded the data an made new observations which invariably conformed to his prejudice. His comparativ data from the civil population consist of material culled from literature which is o very little value for the purpose to which he put it. The unsatisfactory nature of th comparative material is Goring's misfortune and not his fault. The civilian check sam ples used in the present investigation, although gathered especially for the purpos are also inadequate, although much more satisfactory than Goring's borrowings fro literature. Finally, Goring showed the same disregard of the ethnic and racial con plexity of his criminal material which was characteristic of the work of Lombroso. careful scrutiny of Goring's data and of his methods of analysis reveals a larger bod of facts which support the contentions of Lombroso than of evidence which refutes th theories of the Italian School. In the opinion of the present writer Goring's investig tion left the problem of criminal anthropology no nearer to solution than it was at th conclusion of Lombroso's career.

SCOPE AND METHODS OF PRESENT INVESTIGATION
HISTORY AND MATERIAL OF THE SURVEY

The present survey was initiated in the summer of 1926 as an anthropological stud of Massachusetts County Jail prisoners, supplementary to a sociological and psych atric investigation carried on by the Massachusetts State Department of Mental Di eases. The anthropological survey was subsequently extended to include the prison ar reformatory inmates of ten states chosen to represent as adequately as possible th different racial and ethnic elements in the population of the entire country. The states were Massachusetts, Tennessee, Kentucky, Texas, North Carolina, Wisconsi Arizona, Colorado, New Mexico, and Missouri. The total of anthropometric recor analyzed by the survey is 17,077. This number includes some 3,203 civilians mea ured for comparative purposes in Massachusetts, Tennessee, North Carolina, and C orado. The total excludes 604 individuals who were measured and observed b concerning whom parentage data were lacking, or who belonged to ethnic groups t poorly represented for use in statistical analysis. The present volume analyzes on native White criminals of native parentage in prisons and reformatories and the civ ian check samples of similar origin.

The methods of training observers for the field work, the instruments employe the measurements and observations taken, and the sociological data gathered have be described in the Introduction (pages 36–47).

The field observers were graduate students in Physical Anthropology at Harva University, trained by the writer. The instruments used were of standard anthrop netric makes. The measurements taken conform in general to accepted international echniques of anthropometry. Exceptions to this statement have been noted and explained. The sociological observations gathered include marital status, birthplace, nationality and race of subject and of subject's parents, offense, religion, previous convictions, occupation, and education. Psychological and pathological observations are regrettably sparse, except in certain of the groups from Massachusetts institutions.

ANALYSIS OF DATA

The reduction of the data was accomplished by use of the Hollerith electrical sorting and tabulating apparatus. The statistical methods employed were those in general use among biometricians. These have been explained in the Introduction. They include the arithmetic mean, the standard deviation, the coefficients of variation, of correlation, of mean square contingency, the correlation ratio, and the probable errors of constants. Offense subgroups were compared with the total prison series or with a random sample of that series to determine their differentiation or lack of it. The significance of differences in arrays of means or percentages was based upon the expected occurrence in random samples.

PERSONAL EQUATIONS

Personal equations developed by observers in the course of their field work were carefully examined. In measurements this difficulty was investigated by checking the arrays of means of measurements of the two observers upon different but similar groups. As a result of this examination it was found that in three measurements only — head height, ear length, and ear breadth — a serious difference between the observers was manifest. These measurements were analyzed separately according to the series of each observer. The other measurements were combined in a single group.

The morphological observations in which each observer graded his subjects according to qualitative standards were similarly scrutinized. In this case also the entire arrays of the two observers were compared — a process which brought to light all serious personal equations. The morphological observations were then graded into four classes (A, B, C, and D), according to the amount of personal equation displayed by the two observers in each. The two classes of observations in which the differences between observers were found to be serious were discarded entirely (in the case of D observations, except tattooing), or utilized only with the greatest caution (Class C observations). Since it was discovered at an advanced stage of the process of analysis that state differences of physical types were complicating the criminological differences, a method of correcting for state composition was devised. This was based upon the prediction of characters or values expected in any subgroup according to its composition in numbers of individuals from each of the several states, assuming that each state component would exhibit the average development of the measurement, or the percental distribution of the character, found in the total criminal group from that state. Differences independent of state sampling are only those in which offense groups significantly exceed (or fall below) both the mean of the total series and that predicted on the basis of state composition. This prediction also eliminates differences due to the personal equations of the two observers as represented in their own various state series and each other's state series.

GENERAL DISTRIBUTION OF PRISON AND REFORMATORY SERIES

The total prison and reformatory series consists of 10,953 males from ten states. Census data indicate that this series constituted between 11 and 12 per cent of all male prisoners in the United States present on January 1, 1928. It is therefore a numerically adequate sample. Such information as is available suggests that our prison and reformatory group is also representative of the entire prison population in proportions of native born and foreign born Whites, but is slightly high in Negroes and Negroids.

A crude ranking of the frequency of occurrence of the several offenses in the various parentage and racial groups is given in Table II-2, but a serious consideration of racial differences in offense is reserved for a later volume of this report.

The present volume concerns itself with 4212 native White criminals of native parentage from nine states: Massachusetts, Arizona, Colorado, New Mexico, Texas, Wisconsin, Kentucky, Tennessee, and North Carolina. A preponderance of southerners in this series is principally due to the concentration of Old American stocks in the southern states. The disproportionate contributions of various states to the several offense groups are important and must be taken into consideration because each state shows its own differentiated physical type of criminal. Forgery and fraud and versus public welfare are overloaded with Texans, rape with Wisconsin criminals, first degree murder with Kentuckians, and second degree murder with convicts in all three of the East Central mountain states. These irregularities of state distribution in the offense group necessitate the correction for state sampling.

Extraction, or the nationalities of the mothers' and fathers' stocks of these native White prisoners of native parentage, were recorded when known and if other than straight American. Such extractions include 36.85 per cent of the series. Foreign extractions are very low in Kentucky and Tennessee and extremely high in Wisconsin, North Carolina, Massachusetts, and Colorado. No less than 36 per cent of all reported extractions are Irish, and this does not include Scotch-Irish or other mixed Irish strains. English strains comprise 20.68 per cent of the foreign extractions. German strains rank third with 11.66 per cent. Scotch-Irish extractions are fourth with 9.08 per cent. The next in order are French and Scotch. Other extractions reported are insignificant. In the check sample of civilians English lead and Irish take second place, with Scotch a weak third and German a poor fourth.

The comparison of state of birth of prisoners with state of incarceration yields some interesting results with regard to the geographical origin and mobility of this most American category of delinquents. Of the total prison series of native Whites of native parentage only 30.53 per cent are in prison outside of their own native states. Kentucky has the smallest proportion of extra-state inmates and Arizona the largest. In general the western states show higher proportions of criminals born outside of the state, because of the more recent settling of the west. In the old eastern states non-native criminals generally come from adjacent or neighboring states in approximately the order of representation found in the civilian population. Many more states are represented in the criminal population of the west. The direction of population drift is easily ascertainable from the extra-state inmates of the western and southwestern prisons and penitentiaries. Tennessee has the unenviable distinction of contributing the highest proportion of its natives to the prison population of other states. Missouri ranks second. The central position of these states is probably of importance in this connection. But Tennessee contributes proportionately more criminals than civilians to some of these western state populations.

Our series of native White criminals of native parentage does not seem to be a highly migratory group. Most of them are in jail at home, although possibly not at home in jail.

SOCIOLOGY

ETHNIC AND RACIAL ORIGINS OF NATIVE WHITE PRISONERS OF NATIVE PARENTAGE BY STATES

The average age of our native White criminals of native parentage is 30.7 years. The individual range is from 15 to 79 years, but very few are under 18 years of age. We may take 1927 as the central year for the recording of data on age. The average criminal of our series was born in this country about 1896. It seems fair to assume that the native born parents of these criminals were on the average about 30 years of age at the time of the birth of their offspring destined ultimately for incarceration. Therefore it follows that the mean time of residence in this country for the families of the present criminals must be at least 60 years. In other words the greater proportion of the families which gave rise to these criminals must have been in the United States since 1866 or earlier. If our youngest criminal is 15 years old and was born when his mother was 18 years old, then 33 years would be the individual minimum of residence of the criminal family in this country, assuming that the mother of the criminal was born immediately after the immigration of her mother to this country. Possibly then a very few of our criminals may be the descendants of immigrants who arrived no earlier than 1894.

On the whole, it seems probable that the greater part of our series consists of persons of American lineage extending back to the time immediately after the Civil War or much earlier. This is important because it rules out of the ancestry the great bulk of recent immigration from the countries of Central Europe and Southeastern Europe. It leaves us with the following ethnic stocks as the probable reservoirs from which our criminals were drawn: English, Irish, Scotch, Welsh, German, Dutch, French, and Scandinavian. This tallies very well with the reports of extractions of the criminals, which include negligible percentages of Italian, Austrian, Bohemian, Jewish, Polish, Greek, et cetera.

The youngest criminals of our series come from two reformatories, those of Massachusetts and of Colorado. These are both states which have received large increments of aliens in the period of immigration following the Civil War. Doubtless some of our younger criminals are descendants of these comparatively recent immigrants and are responsible for the introduction into our series of minor ethnic elements, apart from the predominantly British and German strains which must comprise the bulk of the national origins. These younger criminals from the reformatories are presumably of urban origin in the majority of instances, and belong to the urban occupations. This circumstance may account in part for the apparently greater diversity of racial strains in such occupations. But actually only 36.85 per cent of our total series have records of foreign extraction. Of the 1552 records of alien ancestry only 40, or 2.58 per cent, admit Spanish, Portuguese, Italian, Polish, Austrian, Bohemian, Jewish, or Greek lineage, and all of these are mixed.

Unless our data on nativity and extraction are wholly unreliable (and I do not consider this to be the case), it seems necessary to conclude that some sort of selection of racial or ethnic types for urban and rural life and for various occupations had taken place in this country prior to the immigration that followed the Civil War, or that some physical types have tended to remain in the country and others to drift into the cities. It is of course possible that urban residence may directly mold physical types in one direction and rural residence in another, but selection seems a much more probable agency.

Apart from the physical differences which are known to appertain to hereditary racial characters, the only clues which we have to the racial and ethnic diversity of our native White criminals of native parentage lie in the data concerning the extraction of about one-third of the series. These show clearly enough that in Massachusetts, for example, there is a strong element of French Canadian origin which is altogether lacking in most of the other states. Again, in Wisconsin there is a marked German strain, and a perceptible Scandinavian element practically absent elsewhere in our series. The proportions of English, Irish, and Scotch blood also vary considerably from state to state.

Further, we must not disregard the possibility that there have crept into our series certain individuals with minor proportions of Negro or Indian blood. The chances of such intermixture are especially favorable in the southern and southwestern states. Of course any obviously mixed individuals were thrown out of the series by the field observers, but small proportions of alien racial blood are often imperceptible, although influencing the total physical combinations. There remains also a suspicion of Mexican admixture in the old White stocks of the Southwest.

Thus it is apparent that this particular series of native White prisoners of native parentage, although derived mainly from English, Irish, and Scotch stocks, must have diversified considerably in the several states according to the varying proportions of the constituents forming the blends, and in conformity with the various minor dashes of alien strains added in different parts of the country.

RELIGIOUS AFFILIATION

The religious affiliations of criminals were recorded, but no analysis of these data has been attempted, beyond the listing of the information by states and by ethnic extraction groups. It was thought that the religious preferences of the large group of Irish ancestry would give some clue as to their northern Irish (Scotch-Irish) or southern Irish origin. In the aggregate of the eight states considered (there are no data on religion from North Carolina) the total Catholics of Irish descent scarcely exceed the Protestants. But in Massachusetts nearly all of the prisoners of Irish descent are Catholics. It seems probable therefore that the Irish from the more western states of our series are predominantly Ulster Irish and that the Massachusetts group is composed almost entirely of southern Irish who are descendants of later immigrants. It is possible, however, that a considerable proportion of the Irish of long residence in this country may have been converted to Protestant faiths.

The most striking fact of the tabulation of religious data is the very high percentage of criminals denying any religious affiliation. This reaches its maximum (31.66 per cent) among the Old Americans. Of this group, by far the largest of the series, only 4.47 per cent is Catholic. Tennessee has a stupendous percentage of persons professing no religion (65.18 per cent of all extractions). Texas has 45.75 per cent of the unaffiliated and Kentucky 14.73 per cent. In the other states there are very few criminals without religious connections.

Altogether this series includes only 14.67 per cent of Catholics. There are 60.36 per cent of Protestants and 24.97 per cent without religious affiliation.

PREVIOUS CONVICTIONS

The data on this subject are defective and include information respecting only 86.8 per cent of the prison and reformatory series. Of these about 39 per cent have recorded previous convictions. This proportion is almost certainly well below the true figure. In some of the states the records were very poor, and in one (North Carolina) no information was secured. When due allowance has been made for state sampling, it is found that first degree murderers, second degree murderers, rapists, other sex offenders, and versus public welfare offenders show marked deficiencies in the percentages with recorded previous convictions, whereas the burglary and larceny group is notable for its high percentage of recidivists.

MARITAL STATUS

On the whole these criminals show a great excess of unmarried men. It is necessary, however, to take into account the influences of age and of state sampling. When these complicating factors have been cleared away, it becomes apparent that first degree murderers show an excess of widowers, second degree murderers of married men, versus public welfare and arson and all other offenders excesses of married men; robbers, burglars, and thieves unduly large proportions of single men, each in comparison with the total criminal series. Rapists and other sex offenders tend to marry in excess of the total criminals, but their differences are not statistically significant when due allowance has been made for state sampling. The most plausible explanation of convict celibacy seems to lie in the obstacles to marriage which the habitual criminal encounters by reason of his frequent imprisonment. Among the married men it seems probable that matrimony frequently provides a motive for crime.

OCCUPATION

Occupational data are considerably complicated by the rural, agricultural character of some of the states and the metropolitan, industrial character of others. When these factors are eliminated the occupational differences between criminals convicted for various kinds of offenses remain very great. These differences are too numerous for recapitulation. Outstanding are the huge excesses of murderers and bootleggers among the persons claiming to belong to the extractive occupations; the substantial excesses of burglars and thieves among laborers, factory operatives, and personal service workers; the excesses of forgery and fraud in the trade, clerical, and professional classes; and the excess of assault among the skilled trades.

On the whole, the occupation of criminals seems to influence strongly the nature of their crimes, since different ways of getting a living offer different kinds of temptation. The predilection of farmers for murder and of skilled tradesmen for assault offer interesting fields for speculation.

The tremendously excessive number of farmers in this series cannot be explained wholly by the largely rural population from which it is derived. Farmers who commit crimes are much more likely to be caught than are city dwellers.

EDUCATION

Our criminals constitute a disgracefully ignorant group. State differences in educational opportunities are very important in the raw educational rankings of the crime groups. After correction for these factors it appears that both classes of murderers are excessively ignorant, and that rapists are distinguished by their lack of high school and college education. Forgery and fraud and robbery are the two best educated groups of criminals. Illiteracy and lack of formal education increase in the successive age groups. Relatively good educational attainment, as defined by reaching eighth grade or the first two years of high school, diminishes in frequency in the advancing age groups. The highest educational attainment — last two years of high school, college and professional school — seems unrelated to age grouping.

Our educational data offer little support for the theory that education is a direct deterrent to crime. On the whole the better educated of our criminal offense groups rank high in previous convictions. Robbers rank third, and forgers and fraudulent offenders fourth. Burglars and thieves, third in education, are easily first in recidivism.

SUMMARY OF SOCIOLOGICAL OBSERVATIONS

All of the offense groups (except perhaps arson and all other offenses) are significant in their sociological deviations from the total series, even when the differences are pared down in order to eliminate the effects of state sampling. Our sociological data are few and crude, but they seem to demonstrate clearly enough that the background of family life, of occupation, of education, and of previous infringement of the law is widely different in various classes of offenders. When we consider the looseness of our offense classification and the probability that many offenders have committed more than one kind of crime at some time or other, there arises the expectation that a precise and exhaustive study of the sociological antecedents of the criminal classified according to his offense would yield an ever sharper differentiation than our material has furnished. At the same time one must not yield to the temptation to interpret directly and causally the associations of these sociological factors with the nature of the offense committed.

STATE DIFFERENTIATION

METRIC AND INDICIAL DIFFERENTIATION BY STATES

The initial assumption in the analysis of our prison data was that all native White males of native parentage, from whatever state, could be combined in one series, providing that the personal equations of the two observers were not such as to make their data incomparable. This procedure seemed justifiable, since the population of two generations' residence in this country has been derived, presumably, from similar ethnic strains, emanating principally from the British Isles and thoroughly mixed. Prison populations were thought to be relatively migratory, as compared with civilian populations, so that the criminal series from any state would be more heterogeneous and cosmopolitan than the civilians of that state. It seemed probable that European settlement in the United States has not been of sufficient duration to develop local physical types, particularly because of migrations caused by pioneering, industrialization, and improved transportation. Again, there are no linguistic or political barriers in this country to restrict free migration from one state to another.

Consequently, the state series were combined, except in certain measurements and indices which showed observational equations. When the various offense groups were compared metrically and indicially each with a random sample of the entire series, and also morphologically with the total of the combined series, they showed remarkable physical differences. It was known, of course, that certain offense groups are heavily weighted with criminals from particular states. For example, there is a tremendous excess of Kentuckians in first degree murder. When it became evident that some of the strongest cases of offense group differentiation occur in the groups which are most heavily overloaded with criminals from some one state, the existence of local state types was clearly indicated. It was then necessary to begin anew and to analyze each state series for the purpose of ascertaining its physical differentiation from the total prison series. From the results of this study of metric and indicial differentiation in the states, a correction for state sampling was devised. This correction eliminates from offense group differences those which are due to accidents of state composition.

The diversity of physical norms in the several states is astounding. Each state series is overwhelmingly distinguished from a random sample of the entire series. The most important deviations of the individual states may be briefly recapitulated.

The Massachusetts criminals are the youngest, the second shortest, lightest, smallest in chest diameters and sitting height, and the narrowest in facial breadth, of all of the state series. They have relatively the longest and narrowest faces and the narrowest jaws.

Tennessee is the least differentiated from the series at large of all of the state groups. Tennessee criminals have the shortest head lengths, the relatively broadest noses, the largest cranial circumferences, and the highest zygo-frontal indices.

Kentucky criminals are slightly below mean weight and mean age but somewhat above mean height, and are especially narrow-shouldered. The breadth of the forehead and the indices employing that diameter are very low. Ear lengths in this state are very short.

Texas is the tallest and the heaviest of all of the groups. All of the breadth diameters of the head and face approach their maxima in this state. Faces are relatively the shortest and broadest.

The North Carolina criminals are considerably below mean age, but above mean height and mean weight. Heads in this group are the longest and narrowest of the series, and head circumferences are smallest. The nose is the shortest in any state and the jaws are very narrow.

Wisconsin is the oldest group, the shortest group, and the second lightest. Head breadth is at the maximum as is also facial breadth; facial and nose heights are also great; relative sitting height is highest of any state and the most leptorrhine mean nasal index is found in this state series.

The combined series from Colorado, New Mexico, and Arizona is notable for excessive upper facial height, great nasal length, and maximum value of the upper facial index.

MORPHOLOGICAL DIFFERENTIATION BY STATES

The percentage of significant deviations in observations of the entire series by states is 69.90, and of measurements and indices 72.29 per cent. Thus, in general, the state series differ from the total series to the same degree in metric and morphological features.

The state contrasts in morphological features are so numerous that only a few of the most important can be mentioned in this summary. Thick beards are most common in Wisconsin and rarest in North Carolina. In the latter state body hair is also most sparse. Texas has the most curved hair and Wisconsin the highest proportion of straight hair. Each state shows some distinctive feature in hair coloring. Massachusetts has the most red-brown hair, the least light brown hair, and the least gray hair. Tennessee has the most light brown hair and the least red-brown hair. Kentucky has the highest proportion of ash-blond hair. Texas shows the maximum of black hair and of red hair. North Carolina yields the most dark brown hair and the least ash-blond. Wisconsin has the most gray hair and the least golden hair. The Southwest is notable for its maximum of golden hair.

Kentucky shows the highest percentage of blue eyes and Wisconsin ranks first in dark brown eyes. Median and external eye folds are commonest in Massachusetts, internal epicanthic folds in Kentucky. Wisconsin shows the fewest eye folds of any kind.

North Carolina has the highest proportion of low foreheads and the Southwest exhibits the opposite extreme of variation. Pronounced forehead slope is most common in Kentucky and rarest in Tennessee.

Nasal root height is greatest in North Carolina and least in Wisconsin. Root breadth is largest in Massachusetts and smallest in Wisconsin. Bridge height seems to be at a maximum in North Carolina. Bridge breadth is greatest in Massachusetts and smallest in Wisconsin. The highest proportion of concave noses occurs in Wisconsin, and of concavo-convex noses in Kentucky. The maximum of straight noses is found in Texas. The thickest nasal tips occur in Massachusetts, while Wisconsin leads in thin nasal extremities. The nasal septum is directed upward most frequently in Wisconsin and downward most frequently in Tennessee. Deflections of the nasal septum are commonest in North Carolina and rarest in Tennessee.

The thinnest membranous lips are found in the North Carolina series. Prognathism was recorded oftenest in Massachusetts and most rarely in the Southwest. Malars, or cheek bones, are oftenest compressed in North Carolina and most prominent in Texas. Jaw angles are also most projecting in the latter state and least so in Tennessee.

Cheek wrinkles are fewest in Massachusetts (the youngest state series) and commonest in Texas (the second oldest series).

North Carolina has the highest proportion of persons who have lost no teeth and Wisconsin of persons who have lost many teeth. North Carolina criminals seem to include also the highest proportion with few dental caries. Here the slight overbite which is normal reaches its maximum. Marked overbites are commonest in Texas, edge-to-edge bites in Tennessee, and underbites in the Southwest.

Small ear lobes are commonest in Massachusetts and large ear lobes in Texas. Attached ear lobes occur most frequently in Massachusetts, while free ear lobes reach their highest proportion in Kentucky. Darwin's point is most frequently absent in North Carolina. This state also records the highest excess of prominent antihelices.

Lambdoid flattening is least common in Texas and most prevalent in the Southwest. Facial asymmetry is commonest in Kentucky and rarest in Wisconsin.

Kentucky is outstanding for short, thick necks and North Carolina for long, thin necks. The latter state also shows the highest frequency of pronounced shoulder slope.

We must recognize the virtual certainty that some of these state differences in morphological features are partially or entirely referable to the personal equations of the field observers. Others are complicated by age changes. In spite of these disturbing factors there is no doubt of the marked differentiation of each state prison group. In the measurements and indices the matter of personal equation is of little importance, except in a few cases. Nevertheless, the aggregate of significant morphological differences does not exceed that of the metrical and indicial deviations. Wisconsin and Tennessee are the only states in which the prison groups deviate from the entire series in a much higher percentage of morphological features than of metric features. These states were not studied by the same observer.

SIGNIFICANCE OF STATE DIFFERENTIATION

In combined metric and morphological features Tennessee, with 59.56 per cent of significant differences, diverges least from the total prison series of native Whites of native parentage. At the other end of the range is Texas with 75.74 per cent of significant differences.

We are now in a position to discuss the meaning of this physical differentiation of the state series. The possible causative factors are: (a) personal equations between the two observers, and variations of each observer's equation from state to state, (b) racial or ethnic heterogeneity of the state series, due either to original diversity of population strains or to continued selective inbreeding of varied ethnic ingredients; (c) the fixation of state types by environmental molding; (d) the overweighting of various state series by this or that offense type of criminal.

It is improbable that the great inter-state physical differences can be attributed exclusively to any one of the factors enumerated above. The probable effect of each must be considered.

In caliper measurements and in their derived indices, consistent differences in the means of the two observers indicate personal equations only in the two ear measurements and in head height. These measurements and indices were analyzed separately for each observer and the deviations of his own state groups were reckoned from the total combined series of that observer. Hence no accumulation of personal equations could contribute to state differentiation in these suspected measurements and indices. Scrupulous examinations of metric data of the same observer gathered in different states reveal no evidence of shifting techniques resulting in inter-state differences. The conclusion reached is that state differences in metric features are effected in a very small degree, if at all, by the personal equations of the two observers.

The morphological observations present a much more difficult problem, which has been discussed in detail in the Introduction.[1] Here there is no doubt of the existence of serious inter-observer personal equations in a considerable proportion of the data. This difficulty has been partially surmounted by the rejection of obviously faulty or disparate observations, and partially by a correction for state sampling. Naturally the correction has been employed in the studies of the offense groups and not in the studies of state differences. The latter have been appraised merely in terms of their probable errors and with due regard to the validity of the original observations.

The comparison of each observer's own variations from state to state reveals differences frequently as marked as in the data of two states measured by different observers. The reader, if he likes, may conclude that each observer shifted his ideal morphological standards from state to state, changing his mind, for example, as to what constitutes a receding forehead, whenever he crossed a state line. I do not believe this to be true. The morphological differences between states of the same or different observers are proportionately no more numerous than are the more reliable metric differences. I have probably overemphasized the seriousness of observational equations in my fear of being misled by them. Nevertheless there can be no doubt that state differences are due in part to this factor.

Variations in the ethnic and racial composition of the several states from which our prisoners are derived must be a potent factor in effecting the state differences between the prison series. Evidence on this point has already been summarized.[2] Nothing short of a genetic miracle could produce physically identical populations in nine states, even if the interbreeding ethnic elements were the same in each. The proportions of the intermingling strains would necessarily vary somewhat from state to state, thus producing differentiated end products. In point of fact, several of the states include minor racial or ethnic strains which are either peculiar to themselves or negligible elsewhere in the material of the survey.

It seems probable, however, that original differences in ethnic composition of the states are not so important as the long continued inbreeding of local ethnic and family strains in the fixation of regional types. Almost all of the states studied include large areas of relative isolation in which agriculture or cattle raising is the basis of subsistence. Intensive inbreeding must have taken place in such regions. This is particularly true of the mountainous parts of Tennessee, Kentucky, and North Carolina. Even in Massachusetts, which has been overrun by immigrants, the native Whites of native parentage are found largely in isolated rural areas and are notoriously inbred. In the Southwestern states a considerable proportion of the native White criminals of native parentage come from other states. Consequently, inbred local types should be fewer. Nevertheless most of the extra-state inmates in the penal institutions of these Southwestern states are derived ultimately from the inbred White stocks of the East Central and Southeastern states. In Texas, at any rate, the huge size of the state and the existence of many isolated areas which have been inhabited by Whites for three or more generations, may well have produced a considerable range of local types.

The degree of metric and indicial diversity in the series of the several states should

[1] Pages 61–67.
[2] Summary p. 257 sqq.

manifest itself in the means of the standard deviations of the measurements and indices. Table XIII–1 presents the results of such a summation. The average standard deviations of measurements and indices are given for each state. The variations from state to state are trivial. Wisconsin alone is distinguished by slightly but definitely higher standard deviations than are found in any other state series. Massachusetts ranks next in magnitude of standard deviations. Since the standard deviation is likely to decrease in any relatively homogeneous sample as the size of the sample becomes larger, it is quite possible that the high rankings of these two states are in some measure due to the

TABLE XIII–1

AVERAGE STANDARD DEVIATIONS FOR STATES

	Measurements (19)	Indices (13)
Massachusetts	5.82	3.63
Tennessee	5.60	3.50
Kentucky	5.73	3.52
Texas	5.73	3.44
North Carolina	5.68	3.57
Wisconsin	6.01	3.80
Southwest	5.75	3.55

small size of their series. Wisconsin has the smallest series and Massachusetts the second smallest. However, we must not overlook the fact that these two northern states have been the recipients of larger and more diversified streams of immigration, flowing in for a longer time, than most of the other states of our series. It is therefore quite possible that native Whites of native parentage in these states may represent a greater variety of racial and ethnic strains than in the other states where the Old American stock is concentrated.

Table II–4 lists the foreign extractions recorded for each state. There are 30 such extractions. Of these varieties the following numbers occur in the several state series: Colorado 19, Wisconsin 18, Massachusetts 15, Texas 14, North Carolina 11, Kentucky 9, Tennessee 9, New Mexico 9, Arizona 6. Colorado, New Mexico, and Arizona have been combined into a Southwestern series because of the small samples from the latter two states. Actually the highest extractive diversity seems to occur in this group, although Wisconsin with a much smaller series presents considerably the highest proportion of prisoners for whom an alien extraction has been reported (83.50 per cent). It seems fair then to conclude that the high ranking standard deviations in Wisconsin are probably due in part to diversity of ethnic origins in the prisoners from that state. Yet it is impossible to say how far this ranking may have been affected by the small size of the Wisconsin sample.

In general it seems to the writer that the most important factor in state differentiation is probably the inbreeding and diversification of local ethnic and racial strains as discussed in the preceding pages.

The third possibility is the fixation of state types by environmental molding. A great many of the criminals of our series are doubtless of Old American lineage. Their ancestors have been in this country for six or seven generations. This is especially probable in the case of the Kentucky and Tennessee mountaineers. Again, a relative immobility of many of our state series is indicated by the predominance of individuals incarcerated in their own native states. If a restricted diet, an identical climate, and virtually unchanged modes of life for several generations can modify human types, one might expect such a phenomenon to occur in the mountain regions of Kentucky and Tennessee. But these states exhibit no uniformity of physical type.

Some anthropologists consider the nasal index as a feature most sensitive to environmental influences. According to this supposition heat and humidity tend to make noses relatively broad, while cold, dry air favors narrow-nosed types. The nasal index is indeed lowest in the two northern states of our series — Wisconsin and Massachusetts — which are also the shortest in stature and lightest in mean weight of all the states.[3] The mean nasal index is highest in Tennessee (68.22), while Kentucky and North Carolina reach the same average figure (66.50). The differences are significant and lend no support to the theory that adjacent areas should yield identical values on account of climatic similarity. Again, Texas has a mean nasal index of 67.74, whereas the nearby states of Colorado, New Mexico and Arizona average only 65.70. Statures in Kentucky, Tennessee, and North Carolina are virtually identical, as are several of the other gross bodily dimensions, but head measurements show very considerable differences.

Since Kentucky and Tennessee are the states reporting by far the smallest percentages of extractions, and hence are presumably those which have the largest proportions of persons long settled in the regions of their imprisonment, we should expect these states to deviate most from the total prison series, if environmental molding of types is important. Actually the ranking in deviations is Kentucky third and Tennessee seventh.

Again, the states with the most extra-state inmates should perhaps fall closest to the means of the entire series. These would be the three combined Southwestern states — Arizona, Colorado, and New Mexico — with about 70 per cent of extra-state inmates, and Texas with about 35 per cent of prisoners born outside of the state of their incarceration. The Southwest actually ranks sixth in magnitude of deviations, but Texas ranks first.

Altogether our data afford little evidence of the existence of environmental types, on the basis of comparisons of groups from contiguous or adjacent states. Nevertheless a small fraction of our state differentiation is probably assignable to environmental causes.

Finally we must consider the extent to which the various state groups may have been overweighted by the predominance of one or more offense group physical types which are distributed disproportionately in the different prison series. It has been sufficiently demonstrated in the body of the text [4] that almost all of the offense groups are strongly differentiated in physical characteristics, even after due allowance has been made for state sampling. Without such allowance the differentiations are overwhelming.

If, in this work, we were principally concerned with the state differences between criminals rather than with offense group differentiations of the entire series, the obvious method of procedure would be to correct the state series for offense group sampling, just as we have corrected the offense groups for state sampling. By this means it would be possible to eliminate the complicating effect of the disproportionate representation

[3] Chapter III, p. 98.
[4] Chapter V, p. 126; Chapter VI, p. 141.

f different kinds of criminals in the several states. However the end would not justify his laborious means of isolating pure state types. We must content ourselves with a urvey of the irregularities of offense group distribution in the state series and with an rgument as to their effect upon the total state samples.

The commonest offense in every state is burglary and larceny. This group comprises 8.27 per cent of all criminals in our series. In the several states it ranges in its propor-on of the entire state series from 33.19 per cent in Kentucky to 53.19 per cent in Ari-ona. Excesses of this strongly differentiated class of criminal occur in Arizona, New Iexico, North Carolina, and Massachusetts. Important deficiencies are found only in entucky and Colorado. Leaving out the combined Southwestern group in which ex-esses of this class of offender in Arizona and New Mexico are offset by a deficiency in olorado, we have North Carolina and Massachusetts with excesses of 13.96 per cent nd 9.95 per cent of thieves and burglars, respectively. Kentucky, the most deficient tate in this category of offense, lacks only 5.08 per cent of the average for the total rison series.

The next offense in order of magnitude is second degree murder. This may be com-ined with first degree murder for the sake of convenience. The total series includes 2.11 per cent of murderers. But the Kentucky series includes no less than 37.49 per ent of murderers, and the Tennessee series 34.28 per cent. On the other hand the Mas-achusetts proportion drops to 9.17 per cent and the Wisconsin series to 9.09 per cent. t is then clear that such inequalities may introduce a considerable variation between tate groups, if the offense types are physically well differentiated.

Assault is a numerically insignificant group, but nearly 10 per cent of all criminals re robbers. In Massachusetts the proportion rises to 15.38 per cent and in North Caro-na it sinks to 4.91 per cent. Forgery and fraud includes 18.91 per cent of Texas pris-ners, but only 4.41 per cent of Massachusetts convicts. Rape ranges from 14.82 per ent in Wisconsin to 1.79 per cent in North Carolina. Versus public welfare offenders clude 16.28 per cent of Texans, but only 1.01 per cent of Wisconsin offenders.

It then seems necessary to conclude that some part of the state group differentiation s due to offense group distributions. Massachusetts criminals are overweighted by urglars, thieves, and robbers; Kentucky and Tennessee criminals by murderers; 'exans by forgers and bootleggers; prisoners in Wisconsin by forgers and rapists; Jorth Carolinians by burglars and thieves. The exact extent to which state differentia-ion is enhanced by this factor cannot be determined by these crude comparisons. It eems probable that the excesses in this or that offense group are hardly sufficient to veight the respective series greatly.

A crude appraisal of the relative importance of two of the main categories of fac-ors which make for state differentiation in physical type may be attempted by consid-ring the average state deviations in pertinent sociological and biological features. Tables XIII–2–3 list the mean percental deviations of each state from the total eries for the various categories of sociological and biological features respectively. These tables disregard the amount of state differentiation which may be due to obser-ational equation, but cover approximately the ground of the possible differentiating auses which have been discussed in the preceding pages under the denominations of acial or ethnic heterogeneity, fixation of state types by environmental molding, and verweighting of state series by various offense groups. Specifically, Table XIII–2 includes the deviations in previous convictions and in offense which together effect whatever of overloading with offense physical types the several state series show, and also the deviations in marital state, occupation, and education, which are the only influences contributing to environmental selection or molding for which we have tangible data. This table also summarizes the mean total sociological deviation of each state and the total average deviation of each sociological factor. The highest deviations are found in previous convictions. In this feature Massachusetts and Wisconsin lead, possibly because of the superiority of their prison records. Offense deviations are much lower. In deviations of this sociological category North Carolina ranks first, with Massachusetts second and Wisconsin third. Deviations in previous convictions enhance state differentiation because recidivists are physically smaller and in some other ways depart from the general norm of total criminals. Again the various offense types are physically differentiated and these contribute their quota to the state differences. The total average deviation of previous convictions is 17.21 per cent and of offense 3.70 per cent. Since the deviations in previous convictions may represent the varying accuracy of prison records more closely than deviations in the proportions of first offenders and recidivists actually occurring in the respective states, the total average deviation probably gives an exaggerated idea of the state physical differentiation attributable to this factor. The relatively small variations in offense support this conclusion.

It is essential to explain briefly how the other sociological deviations in Table XIII–2 may affect the physical type of criminals in different states. Married men are, on the average, older and heavier than single men. Marital state selects physical types partly on the basis of age, and probably partly on the basis of health and economic position. Obviously many occupations exert a stringent physical selection, as is shown

TABLE XIII–2

SOCIOLOGICAL DEVIATIONS OF STATES FROM TOTAL CRIMINAL GROUP EXPRESSED IN
PERCENTAL AVERAGES

	Previous Convictions Per Cent	Marital State Per Cent	Occupation Per Cent	Education Per Cent	Offense Per Cent	Total State Deviation Per Cent
Massachusetts	31.63	9.12	5.81	5.66	4.72	11.39
Tennessee	18.32	1.54	2.61	1.93	2.83	5.45
Kentucky	8.23	2.24	3.56	4.28	3.23	4.31
Texas	15.81	5.18	2.35	2.79	3.60	5.95
North Carolina	(not observed)	1.37	7.10	4.56	5.18	4.55
Wisconsin	21.43	7.84	3.37	3.98	4.00	8.12
Southwest	7.84	5.85	1.63	4.20	2.31	4.37
Total averages	17.21	4.73	3.78	3.91	3.70	6.67

in the study of this subject made in Chapter VIII. Education is a much less potent agency of physical selection, but in these criminals at least, smaller, more slender, and younger men have, in general, better educations.

Altogether the variations in marital state, occupation, and education in the criminal series from the several states must contribute something to the state differentiation which is at any rate more tangible than the sort of environmental molding due to ypothetical climatic or dietetic causes. In fact I should be inclined to restrict the nvironmental causes of state differences in physical type to these three sociological actors just discussed and the previously mentioned effects of deviations in offense and n previous convictions. It should be noted that Massachusetts is the ranking state in nagnitude of combined sociological deviations, possibly because of its urban character. Wisconsin ranks second. Both of these states are high in the deviations of their pre-ious convictions and marital state. Nevertheless in their total physical deviations from he combined series of native White prisoners of native parentage they rank respec-ively fourth and sixth among the nine states. The implication is that their sociolog-al diversity from total criminals has not greatly affected their physiques.

Table XIII–3 records the state and total deviations in extraction, extra-state in-ates, and age. These are, presumably, biological deviations making for state differ-ntiation. Deviations in extraction, of course, imply racial and ethnic diversity. Deviations in proportions of extra-state inmates involve not only racial and ethnic ifferences but also physical differences due to inbreeding and outbreeding and the mi-rations of hypothetical or real environmentally molded or sociologically selected ypes. Age differences are naturally associated with physical variations.

Extractional deviations are very high in most of the states, with Wisconsin far in he lead. The average extractional deviation is 27.26 per cent as compared with 17.21 er cent in previous convictions, the second deviation in average magnitude.

In extra-state inmates the Southwest has by far the highest deviation from the total eries figure, with Kentucky a very poor second and Tennessee a bad last. In age de-iation Wisconsin ranks highest (since its criminals are, on the average, the oldest) nd Massachusetts comes second because of the tender age of its prisoners.

TABLE XIII–3

BIOLOGICAL DEVIATIONS OF STATES FROM TOTAL CRIMINAL GROUP EXPRESSED IN PERCENTAL AVERAGES

	Extractions Per Cent	Extra-State Inmates Per Cent	Age Per Cent	Total State Deviation Per Cent
Massachusetts	31.79	6.86	10.42	16.36
Tennessee	28.10	.27	2.93	10.43
Kentucky	32.64	16.97	3.42	17.68
Texas	2.60	4.22	8.95	5.26
North Carolina	38.37	9.77	7.49	18.54
Wisconsin	46.65	2.25	13.84	20.91
Southwest	10.67	39.34	.32	16.78
Total average deviation	27.26	11.38	6.77	15.14

In total state deviation of these combined biological factors Wisconsin leads easily nd Texas is least divergent from the total series. Nevertheless, in the actual arrays f metric and morphological features the Texas criminals are farthest from the total riminal series. This fact is really quite disastrous for the validity of our test of devi-ting biological factors as listed in Table XIII–3. When we note also that Wiscon-in, which is the leading deviant in biological factors and ranks second in sociological

deviation, is actually sixth in metric and morphological deviations from the total series
it becomes all too apparent that our state sociological and biological deviations, as
listed in Tables XIII–2 and XIII–3, while of considerable interest, are not particu
larly illuminating in defining and evaluating the comparative physical divergences of
separate states from the total series. Practically all that can be said for these average
deviations is that they must be at least partially responsible for state differentiation
although our simple nose-counting of deviations does not square with the actual state
divergences. Certainly we have invoked a sufficiency of causes to explain these state
differences and it seems probable that our carefully considered qualitative estimates
and arguments, as detailed in pages 263–264, possess a greater measure of validity than
a rule-of-thumb appraisal of quantitative deviations of an incomplete list of sociolog
ical and biological factors.

Physical Differentiation of Offense Groups

METRIC AND INDICIAL FEATURES

Are criminals physically differentiated according to the nature of their offenses?
Are the various offense groups of prisoners distinct in bodily characters, each from a
random sample of the entire criminal series? It is essential first to discuss the bearing
of correlation upon this problem. When two variables are significantly correlated an
alteration in the value of one is accompanied by an alteration in the value of the other
but this does not mean that the change in one of the pair causes the change in th
other. In highly correlated variables a prediction of the value of one may be mad
from the known value of the other. Such a prediction cannot be used legitimately as a
correction for the disturbing influence of a correlated character unless it is known that
the correlation is of a causal nature dependent exclusively upon that putative disturb
ing influence. The use of such predictions can be justified in allowing for age differ
ences. Physical features which are subject to age changes show variations between
criminal groups of diverse mean ages which are of no general criminological signifi
cance and should be eliminated. However, the correlation coefficients of age with va
rious metric and indicial features of this series yield only three or four values which
are statistically significant. Weight is only slightly correlated with age, nose height
more markedly, and ear breadth significantly but not closely. Although the correlation
of these features with age are really not high enough to justify the use of corrections
these have been employed in some cases, because it is desirable in this study to make
excessive allowances for factors complicating criminological peculiarities rather than
to incur the accusation of a Lombrosian bias.

Weight is highly correlated with most bodily measurements, but no corrections for
the influence of weight have been made in this study because weight does not cause
size. The same argument applies to most other intercorrelated bodily dimensions and
indices; they vary in correlation because they are similarly and simultaneously affected
by certain growth factors or other agencies of the organism.

Three questions concerning the metric and indicial differentiation of offense groups
must be answered: Are the differences in single characters greater than may be ex
pected to occur through the mere chances of sampling? Are the differences which are
independent of the chances of sampling due to state composition? Is the aggregate c

differences which are independent of sampling and state composition and unaffected by age, large enough to distinguish each offense group from a random sample of the entire series?

Chapter V is devoted to the examination of offense group differences from the total series in each measurement and index. Here it is demonstrated that no single measurement or index displays sufficiently large variations among the offense groups to establish its validity as a sole criterion of physical difference by nature of offense. There is no single infallible diagnostic symptom. This result is epitomized by the correlation ratios of measurements and indices with nature of offense, which are invariably low. The answer to the query as to the existence in single characters of offense group differences supervening the chances of sampling, is that these occur only sporadically and in no case are significant for every offense group of the series.

The questions relating to the effect of state composition upon offense group differences and to the existence of aggregates of significantly deviating measurements and indices in each offense group, clear of sampling effects, state composition, and age influence, may be answered together. Such independent differences, purified also of observational equation, do in fact exist in most of the offense groups.

First degree murderers are differentiated in 25.64 per cent of measurements and indices. They are older, heavier, and taller than criminals *in toto*. They have larger chest diameters, broader jaws, relatively narrower shoulders, relatively shorter trunks, and broader jaws in proportion to facial breadth, than have total criminals.

Second degree murderers are distinguished in 12.82 per cent of measurements and indices. These include excess of age, excess of chest depth, deficiency of head height and of length-height and breadth-height indices.

Criminals convicted of assault are significantly and independently differentiated in only two of 39 metric characters, or 5.13 per cent. These are excess age and excess shoulder breadth. This group is not anthropometrically distinct from the total series, perhaps because of its very small size, which largely increases the probable error of sampling.

Robbers show residual excesses in 5 measurements and indices, or 12.82 per cent. They are below mean age, below mean chest depth, excessive in head height, in face breadth, and in nasal index.

Burglars and thieves are overwhelmingly differentiated from total criminals with 23.08 per cent of residually independent differences. These are deficiencies of age, weight, chest diameters, head length, head circumference, face breadth, and jaw breadth. They show an excess of forehead breadth relative to jaw breadth.

Forgery and fraud has 10.26 per cent of independently distinguished metric features. These are excesses of sitting height, head length, head circumference, and total face height.

Rapists are distinguished by a total of 5 features or 12.82 per cent. They are: excess of mean age, deficiency in stature and sitting height, excesses in chest depth and in relative shoulder breadth.

Other sex offenders are not anthropometrically distinct from the total series.

The versus public welfare group suffers many corrections from state overloading. Residually it is distinguished in 15.38 per cent of metric features: namely, excesses of age, chest depth, face breadth, nose breadth, jaw breadth and cephalo-facial index.

Arson and all other offenses is differentiated in only 3 features, one of which is excess age. It is scarcely an anthropometrically distinct group.

Altogether eight of the ten offense groups are anthropometrically distinct from random samples of the entire criminal series, after deductions have been made for age-affected characters and for the combined influences of state composition and personal equations. The inadequately differentiated groups are other sex, and assault.

Morphological Differentiation by Offense Groups

Morphological differentiation is investigated by methods similar to those utilized in the case of measurements and indices. First the deviations of single subcategories of morphological characters are tabulated and analyzed. These differences are then assembled by offense groups, and the statistical differentiation of each group, or the lack of it, is ascertained on the basis of the percentage of significantly deviating total observations, each of which includes two or more subcategories. The same precautions are employed against the effects of state composition and observational equation. Nine of the ten offense groups prove to be morphologically distinct from the total series. The only undifferentiated group is assault, but other sex offenders are rather feebly distinguished. These are the two small groups which failed to attain distinction in metric features.

Before these conclusions were reached, it was necessary to scrutinize the complicating effects of age differences in the offense groups. There is obviously no great interest attaching to the fact that first degree murderers, for example, have more gray hair than other criminals, if they owe this distinction merely to their superior age. Hence all morphological observations were retabulated by age groups in order to determine the regression of each upon age. These age groupings were then made the basis of predictions which correct for age differences. The final correction serves to isolate the offense group characters which remain significantly deviant after due allowance has been made, not only for state composition, but also for age.

First degree murderers show 7 final differences, or 14.89 per cent of complete morphological observations which include distinctive excesses in their subcategories These are: (1) deficiency of persons with scant body hair; (2) deficiency of narrow nasal bridges; (3) excess of median chins and deficiency of bilateral chins; (4) excess of flat or non-protruding cheek bones; (5) excess of large ear lobes; (6) deficiency of poorly developed antihelices of the ear; and (7) excess of slight shoulder slope.

Second degree murderers have 5 ultimately differentiated morphological characters or 10.64 per cent of the total observations. These are: (1) excess of high nasal bridges; (2) deficiency of median chins and excess of bilateral chins; (3) rarity of absense of cheek wrinkles and excessive presence of this feature; (4) deficiency of teeth showing slight or medium wear; (5) deficiency of teeth without caries.

Assault criminals have but one distinguishing morphological character, or 1.83 per cent, and are hence not morphologically differentiated from a random sample of the total series of the same size. The distinctive morphological character is height of the nasal root, which shows excess of both low and high development and a deficiency of medium.

Robbers retain 7 distinguishing morphological characters, or 14.89 per cen. of total observations. These differentiae are: (1) deficiency of sparse beards; (2) deficiency of straight hair and excess of low waves; (3) excess of diffused irides; (4) excess of median eyefolds; (5) deficiency of wrinkles and excess of their absence; (6) deficiency of edge-to-edge bite; (7) excess of medium ear protrusion and deficiency of pronounced protrusion.

Burglars and thieves preserve 6 differentiated morphological characters, or 12.77 per cent of the total. These consist of :(1) excess of scant body hair; (2) excess of golden head hair; (3) excess of light brown eye color; (4) excess of medium height of the nasal root with a deficiency of high roots; (5) excess of concave nasal profiles; (6) excess of underbite and deficiency of edge-to-edge bite.

Forgery and fraud criminals do not deviate from the mean age of the total series and require no age corrections for their 6 distinguishing morphological characters (12.77 per cent of the total). They are notable for: (1) sparse head hair; (2) lack of sparse beards; (3) excess of medium nasal bridge height and deficiency of pronounced nasal bridge height; (4) scarcity of thin integumental lips; (5) deficiency of thin membranous lips; (6) excess of slight or medium wear of the teeth and deficiency of pronounced wear.

Rapists, after age correction, retain 5 distinguishing morphological characters, or 10.64 per cent. These are ample to distinguish the group morphologically. The differences in question are: (1) excess of blue-gray eye color; (2) excess of speckled sclerae; (3) excess of deflections of the nasal septum to the right and deficiency of no deflection; (4) excess of pronounced alveolar prognathism; and (5) excess of right facial asymmetry.

Other sex offenders are left with 4 differentiated morphological characters or 8.51 per cent — a residuum adequate for general group differentiation. They show: (1) an excess of straight hair and a deficiency of low waves; (2) an excess of thin membranous lips; (3) an excess of thin cheeks; and (4) an excess of right facial asymmetry.

Versus public welfare criminals retain 5 morphological differences, or 10.24 per cent. (1) They are deficient in thin integumental lips; (2) they have an excess of prominent malars and a deficiency of submedium malars; (3) they are deficient in submedium jaw angles; (4) they are, further, deficient in small ear lobes; and (5) they are deficient in attached ear lobes and show an excessive proportion of free ear lobes.

Arson and all other offenders have residually but 3 differentiating morphological features, or 6.38 per cent. They are barely distinguishable as a group. Their three peculiarities are: (1) an excess of ash blond hair, (2) of epicanthic folds, and (3) of slight alveolar prognathism.

When due allowance has been made for accidents of sampling, state composition, and age difference, nine of the ten offense groups are found to be morphologically distinct from random samples of the total series. The exception is the small assault group, which probably owes its lack of differentiation to paucity of numbers. However the miscellaneous arson and all other offenses group is only feebly differentiated, perhaps because of its composite character.

Criminals as a whole are then morphologically differentiated according to the nature of their offenses.

FACTORS CONTRIBUTING TO THE ANTHROPOLOGICAL DIFFERENTIATION
OF THE OFFENSE GROUPS

The etiology of physical differentiation among native White prisoners of native parentage is the crux of our investigation. It may be the part of scientific caution to rest our case upon the mere proof of such differentiation. Nevertheless some interpretation must be essayed, since it is a futile research which yields inexplicable results, especially in the study of a vital sociological problem such as crime. Several possibly causal factors of offense differentiation may be presented for subsequent discussion. The complicating effects of observational equation, state and age differences, and the chances of sampling have been eliminated.

The following factors may determine the physical differentiation of offense groups: (1) inherited mental defect may be accompanied by physical stigmata, the former directly influencing the type of offense, and the latter casually associated with the causative mental state; (2) different racial types or racial blends may present physical variations which are associated with diverse criminal propensities; (3) physical types may be selected for certain occupations and these occupations may condition the nature of the offense committed; (4) constitutional types may determine choice of offense directly or indirectly; (5) urban or rural residence may mold the physique and influence the type of antisocial behavior.

LOMBROSIAN STIGMATA AND RECIDIVISM

The first of the factors mentioned above is virtually the old Lombrosian theory of physical stigmata associated with mental defect. As far as the present investigation is concerned, this possibility can be dismissed summarily. Our criminals present no considerable or imposing array of stigmata of degeneracy or atavistic features, and we know practically nothing about their mental capabilities — at least as regards the present series of native Whites of native parentage. If any such associations do in fact exist, they will have to await demonstration by some more subtle and refined research. The physical stigmata, at any rate, are not obvious to physical anthropologists of the training and ability possessed by our field workers. The writer is confident that such abnormalities, if present in significant numbers of our criminals, would not have been overlooked. The almost complete lack of data on mentality of these criminals is due to the regrettable absence of such information in most prison records and to our financial inability to carry out the requisite tests. The very considerable body of reliable psychiatric material in our possession pertains only to Massachusetts county jail prisoners and to the civil and criminal insane. This material will be correlated with anthropometric measurements in a subsequent volume of this work.

At the center of the entire Lombrosian hypothesis is the conception that the criminal is biologically inferior. The primary test of the validity of such a conception is the comparison of criminals with civilians of the same ethnic origin and similar economic status. A secondary test is provided by an inquiry into the differentiation of habitual criminals from first offenders. If biological inferiority is significantly associated with criminal conduct, it is a reasonable presumption that repeated offenders will show an accentuated deterioration of physique. Further, since there is a well known tendency for habitual or professional criminals to specialize in their types of offense, it may be expected that those convicted of categories of crime which are recognized means of criminal livelihood will be markedly differentiated in physical features because of the excessive numbers of habitual criminals included among them. For this reason an examination of the physical characters of recidivists, in contrast to those of putatively first offenders, is apposite, not only to the general Lombrosian theory of criminal inferiority, but also to our immediate problem of the causation of offense group differences in physical features.

Persons with records of previous convictions comprise 39.12 per cent of the total series, exclusive of North Carolina from which we have no information. Complete records would undoubtedly reveal a higher percentage of recidivists. A comparison of the metric and indicial features of the group previously convicted and of the group of supposed first offenders reveals that the two series are markedly differentiated. Crudely, recidivists are slightly younger, shorter, lighter, narrower-chested, with longer heads, narrower foreheads, relatively longer and narrower faces, shorter noses, narrower jaws, and with faces and foreheads narrower relative to head breadth. They also have higher proportions of dark eyes and dark hair than first offenders possess.

These recidivists come from all of the states studied except North Carolina, but Wisconsin and Massachusetts furnish disproportionately large quotas. This overloading is probably due in part to the inclusion of the Concord reformatory group in the Massachusetts material and in part to the superiority of prison records of previous convictions in Massachusetts and Wisconsin.

The recidivist group is especially recruited from the burglary and larceny class, and also shows excesses of robbers and of forgers. It is notably deficient in murderers and persons convicted of offenses versus public welfare.

Evidently the differences between recidivists and first offenders are conditioned in part by inequalities of state quotas in the two subseries, since each state has its own peculiarities in the physical composition of its criminals. It was therefore necessary to make predictions of expected values on the basis of state composition and to correct the differences between recidivists and first offenders in the light of these predictions. This process reduced 15 initial differences which were statistically significant to 3, or 7.69 per cent of the 39 metric features. Such differences are independent of state sampling. They are inferiority in recidivist weight, chest breadth, and ear index (Observer A). There are no certain differences in hair form between recidivists and first offenders. Light brown hair is uncertainly deficient in recidivists and dark brown hair is insignificantly in excess. Green-brown eyes are commoner and gray-brown and blue-brown eyes are rarer among the recidivists, but all of these pigmental differences are rendered unreliable by state sampling.

In spite of the large number of differences invalidated by corrections for state sampling, the general trend of deviations of prisoners previously convicted from first offenders seems to provide convincing evidence of size inferiority of recidivists. This conclusion is based upon the fact that the actual means of measurements of the recidivists generally fall below those of first offenders to a greater extent than is expected from state predictions. The differences are such as to remove the recidivists farther from the civilian population than are first offenders or total criminals. Since it is not the crime which molds the physique of the criminal, we cannot reasonably refer the ultimate differences between recidivists and first offenders to inequalities of offense group distribution in the two subseries. It is, nevertheless, significant that the repeated offenders with the lowest grade of physique appear in excessive numbers in the predominant burglary and larceny group. The implication is that physical incompetents are economically so ineffectual that many of them attempt to earn their living by stealing rather than by working. Accentuated physical inferiority seems both to encourage recidivism and to select burglary and theft as preferred antisocial activities.

It is unfortunate that the name of Lombroso, even among criminologists, is preeminently associated with the idea that bizarre combinations of physical abnormalities enable one to distinguish various types of criminals from each other and all of them from law-abiding citizens. The lasting contribution of that great Italian to the anthropology of crime lies in his conception of the physical inferiority of criminals *en masse*, not as a direct cause of their delinquency, but as a symptom of the associated weakness of character and mentality which force them into antisocial behavior. The data of Goring and of the present investigation absolutely confirm the main contention of Lombroso in this matter of biological inferiority.

RACIAL AND ETHNIC DIFFERENCES

We may consider next the possibility that different racial types or racial blends may be represented in the offense groups and that the physical variations presented by these types or blends may be associated with diverse criminal tendencies. Do our several offense groups represent different racial types — either pure types or groups in which this or that racial strain is clearly predominant? If this were the case we might expect differences between the offense groups in recognized racial features such as the cephalic index, the nasal index, hair color, eye color, complexion, and, possibly, stature and body build. In most of the metric features the means of offense groups do not present differences which justify such a conclusion. A stock racial character is the cephalic index. Every one of the offense groups presents a range from extreme dolichocephaly to extreme brachycephaly. Every one has a mesocephalic mean index and the maximum difference between means of the offense groups is only .87 index units. Murderers are slightly but significantly more dolichocephalic than other offenders. Yet this difference does not survive the correction for state sampling. Sex offenders are more leptorrhine than other criminals, but again the difference does not withstand correction for state composition. It is obvious, however, that if the several states are differentiated in ethnic and racial composition, our correction for state sampling will have the effect of eliminating or reducing whatever racial and ethnic differences do, in fact, characterize the offense groups. First degree murderers, for example, are overloaded with Kentuckians. If the state proclivity for homicide is due to the predominance of a certain racial type, this causal factor will be obscured, or its effects minimized, by our attempts to smooth out differences in state series by the correction for state composition. Hence in estimating the ethnic and racial factors as possible causes of physical differences in offense groups, it must be borne in mind that in applying state corrections we may have emptied out the baby with the bath.

Nevertheless, if one glances over the tables showing the distribution of pigmentation of hair, skin, and eyes one is struck by the similarity of the distributions of shades in the offense groups rather than by the differences. None of the gross differences which diverse races are supposed to present meet the eye. Each of these offense groups represents a variety of mixtures of different racial types, and by no means radically dissimilar mixtures from group to group. Such simple explanations as an identification of murderers with Nordics, Alpines with thieves, and Mediterraneans with robbers, have no validity.

However, it is impossible to dismiss summarily the postulate that slightly different blends of the various racial elements in the population are represented in individual offense groups. Yet the assemblage of metric and morphological differences give very few clues to any such subtle differences in racial blends. In the next volume of this series, which deals primarily with native Whites of foreign parentage and with foreign Whites, all White prisoners, irrespective of parentage and nationality, have been subjected to an analysis on the basis of stock racial criteria. The results show certain definite correlations of racial types with nature of offense, but the material is racially much more diversified than the present series.

The data on extraction, together with historical records of the colonization of the various states, offer some information concerning the probable ethnic differentiation of the family stocks from which these prisoners are sprung. The evidence is against the supposition that many of them have originated from families which emigrated to this country after 1870. There are two probable exceptions: the youngest of the reformatory prisoners from Massachusetts and Colorado, and some of the younger prisoners of German extraction, especially from Wisconsin.

The Massachusetts criminal stocks are predominantly English and Irish, with a strong admixture of French Canadian. North Carolina was originally settled from Virginia. The leading elements in our criminal stocks from this state, according to history and to records of prisoners' extraction, are English, Irish, and Scotch-Irish. It is impossible to state how much of the Irish is really Ulster Scotch. On the basis of the historical records this element may be in the majority. There is present, in addition, a small German element.

Kentucky was also colonized from Virginia, with Pennsylvania and North Carolina contributing considerable elements. The population is said to have been overwhelmingly English, but there was a perceptible German strain. Our records of foreign extraction include in this state only 4.21 per cent of the criminal series, of which the leading element is Irish and the next German. It is nevertheless probable that the criminal stock here is predominantly English.

Tennessee derived most of its early population from North Carolina, but considerable numbers from Virginia. Grant thinks that the early inhabitants were principally Ulster Scotch.[5] The records of criminal extractions here include only 8.75 per cent of the state series. Again the leading element is Irish. These again may be northern Irish or Ulster Scotch. However the English element is probably very strong here.

Wisconsin was first settled by the Ulster Scotch from Virginia, Kentucky, and Tennessee, and then by agriculturalists from New England and New York. Even before it achieved statehood it had been flooded with foreign immigrants, about half of which were from the British Isles. Soon after this Germans came in great numbers.

[5] Madison Grant, *The Conquest of a Continent*, 1934, pp. 147–149.

Our records of foreign extractions in this state include 83.50 per cent. Here again the Irish are in the lead, with the Germans and the English practically tied for second place, the French third, the Scotch fourth, and the Scotch-Irish fifth. Scandinavian elements are negligible. It would appear that the bulk of our Wisconsin criminals are derived from the earlier Wisconsin immigrants.

Most of the early pioneers of Texas came from Tennessee, Kentucky, and the Lower Mississippi valley. They were predominantly English and Scotch. However Southern and Western Texas attracted a German population from the Upper Rhine as early as 1842. In our Texas extractions, which include 39.45 per cent of the state series, the Irish lead by a huge majority, Scotch-Irish are next, then Germans, English, and Scotch.

Arizona and New Mexico have contributed very small quotas to this series. In both of their extraction records Irish are predominant and Germans next. In Colorado, which is much more diversified ethnically, Irish are twice as numerous as any other nationality in the extraction records; English are second, Germans third, and Scotch fourth.

The very scanty information available concerning the families of these criminals does not indicate a great racial diversity in the populations of the nine states considered. Massachusetts deviates from the other state series in its higher proportion of French Canadians, and Wisconsin in its considerable German element.

DIFFERENTIATION BY OCCUPATION

All of the occupations claimed by criminals have been grouped in 11 categories Each of these includes a miscellaneous assortment. Many of the criminals have probably engaged very little in the occupations which they profess. In a small percentage of cases faulty assignments of occupations to the various categories have been made by the clerical staff. Both of these factors tend to obscure whatever physical differentiation of criminals by occupations may in fact exist. Nevertheless, a surprising degree of differentiation is manifested by the occupational groups. This would be still greater were it not for the fact that many of the occupational categories include very few individuals, whereas the extractive group is huge — comprising nearly one-third of the series. This situation involves very large probable errors of the small groups which in turn require quantitatively huge differentiation from the total series in order to validate their deviations. In the case of the extractive group it is necessary to compare an occupational category with a series of which it comprises 32 per cent. This of course minimizes differences.

The relation between education and occupation is very intimate. It is represented by a coefficient of mean square contingency amounting to .57.

Pigmentation differences in the occupational groups are not very marked. Hair color is lightest in the clerical and professional classes and is darkest among laborers tradesmen, and public servants. Peculiarly enough, eye shades are darkest in the two groups which have the lightest hair. Dark hair is commoner in all classes than dark eyes; while mixed eyes are much commoner than dark hair. Pigmentation in these criminals seems extremely mixed.

We need not discuss here the individual measurements and indices, but it may be well to recapitulate the physical features which distinguish the several occupational groups, noting at the same time variations in educational attainment.

The extractive group is the most ignorant and ranks highest in murder. It is significantly differentiated in physical features, so far as here examined. Differentiae include excess age, deficient head breadth, and deficient forehead breadth. This group contains an excess of tall men of medium weight and ranks highest in blue eyes.

The laborer group is also distinguished by illiterates and poorly educated men. It is significantly differentiated in physical features. Dark brown eyes are in excess and blue eyes are deficient. Laborers are significantly younger, lighter in weight, shorter, narrower in head breadth, smaller in head circumference, more dolichocephalic, than the total series. Short men of medium weight are in excess in this group.

Factory workers, a well educated group, are undistinguished in pigmentation. They are notably younger than the mean and have broader heads, broader foreheads, and higher cephalic indices. Tall-heavy and tall-slender types show dubious excesses in this group, which, on the whole, is physically differentiated from the total series.

The transportation group is very small and is not physically differentiated. This is true also of skilled trades. The trade group is older and broader-headed than the total series and shows probably significant excesses of weight and of head circumference. It is probably differentiated physically from the total series. The public service group shows some interesting deviations, but these are not certainly valid because of the small size of the group. The semi-professional class is most brachycephalic of the occupational groups and displays excessive forehead breadth. It has a probable deficiency of stature and probable excesses of head breadth and head circumference. Although many of its deviations are invalidated by its small size the semi-professional group is, without doubt, physically differentiated from the total series.

The professional group, although tiny, is most remarkably distinct from total criminals. It is the best educated and has next to the lightest hair and next to the darkest eyes. It is the oldest and heaviest group; has the broadest foreheads and faces, and excessive size of cranial circumference.

Personal service is another differentiated group. It has a deficiency of blue eyes, is below mean height and weight, and has an excessively high nasal index.

The clerical group is also distinct. It stands second in education, first in lightness of hair, but at the bottom in lightness of eyes. It is deficient in stature and probably in weight, excessive in head breadth, and the most narrow-nosed of the occupational categories. Short-slender types are disproportionately common in this group.

Thus 7 of 11 occupational groups are certainly physically distinct from the total series. I am confident that the other groups would be similarly differentiated if they included larger assemblages of individuals.

The physical requirements of the various occupations undoubtedly determine to some extent the somatic differentiation. Clerical workers and personal servants are likely to be small and puny men. Farmers are taller and stronger. But, over and beyond these physical requirements, there seems to be operative a racial selection. This is best shown by a number of significant differences in the cephalic index. These are notable for their absence in the offense group differentiation. Thus round-headed, blond men are better educated than most criminals and tend to fall into the clerical and professional occupations. Tall men with narrow heads and blue eyes are especially common among farmers. Laborers tend to be dolichocephalic, dark-eyed, and rather small. Semi-professional workers are the shortest and most brachycephalic of all groups.

The facts point toward a concentration of the tall dolichocephals in the country and in the extractive occupations, of the small, dark dolichocephals in the city among the laboring classes and the personal servants, of the blond brachycephals in the city also and among the learned occupations, of the medium and short brachycephals of darker pigmentation in the city again, in the mechanical and industrial occupations, and probably in trade.

Racial types or racial blends seem to be more closely related to occupation (and probably to urban or rural environment) than to nature of offense. However, the correlations of offense with race, as previously explained, are somewhat obscured by the correction for state sampling. Offense is intimately connected both with urban or rural environment and with occupation. The countryman has a limited range of antisocial opportunities. The latter are ample as regards murder, assault, sex crimes, and offenses against the liquor laws, but rather restricted for robbery, burglary, larceny, fraud, arson. Gainful offenses are less common in the country. From the tall, long-headed, blue-eyed group of farmers there are selected certain inferior types of ignorant men who commit crimes against the person. But all of the more diversified racial types of urbanites have equal opportunities for crimes of personal violence. The city-dwellers then contribute their quota of convictions for murder, sex offenses, and assault, and thereby blur the physical type of the agricultural offender against the person. In urban areas there are not only more physical types than in the country, but more diversified occupations. Educational facilities are abundant and to some extent educational attainment determines the choice of vocation. Social position, economic status of family, and racial and ethnic affinities also play their part in occupational selection. The sum total of these influences results in selection of physical occupational types which are roughly coincident with various racial types and racial blends, although there is considerable overlapping of the occupations. Each of these occupational types has a wide choice of forms of antisocial behavior. First of all they have, in common, personal relationships which may involve crimes of violence. Then each has its special facilities for one or more kinds of crime. Clerical workers have temptations to commit forgery, fraud, and some forms of larceny. Persons in mechanical pursuits are accustomed to the use of tools and electrical devices and are familiar with the intricacies of the automobile engine. They are technically fitted to become safe-blowers, bank-robbers, and other varieties of criminals who employ modern inventions in their profession. Tradesmen and small shopkeepers are sometimes pressed by business difficulties which drive them to commit arson or some sort of fraud. Public servants may accept bribes. Professional men may indulge in malpractice of one sort or another.

It thus seems inevitable that there should be a more stringent operation of physical selection for occupations than for types of antisocial offense. Within any racial or other physical group or within any occupational group, individuals of inferior physique, mentality, and ability, are selected for antisocial behavior. The types of crime they commit depend to some extent upon their opportunities which are restricted by their educations and their vocations. Within any range of criminal opportunity presented to a potential offender, the actual choice of a crime is likely to be determined by the physical and mental peculiarities of the individual himself.

DIFFERENTIATION BY BODY BUILD

Some investigation of the relation of body build types to nature of offense seems necessary in view of the great interest in constitutional types which has been awakened by the work of Kretschmer and others. For purposes of this study the entire criminal series of native Whites of native parentage was separated into stature-weight subgroups. These were obtained by dividing the series into three stature groups on the basis of a medium class comprising all of the individuals within a range of 10 on either side of the mean height. The three classes thus secured were similarly subdivided on the basis of the mean and standard deviation of weight of each. Thus nine stature-weight subgroups were distinguished. These groups vary greatly in size — from 54 individuals in the short-heavy group to 1925 in the medium height-medium weight group.

It was first essayed to determine whether or not these body build subgroups are distinguished in offense. The total of certainly significant differentiations is 14 out of a possible 90, or 15.56 per cent, although the expectation in random samples would be less than 4 per cent. However only 6 of the 9 body build subgroups display differences in excess of three times their probable errors. The lack of certain differentiation in 2 of the 3 groups thus undistinguished is clearly due to their very small size.

Body build differences in previous convictions are marked. Recidivism decreases with increasing weight and stature. The percentage of married, divorced, and widowed men increases with added weight and stature. Nor does this relationship appear to depend markedly upon age. Again, occupation is clearly related to body build. However, this differentiation is not so strong as in the case of offense, since only 8 of 99 instances (8.08 per cent) manifest certain differences. Six of the 9 body build groups are without any question differentiated in occupation.

The body build subgroups also vary in their educational attainments, although each group contains the whole range from illiteracy to college education. On the whole short-slender men are the best educated. Short men of medium weight are at the other end of the scale, with roughly one-fifth of the educational attainment of the former subgroup.

The heavy weights in every stature-weight subgroup are the highest in mean age; the light weights are next in order of age, and the medium weights are lowest in mean age. On the whole the tall stature-weight subgroups are the youngest.

The subgroups were sorted out on the basis of combinations of stature and weight. They are naturally very different each from the other in these two characters. The short men are very short; the tall men are almost gigantic; and the mean subgroup weights range from 111 to 197 pounds.

These body build subgroups are not markedly differentiated in the cephalic index. The short groups have slightly rounder heads and the tall groups are a little more dolichocephalic. Facial indices do not vary widely in the subgroups. In general, the heavy men have relatively the widest and shortest faces. They also have the highest nasal indices.

Hair color shows 7 of 72 differences which are certainly significant, or 9.72 per cent. Yet no body build subgroup even approximates homogeneity in hair pigmentation, and only 4 of the 9 subgroups exhibit certain differences in one or more hair shades. By and large, men of medium height and slender build have the lightest hair, and short, heavy men the darkest.

Significant differences in eye color are found in 6 of 63 instances, or 9.52 per cent. Only three of the body build groups are certainly differentiated. No group is homogeneous. Short-heavy men, and medium height-heavy men have in general the lightest eyes. Short men of medium weight have the darkest eyes. Pigmentation in this criminal series is very mixed. Light hair is far less common than are light eyes.

We may now summarize the general physical and sociological differentiation of the 9 body build subgroups. The short-slender type is smallest, lightest in weight, insignificantly the most round-headed, most often convicted, most addicted to burglary and larceny, least addicted to forgery and robbery, least married, best educated, and most frequently engaged in clerical and other sedentary occupations.

The short-medium weight subgroup has the largest percentage of dark eyes and the smallest percentage of light eyes, but is not otherwise extreme physically. It ties for lowest ranking in first degree murder and is also lowest in versus public welfare offenses. It ranks first in arson. It is second in number of previous convictions. It contains the most laborers and personal servants found in any body build subgroup and the smallest percentage of factory workers. It ranks lowest in educational attainment.

The short-heavy group is oldest, broadest in nose and face, next to the darkest in hair and lightest in eyes. It ranks first in both categories of sex offense and first in assault. It is last in murder and next to the last in robbery. It is near the bottom in previous convictions, near the top in married men, and first in numbers of divorced men and widowers. It is first in professional men, first in transportation, and high in clerical workers. It is in the middle of the educational ranking.

The medium height-slender group is the most leptoprosopic, the most leptorrhine and has the lightest hair. It is not differentiated in offense, but it has the highest proportion of unmarried men and the highest percentage of men in skilled trades. In percentage of laborers it ranks second, and in education third.

The medium height-medium weight subgroup is by far the largest numerically and is physically quite undistinguished. Nor is it notable in offense. In occupation and education it ranks low.

The medium height-heavy subgroup is not particularly outstanding in physical features, but is highest in offenses versus public welfare (largely bootlegging), and second in sex offenses. It is low in burglary and larceny and in previous convictions. Occupationally and educationally it is not individual.

The tall-slender group is small but clearly distinguished. It is the youngest build subgroup and has the second highest proportion of dark hair. It is notably dolichocephalic and leptorrhine. It is first in second degree murder, second in first degree murder, first in robbery, last in burglary and larceny and in both categories of sex offenses. It is especially high in extractive and factory occupations and educationally is exceedingly diverse.

The subgroup designated as tall-medium weight is rather young and ranks second in lightness of hair, because of its large proportion of red-headed men and blonds. It has a large percentage of blue eyes. This subgroup ranks first in forgery and fraud and ties for second place in combined murders. It leads in extractive occupations and rather high in clerical and personal service. It is poorly educated.

The tall-heavy type is above mean age and is lowest in cephalic index. The nasal index is higher than the series average. The subgroup is second darkest in general pigentation of hair and eyes. It ranks first in first degree murder and ties for second in combined murder rankings. It is second in assault, forgery, and other sex. It is very low in burglary and larceny, and next to last in rape. It records the fewest previous convictions, the fewest unmarried men. It ranks first in factory operatives, first in public service, second in transportation, and second in educational attainment.

The state composition of the body build subgroups is of some importance. Massachusetts and Wisconsin contribute significant excesses to the short-slender and short-medium groups. The Southwest is also high in these two body build types. The short-heavy group is significantly deficient only in Tennessee. The medium height-slender subgroup is deficient in Texas and North Carolina and high in Kentucky. The medium height-medium weight group is in excess in Massachusetts and Tennessee and deficient in Wisconsin. The medium height-heavy subgroup is significantly deficient only in Massachusetts. Texas and the Southwest are high in this body type. The tall-slender subgroup is recruited particularly from Tennessee, Texas, and Kentucky. The tall-medium weight group is notably in excess in Texas and notably deficient in Massachusetts. The tall-heavy subgroup is again greatly in excess in Texas and deficient in Massachusetts.

Body build seems to have carried us a step farther than the occupational study. The types isolated, if they can be called types, are not hereditary racial types, but rather individual constitutional types sorted out of various racial blends. Some fairly definite physical-sociological associations seem to have been established. Extreme physical types are extreme in their criminal propensities.

DIFFERENTIATION BY URBAN AND RURAL RESIDENCE

It seems wholly probable that in some European countries the stature of the poorer urban classes has been depressed by generations of slum-dwelling and malnutrition. It possible that some part of the physical differentiation of our criminal offense group is attributable to an urban specialization in physique which is associated with tendencies to commit crimes which are rare in rural districts. Nevertheless it seems unlikely that any of our native White criminals of native parentage have been subjected to any such extreme environmental depression, since the majority of them probably come from small towns rather than congested metropolitan areas and there can scarcely be included in our series any large number of individuals with a long slum heritage.

Of the present series 31.63 per cent are in the extractive occupations (80 per cent agricultural, 16 per cent mining), and of the 17 per cent of laborers, possibly one-half are agricultural. Probably about 40 per cent of the criminals are countrymen. When their ancestors immigrated, farming was the principal occupation in all of the survey states, with the possible exception of Massachusetts. There were no really large cities in these states except Boston. It would appear that our agriculturalists are descended from those immigrant families which stayed upon the land. It would seem to follow that this group would include the most primitive, the most conservative, the most hardy and vigorous, the most inured to manual labor, the most accustomed to firearms, and the least regardful of the economic opportunities of industrial life in the city.

The criminals of our series who belong to the non-extractive occupations are, for the most part, residents of towns or cities. Obviously they are derived either from originally agricultural families or from those which settled in the towns as immigrants. Let us for a moment consider the probable character of those whose families abandoned the land, or who abandoned it themselves, and moved to urban environments. The following reasons for change from rural to urban life may be discussed: physical disqualification for the rigor and drudgery of farm work, dislike of country life; economic failure in farming or other rural occupations; realization of the superior economic possibilities of an urban habitat, including commercial aptitude and desire for education; general restlessness and discontent.

Lack of physical strength to cope successfully with the arduous labor of farm life on the frontier may presumably have driven to the towns some of the smaller, more slender, and weaker offspring of agricultural families. The handicap of physical inferiority, if unaccompanied by an ambition for economic betterment, would be likely to reduce the status of the unfortunate who remained in the country to that of a hired farm laborer. It is probably a fair assumption that agricultural laborers are physically and mentally inferior to the farmers who employ them.

Dislike of country life may result from physical disqualification, from agricultural failure, from ambition, or from a variety of causes. Any physical selection of persons for a change from rural to urban life, on the basis of a distaste for the former, would probably involve the smaller and weaker individuals in larger numbers than the tall, active men.

Economic failure in farming may not result in any considerable migration to cities. The unsuccessful farmer is likely to stay on the land, becoming poorer and poorer, if he really likes farming. Or he may try farming in some new district. It is possible that a certain urge for life in the open, perhaps notable in tall dolichocephalic types of Nordic or mixed Nordic origin, may tend to keep them in rural districts and in extractive occupations, in spite of poverty. On the other hand, it is certain that many recent immigrant stocks — notably the Irish and the Italians — have exchanged a poverty stricken agricultural life in the mother country for whatever the American city may have to offer. Similarly, the migration from the sterile farms of New England must have involved the urbanization of all sorts of types, physically superior and inferior, although the inveterate farmer is likely to have moved farther west to pursue his occupation in more fertile areas.

Again, the descendants of agricultural families who moved to the towns in order to take advantage of the better opportunities afforded by urban industry and commerce and by superior educational facilities, are likely to include both the physically large and superior types and the physically inferior but mentally alert. It seems improbable that such migrants would contribute largely to the criminal population, unless they made failures of urban life. The failures would be those either physically or mentally unfit or both. They would be unable to profit by the educational advantages offered in the city and would gravitate into the lower occupations — unskilled labor, personal service and factory. The most stupid, the most ignorant, and the physically indifferent or inferior would remain at the bottom — in day labor. Taller, stronger, and slightly better educated and more competent men would possibly rise to mechanical work and transportation.

Persons who left the country because of general restlessness and discontent would again include disproportionately large numbers of the physically and mentally inferior and would fall into the lower occupational classes.

On the whole, it seems probable that persons migrating from the country to the city and eventually contributing to the urban criminal classes would be generally shorter, lighter, and weaker than those remaining in the country. They would also be more disinclined to physical exertion, and especially, to physical violence.

Let us now consider the criminals who are descended from families of originally urban residence in this country. In the first place, such families were likely to have been town residents in their home countries — skilled tradesmen, shopkeepers, et cetra. They would have been drawn from those European elements which were physically and temperamentally averse to the adventurous and arduous life of farming on the frontier. They would be in general smaller men, and physically more diversified than the countrymen, because there are always more hereditary strains in cities and towns than in the country. Urban areas are racially and ethnically more heterogeneous than rural areas. Thus, if the country stocks are predominantly dolichocephals of English, Scotch, or Irish extraction, there are sure to be among the city dwellers more brachycephals of non-British origin.

The occupational groupings of the cephalic index indicate a slightly greater prevalence of round-headedness in the urban classes — most marked in the semi-professional, professional, and clerical groups. The extractive class is also taller than any of the urban occupational classes. The evidence concerning pigmentation is confused, since three of the most differentiated urban occupations—professional, semi-professional, and clerical — lead in percentages of dark eyes, but two of them (professional and clerical) also lead in proportions of light hair. This fact suggests that pigmentation in urban areas is more mixed than in the country. The same possibilities of selection between urban and rural life may be applied to the urban European ancestors of the urban bred American criminals, but it seems more probable that over there ethnic and racial factors have operated to determine habitat and occupation. The racial stocks principally involved in our series are tall, blond long-heads (Nordics), tall, dark long-heads (Nordic-Mediterraneans or Atlanto-Mediterraneans), short, dark long-heads (Mediterraneans), short, dark brachycephals (Alpines), short, blond brachycephals (East Baltics), tall, mixed brachycephals (Nordic-Alpines, Nordic-Baltics, Dinarics). All of these were presumably represented in the early American ancestors of this criminal series and all were distributed both in the rural and urban environments. The British stocks were predominantly Nordic and Nordic-Mediterranean, with lesser elements of short, brunet dolichocephals (Mediterranean), and tall, mixed brachycephals (Nordic-Alpine or Dinaric). Of these it seems probable that the Nordics and Nordic-Mediterraneans were especially the rural pioneers, and the shorter long-heads and the round-heads were slightly more numerous in the town and city populations. The German element in the early American population was undoubtedly of principally Alpine, East Baltic, and Nordic-Alpine or Dinaric racial origin, with a minor element of pure Nordic. Most of these Germans went on the land, where they may have added the major part of the shorter brachycephalic elements to the rural population. But some of them undoubtedly settled in the cities or gravitated back into the cities and towns. The French element (almost purely French Canadian) is markedly Alpine, with only slight admixtures of other races, including some strains of American Indian. These French were brunet brachycephals, originally agricultural and rural, but tending in Massachusetts to become urban and industrial.

From the foregoing discussion it seems clear that rural and urban residence in them
selves are likely to effect a selection of physical types. City and town life offer more
ways of gaining a livelihood to weaklings than does the country. It is certain that all o
the families and individuals who have migrated from country to city are not physically
smaller and weaker than those who have remained on the land. However, there is added
to this selection of possibly inferior persons as urban immigrants the further effect o
unfavorable living conditions in the crowded quarters of the cities. No means of esti
mating the intensity of size-depressing factors operative in urban areas are available
from the data of this series. The effect may be considerable or negligible. Moreover
certain ethnic strains exhibit proclivities for urban or rural life according to their tradi
tional occupations in their mother countries, or by simple preference. In this particula
case ethnic predilections seem to accentuate the tallness and dolichocephaly of country
men and variations toward the opposite extremes in the town dwellers.

THE INTERACTION OF VARIABLES CAUSING PHYSICAL DIFFERENTIATION
OF OFFENSE GROUPS

An interpretation of the phenomena of physical differentiation in the offense group
involves the understanding of the simultaneous or consecutive operation of all of the
variables discussed above. Some approach to such a comprehension may be made by
setting forth a few working hypotheses based upon the separate contingencies and re
gressions of offense upon the several anthropological and sociological factors available
from our data. These hypotheses may facilitate the presentation of a rational and
plausible explanation of the grosser facts of offense group differentiation in physica
characters. An actual mathematical solution of this problem of multiple variables —
physical and sociological — would probably require more ample and more precise data
than are here available, if such a solution is possible. It is, at any rate, beyond the abil
ity of the present writer.

Our first proposition is that combinations of stature and weight are related to type
of offense. Homicidal tendencies increase markedly with increments of stature; tenden
cies to commit burglary and larceny decrease. Homicidal tendencies, secondly, increase
slightly with increments of weight, but proclivities toward burglary and larceny more
pronouncedly decrease. Thirdly, tendencies to commit such crimes against property a
forgery and fraud and offenses against liquor laws increase with both increasing stature
and increasing weight. Fourthly, tendencies toward sex crimes decrease with increment
of stature and increase with additions of weight. Possibly the latter statement is tru
also of assault. Lastly, robbery increases slightly with stature but diminishes with in
crements of weight (Cf. Tables IX–7 and IX–8).

The associations, as indicated in Table XIII–4, are not of course unit correlation
but only associative tendencies realized in build combinations, and scarcely perceptible
in mean measurements of offense groups. But from them can be predicted the main of
fense propensities of extreme combinations of height and weight. The influence of stat
ure seems usually to supervene that of weight in contradictory tendencies of the two
physical characters.

The second proposition is that occupation is mainly the resultant of (a) urban o
rural residence, (b) educational qualifications, (c) physical qualifications, (d) per

ɔnal preference and chance. Rural residence restricts occupational choice and educa-
ɔnal qualifications, the exercise of personal preference, and the operation of chance.
t emphasizes physical qualifications. Urban residence extends occupational choice and
ducational advantages, gives more scope to personal preference and chance, and places
ɪore emphasis upon educational qualifications than upon physical qualifications. It
ɔllows as a most important corollary to the foregoing proposition that, in an occupa-

TABLE XIII–4

STATURE — WEIGHT ASSOCIATIONS WITH NATURE OF OFFENSE

	Tall	Short	Slender	Heavy
Against Persons	Homicide Robbery	Sex Assault	Robbery	Sex Assault Homicide
Against Property	Forgery, Fraud Vs. Public Welfare Robbery	Burglary Larceny Arson	Burglary Larceny Robbery	Forgery Fraud Vs. Public Welfare

ɔnal scale beginning with manual labor and ending with the professions, physical se-
·ction decreases in intensity and educational selection increases as the economic level
f the occupation rises.

The third proposition is that occupation, thus determined, is commonly the immedi-
te agency which selects or restricts the type of offense which a criminal commits when
ɪat offense is against property. Indirectly, it affects also types of offenses against
ersons.

Thus far we have the following factors in the order named determining type of of-
ɛnse: (1) a diversity of ethnic and racial types due to heredity, (2) a differential dis-
·ibution of these types in urban and rural environments arising from historical causes
uch as time of ancestral immigration and state of economic and industrial development
f the United States at that time, occupation and residence in mother country, ethnic
:adition, and occupational propensity — individual, familial, or racial; (3) restriction
f rural inhabitants to extractive occupations, physical selection of larger and stronger
ɪdividuals for owner or tenant agriculture and of smaller and weaker individuals for
ired farm labor,[6] limitation of educational opportunities; (4) for urban inhabitants
·ide choice of occupations, ampler educational opportunities, increased stress upon edu-
ational qualifications, decreased stress upon physical qualifications with advance from
nskilled manual labor to highly skilled "mental" occupations; (5) in rural life intensi-
cation of personal relationships due to sparsity of population and isolation, resulting
ι excess of crimes of personal violence; lack of portable wealth and negotiable securi-
es tending to discourage certain offenses against property; (6) in urban life extension
nd diffusion of personal relationships owing to concentration of population, tending to
iminish crimes of personal violence, but tending also to diminish personal responsibil-

[6] I assume, rightly or wrongly, that the physically and mentally inferior, or relatively less efficient, are
ɪore likely to secure employment in rural areas as "hired men" than to work farms themselves.

ity toward fellow men in general and the valuation set upon human life; amplification of opportunities for crimes against property; (7) in rural life inbreeding resulting in physical homogeneity and intensification of mental and physical defects, isolation and brooding of psychopathic individuals, — all tending to increase crimes against persons; (8) in urban life crossbreeding or outbreeding resulting in physical and mental heterogeneity and in consequently intensive physical and mental selection for occupations; as a result unequal distribution of wealth, social unrest and discontent, crimes against property; (9) in rural life sparsity of population and restricted criminal opportunity leading to easy detection and apprehension of persons responsible for crimes; (10) in urban life density of population and difficulty in detecting and apprehending all sorts of offenders; (11) in both rural and urban environments individual differences in mentality and physique, in familial and extra-familial environment, which, in the last analysis select the criminal from the non-criminal.

We may now apply this sequence or conglomeration of causative factors to individual physical combinations in our material. First of all we begin with a diversity of physical types which is implicit in the ethnic heterogeneity of our population. The physical type is antecedent to residence, education, occupation, and ultimate offense. Let us take the case of the short and slender man. He is short either because of his racial inheritance, his familial inheritance, or from the operation of certain growth repressing factors which may be environmental, such as malnutrition, or definitely pathological, such as endocrine disturbances. His slenderness is due to one or other of these same causes.

There are only 64 of these very short and slender men in our sample. Consequently findings concerning them must be interpreted conservatively. First of all, it seems important that there is a great and statistically significant deficiency of this body build type among the extractive occupations. This implies a comparative rarity of short slender men among the rural criminals. It may mean that this type is infrequent in the country population. In this connection the severe physical requirements of agricultural labor are relevant, since they are incompatible with feeble physiques. Evidently this body type discourages rural residence and agricultural occupation. It may be principally a product of urban conditions; it may be reinforced in the cities by migration from the country of those physically unfit for farm work.

The distribution of the short-slender type among the urban occupations ought to be instructive, but the group is so small that its occupational excesses are rarely significant. There is an uncertain deficiency of the type among laborers and an uncertain excess among those engaged in trade. The definite and significant excesses are found in the semi-professional and clerical occupations. In these two categories of occupation the short-slender type easily leads. Since this group is the best educated of all body build types it is obvious that men of this physique are stimulated to acquire enough education to enable them to obtain "white collar" jobs, since they are unsuited for work requiring muscular strength.

We may now consider the offense proclivities of the short-slender type. None of the offense excesses and deficiencies of this group attains statistical significance. Absolutely, however, the type ranks first in burglary and larceny and last in robbery. These facts are quite consistent with the particular opportunities offered by the occupations which short, slender men seem to prefer. It might be inferred that this physical type is disin clined to acts of violence against the person, were it not for the fact that it ranks high in both categories of murder. In this respect it fails to support our assumption concerning the relation of physique to violence. One is tempted to speculate that the murder committed by this group is attributable to the few rural members who maintain the association of agriculture and homicide which is so strong in the entire series of native Whites of native parentage. As a matter of fact, our sortings were not carried to the point of determining within each body build the offenses by occupations.

Short men of medium weight are slightly deficient in the extractive category, but this deficiency is not certainly significant. They are strongly and significantly in excess in the laborer class which is, presumably, in part urban and in part rural. There are no other significant occupational excesses in this class, although it leads all other groups in personal service, which is an urban occupation of low economic status. It is apparent then that this body build type occurs both in city and in country, but is somewhat more common in the former environment. On the whole, this is the most poorly educated of the body build groups. Hence it is not surprising to find it high in unskilled laborers, and in personal service, but low in some of the urban occupations which require more scholastic attainment. This class is surprisingly and significantly deficient in first degree murder and also insignificantly below average in second degree murder, but it exceeds all other body build types save one in rape. It ranks first in arson and second in burglary and larceny.

It is extremely interesting to note that as the weight of these short men increases from slender to medium the entire sociological and criminological complexion of the group alters. Instead of the best educated group we run into the most ignorant. In place of clerical and semi-professional occupational excesses, we find laborers and personal service groups coming to the fore. Murder decreases notably and rape and arson become the outstanding minor offenses, with burglary and larceny maintaining its leading position. These seem to be indications of fundamental differences in temperament, mentality, and physique.

If we pass on to the short-heavy group, which contains only 54 individuals, we observe another astonishing sociological transition. While there are still uncertain indications of a relative scarcity of this type in the country and consequently in extractive and laborer occupations, new urban pursuits become conspicuous. Of these the only absolutely certain excess is in the professional class, but transportation attains its first rank in this build group and clerical occupation its second rank. Educational qualifications fit into the picture insofar as illiteracy is low and there is a significant excess of persons who have attended professional schools. Yet the intermediate educational ranking of this group shows that it contains both ignorant and well schooled persons. Because of the small size of the group, offense excesses fail to attain statistical significance, but it is clear that this group leads in both rape and other sex offenses, rises in forgery and fraud, and drops in burglary and larceny. One must not jump to the conclusion that *all* short, fat, elderly men are prone to commit rape and other sex offenses, especially if they are professional men. There are only two professional men of the 54 in the group, 5 cases of rape, and 4 of other sex offenses. It is hard to escape the conclusion that there is something in the organism of the short, fat man which inclines him to sedentary occupations and sex offenses and something else which makes him averse to homicide — possibly the traditional good humor of the roly-poly. One thing should be noted: there is no indication that it is the greater age of these men which makes them corpulent, although it doubtless has some slightly favoring influence upon this condition. It is quite as likely to be the sedentary nature of their occupations and far more likely to be a matter of constitution. Not all are sedentary; many are not old; but all are short and fat.

Men of medium height and slender build are common in both city and country, although possibly they are found less often in the extractive occupations than in other pursuits. This group shows no important sociological differentiation except a possible predilection for burglary and larceny.

Least of all distinguished in occupation, and presumably in urban or rural residence, is the great group of medium height-medium weight. Yet it is distinctly low in educational qualifications and exhibits a number of offense peculiarities. Since this group includes nearly one-half of the entire series, small excesses are often statistically significant. Thus we have an excess of burglary and larceny and of arson and all other offenses, together with deficiencies of first degree murder, forgery and fraud, and versus public welfare. These seem merely to show slight criminalistic preferences for the cruder gainful offenses on the part of the individuals who are near the mode and the mean of body build.

The medium height-heavy group is also well distributed in the rural and urban occupations. It shows no occupational peculiarities except a deficiency in personal service. It has an excess of college men, but is otherwise undistinguished in education. In offenses it is notable for deficiency in burglary and larceny, for excess in versus public welfare, and possibly in other sex and in murder. These offense peculiarities are not easily explicable on sociological grounds, although it is probable that the uncertain excesses in murder are a part of the rural tradition, and it is a fact that most of the bootlegging in this series has been committed by farmers — especially Texans. Heavy weight is to some slight extent associated with high mean age (which this group exhibits) and also with sex offense — especially other sex offenses. It seems clear that heavy men are lecherous and tall men commit homicide. Here we seem to note the homicidal tendency rising with stature (which increases in the medium height groups from slender weights to heavy weights) and the sexual inclination somewhat diminished by the more powerful impulse to kill.

The tall-slender group represents an extreme of body build and of offense differentiation. Unfortunately the group is so small that many of its divergences are incompletely validated from a statistical point of view. This group is slightly high in farmers, but is by no means restricted to the country. Occupationally it shows no absolutely certain peculiarity except a definite avoidance of personal service. Preferences for factory and extractive categories and aversion to labor are probably indicated. Educational qualifications are not distinctive. Nevertheless these men are extreme in offenses as in physique. Most marked is their low rating in burglary and larceny and in both categories of sex offense, their excessively high rating in robbery and in both kinds of murder. The relation of body build to offense seems to override sociological considerations, although it may be that the tall slim farmers commit most of the murder and the urbanites of this build are the robbers. This group seems to support the short-slender group in indicating a negative association of slenderness with sex offenses.

The tall-medium weight group has the largest proportion of farmers to be found in any build type. Yet this is only 37.30 per cent. It shows no other certain occupational differentiation. It is low in educational attainment, but shows no certainly differentiated category. Nevertheless this group leads all others in forgery and fraud and it is hard to reconcile this circumstance with its educational position. There is also a possibly significant excess of first degree murder in this group — a crime which seems to go with rural residence and tallness. Sex offenses are below average.

Finally, the tall-heavy group is certainly excessively represented in public service, probably in transportation and factory, and seems to be deficient in extractive, laborer, and personal service. It is clearly a more urban group than most other build types considered. It has by far the highest proportion of college men and ranks second in general education. Yet this group is definitely and significantly the leading group in first degree murder. No other offenses are certainly differentiated, although there is a probable deficiency in burglary and larceny, and a probable excess in forgery and fraud.

On the whole, then, it would seem that, to a considerable degree, rural life restricts occupation and education. The occupation selects the physical type in some measure, and at the same time limits the choice of crime. Within these boundaries, physical type seems to influence the ultimate choice of offense. In the city, on the other hand, education is a primary selective agency. To a great extent it determines occupation, although physical type exerts a strong influence also in the lower vocational grades. In the higher categories education is the paramount agency of vocational determination. Occupation, once determined, seems to restrict the choice of crime, but the body build of the individual plays an important part, if it is not actually the decisive factor.

Pigmentation, head form, and other racial characters are not obviously important in this array of factors which influence choice of antisocial behavior. Perhaps race plays its leading rôle in the first act (the immigration of the ancestors of these criminals). Thereafter racial characters are mixed and swapped about until they seem to appear casually and sporadically as indifferent hereditary variations in the offense groups. Yet it will be seen in the next volume that so-called racial combinations of features in individuals actually bear a relationship to offense and to other sociological characters, which is not easily apparent in the crude averaging of means of all of the persons who have been thrust into a single offense category. The influence of race, if real, is subtle, and appears in the present handling of this material only as an occasional hint.

We are now ready to return to the ultimate question of the significance of physical differences in the offense groups. We have first of all the crudely significant differences which are in many cases due to state composition. These physical differences in the several state series are the result of variation in ethnic strains, inbreeding, and urban or rural environment together with its occupational selection of physical types, its diversification of educational and offense opportunities. All of the crude differences in physical composition of the offense groups are explicable in the general light of these various factors. However, when we reach the differences which supervene, or are independent of state sampling, we have at last come to grips with those individual physical features which are or ought to be symptomatic of, or causative to, criminal propensity. Are these differences intelligible or meaningless?

First degree murderers, as compared with total criminals, are older, taller, heavier, larger in chest, broader in jaw, narrower in shoulders relative to their stature, and shorter in relative trunk length. They usually do not have abundant head hair nor scant body hair; narrow nasal bridges are deficient; median chins and flat cheek bones are in excess. Large ear lobes are significantly common, small antihelices rare, and square shoulders frequent. Does this description make sense? I think so. The matter of age may be irrelevant because it depends to some extent upon length of sentence. Here, however, we have physiques considerably superior to those of average criminals, with a suggestion, at any rate, of considerable strength and vigor. When ignorance and the tradition of the frontier are combined with brute force, primitive behavior is not surprising and homicide is natural.

Second degree murderers do not present such a clear picture in their independent differences. They are older than criminals in general and have bigger chests, and lower heads, the latter both absolutely and relative to their head lengths and breadths. Actually they are more dolichocephalic than criminals at large, as are also first degree murderers, but this difference is complicated by state sampling and is reduced to possible insignificance when allowance is made for this factor. Second degree murderers are also characterized by excesses of high nasal bridges, and of bilateral chins, pronounced wrinkling, worn and carious teeth. These differences, surviving state variations, merely sketch roughly a group of men with long heads, low heads, high-bridged noses, wrinkled faces and poor teeth. None of these facts seems particularly significant, except possibly the low head height — a feature which is loosely related to small cranial capacity and inferior intelligence. However, the features mentioned above do distinguish the second degree murderer from the first degree murderer, from whom he appears to differ both physically and criminologically in degree rather than in kind.

Assault criminals are too few to be statistically differentiated. It can be said of them only that they are again older men, and seem to be stocky and broad-shouldered and to have low breadth-height head indices. The broad shoulders point to physical strength and vigor.

Robbers are nearly four years younger than criminals in general. This juvenility is not due to their shorter sentences, but to the fact that the offense seems to be really a crime of reckless youth. They are possibly somewhat more slender than average criminals and certainly have shallower chests and broader faces, and, apparently, shorter ears. Their head heights are excessive. Their nasal indices are higher than those of criminals at large, because the nasal breadth is insignificantly higher than the mean and the nasal height lower. They have heavier beards and more curly hair than the total series. They are peculiar in that the pigment in the iris of the eyes is often diffused and the fold of the upper eyelid overhangs the free edge in the middle of the eye. They are rarely wrinkled; the senile edge-to-edge bite is uncommon; ears are prevailingly of medium protrusion. These independent excesses are almost sufficient to enable one to envisage a type. It is very clearly an urban type, rather weedy, yet with a primitive look about the face as a result of bizygomatic breadth, broad nose, and slit-like eyes with median folds. The heavy beards and curved hair seem to indicate more Mediterranean, Alpine, or other non-Nordic strains than occur in most of these native born criminals of native parentage. The broad faces and noses suggest Alpine elements. The good education of this group is interesting when one takes note of its excessive head height. In some way or other this combination of features seems to describe the gangster.

Burglars and thieves are not only far below mean criminal age, but they are lighter and smaller in almost every dimension. Their only indicial difference is an excess of forehead breadth relative to facial breadth, which would impart a flat-sided appearance to the face. Some descriptive features are partially dependent upon the youthful mean age of this group. These are deficiency of thin head hair, excess of scanty beards, thin body hair, little gray hair, many concave noses and few convex noses, septa prevailingly inclined upward, deficiency of thin lips and wrinkles, of carious and worn teeth, of teeth lost, of edge-to-edge bite, and of large ear lobes. Features which are not dependent upon age are excess of ash-blond and golden hair and rarity of dark hair, absence of pronounced forehead slope, presence of undershot jaws, malars of medium prominence and cheeks of medium fullness, ears with well-rolled helices, absence of facial asymmetry, absence of short thick necks.

The principal impression one derives from this description of the independent peculiarities of thieves and burglars is that of the undersized, undernourished, sneaky individual of slightly infantile or feminine appearance. Some hint of Nordic or East Baltic strains is given by the excess of blondness. This is the class of most frequent recidivism and of most consistent celibacy, of chronic social ineffectiveness, and of marked constitutional inferiority.

Forgery and fraud offenders show a number of excesses which are rendered doubtful by state sampling — among them excessive height, weight, head breadth, head height, forehead breadth, ear length, and ear breadth. But, independently of state sampling they have excessive trunk length, head length, head circumference, and facial height. Excess of sparse head hair and deficiency of scanty beards are not connected with any age differences from the total criminals. Other characteristics are absence of eyefolds, of thin lips, and the prevalently medium height of the nasal bridge. Here is the opposite picture to that presented by the thieves. The fraudulent criminals are larger and have notably bigger heads. We know them to be better educated and suspect them to be more intelligent than most other categories of offenders. Their description seems to correspond more nearly to that of the average, law-abiding citizen than does that of any other offense group. The thin hair is interesting, since early loss of hair is commoner in civilized persons and among those engaged in intellectual pursuits than in savages or in persons of low vocational status.

Rapists are a small and physically peculiar group, considerably influenced by the characteristics of the very large quota furnished by Wisconsin. They are nearly five years older than average, partly because of their long sentences, but it is to be noted in this connection that they are often divorced men or widowers and comparatively rarely single. They are considerably shorter than the run of criminals (but only insignificantly lighter), and have deeper chests and shorter trunks. Their relative shoulder breadths are high. If we are willing to consider, for the sake of a detailed picture, a few differences which are rendered possibly insignificant by state sampling, we observe that these offenders are likely to have also greater relative sitting heights, greater head breadths, slightly rounder heads, longer and relatively narrower noses. They have an excess of blue-gray eyes, pigment-flecked whites of the eyes, protrusive jaws, skewed noses and facial asymmetry.

These rapists create the impression, perhaps, of some degree of physical abnormality, but more especially of a greater infusion of Alpine or other brachycephalic racial strains than is common among these criminals. This suggestion of Alpine blood may be due to the presence of the large Wisconsin contingent, quite possibly of strongly German extraction. In any event, we are brought back to the conception of the short, fat man whom nobody loves. Recall the fact that rapists also are frequently ignorant agriculturists and that they are averse to crimes of bodily violence, except against the weaker sex.

Other sex offenders are not adequately differentiated in the sum total of their physical characters, probably because of their scanty numbers. They are nearly six and one-half years above mean age, possibly significantly short, stout, long and relatively narrow in nose, long of ear, narrow of forehead, small in other head dimensions, but with long faces. Many of these differences are involved in their advanced age. We are left with the picture of lecherous old men who are short, stout, long-nosed, and often well educated. They have straight hair in excess, thin lips, thin cheeks, and right facial asymmetry. Other sex offenses include: incest 25.16 per cent, bigamy 16.08 per cent, sodomy 9.79 per cent, carnal knowledge 9.09 per cent, indecent liberties 9.79 per cent, assault on female 8.39 per cent, seduction 7.69 per cent, and trifling percentages of such acts as pandering, adultery, abortion, et cetera. More than one-third of these offenses are definitely those of perverts.

Versus public welfare offenders are so predominantly Texans that it is hard to get rid of the influence of that state's particular physical features. They are the oldest of all offense groups and are both heavy and tall, but these excesses are largely obliterated by correction for state sampling. However there remain as independent differentiae: excess of chest depth and possibly of chest breadth. The faces of this group are inordinately broad, and the nose breadths and jaw breadths are also excessive. Ears are long, absolutely and relatively, and the facial breadth is great compared with head breadth. Significant descriptive features also pertain to the face: prominent malars, protruding jaw angles, excess of free and large ear lobes. These offenders, then, are large and heavy men with very broad, square faces.

The offenses in versus public welfare to some extent obscure the physical implications of the type. Violation of liquor laws includes 80.33 per cent of these criminals, and violating the Dean law (a 1925 Texas statute concerning the possession of liquor, besides its sale) is the offense of 9.43 per cent. The other offenses are extremely varied and include a number erroneously classified. It should be noted first of all that this group is by no means composed of urban bootleggers. On the contrary, it contains the highest percentage of persons engaged in extractive occupations of any save the two murder groups. Evidently then, it is composed largely of ranchers, farmers, et cetera. While its educational qualifications are, on the whole, poor, it is superior in this respect to any other predominantly extractive offense group. It is lowest in previous convictions and highest in married men. It is then a rural group which, being physically well developed and probably of fair intelligence, tended to find its antisocial outlet in what was one of the most profitable and condoned of illegal activities — that of the illicit liquor traffic. In body build composition the versus public welfare offenders are perhaps closest to the forgery and fraud group, although the former group is particularly notable for its excess of men of medium height and heavy weight, whereas the latter emphasizes tallness with medium weight. This bootlegging group is also somewhat similar to the murder groups in body build composition, but contains relatively fewer short-slender men, and relatively more medium height-heavy individuals. It seems to represent in part the rural equivalent of the physically well developed and moderately intelligent urbanite who commits forgery and fraud, and in part the rather brutal agricultural type, which for various reasons — perhaps superior education and intelligence — has turned from the more primitive crimes of violence to the more sophisticated crimes against property, especially the quasi-respectable offense of bootlegging.

Finally, we have the residual arson and all other offenses group. It is a small miscellany, including 32.67 per cent of men convicted of arson, 14.85 per cent convicted of "confederacy," 7.92 per cent of non-support, 6.93 per cent of child desertion, and a residuum of many scattered and exceptional offenses. We can scarcely expect this offense group to show physical differentiation. As a matter of fact it is independently distinguished in metric features only by superior age, superior chest breadth, inferior forehead breadth, and possibly by long ears. A deficiency in stature is rendered probably insignificant by state correction, as is also a relatively great shoulder breadth. Its morphological excesses are scanty but peculiar. They are excesses of ash-blond hair, of internal epicanthic folds, and of a submedium degree of alveolar prognathism. This group is rather high in previous convictions, decidedly high in married men, and mediocre in education. It contains both rural and urban residents, but is slightly high in the extractive occupations. The only urban occupation in which it shows a probably significant excess (2.55 p.e.) is personal service. If we refer back to our body build types, we find a possibly significant excess of short men of medium weight and a certain excess of medium height-medium weight men in this offense group. The picture is then of small to medium men of probably limited intelligence and rather poor education and generally in the humbler occupations, convicted of various stupid crimes against property — notably arson — of neglect of their family duties, et cetera. The ash-blond hair, the prognathism, and the epicanthic folds suggest an East Baltic strain. The leading state in this offense group is Kentucky (36.89 per cent of the total group), followed by Massachusetts (14.56 per cent) and Wisconsin (10.68 per cent). We then conclude that the rural and agricultural portion of this offense group probably consists of ignorant farmers or farm laborers of inferior physique who burn their own farms or the farms of their employers, or who commit other various, but usually minor, offenses against property. In the city this inferior group, diversely employed, is arrested for confederacy, aiding prisoners to escape, non-support, perjury, abandonment or desertion of wife and children, vagrancy, being a habitual criminal, and arson. These are low grade offenses of physical and mental inferiors.

In this discussion many important influences acting upon the "individual delinquent" have been completely ignored, and necessarily, because we have no data concerning them. Nothing has been said for example concerning the status of the family from which the delinquent originates, whether or not he comes from a "broken home," his place in the fraternity, the character and habits of his parents, his own habits, his mental characteristics, his pathology, et cetera. It is wholly possible that such familial and individual influences and conditions are paramount in determining a career of social usefulness or of crime for the person upon whom they operate. All that we have been able to do is to appraise the physical characteristics of large groups of criminals in the light of some very crude sociological facts, many of which are not even capable of verification. Nevertheless, it has been possible to demonstrate the physical differentiation of criminals according to type of offense and to bring into a rational relationship with such physical differentiation a few of the most important sociological factors.

The variation in physique and body build is certainly causally related to nature of offense. Whether these variations are primarily constitutional and individual, or ethnic and racial, we cannot ascertain from the data in hand. It is wholly possible that the physical, mental, and behavioristic implications of endocrine types may explain, in large part, this apparent relationship of offense to physique. It is, on the other hand, by no means improbable that various types of racial and ethnic blends may be firmly associated with certain types of behavior. Of course, in such case, it would not be the physical combination which determines the type of offense, but the general hereditary combination of factors which would produce simultaneously the physical, mental, and behavioristic differentiae.

On the whole it would appear that such admittedly racial factors as head form and pigmentation are markedly in abeyance when contrasted with constitutional factors which may be largely interracial. On the other hand, it is impossible to overlook the matter of ethnic and social tradition, here obtruding itself most forcibly in the predominance of Irish extraction. The lawless habits of a racial or ethnic group may be persistently linked with its hereditary physique, although in a mainly non-causal relationship. From these nebulous data there emerges, at any rate, a fairly consistent relationship between superior bodily size and vigor and crimes of violence against the person, and between inferior and weak physique and furtive offenses against property.

I must reiterate here that the materials presented in this volume are not classified in such a way as to permit the emergence of racial differences, since the various subgroups are set up on the basis of offense, or according to some other sociological category. This series of native White criminals of native parentage was also selected for the purpose of securing a group as nearly homogeneous as possible in ethnic extraction and in racial composition. The actual investigation of the influence of race demands a primary classification on the basis of combinations in individuals of hereditary physical features. This task is reserved for the second volume of results of this survey.

Morphological Offense Types

The fact that offense groups of criminals exhibit metric and morphological variations sufficiently numerous and of such magnitudes as to distinguish many of the groups from random samples of the total series implies little or nothing as to the existence of individual criminal "type" combinations. The type is the sum total of the observer's impression of the combination of all physical features in an individual. Persons belonging to the same "type" have similar or identical physical combinations. From a zoölogical point of view persons of the same type ought to be closely related, since detailed physical resemblance generally indicates a community of ancestors. We know that our native born criminals of native parentage are considerably diversified in ethnic and racial descent. Unless in some miraculous way persons of common descent were segregated in mutually exclusive offense groups, we could hardly expect individual offense types to exist.

Any attempt to identify or constitute individual morphological types by an arbitrary selection of combinations of features from recorded data is predestined to failure. The certainty of such failure arises from the appalling number of individual combinations which are mathematically possible when any considerable assortment of features, each exhibiting several distinct grades, is taken as the basis of type selec on. The number of different combinations theoretically possible quickly exceeds the um total of individuals in any but the largest anthropometric series.

If each offense group possessed a number of morphological variations peculiar to self, we might entertain some hope of putting these together and establishing indi- idual offense types. But no morphological feature nor any single variation of that eature is the exclusive possession of one offense group. All that we have is a number f significant excesses or deficiencies of certain morphological variations whereby an ffense group is statistically and anthropologically differentiated as a group from the otal criminal series. But these are variations which are found to some extent in every ngle offense group. Anthropologists often distinguish a sort of group "type" based pon the assumption that arithmetic means of measurements and indices, and modes f observational variations, may be strung together to describe average or "typical" idividuals. Such artificial combinations have little or no validity for the diagnosis of idividual type.

The Hollerith sorting apparatus makes possible the mechanical selection of any in- ividual combination, however intricate, which may delimit a type, providing, of course, lat all of the essential variations are tabulated. In order to demonstrate the possi- ility or impossibility of sorting out morphological offense types in individuals the rob- ery group of 414 persons was chosen. First of all, an attempt was made to sort out robber type on the basis of combinations of nine morphological variations in which le robbery offense group shows excesses over the proportions displayed in the entire riminal series. On the sixth sorting an exclusive robber type was indeed obtained — naracterized by a combination of features not found in any individual in any other ffense group. But only one of 414 robbers conforms to this type. By such a process f criminal type identification we might identify one robber and let 413 robbers escape.

Since the order of sorting for successive characters restricts the number of indi- iduals in each sorting by establishing a permutation, it was necessary to sort the rob- ery group for every possible combination of the nine characteristic excess features isplayed by that offense group. Even with a Hollerith sorter this process occupied le full time of an operator for more than six weeks. The number of distinct combi- ations of features possible was 512. The number of different combinations observed as 127, or 24.80 per cent of those possible. Only one individual of the 414 in the roup displays as many as 7 of the 9 excess variations characteristic of the group as whole. Six robbers, or 1.45 per cent of the group, have none of the 9 robber features. hree of the nine excess variations were found to occur in 31.64 per cent of the entire bbery group, two in 27.05 per cent, four in 20.29 per cent. The average occur- nce of these variations or characters is 2.87 per individual. A detailed study of the mbinations of characters actually exhibited in the group suggests that the linkages individuals are entirely fortuitous.

In order to test the frequency of morphological combinations, supposedly charac- ristic of robbers, in other crime groups, nine fourfold combinations were tabulated or all native White criminals of native parentage other than robbers. Most of these mbinations were found to occur much less frequently in non-robbers than in rob- ers. Evidently, all that can be accomplished by sorting for combinations of morpho- gical variations found to occur in excess in any offense group, is to reduce the odds gainst an individual criminal belonging to a specified offense group for which sort-

ings have been made. In so doing one inevitably eliminates most of the members o
the offense group which is to be selected, as well as the vast majority of other offender:
As a matter of fact, it is possible to find a combination of morphological features whic
will be exclusive to an offense group, but such a combination will be found to occur i
only a few individuals of that group. This sorting by arbitrary combinations of ex
cess characters seems then to have no practical utility.

If crime were an exclusively biological phenomenon, we might be able to describ
the physical characteristics of members of various offense groups with the same pre
cision which is possible in the case of a zoölogical characterization of an animal spe
cies. For in that case the nature of the offense would be wholly dependent upon th
hereditary features of the organism. But crime is admittedly a sociological phenom
enon, in part, if not wholly. Hordes of individuals of quite diverse familial, ethni
and racial origins live together in the same society and are subjected to similar er
vironmental stimuli. Many of them are quite unaware of their biological individualit
and of their racial separateness. Opportunities for theft and temptations to homicic
are alike, or virtually alike, for the blond and the brunet, for the Negro and the Whit
It is therefore remarkable that we should be able to demonstrate even a minor o
ganic factor in the intricate web of crime causation.

A priori, it may be concluded that an effective and practical typing of crimina
according to the nature of their offenses is an impossibility. All physical types of me
seem to participate to some extent in every category of crime. Nevertheless, I am
the opinion that a relatively successful typing might be accomplished by a differer
method from that pursued in this work. This would involve a primary separation of a
criminals into physical types on the basis of resemblances and differences and a sul
sequent correlation of these types with offenses. In the present instance we have a
tempted to deduce the type from the offense — to work back from the sociological ar
physical data to the hypothetical type. The method suggested was not employed
this investigation for two reasons: doubt as to the competence of the field observe
to make valid assignments of morphological type in individuals, an incomplete realiz
tion on the part of the writer as to the importance of this method. Actually such
procedure calls for a highly developed and accurate judgment of morphological type
field observations, such as is acquired by the physical anthropologist only after yea
of experience. Such a method carried out in full would, in my judgment, result
the definition of many clear-cut morphological types of criminals. These types wou
probably manifest closer correlations with nature of offense than we have been ab
to demonstrate by our empirical method of working toward a definition of types l
arbitrary physical combinations such as height and weight, or by offense excesses. B
certainly it would never result in delimiting physical types exclusive to offense group
simply because there is no unit correlation of physique with social behavior.

Metric and Indicial Differentiation Between Criminals and Civilians of Similar Parentage

Are criminals physically different from law-abiding citizens of the same ethn
origin? This is a more important question than that of the offense group differenti
tion of criminals. For comparison with the criminals a check sample of civilians

ative birth and native parentage was gathered in Massachusetts and in Tennessee.
he combined civilian series from the two states was compared with the total crimi-
al series. When, however, it become apparent that criminals are physically differ-
ntiated according to the state of their birth, the validity of this comparison with the
stricted check sample became exceedingly dubious. Since it was impossible to re-
en the field work and secure civilian samples from the remaining seven states, the
llowing expedient was adopted. Massachusetts criminals were compared with Mas-
chusetts civilians and Tennessee criminals with Tennessee civilians. Then the values
differences between the total criminal series and the total check sample were ap-
raised in terms of their agreements or disagreements with the two intra-state com-
arisons. There can scarcely be a doubt of the general criminological validity of a
fference between criminals and civilians when it occurs both in Massachusetts and
Tennessee and in the comparison of the total criminal series with the combined
eck sample from the two states.

In the total series comparisons 19 of 33 measurements and indices (57.58 per
nt) showed a significant differentiation between criminals and civilians. Of these
, or 21.21 per cent were fully substantiated in the two state comparisons and a con-
derable number of the other differences were shown to be, in all probability, valid
r criminals in general of this nativity, as compared with civilians of the same
igin.

In appraising the comparisons of the two intra-state series — Massachusetts and
ennessee — with the total series comparison of criminals from nine states with a ci-
lian check sample derived from Massachusetts and Tennessee only, there arose a
ry puzzling problem. When both intra-state comparisons agree with the total com-
arison, one can conclude immediately that the general and common result is valid.
hen one state comparison agrees with the total series and the other differs, it is nec-
ssary to decide which state comparison is the more reliable. Initially it seemed that
e Tennessee comparison of civilians with criminals was less dependable than the
Iassachusetts comparison, because the former state civilian sample was entirely com-
osed of Nashville firemen, a physically and occupationally selected group. Ultimately
is decision was reversed because of the fact that the Massachusetts series compari-
n gave evidence of a certain ethnic and perhaps racial disparity, owing to the pres-
ce in the criminal series of a considerable element of French Canadian extraction.
onsequently, in cases of doubt the evidence of the Tennessee comparison was leaned
pon more heavily. Since the civilian sample considerably exceeds the criminal series
mean age, it was necessary to re-seriate the criminals by age groups, and to com-
are them with civilians of the same age whenever a difference might be considered as
possible effect of disparate age.

Criminals average 3.80 years younger than the civilian check sample. This differ-
nce seems to be the expression of a tendency for antisocial conduct to reach its max-
num in late adolescence and early adult years.

Criminals are inferior to civilians in nearly all of their bodily measurements. These
fferences attain statistical significance and general criminological validity in body
eight, in stature, in biacromial breadth, chest depth, chest breadth, cranial circum-
rence, nose height, ear length, head height, and upper facial height. Criminals also
verge from civilians in having higher fronto-parietal indices, lower facial indices,

higher nasal indices, higher zygo-frontal indices, and greater relative sitting height. These differences appear to be independent of age and of state sampling.

Every individual offense group is anthropometrically differentiated from the total check sample of civilians. Most of the offense groups differ from the civilians in the same direction as does the total criminal series. A few individual offense group peculiarities may be recapitulated here.

First degree murderers are, on the average, older than civilians, are not inferior in stature, but have broader jaws, relatively narrower, longer, and lower heads. In addition they display most of the general inferiorities and excesses which characterize the total criminal comparison with civilians, although these are of lesser magnitude than in the series as a whole. Second degree murderers do not fall significantly below the check sample in age but are markedly inferior in most measurements. They are also relatively longer-headed and lower-headed than civilians and have higher nasal indices.

Assault offenders are less differentiated from civilians, probably because of the small size of this offense group. In addition to several metric inferiorities they are distinguished by relatively broader shoulders than are found in the civilians.

Robbers are 7.75 years younger than civilians and are much slighter in body build. Most of their divergences from the check sample are of the same nature as those manifested by total criminals. Burglars and thieves are 8 years younger, on the average, than civilians, and are inferior to them in every measurement except forehead breadth. They also show many indicial divergences.

The forgery and fraud group is younger and lighter than the civilian check sample and shows similar divergences from the latter to those displayed by the entire criminal series. However these fraudulent offenders exhibit deviations from civilians which are, in general, smaller than those of most other offense groups.

Rapists are the shortest of offenders and are greatly inferior to civilians in every dimension except minimum frontal diameter. Other sex offenders show very similar differences.

Versus public welfare offenders are especially characterized by excessive breadth dimensions of the forehead and of the face, and high index values derived from these measurements. Otherwise they show ordinary criminal divergences from the civilians except in their excess of age, their parity of stature and of ear measurements and indices.

The residual offense group (arson and all others) shows ordinary minus deviations in dimensions, except in notably small stature and relatively great shoulder breadth.

Metrically these criminals are vastly inferior to the civilians. The offense groups differ from each other less markedly than total criminals diverge from law-abiding citizens. In other words, irrespective of nature of offense, criminals present an united front of biological inferiority.

Sociological and morphological differences between criminals and civilians have been tabulated and subjected to a detailed analysis and summary in the body of this work. Nevertheless these differences must be recapitulated, albeit briefly, because it is a sheer impossibility for the reader to retain the mass of minutiae upon which our final argument must rest.

It has been necessary in each sociological and morphological category firstly to

appraise the significance of crude differences between total criminals and the total civilian check sample; secondly to go back to the Massachusetts and Tennessee intra-
state comparisons of criminals and civilians; finally to return to the total series
comparisons and to judge their validity on the basis of state agreements.

These sociological facts seem to represent our yield, after the chaff has been win-
nowed away:

(1) Apart from age considerations, these criminals are less often married, more
often widowed, and more frequently divorced than comparable civilians.

(2) After due allowance is made for the partially rural character of our criminal
series and for the almost exclusively urban provenience of our check sample, there remain in the criminals probable excesses of extractive, laborer, and personal service
occupations, and deficiencies of trade, professional, and clerical occupations.

(3) Criminals are greatly inferior to civilians of the same ethnic origin in educational attainments.

The outstanding morphological differences between criminals and civilians are as
follows:

(1) Tattooing is commoner among criminals than among civilians.

(2) Criminals probably have thinner beard and body hair and thicker head hair.

(3) Criminals have more straight hair and less curved hair.

(4) Criminals have more red-brown hair and less gray and white hair.

(5) Dark eyes and blue eyes are deficient in criminals, and blue-gray and mixed
eyes are in excess. Homogeneous irides are rare in criminals, and zoned and speckled
irides are excessively present. Eyefolds are commoner in criminals and thin eyebrows
occur more frequently.

(6) Low and sloping foreheads are excessively present among criminals.

(7) High narrow nasal roots, high nasal bridges, undulating nasal profiles, nasal
septa inclined upward and deflected laterally, extreme variations in thickness of the
nasal tip, are more frequent in criminals than in civilians.

(8) Thin lips and compressed jaw angles are commoner in criminals.

(9) Marked overbites are rarer in criminals than in civilians.

(10) The ear of the criminal is more likely to have a slightly rolled helix and a perceptible Darwin's point than is that of the civilian. More extreme variations of ear
protrusion are found in criminals than in civilians. The criminal ear tends to be small.

(11) Long, thin necks and sloping shoulders are in excess among criminals.

Many other significant morphological differences between the criminals and the
civilians have been discounted or disregarded because of contradictions or inconsistencies in the state series, because of age complications, or because of the probable
effect of observational equations.

The various offense groups tend to present, for the most part, similar or identical
deviations from the civilian check sample in both sociological and morphological features. Apart from the great bulk of these differences from civilians common to the
total series and to the individual offense groups, the latter are distinguished by some
particular sociological and morphological deviations from the combined civilian check
sample, a few of which may be mentioned here:

(1) First degree murderers are outstanding in their especially large excess of divorced men and widowers, of extractives, of laborers, of illiterates and poorly educated persons. They are also notable in their extremely high proportions of straight hair. In general this class of offender exaggerates the common morphological deviations of the total criminal series.

(2) Second degree murderers parallel the sociological deviations of first degree murderers, but are somewhat less extreme. They are deficient in golden hair, have broad nasal roots and nasal bridges, thick nasal tips, excess of slight alveolar prognathism.

(3) Assault offenders are sociologically distinguished by high percentage of divorced men, of persons in skilled trades and in personal service. They have an excess of olive skin color, and include a disproportionately high number of persons with broad noses, which are high rather than medium or low.

(4) Robbers are notable for their deficiency of married men and for their excess of factory workers. They show excesses of olive skin, and median eye folds.

(5) Burglars and thieves display no important sociological deviations from the check sample which are not shared by the total criminal series. Again there is an excess of olive skin color. Concave noses are common in this group.

(6) The forgery and fraud group exhibits only the general criminological differences from the check sample of civilians.

(7) Rapists are notable for large excesses of divorced men and widowers. Their morphological deviations from civilians are those of the entire criminal group.

(8) Other sex offenders have no sociological peculiarities which distinguish their deviations from the check sample from those of total criminals. Excesses of ruddy skin, of olive skin, and a deficiency of golden hair are perhaps worthy of mention.

(9) Versus public welfare criminals are outstanding in their high percentage of married men. They have excessively thick head hair and thin beard hair in spite of an advanced mean age; they also show excess of red-white skin, of external eye folds, of pronounced malars, of full cheeks.

(10) Arson and all other offenders have a deficiency of single men, excesses of ruddy skin, black hair, ash-blond hair, epicanthic folds, protruding ears.

Table XIII–5 presents a summary and comparison of the totals of differences between all criminals and all civilians and between the two state comparisons in metric sociological, and morphological features (the two latter by subcategories of observations). These are significant but crude differences, with no allowances made for age variations and other complicating factors. In the total series comparison it may be noticed that significant differences between criminals and civilians in categories of sociological features (80.77 per cent) are considerably in excess of the metric differences (57.58 per cent) and of the morphological subcategory differences (61.73 per cent). In the Tennessee comparison the sociological differences (61.54 per cent) are sharply reduced, and in the Massachusetts comparison they sink to 50 per cent. The total series sociological comparison involves the checking of sociological data of criminals from nine states, principally rural in their populations except Massachusetts with an almost exclusively urban civilian sample derived from two states only. In the Tennessee comparison both series are equalized as to state of origin and residence, but the criminals are mixed urban and rural, while the check sample consist of Nashville firemen only. In the Massachusetts comparison both series are urban. It therefore appears that the Massachusetts comparison is most valid in sociological features. Its difference of 50 per cent of characters represents most closely the normal amount of difference between criminals and civilians.

In metric data both state comparisons show the same number and percentages of

TABLE XIII-5

NUMBER AND SIGNIFICANCE OF DEVIATIONS OF TOTAL SERIES AND OF STATE SERIES IN MEASUREMENTS AND INDICES, AND IN SUBCATEGORIES OF SOCIOLOGICAL OBSERVATIONS, AND MORPHOLOGICAL OBSERVATIONS

	Significant		Insignificant		Total Number
	Number	Per Cent	Number	Per Cent	
Total Series					
Measurements and indices	19	57.58	14	42.42	33
Sociological observations	21	80.77	5	19.23	26
Morphological observations ...	100	61.73	62	38.27	162
Massachusetts					
Measurements and indices	21	63.64	12	36.36	33
Sociological observations	13	50.00	13	50.00	26
Morphological observations ...	96	59.26	66	40.74	162
Tennessee					
Measurements and indices	21	63.64	12	36.36	33
Sociological observations	16	61.54	10	38.46	26
Morphological observations ...	71	43.83	91	56.17	162

significant deviations (63.64 per cent), which slightly exceeds the proportion found in the total series comparison (57.58 per cent). Here again, and for the same reasons, the state figures should be more valid than those of the combined series.

In the morphological comparisons the Tennessee data should be the best, since both series were recorded by the same observer and at the same time. On the whole, the safest appraisal of the percentages of the various categories of significant differences which may be taken to apply to all native White criminals of native parentage, as contrasted with sociologically and ethnically comparable civilians would be:

	Per Cent
Measurements and indices	57.58
Sociological observations	50.00
Morphological observations	43.83

This would imply that criminals and civilians are differentiated to about the same extent in physical features as in sociological characters.

Let us now consider the absolutely minimum differences between criminals and civilians, which are significant and in the same direction in both states and in the total series, and are, so far as can be determined, independent of age and other complicating factors.

The left side of Table XIII-6 provides these data which comprise 21.21 per cent of metric and indicial differences, 12.00 per cent of sociological differences and 7.14 per cent of differences in morphological observations. These percentages are, of course, sufficient in each case to differentiate the criminal series from the check sample of civilians. However, this array of differences by no means represents the complete assemblage of valid criminal deviations. For example it disregards the vast educational inferiority in the criminals, merely because of certain eccentricities in the state check samples, whereby one or other state comparison fails to agree with the total series comparison in exhibiting a significant criminal deficiency in each of the several educational grades. Yet there can be no doubt that criminals differ from civilians in educational attainments more strongly than in any other sociological character.

The right side of Table XIII–6 lists also the deviations in which the total series and one state agree in exhibiting significant deviations in the same direction, but in which the other state comparison does not attain statistical significance in its deviation, although the latter agrees in direction. These are almost certainly valid and may be so accepted. The list has been purged of differences which are either seriously affected by age or by some observational equation which raises a doubt as to their correctness. This second list of acceptable general criminological deviations includes 15.15 per cent of metric features, 24.00 of sociological subcategories, 14.93 per cent of subcategories of morphological observations. Thus we have as a total of dependable differences between criminals and civilians 36.36 per cent of measurements and indices, 36 per cent of subcategories of sociological features, 22.07 per cent of subcategories of morphological observations. This may be contrasted with the rough estimate of 57.58 per cent of metric features, 50 per cent of sociological features, and 45.51 per cent of morphological features derived from the optimum choice of the state comparisons and without elimination of age-affected features and certain dubious observations.

Actually there seems little doubt that the larger figures represent the real deviations of criminals from civilians more justly than the diminished percentages. Inadequacies of the civilian check samples and recurrent doubts of the comparability of various observations in which the standards of the field workers appear to have fluctuated have necessitated drastic reductions in the differences. An ideal check sample and a complete elimination of observational equations might well increase the differences rather than diminish them.

CAUSES OF CRIMINAL DIFFERENTIATION FROM CIVILIANS

The outstanding feature of differentiation between criminals and law-abiding citizens of the same ethnic origin is the unanimity of criminal deviation irrespective of offense. Although most of the offense groups are distinct physically and sociologically from the criminal series as a whole, nevertheless the entire body of delinquents presents a uniformity of differences from the civilians which seems to be capable of but one interpretation. Criminals as a group represent an aggregate of sociologically and biologically inferior individuals. The distinctions between civilians and murderers, thieves, rapists, and other categories of offenders are, for the most part, the same indications of criminal inferiority which stigmatize the entire criminal series, irrespective of nature of crime.

Excesses of single men and of divorced men indicate an inability or unwillingness to undertake successfully the normal family responsibilities of the adult male. Deficient educations and low occupational status are bound up with mental inferiority

TABLE XIII-6

NUMBERS AND PERCENTAGES OF SIGNIFICANT CRIMINAL DEVIATIONS FROM CIVILIANS
INDEPENDENT OF AGE

Total Comparisons and State Comparisons Significant and in Same Direction			Total and One State Comparison Significant, All Agreeing in Direction		
Category	Number	Per Cent	Category	Number	Per Cent
Measurements and indices	7	21.21	Measurements and indices	5	15.15
Deficiencies of age, weight, chest breadth, head circumference, upper face height, nose height, ear length			Deficiencies of height, biacromial, chest depth; excesses of nasal and zygo-frontal indices		
Sociological observations	3	12.00	Sociological observations	6	24.00
Excess of divorced men, laborers and personal servants			Deficiencies of married men, of public servants, of students, excesses of extractives and factory operatives, deficiencies of 3rd–4th high		
Morphological observations	11	7.14	Morphological observations	23	14.93
Excess of straight hair, deficiency of low waves, deficiencies of blue eyes and homogeneous irides, excesses of submedium cheek fullness and of submedium gonial angles, deficiency of marked overbite, excess of submedium roll of helix, deficiency of medium and pronounced, deficiency of medium necks and excess of long, thin necks			Deficiency of dark brown eyes, excesses of zoned and speckled irides, excess of submedium forehead height, deficiency of medium nasal root height and excess of pronounced, deficiencies of medium nasal root breadth and nasal bridge breadth, deficiencies of convex and straight noses and excess of concavo-convex, deficiency of medium nasal tip thickness, excess of right nasal septum deflections, excess of slight overbite, deficiency of Darwin's point absent and excess of submedium or medium, deficiency of medium antihelix prominence and excess of pronounced, excess of submedium ear protrusion and deficiency of medium, deficiency of short thick necks, deficiency of medium shoulder slope and excess of pronounced		

lack of industry and stability, and general weakness of character. The fact that criminals as a whole are younger than random samples of the adult male population suggests clearly enough that antisocial tendencies manifest themselves with greatest intensity in the no-man's-land between childhood and maturity, and in that post-adolescent stage when physical powers are fully developed, but when judgment and responsibility lag. Marked deficiencies in gross bodily dimensions and in head and face diameters are unequivocal assertions of undergrowth and poor physical development, since there are in this material no serious racial differences which might confuse the issue. The general lack of important racial criteria among the differentiating metric characters reinforces the conclusion that the great gap between native White criminals of native parentage and civilians of the same origin is not a matter of the selection of certain ethnic blends for antisocial careers. Deficiencies of dark brown eyes and of blue eyes suggest that these criminals include fewer of the relatively pure racial types and more of the mixed types than occur among civilians. Noses broader relative to their height than are characteristic of the civil check sample are an evidence of infantilism or of primitiveness. Poor development of other facial dimensions favors the former interpretation.

Low foreheads, high pinched nasal roots, nasal bridges and tips varying to both extremes of breadth and narrowness, excesses of nasal deflections, compressed faces and narrow jaws, fit well into the picture of general constitutional inferiority. The very small ears with submedium roll of helix, prominent antihelix, and frequent presence of Darwin's point, hint at degeneracy. At the same time it should be noted that the Lombrosian stigmata of auricular deformity are not characteristic of this series.

Our data, of course, provide a complete physical description of the native White American criminal of native parentage. Here we have concerned ourselves principally with those deviations from the presumed law-abiding citizens which set apart the incarcerated offender. But even these differences are sufficiently descriptive to enable us to envisage a sort of general average of criminals of this nativity and parentage. They sketch rather vaguely and with a good many gaps the outline of an Old American type which is smaller, more weedy, and possibly with more degenerative features than would be found in the composite of respectable citizens of the same ethnic origin. This nebular criminal composite can be resolved into offense groups slightly more definite in their physical characterizations. Doubtless it could be broken up into physical combinations which would be real individual types, but these diverse types would be found in each offense group. There would be no type exclusive to a group and embracing the majority of its members. Each individual type would find its counterpart in the civilian population and would doubtless differ from the law-abiding type only in its smaller size and featural inferiority.

Just as there is no single uniform type of the native born American citizen of American parentage, but a diversity of physical types, so there is no unity of type in the American born criminal of American parentage. Individual variation, familial inheritance, inbreeding of certain strains, and diverse blends of various racial and ethnic factors create a wide variety of physical types. In the molding of these types physical environment may well operate with varying intensity. From each of the physical types thus cooperatively produced, the poorer and weaker specimens tend to be selected for antisocial careers and for ultimate incarceration. The dregs of every population draught, pure or mixed, are poured into the prison sinks.

There can be no doubt of the inferior status of the criminal, both in physical and in sociological characters. Can this inferiority be attributed to an unfavorable environment? It is completely obvious that poor housing, lack of nourishing food, absence of medical care, and an unhealthy habitat may deteriorate individuals sprung from healthy stocks, or may even depress the physical status of the entire stock. I am not aware that moral degeneration and the increase of antisocial proclivities are a necessary consequence of such physical depression. Many of our immigrant stocks have been shown to produce offspring of superior size and better constitution in this country than in the homelands where they presumably abode under less favorable environmental conditions. Possibly and probably bodily size and health were there lessened by those depressing factors. The resiliency of the immigrant stock manifests itself in this country by the increments of size in offspring born here. But this increase in the bodily size of children of immigrants is notoriously accompanied by an increase of criminality, rather than a diminution. Criminality in immigrant stocks will be considered in detail in the next volume of this work. I merely cite this instance as an indication of the dubious value of an inference that physiques deteriorated by a poor environment are in themselves necessarily conducive to antisocial behavior. There are innumerable undernourished and under-sized individuals in every population who are not in the least criminalistic.

If we add to the physical depression of an adverse environment such factors as broken homes, criminalistic parents, and vicious associates, together with the corrupting influences of automobiles, the radio, moving pictures, and the tabloid press, we have nearly filled the complement of mainly environmental influences which may be claimed to produce the criminal. Here, however, we are mingling hereditary influences with those which are purely environmental, since at least the character of the home and the social attitudes of the parents are partially the resultants of the quality of germ plasm found in the latter. In other words, family inheritance may to a great extent determine family environment in so far as respect for law and morality are concerned. The criminal who is brought up in a criminalistic home can scarcely be claimed to be an exclusively environmental product.

In this work we have completely neglected the mental status of the criminal, except in so far as it may be indicated by his educational and occupational attainments. Our data upon the intelligence of the native White criminal of native parentage in prisons and reformatories are entirely inadequate for scientific analysis and deduction. Such usable information as we possess pertains to other groups of delinquents and will be discussed in subsequent volumes of this work.

There is, of course, no reason to doubt that this criminal series includes a considerable excess of dull and mentally deficient individuals as compared with the check sample of the normal population. We have, indeed, the intelligence quotients or ratings of 154 men, inmates of the Concord Reformatory in Massachusetts. These were copied from the prison records and are seriated in Table XIII–7. If we assume that an I.Q. of 96 or above indicates normal intelligence, we have only 19.48 per cent of such persons in our tiny sample.

Sheldon and Eleanor T. Glueck secured intelligence ratings upon 466 persons who had been inmates of the Concord Reformatory, and found the following distribution: normal (I.Q. 90–110) 33 per cent, dull (I.Q. 80–90) 24.1 per cent, borderline (I.Q. 70–80) 22.3 per cent, feeble-minded (I.Q. 50–70) 20.6 per cent.[7] That stupidity and mental defect are more potent factors in crime causation than inferior physique and impoverished environment seems undeniable. Actually physical inferiority is so highly correlated with mental defect that there is little doubt that our find-

[7] Sheldon Glueck and Eleanor T. Glueck, *500 Criminal Careers*, p. 156.

ings in regard to the former are principally significant in their implicit association with the latter. There is no inevitable or usual causal relationship between physical defect and mental defect; both are expressions of organic inferiority, whether environmentally induced or inherited.

In every population there are hereditary inferiors in mind and in body, as well as physical and mental deficients whose condition may perhaps be attributed to an unfortunate concatenation of environmental circumstances. Our information definitely

TABLE XIII-7

I.Q. IN CONCORD REFORMATORY

	Number	Per Cent
Estimated low normal or borderline intelligence	3	1.95
45 or under	2	1.30
46–55	3	1.95
56–65	7	4.54
66–75	29	18.83
76–85	40	25.97
86–95	40	25.97
96–105	29	18.83
106–and over	1	.65
Total	154	

proves that it is from the physically inferior element of the population that native born criminals of native parentage are mainly derived. My present hypothesis is that physical inferiority is of principally hereditary origin; that these hereditary inferiors naturally gravitate into unfavorable environmental conditions; and that the worst or weakest of them yield to social stresses which force them into criminal behavior.

Certainly not every individual criminal of our series is mentally deficient or physically inferior. Force of circumstances, evil tradition, and sheer "cussedness" undoubtedly turn the scale in favor of delinquency in many cases. Nevertheless, by and large, within every occupational and educational category, it seems clear that the criminal is inferior to the civilian of corresponding status, either physically or mentally, or both.

Differences in constitutional type, whether of racial origin or due to familial or individual factors of endocrine or other causation, undoubtedly are agents in determining the choice of offense, especially in conjunction with the opportunities afforded by the specific social environment. But in any case these constitutional and environmental factors operate upon the physical and (putatively) mental inferiors, in whatever walk of life.

In this portion of our anthropological survey of criminals we have not investigated racial and ethnic factors in their relation to delinquency, because we have been dealing with a series which is comparatively homogeneous. Only here and there minor indications of possible racial differences in offense types have cropped out. In the next volume devoted to native Whites of foreign parentage by nationality and to foreign Whites of various countries of origin, we shall attack this problem.

Up to this point the results of our investigation cannot be said to have any great practical utility. That is, there are few if any findings which can be put to the use of the police in the detection of criminals. An accurate description of an average gangster will not help to catch a Dillinger. Certain theoretical conclusions are, however, of no little importance. Criminals are organically inferior. Crime is the resultant of the impact of environment upon low grade human organisms. It follows that the elimination of crime can be effected only by the extirpation of the physically, mentally, and morally unfit, or by their complete segregation in a socially aseptic environment.

APPENDIX

Table II-1.   Racial Distribution of Total Prison and Reformatory Series by Offenses

Offense	Native Whites of Native Parentage			Native Whites of Foreign Parentage			Foreign Whites of Foreign Parentage		
	No.	Per Cent of race in offense group	Per Cent of offense in race group	No.	Per Cent of race in offense group	Per Cent of offense in race group	No.	Per Cent of race in offense group	Per Cent of offense in race group
First degree murder	312	37.73	7.41	83	10.04	5.34	75	9.06	6.84
Second degree murder	619	34.01	14.70	116	6.37	7.47	198	10.88	18.05
Assault	80	29.41	1.90	56	20.59	3.61	41	15.07	3.74
Robbery	414	34.97	9.83	216	18.24	13.91	98	8.28	8.93
Burglary and larceny	1612	37.58	38.27	679	15.83	43.72	360	8.39	32.82
Forgery and fraud	467	52.95	11.09	147	16.67	9.47	53	6.01	4.83
Rape	197	32.08	4.68	96	15.64	6.18	137	22.31	12.49
Other sex	151	52.80	3.58	50	17.48	3.22	45	15.73	4.10
Vs. public welfare	257	46.47	6.10	57	10.31	3.67	62	11.21	5.65
Arson and all other	103	45.78	2.44	53	23.56	3.41	28	12.44	2.55
Total	4212	38.46		1553	14.18		1097	10.02	

Offense	Negroids			Negroes			Total	
	No.	Per Cent of race in offense group	Per Cent of offense in race group	No.	Per Cent of race in offense group	Per Cent of offense in race group	No.	Per Cent of offense in race group total
First degree murder	281	33.98	8.45	76	9.19	9.92	827	7.55
Second degree murder	729	40.06	21.92	158	8.68	20.63	1820	16.52
Assault	81	29.78	2.44	14	5.15	1.83	272	2.48
Robbery	374	31.59	11.25	82	6.93	10.70	1184	10.81
Burglary and larceny	1303	30.37	39.19	336	7.83	43.86	4290	39.17
Forgery and fraud	184	20.86	5.53	31	3.52	4.05	882	8.05
Rape	151	24.59	4.54	33	5.38	4.31	614	5.61
Other sex	35	12.24	1.05	5	1.75	0.65	286	2.61
Vs. public welfare	155	28.03	4.66	22	3.98	2.97	553	5.05
Arson and all other	32	14.22	0.96	9	4.00	1.18	225	2.05
Total	3325	30.36		766	6.99		10,953	

Table II-3.

State Distribution by Offenses

State	First Degree Murder No.	Per Cent offense in state	Per Cent state in offense	Second Degree Murder No.	Per Cent offense in state	Per Cent state in offense	Assault No.	Per Cent offense in state	Per Cent state in offense	Robbery No.	Per Cent offense in state	Per Cent state in offense
Massachusetts	2	.59	.64	29	8.58	4.68	8	2.37	10.00	52	15.38	12.56
Tennessee	36	8.51	11.54	109	25.77	17.61	0			50	11.82	12.08
Kentucky	167	14.07	53.53	278	23.42	44.91	16	1.35	20.00	86	7.24	20.77
Texas	42	4.59	13.46	65	7.10	10.50	10	1.09	12.50	88	9.62	21.26
North Carolina	4	.89	1.28	103	22.99	16.64	13	2.90	16.25	22	4.91	5.31
Wisconsin	21	7.07	6.73	6	2.02	.97	15	5.05	18.75	31	10.44	7.49
Arizona	3	6.38	.96	4	8.51	.65	2	4.26	2.50	3	6.38	.72
Colorado	35	7.34	11.22	15	3.14	2.42	16	3.35	20.00	75	15.72	18.12
New Mexico	2	2.50	.64	10	12.50	1.62	0	0	0	7	8.75	1.69
Total	312	7.41		619	14.70		80	1.90		414	9.83	

State	Burglary and Larceny No.	Per Cent offense in state	Per Cent state in offense	Forgery and Fraud No.	Per Cent offense in state	Per Cent state in offense	Rape No.	Per Cent offense in state	Per Cent state in offense	Other Sex Offenses No.	Per Cent offense in state	Per Cent state in offense
Massachusetts	163	48.22	10.11	14	4.14	3.00	29	8.58	14.72	18	5.32	11.92
Tennessee	160	37.82	9.93	29	6.86	6.21	10	2.36	5.08	6	1.42	3.97
Kentucky	394	33.19	24.44	98	8.26	20.98	41	3.45	20.81	38	3.20	25.17
Texas	327	35.74	20.28	173	18.91	37.04	33	3.61	16.75	20	2.19	13.24
North Carolina	234	52.23	14.52	23	5.13	4.92	8	1.79	4.06	28	6.25	18.54
Wisconsin	108	36.36	6.70	40	13.47	8.56	44	14.82	22.34	18	6.06	11.92
Arizona	25	53.19	1.55	7	14.89	1.50	1	2.13	.51	1	2.13	.66
Colorado	161	33.75	9.99	76	15.93	16.27	29	6.08	14.72	20	4.19	13.24
New Mexico	40	50.00	2.48	7	8.75	1.50	2	2.50	1.02	2	2.50	1.32
Total	1612	38.27		467	11.09		197	4.68		151	3.58	

Table II-3 (cont'd).

	Vs. Public Welfare			Arson and All Other Offenses			Total	
	No.	Per Cent offense in state	Per Cent state in offense	No.	Per Cent offense in state	Per Cent state in offense	No.	Per Cent of state in total
Massachusetts	8	2.37	3.11	15	4.44	14.56	338	8.02
Tennessee	14	3.31	5.45	9	2.13	8.74	423	10.04
Kentucky	31	2.61	12.06	38	3.20	36.89	1187	28.18
Texas	149	16.28	57.98	8	.87	7.77	915	21.72
North Carolina	8	1.79	3.11	5	1.12	4.85	448	10.64
Wisconsin	3	1.01	1.17	11	3.70	10.68	297	7.05
Arizona	0	0	0	1	2.13	.97	47	1.12
Colorado	40	8.39	15.56	10	2.10	9.71	477	11.32
New Mexico	4	5.00	1.56	6	7.50	5.83	80	1.90
Total	257	6.10		103	2.44		4212	

Table II-4.

Extraction by States

	Massachusetts	Tennessee	Kentucky	Texas	North Carolina	Wisconsin	Arizona	Colorado	New Mexico	Total	Per Cent
English-American	55	1	6	33	131	51	4	36	4	321	20.68
Welsh-American	-	-	-	-	-	2	1	3	1	6	0.39
Scotch-American	13	3	2	20	20	17	1	21	3	100	6.44
Irish-American	99	18	19	156	101	62	1?	73	18	559	36.02
Danish-American	1	-	-	-	-	1	-	2	1	4	0.26
Swedish-American	-	-	-	2	-	2	-	3	-	8	0.52
Norwegian-American	0	0	-	-	-	4	-	-	-	4	0.26
German-American	10	5	13	34	22	52	7	33	5	181	11.66
Dutch-American	-	1	3	17	13	8	-	14	1	56	3.61
French-American	41	6	2	13	11	21	3	7	1	105	6.77
Spanish-American	1	-	1	2	1	-	-	4	-	9	0.58
Portuguese-American	1	1	-	-	-	-	-	-	-	2	0.13
Italian-American	3	1	2	3	-	-	-	2	-	11	0.71
Polish-American	1	-	-	1	2	5	-	1	1	9	0.58
Austrian-American	-	-	-	1	-	-	-	1	-	2	0.13
Bohemian-American	-	-	-	-	-	3	-	1	-	4	0.26
Greek-American	-	-	-	1	-	-	-	-	-	1	0.06
Jewish-American	1	1	-	-	-	-	-	-	-	2	0.13
Scotch-English	2	-	-	-	-	3	-	2	-	7	0.45
English-German	-	-	-	-	-	-	-	2	-	2	0.13
English-French	-	-	-	-	-	-	-	-	1	1	0.06
Scotch-Irish	2	-	2	77	33	12	2	12	1	141	9.08
Irish-English	1	-	-	-	1	2	-	1	-	4	0.26
Welsh-Irish	-	-	-	-	-	1	-	1	-	1	0.06
Irish-German	-	-	-	-	-	1	-	-	-	1	0.06
Welsh-English	-	-	-	1	-	1	-	-	-	1	0.06
German-Dutch	-	-	-	-	-	-	-	4	-	5	0.32
Dutch-English	1	-	-	-	-	-	-	1	-	2	0.13
Dutch-Irish	-	-	-	-	2	-	-	-	-	2	0.13
French-Irish	-	-	-	-	-	1	-	-	-	1	0.06
Total	232	37	50	361	337	248	30	222	35	1552	
Per cent of total series in each state	68.64	8.75	4.21	39.45	75.22	83.50	63.83	46.54	43.75	36.85	

Table II-6. Religious Affiliation by Extraction

Massachusetts

	Protestant		Catholic		No Religion		Total	
	No.	Per Cent	No.	Per Cent	No.	Per Cent	No.	Per Cent
Old American	51	68.92	19	25.68	4	5.41	74	18.36
Irish-American	8	5.84	125	91.24	4	2.92	137	34.00
English-American	60	76.92	17	21.79	1	1.28	78	19.36
German-American	12	75.00	4	25.00	0	0	16	3.97
Dutch-American	1	20.00	0	0	4	80.00	5	1.24
French-American	6	30.00	14	70.00	0	0	20	4.96
Scotch-American	13	56.52	9	39.13	1	4.35	23	5.71
French-Canadien-American	6	13.33	38	84.44	1	2.22	45	11.17
Italian-American	1	100.00	0	0	0	0	1	0.25
Swedish-American	0	0	1	100.00	0	0	1	0.25
Mexican-American	0	0	1	100.00	0	0	1	0.25
Portuguese-American	0	0	1	100.00	0	0	1	0.25
Lithuanian-American	0	0	1	100.00	0	0	1	0.25
Total	158	39.20	230	57.07	15	3.72	403	

Table II-7.

Religious Affiliation by Extraction

Massachusetts Prison and Reformatory Groups

| | Protestant | | | | Catholic | | | | No Religion | | | | Total |
| | Charlestown Prison | | Concord Reformatory | | Charlestown Prison | | Concord Reformatory | | Charlestown Prison | | Concord Reformatory | | |
	No.	Per Cent	No.	Per Cent	No.	Per Cent	No.	Per Cent	No.	Per Cent	No.	Per Cent	No.
Old American	33	44.59	18	24.32	12	16.22	7	9.46	3	4.05	1	1.35	74
Irish-American	3	2.19	5	3.65	46	33.58	79	57.66	4	2.92	0	0	137
English-American	26	33.33	34	43.59	2	2.56	15	19.23	1	1.28	0	0	78
German-American	8	50.00	4	25.00	0	0	4	25.00	0	0	0	0	16
Dutch-American	1	20.00	0	0	0	0	0	0	4	80.00	0	0	5
French-American	0	0	6	30.00	0	0	14	70.00	0	0	0	0	20
Scotch-American	7	30.43	6	26.09	6	26.09	3	13.04	0	0	1	4.35	23
French-Canadian-American	6	13.33	0	0	15	33.33	23	51.11	1	2.22	0	0	45
Italian-American	1	100.00	0	0	0	0	1	100.00	0	0	0	0	1
Swedish-American	0	0	0	0	0	0	1	100.00	0	0	0	0	1
Mexican-American	0	0	0	0	0	0	0	0	0	0	0	0	1
Portuguese-American	0	0	0	0	1	100.00	0	0	0	0	0	0	1
Lithuanian-American	0	0	0	0	1	100.00	0	0	0	0	0	0	1
Total	85	21.09	73	18.11	83	20.60	147	36.48	13	3.23	2	0.50	403

Table II-8. Religious Affiliation by Extraction

Tennessee

	Protestant		Catholic		No Religion		Total	
	No.	Per Cent	No.	Per Cent	No.	Per Cent	No.	Per Cent
Old American	96	27.99	17	4.96	230	67.06	343	84.69
Irish-American	4	12.12	10	30.30	19	57.58	33	8.15
English-American	1	100.00	0	0	0	0	1	0.25
German-American	2	18.18	1	9.09	8	72.73	11	2.72
Dutch-American	1	33.33	0	0	2	66.67	3	0.74
French-American	3	50.00	2	33.33	1	16.67	6	1.48
Scotch-American	2	40.00	2	40.00	1	20.00	5	1.24
Italian-American	0	0	0	0	2	100.00	2	0.49
Welsh-American	0	0	0	0	1	100.00	1	0.25
Total	109	26.91	32	7.90	264	65.18	405	

Table II-9.

Kentucky

	Protestant		Catholic		No Religion		Total	
	No.	Per Cent	No.	Per Cent	No.	Per Cent	No.	Per Cent
Old American	920	82.29	32	28.62	166	14.85	1118	93.56
Irish-American	18	50.00	15	41.67	3	8.33	36	3.01
English-American	3	75.00	1	25.00	0	0	4	0.34
German-American	15	68.18	4	18.18	3	13.64	22	1.84
Dutch-American	5	83.33	0	0	1	16.67	6	0.50
French-American	4	80.00	0	0	1	20.00	5	0.42
Scotch-American	1	33.33	0	0	2	66.67	3	0.25
Italian-American	0	0	1	100.00	0	0	1	0.08
Total	966	80.84	53	4.44	176	14.73	1195	

Religious Affiliation by Extraction

Table II-10.

Texas

	Protestant		Catholic		No Religion		Total	
	No.	Per Cent	No.	Per Cent	No.	Per Cent	No.	Per Cent
Old American	267	46.52	24	4.18	283	49.30	574	71.75
Irish-American	46	43.81	11	10.48	48	45.71	105	13.12
English-American	15	75.00	0	0	5	25.00	20	2.50
German-American	16	55.17	4	13.79	9	31.03	29	3.62
Dutch-American	5	55.56	1	11.11	3	33.33	9	1.12
French-American	5	45.45	1	9.09	5	45.45	11	1.38
Scotch-American	24	66.67	2	5.56	10	27.78	36	4.50
Italian-American	0	0	1	33.33	2	66.67	3	0.38
Swedish-American	4	100.00	0	0	0	0	4	0.50
Spanish-American	0	0	1	100.00	0	0	1	0.12
Mexican-American	0	0	6	85.71	1	14.29	7	0.88
Polish-American	0	0	1	100.00	0	0	1	0.12
Total	382	47.75	52	6.50	366	45.75	800	

Table II-11.

Wisconsin

	Protestant		Catholic		No Religion		Total	
	No.	Per Cent	No.	Per Cent	No.	Per Cent	No.	Per Cent
Old American	14	73.68	4	21.05	1	5.26	19	13.10
Irish-American	27	64.29	13	30.95	2	4.76	42	28.97
English-American	22	91.67	1	4.17	1	4.17	24	16.55
German-American	15	53.57	11	39.29	2	7.14	28	19.31
Dutch-American	1	100.00	0	0	0	0	1	0.69
French-American	4	44.44	5	55.56	0	0	9	6.21
Scotch-American	6	54.55	5	45.45	0	0	11	7.59
French-Canadian-American	1	33.33	2	66.67	0	0	3	2.07
Swedish-American	1	100.00	0	0	0	0	1	0.69
Norwegian-American	1	100.00	0	0	0	0	1	0.69
Bohemian-American	1	50.00	1	50.00	0	0	2	1.38
Belgian-American	0	0	1	100.00	0	0	1	0.69
Polish-American	0	0	3	100.00	0	0	3	2.07
Total	93	64.14	46	31.72	6	4.14	145	

Table II-12.   Religious Affiliation by Extraction

Southwest

	Protestant		Catholic		No Religion		Total	
	No.	Per Cent	No.	Per Cent	No.	Per Cent	No.	Per Cent
Old American	38	90.48	1	2.38	3	7.14	42	9.72
Irish-American	91	73.39	29	23.39	4	3.23	124	28.70
English-American	40	93.02	3	6.98	0	0	43	9.95
German-American	53	91.38	1	1.72	4	6.90	58	13.43
Dutch-American	10	100.00	0	0	0	0	10	2.32
French-American	8	57.14	3	21.43	3	21.43	14	3.24
Scotch-American	41	80.39	9	17.65	1	1.96	51	11.81
French-Canadian-American	3	42.86	4	57.14	0	0	7	1.62
Italian-American	3	50.00	3	50.00	0	0	6	1.39
Swedish-American	2	100.00	0	0	0	0	2	0.46
Swiss-American	1	100.00	0	0	0	0	1	0.23
Welsh-American	36	94.74	1	2.63	1	2.63	38	8.80
Spanish-American	1	25.00	3	75.00	0	0	4	0.93
Mexican-American	5	15.63	26	81.25	1	3.13	32	7.41
Total	332	76.85	83	19.21	17	3.94	432	

Table II-13.   Religious Affiliation by Extraction - Total Series

| | Protestant | | Catholic | | No Religion | | Total |
	No.	Per Cent	No.	Per Cent	No.	Per Cent	No.
Old American	1386	63.87	97	4.47	687	31.66	2170
Irish-American	194	40.67	203	42.56	80	16.77	477
English-American	141	82.94	22	12.94	7	4.12	170
German-American	113	68.90	25	15.24	26	15.85	164
Dutch-American	23	67.65	1	2.94	10	29.41	34
French-American	30	46.15	25	38.46	10	15.38	65
Scotch-American	87	67.44	27	20.93	15	11.63	129
French-Canadian-American	10	18.18	44	80.00	1	1.82	55
Italian-American	4	30.77	5	38.46	4	30.77	13
Swedish-American	7	87.50	1	12.50	0		8
Swiss-American	1	100.00	0		0		1
Welsh-American	36	92.31	1	2.56	2	5.13	39
Spanish-American	1	20.00	4	80.00	0		5
Mexican-American	5	12.50	33	82.50	2	5.00	40
Norwegian-American	1	100.00	0		0		1
Bohemian-American	1	50.00	1	50.00	0		2
Belgian-American	0		1	100.00	0		1
Portuguese-American	0		1	100.00	0		1
Lithuanian-American	0		1	100.00	0		1
Polish-American	0		4	100.00	0		4
Total	2040	60.36	496	14.67	844	24.97	3380

Table II-14.   Religious Affiliations of Extractions in
Descending Order of Per Cent Represented,
with Total Number of Race Group

Protestant

	Per Cent	Total No.
Swiss-American	100.00	1
Norwegian-American	100.00	1
Welsh-American	92.31	39
Swedish-American	87.50	8
English-American	82.94	170
German-American	68.90	164
Dutch-American	67.65	34
Scotch-American	67.44	129
Old American	63.87	2170
Bohemian-American	50.00	2
French-American	46.15	65
Irish-American	40.67	477
Italian-American	30.77	13
Spanish-American	20.00	5
French-Canadian-American	18.18	55
Mexican-American	12.50	40

Catholic

	Per Cent	Total No.
Belgian-American	100.00	1
Portuguese-American	100.00	1
Lithuanian-American	100.00	1
Polish-American	100.00	1
Mexican-American	82.50	40
Spanish-American	80.00	5
French-Canadian-American	80.00	55
Bohemian-American	50.00	2
Irish-American	42.56	477
French-American	38.46	65
Italian-American	38.46	13
Scotch-American	20.93	129
German-American	15.24	164
English-American	12.94	170
Swedish-American	12.50	8
Old American	4.47	2170
Dutch-American	2.94	34
Welsh-American	2.56	39

No Religion

	Per Cent	Total No.
Old American	31.65	2170
Italian-American	30.77	13
Dutch-American	29.41	34
Irish-American	16.77	477
German-American	15.85	164
French-American	15.38	65
Scotch-American	11.63	129
Welsh-American	5.13	39
Mexican-American	5.00	40
English-American	4.12	170
French-Canadian-American	1.82	55

Table II-15.   Native States of Extra-State Inmates

	Massachusetts (338)	Tennessee (423)	Kentucky (1187)	Texas (915)	North Carolina (448)	Wisconsin (297)	Arizona (47)	Colorado (477)	New Mexico (80)	Totals (4212)	Per Cent
Alabama	-	5	6	21	1	1	-	2	1	37	2.88
Arizona	-	-	-	-	-	1	-	1	-	2	.16
Arkansas	-	9	-	20	-	-	-	13	1	43	3.34
California	2	2	1	11	1	1	-	10	-	28	2.18
Colorado	-	-	2	2	-	-	-	-	2	6	.47
Connecticut	8	-	-	-	1	1	-	-	-	10	.78
Delaware	-	-	1	-	-	-	-	-	-	1	.08
Florida	-	1	2	2	2	1	-	-	-	8	.62
Georgia	-	9	3	11	7	1	-	6	-	37	2.88
Idaho	-	-	-	-	-	-	-	1	-	1	.08
Illinois	3	7	6	17	-	9	2	24	3	71	5.52
Indiana	-	4	15	11	2	7	1	13	2	55	4.28
Iowa	-	-	1	4	-	5	1	23	1	35	2.72
Kansas	-	-	-	8	-	2	3	36	1	50	3.89
Kentucky	1	21	-	21	3	2	2	9	-	59	4.59
Louisiana	-	1	1	17	-	-	1	1	1	22	1.71
Maine	12	-	-	2	-	2	-	1	1	18	1.40
Maryland	2	2	-	1	2	-	-	3	-	10	.78
Massachusetts	-	-	-	-	1	3	-	2	-	6	.47
Michigan	1	3	4	4	-	10	1	5	1	29	2.26
Minnesota	-	-	-	3	-	7	2	1	-	13	1.01
Mississippi	-	17	2	18	-	-	2	2	-	41	3.19
Missouri	1	11	5	26	-	2	1	56	7	109	8.48
Montana	-	-	-	-	-	1	-	1	-	2	.16
Nebraska	-	2	1	1	-	2	-	17	-	23	1.79
New Hampshire	10	-	-	-	-	-	-	-	-	10	.78
New Jersey	4	-	-	1	-	1	-	-	-	6	.47
New Mexico	-	1	-	3	-	1	-	3	-	8	.62
New York	16	1	2	9	3	10	-	14	1	56	4.36
North Carolina	-	-	1	2	-	2	-	6	1	12	.93
North Dakota	-	-	-	-	-	1	-	1	-	2	.16
Ohio	2	9	12	5	1	4	4	12	1	50	3.89
Oklahoma	1	5	1	27	-	-	2	17	4	57	4.43
Oregon	-	-	-	-	-	-	-	1	2	3	.23
Pennsylvania	2	3	6	7	4	3	4	13	2	44	3.42
Rhode Island	5	-	-	-	-	-	-	-	-	5	.39
South Carolina	-	2	1	2	25	-	-	-	1	31	2.41
South Dakota	-	-	-	1	-	-	-	2	-	3	.23
Tennessee	1	-	57	45	23	1	2	7	2	138	10.73
Texas	-	6	6	-	2	1	5	22	17	59	4.59
Utah	-	-	-	-	-	-	-	1	-	1	.08
Vermont	7	-	-	-	-	-	-	-	-	7	.54
Virginia	1	6	11	7	12	2	-	3	1	43	3.34
Washington	-	1	1	4	-	-	-	1	1	8	.62
West Virginia	1	-	11	3	2	-	1	1	1	20	1.56
Wisconsin	-	-	-	2	-	-	-	1	-	3	.23
Wyoming	-	-	-	-	-	-	-	-	1	1	.08
Washington, D. C.	-	-	2	-	1	-	-	-	-	3	.23
Total Extra-state	80	128	161	318	93	84	34	332	56	1286	
Per Cent of Total State	23.67	30.26	13.56	34.75	20.76	28.28	72.34	69.54	70.00	30.53	

Table II-16. Native White Population by State of Residence and State of Birth
(1930)* Compared with Native White Criminals of Native Parentage
(This Series)

	Per Cent Resident in State of Birth	Per Cent Born in Other States	Principal Contributing States in Order
Massachusetts			
Native population	83.9	16.1	Maine, N.Y., N.H., Conn., Vt., R.I.
Native criminals	76.3	23.7	N.Y., Maine, N.H., Conn., Vt., R.I.
Tennessee			
Native population	83.8	16.2	Miss., Ga., Ky., Ala.
Native criminals	69.7	30.3	Ky., Miss., Mo.
Kentucky			
Native population	88.6	11.4	Tenn., Ohio, Ind., Va.
Native criminals	86.4	13.6	Tenn., Ind., Ohio, Va.
Texas			
Native population	79.3	20.7	La., Okla., Ark., Tenn., Ala., Miss., Mo.
Native criminals	65.3	34.7	Tenn., Okla., Mo., Ky., Ala., Ark.
North Carolina			
Native population	90.0	10.0	S.C., Va., Ga.
Native criminals	79.2	20.8	S.C., Tenn., Va.
Wisconsin			
Native population	85.1	14.9	Ill., Minn., Mich., Ia.
Native criminals	71.7	28.3	Mich., N.Y., Ill., Ind., Minn.
Arizona			
Native population	45.2	54.8	Texas, Okla., Mo., Cal., N.M., Ill., Kans.
Native criminals	27.7	72.3	Texas, Ohio, Pa.
Colorado			
Native population	45.0	55.0	Mo., Kans., Neb., Ill., Ia., N.M., Ohio, Okla.
Native criminals	30.5	69.5	Mo., Kans., Ill., Ia., Texas
New Mexico			
Native population	63.6	36.4	Texas, Okla., Mo., Col., Ark., Kansas
Native criminals	30.0	70.0	Texas, Mo., Okla.

Table II-17.   Previous Convictions by Offenses

	Yes		No		
Offense	No.	Per Cent	No.	Per Cent	Total
First degree murder	83	28.23	211	71.77	294
Second degree murder	135	27.00	365	73.00	500
Assault	28	43.08	37	56.92	65
Robbery	161	42.37	219	57.63	380
Burglary and larceny	655	48.77	688	51.23	1343
Forgery and fraud	182	41.74	254	58.26	436
Rape	59	31.89	126	68.11	185
Other sex	34	29.56	81	70.44	115
Vs. public welfare	55	22.45	190	77.55	245
Arson and all other	38	41.30	54	58.70	92
Total	1430	39.12	2225	60.88	3655

Coefficient of mean square contingency = .20

Table II-18.   Previous Convictions by States

	Yes		No		Total
State	No.	Per Cent	No.	Per Cent	No.
Massachusetts	237	70.75	98	29.25	335
Tennessee	88	20.80	335	79.20	423
Kentucky	545	47.35	606	52.65	1151
Texas	207	23.31	681	76.69	888
North Carolina	-	-	-	-	-
Wisconsin	175	60.55	114	39.45	289
Southwest	178	31.28	391	58.72	569
Total	1430	39.12	2225	60.88	3655

Table II-19. Predictions on basis of State Composition and Differences from
Total Series by Offenses

Previous Convictions

Yes

	Predicted Per Cent	Diff. of Subgroup and Predicted Per Cent	Diff. of Subgroup and Total Per Cent ± p.e.	x p.e.
First degree murder	39.93	-11.70	-10.89 ± 1.84	5.92
Second degree murder	39.28	-12.28	-12.12 ± 1.37	8.85
Assault	45.19	-2.11	3.96 ± 4.05	.98
Robbery	39.22	3.15	3.25 ± 1.60	2.03
Burglary and larceny	39.73	9.04	9.65 ± .72	13.40
Forgery and fraud	34.92	6.82	2.62 ± 1.48	1.77
Rape	45.69	-13.80	-7.23 ± 2.36	3.06
Other sex	44.49	-14.93	-9.56 ± 3.02	3.16
Vs. public welfare	29.54	-7.09	-16.67 ± 2.03	8.21
Arson and all other	45.23	-3.93	2.18 ± 3.39	.64

No

	Predicted Per Cent	Diff. of Subgroup and Predicted Per Cent	Diff. of Subgroup and Total Per Cent	x p.e.
First degree murder	60.07	11.70	10.89 ± 1.84	5.92
Second degree murder	60.72	12.28	12.12 ± 1.37	8.85
Assault	54.81	2.11	-3.96 ± 4.05	.98
Robbery	60.77	-3.14	-3.25 ± 1.60	2.03
Burglary and larceny	60.27	-9.04	-9.65 ± .72	13.40
Forgery and fraud	65.08	-6.82	-2.62 ± 1.48	1.77
Rape	54.31	13.80	7.23 ± 2.36	3.06
Other sex	55.50	14.94	9.56 ± 3.02	3.16
Vs. public welfare	70.45	7.10	16.67 ± 2.03	8.21
Arson and all other	54.78	3.92	-2.18 ± 3.39	.64

Significant Differences Independent of State Sampling

Yes

First degree murder: difference	-10.89 (5.92 p.e.)
Second degree murder: difference	-12.12 (8.85 p.e.)
Burglary and larceny: independent difference	9.04 (12.56 p.e.)
Rape: difference	-7.23 (3.06 p.e.)
Other sex: difference	-9.56 (3.16 p.e.)
Vs. public welfare: independent difference	-7.09 (3.49 p.e.)

No

First degree murder: difference	10.89 (5.92 p.e.)
Second degree murder: difference	12.12 (8.85 p.e.)
Burglary and larceny: independent difference	-9.04 (12.56 p.e.)
Rape: difference	7.23 (3.06 p.e.)
Other sex: difference	9.56 (3.16 p.e.)
Vs. public welfare: independent difference	7.10 (3.50 p.e.)

Table II-20.   Marital State by Offenses

Offense	Single		Married		Divorced, Separated		Widower		Total
	No.	Per Cent	No.	Per Cent	No.	Per Cent	No.	Per Cent	
First degree murder	107	34.63	161	52.10	19	6.15	22	7.12	309
Second degree murder	235	38.27	344	56.03	17	2.77	18	2.93	614
Assault	28	35.00	46	57.50	5	6.25	1	1.25	80
Robbery	244	60.25	139	34.32	18	4.44	4	0.99	405
Burglary and larceny	985	61.87	526	33.04	60	3.77	21	1.32	1592
Forgery and fraud	220	47.62	215	46.54	21	4.54	6	1.30	462
Rape	65	33.16	103	52.55	16	8.16	12	6.12	196
Other sex	43	28.67	90	60.00	9	6.00	8	5.33	150
Vs. public welfare	65	25.90	172	68.53	7	2.79	7	2.79	251
Arson and all other	31	30.69	66	65.35	4	3.96	0	0	101
Total	2023	48.63	1862	44.76	176	4.23	99	2.38	4160

Coefficient of mean square contingency = .28

Table II-21.   Marital State by States

State	Single		Married		Divorced, Separated		Widower		Total No.
	No.	Per Cent	No.	Per Cent	No.	Per Cent	No.	Per Cent	
Massachusetts	223	66.57	94	28.06	9	2.69	9	2.69	335
Tennessee	214	50.95	179	42.62	21	5.00	6	1.43	420
Kentucky	544	45.87	584	49.24	36	3.04	22	1.86	1186
Texas	350	39.86	484	55.12	28	3.19	16	1.82	878
North Carolina	209	46.97	203	45.62	14	3.15	19	4.27	445
Wisconsin	121	40.88	109	36.82	51	17.23	15	5.07	296
Southwest	362	60.33	209	34.83	17	2.83	12	2.00	600
Total	2023	48.63	1862	44.76	176	4.23	99	2.38	4160

Table II-22. Predictions on basis of State Composition and Differences from
Total Series by Offenses

Marital State

Single

	Predicted Per Cent	Diff.of Subgroup and Predicted Per Cent	Diff. of Subgroup and Total Per Cent ± p.e.	x p.e.
First degree murder	47.31	-12.68	-14.00 ± 1.85	7.57
Second degree murder	47.92	- 9.65	-10.36 ± 1.25	8.29
Assault	49.68	-14.68	-13.63 ± 3.73	3.65
Robbery	50.46	9.79	11.62 ± 1.59	7.31
Burglary and larceny	49.10	12.77	13.24 ± .66	20.06
Forgery and fraud	46.99	0.63	- 1.01 ± 1.48	0.68
Rape	49.45	-16.29	-15.47 ± 2.35	6.58
Other sex	49.56	-20.89	-19.96 ± 2.70	7.39
Vs. public welfare	45.76	-19.86	-22.73 ± 2.06	11.03
Arson and all other	50.77	-20.08	-17.94 ± 3.31	5.42

Married

	Predicted Per Cent	Diff.of Subgroup and Predicted Per Cent	Diff.of Subgroup and Total Per Cent ± p.e.	x p.e.
First degree murder	46.40	5.70	7.34 ± 1.84	3.99
Second degree murder	46.30	9.73	11.27 ± 1.24	9.09
Assault	41.70	15.80	12.74 ± 3.71	3.43
Robbery	42.95	- 8.63	-10.44 ± 1.58	6.61
Burglary and larceny	44.26	-11.22	-11.72 ± .66	17.76
Forgery and fraud	46.35	0.19	1.78 ± 1.47	1.21
Rape	41.51	11.04	7.79 ± 2.34	3.33
Other sex	42.88	17.12	15.24 ± 2.69	5.66
Vs. public welfare	48.90	19.63	23.77 ± 2.05	11.60
Arson and all other	42.15	23.20	20.59 ± 3.30	6.24

Divorced, Separated

	Predicted Per Cent	Diff.of Subgroup and Predicted Per Cent	Diff.of Subgroup and Total Per Cent ± p.e.	x p.e.
First degree murder	4.21	1.94	2.12 ± .74	2.86
Second degree murder	3.53	- 0.76	- 1.46 ± .51	2.86
Assault	5.66	0.59	2.02 ± 1.50	1.35
Robbery	4.29	0.15	0.21 ± .64	0.33
Burglary and larceny	4.17	- 0.40	- 0.46 ± .27	1.70
Forgery and fraud	4.39	0.15	0.21 ± .59	0.36
Rape	6.25	1.91	3.93 ± .94	4.18
Other sex	4.78	1.22	1.77 ± 1.09	1.62
Vs. public welfare	3.36	- 0.57	- 1.44 ± .83	1.74
Arson and all other	4.66	- 0.70	- 0.27 ± 1.34	0.20

Widower

	Predicted Per Cent	Diff.of Subgroup and Predicted Per Cent	Diff.of Subgroup and Total Per Cent ± p.e.	x p.e.
First degree murder	2.08	5.04	4.74 ± .57	8.32
Second degree murder	2.26	0.67	0.55 ± .38	1.45
Assault	2.96	1.71	- 1.13 ± .49	2.31
Robbery	2.30	- 1.31	- 1.39 ± .49	2.84
Burglary and larceny	2.48	- 1.16	- 1.06 ± .20	5.30
Forgery and fraud	2.26	- 0.96	- 1.08 ± .45	2.40
Rape	2.79	3.33	3.74 ± 1.06	3.53
Other sex	2.79	2.54	2.95 ± .82	3.60
Vs. public welfare	1.98	0.81	0.41 ± .63	0.65
Arson and all other	2.42	- 2.42	- 2.38 ± 1.01	2.36

Table II-22 (Cont'd).

Significant Differences Independent of State Sampling
Single

First degree murder: independent difference	-12.68 (6.85 p.e.)
Second degree murder: independent difference	- 9.65 (7.72 p.e.)
Assault: difference	-13.63 (3.65 p.e.)
Robbery: independent difference	9.79 (6.16 p.e.)
Burglary and larceny: independent difference	12.77 (19.35 p.e.)
Rape: difference	-15.47 (6.58 p.c.)
Other sex: difference	-19.96 (7.39 p.e.)
Vs. public welfare: independent difference	-19.86 (9.64 p.e.)
Arson and all other: difference	-17.94 (5.42 p.e.)

Married

First degree murder: independent difference	5.70 (3.10 p.e.)
Second degree murder: independent difference	9.73 (7.85 p.e.)
Assault: difference	12.74 (3.43 p.e.)
Robbery: independent difference	- 8.63 (5.46 p.e.)
Burglary and larceny: independent difference	-11.22 (17.00 p.e.)
Rape: difference	7.79 (3.33 p.e.)
Other sex: difference	15.24 (5.66 p.e.)
Vs. public welfare: independent difference	19.63 (9.58 p.e.)
Arson and all other: difference	20.59 (6.24 p.e.)

Widower

First degree murder: difference	4.74 (8.32 p.e.)
Burglary and larceny: difference	- 1.06 (5.30 p.e.)
Rape: independent difference	3.33 (3.14 p.e.)
Other sex: independent difference	2.54 (3.10 p.e.)

Differences Rendered Insignificant by State Sampling

Rape: Independent difference	1.91 (2.03 p.e.)

Table II-23.   Marital State by Age Grouping

| Age Group | Single | | Married | | Divorced, Separated | | Widower | | Total |
	No.	Per Cent	No.	Per Cent	No.	Per Cent	No.	Per Cent	No.
15-19	488	86.67	68	12.08	2	.36	5	.89	563
20-24	602	69.51	243	28.06	20	2.30	1	.12	866
25-29	443	47.79	437	47.14	36	3.88	11	1.19	927
30-34	189	32.64	339	58.55	38	6.56	13	2.24	579
35-39	108	26.93	246	61.35	28	6.98	19	4.74	401
40-44	76	26.95	184	65.25	17	6.03	5	1.77	282
45-49	38	21.35	119	66.85	13	7.30	8	4.49	178
50-54	28	18.30	103	67.32	5	3.27	17	11.11	153
55-59	16	21.92	49	67.12	1	1.37	7	9.59	73
60-64	13	20.00	42	64.62	4	6.15	6	9.23	65
65-69	13	26.00	26	52.00	5	10.00	6	12.00	50
Total	2014	48.68	1856	44.86	169	4.08	98	2.37	4137

Table II-24.   Predictions on basis of Age Grouping and Differences
from Total Series by Offenses

Marital State

Single

	Predicted Per Cent	Diff.of Subgroup and Predicted Per Cent	x p.e.	Diff.of Subgroup and Total Per Cent ± p.e.	x p.e.
First degree murder	36.30	- 1.67	.90	-14.00 ± 1.85	7.57
Second degree murder	42.57	- 4.30	3.44	-10.36 ± 1.25	8.29
Assault	41.52	- 6.52	1.75	-13.63 ± 3.73	3.65
Robbery	54.26	5.99	3.77	11.62 ± 1.59	7.31
Burglary and larceny	56.81	5.06	7.67	13.24 ± .66	20.06
Rape	38.71	- 5.55	2.36	-15.47 ± 2.35	6.58
Other sex	38.13	- 9.46	3.50	-19.96 ± 2.70	7.39
Vs. public welfare	35.04	- 9.14	4.44	-22.73 ± 2.06	11.03
Arson and all other	42.56	-11.87	3.59	-17.94 ± 3.31	5.42

Married

	Predicted Per Cent	Diff.of Subgroup and Predicted Per Cent	x p.e.	Diff.of Subgroup and Total Per Cent ± p.e.	x p.e.
First degree murder	54.74	- 2.64	1.44	7.34 ± 1.84	3.99
Second degree murder	49.78	6.25	5.04	11.27 ± 1.24	9.09
Assault	50.74	6.76	1.82	12.74 ± 3.71	3.43
Robbery	40.64	- 6.32	4.00	-10.44 ± 1.58	6.61
Burglary and larceny	38.24	- 5.20	7.88	-11.72 ± .66	17.76
Rape	52.79	- .24	.10	7.79 ± 2.34	3.33
Other sex	53.42	6.58	2.45	15.24 ± 2.69	5.66
Vs. public welfare	55.62	12.91	6.30	23.77 ± 2.05	11.60
Arson and all other	49.98	15.37	4.66	20.59 ± 3.30	6.24

Widower

	Predicted Per Cent	Diff.of Subgroup and Predicted Per Cent	x p.e.	Diff.of Subgroup and Total Per Cent ± p.e.	x p.e.
First degree murder	3.81	3.31	5.81	4.74 ± .57	8.32
Burglary and larceny	1.55	- .23	1.15	- 1.06 ± .20	5.30
Rape	3.54	2.58	2.43	3.74 ± .73	5.12
Other sex	3.78	1.55	1.89	2.95 ± .82	3.50

Table II-25. Summary of Differences by Offenses on basis of Age Grouping

Marital State

Offense	Significant and Independent of Age Sampling		Crude Differences Invalidated by Age Sampling		Insignificant Differences	
	Diff.	x p.e.	Diff.	x p.e.	Diff.	x p.e.
First degree murder						
Marital state						
Single	-	-	-14.00	7.57	(- 1.67	.90)
Married	-	-	7.34	3.99	(- 2.64	1.44)
Widower	3.31*	5.81*	-	-	-	-
Second degree murder						
Marital state						
Single	- 4.30*	3.44*	-	-	-	-
Married	6.25*	5.04*	-	-	-	-
Assault						
Marital state						
Single	-	-	-13.63	3.65	(- 6.52	1.75)
Married	-	-	12.74	3.43	(6.76	1.82)
Robbery						
Marital state						
Single	5.99*	3.77*	-	-	-	-
Married	- 6.32*	4.00*	-	-	-	-
Burglary and larceny						
Marital state						
Single	5.06*	7.67*	-	-	-	-
Married	- 5.20*	7.88*	-	-	-	-
Widower	-	-	- 1.06	5.30	(- .23	1.15)
Rape						
Marital state						
Single	-	-	-15.47	6.58	(- 5.55	2.36)
Married	-	-	7.79	3.33	(- .24	.10)
Widower	-	-	3.74	3.53	(2.58	2.43)
Other sex						
Marital state						
Single	- 9.46*	3.50*	-	-	-	-
Married	-	-	15.24	5.66	(6.58	2.45)
Widower	-	-	2.95	3.60	(1.55	1.89)
Vs. public welfare						
Marital state						
Single	- 9.14*	4.44*	-	-	-	-
Married	12.91*	6.30*	-	-	-	-
Arson and all other						
Marital state						
Single	-11.87*	3.59*	-	-	-	-
Married	15.37*	4.66*	-	-	-	-

Summary

No.	No.	Per Cent	No.	Per Cent		
22	12	54.54	10	45.46		

*Independent difference corrected for age sampling

Table II-26.

Occupation by Offenses

Offense	Extractive No.	Per Cent	Laborer No.	Per Cent	Factory No.	Per Cent	Transportation No.	Per Cent	Skilled Trades No.	Per Cent	Trade No.	Per Cent
First degree murder	155	51.16	34	11.22	31	10.23	23	7.59	24	7.92	15	4.95
Second degree murder	319	52.30	102	16.72	62	10.16	35	5.74	30	4.92	28	4.59
Assault	17	21.80	16	20.51	10	12.82	8	10.26	15	19.23	3	3.85
Robbery	53	13.45	54	13.71	112	28.43	32	8.12	45	11.42	28	7.11
Burglary and larceny	364	23.05	337	21.34	33C	20.90	119	7.54	154	9.75	61	3.86
Forgery and fraud	117	25.49	48	10.46	71	15.47	38	8.28	47	10.24	41	8.93
Rape	71	36.79	31	16.06	26	13.47	.9	9.84	21	10.88	6	3.11
Other sex	45	30.40	28	18.92	23	15.54	6	4.05	11	7.43	11	7.43
Vs. public welfare	125	49.60	24	9.52	37	14.68	13	5.16	18	7.14	18	7.14
Arson and all other	36	36.00	14	14.00	14	14.00	8	8.00	9	9.00	4	4.00
Total	1302	31.63	688	16.72	716	17.40	301	7.31	374	9.09	215	5.22

Offense	Public Service No.	Per Cent	Semi-professional No.	Per Cent	Professional No.	Per Cent	Personal Service No.	Per Cent	Clerical No.	Per Cent	Total
First degree murder	1	0.33	1	0.33	2	0.66	14	4.62	3	0.99	303
Second degree murder	7	1.15	2	0.33	3	0.49	17	2.79	5	0.82	610
Assault	0	0	2	2.56	0	0	6	7.69	1	1.28	78
Robbery	3	0.76	9	2.28	4	1.02	35	8.88	19	4.82	394
Burglary and larceny	7	0.44	40	2.53	3	0.19	128	8.11	36	2.28	1579
Forgery and fraud	3	0.65	9	1.96	8	1.74	36	7.84	41	8.93	459
Rape	3	1.55	3	1.55	0	0	11	5.70	2	1.04	193
Other sex	2	1.35	1	0.68	5	3.38	10	6.76	6	4.05	148
Vs. public welfare	1	0.40	1	0.40	1	0.40	11	4.36	3	1.19	252
Arson and all other	0	0	1	1.00	2	2.00	11	11.00	1	1.00	100
Total	27	0.66	69	1.68	28	0.68	279	6.78	117	2.84	4116

Coefficient of mean square contingency = .36

Table II-27.

Occupation by States

State	Extractive		Laborer		Factory		Transportation		Skilled Trades		Trade	
	No.	Per Cent	No.	Per Cent	No.	Per Cent	No.	Per Cent	No.	Per Cent	No.	Per Cent
Massachusetts	8	2.53	44	13.92	81	25.63	50	15.82	42	13.29	32	10.13
Tennessee	169	41.42	32	7.84	84	20.59	26	6.37	27	6.62	24	5.88
Kentucky	590	50.91	138	11.91	122	10.53	76	6.56	98	8.46	54	4.66
Texas	250	27.87	81	9.03	219	24.42	60	6.69	99	11.04	43	4.79
North Carolina	59	13.20	241	53.91	86	19.24	3	.67	29	6.49	14	3.13
Wisconsin	60	20.34	65	22.03	32	10.85	26	8.81	29	9.83	18	6.10
Southwest	166	27.95	87	14.65	92	15.49	60	10.10	50	8.42	30	5.05
Total	1302	31.63	688	16.72	716	17.40	301	7.31	374	9.09	215	5.22

State	Public Service		Semi-professional		Professional		Personal Service		Clerical		Total
	No.	Per Cent	No.	Per Cent	No.	Per Cent	No.	Per Cent	No.	Per Cent	
Massachusetts	5	1.58	12	3.80	2	.63	24	7.60	16	5.06	316
Tennessee	3	.74	9	2.21	2	.49	20	4.90	12	2.94	408
Kentucky	11	.95	7	.60	6	.52	41	3.54	16	1.38	1159
Texas	2	.22	17	1.90	9	1.00	90	10.03	27	3.01	897
North Carolina	1	.22	0	0	2	.45	8	1.79	4	.90	447
Wisconsin	4	1.36	9	3.05	0	0	33	11.19	19	6.44	295
Southwest	1	.17	15	2.52	7	1.18	63	10.61	23	3.87	594
Total	27	0.66	69	1.68	28	0.68	279	6.78	117	2.84	4116

Table II-30. Predictions on basis of State Composition and Differences from
Total Series by Offenses

Occupation

Extractive

	Predicted Per Cent	Diff.of Subgroup and Predicted Per Cent	Diff.of Subgroup and Total Per Cent ± p.e.	x p.e.
First degree murder	40.92	10.24	19.53 ± 1.73	11.29
Second degree murder	36.91	15.39	20.67 ± 1.17	17.67
Assault	26.17	- 4.37	- 9.83 ± 3.52	2.79
Robbery	29.78	-16.33	-18.18 ± 1.50	12.12
Burglary and larceny	29.66	- 6.61	- 8.58 ± .62	13.84
Forgery and fraud	31.44	- 5.95	- 6.14 ± 1.38	4.45
Rape	27.36	9.43	5.16 ± 2.21	2.34
Other sex	27.58	2.82	- 1.23 ± 2.53	.49
Vs. public welfare	30.07	19.53	17.97 ± 1.92	9.36
Arson and all other	32.36	3.64	4.37 ± 3.10	1.41

Laborer

	Predicted Per Cent	Diff.of Subgroup and Predicted Per Cent	Diff.of Subgroup and Total Per Cent ± p.e.	x p.e.
First degree murder	12.64	- 1.42	- 5.50 ± 1.39	3.96
Second degree murder	18.20	- 1.48	0.00 ± .94	0.00
Assault	21.09	- 0.58	3.79 ± 2.82	1.34
Robbery	14.61	- 0.90	- 3.01 ± 1.21	2.49
Burglary and larceny	18.28	3.06	4.62 ± .50	9.24
Forgery and fraud	14.11	- 3.65	- 6.26 ± 1.11	5.64
Rape	15.93	0.13	- .66 ± 1.77	.37
Other sex	21.02	- 2.10	2.20 ± 2.03	1.08
Vs. public welfare	11.98	- 2.46	- 7.20 ± 1.54	4.68
Arson and all other	15.20	- 1.20	- 2.72 ± 2.48	1.10

Factory

	Predicted Per Cent	Diff.of Subgroup and Predicted Per Cent	Diff.of Subgroup and Total Per Cent ± p.e.	x p.e.
First degree murder	14.43	- 4.20	- 7.17 ± 1.42	5.05
Second degree murder	16.15	- 5.99	- 7.24 ± .96	7.54
Assault	16.37	- 3.55	- 4.58 ± 2.87	1.60
Robbery	18.10	10.33	11.03 ± 1.23	8.97
Burglary and larceny	17.85	3.05	3.50 ± .51	6.86
Forgery and fraud	18.16	- 2.69	- 1.93 ± 1.13	1.71
Rape	16.82	- 3.35	- 3.93 ± 1.79	2.20
Other sex	16.98	- 1.44	- 1.86 ± 2.06	.90
Vs. public welfare	20.72	- 6.04	- 2.72 ± 1.56	1.74
Arson and all other	15.96	- 1.96	- 3.40 ± 2.52	1.35

Table II-30 (cont'd).

	Predicted Per Cent	Transportation Diff. of Subgroup and Predicted Per Cent	Diff. of Subgroup and Total Per Cent ± p.e.	x p.e.
First degree murder	7.14	0.45	.28 ± .97	.29
Second degree murder	6.18	- 0.44	- 1.57 ± .66	2.38
Assault	7.76	2.50	2.95 ± 1.97	1.50
Robbery	8.31	- 0.19	.81 ± .84	.96
Burglary and larceny	7.30	0.24	.23 ± .34	.68
Forgery and fraud	7.46	0.82	.97 ± .77	1.26
Rape	8.77	1.07	2.53 ± 1.23	2.06
Other sex	7.39	- 3.34	- 3.26 ± 1.42	2.30
Vs. public welfare	7.36	- 2.20	- 2.15 ± 1.07	2.01
Arson and all other	8.44	- 0.44	.69 ± 1.73	.40

	Predicted Per Cent	Skilled Trade Diff. of Subgroup and Predicted Per Cent	Diff. of Subgroup and Total Per Cent ± p.e.	x p.e.
First degree murder	8.69	- 0.77	- 1.17 ± 1.07	1.09
Second degree murder	8.32	- 3.40	- 4.17 ± .72	5.79
Assault	9.19	10.14	10.14 ± 2.17	4.67
Robbery	9.38	2.04	2.33 ± .93	2.50
Burglary and larceny	9.09	0.66	.66 ± .38	1.74
Forgery and fraud	9.46	0.78	1.15 ± .85	1.35
Rape	9.73	1.15	1.79 ± 1.36	1.32
Other sex	9.10	- 1.67	- 1.66 ± 1.56	1.06
Vs. public welfare	9.95	- 2.81	- 1.95 ± 1.19	1.64
Arson and all other	9.25	- 0.25	- .09 ± 1.92	.05

	Predicted Per Cent	Trade Diff. of Subgroup and Predicted Per Cent	Diff. of Subgroup and Total Per Cent ± p.e.	x p.e.
First degree murder	4.98	- 0.03	- .27 ± .83	.32
Second degree murder	4.92	- 0.33	- .63 ± .56	1.12
Assault	5.33	- 1.48	- 1.37 ± 1.69	.81
Robbery	5.63	1.48	1.89 ± .72	2.62
Burglary and larceny	5.29	- 1.43	- 1.36 ± .30	4.53
Forgery and fraud	5.07	3.86	3.71 ± .66	5.62
Rape	5.87	- 2.76	- 2.11 ± 1.05	2.01
Other sex	5.32	2.11	1.92 ± .92	2.09
Arson and all other	5.72	- 1.72	- 1.22 ± 1.48	.82

Table II-30 (cont'd).

	Public Service Predicted Per Cent	Diff.of Subgroup and Predicted Per Cent	Diff.of Subgroup and Total Per Cent ± p.e.	x p.e.
First degree murder	0.75	- 0.42	- 0.33 ± 0.30	1.10
Second degree murder	0.71	0.44	0.49 ± 0.20	2.45
Assault	0.70	- 0.70	- 0.66 ± 0.61	1.08
Robbery	0.68	0.08	0.10 ± 0.26	0.38
Burglary and larceny	0.66	- 0.22	- 0.22 ± 0.12	1.83
Forgery and fraud	0.53	0.12	- 0.01 ± 0.24	0.04
Rape	0.84	0.71	0.89 ± 0.38	2.34
Other sex	0.72	0.63	0.69 ± 0.44	1.57
Vs. public welfare	0.38	0.02	- 0.26 ± 0.34	0.76
Arson and all other	0.85	- 0.85	- 0.66 ± 0.54	1.22

	Semi-professional Predicted Per Cent	Diff.of Subgroup and Predicted Per Cent	Diff.of Subgroup and Total Per Cent ± p.e.	x p.e.
First degree murder	1.38	- 1.05	- 1.35 ± 0.48	2.81
Second degree murder	1.18	- 0.85	- 1.35 ± 0.32	4.22
Assault	1.88	0.68	0.88 ± 0.97	0.91
Robbery	2.02	0.26	0.60 ± 0.42	1.43
Burglary and larceny	1.69	0.84	0.85 ± 0.16	5.31
Forgery and fraud	1.83	0.13	0.28 ± 0.38	0.74
Rape	2.20	- 0.65	- 0.13 ± 0.61	0.21
Other sex	1.69	- 1.01	- 1.00 ± 0.70	1.43
Vs. public welfare	1.88	- 1.48	- 1.28 ± 0.53	2.42
Arson and all other	1.86	- 0.86	- 0.68 ± 0.86	0.79

	Professional Predicted Per Cent	Diff.of Subgroup and Predicted Per Cent	Diff. of Subgroup and Total Per Cent ± p.e.	x p.e.
First degree murder	0.63	0.03	- .02 ± .31	.06
Second degree murder	0.58	- 0.09	- .19 ± .22	.86
Assault	0.63	- 0.63	- .68 ± .63	1.08
Robbery	0.72	0.30	.34 ± .27	1.26
Burglary and larceny	0.67	- 0.48	- .49 ± .12	4.08
Forgery and fraud	0.78	0.96	1.06 ± .24	4.42
Rape	0.60	- 0.60	- .68 ± .39	1.74
Other sex	0.62	2.76	2.70 ± .44	6.14
Vs. public welfare	0.90	- 0.50	- .28 ± .34	.82
Arson and all other	0.62	1.38	1.32 ± .55	2.40

Table II-30 (cont'd).

Personal Service

	Predicted Per Cent	Diff.of Subgroup and Predicted Per Cent	Diff.of Subgroup and Total Per Cent ± p.e.	x p.e.
First degree murder	6.00	- 1.38	- 2.16 ± 0.94	2.30
Second degree murder	4.76	- 1.97	- 3.99 ± 0.63	6.33
Assault	7.50	0.19	0.91 ± 1.90	0.48
Robbery	7.52	1.36	2.10 ± 0.81	2.59
Burglary and larceny	6.65	1.46	1.33 ± 0.34	3.91
Forgery and fraud	8.08	- 0.24	1.06 ± 0.74	1.43
Rape	8.08	- 2.38	- 1.08 ± 1.19	0.91
Other sex	6.60	0.16	- 0.02 ± 1.37	0.02
Vs. public welfare	8.75	- 4.39	- 2.42 ± 1.03	2.35
Arson and all other	6.65	4.35	4.22 ± 1.67	2.53

Clerical

	Predicted Per Cent	Diff.of Subgroup and Predicted Per Cent	Diff.of Subgroup and Total Per Cent ± p.e.	x p.e.
First degree murder	2.46	- 1.47	- 1.85 ± .62	2.98
Second degree murder	2.08	- 1.26	- 2.02 ± .42	4.81
Assault	3.38	- 2.10	- 1.56 ± 1.25	1.25
Robbery	3.24	1.58	1.98 ± .53	3.74
Burglary and larceny	2.86	- 0.58	- .56 ± .22	2.54
Forgery and fraud	3.08	5.85	6.09 ± .49	12.43
Rape	3.79	- 2.75	- 1.80 ± .79	2.28
Other sex	2.99	1.06	1.21 ± .90	1.34
Vs. public welfare	3.00	- 1.81	- 1.65 ± .69	2.39
Arson and all other	3.11	- 2.11	- 1.84 ± 1.11	1.66

Significant Differences Independent of State Sampling

Extractive

First degree murder: independent difference	10.24 (5.91 p.e.)
Second degree murder: independent difference	15.39 (13.15 p.e.)
Robbery: independent difference	-16.33 (10.89 p.e.)
Burglary and larceny: independent difference	- 6.61 (10.66 p.e.)
Forgery and fraud: independent difference	- 5.95 (4.31 p.e.)
Vs. public welfare: difference	17.97 (9.36 p.e.)

Laborer

Burglary and larceny: independent difference	3.06 (6.12 p.e.)
Forgery and fraud: independent difference	- 3.65 (3.28 p.e.)

Factory

Second degree murder: independent difference	- 5.99 (6.24 p.e.)
Robbery: independent difference	10.33 (8.39 p.e.)
Burglary and larceny: independent difference	3.05 (5.98 p.e.)

Skilled Trades

Second degree murder: independent difference	- 3.40 (4.72 p.e.)
Assault: difference	10.14 (4.67 p.e.)

Table II-30 (cont'd).

Trade

Burglary and larceny: difference	- 1.36 (4.53 p.e.)
Forgery and fraud: difference	3.71 (5.62 p.e.)

Semi-professional

Burglary and larceny: independent difference	.84 (5.25 p.e.)

Professional

Burglary and larceny: independent difference	- .48 (4.00 p.e.)
Forgery and fraud: independent difference	.96 (4.00 p.e.)
Other sex: difference	2.70 (6.14 p.e.)

Personal Service

Second degree murder: independent difference	- 1.97 (3.13 p.e.)
Burglary and larceny: difference	1.33 (3.91 p.e.)

Clerical

Second degree murder: independent difference	- 1.26 (3.00 p.e.)
Forgery and fraud: independent difference	5.85 (11.94 p.e.)

Significant Differences Invalidated by State Sampling

Laborer

First degree murder: independent difference	- 1.42 (1.02 p.e.)
Vs. public welfare: independent difference	- 2.46 (1.60 p.e.)

Factory

First degree murder: independent difference	- 4.20 (2.96 p.e.)

Semi-professional

Second degree murder: independent difference	- .85 (2.66 p.e.)

Clerical

Robbery: independent difference	1.58 (2.98 p.e.)

Table II-31.

Occupation by Age Grouping

Age Group	Extractive		Laborer		Factory		Transportation		Skilled Trades		Trade	
	No.	Per Cent	No.	Per Cent	No.	Per Cent	No.	Per Cent	No.	Per Cent	No.	Per Cent
15-19	167	31.10	137	25.51	95	17.69	43	8.01	36	6.70	11	2.05
20-24	246	28.87	160	18.78	172	20.19	54	6.34	81	9.51	46	5.40
25-29	268	29.07	141	15.29	195	21.15	77	8.35	73	7.92	37	4.01
30-34	176	30.19	83	14.24	89	15.27	42	7.20	69	11.84	29	4.97
35-39	132	33.42	52	13.16	69	17.47	35	8.86	34	8.61	27	6.84
40-44	96	33.68	38	13.33	35	12.28	20	7.02	31	10.88	21	7.37
45-49	65	36.31	21	11.73	26	14.52	10	5.59	18	10.06	13	7.26
50-54	64	41.03	20	12.82	19	12.18	6	3.85	19	12.18	12	7.69
55-59	33	45.20	13	17.81	7	9.59	2	2.74	4	5.48	6	8.22
60-64	27	41.54	7	10.77	6	9.23	4	6.15	4	6.15	5	7.69
65-69	23	46.94	12	24.49	2	4.08	1	2.04	2	4.08	5	10.20
Total	1297	31.66	684	16.70	715	17.46	294	7.18	371	9.06	212	5.18

Age Group	Public Service		Semi-professional		Professional		Personal Service		Clerical		Student		Total No.
	No.	Per Cent	No.	Per Cent	No.	Per Cent	No.	Per Cent	No.	Per Cent	No.	Per Cent	
15-19	2	.37	7	1.30	0	0	30	5.59	8	1.50	1	.19	537
20-24	3	.35	16	1.88	2	.23	54	6.34	18	2.11	0	0	852
25-29	6	.65	15	1.63	5	.54	66	7.16	38	4.12	1	.11	922
30-34	6	1.03	16	2.74	1	.17	53	9.09	18	3.09	1	.17	583
35-39	3	.76	2	.51	4	1.01	29	7.34	8	2.02	0	0	395
40-44	3	1.05	6	2.10	3	1.05	20	7.02	12	4.21	0	0	285
45-49	3	1.68	3	1.68	1	.56	15	8.38	4	2.23	0	0	179
50-54	0	0	2	1.28	2	1.28	5	3.20	7	4.49	0	0	156
55-59	0	0	0	0	3	4.11	5	6.85	0	0	0	0	73
60-64	1	1.54	0	0	3	4.62	3	4.62	5	7.69	0	0	65
65-69	1	2.04	1	2.04	1	2.04	1	2.04	0	0	0	0	49
Total	28	.68	68	1.66	25	.61	281	6.86	118	2.88	3	.07	4096

Table II-32.

Education by Offenses

Offense	Illiterate No.	Per Cent	Read, Write No.	Per Cent	1-5th Grade No.	Per Cent	6th Grade No.	Per Cent	7th Grade No.	Per Cent	8th Grade No.	Per Cent
First degree murder	50	16.23	26	8.44	100	32.47	34	11.04	17	5.52	50	16.23
Second degree murder	127	20.55	33	5.34	215	34.79	54	8.74	47	7.60	73	11.81
Assault	8	10.00	1	1.25	20	25.00	9	11.25	9	11.25	19	23.75
Robbery	15	3.65	7	1.70	66	16.06	30	7.30	55	13.38	109	26.52
Burglary and larceny	133	8.32	46	2.88	400	25.03	149	9.32	191	11.95	306	19.15
Forgery and fraud	20	4.31	19	4.10	62	13.36	33	7.11	48	10.34	97	20.90
Rape	22	11.22	10	5.10	59	30.10	33	10.20	18	9.18	45	22.96
Other sex	22	14.76	10	6.71	34	22.82	8	5.37	16	10.74	29	19.46
Vs. public welfare	18	7.06	20	7.84	72	28.24	28	10.98	29	11.37	45	17.65
Arson and all other	10	9.90	4	3.96	27	26.73	12	11.88	6	5.94	23	22.77
Total	425	10.16	176	4.21	1055	25.24	377	9.02	436	10.43	795	19.04

Offense	1st-2nd High No.	Per Cent	3rd-4th High No.	Per Cent	College No.	Per Cent	Professional School No.	Per Cent	Total No.
First degree murder	23	7.47	6	1.95	2	.65	0	0	308
Second degree murder	52	8.41	6	.97	11	1.78	0	0	618
Assault	9	11.25	3	3.75	1	1.25	1	1.25	80
Robbery	85	20.68	30	7.30	13	3.16	1	.24	411
Burglary and larceny	257	16.08	80	5.01	36	2.25	0	0	1598
Forgery and fraud	95	20.47	32	6.90	56	12.07	2	.43	464
Rape	14	7.14	8	4.08	0	0	0	0	196
Other sex	15	10.07	7	4.70	8	5.37	0	0	149
Vs. public welfare	29	11.37	11	4.31	3	1.18	0	0	255
Arson and all other	13	12.87	3	2.97	1	.99	2	1.98	101
Total	592	14.16	186	4.45	131	3.13	6	.14	4180

Coefficient of mean square contingency = .35

Table II-33. Illiteracy of Native White Prisoners (1910)* Compared with
             Native White Criminals of Native Parentage (This Series)

Region	Criminals	Per Cent
New England		
Massachusetts	1910 series	2.8
	this series	0.60
East South Central		
(Kentucky, Tennessee, Alabama, Mississippi)	1910 series	13.4
Tennessee	this series	13.51
Kentucky	this series	19.83
West South Central		
(Arkansas, Louisiana, Oklahoma, Texas)	1910 series	12.2
Texas	this series	3.84
South Atlantic		
(Delaware, Maryland, District of Columbia,		
Virginia, West Virginia, North Carolina,		
South Carolina, Georgia, Florida)	1910 series	12.2
North Carolina	this series	16.03
East North Central		
(Ohio, Indiana, Illinois, Michigan,		
Wisconsin)	1910 series	4.2
Wisconsin	this series	2.72
Mountain		
(Montana, Idaho, Wyoming, Colorado, New		
Mexico, Arizona, Utah, Nevada)	1910 series	7.1
Arizona, Colorado, New Mexico	this series	3.03

*Prisoners and Juvenile Delinquents in the United States, 1910, Department of Commerce,
Bureau of the Census, Washington, D.C., 1918, p. 148.

Table II-34.

Education by States

State	Illiterate No.	Per Cent	Read, Write No.	Per Cent	1st-5th Grade No.	Per Cent	6th Grade No.	Per Cent	7th Grade No.	Per Cent	8th Grade No.	Per Cent
Massachusetts	2	.60	2	.60	34	10.12	33	9.82	50	14.88	99	29.46
Tennessee	57	13.51	11	2.61	106	25.12	30	7.11	24	5.69	89	21.09
Kentucky	234	19.83	72	6.10	414	35.08	100	8.47	90	7.63	166	14.07
Texas	35	3.84	71	7.79	185	20.31	80	8.78	122	13.39	151	16.58
North Carolina	71	16.03	6	1.35	176	39.73	37	8.35	57	12.87	35	7.90
Wisconsin	8	2.72	6	2.04	48	16.33	34	11.56	33	11.22	93	31.63
Southwest	18	3.03	8	1.35	92	15.49	63	10.61	60	10.10	163	27.44
Total	425	10.16	176	4.21	1055	25.24	377	9.02	436	10.43	796	19.04

State	1st-2nd High No.	Per Cent	3rd-4th High No.	Per Cent	College No.	Per Cent	Professional School No.	Per Cent	Total No.
Massachusetts	68	20.24	35	10.42	11	3.27	2	.60	336
Tennessee	74	17.54	14	3.32	17	4.03	0	0	422
Kentucky	80	6.78	12	1.02	12	1.02	0	0	1180
Texas	160	17.56	66	7.24	39	4.28	2	.22	911
North Carolina	38	8.58	15	3.39	8	1.81	0	0	443
Wisconsin	38	12.92	23	7.82	11	3.74	0	0	294
Southwest	134	22.56	21	3.54	33	5.56	2	.34	594
Total	592	14.16	186	4.45	131	3.13	6	.14	4180

Table II-37. Predictions on basis of State Composition and Differences
from Total Series by Offenses

Education

Illiterate

	Predicted Per Cent	Diff.of Subgroup and Predicted Per Cent	Diff.of Subgroup and Total Per Cent ± p.e.	x p.e.
First degree murder	13.47	2.76	6.07 ± 1.12	5.42
Second degree murder	14.55	6.00	10.39 ± .76	13.67
Assault	8.30	1.70	- 0.16 ± 2.25	0.07
Robbery	8.32	- 4.67	- 6.51 ± .95	6.85
Burglary and larceny	9.96	- 1.64	- 1.84 ± .40	4.60
Forgery and fraud	8.05	- 3.74	- 5.85 ± .89	6.57
Rape	7.30	3.92	1.06 ± 1.42	0.75
Other sex	9.86	4.90	4.60 ± 1.64	2.80
Vs. public welfare	6.42	0.64	- 3.10 ± 1.23	2.52
Arson and all other	10.45	- 0.55	- 0.26 ± 2.00	0.13

Read and Write

	Predicted Per Cent	Diff.of Subgroup and Predicted Per Cent	Diff.of Subgroup and Total Per Cent ± p.e.	x p.e.
First degree murder	4.94	3.50	4.23 ± .74	5.72
Second degree murder	4.35	0.99	1.13 ± .51	2.22
Assault	3.16	- 1.91	- 2.96 ± 1.50	1.97
Robbery	3.81	- 2.11	- 2.51 ± .63	3.98
Burglary and larceny	3.91	- 1.03	- 1.33 ± .27	4.93
Forgery and fraud	4.84	- 0.74	- 0.11 ± .59	0.19
Rape	3.52	1.58	0.89 ± .94	0.95
Other sex	3.44	3.27	2.50 ± 1.09	2.29
Vs. public welfare	5.70	2.14	3.63 ± .82	4.43
Arson and all other	3.68	0.28	- 0.25 ± 1.33	0.19

1-5th Grade

	Predicted Per Cent	Diff.of Subgroup and Predicted Per Cent	Diff.of Subgroup and Total Per Cent ± p.e.	x p.e.
First degree murder	28.07	4.40	7.23 ± 1.60	4.52
Second degree murder	30.28	4.51	9.55 ± 1.09	8.76
Assault	21.58	3.42	- 0.24 ± 3.24	0.07
Robbery	22.42	- 6.36	- 9.18 ± 1.38	6.65
Burglary and larceny	25.24	- 0.21	- 0.21 ± .57	0.37
Forgery and fraud	23.09	- 9.73	-11.88 ± 1.28	9.28
Rape	21.24	8.86	4.86 ± 2.04	2.38
Other sex	25.40	- 2.58	- 2.42 ± 2.35	1.03
Vs. public welfare	21.77	6.47	3.00 ± 1.78	1.68
Arson and all other	24.42	2.31	1.49 ± 2.88	0.52

Table II-37 (cont'd).

	Predicted Per Cent	6th Grade Diff.of Subgroup and Predicted Per Cent	Diff.of Subgroup and Total Per Cent ± p.e.	x p.e.
First degree murder	8.84	2.20	2.02 ± 1.06	1.91
Second degree murder	8.44	0.30	- 0.28 ± .72	0.39
Assault	9.68	1.57	2.23 ± 2.14	1.04
Robbery	9.21	- 1.91	- 1.72 ± .90	1.91
Burglary and larceny	9.02	0.30	0.30 ± .38	0.79
Forgery and fraud	9.21	- 2.10	- 1.91 ± .84	2.27
Rape	9.68	0.52	1.18 ± 1.35	0.87
Other sex	9.29	- 3.92	- 3.65 ± 1.55	2.36
Vs. public welfare	9.02	1.96	1.96 ± 1.17	1.68
Arson and all other	9.25	2.63	2.86 ± 1.90	1.50

	Predicted Per Cent	7th Grade Diff.of Subgroup and Predicted Per Cent	Diff.of Subgroup and Total Per Cent ± p.e.	x p.e.
First degree murder	8.85	- 3.33	- 4.91 ± 1.13	4.34
Second degree murder	9.26	- 1.66	- 2.83 ± .77	3.68
Assault	11.16	0.09	0.82 ± 2.28	0.36
Robbery	10.58	2.80	2.95 ± .96	3.07
Burglary and larceny	10.69	1.26	1.52 ± .40	3.80
Forgery and fraud	10.90	- 0.56	- 0.09 ± .90	0.10
Rape	10.98	- 1.80	- 1.25 ± 1.44	0.87
Other sex	10.96	- 0.22	0.31 ± 1.66	0.19
Vs. public welfare	11.72	- 0.35	0.94 ± 1.25	0.75
Arson and all other	10.01	- 4.07	- 4.49 ± 2.02	2.22

	Predicted Per Cent	8th Grade Diff.of Subgroup and Predicted Per Cent	Diff.of Subgroup and Total Per Cent ± p.e.	x p.e.
First degree murder	18.13	- 1.90	- 2.81 ± 1.45	1.94
Second degree murder	16.06	- 4.25	- 7.23 ± .98	7.38
Assault	21.22	2.53	4.71 ± 2.93	1.61
Robbery	21.12	5.40	7.48 ± 1.24	6.03
Burglary and larceny	18.99	0.16	0.11 ± .53	0.21
Forgery and fraud	19.67	1.23	1.86 ± 1.16	1.60
Rape	22.96	0	3.92 ± 1.85	2.12
Other sex	19.50	- 0.04	0.42 ± 2.13	0.20
Vs. public welfare	18.69	- 1.04	- 1.39 ± 1.60	0.87
Arson and all other	20.90	1.87	3.73 ± 2.60	1.44

Table II-37 (cont'd).

	Predicted Per Cent	1st-2nd High Diff.of Subgroup and Predicted Per Cent	Diff.of Subgroup and Total Per Cent ± p.e.	x p.e.
First degree murder	12.02	- 4.55	- 6.69 ± 1.29	5.19
Second degree murder	11.54	- 3.13	- 5.75 ± .88	6.53
Assault	14.47	- 3.22	- 2.91 ± 2.60	1.12
Robbery	15.86	4.82	6.52 ± 1.10	5.93
Burglary and larceny	14.28	1.80	1.92 ± .46	4.17
Forgery and fraud	15.50	4.97	6.31 ± 1.03	6.13
Rape	15.12	- 7.98	- 7.02 ± 1.64	4.28
Other sex	13.71	- 3.64	- 4.09 ± 1.89	2.16
Vs. public welfare	16.86	- 5.49	- 2.79 ± 1.43	1.95
Arson and all other	13.86	- 0.99	- 1.29 ± 2.31	0.56

	Predicted Per Cent	3rd-4th High Diff.of Subgroup and Predicted Per Cent	Diff.of Subgroup and Total Per Cent ± p.e.	x p.e.
First degree murder	2.99	- 1.04	- 2.50 ± .76	3.29
Second degree murder	3.10	- 2.13	- 3.48 ± .52	6.69
Assault	4.96	- 1.21	- 0.70 ± 1.54	0.45
Robbery	4.95	2.35	2.85 ± .65	4.38
Burglary and larceny	4.61	0.40	0.56 ± .27	2.07
Forgery and fraud	4.93	1.97	2.45 ± .61	4.02
Rape	5.59	- 1.51	- 0.37 ± .97	0.38
Other sex	4.69	0.01	0.25 ± 1.12	0.22
Vs. public welfare	5.63	- 1.32	- 0.14 ± .84	0.17
Arson and all other	4.33	- 1.36	- 1.48 ± 1.37	1.08

	Predicted Per Cent	College Diff.of Subgroup and Predicted Per Cent	Diff.of Subgroup and Total Per Cent ± p.e.	x p.e.
First degree murder	2.60	- 1.95	- 2.48 ± .64	3.88
Second degree murder	2.37	- 0.59	- 1.35 ± .44	3.07
Assault	3.31	- 2.06	- 1.88 ± 1.30	1.45
Robbery	3.54	- 0.38	0.03 ± .55	0.05
Burglary and larceny	3.14	- 0.89	- 0.88 ± .24	3.67
Forgery and fraud	3.63	8.44	8.94 ± .51	17.53
Rape	3.43	- 3.43	- 3.13 ± .82	3.82
Other sex	3.00	2.37	2.24 ± .94	2.38
Vs. public welfare	3.98	- 2.80	- 1.95 ± .72	2.71
Arson and all other	2.94	- 1.95	- 2.14 ± 1.15	1.86

Table II-37 (cont'd).

Significant Differences Independent of State Sampling

Illiterate

Second degree murder: independent difference	6.00 (7.90 p.e.)
Robbery: independent difference	- 4.67 (4.92 p.e.)
Burglary and larceny: independent difference	- 1.64 (4.10 p.e.)
Forgery and fraud: independent difference	- 3.74 (4.20 p.e.)

Read, Write

First degree murder: independent difference	3.50 (4.73 p.e.)
Robbery: independent difference	- 2.11 (3.35 p.e.)
Burglary and larceny: independent difference	- 1.03 (3.82 p.e.)

1-5th Grade

Second degree murder: independent difference	4.51 (4.14 p.e.)
Robbery: independent difference	- 6.36 (4.61 p.e.)
Forgery and fraud: independent difference	- 9.73 (7.60 p.e.)

7th Grade

Burglary and larceny: independent difference	1.26 (3.15 p.e.)

8th Grade

Second degree murder: independent difference	- 4.25 (4.34 p.e.)
Robbery: independent difference	5.40 (4.36 p.e.)

1st-2nd High

First degree murder: independent difference	- 4.55 (3.53 p.e.)
Second degree murder: independent difference	- 3.13 (3.56 p.e.)
Robbery: independent difference	4.82 (4.38 p.e.)
Burglary and larceny: independent difference	1.80 (3.91 p.e.)
Forgery and fraud: independent difference	4.97 (4.82 p.e.)
Rape: difference	- 7.02 (4.28 p.e.)

3rd-4th High

Second degree murder: independent difference	- 2.13 (4.10 p.e.)
Robbery: independent difference	2.35 (3.62 p.e.)
Forgery and fraud: independent difference	1.97 (3.23 p.e.)

College

First degree murder: independent difference	- 1.95 (3.05 p.e.)
Burglary and larceny: difference	- 0.88 (3.67 p.e.)
Forgery and fraud: independent difference	8.44 (16.55 p.e.)
Rape: difference	- 3.13 (3.82 p.e.)

Differences Rendered Insignificant by State Sampling

Illiterate

First degree murder: independent difference	2.76 (2.46 p.e.)

Read, Write

Vs. public welfare: independent difference	2.14 (2.61 p.e.)

1-5th Grade

First degree murder: independent difference	4.40 (2.75 p.e.)

7th Grade

First degree murder: independent difference	- 3.33 (2.95 p.e.)
Second degree murder: independent difference	- 1.66 (2.16 p.e.)
Robbery: independent difference	2.80 (2.92 p.e.)

Table II-37 (cont'd).

3rd-4th High
First degree murder: independent difference   - 1.04 (1.37 p.e.)

College
Second degree murder: independent difference   - 0.59 (1.34 p.e.)

Table II-38

Education by Age Grouping

Age Group	Illiterate No.	Per Cent	Read, Write No.	Per Cent	1st-5th Grade No.	Per Cent	6th Grade No.	Per Cent	7th Grade No.	Per Cent
15-19	51	9.06	13	2.31	146	25.93	58	10.30	71	12.61
20-24	82	9.48	24	2.77	197	22.77	82	9.48	107	12.37
25-29	66	7.05	34	3.63	231	24.68	74	7.91	88	9.40
30-34	60	10.25	20	3.42	146	24.95	60	10.25	63	10.77
35-39	39	9.68	22	5.46	109	27.05	35	8.68	39	9.68
40-44	34	11.80	21	7.29	73	25.35	25	8.68	29	10.07
45-49	26	14.52	10	5.59	53	29.61	18	10.06	15	8.38
50-54	27	17.42	12	7.74	45	29.03	14	9.03	10	6.45
55-59	12	16.22	12	16.22	21	28.38	4	5.40	6	8.11
60-64	10	15.38	4	6.15	18	27.69	5	7.69	7	10.77
65-69	14	29.17	4	8.33	11	22.92	4	8.33	1	2.08
Total	421	10.12	176	4.23	1050	25.23	379	9.11	436	10.48

Age Group	8th Grade No.	Per Cent	1st-2nd High No.	Per Cent	3rd-4th High No.	Per Cent	College No.	Per Cent	Professional School No.	Per Cent	Total No.
15-19	114	20.25	83	14.74	22	3.91	5	.89	0	0	563
20-24	171	19.77	138	15.95	48	5.55	16	1.85	0	0	865
25-29	192	20.51	167	17.84	47	5.02	35	3.74	2	.21	936
30-34	102	17.43	84	14.36	26	4.44	24	4.10	0	0	585
35-39	90	22.33	44	10.92	10	2.48	15	3.72	0	0	403
40-44	54	18.75	32	11.11	5	1.74	14	4.86	1	.35	288
45-49	24	13.41	15	8.38	12	6.70	5	2.79	1	.56	179
50-54	19	12.26	12	7.74	8	5.16	6	3.87	2	1.29	155
55-59	5	6.76	6	8.11	3	4.05	4	5.40	1	1.35	74
60-64	7	10.77	4	6.15	5	7.69	5	7.69	0	0	65
65-69	8	16.67	4	8.33	1	2.08	1	2.08	0	0	48
Total	786	18.89	589	14.16	187	4.49	130	3.12	7	.17	4161

Table II-39. Summary of Differences on basis of State Composition of
Sociological Observations

First Degree Murder

	Significant and Independent of State Sampling		Crude Differences Invalidated by State Sampling		Insignificant Differences	
	Diff.	x p.e.	Diff.	x p.e.	Diff.	x p.e.
Previous convictions						
Yes	-10.89	5.92	-	-	-	-
No	10.89	5.92	-	-	-	-
Marital state						
Single	-12.68*	6.85*	-	-	-	-
Married	5.70*	3.10*	-	-	-	-
Divorced,separated	-	-	-	-	2.12	2.86
Widower	4.74	8.32	-	-	-	-
Occupation						
Extractive	10.24*	5.91*	-	-	-	-
Laborer	-	-	- 5.50	3.96	(- 1.42	1.02)*
Factory	-	-	- 7.17	5.05	(- 4.20	2.96)*
Transportation	-	-	-	-	0.28	0.29
Skilled trades	-	-	-	-	- 1.17	1.09
Trade	-	-	-	-	- 0.27	0.32
Public service	-	-	-	-	- 0.33	1.10
Semi-professional	-	-	-	-	- 1.35	2.81
Professional	-	-	-	-	- 0.02	0.06
Personal service	-	-	-	-	- 2.16	2.30
Clerical	-	-	-	-	- 1.85	2.98
Education						
Illiterate	-	-	6.07	5.42	(2.76	2.46)*
Read, write	3.50*	4.73*	-	-	-	-
1st-5th grade	-	-	7.23	4.52	(4.40	2.75)*
6th grade	-	-	-	-	2.02	1.91
7th grade	-	-	- 4.91	4.34	(- 3.33	2.95)*
8th grade	-	-	-	-	- 2.81	1.94
1st-2nd high	- 4.55*	3.53*	-	-	-	-
3rd-4th high	-	-	- 2.50	3.29	(- 1.04	1.37)*
College	- 1.95*	3.05*	-	-	-	-

*Independent difference corrected for state sampling.

Table II-40. Summary of Differences on basis of State Composition of
Sociological Observations

Second Degree Murder

	Significant and Independent of State Sampling		Crude Differences Invalidated by State Sampling		Insignificant Differences	
	Diff.	x p.e.	Diff.	x p.e.	Diff.	x p.e.
Previous convictions						
Yes	-12.12	8.85				
No	12.12	8.85				
Marital state						
Single	- 9.65*	7.72*	-	-	-	-
Married	9.73*	7.85*	-	-	-	-
Divorced,separated	-	-	-	-	- 1.46	2.86
Widower	-	-	-	-	0.55	1.45
Occupation						
Extractive	15.39*	13.15*	-	-	-	-
Laborer	-	-	-	-	0.00	0.00
Factory	- 5.99*	6.24*	-	-	-	-
Transportation	-	-	-	-	- 1.57	2.38
Skilled trades	- 3.40*	4.72*	-	-	-	-
Trade	-	-	-	-	- 0.63	1.12
Public service	-	-	-	-	0.49	2.45
Semi-professional	-	-	- 1.35	4.22	(- 0.85	2.66)*
Professional	-	-	-	-	- 0.19	0.86
Personal service	- 1.97*	3.13*	-	-	-	-
Clerical	- 1.26*	3.00*	-	-	-	-
Education						
Illiterate	6.00*	7.90*	-	-	-	-
Read, write	-	-	-	-	1.13	2.22
1st-5th grade	4.51*	4.14*	-	-	-	-
6th grade	-	-	-	-	- 0.28	0.39
7th grade	-	-	- 2.83	3.68	(- 1.66	2.16)*
8th grade	- 4.25*	4.34*	-	-	-	-
1st-2nd high	- 3.13*	3.56*	-	-	-	-
3rd-4th high	- 2.13*	4.10*	-	-	-	-
College	-	-	- 1.35	3.07	(- 0.59	1.34)*

*Independent difference corrected for state sampling.

Table II-41. Summary of Differences on basis of State Composition of
Sociological Observations

Assault

	Significant and Independent of State Sampling		Crude Differences Invalidated by State Sampling		Insignificant Differences	
	Diff.	x p.e.	Diff.	x p.e.	Diff.	x p.e.
Previous convictions						
Yes	-	-	-	-	3.96	0.98
No	-	-	-	-	- 3.96	0.98
Marital state						
Single	-13.63	3.65	-	-	-	-
Married	12.74	3.43	-	-	-	-
Divorced,separated	-	-	-	-	2.02	1.35
Widower	-	-	-	-	- 1.13	2.31
Occupation						
Extractive	-	-	-	-	- 9.83	2.79
Laborer	-	-	-	-	3.79	1.34
Factory	-	-	-	-	- 4.58	1.60
Transportation	-	-	-	-	2.95	1.50
Skilled trades	10.14	4.67	-	-	-	-
Trade	-	-	-	-	- 1.37	0.81
Public service	-	-	-	-	- 0.66	1.08
Semi-professional	-	-	-	-	0.88	0.91
Professional	-	-	-	-	- 0.68	1.08
Personal service	-	-	-	-	0.91	0.48
Clerical	-	-	-	-	- 1.56	1.25
Education						
Illiterate	-	-	-	-	- 0.16	0.07
Read, write	-	-	-	-	- 2.96	1.97
1st-5th grade	-	-	-	-	- 0.24	0.07
6th grade	-	-	-	-	2.23	1.04
7th grade	-	-	-	-	0.82	0.36
8th grade	-	-	-	-	4.71	1.61
1st-2nd high	-	-	-	-	- 2.91	1.12
3rd-4th high	-	-	-	-	- 0.70	0.45
College	-	-	-	-	- 1.88	1.45

*Independent difference corrected for state sampling.

Table II-42   Summary of Differences on basis of State Composition of
Sociological Observations

Robbery

	Significant and Independent of State Sampling		Crude Differences Invalidated by State Sampling		Insignificant Differences	
	Diff.	x p.e.	Diff.	x p.e.	Diff.	x p.e.
Previous convictions						
Yes	-	-	-	-	3.25	2.03
No	-	-	-	-	- 3.25	2.03
Marital state						
Single	9.79*	6.16*	-	-	-	-
Married	- 8.63*	5.46*	-	-	-	-
Divorced, separated	-	-	-	-	0.21	0.33
Widower	-	-	-	-	- 1.39	2.84
Occupation						
Extractive	-16.33*	10.89*	-	-	-	-
Laborer	-	-	-	-	- 3.01	2.49
Factory	10.33*	8.39*	-	-	-	-
Transportation	-	-	-	-	0.81	0.96
Skilled trades	-	-	-	-	2.33	2.50
Trade	-	-	-	-	1.89	2.62
Public service	-	-	-	-	0.10	0.38
Semi-professional	-	-	-	-	0.60	1.43
Professional	-	-	-	-	0.34	1.26
Personal service	-	-	-	-	2.10	2.59
Clerical	-	-	1.98	3.74	(1.58	2.98)*
Education						
Illiterate	- 4.67*	4.92*	-	-	-	-
Read, write	- 2.11*	3.35*	-	-	-	-
1st-5th grade	- 6.36*	4.61*	-	-	-	-
6th grade	-	-	-	-	- 1.72	1.91
7th grade	-	-	2.95	3.07	(2.80	2.92)*
8th grade	5.40*	4.36*	-	-	-	-
1st-2nd high	4.82*	4.38*	-	-	-	-
3rd-4th high	2.35*	3.62*	-	-	-	-
College	-	-	-	-	- 0.03	0.05

*Independent difference corrected for state sampling

Table II-43. Summary of Differences on basis of State Composition of
Sociological Observations

Burglary and Larceny

	Significant and Independent of State Sampling		Crude Differences Invalidated by State Sampling		Insignificant Difference	
	Diff.	x p.e.	Diff.	x p.e.	Diff.	x p.e.
Previous convictions						
Yes	9.04*	12.56*				
No	- 9.04*	12.56*				
Marital state						
Single	12.77*	19.35*	-	-	-	-
Married	-11.22*	17.00*	-	-	-	-
Divorced,separated	-	-	-	-	- 0.46	1.70
Widower	- 1.06	5.30	-	-	-	-
Occupation						
Extractive	- 6.61*	10.66*	-	-	-	-
Laborer	3.06*	6.12*	-	-	-	-
Factory	3.05*	5.98*	-	-	-	-
Transportation	-	-	-	-	-	-
Skilled trades	-	-	-	-	0.23	0.68
Trade	- 1.36	4.53	-	-	0.66	1.74
Public service	-	-	-	-	-	-
Semi-professional	0.84*	5.25*	-	.	- 0.22	1.83
Professional	- 0.48*	4.00*	-	-	-	-
Personal service	1.33	3.91	-	-	-	-
Clerical	-	-	-	-	- 0.56	2.54
Education						
Illiterate	- 1.64*	4.10*	-	-	-	-
Read, write	- 1.03*	3.82*	-	-	-	-
1st-5th grade	-	-	-	-	- 0.21	0.37
6th grade	-	-	-	-	0.30	0.79
7th grade	1.26*	3.15*	-	-	-	-
8th grade	-	-	-	-	0.11	0.21
1st-2nd high	1.80*	3.91*	-	-	-	-
3rd-4th high	-	-	-	-	0.56	2.07
College	- 0.88	3.67	-	-	-	-

*Independent difference corrected for state sampling.

Table II-44. Summary of Differences on basis of State Composition of Sociological Observations

Forgery and Fraud

	Significant and Independent of State Sampling		Crude Differences Invalidated by State Sampling		Insignificant Differences	
	Diff.	x p.e.	Diff.	x p.e.	Diff.	x p.e.
Previous convictions						
Yes	-	-	-	-	2.62	1.77
No	-	-	-	-	- 2.62	1.77
Marital state						
Single	-	-	-	-	- 1.01	0.68
Married	-	-	-	-	1.78	1.21
Divorced,separated	-	-	-	-	0.21	0.36
Widower	-	-	-	-	- 1.08	2.40
Occupation						
Extractive	- 5.95*	4.31*	-	-	-	-
Laborer	- 3.65*	3.28*	-	-	- 1.93	1.71
Factory	-	-	-	-	0.97	1.26
Transportation	-	-	-	-	1.15	1.35
Skilled trades	-	-	-	-	-	-
Trade	3.71	5.62	-	-	- 0.01	0.04
Public service	-	-	-	-	0.28	0.74
Semi-professional	-	-	-	-	-	-
Professional	0.96*	4.00*	-	-	1.06	1.43
Personal service	-	-	-	-	-	-
Clerical	5.85*	11.94*	-	-	-	-
Education						
Illiterate	- 3.74*	4.20*	-	-	-	
Read, write	-	-	-	-	- 0.11	0.19
1st-5th grade	- 9.73*	7.60*	-	-	-	-
6th grade	-	-	-	-	- 1.91	2.27
7th grade	-	-	-	-	- 0.09	0.10
8th grade	-	-	-	-	1.86	1.60
1st-2nd high	4.97*	4.82*	-	-	-	-
3rd-4th high	1.97*	3.23*	-	-	-	-
College	8.44*	16.55*	-	-	-	-

*Independent difference corrected for state sampling.

Table II-45. Summary of Differences on basis of State Composition of
Sociological Observations

Rape

	Significant and Independent of State Sampling		Crude Differences Invalidated by State Sampling		Insignificant Differences	
	Diff.	x p.e.	Diff.	x p.e.	Diff.	x p.e.
Previous convictions						
Yes	- 7.23	3.06	-	-	-	-
No	7.23	3.06	-	-	-	-
Marital state						
Single	-15.47	6.58	-	-	-	-
Married	7.79	3.33	-	-	-	-
Divorced,separated	-	-	3.93	4.18	(1.91	2.03)*
Widower	3.33*	3.14*	-	-	-	-
Occupation						
Extractive	-	-	-	-	5.16	2.34
Laborer	-	-	-	-	- 0.66	0.37
Factory	-	-	-	-	- 3.93	2.20
Transportation	-	-	-	-	2.53	2.06
Skilled trades	-	-	-	-	1.79	1.32
Trade	-	-	-	-	- 2.11	2.01
Public service	-	-	-	-	0.89	2.34
Semi-professional	-	-	-	-	- 0.13	0.21
Professional	-	-	-	-	- 0.68	1.74
Personal service	-	-	-	-	- 1.08	0.91
Clerical	-	-	-	-	- 1.80	2.28
Education						
Illiterate	-	-	-	-	1.06	0.75
Read, write	-	-	-	-	0.89	0.95
1st-5th grade	-	-	-	-	4.86	2.38
6th grade	-	-	-	-	1.18	0.87
7th grade	-	-	-	-	- 1.25	0.87
8th grade	-	-	-	-	3.92	2.12
1st-2nd high	- 7.02	4.28	-	-	-	-
3rd-4th high	-	-	-	-	- 0.37	0.38
College	- 3.13	3.82	-	-	-	-

*Independent difference corrected for state sampling.

Table II-46. Summary of Differences on basis of State Composition of
Sociological Observations

Other Sex Offenses

	Significant and Independent of State Sampling		Crude Differences Invalidated by State Sampling		Insignificant Differences	
	Diff.	x p.e.	Diff.	x p.e.	Diff.	x p.e.
Previous convictions						
Yes	- 9.56	3.16				
No	9.56	3.16				
Marital state						
Single	-19.96	7.39	-	-	-	-
Married	15.24	5.66	-	-	-	-
Divorced,separated	-	-	-	-	1.77	1.62
Widower	2.54*	3.10*	-	-	-	-
Occupation						
Extractive	-	-	-	-	- 1.23	0.49
Laborer	-	-	-	-	2.20	1.08
Factory	-	-	-	-	- 1.86	0.90
Transportation	-	-	-	-	- 3.26	2.30
Skilled trades	-	-	-	-	- 1.66	1.06
Trade	-	-	-	-	2.21	1.83
Public service	-	-	-	-	0.69	1.57
Semi-professional	-	-	-	-	- 1.00	1.43
Professional	2.70	6.14	-	-	-	-
Personal service	-	-	-	-	- 0.02	0.02
Clerical	-	-	-	-	1.21	1.34
Education						
Illiterate	-	-	-	-	4.60	2.80
Read, write	-	-	-	-	2.50	2.29
1st-5th grade	-	-	-	-	- 2.48	1.03
6th grade	-	-	-	-	- 3.65	2.36
7th grade	-	-	-	-	0.31	0.19
8th grade	-	-	-	-	0.42	0.20
1st-2nd high	-	-	-	-	- 4.09	2.16
3rd-4th high	-	-	-	-	0.25	0.22
College	-	-	-	-	2.24	2.38

*Independent difference corrected for state sampling.

Table II-47. Summary of Differences on basis of State Composition of
Sociological Observations

Versus Public Welfare

	Significant and Independent of State Sampling		Crude Differences Invalidated by State Sampling		Insignificant Difference	
	Diff.	x p.e.	Diff.	x p.e.	Diff.	x p.e.
Previous convictions						
Yes	- 7.09*	3.49*	-	-	-	-
No	7.09*	3.49*	-	-	-	-
Marital state						
Single	-19.86*	9.64*	-	-	-	-
Married	19.63*	9.58*	-	-	-	-
Divorced,separated	-	-	-	-	- 1.44	1.74
Widower	-	-	-	-	0.41	0.65
Occupation						
Extractive	17.97	9.36	-	-	-	-
Laborer	-	-	- 7.20	1.68	(- 2.46	1.60)*
Factory	-	-	-	-	- 2.72	1.74
Transportation	-	-	-	-	- 2.15	2.01
Skilled trades	-	-	-	-	- 1.95	1.64
Trade	-	-	-	-	1.92	2.09
Public service	-	-	-	-	- 0.26	0.76
Semi-professional	-	-	-	-	- 1.28	2.42
Professional	-	-	-	-	- 0.28	0.82
Personal service	-	-	-	-	- 2.42	2.35
Clerical	-	-	-	-	- 1.65	2.39
Education						
Illiterate	-	-	-	-	- 3.10	2.52
Read, write	-	-	3.63	4.43	(2.14	2.61)*
1st-5th grade	-	-	-	-	3.00	1.68
6th grade	-	-	-	-	1.96	1.68
7th grade	-	-	-	-	0.94	0.75
8th grade	-	-	-	-	- 1.39	0.87
1st-2nd high	-	-	-	-	- 2.79	1.95
3rd-4th high	-	-	-	-	- 0.14	0.17
College	-	-	-	-	- 1.95	2.71

*Independent difference corrected for state sampling.

Table II-48. Summary of Differences on basis of State Composition of
Sociological Observations

Arson and All Other Offenses

	Significant and Independent of State Sampling		Crude Differences Invalidated by State Sampling		Insignificant Difference	
	Diff.	x p.e.	Diff.	x p.e.	Diff.	x p.e.
Previous convictions						
Yes	-	-	-	-	2.18	0.64
No	-	-	-	-	- 2.18	0.64
Marital state						
Single	-17.94	5.42	-	-	-	-
Married	20.59	6.24	-	-	-	-
Divorced,separated	-	-	-	-	- 0.27	0.20
Widower	-	-	-	-	- 2.38	2.36
Occupation						
Extractive	-	-	-	-	4.37	1.41
Laborer	-	-	-	-	- 2.72	1.10
Factory	-	-	-	-	- 3.40	1.35
Transportation	-	-	-	-	0.69	0.40
Skilled trades	-	-	-	-	- 0.09	0.05
Trade	-	-	-	-	- 1.22	0.82
Public service	-	-	-	-	- 0.66	1.22
Semi-professional	-	-	-	-	- 0.68	0.79
Professional	-	-	-	-	1.32	2.40
Personal service	-	-	-	-	4.22	2.53
Clerical	-	-	-	-	- 1.84	1.66
Education						
Illiterate	-	-	-	-	- 0.26	0.13
Read,write	-	-	-	-	- 0.25	0.19
1st-5th grade	-	-	-	-	1.49	0.52
6th grade	-	-	-	-	2.86	1.50
7th grade	-	-	-	-	- 4.49	2.22
8th grade	-	-	-	-	3.73	1.44
1st-2nd high	-	-	-	-	- 1.29	0.56
3rd-4th high	-	-	-	-	- 1.48	1.08
College	-	-	-	-	- 2.14	1.86

*Independent difference corrected for state sampling.

Table II-49   Number of Significant and Insignificant Sociological
                         Differences on basis of State Composition
                                       by Offenses

	Total Number of Observations	Significant Differences Independent of State Sampling		Crude Differences Invalidated by State Sampling		Insignificant Differences	
		No.	Per Cent	No.	Per Cent	No.	Per Cent
First degree murder	26	9	34.62	6	23.08	11	42.31
Second degree murder	26	14	53.85	3	11.54	9	34.62
Assault	26	3	11.54	0	0	23	88.46
Robbery	26	10	38.46	2	7.69	14	53.85
Burglary and larceny	26	17	65.38	0	0	9	34.62
Forgery and fraud	26	10	38.46	0	0	16	61.54
Rape	26	7	26.92	1	3.85	18	69.23
Other sex	26	6	23.08	0	0	20	76.92
Vs. public welfare	26	5	19.23	2	7.69	19	73.08
Arson and all other	26	2	7.69	0	0	24	92.31

Table II-50. Differentiation of Offense Groups in Total Sociological Characters

	Significantly Differentiated No.	Undifferentiated No.	Total
First degree murder	4	0	4
Second degree murder	4	0	4
Assault	2	2	4
Robbery	3	1	4
Burglary and larceny	4	0	4
Forgery and fraud	2	2	4
Rape	3	1	4
Other sex offenses	3	1	4
Versus public welfare	3	1	4
Arson and all other offenses	1	3	4
Totals No.	29	11	40
Per Cent	72.50	27.50	

Table III-1.   Age by States

	No.	Range	Mean	S. D.	V.
Massachusetts	336	15-64	27.50 ± .38	10.20 ± .26	37.09 ± .97
Tennessee	423	15-69	29.80 ± .39	11.90 ± .28	39.93 ± .93
Kentucky	1185	15-69	29.65 ± .21	10.60 ± .15	35.75 ± .50
Texas	914	15-79	33.45 ± .25	11.15 ± .18	33.33 ± .53
North Carolina	445	15-79	28.40 ± .36	11.40 ± .26	40.14 ± .91
Wisconsin	296	15-69	34.95 ± .44	11.30 ± .31	32.33 ± .90
Southwest	589	15-74	30.60 ± .34	12.20 ± .24	39.87 ± .78
Total	4188	15-79	30.70 ± .12	11.40 ± .08	37.13 ± .27

Table III-2.   Weight by States

	No.	Range	Mean	S. D.	V.
Massachusetts	338	101-240	145.90 ± .72	19.50 ± .51	13.36 ± .35
Tennessee	420	91-230	150.60 ± .62	19.00 ± .44	12.62 ± .29
Kentucky	1131	101-270	149.80 ± .41	20.50 ± .29	13.68 ± .19
Texas	890	91-250	154.50 ± .45	20.10 ± .32	13.01 ± .21
North Carolina	446	101-240	152.70 ± .61	19.20 ± .43	12.57 ± .28
Wisconsin	296	101-220	147.30 ± .83	21.10 ± .58	14.32 ± .40
Southwest	398	91-230	150.80 ± .69	20.40 ± .49	13.53 ± .32
Total	3919	91-270	150.90 ± .22	20.20 ± .15	13.39 ± .10

Table III-4.   Height by States

	No.	Range	Mean	S. D.	V.
Massachusetts	337	155-187	169.77 ± .22	5.97 ± .16	3.52 ± .09
Tennessee	422	155-190	172.35 ± .19	5.76 ± .13	3.34 ± .08
Kentucky	1186	149-190	172.29 ± .12	6.06 ± .08	3.52 ± .05
Texas	911	149-190	173.13 ± .14	6.12 ± .10	3.54 ± .06
North Carolina	447	149-196	172.38 ± .21	6.51 ± .15	3.78 ± .08
Wisconsin	297	149-190	169.47 ± .31	7.83 ± .22	4.62 ± .13
Southwest	602	137-196	170.94 ± .19	6.87 ± .13	4.02 ± .08
Total	4202	137-196	171.90 ± .07	6.45 ± .05	3.75 ± .03

Table III-5.   Biacromial Diameter by States

	No.	Range	Mean	S. D.	V.
Massachusetts	337	31-45	37.88 ± .09	2.34 ± .06	6.18 ± .16
Tennessee	422	31-45	38.18 ± .07	2.07 ± .05	5.42 ± .13
Kentucky	1185	31-45	37.91 ± .04	2.19 ± .03	5.78 ± .08
Texas	908	31-45	38.33 ± .05	2.13 ± .03	5.56 ± .09
North Carolina	446	28-48	38.09 ± .08	2.43 ± .05	6.38 ± .14
Wisconsin	296	28-45	38.36 ± .09	2.31 ± .06	6.02 ± .17
Southwest	602	28-45	38.30 ± .06	2.37 ± .05	6.19 ± .12
Total	4196	28-48	38.12 ± .02	2.25 ± .02	5.90 ± .04

Table III-6.   Chest Depth by States

	No.	Range	Mean	S. D.	V.
Massachusetts	333	16-27	21.14 ± .05	1.46 ± .04	6.91 ± .18
Tennessee	420	18-27	21.08 ± .05	1.60 ± .04	7.59 ± .18
Kentucky	1176	16-27	21.24 ± .03	1.62 ± .02	7.63 ± .11
Texas	909	16-29	21.30 ± .04	1.66 ± .03	7.79 ± .12
North Carolina	448	16-29	20.22 ± .06	1.84 ± .04	9.10 ± .20
Wisconsin	296	16-27	20.72 ± .07	1.84 ± .05	8.88 ± .25
Southwest	603	16-27	20.94 ± .05	1.86 ± .04	8.88 ± .17
Total	4185	16-29	21.04 ± .02	1.74 ± .01	8.27 ± .06

Table III-7.   Chest Breadth by States

	No.	Range	Mean	S. D.	V.
Massachusetts	332	20-34	26.67 ± .07	1.92 ± .05	7.20 ± .19
Tennessee	421	23-34	27.69 ± .06	1.71 ± .04	6.18 ± .14
Kentucky	1175	20-40	27.63 ± .04	1.92 ± .03	6.95 ± .10
Texas	907	20-37	27.60 ± .04	1.83 ± .03	6.63 ± .10
North Carolina	448	20-34	27.42 ± .06	1.89 ± .04	6.89 ± .16
Wisconsin	296	23-34	27.36 ± .08	2.10 ± .06	7.68 ± .21
Southwest	603	20-34	27.48 ± .05	1.86 ± .04	6.77 ± .13
Total	4182	20-40	27.48 ± .02	1.89 ± .01	6.88 ± .05

Table III-8.   Sitting Height by States

	No.	Range	Mean	S. D.	V.
Massachusetts	337	81- 98	89.05 ± .13	3.42 ± .09	3.84 ± .10
Tennessee	414	78-101	89.62 ± .11	3.30 ± .08	3.68 ± .09
Kentucky	1181	78-104	90.01 ± .06	3.33 ± .05	3.70 ± .05
Texas	896	81-101	90.91 ± .08	3.42 ± .05	3.76 ± .06
North Carolina	448	81-101	90.97 ± .10	3.30 ± .07	3.63 ± .08
Wisconsin	297	81-104	90.70 ± .14	3.54 ± .10	3.90 ± .11
Southwest	604	72-101	90.28 ± .10	3.63 ± .07	4.02 ± .08
Total	4177	72-104	90.28 ± .04	3.45 ± .02	3.82 ± .03

Table III-9.   Head Length by States

	No.	Range	Mean	S. D.	V.
Massachusetts	338	176-211	192.43 ± .24	6.60 ± .17	3.43 ± .09
Tennessee	423	170-211	192.00 ± .22	6.69 ± .16	3.48 ± .08
Kentucky	1187	173-217	194.67 ± .13	6.42 ± .09	3.30 ± .05
Texas	913	173-220	193.02 ± .14	6.51 ± .10	3.37 ± .05
North Carolina	447	176-214	194.70 ± .20	6.33 ± .14	3.25 ± .07
Wisconsin	297	176-214	194.22 ± .24	6.21 ± .17	3.20 ± .09
Southwest	604	167-223	194.61 ± .18	6.51 ± .13	3.34 ± .06
Total	4209	167-223	193.89 ± .07	6.48 ± .05	3.34 ± .02

Table III-10.   Head Breadth by States

	No.	Range	Mean	S. D.	V.
Massachusetts	338	129-170	151.78 ± .21	5.79 ± .15	3.82 ± .10
Tennessee	422	135-167	152.32 ± .17	5.31 ± .12	3.49 ± .08
Kentucky	1187	135-173	151.63 ± .10	5.25 ± .07	3.46 ± .05
Texas	914	138-170	152.47 ± .12	5.22 ± .08	3.42 ± .05
North Carolina	447	129-170	151.60 ± .18	5.52 ± .12	3.64 ± .08
Wisconsin	297	129-170	153.76 ± .21	5.43 ± .15	3.53 ± .10
Southwest	603	135-170	152.38 ± .15	5.31 ± .10	3.48 ± .07
Total	4208	129-173	152.14 ± .06	5.40 ± .04	3.55 ± .03

Table III-11.   Head Height (Observer A) by States

	No	Range	Mean	S. D.	V.
Massachusetts	336	113-148	133.38 ± .20	5.43 ± .14	4.07 ± .11
Tennessee	423	116-151	133.38 ± .18	5.55 ± .13	4.16 ± .10
Kentucky	1185	110-148	131.88 ± .11	5.64 ± .08	4.28 ± .06
Texas	913	119-154	133.11 ± .12	5.43 ± .09	4.08 ± .06
Total-Observer A	2857	110-154	132.66 ± .07	5.52 ± .05	4.16 ± .04

Table III-12.   Head Height (Observer B) by States

	No.	Range	Mean	S. D.	V.
North Carolina	448	101-136	118.68 ± .20	6.12 ± .14	5.16 ± .12
Wisconsin	297	104-139	123.06 ± .23	5.88 ± .16	4.78 ± .13
Southwest	602	104-148	122.31 ± .15	5.37 ± .10	4.39 ± .08
Total-Observer B	1347	101-148	121.26 ± .11	6.03 ± .08	4.97 ± .06

Table III-13.   Head Circumference by States

	No.	Range	Mean	S. D.	V.
Massachusetts	337	514-621	561.50 ± .62	16.80 ± .44	2.99 ± .08
Tennessee	188	526-621	568.46 ± .73	14.76 ± .52	2.60 ± .09
Kentucky	1187	514-621	566.90 ± .32	15.84 ± .22	2.79 ± .04
Texas	915	514-621	568.22 ± .33	15.00 ± .24	2.64 ± .04
North Carolina	448	502-609	557.30 ± .48	15.12 ± .34	2.71 ± .06
Wisconsin	213	514-609	559.10 ± .68	14.76 ± .48	2.64 ± .09
Southwest	602	502-609	557.90 ± .41	14.76 ± .29	2.65 ± .05
Total	3890	502-621	563.90 ± .17	16.08 ± .12	2.85 ± .02

Table III-14. Minimum Frontal Diameter by States

	No.	Range	Mean	S. D.	V.
Massachusetts	337	97-128	110.42 ± .17	4.68 ± .12	4.24 ± .11
Tennessee	423	101-128	113.06 ± .15	4.48 ± .10	3.96 ± .09
Kentucky	1186	93-124	109.30 ± .09	4.48 ± .06	4.10 ± .06
Texas	914	97-128	113.14 ± .10	4.40 ± .07	3.89 ± .06
North Carolina	448	101-128	112.74 ± .15	4.84 ± .11	4.29 ± .10
Wisconsin	297	97-128	111.90 ± .20	5.12 ± .14	4.58 ± .13
Southwest	603	97-128	112.22 ± .13	4.64 ± .09	4.14 ± .08
Total	4208	93-128	111.58 ± .05	4.88 ± .04	4.37 ± .03

Table III-15. Bizygomatic Diameter by States

	No.	Range	Mean	S. D.	V.
Massachusetts	338	120-154	137.30 ± .20	5.55 ± .14	4.04 ± .10
Tennessee	423	120-159	138.85 ± .17	5.20 ± .12	3.74 ± .09
Kentucky	1187	120-159	138.00 ± .11	5.30 ± .07	3.84 ± .05
Texas	915	115-159	139.50 ± .12	5.20 ± .08	3.73 ± .06
North Carolina	448	125-159	138.65 ± .17	5.40 ± .12	3.90 ± .09
Wisconsin	297	125-159	139.55 ± .21	5.35 ± .15	3.83 ± .11
Southwest	603	115-159	138.55 ± .14	5.15 ± .10	3.72 ± .07
Total	4211	115-159	138.60 ± .06	5.35 ± .04	3.86 ± .03

Table III-16. Total Face Height by States

	No.	Range	Mean	S. D.	V.
Massachusetts	338	100-144	122.90 ± .24	6.60 ± .17	5.37 ± .14
Tennessee	423	105-144	121.80 ± .21	6.45 ± .15	5.30 ± .12
Kentucky	1186	100-154	121.50 ± .13	6.65 ± .09	5.47 ± .08
Texas	914	100-149	121.10 ± .14	6.25 ± .10	5.16 ± .08
North Carolina	448	100-139	120.70 ± .20	6.35 ± .14	5.26 ± .12
Wisconsin	297	105-149	122.20 ± .27	6.90 ± .19	5.65 ± .16
Southwest	603	100-144	122.30 ± .18	6.40 ± .12	5.23 ± .10
Total	4209	100-154	121.60 ± .07	6.50 ± .05	5.34 ± .04

Table III-17. Upper Face Height by States

	No.	Range	Mean	S. D.	V.
Massachusetts	337	50-84	68.80 ± .17	4.55 ± .12	6.61 ± .17
Tennessee	423	50-84	68.65 ± .14	4.40 ± .10	6.41 ± .15
Kentucky	1185	50-84	69.00 ± .08	4.35 ± .06	6.30 ± .09
Texas	915	55-94	68.40 ± .10	4.40 ± .07	6.43 ± .10
North Carolina	448	55-94	70.20 ± .14	4.50 ± .10	6.41 ± .14
Wisconsin	297	55-94	70.70 ± .20	5.10 ± .14	7.21 ± .20
Southwest	604	55-84	71.25 ± .12	4.40 ± .08	6.18 ± .12
Total	4209	50-94	69.40 ± .05	4.55 ± .03	6.56 ± .05

Table III-18.   Nose Height by States

	No.	Range	Mean	S. D.	V.
Massachusetts	338	36-67	51.90 ± .16	4.28 ± .11	8.25 ± .21
Tennessee	423	44-63	51.98 ± .12	3.72 ± .09	7.16 ± .17
Kentucky	1185	40-67	51.82 ± .08	3.88 ± .05	7.49 ± .10
Texas	910	40-71	52.38 ± .08	3.52 ± .06	6.72 ± .11
North Carolina	448	36-63	50.98 ± .12	3.92 ± .09	7.69 ± .17
Wisconsin	297	40-71	53.78 ± .17	4.28 ± .12	7.96 ± .22
Southwest	602	40-63	53.50 ± .10	3.72 ± .07	6.95 ± .14
Total	4203	36-71	52.26 ± .04	3.92 ± .03	7.50 ± .06

Table III-19.   Nose Breadth by States

	No.	Range	Mean	S. D.	V.
Massachusetts	336	28-48	34.01 ± .10	2.79 ± .07	8.20 ± .21
Tennessee	422	22-48	35.30 ± .09	2.79 ± .06	7.90 ± .18
Kentucky	1183	25-45	34.40 ± .05	2.61 ± .04	7.59 ± .11
Texas	912	28-48	35.45 ± .06	2.67 ± .04	7.53 ± .12
North Carolina	448	25-45	33.92 ± .09	2.79 ± .06	8.22 ± .18
Wisconsin	297	25-45	34.79 ± .11	2.88 ± .08	8.28 ± .23
Southwest	603	25-48	35.18 ± .08	3.00 ± .06	8.53 ± .17
Total	4201	22-48	34.76 ± .03	2.79 ± .02	8.03 ± .06

Table III-20.   Bigonial Diameter by States

	No.	Range	Mean	S. D.	V.
Massachusetts	337	90-125	106.06 ± .20	5.40 ± .14	5.09 ± .13
Tennessee	423	90-125	108.30 ± .19	5.68 ± .13	5.24 ± .12
Kentucky	1185	86-129	107.78 ± .11	5.52 ± .08	5.12 ± .07
Texas	914	86-129	109.18 ± .13	5.68 ± .09	5.20 ± .08
North Carolina	447	90-125	106.42 ± .17	5.32 ± .12	5.00 ± .11
Wisconsin	296	90-121	107.78 ± .23	5.80 ± .16	5.38 ± .15
Southwest	604	90-125	107.30 ± .16	5.72 ± .11	5.33 ± .10
Total	4206	86-129	107.78 ± .06	5.68 ± .04	5.27 ± .04

Table III-22.   Ear Length (Observer A) by States

	No.	Range	Mean	S. D.	V.
Massachusetts	336	44-79	61.22 ± .17	4.64 ± .12	7.58 ± .20
Tennessee	423	48-79	61.82 ± .15	4.60 ± .11	7.44 ± .17
Kentucky	1186	44-79	60.34 ± .09	4.72 ± .06	7.82 ± .11
Texas	909	48-79	63.50 ± .15	6.76 ± .11	10.65 ± .17
Total	2854	44-79	61.66 ± .06	4.84 ± .04	7.85 ± .07

Table III-23.   Ear Length (Observer B) by States

	No.	Range	Mean	S. D.	V.
North Carolina	448	44-75	58.38 ± .13	4.00 ± .09	6.85 ± .15
Wisconsin	297	44-75	58.98 ± .18	4.72 ± .13	8.00 ± .22
Southwest	604	40-75	57.86 ± .13	4.68 ± .09	8.09 ± .16
Total	1349	40-75	58.30 ± .08	4.48 ± .06	7.68 ± .10

Table III-24.   Ear Breadth (Observer A) by States

	No.	Range	Mean	S. D.	V.
Massachusetts	336	29-46	36.72 ± .10	2.76 ± .07	7.52 ± .20
Tennessee	423	29-49	38.52 ± .11	3.24 ± .08	8.41 ± .20
Kentucky	1186	26-49	37.47 ± .05	2.67 ± .04	7.13 ± .10
Texas	909	29-49	38.22 ± .06	2.52 ± .04	6.59 ± .10
Total	2854	26-49	37.77 ± .04	2.79 ± .02	7.39 ± .07

Table III-25.   Ear Breadth (Observer B) by States

	No.	Range	Mean	S. D.	V.
North Carolina	448	29-46	35.34 ± .08	2.64 ± .06	7.47 ± .17
Wisconsin	296	29-46	36.75 ± .12	3.00 ± .08	8.16 ± .23
Southwest	604	29-46	36.27 ± .07	2.67 ± .05	7.36 ± .14
Total	1348	29-46	36.02 ± .05	2.76 ± .04	7.66 ± .10

Table III-26.   Relative Shoulder Breadth by States

	No.	Range	Mean	S. D.	V.
Massachusetts	337	18-29	22.62 ± .06	1.56 ± .04	6.90 ± .18
Tennessee	421	14-27	21.82 ± .05	1.58 ± .04	7.24 ± .17
Kentucky	1184	16-27	22.04 ± .03	1.28 ± .02	5.81 ± .08
Texas	907	18-27	22.10 ± .03	1.22 ± .02	5.52 ± .09
North Carolina	445	16-27	22.02 ± .04	1.38 ± .03	6.27 ± .14
Wisconsin	296	18-27	22.72 ± .05	1.38 ± .04	6.07 ± .17
Southwest	602	16-29	22.42 ± .04	1.32 ± .03	5.89 ± .11
Total	4192	14-29	22.18 ± .01	1.38 ± .01	6.22 ± .05

Table III-27.   Relative Sitting Height by States

	No.	Range	Mean	S. D.	V.
Massachusetts	336	48-59	52.42 ± .05	1.48 ± .04	2.82 ± .07
Tennessee	414	48-59	51.94 ± .05	1.50 ± .04	2.89 ± .07
Kentucky	1181	46-59	52.30 ± .03	1.44 ± .02	2.75 ± .04
Texas	896	48-61	52.50 ± .03	1.38 ± .02	2.63 ± .04
North Carolina	447	42-59	52.74 ± .05	1.56 ± .04	2.96 ± .07
Wisconsin	297	48-61	53.50 ± .07	1.74 ± .05	3.25 ± .09
Southwest	603	42-59	52.78 ± .04	1.64 ± .03	3.11 ± .06
Total	4174	42-61	52.52 ± .02	1.56 ± .01	2.97 ± .02

Table III-28.   Cephalic Index by States

	No.	Range	Mean	S. D.	V.
Massachusetts	337	68-91	79.02 ± .13	3.45 ± .09	4.37 ± .11
Tennessee	422	68-91	79.32 ± .11	3.24 ± .08	4.08 ± .10
Kentucky	1186	68-91	78.01 ± .06	3.09 ± .04	3.96 ± .06
Texas	912	65-91	79.02 ± .07	3.18 ± .05	4.02 ± .06
North Carolina	447	65-91	77.91 ± .11	3.42 ± .08	4.39 ± .10
Wisconsin	297	65-94	79.29 ± .14	3.69 ± .10	4.65 ± .13
Southwest	603	65-91	78.33 ± .09	3.33 ± .06	4.25 ± .08
Total	4204	65-94	78.57 ± .03	3.30 ± .02	4.20 ± .03

Table III-29.   Cephalo-facial Index by States

	No.	Range	Mean	S. D.	V.
Massachusetts	338	79- 99	90.14 ± .11	3.03 ± .08	3.36 ± .09
Tennessee	422	82-102	91.07 ± .10	3.09 ± .07	3.39 ± .08
Kentucky	1187	76-102	91.01 ± .06	3.03 ± .04	3.33 ± .05
Texas	913	70-102	91.37 ± .07	3.30 ± .05	3.61 ± .06
North Carolina	446	82-102	91.46 ± .10	3.09 ± .07	3.39 ± .08
Wisconsin	296	82-102	91.04 ± .12	3.12 ± .09	3.43 ± .10
Southwest	601	82-102	91.13 ± .08	2.91 ± .06	3.19 ± .06
Total	4203	70-102	91.10 ± .03	3.09 ± .02	3.39 ± .03

Table III-30.   Length-Height Index (Observer A) by States

	No.	Range	Mean	S. D.	V.
Massachusetts	336	61-81	69.35 ± .12	3.12 ± .08	4.50 ± .12
Tennessee	423	61-81	69.53 ± .10	3.06 ± .07	4.40 ± .10
Kentucky	1186	55-78	67.76 ± .06	3.12 ± .04	4.60 ± .06
Texas	912	58-81	69.02 ± .07	3.18 ± .05	4.61 ± .07
Total	2857	55-81	68.60 ± .04	3.21 ± .03	4.68 ± .04

Table III-31.   Length-Height Index (Observer B) by States

	No.	Range	Mean	S. D.	V.
North Carolina	447	52-78	61.01 ± .11	3.42 ± .08	5.61 ± .13
Wisconsin	297	52-78	63.47 ± .13	3.30 ± .09	5.20 ± .14
Southwest	601	52-78	62.93 ± .08	3.09 ± .06	4.91 ± .10
Total	1345	52-78	62.42 ± .06	3.39 ± .04	5.43 ± .07

Table III-32.   Breadth-Height Index (Observer A) by States

	No.	Range	Mean	S. D.	V.
Massachusetts	336	76- 99	87.92 ± .14	3.84 ± .10	4.37 ± .11
Tennessee	422	79- 99	87.59 ± .12	3.66 ± .08	4.18 ± .10
Kentucky	1186	76-102	87.02 ± .08	3.87 ± .05	4.45 ± .06
Texas	913	73- 99	87.32 ± .08	3.78 ± .06	4.33 ± .07
Total	2857	73-102	87.32 ± .05	3.84 ± .03	4.40 ± .04

Table III-33.   Breadth-Height Index (Observer B) by States

	No.	Range	Mean	S. D.	V.
North Carolina	447	70-90	78.38 ± .12	3.90 ± .09	4.98 ± .11
Wisconsin	297	64-96	80.30 ± .17	4.26 ± .12	5.30 ± .15
Southwest	601	70-96	80.36 ± .10	3.54 ± .07	4.40 ± .09
Total	1345	64-96	79.70 ± .07	3.90 ± .05	4.89 ± .06

Table III-34.   Facial Index by States

	No.	Range	Mean	S. D.	V.
Massachusetts	338	74-105	89.78 ± .19	5.24 ± .14	5.84 ± .15
Tennessee	423	74-105	87.90 ± .17	5.28 ± .12	6.01 ± .14
Kentucky	1185	74-105	88.06 ± .10	5.32 ± .07	6.04 ± .08
Texas	915	70-105	86.90 ± .11	4.96 ± .08	5.71 ± .09
North Carolina	448	70-105	87.14 ± .16	5.00 ± .11	5.74 ± .13
Wisconsin	297	70-105	87.66 ± .21	5.28 ± .15	6.02 ± .17
Southwest	603	74-109	88.18 ± .14	5.28 ± .10	5.99 ± .12
Total	4209	70-109	87.82 ± .06	5.28 ± .04	6.01 ± .04

Table III-35.   Upper Facial Index by States

	No.	Range	Mean	S. D.	V.
Massachusetts	338	37-63	50.36 ± .13	3.42 ± .09	6.79 ± .18
Tennessee	423	40-60	49.58 ± .11	3.42 ± .08	6.90 ± .16
Kentucky	1185	37-66	50.06 ± .07	3.57 ± .05	7.13 ± .10
Texas	915	37-66	49.10 ± .08	3.42 ± .05	6.96 ± .11
North Carolina	448	40-63	50.69 ± .11	3.42 ± .08	6.75 ± .15
Wisconsin	297	37-63	50.75 ± .14	3.66 ± .10	7.21 ± .20
Southwest	60?	40-66	51.35 ± .09	3.39 ± .07	6.60 ± .13
Total	4209	37-66	50.12 ± .04	3.54 ± .03	7.06 ± .05

Table III-36.   Nasal Index by States

	No.	Range	Mean	S. D.	V.
Massachusetts	336	44-99	65.46 ± .26	6.92 ± .18	10.57 ± .28
Tennessee	422	44-99	68.22 ± .26	6.88 ± .16	10.08 ± .23
Kentucky	1183	44-95	66.50 ± .13	6.64 ± .09	9.98 ± .14
Texas	910	44-91	67.74 ± .14	6.24 ± .10	9.21 ± .15
North Carolina	448	44-91	66.50 ± .22	7.00 ± .16	10.53 ± .24
Wisconsin	297	44-91	65.02 ± .28	7.28 ± .20	11.20 ± .31
Southwest	602	48-99	65.70 ± .19	6.88 ± .13	10.47 ± .20
Total	4198	44-99	66.62 ± .07	6.80 ± .05	10.21 ± .08

Table III-37.   Ear Index (Observer A) by States

	No.	Range	Mean	S. D.	V.
Massachusetts	336	45-88	60.26 ± .19	5.08 ± .13	8.43 ± .22
Tennessee	423	49-84	61.70 ± .14	4.24 ± .10	6.87 ± .16
Kentucky	1186	45-84	62.06 ± .09	4.72 ± .06	7.61 ± .10
Texas	908	45-80	60.46 ± .10	4.48 ± .07	7.41 ± .12
Total	2853	45-88	61.30 ± .06	4.64 ± .04	7.57 ± .07

Table III-38.   Ear Index (Observer B) by States

	No.	Range	Mean	S. D.	V.
North Carolina	448	45-80	60.58 ± .16	4.88 ± .11	8.06 ± .18
Wisconsin	296	49-80	62.66 ± .20	5.04 ± .14	8.04 ± .22
Southwest	604	49-88	63.06 ± .14	5.12 ± .10	8.12 ± .16
Total	1348	45-88	62.18 ± .09	5.12 ± .07	8.23 ± .11

Table III-39   Zygo-frontal Index by States

	No.	Range	Mean	S. D.	V.
Massachusetts	337	72-99	80.74 ± .12	3.20 ± .08	3.96 ± .10
Tennessee	423	72-91	81.58 ± .10	3.00 ± .07	3.68 ± .08
Kentucky	1186	64-87	79.26 ± .06	3.12 ± .04	3.94 ± .05
Texas	914	68-95	81.10 ± .07	3.00 ± .05	3.70 ± .06
North Carolina	448	72-91	81.26 ± .09	2.96 ± .07	3.64 ± .08
Wisconsin	297	68-95	80.26 ± .13	3.32 ± .09	4.14 ± .11
Southwest	602	72-91	80.98 ± .08	3.04 ± .06	3.75 ± .07
Total	4207	64-99	80.54 ± .03	3.16 ± .02	3.92 ± .03

Table III-40.   Fronto-parietal Index by States

	No.	Range	Mean	S. D.	V.
Massachusetts	337	63-80	72.85 ± .10	2.82 ± .07	3.87 ± .10
Tennessee	422	66-86	74.29 ± .10	3.00 ± .07	4.04 ± .09
Kentucky	1186	60-86	72.22 ± .06	3.03 ± .04	4.20 ± .06
Texas	913	66-86	74.26 ± .07	2.94 ± .05	3.96 ± .06
North Carolina	447	66-86	74.41 ± .10	3.00 ± .07	4.03 ± .09
Wisconsin	297	63-86	72.94 ± .14	3.54 ± .10	4.85 ± .13
Southwest	603	63-83	73.78 ± .08	2.94 ± .06	3.98 ± .08
Total	4205	60-86	73.42 ± .03	3.15 ± .02	4.29 ± .03

Table III-41.   Zygo-gonial Index by States

	No.	Range	Mean	S. D.	V.
Massachusetts	337	66-92	77.53 ± .15	4.02 ± .10	5.18 ± .14
Tennessee	423	69-89	78.04 ± .12	3.57 ± .08	4.58 ± .11
Kentucky	1186	60-89	78.07 ± .07	3.57 ± .05	4.57 ± .06
Texas	915	66-92	78.25 ± .08	3.66 ± .06	4.68 ± .07
North Carolina	447	66-89	76.69 ± .11	3.42 ± .08	4.46 ± .10
Wisconsin	297	66-89	77.14 ± .15	3.78 ± .10	4.90 ± .14
Southwest	604	63-89	77.32 ± .10	3.72 ± .07	4.81 ± .09
Total	4209	60-92	77.74 ± .04	3.69 ± .03	4.75 ± .04

Table III-42.   Differences of Means with Value in Terms of the Probable
Error of State Subgroups and Total Series

	Massachusetts		Tennessee		Kentucky	
	Diff.	x p.e.	Diff.	x p.e.	Diff.	x p.e.
Age	- 3.20	7.62	- 0.90	2.43	- 1.05	4.77
Weight	- 5.00	6.76	- 0.30	-.45	- 1.10	2.75
Height	- 2.13	8.88	0.45	2.14	0.39	3.00
Biacromial diameter	- 0.24	3.00	0.06	0.86	- 0.21	5.25
Chest depth	0.10	1.67	0.04	0.67	0.20	6.67
Chest breadth	- 0.81	11.57	0.21	3.50	0.15	3.75
Sitting height	- 1.23	9.46	- 0.66	6.00	- 0.27	3.86
Head length	- 1.41	5.88	- 1.89	9.00	0.78	6.00
Head breadth	- 0.36	1.80	0.18	1.00	- 0.51	4.64
Head height (Observer A)	0.72	3.60	0.72	4.00	- 0.78	7.09
Head circumference	- 2.40	4.07	4.56	5.77	3.00	9.38
Minimum frontal diameter	- 1.16	6.44	1.48	9.25	- 2.28	22.80
Bizygomatic diameter	- 1.30	6.50	0.25	1.39	- 0.60	6.00
Total face height	1.30	5.42	0.20	0.95	- 0.10	0.77
Upper face height	- 0.60	3.53	- 0.75	5.00	- 0.40	4.44
Nose height	- 0.36	2.57	- 0.28	2.15	- 0.44	5.50
Nose breadth	- 0.75	7.50	0.54	6.00	- 0.36	6.00
Bigonial diameter	- 1.72	8.19	0.52	2.74	0	0
Ear length (Observer A)	- 0.44	2.44	0.16	1.00	- 1.32	13.20
Ear breadth (Observer A)	- 1.05	10.50	0.75	8.33	- 0.30	5.00
Relative shoulder breadth	0.44	8.80	- 0.36	9.00	- 0.14	4.67
Relative sitting height	- 0.10	1.67	- 0.58	11.60	- 0.22	7.33
Cephalic index	0.45	3.75	0.75	6.82	- 0.56	9.33
Cephalo-facial index	- 0.96	8.73	- 0.03	0.30	- 0.09	1.50
Length-height index (Observer A)	0.75	6.25	0.93	9.30	- 0.84	14.00
Breadth-height index (Observer A)	0.60	4.29	0.27	2.08	- 0.30	3.75
Facial index	1.96	10.32	0.08	0.47	0.24	2.40
Upper facial index	0.24	1.85	- 0.54	4.50	- 0.06	0.86
Nasal index	- 1.16	4.64	1.60	7.27	- 0.12	0.92
Ear index (Observer A)	- 1.04	6.12	0.40	2.67	0.76	8.44
Zygo-frontal index	0.20	1.67	1.04	10.40	- 1.28	21.33
Fronto-parietal index	- 0.57	4.75	0.87	8.70	- 1.20	20.00
Zygo-gonial index	- 0.21	1.50	0.30	2.50	0.33	4.71

Table III-42 (cont'd).

	Texas Diff.	x p.e.	North Carolina Diff.	x p.e.	Wisconsin Diff.	x p.e.	Southwest Diff.	x p.e.
Age	2.75	11.00	- 2.30	6.39	4.25	9.44	- 0.10	0.31
Weight	3.60	7.83	1.80	2.81	- 3.60	4.56	- 0.10	0.15
Height	1.23	8.79	0.48	2.29	- 2.43	9.72	- 0.96	5.33
Biacromial diameter	0.21	4.20	- 0.03	0.43	0.24	2.67	0.18	3.00
Chest depth	0.26	6.50	- 0.82	13.67	- 0.32	4.57	- 0.10	2.00
Chest breadth	0.12	3.00	- 0.06	1.00	- 0.12	1.71	0	0
Sitting height	0.63	7.88	0.69	6.27	0.42	3.00	0	0
Head length	- 0.87	6.21	0.81	3.86	0.33	1.32	0.72	4.00
Head breadth	0.33	2.75	- 0.54	3.18	1.62	7.71	0.24	1.60
Head height								
(Observer A)	0.45	3.75						
(Observer B)			- 2.58	13.58	1.80	7.50	1.05	6.18
Head circumference	4.32	12.00	- 6.60	12.94	- 4.80	6.49	- 6.00	13.64
Minimum frontal diameter	1.56	14.18	1.16	7.25	0.32	1.68	0.64	4.92
Bizygomatic diameter	0.90	7.50	0.05	0.29	0.95	4.52	- 0.05	0.33
Total face height	- 0.50	3.57	- 0.90	4.29	0.60	2.40	0.70	3.89
Upper face height	- 1.00	10.00	0.80	5.71	1.30	7.22	1.85	15.42
Nose height	0.12	1.33	- 1.28	10.67	1.52	10.13	1.24	11.27
Nose breadth	0.69	11.50	- 0.84	9.33	0.03	0.27	0.42	5.25
Bigonial diameter	1.40	10.77	- 1.36	7.56	0	0	- 0.48	3.00
Ear length								
(Observer A)	1.84	16.73						
(Observer B)			0.08	0.57	0.68	3.78	- 0.44	3.67
Ear breadth								
(Observer A)	0.45	7.50						
(Observer B)			- 0.68	7.56	0.73	6.64	0.25	3.12
Relative shoulder breadth	- 0.08	2.67	- 0.16	4.00	0.54	10.80	0.24	6.00
Relative sitting height	- 0.02	0.50	0.22	4.40	0.98	16.33	0.26	6.50
Cephalic index	0.45	6.43	- 0.66	6.60	0.72	5.54	- 0.24	2.67
Cephalo-facial index	0.27	3.86	0.36	3.60	- 0.06	0.50	0.03	0.38
Length-height index								
(Observer A)	0.42	6.00						
(Observer B)			- 1.41	12.82	1.05	8.08	0.51	5.67
Breadth-height index								
(Observer A)	0	0						
(Observer B)			- 1.32	11.00	0.60	4.00	0.66	6.00
Facial index	- 0.92	7.67	- 0.68	4.00	- 0.16	0.76	0.36	2.57
Upper facial index	- 1.02	12.75	0.57	5.18	0.63	4.50	1.23	12.30
Nasal index	1.12	7.47	- 0.12	0.54	- 1.60	5.93	- 0.92	4.84
Ear Index								
(Observer A)	- 0.84	8.40						
(Observer B)			- 1.60	10.00	0.48	2.40	0.88	6.29
Zygo-frontal index	0.56	8.00	0.72	7.20	- 0.28	2.33	0.44	4.89
Fronto-parietal index	0.84	12.00	0.99	9.90	- 0.48	4.00	0.36	4.00
Zygo-gonial index	0.51	6.38	- 1.05	8.75	- 0.60	4.29	- 0.42	4.20

Table III-43. Distribution of State Means Differences in Terms of the Probable
Error Compared with Distribution Expected in Random Sample

Measurements

	x - 1 p.e. No.	1 - 2 p.e. No.	2 - 3 p.e. No.	3 - 4 p.e. No.	4 - 5 p.e. No.	5 - 6 p.e. No.	Total No.
Expected in random sample	10.00	6.45	2.69	0.72	0.12	0.01	20
Observed in							
Massachusetts	0	2	2	3	1	12	20
Tennessee	4	3	4	1	1	7	20
Kentucky	2	0	1	3	3	11	20
Texas	0	1	1	3	1	14	20
North Carolina	3	1	2	2	1	11	20
Wisconsin	2	3	2	2	3	8	20
Southwest	5	1	1	5	2	6	20
Total expected	70.00	45.18	18.80	5.04	0.87	0	140
Total observed	16	11	13	19	12	69	140

Indices

	x - 1 p.e. No.	1 - 2 p.e. No.	2 - 3 p.e. No.	3 - 4 p.e. No.	4 - 5 p.e. No.	5 - 6 p.e. No.	Total No.
Expected in random sample	6.50	4.20	1.75	0.47	0.08	0.01	13
Observed in							
Massachusetts	0	4	0	1	3	5	13
Tennessee	2	0	3	0	1	7	13
Kentucky	2	1	1	1	2	6	13
Texas	2	0	1	1	0	9	13
North Carolina	1	0	0	1	3	8	13
Wisconsin	2	0	2	0	4	5	13
Southwest	1	0	2	0	4	6	13
Total expected	45.50	29.37	12.22	3.28	0.06	0	91
Total observed	10	5	9	4	17	46	91

Table IV-2.   Hair Quantity by States

Head

	Small		Medium		Large		
	No.	Per Cent	No.	Per Cent	No.	Per Cent	Total
Massachusetts	27	8.01	286	84.87	24	7.12	337
Tennessee	39	9.24	312	73.93	71	16.82	422
Kentucky	135	11.39	748	63.12	302	25.48	1185
Texas	130	14.21	488	53.33	297	32.46	915
North Carolina	30	6.73	380	85.20	36	8.07	446
Wisconsin	39	13.13	258	86.87	0	0	297
Southwest	43	7.12	511	84.60	50	8.28	604
Total	443	10.53	2983	70.92	780	18.54	4206

Beard

	Small		Medium		Large		
	No.	Per Cent	No.	Per Cent	No.	Per Cent	Total
Massachusetts	46	13.65	228	67.66	63	18.69	337
Tennessee	292	69.19	98	23.22	32	7.58	422
Kentucky	171	14.42	929	78.33	86	7.25	1186
Texas	231	25.27	499	54.60	184	20.13	914
North Carolina	314	70.25	102	22.82	31	6.94	447
Wisconsin	114	38.38	114	38.38	69	23.23	297
Southwest	314	52.25	186	30.95	101	16.80	601
Total	1482	35.25	2156	51.28	566	13.46	4204

Body

	Small		Medium		Large		
	No.	Per Cent	No.	Per Cent	No.	Per Cent	Total
Massachusetts	76	22.69	237	70.75	22	6.57	335
Tennessee	275	65.32	104	24.70	42	9.98	421
Kentucky	385	32.46	600	50.59	201	16.95	1186
Texas	380	41.58	359	39.28	175	19.15	914
North Carolina	354	79.20	75	16.78	18	4.03	447
Wisconsin	162	54.54	96	32.32	39	13.13	297
Southwest	374	64.15	130	22.30	79	13.55	583
Total	2006	47.96	1601	38.27	576	13.77	4183

Table IV-3. Differences between State Subgroups and Total Series with Value
in Terms of the Probable Error

Hair Quantity

Head

	Small Per Cent	x p.e.	Large Per Cent	x p.e.
Massachusetts	- 2.52 ± 1.08	2.33	-11.42 ± 1.37	8.34
Tennessee	- 1.29 ± .96	1.34	- 1.72 ± 1.21	1.42
Kentucky	.86 ± .51	1.69	6.94 ± .65	10.68
Texas	3.68 ± .61	6.03	13.92 ± .77	18.08
North Carolina	- 3.80 ± .93	4.09	-10.47 ± 1.17	8.95
Wisconsin	2.60 ± 1.16	2.24	-18.54 ± 1.47	12.61
Southwest	- 3.41 ± .78	4.37	-10.26 ± .98	10.47

Beard

	Small Per Cent	x p.e.	Large Per Cent	x p.e.
Massachusetts	-21.60 ± 1.69	12.78	5.23 ± 1.20	4.36
Tennessee	33.94 ± 1.49	22.78	- 5.88 ± 1.07	5.50
Kentucky	-20.83 ± .80	26.04	- 6.21 ± .57	10.90
Texas	- 9.98 ± .94	10.62	6.67 ± .67	9.96
North Carolina	35.00 ± 1.44	24.30	- 6.52 ± 1.03	6.33
Wisconsin	3.13 ± 1.80	1.74	9.77 ± 1.29	7.57
Southwest	17.00 ± 1.22	13.93	3.34 ± .87	3.84

Body

	Small Per Cent	x p.e.	Large Per Cent	x p.e.
Massachusetts	-25.27 ± 1.77	14.28	- 7.20 ± 1.22	5.90
Tennessee	17.36 ± 1.56	11.13	- 3.79 ± 1.07	3.54
Kentucky	-15.50 ± .83	18.68	3.18 ± .57	5.58
Texas	- 6.38 ± .98	6.51	5.38 ± .68	7.91
North Carolina	31.24 ± 1.50	20.83	- 9.74 ± 1.04	9.36
Wisconsin	6.58 ± 1.89	3.48	- .64 ± 1.30	.49
Southwest	16.19 ± 1.30	12.45	- .22 ± .89	.25

Table IV-6.   Skin Color by States

	Red White No.	Per Cent	Pale White No.	Per Cent	Ruddy No.	Per Cent	Olive No.	Per Cent
Massachusetts	103	30.47	216	63.90	11	3.25	7	2.07
Tennessee	154	36.41	267	63.12	2	0.48	0	0
Kentucky	456	38.42	711	59.90	2	0.17	18	1.52
Texas	418	45.68	485	53.00	3	0.33	9	0.98
North Carolina	145	32.44	171	38.26	2	0.45	31	6.94
Wisconsin	4	1.35	289	97.31	3	1.01	1	0.34
Southwest	48	7.95	477	78.97	7	1.16	60	9.93
Total	1328	31.54	2616	62.12	30	.71	126	2.99

	Light Yellow-brown No.	Per Cent	Light Brown No.	Per Cent	Medium Red-brown No.	Per Cent	Total
Massachusetts	1	0.30	0	0	0	0	338
Tennessee	0	0	0	0	0	0	423
Kentucky	0	0	0	0	0	0	1187
Texas	0	0	0	0	0	0	915
North Carolina	1	0.22	96	21.48	1	0.22	447
Wisconsin	0	0	0	0	0	0	297
Southwest	1	0.17	11	1.82	0	0	604
Total	3	0.07	107	2.54	1	0.02	4211

Table IV-7. Hair Form by States

	Straight		Low Waves		Deep Waves		Curly		Frizzly		Total
	No.	Per Cent	No.	Per Cent	No.	Per Cent	No.	Per Cent	No.	Per Cent	No.
Massachusetts	273	81.25	27	8.04	18	5.36	18	5.36	0	0	336
Tennessee	372	88.15	29	6.87	13	3.08	8	1.90	0	0	422
Kentucky	1023	86.55	70	5.92	58	4.91	30	2.54	1	0.08	1182
Texas	702	76.72	131	14.32	52	5.68	29	3.17	1	0.11	915
North Carolina	388	87.19	39	8.76	13	2.92	3	0.67	2	0.45	445
Wisconsin	286	96.30	11	3.70	0	0	0	0	0	0	297
Southwest	539	89.68	45	7.49	14	2.33	3	0.50	0	0	601
Total	3583	85.35	352	8.38	168	4.00	91	2.17	4	0.10	4198

Table IV-8. Differences between State Subgroups and Total Series with Value in Terms of the Probable Error

Hair Form

	Straight Per Cent	x p.e.	Low Waves Per Cent	x p.e.
Massachusetts	- 4.10 ± 1.25	3.28	- .34 ± .98	.35
Tennessee	2.80 ± 1.10	2.54	- 1.51 ± .86	1.76
Kentucky	1.20 ± .59	2.03	- 2.46 ± .46	5.35
Texas	- 8.63 ± .70	12.33	5.94 ± .55	10.80
North Carolina	1.84 ± 1.07	1.72	- .38 ± .84	.45
Wisconsin	10.95 ± 1.34	8.17	- 4.68 ± 1.04	4.50
Southwest	4.33 ± .90	4.81	- .89 ± .71	1.25

Table IV-9.   Hair Color by States

| | Black | | .Dark Brown | | Reddish Brown | | Light Brown | |
	No.	Per Cent	No.	Par Cent	No.	Per Cent	No.	Per Cent
Massachusetts	14	4.19	112	33.53	119	35.63	48	14.37
Tennessee	21	5.06	117	28.19	27	6.51	185	44.58
Kentucky	65	5.53	434	36.94	232	19.74	284	24.17
Texas	64	7.14	271	30.25	208	23.21	186	20.76
North Carolina	24	5.36	209	46.65	58	12.95	121	27.01
Wisconsin	16	5.39	129	43.43	47	15.82	54	18.18
Southwest	5	0.83	166	27.62	142	23.63	200	33.28
Total	209	5.02	1438	34.52	833	20.00	1078	25.88

| | Ash-blond | | Golden | | Red | | Gray, White | | Total |
	No.	Per Cent	No.	Per Cent	No.	Per Cent	No.	Per Cent	No.
Massachusetts	10	2.99	13	3.89	13	3.89	5	1.50	334
Tennessee	7	1.69	16	3.86	19	4.58	23	5.54	415
Kentucky	42	3.57	36	3.06	37	3.15	45	3.83	1175
Texas	18	2.01	31	3.46	63	7.03	55	6.14	896
North Carolina	1	0.22	14	3.12	9	2.01	12	2.68	448
Wisconsin	5	1.68	3	1.01	3	1.01	40	13.47	297
Southwest	8	1.33	32	5.32	17	2.83	31	5.16	601
Total	91	2.18	145	3.48	161	3.86	211	5.06	4166

Table IV-10.

Differences between State Subgroups and Total Series
with Value in Terms of the Probable Error

Hair Color

	Black Per Cent	x p.e.	Dark Brown Per Cent	x p.e.	Reddish Brown Per Cent	x p.e.	Light Brown Per Cent	x p.e.
Massachusetts	- .83 ± .77	1.08	- .99 ± 1.68	.59	15.63 ± 1.42	11.01	-11.51 ± 1.55	7.43
Tennessee	.04 ± .69	.06	- 6.33 ± 1.49	4.25	-13.49 ± 1.25	10.79	18.70 ± 1.38	13.55
Kentucky	.51 ± .36	1.42	2.42 ± .80	3.02	- .26 ± .67	.39	- 1.71 ± .73	2.34
Texas	2.12 ± .44	4.82	- 4.27 ± .95	4.50	3.21 ± .80	4.01	- 5.12 ± .88	5.82
North Carolina	- .34 ± .66	.52	12.13 ± 1.43	8.48	- 7.05 ± 1.21	5.83	1.13 ± 1.32	.86
Wisconsin	- .37 ± .82	.45	8.91 ± 1.79	4.98	- 4.18 ± 1.51	2.77	- 7.70 ± 1.65	4.57
Southwest	- 4.19 ± .55	7.62	- 6.90 ± 1.21	5.70	3.63 ± 1.02	3.56	7.40 ± 1.11	6.57

	Ash-blond Per Cent	x p.e.	Golden Per Cent	x p.e.	Red Per Cent	x p.e.	Gray, White Per Cent	x p.e.
Massachusetts	.81 ± .51	1.59	.41 ± .65	.63	.03 ± .68	.04	- 3.56 ± .78	4.56
Tennessee	.49 ± .46	1.06	.38 ± .57	.67	.72 ± .60	1.20	- .48 ± .69	.70
Kentucky	1.39 ± .24	5.79	- .42 ± .30	1.40	- .71 ± .32	2.22	- 1.23 ± .36	3.42
Texas	- .17 ± .30	.57	- .02 ± .36	.06	3.17 ± .38	8.34	1.08 ± .44	2.45
North Carolina	- 1.96 ± .44	4.45	- .36 ± .55	.65	- 1.85 ± .58	3.19	- 2.38 ± .66	3.61
Wisconsin	- .50 ± .55	.91	- 2.47 ± .69	3.58	- 2.85 ± .73	3.90	8.41 ± .82	10.26
Southwest	- .85 ± .37	2.30	1.84 ± .46	4.00	- 1.03 ± .49	2.10	- .10 ± .55	.18

Table IV-12.   Eye Color by States

| | Dark Brown | | Light Brown | | Blue-brown | | Gray-brown | |
	No.	Per Cent	No.	Per Cent	No.	Per Cent	No.	Per Cent
Massachusetts	19	5.66	4	1.19	62	18.45	25	7.44
Tennessee	4	0.95	16	3.80	220	52.26	55	13.06
Kentucky	37	3.14	9	0.76	178	15.08	251	21.27
Texas	24	2.63	17	1.86	144	15.76	381.	41.68
North Carolina	16	3.57	7	1.56	101	22.54	6	1.34
Wisconsin	19	6.40	10	3.37	61	20.54	0	0
Southwest	21	3.48	65	10.76	87	14.40	12	1.99
Total	140	3.33	128	3.05	853	20.31	730	17.38

| | Green-brown | | Blue | | Blue-gray | | Total |
	No	Per Cent	No.	Per Cent	No.	Per Cent	No.
Massachusetts	116	34.52	56	16.67	54	16.07	336
Tennessee	64	15.20	54	12.83	8	1.90	421
Kentucky	345	29.24	313	26.52	47	3.98	1180
Texas	117	12.80	190	20.79	41	4.49	914
North Carolina	174	38.84	59	13.17	85	18.97	448
Wisconsin	92	30.98	48	16.16	67	22.56	297
Southwest	229	37.91	82	13.58	108	17.88	604
Total	1137	27.07	802	19.10	410	9.76	4200

Table IV-13. Differences between State Subgroups and Total Series with Value in Terms of the Probable Error

Eye Color

	Dark Brown Per Cent	x p.e.	Light Brown Per Cent	x p.e.	Blue-brown Per Cent	x p.e.	Gray-brown Per Cent	x p.e.
Massachusetts	2.33 ± .63	3.70	- 1.86 ± .61	3.05	- 1.86 ± 1.42	1.31	- 9.94 ± 1.34	7.42
Tennessee	- 2.38 ± .56	4.25	.75 ± .53	1.42	31.95 ± 1.25	25.56	- 4.32 ± 1.18	3.66
Kentucky	- .19 ± .30	.63	- 2.29 ± .28	8.18	- 5.23 ± .67	7.81	3.89 ± .63	6.18
Texas	- .70 ± .36	1.94	- 1.19 ± .34	3.50	- 4.55 ± .80	5.69	24.30 ± .75	32.40
North Carolina	- .24 ± .54	.44	- 1.49 ± .52	2.86	2.23 ± 1.21	1.84	-16.04 ± 1.14	14.07
Wisconsin	3.07 ± .67	4.58	.32 ± .65	.49	- .23 ± 1.52	.15	-17.38 ± 1.43	12.15
Southwest	.15 ± .46	.33	7.71 ± .44	17.52	- 5.91 ± 1.02	5.79	-15.39 ± .96	16.03

	Green-brown Per Cent	x p.e.	Blue Per Cent	x p.e.	Blue-gray Per Cent	x p.e.
Massachusetts	7.45 ± 1.57	4.74	- 2.43 ± 1.39	1.75	6.31 ± 1.04	6.07
Tennessee	-11.87 ± 1.38	8.60	- 6.27 ± 1.23	5.10	- 7.86 ± .92	8.54
Kentucky	2.17 ± .74	2.93	7.42 ± .65	11.42	- 5.78 ± .50	11.56
Texas	-14.27 ± .88	16.22	1.69 ± .78	2.17	- 5.27 ± .59	8.93
North Carolina	11.77 ± 1.34	8.78	- 5.93 ± 1.19	4.98	9.21 ± .90	10.23
Wisconsin	3.91 ± 1.68	2.33	- 2.94 ± 1.48	1.99	12.80 ± 1.12	11.43
Southwest	10.84 ± 1.13	9.59	- 5.52 ± 1.00	5.52	8.12 ± .76	10.68

Table IV-16.   Sclera by States

| | Clear | | Speckled | | Yellow | | |
	No.	Per Cent	No.	Per Cent	No.	Per Cent	Total
Massachusetts	256	77.11	72	21.69	4	1.20	332
Tennessee	384	92.31	26	6.25	6	1.44	416
Kentucky	1100	95.57	44	3.82	7	0.61	1151
Texas	858	96.08	32	3.58	3	0.34	893
North Carolina	447	99.78	1	0.22	0	0	448
Wisconsin	295	99.32	2	0.67	0	0	297
Southwest	593	98.34	10	1.66	0	0	603
Total	3933	95.00	187	4.52	20	0.48	4140

Table IV-17.   Differences between State Subgroups and Total Series
                    with Value in Terms of the Probable Error

                                  Sclera

	Clear Per Cent	x p.e.	Speckled Per Cent	x p.e.
Massachusetts	-17.89 ± .78	22.94	17.17 ± .74	23.20
Tennessee	- 2.69 ± .69	3.90	1.73 ± .65	2.66
Kentucky	.57 ± .37	1.54	- .70 ± .35	2.00
Texas	1.08 ± .44	2.45	- .94 ± .42	2.24
North Carolina	4.78 ± .66	7.24	- 4.30 ± .63	6.82
Wisconsin	4.32 ± .82	5.27	- 3.85 ± .78	4.94
Southwest	3.34 ± .55	4.75	- 2.86 ± .53	5.40

Table IV-18.

Iris by States

	Homogeneous		Rayed		Zoned		Speckled		Diffused		Total
	No.	Per Cent	No.	Per Cent	No.	Per Cent	No.	Per Cent	No.	Per Cent	No.
Massachusetts	24	7.21	165	49.55	91	27.33	40	12.01	13	3.90	333
Tennessee	30	7.11	37	8.77	143	33.89	161	38.15	51	12.08	422
Kentucky	107	9.04	361	30.52	272	22.99	325	27.47	118	9.98	1183
Texas	59	6.48	170	18.66	389	42.70	191	20.97	102	11.20	911
North Carolina	16	3.58	133	29.75	103	23.04	167	37.36	28	6.26	447
Wisconsin	30	10.10	44	14.82	180	60.61	36	12.12	7	2.36	297
Southwest	58	9.60	224	37.09	121	20.03	159	26.32	42	6.95	604
Total	324	7.72	1134	27.02	1299	30.95	1079	25.71	361	8.60	4197

Table IV-19.   Differences between State Subgroups and Total Series with Value in Terms of the Probable Error

Iris

	Homogeneous		Rayed		Zoned		Speckled		Diffused	
	Per Cent	x p.e.	Per Cent	x p.e.	Per Cent	x p.e.	Per Cent	x p.e.	Per Cent	x p.e.
Massachusetts	- .51 ± .94	.54	22.53 ± 1.57	14.35	- 3.62 ± 1.64	2.21	-13.70 ± 1.55	8.84	- 4.70 ± .99	4.75
Tennessee	- .61 ± .83	.74	-18.25 ± 1.38	13.22	- 2.94 ± 1.44	2.04	12.44 ± 1.36	9.15	3.48 ± .88	3.95
Kentucky	1.32 ± .44	3.00	3.50 ± .74	4.73	- 7.96 ± .77	10.34	1.76 ± .73	2.41	1.38 ± .46	3.00
Texas	- 1.24 ± .53	2.34	- 8.36 ± .88	9.50	11.75 ± .92	12.77	- 4.74 ± .86	5.51	2.60 ± .55	4.73
North Carolina	- 4.14 ± .80	5.18	2.73 ± 1.34	2.04	- 7.91 ± 1.40	5.65	11.65 ± 1.32	8.83	- 2.34 ± .84	2.79
Wisconsin	2.38 ± 1.00	2.38	-12.20 ± 1.67	7.30	29.66 ± 1.75	16.95	-13.59 ± 1.65	8.24	- 6.24 ± 1.06	5.89
Southwest	1.88 ± .67	2.81	10.07 ± 1.13	8.91	-10.92 ± 1.17	9.33.	.61 ± 1.11	.55	- 1.65 ± .71	2.32

Table IV-20.   Eye Folds by States

| | Epicanthus | | Median | | External | | Absent | | |
	No.	Per Cent	No.	Per Cent	No.	Per Cent	No.	Per Cent	Total
Massachusetts	6	1.79	68	20.30	64	19.10	197	58.81	335
Tennessee	9	2.13	25	5.92	25	5.92	363	86.02	422
Kentucky	125	10.58	176	14.90	96	8.13	784	66.38	1181
Texas	16	1.75	93	10.18	84	9.19	721	78.88	914
North Carolina	16	3.58	66	14.76	37	8.28	328	73.38	447
Wisconsin	3	1.01	10	3.37	22	7.41	262	88.22	297
Southwest	10	1.66	102	16.89	54	8.94	438	72.52	604
Total	185	4.40	540	12.86	382	9.10	3093	73.64	4200

Table IV-21.   Differences between State Subgroups and Total Series
with Value in Terms of the Probable Error

Eye Folds

	Epicanthus Per Cent	x p.e.	Median Per Cent	x p.e.	External Per Cent	x p.e.
Massachusetts	- 2.61 ± .73	3.58	7.44 ± 1.19	6.25	10.00 ± 1.02	9.80
Tennessee	- 2.27 ± .64	3.55	- 6.94 ± 1.05	6.61	- 3.18 ± .90	3.53
Kentucky	6.18 ± .34	18.18	2.04 ± .55	3.71	- .97 ± .48	2.02
Texas	- 2.65 ± .40	6.62	- 2.68 ± .66	4.06	.09 ± .57	.16
North Carolina	- .82 ± .62	1.32	1.90 ± 1.01	1.88	- .82 ± .86	.95
Wisconsin	- 3.39 ± .78	4.35	- 9.49 ± 1.26	7.53	- 1.69 ± 1.09	1.55
Southwest	- 2.74 ± .53	5.17	4.03 ± .85	4.74	- .16 ± .73	.22

Table IV-22.   Eyebrow Thickness by States

| | Submedium | | Medium | | Pronounced | | Total |
	No.	Per Cent	No.	Per Cent	No.	Per Cent	No.
Massachusetts	21	6.25	235	69.94	80	23.81	336
Tennessee	5	1.18	341	80.62	77	18.20	423
Kentucky	101	8.52	692	58.35	393	33.14	1186
Texas	40	4.38	581	63.64	292	31.98	913
North Carolina	5	1.12	272	60.71	171	38.17	448
Wisconsin	5	1.68	196	65.99	96	32.32	297
Southwest	7	1.16	353	58.44	244	40.40	604
Total	184	4.37	2670	63.47	1353	32.16	4207

Table IV-23. Differences between State Subgroups and Total Series
with Value in Terms of the Probable Error

Eyebrow Thickness

	Submedium Per Cent	x p.e.	Pronounced Per Cent	x p.e.
Massachusetts	1.88 ± .72	2.61	- 8.35 ± 1.65	5.06
Tennessee	- 3.19 ± .63	5.06	-13.96 ± 1.45	9.63
Kentucky	4.15 ± .34	12.21	.98 ± .78	1.26
Texas	.01 ± .40	.02	- .18 ± .92	.20
North Carolina	- 3.25 ± .61	5.33	6.01 ± 1.41	4.26
Wisconsin	- 2.69 ± .77	3.49	.16 ± 1.76	.09
Southwest	- 3.21 ± .52	6.17	8.24 ± 1.19	6.92

Table IV-24.　　　　　　　　Forehead Height by States

| | Submedium | | Medium | | Pronounced | | Total |
	No.	Per Cent	No.	Per Cent	No.	Per Cent	No.
Massachusetts	35	10.36	212	62.72	91	26.92	338
Tennessee	21	4.98	340	80.57	61	14.45	422
Kentucky	207	17.45	697	58.77	282	23.78	1186
Texas	78	8.52	669	73.12	168	18.36	915
North Carolina	116	25.89	213	47.54	119	26.56	448
Wisconsin	5	1.68	195	65.66	97	32.66	297
Southwest	70	11.59	322	53.31	212	35.10	604
Total	532	12.64	2648	62.90	1030	24.46	4210

Table IV-25. Differences between State Subgroups and Total Series
with Value in Terms of the Probable Error

Forehead Height

	Submedium Per Cent	x p.e.	Pronounced	x p.e.
Massachusetts	- 2.28 ± 1.17	1.95	2.46 ± 1.51	1.63
Tennessee	- 7.66 ± 1.03	7.44	-10.01 ± 1.34	7.47
Kentucky	4.81 ± .55	8.74	- .68 ± .72	.94
Texas	- 4.12 ± .65	6.34	- 6.10 ± .85	7.18
North Carolina	13.25 ± 1.00	13.25	2.10 ± 1.30	1.62
Wisconsin	-10.96 ± 1.25	8.77	8.20 ± 1.62	5.06
Southwest	- 1.05 ± .84	1.25	10.64 ± 1.09	9.76

Table IV-26.　　　　　　　　Forehead Slope by States

| | Absent, Submedium | | Medium | | Pronounced | | Total |
	No.	Per Cent	No.	Per Cent	No.	Per Cent	No.
Massachusetts	3	0.89	235	69.53	100	29.59	338
Tennessee	100	23.70	226	53.55	96	22.75	422
Kentucky	94	7.92	536	45.16	557	46.92	1187
Texas	19	2.08	658	71.91	238	26.01	915
North Carolina	49	10.94	223	49.78	176	39.29	448
Wisconsin	38	12.80	160	53.87	99	33.33	297
Southwest	40	6.62	376	62.25	188	31.13	604
Total	343	8.14	2414	57.33	1454	34.53	4211

Table IV-27. Differences between State Subgroups and Total Series
with Value in Terms of the Probable Error

Forehead Slope

	Absent, Submedium Per Cent	x p.e.	Pronounced Per Cent	x p.e.
Massachusetts	- 7.25 ± .96	7.55	- 4.94 ± 1.67	2.96
Tennessee	15.56 ± .85	18.31	-11.78 ± 1.48	7.96
Kentucky	- .22 ± .45	.49	12.39 ± .79	15.68
Texas	- 6.06 ± .54	11.22	- 8.52 ± .94	9.06
North Carolina	2.80 ± .82	3.42	4.76 ± 1.43	3.33
Wisconsin	4.66 ± 1.03	4.52	- 1.20 ± 1.79	.67
Southwest	- 1.52 ± .69	2.20	- 3.40 ± 1.21	2.81

Table IV-28.   Nasion Depression by States

	Absent		Submedium		Medium		Pronounced		Total
	No.	Per Cent	No.	Per Cent	No.	Per Cent	No.	Per Cent	No.
Massachusetts	0	0	13	3.85	247	73.08	78	23.08	338
Tennessee	0	0	14	3.31	358	84.63	51	12.06	423
Kentucky	2	0.17	146	12.33	623	52.62	413	34.88	1184
Texas	0	0	11	1.20	760	83.24	142	15.55	913
North Carolina	2	0.45	129	28.80	281	62.72	36	8.04	448
Wisconsin	0	0	16	5.39	277	93.27	4	1.35	297
Southwest	0	0	59	9.77	504	83.44	41	6.79	604
Total	4	0.10	388	9.22	3050	72.50	765	18.18	4207

Table IV-29.   Nasal Root Height by States

| | Submedium | | Medium | | Pronounced | | Total |
	No.	Per Cent	No.	Per Cent	No.	Per Cent	No.
Massachusetts	2	0.59	229	67.75	107	31.66	338
Tennessee	4	0.95	394	93.14	25	5.91	423
Kentucky	33	2.78	914	77.00	240	20.22	1187
Texas	14	1.53	796	86.99	105	11.48	915
North Carolina	8	1.79	240	53.57	200	44.64	448
Wisconsin	9	3.03	257	86.53	31	10.44	297
Southwest	9	1.49	514	85.10	81	13.41	604
Total	79	1.88	3344	79.39	789	18.73	4212

Table IV-30. Differences between State Subgroups and Total Series
with Value in Terms of the Probable Error

Nasal Root Height

	Submedium Per Cent	x p.e.	Pronounced Per Cent	x p.e.
Massachusetts	- 1.29 ± .48	2.69	12.93 ± 1.38	9.37
Tennessee	- .93 ± .42	2.21	-12.82 ± 1.21	10.60
Kentucky	.90 ± .22	4.09	1.49 ± .65	2.29
Texas	- .35 ± .27	1.30	- 7.25 ± .77	9.42
North Carolina	· .09 ± .41	.22	25.91 ± 1.17	22.14
Wisconsin	1.15 ± .51	2.26	- 8.29 ± 1.47	5.64
Southwest	- .39 ± .34	1.15	- 5.32 ± .99	5.37

Table IV-31.   Nasal Root Breadth by States

| | Submedium | | Medium | | Pronounced | | Total |
	No.	Per Cent	No.	Per Cent	No.	Per Cent	No.
Massachusetts	2	0.59	215	63.61	121	35.80	338
Tennessee	6	1.43	417	98.58	0	0	423
Kentucky	13	1.10	1076	90.72	97	8.19	1185
Texas	1	0.11	875	95.63	39	4.26	915
North Carolina	48	10.71	374	83.48	26	5.80	448
Wisconsin	99	33.33	179	60.27	19	6.40	297
Southwest	36	5.96	463	76.66	105	17.38	604
Total	205	4.87	3598	85.46	407	9.67	4210

Table IV-32. Differences between State Subgroups and Total Series
with Value in Terms of the Probable Error

Nasal Root Breadth

	Submedium Per Cent	x p.e.	Pronounced Per Cent	x p.e.
Massachusetts	- 4.28 ± .85	5.04	26.13 ± 1.04	25.12
Tennessee	- 3.44 ± .67	5.13	- 9.67 ± .92	10.51
Kentucky	- 3.77 ± .36	10.47	- 1.48 ± .49	3.02
Texas	- 4.76 ± .42	11.33	- 5.41 ± .59	9.17
North Carolina	5.84 ± .65	8.98	- 3.87 ± .89	4.35
Wisconsin	28.46 ± .81	35.14	- 3.27 ± 1.12	2.92
Southwest	1.09 ± .55	1.98	7.71 ± .75	10.28

Table IV-33.   Nasal Bridge Height by States

| | Submedium | | Medium | | Pronounced | | Total |
	No.	Per Cent	No.	Per Cent	No.	Per Cent	No.
Massachusetts	1	0.30	158	46.75	179	52.96	338
Tennessee	0	0	332	78.49	91	21.51	423
Kentucky	7	0.59	424	35.72	756	63.69	1187
Texas	1	0.11	628	3.63	286	31.26	915
North Carolina	0	0	159	5.49	289	64.51	448
Wisconsin	4	1.35	237	79.80	56	18.86	297
Southwest	1	0.17	360	59.60	243	40.23	604
Total	14	0.33	2298	54.56	1900	45.11	4212

Table IV-34.   Differences between State Subgroups and Total Series
with Value in Terms of the Probable Error

Nasal Bridge Height

	*Pronounced Per Cent	x p.e.
Massachusetts	7.85 ± 1.75	4.49
Tennessee	-23.60 ± 1.55	15.23
Kentucky	18.58 ± .82	22.66
Texas	-13.85 ± .98	14.13
North Carolina	19.40 ± 1.50	12.93
Wisconsin	-26.25 ± 1.88	13.96
Southwest	- 4.88 ± 1.26	3.87

*Since there is practically nothing in the submedium group and the excesses in pronounced are reflected in the means, the probable errors were calculated for the pronounced group only.

Table IV-35.   Nasal Bridge Breadth by States

| | Submedium | | Medium | | Pronounced | | Total |
	No.	Per Cent	No.	Per Cent	No.	Per Cent	No.
Massachusetts	2	0.59	218	64.50	118	34.91	338
Tennessee	6	1.42	387	91.71	29	6.87	422
Kentucky	11	0.93	1031	87.00	143	12.07	1185
Texas	3	0.33	821	89.82	90	9.85	914
North Carolina	22	4.91	372	83.04	54	12.05	448
Wisconsin	89	29.97	185	62.29	23	7.74	297
Southwest	18	2.98	385	63.74	201	33.28	604
Total	151	3.59	3399	80.77	658	15.64	4208

Table IV-36. Differences between State Subgroups and Total Series
with Value in Terms of the Probable Error

Nasal Bridge Breadth

	Submedium Per Cent	x p.e.	Pronounced Per Cent	x p.e.
Massachusetts	- 3.00 ± .65	4.62	19.27 ± 1.28	15.06
Tennessee	- 2.17 ± .58	3.74	- 8.77 ± 1.13	7.76
Kentucky	- 2.66 ± .31	8.58	- 3.57 ± .60	5.95
Texas	- 3.26 ± .37	8.81	- 5.79 ± .72	8.04
North Carolina	1.32 ± .56	2.36	- 3.59 ± 1.09	3.29
Wisconsin	26.38 ± .70	37.69	- 7.90 ± 1.37	5.77
Southwest	- .61 ± .47	1.30	17.64 ± .92	19.17

Table IV-37. Nasal Profile by States

	No.	Concave Per Cent	Straight No.	Straight Per Cent	Convex No.	Convex Per Cent	Concavo-convex No.	Concavo-convex Per Cent	Total No.
Massachusetts	91	27.25	46	13.77	55	16.47	142	42.52	334
Tennessee	102	24.11	45	10.64	95	22.46	181	42.79	423
Kentucky	219	18.50	147	12.42	126	10.64	692	58.45	1184
Texas	162	17.74	178	19.50	177	19.39	396	43.37	913
North Carolina	120	26.79	29	6.47	138	30.80	161	35.94	448
Wisconsin	96	32.32	10	3.37	99	33.33	92	30.98	297
Southwest	142	23.51	23	3.81	192	31.79	247	40.89	604
Total	932	22.18	478	11.37	882	20.98	1911	45.47	4203

Table IV-38. Differences between State Subgroups and Total Series with Value in Terms of the Probable Error

Nasal Profile

	Concave Per Cent	x p.e.	Straight Per Cent	x p.e.	Convex Per Cent	x p.e.	Concavo-convex Per Cent	x p.e.
Massachusetts	5.07 ± 1.47	3.45	2.40 ± 1.13	2.12	- 4.51 ± 1.44	3.13	- 2.95 ± 1.77	1.67
Tennessee	1.93 ± 1.30	1.48	- .73 ± .98	.74	1.48 ± 1.27	1.16	- 2.68 ± 1.55	1.73
Kentucky	- 3.68 ± .69	5.33	- 1.05 ± .53	1.98	-10.34 ± .67	15.43	12.98 ± .82	15.83
Texas	- 4.44 ± .82	5.42	8.13 ± .63	12.90	- 1.59 ± .80	1.99	- 2.10 ± .98	2.14
North Carolina	4.61 ± 1.25	3.69	- 4.90 ± .96	5.10	9.82 ± 1.23	7.98	- 9.53 ± 1.50	6.35
Wisconsin	10.14 ± 1.56	6.50	- 8.00 ± 1.20	6.67	12.35 ± 1.54	8.02	-14.49 ± 1.88	7.71
Southwest	1.33 ± 1.05	1.27	- 7.56 ± .81	9.33	10.81 ± 1.03	10.50	- 4.58 ± 1.27	3.61

Table IV-40.   Nasal Tip Thickness by States

| | Submedium | | Medium | | Pronounced | | Total |
	No.	Per Cent	No.	Per Cent	No.	Per Cent	No.
Massachusetts	4	1.20	203	60.96	126	37.84	333
Tennessee	16	3.78	364	86.05	43	10.16	423
Kentucky	187	15.78	763	64.39	235	19.83	1185
Texas	6	0.66	693	75.90	214	23.44	913
North Carolina	111	24.78	278	62.05	59	13.17	448
Wisconsin	71	23.91	201	67.68	25	8.42	297
Southwest	25	4.14	399	66.06	180	29.80	604
Total	420	9.99	2901	69.02	882	20.98	4203

Table IV-41. Differences between State Subgroups and Total Series
with Value in Terms of the Probable Error

Nasal Tip Thickness

	Submedium Per Cent	x p.e.	Pronounced Per Cent	x p.e.
Massachusetts	- 8.79 ± 1.07	8.22	16.86 ± 1.44	11.71
Tennessee	- 6.21 ± .93	6.68	-10.82 ± 1.27	8.52
Kentucky	5.79 ± .50	11.58	- 1.15 ± .67	1.72
Texas	- 9.33 ± .59	15.81	2.46 ± .80	3.08
North Carolina	14.79 ± .90	16.43	- 7.81 ± 1.23	6.35
Wisconsin	13.92 ± 1.13	12.32	-12.56 ± 1.54	8.16
Southwest	- 5.85 ± .76	7.70	8.82 ± 1.03	8.56

Table IV-42.   Nasal Septum Inclination by States

| | Up | | Down | | Absent | | Total |
	No.	Per Cent	No.	Per Cent	No.	Per Cent	No.
Massachusetts	227	69.00	101	30.70	1	0.30	329
Tennessee	184	43.50	238	56.26	1	0.24	423
Kentucky	897	76.08	271	22.99	11	0.93	1179
Texas	524	57.33	387	42.34	3	0.33	914
North Carolina	380	84.82	67	14.96	1	0.22	448
Wisconsin	254	85.52	43	14.48	0	0	297
Southwest	392	64.90	211	34.93	1	0.17	604
Total	2858	68.14	1318	31.43	18	0.43	4194

Table IV-43. Differences between State Subgroups and Total Series
with Value in Terms of the Probable Error

Nasal Septum Inclination

	Up Per Cent	x p.e.	Down Per Cent	x p.e.
Massachusetts	.86 ± 1.67	.52	- .73 ± 1.66	.44
Tennessee	-24.64 ± 1.45	16.99	24.83 ± 1.44	17.24
Kentucky	7.94 ± .78	10.18	- 8.44 ± .77	10.96
Texas	-10.81 ± .92	11.75	10.91 ± .92	11.86
North Carolina	16.68 ± 1.40	11.91	-16.47 ± 1.40	11.76
Wisconsin	17.38 ± 1.78	9.88	-16.95 ± 1.75	9.69
Southwest	- 3.24 ± 1 19	2.72	3.50 ± 1.18	2.97

Table IV-44.   Septum Deflection by States

| | Right | | Left | | Absent | | Total |
	No.	Per Cent	No.	Per Cent	No.	Per Cent	No.
Massachusetts	111	33.23	17	5.09	206	61.68	334
Tennessee	40	9.46	9	2.13	374	88.42	423
Kentucky	398	33.62	149	12.58	637	53.80	1184
Texas	64	7.00	43	4.70	807	88.29	914
North Carolina	188	42.15	94	21.08	164	36.77	446
Wisconsin	99	33.33	48	16.16	150	50.50	297
Southwest	87	14.40	43	7.12	474	78.48	604
Total	987	23.49	403	9.59	2812	66.92	4202

Table IV-45.   Differences between State Subgroups and Total Series
with Value in Terms of the Probable Error

Septum Deflection

| | Right | | Left | | Absent | |
	Per Cent	x p.e.	Per Cent	x p.e.	Per Cent	x p.e.
Massachusetts	9.74 ± 1.50	6.49	- 4.50 ± 1.04	4.33	- 5.24 ± 1.67	3.14
Tennessee	-14.03 ± 1.32	10.63	- 7.46 ± .92	8.11	21.50 ± 1.46	14.73
Kentucky	10.13 ± .70	14.47	2.99 ± .49	6.10	-13.12 ± .78	16.82
Texas	-16.49 ± .84	19.63	- 4.89 ± .58	8.43	21.37 ± .93	22.98
North Carolina	18.66 ± 1.28	14.58	11.49 ± .89	12.91	-30.15 ± 1.42	21.23
Wisconsin	9.84 ± 1.60	6.15	6.57 ± 1.11	5.92	-16.42 ± 1.77	9.28
Southwest	- 9.09 ± 1.08	8.42	- 2.47 ± .75	3.29	11.56 ± 1.19	9.71

Table IV-46.   Lips Integumental Thickness by States

| | Submedium | | Medium | | Pronounced | | Total |
	No.	Per Cent	No.	Per Cent	No.	Per Cent	No.
Massachusetts	126	38.30	194	58.97	9	2.74	329
Tennessee	6	1.43	408	96.45	9	2.13	423
Kentucky	265	22.32	835	70.34	87	7.33	1187
Texas	71	7.78	837	91.68	5	0.55	913
North Carolina	34	7.59	398	88.84	16	3.57	448
Wisconsin	8	2.69	282	94.95	7	2.36	297
Southwest	30	4.97	470	77.81	104	17.22	604
Total	540	12.85	3424	81.50	237	5.64	4201

Table IV-47. Differences between State Subgroups and Total Series
with Value in Terms of the Probable Error

Lips Integumental Thickness

| | Submedium | | Pronounced | |
	Per Cent	x p.e.	Per Cent	x p.e.
Massachusetts	25.45 ± 1.19	21.39	- 2.90 ± .82	3.54
Tennessee	-11.42 ± 1.04	10.98	- 3.51 ± .72	4.88
Kentucky	9.47 ± .55	17.22	1.69 ± .38	4.45
Texas	- 5.07 ± .66	7.68	- 5.09 ± .46	11.06
North Carolina	- 5.26 ± 1.00	5.26	- 2.07 ± .70	2.96
Wisconsin	-10.16 ± 1.26	8.06	- 3.28 ± .87	3.77
Southwest	- 7.88 ± .85	9.27	11.58 ± .59	19.63

Table IV-48. Lips Membranous Thickness

| | Submedium | | Medium | | Upper,Submedium Lower,Pronounced | | Pronounced | | Total |
	No.	Per Cent	No.	Per Cent	No.	Per Cent	No.	Per Cent	No.
Massachusetts	39	11.68	207	61.98	76	22.75	12	3.59	334
Tennessee	34	8.04	359	84.87	23	5.44	7	1.66	423
Kentucky	175	14.74	908	76.50	43	3.62	61	5.14	1187
Texas	87	9.53	655	71.74	148	16.21	23	2.52	913
North Carolina	153	34.15	212	47.32	82	18.30	1	0.22	448
Wisconsin	97	32.66	148	49.83	51	17.17	1	0.34	297
Southwest	116	19.20	368	60.93	104	17.22	16	2.65	604
Total	701	16.67	2857	67.93	527	12.53	121	2.88	4206

Table IV-49. Differences between State Subgroups and Total Series
with Value in Terms of the Probable Error

Lips Membranous Thickness

	Submedium Per Cent	x p.e.	Upper Submedium Lower Pronounced Per Cent	x p.e.	Pronounced Per Cent	x p.e.
Massachusetts	- 4.99 ± 1.32	3.78	10.22 ± 1.17	8.74	.71 ± .59	1.20
Tennessee	- 8.63 ± 1.16	7.44	- 7.09 ± 1.03	6.88	- 1.22 ± .53	2.30
Kentucky	- 1.93 ± .62	3.11	- 8.91 ± .55	16.20	2.26 ± .28	8.07
Texas	- 7.14 ± .74	9.65	3.68 ± .65	5.66	- .36 ± .33	1.09
North Carolina	17.48 ± 1.12	15.61	5.77 ± 1.00	5.77	- 2.66 ± .51	5.22
Wisconsin	15.99 ± 1.41	11.34	4.64 ± 1.24	3.74	- 2.54 ± .63	4.03
Southwest	2.53 ± .94	2.69	4.69 ± .84	5.58	- .23 ± .42	.55

Table IV-50. Lip Seam by States

| | Absent, Submedium | | Medium | | Pronounced | | Total |
	No.	Per Cent	No.	Per Cent	No.	Per Cent	No.
Massachusetts	27	8.23	246	75.00	55	16.77	328
Tennessee	64	15.13	271	64.07	88	20.80	423
Kentucky	103	8.68	789	66.53	294	24.79	1186
Texas	219	23.96	508	55.58	187	20.46	914
North Carolina	73	16.30	275	61.38	100	22.32	448
Wisconsin	19	6.40	261	87.88	17	5.72	297
Southwest	103	17.05	437	72.35	64	10.60	604
Total	608	14.48	2787	66.36	805	19.17	4200

Table IV-51. Differences between State Subgroups and Total Series
with Value in Terms of the Probable Error

Lip Seam

	Absent,Submedium Per Cent	x p.e.	Pronounced Per Cent	x p.e.
Massachusetts	- 6.25 ± 1.26	4.96	- 2.40 ± 1.41	1.70
Tennessee	.65 ± 1.09	.60	1.63 ± 1.23	1.32
Kentucky	- 5.80 ± .59	9.83	5.62 ± .65	8.65
Texas	9.48 ± .70	13.54	1.29 ± .78	1.65
North Carolina	1.82 ± 1.06	1.72	3.15 ± 1.19	2.65
Wisconsin	- 8.08 ± 1.33	6.08	-13.45 ± 1.48	9.09
Southwest	2.57 ± .90	2.86	- 8.57 ± 1.00	8.57

Table IV-52.   Alveolar Prognathism by States

	Absent		Submedium		Medium		Pronounced		Total
	No.	Per Cent	No.	Per Cent	No.	Per Cent	No.	Per Cent	No.
Massachusetts	226	66.86	79	23.37	31	9.17	2	0.59	338
Tennessee	358	84.63	38	8.98	22	5.20	5	1.18	423
Kentucky	889	74.96	231	19.48	65	5.48	1	0.08	1186
Texas	720	78.77	154	16.85	35	3.83	5	0.55	914
North Carolina	426	95.09	15	3.35	7	1.56	0	0	448
Wisconsin	266	89.56	17	5.72	11	3.70	3	1.01	297
Southwest	584	96.69	15	2.48	3	0.50	2	0.33	604
Total	3469	82.40	549	13.04	174	4.13	18	0.43	4210

Table IV-53. Differences between State Subgroups and Total Series
with Valu⸗ in Terms of the Probable Error

Alveolar Prognathism

	Submedium Per Cent	x p.e.	Medium Per Cent	x p.e.
Massachusetts	10.33 ± 1.19	8.68	5.04 ± .70	7.20
Tennessee	- 4.06 ± 1.04	3.90	1.07 ± .59	1.81
Kentucky	6.44 ± .56	11.50	1.35 ± .32	4.22
Texas	3.81 ± .66	5.77	- .30 ± .38	.79
North Carolina	- 9.69 ± 1.01	9.59	- 2.57 ± .57	4.51
Wisconsin	- 7.32 ± 1.27	5.76	- .43 ± .72	.60
Southwest	-10.56 ± .86	12.28	- 3.63 ± .51	7.12

Table IV-54.   Facial Prognathism by States

	Absent		Submedium		Medium		Pronounced		Total
	No.	Per Cent	No.	Per Cent	No.	Per Cent	No.	Per Cent	No.
Massachusetts	248	73.37	40	11.83	34	10.06	16	4.73	338
Tennessee	368	87.00	40	9.46	13	3.07	2	0.47	423
Kentucky	1000	84.39	106	8.94	70	5.91	9	0.76	1185
Texas	798	87.31	70	7.66	41	4.49	5	0.55	914
North Carolina	423	94.42	17	3.80	8	1.79	0	0	448
Wisconsin	269	90.57	15	5.05	10	3.37	3	1.01	297
Southwest	585	96.85	12	1.99	7	1.16	0	0	604
Total	3691	87.69	300	7.13	183	4.35	5	0.83	4209

Table IV-55.   Differences between State Subgroups and Total Series
with Value in Terms of the Probable Error

Facial Prognathism

	Submedium Per Cent	x p.e.	Medium Per Cent	x p.e.	Pronounced Per Cent	x p.e.
Massachusetts	4.70 ± .90	5.22	5.71 ± .72	7.93	3.90 ± .32	12.19
Tennessee	2.33 ± .80	2.91	1.28 ± .63	2.03	- .36 ± .28	1.29
Kentucky	1.81 ± .42	4.31	1.56 ± .34	4.59	- .07 ± .15	.47
Texas	.53 ± .51	1.04	.14 ± .40	.35	- .28 ± .18	1.56
North Carolina	- 3.33 ± .78	4.27	- 2.56 ± .61	4.20	- .83 ± .27	3.07
Wisconsin	- 2.08 ± .97	2.14	- .98 ± .77	1.27	.18 ± .34	.53
Southwest	- 5.14 ± .65	7.91	- 3.19 ± .52	6.14	- .83 ± .24	3.46

Table IV-56.   Chin Form by States

| | Median | | Bilateral | | Total |
	No.	Per Cent	No.	Per Cent	No.
Massachusetts	218	64.50	120	35.50	338
Tennessee	299	70.69	124	29.31	423
Kentucky	628	53.08	555	46.92	1183
Texas	471	51.76	439	48.24	910
North Carolina	228	50.89	220	49.11	448
Wisconsin	212	71.38	85	28.62	297
Southwest	313	51.82	291	48.18	604
Total	2369	56.36	1834	43.64	4203

Table IV-57. Differences between State Subgroups and Total Series
with Value in Terms of the Probable Error

Chin Form

	Median Per Cent	x p.e.	Bilateral Per Cent	x p.e.
Massachusetts	8.14 ± 1.75	4.65	- 8.14 ± 1.75	4.65
Tennessee	14.33 ± 1.54	9.30	-14.33 ± 1.54	9.30
Kentucky	- 3.28 ± .82	4.00	3.28 ± .82	4.00
Texas	- 4.60 ± .98	4.69	4.60 ± .98	4.69
North Carolina	- 5.47 ± 1.50	3.65	5.47 ± 1.50	3.65
Wisconsin	15.02 ± 1.88	7.99	-15.02 ± 1.88	7.99
Southwest	- 4.54 ± 1.26	3.60	4.54 ± 1.26	3.60

Table IV-58.   Malars Prominence by States

| | Submedium | | Medium | | Pronounced | | Total |
	No.	Per Cent	No.	Per Cent	No.	Per Cent	No.
Massachusetts	7	2.17	257	79.57	59	18.27	323
Tennessee	12	2.84	322	76.30	88	20.85	422
Kentucky	108	9.12	821	69.34	255	21.54	1184
Texas	7	.77	420	46.10	484	53.13	911
North Carolina	75	16.74	308	68.75	65	14.51	448
Wisconsin	1	.34	284	95.62	12	4.04	297
Southwest	27	4.47	475	78.64	102	16.99	604
Total	237	5.66	2887	68.92	1065	25.42	4189

Table IV-59. Differences between State Subgroups and Total Series
with Value in Terms of the Probable Error

Malars Prominence

	Submedium Per Cent	x p.e	Pronounced Per Cent	x p.e.
Massachusetts	- 3.49 ± .84	4.15	- 7.15 ± 1.57	4.55
Tennessee	- 2.82 ± .72	3.92	- 4.57 ± 1.36	3.36
Kentucky	3.46 ± .38	9.10	- 3.88 ± .72	5.39
Texas	- 4.89 ± .46	10.63	27.71 ± .86	32.22
North Carolina	11.08 ± .70	15.83	-10.91 ± 1.31	8.33
Wisconsin	- 5.32 ± .87	6.11	-21.38 ± 1.65	12.96
Southwest	- 1.19 ± .59	2.02	- 8.53 ± 1.11	7.68

Table IV-60. Cheek Fullness by States

| | Submedium | | Medium | | Pronounced | | Total |
	No.	Per Cent	No.	Per Cent	No.	Per Cent	No.
Massachusetts	62	18.34	210	62.13	66	19.53	338
Tennessee	61	14.52	319	75.95	40	9.52	420
Kentucky	271	22.93	738	62.44	173	14.64	1182
Texas	54	5.91	504	55.14	356	38.95	914
North Carolina	198	44.40	208	46.64	40	8.97	446
Wisconsin	137	46.13	141	47.48	19	6.40	297
Southwest	241	39.97	300	49.75	62	10.28	603
Total	1024	24.38	2420	57.62	756	18.00	4200

Table IV-61. Differences between State Subgroups and Total Series
with Value in Terms of the Probable Error

Cheek Fullness

	Submedium Per Cent	x p.e.	Pronounced Per Cent	x p.e.
Massachusetts	- 6.04 ± 1.51	4.00	1.53 ± 1.35	1.13
Tennessee	- 9.86 ± 1.34	7.36	- 8.48 ± 1.20	7.07
Kentucky	- 1.45 ± .72	2.01	- 3.36 ± .64	5.25
Texas	-18.47 ± .85	21.73	20.95 ± .76	27.57
North Carolina	20.02 ± 1.30	15.40	- 9.03 ± 1.16	7.78
Wisconsin	21.75 ± 1.62	13.43	-11.60 ± 1.45	8.00
Southwest	15.59 ± 1.09	14.30	- 7.72 ± .98	7.88

Table IV-62. Gonial Angles by States

| | Submedium | | Medium | | Pronounced | | Total |
	No.	Per Cent	No.	Per Cent	No.	Per Cent	No.
Massachusetts	51	15.09	261	77.22	26	7.69	338
Tennessee	98	23.33	259	61.67	63	15.00	420
Kentucky	137	11.56	872	73.59	176	14.85	1185
Texas	87	9.53	514	56.30	312	34.17	913
North Carolina	74	16.52	317	70.76	57	12.72	448
Wisconsin	8	2.69	277	93.27	12	4.04	297
Southwest	60	9.93	453	75.00	91	15.07	604
Total	515	12.25	2953	70.22	737	17.53	4205

Table IV-63. Differences between State Subgroups and Total Series
with Value in Terms of the Probable Error

Gonial Angles

	Submedium Per Cent	x p.e.	Pronounced Per Cent	x p.e.
Massachusetts	2.84 ± 1.15	2.47	- 9.84 ± 1.34	7.34
Tennessee	11.08 ± 1.02	10.86	- 2.53 ± 1.19	2.13
Kentucky	- .69 ± .55	1.25	- 2.68 ± .63	4.25
Texas	- 2.72 ± .65	4.18	16.64 ± .75	22.19
North Carolina	4.27 ± .98	4.36	- 4.81 ± 1.15	4.18
Wisconsin	- 9.56 ± 1.23	7.77	-13.49 ± 1.44	9.37
Southwest	- 2.32 ± .83	2.80	- 2.46 ± .96	2.56

Table IV-64.   Cheeks Wrinkling by States

| | Absent | | Slight,medium | | Pronounced | | Total |
	No.	Per Cent	No.	Per Cent	No.	Per Cent	No.
Massachusetts	268	79.76	62	18.45	6	1.79	336
Tennessee	145	34.77	204	48.92	68	16.31	417
Kentucky	637	53.85	404	34.15	142	12.00	1183
Texas	318	35.02	422	46.48	168	18.50	908
North Carolina	249	55.58	150	33.48	49	10.94	448
Wisconsin	211	71.04	66	22.22	20	6.73	297
Southwest	336	55.63	168	27.81	100	16.56	604
Total	2164	51.61	1476	35.20	553	13.19	4193

Table IV-65.   Teeth Wear by States

| | None | | Slight,medium | | Pronounced | | Total |
	No.	Per Cent	No.	Per Cent	No.	Per Cent	No.
Massachusetts	0	0	275	86.48	43	13.52	318
Tennessee	38	9.38	278	68.64	89	21.98	405
Kentucky	2	.17	950	82.04	206	17.79	1158
Texas	1	.11	744	84.16	139	15.72	884
North Carolina	2	.45	381	86.20	59	13.35	442
Wisconsin	0	0	244	87.14	36	12.86	280
Southwest	0	0	496	86.71	76	13.29	572
Total	43	1.06	3368	82.98	648	15.96	4059

Table IV-66.   Teeth Caries by States

| | None | | Few | | Many | | Total |
	No.	Per Cent	No.	Per Cent	No.	Per Cent	No.
Massachusetts	17	5.33	153	47.96	149	46.71	319
Tennessee	15	3.70	238	58.76	152	37.53	405
Kentucky	40	3.45	902	77.76	218	18.79	1160
Texas	25	2.81	464	52.19	400	44.99	889
North Carolina	2	.45	399	90.27	41	9.28	442
Wisconsin	0	0	238	85.00	42	15.00	280
Southwest	1	.18	502	87.76	69	12.06	572
Total	100	2.46	2896	71.21	1071	26.33	4067

Table IV-67. Differences between State Subgroups and Total Series
with Value in Terms of the Probable Error

Teeth Caries

	Many Per Cent	x p.e.
Massachusetts	20.38 ± 1.60	12.74
Tennessee	11.20 ± 1.40	8.00
Kentucky	- 7.54 ± .74	10.19
Texas	18.66 ± .88	21.20
North Carolina	-17.05 ± 1.34	12.72
Wisconsin	-11.33 ± 1.71	6.63
Southwest	-14.27 ± 1.15	12.41

Table IV-68.   Teeth Lost by States

| | None | | Few | | Many | | Total |
	No.	Per Cent	No.	Per Cent	No.	Per Cent	No.
Massachusetts	36	10.75	210	62.69	89	26.57	335
Tennessee	107	25.42	224	53.21	90	21.38	421
Kentucky	285	24.19	617	52.38	276	23.43	1178
Texas	274	30.08	406	44.57	231	25.36	911
North Carolina	165	37.25	192	43.34	86	19.41	443
Wisconsin	43	14.93	131	45.49	114	39.58	288
Southwest	201	33.44	254	42.26	146	24.29	601
Total	1111	26.60	2034	48.70	1032	24.71	4177

Table IV-69. Differences between State Subgroups and Total Series
with Value in Terms of the Probable Error

Teeth Lost

| | None | | Many | |
	Per Cent	x p.e.	Per Cent	x p.e.
Massachusetts	-15.85 ± 1.56	10.16	1.86 ± 1.52	1.22
Tennessee	- 1.18 ± 1.38	.86	- 3.33 ± 1.34	2.48
Kentucky	- 2.41 ± .74	3.26	- 1.28 ± .72	1.78
Texas	3.48 ± .88	3.95	.65 ± .85	.76
North Carolina	10.65 ± 1.34	7.95	- 5.30 ± 1.31	4.05
Wisconsin	-11.67 ± 1.69	6.90	14.87 ± 1.65	9.01
Southwest	6.84 ± 1.13	6.05	- .42 ± 1.10	.38

Table IV-70.   Bite by States

| | Under | | Edge-to-edge | | Slight over | | Marked over | | Total |
	No.	Per Cent	No.	Per Cent	No.	Per Cent	No.	Per Cent	No.
Massachusetts	14	4.76	39	13.26	160	54.42	81	27.55	294
Tennessee	14	3.75	100	26.81	197	52.82	62	16.62	373
Kentucky	24	2.22	224	20.68	584	53.92	251	23.18	1083
Texas	8	.98	104	12.81	417	51.35	283	34.85	812
North Carolina	1	.24	93	22.20	251	59.90	74	17.66	419
Wisconsin	6	2.26	51	19.17	158	59.40	51	19.17	266
Southwest	42	7.62	98	17.79	309	56.08	102	18.51	551
Total	109	2.87	709	18.67	2076	54.66	904	23.80	3798

Table IV-71.   Differences between State Subgroups and Total Series
with Value in Terms of the Probable Error

| | Under | | Edge-to-edge | | Marked over | |
	Per Cent	x p.e.	Per Cent	x p.e.	Per Cent	x p.e.
Massachusetts	1.89 ± .63	3.00	- 5.41 ± 1.47	3.68	3.75 ± 1.60	2.34
Tennessee	.88 ± .55	1.60	8.14 ± 1.30	6.26	- 7.18 ± 1.42	5.06
Kentucky	- .65 ± .28	2.32	2.01 ± .67	3.00	- .62 ± .74	.84
Texas	- 1.89 ± .35	5.40	- 5.86 ± .82	7.15	11.05 ± .90	12.28
North Carolina	- 2.63 ± .52	5.06	3.53 ± 1.21	2.92	- 6.14 ± 1.32	4.65
Wisconsin	- .61 ± .67	.91	.50 ± 1.55	.32	- 4.63 ± 1.70	2.72
Southwest	4.75 ± .44	10.80	- .88 ± 1.04	.85	- 5.29 ± 1.13	4.68

Table IV-72. Ear Lobes by States

	Submedium		Medium		Pronounced		Total
	No.	Per Cent	No.	Per Cent	No.	Per Cent	No.
Massachusetts	82	24.40	207	61.61	47	13.99	336
Tennessee	14	3.31	383	90.76	25	5.92	422
Kentucky	175	14.78	750	63.34	259	21.88	1184
Texas	41	4.49	668	73.16	204	22.34	913
North Carolina	29	6.47	349	77.90	70	15.62	448
Wisconsin	18	6.06	247	83.16	32	10.77	297
Southwest	107	17.72	394	65.23	103	17.05	604
Total	466	11.08	2998	71.31	740	17.60	4204

Table IV-73. Differences between State Subgroups and Total Series
with Value in Terms of the Probable Error

Ear Lobes

	Submedium Per Cent	x p.e.	Pronounced Per Cent	x p.e.
Massachusetts	13.32 ± 1.11	12.00	- 3.61 ± 1.34	2.69
Tennessee	- 7.77 ± .98	7.93	-11.68 ± 1.19	9.82
Kentucky	3.70 ± .53	6.98	4.28 ± .63	6.79
Texas	- 6.59 ± .62	10.63	4.74 ± .75	6.32
North Carolina	- 4.61 ± .94	4.90	- 1.98 ± 1.15	1.72
Wisconsin	- 5.02 ± 1.19	4.22	- 6.83 ± 1.44	4.74
Southwest	6.64 ± .80	8.30	- .55 ± .97	.57

Table IV-74. Ear Lobe Attachment by States

	Attached		Free		Notched,divided		Total
	No.	Per Cent	No.	Per Cent	No.	Per Cent	No.
Massachusetts	166	50.61	162	49.39	0		328
Tennessee	149	35.31	273	64.59	0		422
Kentucky	417	35.28	765	64.72	0		1182
Texas	338	37.14	572	62.86	0		910
North Carolina	191	42.63	256	57.14	1	.22	448
Wisconsin	118	39.73	179	60.27	0		297
Southwest	247	40.89	356	58.94	1	.17	604
Total	1626	38.80	2563	61.15	2	.05	4191

Table IV-75. Differences between State Subgroups and Total Series
with Value in Terms of the Probable Error

Ear Lobe Attachment

	Attached Per Cent	x p.e.
Massachusetts	11.81 ± 1.74	6.79
Tennessee	- 3.49 ± 1.52	2.30
Kentucky	- 3.52 ± .81	4.35
Texas	- 1.66 ± .96	1.73
North Carolina	3.83 ± 1.47	2.60
Wisconsin	.93 ± 1.84	.50
Southwest	2.09 ± 1.23	1.70

Table IV-76.   Roll of Helix by States

	Absent		Submedium		Medium,pronounced		Total
	No.	Per Cent	No.	Per Cent	No.	Per Cent	No.
Massachusetts	0		96	29.09	234	70.91	330
Tennessee	1	.24	130	30.88	290	68.88	421
Kentucky	2	.17	440	37.16	742	62.67	1184
Texas	1	0.11	293	32.02	621	67.87	915
North Carolina	0		152	33.93	296	66.07	448
Wisconsin	0		51	17.17	246	82.83	297
Southwest	0		187	30.96	417	69.04	604
Total	4	.10	1349	32.13	2846	67.78	4199

Table IV-77. Differences between State Subgroups and Total Series
with Value in Terms of the Probable Error

Roll of Helix

	Submedium Per Cent	x p.e.
Massachusetts	- 3.04 ± 1.67	1.82
Tennessee	- 1.25 ± 1.46	.86
Kentucky	5.03 ± .78	6.45
Texas	- .11 ± .92	.12
North Carolina	1.80 ± 1.41	1.28
Wisconsin	-14.96 ± 1.76	8.50
Southwest	- 1.17 ± 1.19	.98

Table IV-78.   Darwin's Point by States

	Absent		Small,medium		Pronounced		Total
	No.	Per Cent	No.	Per Cent	No.	Per Cent	No.
Massachusetts	183	55.62	117	35.56	29	8.81	329
Tennessee	240	56.87	114	27.01	68	16.11	422
Kentucky	621	52.45	326	27.53	237	20.02	1184
Texas	568	62.14	161	17.62	185	20.24	914
North Carolina	348	77.68	92	20.54	8	1.79	448
Wisconsin	204	68.69	91	30.64	2	.67	297
Southwest	309	51.16	279	46.19	16	2.65	604
Total	2473	58.91	1180	28.11	545	12.98	4198

Table IV-79. Differences between State Subgroups and Total Series
with Value in Terms of the Probable Error

Darwin's Point

	Absent Per Cent	x p.e.	Pronounced Per Cent	x p.e.
Massachusetts	- 3.29 ± 1.75	1.88	- 4.17 ± 1.20	3.48
Tennessee	- 2.04 ± 1.53	1.33	3.13 ± 1.05	2.98
Kentucky	- 6.46 ± .82	7.88	7.04 ± .56	12.57
Texas	3.23 ± .97	3.33	7.26 ± .66	11.00
North Carolina	18.77 ± 1.48	12.68	-11.19 ± 1.01	11.08
Wisconsin	9.78 ± 1.85	5.29	-12.31 ± 1.27	9.69
Southwest	- 7.75 ± 1.25	6.20	-10.33 ± .85	12.15

Table IV-80.   Antihelix Prominence by States

	Submedium		Medium		Pronounced		Total
	No.	Per Cent	No.	Per Cent	No.	Per Cent	No.
Massachusetts	43	13.03	221	66.97	66	20.00	330
Tennessee	25	5.94	393	93.35	3	.71	421
Kentucky	95	8.01	981	82.72	110	9.28	1186
Texas	94	10.30	747	81.82	72	7.88	913
North Carolina	36	8.05	283	63.31	128	28.64	447
Wisconsin	23	7.74	205	69.02	69	23.23	297
Southwest	25	4.14	421	69.70	158	26.16	604
Total	341	8.12	3251	77.44	606	14.44	4198

Table IV-81. Differences between State Subgroups and Total Series
with Value in Terms of the Probable Error

Antihelix Prominence

	Submedium Per Cent	x p.e.	Pronounced Per Cent	x p.e.
Massachusetts	4.91 ± .97	5.06	5.56 ± 1.25	4.45
Tennessee	- 2.18 ± .85	2.56	-13.73 ± 1.09	12.60
Kentucky	- .11 ± .45	.24	- 5.16 ± .59	8.75
Texas	2.18 ± .54	4.04	- 6.56 ± .70	9.37
North Carolina	- .07 ± .82	.08	14.20 ± 1.06	13.40
Wisconsin	- .38 ± 1.03	.37	8.79 ± 1.33	6.61
Southwest	- 3.98 ± .70	5.69	11.72 ± .89	13.17

Table IV-82.   Ear Protrusion by States

	Submedium		Medium		Pronounced		Total
	No.	Per Cent	No.	Per Cent	No.	Per Cent	No.
Massachusetts	33	9.82	222	66.07	81	24.11	336
Tennessee	34	8.06	329	77.96	59	13.98	422
Kentucky	136	11.48	489	41.27	560	47.26	1185
Texas	38	4.15	574	62.73	303	33.12	915
North Carolina	34	7.59	228	50.89	186	41.52	448
Wisconsin	3	1.01	245	82.49	49	16.50	297
Southwest	37	6.13	314	51.99	253	41.89	604
Total	315	7.49	2401	57.07	1491	35.44	4207

Table IV-83. Differences between State Subgroups and Total Series
with Value in Terms of the Probable Error

Ear Protrusion

	Submedium Per Cent	x p.e.	Pronounced Per Cent	x p.e.
Massachusetts	2.33 ± .93	2.50	-11.33 ± 1.69	6.70
Tennessee	.57 ± .82	.70	-21.45 ± 1.49	14.40
Kentucky	3.99 ± .44	9.07	11.82 ± .80	14.78
Texas	- 3.34 ± .52	6.42	- 2.32 ± .94	2.47
North Carolina	.10 ± .80	.12	6.08 ± 1.44	4.22
Wisconsin	- 6.48 ± .99	6.54	-18.94 ± 1.81	10.46
Southwest	- 1.36 ± .67	2.03	6.45 ± 1.21	5.33

Table IV-84.   Temporal Fullness by States

	Submedium		Medium		Pronounced		Total
	No.	Per Cent	No.	Per Cent	No.	Per Cent	No.
Massachusetts	7	2.11	321	96.69	4	1.20	332
Tennessee	121	28.81	273	65.00	26	6.19	420
Kentucky	277	23.38	728	61.43	180	15.19	1185
Texas	292	31.95	590	64.55	32	3.50	914
North Carolina	23	5.13	323	72.10	102	22.77	448
Wisconsin	8	2.70	287	96.96	1	.34	296
Southwest	14	2.32	530	87.89	59	9.78	603
Total	742	17.68	3052	72.70	404	9.62	4198

Table IV-85. Differences between State Subgroups and Total Series
with Value in Terms of the Probable Error

Temporal Fullness

	Submedium Per Cent	x p.e.	Pronounced Per Cent	x p.e.
Massachusetts	-15.57 ± 1.36	11.45	- 8.42 ± 1.05	8.02
Tennessee	11.13 ± 1.19	9.35	- 3.43 ± .92	3.73
Kentucky	5.70 ± .63	9.05	5.57 ± .49	11.37
Texas	14.27 ± .75	19.03	- 6.12 ± .58	10.55
North Carolina	-12.55 ± 1.15	10.91	13.15 ± .89	14.78
Wisconsin	-14.98 ± 1.44	10.40	- 9.28 ± 1.11	8.36
Southwest	-15.36 ± .97	15.84	.16 ± .75	.21

Table IV-86.   Lambdoid Flattening by States

	Absent		Present		Total
	No.	Per Cent	No.	Per Cent	No.
Massachusetts	283	84.98	50	15.02	333
Tennessee	383	91.19	37	8.81	420
Kentucky	708	60.05	471	39.95	1179
Texas	867	94.96	46	5.04	913
North Carolina	226	50.45	222	49.55	448
Wisconsin	165	55.56	132	44.44	297
Southwest	164	27.29	437	72.71	601
Total	2796	66.71	1395	33.29	4191

Table IV-87.   Asymmetry by States

	Right		Left		None		Total
	No.	Per Cent	No.	Per Cent	No.	Per Cent	No.
Massachusetts	60	17.86	33	9.82	243	72.32	336
Tennessee	39	9.42	87	21.01	288	69.56	414
Kentucky	224	18.97	154	13.04	803	67.99	1181
Texas	100	11.86	127	15.06	616	73.07	843
North Carolina	82	18.72	54	12.33	302	68.95	438
Wisconsin	23	7.80	14	4.75	258	87.46	295
Southwest	29	5.41	60	11.19	447	83.40	536
Total	557	13.78	529	13.08	2957	73.14	4043

Table IV-88.   Differences between State Subgroups and Total Series
with Value in Terms of the Probable Error

Asymmetry

	Right Per Cent	x p.e.	Left Per Cent	x p.e.	None Per Cent	x p.e.
Massachusetts	4.08 ± 1.21	3.37	- 3.26 ± 1.19	2.74	- .82 ± 1.56	.53
Tennessee	- 4.36 ± 1.09	4.00	7.93 ± 1.06	7.48	- 3.58 ± 1.39	2.58
Kentucky	5.19 ± .57	9.10	- .04 ± .55	.07	- 5.15 ± .74	6.96
Texas	- 1.92 ± .72	2.67	1.98 ± .70	2.83	- .07 ± .92	.08
North Carolina	4.94 ± 1.05	4.70	- .75 ± 1.02	.74	- 4.19 ± 1.35	3.10
Wisconsin	- 5.98 ± 1.30	4.60	- 8.33 ± 1.28	6.51	14.32 ± 1.67	8.58
Southwest	- 8.37 ± .94	8.90	- 1.89 ± .92	2.05	10.26 ± 1.20	8.55

Table IV-89.   Neck by States

	Medium Length,Breadth		Long,Thin		Short,Thick		Total
	No.	Per Cent	No.	Per Cent	No.	Per Cent	No.
Massachusetts	279	82.79	42	12.46	16	4.75	337
Tennessee	223	53.48	181	43.40	13	3.12	417
Kentucky	711	60.25	387	32.80	82	6.95	1180
Texas	662	72.67	204	22.39	45	4.94	911
North Carolina	232	52.37	199	44.92	12	2.71	443
Wisconsin	280	94.28	16	5.39	1	.34	297
Southwest	432	71.52	137	22.68	35	5.80	604
Total	2819	67.30	1166	27.83	204	4.87	4189

Table IV-90.   Differences between State Subgroups and Total Series
with Value in Terms of the Probable Error

Neck

	Medium Length,Breadth Per Cent	x p.e.	Long,Thin Per Cent	x p.e.	Short,Thick Per Cent	x p.e.
Massachusetts	15.49 ± 1.65	9.39	-15.37 ± 1.58	9.73	- .12 ± .76	.16
Tennessee	-13.82 ± 1.47	9.40	15.57 ± 1.40	11.12	- 1.75 ± .67	2.61
Kentucky	- 7.05 ± .78	9.04	4.97 ± .74	6.72	2.08 ± .36	5.78
Texas	5.37 ± .93	5.77	- 5.44 ± .88	6.18	.07 ± .42	.17
North Carolina	-14.93 ± 1.42	10.51	17.09 ± 1.36	12.57	- 2.16 ± .65	3.32
Wisconsin	26.98 ± 1.77	15.24	-22.44 ± 1.69	13.28	- 4.53 ± .81	5.59
Southwest	4.22 ± 1.19	3.55	- 5.15 ± 1.13	4.56	.93 ± .55	1.69

Table IV-91.   Shoulder Slope by States

| | Slight | | Medium | | Pronounced | | Total |
	No.	Per Cent	No.	Per Cent	No.	Per Cent	No.
Massachusetts	9	2.68	313	93.16	14	4.17	336
Tennessee	12	2.86	327	78.04	80	19.09	419
Kentucky	33	2.78	782	65.94	371	31.28	1186
Texas	2	.22	766	84.27	141	15.51	909
North Carolina	18	4.02	264	58.93	166	37.05	448
Wisconsin	13	4.38	269	90.57	15	5.05	297
Southwest	22	3.65	475	79.04	104	17.30	601
Total	109	2.60	3196	76.17	891	21.23	4196

Table IV-92   Differences between State Subgroups and Total Series
with Value in Terms of the Probable Error

Shoulder Slope

	Slight Per Cent	x p.e.	Pronounced Per Cent	x p.e.
Massachusetts	.08 ± .56	.14	-17.06 ± 1.44	11.85
Tennessee	.26 ± .50	.52	- 2.14 ± 1.28	1.67
Kentucky	.18 ± .26	.69	10.05 ± .67	15.00
Texas	- 2.38 ± .32	7.44	- 5.72 ± .81	7.06
North Carolina	1.42 ± .48	2.96	15.82 ± 1.23	12.86
Wisconsin	1.78 ± .60	2.97	-16.18 ± 1.54	10.51
Southwest	1.06 ± .40	2.65	- 3.93 ± 1.04	3.78

Table IV-94. Summary of Morphological Differentiation of States
from Total Series

Massachusetts

	Significant Differences		Insignificant Differences		Observations not Differentiated	
	Diff.	x p.e.	Diff.	x p.e.	Per Cent	Excess or deficiency
Hair quantity, head						
Small	-	-	- 2.52	2.33	-	-
Medium	-	-	-	-	84.87	excess
Large	-11.42	8.34	-	-	-	-
Hair quantity, beard						
Small	-21.60	12.78	-	-	-	-
Medium	-	-	-	-	67.66	excess
Large	5.23	4.36	-	-	-	-
Hair quantity, body						
Small	-25.27	14.28	-	-	-	-
Medium	-	-	-	-	70.75	excess
Large	- 7.20	5.90	-	-	-	-
Skin color						
Red white	-	-	-	-	30.47	deficiency
Pale white	-	-	-	-	63.90	excess
Ruddy	-	-	-	-	3.25	excess
Olive	-	-	-	-	2.07	deficiency
Light yellow-brown	-	-	-	-	0.30	excess
Hair form						
Straight	- 4.10	3.28	-	-	-	-
Low waves	-	-	- 0.34	0.35	-	-
Deep waves	-	-	-	-	5.36	excess
Hair color						
Black	-	-	- 0.83	1.08	-	-
Dark brown	-	-	- 0.99	0.59	-	-
Reddish brown	15.63	11.01	-	-	-	-
Light brown	-11.51	7.43	-	-	-	-
Ash-blond	-	-	0.81	1.59	-	-
Golden	-	-	0.41	0.63	-	-
Red	-	-	0.03	0.04	-	-
Gray,white	- 3.56	4.56	-	-	-	-
Eye color						
Dark brown	2.33	3.70	-	-	-	-
Light brown	- 1.86	3.05	-	-	-	-
Blue-brown	-	-	- 1.86	1.31	-	-
Gray-brown	- 9.94	7.42	-	-	-	-
Green-brown	7.45	4.74	-	-	-	-
Blue	-	-	- 2.43	1.75	-	-
Blue-gray	6.31	6.07	-	-	-	-
Sclera						
Clear	-17.89	22.94	-	-	-	-
Speckled	17.17	23.20	-	-	-	-
Yellow	-	-	-	-	1.20	excess
Iris						
Homogeneous	-	-	- 0.51	0.54	-	-
Rayed	22.53	14.35	-	-	-	-
Zoned	-	-	- 3.62	2.21	-	-
Speckled	-13.70	8.84	-	-	-	-
Diffused	- 4.70	4.75	-	-	-	-
Eye folds						
Epicanthus	- 2.61	3.58	-	-	-	-
Median	7.44	6.25	-	-	-	-
External	10.00	9.80	-	-	-	-
Absent	-	-	-	-	58.81	deficiency

Table IV-94 (cont'd).

	Significant Differences		Insignificant Differences		Observations not Differentiated	
	Diff.	x p.e.	Diff.	x p.e.	Per Cent	Excess or deficiency
Eyebrow thickness					-	-
Submedium	-	-	1.88	2.61	69.94	excess
Medium	-	-	-	-		
Pronounced	- 9.35	5.06	-	-	-	-
Forehead height					-	-
Submedium	-	-	- 2.28	1.95	62.72	deficiency
Medium	-	-	-	-		
Pronounced	-	-	2.46	1.63	-	-
Forehead slope					-	-
Absent, submedium	- 7.25	7.55	-	-	69.53	excess
Medium	-	-	-	-		
Pronounced	-	-	- 4.94	2.96	-	-
Nasion depression			-	-	3.85	deficiency
Submedium	-	-	-	-	73.08	excess
Medium	-	-	-	-	23.08	excess
Pronounced	-	-	-	-		
Nasal root height					-	-
Submedium	-	-	- 1.29	2.69	67.75	deficiency
Medium	-	-	-	-		
Pronounced	12.93	9.37	-	-	-	-
Nasal root breadth						
Submedium	- 4.28	5.04	-	-	-	-
Medium	-	-	-	-	63.61	deficiency
Pronounced	26.13	25.12	-	-	-	-
Nasal bridge height			-	-	0.30	deficiency
Submedium	-	-	-	-	46.75	deficiency
Medium	-	-	-	-		
Pronounced	7.85	4.49	-	-	-	-
Nasal bridge breadth					-	-
Submedium	- 3.00	4.62	-	-	64.50	deficiency
Medium	-	-	-	-		
Pronounced	19.27	15.06	-	-	-	-
Nasal profile					-	-
Concave	5.07	3.45	-	-	-	-
Straight	-	-	2.40	2.12	-	-
Convex	- 4.51	3.13	-	-	-	-
Concavo-convex	-	-	- 2.95	1.67	-	-
Nasal tip thickness					-	-
Submedium	- 8.79	8.22	-	-	60.96	deficiency
Medium	-	-	-	-		
Pronounced	16.86	11.71	-	-	-	-
Nasal septum inclination			0.86	0.52	-	-
Up	-	-	- 0.73	0.44	-	-
Down	-	-	-	-	0.30	deficiency
Absent	-	-	-	-		
Septum deflection					-	-
Right	9.74	6.49	-	-	-	-
Left	- 4.50	4.33	-	-	-	-
Absent	- 5.24	3.14	-	-		
Lips integumental thickness					-	-
Submedium	25.45	21.39	-	-	58.97	deficiency
Medium	-	-	-	-		
Pronounced	- 2.90	3.54	-	-	-	-

Table IV-94 (cont'd).

	Significant Differences		Insignificant Differences		Observations not Differentiated	
	Diff.	x p.e.	Diff.	x p.e.	Per Cent	Excess or deficiency
Lips membranous thickness						
Submedium	- 4.99	3.78	-	-	-	-
Medium	-	-	-	-	61.98	deficiency
Upper,submedium; lower,pronounced	10.22	8.74	-	-	-	-
Pronounced	-	-	0.71	1.20	-	-
Lip seam						
Absent,submedium	- 6.25	4.96	-	-	-	-
Medium	-	-	-	-	75.00	excess
Pronounced	-	-	- 2.40	1.70	-	-
Alveolar prognathism						
Absent					66.86	deficiency
Submedium	10.33	8.68	-	-	-	-
Medium	5.04	7.20	-	-	-	-
Pronounced	-	-	-	-	0.59	excess
Facial prognathism						
Absent	-	-	-	-	73.37	deficiency
Submedium	4.70	5.22	-	-	-	-
Medium	5.71	7.93	-	-	-	-
Pronounced	3.90	12.19	-	-	-	-
Chin Form						
Median	8.14	4.65	-	-	-	-
Bilateral	- 8.14	4.65	-	-	-	-
Malars prominence						
Submedium	- 3.49	4.15	-	-	-	-
Medium	-	-	-	-	79.57	excess
Pronounced	- 7.15	4.55	-	-	-	-
Cheeks fullness						
Submedium	- 6.04	4.00	-	-	-	-
Medium	-	-	-	-	62.13	excess
Pronounced	-	-	1.53	1.13	-	-
Gonial angles						
Submedium	-	-	2.84	2.47	-	-
Medium	-	-	-	-	77.22	excess
Pronounced	- 9.84	7.34	-	-	-	-
Cheeks wrinkling						
Absent	-	-	-	-	79.76	excess
Slight,medium	-	-	-	-	18.45	deficiency
Pronounced	-	-	-	-	1.79	deficiency
Teeth wear						
Slight,medium	-	-	-	-	86.48	excess
Pronounced	-	-	-	-	13.52	deficiency
Teeth caries						
None	-	-	-	-	5.33	excess
Few	-	-	-	-	47.96	deficiency
Many	20.38	12.74	-	-	-	-
Teeth lost						
None	-15.85	10.16	-	-	-	-
Few	-	-	-	-	62.69	excess
Many	-	-	1.86	1.22	-	-
Bite						
Under	1.89	3.00	-	-	-	-
Edge-to-edge	- 5.41	3.68	-	-	-	-
Slight over	-	-	-	-	54.42	deficiency
Marked over	-	-	3.75	2.34	-	-

Table IV-94 (cont'd).

	Significant Differences		Insignificant Differences		Observations not Differentiated	
	Diff.	x p.e.	Diff.	x p.e.	Per Cent	Excess or deficiency
Ear lobes						
Submedium	13.32	12.00	-	-	-	-
Medium	-	-	-	-	61.61	deficiency
Pronounced	-	-	- 3.61	2.69	-	-
Ear lobe attachment						
Attached	11.81	6.79	-	-	-	-
Free	-	-	-	-	49.39	deficiency
Roll of Helix						
Submedium	-	-	- 3.04	1.82	-	-
Medium,pronounced	-	-	-	-	70.91	excess
Darwin's point						
Absent	-	-	- 3.29	1.88	-	-
Small,medium	-	-	-	-	35.56	excess
Pronounced	- 4.17	- 3.48	-	-	-	-
Antihelix prominence						
Submedium	4.91	5.06	-	-	-	-
Medium	-	-	-	-	66.97	deficiency
Pronounced	5.56	4.45	-	-	-	-
Ear protrusion						
Submedium	-	-	2.33	2.50	-	-
Medium	-	-	-	-	66.07	excess
Pronounced	-11.33	6.70	-	-	-	-
Temporal fullness						
Submedium	-15.57	11.45	-	-	-	-
Medium	-	-	-	-	96.59	excess
Pronounced	- 8.42	8.02	-	-	-	-
Lambdoid flattening						
Absent	-	-	-	-	84.98	excess
Present	-	-	-	-	15.02	deficiency
Asymmetry						
Right	4.08	3.37	-	-	-	-
Left	-	-	- 3.25	2.74	-	-
None	-	-	- 0.82	0.53	-	-
Neck						
Medium length and breadth	15.49	9.39	-	-	-	-
Long, thin	-15.37	9.73	-	-	-	-
Short, thick	-	-	- 0.12	0.16	-	-
Shoulder slope						
Slight	-	-	0.08	0.14	-	-
Medium	-	-	-	-	93.16	excess
Pronounced	-17.06	11.85	-	-	-	-

Table IV-95   Summary of Morphological Differentiation of States
from Total Series

Tennessee

	Significant Differences		Insignificant Differences		Observations not Differentiated	
	Diff.	x p.e.	Diff.	x p.e.	Per Cent	Excess or deficiency
Hair quantity, head						
Small	-	-	- 1.29	1.34	-	-
Medium	-	-	-	-	73.93	excess
Large	-	-	- 1.72	1.42	-	-
Hair quantity, beard						
Small	33.94	22.78	-	-	-	-
Medium	-	-	-	-	23.22	deficiency
Large	- 5.88	5.50	-	-	-	-
Hair quantity, body						
Small	17.36	11.13	-	-	-	-
Medium	-	-	-	-	24.70	deficiency
Large	- 3.79	3.54	-	-	-	-
Skin color						
Red white	-	-	-	-	36.41	excess
Pale white	-	-	-	-	63.12	excess
Ruddy	-	-	-	-	0.48	deficiency
Hair form						
Straight	-	-	2.80	2.54	-	-
Low waves	-	-	- 1.51	1.76	-	-
Deep waves	-	-	-	-	3.08	deficiency
Curly	-	-	-	-	1.90	deficiency
Hair color						
Black	-	-	0.04	0.06	-	-
Dark brown	- 6.33	4.25	-	-	-	-
Reddish brown	-13.49	10.79	-	-	-	-
Light brown	18.70	13.55	-	-	-	-
Ash-blond	-	-	- 0.49	1.06	-	-
Golden	-	-	0.38	0.57	-	-
Red	-	-	0.72	1.20	-	-
Gray, white	-	-	0.48	0.70	-	-
Eye color						
Dark brown	- 2.38	4.25	-	-	-	-
Light brown	-	-	0.75	1.42	-	-
Blue-brown	31.95	25.56	-	-	-	-
Gray-brown	- 4.32	3.66	-	-	-	-
Green-brown	-11.87	8.50	-	-	-	-
Blue	- 6.27	5.10	-	-	-	-
Blue-gray	- 7.86	8.54	-	-	-	-
Sclera						
Clear	- 2.69	3.90	-	-	-	-
Speckled	-	-	1.73	2.66	-	-
Yellow	-	-	-	-	1.44	excess
Iris						
Homogeneous	-	-	- 0.61	0.74	-	-
Rayed	-18.25	13.22	-	-	-	-
Zoned	-	-	2.94	2.04	-	-
Speckled	12.44	9.15	-	-	-	-
Diffused	3.48	3.95	-	-	-	-

Table IV-95 (cont'd).

	Significant Differences		Insignificant Differences		Observations not Differentiated	
	Diff.	x p.e.	Diff.	x p.e.	Per Cent	Excess or deficiency
Eye folds						
Epicanthus	- 2.27	3.55	-	-	-	-
Median	- 6.94	6.61	-	-	-	-
External	- 3.18	3.53	-	-	-	-
Absent	-	-	-	-	86.02	excess
Eyebrows thickness						
Submedium	- 3.19	5.06	-	-	-	-
Medium	-	-	-	-	80.62	excess
Pronounced	-13.96	9.63	-	-	-	-
Forehead height						
Submedium	- 7.66	7.44	-	-	-	-
Medium	-	-	-	-	80.57	excess
Pronounced	-10.01	7.47	-	-	-	-
Forehead slope						
Absent, submedium	15.56	18.31	-	-	-	-
Medium	-	-	-	-	53.55	deficiency
Pronounced	-11.78	7.96	-	-	-	-
Nasion depression						
	-	-	-	-	3.31	deficiency
Submedium	-	-	-	-	84.63	excess
Medium	-	-	-	-	12.06	deficiency
Pronounced	-	-	-	-		
Nasal root height						
	-	-	- 0.93	2.21	-	-
Submedium	-	-	-	-	93.14	excess
Medium	-	-	-	-	-	-
Pronounced	-12.82	10.60	-	-		
Nasal root breadth						
Submedium	- 3.44	5.13	-	-	-	-
Medium	-	-	-	-	98.58	excess
Pronounced	- 9.67	10.51	-	-	-	-
Nasal bridge height						
Medium	-	-	-	-	78.49	excess
Pronounced	-23.60	15.23	-	-	-	-
Nasal bridge breadth						
Submedium	- 2.17	3.74	-	-	-	-
Medium	-	-	-	-	91.71	excess
Pronounced	- 8.77	7.76	-	-	-	-
Nasal profile						
Concave	-	-	1.93	1.48	-	-
Straight	-	-	- 0.73	0.74	-	-
Convex	-	-	1.48	1.16	-	-
Concavo-convex	-	-	- 2.68	1.73	-	-
Nasal tip thickness						
Submedium	- 6.21	6.68	-	-	-	-
Medium	-	-	-	-	86.05	excess
Pronounced	-10.82	8.52	-	-	-	-
Nasal septum inclination						
Up	-24.64	16.99	-	-	-	-
Down	24.83	17.24	-	-	-	-
Absent	-	-	-	-	0.24	deficiency
Septum deflection						
Right	-14.03	10.63	-	-	-	-
Left	- 7.46	8.11	-	-	-	-
Absent	21.50	14.73	-	-	-	-

Table IV-95 (cont'd).

	Significant Differences		Insignificant Differences		Observations not Differentiated	
	Diff.	x p.e.	Diff.	x p.e.	Per Cent	Excess or deficiency
Lips integumental thickness						
Submedium	-11.42	10.98	-	-	-	-
Medium	-	-	-	-	96.45	excess
Pronounced	- 3.51	4.88	-	-	-	-
Lips membranous thickness						
Submedium	- 8.63	7.44	-	-	-	-
Medium	-	-	-	-	84.87	excess
Upper,submedium; lower, pronounced	- 7.09	6.88	-	-	-	-
Pronounced	-	-	- 1.22	2.30	-	-
Lip seam						
Absent, submedium	-	-	0.65	0.60	-	-
Medium	-	-	-	-	64.07	deficiency
Pronounced	-	-	.1.63	1.32	-	-
Alveolar prognathism						
Absent	-	-	-	-	84.63	excess
Submedium	- 4.06	3.90	-	-	-	-
Medium	-	-	1.07	1.81	-	-
Pronounced	-	-	-	-	1.18	excess
Facial prognathism						
Absent	-	-	-	-	87.00	deficiency
Submedium	-	-	2.33	2.91	-	-
Medium	-	-	- 1.28	2.03	-	-
Pronounced	-	-	- 0.36	1.29	-	-
Chin form						
Median	14.33	9.30	-	-	-	-
Bilateral	-14.33	9.30	-	-	-	-
Malars prominence						
Submedium	- 2.82	3.92	-	-	-	-
Medium	-	-	-	-	76.30	excess
Pronounced	- 4.57	3.36	-	-	-	-
Cheeks fullness						
Submedium	- 9.86	7.36	-	-	-	-
Medium	-	-	-	-	75.95	excess
Pronounced	- 8.48	4.07	-	-	-	-
Gonial angles						
Submedium	11.08	10.86	-	-	-	-
Medium	-	-	-	-	61.67	deficiency
Pronounced	-	-	- 2.53	2.13	-	-
Cheeks wrinkling						
Absent	-	-	-	-	34.77	deficiency
Slight, medium	-	-	-	-	48.92	excess
Pronounced	-	-	-	-	16.31	excess
Teeth wear						
None	-	-	-	-	9.38	excess
Slight, medium	-	-	-	-	68.64	deficiency
Pronounced	-	-	-	-	21.98	excess
Teeth caries						
None	-	-	-	-	3.70	excess
Few	-	-	-	-	58.76	deficiency
Many	11.20	8.00	-	-	-	-

Table IV-95 (cont'd).

	Significant Differences		Insignificant Differences		Observations not Differentiated	
	Diff.	x p.e.	Diff.	x p.e.	Per Cent	Excess or deficiency
Teeth lost						
None	-	-	- 1.18	0.86	-	-
Few	-	-	-	-	53.21	excess
Many	-	-	- 3.33	2.48	-	-
Bite						
Under	-	-	0.88	1.60	-	-
Edge-to-edge	8.14	6.26	-	-	-	-
Slight over	-	-	-	-	52.82	deficiency
Marked over	- 7.18	5.06	-	-	-	-
Ear lobes						
Submedium	- 7.77	7.93	-	-	-	-
Medium	-	-	-	-	90.76	excess
Pronounced	-11.68	9.82	-	-	-	-
Ear lobe attachment						
Attached	-	-	- 3.49	2.30	-	-
Free	-	-	-	-	64.69	excess
Roll of helix						
Absent	-	-	-	-	0.24	excess
Submedium	-	-	- 1.25	0.86	-	-
Medium, pronounced	-	-	-	-	68.88	excess
Darwin's point						
Absent	-	-	- 2.04	1.33	-	-
Small, medium	-	-	-	-	27.01	deficiency
Pronounced	-	-	3.13	1.05	-	-
Antihelix prominence						
Submedium	-	-	- 2.18	2.56	-	-
Medium	-	-	-	-	93.35	excess
Pronounced	-13.73	12.60	-	-	-	-
Ear protrusion						
Submedium	-	-	0.57	0.70	-	-
Medium	-	-	-	╲	77.96	excess
Pronounced	-21.46	14.40	-	-	-	-
Temporal fullness						
Submedium	11.13	9.35	-	-	-	-
Medium	-	-	-	-	65.00	deficiency
Pronounced	- 3.43	3.73	-	-	-	-
Lambdoid flattening						
Absent	-	-	-	-	91.19	excess
Present	-	-	-	-	8.81	deficiency
Asymmetry						
Right	- 4.36	4.00	-	-	-	-
Left	7.93	7.48	-	-	-	-
None	-	-	- 3.58	2.58	-	-
Neck						
Medium length and breadth	-13.82	9.40	-	-	-	-
Long and thick	15.57	11.12	-	-	-	-
Short and thick	-	-	- 1.75	2.61	-	-
Shoulder slope						
Slight	-	-	0.26	0.52	-	-
Medium	-	-	-	-	78.04	excess
Pronounced	-	-	- 2.14	1.67	-	-

Table IV-96.   Summary of Morphological Differentiation of States
from Total Series

Kentucky

	Significant Differences		Insignificant Differences		Observations not Differentiated	
	Diff.	x p.e.	Diff.	x p.e.	Per Cent	Excess or deficiency
Hair quantity, head						
Small	-	-	0.86	1.69	-	-
Medium	-	-	-	-	63.12	deficiency
Large	6.94	10.68	-	-	-	-
Hair quantity, beard						
Small	-20.83	26.04	-	-	-	-
Medium	-	-	-	-	78.33	excess
Large	- 6.21	10.90	-	-	-	-
Hair quantity, body						
Small	-15.50	18.68	-	-	-	-
Medium	-	-	-	-	50.59	excess
Large	3.18	5.58	-	-	-	-
Skin color						
Red white	-	-	-	-	38.42	excess
Pale white	-	-	-	-	59.90	deficiency
Ruddy	-	-	-	-	0.17	deficiency
Olive	-	-	-	-	1.52	deficiency
Hair form						
Straight	-	-	1.20	2.03	-	-
Low waves	- 2.46	5.35	-	-	-	-
Deep waves	-	-	-	-	4.91	excess
Curly	-	-	-	-	2.54	excess
Frizzly	-	-	-	-	0.08	deficiency
Hair color						
Black	-	-	0.51	1.42	-	-
Dark brown	2.42	3.02	-	-	-	-
Reddish brown	-	-	- 0.26	0.39	-	-
Light brown	-	-	- 1.71	2.34	-	-
Ash-blond	1.39	5.79	-	-	-	-
Golden	-	-	- 0.42	1.40	-	-
Red	-	-	- 0.71	2.22	-	-
Gray, white	- 1.23	3.42	-	-	-	-
Eye color						
Dark brown	-	-	- 0.19	0.63	-	-
Light brown	- 2.29	8.18	-	-	-	-
Blue-brown	- 5.23	7.81	-	-	-	-
Gray-brown	3.89	6.18	-	-	-	-
Green-brown	-	-	2.17	2.93	-	-
Blue	7.42	11.42	-	-	-	-
Blue-gray	- 5.78	11.56	-	-	-	-
Sclera						
Clear	-	-	0.57	1.54	-	-
Speckled	-	-	- 0.70	2.00	-	-
Yellow	-	-	-	-	0.61	excess
Iris						
Homogeneous	1.32	3.00	-	-	-	-
Rayed	3.50	4.73	-	-	-	-
Zoned	- 7.96	10.34	-	-	-	-
Speckled	-	-	1.76	2.41	-	-
Diffused	1.38	3.00	-	-	-	-

Table IV-96 (cont'd).

	Significant Differences		Insignificant Differences		Observations not Differentiated	
	Diff.	x p.e.	Diff.	x p.e.	Per Cent	Excess or deficiency
Eye folds						
Epicanthus	6.18	18.18	-	-	-	-
Median	2.04	3.71	-	-	-	-
External	-	-	- 0.97	2.02	66.38	deficiency
Absent	-	-	-	-		
Eyebrow thickness					-	-
Submedium	4.15	12.21	-	-	58.35	deficiency
Medium	-	-	-	-		
Pronounced	-	-	0.98	1.26	-	-
Forehead height					-	-
Submedium	4.81	8.74	-	-	58.77	deficiency
Medium	-	-	-	-		
Pronounced	-	-	- 0.68	0.94	-	-
Forehead slope			- 0.22	0.49	-	-
Absent, submedium	-	-	-	-	45.16	deficiency
Medium	-	-	-	-	-	-
Pronounced	12.39	15.68	-	-		
Nasion depression					0.17	excess
Absent	-	-	-	-	12.33	excess
Submedium	-	-	-	-	52.62	deficiency
Medium	-	-	-	-	34.88	excess
Pronounced	-	-	-	-		
Nasal root height					-	-
Submedium	0.90	4.09	-	-	77.00	deficiency
Medium	-	-	-	-		
Pronounced	-	-	1.49	2.29	-	-
Nasal root breadth					-	-
Submedium	- 3.77	10.47	-	-	90.72	excess
Medium	-	-	-	-		
Pronounced	- 1.48	3.02	-	-	-	-
Nasal bridge height					0.59	excess
Submedium	-	-	-	-	35.72	deficiency
Medium	-	-	-	-		
Pronounced	18.58	22.66	-	-	-	-
Nasal bridge breadth					-	-
Submedium	- 2.66	8.58	-	-	87.00	excess
Medium	-	-	-	-		
Pronounced	- 3.58	5.95	-	-	-	-
Nasal profile						
Concave	- 3.68	5.33	-	-	-	-
Straight	-	-	1.05	1.98	-	-
Convex	-10.34	15.43	-	-	-	-
Concavo-convex	12.98	15.83	-	-	-	-
Nasal tip thickness						
Submedium	5.79	11.58	-	-	64.39	deficiency
Medium	-	-	-	-		
Pronounced	-	-	- 1.15	1.72	-	-
Nasal septum inclination					-	-
Up	7.94	10.18	-	-	-	-
Down	- 8.44	10.96	-	-		
Absent	-	-	-	-	0.93	excess
Septum deflection					-	-
Right	10.13	14.47	-	-	-	-
Left	2.99	6.10	-	-	-	-
Absent	-13.12	16.82	-	-	-	-

Table IV-96 (cont'd)

	Significant Differences		Insignificant Differences		Observations not Differentiated	
	Diff.	x p.e.	Diff.	x p.e.	Per Cent	Excess or deficiency
Lips integumental thickness						
Submedium	9.47	17.22	-	-	-	-
Medium	-	-	-	-	70.34	deficiency
Pronounced	1.69	4.45	-	-	-	-
Lips membranous thickness						
Submedium	- 1.93	3.11	-	-	-	-
Medium	-	-	-	-	76.50	excess
Upper, submedium; lower, pronounced	- 8.91	16.20	-	-	-	-
Pronounced	2.26	8.07	-	-	-	-
Lip seam						
Absent, submedium	- 5.80	9.83	-	-	-	-
Medium	-	-	-	-	66.53	excess
Pronounced	5.62	8.65	-	-	-	-
Alveolar prognathism						
Absent	-	-	-	-	74.96	deficiency
Submedium	6.44	11.50	-	-	-	-
Medium	1.35	4.22	-	-	-	-
Pronounced	-	-	-	-	0.08	deficiency
Facial prognathism						
Absent	-	-	-	-	84.39	deficiency
Submedium	1.81	4.31	-	-	-	-
Medium	1.56	4.59	-	-	-	-
Pronounced	-	-	- 0.07	0.47	-	-
Chin form						
Median	- 3.28	4.00	-	-	-	-
Bilateral	3.28	4.00	-	-	-	-
Malars prominence						
Submedium	3.46	9.10	-	-	-	-
Medium	-	-	-	-	69.34	excess
Pronounced	- 3.88	5.39	-	-	-	-
Cheeks fullness						
Submedium	-	-	- 1.45	2.01	-	-
Medium	-	-	-	-	62.44	excess
Pronounced	- 3.36	5.25	-	-	-	-
Gonial angles						
Submedium	-	-	- 0.69	1.25	-	-
Medium	-	-	-	-	73.59	excess
Pronounced	- 2.68	4.25	-	-	-	-
Cheeks wrinkling						
Absent	-	-	-	-	53.85	excess
Slight, medium	-	-	-	-	34.15	deficiency
Pronounced	-	-	-	-	12.00	deficiency
Teeth wear						
None	-	-	-	-	0.17	deficiency
Slight, medium	-	-	-	-	82.04	deficiency
Pronounced	-	-	-	-	17.79	excess
Teeth caries						
None	-	-	-	-	3.45	excess
Few	-	-	-	-	77.76	excess
Many	- 7.54	10.19	-	-	-	-

Table IV-96 (cont'd).

	Significant Differences		Insignificant Differences		Observations not Differentiated	
	Diff.	x p.e.	Diff.	x p.e.	Per Cent	Excess or deficiency
Teeth lost						
None	- 2.41	3.26	-	-	-	-
Few	-	-	-	-	52.38	excess
Many	-	-	- 1.28	1.78	-	-
Bite						
Under	-	-	- 0.65	2.32	-	-
Edge-to-edge	2.01	3.00	-	-	-	-
Slight over	-	-	-	-	53.92	deficiency
Marked over	-	-	- 0.62	0.84	-	-
Ear lobes						
Submedium	3.70	6.98	-	-	-	-
Medium	-	-	-	-	63.34	deficiency
Pronounced	4.28	6.79	-	-	-	-
Ear lobe attachment						
Attached	- 3.52	4.35	-	-	-	-
Free	-	-	-	-	64.72	excess
Roll of helix						
Absent	-	-	-	-	0.17	excess
Submedium	5.03	6.45	-	-	-	-
Medium, pronounced	-	-	-	-	62.67	deficiency
Darwin's point						
Absent	- 6.46	7.88	-	-	-	-
Small, medium	-	-	-	-	27.53	excess
Pronounced	7.04	12.57	-	-	-	-
Antihelix prominence						
Submedium	-	-	- 0.11	0.24	-	-
Medium	-	-	-	-	82.72	excess
Pronounced	- 5.16	8.75	-	-	-	-
Ear protrusion						
Submedium	3.99	9.07	-	-	-	-
Medium	-	- .	-	-	41.27	deficiency
Pronounced	11.82	14.78	-	-	-	-
Temporal fullness						
Submedium	5.70	9.05	-	-	-	-
Medium	-	-	-	-	61.43	deficiency
Pronounced	5.57	11.37	-	-	-	-
Lambdoid flattening						
Absent	-	-	-	-	60.05	deficiency
Present	-	-	-	-	39.95	excess
Asymmetry						
Right	5.19	9.10	-	-	-	-
Left	-	-	- 0.04	0.07	-	-
None	- 5.15	6.96	-	-	-	-
Neck						
Medium length and breadth	- 7.05	9.04	-	-	-	-
Long and thin	4.97	6.72	-	-	-	-
Short and thick	2.08	5.78	-	-	-	-
Shoulder slope						
Slight	-	-	0.18	0.69	-	-
Medium	-	-	-	-	65.94	deficiency
Pronounced	10.05	15.00	-	-	-	-

Table IV-97.   Summary of Morphological Differentiation of States
from Total Series

Texas

	Significant Differences		Insignificant Differences		Observations not Differentiated	
						Excess or
	Diff.	x p.e.	Diff.	x p.e.	Per Cent	deficiency
Hair quantity, head						
Small	3.68	6.03	-	-	-	-
Medium	-	-	-	-	53.33	deficiency
Large	13.92	18.08	-	-	-	-
Hair quantity, beard						
Small	- 9.98	10.62	-	-	-	-
Medium	-	-	-	-	54.60	excess
Large	6.67	9.96	-	-	-	-
Hair quantity, body						
Small	- 6.38	6.51	-	-	-	-
Medium	-	-	-	-	39.28	excess
Large	5.38	7.91	-	-	-	-
Skin color						
Red white	-	-	-	-	45.68	excess
Pale white	-	-	-	-	53.00	deficiency
Ruddy	-	-	-	-	0.33	deficiency
Olive	-	-	-	-	0.98	deficiency
Hair form						
Straight	- 8.63	12.33	-	-	-	-
Low waves	5.94	10.80	-	-	-	-
Deep waves	-	-	-	-	5.68	excess
Curly	-	-	-	-	3.17	excess
Frizzly	-	-	-	-	0.11	excess
Hair color						
Black	2.12	4.82	-	-	-	-
Dark brown	- 4.27	4.50	-	-	-	-
Reddish brown	3.21	4.01	-	-	-	-
Light brown	- 5.12	5.82	-	-	-	-
Ash-blond	-	-	- 0.17	0.57	-	-
Golden	-	-	- 0.02	0.06	-	-
Red	3.17	8.34	-	-	-	-
Gray, white	-	-	1.08	2.45	-	-
Eye color						
Dark brown	-	-	- 0.70	1.94	-	-
Light brown	- 1.19	3.50	-	-	-	-
Blue-brown	- 4.55	5.69	-	-	-	-
Gray-brown	24.30	32.40	-	-	-	-
Green-brown	-14.27	16.22	-	-	-	-
Blue	-	-	1.69	2.17	-	-
Blue-gray	- 5.27	8.93	-	-	-	-
Sclera						
Clear	-	-	1.08	2.45	-	-
Speckled	-	-	- 0.94	2.24	-	-
Yellow	-	-	-	-	0.34	deficiency
Iris						
Homogeneous	-	-	- 1.24	2.34	-	-
Rayed	- 8.36	9.50	-	-	-	-
Zoned	11.75	12.77	-	-	-	-
Speckled	- 4.74	5.51	-	-	-	-
Diffused	2.60	4.73	-	-	-	-

Table IV-97 (cont'd).

	Significant Differences		Insignificant Differences		Observations not Differentiated	
	Diff.	x p.e.	Diff.	x p.e.	Per Cent	Excess or deficiency
Eye folds						
Epicanthus	- 2.65	6.62	-	-	-	-
Median	- 2.68	4.06	-	-	-	-
External			0.09	0.16	-	-
Absent	-	-	-	-	78.88	excess
Eyebrow thickness						
Submedium	-	-	0.01	0.02	-	-
Medium	-	-	-	-	63.64	excess
Pronounced	-	-	- 0.18	0.20	-	-
Forehead height						
Submedium	- 4.12	6.34	-	-	-	-
Medium	-	-	-	-	73.12	excess
Pronounced	- 6.10	7.18	-	-	-	-
Forehead slope						
Absent, submedium	- 6.06	11.22	-	-	-	-
Medium	-	-	-	-	71.91	excess
Pronounced	- 8.52	9.06	-	-	-	-
Nasion depression						
Submedium	-	-	-	-	1.20	deficiency
Medium	-	-	-	-	83.24	excess
Pronounced	-	-	-	-	15.55	deficiency
Nasal root height						
Submedium	-	-	- 0.35	1.30	-	-
Medium	-	-	-	-	86.99	excess
Pronounced	- 7.25	9.42	-	-	-	-
Nasal root breadth						
Submedium	- 4.76	11.33	-	-	-	-
Medium	-	-	-	-	95.63	excess
Pronounced	- 5.41	9.17	-	-	-	-
Nasal bridge height						
Submedium	-	-	-	-	0.11	deficiency
Medium	-	-	-	-	68.63	excess
Pronounced	-13.85	14.13	-	-	-	-
Nasal bridge breadth						
Submedium	- 3.26	8.81	-	-	-	-
Medium	-	-	-	-	89.82	excess
Pronounced	- 5.79	8.04	-	-	-	-
Nasal profile						
Concave	- 4.44	5.42	-	-	-	-
Straight	8.13	12.90	-	-	-	-
Convex	-	-	- 1.59	1.99	-	-
Concavo-convex	-	-	- 2.10	2.14	-	-
Nasal tip thickness						
Submedium	- 9.33	15.81	-	-	-	-
Medium	-	-	-	-	75.90	excess
Pronounced	2.46	3.08	-	-	-	-
Nasal septum inclination						
Up	-10.81	11.75	-	-	-	-
Down	10.91	11.86	-	-	-	-
Absent	-	-	-	-	0.33	deficiency
Septum deflection						
Right	-16.49	19.63	-	-	-	-
Left	- 4.89	8.43	-	-	-	-
Absent	21.37	22.98	-	-	-	-

Table IV-97 (cont'd).

	Significant Differences		Insignificant Differences		Observations not Differentiated	
	Diff.	x p.e.	Diff.	x p.e.	Per Cent	Excess or deficiency
Lips integumental thickness						
Submedium	- 5.07	7.68	-	-	-	-
Medium	-	-	-	-	91.68	excess
Pronounced	- 5.09	11.06	-	-	-	-
Lips membranous thickness						
Submedium	- 7.14	9.65	-	-	-	-
Medium	-	-	-	-	71.74	excess
Upper, submedium; lower, pronounced	3.68	5.66	-	-	-	-
Pronounced	-	-	- 0.36	1.09	-	-
Lip seam						
Absent, submedium	9.48	13.54	-	-	-	-
Medium	-	-	-	-	55.58	deficiency
Pronounced	-	-	1.29	1.65	-	-
Alveolar prognathism						
Absent	-	-	-	-	78.77	deficiency
Submedium	3.81	5.77	-	-	-	-
Medium	-	-	- 0.30	0.79	-	-
Pronounced	-	-	-	-	0.55	excess
Facial prognathism						
Absent	-	-	-	-	87.31	deficiency
Submedium	-	-	0.53	1.04	-	-
Medium	-	-	0.14	0.35	-	-
Pronounced	-	-	- 0.28	1.56	-	-
Chin form						
Median	- 4.60	4.69	-	-	-	-
Bilateral	4.60	4.69	-	-	-	-
Malars prominence						
Submedium	- 4.89	10.63	-	-	-	-
Medium	-	-	-	-	46.10	deficiency
Pronounced	27.71	32.22	-	-	-	-
Cheeks fullness						
Submedium	-18.47	21.73	-	-	-	-
Medium	-	-	-	-	55.14	deficiency
Pronounced	20.95	27.57	-	-	-	-
Gonial angles						
Submedium	- 2.72	4.18	-	-	-	-
Medium	-	-	-	-	56.30	deficiency
Pronounced	16.64	22.19	-	-	-	-
Cheeks wrinkling						
Absent	-	-	-	-	35.02	deficiency
Slight, medium	-	-	-	-	46.48	excess
Pronounced	-	-	-	-	18.50	excess
Teeth wear						
None	-	-	-	-	0.11	deficiency
Slight, medium	-	-	-	-	84.16	excess
Pronounced	-	-	-	-	15.72	deficiency
Teeth caries						
None	-	-	-	-	2.81	excess
Few	-	-	-	-	52.19	deficiency
Many	18.66	21.20	-	-	-	-

Table IV-97 (cont'd).

	Significant Differences		Insignificant Differences		Observations not Differentiated	
	Diff.	x p.e.	Diff.	x p.e.	Per Cent	Excess or deficiency
Teeth lost						
None	3.48	3.95	-	-	-	-
Few	-	-	-	-	44.57	deficiency
Many	-	-	0.65	0.76	-	-
Bite						
Under	- 1.89	5.40	-	-	-	-
Edge-to-edge	- 5.86	7.15	-	-	-	-
Slight over	-	-	-	-	51.35	deficiency
Marked over	11.05	12.28	-	-	-	-
Ear lobes						
Submedium	- 6.59	10.63	-	-	-	-
Medium	-	-	-	-	73.16	excess
Pronounced	4.74	6.32	-	-	-	-
Ear lobe attachment						
Attached	-	-	- 1.66	1.73	-	-
Free	-	-	-	-	62.86	excess
Roll of helix						
Absent	-	-	-	-	1.09	excess
Submedium	-	-	- 0.11	0.12	-	-
Medium, pronounced	-	-	-	-	67.87	excess
Darwin's point						
Absent	3.23	3.33			-	-
Small, medium	-	-	-	-	17.62	deficiency
Pronounced	7.26	11.00	-	-	-	-
Antihelix prominence						
Submedium	2.18	4.04	-	-	-	-
Medium	-	-	-	-	81.82	excess
Pronounced	- 6.56	9.37	-	-	-	-
Ear protrusion						
Submedium	- 3.34	6.42	-	-	-	-
Medium	-	-	-	-	62.73	excess
Pronounced	-	-	- 2.32	2.47	-	-
Temporal fullness						
Submedium	14.27	19.03	-	-	-	-
Medium	-	-	-	-	64.55	deficiency
Pronounced	- 6.12	10.55	-	-	-	-
Lambdoid flattening						
Absent	-	-	-	-	94.96	excess
Present	-	-	-	-	5.04	deficiency
Asymmetry						
Right	-	-	- 1.92	2.67	-	-
Left	-	-	1.98	2.83	-	-
None	-	-	- 0.07	0.08	-	-
Neck						
Medium length and breadth	5.37	5.77	-	-	-	-
Long and thin	- 5.44	6.18	-	-	-	-
Short and thick	-	-	0.07	0.17	-	-
Shoulder slope						
Slight	- 2.38	7.44	-	-	-	-
Medium	-	-	-	-	84.27	excess
Pronounced	- 5.72	7.06	-	-	-	-

Table IV-98.   Summary of Morphological Differentiation of States
from Total Series

North Carolina

	Significant Differences		Insignificant Differences		Observations not Differentiated	
	Diff.	x p.e.	Diff.	x p.e.	Per Cent	Excess or deficiency
Hair quantity, head						
Small	- 3.80	4.09	-	-	-	-
Medium	-	-	-	-	85.20	excess
Large	-10.47	8.95	-	-	-	-
Hair quantity, beard						
Small	35.00	24.30	-	-	-	-
Medium	-	-	-	-	22.82	deficiency
Large	- 6.52	6.33	-	-	-	-
Hair quantity, body						
Small	31.24	20.83	-	-	-	-
Medium	-	-	-	-	16.78	deficiency
Large	- 9.74	9.36	-	-	-	-
Skin color						
Red white	-	-	-	-	32.44	excess
Pale white	-	-	-	-	38.26	deficiency
Ruddy	-	-	-	-	0.45	deficiency
Olive	-	-	-	-	6.94	excess
Light yellow-brown	-	-	-	-	0.22	excess
Light brown	-	-	-	-	21.48	excess
Medium red-brown	-	-	-	-	0.22	excess
Hair form						
Straight	-	-	1.84	1.72	-	-
Low waves	-	-	0.38	0.45	-	-
Deep waves	-	-	-	-	2.92	deficiency
Curly	-	-	-	-	0.67	deficiency
Frizzly	-	-	-	-	0.45	excess
Hair color						
Black	-	-	0.34	0.52	-	-
Dark brown	12.13	8.48	-	-	-	-
Reddish brown	- 7.05	5.83	-	-	-	-
Light brown	-	-	1.13	0.86	-	-
Ash-blond	- 1.96	4.45	-	-	-	-
Golden	-	-	- 0.36	0.65	-	-
Red	- 1.85	3.19	-	-	-	-
Gray, white	- 2.38	3.61	-	-	-	-
Eye color						
Dark brown	-	-	0.24	0.44	-	-
Light brown	-	-	- 1.49	2.86	-	-
Blue-brown	-	-	2.23	1.84	-	-
Gray-brown	-16.04	14.07	-	-	-	-
Green-brown	11.77	8.78	-	-	-	-
Blue	- 5.93	4.98	-	-	-	-
Blue-gray	9.21	10.23	-	-	-	-
Sclera						
Clear	4.78	7.24	-	-	-	-
Speckled	- 4.30	6.82	-	-	-	-
Iris						
Homogeneous	- 4.14	5.18	-	-	-	-
Rayed	-	-	2.73	2.04	-	-
Zoned	- 7.91	5.65	-	-	-	-
Speckled	11.65	8.83	-	-	-	-
Diffused	-	-	- 2.34	2.79	-	-

Table IV-98 (cont'd).

	Significant Differences		Insignificant Differences		Observations not Differentiated	
	Diff.	x p.e.	Diff.	x p.e.	Per Cent	Excess or deficiency
Eye folds					-	-
Epicanthus	-	-	- 0.82	1.32	-	-
Median	-	-	1.90	1.88	-	-
External	-	-	- 0.82	0.95	-	-
Absent	-	-	-	-	73.38	deficiency
Eyebrows thickness					-	-
Submedium	- 3.25	5.33	-	-	-	-
Medium	-	-	-	-	60.71	deficiency
Pronounced	6.01	4.26	-	-	-	-
Forehead height					-	-
Submedium	13.25	13.25	-	-	-	-
Medium	-	-	-	-	47.54	deficiency
Pronounced	-	-	2.10	1.62	-	-
Forehead slope						
Absent, submedium	2.80	3.42	-	-	-	-
Medium	-	-	-	-	49.78	deficiency
Pronounced	4.76	3.33	-	-	-	-
Nasion depression						
Absent	-	-	-	-	0.45	excess
Submedium	-	-	-	-	28.80	excess
Medium	-	-	-	-	62.72	deficiency
Pronounced	-	-	-	-	8.04	deficiency
Nasal root height						
Submedium	-	-	- 0.09	0.22	-	-
Medium	-	-	-	-	53.57	deficiency
Pronounced	25.91	22.14	-	-	-	-
Nasal root breadth					-	-
Submedium	5.84	8.98	-	-	-	-
Medium	-	-	-	-	83.48	deficiency
Pronounced	- 3.87	4.35	-	-	-	-
Nasal bridge height		-			35.49	deficiency
Medium	-	-	-	-	-	-
Pronounced	19.40	12.93	-	-	-	-
Nasal bridge breadth					-	-
Submedium	-	-	1.32	2.36	-	-
Medium	-	-	-	-	83.04	excess
Pronounced	- 3.59	3.29	-	-	-	-
Nasal profile						
Concave	4.61	3.69	-	-	-	-
Straight	- 4.90	5.10	-	-	-	-
Convex	9.82	7.98	-	-	-	-
Concavo-convex	- 9.53	6.35	-	-	-	-
Nasal tip thickness					-	-
Submedium	14.79	16.43	-	-	-	-
Medium	-	-	-	-	62.05	deficiency
Pronounced	- 7.81	6.35	-	-	-	-
Nasal septum inclination					-	-
Up	16.68	11.91	-	-	-	-
Down	-16.47	11.76	-	-	-	-
Absent	-	-	-	-	0.22	deficiency
Septum deflection					-	-
Right	18.66	14.58	-	-	-	-
Left	11.49	12.91	-	-	-	-
Absent	-30.15	21.23	-	-	-	-

Table IV-98 (cont'd).

	Significant Differences		Insignificant Differences		Observations not Differentiated	
	Diff.	x p.e.	Diff.	x p.e.	Per Cent	Excess or deficiency
Lips integumental thickness						
Submedium	- 5.26	5.26	-	-	-	-
Medium	-	-	-	-	88.84	excess
Pronounced	-	-	- 2.07	2.96	-	-
Lips membranous thickness						
Submedium	17.48	15.61	-	-	-	-
Medium	-	-	-	-	47.32	deficiency
Upper, submedium; lower, pronounced	5.77	5.77	-	-	-	-
Pronounced	- 2.66	5.22	-	-	-	-
Lip seam						
Absent, submedium	-	-	1.82	1.72	-	-
Medium	-	-	-	-	61.38	deficiency
Pronounced	-	-	3.15	2.65	-	-
Alveolar prognathism						
Absent	-	-	-	-	95.09	excess
Submedium	- 9.69	9.59	-	-	-	-
Medium	- 2.57	4.51	-	-	-	-
Facial prognathism						
Absent	-	-	-	-	94.42	excess
Submedium	- 3.33	4.27	-	-	-	-
Medium	- 2.56	4.20	-	-	-	-
Pronounced	- 0.83	3.07	-	-	-	-
Chin form						
Median	- 5.47	3.65	-	-	-	-
Bilateral	5.47	3.65	-	-	-	-
Malars prominence						
Submedium	11.08	15.83	-	-	-	-
Medium	-	-	-	-	68.75	excess
Pronounced	-10.91	8.33	-	-	-	-
Cheeks fullness						
Submedium	20.02	15.40	-	-	-	-
Medium	-	-	-	-	46.64	deficiency
Pronounced	- 9.03	7.78	-	-	-	-
Gonial angles						
Submedium	4.27	4.36	-	-	-	-
Medium	-	-	-	-	70.76	excess
Pronounced	- 4.81	4.18	-	-	-	-
Cheeks wrinkling						
Absent	-	-	-	-	55.58	excess
Slight, medium	-	-	-	-	33.48	deficiency
Pronounced	-	-	-	-	10.94	deficiency
Teeth wear						
None	-	-	-	-	0.45	deficiency
Slight, medium	-	-	-	-	85.20	excess
Pronounced	-	-	-	-	13.35	deficiency
Teeth caries						
None	-	-	-	-	0.45	deficiency
Few	-	-	-	-	90.27	excess
Many	-17.05	12.72	-	-	-	-

Table IV-98 (cont'd).

	Significant Differences		Insignificant Differences		Observations not Differentiated	
	Diff.	x p.e.	Diff.	x p.e.	Per Cent	Excess or deficiency
Teeth lost	-	-	-	-	-	-
None	10.65	7.95	-	-	43.34	deficiency
Few	-	-	-	-	-	-
Many	- 5.30	4.05	-	-	-	-
Bite	-	-	-	-	-	-
Under	- 2.63	5.06	-	-	-	-
Edge-to-edge	-	-	3.53	2.92	59.90	excess
Slight over	-	-	-	-	-	-
Marked over	- 6.14	4.65	-	-	-	-
Ear lobes	-	-	-	-	-	-
Submedium	- 4.61	4.90	-	-	77.90	excess
Medium	-	-	-	-	-	-
Pronounced	-	-	- 1.98	1.72	-	-
Ear lobe attachment	-	-	-	-	-	-
Attached	-	-	3.83	2.60	57.14	deficiency
Free	-	-	-	-	0.22	excess
Notched, divided	-	-	-	-	-	-
Roll of helix	-	-	-	-	-	-
Submedium	-	-	1.80	1.28	66.07	deficiency
Medium, pronounced	-	-	-	-	-	-
Darwin's point	-	-	-	-	-	-
Absent	18.77	12.68	-	-	20.54	deficiency
Small, medium	-	-	-	-	-	-
Pronounced	-11.19	11.08	-	-	-	-
Antihelix prominence	-	-	-	-	-	-
Submedium	-	-	- 0.07	0.08	63.31	deficiency
Medium	-	-	-	-	-	-
Pronounced	14.20	13.40	-	-	-	-
Ear protrusion	-	-	-	-	-	-
Submedium	-	-	0.10	0.12	50.89	deficiency
Medium	-	-	-	-	-	-
Pronounced	6.08	4.22	-	-	-	-
Temporal fullness	-	-	-	-	-	-
Submedium	-12.55	10.91	-	-	72.10	deficiency
Medium	-	-	-	-	-	-
Pronounced	13.15	14.78	-	-	-	-
Lambdoid flattening			-	-	50.45	deficiency
Absent	-	-	-	-	49.55	excess
Present	-	-	-	-	-	-
Asymmetry	-	-	-	-	-	-
Right	4.94	4.70	-	-	-	-
Left	-	-	- 0.75	0.74	-	?
None	- 4.19	3.10	-	-	-	-
Neck	-	-	-	-	-	-
Medium length and breadth	-14.93	10.51	-	-	-	-
Long and thin	17.09	12.57	-	-	-	-
Short and thick	- 2.16	3.32	-	-	-	-
Shoulder slope	-	-	-	-	-	-
Slight	-	-	1.42	2.96	58.93	deficiency
Medium	-	-	-	-	-	-
Pronounced	15.82	12.86	-	-	-	-

Table IV-99.   Summary of Morphological Differentiation of States
from Total Series

Wisconsin

	Significant Differences		Insignificant Differences		Observations not Differentiated	
	Diff.	x p.e.	Diff.	x p.e.	Per Cent	Excess or deficiency
Hair quantity, head						
Small	-	-	2.60	2.24	-	-
Medium	-	-	-	-	86.87	excess
Large	-18.54	12.61	-	-	-	-
Hair quantity, beard						
Small	-	-	3.13	1.74	-	-
Medium	-	-	-	-	38.38	deficiency
Large	9.77	7.57	-	-	-	-
Hair quantity, body						
Small	6.58	3.48	-	-	-	-
Medium	-	-	-	-	32.32	deficiency
Large	-	-	- 0.64	0.49	-	-
Skin color						
Red white	-	-	-	-	1.35	deficiency
Pale white	-	-	-	-	97.31	excess
Ruddy	-	-	-	-	1.01	excess
Olive	-	-	-	-	0.34	deficiency
Hair form						
Straight	10.95	8.17	-	-	-	-
Low waves	- 4.68	4.50	-	-	-	-
Hair color						
Black	-	-	0.37	0.45	-	-
Dark brown	8.91	4.98	-	-	-	-
Reddish brown	-	-	- 4.18	2.77	-	-
Light brown	- 7.70	4.67	-	-	-	-
Ash-blond	-	-	- 0.50	0.91	-	-
Golden	- 2.47	3.58	-	-	-	-
Red	- 2.85	3.90	-	-	-	-
Gray, white	8.41	10.26	-	-	-	-
Eye color						
Dark brown	3.07	4.58	-	-	-	-
Light brown	-	-	0.32	0.49	-	-
Blue-brown	-	-	0.23	0.15	-	-
Gray-brown	-17.38	12.15	-	-	-	-
Green-brown	-	-	3.91	2.33	-	-
Blue	-	-	- 2.94	1.99	-	-
Blue-gray	12.80	11.43	-	-	-	-
Sclera						
Clear	4.32	5.27	-	-	-	-
Speckled	- 3.85	4.94	-	-	-	-
Iris						
Homogeneous	-	-	2.38	2.38	-	-
Rayed	-12.20	7.30	-	-	-	-
Zoned	29.66	16.95	-	-	-	-
Speckled	-13.59	8.24	-	-	-	-
Diffused	- 6.24	5.89	-	-	-	-
Eye folds						
Epicanthus	- 3.39	4.35	-	-	-	-
Median	- 9.49	7.53	-	-	-	-
External	-	-	- 1.69	1.55	-	-
Absent	-	-	-	-	88.22	excess

Table IV-99 (cont'd).

	Significant Differences		Insignificant Differences		Observations not Differentiated	
	Diff.	x p.e.	Diff.	x p.e.	Per Cent	Excess or deficiency
Eyebrow thickness						
Submedium	- 2.69	3.49	-	-	-	-
Medium	-	-	-	-	65.99	excess
Pronounced	-	-	0.16	0.09	-	-
Forehead height						
Submedium	10.96	8.77	-	-	-	-
Medium	-	-	-	-	65.66	excess
Pronounced	8.20	5.06	-	-	-	-
Forehead slope						
Absent, submedium	4.66	4.52	-	-	-	-
Medium	-	-	-	-	53.87	deficiency
Pronounced	-	-	- 1.20	0.67	-	-
Nasion depression						
Submedium	-	-	-	-	5.39	deficiency
Medium	-	-	-	-	93.27	excess
Pronounced	-	-	-	-	1.35	deficiency
Nasal root height						
Submedium	-	-	1.15	2.26	-	-
Medium	-	-	-	-	86.53	excess
Pronounced	- 8.29	5.64	-	-	-	-
Nasal root breadth						
Submedium	28.46	35.14	-	-	-	-
Medium	-	-	-	-	60.27	deficiency
Pronounced	-	-	- 3.27	2.92	-	-
Nasal bridge height						
Submedium	-	-	-	-	1.35	excess
Medium	-	-	-	-	79.80	excess
Pronounced	-26.25	13.96	-	-	-	-
Nasal bridge breadth						
Submedium	26.38	37.69	-	-	-	-
Medium	-	-	-	-	62.29	deficiency
Pronounced	- 7.90	5.77	-	-	-	-
Nasal profile						
Concave	10.14	6.50	-	-	-	-
Straight	- 8.00	6.67	-	-	-	-
Convex	12.35	8.02	-	-	-	-
Concavo-convex	-14.49	7.71	-	-	-	-
Nasal tip thickness						
Submedium	13.92	12.32	-	-	-	-
Medium	-	-	-	-	67.68	deficiency
Pronounced	-12.56	8.16	-	-	-	-
Nasal septum inclination						
Up	17.38	9.88	-	-	-	-
Down	-16.95	9.69	-	-	-	-
Septum deflection						
Right	9.84	6.15	-	-	-	-
Left	6.57	5.92	-	-	-	-
Absent	-16.42	9.28	-	-	-	-
Lips integumental thickness						
Submedium	-10.16	8.06	-	-	-	-
Medium	-	-	-	-	94.95	excess
Pronounced	- 3.29	3.77	-	-	-	-

Table IV-99 (cont'd).

	Significant Differences		Insignificant Differences		Observations not Differentiated	
	Diff.	x p.e.	Diff.	x p.e.	Per Cent	Excess or deficiency
Lips membranous thickness						
Submedium	15.99	11.34	-	-	-	-
Medium	-	-	-	-	49.83	deficiency
Upper, submedium; lower, pronounced	4.64	3.74	-	-	-	-
Pronounced	- 2.54	4.03	-	-	-	-
Lip seam						
Absent, submedium	- 8.08	6.08	-	-	-	-
Medium	-	-	-	-	87.88	excess
Pronounced	-13.45	9.09	-	-	-	-
Alveolar prognathism						
Absent	-	-	-	-	89.56	excess
Submedium	- 7.32	5.76	-	-	-	-
Medium	-	-	- 0.43	0.60	-	-
Pronounced	-	-	-	-	1.01	excess
Facial prognathism						
Absent	-	-	-	-	90.57	excess
Submedium	-	-	- 2.08	2.14	-	-
Medium	-	-	- 0.98	1.27	-	-
Pronounced	-	-	0.18	0.53	-	-
Chin form						
Median	15.02	7.99	-	-	-	-
Bilateral	-15.02	7.99	-	-	-	-
Malars prominence						
Submedium	- 5.32	6.11	-	-	-	-
Medium	-	-	-	-	95.62	excess
Pronounced	-21.38	12.96	-	-	-	-
Cheeks fullness						
Submedium	21.75	13.43	-	-	-	-
Medium	-	-	-	-	47.48	deficiency
Pronounced	-11.60	8.00	-	-	-	-
Gonial angles						
Submedium	- 9.56	7.77	-	-	-	-
Medium	-	-	-	-	93.27	excess
Pronounced	-13.49	9.37	-	-	-	-
Cheeks wrinkling						
Absent	-	-	-	-	71.04	excess
Slight, medium	-	-	-	-	22.22	deficiency
Pronounced	-	-	-	-	6.73	deficiency
Teeth wear						
Slight, medium	-	-	-	-	87.14	excess
Pronounced	-	-	-	-	12.86	deficiency
Teeth caries						
Few	-	-	-	-	85.00	excess
Many	-11.33	6.63	-	-	-	-
Teeth lost						
None	-11.67	6.90	-	-	-	-
Few	-	-	-	-	45.49	deficiency
Many	14.87	9.01	-	-	-	-
Bite						
Under	-	-	- 0.61	0.91	-	-
Edge-to-edge	-	-	0.50	0.32	-	-
Slight over	-	-	-	-	59.40	excess
Marked over	-	-	- 4.63	2.72	-	-

Table IV-99 (cont'd).

	Significant Differences		Insignificant Differences		Observations not Differentiated	
	Diff.	x p.e.	Diff.	x p.e.	Per Cent	Excess or deficiency
Ear lobes	-	-	-	-	-	-
Submedium	- 5.02	4.22	-	-	-	-
Medium	-	-	-	-	83.16	excess
Pronounced	- 6.83	4.74	-	-	-	-
Ear lobe attachment			0.93	0.50	-	-
Attached	-	-	0.93	0.50	-	-
Free	-	-	-	-	60.27	deficiency
Roll of helix					-	-
Submedium	-14.96	8.50	-	-	-	-
Medium, pronounced	-	-	-	-	82.83	excess
Darwin's point					-	-
Absent	9.78	5.29	-	-	-	-
Small, medium	-	-	-	-	30.64	excess
Pronounced	-12.31	9.69	-	-	-	-
Antihelix prominence			- 0.38	0.37	-	-
Submedium	-	-	- 0.38	0.37	-	-
Medium	-	-	-	-	69.02	deficiency
Pronounced	8.79	6.61	-	-	-	-
Ear protrusion					-	-
Submedium	- 6.48	6.54	-	-	-	-
Medium	-	-	-	-	82.49	excess
Pronounced	-18.94	10.46	-	-	-	-
Temporal fullness					-	-
Submedium	-14.98	10.40	-	-	-	-
Medium	-	-	-	-	96.96	excess
Pronounced	- 9.28	8.36	-	-	-	-
Lambdoid flattening					55.56	deficiency
Absent	-	-	-	-	55.56	deficiency
Present	-	-	-	..	44.44	excess
Asymmetry						
Right	- 5.98	4.60	-	-	-	-
Left	- 8.33	6.51	-	-	-	-
None	14.32	8.58	-	-	-	-
Neck						
Medium length and breadth	26.98	15.24	-	-	-	-
Long and thin	-22.44	13.28	-	-	-	-
Short and thick	- 4.53	5.59	-	-	-	-
Shoulder slope			1.78	2.97	-	-
Slight	-	-	1.78	2.97	-	-
Medium	-	-	-	-	90.57	excess
Pronounced	-16.18	10.51	-	-	-	-

Table IV-100.   Summary of Morphological Differentiation of States
from Total Series

Southwest

	Significant Differences		Insignificant Differences		Observations not Differentiated	
	Diff.	x p.e.	Diff.	x p.e.	Per Cent	Excess or deficiency
Hair quantity, head						
Small	- 3.41	4.37	-	-	-	-
Medium	-	-	-	-	84.60	excess
Large	-10.26	10.47	-	-	-	-
Hair quantity, beard						
Small	17.00	13.93	-	-	-	-
Medium	-	-	-	-	30.95	deficiency
Large	3.34	3.84	-	-	-	-
Hair quantity, body						
Small	16.19	12.45	-	-	-	-
Medium	-	-	-	-	22.30	deficiency
Large	-	-	- 0.22	0.25	-	-
Skin color						
Red white	-	-	-	-	7.95	deficiency
Pale white	-	-	-	-	78.97	excess
Ruddy	-	-	-	-	1.16	excess
Olive	-	-	-	-	9.93	excess
Light yellow-brown	-	-	-	-	0.17	excess
Light brown	-	-	-	-	1.82	deficiency
Hair form						
Straight	4.33	4.81	-	-	-	-
Low waves	-	-	- 0.89	1.25	-	-
Deep waves	-	-	-	-	2.33	deficiency
Curly	-	-	-	-	0.50	deficiency
Hair color						
Black	- 4.19	7.62	-	-	-	-
Dark brown	- 6.90	5.70	-	-	-	-
Reddish brown	3.63	3.56	-	-	-	-
Light brown	7.40	6.67	-	-	-	-
Ash-blond	-	-	- 0.85	2.30	-	-
Golden	1.84	4.00	-	-	-	-
Red	-	-	- 1.03	2.10	-	-
Gray, white	-	-	0.10	0.18	-	-
Eye color						
Dark brown	-	-	0.15	0.33	-	-
Light brown	7.71	17.52	-	-	-	-
Blue-brown	- 5.91	5.79	-	-	-	-
Gray-brown	-15.39	16.03	-	-	-	-
Green-brown	10.84	9.59	-	-	-	-
Blue	- 5.52	5.52	-	-	-	-
Blue-gray	8.12	10.68	-	-	-	-
Sclera						
Clear	3.34	4.75	-	-	-	-
Speckled	- 2.86	5.40	-	-	-	-
Iris						
Homogeneous	-	-	1.88	2.81	-	-
Rayed	10.07	8.91	-	-	-	-
Zoned	-10.92	9.33	-	-	-	-
Speckled	-	-	0.61	0.55	-	-
Diffused	-	-	- 1.65	2.32	-	-

Table IV-100 (cont'd).

	Significant Differences		Insignificant Differences		Observations not Differentiated	
	Diff.	x p.e.	Diff.	x p.e.	Per Cent	Excess or deficiency
Eye folds						
Epicanthus	- 2.74	5.17	-	-	-	-
Median	4.03	4.74	-	-	-	-
External	-	-	- 0.16	0.22	-	-
Absent	-	-	-	-	72.52	deficiency
Eyebrow thickness						
Submedium	- 3.21	6.17	-	-	-	-
Medium	-	-	-	-	58.44	deficiency
Pronounced	8.24	6.92	-	-	-	-
Forehead height						
Submedium	-	-	- 1.05	1.25	-	-
Medium	-	-	-	-	53.31	deficiency
Pronounced	10.64	9.76	-	-	-	-
Forehead slope						
Absent, submedium	-	-	- 1.52	2.20	-	-
Medium	-	-	-	-	62.25	excess
Pronounced	-	-	- 3.40	2.81	-	-
Nasion depression						
Submedium	-	-	-	-	9.77	excess
Medium	-	-	-	-	83.44	excess
Pronounced	-	-	-	-	6.79	deficiency
Nasal root height						
Submedium	-	-	- 0.39	1.15	-	-
Medium	-	-	-	-	85.10	excess
Pronounced	- 5.32	5.37	-	-	-	-
Nasal root breadth						
Submedium	-	-	1.09	1.98	-	-
Medium	-	-	-	-	76.66	deficiency
Pronounced	7.71	10.28	-	-	-	-
Nasal bridge height						
Submedium	-	-	-	-	0.17	deficiency
Medium	-	-	-	-	59.60	excess
Pronounced	- 4.88	3.87	-	-	-	-
Nasal bridge breadth						
Submedium	-	-	- 0.61	1.30	-	-
Medium	-	-	-	-	63.74	deficiency
Pronounced	17.64	19.17	-	-	-	-
Nasal profile						
Concave	-	-	1.33	1.27	-	-
Straight	- 7.56	9.33	-	-	-	-
Convex	10.81	10.50	-	-	-	-
Concavo-convex	- 4.58	3.61	-	-	-	-
Nasal tip thickness						
Submedium	- 5.85	7.70	-	-	-	-
Medium	-	-	-	-	66.06	deficiency
Pronounced	8.82	8.56	-	-	-	-
Nasal septum inclination						
Up	-	-	- 3.24	2.72	-	-
Down	-	-	3.50	2.97	-	-
Absent	-	-	-	-	0.17	deficiency
Septum deflection						
Right	- 9.09	8.42	-	-	-	-
Left	- 2.47	3.29	-	-	-	-
Absent	11.56	9.71	-	-	-	-

Table IV-100 (cont'd).

	Significant Differences		Insignificant Differences		Observations not Differentiated	
	Diff.	x p.e.	Diff.	x p.e.	Per Cent	Excess or deficiency
Lips integumental thickness						
Submedium	- 7.88	9.27	-	-	-	-
Medium	-	-	-	-	77.81	deficiency
Pronounced	11.58	19.63	-	-	-	-
Lips membranous thickness						
Submedium	-	-	2.53	2.69	-	-
Medium	-	-	-	-	60.93	deficiency
Upper, submedium; lower, pronounced	4.69	5.58	-	-	-	-
Pronounced	-	-	- 0.23	0.55	-	-
Lip seam						
Absent, submedium	-	-	2.57	2.86	-	-
Medium	-	-	-	-	72.35	excess
Pronounced	- 8.57	8.57	-	-	-	-
Alveolar prognathism						
Absent	-	-	-	-	96.69	excess
Submedium	-10.56	12.28	-	-	-	-
Medium	- 3.63	7.12	-	-	-	-
Pronounced	-	-	-	-	0.33	deficiency
Facial prognathism						
Absent	-	-	-	-	96.85	excess
Submedium	- 5.14	7.91	-	-	-	-
Medium	- 3.19	6.14	-	-	-	-
Pronounced	- 0.83	3.46	-	-	-	-
Chin form						
Median	- 4.54	3.60	-	-	-	-
Bilateral	4.54	3.60	-	-	-	-
Malars prominence						
Submedium	-	-	- 1.19	2.02	-	-
Medium	-	-	-	-	78.64	excess
Pronounced	- 8.53	7.68	-	-	-	-
Cheeks fullness						
Submedium	15.59	14.30	-	-	-	-
Medium	-	-	-	-	49.75	deficiency
Pronounced	- 7.72	7.88	-	-	-	-
Gonial angles						
Submedium	-	-	- 2.32	2.80	-	-
Medium	-	-	-	-	75.00	excess
Pronounced	-	-	- 2.46	2.56	-	-
Cheeks wrinkling						
Absent	-	-	-	-	55.63	excess
Slight, medium	-	-	-	-	27.81	deficiency
Pronounced	-	-	-	-	16.56	excess
Teeth wear						
Slight, medium	-	-	-	-	86.71	excess
Pronounced	-	-	-	-	13.29	deficiency
Teeth caries						
None	-	-	-	-	0.18	deficiency
Few	-	-	-	-	87.76	excess
Many	-14.27	12.41	-	-	-	-

Table IV-100 (cont'd)

	Significant Differences		Insignificant Differences		Observations not Differentiated	
	Diff.	x p.e.	Diff.	x p.e.	Per Cent	Excess or deficiency
Teeth lost						
None	6.84	6.05	-	-	-	-
Few	-	-	-	-	42.26	deficiency
Many	-	-	- 0.42	0.38	-	-
Bite						
Under	4.75	10.80	-	-	-	-
Edge-to-edge	-	-	- 0.88	0.85	-	-
Slight over	-	-	-	-	56.08	excess
Marked over	- 5.29	4.68	-	-	-	-
Ear lobes						
Submedium	6.64	8.30	-	-	-	-
Medium	-	-	-	-	65.23	deficiency
Pronounced	-	-	- 0.55	0.57	-	-
Ear lobe attachment						
Attached	-	-	2.09	1.70	-	-
Free	-	-	-	-	58.94	deficiency
Notched, divided	-	-	-	-	0.17	excess
Roll of helix						
Submedium	-	-	- 1.17	0.98	-	-
Medium, pronounced	-	-	-	-	69.04	excess
Darwin's point						
Absent	- 7.75	6.20	-	-	-	-
Small, medium	-	-	-	-	46.19	excess
Pronounced	-10.33	12.15	-	-	-	-
Antihelix prominence						
Submedium	- 3.98	5.69	-	-	-	-
Medium	-	-	-	-	69.70	deficiency
Pronounced	11.72	13.17	-	-	-	-
Ear protrusion						
Submedium	-	-	- 1.36	2.03	-	-
Medium	-	-	-	-	51.99	deficiency
Pronounced	6.45	5.33	-	-	-	-
Temporal fullness						
Submedium	-15.36	15.84	-	-	-	-
Medium	-	-	-	-	87.89	excess
Pronounced	-	-	0.16	0.21	-	-
Lambdoid flattening						
Absent	-	-	-	-	27.29	deficiency
Present	-	-	-	-	72.71	excess
Asymmetry						
Right	- 8.37	8.90	-	-	-	-
Left	-	-	- 1.89	2.05	-	-
None	10.26	8.55	-	-	-	-
Neck						
Medium length and breadth	4.22	3.55	-	-	-	-
Long and thin	- 5.15	4.56	-	-	-	-
Short and thick	-	-	0.93	1.69	-	-
Shoulder slope						
Slight	-	-	1.06	2.65	-	-
Medium	-	-	-	-	79.04	excess
Pronounced	- 3.93	3.78	-	-	-	-

Table IV-101.   Differentiation by States in Terms of Deviations of Complete
Morphological Characters from the Total Series

| | Differentiated | | Undifferentiated | | Total |
	No.	Per Cent	No.	Per Cent	No.
Massachusetts	39	82.98	8	17.02	47
Tennessee	32	68.09	15	31.91	47
Kentucky	41	87.23	6	12.77	47
Texas	36	76.60	11	23.40	47
North Carolina	37	78.72	10	21.28	47
Wisconsin	39	82.98	8	17.02	47
Southwest	37	78.72	10	21.28	47
Total	261	79.33	68	20.67	329

Table V-1.　　　Coefficients of Correlation of Age with Metric
and Indicial Features

	r		r
Weight	.13 ± .01	Nose breadth	.18 ± .01
Height	- .03 ± .01	Ear length (Observer A)	.35 ± .01
Biacromial diameter	- .02 ± .01	Ear length (Observer B)	.28 ± .02
Head length	.03 ± .01	Ear breadth (Observer A)	.21 ± .01
Head breadth	.08 ± .01	Ear breadth (Observer B)	.25 ± .02
Head height (Observer A)	- .04 ± .01	Ear index (Observer A)	- .15 ± .01
Head height (Observer B)	- .01 ± .02	Ear index (Observer B)	- .12 ± .02
Bizygomatic diameter	.10 ± .01	Relative sitting height	.01 ± .01
Total face height	- .04 ± .01	Cephalic index	.04 ± .01
Upper face height	- .01 ± .01	Total facial index	- .10 ± .01
Sitting height	- .04 ± .01	Upper facial index	- .07 ± .01
Nose height	.26 ± .01	Nasal index	- .03 ± .01

Table V-2.　　　Coefficients of Correlation of Weight with Metric
and Indicial Features

	r		r
Age	.13 ± .01	Circumference	.41 ± .01
Height	.48 ± .01	Bizygomatic diameter	.47 ± .01
Biacromial diameter	.41 ± .01	Total face height	.22 ± .01
Chest depth	.55 ± .01	Nose breadth	.28 ± .01
Chest breadth	.57 ± .01	Bigonial diameter	.37 ± .01
Sitting height	.45 ± .01	Relative shoulder breadth	.09 ± .01
Head length	.34 ± .01	Relative sitting height	- .01 ± .01
Head breadth	.31 ± .01	Cephalic index	- .04 ± .01
Head height (Observer A)	.22 ± .01	Total facial index	.11 ± .01
Head height (Observer B)	.21 ± .02	Nasal index	- .10 ± .01

Table V-3.　　　Coefficients of Correlation of Height with Metric
and Indicial Features

	r		r
Age	- .03 ± .01	Total face height	.24 ± .01
Biacromial diameter	.30 ± .01	Weight	.48 ± .01
Chest depth	.21 ± .01	Ear length (Observer A)	.24 ± .01
Sitting height	.70 ± .01	Ear length (Observer B)	.24 ± .02
Head length	.26 ± .01	Cephalic index	- .09 ± .01
Head breadth	.15 ± .01	Length-height index	
Head height (Observer A)	.24 ± .01	(Observer A)	.03 ± .01
Head height (Observer B)	.15 ± .02	(Observer B)	- .03 ± .02
Head circumference	.31 ± .01	Facial index	.05 ± .01
Minimum frontal diameter	.20 ± .01	Nasal index	- .03 ± .01
Bizygomatic diameter	.25 ± .01	Ear index (Observer A)	- .06 ± .01
		Ear index (Observer B)	- .07 ± .02

Table V-4.   Coefficients of Correlation of Head Length with Metric
and Indicial Features

	r		r
Age	.03 ± .01	Ear length (Observer A)	.15 ± .01
Weight	.34 ± .01	Ear length (Observer B)	.18 ± .02
Height	.26 ± .01	Relative shoulder breadth	.01 ± .01
Minimum frontal diameter	.22 ± .01	Total facial index	.02 ± .01
Total face height	.24 ± .01	Nasal index	.04 ± .01
Upper face height	.22 ± .01	Ear index (Observer A)	- .01 ± .01
Nose height	.10 ± .01	Ear index (Observer B)	- .06 ± .02

Table V-5.   Coefficients of Correlation of Head Breadth with Metric
and Indicial Features

	r		r
Age	.08 ± .01	Nose breadth	.19 ± .01
Weight	.31 ± .01	Ear breadth (Observer A)	.13 ± .01
Height	.15 ± .01	Ear breadth (Observer B)	.17 ± .01
		Biacromial diameter	.17 ± .01

Table V-6.   Coefficients of Correlation of Nose Height and Nose Breadth
with Metric and Indicial Features

Nose Height	r	Nose Breadth	r
Age	.26 ± .01	Age	.18 ± .01
Cephalic index	- .01 ± .01	Weight	.28 ± .01
Upper facial index	.46 ± .01	Head breadth	.19 ± .01
Ear length (Observer A)	.18 ± .01	Bigonial diameter	.22 ± .01
Ear length (Observer B)	.18 ± .02	Cephalic index	.03 ± .01
Head length	.10 ± .01	Bizygomatic diameter	.27 ± .01

Table V-7.   Coefficients of Correlation of Cephalic Index with Metric
and Indicial Features

	r		r
Age	.04 ± .01	Biacromial diameter	.02 ± .01
Weight	- .04 ± .01	Nose breadth	.03 ± .01
Height	- .09 ± .01	Nose height	- .01 ± .01

Table V-8. Miscellaneous Coefficients of Correlation

	r
Chest depth with chest breadth	.33 ± .01
Biacromial diameter with sitting height	.28 ± .01
Biacromial diameter with bizygomatic diameter	.27 ± .01
Facial index with nasal index	- .45 ± .01
Facial index with cephalo-facial index	- .23 ± .01
Nasal index with fronto-parietal index	.07 ± .01
Nasal index with ear index	.01 ± .01

Table V-9. Age by Offenses

	No.	Range	Mean	S. D.	V.
First degree murder	310	15-79	37.80 ± .49	12.85 ± .35	33.99 ± .92
Second degree murder	614	15-79	34.05 ± .34	12.50 ± .24	36.71 ± .71
Assault	78	15-69	34.00 ± .89	11.60 ± .63	34.12 ± 1.84
Robbery	411	15-64	26.75 ± .25	7.50 ± .18	28.04 ± .66
Burglary and larceny	1606	15-74	26.50 ± .15	8.85 ± .10	33.40 ± .40
Forgery and fraud	465	15-69	30.25 ± .32	10.15 ± .22	33.55 ± .74
Rape	197	15-69	36.10 ± .60	12.50 ± .42	34.63 ± 1.18
Other sex	149	15-69	37.10 ± .71	12.85 ± .50	34.64 ± 1.35
Vs. public welfare	257	15-69	38.25 ± .52	12.45 ± .37	32.55 ± .97
Arson and all other	101	15-69	33.05 ± .74	10.95 ± .52	33.13 ± 1.57
Total	4188	15-79	30.70 ± .12	11.40 ± .08	37.13 ± .27

Correlation ratio = .40 ± .01

Table V-10. Predictions on Basis of State Composition and Differences from Random Sample of Total Series by Offenses

Age

	Predicted Mean	Diff.of Subgroup and Predicted Mean	Diff.of Subgroup and Total Mean ± p.e.	x p.e.
First degree murder	30.63	7.17	7.10 ± .44	16.14
Second degree murder	29.86	4.19	3.35 ± .31	10.81
Assault	30.91	3.09	3.30 ± .87	3.79
Robbery	30.73	- 3.98	- 3.95 ± .38	10.40
Burglary and larceny	30.52	- 4.02	- 4.20 ± .19	22.10
Forgery and fraud	31.58	- 1.33	- 0.45 ± .36	1.25
Rape	31.26	4.84	5.40 ± .55	9.82
Other sex	30.45	6.65	6.40 ± .63	10.16
Vs. public welfare	31.98	6.27	7.55 ± .48	15.73
Arson and all other	30.31	2.74	2.35 ± .76	3.09

Significant Differences Independent of State Sampling

First degree murder: difference	7.10 (16.14 p.e.)
Second degree murder: difference	3.35 (10.81 p.e.)
Assault: independent difference	3.09 (3.55 p.e.)
Robbery: difference	- 3.95 (10.40 p.e.)
Burglary and larceny: independent difference	- 4.02 (21.16 p.e.)
Rape: independent difference	4.84 (8.80 p.e.)
Other sex: difference	6.40 (10.16 p.e.)
Vs. public welfare: independent difference	6.27 (13.06 p.e.)
Arson and all other: difference	2.35 (3.09 p.e.)

Table V-11.   Weight by Offenses

	No.	Range	Mean	S. D.	V.
First degree murder	276	101-270	155.50 ± .95	23.50 ± .68	15.11 ± .43
Second degree murder	588	91-250	152.10 ± .60	21.60 ± .42	14.20 ± .28
Assault	72	111-230	151.70 ± 1.72	21.70 ± 1.22	14.30 ± .80
Robbery	378	101-230	149.40 ± .61	17.60 ± .43	11.78 ± .29
Burglary and larceny	1522	91-240	148.90 ± .33	18.60 ± .23	12.49 ± .16
Forgery and fraud	427	101-240	153.20 ± .67	20.50 ± .47	13.38 ± .31
Rape	182	101-230	149.20 ± 1.03	20.60 ± .73	13.81 ± .49
Other sex	143	101-260	152.70 ± 1.34	23.80 ± .95	15.59 ± .52
Vs. public welfare	235	101-250	154.30 ± .97	22.10 ± .69	14.32 ± .44
Arson and all other	96	111-190	148.20 ± 1.03	14.90 ± .72	10.05 ± .49
Total	3919	91-270	150.90 ± .22	20.20 ± .15	13.39 ± .10

Correlation ratio = .11 ± .01

Table V-13. Predictions on Basis of State Composition and Differences
from Random Sample of Total Series by Offenses

Weight

	Predicted Mean	Diff.of Subgroup and Predicted Mean	Diff.of Subgroup and Total Mean ± p.e.	x p.e.
First degree murder	150.50	5.00	4.60 ± .82	5.61
Second degree murder	150.75	1.34	1.20 ± .56	2.14
Assault	150.22	1.48	0.80 ± 1.61	0.50
Robbery	150.58	- 1.18	- 1.50 ± .70	2.14
Burglary and larceny	150.83	- 1.93	- 2.00 ± .36	5.56
Forgery and fraud	151.60	1.60	2.30 ± .66	3.48
Rape	149.78	- 0.58	- 1.70 ± 1.01	1.68
Other sex	150.38	2.32	1.80 ± 1.14	1.58
Vs. public welfare	152.68	1.62	3.40 ± .89	3.82
Arson and all other	149.71	- 1.51	- 2.70 ± 1.39	1.94

Differences Significant and Independent of State Sampling

First degree murder: difference   4.60 (5.61 p.e.)
Burglary and larceny: independent difference   - 1.93 (5.36 p.e.)

Differences Rendered Insignificant by State Sampling

Forgery and fraud: independent difference   1.60 (2.42 p.e.)
Vs. public welfare: independent difference   1.62 (1.82 p.e.)

Table V-14.   Height by Offenses

	No.	Range	Mean	S. D.	V.
First degree murder	311	155-190	173.10 ± .24	6.18 ± .17	3.57 ± .10
Second degree murder	616	146-190	172.14 ± .17	6.18 ± .12	3.59 ± .07
Assault	80	152-190	171.66 ± .49	6.54 ± .35	3.81 ± .20
Robbery	414	152-196	172.02 ± .21	6.24 ± .15	3.63 ± .08
Burglary and larceny	1608	137-190	171.60 ± .11	6.42 ± .08	3.74 ± .04
Forgery and fraud	467	149-196	172.53 ± .22	6.96 ± .15	4.03 ± .09
Rape	196	152-190	170.19 ± .32	6.63 ± .23	3.90 ± .13
Other sex	151	146-190	171.00 ± .38	6.87 ± .27	4.02 ± .16
Vs. public welfare	257	155-190	172.92 ± .26	6.06 ± .18	3.50 ± .10
Arson and all other	101	137-184	170.40 ± .45	6.66 ± .32	3.91 ± .19
Total	4201	137-196	171.90 ± .07	6.45 ± .05	3.75 ± .03

Correlation ratio = .11 ± .01

Table V-15. Predictions on Basis of State Composition and Differences
from Random Sample of Total Series by Offenses

Height

	Predicted Mean	Diff.of Subgroup and Predicted Mean	Diff.of Subgroup and Total Mean ± p.e.	x p.e.
First degree murder	172.03	1.07	1.20 ± .25	4.80
Second degree murder	172.20	- 0.06	0.24 ± .18	1.33
Assault	171.32	0.34	- 0.24 ± .49	0.49
Robbery	171.68	0.34	0.12 ± .21	0.57
Burglary and larceny	171.85	- 0.25	- 0.30 ± .11	2.73
Forgery and fraud	172.03	0.50	0.63 ± .20	3.15
Rape	171.22	- 1.03	- 1.71 ± .31	5.52
Other sex	171.58	- 0.58	- 0.90 ± .35	2.57
Vs. public welfare	172.44	0.48	1.02 ± .27	3.78
Arson and all other	171.47	- 1.07	- 1.50 ± .43	3.49

Significant Differences Independent of State Sampling

First degree murder: independent difference   1.07 (4.28 p.e.)
Rape: independent difference   - 1.03 (3.32 p.e.)

Differences Rendered Insignificant by State Sampling

Forgery and fraud: independent difference   0.50 (2.50 p.e.)
Vs. public welfare: independent difference   0.48 (1.78 p.e.)
Arson and all other: independent difference   - 1.07 (2.49 p.e.)

Table V-16.   Biacromial Diameter by Offenses

	No.	Range	Mean	S. D.	V.
First degree murder	308	28-45	38.15 ± .09	2.37 ± .06	6.21 ± .17
Second degree murder	615	28-45	38.00 ± .06	2.28 ± .04	6.00 ± .12
Assault	80	34-45	38.75 ± .18	2.37 ± .13	6.12 ± .33
Robbery	413	31-45	38.18 ± .08	2.28 ± .05	5.97 ± .14
Burglary and larceny	1607	28-45	38.03 ± .04	2.16 ± .03	5.68 ± .07
Forgery and fraud	466	31-48	38.30 ± .07	2.31 ± .05	6.03 ± .13
Rape	197	28-45	38.09 ± .11	2.28 ± .08	5.99 ± .20
Other sex	150	34-45	38.42 ± .12	2.25 ± .09	5.86 ± .23
Vs. public welfare	257	31-45	38.27 ± .09	2.16 ± .06	5.64 ± .17
Arson and all other	103	31-42	38.27 ± .14	2.10 ± .10	5.49 ± .26
Total	4196	28-48	38.12 ± .02	2.25 ± .02	5.90 ± .04

Correlation ratio = .06 ± .01

**Table V-17. Predictions on Basis of State Composition and Differences from
Random Sample of Total Series by Offenses**

Biacromial Diameter

	Predicted Mean	Diff.of Subgroup and Predicted Mean	Diff.of Subgroup and Total Mean ± p.e.	x p.e.
First degree murder	38.08	0.07	0.03 ± .09	0.33
Second degree murder	38.05	- 0.05	- 0.12 ± .06	2.00
Assault	38.16	0.59	0.63 ± .17	3.71
Robbery	38.15	0.03	0.06 ± .08	0.75
Burglary and larceny	38.13	- 0.10	- 0.09 ± .04	2.25
Forgery and fraud	38.20	0.10	0.18 ± .07	2.57
Rape	38.16	- 0.07	- 0.03 ± .11	0.27
Other sex	38.12	0.30	0.30 ± .12	2.50
Vs. public welfare	38.24	0.03	0.15 ± .10	1.50
Arson and all other	38.08	0.19	0.15 ± .15	1.00

Significant Differences Independent of State Sampling

Assault: independent difference   .59 (3.47 p.e.)

Table V-18.   Chest Depth by Offenses

	No.	Range	Mean	S. D.	V.
First degree murder	309	16-27	21.64 ± .07	1.86 ± .05	8.60 ± .23
Second degree murder	608	16-29	21.28 ± .05	1.80 ± .04	8.46 ± .16
Assault	80	18-27	21.30 ± .13	1.72 ± .09	8.08 ± .43
Robbery	413	16-27	20.74 ± .05	1.54 ± .04	7.42 ± .17
Burglary and larceny	1605	16-27	20.78 ± .03	1.50 ± .02	7.70 ± .09
Forgery and fraud	466	16-27	20.98 ± .06	1.76 ± .04	8.39 ± .18
Rape	197	16-29	21.38 ± .09	1.80 ± .06	8.42 ± .29
Other sex	151	16-25	21.26 ± .10	1.74 ± .07	8.18 ± .32
Vs. public welfare	255	18-29	21.52 ± .09	2.08 ± .06	9.66 ± .29
Arson and all other	101	16-25	20.94 ± .10	1.56 ± .07	7.45 ± .35
Total	4185	16-29	21.04 ± .02	1.74 ± .01	8.27 ± .06

Correlation ratio = .17 ± .01

Table V-19.   Predictions on Basis of State Composition and Differences
from Random Sample of Total Series by Offenses

Chest Depth

	Predicted Mean	Diff.of Subgroup and Predicted Mean	Diff.of Subgroup and Total Mean ± p.e.	x p.e.
First degree murder	21.14	0.50	0.60 ± .07	8.57
Second degree murder	21.02	0.26	0.24 ± .05	4.80
Assault	20.91	0.39	0.26 ± .13	2.00
Robbery	21.07	- 0.33	- 0.30 ± .06	5.00
Burglary and larceny	21.00	- 0.22	- 0.26 ± .03	8.57
Forgery and fraud	21.10	- 0.12	- 0.06 ± .05	1.20
Rape	21.02	0.36	0.34 ± .08	4.25
Other sex	20.93	0.33	0.22 ± .10	2.20
Vs. public welfare	21.17	0.35	0.48 ± .07	6.86
Arson and all other	21.06	- 0.12	- 0.10 ± .12	0.83

Significant Differences Independent of State Sampling

First degree murder: independent difference	0.50 (7.14 p.e.)
Second degree murder: difference	0.24 (4.80 p.e.)
Robbery: difference	- 0.30 (5.00 p.e.)
Burglary and larceny: independent difference	- 0.22 (7.33 p.e.)
Rape: difference	0.34 (4.25 p.e.)
Vs. public welfare: independent difference	0.35 (5.00 p.e.)

Table V-20.   Chest Breadth by Offenses

	No.	Range	Mean	S. D.	V.
First degree murder	308	20-40	27.81 ± .08	2.10 ± .06	7.55 ± .20
Second degree murder	609	20-37	27.63 ± .05	1.92 ± .04	6.95 ± .13
Assault	80	23-34	27.84 ± .15	1.95 ± .10	7.00 ± .37
Robbery	413	20-34	27.39 ± .06	1.74 ± .04	6.35 ± .15
Burglary and larceny	1604	20-37	27.27 ± .03	1.83 ± .02	6.71 ± .08
Forgery and fraud	466	20-34	27.51 ± .06	1.92 ± .04	6.98 ± .15
Rape	197	20-34	27.54 ± .09	1.95 ± .07	7.08 ± .24
Other sex	151	23-34	27.60 ± .11	2.04 ± .08	7.39 ± .29
Vs. public welfare	254	23-34	27.78 ± .08	1.80 ± .05	6.48 ± .19
Arson and all other	100	23-37	28.50 ± .15	2.19 ± .10	7.68 ± .37
Total	4182	20-40	27.48 ± .02	1.89 ± .01	6.88 ± .05

Correlation ratio = .13 ± .01

Table V-21. Predictions on Basis of State Composition and Differences
from Random Sample of Total Series by Offenses

Chest Breadth

	Predicted Mean	Diff. of Subgroup and Predicted Mean	Diff. of Subgroup and Total Mean ± p.e.	x p.e.
First degree murder	27.59	0.22	0.33 ± .07	4.71
Second degree murder	27.55	0.08	0.15 ± .05	3.00
Assault	27.41	0.43	0.36 ± .14	2.57
Robbery	27.45	- 0.06	- 0.09 ± .06	1.50
Burglary and larceny	27.46	- 0.19	- 0.21 ± .03	7.00
Forgery and fraud	27.53	- 0.02	0.03 ± .06	0.50
Rape	27.39	0.15	0.06 ± .09	0.67
Other sex	27.42	0.18	0.12 ± .10	1.20
Vs. public welfare	27.55	0.23	0.30 ± .08	3.75
Arson and all other	27.43	1.07	1.02 ± .13	7.85

Significant Differences Independent of State Sampling

First degree murder: independent difference	0.22 (3.14 p.e.)
Burglary and larceny: independent difference	- 0.19 (6.33 p.e.)
Arson and all other: difference	1.02 (7.85 p.e.)

Differences Rendered Insignificant by State Sampling

| Second degree murder: independent difference | 0.08 (1.60 p.e.) |
| Vs. public welfare: independent difference | 0.23 (2.88 p.e.) |

Table V-22.   Sitting Height by Offenses

	No.	Range	Mean	S. D.	V.
First degree murder	309	81-101	90.31 ± .13	3.45 ± .09	3.82 ± .10
Second degree murder	611	78-101	90.19 ± .09	3.27 ± .06	3.63 ± .07
Assault	80	72-101	90.40 ± .30	3.99 ± .21	4.41 ± .24
Robbery	408	78-101	90.55 ± .11	3.36 ± .08	3.71 ± .09
Burglary and larceny	1607	78-104	90.16 ± .06	3.51 ± .04	3.89 ± .05
Forgery and fraud	462	78-101	90.88 ± .11	3.57 ± .08	3.93 ± .09
Rape	195	78-101	89.71 ± .18	3.66 ± .12	4.08 ± .14
Other sex	149	78-101	89.98 ± .19	3.39 ± .13	3.77 ± .15
Vs. public welfare	254	81-104	90.40 ± .14	3.36 ± .10	3.72 ± .11
Arson and all other	103	81- 98	89.80 ± .22	3.24 ± .15	3.61 ± .17
Total	4178	72-104	90.28 ± .04	3.45 ± .02	3.82 ± .03

Correlation ratio = .08 ± .01

Table V-23.   Predictions on Basis of State Composition and Differences
from Random Sample of Total Series by Offenses

Sitting Height

	Predicted Mean	Diff.of Subgroup and Predicted Mean	Diff.of Subgroup and Total Mean ± p.e.	x p.e.
First degree murder	90.17	0.14	0.03 ± .13	0.23
Second degree murder	90.17	0.02	- 0.09 ± .09	1.00
Assault	90.37	0.03	0.12 ± .26	0.46
Robbery	90.19	0.36	0.27 ± .12	2.25
Burglary and larceny	90.28	- 0.12	- 0.12 ± .06	2.00
Forgery and fraud	90.45	0.43	0.60 ± .11	5.45
Rape	90.24	- 0.53	- 0.57 ± .17	3.35
Other sex	90.30	- 0.32	- 0.30 ± .19	1.58
Vs. public welfare	90.56	- 0.16	0.12 ± .15	0.80
Arson and all other	90.07	- 0.27	- 0.48 ± .23	2.09

Significant Differences Independent of State Sampling

Forgery and fraud: independent difference   0.43 (3.91 p.e.)
Rape: independent difference   - 0.53 (3.12 p.e.)

Table V-24.   Head Length by Offenses

	No.	Range	Mean	S. D.	V.
First degree murder	311	167-217	194.46 ± .26	6.93 ± .19	3.56 ± .10
Second degree murder	618	176-217	194.10 ± .17	6.30 ± .12	3.25 ± .06
Assault	80	182-211	194.13 ± .47	6.27 ± .33	3.23 ± .17
Robbery	414	176-214	194.25 ± .21	6.39 ± .15	3.29 ± .08
Burglary and larceny	1611	170-223	193.44 ± .11	6.57 ± .08	3.40 ± .04
Forgery and fraud	467	173-220	194.93 ± .21	6.84 ± .15	3.51 ± .08
Rape	196	176-214	193.85 ± .31	6.48 ± .22	3.34 ± .11
Other sex	151	176-211	193.65 ± .35	6.42 ± .25	3.32 ± .13
Vs. public welfare	257	176-211	193.68 ± .27	6.45 ± .19	3.33 ± .10
Arson and all other	103	173-208	193.44 ± .40	5.94 ± .28	3.07 ± .14
Total	4208	167-223	193.89 ± .07	6.48 ± .05	3.34 ± .02

Correlation ratio = .08 ± .01

Table V-25.   Predictions on Basis of State Composition and Differences
from Random Sample of Total Series by Offenses

Head Length

	Predicted Mean	Diff. of Subgroup and Predicted Mean	Diff. of Subgroup and Total Mean ± p.e.	x p.e.
First degree murder	194.09	0.37	0.57 ± .25	2.28
Second degree murder	193.92	0.18	0.21 ± .18	1.17
Assault	194.15	- 0.02	0.24 ± .49	0.49
Robbery	193.68	0.57	0.36 ± .22	1.64
Burglary and larceny	193.82	- 0.38	- 0.45 ± .11	4.09
Forgery and fraud	193.78	1.15	1.04 ± .20	5.20
Rape	193.83	0.02	- 0.04 ± .31	0.13
Other sex	194.03	- 0.38	- 0.24 ± .36	0.67
Vs. public welfare	193.48	0.20	- 0.21 ± .27	0.78
Arson and all other	193.93	- 0.49	- 0.45 ± .43	1.05

Significant Differences Independent of State Sampling

Burglary and larceny: independent difference	- 0.38 (3.45 p.e.)
Forgery and fraud: difference	1.04 (5.20 p.e.)

Table V-26.   Head Breadth by Offenses

	No.	Range	Mean	S. D.	V.
First degree murder	311	135-170	152.08 ± .20	5.22 ± .14	3.43 ± .09
Second degree murder	617	129-167	151.87 ± .15	5.37 ± .10	3.54 ± .07
Assault	80	135-164	151.54 ± .46	6.03 ± .32	3.98 ± .21
Robbery	414	138-170	152.47 ± .17	5.13 ± .12	3.36 ± .08
Burglary and larceny	1612	129-170	151.90 ± .09	5.52 ± .07	3.63 ± .04
Forgery and fraud	466	135-173	152.77 ± .17	5.40 ± .12	3.54 ± .08
Rape	197	135-173	152.62 ± .26	5.40 ± .18	3.54 ± .12
Other sex	151	135-164	152.02 ± .30	5.40 ± .21	3.55 ± .14
Vs. public welfare	257	138-167	152.53 ± .21	5.04 ± .15	3.30 ± .10
Arson and all other	103	141-164	152.02 ± .34	5.10 ± .24	3.36 ± .16
Total	4208	129-173	152.14 ± .06	5.40 ± .04	3.55 ± .03

Correlation ratio =   .06 ± .01

Table V-27.   Predictions on Basis of State Composition and Differences
from Random Sample of Total Series by Offenses

Head Breadth

	Predicted Mean	Diff. of Subgroup and Predicted Mean	Diff. of Subgroup and Total Mean ± p.e.	x p.e.
First degree murder	152.06	0.02	- 0.06 ± .21	0.29
Second degree murder	151.90	- 0.03	÷ 0.27 ± .15	1.80
Assault	152.31	- 0.77	- 0.60 ± .41	1.46
Robbery	152.22	0.25	0.33 ± .18	1.83
Burglary and larceny	152.13	- 0.23	- 0.24 ± .09	2.67
Forgery and fraud	152.31	0.46	0.63 ± .17	˥ 71
Rape	152.42	0.20	0.48 ± .26	1.85
Other sex	152.15	- 0.13	- 0.12 ± .30	0.40
Vs. public welfare	152.31	0.22	0.39 ± .23	1.70
Arson and all other	152.13	- 0.11	- 0.12 ± .36	0.33

Differences Rendered Insignificant by State Sampling

Forgery and fraud: independent difference   0.46 (2.71 p.e.)

Table V-28.   Head Height (Observer A) by Offenses

	No.	Range	Mean	S. D.	V.
First degree murder	247	116-148	132.30 ± .24	5.58 ± .17	4.22 ± .13
Second degree murder	479	119-145	131.88 ± .17	5.34 ± .12	4.05 ± .09
Assault	34	119-142	131.22 ± .64	5.58 ± .46	4.25 ± .35
Robbery	276	119-148	133.71 ± .21	5.16 ± .15	3.86 ± .11
Burglary and larceny	1042	110-148	132.66 ± .12	5.55 ± .08	4.18 ± .06
Forgery and fraud	313	116-154	133.35 ± .22	5.76 ± .16	4.32 ± .12
Rape	113	119-145	132.87 ± .35	5.52 ± .25	4.15 ± .19
Other sex	81	116-151	132.42 ± .44	5.82 ± .31	4.40 ± .23
Vs. public welfare	202	119-145	132.66 ± .24	5.13 ± .17	3.87 ± .13
Arson and all other	70	122-148	132.51 ± .43	5.28 ± .30	3.98 ± .23
Total	2857	110-154	132.66 ± .07	5.52 ± .05	4.16 ± .05

Correlation ratio = .10 ± .01

Head Height (Observer B) by Offenses

	No.	Range	Mean	S. D.	V.
First degree murder	65	104-136	121.47 ± .43	5.13 ± .30	4.22 ± .25
Second degree murder	138	104-133	119.70 ± .35	6.06 ± .25	5.06 ± .20
Assault	46	104-136	120.90 ± .66	6.60 ± .46	5.46 ± .38
Robbery	138	107-148	122.46 ± .36	6.27 ± .26	5.12 ± .21
Burglary and larceny	567	104-139	121.11 ± .17	6.06 ± .12	5.00 ± .10
Forgery and fraud	153	104-136	122.76 ± .31	5.61 ± .22	4.57 ± .18
Rape	83	104-136	121.35 ± .44	5.94 ± .31	4.90 ± .26
Other sex	69	101-136	120.42 ± .55	6.81 ± .39	5.66 ± .32
Vs. public welfare	55	110-133	121.35 ± .44	4.83 ± .31	3.98 ± .26
Arson and all other	33	110-130	120.36 ± .51	4.35 ± .36	3.61 ± .30
Total	1347	101-148	121.26 ± .11	6.03 ± .08	4.97 ± .06

Correlation ratio = .14 ± .02

Table V-29.   Predictions on Basis of State Composition and Differences
from Random Sample of Total Series by Offenses

Head Height (Observer A)

	Predicted Mean	Diff. of Subgroup and Predicted Mean	Diff. of Subgroup and Total Mean ± p.e.	x p.e.
First degree murder	132.32	- 0.02	- 0.36 ± .24	1.50
Second degree murder	132.48	- 0.60	- 0.78 ± .17	4.59
Assault	132.60	- 1.38	- 1.44 ± .64	2.25
Robbery	132.83	0.88	1.05 ± .21	4.77
Burglary and larceny	132.73	- 0.07	0 ± .12	0
Forgery and fraud	132.76	0.59	0.69 ± .21	3.29
Rape	132.76	0.11	0.21 ± .35	0.60
Other sex	132.62	- 0.20	- 0.24 ± .41	0.58
Vs. public welfare	132.95	- 0.29	0 ± .26	0
Arson and all other	132.54	- 0.03	- 0.15 ± .44	0.34

Table V-29 (cont'd).

Significant Differences Independent of State Sampling

Second degree murder: independent difference	- 0.60 (3.53 p.e.)
Robbery: independent difference	0.88 (4.00 p.e.)

Differences Rendered Insignificant by State Sampling

Forgery and fraud: independent difference	0.59 (2.81 p.e.)

Head Height (Observer B)

	Predicted Mean	Diff.of Actual and Predicted Mean	Diff.of Subgroup and Total Mean ± p.e.	x p.e.
First degree murder	122.33	- 0.86	0.21 ± .50	0.42
Second degree murder	119.63	0.07	- 1.56 ± .35	4.46
Assault	121.53	- 0.63	- 0.36 ± .60	0.60
Robbery	121.90	0.56	1.20 ± .35	3.43
Burglary and larceny	120.96	0.15	- 0.15 ± .17	0.88
Forgery and fraud	121.96	0.80	1.50 ± .33	4.54
Rape	122.36	- 1.01	0.09 ± .45	0.20
Other sex	121.03	- 0.61	- 0.84 ± .49	1.71
Vs. public welfare	121.82	- 0.47	0.09 ± .55	0.16
Arson and all other	122.01	- 1.65	- 0.90 ± .71	1.27

Differences Rendered Insignificant by State Sampling

Second degree murder: independent difference	0.07 (0.20 p.e.)
Robbery: independent difference	0.56 (1.60 p.e.)
Forgery and fraud: independent difference	0.80 (2.42 p.e.)

Table V-30.   Head Circumference by Offenses

	No.	Range	Mean	S. D.	V.
First degree murder	287	514-621	566.66 ± .54	13.68 ± .38	2.41 ± .07
Second degree murder	565	514-609	564.62 ± .45	15.72 ± .32	2.78 ± .06
Assault	74	526-609	560.66 ± 1.29	16.44 ± .91	2.93 ± .15
Robbery	365	514-621	564.98 ± .53	15.12 ± .38	2.68 ± .07
Burglary and larceny	1491	502-621	562.45 ± .28	16.20 ± .20	2.88 ± .04
Forgery and fraud	443	514-621	566.42 ± .52	16.32 ± .37	2.88 ± .06
Rape	173	502-609	561.38 ± .78	15.12 ± .55	2.69 ± .10
Other sex	146	502-597	561.74 ± .87	15.60 ± .62	2.78 ± .11
Vs. public welfare	250	514-609	566.06 ± .67	15.72 ± .47	2.78 ± .08
Arson and all other	96	514-609	562.58 ± 1.16	16.92 ± .82	3.01 ± .15
Total	3890	502-621	563.90 ± .17	16.08 ± .12	2.85 ± .02

Correlation ratio = .11 ± .01

Table V-31.   Predictions on Basis of State Composition and Differences
from Random Sample of Total Series by Offenses

Head Circumference

	Predicted Mean	Diff.of Subgroup and Predicted Mean	Diff.of Subgroup and Total Mean ± p.e.	x p.e.
First degree murder	565.42	1.24	2.76 ± .64	4.31
Second degree murder	564.97	- 0.35	0.72 ± .46	1.56
Assault	561.48	- 0.82	- 3.24 ± 1.26	2.57
Robbery	563.75	1.23	1.08 ± .57	1.90
Burglary and larceny	563.60	- 1.14	- 1.44 ± .28	5.14
Forgery and fraud	564.45	1.97	2.52 ± .52	4.85
Rape	562.81	- 1.43	- 2.52 ± .82	3.07
Other sex	562.41	- 0.67	- 2.16 ± .90	2.40
Vs. public welfare	565.65	0.41	2.16 ± .69	3.13
Arson and all other	563.57	- 0.99	- 1.32 ± 1.11	1.19

Significant Differences Independent of State Sampling

Burglary and larceny: independent difference	- 1.14 (4.07 p.e.)
Forgery and fraud: independent difference	1.97 (3.79 p.e.)

Differences Rendered Insignificant by State Sampling

First degree murder: independent difference	1.24 (1.94 p.e.)
Rape: independent difference	- 1.43 (1.74 p.e.)
Vs. public welfare: independent difference	0.41 (0.59 p.e.)

Table V-32.   Minimum Frontal Diameter by Offenses

	No.	Range	Mean	S. D.	V.
First degree murder	311	97-124	110.74 ± .17	4.56 ± .12	4.12 ± .11
Second degree murder	619	97-128	111.06 ± .14	5.04 ± .10	4.54 ± .09
Assault	80	97-124	111.46 ± .36	4.72 ± .25	4.24 ± .23
Robbery	414	97-128	112.06 ± .14	4.36 ± .10	3.89 ± .09
Burglary and larceny	1610	93-128	111.62 ± .08	4.88 ± .06	4.37 ± .05
Forgery and fraud	467	97-128	112.18 ± .15	4.92 ± .11	4.39 ± .10
Rape	197	97-128	111.34 ± .23	4.76 ± .16	4.28 ± .14
Other sex	150	97-124	110.86 ± .27	4.96 ± .19	4.47 ± .17
Vs. public welfare	257	97-128	112.58 ± .20	4.88 ± .14	4.33 ± .13
Arson and all other	103	97-124	110.42 ± .35	5.28 ± .25	4.78 ± .22
Total	4208	93-128	111.58 ± .05	4.88 ± .04	4.37 ± .03

Correlation ratio =   .09 ± .01

Table V-33.   Predictions on Basis of State Composition and Differences
from Random Sample of Total Series by Offenses

Minimum Frontal Diameter

	Predicted Mean	Diff.of Subgroup and Predicted Mean	Diff.of Subgroup and Total Mean ± p.e.	x p.e.
First degree murder	110.85	- 0.11	- 0.84 ± .19	4.42
Second degree murder	111.15	- 0.09	- 0.52 ± .13	4.00
Assault	111.60	- 0.14	- 0.12 ± .37	0.32
Robbery	111.69	0.37	0.48 ± .16	3.00
Burglary and larceny	111.65	- 0.03	0.04 ± .08	0.50
Forgery and fraud	111.94	0.24	0.60 ± .15	4.00
Rape	111.49	- 0.15	- 0.24 ± .23	1.04
Other sex	111.48	- 0.62	- 0.72 ± .27	2.67
Vs. public welfare	112.40	0.18	1.00 ± .20	5.00
Arson and all other	112.43	- 2.01	- 1.16 ± .32	3.62

Significant Differences Independent of State Sampling

Arson and all other: difference   - 1.16 (3.62 p.e.)

Differences Rendered Insignificant by State Sampling

First degree murder: independent difference   - 0.11 (0.58 p.e.)
Second degree murder: independent difference   - 0.09 (0.69 p.e.)
Robbery: independent difference   0.37 (2.31 p.e.)
Forgery and fraud: independent difference   0.24 (1.60 p.e.)
Vs. public welfare: independent difference   0.18 (0.90 p.e.)

Table V-34.   Bizygomatic Diameter by Offenses

	No.	Range	Mean	S. D.	V.
First degree murder	311	120-159	138.85 ± .21	5.55 ± .15	3.99 ± .11
Second degree murder	619	125-159	138.55 ± .14	5.20 ± .10	3.75 ± .07
Assault	80	120-154	139.20 ± .41	5.40 ± .29	3.88 ± .21
Robbery	414	125-159	139.25 ± .18	5.30 ± .12	3.81 ± .09
Burglary and larceny	1612	120-159	138.15 ± .09	5.30 ± .06	3.84 ± .05
Forgery and fraud	467	125-159	138.95 ± .16	5.15 ± .11	3.71 ± .08
Rape	197	115-154	138.60 ± .25	5.25 ± .18	3.79 ± .13
Other sex	151	125-154	138.70 ± .31	5.60 ± .22	4.04 ± .16
Vs. public welfare	257	115-154	139.75 ± .24	5.60 ± .17	4.01 ± .12
Arson and all other	103	125-149	138.20 ± .34	5.15 ± .24	3.73 ± .18
Total	4211	115-159	138.60 ± .06	5.35 ± .04	3.86 ± .03

Correlation ratio = .09 ± .01

Table V-35.   Predictions on Basis of State Composition and Differences
from Random Sample of Total Series by Offenses

Bizygomatic Diameter

	Predicted Mean	Diff.of Subgroup and Predicted Mean	Diff.of Subgroup and Total Mean ± p.e.	x p.e.
First degree murder	138.48	0.37	0.25 ± .20	1.25
Second degree murder	138.42	0.13	- 0.05 ± .14	0.36
Assault	138.64	0.56	0.60 ± .40	1.50
Robbery	138.60	0.65	0.65 ± .18	3.61
Burglary and larceny	138.59	- 0.44	- 0.45 ± .09	5.00
Forgery and fraud	138.86	0.09	0.35 ± .17	2.06
Rape	138.65	- 0.05	0 ± .26	0
Other sex	138.54	0.16	0.10 ± .29	0.34
Vs. public welfare	139.03	0.72	1.15 ± .22	5.23
Arson and all other	138.38	- 0.18	- 0.40 ± .36	1.11

Significant Differences Independent of State Sampling

Robbery: difference	0.65 (3.61 p.e.)
Burglary and larceny: independent difference	- 0.44 (4.89 p.e.)
Vs. public welfare: independent difference	0.72 (3.27 p.e.)

Table V-36.   Total Face Height by Offenses

	No.	Range	Mean	S. D.	V.
First degree murder	311	100-144	121.95 ± .24	6.40 ± .17	5.25 ± .14
Second degree murder	618	100-154	121.35 ± .18	6.50 ± .13	5.44 ± .10
Assault	80	100-144	122.00 ± .54	7.20 ± .38	5.90 ± .32
Robbery	414	100-139	121.60 ± .21	6.20 ± .14	5.10 ± .12
Burglary and larceny	1611	100-149	121.35 ± .11	6.30 ± .07	5.19 ± .06
Forgery and fraud	467	100-144	122.35 ± .20	6.50 ± .14	5.31 ± .12
Rape	197	100-139	121.95 ± .32	6.70 ± .23	5.49 ± .19
Other sex	151	100-149	122.35 ± .40	7.35 ± .28	6.01 ± .23
Vs. public welfare	257	100-149	121.55 ± .2(	6.95 ± .21	5.72 ± .17
Arson and all other	103	105-144	121.80 ± .44	6.60 ± .31	5.42 ± .26
Total	4209	100-154	121.60 ± .07	6.50 ± .05	5.34 ± .04

Correlation ratio = .06 ± .01

Table V-37.   Predictions on Basis of State Composition and Differences
from Random Sample of Total Series by Offenses

Total Face Height

	Predicted Mean	Diff. of Subgroup and Predicted Mean	Diff. of Subgroup and Total Mean ± p.e.	x p.e.
First degree murder	121.63	0.32	0.35 ± .25	1.40
Second degree murder	121.49	- 0.14	- 0.25 ± .18	1.39
Assault	121.77	0.23	0.40 ± .49	0.82
Robbery	121.80	- 0.20	0 ± .22	0
Burglary and larceny	121.63	- 0.28	- 0.25 ± .11	2.27
Forgery and fraud	121.59	0.76	0.75 ± .20	3.75
Rape	121.91	0.04	0.35 ± .31	1.13
Other sex	121.68	0.67	0.75 ± .36	2.08
Vs. public welfare	121.45	0.10	- 0.05 ± .27	0.18
Arson and all other	121.87	- 0.07	0.20 ± .43	0.46

Significant Differences Independent of State Sampling

Forgery and fraud: difference   0.75 (3.75 p.e.)

Table V-38.   Upper Face Height by Offenses

	No.	Range	Mean	S. D.	V.
First degree murder	312	50-89	69.70 ± .18	4.80 ± .13	6.89 ± .19
Second degree murder	618	50-84	69.20 ± .12	4.55 ± .09	6.58 ± .13
Assault	80	55-84	69.60 ± .35	4.60 ± .24	6.61 ± .35
Robbery	414	55-84	69.35 ± .14	4.25 ± .10	6.13 ± .14
Burglary and larceny	1611	50-94	69.25 ± .07	4.45 ± .05	6.43 ± .08
Forgery and fraud	466	55-94	69.70 ± .14	4.55 ± .10	6.53 ± .14
Rape	197	55-79	69.70 ± .24	4.90 ± .17	7.03 ± .24
Other sex	151	55-94	69.85 ± .28	5.20 ± .20	7.44 ± .29
Vs. public welfare	257	55-94	69.25 ± .20	4.80 ± .14	6.93 ± .21
Arson and all other	103	55-84	69.85 ± .32	4.80 ± .23	6.87 ± .32
Total	4209	50-94	69.40 ± .05	4.55 ± .03	6.56 ± .05

Correlation ratio = .05 ± .01

Table V-39. Predictions on Basis of State Composition and Differences
from Random Sample of Total Series by Offenses

Upper Face Height

	Predicted Mean	Diff.of Subgroup and Predicted Mean	Diff.of Subgroup and Total Mean ± p.e.	x p.e.
First degree murder	69.30	0.40	0.30 ± .17	1.76
Second degree murder	69.19	0.01	- 0.20 ± .12	1.67
Assault	69.92	- 0.32	0.20 ± .35	0.59
Robbery	69.46	- 0.11	- 0.05 ± .15	0.33
Burglary and larceny	69.43	- 0.18	- 0.15 ± .08	1.88
Forgery and fraud	69.39	0.31	0.30 ± .14	2.14
Rape	69.65	0.05	0.30 ± .22	1.36
Other sex	69.65	0.20	0.45 ± .25	1.80
Vs. public welfare	69.07	0.18	- 0.15 ± .19	0.79
Arson and all other	69.50	0.35	0.45 ± .31	1.45

Table V-40.   Nose Height by Offenses

	No.	Range	Mean	S. D.	V.
First degree murder	312	40-71	53.06 ± .16	4.08 ± .11	7.69 ± .21
Second degree murder	618	40-57	52.34 ± .11	3.96 ± .08	7.57 ± .14
Assault	80	40-63	52.74 ± .31	4.08 ± .22	7.74 ± .41
Robbery	412	44-63	51.90 ± .12	3.56 ± .08	6.86 ± .16
Burglary and larceny	1611	36-67	51.74 ± .06	3.84 ± .05	7.42 ± .09
Forgery and fraud	464	40-71	52.50 ± .12	3.92 ± .09	7.47 ± .16
Rape	197	40-63	52.90 ± .20	4.12 ± .14	7.79 ± .26
Other sex	151	40-71	53.06 ± .22	4.08 ± .16	7.69 ± .30
Vs. public welfare	256	36-63	52.66 ± .17	3.96 ± .12	7.52 ± .22
Arson and all other	103	40-63	52.86 ± .30	4.48 ± .21	8.48 ± .40
Total	4204	36-71	52.26 ± .04	3.92 ± .03	7.50 ± .06

Correlation ratio = .12 ± .01

Table V-41   Age Correction for Nose Height

	Mean Age	Predicted Nose Height Mean	Observed Nose Height Mean	Difference	x p.e.
First degree murder	37.80	52.90 ± .14	53.06	0.16	1.14
Second degree murder	34.05	52.56 ± .10	52.34	- 0.22	2.20
Assault	34.00	52.36 ± .29	52.74	0.18	0.62
Robbery	26.75	51.90 ± .13	51.90	- 0.01	0.08
Burglary and larceny	26.50	51.88 ± .06	51.74	- 0.14	2.33
Forgery and fraud	30.25	52.22 ± .12	52.50	0.28	2.33
Rape	36.10	52.74 ± .18	52.90	0.16	0.89
Other sex	37.10	52.83 ± .21	53.06	0.23	1.10
Vs. public welfare	38.25	52.94 ± .16	52.66	- 0.28	1.75
Arson and all other	33.05	52.47 ± .25	52.86	0.39	1.56

Table V-42. Predictions on Basis of State Composition and Differences
from Random Sample of Total Series by Offenses

	Predicted Mean	Diff. of Subgroup and Predicted Mean	Diff. of Subgroup and Total Mean ± p.e.	x p.e.
First degree murder	52.25	0.81	0.80 ± .15	5.33
Second degree murder	51.87	0.47	0.08 ± .11	0.73
Assault	52.51	0.23	0.48 ± .30	1.60
Robbery	52.42	- 0.52	- 0.36 ± .13	2.77
Burglary and larceny	52.20	- 0.46	- 0.52 ± .07	7.43
Forgery and fraud	52.49	0.01	0.24 ± .12	2.00
Rape	52.61	0.29	0.64 ± .19	3.37
Other sex	52.24	0.82	0.80 ± .22	3.64
Vs. public welfare	52.44	0.22	0.40 ± .16	2.50
Arson and all other	52.34	0.52	0.60 ± .26	2.31

Significant Differences Independent of State Sampling

First degree murder: difference   0.80 (5.33 p.e.)
Burglary and larceny: independent difference   - 0.46 (6.57 p.e.)
Other sex: difference   0.80 (3.64 p.e.)

Differences Rendered Insignificant by State Sampling

Rape: independent difference   0.29 (1.52 p.e.)

Table V-43.   Nose Breadth by Offenses

	No.	Range	Mean	S. D.	V.
First degree murder	311	28-42	34.91 ± .10	2.61 ± .07	7.48 ± .20
Second degree murder	618	22-48	34.76 ± .08	2.97 ± .06	8.54 ± .16
Assault	80	28-45	34.73 ± .22	2.85 ± .15	8.21 ± .44
Robbery	413	28-45	34.97 ± .09	2.79 ± .07	7.98 ± .19
Burglary and larceny	1610	25-48	34.55 ± .05	2.73 ± .03	7.90 ± .09
Forgery and fraud	464	25-48	34.82 ± .09	2.79 ± .06	8.01 ± .18
Rape	196	28-45	34.70 ± .13	2.79 ± .10	8.04 ± .27
Other sex	151	28-48	34.91 ± .17	3.15 ± .12	9.02 ± .35
Vs. public welfare	255	28-45	35.54 ± .12	2.73 ± .08	7.68 ± .23
Arson and all other	103	28-42	34.76 ± .19	2.82 ± .13	8.11 ± .38
Total	4201	22-48	34.76 ± .03	2.79 ± .02	8.03 ± .06

Correlation ratio = .09 ± .01

Table V-44   Age Correction for Nose Breadth

	Mean Age	Predicted Nose Breadth Mean	Observed Nose Breadth Mean	Differ-ence	x p.e.
First degree murder	37.80	35.07 ± .10	34.91	- 0.16	1.60
Second degree murder	34.05	34.91 ± .07	34.76	- 0.15	2.14
Assault	34.00	34.91 ± .21	34.73	- 0.18	0.86
Robbery	26.75	34.59 ± .09	34.97	0.38	4.22
Burglary and larceny	26.50	34.58 ± .05	34.55	- 0.03	0.60
Forgery and fraud	30.25	34.74 ± .09	34.82	0.08	0.89
Rape	36.10	35.00 ± .13	34.70	- 0.30	2.31
Other sex	37.10	35.04 ± .15	34.91	- 0.13	0.87
Vs. public welfare	38.25	35.09 ± .12	35.54	0.45	3.75
Arson and all other	33.05	34.86 ± .18	34.76	- 0.10	0.56

Table V-45. Predictions on Basis of State Composition and Differences
from Random Sample of Total Series by Offenses

Nose Breadth

	Predicted Mean	Diff.of Subgroup and Predicted Mean	Diff.of Subgroup and Total Mean ± p.e.	x p.e.
First degree murder	34.76	0.15	0.15 ± .11	1.36
Second degree murder	34.61	0.15	0 ± .08	0
Assault	34.66	0.0	- 0.03 ± .21	0.14
Robbery	34.85	0.12	0.21 ± .09	2.33
Burglary and larceny	34.73	- 0.18	- 0.21 ± .05	4.20
Forgery and fraud	34.99	- 0.17	0.06 ± .09	0.67
Rape	34.76	- 0.06	- 0.06 ± .13	0.46
Other sex	34.60	0.31	0.15 ± .15	1.00
Vs. public welfare	35.17	0.37	0.78 ± .12	6.50
Arson and all other	34.65	0.11	0 ± .18	0

Significant Differences Independent of State Sampling

Burglary and larceny: independent difference   - 0.18 (3.60 p.e.)
Vs. public welfare: independent difference   0.37 (3.08 p.e.)

Table V-46.   Bigonial Diameter by Offenses

	No.	Range	Mean	S. D.	V.
First degree murder	312	86-129	108.94 ± .21	5.60 ± .15	5.14 ± .14
Second degree murder	618	90-129	108.06 ± .15	5.56 ± .11	5.14 ± .10
Assault	80	94-121	107.74 ± .38	5.04 ± .27	4.68 ± .25
Robbery	413	94-125	107.82 ± .19	5.60 ± .13	5.19 ± .12
Burglary and larceny	1609	86-129	107.26 ± .10	5.76 ± .07	5.37 ± .06
Forgery and fraud	466	90-125	108.06 ± .17	5.56 ± .12	5.14 ± .11
Rape	197	90-121	107.06 ± .26	5.32 ± .18	4.97 ± .17
Other sex	151	90-125	107.54 ± .31	5.60 ± .22	5.21 ± .20
Vs. public welfare	257	90-129	109.42 ± .25	5.88 ± .18	5.37 ± .16
Arson and all other	103	94-121	107.30 ± .37	5.52 ± .26	5.14 ± .24
Total	4206	86-129	107.78 ± .06	5.68 ± .04	5.27 ± .04

Correlation ratio = .11 ± .01

Table V-47. Predictions on Basis of State Composition and Differences
from Random Sample of Total Series by Offenses

Bigonial Diameter

	Predicted Mean	Diff.of Subgroup and Predicted Mean	Diff.of Subgroup and Total Mean ± p.e.	x p.e.
First degree murder	107.94	1.00	1.16 ± .22	5.27
Second degree murder	107.69	0.37	0.28 ± .15	1.87
Assault	107.45	0.29	- 0.04 ± .43	0.09
Robbery	107.75	0.07	0.04 ± .19	0.21
Burglary and larceny	107.68	- 0.42	- 0.52 ± .10	5.20
Forgery and fraud	108.12	- 0.06	0.28 ± .18	1.56
Rape	107.65	- 0.59	- 0.72 ± .27	2.67
Other sex	107.46	0.08	- 0.24 ± .31	0.77
Vs. public welfare	108.44	0.98	1.64 ± .24	6.83
Arson and all other	107.54	- 0.24	- 0.48 ± .35	1.37

Significant Differences Independent of State Sampling

First degree murder: independent difference	1.00 (4.54 p.e.)
Burglary and larceny: independent difference	- 0.42 (4.20 p.e.)
Vs. public welfare: independent difference	0.98 (4.08 p.e.)

Table V-48.   Ear Length (Observer A) by Offenses

	No.	Range	Mean	S. D.	V.
First degree murder	247	44-79	61.66 ± .23	5.36 ± .16	8.69 ± .26
Second degree murder	479	44-75	61.46 ± .15	4.88 ± .11	7.94 ± .17
Assault	34	44-79	61.74 ± .68	5.84 ± .48	9.46 ± .77
Robbery	275	48-79	61.34 ± .18	4.48 ± .13	7.30 ± .21
Burglary and larceny	1043	44-79	61.10 ± .10	4.56 ± .07	7.46 ± .11
Forgery and fraud	312	48-79	62.22 ± .18	4.76 ± .13	7.65 ± .21
Rape	112	52-75	62.30 ± .30	4.64 ± .21	7.45 ± .34
Other sex	82	52-79	62.38 ± .37	4.96 ± .26	7.95 ± .42
Vs. public welfare	200	52-79	63.90 ± .24	4.92 ± .17	7.70 ± .26
Arson and all other	70	52-79	61.90 ± .38	4.72 ± .27	7.62 ± .43
Total	2854	44-79	61.66 ± .06	4.84 ± .04	7.85 ± .07

Correlation ratio = .15 ± .01

Ear Length (Observer B) by Offenses

	No.	Range	Mean	S. D.	V.
First degree murder	65	48-75	60.46 ± .40	4.76 ± .28	7.87 ± .47
Second degree murder	138	44-75	58.38 ± .27	4.68 ± .19	8.02 ± .33
Assault	46	48-71	58.54 ± .46	4.60 ± .32	7.86 ± .55
Robbery	138	44-75	57.18 ± .24	4.24 ± .17	7.42 ± .30
Burglary and larceny	568	40-81	57.86 ± .12	4.16 ± .08	7.19 ± .14
Forgery and fraud	153	44-71	58.06 ± .26	4.76 ± .18	8.20 ± .32
Rape	84	44-75	59.26 ± .33	4.44 ± .23	7.49 ± .39
Other sex	69	48-71	59.06 ± .36	4.44 ± .26	7.52 ± .43
Vs. public welfare	55	48-75	59.30 ± .40	4.44 ± .29	7.49 ± .48
Arson and all other	33	48-71	60.18 ± .56	4.80 ± .40	7.98 ± .66
Total	1349	40-81	58.30 ± .08	4.48 ± .06	7.68 ± .10

Correlation ratio = .18 ± .02

Table V-49. Predictions on Basis of State Composition and Differences
from Random Sample of Total Series by Offenses

Ear Length (Observer A)

	Predicted Mean	Diff. of Subgroup and Predicted Mean	Diff. of Subgroup and Total Mean ± p.e.	x p.e.
First degree murder	61.10	0.56	0 ± .21	0
Second degree murder	61.16	0.30	- 0.20 ± .15	1.33
Assault	61.48	0.26	0.08 ± .56	0.14
Robbery	61.78	- 0.44	- 0.32 ± .20	1.60
Burglary and larceny	61.69	- 0.59	- 0.56 ± .10	5.60
Forgery and fraud	62.26	- 0.04	0.56 ± .18	3.11
Rape	61.62	0.68	0.64 ± .31	2.06
Other sex	61.41	0.97	0.72 ± .36	2.00
Vs. public welfare	62.81	1.09	2.24 ± .23	9.74
Arson and all other	61.08	0.82	0.24 ± .39	0.62

Significant Differences Independent of State Sampling

Burglary and larceny: difference   - 0.56 (5.60 p.e.)
Vs. public welfare: independent difference   1.09 (4.74 p.e.)

Differences Rendered Insignificant by State Sampling

Forgery and fraud: independent difference   - 0.04 (0.22 p.e.)

Table V-49 (cont'd).   Ear Length (Observer B)

	Predicted Mean	Diff.of Subgroup and Predicted Mean	Diff.of Subgroup and Total Mean ± p.e.	x p.e.
First degree murder	58.25	2.21	2.16 ± .37	5.84
Second degree murder	58.30	0.08	0.08 ± .26	0.31
Assault	58.37	0.17	0.24 ± .45	0.53
Robbery	58.19	- 1.01	- 1.12 ± .26	4.31
Burglary and larceny	58.29	- 0.43	- 0.44 ± .13	3.38
Forgery and fraud	58.23	- 0.17	- 0.24 ± .24	1.00
Rape	58.50	0.76	0.96 ± .33	2.91
Other sex	58.36	0.70	0.76 ± .36	2.11
Vs. public welfare	58.00	1.30	1.00 ± .41	2.44
Arson and all other	58.31	1.87	1.88 ± .53	3.55

Significant Differences Independent of State Sampling

First degree murder: difference	2.16 (5.84 p.e.)
Robbery: independent difference	- 1.01 (3.88 p.e.)
Burglary and larceny: independent difference	- 0.43 (3.31 p.e.)
Arson and all other: independent difference	1.87 (3.53 p.e.)

Table V-50.   Ear Breadth (Observer A) by Offenses

	No.	Range	Mean	S. D.	V.
First degree murder	247	29-49	38.82 ± .15	3.57 ± .11	9.20 ± .28
Second degree murder	478	29-46	37.68 ± .09	2.79 ± .06	8.13 ± .18
Assault	34	32-46	37.41 ± .28	2.43 ± .20	6.50 ± .53
Robbery	275	32-46	37.68 ± .10	2.46 ± .07	6.53 ± .19
Burglary and larceny	104?	29-49	37.50 ± .05	2.61 ± .04	6.96 ± .10
Forgery and fraud	31?	29-4	38.10 ± .10	2.61 ± .07	6.85 ± .18
Rape	112	32-4.	37.86 ± .18	2.79 ± .13	7.37 ± .33
Other sex	82	26-46	37.35 ± .24	3.18 ± .17	8.51 ± .45
Vs. public welfare	201	29-49	38.07 ± .13	2.79 ± .09	7.33 ± .25
Arson and all other	70	32-46	37.71 ± .21	2.55 ± .14	6.76 ± .38
Total	2854	26-49	37.77 ± .04	2.79 ± .02	7.39 ± .07

Correlation ratio = .14 ± .01

Ear Breadth (Observer B) by Offenses

	No.	Range	Mean	S. D.	V.
First degree murder	65	32-46	36.87 ± .22	2.73 ± .16	7.40 ± .44
Second degree murder	138	29-43	35.88 ± .10	1.65 ± .07	4.60 ± .19
Assault	45	32-43	36.60 ± .29	2.88 ± .20	7.87 ± .56
Robbery	138	29-43	35.64 ± .16	2.70 ± .11	7.58 ± .31
Burglary and larceny	568	29-46	35.73 ± .08	2.73 ± .06	7.64 ± .15
Forgery and fraud	153	29-43	36.27 ± .14	2.61 ± .10	7.20 ± .28
Rape	84	29-46	36.33 ± .22	2.97 ± .16	8.18 ± .43
Other sex	69	29-43	36.36 ± .20	2.43 ± .14	6.68 ± .38
Vs. public welfare	55	29-43	36.81 ± .29	3.15 ± .20	8.56 ± .55
Arson and all other	33	29-43	36.36 ± .32	2.76 ± .23	7.59 ± .63
Total	1348	29-46	36.02 ± .05	2.76 ± .04	7.66 ± .10

Correlation ratio = .14 ± .02

Table V-51.   Predictions on Basis of State Composition and Differences
from Random Sample of Total Series by Offenses

Ear Breadth (Observer A)

	Predicted Mean	Diff. of Subgroup and Predicted Mean	Diff. of Subgroup and Total Mean ± p.e.	x p.e.
First degree murder	37.74	1.08	1.05 ± .12	8.75
Second degree murder	37.76	- 0.08	- 0.09 ± .09	1.00
Assault	37.51	- 0.10	- 0.36 ± .32	1.12
Robbery	37.76	- 0.08	- 0.09 ± .11	0.82
Burglary and larceny	37.75	- 0.25	- 0.27 ± .06	4.50
Forgery and fraud	37.95	0.15	0.33 ± .11	3.00
Rape	37.59	0.27	0.09 ± .18	0.50
Other sex	37.56	- 0.21	- 0.42 ± .21	2.00
Vs. public welfare	38.07	0	0.30 ± .13	2.31
Arson and all other	37.53	0.18	- 0.06 ± .22	0.27

Significant Differences Independent of State Sampling

First degree murder: difference   1.05 (8.75 p.e.)
Burglary and larceny: independent difference   - 0.25 (4.17 p.e.)

Differences Rendered Insignificant by State Sampling

Forgery and fraud: independent difference   0.15 (1.36 p.e.)

Ear Breadth (Observer B)

	Predicted Mean	Diff. of Subgroup and Predicted Mean	Diff. of Subgroup and Total Mean ± p.e.	x p.e.
First degree murder	36.37	0.50	0.85 ± .23	3.70
Second degree murder	35.60	0.28	- 0.14 ± .16	0.88
Assault	36.16	0.44	0.58 ± .28	2.07
Robbery	36.23	- 0.59	- 0.38 ± .16	2.38
Burglary and larceny	35.98	- 0.25	- 0.29 ± .08	3.62
Forgery and fraud	36.26	0.01	0.25 ± .15	1.57
Rape	36.43	- 0.10	0.31 ± .20	1.55
Other sex	36.02	0.34	0.34 ± .22	1.55
Vs. public welfare	36.16	0.65	0.79 ± .25	3.16
Arson and all other	36.29	0.07	0.34 ± .32	1.06

Significant Differences Independent of State Sampling

Burglary and larceny: independent difference   - 0.25 (3.12 p.e.)

Differences Rendered Insignificant by State Sampling

First degree murder: independent difference   0.50 (2.17 p.e.)
Vs. public welfare: independent difference   0.65 (2.60 p.e.)

Table V-52.   Relative Shoulder Breadth by Offenses

	No.	Range	Mean	S. D.	V.
First degree murder	308	14-27	21.64 ± .07	1.84 ± .05	8.50 ± .23
Second degree murder	614	18-27	22.12 ± .02	1.32 ± .02	5.97 ± .12
Assault	80	20-25	22.52 ± .09	1.24 ± .07	5.51 ± .29
Robbery	413	18-29	22.32 ± .05	1.42 ± .03	6.36 ± .15
Burglary and larceny	1605	16-29	22.16 ± .02	1.28 ± .02	5.78 ± .07
Forgery and fraud	466	18-29	22.20 ± .04	1.38 ± .03	6.22 ± .14
Rape	196	18-27	22.56 ± .06	1.34 ± .05	5.94 ± .20
Other sex	150	18-25	22.36 ± .07	1.32 ± .05	5.90 ± .23
Vs. public welfare	257	18-27	22.12 ± .05	1.24 ± .04	5.61 ± .17
Arson and all other	103	20-27	22.46 ± .06	0.96 ± .04	4.27 ± .20
Total	4192	14-29	22.18 ± .01	1.38 ± .01	6.22 ± .05

Correlation ratio = .14 ± .01

Table V-53.   Predictions on Basis of State Composition and Differences
from Random Sample of Total Series by Offenses

Relative Shoulder Breadth

	Predicted Mean	Diff.of Subgroup and Predicted Mean	Diff.of Subgroup and Total Mean ± p.e.	x p.e.
First degree murder	22.12	- 0.48	- 0.54 ± .05	10.80
Second degree murder	22.06	0.06	- 0.06 ± .04	1.50
Assault	22.32	0.20	0.34 ± .10	3.40
Robbery	22.23	0.09	0.14 ± .05	2.80
Burglary and larceny	22.18	- 0.02	- 0.02 ± .02	1.00
Forgery and fraud	22.20	0	0.02 ± .04	0.50
Rape	22.34	0.22	0.38 ± .07	5.43
Other sex	22.24	0.12	0.13 ± .08	2.25
Vs. public welfare	22.15	- 0.03	- 0.06 ± .06	1.00
Arson and all other	22.24	0.22	0.28 ± .09	3.11

Significant Differences Independent of State Sampling

First degree murder: independent difference   - 0.48 (9.60 p.e.)
Rape: independent difference   0.22 (3.14 p.e.)

Differences Rendered Insignificant by State Sampling

Assault: independent difference   0.20 (2.00 p.e.)
Arson and all other: independent difference   0.22 (2.44 p.e.)

Table V-54.   Relative Sitting Height by Offenses

	No.	Range	Mean	S. D.	V.
First degree murder	309	46-57	52.14 ± .06	1.48 ± .04	2.84 ± .08
Second degree murder	610	46-59	52.40 ± .04	1.52 ± .03	2.90 ± .06
Assault	80	42-59	52.54 ± .13	1.76 ± .09	3.35 ± .18
Robbery	408	48-61	52.60 ± .05	1.48 ± .04	2.81 ± .07
Burglary and larceny	1604	46-61	52.56 ± .03	1.58 ± .02	3.01 ± .04
Forgery and fraud	462	42-57	52.52 ± .05	1.60 ± .04	3.04 ± .07
Rape	195	50-57	52.92 ± .08	1.56 ± .05	2.95 ± .10
Other sex	149	48-59	52.52 ± .09	1.62 ± .06	3.08 ± .12
Vs. public welfare	254	48-59	52.34 ± .06	1.34 ± .04	2.56 ± .08
Arson and all other	103	50-57	52.48 ± .10	1.48 ± .07	2.82 ± .13
Total	4174	42-61	52.52 ± .02	1.56 ± .01	2.97 ± .02

Correlation ratio = .09 ± .01

Table V-55. Predictions on Basis of State Composition and Differences
from Random Sample of Total Series by Offenses

	Predicted Mean	Diff. of Subgroup and Predicted Mean	Diff. of Subgroup and Total Mean ± p.e.	x p.e.
First degree murder	52.43	- 0.29	- 0.38 ± .06	6.33
Second degree murder	52.37	0.03	- 0.12 ± .04	3.00
Assault	52.74	- 0.20	0.02 ± .12	0.17
Robbery	52.53	0.07	0.08 ± .05	1.60
Burglary and larceny	52.53	0.03	0.04 ± .03	1.33
Forgery and fraud	52.57	0.05	0.10 ± .05	2.00
Rape	52.70	0.22	0.40 ± .08	5.00
Other sex	52.62	- 0.10	0 ± .09	0
Vs. public welfare	52.51	- 0.17	- 0.18 ± .07	2.57
Arson and all other	52.53	- 0.05	- 0.04 ± .10	0.40

Significant Differences Independent of State Sampling

First degree murder: independent difference   - 0.29 (4.83 p.e.)

Differences Rendered Insignificant by State Sampling

Second degree murder: independent difference   0.03 (0.75 p.e.)
Rape: independent difference   0.22 (2.75 p.e.)

Table V-56.   Cephalic Index by Offenses

	No.	Range	Mean	S. D.	V.
First degree murder	310	65-91	78.15 ± .13	3.33 ± .09	4.26 ± .12
Second degree murder	617	65-91	78.30 ± .09	3.27 ± .06	4.18 ± .08
Assault	80	71-91	78.66 ± .24	3.21 ± .17	4.08 ± .22
Robbery	414	71-91	78.66 ± .12	3.48 ± .08	4.42 ± .10
Burglary and larceny	1609	68-94	78.66 ± .06	3.30 ± .04	4.20 ± .05
Forgery and fraud	466	65-88	78.54 ± .11	3.39 ± .08	4.32 ± .10
Rape	197	71-88	79.02 ± .16	3.42 ± .12	4.33 ± .15
Other sex	151	68-91	78.54 ± .18	3.18 ± .12	4.05 ± .16
Vs. public welfare	257	71-88	78.72 ± .12	2.91 ± .09	3.70 ± .11
Arson and all other	103	71-91	78.87 ± .22	3.30 ± .16	4.18 ± .20
Total	4204	65-94	78.57 ± .03	3.30 ± .02	4.20 ± .03

Correlation ratio = .06 ± .01

Table V-57.   Predictions on Basis of State Composition and Differences
from Random Sample of Total Series by Offenses

Cephalic Index

	Predicted Mean	Diff.of Subgroup and Predicted Mean	Diff.of Subgroup and Total Mean ± p.e.	x p.e.
First degree murder	78.43	- 0.28	- 0.42 ± .13	3.23
Second degree murder	78.40	- 0.10	- 0.27 ± .09	3.00
Assault	78.53	0.13	0.09 ± .25	0.36
Robbery	78.67	- 0.01	0.09 ± .11	0.82
Burglary and larceny	78.56	0.10	0.09 ± .06	1.50
Forgery and fraud	78.66	- 0.12	- 0.03 ± .10	0.30
Rape	78.73	0.29	0.45 ± .16	2.81
Other sex	78.50	0.04	- 0.03 ± .18	0.17
Vs. public welfare	78.76	- 0.04	0.15 ± .14	1.07
Arson and all other	78.54	0.33	0.30 ± .22	1.36

Differences Rendered Insignificant by State Sampling

First degree murder: independent difference   - 0.28 (2.15 p.e.)
Second degree murder: independent difference   - 0.10 (1.11 p.e.)

Table V-58.   Cephalo-facial Index by Offenses

	No.	Range	Mean	S. D.	V.
First degree murder	310	76-102	91.34 ± .13	3.30 ± .09	3.61 ± .10
Second degree murder	616	82-102	91.16 ± .08	3.06 ± .06	3.36 ± .06
Assault	80	82- 99	91.28 ± .25	3.33 ± .18	3.65 ± .20
Robbery	414	72- 99	91.16 ± .10	3.15 ± .07	3.46 ± .08
Burglary and larceny	1609	70-102	90.98 ± .05	3.06 ± .04	3.36 ± .04
Forgery and fraud	466	79-102	90.98 ± .10	3.00 ± .07	3.30 ± .07
Rape	197	72- 99	90.86 ± .16	3.24 ± .11	3.57 ± .12
Other sex	151	85- 99	91.04 ± .18	3.30 ± .13	3.62 ± .14
Vs. public welfare	257	82-102	91.64 ± .13	3.03 ± .09	3.31 ± .10
Arson and all other	103	82- 99	90.89 ± .20	2.94 ± .14	3.24 ± .15
Total	4203	70-102	91.10 ± .03	3.09 ± .02	3.39 ± .02

Correlation ratio = .06 ± .01

Table V-59.   Predictions on Basis of State Composition and Differences
from Random Sample of Total Series by Offenses

Cephalo-facial Index

	Predicted Mean	Diff.of Subgroup and Predicted Mean	Diff.of Subgroup and Total Mean ± p.e.	x p.e.
First degree murder	91.08	0.26	0.24 ± .12	2.00
Second degree murder	91.10	0.06	0.06 ± .08	0.75
Assault	91.07	0.21	0.18 ± .23	0.78
Robbery	91.04	0.12	0.06 ± .10	0.60
Burglary and larceny	91.08	- 0.10	- 0.12 ± .05	2.40
Forgery and fraud	91.17	- 0.19	- 0.12 ± .10	1.20
Rape	90.99	- 0.13	- 0.24 ± .15	1.60
Other sex	91.06	- 0.02	- 0.06 ± .17	0.35
Vs. public welfare	91.23	0.41	0.54 ± .13	4.15
Arson and all other	90.96	- 0.07	- 0.21 ± .20	1.05

Significant Differences Independent of State Sampling

Vs. public welfare: independent difference   0.41 (3.15 p.e.)

Table V-60.   Length-Height Index (Observer A) by Offenses

	No.	Range	Mean	S. D.	V.
First degree murder	246	58-78	68.15 ± .14	3.36 ± .10	4.93 ± .15
Second degree murder	480	58-78	68.00 ± .10	3.15 ± .07	4.63 ± .10
Assault	34	61-75	67.91 ± .40	3.45 ± .28	5.08 ± .42
Robbery	276	55-78	68.90 ± .13	3.21 ± .09	4.66 ± .13
Burglary and larceny	1041	58-81	68.78 ± .06	3.12 ± .05	4.54 ± .07
Forgery and fraud	313	58-81	68.93 ± .13	3.30 ± .09	4.79 ± .13
Rape	113	58-78	68.81 ± .22	3.45 ± .16	5.01 ± .22
Other sex	82	61-78	68.81 ± .23	3.12 ± .16	4.53 ± .24
Vs. public welfare	202	61-78	68.66 ± .15	3.18 ± .11	4.63 ± .16
Arson and all other	70	61-75	68.72 ± .24	2.94 ± .17	4.28 ± .24
Total	2857	55-81	68.60 ± .04	3.21 ± .03	4.68 ± .04

Correlation ratio = .11 ± .01

Length-Height Index (Observer B) by Offenses

	No.	Range	Mean	S. D.	V.
First degree murder	64	52-78	62.84 ± .32	3.84 ± .23	6.11 ± .36
Second degree murder	137	52-69	61.77 ± .19	3.30 ± .13	5.34 ± .22
Assault	46	52-72	62.18 ± .33	3.33 ± .23	5.36 ± .38
Robbery	138	52-72	62.66 ± .20	3.54 ± .14	5.65 ± .23
Burglary and larceny	567	52-78	62.42 ± .10	3.42 ± .07	5.48 ± .11
Forgery and fraud	153	52-78	62.78 ± .19	3.42 ± .13	5.45 ± .21
Rape	83	52-69	62.72 ± .23	3.09 ± .16	4.93 ± .26
Other sex	69	52-72	62.09 ± .27	3.30 ± .19	5.32 ± .30
Vs. public welfare	55	55-75	62.42 ± .26	2.88 ± .18	4.61 ± .30
Arson and all other	33	55-69	61.55 ± .31	2.67 ± .22	4.34 ± .36
Total	1345	52-78	62.42 ± .06	3.39 ± .04	5.43 ± .07

Correlation ratio = .09 ± .02

Table V-61.   Predictions on Basis of State Composition and Differences
from Random Sample of Total Series by Offenses

Length-Height Index (Observer A)

	Predicted Mean	Diff.of Subgroup and Predicted Mean	Diff.of Subgroup and Total Mean ± p.e.	x p.e.
First degree murder	68.24	- 0.09	- 0.45 ± .14	3.21
Second degree murder	68.43	- 0.43	- 0.60 ± .10	6.00
Assault	68.50	- 0.59	- 0.69 ± .37	1.86
Robbery	68.78	0.12	0.30 ± .13	2.31
Burglary and larceny	68.67	0.11	0.18 ± .07	2.57
Forgery and fraud	68.69	0.24	0.33 ± .12	2.75
Rape	68.69	0.12	0.21 ± .20	1.05
Other sex	68.55	0.26	0.21 ± .24	0.88
Vs. public welfare	68.88	- 0.22	0.06 ± .15	0.40
Arson and all other	68.47	0.25	0.12 ± .26	0.46

Significant Differences Independent of State Sampling

Second degree murder: independent difference   - 0.43 (4.30 p.e.)

Differences Rendered Insignificant by State Sampling

First degree murder: independent difference   - 0.09 (0.64 p.e.)

Table V-61 (cont'd).   Length-Height Index (Observer B)

	Predicted Mean	Diff.of Subgroup and Predicted Mean	Diff.of Subgroup and Total Mean ± p.e.	x p.e.
First degree murder	62.99	- 0.15	0.42 ± .29	1.45
Second degree murder	61.52	0.25	- 0.65 ± .20	3.25
Assault	62.56	- 0.38	- 0.24 ± .34	0.71
Robbery	62.74	- 0.08	0.24 ± .20	1.20
Burglary and larceny	62.24	0.18	0 ± .10	0
Forgery and fraud	62.78	0	0.36 ± .18	2.00
Rape	63.03	- 0.31	0.30 ± .25	1.20
Other sex	62.29	- 0.20	- 0.33 ± .28	1.18
Vs. public welfare	62.68	- 0.26	0 ± .31	0
Arson and all other	62.82	- 1.27	- 0.87 ± .40	2.18

Differences Rendered Insignificant by State Sampling

Second degree murder: independent difference   0.25 (1.25 p.e.)

Table V-62.   Breadth-Height Index (Observer A) by Offenses

	No.	Range	Mean	S. D.	V.
First degree murder	247	76-102	87.29 ± .17	3.96 ± .12	4.54 ± .14
Second degree murder	479	76-102	86.75 ± .12	3.72 ± .08	4.29 ± .09
Assault	34	76- 95	85.63 ± .52	4.47 ± .37	5.22 ± .43
Robbery	276	79- 99	87.80 ± .16	3.81 ± .11	4.34 ± .12
Burglary and larceny	1042	76- 99	87.53 ± .08	3.78 ± .06	4.32 ± .06
Forgery and fraud	312	76- 99	87.53 ± .14	3.75 ± .10	4.28 ± .12
Rape	113	73- 99	87.08 ± .26	4.08 ± .18	4.68 ± .21
Other sex	82	73- 96	87.14 ± .30	4.05 ± .21	4.65 ± .24
Vs. public welfare	202	76- 99	86.99 ± .19	3.90 ± .13	4.48 ± .15
Arson and all other	70	76- 93	86.93 ± .24	3.00 ± .17	3.45 ± .20
Total	2857	73-102	87.32 ± .05	3.84 ± .03	4.40 ± .04

Correlation ratio = .10 ± .01

Breadth-Height Index (Observer B) by Offenses

	No.	Range	Mean	S. D.	V.
First degree murder	64	70-93	79.31 ± .29	3.39 ± .20	4.27 ± .25
Second degree murder	137	70-90	79.34 ± .22	3.90 ± .16	4.92 ± .20
Assault	46	70-87	79.10 ± .35	3.48 ± .24	4.40 ± .31
Robbery	138	70-93	80.00 ± .22	3.84 ± .16	4.80 ± .20
Burglary and larceny	567	70-96	79.64 ± .11	3.93 ± .08	4.94 ± .10
Forgery and fraud	153	70-90	80.54 ± .20	3.72 ± .14	4.62 ± .18
Rape	83	70-90	79.46 ± .27	3.69 ± .19	4.64 ± .24
Other sex	69	64-90	79.10 ± .32	3.99 ± .23	5.04 ± .29
Vs. public welfare	55	70-96	80.21 ± .41	4.50 ± .29	5.61 ± .36
Arson and all other	33	73-96	80.00 ± .51	4.38 ± .36	5.48 ± .46
Total	1345	64-96	79.70 ± .07	3.90 ± .05	4.89 ± .06

Correlation ratio = .10 ± .02

Table V-63.   Predictions on Basis of State Composition and Differences
from Random Sample of Total Series by Offenses

Breadth-Height Index (Observer A)

	Predicted Mean	Diff.of Subgroup and Predicted Mean	Diff.of Subgroup and Total Mean ± p.e.	x p.e.
First degree murder	87.16	0.13	- 0.03 ± .16	0.19
Second degree murder	87.24	- 0.49	- 0.57 ± .12	4.75
Assault	87.32	- 1.69	- 1.69 ± .44	3.84
Robbery	87.39	0.41	0.48 ± .16	3.00
Burglary and larceny	87.34	0.19	0.21 ± .08	2.62
Forgery and fraud	87.28	0.25	0.21 ± .15	1.40
Rape	87.39	- 0.31	- 0.24 ± .24	1.00
Other sex	87.33	- 0.19	- 0.18 ± .29	0.62
Vs. public welfare	87.32	- 0.33	- 0.33 ± .18	1.83
Arson and all other	87.32	- 0.39	- 0.39 ± .31	1.26

Significant Differences Independent of State Sampling

Second degree murder: independent difference	- 0.49 (4.08 p.e.)
Assault: difference	- 1.69 (3.84 p.e.)

Differences Rendered Insignificant by State Sampling

Robbery: independent difference	0.41 (2.56 p.e.)

Breadth-Height Index (Observer B)

	Predicted Mean	Diff.of Subgroup and Predicted Mean	Diff.of Subgroup and Total Mean ± p.e.	x p.e.
First degree murder	80.22	- 0.91	- 0.39 ± .33	1.18
Second degree murder	78.88	0.46	- 0.36 ± .22	1.64
Assault	79.78	- 0.68	- 0.60 ± .39	1.54
Robbery	80.03	- 0.03	0.30 ± .22	1.36
Burglary and larceny	79.53	0.11	- 0.06 ± .11	0.54
Forgery and fraud	80.05	0.49	0.84 ± .21	4.00
Rape	80.14	- 0.68	- 0.24 ± .29	0.83
Other sex	79.54	- 0.44	- 0.60 ± .32	1.88
Vs. public welfare	80.07	0.14	0.51 ± .35	1.46
Arson and all other	80.04	- 0.04	0.30 ± .46	0.65

Differences Rendered Insignificant by State Sampling

Forgery and fraud: independent difference	0.49 (2.33 p.e.)

Table V-64.   Facial Index by Offenses

	No.	Range	Mean	S. D.	V.
First degree murder	311	74-105	87.86 ± .20	5.20 ± .14	5.92 ± .16
Second degree murder	618	74-105	87.66 ± .14	5.20 ± .10	5.93 ± .11
Assault	80	78-105	87.98 ± .39	5.20 ± .28	5.91 ± .32
Robbery	413	74-105	87.58 ± .17	5.08 ± .12	5.80 ± .14
Burglary and larceny	1612	70-105	87.90 ± .09	5.16 ± .06	5.87 ± .07
Forgery and fraud	467	74-105	88.10 ± .16	5.16 ± .11	5.85 ± .13
Rape	197	70-109	87.82 ± .27	5.68 ± .19	6.47 ± .22
Other sex	151	70-109	88.14 ± .32	5.84 ± .23	6.63 ± .26
Vs. public welfare	257	74-105	86.86 ± .23	5.36 ± .16	6.17 ± .18
Arson and all other	103	74-105	88.58 ± .37	5.60 ± .26	6.32 ± .30
Total	4209	70-109	87.82 ± .06	5.28 ± .04	6.01 ± .04

Correlation ratio = .06 ± .01

Table V-65.   Predictions on Basis of State Composition and Differences
from Random Sample of Total Series by Offenses

Facial Index

	Predicted Mean	Diff. of Subgroup and Predicted Mean	Diff. of Subgroup and Total Mean ± p.e.	x p.e.
First degree murder	87.87	- 0.01	0.04 ± .20	0.20
Second degree murder	87.84	- 0.18	- 0.16 ± .14	1.14
Assault	87.89	0.09	0.16 ± .40	0.40
Robbery	87.96	- 0.38	- 0.24 ± .18	1.33
Burglary and larceny	87.84	0.06	0.08 ± .09	0.89
Forgery and fraud	87.62	0.48	0.28 ± .16	1.75
Rape	88.00	- 0.18	0 ± .25	0
Other sex	87.90	0.24	0.32 ± .29	1.10
Vs. public welfare	87.42	- 0.56	- 0.96 ± .22	4.36
Arson and all other	88.14	0.44	0.76 ± .35	2.17

Differences Rendered Insignificant by State Sampling

Vs. public welfare: independent difference   - 0.56 (2.54 p.e.)

Table V-66.   Upper Facial Index by Offenses

	No.	Range	Mean	S. D.	V.
First degree murder	311	37-60	50.36 ± .13	3.51 ± .10	6.97 ± .19
Second degree murder	618	40-63	50.03 ± .10	3.60 ± .07	7.20 ± .14
Assault	80	40-60	50.30 ± .28	3.78 ± .20	7.52 ± .40
Robbery	414	40-60	49.97 ± .11	3.27 ± .08	6.54 ± .15
Burglary and larceny	1611	37-66	50.15 ± .06	3.42 ± .04	6.82 ± .08
Forgery and fraud	467	40-66	50.21 ± .11	3.57 ± .08	7.11 ± .16
Rape	197	37-66	50.21 ± .19	3.93 ± .13	7.83 ± .27
Other sex	151	43-63	50.60 ± .21	3.84 ± .15	7.59 ± .30
Vs. public welfare	257	40-66	49.61 ± .16	3.84 ± .11	7.74 ± .23
Arson and all other	103	40-63	50.66 ± .25	3.81 ± .18	7.52 ± .35
Total	4209	37-66	50.12 ± .04	3.54 ± .03	7.06 ± .05

Correlation ratio = .06 ± .01

Table V-67.   Predictions on Basis of State Composition and Differences
from Random Sample of Total Series by Offenses

Upper Facial Index

	Predicted Mean	Diff.of Subgroup and Predicted Mean	Diff.of Subgroup and Total Mean ± p.e.	x p.e.
First degree murder	50.10	0.26	0.24 ± .14	1.71
Second degree murder	50.06	- 0.03	- 0.09 ± .10	0.90
Assault	50.49	- 0.19	0.18 ± .27	0.67
Robbery	50.19	- 0.22	- 0.15 ± .12	1.25
Burglary and larceny	50.17	- 0.02	0.03 ± .06	0.50
Forgery and fraud	50.02	0.19	0.09 ± .11	0.82
Rape	50.31	- 0.10	0.09 ± .17	0.53
Other sex	50.34	0.26	0.48 ± .19	2.53
Vs. public welfare	49.74	- 0.13	- 0.51 ± .15	3.40
Arson and all other	50.30	0.36	0.54 ± .24	2.25

Differences Rendered Insignificant by State Sampling

Vs. public welfare: independent difference   - 0.13 (0.86 p.e.)

Table V-68.   Nasal Index by Offenses

	No.	Range	Mean	S. D.	V.
First degree murder	311	44-91	65.86 ± .24	6.28 ± .17	9.54 ± .26
Second degree murder	618	44-99	66.50 ± .18	6.76 ± .13	10.16 ± .20
Assault	80	48-91	66.30 ± .60	7.92 ± .42	11.95 ± .64
Robbery	413	44-87	67.50 ± .23	6.84 ± .16	10.13 ± .24
Burglary and larceny	1610	44-99	66.90 ± .12	6.84 ± .08	10.22 ± .12
Forgery and fraud	463	48-99	66.38 ± .20	6.48 ± .14	9.76 ± .22
Rape	196	44-87	65.62 ± .33	6.84 ± .23	10.42 ± .36
Other sex	151	48-95	65.42 ± .39	7.04 ± .27	10.78 ± .42
Vs. public welfare	254	52-91	67.06 ± .27	6.44 ± .19	9.60 ± .29
Arson and all other	103	48-83	66.02 ± .47	7.12 ± .33	10.78 ± .51
Total	4199	44-99	66.62 ± .07	6.80 ± .05	10.21 ± .08

Correlation ratio = .08 ± .01

Table V-69.   Predictions on Basis of State Composition and Difference
from Random Sample of Total Series by Offenses

Nasal Index

	Predicted Mean	Diff.of Subgroup and Predicted Mean	Diff.of Subgroup and Total Mean ± p.e.	x p.e.
First degree murder	66.66	- 0.80	- 0.76 ± .26	2.92
Second degree murder	66.83	- 0.33	- 0.12 ± .18	0.67
Assault	66.09	0.21	- 0.32 ± .51	0.63
Robbery	66.57	0.93	0.88 ± .23	3.83
Burglary and larceny	66.61	0.29	0.28 ± .11	2.54
Forgery and fraud	66.75	- 0.37	- 0.24 ± .21	1.14
Rape	66.18	- 0.56	- 1.00 ± .33	3.03
Other sex	66.31	- 0.89	- 1.20 ± .37	3.24
Vs. public welfare	67.13	- 0.07	0.44 ± .29	1.52
Arson and all other	66.30	- 0.28	- 0.60 ± .45	1.33

Significant Differences Independent of State Sampling

Robbery: difference   0.88 (3.83 p.e.)

Differences Rendered Insignificant by State Sampling

Rape: independent difference   - 0.56 (1.70 p.e.)
Other sex: independent difference   - 0.89 (2.40 p.e.)

Table V-70.   Ear Index (Observer A) by Offenses

	No.	Range	Mean	S. D.	V.
First degree murder	247	45-84	61.74 ± .22	5.04 ± .15	8.16 ± .25
Second degree murder	478	45-76	61.34 ± .14	4.44 ± .10	7.24 ± .16
Assault	34	53-76	61.10 ± .56	4.84 ± .40	7.92 ± .65
Robbery	275	45-76	61.62 ± .20	4.80 ± .14	7.79 ± .22
Burglary and larceny	1043	49-88	61.50 ± .09	4.48 ± .07	7.28 ± .11
Forgery and fraud	312	45-80	61.42 ± .18	4.76 ± .13	7.75 ± .21
Rape	112	49-72	60.70 ± .30	4.64 ± .21	7.64 ± .34
Other sex	82	45-68	59.90 ± .33	4.44 ± .23	7.41 ± .39
Vs. public welfare	200	45-75	59.86 ± .24	4.92 ± .17	8.22 ± .28
Arson and all other	70	49-72	61.06 ± .34	4.24 ± .24	6.94 ± .40
Total	2853	45-88	61.30 ± .06	4.64 ± .04	7.57 ± .07

Correlation ratio = .11 ± .01

Ear Index (Observer B) by Offenses

	No.	Range	Mean	S. D.	V.
First degree murder	65	49-76	60.90 ± .42	5.08 ± .30	8.34 ± .49
Second degree murder	138	45-58	61.58 ± .32	5.60 ± .23	9.09 ± .37
Assault	45	53-72	62.94 ± .43	4.32 ± .31	6.86 ± .49
Robbery	138	49-76	62.86 ± .27	4.68 ± .19	7.44 ± .30
Burglary and larceny	568	45-88	62.25 ± .14	5.12 ± .10	8.22 ± .16
Forgery and fraud	153	53-80	62.90 ± .19	5.04 ± .19	8.01 ± .31
Rape	84	49-80	61.34 ± .39	5.36 ± .28	8.74 ± .46
Other sex	69	49-76	63.26 ± .42	5.20 ± .30	8.22 ± .47
Vs. public welfare	55	49-76	62.14 ± .44	4.88 ± .31	7.85 ± .50
Arson and all other	33	53-76	61.18 ± .59	5.00 ± .42	8.17 ± .68
Total	1348	45-88	62.18 ± .09	5.12 ± .07	8.23 ± .11

Correlation ratio = .12 ± .02

Table V-71.   Predictions on Basis of State Composition and Differences
from Random Sample of Total Series by Offenses

Ear Index (Observer A)

	Predicted Mean	Diff.of Subgroup and Predicted Mean	Diff.of Subgroup and Total Mean ± p.e.	x p.e.
First degree murder	61.72	0.02	0.44 ± .20	2.20
Second degree murder	61.65	- 0.31	0.04 ± .14	0.29
Assault	61.17	- 0.07	- 0.20 ± .54	0.37
Robbery	61.15	0.47	0.32 ± .19	1.68
Burglary and larceny	61.22	0.28	0.20 ± .10	2.00
Forgery and fraud	61.06	0.35	0.12 ± .18	0.67
Rape	61.10	- 0.40	- 0.60 ± .30	2.00
Other sex	61.25	- 1.35	- 1.40 ± .35	4.00
Vs. public welfare	60.78	- 0.92	- 1.44 ± .22	6.54
Arson and all other	61.44	- 0.38	- 0.24 ± .37	0.65

Significant Differences Independent of State Sampling

Other sex: independent difference   - 1.35 (3.86 p.e.)
Vs. public welfare: independent difference   - 0.92 (4.18 p.e.)

Table V-71 (cont'd).   **Ear** Index (Observer B)

	Predicted Mean	Diff.of Subgroup and Predicted Mean	Diff.of Subgroup and Total Mean ± p.e.	x p.e.
First degree murder	62.78	- 1.88	- 1.28 ± .43	2.98
Second degree murder	61.19	0.39	- 0.60 ± .29	2.07
Assault	62.23	0.71	0.76 ± .51	1.49
Robbery	62.58	0.28	0.68 ± .29	2.34
Burglary and larceny	61.96	0.30	0.08 ± .14	0.57
Forgery and fraud	62.58	0.32	0.72 ± .28	2.57
Rape	62.61	- 1.27	- 0.84 ± .38	2.21
Other sex	61.95	1.31	1.08 ± .42	2.57
Vs. public welfare	62.68	- 0.54	- 0.04 ± .47	0.08
Arson and all other	62.55	- 1.37	- 1.00 ± .60	1.67

Table V-72.   Zygo-frontal Index by Offenses

	No.	Range	Mean	S. D.	V.
First degree murder	310	68-91	79.74 ± .12	2.96 ± .08	3.71 ± .10
Second degree murder	619	64-91	80.18 ± .06	3.24 ± .06	4.04 ± .08
Assault	80	72-87	80.38 ± .25	3.28 ± .18	4.08 ± .22
Robbery	414	72-91	80.74 ± .09	2.84 ± .07	3.52 ± .08
Burglary and larceny	1610	68-99	80.86 ± .05	3.12 ± .04	3.86 ± .05
Forgery and fraud	467	64-91	80.66 ± .10	3.28 ± .07	4.07 ± .09
Rape	197	72-91	80.38 ± .16	3.40 ± .12	4.23 ± .14
Other sex	150	72-91	80.22 ± .17	3.04 ± .12	3.79 ± .15
Vs. public welfare	257	68-95	80.54 ± .14	3.32 ± .10	4.12 ± .12
Arson and all other	103	68-95	79.94 ± .25	3.80 ± .18	4.75 ± .22
Total	4207	64-99	80.54 ± .03	3.16 ± .02	3.92 ± .03

Correlation ratio = .11 ± .01

Table V-73.   Predictions on Basis of State Composition and Differences
from Random Sample of Total Series by Offenses

	Predicted Mean	Diff.of Subgroup and Predicted Mean	Diff.of Subgroup and Total Mean ± p.e.	x p.e.
First degree murder	80.10	- 0.36	- 0.80 ± .12	6.67
Second degree murder	80.35	- 0.17	- 0.36 ± .09	4.00
Assault	80.54	- 0.16	- 0.16 ± .24	0.67
Robbery	80.65	0.09	0.20 ± .10	2.00
Burglary and larceny	80.61	0.25	0.32 ± .05	6.40
Forgery and fraud	80.65	0.01	0.12 ± .10	1.20
Rape	80.49	- 0.11	- 0.16 ± .15	1.07
Other sex	80.52	- 0.30	- 0.32 ± .17	1.88
Vs. public welfare	80.87	- 0.33	0 ± .13	0
Arson and all other	80.31	- 0.37	- 0.60 ± .21	2.86

Significant Differences Independent of State Sampling

First degree Murder: independent difference   - 0.36 (3.00 p.e.)
Burglary and larceny: independent difference   0.25 (5.00 p.e.)

Differences Rendered Insignificant by State Sampling

Second degree murder: independent difference   - 0.17 (1.89 p.e.)

Table V-74.   Fronto-parietal Index by Offenses

	No.	Range	Mean	S. D.	V.
First degree murder	311	60-86	72.94 ± .12	3.24 ± .09	4.44 ± .12
Second degree murder	617	63-86	73.18 ± .09	3.18 ± .06	4.34 ± .08
Assault	80	66-83	73.15 ± .27	3.54 ± .19	4.84 ± .26
Robbery	414	66-83	73.60 ± .09	2.82 ± .07	3.83 ± .09
Burglary and larceny	1610	63-86	73.57 ± .05	3.12 ± .04	4.24 ± .05
Forgery and fraud	466	63-83	73.57 ± .10	3.24 ± .07	4.40 ± .10
Rape	197	66-86	73.06 ± .15	3.12 ± .11	4.27 ± .14
Other sex	150	63-80	73.21 ± .18	3.24 ± .13	4.43 ± .17
Vs. public welfare	257	66-86	73.96 ± .13	3.15 ± .09	4.26 ± .13
Arson and all other	103	66-83	72.76 ± .21	3.12 ± .15	4.29 ± .20
Total	4205	60-86	73.42 ± .03	3.15 ± .02	4.29 ± .03

Correlation ratio = .09 ± .01

Table V-75.   Predictions on Basis of State Composition and Differences
from Random Sample of Total Series by Offenses

Fronto-parietal Index

	Predicted Mean	Diff. of Subgroup and Predicted Mean	Diff. of Subgroup and Total Mean ± p.e.	x p.e.
First degree murder	73.01	- 0.07	- 0.48 ± .12	4.00
Second degree murder	73.27	- 0.09	- 0.24 ± .09	2.67
Assault	73.38	- 0.23	- 0.27 ± .24	1.12
Robbery	73.47	0.13	0.18 ± .10	1.80
Burglary and larceny	73.49	0.08	0.15 ± .05	3.00
Forgery and fraud	73.59	- 0.02	0.15 ± .10	1.50
Rape	73.26	- 0.20	- 0.36 ± .15	2.40
Other sex	73.38	- 0.17	- 0.21 ± .17	1.24
Vs. public welfare	73.88	0.08	0.54 ± .13	4.15
Arson and all other	73.09	- 0.33	- 0.66 ± .21	3.14

Differences Rendered Insignificant by State Sampling

First degree murder: independent difference	- 0.07 (0.58 p.e.)
Burglary and larceny: independent difference	0.08 (1.60 p.e.)
Vs. public welfare: independent difference	0.08 (0.62 p.e.)
Arson and all other: independent difference	- 0.33 (1.57 p.e.)

Table V-76.   Zygo-gonial Index by Offenses

	No.	Range	Mean	S. D.	V.
First degree murder	310	60-89	78.55 ± .14	3.72 ± .10	4.74 ± .13
Second degree murder	618	66-89	77.86 ± .09	3.45 ± .07	4.43 ± .08
Assault	80	66-86	77.20 ± .28	3.72 ± .20	4.82 ± .26
Robbery	414	66-92	77.56 ± .12	3.72 ± .09	4.80 ± .11
Burglary and larceny	1610	63-92	77.62 ± .06	3.72 ± .04	4.79 ± .06
Forgery and fraud	467	66-92	77.80 ± .12	3.75 ± .08	4.82 ± .11
Rape	197	69-89	77.26 ± .17	3.60 ± .12	4.66 ± .16
Other sex	150	69-92	77.80 ± .22	3.90 ± .15	5.01 ± .20
Vs. public welfare	257	66-89	78.13 ± .15	3.57 ± .11	4.57 ± .14
Arson and all other	103	63-86	77.65 ± .26	3.90 ± .18	5.02 ± .24
Total	4206	60-92	77.74 ± .04	3.69 ± .03	4.75 ± .04

Correlation ratio = .08 ± .01

Table V-77. Predictions on Basis of State Composition and Difference
from Random Sample of Total Series by Offenses

Zygo-gonial Index

	Predicted Mean	Diff.of Subgroup and Predicted Mean	Diff.of Subgroup and Total Mean ± p.e.	x p.e.
First degree murder	77.91	0.64	0.81 ± .14	5.79
Second degree murder	77.78	0.08	0.12 ± .10	1.20
Assault	77.47	- 0.27	- 0.54 ± .28	1.93
Robbery	77.74	- 0.18	- 0.18 ± .12	1.50
Burglary and larceny	77.68	- 0.06	- 0.12 ± .06	2.00
Forgery and fraud	77.83	- 0.03	0.06 ± .12	0.50
Rape	77.63	- 0.37	- 0.48 ± .18	2.67
Other sex	77.55	0.25	0.06 ± .20	0.30
Vs. public welfare	77.97	0.16	0.39 ± .16	2.44
Arson and all other	77.71	- 0.06	- 0.09 ± .24	0.38

Significant Differences Independent of State Sampling

First degree murder: independent difference   0.64 (4.57 p.e.)

Table V-78. Summary of Correlation Ratios with Offense

Measurements

Age	.40 ± .01	Head circumference	.11 ± .01
Weight	.11 ± .01	Minimum frontal diameter	.09 ± .01
Height	.11 ± .01	Bizygomatic diameter	.09 ± .01
Biacromial diameter	.06 ± .01	Total face height	.06 ± .01
Chest depth	.17 ± .01	Upper face height	.05 ± .01
Chest breadth	.13 ± .01	Nose height	.12 ± .01
Sitting height	.08 ± .01	Nose breadth	.09 ± .01
Head length	.08 ± .01	Bigonial diameter	.11 ± .01
Head breadth	.06 ± .01	Ear length (Observer A)	.15 ± .01
Head height (Observer A)	.10 ± .01	Ear length (Observer B)	.18 ± .01
Head height (Observer B)	.14 ± .02	Ear breadth (Observer A)	.14 ± .01
		Ear breadth (Observer B)	.14 ± .02

Indices

Relative shoulder breadth	.14 ± .01	Facial index	.06 ± .01
Relative sitting height	.09 ± .01	Upper facial index	.06 ± .01
Cephalic index	.06 ± .01	Nasal index	.08 ± .01
Cephalo-facial index	.06 ± .01	Ear index (Observer A)	.11 ± .01
Length-height index (Observer A)	.11 ± .01	Ear index (Observer B)	.12 ± .02
Length-height index (Observer B)	.09 ± .02	Zygo-frontal index	.11 ± .01
Breadth-height index (Observer A)	.10 ± .01	Fronto-parietal index	.09 ± .01
Breadth-height index (Observer B)	.10 ± .02	Zygo-gonial index	.08 ± .01

Table V-79. Summary of Metric and Indicial Differentiation of Offenses
from Random Sample of Total Series on Basis of State Composition

First Degree Murder

	Significant and Independent of State Sampling		Crude Differences Invalidated by State Sampling		Insignificant Differences	
	Diff.	x p.e.	Diff.	x p.e.	Diff.	x p.e.
Age	7.10	16.14	-	-	-	-
Weight	4.60	5.61	-	-	-	-
Height	1.07*	4.28*	-	-	-	-
Biacromial diameter	-	-	-	-	0.03	0.33
Chest depth	0.50*	7.14*	-	-	-	-
Chest breadth	0.22*	3.14*	-	-	-	-
Sitting height	-	-	-	-	0.03	0.23
Head length	-	-	-	-	0.57	2.28
Head breadth	-	-	-	-	- 0.06	0.29
Head height (Observer A)	-	-	-	-	- 0.36	1.50
Head height (Observer B)	-	-	-	-	0.21	0.42
Head circumference	-	-	2.76	4.31	(1.24	1.94)
Minimum frontal diameter	-	-	- 0.84	4.42	(- 0.11	0.58)
Bizygomatic diameter	-	-	-	-	0.25	1.25
Total face height	-	-	-	-	0.35	1.40
Upper face height	-	-	-	-	0.30	1.76
Nose height	0.80	5.33	-	-	-	-
Nose breadth	-	-	-	-	0.15	1.36
Bigonial diameter	1.00*	4.54*	-	-	-	-
Ear length (Observer A)	-	-	-	-	0 .	0
Ear length (Observer B)	2.16	5.68	-	-	-	-
Ear breadth (Observer A)	1.05	8.75	-	-	-	-
Ear breadth (Observer B)	-	-	0.85	3.70	(0.50	2.17)
Relative shoulder breadth	- 0.48*	9.60*	-	-	-	-
Relative sitting height	- 0.29*	4.83*	-	-	-	-
Cephalic index	-	-	- 0.42	3.23	(- 0.28	2.15)
Cephalo-facial index	-	-	-	-	0.24	2.00
Length-height index						
(Observer A)	-	-	- 0.45	3.21	(- 0.09	0.64)
(Observer B)	-	-	-	-	0.42	1.45
Breadth-height index						
(Observer A)	-	-	-	-	- 0.03	0.19
(Observer B)	-	-	-	-	- 0.39	1.18
Facial index	-	-	-	-	0.04	0.20
Upper facial index	-	-	-	-	0.24	1.71
Nasal index	-	-	-	-	- 0.76	2.92
Ear index (Observer A)	-	-	-	-	0.44	2.20
Ear index (Observer B)	-	-	-	-	- 1.28	2.98
Zygo-frontal index	- 0.36*	3.00*	-	-	-	-
Fronto-parietal index	-	-	- 0.48	4.00	(- 0.07	0.58)
Zygo-gonial index	0.64*	4.57*	-	-	-	-

Measurements				
Number	9		3	11
Per Cent	39.13		13.04	47.83
Indices				
Number	4		3	9
Per Cent	25.00		18.75	56.25

*Independent difference corrected for state sampling.

Table V-80. Summary of Metric and Indicial Differentiation of Offenses from
Random Sample of Total Series on Basis of State Composition

Second Degree Murder

	Significant and Independent of State Sampling		Crude Differences Invalidated by State Sampling		Insignificant Differences	
	Diff.	x p.e.	Diff.	x p.e.	Diff.	x p.e.
Age	3.35	10.81	-	-	-	-
Weight	-	-	-	-	1.20	2.14
Height	-	-	-	-	0.24	1.33
Biacromial diameter	-	-	-	-	- 0.12	2.00
Chest depth	0.24	4.80	-	-	-	-
Chest breadth	-	-	0.15	3.00	(0.08	1.60)
Sitting height	-	-	-	-	- 0.09	1.00
Head length	-	-	-	-	0.21	1.17
Head breadth	-	-	-	-	- 0.27	1.80
Head height (Observer A)	- 0.60*	3.53*	-	-	-	-
Head height (Observer B)	-	-	- 1.56	4.46	(0.07	0.20)
Head circumference	-	-	-	-	0.72	1.56
Minimum frontal diameter	-	-	- 0.52	4.00	(- 0.09	0.69)
Bizygomatic diameter	-	-	-	-	- 0.05	0.36
Total face height	-	-	-	-	- 0.25	1.39
Upper face height	-	-	-	-	- 0.20	1.67
Nose height	-	-	-	-	0.08	0.73
Nose breadth	-	-	-	-	0	0
Bigonial diameter	-	-	-	-	0.28	1.87
Ear length (Observer A)	-	-	-	-	- 0.20	1.33
Ear length (Observer B)	-	-	-	-	0.08	0.31
Ear breadth (Observer A)	-	-	-	-	- 0.09	1.00
Ear breadth (Observer B)	-	-	-	-	- 0.16	1.00
Relative shoulder breadth	-	-	-	-	- 0.06	1.50
Relative sitting height	-	-	- 0.12	3.00	(0.03	0.75)
Cephalic index	-	-	- 0.27	3.00	(- 0.10	1.11)
Cephalo-facial index	-	-	-	-	0.06	0.75
Length-height index						
(Observer A)	- 0.43*	4.30*	-	-	-	-
(Observer B)	-	-	- 0.65	3.25	(- 0.25	1.25)
Breadth-height index						
(Observer A)	- 0.49*	4.08*	-	-	-	-
(Observer B)	-	-	-	-	- 0.36	1.64
Facial index	-	-	-	-	- 0.16	1.14
Upper facial index	-	-	-	-	- 0.09	0.90
Nasal index	-	-	-	-	- 0.12	0.67
Ear index (Observer A)	-	-	-	-	0.04	0.29
Ear index (Observer B)	-	-	-	-	- 0.60	2.07
Zygo-frontal index	-	-	- 0.36	4.00	(- 0.17	1.89)
Fronto-parietal index	-	-	-	-	- 0.24	2.67
Zygo-gonial index	-	-	-	-	0.12	1.20
Measurements						
Number	3		3		17	
Per Cent	13.04		13.04		73.91	
Indices						
Number	2		4		10	
Per Cent	12.50		25.00		62.50	

*Independent difference corrected for state sampling.

Table V-81   Summary of Metric and Indicial Differentiation of Offenses from
Random Sample of Total Series on Basis of State Composition

Assault

	Significant and Independent of State Sampling		Crude Differences Invalidated by State Sampling		Insignificant Differences	
	Diff.	x p.e.	Diff.	x p.e.	Diff.	x p.e.
Age	3.09*	3.55*	-	-	-	-
Weight	-	-	-	-	0.80	0.50
Height	-	-	-	-	- 0.24	0.49
Biacromial diameter	0.59*	3.47*	-	-	-	-
Chest depth	-	-	-	-	0.26	2.00
Chest breadth	-	-	-	-	0.36	2.57
Sitting height	-	-	-	-	0.12	0.46
Head length	-	-	-	-	0.24	0.49
Head breadth	-	-	-	-	- 0.60	1.46
Head height (Observer A)	-	-	-	-	- 1.44	2.25
Head Height (Observer B)	-	-	-	-	- 0.36	0.60
Head circumference	-	-	-	-	- 3.24	2.57
Minimum frontal diameter	-	-	-	-	- 0.12	0.32
Bizygomatic diameter	-	-	-	-	0.60	1.50
Total face height	-	-	-	-	0.40	0.82
Upper face height	-	-	-	-	0.20	0.59
Nose height	-	-	-	-	0.48	1.60
Nose breadth	-	-	-	-	- 0.03	0.14
Bigonial diameter	-	-	-	-	- 0.04	0.09
Ear length (Observer A)	-	-	-	-	0.08	0.14
Ear length (Observer B)	-	-	-	-	0.24	0.53
Ear breadth (Observer A)	-	-	-	-	- 0.36	1.12
Ear breadth (Observer B)	-	-	-	-	0.58	2.07
Relative shoulder breadth	-	-	0.34	3.40	(0.20	2.00)
Relative sitting height	-	-	-	-	0.02	0.17
Cephalic index	-	-	-	-	0.09	0.36
Cephalo-facial index	-	-	-	-	0.18	0.78
Length-height index						
(Observer A)	-	-	-	-	- 0.69	1.86
(Observer B)	-	-	-	-	- 0.24	0.71
Breadth-height index						
(Observer A)	- 1.69	3.84	-	-	-	-
(Observer B)	-	-	-	-	- 0.60	1.54
Facial index	-	-	-	-	0.16	0.40
Upper facial index	-	-	-	-	0.18	0.67
Nasal index	-	-	-	-	- 0.32	0.63
Ear index (Observer A)	-	-	-	-	- 0.20	0.37
Ear index (Observer B)	-	-	-	-	0.76	1.49
Zygo-frontal index	-	-	-	-	- 0.16	0.67
Fronto-parietal index	-	-	-	-	- 0.27	1.12
Zygo-gonial index	-	-	-	-	- 0.54	1.93
Measurements						
Number	2		0		21	
Per Cent	8.70		0		91.30	
Indices						
Number	1		1		14	
Per Cent	6.25		6.25		87.50	

*Independent difference corrected for state sampling.

Table V-82.   Summary of Metric and Indicial Differentiation of Offenses from
Random Sample of Total Series on Basis of State Composition

Robbery

	Significant and Independent of State Sampling		Crude Differences Invalidated by State Sampling		Insignificant Differences	
	Diff.	x p.e.	Diff.	x p.e.	Diff.	x p.e.
Age	- 3.95	10.40	-	-	-	-
Weight	-	-	-	-	- 1.50	2.14
Height	-	-	-	-	0.12	0.57
Biacromial diameter	-	-	-	-	0.06	0.75
Chest depth	- 0.30	5.00	-	-	-	-
Chest breadth	-	-	-	-	- 0.09	1.50
Sitting height	-	-	-	-	0.27	2.25
Head length	-	-	-	-	0.35	1.64
Head breadth	-	-	-	-	0.33	1.83
Head height (Observer A)	0.88*	4.00*	-	-	-	-
Head height (Observer B)	-	-	1.20	3.43	(0.56	1.60)
Head circumference	-	-	-	-	1.08	1.90
Minimum frontal diameter	-	-	0.48	3.00	(0.37	2.31)
Bizygomatic diameter	0.65	3.61	-	-	-	-
Total face height	-	-	-	-	0	0
Upper face height	-	-	-	-	- 0.05	0.33
Nose height	-	-	-	-	- 0.36	2.77
Nose breadth	-	-	-	-	0.21	2.33
Bigonial diameter	-	-	-	-	0.04	0.21
Ear length (Observer A)	-	-	-	-	- 0.32	1.60
Ear length (Observer B)	- 1.01*	3.88*	-	-	-	-
Ear breadth (Observer A)	-	-	-	-	- 0.09	0.82
Ear breadth (Observer B)	-	-	-	-	- 0.38	2.38
Relative shoulder breadth	-	-	-	-	0.14	2.80
Relative sitting height	-	-	-	-	0.08	1.60
Cephalic index	-	-	-	-	0.09	0.82
Cephalo-facial index	-	-	-	-	0.06	0.60
Length-height index						
(Observer A)	-	-	-	-	0.30	2.31
(Observer B)	-	-	-	-	0.24	1.20
Breadth-height index						
(Observer A)	-	-	0.48	3.00	(0.41	2.56)
(Observer B)	-	-	-	-	0.30	1.36
Facial index	-	-	-	-	- 0.24	1.33
Upper facial index	-	-	-	-	- 0.15	1.25
Nasal index	0.88	3.83	-	-	-	-
Ear index (Observer A)	-	-	-	-	0.32	1.68
Ear index (Observer B)	-	-	-	-	0.68	2.34
Zygo-frontal index	-	-	-	-	0.20	2.00
Fronto-parietal index	-	-	-	-	0.18	1.80
Zygo-gonial index	-	-	-	-	- 0.18	1.50
Measurements						
Number	5		2		16	
Per Cent	21.74		8.70		69.57	
Indices						
Number	1		1		14	
Per Cent	6.25		6.25		87.50	

*Independent difference corrected for state sampling.

Table V-83.　Summary of Metric and Indicial Differentiation of Offenses from
Random Sample of Total Series on Basis of State Composition

Burglary and Larceny

	Significant and Independent of State Sampling		Crude Differences Invalidated by State Sampling		Insignificant Differences	
	Diff.	x p.e.	Diff.	x p.e.	Diff.	x p.e.
Age	- 4.02*	21.16*	-	-	-	-
Weight	- 1.93*	5.36*	-	-	-	-
Height	-	-	-	-	- 0.30	2.73
Biacromial diameter	-	-	-	-	- 0.09	2.25
Chest depth	- 0.22*	7.33*	-	-	-	-
Chest breadth	- 0.19*	6.33*	-	-	-	-
Sitting height	-	-	-	-	- 0.12	2.00
Head length	- 0.38*	3.45*	-	-	-	-
Head breadth	-	-	-	-	- 0.24	2.67
Head height (Observer A)	-	-	-	-	0	0
Head height (Observer B)	-	-	-	-	- 0.15	0.88
Head circumference	- 1.14*	4.07*	-	-	-	-
Minimum frontal diameter	-	-	-	-	0.04	0.50
Bizygomatic diameter	- 0.44*	4.89*	-	-	-	-
Total face height	-	-	-	-	- 0.25	2.27
Upper face height	-	-	-	-	- 0.15	1.88
Nose height	- 0.46*	6.57*	-	-	-	-
Nose breadth	- 0.18*	3.60*	-	-	-	-
Bigonial diameter	- 0.42*	4.20*	-	-	-	-
Ear length (Observer A)	- 0.56	5.60	-	-	-	-
Ear length (Observer B)	- 0.43	3.31	-	-	-	-
Ear breadth (Observer A)	- 0.25*	4.17*	-	-	-	-
Ear breadth (Observer B)	- 0.25*	3.12*	-	-	-	-
Relative shoulder breadth	-	-	-	-	- 0.02	1.00
Relative sitting height	-	-	-	-	0.04	1.33
Cephalic index	-	-	-	-	0.09	1.50
Cephalo-facial index	-	-	-	-	- 0.12	2.40
Length-height index						
(Observer A)	-	-	-	-	0.18	2.57
(Observer B)	-	-	-	-	0	0
Breadth-height index						
(Observer A)	-	-	-	-	0.21	2.62
(Observer B)	-	-	-	-	- 0.06	0.54
Facial index	-	-	-	-	0.08	0.89
Upper facial index	-	-	-	-	0.03	0.50
Nasal index	-	-	-	-	0.28	2.54
Ear index (Observer A)	-	-	-	-	0.20	2.00
Ear index (Observer B)	-	-	-	-	0.08	0.57
Zygo-frontal index	0.25*	5.00*	-	-	-	-
Fronto-parietal index	-	-	0.15	3.00	(0.08	1.60)
Zygo-gonial index	-	-	-	-	- 0.12	2.00
Measurements						
Number	14		0		9	
Per Cent	60.87		0		39.13	
Indices						
Number	1		1		14	
Per Cent	6.25		6.25		87.50	

*Independent difference corrected for state sampling.

Table V-84. Summary of Metric and Indicial Differentiation of Offenses from
Random Sample of Total Series on Basis of State Composition

Forgery and Fraud

	Significant and Independent of State Sampling		Crude Differences Invalidated by State Sampling		Insignificant Differences	
	Diff.	x p.e.	Diff.	x p.e.	Diff.	x p.e.
Age	-	-	-	-	- 0.45	1.25
Weight	-	-	2.30	3.48	(1.60	2.42)
Height	-	-	0.63	3.15	(0.50	2.50)
Biacromial diameter	-	-	-	-	0.18	2.57
Chest depth	-	-	-	-	- 0.06	1.20
Chest breadth	-	-	-	-	0.03	0.50
Sitting height	0.43*	3.91*	-	-	-	-
Head length	1.04	5.20	-	-	-	-
Head breadth	-	-	0.63	3.71	(0.46	2.71)
Head height (Observer A)	-	-	0.69	3.29	(0.59	2.81)
Head height (Observer B)	-	-	1.50	4.54	(0.80	2.42)
Head circumference	1.97*	3.79*	-	-	-	-
Minimum frontal diameter	-	-	0.60	4.00	(0.24	1.69)
Bizygomatic diameter	-	-	-	-	0.25	1.47
Total face height	0.75	3.75	-	-	-	-
Upper face height	-	-	-	-	0.30	2.14
Nose height	-	-	-	-	0.24	2.00
Nose breadth	-	-	-	-	0.06	0.67
Bigonial diameter	-	-	-	-	0.28	1.56
Ear length (Observer A)	-	-	0.56	3.11	(- 0.04	0.22)
Ear length (Observer B)	-	-	-	-	- 0.24	1.00
Ear breadth (Observer A)	-	-	0.33	3.00	(0.15	1.36)
Ear breadth (Observer B)	-	-	-	-	0.25	1.67
Relative shoulder breadth	-	-	-	-	0.02	0.50
Relative sitting height	-	-	-	-	0.10	2.00
Cephalic index	-	-	-	-	- 0.03	0.30
Cephalo-facial index	-	-	-	-	- 0.12	1.20
Length-height index						
(Observer A)	-	-	-	-	0.33	2.75
(Observer B)	-	-	-	-	0.36	2.00
Breadth-height						
(Observer A)	-	-	-	-	0.21	1.40
(Observer B)	-	-	0.84	4.00	(0.49	2.33)
Facial index	-	-	-	-	0.28	1.75
Upper facial index	-	-	-	-	0.09	0.82
Nasal index	-	-	-	-	- 0.24	1.14
Ear index (Observer A)	-	-	-	-	0.12	0.67
Ear index (Observer B)	-	-	-	-	0.72	2.57
Zygo-frontal index	-	-	-	-	0.12	1.20
Fronto-parietal index	-	-	-	-	0.15	1.50
Zygo-gonial index	-	-	-	-	0.06	0.50
Measurements						
Number	4		8		11	
Per Cent	17.39		34.78		47.83	
Indices						
Number	0		1		15	
Per Cent	0		6.25		93.75	

*Significant difference corrected for state sampling.

Table V-85. Summary of Metric and Indicial Differentiation of Offenses from
Random Sample of Total Series on Basis of State Composition

Rape

	Significant and Independent of State Sampling		Crude Differences Invalidated by State Sampling		Insignificant Differences	
	Diff.	x p.e.	Diff.	x p.e.	Diff.	x p.e.
Age	4.84*	8.80*	-	-	-	-
Weight	-	-	-	-	- 1.70	1.68
Height	- 1.03	3.32	-	-	-	-
Biacromial diameter	-	-	-	-	- 0.03	0.27
Chest depth	0.34	4.25	-	-	-	-
Chest breadth	-	-	-	-	0.06	0.67
Sitting height	- 0.53*	3.12*	-	-	-	-
Head length	-	-	-	-	- 0.04	0.13
Head breadth	-	-	-	-	0.48	1.85
Head height (Observer A)	-	-	-	-	0.21	0.60
Head height (Observer B)	-	-	-	-	0.09	0.20
Head circumference	-	-	- 2.52	3.07	(- 1.43	1.74)
Minimum frontal diameter	-	-	-	-	- 0.24	1.04
Bizygomatic diameter	-	-	-	-	0	0
Total face height	-	-	-	-	0.35	1.13
Upper face height	-	-	-	-	0.30	1.36
Nose height	-	-	0.54	3.37	(0.29	1.53)
Nose breadth	-	-	-	-	- 0.06	0.46
Bigonial diameter	-	-	-	-	- 0.72	2.57
Ear length (Observer A)	-	-	-	-	0.64	2.06
Ear length (Observer B)	-	-	-	-	0.96	2.91
Ear breadth (Observer A)	-	-	-	-	0.09	0.50
Ear breadth (Observer B)	-	-	-	-	0.31	1.55
Relative shoulder breadth	0.22*	3.14*	-	-	-	-
Relative sitting height	-	-	0.40	5.00	0.22	2.75)
Cephalic index	-	-	-	-	0.45	2.81
Cephalo-facial index	-	-	-	-	- 0.24	1.60
Length-height index						
(Observer A)	-	-	-	-	0.21	1.05
(Observer B)	-	-	-	-	0.30	1.20
Breadth-height index						
(Observer A)	-	-	-	-	- 0.24	1.00
(Observer B)	-	-	-	-	- 0.24	0.83
Facial index	-	-	-	-	0	0
Upper facial index	-	-	-	-	0.09	0.53
Nasal index	-	-	- 1.00	3.03	(- 0.56	1.70)
Ear index (Observer A)	-	-	-	-	- 0.60	2.00
Ear index (Observer B)	-	-	-	-	- 0.84	2.21
Zygo-frontal index	-	-	-	-	- 0.16	1.07
Fronto-parietal index	-	-	-	-	- 0.36	2.40
Zygo-gonial index	-	-	-	-	- 0.48	2.57
Measurements						
Number	4		2		17	
Per Cent	17.39		8.70		73.91	
Indices						
Number	1		2		13	
Per Cent	6.25		12.50		81.25	

*Significant difference corrected for state sampling.

Table V-86. Summary of Metric and Indicial Differentiation of Offenses from
Random Sample of Total Series on Basis of State Composition

Other Sex Offenses

	Significant and Independent of State Sampling		Crude Differences Invalidated by State Sampling		Insignificant Differences	
	Diff.	x p.e.	Diff.	x p.e.	Diff.	x p.e.
Age	6.40	10.16	-	-	-	-
Weight	-	-	-	-	1.80	1.58
Height	-	-	-	-	- 0.90	2.57
Biacromial diameter	-	-	-	-	0.30	2.50
Chest depth	-	-	-	-	0.22	2.20
Chest breadth	-	-	-	-	0.12	1.20
Sitting heigh	-	-	-	-	- 0.30	1.58
Head length	-	-	-	-	- 0.24	0.67
Head breadth	-	-	-	-	- 0.12	0.40
Head height (Observer A)	-	-	-	-	- 0.24	0.58
Head height (Observer B)	-	-	-	-	- 0.84	1.71
Head circumference	-	-	-	-	- 2.16	2.40
Minimum frontal diameter	-	-	-	-	- 0.72	2.67
Bizygomatic diameter	-	-	-	-	0.10	0.34
Total face height	-	-	-	-	0.75	2.08
Upper face height	-	-	-	-	0.45	1.90
Nose height	0.80	3.64	-	-	-	-
Nose breadth	-	-	-	-	0.15	1.00
Bigonial diameter	-	-	-	-	- 0.24	0.77
Ear length (Observer A)	-	-	-	-	0.72	2.00
Ear length (Observer B)	-	-	-	-	0.76	2.11
Ear breadth (Observer A)	-	-	-	-	- 0.42	2.00
Ear breadth (Observer B)	-	-	-	-	0.34	1.48
Relative shoulder breadth	-	-	-	-	0.18	2.2:
Relative sitting height	-	-	-	-	0	0
Cephalic index	-	-	-	-	- 0.03	0.17
Cephalo-facial index	-	-	-	-	- 0.06	0.35
Length-height index						
(Observer A)	-	-	-	-	0.21	0.88
(Observer B)	-	-	-	-	- 0.33	1.18
Breadth-height						
(Observer A)	-	-	-	-	- 0.18	0.52
(Observer B)	-	-	-	-	- 0.60	1.98
Facial index	-	-	-	-	0.32	1.10
Upper facial index	-	-	-	-	0.48	2.53
Nasal index	-	-	- 1.20	3.24	(0.89	2.40)
Ear index (Observer A)	- 1.35*	3.86*	-	-	-	-
Ear index (Observer B)	-	-	-	-	1.08	2.57
Zygo-frontal index	-	-	-	-	- 0.32	1.88
Fronto-perietal index	-	-	-	-	- 0.21	1.24
Zygo-gonial index	ד	-	-	-	0.06	0.30
Measurements						
Number	2		0		21	
Per Cent	8.70		0		91.30	
Indices						
Number	1		1		14	
Per Cent	6.25		6.25		87.50	

*Significant difference corrected for state sampling.

Table V-87. Summary of Metric and Indicial Differentiation of Offenses from
Random Sample of Total Series on Basis of State Composition

Versus Public Welfare

	Significant and Independent of State Sampling		Crude Differences Invalidated by State Sampling		Insignificant Differences	
	Diff.	x p.e.	Diff.	x p.e.	Diff.	x p.e.
Age	6.27*	13.06*	-	-	-	-
Weight	-	-	3.40	3.82	(1.62	1.82)
Height	-	-	1.02	3.78	(0.48	1.78)
Biacromial diameter	-	-	-	-	0.15	1.50
Chest depth	0.35*	5.00*	-	-	-	-
Chest breadth	-	-	0.30	3.75	(0.23	2.88)
Sitting height	-	-	-	-	0.12	0.80
Head length	-	-	-	-	- 0.21	0.78
Head breadth	-	-	-	-	0.39	1.70
Head height (Observer A)	-	-	-	-	0	0
Head height (Observer B)	-	-	-	-	0.09	0.16
Head circumference	-	-	2.16	3.13	(0.41	0.59)
Minimum frontal diameter	-	-	1.00	5.00	(0.18	0.90)
Bizygomatic diameter	0.72*	3.27*	-	-	-	-
Total face height	-	-	-	-	- 0.05	0.18
Upper face height	-	-	-	-	- 0.15	0.79
Nose height	-	-	-	-	0.40	2.50
Nose breadth	0.37*	3.08*	-	-	-	-
Bigonial diameter	0.98*	4.08*	-	-	-	-
Ear length (Observer A)	1.09*	4.74*	-	-	-	-
Ear length (Observer B)	-	-	-	-	1.00	2.44
Ear breadth (Observer A)	-	-	-	-	0.30	2.31
Ear breadth (Observer B)	-	-	0.79	3.16	(0.65	2.60)
Relative shoulder breadth	-	-	-	-	- 0.06	1.00
Relative sitting height	-	-	-	-	- 0.18	2.57
Cephalic index	-	-	-	-	0.15	1.07
Cephalo-facial index	0.41*	3.15*	-	-	-	-
Length-height index						
(Observer A)	-	-	-	-	0.06	0.40
(Observer B)	-	-	-	-	0	0
Breadth-height index						
(Observer A)	-	-	-	-	- 0.33	1.83
(Observer B)	-	-	-	-	0.51	1.42
Facial index	-	-	- 0.96	4.36	(0.56	2.54)
Upper facial index	-	-	- 0.51	3.40	(- 0.13	0.87)
Nasal index	-	-	-	-	0.44	1.52
Ear index (Observer A)	- 0.92*	4.18*	-	-	-	-
Ear index (Observer B)	-	-	-	-	- 0.04	0.08
Zygo-frontal index	-	-	-	-	0	0
Fronto-parietal index	-	-	0.54	4.15	(0.08	0.62)
Zygo-gonial index	-	-	-	-	0.39	2.44
Measurements						
Number	6		6		11	
Per Cent	26.09		26.09		47.83	
Indices						
Number	2		3		11	
Per Cent	12.50		18.75		68.75	

*Significant difference corrected for state sampling.

Table V-88. Summary of Metric and Indicial Differentiation of Offenses from
Random Sample of Total Series on Basis of State Composition

Arson and All Other Offenses

	Significant and Independent of State Sampling		Crude Differences Invalidated by State Sampling		Insignificant Differences	
	Diff.	x p.e.	Diff.	x p.e.	Diff.	x p.e.
Age	2.35	3.09	-	-	-	-
Weight	-	-	-	-	- 2.70	1.94
Height	-	-	- 1.50	3.49	(- 1.07	2.49)
Biacromial diameter	-	-	-	-	0.15	1.00
Chest depth	-	-	-	-	- 0.10	0.83
Chest breadth	1.02	7.85	-	-	-	-
Sitting height	-	-	-	-	- 0.48	2.09
Head length	-	-	-	-	- 0.45	1.05
Head breadth	-	-	-	-	- 0.12	0.33
Head height (Observer A)	-	-	-	-	- 0.15	0.34
Head height (Observer B)	-	-	-	-	- 0.90	1.27
Head circumference	-	-	-	-	- 1.32	1.19
Minimum frontal diameter	- 1.16	3.62	-	-	-	-
Bizygomatic diameter	-	-	-	-	- 0.40	1.11
Total face height	-	-	-	-	0.20	0.46
Upper face height	-	-	-	-	0.45	1.45
Nose height	-	-	-	-	0.60	2.31
Nose breadth	-	-	-	-	0	0
Bigonial diameter	-	-	-	-	- 0.48	1.37
Ear length (Observer A)	-	-	-	-	0.24	0.62
Ear length (Observer B)	1.88	3.53	-	-	-	-
Ear breadth (Observer A)	-	-	-	-	- 0.06	0.27
Ear breadth (Observer B)	-	-	-	-	0.34	1.03
Relative shoulder breadth	-	-	0.28	3.11	(0.22	2.44)
Relative sitting height	-	-	-	-	- 0.04	0.40
Cephalic index	-	-	-	-	0.30	1.36
Cephalo-facial	-	-	-	-	- 0.21	1.05
Length-height index						
(Observer A)	-	-	-	-	0.12	0.46
(Observer B)	-	-	-	-	- 0.87	2.18
Breadth-height index						
(Observer A)	-	-	-	-	- 0.39	1.26
(Observer B)	-	-	-	-	0.30	0.65
Facial index	-	-	-	-	0.76	2.17
Upper facial index	-	-	-	-	0.54	2.25
Nasal index	-	-	-	-	- 0.60	1.33
Ear index (Observer A)	-	-	-	-	- 0.24	0.65
Ear index (Observer B)	-	-	-	-	- 1.00	1.67
Zygo-frontal index	-	-	-	-	- 0.60	2.86
Fronto-parietal index	-	-	- 0.66	3.14	(0.33	1.57)
Zygo-gonial index	-	-	-	-	- 0.09	0.38
Measurements						
Number	4		1		18	
Per Cent	17.39		4.35		78.26	
Indices						
Number	0		2		14	
Per Cent	0		12.50		87.50	

*Significant difference corrected for state sampling.

Table V-89. Distribution of Offense Differences in Terms of the Probable Error
on Basis of State Composition Compared with Distribution Expected
in Random Sample

Measurements

	Less than 1 p.e.	1 p.e. to 2 p.e.	2 p.e. to 3 p.e.	3 p.e. to 4 p.e.	4 p.e. to 5 p.e.	Total
	No.	No.	No.	No.	No.	
Expectation in Random Sample	11.50	7.42	3.09	0.83	0.16	23
First degree murder	6	6	2	1	8	23
Second degree murder	6	12	2	1	2	23
Assault	12	4	5	2	0	23
Robbery	6	6	6	2	3	23
Burglary and larceny	3	1	5	4	10	23
Forgery and fraud	3	8	8	3	1	23
Rape	8	8	3	2	2	23
Other sex	5	7	9	1	1	23
Vs. public welfare	8	4	5	2	4	23
Arson and all other	7	9	3	3	1	23
Expectation in Random Samples	115	74.2	30.9	8.3	1.6	230
Total	64	65	48	21	32	230

Indices

	Less than 1 p.e.	1 p.e. to 2 p.e.	2 p.e. to 3 p.e.	3 p.e. to 4 p.e.	4 p.e. to 5 p.e.	Total
	No.	No.	No.	No.	No.	
Expectation in Random Sample	8.00	5.16	2.15	0.58	0.11	16
First degree murder	4	3	5	1	3	16
Second degree murder	5	7	2	0	2	16
Assault	9	5	1	1	0	16
Robbery	2	8	5	1	0	16
Burglary and larceny	5	4	6	0	1	16
Forgery and fraud	5	6	5	0	0	16
Rape	3	6	6	1	0	16
Other sex	6	5	4	1	0	16
Vs. public welfare	6	5	3	1	1	16
Arson and all other	5	6	5	0	0	16
Expectation in Random Samples	80	51.6	21.5	5.8	1.1	160
Total	50	55	42	6	7	160

·Table V-90.　　　Number of Significant and Insignificant Metric and Indicial
Differences on Basis of State Composition by Offenses

Measurements

	Total Number of Measurements in Crime Group	Significant Differences Independent of State Sampling		Crude Differences Invalidated by State Sampling		Insignificant Differences	
		No.	Per Cent	No.	Per Cent	No.	Per Cent
First degree murder	23	9	39.13	3	13.04	11	47.83
Second degree murder	23	3	13.04	3	13.04	17	73.91
Assault	23	2	8.70	0	0	21	91.30
Robbery	23	5	21.74	2	8.70	16	69.57
Burglary and larceny	23	14	60.87	0	0	9	39.13
Forgery and fraud	23	4	17.39	8	34.78	11	47.83
Rape	23	4	17.39	2	8.70	17	73.91
Other sex	23	2	8.70	0	0	21	91.30
Vs. public welfare	23	6	26.09	6	26.09	11	47.83
Arson and all other	23	4	17.39	1	4.35	18	78.26

Indices

	Total Number of Indices in Crime Group	Significant Differences Independent of State Sampling		Crude Differences Invalidated by State Sampling		Insignificant Differences	
		No.	Per Cent	No.	Per Cent	No.	Per Cent
First degree murder	16	4	25.00	3	18.75	9	56.25
Second degree murder	16	2	12.50	4	25.00	10	62.50
Assault	16	1	6.25	1	6.25	14	87.50
Robbery	16	1	6.25	1	6.25	14	87.50
Burglary and larceny	16	1	6.25	1	6.25	14	87.50
Forgery and fraud	16	0	0	1	6.25	15	93.75
Rape	16	1	6.25	2	12.50	13	81.25
Other sex	16	1	6.25	1	6.25	14	87.50
Vs. public welfare	16	2	12.50	3	18.75	11	68.75
Arson and all other	16	0	0	2	12.50	14	87.50

Table V-91. Summary of Metric and Indicial Differentiation by Offenses
on Basis of Age Grouping

Measurements

	Independent of State Sampling		Affected by Age or Observational Equation		Independent of State Sampling and Age	
	No.	Per Cent	No.	Per Cent	No.	Per Cent
First degree murder	9	39.13	3	13.04	6	26.09
Second degree murder	3	13.04	0	0	3	13.04
Assault	2	8.70	0	0	2	8.70
Robbery	5	21.74	1	4.35	4	17.39
Burglary and larceny	14	60.87	6	26.09	8	34.78
Forgery and fraud	4	17.39	0	0	4	17.39
Rape	4	17.39	0	0	4	17.39
Other sex	2	8.70	1	4.35	1	4.35
Vs. public welfare	6	26.09	1	4.35	5	21.74
Arson and all other	4	13.04	1	4.35	3	13.04
Total	53	23.04	13	5.65	40	17.39

Indices

	Independent of State Sampling		Affected by Age or Observational Equation		Independent of State Sampling and Age	
	No.	Per Cent	No.	Per Cent	No.	Per Cent
First degree murder	4	25.00	0	0	4	25.00
Second degree murder	2	12.50	0	0	2	12.50
Assault	1	6.25	1	6.25	0	0
Robbery	1	6.25	0	0	1	6.25
Burglary and larceny	1	6.25	0	0	1	6.25
Forgery and fraud	0	0	0	0	0	0
Rape	1	6.25	0	0	1	6.25
Other sex	1	6.25	1	6.25	0	0
Vs. public welfare	2	12.50	1	6.25	1	6.25
Arson and all other	0	0	0	0	0	0
Total	13	8.13	3	1.87	10	6.25

Total Measurements and Indices Independently Differentiated

	No.	Per Cent
First degree murder	10	25.64
Second degree murder	5	12.82
Assault	2	5.13
Robbery	5	12.82
Burglary and larceny	9	23.08
Forgery and fraud	4	10.26
Rape	5	12.82
Other sex	1	2.56
Vs. public welfare	6	15.38
Arson and all other	3	7.69
Total	50	12.82

Table VI-1.   Tattooing (Observer A) by Offenses

	None		Some		Extensive		Total
	No.	Per Cent	No.	Per Cent	No.	Per Cent	
First degree murder	225	91.84	19	7.76	1	0.41	245
Second degree murder	438	91.63	31	6.48	9	1.88	478
Assault	29	85.29	3	8.82	2	5.88	34
Robbery	211	76.45	51	18.48	14	5.07	276
Burglary and larceny	852	81.61	154	14.75	38	3.64	1044
Forgery and fraud	266	84.98	42	13.42	5	1.60	313
Rape	98	86.73	13	11.50	2	1.77	113
Other sex	68	82.93	14	17.07	0	0	82
Vs. public welfare	178	88.12	19	9.41	5	2.48	202
Arson and all other	61	87.14	7	10.00	2	2.86	70
Total	2426	84.91	353	12.36	78	2.73	2857

Table VI-2.   Differences of Offense Subgroups and Total Series with Value
in Terms of the Probable Error

Tattooing

None

	Per Cent	x p.e.
First degree murder	6.93 ± 1.48	4.68
Second degree murder	6.72 ± 1.00	6.72
Assault	0.38 ± 4.11	0.09
Robbery	− 8.46 ± 1.38	6.13
Burglary and larceny	− 3.30 ± .59	5.59
Forgery and fraud	0.07 ± 1.29	0.05
Rape	1.82 ± 2.23	0.82
Other sex	− 1.98 ± 2.63	0.75
Vs. public welfare	3.21 ± 1.64	1.96
Arson and all other	2.23 ± 2.85	0.78

Table VI-3.   Hair Quantity by Offenses

Head

	Small		Medium		Large		Total
	No.	Per Cent	No.	Per Cent	No.	Per Cent	No.
First degree murder	55	17.68	204	65.59	52	16.72	311
Second degree murder	75	12.16	426	69.04	116	18.80	617
Assault	6	7.50	66	82.50	8	10.00	80
Robbery	30	7.26	296	71.67	87	21.07	413
Burglary and larceny	123	7.64	1174	72.87	314	19.49	1611
Forgery and fraud	68	14.56	319	68.31	80	17.13	467
Rape	30	15.23	149	75.63	18	9.14	197
Other sex	22	14.57	104	68.87	25	16.56	151
Vs. public welfare	45	17.51	153	59.53	59	22.96	257
Arson and all other	12	11.65	76	73.79	15	14.56	103
Total	466	11.08	2967	70.52	774	18.40	4207

Coefficient of mean square contingency = .14

Beard

	Small		Medium		Large		Total
	No.	Per Cent	No.	Per Cent	No.	Per Cent	No.
First degree murder	73	23.47	191	61.41	47	15.11	311
Second degree murder	236	38.19	330	53.40	52	8.41	618
Assault	27	33.75	46	57.50	7	8.75	80
Robbery	125	30.34	219	53.16	68	16.50	412
Burglary and larceny	645	40.06	749	46.52	216	13.42	1610
Forgery	128	27.41	261	55.89	78	16.70	467
Rape	76	38.97	96	49.23	23	11.79	195
Other sex	49	32.45	80	52.98	22	14.57	151
Vs. public welfare	89	34.63	130	50.58	38	14.79	257
Arson and all other	34	33.01	54	52.43	15	14.56	103
Total	1482	35.25	2156	51.28	566	13.46	4204

Coefficient of mean square contingency = .10

Body

	Small		Medium		Large		Total
	No.	Per Cent	No.	Per Cent	No.	Per Cent	No.
First degree murder	97	31.49	155	50.32	56	18.18	308
Second degree murder	252	40.91	273	44.32	91	14.77	616
Assault	36	45.00	31	38.75	13	16.25	80
Robbery	206	50.00	152	36.89	54	13.11	412
Burglary and larceny	913	57.03	526	32.85	162	10.12	1601
Forgery	229	49.35	159	34.27	76	16.38	464
Rape	72	37.31	89	46.11	32	16.58	193
Other sex	56	37.09	70	46.36	25	16.56	151
Vs. public welfare	94	36.72	118	46.09	44	17.19	256
Arson and all other	49	47.57	40	38.84	14	13.59	103
Total	2004	47.90	1613	38.55	567	13.55	4184

Coefficient of mean square contingency = .10

Table VI-4. Predictions on Basis of State Composition and Differences
from Total Series by Offenses

Hair Quantity, Head

	Predicted Per Cent	Small Diff.of Subgroup and Predicted Per Cent	Diff.of Subgroup and Total Per Cent ± p.e.	x p.e.
First degree murder	11.04	6.64	6.60 ± 1.15	5.74
Second degree murder	10.22	1.94	1.08 ± .79	1.37
Assault	10.01	- 2.51	- 3.58 ± 2.36	1.52
Robbery	10.34	- 3.08	- 3.82 ± .99	3.86
Burglary and larceny	10.26	- 2.62	- 3.44 ± .42	8.19
Forgery and fraud	11.30	3.26	3.48 ± .92	3.78
Rape	10.76	4.47	4.15 ± 1.47	2.82
Other sex	9.97	4.60	3.49 ± 1.69	2.06
Vs. public welfare	11.95	5.56	6.43 ± 1.28	5.02
Arson and all other	10.18	1.47	0.57 ± 2.06	0.28

	Predicted Per Cent	Large Diff.of Subgroup and Predicted Per Cent	Diff.of Subgroup and Total Per Cent ± p.e.	x p.e.
First degree murder	21.23	- 9.51	- 1.68 ± 1.42	1.18
Second degree murder	19.94	- 1.14	0.40 ± .97	0.41
Assault	13.04	- 3.04	- 8.40 ± 2.89	2.91
Robbery	17.29	3.78	2.67 ± 1.22	2.19
Burglary and larceny	17.54	1.95	1.09 ± .51	2.14
Forgery and fraud	20.62	- 3.49	- 1.27 ± 1.14	1.11
Rape	14.32	- 5.18	- 9.26 ± 1.81	5.12
Other sex	14.99	1.57	- 1.84 ± 2.09	0.88
Vs. public welfare	24.70	- 1.74	4.56 ± 1.58	2.89
Arson and all other	16.19	- 1.63	- 3.84 ± 2.54	1.51

Significant Differences Independent of State Sampling

Small

First degree murder: difference	6.60 (5.74 p.e.)
Robbery: independent difference	- 3.08 (3.11 p.e.)
Burglary and larceny: independent difference	- 2.62 (6.24 p.e.)
Forgery and fraud: independent difference	3.26 (3.54 p.e.)
Vs. public welfare: independent difference	5.56 (4.34 p.e.)

Differences Rendered Insignificant by State Sampling

Large

Rape: independent difference:	- 5.18 (2.86 p.e.)

Table VI-4 (cont'd). Hair Quantity, Beard

	Predicted Per Cent	Small Diff. of Subgroup and Predicted Per Cent	Diff. of Subgroup and Total Per Cent ± p.e.	x p.e.
First degree murder	22.82	0.65	-11.78 ± 1.76	6.69
Second degree murder	36.52	1.67	2.94 ± 1.20	2.45
Assault	37.78	- 4.03	- 1.50 ± 3.57	.42
Robbery	35.95	- 5.61	- 4.91 ± 1.51	3.25
Burglary and larceny	37.04	3.02	4.81 ± .63	7.64
Forgery and fraud	33.91	- 6.50	- 7.84 ± 1.40	5.60
Rape	33.00	5.97	3.72 ± 2.25	1.65
Other sex	36.91	- 4.46	- 2.80 ± 2.56	1.09
Vs. public welfare	32.16	2.47	- 0.62 ± 1.95	.32
Arson and all other	31.45	1.56	- 2.24 ± 3.14	.71

	Predicted Per Cent	Large Diff. of Subgroup and Predicted Per Cent	Diff. of Subgroup and Total Per Cent ± p.e.	x p.e.
First degree murder	11.39	3.72	1.65 ± 1.26	1.31
Second degree murder	9.75	- 1.34	- 5.05 ± .86	5.87
Assault	15.10	- 6.35	- 4.71 ± 2.55	1.85
Robbery	14.60	1.90	3.04 ± 1.08	2.82
Burglary and larceny	13.42	0	- 0.04 ± .45	.09
Forgery and fraud	15.58	1.12	3.24 ± 1.00	3.24
Rape	16.22	- 4.43	- 1.67 ± 1.63	1.04
Other sex	13.64	0.93	1.11 ± 1.84	.60
Vs. public welfare	16.90	- 2.11	1.33 ± 1.39	.96
Arson and all other	13.21	1.35	1.10 ± 2.24	0.49

Significant Differences Independent of State Sampling

Small

Robbery: difference	- 4.91 (3.25 p.e.)
Burglary and larceny: independent difference	3.02 (4.79 p.e.)
Forgery and fraud: independent difference	- 6.50 (4.64 p.e.)

Differences Rendered Insignificant by State Sampling

Small

First degree murder: independent difference	0.65 (0.37 p.e.)*

Large

Second degree murder: independent difference	- 1.34 (1.56 p.e.)
Forgery and fraud: independent difference	1.12 (1.12 p.e.)

*Signs are opposite

Table VI-4 (cont'd).   Hair Quantity, Body

	Predicted Per Cent	Small Diff. of Subgroup and Predicted Per Cent	Diff. of Subgroup and Total Per Cent ± p.e.	x p.e.
First degree murder	43.56	-12.07	-16.41 ± 1.85	8.87
Second degree murder	48.22	- 7.31	- 6.99 ± 1.26	5.55
Assault	51.49	- 6.49	- 2.90 ± 3.73	.78
Robbery	47.78	2.22	2.10 ± 1.58	1.33
Burglary and larceny	49.29	7.74	9.13 ± .66	13.83
Forgery and fraud	47.89	1.46	1.45 ± 1.48	.98
Rape	46.20	- 8.89	-10.59 ± 2.37	4.47
Other sex	49.94	-12.85	-10.81 ± 2.69	4.02
Vs. public welfare	46.37	- 9.65	-11.18 ± 2.04	5.48
Arson and all other	44.47	3.10	- 0.33 ± 3.28	.10

	Predicted Per Cent	Large Diff. of Subgroup and Predicted Per Cent	Diff. of Subgroup and Total Per Cent ± p.e.	x p.e.
First degree murder	15.52	2.66	4.63 ± 1.27	3.65
Second degree murder	13.12	1.65	1.22 ± .86	1.42
Assault	12.61	3.64	2.70 ± 2.56	1.06
Robbery	13.60	- 0.49	- 0.44 ± 1.08	.41
Burglary and larceny	13.05	- 2.93	- 3.43 ± .45	7.62
Forgery and fraud	15.40	0.98	2.83 ± 1.01	2.80
Rape	13.51	3.07	3.03 ± 1.63	1.86
Other sex	12.36	4.20	3.01 ± 1.85	1.63
Vs. public welfare	16.49	0.70	3.64 ± 1.40	2.60
Arson and all other	13.40	0.19	0.04 ± 2.25	.02

Significant Difference Independent of State Sampling
Small

First degree murder: independent difference	-12.07 (6.52 p.e.)
Second degree murder: difference	- 6.99 (5.55 p.e.)
Burglary and larceny: independent difference	7.74 (11.73 p.e.)
Rape: independent difference	- 8.89 (3.75 p.e.)
Other sex: difference	-10.81 (4.02 p.e.)
Vs. public welfare: independent difference	- 9.65 (4.73 p.e.)

Large

Burglary and larceny: independent difference	- 2.93 (6.51 p.e.)

Differences Rendered Insignificant by State Sampling

Large

First degree murder: independent difference	2.66 (2.09 p.e.)

Table VI-5.   Skin Color by Offenses

| | Red White | | Pale White | | Ruddy | | Olive | |
	No.	Per Cent	No.	Per Cent	No.	Per Cent	No.	Per Cent
First degree murder	108	34.62	198	63.46	0	0	4	1.28
Second degree murder	216	34.89	347	56.06	2	0.32	22	3.56
Assault	18	22.50	55	68.75	1	1.25	3	3.75
Robbery	116	28.09	276	66.83	2	0.48	12	2.91
Burglary and larceny	497	30.83	996	61.79	14	0.87	52	3.23
Forgery and fraud	144	30.84	300	64.24	5	1.07	15	3.21
Rape	51	25.89	135	68.53	2	1.02	7	3.55
Other sex	43	28.48	98	64.90	2	1.32	3	1.99
Vs. public welfare	105	40.86	144	56.03	1	0.39	5	1.95
Arson and all other	30	29.13	67	65.05	1	0.97	3	2.91
Total	1328	31.54	2616	62.12	30	0.71	126	2.99

| | Light Yellow Brown | | Light Brown | | Medium Red Brown | | Total | |
	No.	Per Cent	No.	Per Cent	No.	Per Cent	No.	
First degree murder	0	0	2	0.64	0	0	312	
Second degree murder	0	0	32	5.17	0	0	619	
Assault	0	0	3	3.75	0	0	80	
Robbery	0	0	6	1.45	1	0.24	413	
Burglary and larceny	1	0.06	52	3.23	0	0	1612	
Forgery and fraud	0	0	3	0.64	0	0	467	
Rape	0	0	2	1.02	0	0	197	
Other sex	0	0	5	3.31	0	0	151	
Vs. public welfare	1	0.39	1	0.39	0	0	257	
Arson and all other	1	0.97	1	0.97	0	0	103	
Total	3	0.07	107	2.54	1	0.02	4211	

Table VI-6. Predictions on Basis of State Composition and Differences
from Total Series by Offenses

Skin Color

| | | Red White | | |
	Predicted Per Cent	Diff. of Subgroup and Predicted Per Cent	Diff. of Subgroup and Total Per Cent ± p.e.	x p.e.
First degree murder	32.64	1.98	3.08 ± 1.71	1.80
Second degree murder	35.67	- 0.78	3.35 ± 1.17	2.86
Assault	23.75	- 1.25	- 9.04 ± 3.47	2.60
Robbery	29.37	- 1.28	- 3.45 ± 1.46	2.36
Rape	24.89	1.00	- 5.65 ± 2.18	2.59
Other sex	28.18	0.30	- 3.06 ± 2.50	1.22
Vs. public welfare	36.44	4.42	9.32 ± 1.90	4.90

Table VI-6 (cont'd).

Pale White

	Predicted Per Cent	Diff.of Subgroup and Predicted Per Cent	Diff.of Subgroup and Total Per Cent ± p.e.	x p.e.
Second degree murder	57.58	- 1.52	- 6.06 ± 1.21	5.01
Assault	67.23	1.52	6.63 ± 3.62	1.83
Robbery	64.89	1.94	4.71 ± 1.53	3.08
Forgery and fraud	63.48	0.76	2.12 ± 1.43	1.48
Rape	70.07	- 1.54	6.41 ± 2.27	2.82
Other sex	62.94	1.96	2.78 ± 2.62	1.06
Vs. public welfare	59.23	- 3.20	- 6.09 ± 1.98	3.08
Arson and all other	66.32	- 1.27	2.93 ± 3.18	0.92

Ruddy

	Predicted Per Cent	Diff.of Subgroup and Predicted Per Cent	Diff.of Subgroup and Total Per Cent
First degree murder	0.43	- 0.43	- 0.71
Second degree murder	0.49	- 0.17	- 0.39
Assault	0.92	0.33	0.54
Forgery and fraud	0.62	0.45	0.36
Rape	1.02	0	0.31
Other sex	0.87	0.45	0.61

Olive

	Predicted Per Cent	Diff.of Subgroup and Predicted Per Cent	Diff.of Subgroup and Total Per Cent
First degree murder	2.34	- 1.06	- 1.71
Second degree murder	2.51	1.05	0.57
Assault	4.06	- 0.31	0.76
Burglary and larceny	3.20	0.03	0.24
Rape	2.76	0.79	0.56
Other sex	3.60	- 1.61	- 1.00
Vs. public welfare	2.74	- 0.79	- 1.04

Light Brown

	Predicted Per Cent	Diff.of Subgroup and Predicted Per Cent	Diff.of Subgroup and Total Per Cent
First degree murder	0.51	0.13	- 1.90
Second degree murder	3.66	1.51	2.63
Assault	3.90	- 0.15	1.21
Robbery	1.52	- 0.07	- 1.09
Burglary and larceny	3.37	- 0.14	0.69
Forgery and fraud	1.41	- 0.77	- 1.90

Differences Rendered Insignificant by State Sampling

Red White

Vs. public welfare: independent difference   4.42 (2.33 p.e.)

Pale White

Second degree murder: independent difference   - 1.52 (1.26 p.e.)

Robbery: independent difference   1.94 (1.27 p.e.)

Vs. public welfare: independent difference   - 3.20 (1.62 p.e.)

Table VI-7.   Hair Form by Offenses

	Straight		Low Waves		Deep Waves	
	No.	Per Cent	No.	Per Cent	No.	Per Cent
First degree murder	279	89.71	16	5.14	10	3.22
Second degree murder	524	84.91	55	8.91	27	4.38
Assault	65	81.25	8	10.00	4	5.00
Robbery	330	80.49	48	11.71	23	5.61
Burglary and larceny	1379	85.81	123	7.65	68	4.23
Forgery and fraud	394	84.37	45	9.64	15	3.21
Rape	176	89.34	14	7.11	2	1.02
Other sex	140	93.33	3	2.00	6	4.00
Vs. public welfare	214	83.59	26	10.16	9	3.52
Arson and all other	82	79.61	14	13.59	3	2.91
Total	3583	85.35	352	8.38	167	3.98

	Curly		Frizzly		Total
	No.	Per Cent	No.	Per Cent	No.
First degree murder	6	1.93	0	0	311
Second degree murder	11	1.78	0	0	617
Assault	3	3.75	0	0	80
Robbery	9	2.20	0	0	410
Burglary and larceny	36	2.24	1	0.06	1607
Forgery and fraud	11	2.36	2	0.43	467
Rape	5	2.54	0	0	197
Other sex	1	0.67	0	0	150
Vs. public welfare	6	2.34	1	0.39	256
Arson and all other	4	3.88	0	0	103
Total	92	2.19	4	0.10	4198

Coefficient of mean square contingency = .10

Table VI-8. Predictions on Basis of State Composition and Differences
from Total Series by Offenses

Hair Form

		Straight		
	Predicted Per Cent	Diff.of Subgroup and Predicted Per Cent	Diff.of Subgroup and Total Per Cent ± p.e.	x p.e.
First degree murder	86.44	3.27	4.36 ± 1.30	3.35
Second degree murder	85.90	- 0.97	- 0.42 ± .89	0.47
Assault	87.43	- 6.18	- 4.10 ± 2.64	1.55
Robbery	85.40	- 4.91	- 4.86 ± 1.12	4.34
Burglary and larceny	85.36	0.45	0.46 ± .46	1.00
Forgery and fraud	84.32	0.05	- 0.98 ± 1.04	0.94
Rape	86.92	2.42	3.99 ± 1.66	2.40
Other sex	86.44	6.89	7.98 ± 1.92	4.16
Vs. public welfare	81.44	2.15	- 1.76 ± 1.44	1.22
Arson and all other	86.74	- 7.13	- 5.74 ± 2.32	2.47

Table VI-8 (cont'd).

	Predicted Per Cent	Low Waves Diff.of Subgroup and Predicted Per Cent	Diff.of Subgroup and Total Per Cent ± p.e.	x p.e.
First degree murder	7.26	2.12	- 3.24 ± 1.02	3.18
Second degree murder	7.59	1.32	0.53 ± .70	0.76
Assault	7.58	2.42	1.62 ± 2.07	0.78
Robbery	8.39	3.32	3.33 ± .88	3.78
Burglary and larceny	8.42	- 0.77	- 0.73 ± .37	1.97
Forgery and fraud	9.41	0.23	1.26 ± .82	1.54
Rape	7.56	- 0.45	- 1.27 ± 1.30	0.98
Other sex	7.82	- 5.82	- 6.38 ± 1.50	4.25
Vs. public welfare	11.24	- 1.08	1.78 ± 1.13	1.58
Arson and all other	7.12	6.47	5.21 ± 1.82	2.86

	Predicted Per Cent	Deep Waves Diff.of Subgroup and Predicted Per Cent	Diff.of Subgroup and Total Per Cent ± p.e.	x p.e.
First degree murder	4.12	- 0.90	- 0.76 ± .72	1.06
Second degree murder	4.19	0.19	0.40 ± .49	0.82
Assault	3.23	1.77	1.02 ± 1.46	0.70
Robbery	3.91	1.70	1.63 ± .62	2.63
Burglary and larceny	3.95	0.28	0.25 ± .26	0.96
Forgery and fraud	4.08	- 0.87	- 0.77 ± .57	1.35
Rape	3.42	- 2.40	- 2.96 ± .92	3.22
Other sex	3.65	0.35	0.02 ± 1.06	0.02
Vs. public welfare	4.71	- 1.19	- 0.46 ± .80	0.58
Arson and all other	3.83	- 0.92	- 1.07 ± 1.28	0.84

	Predicted Per Cent	Curly Diff.of Subgroup and Predicted Per Cent	Diff.of Subgroup and Total Per Cent ± p.e.	x p.e.
First degree murder	2.11	- 0.18	- 0.26 ± .54	0.48
Second degree murder	2.19	- 0.41	- 0.41 ± .37	1.11
Assault	1.66	2.09	1.56 ± 1.09	1.43
Robbery	2.24	- 0.04	0.01 ± .46	0.02
Burglary and larceny	2.16	0.08	0.05 ± .19	0.26
Forgery and fraud	2.12	0.24	0.17 ± .43	0.40
Rape	2.05	0.49	0.35 ± .69	0.51
Other sex	1.97	- 1.30	- 1.52 ± .80	1.90
Vs. public welfare	2.52	- 0.18	0.15 ± .59	0.25
Arson and all other	2.24	1.64	1.69 ± .96	1.76

Significant Differences Independent of State Sampling

Straight

Robbery: difference — 4.86 (4.34 p.e.)
Other sex: independent difference 6.89 (3.59 p.e.)

Low Waves

Robbery: independent difference 3.32 (3.77 p.e.)
Other sex: independent difference - 5.82 (3.88 p.e.)

Differences Rendered Insignificant by State Sampling

Straight

First degree murder: independent difference 3.27 (2.52 p.e.)

Low Waves

First degree murder: independent difference - 2.12 (2.08 p.e.)

Deep Waves

Rape: independent difference - 2.40 (2.61 p.e.)

Table VI-9.   Hair Color by Offenses

| | Black | | Dark Brown | | Reddish Brown | | Light Brown | |
	No.	Per Cent	No.	Per Cent	No.	Per Cent	No.	Per Cent
First degree murder	16	5.14	111	35.69	60	19.29	74	23.79
Second degree murder	40	6.56	228	37.38	106	17.38	155	25.41
Assault	2	2.53	31	39.24	17	21.52	16	20.25
Robbery	15	3.63	135	32.69	93	22.52	126	30.51
Burglary and larceny	63	3.96	552	34.67	330	20.73	417	26.19
Forgery and fraud	28	6.09	150	32.61	84	18.26	124	26.96
Rape	10	5.13	70	35.90	37	18.97	44	22.56
Other sex	10	6.62	56	37.09	34	22.52	27	17.88
Vs. public welfare	16	6.35	71	28.17	52	20.63	66	26.19
Arson and all other	9	8.74	34	33.01	20	19.42	24	23.30
Total	209	5.02	1438	34.52	833	20.00	1073	25.76

| | Ash-blond | | Golden | | Red | | Gray, White | | Total |
	No.	Per Cent	No.	Per Cent	No.	Per Cent	No.	Per Cent	No.
First degree murder	4	1.29	7	2.25	5	1.61	34	10.93	311
Second degree murder	9	1.48	11	1.80	18	2.95	43	7.05	610
Assault	1	1.27	1	1.27	6	7.59	5	6.33	79
Robbery	6	1.45	10	2.42	20	4.84	8	1.94	413
Burglary and larceny	50	3.14	77	4.84	69	4.33	34	2.14	1592
Forgery and fraud	16	3.48	22	4.78	19	4.13	17	3.70	460
Rape	3	1.54	6	3.08	4	2.05	21	10.77	195
Other sex	0	0	1	0.66	6	3.97	17	11.26	151
Vs. public welfare	1	0.40	8	3.17	13	5.16	25	9.92	252
Arson and all other	6	5.82	2	1.94	1	0.97	7	6.80	103
Total	96	2.30	145	3.48	161	3.86	211	5.06	4166

Coefficient of mean square contingency = .22

Table VI-10. Predictions on Basis of State Composition and Differences
from Total Series by Offenses

	Predicted Per Cent	Black Diff.of Subgroup and Predicted Per Cent	Diff.of Subgroup and Total Per Cent ± p.e.	x p.e.
First degree murder	5.07	0.07	0.12 ± .80	.15
Second degree murder	5.30	1.26	1.54 ± .55	2.80
Assault	4.49	- 1.96	- 2.49 ± 1.64	1.52
Robbery	4.66	- 1.03	- 1.39 ± .69	2.01
Burglary and larceny	4.98	- 1.02	- 1.06 ± .28	3.79
Forgery and fraud	5.13	0.96	1.07 ± .65	1.65
Rape	4.78	0.35	0.11 ± 1.03	.11
Other sex	4.80	1.82	1.60 ± 1.17	1.37
Vs. public welfare	5.58	0.77	1.33 ± .90	1.48
Arson and all other	4.62	4.12	3.72 ± 1.44	2.58

Table VI-10 (cont'd).

		Dark Brown		
	Predicted Per Cent	Diff.of Subgroup and Predicted Per Cent	Diff.of Subgroup and Total Per Cent ± p.e.	x p.e.
First degree murder	34.37	1.32	1.17 ± 1.75	.67
Second degree murder	35.78	1.60	2.86 ± 1.20	2.38
Assault	36.46	2.78	4.72 ± 3.58	1.32
Robbery	33.12	- 0.43	- 1.83 ± 1.50	1.22
Burglary and larceny	34.91	- 0.24	0.15 ± .63	.24
Forgery and fraud	33.05	- 0.44	- 1.91 ± 1.41	1.36
Rape	35.20	0.70	1.38 ± 2.24	.62
Other sex	36.45	0.64	2.57 ± 2.56	1.00
Vs. public welfare	31.26	- 3.09	- 6.35 ± 1.96	3.24
Arson and all other	34.78	- 1.77	- 1.51 ± 3.12	.48

		Reddish Brown		
	Predicted Per Cent	Diff.of Subgroup and Predicted Per Cent	Diff.of Subgroup and Total Per Cent ± p.e.	x p.e.
First degree murder	18.93	0.36	- 0.71 ± 1.47	0.48
Second degree murder	17.53	- 0.15	- 2.62 ± 1.01	2.59
Assault	20.80	0.72	1.52 ± 3.01	0.50
Robbery	21.02	1.50	2.52 ± 1.26	2.00
Burglary and larceny	20.04	0.69	0.73 ± .53	1.38
Forgery and fraud	20.76	- 2.50	- 1.74 ± 1.19	1.46
Rape	21.47	- 2.50	- 1.03 ± 1.89	0.54
Other sex	20.43	2.09	2.52 ± 2.15	1.17
Vs. public welfare	21.93	- 1.30	0.63 ± 1.65	0.38
Arson and all other	21.06	- 1.64	- 0.58 ± 2.62	0.22

		Light Brown		
	Predicted Per Cent	Diff.of Subgroup and Predicted Per Cent	Diff.of Subgroup and Total Per Cent ± p.e.	x p.e.
First degree murder	26.80	- 3.01	- 1.97 ± 1.60	1.23
Second degree murder	27.79	- 2.38	- 0.35 ± 1.11	0.32
Assault	24.15	- 3.90	- 5.51 ± 3.28	1.68
Robbery	26.25	4.26	4.75 ± 1.38	3.44
Burglary and larceny	25.80	0.39	0.43 ± .58	0.74
Forgery and fraud	25.26	1.70	1.20 ± 1.30	0.92
Rape	23.45	- 0.89	- 3.20 ± 2.06	1.55
Other sex	24.56	- 6.68	- 7.88 ± 2.35	3.35
Vs. public welfare	24.58	1.61	0.43 ± 1.80	0.24
Arson and all other	25.26	- 1.96	- 2.46 ± 2.87	0.86

Table VI-10 (cont'd).

	Predicted Per Cent	Ash-blond Diff. of Subgroup and Predicted Per Cent	Diff. of Subgroup and Total Per Cent ± p.e.	x p.e.
First degree murder	2.68	- 1.39	- 1.01 ± .55	1.84
Second degree murder	2.37	- 0.89	- 0.82 ± .38	2.16
Assault	1.91	- 0.64	- 1.03 ± 1.13	0.91
Robbery	2.16	- 0.71	- 0.85 ± .47	1.81
Burglary and larceny	2.08	1.06	0.84 ± .20	4.20
Forgery and fraud	2.10	1.38	1.18 ± .44	2.68
Rape	2.21	- 0.67	- 0.76 ± .71	1.07
Other sex	2.03	- 2.03	- 2.30 ± .81	2.84
Vs. public welfare	2.04	- 1.64	- 1.90 ± .62	3.06
Arson and all other	2.47	3.35	3.52 ± .99	3.56

	Predicted Per Cent	Golden Diff. of Subgroup and Predicted Per Cent	Diff. of Subgroup and Total Per Cent ± p.e.	x p.e.
First degree murder	3.36	- 1.11	- 1.23 ± .67	1.84
Second degree murder	3.38	- 1.58	- 1.68 ± .46	3.65
Assault	3.33	- 2.06	- 2.21 ± 1.38	1.60
Robbery	3.66	- 1.24	- 1.06 ± .57	1.86
Burglary and larceny	3.49	1.35	1.36 ± .24	5.67
Forgery and fraud	3.55	1.23	1.30 ± .55	2.36
Rape	3.20	- 0.12	- 0.40 ± .87	0.46
Other sex	3.36	- 2.70	- 2.82 ± .99	2.85
Vs. public welfare	3.73	- 0.56	- 0.31 ± .76	0.41
Arson and all other	3.44	- 1.50	- 1.54 ± 1.20	1.28

	Predicted Per Cent	Red Diff. of Subgroup and Predicted Per Cent	Diff. of Subgroup and Total Per Cent ± p.e.	x p.e.
First degree murder	3.64	- 2.03	- 2.25 ± .71	3.17
Second degree murder	3.62	- 0.67	- 0.91 ± .49	1.86
Assault	3.05	4.54	3.73 ± 1.45	2.57
Robbery	3.95	0.89	0.98 ± .61	1.61
Burglary and larceny	3.80	0.53	0.47 ± .25	1.88
Forgery and fraud	4.40	- 0.27	0.27 ± .57	0.47
Rape	3.40	- 1.35	- 1.81 ± .90	2.01
Other sex	3.29	0.68	0.11 ± 1.04	0.11
Vs. public welfare	5.38	- 0.22	1.30 ± .80	1.62
Arson and all other	3.35	- 2.38	- 2.89 ± 1.26	2.29

Table VI-10 (cont'd).

	Predicted Per Cent	Gray, White Diff.of Subgroup and Predicted Per Cent	Diff.of Subgroup and Total Per Cent ± p.e.	x p.e.
First degree murder	5.13	5.80	5.87 ± .81	7.25
Second degree murder	4.23	2.82	1.99 ± .55	3.62
Assault	5.81	0.52	1.27 ± 1.65	0.77
Robbery	5.17	- 3.23	- 3.12 ± .69	4.52
Burglary and larceny	4.90	- 2.76	- 2.92 ± .30	9.73
Forgery and fraud	5.75	- 2.05	- 1.36 ± .65	2.09
Rape	6.28	4.49	5.71 ± 1.03	5.54
Other sex	5.06	6.20	6.20 ± 1.18	5.25
Vs. public welfare	5.49	4.43	4.86 ± .90	5.40
Arson and all other	5.01	1.79	1.74 ± 1.44	1.21

Significant Differences Independent of State Sampling

Black
Burglary and larceny: independent difference — - 1.02 (3.64 p.e.)

Light Brown
Robbery: independent difference — 4.26 (3.09 p.e.)

Ash-blond
Burglary and larceny: difference — .84 (4.20 p.e.)
Arson and all other: independent difference — 3.35 (3.38 p.e.)

Golden
Second degree murder: independent difference — - 1.58 (3.43 p.e.)
Burglary and larceny: independent difference — 1.35 (5.62 p.e.)

Gray
First degree murder: independent difference — 5.80 (7.16 p.e.)
Second degree murder: difference — 1.99 (3.62 p.e.)
Robbery: difference — - 3.12 (4.52 p.e.)
Burglary and larceny: independent difference — - 2.76 (9.20 p.e.)
Rape: independent difference — 4.49 (4.36 p.e.)
Other sex: independent difference — 6.20 (5.25 p.e.)
Vs. public welfare: independent difference — 4.43 (4.92 p.e.)

Differences Rendered Insignificant by State Sampling

Dark Brown
Vs. public welfare: independent difference — - 3.09 (1.58 p.e.)

Light Brown
Other sex: independent difference — - 6.68 (2.84 p.e.)

Ash-blond
Vs. plic welfare: independent difference — - 1.64 (2.64 p.e.)

Red
First degree murder: independent difference — - 2.03 (2.86 p.e.)

Table VI-11.   Eye Color by Offenses

| | Dark Brown | | Light Brown | | Blue-brown | | Gray-brown | |
	No.	Per Cent	No.	Per Cent	No.	Per Cent	No.	Per Cent
First degree murder	8	2.57	7	2.25	73	23.47	62	19.94
Second degree murder	19	3.08	13	2.11	146	23.66	109	17.67
Assault	6	7.50	3	3.75	18	22.50	6	7.50
Robbery	13	3.16	22	5.34	85	20.63	74	17.96
Burglary and larceny	56	3.48	64	3.98	318	19.75	266	16.52
Forgery and fraud	13	2.78	9	1.93	88	18.84	86	18.42
Rape	9	4.66	5	2.59	35	18.13	20	10.36
Other sex	6	4.00	1	0.67	28	18.67	21	14.00
Vs. public welfare	6	2.33	3	1.17	42	16.34	71	27.63
Arson and all other	3	2.91	2	1.94	20	19.42	15	14.56
Total	139	3.31	129	3.07	853	20.31	730	17.38

| | Green-brown | | Blue | | Blue-gray | | Total | |
	No.	Per Cent	No.	Per Cent	No.	Per Cent	No.	
First degree murder	77	24.75	63	20.26	21	6.75	311	
Second degree murder	169	27.39	118	19.12	43	6.97	617	
Assault	24	30.00	14	17.50	9	11.25	80	
Robbery	118	28.64	64	15.53	36	8.74	412	
Burglary and larceny	445	27.64	294	18.26	167	10.37	1610	
Forgery and fraud	122	26.12	105	22.48	44	9.42	467	
Rape	52	26.94	35	18.13	37	19.17	193	
Other sex	41	27.34	34	22.67	19	12.67	150	
Vs. public welfare	54	21.01	54	21.01	27	10.51	257	
Arson and all other	35	33.98	21	20.39	7	6.80	103	
Total	1137	27.07	802	19.10	410	9.76	4200	

Coefficient of mean square contingency = .14.

Table VI-12. Predictions on Basis of State Composition and Differences
from Total Series by Offenses

	Predicted Per Cent	Dark Brown Diff.of Subgroup and Predicted Per Cent	Diff.of Subgroup and Total Per Cent ± p.e.	x p.e.
First degree murder	3.10	- 0.53	- 0.74 ± .65	1.14
Second degree murder	2.94	0.14	- 0.23 ± .45	0.51
Assault	4.09	3.41	4.19 ± 1.34	3.13
Robbery	3.42	- 0.25	- 0.15 ± .57	0.26
Burglary and larceny	3.40	0.08	0.17 ± .24	0.71
Forgery and fraud	3.26	- 0.48	- 0.53 ± .53	1.00
Rape	4.12	0.54	1.35 ± .85	1.59
Other sex	3.81	0.19	0.69 ± .97	0.71
Vs. public welfare	2.91	- 0.58	- 0.98 ± .73	1.34
Arson and all other	3.70	- 0.79	- 0.40 ± 1.17	0.34

Table VI-12 (cont'd).

Light Brown

	Predicted Per Cent	Diff.of Subgroup and Predicted Per Cent	Diff.of Subgroup and Total Per Cent ± p.e.	x p.e.
First degree murder	2.73	- 0.48	- 0.82 ± .63	1.30
Second degree murder	2.06	0.05	- 0.96 ± .43	2.23
Assault	3.81	- 0.06	0.68 ± 1.29	0.53
Robbery	3.71	1.63	2.27 ± .55	4.13
Burglary and larceny	3.02	0.96	0.91 ± .22	4.14
Forgery and fraud	3.56	- 1.63	- 1.14 ± .51	2.24
Rape	3.40	- 0.81	- 0.48 ± .82	0.59
Other sex	3.06	- 2.39	- 2.40 ± .93	2.58
Vs. public welfare	3.34	- 2.17	- 1.90 ± .70	2.71
Arson and all other	3.14	- 1.20	- 1.13 ± 1.13	1.00

Blue-brown

	Predicted Per Cent	Diff.of Subgroup and Predicted Per Cent	Diff.of Subgroup and Total Per Cent ± p.e.	x p.e.
First degree murder	19.86	3.61	3.16 ± 1.48	2.14
Second degree murder	23.12	0.54	3.35 ± 1.01	3.32
Assault	17.58	4.92	2.19 ± 3.00	0.73
Robbery	20.80	- 0.17	0.32 ± 1.27	0.25
Burglary and larceny	20.60	- 0.85	- 0.56 ± .53	1.06
Forgery and fraud	18.45	0.39	- 1.47 ± 1.18	1.25
Rape	18.99	- 0.86	- 2.18 ± 1.91	1.14
Other sex	18.98	- 0.31	- 1.64 ± 2.17	0.76
Vs. public welfare	17.78	- 1.44	- 3.97 ± 1.64	2.42
Arson and all other	19.70	- 0.28	- 0.89 ± 2.57	0.35

Gray-brown

	Predicted Per Cent	Diff.of Subgroup and Predicted Per Cent	Diff.of Subgroup and Total Per Cent ± p.e.	x p.e.
First degree murder	18.82	1.12	2.56 ± 1.40	1.83
Second degree murder	16.89	0.78	0.29 ± .95	0.31
Assault	10.87	- 3.37	- 9.88 ± 2.83	3.49
Robbery	16.27	1.69	0.58 ± 1.19	0.49
Burglary and larceny	16.18	0.34	- 0.86 ± .50	1.72
Forgery and fraud	21.39	- 2.97	1.04 ± 1.11	0.94
Rape	13.54	- 3.18	- 7.02 ± 1.79	3.92
Other sex	12.83	1.17	- 3.38 ± 2.05	1.65
Vs. public welfare	28.06	- 0.43	10.25 ± 1.54	6.66
Arson and all other	13.70	0.86	- 2.82 ± 2.49	1.13

Table VI-12 (cont'd).

Green-brown

	Predicted Per Cent	Diff.of Subgroup and Predicted Per Cent	Diff.of Subgroup and Total Per Cent ± p.e.	x p.e.
First degree murder	26.79	- 2.04	- 2.32 ± 1.63	1.42
Second degree murder	27.31	0.08	0.32 ± 1.11	0.29
Assault	31.55	- 1.55	2.93 ± 3.32	0.88
Robbery	27.13	1.51	1.57 ± 1.40	1.12
Burglary and larceny	27.77	- 0.13	0.57 ± .59	0.97
Forgery and fraud	24.73	1.39	- 0.95 ± 1.31	0.73
Rape	28.74	- 1.80	- 0.13 ± 2.10	0.06
Other sex	30.44	- 3.10	0.27 ± 2.40	0.11
Vs. public welfare	20.91	0.10	- 6.06 ± 1.81	3.35
Arson and all other	29.59	4.39	6.91 ± 2.91	2.37

Blue

	Predicted Per Cent	Diff.of Subgroup and Predicted Per Cent	Diff.of Subgroup and Total Per Cent ± p.e.	x p.e.
First degree murder	21.58	- 1.32	1.16 ± 1.44	0.81
Second degree murder	20.12	- 1.00	0.02 ± .98	0.02
Assault	17.80	- 0.30	- 1.60 ± 2.93	0.55
Robbery	18.27	- 2.74	- 3.57 ± 1.24	2.88
Burglary and larceny	18.56	- 0.30	- 0.84 ± .52	1.62
Forgery and fraud	19.21	3.27	3.38 ± 1.15	2.94
Rape	18.46	- 0.33	- 0.97 ± 1.86	0.52
Other sex	18.36	4.31	3.57 ± 2.12	1.68
Vs. public welfare	19.39	1.62	1.91 ± 1.60	1.19
Arson and all other	19.55	0.84	1.29 ± 2.58	0.50

Blue-gray

	Predicted Per Cent	Diff.of Subgroup and Predicted Per Cent	Diff.of Subgroup and Total Per Cent ± p.e.	x p.e.
First degree murder	7.11	- 0.36	- 3.01 ± 1.09	2.76
Second degree murder	7.56	- 0.59	- 2.79 ± .74	3.77
Assault	14.30	- 3.05	1.49 ± 2.21	0.67
Robbery	10.40	- 1.66	- 1.02 ± .94	1.09
Burglary and larceny	10.47	- 0.10	0.61 ± .39	1.56
Forgery and fraud	9.41	0.01	- 0.34 ± .87	0.39
Rape	12.76	6.41	9.41 ± 1.41	6.67
Other sex	12.52	0.15	2.91 ± 1.61	1.81
Vs. public welfare	7.60	2.91	0.75 ± 1.21	0.62
Arson and all other	10.60	- 3.80	- 2.96 ± 1.95	1.52

Significant Differences Independent of State Sampling

Light Brown

Burglary and larceny: difference   .91 (4.14 p.e.)

Blue-gray

Rape: independent difference   6.41 (4.55 p.e.)

Differences Rendered Insignificant by State Sampling

Dark Brown

Assault: independent difference   3.41 (2.54 p.e.)

Table VI-12 (cont'd).   Light Brown

Robbery: independent difference   1.63 (2.96 p.e.)

                               Blue-brown
Second degree murder: independent difference   .54 (.53 p.e.)

                               Gray-brown
Assault: independent difference   - 3.37 (1.19 p.e.)
Rape: independent difference   - 3.18 (1.78 p.e.)
Vs. public welfare: independent difference   - 0.43 (.28 p.e.)*

                               Green-brown
Vs. public welfare: independent difference   .10 (.06 p.e.)*

                               Blue-gray
Second degree murder: independent difference   - .59 (.80 p.e.)

Table VI-13.   Sclera by Offenses

	Clear		Speckled		Yellow		Total
	No.	Per Cent	No.	Per Cent	No.	Per Cent	No.
First degree murder	290	93.25	19	6.11	2	0.64	311
Second degree murder	581	95.56	22	3.52	5	0.82	608
Assault	75	93.75	5	6.25	0	0	80
Robbery	387	95.56	17	4.20	1	0.24	405
Burglary and larceny	1511	95.15	70	4.41	7	0.44	1588
Forgery and fraud	442	96.51	12	2.62	4	0.87	458
Rape	177	91.71	16	8.29	0	0	193
Other sex	143	97.28	4	2.72	0	0	147
Vs. public welfare	233	93.20	15	6.00	2	0.80	250
Arson and all other	94	92.16	7	6.86	1	0.98	102
Total	3933	94.95	187	4.52	22	0.53	4142

Coefficient of mean square contingency = .10

                Predictions on Basis of State Composition and Differences
                        from Total Series by Offenses

		Speckled		
	Predicted Per Cent	Diff. of Subgroup and Predicted Per Cent	Diff. of Subgroup and Total Per Cent ± p.e.	x p.e.
Rape	5.33	2.96	3.77 ± .98	3.85

        Rape: independent difference   2.96 (3.02 p.e.)

Table VI-14.   Iris by Offenses

	Homogeneous		Rayed		Zoned	
	No.	Per Cent	No.	Per Cent	No.	Per Cent
First degree murder	25	8.06	81	26.13	90	29.03
Second degree murder	46	7.43	179	28.92	152	24.56
Assault	11	13.75	21	26.25	24	30.00
Robbery	32	7.82	100	24.45	136	33.25
Burglary and larceny	120	7.47	430	26.76	501	31.18
Forgery and fraud	36	7.71	117	25.05	168	35.97
Rape	13	6.67	58	29.74	72	36.92
Other sex	16	10.60	46	30.46	40	26.49
Vs. public welfare	16	6.25	72	28.12	88	34.38
Arson and all other	9	8.74	30	29.13	28	27.18
Total	324	7.72	1134	27.02	1299	30.95

	Speckled		Diffused		Total
	No.	Per Cent	No.	Per Cent	No.
First degree murder	88	28.39	26	8.39	310
Second degree murder	192	31.02	50	8.08	619
Assault	17	21.25	7	8.75	80
Robbery	93	22.74	48	11.74	409
Burglary and larceny	419	26.07	137	8.53	1607
Forgery and fraud	102	21.84	44	9.42	467
Rape	37	18.97	15	7.69	195
Other sex	42	27.81	7	4.64	151
Vs. public welfare	62	24.22	18	7.03	256
Arson and all other	27	26.21	9	8.74	103
Total	1079	25.71	361	8.60	4197

Coefficient of mean square contingency - .10

Table VI-15.   Predictions on Basis of State Composition and Differences
from Total Series by Offenses

Iris

		Homogeneous		
	Predicted Per Cent	Diff. of Subgroup and Predicted Per Cent	Diff. of Subgroup and Total Per Cent $\pm$ p.e.	x p.e.
First degree murder	8.53	- 0.47	0.34 $\pm$ .98	0.35
Second degree murder	7.47	- 0.04	- 0.29 $\pm$ .67	0.43
Assault	7.97	5.78	6.03 $\pm$ 2.00	3.02
Robbery	7.94	- 0.12	0.10 $\pm$ .84	0.12
Burglary and larceny	7.50	- 0.03	- 0.25 $\pm$ .35	0.71
Forgery and fraud	7.85	- 0.14	- 0.01 $\pm$ .79	0.01
Rape	8.35	- 1.68	- 1.05 $\pm$ 1.26	0.83
Other sex	7.60	3.00	2.88 $\pm$ 1.44	2.00
Vs. public welfare	7.33	- 1.08	- 1.47 $\pm$ 1.09	1.35
Arson and all other	8.35	0.39	1.02 $\pm$ 1.75	0.58

Table VI-15 (cont'd).

	Predicted Per Cent	Rayed Diff. of Subgroup and Predicted Per Cent	Diff. of Subgroup and Total Per Cent ± p.e.	x p.e.
First degree murder	26.31	- 0.18	- 0.89 ± 1.64	0.54
Second degree murder	26.36	2.56	1.90 ± 1.11	1.71
Assault	29.35	- 3.10	- 0.77 ± 3.32	0.23
Robbery	27.90	- 3.45	- 2.57 ± 1.41	1.82
Burglary and larceny	27.64	- 0.88	- 0.26 ± .59	0.44
Forgery and fraud	25.23	- 0.18	- 1.97 ± 1.31	1.50
Rape	27.76	1.98	2.72 ± 2.09	1.30
Other sex	29.34	1.12	3.44 ± 2.39	1.44
Vs. public welfare	23.97	4.15	1.10 ± 1.81	0.61
Arson and all other	29.84	- 0.71	2.11 ± 2.91	0.72

	Predicted Per Cent	Zoned Diff. of Subgroup and Predicted Per Cent	Diff. of Subgroup and Total Per Cent ± p.e.	x p.e.
First degree murder	29.08	- 0.05	- 1.92 ± 1.71	1.12
Second degree murder	27.42	- 2.86	- 6.39 ± 1.16	5.51
Assault	32.28	- 2.28	- 0.95 ± 3.45	0.28
Robbery	31.25	2.00	2.30 ± 1.46	1.58
Burglary and larceny	30.62	0.56	0.23 ± .61	0.38
Forgery and fraud	33.75	2.22	5.02 ± 1.36	3.69
Rape	35.41	1.51	5.97 ± 2.18	2.74
Other sex	30.59	- 4.10	- 4.46 ± 2.49	1.79
Vs. public welfare	35.08	- 0.70	3.43 ± 1.88	1.82
Arson and all other	29.64	- 2.46	- 3.77 ± 3.04	1.24

	Predicted Per Cent	Speckled Diff. of Subgroup and Predicted Per Cent	Diff. of Subgroup and Total Per Cent ± p.e.	x p.e.
First degree murder	26.67	1.72	2.68 ± 1.61	1.66
Second degree murder	29.39	1.63	5.31 ± 1.09	4.87
Assault	23.58	- 2.33	- 4.46 ± 3.26	1.37
Robbery	24.58	- 1.84	- 2.97 ± 1.38	2.15
Burglary and larceny	25.89	0.18	0.36 ± .57	0.63
Forgery and fraud	24.21	- 2.37	- 3.87 ± 1.29	3.00
Rape	21.43	- 2.46	- 6.74 ± 2.05	3.29
Other sex	25.02	2.79	2.10 ± 2.34	0.90
Vs. public welfare	23.73	0.49	- 1.49 ± 1.78	0.84
Arson and all other	24.30	1.91	0.50 ± 2.85	0.18

Table VI-15 (cont'd).

	Predicted Per Cent	Diffused Diff.of Subgroup and Predicted Per Cent	Diff.of Subgroup and Total Per Cent ± p.e.	x p.e.
First degree murder	9.40	- 1.01	- 0.21 ± 1.03	0.20
Second degree murder	9.36	- 1.28	- 0.52 ± .70	0.74
Assault	6.81	1.94	0.15 ± 2.09	0.07
Robbery	8.54	3.40	3.14 ± .89	3.53
Burglary and larceny	8.35	0.18	- 0.07 ± .37	0.19
Forgery and fraud	8.96	0.46	0.82 ± .82	1.00
Rape	7.05	0.64	- 0.91 ± 1.32	0.69
Other sex	7.44	- 2.80	- 3.96 ± 1.51	2.62
Vs. public welfare	9.89	- 2.86	- 1.57 ± 1.15	1.36
Arson and all other	7.88	0.86	0.14 ± 1.84	0.08

Significant Differences Independent of State Sampling

Diffused

Robbery: difference   3.14 (3.53 p.e.)

Differences Rendered Insignificant by State Sampling

Homogeneous

Assault: independent difference   5.78 (2.89 p.e.)

Zoned

Second degree murder: independent difference   - 2.86 (2.47 p.e.)
Forgery and fraud: independent difference   2.22 (1.63 p.e.)

Speckled

Second degree murder: independent difference   1.63 (1.50 p.e.)
Forgery and fraud: independent difference   - 2.37 (1.84 p.e.)
Rape: independent difference   - 2.46 (1.18 p.e.)

Table VI-16.   Eye Folds by Offenses

	Epicanthus No.	Per Cent	Median No.	Per Cent	External No.	Per Cent	Absent No.	Per Cent	Total No.
First degree murder	20	6.41	29	9.29	30	9.62	233	74.68	312
Second degree murder	29	4.71	69	11.20	60	9.74	458	74.35	616
Assault	4	5.00	11	13.75	10	12.50	55	68.75	80
Robbery	16	3.89	75	18.25	31	7.54	289	70.32	411
Burglary and larceny	68	4.23	228	14.18	136	8.46	1176	73.13	1608
Forgery and fraud	14	3.00	58	12.42	32	6.85	363	77.73	467
Rape	6	3.05	19	9.64	22	11.17	150	76.14	197
Other sex	9	6.00	15	10.00	15	10.00	111	74.00	150
Vs. public welfare	9	3.52	25	9.77	30	11.72	192	75.00	256
Arson and all other	10	9.71	11	10.68	10	9.71	72	69.90	103
Total	185	4.40	540	12.86	376	8.95	3099	73.79	4200

Coefficient of mean square contingency = .10

Table VI-17.   Predictions on Basis of State Composition and Differences
from Total Series by Offenses

Eye Folds

	Predicted Per Cent	Epicanthus Diff.of Subgroup and Predicted Per Cent	Diff.of Subgroup and Total Per Cent ± p.e.	x p.e.
First degree murder	6.48	- 0.07	2.01 ± .76	2.64
Second degree murder	6.08	- 1.37	0.31 ± .51	0.61
Assault	3.66	1.34	0.60 ± 1.53	0.39
Robbery	3.66	0.23	- 0.51 ± .65	0.78
Burglary and larceny	4.15	0.08	- 0.17 ± .27	0.63
Forgery and fraud	3.64	- 0.64	- 1.40 ± .60	2.33
Rape	3.51	- 0.46	- 1.35 ± .96	1.41
Other sex	4.23	1.77	1.60 ± 1.11	1.44
Vs. public welfare	2.87	0.65	- 0.88 ± .84	1.05
Arson and all other	5.04	4.67	5.31 ± 1.35	3.93

	Predicted Per Cent	Median Diff.of Subgroup and Predicted Per Cent	Diff.of Subgroup and Total Per Cent ± p.e.	x p.e.
First degree murder	12.74	- 3.45	- 3.57 ± 1.23	2.90
Second degree murder	13.03	- 1.83	- 1.66 ± .84	1.98
Assault	13.11	0.64	0.89 ± 2.50	0.36
Robbery	13.03	5.22	5.39 ± 1.06	5.08
Burglary and larceny	13.08	1.10	1.32 ± .44	3.00
Forgery and fraud	12.14	0.28	- 0.44 ± .98	0.45
Rape	12.19	- 2.55	- 3.22 ± 1.57	2.05
Other sex	13.46	- 3.46	- 2.86 ± 1.81	1.58
Vs. public welfare	12.04	- 2.27	- 3.09 ± 1.37	2.26
Arson and all other	13.62	- 2.94	- 2.18 ± 2.20	0.99

	Predicted Per Cent	External Diff.of Subgroup and Predicted Per Cent	Diff.of Subgroup and Total Per Cent ± p.e.	x p.e.
First degree murder	8.14	1.48	0.67 ± 1.05	0.64
Second degree murder	8.42	1.32	0.79 ± .72	1.10
Assault	9.43	3.07	3.55 ± 2.13	1.67
Robbery	9.59	- 2.05	- 1.41 ± .90	1.57
Burglary and larceny	9.32	- 0.86	- 0.49 ± .38	1.29
Forgery and fraud	8.82	- 1.97	- 2.10 ± .84	2.50
Rape	9.79	1.38	2.22 ± 1.34	1.66
Other sex	9.56	0.44	1.05 ± 1.54	0.68
Vs. public welfare	9.10	2.62	2.77 ± 1.17	2.37
Arson and all other	9.68	0.03	0.76 ± 1.88	0.40

Table VI-17 (cont'd).

	Predicted Per Cent	Absent Diff.of Subgroup and Predicted Per Cent	Diff.of Subgroup and Total Per Cent ± p.e.	x p.e.
First degree murder	72.63	2.05	0.89 ± 1.62	0.55
Second degree murder	72.46	1.89	0.56 ± 1.11	0.50
Assault	73.80	- 5.05	- 5.04 ± 3.28	1.54
Robbery	73.73	- 3.41	- 3.47 ± 1.39	2.50
Burglary and larceny	73.44	- 0.31	- 0.66 ± .58	1.14
Forgery and fraud	75.40	2.33	3.94 ± 1.29	3.05
Rape	74.52	1.62	2.35 ± 2.05	1.15
Other sex	72.75	1.25	0.21 ± 2.38	0.09
Vs. public welfare	75.98	- 0.98	1.21 ± 1.78	0.68
Arson and all other	71.65	- 1.75	- 3.89 ± 2.89	1.35

Significant Differences Independent of State Sampling

Epicanthus

Arson and all other: independent difference   4.67 (3.46 p.e.)

Median

Robbery: independent difference   5.22 (4.92 p.e.)

Differences Rendered Insignificant by State Sampling

Median

Burglary and larceny: independent difference   1.10 (' 2.50 p.e.)

Absent

Forgery and fraud: independent difference   2.33 (1.81 p.e.)

Table VI-18.   Eyebrows Thickness by Offenses

	Submedium		Medium		Pronounced		Total
	No.	Per Cent	No.	Per Cent	No.	Per Cent	No.
First degree murder	16	5.13	189	60.58	107	34.29	312
Second degree murder	31	5.02	398	64.40	189	30.58	618
Assault	4	5.00	46	57.50	30	37.50	80
Robbery	12	2.91	267	64.65	134	32.46	413
Burglary and larceny	61	3.79	1030	63.98	519	32.24	1610
Forgery and fraud	21	4.51	303	65.02	142	30.47	466
Rape	9	4.57	131	66.50	57	28.93	197
Other sex	8	5.30	89	58.94	54	35.76	151
Vs. public welfare	16	6.23	154	59.92	87	33.85	257
Arson and all other	6	5.82	58	56.31	39	37.86	103
Total	184	4.37	2665	63.35	1358	32.28	4207

Coefficient of mean square contingency = .06

Table VI-19. Predictions on Basis of State Composition and Differences
from Total Series by Offenses

Eyebrows Thickness

	Predicted Per Cent	Submedium Diff.of Subgroup and Predicted Per Cent	Diff.of Subgroup and Total Per Cent ± p.e.	x p.e.
First degree murder	5.60	- 0.47	0.76 ± .75	1.01
Second degree murder	5.04	- 0.02	0.65 ± .51	1.27
Assault	3.63	1.37	0.63 ± 1.52	.41
Robbery	4.05	- 1.14	- 1.46 ± .64	2.28
Burglary and larceny	4.16	- 0.37	- 0.58 ± .27	2.15
Forgery and fraud	4.09	0.42	0.14 ± .60	.23
Rape	4.10	0.47	0.20 ± .96	.21
Other sex	4.10	1.20	0.93 ± 1.10	.84
Vs. public welfare	4.08	2.15	1.86 ± .84	2.21
Arson and all other	4.92	0.90	1.45 ± 1.34	1.08

	Predicted Per Cent	Pronounced Diff.of Subgroup and Predicted Per Cent	Diff.of Subgroup and Total Per Cent ± p.e.	x p.e.
First degree murder	32.14	2.15	2.01 ± 1.72	1.17
Second degree murder	31.12	- 0.54	- 1.70 ± 1.17	1.45
Assault	34.36	3.14	5.22 ± 3.49	1.50
Robbery	31.61	0.85	0.18 ± 1.47	.12
Burglary and larceny	32.17	0.07	- 0.04 ± .62	.06
Forgery and fraud	33.08	- 2.61	- 1.81 ± 1.38	1.31
Rape	32.01	- 3.08	- 3.35 ± 2.19	1.53
Other sex	32.54	3.22	3.48 ± 2.52	1.39
Vs. public welfare	32.75	1.10	1.57 ± 1.91	.82
Arson and all other	31.74	6.12	5.58 ± 3.07	1.82

Table VI-20.   Forehead Height by Offenses

	Submedium No.	Per Cent	Medium No.	Per Cent	Pronounced No.	Per Cent	Total No.
First degree murder	40	12.82	188	60.26	84	26.92	312
Second degree murder	96	15.51	383	61.87	140	22.62	619
Assault	10	12.50	46	57.50	24	30.00	80
Robbery	44	10.63	280	67.63	90	21.74	414
Burglary and larceny	212	13.17	1026	63.73	372	23.11	1610
Forgery and fraud	43	9.21	299	64.03	125	26.77	467
Rape	22	11.17	115	58.38	60	30.46	197
Other sex	19	12.58	93	61.59	39	25.83	151
Vs. public welfare	33	12.84	156	60.70	68	26.46	257
Arson and all other	13	12.62	32	60.20	28	27.18	103
Total	532	12.64	2648	62.90	1030	24.47	4210

Coefficient of mean square contingency = .08

Table VI-21. Predictions on Basis of State Composition and Differences
from Total Series by Offenses

Forehead Height

	Predicted Per Cent	Submedium Diff. of Subgroup and Predicted Per Cent	Diff. of Subgroup and Total Per Cent ± p.e.	x p.e.
First degree murder	13.06	- 0.24	0.18 ± 1.22	.15
Second degree murder	14.96	0.55	2.87 ± .83	3.46
Assault	12.72	- 0.22	- 0.14 ± 2.48	.06
Robbery	11.22	- 0.59	- 2.01 ± 1.04	1.93
Burglary and larceny	13.03	0.14	0.53 ± .44	1.20
Forgery and fraud	11.09	- 1.88	- 3.43 ± .98	3.50
Rape	10.15	1.02	- 1.47 ± 1.55	.94
Other sex	13.72	- 1.14	- 0.06 ± 1.79	.03
Vs. public welfare	10.45	2.39	0.20 ± 1.36	.15
Arson and all other	12.39	0.23	- 0.02 ± 2.18	.01

	Predicted Per Cent	Medium Diff. of Subgroup and Predicted Per Cent	Diff. of Subgroup and Total Per Cent ± p.e.	x p.e.
First degree murder	62.86	- 2.60	- 2.64 ± 1.77	1.49
Second degree murder	62.24	- 0.37	- 1.03 ± 1.21	.85
Assault	59.20	- 1.70	- 5.40 ± 3.61	1.50
Robbery	63.75	3.88	4.73 ± 1.52	3.11
Burglary and larceny	62.31	1.42	0.83 ± .64	1.30
Forgery and fraud	64.54	- 0.51	1.13 ± 1.42	.80
Rape	63.06	- 4.68	- 4.52 ± 2.27	1.99
Other sex	59.92	1.67	- 1.31 ± 2.60	.50
Vs. public welfare	67.20	- 6.50	- 2.20 ± 1.97	1.12
Arson and all other	61.65	- 1.45	- 2.70 ± 3.17	.85

	Predicted Per Cent	Pronounced Diff. of Subgroup and Predicted Per Cent	Diff. of Subgroup and Total Per Cent ± p.e.	x p.e.
First degree murder	24.08	2.84	2.45 ± 1.58	1.55
Second degree murder	22.79	- 0.17	- 1.85 ± 1.08	1.71
Assault	28.08	1.92	5.53 ± 3.21	1.72
Robbery	25.03	- 3.29	- 2.73 ± 1.35	2.02
Burglary and larceny	24.66	- 1.55	- 1.36 ± .57	2.39
Forgery and fraud	24.37	2.40	2.30 ± 1.27	1.81
Rape	26.80	3.66	5.99 ± 2.02	2.96
Other sex	26.36	- 0.53	1.36 ± 2.32	.59
Vs. public welfare	22.36	4.10	1.99 ± 1.75	1.14
Arson and all other	25.95	1.23	2.71 ± 2.82	0.96

Differences Rendered Insignificant by State Sampling

Submedium
Second degree murder: independent difference   .55 (.66 p.e.)
Forgery and fraud: independent difference   - 1.88 (1.92 p.e.)
Medium
Robbery: independent difference   3.88 (2.55 p.e.)

Table VI-22.   Forehead Slope by Offenses

| | Absent Submedium | | Medium | | Pronounced | | Total |
	No.	Per Cent	No.	Per Cent	No.	Per Cent	No.
First degree murder	30	9.61	161	51.60	121	38.78	312
Second degree murder	57	9.21	309	49.92	253	40.87	619
Assault	4	5.00	48	60.00	28	35.00	80
Robbery	31	7.49	249	60.14	134	32.38	414
Burglary and larceny	140	8.69	952	59.09	519	32.22	1611
Forgery and fraud	29	6.21	286	61.24	152	32.55	467
Rape	18	9.14	111	56.35	68	34.52	197
Other sex	13	8.61	80	52.98	58	38.41	151
Vs. public welfare	11	4.28	159	61.87	87	33.85	257
Arson and all other	10	9.71	59	57.28	34	33.01	103
Total	343	8.14	2414	57.33	1454	34.53	4211

Coefficient of mean square contingency = .10

Table VI-23. Predictions on Basis of State Composition and Differences
from Total Series by Offenses

Forehead Slope

Absent, Submedium

	Predicted Per Cent	Diff.of Subgroup and Predicted Per Cent	Diff.of Subgroup and Total Per Cent ± p.e.	x p.e.
First degree murder	9.11	0.50	1.47 ± 1.01	1.46
Second degree murder	10.24	- 1.03	1.07 ± .69	1.55
Assault	7.60	- 2.60	- 3.14 ± 2.04	1.54
Robbery	7.96	- 0.47	- 0.65 ± .86	.75
Burglary and larceny	8.17	0.52	0.55 ± .36	1.53
Forgery and fraud	6.84	- 0.63	- 1.93 ± .80	2.41
Rape	7.71	1.43	1.00 ± 1.28	.78
Other sex	7.88	0.73	0.47 ± 1.48	0.32
Vs. public welfare	5.10	- 0.82	- 3.86 ± 1.11	3.48
Arson and all other	8.27	1.44	1.57 ± 1.79	0.88

Medium

	Predicted Per Cent	Diff.of Subgroup and Predicted Per Cent	Diff.of Subgroup and Total Per Cent ± p.e.	x p.e.
First degree murder	52.72	- 1.12	- 5.73 ± 1.81	3.17
Second degree murder	52.24	- 2.32	- 7.41 ± 1.24	5.98
Assault	57.17	2.83	2.67 ± 3.70	.72
Robbery	59.33	0.81	2.81 ± 1.56	1.80
Burglary and larceny	57.53	1.56	1.76 ± .65	2.71
Forgery and fraud	60.59	0.65	3.91 ± 1.46	2.68
Rape	58.56	- 2.21	- 0.98 ± 2.32	.42
Other sex	56.44	- 3.46	- 4.35 ± 2.66	1.64
Vs. public welfare	65.06	- 3.19	4.54 ± 2.02	2.25
Arson and all other	55.50	1.78	- 0.05 ± 3.24	.02

Table VI-23 (cont'd).

	Predicted Per Cent	Pronounced Diff.of Subgroup and Predicted Per Cent	Diff.of Subgroup and Total Per Cent ± p.e.	x p.e.
First degree murder	38.17	0.61	4.25 ± 1.75	2.43
Second degree murder	37.52	3.35	6.34 ± 1.19	5.33
Assault	35.23	- 0.23	0.47 ± 3.55	.13
Robbery	32.71	- 0.33	- 2.15 ± 1.50	1.43
Burglary and larceny	34.30	- 2.08	- 2.31 ± .63	3.67
Forgery and fraud	32.57	- 0.02	- 1.98 ± 1.40	1.41
Rape	33.73	0.79	- 0.01 ± 2.23	0
Other sex	35.68	2.73	3.88 ± 2.56	1.52
Vs. public welfare	29.84	4.01	- 0.68 ± 1.94	.35
Arson and all other	36.23	- 3.22	- 1.52 ± 3.12	.49

Significant Differences Independent of State Sampling

Pronounced

Burglary and larceny: independent difference   - 2.08 (3.30 p.e.)

Differences Rendered Insignificant by State Sampling

Absent, Submedium

Vs. public welfare: independent difference   - .82 (.74 p.e.)

Medium

First degree murder: independent difference   - 1.12 (.62 p.e.)
Second degree murder: independent difference   - 2.32 (1.87 p.e.)

Pronounced

Second degree murder: independent difference   3.35 (2.82 p.e.)

Table VI-24.   Nasion Depression by Offenses

	Absent No.	Per Cent	Submedium No.	Per Cent	Medium No.	Per Cent	Pronounced No.	Per Cent	Total No.
First degree murder	1	0.32	26	8.33	212	67.95	73	23.40	312
Second degree murder	1	0.16	70	11.33	398	64.40	149	24.11	618
Assault	0	0	13	16.25	52	65.00	15	18.75	80
Robbery	1	0.24	27	6.54	318	77.00	67	15.22	413
Burglary and larceny	1	0.06	179	11.11	1161	72.07	270	16.76	1611
Forgery and fraud	0	0	30	6.42	374	80.09	63	13.49	467
Rape	0	0	10	5.10	149	76.02	37	18.88	195
Other sex	0	0	17	11.33	104	69.33	29	19.33	150
Vs. public welfare	0	0	9	3.50	210	81.71	38	14.79	257
Arson and all other	0	0	7	6.80	72	69.90	24	23.30	103
Total	4	0.10	388	9.22	3050	72.50	765	18.18	4207

Table VI-25. Predictions on Basis of State Composition and Differences
from Total Series by Offenses

Nasion Depression

	Predicted Per Cent	Submedium Diff.of Subgroup and Predicted Per Cent	Diff.of Subgroup and Total Per Cent ± p.e.	x p.e.
Second degree murder	11.73	- 0.40	2.11 ± .73	2.89
Assault	10.89	5.36	7.03 ± 2.16	3.26
Robbery	7.64	- 1.10	- 2.68 ± .91	2.94
Forgery and fraud	7.12	- 0.70	- 2.90 ± .85	3.29
Rape	7.46	- 2.36	- 4.12 ± 1.36	3.03
Vs. public welfare	5.12	- 1.62	- 5.72 ± 1.18	4.85

	Predicted Per Cent	Medium Diff.of Subgroup and Predicted Per Cent	Diff.of Subgroup and Total Per Cent ± p.e.	x p.e.
First degree murder	67.38	0.57	- 4.55 ± 1.64	2.77
Second degree murder	65.95	- 1.55	- 8.10 ± 1.12	7.23
Assault	74.69	- 9.69	- 7.50 ± 3.33	2.25
Robbery	75.47	1.53	4.50 ± 1.40	3.21
Forgery and fraud	76.48	3.61	7.59 ± 1.32	5.75
Rape	76.88	- 0.86	3.52 ± 2.10	1.58
Vs. public welfare	78.82	2.89	9.21 ± 1.82	5.06

	Predicted Per Cent	Pronounced Diff.of Subgroup and Predicted Per Cent	Diff.of Subgroup and Total Per Cent ± p.e.	x p.e.
First degree murder	23.37	0.03	5.22 ± 1.42	3.68
Second degree murder	22.17	1.94	5.93 ± .96	6.18
Forgery and fraud	16.34	- 2.85	- 4.69 ± 1.13	4.15
Vs. public welfare	16.03	- 1.24	- 3.39 ± 1.57	2.16
Arson and all other	20.15	3.15	5.12 ± 2.53	2.02

Differences Rendered Insignificant by State Sampling

Submedium

Assault: independent difference	5.36 (2.48 p.e.)
Forgery and fraud: independent difference	- .70 (.82 p.e.)
Rape: independent difference	- 2.36 (1.74 p.e.)
Vs. public welfare: independent difference	- 1.62 (1.37 p.e.)

Medium

Second degree murder: independent difference	- 1.55 (1.38 p.e.)
Robbery: independent difference	1.53 (1.09 p.e.)
Forgery and fraud: independent difference	3.61 (2.74 p.e.)
Vs. public welfare: independent difference	2.99 (1.59 p.e.)

Pronounced

First degree murder: independent difference	.03 (.02 p.e.)
Second degree murder: independent difference	1.94 (2.02 p.e.)
Forgery and fraud: independent difference	- 2.85 (2.52 p.e.)

Table VI-26.   Nasal Root Height by Offenses

| | Submedium | | Medium | | Pronounced | | Total |
	No.	Per Cent	No.	Per Cent	No.	Per Cent	No.
First degree murder	9	2.88	241	77.24	62	19.87	312
Second degree murder	12	1.94	485	78.35	122	19.71	619
Assault	4	5.00	50	62.50	26	32.50	80
Robbery	6	1.45	342	82.61	66	15.94	414
Burglary and larceny	23	1.43	1369	84.93	220	13.65	1612
Forgery and fraud	4	0.86	394	84.37	69	14.78	467
Rape	5	2.54	158	80.20	34	17.26	197
Other sex	2	1.32	112	74.17	37	24.50	151
Vs. public welfare	2	0.78	217	84.44	38	14.79	257
Arson and all other	1	0.97	81	78.64	21	20.39	103
Total	68	1.61	3449	81.88	695	16.50	4212

Coefficient of mean square contingency = .14

Table VI-27. Predictions on Basis of State Composition and Differences
from Total Series by Offenses

Nasal Root Height

| | | Submedium | | |
	Predicted Per Cent	Diff.of Subgroup and Predicted Per Cent	Diff.of Subgroup and Total Per Cent ± p.e.	x p.e.
First degree murder	2.22	0.66	1.27 ± .46	2.76
Second degree murder	2.00	- 0.06	0.33 ± .32	1.03
Assault	2.00	3.00	3.39 ± .94	3.61
Robbery	1.72	- 0.27	- 0.16 ± .39	0.41
Burglary and larceny	1.82	- 0.39	- 0.18 ± .16	1.12
Forgery and fraud	1.86	- 1.00	- 0.75 ± .37	2.03
Rape	1.96	0.58	0.93 ± .59	1.58
Other sex	1.93	- 0.61	- 0.29 ± .67	0.43
Vs. public welfare	1.64	- 0.86	- 0.83 ± .51	1.63
Arson and all other	1.97	- 1.00	- 0.64 ± .82	0.78

| | | Medium | | |
	Predicted Per Cent	Diff.of Subgroup and Predicted Per Cent	Diff.of Subgroup and Total Per Cent ± p.e.	x p.e.
First degree murder	81.53	- 4.29	- 4.64 ± 1.42	2.14
Second degree murder	77.03	1.32	- 3.53 ± .96	3.68
Assault	77.13	-14.63	-19.38 ± 2.88	6.73
Robbery	81.04	1.57	0.73 ± 1.21	0.60
Burglary and larceny	78.07	6.86	3.05 ± .51	5.98
Forgery and fraud	82.65	1.72	2.49 ± 1.13	2.20
Rape	80.62	- 0.42	- 1.68 ± 1.81	0.93
Other sex	75.89	- 1.72	- 7.71 ± 2.08	3.71
Vs. public welfare	84.15	0.29	2.56 ± 1.57	1.63
Arson and all other	79.06	- 0.42	- 3.24 ± 2.53	1.28

Table VI-27 (cont'd).

	Predicted Per Cent	Pronounced Diff.of Subgroup and Predicted Per Cent	Diff.of Subgroup and Total Per Cent ± p.e.	x p.e.
First degree murder	16.25	3.62	3.37 ± 1.36	2.48
Second degree murder	20.97	- 1.26	3.21 ± .93	3.45
Assault	20.87	11.63	16.00 ± 2.77	5.78
Robbery	17.24	- 1.30	- 0.56 ± 1.17	0.48
Burglary and larceny	20.12	- 6.47	- 2.85 ± .49	5.82
Forgery and fraud	15.49	- 0.71	- 1.72 ± 1.09	1.58
Rape	17.42	- 0.16	0.76 ± 1.74	0.44
Other sex	22.18	2.32	8.00 ± 2.00	4.00
Vs. public welfare	14.21	0.58	- 1.71 ± 1.51	1.13
Arson and all other	18.97	1.42	3.89 ± 2.44	1.59

Significant Differences Independent of State Sampling

Submedium

Assault: independent difference   3.00 (3.19 p.e.)

Medium

Assault: independent difference   -14.63 (5.08 p.e.)
Burglary and larceny: difference   3.05 (5.98 p.e.)

Pronounced

Assault: independent difference   11.63 (4.20 p.e.)
Burglary and larceny: difference   - 2.85 (5.82 p.e.)

Differences Rendered Insignificant by State Sampling

Medium

Second degree murder: independent difference   1.32 (1.38 p.e.)*
Other sex: independent difference   - 1.72 (.83 p.e.)

Pronounced

Second degree murder: independent difference   - 1.26 (1.36 p.e.)*
Other sex: independent difference   2.32 (1.16 p.e.)

*Signs are opposite

Table VI-28.   Nasal Root Breadth by Offenses

	Submedium No.	Per Cent	Medium No.	Per Cent	Pronounced No.	Per Cent	Total No.
First degree murder	9	2.88	279	89.42	24	7.69	312
Second degree murder	22	3.56	546	88.35	50	8.09	618
Assault	8	10.00	62	77.50	10	12.50	80
Robbery	22	5.31	355	85.75	37	8.94	414
Burglary and larceny	80	4.96	1369	84.93	163	10.11	1612
Forgery and fraud	27	5.78	406	86.94	34	7.28	467
Rape	19	9.69	149	76.02	28	14.29	196
Other sex	6	3.97	125	82.78	20	13.24	151
Vs. public welfare	4	1.56	237	92.22	16	6.23	257
Arson and all other	7	6.80	82	79.61	14	13.59	103
Total	204	4.84	3610	85.75	396	9.41	4210

Coefficient of mean square contingency = .10

Table VI-29. Predictions on Basis of State Composition and Differences
from Total Series by Offenses

Nasal Root Breadth

Submedium

	Predicted Per Cent	Diff.of Subgroup and Predicted Per Cent	Diff.of Subgroup and Total Per Cent ± p.e.	x p.e.
First degree murder	3.92	- 1.04	- 1.96 ± .79	2.48
Second degree murder	3.17	0.39	- 1.28 ± .54	2.37
Assault	9.62	0.38	5.16 ± 1.60	3.22
Robbery	4.79	0.52	0.47 ± .67	0.70
Burglary and larceny	5.12	- 0.16	0.12 ± .28	0.43
Forgery and fraud	4.91	0.87	0.94 ± .63	1.49
Rape	9.25	0.44	4.85 ± 1.01	4.80
Other sex	7.28	- 3.31	- 0.87 ± 1.16	0.75
Vs. public welfare	2.04	- 0.48	- 3.28 ± 0.88	3.73
Arson and all other	5.69	1.11	1.96 ± 1.41	1.39

Medium

	Predicted Per Cent	Diff.of Subgroup and Predicted Per Cent	Diff.of Subgroup and Total Per Cent ± p.e.	x p.e.
First degree murder	88.17	1.25	3.67 ± 1.28	2.87
Second degree murder	89.19	- 0.84	2.60 ± .88	2.95
Assault	78.57	1.07	- 8.25 ± 2.61	3.16
Robbery	83.76	1.99	0 ± 1.10	0
Burglary and larceny	84.69	0.24	- 0.82 ± .46	1.78
Forgery and fraud	86.54	0.40	1.19 ± 1.03	1.16
Rape	78.57	- 2.55	- 9.73 ± 1.65	5.90
Other sex	81.34	1.44	- 2.97 ± 1.88	1.58
Vs. public welfare	90.16	2.06	6.47 ± 1.42	4.56
Arson and all other	81.92	- 2.31	- 6.14 ± 2.29	2.68

Pronounced

	Predicted Per Cent	Diff.of Subgroup and Predicted Per Cent	Diff.of Subgroup and Total Per Cent ± p.e.	x p.e.
First degree murder	7.92	- 0.23	- 1.72 ± 1.07	1.61
Second degree murder	7.64	0.45	- 1.32 ± .74	1.78
Assault	11.80	0.70	3.09 ± 2.18	1.42
Robbery	11.46	- 2.52	- 0.47 ± .92	0.51
Burglary and larceny	10.19	- 0.08	0.70 ± .38	1.84
Forgery and fraud	8.55	- 1.27	- 2.13 ± .86	2.48
Rape	12.18	2.11	4.88 ± 1.38	3.54
Other sex	11.38	1.86	3.83 ± 1.57	2.44
Vs. public welfare	7.80	- 1.57	- 3.18 ± 1.19	2.67
Arson and all other	12.40	1.19	4.18 ± 1.90	2.20

Table VI-29 (cont'd).
Differences Rendered Insignificant by State Sampling

Submedium

Assault: independent difference	.38 (.24 p.e ,
Rape: independent difference	.44 (.44 p.e.)
Vs. public welfare: independent difference	- .48 (.55 p.e.)

Medium

Assault: independent difference	- 1.07 (.41 p.e.)
Rape: independent difference	- 2.55 (1.54 p.e.)
Vs. public welfare: independent difference	2.06 (1.45 p.e.)

Pronounced

Rape: independent difference	2.11 (1.53 p.e.)

Table VI-30.   Nasal Bridge Height by Offenses

	Submedium		Medium		Pronounced		Total
	No.	Per Cent	No.	Per Cent	No.	Per Cent	No.
First degree murder	3	0.96	159	48.08	150	50.96	312
Second degree murder	1	0.16	326	52.67	292	47.17	619
Assault	0	0	41	51.25	39	48.75	80
Robbery	2	0.48	267	64.49	145	35.02	414
Burglary and larceny	5	0.31	976	60.55	631	39.14	1612
Forgery and fraud	1	0.21	315	67.45	151	32.33	467
Rape	1	0.51	115	58.38	81	41.12	197
Other sex	0	0	78	51.56	73	48.34	151
Vs. public welfare	1	0.39	158	61.48	98	38.13	257
Arson and all other	0	0	63	61.17	40	38.84	103
Total	14	0.33	2498	59.31	1700	40.36	4212

Coefficient of mean square contingency = .14

Table VI-31. Predictions on Basis of State Composition and Differences
from Total Series by Offenses

Nasal Bridge Height

	Predicted Per Cent	Medium Diff.of Subgroup and Predicted Per Cent	Diff.of Subgroup and Total Per Cent ± p.e.	x p.e.
First degree murder	51.18	- 3.10	-11.23 ± 1.81	6.20
Second degree murder	48.73	3.94	- 6.64 ± 1.23	5.40
Assault	54.54	- 3.29	- 8.06 ± 3.67	2.20
Robbery	57.46	7.03	5.18 ± 1.54	3.36
Burglary and larceny	54.02	6.53	1.24 ± .65	1.91
Forgery and fraud	59.26	8.19	8.14 ± 1.44	5.65
Rape	58.74	- 0.36	- 0.93 ± 2.31	0.40
Other sex	51.94	- 0.28	- 7.65 ± 2.58	2.96
Vs. public welfare	62.07	- 0.59	2.17 ± 2.00	1.08
Arson and all other	52.26	8.91	1.86 ± 3.22	0.58

Table VI-31 (cont'd).

	Predicted Per Cent	Pronounced Diff.of Subgroup and Predicted Per Cent	Diff.of Subgroup and Total Per Cent ± p.e.	x p.e.
First degree murder	48.37	2.59	10.60 ± 1.80	5.89
Second degree murder	50.96	- 3.79	6.91 ± 1.23	5.54
Assault	45.01	3.74	8.39 ± 3.66	2.29
Robbery	42.22	- 7.20	- 5.34 ± 1.54	3.47
Burglary and larceny	45.67	- 6.53	- 1.22 ± .65	1.88
Forgery and fraud	40.42	- 8.09	- 8.03 ± 1.44	5.58
Rape	40.75	0.37	0.76 ± 2.30	0.33
Other sex	47.67	0.67	7.98 ± 2.54	3.02
Vs. public welfare	37.74	0.39	- 2.23 ± 2.00	1.12
Arson and all other	47.30	- 8.46	- 1.52 ± 3.22	0.47

Significant Differences Independent of State Sampling

Medium

Second degree murder: independent difference	3.94 (3.20 p.e.)*
Robbery: difference	5.13 (3.36 p.e.)
Forgery and fraud: difference	8.14 (5.65 p.e.)

Pronounced

Second degree murder: independent difference	3.79 (3.08 p.e.)
Robbery: difference	- 5.34 (3.47 p.e.)
Forgery and fraud: difference	- 8.03 (5.58 p.e.)

Differences Rendered Insignificant by State Sampling

Medium

First degree murder: independent difference	- 3.10 (1.71 p.e.)

Pronounced

First degree murder: independent difference	2.59 (1.44 p.e.)
Other sex: independent difference	.67 (.25 p.e.)

Table VI-32.   Nasal Bridge Breadth by Offenses

	Submedium No.	Per Cent	Medium No.	Per Cent	Pronounced No.	Per Cent	Total No.
First degree murder	2	0.64	260	83.60	49	15.76	311
Second degree murder	11	1.78	522	84.33	86	13.89	619
Assault	2	2.50	62	77.50	16	20.00	80
Robbery	17	4.13	322	78.16	73	17.72	412
Burglary and larceny	67	4.16	1291	80.09	254	15.76	1612
Forgery and fraud	21	4.50	380	81.37	66	14.13	467
Rape	14	7.14	141	71.94	41	20.92	196
Other sex	4	2.65	124	82.12	23	15.23	151
Vs. public welfare	3	1.17	214	83.27	40	15.56	257
Arson and all other	5	4.85	79	76.70	19	18.45	103
Total	146	3.47	3395	80.68	667	15.85	4208

Coefficient of mean square contingency = .10

Table VI-33. Predictions on Basis of State Composition and Differences from Total Series by Offenses

Nasal Bridge Breadth

	Predicted Per Cent	Submedium Diff.of Subgroup and Predicted Per Cent	Diff.of Subgroup and Total Per Cent ± p.e.	x p.e.
First degree murder	3.17	- 2.53	- 2.83 ± .67	4.22
Second degree murder	1.98	- 0.20	- 1.69 ± .47	3.60
Assault	7.37	- 4.87	- 0.97 ± 1.36	0.71
Robbery	3.63	0.50	0.66 ± .57	1.16
Burglary and larceny	3.53	0.53	0.69 ± .24	2.88
Forgery and fraud	3.81	0.69	1.03 ± .54	1.91
Rape	7.78	- 0.64	3.67 ± .86	4.27
Other sex	5.34	- 2.59	- 0.92 ± .98	0.94
Vs. public welfare	1.41	- 0.24	- 2.30 ± .74	3.11
Arson and all other	4.51	0.34	1.38 ± 1.20	1.15

	Predicted Per Cent	Pronounced Diff.of Subgroup and Predicted Per Cent	Diff.of Subgroup and Total Per Cent ± p.e.	x p.e.
First degree murder	13.74	2.02	- 0.09 ± 1.34	0.07
Second degree murder	12.94	0.95	- 1.96 ± .92	2.13
Assault	18.03	1.97	4.15 ± 2.72	1.53
Robbery	17.87	- 0.15	1.87 ± 1.15	1.53
Burglary and larceny	16.09	- 0.33	- 0.09 ± .48	0.19
Forgery and fraud	15.32	- 1.19	- 1.72 ± 1.07	1.61
Rape	17.27	3.65	5.07 ± 1.72	2.95
Other sex	17.00	- 1.77	- 0.62 ± 1.96	0.32
Vs. public welfare	14.79	0.77	- 0.29 ± 1.49	0.19
Arson and all other	17.81	0.64	2.60 ± 2.39	1.09

Significant Differences Independent of State Sampling

Submedium
First degree murder: independent difference   - 2.53 (3.78 p.e.)

Differences Rendered Insignificant by State Sampling

Submedium
Second degree murder: independent difference   - .20 (.43 p.e.)
Rape: independent difference   - .64 (.74 p.e.)*
Vs. public welfare: independent difference   - .24 (.32 p.e.)

*Signs are opposite

Table VI-34.   Nasal Profile by Offenses

| | Concave | | Straight | | Convex | | Concavo-convex | | Total |
	No.	Per Cent	No.	Per Cent	No.	Per Cent	No.	Per Cent	No.
First degree murder	49	15.76	33	10.61	71	22.83	158	50.80	311
Second degree murder	111	17.96	65	10.52	139	22.49	303	49.03	618
Assault	17	21.25	5	6.25	21	26.25	37	46.25	80
Robbery	102	24.70	47	11.38	81	19.61	183	44.31	413
Burglary and larceny	422	26.19	180	11.17	287	17.82	722	44.82	1611
Forgery and fraud	104	22.32	55	11.80	98	21.03	209	44.85	466
Rape	32	16.33	24	12.24	55	28.06	85	43.37	196
Other sex	37	24.67	15	10.00	37	24.67	61	40.67	150
Vs. public welfare	41	16.08	39	15.29	61	23.92	114	44.70	255
Arson and all other	21	20.39	11	10.68	26	25.24	45	43.69	103
Total	936	22.27	474	11.28	876	20.84	1917	45.61	4203

Coefficient of mean square contingency = .10

Table VI-35. Predictions on Basis of State Composition and Differences
from Total Series by Offenses

Nasal Profile

| | Concave | | | |
	Predicted Per Cent	Diff.of Subgroup and Predicted Per Cent	Diff.of Subgroup and Total Per Cent ± p.e.	x p.e.
First degree murder	20.78	− 5.02	− 6.51 ± 1.53	4.26
Second degree murder	21.57	− 3.61	− 4.31 ± 1.05	4.10
Assault	24.35	− 3.10	− 1.02 ± 3.11	0.33
Robbery	22.62	2.08	2.43 ± 1.31	1.86
Burglary and larceny	22.62	3.57	3.92 ± .55	7.13
Forgery and fraud	21.39	0.93	0.05 ± 1.23	0.04
Rape	24.18	− 7.85	− 5.94 ± 1.96	3.03
Other sex	23.61	1.06	2.40 ± 2.25	1.07
Vs. public welfare	19.91	− 3.83	− 6.19 ± 1.71	3.62
Arson and all other	22.91	− 2.52	− 1.88 ± 2.73	0.69

| | Straight | | | |
	Predicted Per Cent	Diff.of Subgroup and Predicted Per Cent	Diff.of Subgroup and Total Per Cent ± p.e.	x p.e.
First degree murder	11.39	− 0.78	− 0.67 ± 1.17	0.57
Second degree murder	11.43	− 0.91	− 0.76 ± .80	0.95
Assault	8.84	− 2.59	− 5.03 ± 2.36	2.13
Robbery	11.12	0.26	0.10 ± 1.00	0.10
Burglary and larceny	11.14	0.03	− 0.11 ± .42	0.26
Forgery and fraud	12.24	− 0.44	0.52 ± .93	0.56
Rape	10.05	2.19	0.96 ± 1.49	0.64
Other sex	9.95	0.05	− 1.28 ± 1.71	0.75
Vs. public welfare	14.70	0.59	4.01 ± 1.30	3.08
Arson and all other	10.33	0.35	− 0.60 ± 2.08	0.29

Table VI-35 (cont'd).

	Predicted Per Cent	Convex Diff. of Subgroup and Predicted Per Cent	Diff. of Subgroup and Total Per Cent ± p.e.	x p.e.
First degree murder	17.72	5.11	1.99 ± 1.50	1.33
Second degree murder	18.48	4.01	1.65 ± 1.02	1.62
Assault	24.61	1.64	5.41 ± 3.04	1.78
Robbery	21.77	- 2.16	- 1.23 ± 1.28	0.96
Burglary and larceny	21.59	- 3.77	- 3.02 ± .53	5.70
Forgery and fraud	21.80	- 0.77	0.19 ± 1.20	0.16
Rape	22.89	5.17	7.22 ± 1.91	3.78
Other sex	22.63	2.04	3.83 ± 2.20	1.74
Vs. public welfare	21.05	2.87	3.08 ± 1.67	1.84
Arson and all other	20.09	5.15	4.40 ± 2.67	1.65

	Predicted Per Cent	Concavo-convex Diff. of Subgroup and Predicted Per Cent	Diff. of Subgroup and Total Per Cent ± p.e.	x p.e.
First degree murder	50.12	0.68	5.19 ± 1.84	2.82
Second degree murder	48.53	0.50	3.42 ± 1.25	2.74
Assault	42.21	4.04	0.64 ± 3.72	0.17
Robbery	44.49	- 0.18	- 1.30 ± 1.57	0.83
Burglary and larceny	44.66	0.16	- 0.79 ± .66	1.20
Forgery and fraud	44.57	0.28	- 0.76 ± 1.47	0.52
Rape	42.88	0.49	- 2.24 ± 2.34	0.96
Other sex	43.81	- 3.14	- 4.94 ± 2.69	1.84
Vs. public welfare	44.33	0.37	- 0.91 ± 2.04	0.45
Arson and all other	46.67	- 2.98	- 1.92 ± 3.27	0.59

Significant Differences Independent of State Sampling

Concave
First degree murder: independent difference   - 5.02 (3.28 p.e.)
Second degree murder: independent difference   - 3.61 (3.44 p.e.)
Burglary and larceny: independent difference   3.57 (6.49 p.e.)
Rape: difference   - 5.94 (3.03 p.e.)

Convex
Burglary and larceny: difference   - 3.02 (5.70 p.e.)

Differences Rendered Insignificant by State Sampling

Concave
Vs. public welfare: independent difference   - 3.83 (2.24 p.e.)

Straight
Vs. public welfare: independent difference   .59 (.45 p.e.)

Convex
Rape: independent difference   5.17 (2.71 p.e.)

Table VI-36.　　　　　　　Nasal Tip Thickness by Offenses

	Submedium		Medium		Pronounced		Total
	No.	Per Cent	No.	Per Cent	No.	Per Cent	No.
First degree murder	39	12.54	213	68.49	59	18.97	311
Second degree murder	88	14.24	401	64.89	129	20.87	618
Assault	5	6.25	57	71.25	18	22.50	80
Robbery	39	9.47	283	68.69	90	21.84	412
Burglary and larceny	154	9.56	1133	70.33	324	20.11	1611
Forgery and fraud	44	9.44	332	71.24	90	19.31	466
Rape	24	12.24	126	64.29	46	23.47	196
Other sex	16	10.67	106	70.67	28	18.67	150
Vs. public welfare	4	1.56	182	71.09	70	27.34	256
Arson and all other	7	6.80	68	66.02	28	27.18	103
Total	420	9.99	2901	69.02	882	20.98	4203

Coefficient of mean square contingency = .10

Table VI-37. Predictions on Basis of State Composition and Differences
from Total Series by Offenses

Nasal Tip Thickness

	Predicted Per Cent	Submedium Diff.of Subgroup and Predicted Per Cent	Diff.of Subgroup and Total Per Cent ± p.e.	x p.e.
First degree murder	11.44	1.10	2.55 ± 1.11	2.30
Second degree murder	12.43	1.81	4.25 ± .75	5.67
Assault	12.80	- 6.55	- 3.74 ± 2.24	1.67
Robbery	7.98	1.49	- 0.52 ± .94	0.55
Burglary and larceny	10.27	- 0.71	- 0.43 ± .39	1.10
Forgery and fraud	7.89	1.55	- 0.55 ± .88	0.62
Rape	10.78	1.46	2.25 ± 1.41	1.60
Other sex	12.43	- 1.76	0.68 ± 1.62	0.42
Vs. public welfare	4.29	- 2.73	- 8.43 ± 1.23	6.85
Arson and all other	10.82	- 4.02	- 3.19 ± 1.97	1.62

	Predicted Per Cent	Medium Diff.of Subgroup and Predicted Per Cent	Diff.of Subgroup and Total Per Cent ± p.e.	x p.e.
First degree murder	68.82	- 0.33	- 0.53 ± 1.70	0.31
Second degree murder	68.97	- 4.08	- 4.13 ± 1.16	3.56
Assault	66.10	5.15	2.23 ± 3.45	0.65
Robbery	69.49	- 0.80	- 0.33 ± 1.46	0.23
Burglary and larceny	68.64	1.69	1.31 ± .61	2.15
Forgery and fraud	70.38	0.86	2.22 ± 1.36	1.63
Rape	67.82	- 3.53	- 4.73 ± 2.17	2.18
Other sex	66.58	4.09	1.65 ± 2.48	0.67
Vs. public welfare	72.39	- 1.30	2.07 ± 1.89	1.10
Arson and all other	67.19	- 1.17	- 3.00 ± 3.04	0.99

Table VI-37 (cont'd).

	Predicted Per Cent	Pronounced Diff. of Subgroup and Predicted Per Cent	Diff. of Subgroup and Total Per Cent ± p.e.	x p.e.
First degree murder	19.74	- 0.77	- 2.01 ± 1.50	1.34
Second degree murder	18.60	2.27	- 0.11 ± 1.02	0.11
Assault	21.10	1.40	1.52 ± 3.04	0.50
Robbery	22.53	- 0.69	0.86 ± 1.28	0.67
Burglary and larceny	21.09	- 0.98	- 0.87 ± .54	1.61
Forgery and fraud	21.72	- 2.41	- 1.67 ± 1.20	1.39
Rape	21.40	2.07	2.49 ± 1.92	1.30
Other sex	20.99	- 2.32	- 2.31 ± 2.20	1.05
Vs. public welfare	23.32	4.02	6.36 ± 1.67	3.81
Arson and all other	21.99	5.19	6.20 ± 2.67	2.32

Significant Differences Independent of State Sampling

Medium

Second degree murder: independent difference   - 4.08 (3.52 p.e.)

Differences Rendered Insignificant by State Sampling

Submedium

Second degree murder: independent difference   1.81 (2.41 p.e.)
Vs. public welfare: independent difference   - 2.73 (2.22 p.e.)

Pronounced

Vs. public welfare: independent difference   4.02 (2.41 p.e.)

Table VI-38.   Nasal Septum Inclination by Offenses

	Up		Down		Absent		Total
	No.	Per Cent	No.	Per Cent	No.	Per Cent	No.
First degree murder	193	61.86	114	36.54	5	1.60	312
Second degree murder	386	62.66	226	36.69	4	0.65	616
Assault	54	67.50	26	32.50	0	0	80
Robbery	292	70.70	121	29.30	0	0	413
Burglary and larceny	1178	73.44	423	26.37	3	0.19	1604
Forgery and fraud	315	67.89	148	31.90	1	0.22	464
Rape	124	63.27	70	35.71	2	1.02	196
Other sex	100	66.67	49	32.67	1	0.67	150
Vs. public welfare	150	58.59	105	41.02	1	0.39	256
Arson and all other	66	64.08	36	34.95	1	0.97	103
Total	2858	68.14	1318	31.42	18	0.43	4194

Coefficient of mean square contingency = .14

Table VI-39. Predictions on Basis of State Composition and Differences
from Total Series by Offenses

Nasal Septum Inclination

Up

	Predicted Per Cent	Diff.of Subgroup and Predicted Per Cent	Diff.of Subgroup and Total Per Cent ± p.e.	x p.e.
First degree murder	69.06	- 7.20	- 6.28 ± 1.71	3.67
Second degree murder	69.06	- 6.40	- 5.48 ± 1.17	4.68
Assault	73.70	- 6.20	- 0.64 ± 3.48	0.18
Robbery	66.15	4.55	2.56 ± 1.47	1.74
Burglary and larceny	68.66	4.78	5.30 ± .62	8.55
Forgery and fraud	65.98	1.91	- 0.25 ± 1.58	0.18
Rape	70.89	- 7.62	- 4.87 ± 2.19	2.22
Other sex	72.50	- 5.83	- 1.47 ± 2.52	0.58
Vs. public welfare	61.68	- 3.09	- 9.55 ± 1.90	5.03
Arson and all other	70.33	- 6.25	- 4.06 ± 3.06	1.33

Down

	Predicted Per Cent	Diff.of Subgroup and Predicted Per Cent	Diff.of Subgroup and Total Per Cent ± p.e.	x p.e.
First degree murder	30.34	6.20	5.12 ± 1.71	2.99
Second degree murder	30.38	6.31	5.27 ± 1.17	4.50
Assault	25.97	6.53	1.08 ± 3.47	0.31
Robbery	33.48	- 4.18	- 2.12 ± 1.46	1.45
Burglary and larceny	30.94	- 4.57	- 5.05 ± .61	8.28
Forgery and fraud	33.63	- 1.73	0.48 ± 1.37	0.35
Rape	28.77	6.94	4.29 ± 2.18	1.97
Other sex	27.11	5.56	1.25 ± 2.51	0.50
Vs. public welfare	37.96	3.06	9.60 ± 1.90	5.05
Arson and all other	29.20	5.75	3.53 ± 3.05	1.16

Significant Differences Independent of State Sampling

Up

First degree murder: difference	- 6.28 (3.67 p.e.)
Second degree murder: difference	- 5.48 (4.68 p.e.)
Burglary and larceny: independent difference	4.78 (7.71 p.e.)

Down

Second degree murder: difference	5.27 (4.50 p.e.)
Burglary and larceny: independent difference	- 4.57 (7.49 p.e.)

Differences Rendered Insignificant by State Sampling

Up

Vs. public welfare: independent difference	- 3.09 (1.63 p.e.)

Down

Vs. public welfare: independent difference	3.06 (1.61 p.e.)

Table VI-40.   Nasal Septum Deflection by Offenses

| | Right | | Left | | Absent | | Total |
	No.	Per Cent	No.	Per Cent	No.	Per Cent	No.
First degree murder	69	22.13	39	12.50	204	65.38	312
Second degree murder	173	27.99	73	11.81	372	60.19	618
Assault	18	22.50	12	15.00	50	62.50	80
Robbery	100	24.15	31	7.49	283	68.36	414
Burglary and larceny	374	23.24	136	8.45	1099	68.30	1609
Forgery and fraud	81	17.38	38	8.15	347	74.46	466
Rape	61	31.28	21	10.77	113	57.95	195
Other sex	50	33.78	18	12.16	80	54.05	148
Vs. public welfare	37	14.40	22	8.56	198	77.04	257
Arson and all other	24	23.53	12	11.76	66	64.71	102
Total	987	23.49	402	9.57	2812	66.94	4201

Table VI-41.   Predictions on Basis of State Composition and Differences
from Total Series by Offenses

Nasal Septum Deflection

| | | Right | | |
	Predicted Per Cent	Diff.of Subgroup and Predicted Per Cent	Diff.of Subgroup and Total Per Cent ± p.e.	x p.e.
First degree murder	24.87	- 2.74	· 1.36 ± 1.56	0.87
Second degree murder	27.07	0.92	4.50 ± 1.07	4.21
Assault	27.26	- 4.76	- 0.99 ± 3.16	0.31
Robbery	21.48	2.67	0.66 ± 1.34	0.49
Burglary and larceny	24.31	- 1.07	- 0.25 ± .56	0.45
Forgery and fraud	18.94	- 1.56	- 6.11 ± 1.25	4.89
Rape	25.04	6.24	7.79 ± 2.00	3.90
Other sex	27.71	6.07	10.29 ± 2.31	4.45
Vs. public welfare	13.83	0.57	- 9.09 ± 1.73	5.25
Arson and all other	26.60	- 3.07	0.04 ± 2.80	0.01

| | | Left | | |
	Predicted Per Cent	Diff.of Subgroup and Predicted Per Cent	Diff.of Subgroup and Total Per Cent ± p.e.	x p.e.
First degree murder	14.73	- 2.23	2.93 ± 1.08	2.71
Second degree murder	14.80	- 2.99	2.24 ± .74	3.03
Assault	13.47	1.53	5.43 ± 2.20	2.47
Robbery	10.17	- 2.58	- 2.08 ± .92	2.26
Burglary and larceny	12.10	- 3.65	- 1.12 ± .38	2.95
Forgery and fraud	10.35	- 2.20	- 1.42 ± .86	1.65
Rape	11.76	- 0.99	1.20 ± 1.39	0.86
Other sex	13.66	- 1.50	2.59 ± 1.60	1.62
Vs. public welfare	7.67	0.89	- 1.01 ± 1.20	0.84
Arson and all other	13.18	- 1.42	2.19 ± 1.94	1.13

Table VI-41 (cont'd).

	Predicted Per Cent	Absent Diff.of Subgroup and Predicted Per Cent	Diff.of Subgroup and Total Per Cent ± p.e.	x p.e.
First degree murder	65.21	0.17	- 1.56 ± 1.73	0.90
Second degree murder	62.18	- 1.99	- 6.75 ± 1.18	5.72
Assault	61.07	1.43	- 4.44 ± 3.51	1.26
Robbery	70.22	- 1.86	1.42 ± 1.48	0.96
Burglary and larceny	65.80	2.50	1.36 ± 0.62	2.19
Forgery and fraud	72.60	1.86	7.52 ± 1.38	5.45
Rape	65.08	- 7.13	- 8.99 ± 2.22	4.05
Other sex	60.89	- 6.84	-12.89 ± 2.56	5.04
Vs. public welfare	79.58	- 2.54	10.10 ± 1.92	5.26
Arson and all other	63.55	1.16	- 2.23 ± 3.10	0.72

Significant Differences Independent of State Sampling

Right

Rape: independent difference   6.24 (3.12 p.e.)

Absent

Rape: independent difference   - 7.13 (3.21 p.e.)

Differences Rendered Insignificant by State Sampling

Right

Second degree murder: independent difference   .92 (.86 p.e.)
Forgery and fraud: independent difference   - 1.56 (1.25 p.e.)
Other sex: independent difference   6.07 (2.63 p.e.)
Vs. public welfare: independent difference   0.57 (.33 p.e.)*

Left

Second degree murder: independent difference   - 2.99 (4.04 p.e.)*

Absent

Second degree murder: independent difference   - 1.99 (1.69 p.e.)
Forgery and fraud: independent difference   1.86 (1.35 p.e.)
Other sex: independent difference   - 6.84 (2.67 p.e.)
Vs. public welfare: independent difference   - 2.54 (1.32 p.e.)*
*Signs are opposite

Table VI-42.   Lips Integumental Thickness by Offenses

	Submedium No.	Submedium Per Cent	Medium No.	Medium Per Cent	Pronounced No.	Pronounced Per Cent	Total No.
First degree murder	40	12.82	248	79.49	24	7.69	312
Second degree murder	97	15.70	479	77.51	42	6.80	618
Assault	13	16.25	59	73.75	8	10.00	80
Robbery	49	11.86	338	81.84	26	6.30	413
Burglary and larceny	201	12.51	1339	83.32	67	4.17	1607
Forgery and fraud	34	7.30	407	87.34	25	5.36	466
Rape	28	14.29	150	76.53	18	9.18	196
Other sex	15	10.00	130	86.67	5	3.34	150
Vs. public welfare	13	5.08	230	89.84	13	5.08	256
Arson and all other	19	18.45	75	72.82	9	8.74	103
Total	509	12.12	3455	82.24	237	5.64	4201

Coefficient of mean square contingency = .10

Table VI-43. Predictions on Basis of State Composition and Differences
from Total Series by Offenses

Lips Integumental Thickness

Submedium

	Predicted Per Cent	Diff.of Subgroup and Predicted Per Cent	Diff.of Subgroup and Total Per Cent ± p.e.	x p.e.
First degree murder	14.32	- 1.50	0.70 ± 1.20	.58
Second degree murder	14.41	1.29	3.58 ± .82	4.37
Assault	12.12	4.13	4.13 ± 2.44	1.69
Robbery	12.90	- 1.04	- 0.26 ± 1.02	.26
Burglary and larceny	13.03	- 0.52	0.39 ± .43	.91
Forgery and fraud	10.36	- 3.06	- 4.82 ± .96	5.02
Rape	13.38	0.91	2.17 ± 1.54	1.41
Other sex	13.76	- 3.76	- 2.12 ± 1.77	1.20
Vs. public welfare	9.59	- 4.51	- 7.04 ± 1.34	5.25
Arson and all other	16.02	2.43	6.33 ± 2.14	2.96

Medium

	Predicted Per Cent	Diff.of Subgroup and Predicted Per Cent	Diff.of Subgroup and Total Per Cent ± p.e.	x p.e.
First degree murder	79.00	0.49	- 2.75 ± 1.40	1.96
Second degree murder	80.31	- 2.80	- 4.73 ± .96	4.93
Assault	81.17	- 7.42	- 8.49 ± 2.85	2.98
Robbery	80.96	0.88	- 0.40 ± 1.21	.33
Burglary and larceny	81.49	1.83	1.08 ± .51	2.12
Forgery and fraud	83.98	3.36	5.10 ± 1.13	4.51
Rape	81.03	- 4.50	- 5.71 ± 1.79	3.19
Other sex	80.35	6.32	4.43 ± 2.06	2.15
Vs. public welfare	85.92	3.92	7.60 ± 1.56	4.87
Arson and all other	77.38	- 4.56	- 9.42 ± 2.51	3.75

Pronounced

	Predicted Per Cent	Diff.of Subgroup and Predicted Per Cent	Diff.of Subgroup and Total Per Cent ± p.e.	x p.e.
First degree murder	6.67	1.02	2.05 ± .84	2.44
Second degree murder	5.28	1.52	1.16 ± .57	2.04
Assault	6.71	3.29	4.36 ± 1.72	2.54
Robbery	6.14	0.16	0.66 ± .73	.90
Burglary and larceny	5.48	- 1.31	- 1.47 ± .30	4.90
Forgery and fraud	5.65	- 0.29	- 0.28 ± .68	.41
Rape	5.60	3.58	3.54 ± 1.09	3.25
Other sex	5.89	- 2.55	- 2.30 ± 1.25	1.84
Vs. public welfare	4.49	0.59	- 0.56 ± .94	.60
Arson and all other	6.60	2.14	3.10 ± 1.51	2.05

Table VI-43 (cont'd).
　　Significant Differences Independent of State Sampling

	Submedium
Forgery and fraud: independent difference	- 3.06 (3.19 p.e.)
Vs. public welfare: independent difference	- 4.51 (3.37 p.e.)

	Pronounced
Burglary and larceny: independent difference	- 1.31 (4.37 p.e.)
Rape: difference	3.54 (3.25 p.e.)

　　Differences Rendered Insignificant by State Sampling

	Submedium
Second degree murder: independent difference	1.29 (1.57 p.e.)

	Medium
Second degree murder: independent difference	- 2.80 (2.92 p.e.)
Forgery and fraud: independent difference	3.36 (2.97 p.e.)
Rape: independent difference	- 4.50 (2.51 p.e.)
Vs. public welfare: independent difference	3.92 (2.51 p.e.)
Arson and all other: independent difference	- 4.56 (1.82 p.e.)

Table VI-44.　　　　　Lips Membranous Thickness by Offenses

	Submedium		Medium		Upper,Submedium Lower,Pronounced		Pronounced		Total
	No.	Per Cent	No.	Per Cent	No.	Per Cent	No.	Per Cent	No.
First degree murder	64	20.51	211	67.63	28	8.97	9	2.88	312
Second degree murder	124	20.03	428	69.14	51	8.24	16	2.58	619
Assault	20	25.00	44	55.00	13	16.25	3	3.75	80
Robbery	50	12.08	300	72.46	47	11.35	17	4.11	414
Burglary and larceny	231	14.37	1105	68.72	225	13.99	47	2.92	1608
Forgery and fraud	53	11.35	328	70.24	73	15.63	13	2.78	467
Rape	47	23.98	113	57.65	31	15.82	5	2.55	196
Other sex	44	29.14	85	56.29	17	11.26	5	3.31	151
Vs. public welfare	48	18.75	171	66.80	34	13.28	3	1.17	256
Arson and all other	20	19.42	72	69.90	8	7.77	3	2.91	103
Total	701	16.67	2857	67.93	527	12.53	121	2.88	4206

Coefficient of mean square contingency = .14

Table VI-45. Predictions on Basis of State Composition and Differences
from Total Series by Offenses

Lips Membranous Thickness

	Predicted Per Cent	Submedium Diff.of Subgroup and Predicted Per Cent	Diff.of Subgroup and Total Per Cent ± p.e.	x p.e.
First degree murder	15.27	5.24	3.84 ± 1.37	2.80
Second degree murder	16.48	3.55	3.36 ± .93	3.61
Assault	21.30	3.70	8.33 ± 2.79	2.99
Robbery	15.73	- 3.65	- 4.59 ± 1.17	3.92
Burglary and larceny	17.35	- 2.98	- 2.30 ± .49	4.59
Forgery and fraud	15.65	- 4.30	- 5.32 ± 1.09	4.88
Rape	18.59	5.39	7.31 ± 1.75	4.18
Other sex	19.83	9.31	12.47 ± 2.00	6.24
Vs. public welfare	12.84	5.91	2.08 ± 1.52	1.37
Arson and all other	16.90	2.52	2.75 ± 2.45	1.12

	Predicted Per Cent	Medium Diff.of Subgroup and Predicted Per Cent	Diff.of Subgroup and Total Per Cent ± p.e.	x p.e.
First degree murder	72.57	- 4.94	- 0.30 ± 1.71	.18
Second degree murder	70.95	- 1.81	1.21 ± 1.17	1.03
Assault	61.21	- 6.21	-12.93 ± 3.49	3.70
Robbery	67.93	4.53	4.53 ± 1.47	3.08
Burglary and larceny	66.69	2.03	0.79 ± .62	1.27
Forgery and fraud	68.10	2.14	2.31 ± 1.38	1.67
Rape	64.32	- 6.67	-10.28 ± 2.19	4.69
Other sex	63.51	- 7.22	-11.64 ± 2.52	4.62
Vs. public welfare	69.86	- 3.06	- 1.13 ± 1.90	.50
Arson and all other	67.91	1.99	1.97 ± 3.06	.64

	Predicted Per Cent	Upper Submedium, Lower Pronounced Diff.of Subgroup and Predicted Per Cent	Diff.of Subgroup and Total Per Cent ± p.e.	x p.e.
First degree murder	8.49	0.48	- 3.56 ± 1.21	2.94
Second degree murder	9.37	- 1.13	- 4.29 ± .83	5.17
Assault	15.09	1.16	3.72 ± 2.48	1.50
Robbery	13.51	- 2.16	- 1.18 ± 1.04	1.14
Burglary and larceny	13.23	0.76	1.46 ± .44	3.32
Forgery and fraud	13.48	2.15	3.10 ± .98	3.16
Rape	14.47	1.35	3.29 ± 1.56	2.11
Other sex	14.05	- 2.79	- 1.27 ± 1.79	.71
Vs. public welfare	14.56	- 1.28	0.75 ± 1.35	.56
Arson and all other	11.95	- 4.18	- 4.76 ± 2.17	2.19

Table VI-45 (cont'd).

	Predicted Per Cent	Pronounced Diff.of Subgroup and Predicted Per Cent	Diff.of Subgroup and Total Per Cent ± p.e.	x p.e.
First degree murder	3.67	- 0.79	0 ± .61	0
Second degree murder	3.20	- 0.62	- 0.30 ± .42	.71
Assault	2.40	1.35	0.87 ± 1.24	.70
Robbery	2.84	1.27	1.23 ± .53	2.32
Burglary and larceny	2.72	0.20	0.04 ± .22	.18
Forgery and fraud	2.77	0.01	- 0.10 ± .49	.20
Rape	2.62	- 0.07	- 0.33 ± .79	.42
Other sex	2.61	0.70	0.43 ± .92	0.47
Vs. public welfare	2.75	- 1.58	- 1.71 ± .69	2.48
Arson and all other	3.24	- 0.33	0.03 ± 1.10	.03

Significant Differences Independent of State Sampling

Submedium

Second degree murder: difference	3.35 (3.61 p.e.)
Robbery: independent difference	- 3.65 (3.12 p.e.)
Burglary and larceny: difference	- 2.30 (4.69 p.e.)
Forgery and fraud: independent difference	- 4.30 (3.94 p.e.)
Rape: independent difference	5.39 (3.08 p.e.)
Other sex: independent difference	9.31 (4.65 p.e.)

Medium

Robbery: difference	4.53 (3.08 p.e.)
Rape: independent difference	- 6.67 (3.05 p.e.)

Differences Rendered Insignificant by State Sampling

Medium

Assault: independent difference	- 6.21 (1.78 p.e.)
Other sex: independent difference	- 7.22 (2.87 p.e.)

Upper Submedium, Lower Pronounced

Second degree murder: independent difference	- 1.13 (1.36 p.e.)
Burglary and larceny: independent difference	.76 (1.73 p.e.)
Forgery and fraud: independent difference	2.15 (2.19 p.e.)

Table VI-46.   Lip Seam by Offenses

	Absent, Submedium No.	Per Cent	Medium No.	Per Cent	Pronounced No.	Per Cent	Total No.
First degree murder	54	17.31	199	63.78	59	18.91	312
Second degree murder	103	16.72	376	61.04	137	22.24	616
Assault	8	10.00	54	67.50	18	22.50	80
Robbery	39	9.44	298	72.15	76	18.40	413
Burglary and larceny	197	12.26	1091	67.90	319	19.85	1607
Forgery and fraud	72	15.42	321	68.74	74	15.85	467
Rape	41	20.92	126	64.29	29	14.80	196
Other sex	25	16.67	91	60.67	34	22.67	150
Vs. public welfare	60	23.44	154	60.16	42	16.41	256
Arson and all other	9	8.74	77	74.76	17	16.50	103
Total	608	14.48	2787	66.36	805	19.17	4200

Coefficient of mean square contingency = .10

Table VI-47. Predictions on Basis of State Composition and Differences
from Total Series by Offenses

Lip Seam

Absent, Submedium

	Predicted Per Cent	Diff.of Subgroup and Predicted Per Cent	Diff.of Subgroup and Total Per Cent ± p.e.	x p.e.
First degree murder	12.50	4.81	2.83 ± 1.30	2.18
Second degree murder	13.04	3.58	2.24 ± .88	2.54
Assault	13.24	− 3.24	− 4.48 ± 2.63	1.70
Robbery	14.50	− 5.16	− 5.04 ± 1.11	4.54
Burglary and larceny	14.50	− 2.24	− 2.22 ± .46	4.83
Forgery and fraud	16.52	− 1.10	0.94 ± 1.04	.90
Rape	12.66	8.26	6.44 ± 1.65	3.90
Other sex	13.32	3.35	2.19 ± 1.90	1.15
Vs. public welfare	19.52	3.92	8.96 ± 1.44	6.22
Arson and all other	11.87	− 3.13	− 5.74 ± 2.31	2.48

Medium

	Predicted Per Cent	Diff.of Subgroup and Predicted Per Cent	Diff.of Subgroup and Total Per Cent ± p.e.	x p.e.
First degree murder	66.94	− 3.16	− 2.58 ± 1.73	1.49
Second degree murder	64.97	− 3.93	− 5.32 ± 1.19	4.47
Assault	70.48	− 2.98	1.14 ± 3.53	.32
Robbery	67.49	4.66	5.79 ± 1.49	3.89
Burglary and larceny	66.42	1.48	1.54 ± .63	2.44
Forgery and fraud	65.27	3.47	2.38 ± 1.39	1.71
Rape	71.32	− 7.03	− 2.07 ± 2.23	.93
Other sex	68.47	− 7.80	− 5.69 ± 2.56	2.22
Vs. public welfare	61.40	− 1.24	− 6.20 ± 1.93	3.21
Arson and all other	69.69	5.07	8.40 ± 3.10	2.71

Pronounced

	Predicted Per Cent	Diff.of Subgroup and Predicted Per Cent	Diff.of Subgroup and Total Per Cent ± p.e.	x p.e.
First degree murder	20.56	− 1.65	− 0.26 ± 1.44	.18
Second degree murder	22.00	0.24	3.07 ± .99	3.10
Assault	16.28	6.22	3.33 ± 2.94	1.13
Robbery	17.91	0.49	− 0.77 ± 1.24	.62
Burglary and larceny	19.08	0.77	0.68 ± .53	1.28
Forgery and fraud	18.21	− 2.36	− 3.32 ± 1.16	2.86
Rape	16.02	− 1.22	− 4.37 ± 1.85	2.36
Other sex	18.21	4.46	3.50 ± 2.13	1.64
Vs. public welfare	19.08	− 2.67	− 2.76 ± 1.60	1.72
Arson and all other	18.44	− 1.94	− 2.67 ± 2.58	1.04

Table **VI-47** (cont'd).
Significant Differences Independent of State Sampling

Absent, Submedium

Robbery: difference	- 5.04 (4.54 p.e.)
Burglary and larceny: difference	- 2.22 (4.83 p.e.)
Rape: difference	6.44 (3.90 p.e.)

Medium

Second degree murder: independent difference	- 3.93 (3.30 p.e.)
Robbery: independent difference	4.66 (3.13 p.e.)

Differences Rendered Insignificant by State Sampling

Absent, Submedium

Vs. public welfare: independent difference	3.92 (2.72 p.e.)

Medium

Vs. public welfare: independent difference	- 1.24 (.64 p.e.)

Pronounced

Second degree murder: independent difference	.24 (.24 p.e.)

Table VI-48.   Alveolar Prognathism by Offenses

	Absent		Submedium		Medium		Pronounced		Total
	No.	Per Cent	No.	Per Cent	No.	Per Cent	No.	Per Cent	No.
First degree murder	253	81.09	51	16.35	8	2.56	0	0	312
Second degree murder	519	83.98	75	12.14	23	3.72	1	0.16	618
Assault	67	83.75	7	8.75	5	6.25	1	1.25	80
Robbery	339	81.88	59	14.25	15	3.62	1	0.24	414
Burglary and larceny	1336	82.93	190	11.79	77	4.78	8	0.50	1611
Forgery and fraud	382	81.80	65	13.92	17	3.64	3	0.64	467
Rape	162	82.23	25	12.69	7	3.55	3	1.52	197
Other sex	116	76.82	26	17.22	9	5.96	0	0	151
Vs. public welfare	217	84.44	29	11.28	11	4.28	0	0	257
Arson and all other	78	75.73	23	22.33	1	0.97	1	0.97	103
Total	3469	82.40	550	13.06	173	4.11	18	0.43	4210

Coefficient of mean square contingency = .10

Table VI-49. Predictions on Basis of State Composition and Differences
from Total Series by Offenses

Alveolar Prognathism

Absent

	Predicted Per Cent	Diff.of Subgroup and Predicted Per Cent	Diff.of Subgroup and Total Per Cent ± p.e.	x p.e.
First degree murder	80.56	0.53	- 1.31 ± 1.40	.94
Second degree murder	81.19	2.79	1.58 ± .95	1.66
Assault	85.52	- 1.77	1.35 ± 2.85	.47
Robbery	82.54	- 0.66	- 0.52 ± 1.20	.43
Burglary and larceny	82.82	0.11	0.53 ± .51	1.04
Forgery and fraud	83.16	- 1.36	- 0.60 ± 1.12	.54
Rape	82.50	- 0.27	- 0.17 ± 1.79	.10
Other sex	83.67	- 6.85	- 5.58 ± 2.05	2.72
Vs. public welfare	81.96	2.48	2.04 ± 1.55	1.32
Arson and all other	81.04	- 5.31	- 6.67 ± 2.50	2.67

Submedium

	Predicted Per Cent	Diff.of Subgroup and Predicted Per Cent	Diff.of Subgroup and Total Per Cent ± p.e.	x p.e.
First degree murder	14.63	1.72	3.29 ± 1.24	2.65
Second degree murder	13.92	- 1.78	- 0.92 ± .84	1.10
Assault	10.51	- 1.76	- 4.31 ± 2.52	1.71
Robbery	12.76	1.49	1.19 ± 1.06	1.12
Burglary and larceny	12.65	- 0.86	- 1.27 ± .44	2.89
Forgery and fraud	12.72	1.20	0.86 ± .99	.87
Rape	12.59	0.10	- 0.37 ± 1.58	.23
Other sex	11.96	5.26	4.16 ± 1.81	2.30
Vs. public welfare	13.93	- 2.65	- 1.78 ± 1.38	1.29
Arson and all other	13.87	8.46	9.27 ± 2.21	4.20

Medium

	Predicted Per Cent	Diff.of Subgroup and Predicted Per Cent	Diff.of Subgroup and Total Per Cent ± p.e.	x p.e.
First degree murder	4.44	- 1.88	- 1.55 ± .73	2.12
Second degree murder	4.53	- 0.81	- 0.39 ± .50	.78
Assault	3.55	2.70	2.14 ± 1.48	1.44
Robbery	4.20	- 0.58	- 0.49 ± .63	.78
Burglary and larceny	4.00	0.68	0.67 ± .26	2.58
Forgery and fraud	3.66	- 0.02	- 0.47 ± .59	.80
Rape	4.37	- 0.82	- 0.56 ± .93	.60
Other sex	3.99	1.97	1.85 ± 1.07	1.73
Vs. public welfare	3.63	0.65	0.17 ± .81	.21
Arson and all other	4.66	- 3.69	- 3.14 ± 1.30	2.42

Pronounced

	Predicted Per Cent	Diff.of Subgroup and Predicted Per Cent	Diff.of Subgroup and Total Per Cent ± p.e.	x p.e.
Rape	0.54	0.98	1.09 ± .30	3.63

Table VI-49 (cont'd).
Significant Differences Independent of State Sampling

Submedium
Arson and all other: independent difference   8.46 (3.83 p.e.)

Pronounced
Rape: independent difference   .98 (3.27 p.e.)

Table VI-50.   Facial Prognathism by Offenses

| | Absent | | Submedium | | Medium | | Pronounced | | Total |
	No.	Per Cent	No.	Per Cent	No.	Per Cent	No.	Per Cent	No.
First degree murder	280	90.03	22	7.07	9	2.89	0	0	311
Second degree murder	551	89.16	44	7.12	22	3.56	1	0.16	618
Assault	71	88.75	6	7.50	2	2.50	1	1.25	80
Robbery	363	87.68	36	8.70	13	3.14	2	0.48	414
Burglary and larceny	1406	87.28	116	7.20	79	4.90	10	0.62	1611
Forgery and fraud	417	89.29	28	6.00	21	4.50	1	0.21	467
Rape	175	88.83	9	4.57	12	6.09	1	0.51	197
Other sex	130	86.09	10	6.62	10	6.62	1	0.66	151
Vs. public welfare	226	87.94	17	6.62	11	4.28	3	1.17	257
Arson and all other	87	84.47	12	11.65	4	3.88	0	0	103
Total	3706	88.05	300	7.13	183	4.35	20	0.48	4209

Coefficient of mean square contingency = .10

Table VI-51. Predictions on Basis of State Composition and Differences
from Total Series by Offenses

Facial Prognathism

	Predicted Per Cent	Submedium Diff.of Subgroup and Predicted Per Cent	Diff.of Subgroup and Total Per Cent ± p.e.	x p.e.
Robbery	7.15	1.55	1.57 ± .81	1.94
Arson and all other	7.50	4.15	4.52 ± 1.67	2.67

	Predicted Per Cent	Medium Diff.of Subgroup and Predicted Per Cent	Diff.of Subgroup and Total Per Cent ± p.e.	x p.e.
Rape	4.63	1.46	1.74 ± .96	1.81
Other sex	4.31	2.31	2.27 ± 1.10	2.06

The differences above are independent of state sampling, but are not large enough to be significant.

Table VI-52.   Chin Form by Offenses

	Median No.	Median Per Cent	Bilateral No.	Bilateral Per Cent	Total No.
First degree murder	201	64.63	110	35.37	311
Second degree murder	316	51.22	301	48.78	617
Assault	45	56.25	35	43.75	80
Robbery	234	56.66	179	43.34	413
Burglary and larceny	938	58.26	672	41.74	1610
Forgery and fraud	257	55.03	210	44.97	467
Rape	123	62.76	73	37.24	196
Other sex	86	57.33	64	42.67	150
Vs. public welfare	130	50.78	126	49.22	256
Arson and all other	60	58.25	43	41.75	103
Total	2390	56.86	1813	43.14	4203

Coefficient of mean square contingency = .10

Table VI-53. Predictions on Basis of State Composition and Differences
from Total Series by Offenses

Chin Form

Median

	Predicted Per Cent	Diff.of Subgroup and Predicted Per Cent	Diff.of Subgroup and Total Per Cent ± p.e.	x p.e.
First degree murder	56.05	8.58	7.77 ± 1.82	4.27
Second degree murder	56.33	- 5.11	- 5.64 ± 1.24	4.55
Assault	56.85	- 0.60	- 0.61 ± 3.70	.16
Robbery	57.36	- 0.70	- 0.20 ± 1.56	.13
Burglary and larceny	56.45	1.81	1.40 ± .65	2.15
Forgery and fraud	55.24	- 0.21	- 1.83 ± 1.46	1.25
Rape	59.23	3.53	5.90 ± 2.33	2.53
Other sex	56.55	0.78	0.47 ± 2.68	.18
Vs. public welfare	53.56	- 2.78	- 6.08 ± 2.02	3.01
Arson and all other	57.82	0.43	1.39 ± 3.25	.43

Bilateral

	Predicted Per Cent	Diff.of Subgroup and Predicted Per Cent	Diff.of Subgroup and Total Per Cent ± p.e.	x p.e.
First degree murder	43.95	- 8.58	- 7.77 ± 1.82	4.27
Second degree murder	43.67	5.11	5.64 ± 1.24	4.55
Assault	43.15	0.60	0.61 ± 3.70	.16
Robbery	42.64	0.70	0.20 ± 1.56	.13
Burglary and larceny	43.55	- 1.81	- 1.40 ± .65	2.15
Forgery and fraud	44.76	0.21	1.83 ± 1.46	1.25
Rape	40.77	- 3.53	- 5.90 ± 2.33	2.53
Other sex	43.45	- 0.78	- 0.47 ± 2.68	.18
Vs. public welfare	46.44	2.78	6.08 ± 2.02	3.01
Arson and all other	42.18	- 0.43	- 1.39 ± 3.25	.43

Table VI-53 (cont'd).

Significant Differences Independent of State Sampling

Median

| First degree murder: difference | 7.77 (4.27 p.e.) |
| Second degree murder: independent difference | - 5.11 (4.12 p.e.) |

Bilateral

| First degree murder: difference | - 7.77 (4.27 p.e.) |
| Second degree murder: independent difference | 5.11 (4.12 p.e.) |

Differences Rendered Insignificant by State Sampling

Median

| Vs. public welfare: independent difference | - 2.78 (1.38 p.e.) |

Bilateral

| Vs. public welfare: independent difference | 2.78 (1.38 p.e.) |

Table VI-54. Malars Prominence by Offenses

| | Submedium | | Medium | | Pronounced | | Total |
	No.	Per Cent	No.	Per Cent	No.	Per Cent	No.
First degree murder	30	9.65	209	67.20	72	23.15	311
Second degree murder	52	8.43	413	66.94	152	24.64	617
Assault	5	6.25	58	72.50	17	21.25	80
Robbery	17	4.11	294	71.01	103	24.88	414
Burglary and larceny	85	5.28	1150	71.47	374	23.24	1609
Forgery and fraud	20	4.29	319	68.45	127	27.25	466
Rape	7	3.55	138	70.05	52	26.40	197
Other sex	8	5.30	112	74.17	31	20.53	151
Vs. public welfare	8	3.14	133	52.16	114	44.70	255
Arson and all other	6	5.82	71	68.93	26	25.24	103
Total	238	5.66	2897	68.93	1068	25.41	4203

Coefficient of mean square contingency = .14

Table VI-55. Predictions on Basis of State Composition and Differences
from Total Series by Offenses

Malars Prominence

	Predicted Per Cent	Submedium Diff. of Subgroup and Predicted Per Cent	Diff. of Subgroup and Total Per Cent ± p.e.	x p.e.
First degree murder	6.14	3.51	3.99 ± .85	4.69
Second degree murder	7.78	0.65	2.77 ± .58	4.78
Assault	5.93	0.32	0.59 ± 1.73	0.34
Robbery	4.51	- 0.40	- 1.55 ± .73	2.12
Burglary and larceny	5.97	- 0.69	- 0.38 ± .30	1.27
Forgery and fraud	4.16	0.13	- 1.37 ± .68	2.02
Rape	3.97	- 0.42	- 2.11 ± 1.09	1.94
Other sex	6.59	- 1.29	- 0.36 ± 1.25	0.29
Vs. public welfare	3.06	0.08	- 2.52 ± .94	2.68
Arson and all other	5.58	0.24	0.16 + 1.52	0.10

Table VI-55 (cont'd).

	Predicted Per Cent	Medium Diff.of Subgroup and Predicted Per Cent	Diff.of Subgroup and Total Per Cent ± p.e.	x p.e.
First degree murder	70.03	- 2.83	- 1.73 ± 1.71	1.01
Second degree murder	69.20	- 2.26	- 1.99 ± 1.16	1.72
Assault	74.38	- 1.88	3.57 ± 3.45	1.04
Robbery	70.37	0.64	2.08 ± 1.46	1.42
Burglary and larceny	69.33	2.14	2.54 ± .61	4.16
Forgery and fraud	65.48	2.97	- 0.48 ± 1.36	0.35
Rape	74.66	- 4.61	1.12 ± 2.17	0.52
Other sex	72.20	1.97	5.24 ± 2.50	2.10
Vs. public welfare	58.44	- 6.28	-16.77 ± 1.90	8.83
Arson and all other	73.95	- 5.02	0 ± 3.04	0

	Predicted Per Cent	Pronounced Diff.of Subgroup and Predicted Per Cent	Diff.of Subgroup and Total Per Cent ± p.e.	x p.e.
First degree murder	23.83	- 0.68	- 2.26 ± 1.60	1.41
Second degree murder	23.02	1.62	- 0.77 ± 1.09	0.71
Assault	19.69	1.56	- 4.16 ± 3.25	1.28
Robbery	25.12	- 0.24	- 0.53 ± 1.37	0.39
Burglary and larceny	24.70	- 1.46	- 2.17 ± .57	3.81
Forgery and fraud	30.36	- 3.11	1.84 ± 1.28	1.44
Rape	21.37	5.03	0.99 ± 2.04	0.48
Other sex	21.21	- 0.68	- 4.88 ± 2.35	2.08
Vs. public welfare	38.50	6.20	19.29 ± 1.78	10.84
Arson and all other	20.48	4.76	- 0.17 ± 2.86	0.06

Significant Differences Independent of State Sampling

Submedium

First degree murder: independent difference   3.51 (4.13 p.e.)

Medium

Burglary and larceny: independent difference   2.14 (3.51 p.e.)
Vs. public welfare: independent difference   - 6.28 (3.30 p.e.)

Pronounced

Vs. public welfare: independent difference   6.20 (3.48 p.e.)

Differences Rendered Insignificant by State Sampling

Submedium

Second degree murder: independent difference   .65 (1.12 p.e.)

Pronounced

Burglary and larceny: independent difference   - 1.46 (2.56 p.e.)

Table VI-56.   Cheeks Fullness by Offenses

	Submedium		Medium		Pronounced		Total
	No.	Per Cent	No.	Per Cent	No.	Per Cent	No.
First degree murder	94	30.42	169	54.69	46	14.89	309
Second degree murder	145	23.54	365	59.25	106	17.21	616
Assault	29	36.25	38	47.50	13	16.25	80
Robbery	98	23.67	246	59.42	70	16.91	414
Burglary and larceny	359	22.33	960	59.70	289	17.97	1608
Forgery and fraud	112	23.98	260	55.67	95	20.34	467
Rape	60	30.46	110	55.84	27	13.71	197
Other sex	55	36.67	79	52.67	16	10.67	150
Vs. public welfare	44	17.12	137	53.31	76	29.57	257
Arson and all other	28	27.45	56	54.90	18	17.65	102
Total	1024	24.38	2420	57.62	756	18.00	4200

Table VI-57.   Predictions on Basis of State Composition and Differences
from Total Series by Offenses

Cheeks Fullness

	Predicted Per Cent	Submedium Diff.of Subgroup and Predicted Per Cent	Diff.of Subgroup and Total Per Cent ± p.e.	x p.e.
First degree murder	23.66	6.76	6.04 ± 1.58	3.82
Second degree murder	24.04	- 0.50	- 0.84 ± 1.07	0.78
Assault	32.02	4.23	11.87 ± 3.21	3.70
Robbery	24.10	- 0.43	- 0.71 ± 1.35	0.53
Burglary and larceny	25.24	- 2.91	- 2.05 ± .57	3.60
Forgery and fraud	22.29	1.69	- 0.40 ± 1.26	0.32
Rape	27.80	2.66	6.08 ± 2.02	3.01
Other sex	29.14	7.53	12.29 ± 2.32	5.30
Vs. public welfare	16.32	0.80	- 7.26 ± 1.75	4.15
Arson and all other	26.54	0.91	3.07 ± 2.83	1.08

	Predicted Per Cent	Medium Diff.of Subgroup and Predicted Per Cent	Diff.of Subgroup and Total Per Cent ± p.e.	x p.e.
First degree murder	60.18	- 5.49	- 2.93 ± 1.83	1.60
Second degree murder	60.67	- 1.42	1.63 ± 1.24	1.31
Assault	53.27	- 5.77	-10.12 ± 3.69	2.74
Robbery	57.92	1.50	1.80 ± 1.56	1.15
Burglary and larceny	57.19	2.51	2.08 ± .65	3.20
Forgery and fraud	56.06	- 0.39	- 1.95 ± 1.46	1.34
Rape	55.81	0.03	- 1.78 ± 2.32	0.77
Other sex	55.33	- 2.56	- 4.95 ± 2.67	1.85
Vs. public welfare	56.10	- 2.79	- 4.31 ± 2.02	2.13
Arson and all other	58.55	- 3.65	- 2.72 ± 3.26	0.83

Table VI-57 (cont'd).

	Predicted Per Cent	Pronounced Diff.of Subgroup and Predicted Per Cent	Diff.of Subgroup and Total Per Cent ± p.e.	x p.e.
First degree murder	13.20	1.69	- 3.11 ± 1.42	2.19
Second degree murder	15.29	1.92	- 0.79 ± .96	0.82
Assault	14.72	1.53	- 1.75 ± 2.87	0.61
Robbery	17.99	- 1.08	- 1.09 ± 1.21	0.90
Burglary and larceny	17.57	0.40	- 0.03 ± .51	0.06
Forgery and fraud	21.65	- 1.31	2.34 ± 1.13	2.07
Rape	16.39	- 2.68	- 4.29 ± 1.80	2.38
Other sex	15.54	- 4.87	- 7.33 ± 2.08	3.52
Vs. public welfare	27.59	1.98	11.57 ± 1.56	7.42
Arson and all other	14.92	2.73	- 0.35 ± 2.54	0.14

Significant Differences Independent of State Sampling

Submedium

First degree murder: difference	6.04 (3.82 p.e.)
Burglary and larceny: difference	- 2.05 (3.60 p.e.)
Other sex: independent difference	7.53 (3.25 p.e.)

Medium

Burglary and larceny: difference	2.08 (3.20 p.e.)

Differences Rendered Insignificant by State Sampling

Submedium

Assault: independent difference	4.23 (1.32 p.e.)
Rape: independent difference	2.66 (1.32 p.e.)
Vs. public welfare: independent difference	0.80 (0.46 p.e.)*

Pronounced

Other sex: independent difference	- 4.87 (2.34 p.e.)
Vs. public welfare: independent difference	1.98 (1.27 p.e.)

Table VI-58.   Gonial Angles by Offenses

	Submedium		Medium		Pronounced		Total
	No.	Per Cent	No.	Per Cent	No.	Per Cent	No.
First degree murder	35	11.22	220	70.51	57	18.27	312
Second degree murder	75	12.16	424	68.72	118	19.12	617
Assault	7	8.75	61	76.25	12	15.00	80
Robbery	53	12.80	303	73.19	58	14.01	414
Burglary and larceny	220	13.67	1132	70.35	257	15.97	1609
Forgery and fraud	50	10.71	321	68.74	96	20.56	467
Rape	21	10.66	143	72.59	33	16.75	197
Other sex	24	16.00	102	68.00	24	16.00	150
Vs. public welfare	10	4.02	179	71.89	60	24.10	249
Arson and all other	6	5.88	83	81.37	13	12.74	102
Total	501	11.94	2968	70.72	728	17.35	4197

Coefficient of mean square contingency = .10

*Signs are opposite

Table VI-59. Predictions on Basis of State Composition and Differences
from Total Series by Offenses

Gonial Angles

	Predicted Per Cent	Submedium Diff.of Subgroup and Predicted Per Cent	Diff.of Subgroup and Total Per Cent ± p.e.	x p.e.
First degree murder	11.92	- 0.70	- 0.72 ± 1.19	0.60
Second degree murder	14.25	- 2.09	0.22 ± .81	0.27
Assault	10.44	- 1.69	- 3.19 ± 2.42	1.32
Robbery	12.26	0.54	0.86 ± 1.02	0.84
Burglary and larceny	12.57	1.10	1.73 ± .42	4.12
Forgery and fraud	10.82	- 0.11	- 1.23 ± .95	1.30
Rape	10.29	0.37	- 1.28 ± 1.52	0.84
Other sex	11.79	4.21	4.06 ± 1.75	2.32
Vs. public welfare	10.91	- 6.89	- 7.92 ± 1.34	5.91
Arson and all other	11.97	- 6.09	- 6.06 ± 2.14	2.83

	Predicted Per Cent	Pronounced Diff.of Subgroup and Predicted Per Cent	Diff.of Subgroup and Total Per Cent ± p.e.	x p.e.
First degree murder	16.70	1.57	0.92 ± 1.39	0.66
Second degree murder	16.12	3.00	1.77 ± .95	1.86
Assault	14.23	0.77	- 2.35 ± 2.83	0.83
Robbery	17.20	- 3.19	- 3.34 ± 1.19	2.81
Burglary and larceny	17.06	- 1.09	- 1.38 ± .50	2.76
Forgery and fraud	20.81	- 0.25	3.21 ± 1.11	2.89
Rape	14.58	2.17	- 0.60 ± 1.77	0.34
Other sex	14.91	1.09	- 1.35 ± 2.05	0.66
Vs. public welfare	25.68	- 1.58	6.75 ± 1.57	4.30

Significant Differences Independent of State Sampling

Submedium
Vs. public welfare: independent difference   - 6.89 (5.14 p.e.)

Differences Rendered Insignificant by State Sampling

Submedium
Burglary and larceny: independent difference   1.10 (2.62 p.e.)

Pronounced
Vs. public welfare: independent difference   - 1.58 (1.01 p.e.)*

*Signs are opposite

Table VI-60.   Cheeks Wrinkling by Offenses

	Absent No.	Absent Per Cent	Slight, Medium No.	Slight, Medium Per Cent	Pronounced No.	Pronounced Per Cent	Total No.
First degree murder	122	39.23	112	36.01	77	24.76	311
Second degree murder	236	38.37	254	41.30	125	20.32	615
Assault	39	48.75	31	38.75	10	12.50	80
Robbery	269	64.98	122	29.47	23	5.56	414
Burglary and larceny	986	61.47	508	31.67	110	6.86	1604
Forgery and fraud	227	49.03	187	40.39	49	10.58	463
Rape	87	44.16	71	36.04	39	19.80	197
Other sex	59	39.33	51	34.00	40	26.57	150
Vs. public welfare	84	32.68	108	42.02	65	25.29	257
Arson and all other	54	52.94	33	32.35	15	14.71	102
Total	2163	51.59	1477	35.22	553	13.19	4193

Coefficient of mean square contingency = .26

Table VI-61. Predictions on Basis of State Composition and Differences
from Total Series by Offenses

Cheeks Wrinkling

	Predicted Per Cent	Absent Diff.of Subgroup and Predicted Per Cent	Diff.of Subgroup and Total Per Cent ± p.e.	x p.e.
First degree murder	50.69	-11.46	-12.36 ± 1.84	6.72
Second degree murder	50.26	-11.89	-13.22 ± 1.26	10.49
Assault	57.99	- 9.24	- 2.84 ± 3.73	0.76
Robbery	52.54	12.44	13.39 ± 1.57	8.53
Burglary and larceny	52.41	9.06	9.88 ± .66	14.97
Forgery and fraud	48.37	0.66	- 2.56 ± 1.48	1.73
Rape	57.74	-13.58	- 7.43 ± 2.35	3.16
Other sex	56.33	-17.00	-12.26 ± 2.70	4.54
Vs. public welfare	43.26	-10.58	-18.91 ± 2.04	9.27
Arson and all other	56.71	- 3.77	1.35 ± 3.30	0.41

	Predicted Per Cent	Slight, Medium Diff.of Subgroup and Predicted Per Cent	Diff.of Subgroup and Total Per Cent ± p.e.	x p.e.
First degree murder	35.79	0.22	0.79 ± 1.76	0.45
Second degree murder	36.79	4.51	6.08 ± 1.20	5.07
Assault	30.35	8.40	3.53 ± 3.57	0.99
Robbery	34.35	- 4.88	- 5.75 ± 1.50	3.83
Burglary and larceny	34.74	- 3.07	- 3.55 ± .63	5.64
Forgery and fraud	36.89	3.50	5.17 ± 1.41	3.67
Rape	30.93	5.11	0.82 ± 2.24	0.37
Other sex	31.99	2.01	- 1.22 ± 2.58	0.47
Vs. public welfare	40.37	1.65	6.80 ± 1.95	3.49
Arson and all other	31.76	0.59	- 2.87 ± 3.15	0.91

Table VI-61 (cont'd).

	Predicted Per Cent	Pronounced Diff.of Subgroup and Predicted Per Cent	Diff.of Subgroup and Total Per Cent ± p.e.	x p.e.
First degree murder	13.52	11.24	11.57 ± 1.25	9.26
Second degree murder	12.95	7.37	7.13 ± .85	8.39
Assault	11.66	0.84	- 0.69 ± 2.53	0.27
Robbery	13.10	- 7.54	- 7.63 ± 1.07	7.13
Burglary and larceny	12.85	- 5.99	- 6.33 ± 0.44	14.39
Forgery and fraud	14.74	- 4.16	- 2.61 ± 1.00	2.61
Rape	11.32	8.48	6.61 ± 1.58	4.18
Other sex	11.68	14.99	13.48 ± 1.83	7.37
Vs. public welfare	16.37	8.92	12.10 ± 1.38	8.77
Arson and all other	11.53	3.18	- 1.52 ± 2.23	0.68

Significant Differences Independent of State Sampling

Absent

First degree murder: independent difference	-11.46 (6.23 p.e.)
Second degree murder: independent difference	-11.89 (9.44 p.e.)
Robbery: independent difference	12.44 (7.92 p.e.)
Burglary and larceny: independent difference	9.06 (13.73 p.e.)
Rape: difference	- 7.43 (3.16 p.e.)
Other sex: difference	-12.26 (4.54 p.e.)
Vs. public welfare: independent difference	-10.58 (5.19 p.e.)

Slight, Medium

Second degree murder: independent difference	4.51 (3.76 p.e.)
Robbery: independent difference	- 4.88 (3.25 p.e.)
Burglary and larceny: independent difference	- 3.07 (4.87 p.e.)

Pronounced

First degree murder: independent difference	11.24 (8.99 p.e.)
Second degree murder: difference	7.13 (8.39 p.e.)
Robbery: independent difference	- 7.54 (7.05 p.e.)
Burglary and larceny: independent difference	- 5.99 (13.61 p.e.)
Rape: difference	6.61 (4.18 p.e.)
Other sex: difference	13.48 (7.37 p.e.)
Vs. public welfare: independent difference	8.92 (6.46 p.e.)

Differences Rendered Insignificant by State Sampling

Slight, Medium

Forgery and fraud: independent difference	3.50 (2.48 p.e.)
Vs. public welfare: independent difference	1.65 (.85 p.e.)

Table VI-62.   Teeth Wear by Offenses

	None		Slight, Medium		Pronounced		Total
	No.	Per Cent	No.	Per Cent	No.	Per Cent	No.
First degree murder	0	0	215	74.14	75	25.86	290
Second degree murder	11	1.86	442	74.54	140	23.61	593
Assault	0	0	62	80.52	15	19.48	77
Robbery	5	1.23	371	90.93	32	7.84	408
Burglary and larceny	23	1.46	1383	87.64	172	10.90	1578
Forgery and fraud	2	0.45	391	87.28	55	12.28	448
Rape	0	0	147	79.03	39	20.97	186
Other sex	0	0	101	72.66	38	27.34	139
Vs. public welfare	1	0.41	178	73.25	64	26.34	243
Arson and all other	1	1.03	77	79.38	19	19.59	97
Total	43	1.06	3367	82.95	649	15.99	4059

Coefficient of mean square contingency = .20

Table VI-63. Predictions on Basis of State Composition and Differences
from Total Series by Offenses

Teeth Wear

Slight, Medium

	Predicted Per Cent	Diff.of Subgroup and Predicted Per Cent	Diff.of Subgroup and Total Per Cent ± p.e.	x p.e.
First degree murder	81.80	· 7.66	- 8.81 ± 1.44	6.12
Second degree murder	81.07	· 6.53	- 8.41 ± .96	8.76
Assault	85.43	- 4.91	- 2.43 ± 2.86	0.85
Robbery	82.99	7.94	7.98 ± 1.19	6.71
Burglary and larceny	83.19	4.45	4.69 ± .50	9.38
Forgery and fraud	83.67	3.61	4.33 ± 1.13	3.83
Rape	84.44	- 5.41	- 3.92 ± 1.81	2.17
Other sex	84.41	-11.75	-10.29 ± 2.11	4.88
Vs. public welfare	83.67	-10.42	- 9.70 ± 1.58	6.14
Arson and all other	83.20	- 3.82	- 3.57 ± 2.54	1.41

Pronounced

	Predicted Per Cent	Diff.of Subgroup and Predicted Per Cent	Diff.of Subgroup and Total Per Cent ± p.e.	x p.e.
First degree murder	17.00	8.86	9.87 ± 1.40	7.05
Second degree murder	17.11	6.50	7.62 ± .94	8.11
Assault	14.45	5.03	3.49 ± 2.79	1.25
Robbery	15.79	- 7.95	- 8.15 ± 1.16	7.03
Burglary and larceny	15.75	- 4.85	- 5.09 ± .49	10.39
Forgery and fraud	15.65	- 3.37	- 3.71 ± 1.10	3.37
Rape	15.02	5.95	4.98 ± 1.77	2.81
Other sex	15.08	12.26	11.35 ± 2.06	5.51
Vs. public welfare	15.72	10.62	10.35 ± 1.54	6.72
Arson and all other	15.89	3.70	3.60 ± 2.48	1.45

Table VI-63 (cont'd).
Significant Differences Independent of State Sampling

Slight, Medium

First degree murder: independent difference	- 7.66 (5.32 p.e.)
Second degree murder: independent difference	- 6.53 (6.80 p.e.)
Robbery: independent difference	7.94 (6.67 p.e.)
Burglary and larceny: independent difference	4.45 (8.90 p.e.)
Forgery and fraud: independent difference	3.61 (3.20 p.e.)
Other sex: difference	-10.29 (4.88 p.e.)
Vs. public welfare: difference	- 9.70 (6.14 p.e.)

Pronounced

First degree murder: independent difference	8.86 (6.33 p.e.)
Second degree murder: independent difference	6.50 (6.92 p.e.)
Robbery: independent difference	- 7.95 (6.85 p.e.)
Burglary and larceny: independent difference	- 4.85 (9.90 p.e.)
Forgery and fraud: independent difference	- 3.37 (3.06 p.e.)
Other sex: difference	11.35 (5.51 p.e.)
Vs. public welfare: difference	10.35 (6.72 p.e.)

Table VI-64.   Teeth Caries by Offenses

	None		Few		Many		Total
	No.	Per Cent	No.	Per Cent	No.	Per Cent	No.
First degree murder	6	2.06	181	62.20	104	35.74	291
Second degree murder	26	4.36	403	67.50	168	28.14	597
Assault	2	2.60	54	70.13	21	27.27	77
Robbery	10	2.45	297	72.79	101	24.76	408
Burglary and larceny	36	2.28	1218	77.19	324	20.53	1578
Forgery and fraud	13	2.90	321	71.49	115	25.61	449
Rape	1	0.54	128	68.45	58	31.02	187
Other sex	0	0	86	61.87	53	38.13	139
Vs. public welfare	4	1.64	138	56.56	102	41.80	244
Arson and all other	2	2.06	70	72.16	25	25.77	97
Total	100	2.46	2896	71.21	1071	26.33	4067

Table VI-65. Predictions on Basis of State Composition and Differences
from Total Series by Offenses

Teeth Caries

		None		
	Predicted Per Cent	Diff.of Subgroup and Predicted Per Cent	Diff.of Subgroup and Total Per Cent ± p.e.	x p.e.
Second degree murder	2.83	1.53	1.90 ± .39	4.87
Rape	2.21	- 1.67	- 1.92 ± .74	2.59

Table VI-65 (cont'd).

Few

	Predicted Per Cent	Diff.of Subgroup and Predicted Per Cent	Diff.of Subgroup and Total Per Cent ± p.e.	x p.e.
First degree murder	73.86	-11.66	- 9.01 ± 1.73	5.21
Second degree murder	72.95	- 5.45	- 3.71 ± 1.15	3.23
Burglary and larceny	71.38	5.81	5.98 ± .60	9.97
Other sex	74.77	-12.90	- 9.34 ± 2.54	3.68
Vs. public welfare	63.16	- 6.60	-14.65 ± 1.90	7.71

Many

	Predicted Per Cent	Diff.of Subgroup and Predicted Per Cent	Diff.of Subgroup and Total Per Cent ± p.e.	x p.e.
First degree murder	23.42	12.32	9.41 ± 1.68	5.60
Burglary and larceny	26.21	- 5.68	- 5.80 ± .59	9.83
Rape	25.91	5.11	4.69 ± 2.12	2.21
Other sex	23.09	15.04	11.80 ± 2.48	4.76
Vs. public welfare	34.38	7.42	15.47 ± 1.84	8.41

Significant Differences Independent of State Sampling

None

Second degree murder: independent difference	1.53 (3.92 p.e.)

Few

First degree murder: difference	- 9.01 (5.21 p.e.)
Second degree murder: difference	- 3.71 (3.23 p.e.)
Burglary and larceny: independent difference	5.81 (9.68 p.e.)
Other sex: difference	- 9.34 (3.68 p.e.)
Vs. public welfare: independent difference	- 6.60 (3.47 p.e.)

Many

First degree murder: difference	9.41 (5.60 p.e.)
Burglary and larceny: independent difference	- 5.68 (9.63 p.e.)
Other sex: difference	11.80 (4.76 p.e.)
Vs. public welfare: independent difference	7.42 (4.03 p.e.)

Table VI-66.   Teeth Lost by Offenses

	None		Few		Many		Total
	No.	Per Cent	No.	Per Cent	No.	Per Cent	No.
First degree murder	57	18.45	142	45.96	110	35.60	309
Second degree murder	144	23.61	303	49.67	163	26.72	610
Assault	14	17.50	45	56.25	21	26.25	80
Robbery	99	24.09	229	55.72	83	20.20	411
Burglary and larceny	516	32.13	806	50.19	284	17.68	1606
Forgery and fraud	135	29.16	208	44.92	120	25.92	463
Rape	37	18.88	86	43.88	73	37.24	196
Other sex	24	16.00	65	43.33	61	40.67	150
Vs. public welfare	66	25.78	102	39.84	88	34.38	256
Arson and all other	19	18.81	48	47.52	34	33.66	101
Total	1111	26.57	2034	48.64	1037	24.80	4182

Coefficient of mean square contingency = .20

Table VI-67. Predictions on Basis of State Composition and Differences
from Total Series by Offenses

Teeth Lost

None

	Predicted Per Cent	Diff.of Subgroup and Predicted Per Cent	Diff.of Subgroup and Total Per Cent ± p.e.	x p.e.
First degree murder	25.77	- 7.32	- 8.12 ± 1.63	4.98
Second degree murder	26.91	- 3.30	- 2.96 ± 1.11	2.67
Assault	26.05	- 8.55	- 9.07 ± 3.30	2.75
Robbery	25.80	- 1.71	- 2.48 ± 1.40	1.77
Burglary and larceny	26.72	5.41	5.56 ± .59	9.42
Forgery and fraud	27.68	1.48	2.59 ± 1.31	1.98
Rape	23.22	- 4.34	- 7.69 ± 2.08	3.70
Other sex	26.14	-10.14	-10.57 ± 2.39	4.42
Vs. public welfare	29.14	- 3.36	- 0.79 ± 1.80	0.44
Arson and all other	23.97	- 5.16	- 7.76 ± 2.93	2.65

Few

	Predicted Per Cent	Diff.of Subgroup and Predicted Per Cent	Diff.of Subgroup and Total Per Cent ± p.e.	x p.e.
First degree murder	49.61	- 3.65	- 2.68 ± 1.85	1.45
Second degree murder	50.14	- 0.47	1.03 ± 1.26	0.82
Assault	47.40	8.85	7.61 ± 3.73	2.04
Robbery	49.04	6.68	7.08 ± 1.58	4.48
Burglary and larceny	48.73	1.46	1.55 ± .66	2.35
Forgery and fraud	46.86	- 1.94	- 3.72 ± 1.48	2.51
Rape	49.08	- 5.20	- 4.76 ± 2.35	2.03
Other sex	48.57	- 5.24	- 5.31 ± 2.70	1.97
Vs. public welfare	46.12	- 6.28	- 8.80 ± 2.04	4.31
Arson and all other	50.50	- 2.98	- 1.12 ± 3.31	0.34

Many

	Predicted Per Cent	Diff.of Subgroup and Predicted Per Cent	Diff.of Subgroup and Total Per Cent ± p.e.	x p.e.
First degree murder	24.62	10.98	10.80 ± 1.59	6.79
Second degree murder	22.95	3.77	1.92 ± 1.09	1.76
Assault	26.55	- 0.30	1.45 ± 3.22	0.45
Robbery	25.16	- 4.96	- 4.60 ± 1.36	3.38
Burglary and larceny	24.55	- 6.87	- 7.12 ± .57	12.49
Forgery and fraud	25.46	0.46	1.12 ± 1.28	0.88
Rape	27.70	9.54	12.44 ± 2.03	6.13
Other sex	25.29	15.38	15.87 ± 2.33	6.81
Vs. public welfare	24.75	9.63	9.58 ± 1.77	5.41
Arson and all other	25.53	8.13	8.86 ± 2.86	3.10

Table VI-67 (cont'd).
Significant Differences Independent of State Sampling

None
First degree murder: independent difference   - 7.32 (4.49 p.e.)
Burglary and larceny: independent difference   5.41 (9.17 p.e.)
Other sex: independent difference   -10.14 (4.24 p.e.)

Few
Robbery: independent difference   6.68 (4.23 p.e.)
Vs. public welfare: independent difference   - 6.28 (3.08 p.e.)

Many
First degree murder: difference   10.80 (6.79 p.e.)
Robbery: difference   - 4.60 (3.38 p.e.)
Burglary and larceny: independent difference   - 6.87 (12.05 p.e.)
Rape: independent difference   9.54 (4.70 p.e.)
Other sex: independent difference   15.38 (6.60 p.e.)
Vs. public welfare: difference   9.58 (5.41 p.e.)

Differences Rendered Insignificant by State Sampling

None
Rape: independent difference   - 4.34 (2.09 p.e.)

Many
Arson and all other: independent difference   8.13 (2.84 p.e.)

Table VI-68.   Bite by Offenses

| | Under | | Edge-to-edge | | Slight Over | | Marked Over | | Total |
	No.	Per Cent	No.	Per Cent	No.	Per Cent	No.	Per Cent	No.
First degree murder	5	1.98	65	25.69	127	50.20	56	22.13	253
Second degree murder	8	1.45	140	25.45	269	48.91	133	24.18	550
Assault	1	1.39	15	20.83	39	54.17	17	23.61	72
Robbery	4	1.04	51	13.21	234	60.62	97	25.13	386
Burglary and larceny	65	4.30	227	15.00	868	57.37	353	23.33	1513
Forgery and fraud	14	3.32	73	17.30	236	55.92	99	23.46	422
Rape	4	2.41	39	23.49	87	52.41	36	21.69	166
Other sex	1	0.79	33	25.98	63	49.61	30	23.62	127
Vs. public welfare	2	0.92	50	23.04	104	47.93	61	28.11	217
Arson and all other	4	4.35	16	17.39	51	55.44	21	22.83	92
Total	108	2.84	709	18.67	2078	54.71	903	23.78	37°8

Coefficient of mean square contingency = .14

Table VI-69. Predictions on Basis of State Composition and Differences
from Total Series by Offenses

Bite

	Predicted Per Cent	Under Diff.of Subgroup and Predicted Per Cent	Diff.of Subgroup and Total Per Cent ± p.e.	x p.e.
Burglary and larceny	2.85	1.45	1.46 ± .22	6.64
Forgery and fraud	2.88	0.44	0.48 ± .51	0.94
Arson and all other	3.43	0.92	1.51 ± 1.15	1.31

Table VI-69 (cont'd).

Edge-to-edge

	Predicted Per Cent	Diff. of Subgroup and Predicted Per Cent	Diff. of Subgroup and Total Per Cent ± p.e.	x p.e.
First degree murder	19.83	5.86	7.02 ± 1.60	4.39
Second degree murder	20.69	4.76	6.78 ± 1.04	6.52
Robbery	18.19	- 4.98	- 5.46 ± 1.27	4.30
Burglary and larceny	18.66	- 3.66	- 3.67 ± .53	6.92
Rape	17.84	5.65	4.82 ± 2.00	2.41
Other sex	18.66	7.32	7.31 ± 2.29	3.19
Vs. public welfare	15.76	7.28	4.37 ± 1.73	2.53

Slight Over

	Predicted Per Cent	Diff. of Subgroup and Predicted Per Cent	Diff. of Subgroup and Total Per Cent ± p.e.	x p.e.
First degree murder	54.17	- 3.97	- 4.51 ± 2.04	2.21
Second degree murder	54.63	- 5.72	- 5.80 ± 1.32	4.39
Robbery	54.48	6.14	5.91 ± 1.62	3.65
Other sex	55.69	- 6.08	- 5.10 ± 2.93	1.74
Vs. public welfare	53.01	- 5.08	- 6.78 ± 2.21	3.07

Marked Over

	Predicted Per Cent	Diff. of Subgroup and Predicted Per Cent	Diff. of Subgroup and Total Per Cent ± p.e.	x p.e.
Rape	23.57	- 1.88	- 2.09 ± 2.18	0.96
Vs. public welfare	28.71	- 0.60	4.33 ± 1.90	2.28

Significant Differences Independent of State Sampling

Under

Burglary and larceny: independent difference   1.45 (6.59 p.e.)

Edge-to-edge

First degree murder: independent difference   5.86 (3.66 p.e.)
Second degree murder: independent difference   4.76 (4.58 p.e.)
Robbery: independent difference   - 4.98 (3.92 p.e.)
Burglary and larceny: independent difference   - 3.66 (6.91 p.e.)
Other sex: difference   7.31 (3.19 p.e.)

Slight Over

Second degree murder: independent difference   - 5.72 (4.33 p.e.)
Robbery: difference   5.91 (3.65 p.e.)

Differences Rendered Insignificant by State Sampling

Slight Over

Vs. public welfare: independent difference   - 5.08 (2.30 p.e.)

Table VI-70.   Ear Lobes by Offenses

| | Submedium | | Medium | | Pronounced | | Total |
	No.	Per Cent	No.	Per Cent	No.	Per Cent	No.
First degree murder	35	11.25	201	64.63	75	24.12	311
Second degree murder	63	10.19	445	72.00	110	17.80	618
Assault	14	17.50	52	65.00	14	17.50	80
Robbery	55	13.28	302	72.95	57	13.77	414
Burglary and larceny	196	12.18	1170	72.72	243	15.10	1609
Forgery and fraud	38	8.15	329	70.60	99	21.24	466
Rape	26	13.33	131	67.18	38	19.49	195
Other sex	15	9.93	110	72.85	26	17.22	151
Vs. public welfare	11	4.28	191	74.32	55	21.40	257
Arson and all other	13	12.62	67	65.05	23	22.33	103
Total	466	11.08	2998	71.31	740	17.60	4204

Coefficient of mean square contingency = .10

Table VI-71. Predictions on Basis of State Composition and Differences
                   from Total Series by Offenses

Ear Lobes

Submedium

	Predicted Per Cent	Diff.of Subgroup and Predicted Per Cent	Diff.of Subgroup and Total Per Cent ± p.e.	x p.e.
First degree murder	11.82	- 0.57	0.17 ± 1.15	0.15
Second degree murder	10.80	- 0.61	- 0.89 ± .79	1.13
Assault	12.13	5.37	6.42 ± 2.35	2.73
Robbery	11.92	1.36	2.20 ± .98	2.24
Burglary and larceny	11.15	1.03	1.10 ± .42	2.62
Forgery and fraud	9.96	- 1.81	- 2.93 ± .92	3.18
Rape	12.08	1.25	2.25 ± 1.48	1.52
Other sex	11.98	- 2.05	- 1.15 ± 1.69	0.68
Vs. public welfare	8.63	- 4.35	- 6.80 ± 1.28	5.31
Arson and all other	13.53	- 0.91	1.54 ± 2.06	0.75

Medium

	Predicted Per Cent	Diff.of Subgroup and Predicted Per Cent	Diff.of Subgroup and Total Per Cent ± p.e.	x p.e.
First degree murder	69.58	- 4.95	- 6.68 ± 1.67	4.00
Second degree murder	71.82	0.18	0.69 ± 1.13	0.61
Assault	70.90	- 5.90	- 6.31 ± 3.38	1.87
Robbery	71.17	1.78	1.64 ± 1.42	1.16
Burglary and larceny	71.58	1.14	1.41 ± .59	2.39
Forgery and fraud	71.41	- 0.81	- 0.71 ± 1.34	0.53
Rape	71.45	- 4.27	- 4.13 ± 2.13	1.94
Other sex	70.87	1.98	1.54 ± 2.44	0.63
Vs. public welfare	71.48	2.84	3.01 ± 1.85	1.63
Arson and all other	69.38	- 4.33	- 6.26 ± 2.97	2.11

Table VI-71 (cont'd).

	Predicted Per Cent	Pronounced Diff.of Subgroup and Predicted Per Cent	Diff.of Subgroup and Total Per Cent ± p.e.	x p.e.
First degree murder	18.60	5.52	6.52 ± 1.40	4.65
Second degree murder	17.37	0.43	0.20 ± .95	0.21
Assault	16.96	0.54	- 0.10 ± 2.85	0.04
Robbery	16.90	- 3.13	- 3.83 ± 1.20	3.19
Burglary and larceny	17.26	- 2.16	- 2.50 ± .51	4.90
Forgery and fraud	18.63	2.61	3.64 ± 1.12	3.25
Rape	16.46	3.03	1.89 ± 1.79	1.06
Other sex	17.14	0.08	- 0.38 ± 2.05	0.18
Vs. public welfare	19.88	1.52	3.80 ± 1.55	2.45
Arson and all other	17.08	5.25	4.73 ± 2.50	1.89

Significant Differences Independent of State Sampling

Submedium

Vs. public welfare: independent difference   - 4.35 (3.40 p.e.)

Pronounced

First degree murder: independent difference   5.52 (3.94 p.e.)
Burglary and larceny: independent difference   - 2.16 (4.24 p.e.)

Differences Rendered Insignificant by State Sampling

Submedium

Forgery and fraud: independent difference   - 1.81 (1.97 p.e.)

Medium

First degree murder: independent difference   - 4.95 (2.96 p.e.)

Pronounced

Robbery: independent difference   - 3.13 (2.61 p.e.)
Forgery and fraud: independent difference   2.61 (2.33 p.e.)

Table VI-72.   Ear Lobe Attachment by Offenses

	Attached No.	Per Cent	Free No.	Per Cent	Notched,Divided No.	Per Cent	Total No.
First degree murder	105	33.76	206	66.24	0	0	311
Second degree murder	240	38.84	377	61.00	1	0.16	618
Assault	32	40.00	48	60.00	0	0	80
Robbery	182	44.07	231	55.93	0	0	413
Burglary and larceny	661	41.29	939	58.65	1	0.06	1601
Forgery and fraud	176	37.93	288	62.07	0	0	464
Rape	64	33.16	129	66.84	0	0	193
Other sex	49	32.45	102	67.55	0	0	151
Vs. public welfare	77	29.96	180	70.04	0	0	257
Arson and all other	40	38.84	63	61.16	0	0	103
Total	1626	38.80	2563	61.16	2	0.05	4191

Coefficient of mean square contingency = .10

Table VI-73.   Predictions on Basis of State Composition and Differences
from Total Series by Offenses

Ear Lobe Attachment

	Predicted Per Cent	Attached Diff. of Subgroup and Predicted Per Cent	Diff. of Subgroup and Total Per Cent ± p.e.	x p.e.
First degree murder	36.74	- 2.98	- 5.04 ± 1.79	2.82
Second degree murder	37.73	1.11	0.04 ± 1.22	0.03
Assault	40.34	- 0.34	1.20 ± 3.64	0.33
Robbery	39.48	4.59	5.27 ± 1.54	3.42
Burglary and larceny	39.36	1.93	2.49 ± .65	3.83
Forgery and fraud	38.26	- 0.33	- 0.87 ± 1.44	0.60
Rape	40.05	- 6.89	- 5.64 ± 2.31	2.44
Other sex	40.10	- 7.65	- 6.35 ± 2.62	2.42
Vs. public welfare	38.08	- 8.12	- 8.84 ± 1.98	4.46
Arson and all other	39.42	- 0.58	0.04 ± 3.20	0.01

	Predicted Per Cent	Free Diff. of Subgroup and Predicted Per Cent	Diff. of Subgroup and Total Per Cent ± p.e.	x p.e.
First degree murder	63.23	3.01	5.08 ± 1.79	2.84
Second degree murder	62.23	- 1.23	- 0.16 ± 1.22	0.13
Assault	59.59	0.41	- 1.16 ± 3.64	0.32
Robbery	60.47	- 4.54	- 5.23 ± 1.54	3.40
Burglary and larceny	60.58	- 1.93	- 2.51 ± .65	3.85
Forgery and fraud	61.70	0.37	0.91 ± 1.44	0.63
Rape	59.91	6.93	5.68 ± 2.31	2.46
Other sex	59.83	7.72	6.39 ± 2.52	2.44
Vs. public welfare	61.88	8.16	8.88 ± 1.99	4.46
Arson and all other	60.54	0.62	0 ± 3.20	0

Significant Differences Independent of State Sampling

Attached

Vs. public welfare: independent difference   - 8.12 (4.10 p.e.)

Free

Vs. public welfare: 8.15 (4.10 p.e.)

Differences Rendered Insignificant by State Sampling

Attached

Robbery: independent difference   4.59 (2.98 p.e.)
Burglary and larceny: independent difference   1.93 (2.97 p.e.)

Free

Robbery: independent difference   - 4.54 (2.95 p.e.)
Burglary and larceny: independent difference   - 1.93 (2.97 p.e.)

Table VI-74.   Roll of Helix by Offenses

	Absent		Submedium		Medium, Pronounced		Total
	No.	Per Cent	No.	Per Cent	No.	Pér Cent	No.
First degree murder	0	0	106	34.08	205	65.92	311
Second degree murder	0	0	229	37.06	389	62.94	618
Assault	0	0	27	34.18	52	65.82	79
Robbery	2	0.48	125	30.27	286	69.25	413
Burglary and larceny	0	0	486	30.22	1122	69.78	1608
Forgery and fraud	1	0.21	139	29.83	326	69.96	466
Rape	0	0	68	34.69	128	65.31	196
Other sex	0	0	48	32.22	101	67.78	149
Vs. public welfare	0	0	84	32.81	172	67.19	256
Arson and all other	1	0.97	37	35.92	65	63.11	103
Total	4	0.10	1349	32.13	2846	67.78	4199

Coefficient of mean square contingency = .10

Table VI-75. Predictions on Basis of State Composition and Differences
from Total Series by Offenses

Roll of Helix

		Submedium		
	Predicted Per Cent	Diff.of Subgroup and Predicted Per Cent	Diff.of Subgroup and Total Per Cent ± p.e.	x p.e.
First degree murder	33.51	0.57	1.95 ± 1.72	1.13
Second degree murder	34.12	2.94	4.93 ± 1.17	4.21
Assault	30.04	4.14	2.05 ± 3.51	0.58
Robbery	31.35	- 1.08	- 1.86 ± 1.47	1.26
Burglary and larceny	32.00	- 1.78	- 1.91 ± .62	3.08
Forgery and fraud	31.56	- 1.73	- 2.30 ± 1.38	1.67
Rape	29.19	5.50	2.56 ± 2.20	1.16
Other sex	31.34	0.88	0.09 ± 2.54	0.04
Vs. public welfare	32.19	0.62	0.68 ± 1.91	0.36
Arson and all other	31.72	4.20	3.79 ± 3.06	1.24

		Medium, Pronounced		
	Predicted Per Cent	Diff.of Subgroup and Predicted Per Cent	Diff.of Subgroup and Total Per Cent ± p.e.	x p.e.
First degree murder	66.36	- 0.44	- 1.86 ± 1.72	1.08
Second degree murder	65.76	- 2.82	- 4.94 ± 1.17	4.14
Assault	69.91	- 4.09	- 1.96 ± 3.51	0.56
Robbery	68.56	0.69	1.47 ± 1.47	1.00
Burglary and larceny	67.91	1.87	2.00 ± .62	3.23
Forgery and fraud	68.35	1.61	2.18 ± 1.38	1.58
Rape	70.74	- 5.43	- 2.47 ± 2.20	1.12
Other sex	68.59	- 0.81	0 ± 2.54	0
Vs. public welfare	67.71	- 0.52	- 0.59 ± 1.91	0.31
Arson and all other	68.19	- 5.08	- 4.67 ± 3.07	1.52

Table VI-75 (cont'd).
Significant Differences Independent of State Sampling

Medium, Pronounced
Burglary and larceny: independent difference   1.87 (3.02 p.e.)

Differences Rendered Insignificant by State Sampling

Submedium
Second degree murder: independent difference   2.94 (2.51 p.e.)
Burglary and larceny: independent difference   - 1.78 (2.87 p.e.)

Medium, Pronounced
Second degree murder: independent difference   - 2.82 (2.41 p.e.)

Table VI-76.   Darwin's Point by Offenses

	Absent		Submedium, Medium		Pronounced		Total
	No.	Per Cent	No.	Per Cent	No.	Per Cent	No.
First degree murder	174	55.95	99	31.83	38	12.22	311
Second degree murder	370	59.87	169	27.35	79	12.78	618
Assault	50	63.29	25	31.65	4	5.06	79
Robbery	223	54.13	130	31.55	59	14.32	412
Burglary and larceny	967	60.10	424	26.35	218	13.55	1609
Forgery and fraud	275	59.01	132	28.33	59	12.66	466
Rape	114	58.46	60	30.77	21	10.77	195
Other sex	91	61.07	39	26.17	19	12.75	149
Vs. public welfare	149	57.98	67	26.07	41	15.95	257
Arson and all other	60	58.82	35	34.31	7	6.86	102
Total	2473	58.91	1180	28.11	545	12.98	4198

Coefficient of mean square contingency = .07

Table VI-77. Predictions on Basis of State Composition and Differences
from Total Series by Offenses

Darwin's Point

	Predicted Per Cent	Absent Diff.of Subgroup and Predicted Per Cent	Diff.of Subgroup and Total Per Cent ± p.e.	x p.e.
First degree murder	55.54	0.41	- 2.96 ± 1.81	1.64
Second degree murder	58.69	1.18	0.96 ± 1.23	0.78
Assault	60.83	2.46	4.38 ± 3.70	1.18
Robbery	57.73	- 3.60	- 4.78 ± 1.55	3.08
Burglary and larceny	59.74	0.36	1.19 ± .65	1.83
Forgery and fraud	58.79	0.22	0.10 ± 1.45	0.07
Rape	59.21	- 0.75	- 0.45 ± 2.32	0.19
Other sex	60.70	0.37	2.15 ± 2.67	0.81
Vs. public welfare	59.16	- 1.18	- 0.93 ± 2.00	0.46
Arson and all other	56.80	2.02	- 0.09 ± 3.24	0.03

Table VI-77 (cont'd).

	Predicted Per Cent	Submedium Diff.of Subgroup and Predicted Per Cent	Diff.of Subgroup and Total Per Cent ± p.e.	x p.e.
First degree murder	28.70	3.13	3.72 ± 1.65	2.25
Second degree murder	26.52	0.83	- 0.76 ± 1.13	0.67
Assault	30.74	0.91	3.54 ± 3.38	1.05
Robbery	30.06	1.49	3.44 ± 1.42	2.42
Burglary and larceny	28.09	- 1.74	- 1.76 ± .59	2.98
Forgery and fraud	27.59	0.74	0.22 ± 1.32	0.17
Rape	30.47	0.30	2.66 ± 2.12	1.26
Other sex	29.07	- 2.90	- 1.94 ± 2.44	0.80
Vs. public welfare	25.02	1.05	- 2.04 ± 1.84	1.11
Arson and all other	30.96	3.35	6.20 ± 2.97	2.09

	Predicted Per Cent	Pronounced Diff.of Subgroup and Predicted Per Cent	Diff.of Subgroup and Total Per Cent ± p.e.	x p.e.
First degree murder	15.76	- 3.54	- 0.76 ± 1.23	0.62
Second degree murder	14.80	- 2.02	- 0.20 ± .84	0.24
Assault	8.43	- 3.37	- 7.92 ± 2.53	3.13
Robbery	12.20	2.12	1.34 ± 1.06	1.26
Burglary and larceny	12.16	1.39	0.57 ± .44	1.30
Forgery and fraud	13.62	- 0.96	- 0.32 ± .99	0.32
Rape	10.32	0.45	- 2.21 ± 1.58	1.40
Other sex	10.22	2.53	- 0.23 ± 1.83	0.13
Vs. public welfare	15.82	0.13	2.97 ± 1.37	2.17
Arson and all other	12.24	- 5.38	- 6.12 ± 2.22	2.76

Differences Rendered Insignificant by State Sampling

Absent

Robbery: independent difference   - 3.50 (2.32 p.e.)

Pronounced

Assault: independent difference   - 3.37 (1.33 p.e.)

Table VI-78.   Antihelix Prominence by Offenses

	Submedium No.	Per Cent	Medium No.	Per Cent	Pronounced No.	Per Cent	Total No.
First degree murder	13	4.18	257	82.64	41	13.18	311
Second degree murder	62	10.03	474	76.70	82	13.27	618
Assault	7	8.86	56	70.89	16	20.25	79
Robbery	30	7.26	321	77.72	62	15.01	413
Burglary and larceny	141	8.77	1236	76.87	231	14.36	1608
Forgery and fraud	30	6.44	369	79.18	67	14.38	466
Rape	16	8.20	146	74.87	33	16.92	195
Other sex	12	8.05	115	77.18	22	14.76	149
Vs. public welfare	26	10.16	198	77.34	32	12.50	256
Arson and all other	4	3.88	79	76.70	20	19.42	103
Total	341	8.12	3251	77.44	606	14.44	4198

Table VI-79. Predictions on Basis of State Composition and Differences
from Total Series by Offenses

Antihelix Prominence

	Predicted Per Cent	Submedium Diff.of Subgroup and Predicted Per Cent	Diff.of Subgroup and Total Per Cent ± p.e.	x p.e.
First degree murder	7.60	- 3.42	- 3.94 ± 1.00	3.94
Second degree murder	7.94	2.09	1.91 ± .69	2.77
Forgery and fraud	8.11	- 1.67	- 1.68 ± .80	2.10
Vs. public welfare	8.72	1.44	2.04 ± 1.12	1.82
Arson and all other	8.07	- 4.19	- 4.24 ± 1.79	2.37

	Predicted Per Cent	Medium Diff.of Subgroup and Predicted Per Cent	Diff.of Subgroup and Total Per Cent ± p.e.	x p.e.
First degree murder	80.89	1.75	5.20 ± 1.54	3.38
Assault	72.38	- 1.49	- 6.55 ± 3.14	2.08
Rape	74.83	0.04	- 2.57 ± 1.97	1.30

	Predicted Per Cent	Pronounced Diff.of Subgroup and Predicted Per Cent	Diff.of Subgroup and Total Per Cent ± p.e.	x p.e.
Assault	19.74	0.51	5.81 ± 2.64	2.20
Rape	16.83	0.09	2.48 ± 1.66	1.49
Vs. public welfare	11.99	0.51	- 1.94 ± 1.44	1.35
Arson and all other	15.20	4.22	4.98 ± 2.31	2.16

Significant Differences Independent of State Sampling

Submedium

First degree murder: independent difference   - 3.42 (3.42 p.e.)

Differences Rendered Insignificant by State Sampling

Medium

First degree murder: independent difference   1.75 (1.14 p.e.)

Table VI-80.   Ear Protrusion by Offenses

	Submedium		Medium		Pronounced		Total
	No.	Per Cent	No.	Per Cent	No.	Per Cent	No.
First degree murder	33	10.61	151	48.55	127	40.84	311
Second degree murder	54	8.72	338	54.60	227	36.67	619
Assault	4	5.00	42	52.50	34	42.50	80
Robbery	29	7.00	265	64.01	120	28.99	414
Burglary and larceny	119	7.39	925	57.45	566	35.16	1610
Forgery and fraud	27	5.78	281	60.17	159	34.05	467
Rape	11	5.61	107	54.59	78	39.80	196
Other sex	13	8.61	87	57.62	51	33.78	151
Vs. public welfare	19	7.39	148	57.59	90	35.02	257
Arson and all other	6	5.88	57	55.88	39	38.24	102
Total	315	7.49	2401	57.07	1491	35.44	4207

Coefficient of mean square contingency = .10

Table VI-81. Predictions on Basis of State Composition and Differences
from Total Series by Offenses

Ear Protrusion

	Predicted Per Cent	Submedium Diff.of Subgroup and Predicted Per Cent	Diff.of Subgroup and Total Per Cent ± p.e.	x p.e.
First degree murder	8.65	1.96	3.12 ± .97	3.22
Second degree murder	9.03	- 0.31	1.23 ± .66	1.86
Assault	6.60	- 1.60	- 2.49 ± 1.97	1.26
Robbery	7.21	- 0.21	- 0.49 ± .83	0.59
Burglary and larceny	7.47	- 0.08	- 0.10 ± .35	0.29
Forgery and fraud	6.38	- 0.60	- 1.71 ± .78	2.19
Rape	6.47	- 0.86	- 1.88 ± 1.24	1.52
Other sex	7.39	1.22	1.12 ± 1.42	0.79
Vs. public welfare	5.83	1.56	- 0.10 ± 1.07	0.09
Arson and all other	8.18	- 2.30	- 1.61 ± 1.74	0.92

	Predicted Per Cent	Medium Diff.of Subgroup and Predicted Per Cent	Diff.of Subgroup and Total Per Cent ± p.e.	x p.e.
First degree murder	52.82	- 4.27	- 8.52 ± 1.82	4.68
Second degree murder	53.65	0.95	- 2.47 ± 1.24	1.99
Assault	58.14	- 5.64	- 4.57 ± 3.70	1.69
Robbery	59.18	4.83	6.94 ± 1.56	4.45
Burglary and larceny	57.43	0.02	0.38 ± .65	0.58
Forgery and fraud	58.31	1.86	3.10 ± 1.46	2.12
Rape	61.72	- 7.13	- 2.48 ± 2.33	1.06
Other sex	56.86	0.76	0.55 ± 2.67	0.21
Vs. public welfare	59.10	- 1.51	0.52 ± 2.02	0.26
Arson and all other	56.39	- 0.51	- 1.19 ± 3.26	0.36

	Predicted Per Cent	Pronounced Diff.of Subgroup and Predicted Per Cent	Diff.of Subgroup and Total Per Cent ± p.e.	x p.e.
First degree murder	38.54	2.30	5.40 ± 1.76	3.07
Second degree murder	37.32	- 0.65	1.23 ± 1.20	1.02
Assault	35.27	7.23	7.06 ± 3.58	1.97
Robbery	33.62	- 4.63	- 6.45 ± 1.50	4.30
Burglary and larceny	35.10	0.06	- 0.28 ± .63	0.44
Forgery and fraud	35.31	- 1.26	- 1.39 ± 1.41	0.99
Rape	31.82	7.98	4.36 ± 2.25	1.94
Other sex	35.76	- 1.98	- 1.66 ± 2.58	0.64
Vs. public welfare	35.07	- 0.05	- 0.42 ± 1.95	0.22
Arson and all other	35.43	2.81	2.80 ± 3.15	0.89

Table VI-81 (cont'd).
Significant Differences Independent of State Sampling

Medium

Robbery: independent difference   4.83 (3.10 p.e.)

Pronounced

Robbery: independent difference   - 4.63 (3.09 p.e.)

Differences Rendered Insignificant by State Sampling

Submedium

First degree murder: independent difference   1.96 (2.02 p.e.)

Medium

First degree murder: independent difference   - 4.27 (2.35 p.e.)

Pronounced

First degree murder: independent difference   2.30 (1.31 p.e.)

Table VI-82.   Temporal Fullness by Offenses

| | Submedium | | Medium | | Pronounced | | Total |
	No.	Per Cent	No.	Per Cent	No.	Per Cent	No.
First degree murder	54	17.36	228	73.31	29	9.32	311
Second degree murder	95	15.37	445	72.01	78	12.62	618
Assault	11	13.75	64	80.00	5	6.25	80
Robbery	72	17.48	309	75.00	31	7.52	412
Burglary and larceny	271	16.87	1165	72.54	170	10.58	1606
Forgery and fraud	100	21.55	333	71.77	31	6.68	464
Rape	22	11.22	160	81.63	14	7.14	196
Other sex	20	13.24	110	72.85	21	13.91	151
Vs. public welfare	72	28.02	169	65.76	16	6.22	257
Arson and all other	25	24.27	69	66.99	9	8.74	103
Total	742	17.68	3052	72.70	404	9.62	4198

Table VI-83. Predictions on Basis of State Composition and Differences
from Total Series by Offenses

Temporal Fullness

	Predicted Per Cent	Submedium Diff.of Subgroup and Predicted Per Cent	Diff.of Subgroup and Total Per Cent ± p.e.	x p.e.
Assault	10.74	3.01	- 3.93 ± 2.85	1.38
Forgery and fraud	19.53	2.02	3.87 ± 1.13	3.42
Rape	13.18	- 1.96	- 6.46 ± 1.79	3.61
Other sex	13.14	0.10	- 4.44 ± 2.06	2.16
Vs. public welfare	23.57	4.45	10.34 ± 1.56	6.63
Arson and all other	14.85	9.42	6.59 ± 2.50	2.64

Table VI-83 (cont'd).

Medium

	Predicted Per Cent	Diff. of Subgroup and Predicted Per Cent	Diff. of Subgroup and Total Per Cent ± p.e.	x p.e.
Assault	79.70	0.03	7.30 ± 3.32	2.20
Rape	79.99	1.64	8.93 ± 2.10	4.25
Vs. public welfare	69.81	- 4.05	- 6.94 ± 1.81	3.83
Arson and all other	75.80	- 8.81	- 5.71 ± 2.92	1.96

Pronounced

	Predicted Per Cent	Diff. of Subgroup and Predicted Per Cent	Diff. of Subgroup and Total Per Cent ± p.e.	x p.e.
Second degree murder	12.59	0.03	3.00 ± .74	4.05
Assault	9.56	- 3.31	- 3.37 ± 2.21	1.52
Other sex	10.43	3.48	4.29 ± 1.59	2.70
Vs. public welfare	6.62	- 0.40	- 3.40 ± 1.20	2.83

Differences Rendered Insignificant by State Sampling

Submedium

Forgery and fraud: independent difference	2.02 (1.79 p.e.)
Rape: independent difference	- 1.96 (1.10 p.e.)
Vs. public welfare: independent difference	4.45 (2.85 p.e.)

Medium

Rape: independent difference	1.64 (.78 p.e.)
Vs. public welfare: independent difference	- 4.05 (2.24 p.e.)

Pronounced

Second degree murder: independent difference	.03 (.04 p.e.)

Table VI-84.   Lambdoid Flattening by Offenses

	Absent No.	Absent Per Cent	Present No.	Present Per Cent	Total No.
First degree murder	188	60.64	122	39.36	310
Second degree murder	399	64.67	218	35.33	617
Assault	42	53.16	37	46.84	79
Robbery	271	66.26	138	33.74	409
Burglary and larceny	1096	68.16	512	31.84	1608
Forgery and fraud	309	66.74	154	33.26	463
Rape	124	63.26	72	36.74	196
Other sex	99	65.56	52	34.44	151
Vs. public welfare	201	78.21	56	21.79	257
Arson and all other	67	66.34	34	33.66	101
Total	2796	66.71	1395	33.29	4191

Coefficient of mean square contingency = .10

Table VI-85. Predictions on Basis of State Composition and Differences
from Total Series by Offenses

Lambdoid Flattening

Absent

	Predicted Per Cent	Diff.of Subgroup and Predicted Per Cent	Diff.of Subgroup and Total Per Cent ± p.e.	x p.e.
First degree murder	63.88	- 3.24	- 6.07 ± 1.76	3.45
Second degree murder	67.19	- 2.52	- 2.04 ± 1.18	1.73
Assault	63.36	-10.20	-13.55 ± 3.56	3.81
Robbery	66.79	- 0.53	- 0.45 ± 1.49	0.30
Burglary and larceny	66.46	1.70	1.45 ± .62	2.34
Forgery and fraud	66.46	0.28	0.03 ± 1.40	0.02
Rape	64.43	- 1.17	- 3.45 ± 2.22	1.55
Other sex	61.58	3.98	- 1.15 ± 2.54	0.45
Vs. public welfare	76.80	1.41	11.50 ± 1.92	5.99
Arson and all other	62.76	3.58	- 0.37 ± 3.12	0.12

Present

	Predicted Per Cent	Diff.of Subgroup and Predicted Per Cent	Diff.of Subgroup and Total Per Cent ± p.e.	x p.e.
First degree murder	36.12	3.24	6.07 ± 1.76	3.45
Second degree murder	32.81	2.52	2.04 ± 1.18	1.73
Assault	36.64	10.20	13.55 ± 3.56	3.81
Robbery	33.21	.53	0.45 ± 1.49	0.30
Burglary and larceny	33.54	- 1.70	- 1.45 ± .62	2.34
Forgery and fraud	33.54	- .28	- 0.03 ± 1.40	0.02
Rape	35.57	1.17	3.45 ± 2.22	1.55
Other sex	38.42	- 3.98	1.15 ± 2.54	0.45
Vs. public welfare	23.20	- 1.41	-11.50 ± 1.92	5.99
Arson and all other	37.24	- 3.58	0.37 ± 3.12	0.12

Differences Rendered Insignificant by State Sampling

Absent

First degree murder: independent difference	- 3.24 (1.84 p.e.)
Assault: independent difference	-10.20 (2.86 p.e.)
Vs. public welfare: independent difference	1.41 (.73 p.e.)

Present

First degree murder: independent difference	3.24 (1.84 p.e.)
Assault: independent difference	10.20 (2.86 p.e.)
Vs. public welfare: independent difference	- 1.41 (.73 p.e.)

Table VI-86.   Asymmetry by Offenses

| | Right | | Left | | None | | Total |
	No.	Per Cent	No.	Per Cent	No.	Per Cent	No.
First degree murder	54	17.76	51	16.78	199	65.46	304
Second degree murder	87	14.26	101	16.56	422	69.18	610
Assault	12	15.38	11	14.10	55	70.51	78
Robbery	49	12.34	41	10.33	307	77.33	397
Burglary and larceny	193	12.55	178	11.57	1167	75.88	1538
Forgery and fraud	53	12.24	52	12.00	328	75.75	433
Rape	38	20.00	22	11.58	130	68.42	190
Other sex	32	21.33	17	11.33	101	67.33	150
Vs. public welfare	26	10.70	41	16.87	176	72.43	243
Arson and all other	14	14.00	13	13.00	73	73.00	100
Total	558	13.80	527	13.03	2958	73.16	4043

Coefficient of mean square contingency = .10

Table VI-87. Predictions on Basis of State Composition and Differences
from Total Series by Offenses

Asymmetry

	Predicted Por Cent	Right Diff.of Subgroup and Predicted Per Cent	Diff.of Subgroup and Total Per Cent ± p.e.	x p.e.
First degree murder	14.41	3.35	3.96 ± 1.28	3.09
Second degree murder	15.70	- 1.44	0.46 ± .87	0.53
Assault	12.78	2.60	1.58 ± 2.61	0.60
Robbery	12.53	- 0.19	- 1.46 ± 1.11	1.32
Burglary and larceny	13.78	- 1.23	- 1.25 ± .46	2.72
Forgery and fraud	12.13	0.11	- 1.56 ± 1.05	1.49
Rape	12.42	7.58	6.20 ± 1.65	3.76
Other sex	14.07	7.26	7.53 ± 1.86	4.05
Vs. public welfare	11.83	- 1.13	- 3.10 ± 1.44	2.15
Arson and all other	13.98	0.02	0.20 ± 2.30	0.09

	Predicted Per Cent	Left Diff.of Subgroup and Predicted Per Cent	Diff.of Subgroup and Total Per Cent ± p.e.	x p.e.
First degree murder	13.41	3.37	3.75 ± 1.25	3.00
Second degree murder	14.22	2.34	3.53 ± .85	4.15
Assault	10.88	3.22	1.07 ± 2.54	0.42
Robbery	12.99	- 2.66	- 2.70 ± 1.08	2.50
Burglary and larceny	13.00	- 1.43	- 1.46 ± .46	3.17
Forgery and fraud	13.08	- 1.08	- 1.03 ± 1.03	1.00
Rape	11.13	0.45	- 1.45 ± 1.60	0.91
Other sex	11.84	- 0.51	- 1.70 ± 1.82	0.93
Vs. public welfare	14.11	2.76	3.84 ± 1.41	2.72
Arson and all other	12.20	0.80	- 0.03 ± 2.24	0.01

Table VI-87 (cont'd).

	Predicted Per Cent	None Diff. of Subgroup and Predicted Per Cent	Diff. of Subgroup and Total Per Cent ± p.e.	x p.e.
First degree murder	72.18	- 6.72	- 7.70 ± 1.65	4.67
Second degree murder	70.07	- 0.89	- 3.98 ± 1.11	3.59
Assault	76.33	- 5.82	- 2.65 ± 3.35	0.79
Robbery	74.48	2.85	4.17 ± 1.42	2.94
Burglary and larceny	73.22	2.66	2.72 ± .60	4.53
Forgery and fraud	74.78	0.97	2.59 ± 1.36	1.90
Rape	76.45	- 8.03	- 4.74 ± 2.12	2.24
Other sex	74.09	- 6.76	- 5.83 ± 2.39	2.44
Vs. public welfare	74.05	- 1.62	- 0.73 ± 1.86	0.39
Arson and all other	73.82	- 0.82	- 0.16 ± 2.95	0.05

Significant Differences Independent of State Sampling

Right

Rape: difference — 6.20 (3.76 p.e.)
Other sex: independent difference — 7.26 (3.90 p.e.)

Left

Burglary and larceny: independent difference — - 1.43 (3.11 p.e.)

None

First degree murder: independent difference — - 6.72 (3.07 p.e.)
Burglary and larceny: independent difference — 2.66 (4.43 p.e.)

Differences Rendered Insignificant by State Sampling

Right

First degree murder: independent difference — 3.35 (2.62 p.e.)

Left

First degree murder: independent difference — 3.37 (2.70 p.e.)
Second degree murder: independent difference — 2.34 (2.75 p.e.)

None

Second degree murder: independent difference — - .89 (.80 p.e.)

Table VI-88.   Neck by Offenses

	Medium in Length, Breadth No.	Per Cent	Long, Thin No.	Per Cent	Short, Thick No.	Per Cent	Total No.
First degree murder	201	64.63	91	29.26	19	6.11	311
Second degree murder	369	59.90	209	33.93	38	6.17	616
Assault	55	68.75	22	27.50	3	3.75	80
Robbery	286	69.08	105	25.36	23	5.56	414
Burglary and larceny	1093	68.18	448	27.95	62	3.87	1603
Forgery and fraud	319	68.60	119	25.59	27	5.81	465
Rape	140	71.80	47	24.10	8	4.10	195
Other sex	102	67.55	44	29.14	5	3.31	151
Vs. public welfare	183	71.76	57	22.35	15	5.88	255
Arson and all other	75	72.82	24	23.30	4	3.88	103
Total	2823	67.33	1166	27.81	204	4.86	4193

Coefficient of mean square contingency = .10

Table VI-89. Predictions on Basis of State Composition and Differences
from Total Series by Offenses

Neck

Medium in Length, Breadth

	Predicted Per Cent	Diff.of Subgroup and Predicted Per Cent	Diff.of Subgroup and Total Per Cent ± p.e.	x p.e.
First degree murder	64.92	- 0.29	- 2.70 ± 1.73	1.56
Second degree murder	60.96	- 1.06	- 7.43 ± 1.18	6.30
Assault	71.69	- 2.94	1.42 ± 3.50	.41
Robbery	69.35	- 0.27	1.75 ± 1.48	1.18
Burglary and larceny	67.09	1.09	0.85 ± .62	1.37
Forgery and fraud	69.80	- 1.20	1.27 ± 1.38	.92
Rape	74.42	- 2.62	4.47 ± 2.21	2.02
Other sex	68.62	- 1.07	0.22 ± 2.53	.09
Vs. public welfare	69.85	1.90	4.43 ± 1.92	2.31
Arson and all other	69.02	3.80	5.49 ± 3.08	1.78

Long, Thin

	Predicted Per Cent	Diff.of Subgroup and Predicted Per Cent	Diff.of Subgroup and Total Per Cent ± p.e.	x p.e.
First degree murder	29.50	- 0.24	1.45 ± 1.65	.88
Second degree murder	33.90	0.03	6.12 ± 1.13	5.42
Assault	24.02	3.48	- 0.31 ± 3.35	.09
Robbery	22.79	2.57	- 2.45 ± 1.41	1.74
Burglary and larceny	28.19	- 0.24	0.14 ± .59	.24
Forgery and fraud	25.29	0.30	- 2.22 ± 1.32	1.68
Rape	21.33	2.77	- 3.71 ± 2.11	1.76
Other sex	26.86	2.28	1.33 ± 2.42	0.55
Vs. public welfare	25.03	- 2.68	- 5.46 ± 1.84	2.97
Arson and all other	25.95	- 2.65	- 4.51 ± 2.94	1.53

Short, Thick

	Predicted Per Cent	Diff.of Subgroup and Predicted Per Cent	Diff.of Subgroup and Total Per Cent ± p.e.	x p.e.
First degree murder	5.58	0.53	1.25 ± .80	1.56
Second degree murder	5.14	1.03	1.31 ± .54	2.43
Assault	4.29	- 0.54	- 1.11 ± 1.60	.69
Robbery	4.83	0.73	0.70 ± .67	1.04
Burglary and larceny	4.72	- 0.85	- 0.99 ± .28	3.54
Forgery and fraud	4.90	0.91	0.95 ± .63	1.51
Rape	4.26	- 0.16	- 0.76 ± 1.01	.75
Other sex	4.52	- 1.21	- 1.55 ± 1.16	1.34
Vs. public welfare	5.10	0.78	1.02 ± .88	1.16
Arson and all other	5.04	- 1.16	- 0.98 ± 1.41	.70

Table VI-89 (cont'd).
Significant Differences Independent of State Sampling

Short, Thick
Burglary and larceny: independent difference   - .85 (3.04 p.e.)

Differences Rendered Insignificant by State Sampling

Medium in Length, Breadth
Second degree murder: independent difference   - 1.06 (.90 p.e.)

Long, Thin
Second degree murder: independent difference   .03 (.03 p.e.)

Table VI-90.   Shoulders Slope by Offenses

| | Slight | | Medium | | Pronounced | | Total |
	No.	Per Cent	No.	Per Cent	No.	Per Cent	No.
First degree murder	17	5.47	223	71.70	71	22.83	311
Second degree murder	17	2.76	433	70.18	167	27.07	617
Assault	1	1.25	69	86.25	10	12.50	80
Robbery	12	2.91	324	78.64	76	18.45	412
Burglary and larceny	37	2.30	1214	75.59	355	22.10	1606
Forgery and fraud	9	1.93	362	77.68	95	20.39	466
Rape	6	3.08	163	83.59	26	13.33	195
Other sex	3	1.99	120	79.47	28	18.54	151
Vs. public welfare	6	2.35	205	80.38	44	17.25	255
Arson and all other	1	0.97	83	80.58	19	18.45	103
Total	109	2.60	3196	76.17	891	21.23	4196

Coefficient of mean square contingency = .10

Table VI-91. Predictions on Basis of State Composition and Differences
from Total Series by Offenses

Shoulders Slope

	Predicted Per Cent	Slight Diff.of Subgroup and Predicted Per Cent	Diff.of Subgroup and Total Per Cent ± p.e.	x p.e.
First degree murder	2.68	2.79	2.87 ± .59	4.86

	Predicted Per Cent	Medium Diff.of Subgroup and Predicted Per Cent	Diff.of Subgroup and Total Per Cent ± p.e.	x p.e.
First degree murder	73.23	- 1.53	- 4.47 ± 1.56	2.86
Second degree murder	70.96	- 0.78	- 5.99 ± 1.07	5.60
Assault	77.38	8.87	10.08 ± 3.18	3.17
Robbery	78.88	- 0.24	2.47 ± 1.34	1.84
Burglary and larceny	76.08	- 0.49	- 0.58 ± .57	1.02
Forgery and fraud	78.59	- 0.91	1.51 ± 1.25	1.21
Rape	80.98	2.61	7.42 ± 2.01	3.59
Other sex	75.72	3.75	3.30 ± 2.29	1.44
Vs. public welfare	80.39	- 0.01	4.21 ± 1.74	2.42
Arson and all other	76.84	3.74	4.41 ± 2.80	1.58

Table VI-91 (cont'd).

	Predicted Per Cent	Pronounced Diff. of Subgroup and Predicted Per Cent	Diff. of Subgroup and Total Per Cent ± p.e.	x p.e.
First degree murder	24.09	- 1.26	1.60 ± 1.50	1.07
Second degree murder	26.26	0.81	5.84 ± 1.02	5.72
Assault	19.47	- 6.97	- 8.73 ± 3.06	2.85
Robbery	18.52	- 0.07	- 2.78 ± 1.29	2.16
Burglary and larceny	21.25	0.85	0.87 ± .54	1.61
Forgery and fraud	19.21	1.18	- 0.84 ± 1.21	0.69
Rape	16.13	- 2.80	- 7.90 ± 1.93	4.09
Other sex	21.29	- 2.75	- 2.69 ± 2.21	1.22
Vs. public welfare	18.11	- 0.86	- 3.98 ± 1.67	2.38
Arson and all other	20.21	- 1.76	- 2.79 ± 2.68	1.04

Significant Difference Independent of State Sampling

Slight

First degree murder: independent difference   2.79 (4.73 p.e.)

Differences Rendered Insignificant by State Sampling

Medium

Second degree murder: independent difference   - .78 (.73 p.e.)
Assault: independent difference   8.87 (2.79 p.e.)
Rape: independent difference   2.61 (1.30 p.e.)

Pronounced

Second degree murder: independent difference   .81 (.79 p.e.)
Rape: independent difference   - 2.80 (1.45 p.e.)

Table VI-92.   Summary of Contingencies of Observation with Offense

Class A.

Hair form	.10
Hair color	.22
Iris	.10
Eye folds	.10
Forehead slope	.10
Nasal root height	.14
Nasal bridge height	.14
Nasal septum inclination	.14
Chin form	.10
Cheeks wrinkling	.26
Teeth wear	.20
Teeth lost	.20
Bite	.14
Ear lobes development	.10
Ear lobes attachment	.10
Roll of helix	.10
Ear protrusion	.10
Neck	.10
Shoulder slope	.10

Class B.

Eye color	.14
Sclera	.10
Eyebrow thickness	.06
Forehead height	.08
Nasal root breadth	.10
Nasal profile	.10
Nasal tip thickness	.10
Nasal septum deflection	.10
Lips integumental thickness	.10
Lip seam	.10
Facial prognathism	.10
Gonial angles	.10
Asymmetry	.10

Class C.

Hair quantity, head	.14
Hair quantity, beard	.10
Hair quantity, body	.10
Nasal bridge breadth	.10
Lips membranous thickness	.14
Alveolar prognathism	.10
Malars prominence	.14
Darwin's point	.07
Lambdoid flattening	.10

Table VI-93. Summary of Morphological Differentiation of Offenses from
Total Series on Basis of State Composition

First Degree Murder

	Significant Independent of State Sampling		Crude Differences Invalidated by State Sampling		Insignificant Difference	
	Diff.	x p.e.	Diff.	x p.e.	Diff.	x p.e.
Hair quantity, head						
Small	6.60	5.74	-	-	-	-
Large	-	-	-	-	- 1.68	1.18
Hair quantity, beard						
Small	-	-	-11.78	6.69	(0.65	0.37)*
Large	-	-	-	-	1.65	1.31
Hair quantity, body						
Small	-12.07*	6.52	-	-	-	-
Large	-	-	4.63	3.65	(2.66	2.09)*
Skin color						
Red white	-	-	-	-	3.08	1.80
Hair form						
Straight	-	-	4.36	3.35	(3.27	2.52)*
Low waves	-	-	- 3.24	3.18	(- 2.12	2.08)*
Deep waves	-	-	-	-	0.76	1.06
Curly	-	-	-	-	- 0.26	0.48
Hair color						
Black	-	-	-	-	0.12	0.15
Dark brown	-	-	-	-	1.17	0.67
Reddish brown	-	-	-	-	- 0.71	0.48
Light brown	-	-	-	-	- 1.97	1.23
Ash-blond	-	-	-	-	- 1.01	1.84
Golden	-	-	-	-	- 1.23	1.84
Red	-	-	- 2.25	3.17	(- 2.03	2.86)*
Gray, white	5.80*	7.16*	-	-	-	-
Eye color						
Dark brown	-	-	-	-	- 0.74	1.14
Light brown	-	-	-	-	- 0.82	1.30
Blue-brown	-	-	-	-	3.16	2.14
Gray-brown	-	-	-	-	2.56	1.83
Green-brown	-	-	-	-	- 2.32	1.42
Blue	-	-	-	-	1.16	0.81
Blue-gray	-	-	-	-	- 3.01	2.76
Iris						
Homogeneous	-	-	-	-	0.34	0.35
Rayed	-	-	-	-	- 0.89	0.54
Zoned	-	-	-	-	- 1.92	1.12
Speckled	-	-	-	-	2.68	1.66
Diffused	-	-	-	-	- 0.21	0.20
Eye folds						
Epicanthus	-	-	-	-	2.01	2.64
Median	-	-	-	-	- 3.57	2.90
External	-	-	-	-	0.67	0.64
Absent	-	-	-	-	0.89	0.55
Eyebrows thickness						
Submedium	-	-	-	-	0.76	1.01
Pronounced	-	-	-	-	2.01	1.17
Forehead height						
Submedium	-	-	-	-	0.18	0.15
Medium	-	-	-	-	- 2.64	1.49
Pronounced	-	-	-	-	2.45	1.55

*Independent difference corrected for state sampling.

Table VI-93 (cont'd).

	Significant and Independent of State Sampling		Crude Differences Invalidated by State Sampling		Insignificant Difference	
	Diff.	x p.e.	Diff.	x p.e.	Diff.	x p.e.
Forehead slope						
Absent, submedium	-	-	-	-	1.47	1.46
Medium	-	-	- 5.73	3.17	(- 1.12	0.62)*
Pronounced	-	-	-	-	4.25	2.43
Nasion depression						
Medium	-	-	-	-	- 4.55	2.77
Pronounced	-	-	5.22	3.68	(0.03	0.02)*
Nasal root height						
Submedium	-	-	-	-	1.27	2.76
Medium	- 4.29*	3.02*	-	-	-	-
Pronounced	-	-	-	-	3.37	2.48
Nasal root breadth						
Submedium	-	-	-	-	- 1.96	2.48
Medium	-	-	-	-	3.67	2.87
Pronounced	-	-	-	-	- 1.72	1.61
Nasal bridge height						
Medium	-	-	-11.23	6.20	(- 3.10	1.71)*
Pronounced	-	-	10.60	5.89	(2.59	1.44)*
Nasal bridge breadth						
Submedium	- 2.53*	3.78*	-	-	-	-
Pronounced	-	-	-	-	- 0.09	0.07
Nasal profile						
Concave	- 5.02*	3.28*	-	-	-	-
Straight	-	-	-	-	- 0.67	0.57
Convex	-	-	-	-	1.99 ⌐	1.33
Concavo-convex	-	-	-	-	5.19	2.82
Nasal tip thickness						
Submedium	-	-	-	-	2.55	2.30
Medium	-	-	-	-	- 0.53	0.31
Pronounced	-	-	-	-	- 2.01	1.34
Nasal septum inclination						
Up	- 6.28	3.67	-	-	-	-
Down	-	-	-	-	5.12	2.99
Nasal septum deflection						
Right	-	-	-	-	- 1.36	0.87
Left	-	-	-	-	2.93	2.71
Absent	-	-	-	-	- 1.56	0.90
Lips integumental thickness						
Submedium	-	-	-	-	0.70	0.58
Medium	-	-	-	-	- 2.75	1.96
Pronounced	-	-	-	-	2.05	2.44
Lips membranous thickness						
Submedium	-	-	-	-	3.84	2.80
Medium	-	-	-	-	- 0.30	0.18
Upper, small; lower, pronounced	-	-	-	-	- 3.56	2.94
Pronounced	-	-	-	-	0	0
Lip seam						
Absent, submedium	-	-	-	-	2.83	2.18
Medium	-	-	-	-	- 2.58	1.49
Pronounced	-	-	-	-	- 0.26	0.18

*Independent difference corrected for state sampling.

Table VI-93 (cont'd).

	Significant and Independent of State Sampling		Crude Differences Invalidated by State Sampling		Insignificant Difference	
	Diff.	λ p.e.	Diff.	x p.e.	Diff.	x p.e.
Alveolar prognathism						
Absent	-	-	-	-	- 1.31	.94
Submedium	-	-	-	-	3.29	2.65
Medium	-	-	-	-	- 1.55	2.12
Chin form						
Median	7.77	4.27	-	-	-	-
Bilateral	- 7.77	4.27	-	-	-	-
Malars prominence						
Submedium	3.51*	4.13*	-	-	-	-
Medium	-	-	-	-	- 1.73	1.01
Pronounced	-	-	-	-	- 2.26	1.41
Cheeks fullness						
Submedium	6.04	3.82	-	-	-	-
Medium	-	-	-	-	- 2.93	1.60
Pronounced	-	-	-	-	- 3.11	2.19
Gonial angles						
Submedium	-	-	-	-	- 0.72	0.60
Pronounced	-	-	-	-	0.92	0.66
Cheeks wrinkling						
Absent	-11.46*	6.23*	-	-	-	-
Slight, medium	-	-	-	-	0.79	0.45
Pronounced	11.24*	8.99*	-	-	-	-
Teeth wear						
Slight, medium	- 7.66*	5.32*	-	-	-	-
Pronounced	8.86*	6.33*	-	-	-	-
Teeth caries						
Few	- 9.01	5.21	-	-	-	-
Many	9.41	5.60	-	-	-	-
Teeth lost						
None	- 7.32*	4.49*	-	-	-	-
Few	-	-	-	-	- 2.68	1.45
Many	10.80	6.79	-	-	-	-
Bite						
Edge-to-edge	5.86*	3.66*	-	-	-	-
Slight over	-	-	-	-	- 4.51	2.21
Ear lobes						
Submedium	-	-	-	-	0.17	0.15
Medium	-	-	- 6.68	4.00	(- 4.95	2.96)*
Pronounced	5.52*	3.94*	-	-	-	-
Ear lobe attachment						
Attached	-	-	-	-	- 5.04	2.82
Free	-	-	-	-	5.08	2.84
Roll of helix						
Submedium	-	-	-	-	1.95	1.13
Medium, pronounced	-	-	-	-	- 1.86	1.08
Darwin's point						
Absent	-	-	-	-	- 2.96	1.64
Submedium	-	-	-	-	3.72	2.25
Pronounced	-	-	-	-	- 0.76	0.62
Antihelix prominence						
Submedium	- 3.42	3.42	-	-	-	-
Medium	-	-	5.20	3.38	(1.75	1.14)*

*Independent difference corrected for state sampling.

Table VI-93 (cont'd).

	Significant and Independent of State Sampling		Crude Differences Invalidated by State Sampling		Insignificant Difference	
	Diff.	x p.e.	Diff.	x p.e.	Diff.	x p.e.
Ear protrusion						
Submedium	-	-	3.12	3.22	(1.96	2.02)*
Medium	-	-	- 8.52	4.68	(- 4.27	2.35)*
Pronounced	-	-	5.40	3.07	(2.30	1.31)*
Lambdoid flattening						
Absent	-	-	- 6.07	3.45	(- 3.24	1.84)*
Present	-	-	6.07	3.45	(3.24	1.84)*
Asymmetry						
Right	-	-	3.96	3.09	(3.35	2.62)*
Left	-	-	3.75	3.00	(3.37	2.70)*
None	- 6.72	3.07	-	-	-	-
Neck						
Medium length,breadth	-	-	-	-	- 2.70	1.56
Long and thin	-	-	-	-	1.45	0.88
Short and thick	-	-	-	-	1.25	1.56
Shoulders slope						
Slight	2.79*	4.73*	-	-	-	-
Medium	-	-	-	-	- 4.47	2.86
Pronounced	-	-	-	-	1.60	1.07

Table VI-94. Summary of Morphological Differentiation of Offenses from
Total Series on Basis of State Composition

Second Degree Murder

	Significant and Independent of State Sampling		Crude Differences Invalidated by State Sampling		Insignificant Differences	
	Diff.	x p.e.	Diff.	x p.e.	Diff.	x p.e.
Hair quantity, head						
Small	-	-	-	-	1.08	1.37
Large	-	-	-	-	0.40	0.41
Hair quantity, beard						
Small	-	-	-	-	2.94	2.45
Large	-	-	- 5.05	5.87	(- 1.34	1.56)*
Hair quantity, body						
Small	- 6.99	5.55	-	-	-	-
Large	-	-	-	-	1.22	1.42
Skin color						
Red white	-	-	-	-	3.35	2.86
Pale white	-	-	- 6.06	5.01	(- 1.52	1.26)
Hair form						
Straight	-	-	-	-	- 0.42	0.47
Low waves	-	-	-	-	0.53	0.76
Deep waves	-	-	-	-	0.40	0.82
Curly	-	-	-	-	- 0.41	1.11

*Independent difference corrected for state sampling.

Table VI-94 (cont'd).	Significant and Independent of State Sampling		Crude Differences Invalidated by State Sampling		Insignificant Difference	
	Diff.	x p.e.	Diff.	x p.e.	Diff.	x p.e.
Hair color						
Black	-	-	-	-	1.54	2.80
Dark brown	-	-	-	-	2.86	2.38
Reddish brown	-	-	-	-	- 2.62	2.59
Light brown	-	-	-	-	- 0.35	0.32
Ash-blond	-	-	-	-	- 0.92	2.16
Golden	- 1.58*	3.43*	-	-	-	-
Red	-	-	-	-	- 0.91	1.86
Gray, white	1.99	3.62	-	-	-	-
Eye color						
Dark brown	-	-	-	-	- 0.23	0.51
Light brown	-	-	-	-	- 0.96	2.23
Blue-brown	-	-	3.35	3.32	(0.54	0.53)*
Gray-brown	-	-	-	-	0.29	0.31
Green-brown	-	-	-	-	0.32	0.29
Blue	-	-	-	-	0.02	0.02
Blue-gray	-	-	- 2.79	3.77	(- 0.59	0.80)*
Iris						
Homogeneous	-	-	-	-	- 0.29	0.43
Rayed	-	-	-	-	1.90	1.71
Zoned	-	-	- 6.39	5.51	(- 2.86	2.47)*
Speckled	-	-	5.31	4.87	(1.63	1.50)*
Diffused	-	-	-	-	- 0.52	0.74
Eye folds						
Epicanthus	-	-	-	-	0.31	0.61
Median	-	-	-	-	- 1.66	1.98
External	-	-	-	-	0.79	1.10
Absent	-	-	-	-	0.56	0.50
Eyebrows thickness						
Submedium	-	-	-	-	0.65	1.27
Pronounced	-	-	-	-	- 1.70	1.45
Forehead height						
Submedium	-	-	2.87	3.46	(0.55	0.66)*
Medium	-	-	-	-	- 1.03	0.85
Pronounced	-	-	-	-	- 1.85	1.71
Forehead slope						
Absent, submedium	-	-	-	-	1.07	1.55
Medium	-	-	- 7.41	5.98	(- 2.32	1.87)*
Pronounced	-	-	6.34	5.33	(3.35	2.82)*
Nasion depression						
Submedium	-	-	-	-	2.11	2.89
Medium	-	-	- 8.10	7.23	(- 1.55	1.38)*
Pronounced	-	-	5.93	6.18	(1.94	2.02)*
Nasal root height						
Submedium	-	-	-	-	0.33	1.03
Medium	-	-	- 3.53	3.68	(1.32	1.38)*
Pronounced	-	-	3.21	3.45	(- 1.26	1.36)*
Nasal root breadth						
Submedium	-	-	-	-	1.28	2.37
Medium	-	-	-	-	2.50	2.95
Pronounced	-	-	-	-	- 1.32	1.78
Nasal bridge height						
Medium	-	-	- 6.54	5.40	(3.94	3.20)*
Pronounced	3.79	3.08	-	-	-	-

*Independent difference corrected for state sampling.

Table VI-94 (cont'd).	Significant and Independent of State Sampling		Crude Differences Invalidated by State Sampling		Insignificant Difference	
	Diff.	x p.e.	Diff.	x p.e.	Diff.	x p.e.
Nasal bridge breadth						
Submedium	-	-	- 1.69	3.67	(- 0.20	0.43)*
Pronounced	-	-	-	-	- 1.96	2.13
Nasal profile						
Concave	- 3.61*	3.44*	-	-	-	-
Straight	-	-	-	-	- 0.76	0.95
Convex	-	-	-	-	1.65	1.62
Concavo-convex	-	-	-	-	3.42	2.74
Nasal tip thickness						
Submedium	-	-	4.25	5.67	(1.81	2.41)*
Medium	- 4.08	3.52	-	-	-	-
Pronounced	-	-	-	-	- 0.11	0.11
Nasal septum inclination						
Up	- 5.48	4.68	-	-	-	-
Down	5.27	4.50	-	-	-	-
Nasal septum deflection						
Right	-	-	4.50	4.21	(0.92	0.86)*
Left	-	-	2.24	3.03	(- 2.99	4.04)*
Absent	-	-	- 6.75	5.72	(- 1.99	1.69)*
Lips integumental thickness						
Submedium	-	-	3.58	4.37	(1.29	1.57)*
Medium	-	-	- 4.73	4.93	(- 2.80	2.92)*
Pronounced	-	-	-	-	1.16	2.04
Lips membranous thickness						
Submedium	3.36	3.61	-	-	-	-
Medium	-	-	-	-	1.21	1.03
Upper, small; lower, pronounced	-	-	- 4.29	5.17	(- 1.13	1.36)*
Pronounced	-	-	-	-	- 0.30	0.71
Lip seam						
Absent, submedium	-	-	-	-	2.24	2.54
Medium	- 3.93*	3.30*	-	-	-	-
Pronounced	-	-	3.07	3.10	(0.24	0.24)*
Alveolar prognathism						
Absent	-	-	-	-	1.58	1.66
Submedium	-	-	-	-	- 0.92	1.10
Medium	-	-	-	-	- 0.39	0.78
Chin form						
Median	- 5.11*	4.12*	-	-	-	-
Bilateral	5.11*	4.12*	-	-	-	-
Malars prominence						
Submedium	-	-	2.77	4.78	(0.65	1.12)*
Medium	-	-	-	-	- 1.99	1.72
Pronounced	-	-	-	-	- 0.77	0.71
Cheeks fullness						
Submedium	-	-	-	-	- 0.84	0.78
Medium	-	-	-	-	1.63	1.31
Pronounced	-	-	-	-	- 0.79	0.82
Gonial angles						
Submedium	-	-	-	-	0.22	0.27
Pronounced	-	-	-	-	1.77	1.86
Cheeks wrinkling						
Absent	-11.89*	9.44*	-	-	-	-
Slight, medium	4.51*	3.76*	-	-	-	-
Pronounced	7.13	8.39	-	-	-	-

*Independent difference corrected for state sampling.

Table VI-94 (cont'd).

	Significant and Independent of State Sampling		Crude Differences Invalidated by State Sampling		Insignificant Difference	
	Diff.	x p.e.	Diff.	x p.e.	Diff.	x p.e.
Teeth wear						
Slight, medium	- 6.53*	6.80*	-	-	-	-
Pronounced	6.50*	6.92*	-	-	-	-
Teeth caries						
None	1.53*	3.92*	-	-	-	-
Few	- 3.71	3.23	-	-	-	-
Teeth lost						
None	-	-	-	-	- 2.96	2.67
Few	-	-	-	-	1.03	0.82
Many	-	-	-	-	1.92	1.76
Bite						
Edge-to-edge	4.76*	4.58*	-	-	-	-
Slight over	- 5.72*	4.33*	-	-	-	-
Ear lobes						
Submedium	-	-	-	-	- 0.89	1.13
Medium	-	-	-	-	0.69	0.61
Pronounced	-	-	-	-	0.20	0.21
Ear lobe attachment						
Attached	-	-	-	-	0.04	0.03
Free	-	-	-	-	- 0.15	0.13
Roll of helix						
Submedium	-	-	4.93	4.21	(2.94	2.51)*
Medium, pronounced	-	-	- 4.84	4.14	(- 2.82	2.41)*
Darwin's point						
Absent	-	-	-	-	0.96	0.78
Submedium	-	-	-	-	- 0.76	0.67
Pronounced	-	-	-	-	- 0.20	0.24
Antihelix prominence						
Submedium	-	-	-	-	1.91	2.77
Ear protrusion						
Submedium	-	-	-	-	1.23	1.86
Medium	-	-	-	-	- 2.47	1.99
Pronounced	-	-	-	-	1.23	1.02
Temporal fullness						
Pronounced	-	-	3.00	4.05	(0.03	0.04)*
Lambdoid flattening						
Absent	-	-	-	-	- 2.04	1.73
Present	-	-	-	-	2.04	1.73
Asymmetry						
Right	-	-	-	-	0.46	0.53
Left	-	-	3.53	4.15	2.34	2.75
None	-	-	- 3.98	3.59	(- 0.89	0.80)*
Neck						
Medium in length, breadth	-	-	- 7.43	6.30	(- 1.06	0.90)*
Long and thin	-	-	6.12	5.42	(0.03	0.03)*
Short and thick	-	-	-	-	1.31	2.43
Shoulders slope						
Medium	-	-	- 5.99	5.60	(- 0.78	0.73)*
Pronounced	-	-	5.84	5.72	(0.81	0.79)*

*Independent difference corrected for state sampling.

Table VI-95. Summary of Morphological Differentiation of Offenses from
Total Series on Basis of State Composition

Assault

	Significant and Independent of State Sampling		Crude Differences Invalidated by State Sampling		Insignificant Difference	
	Diff.	x p.e.	Diff.	x p.e.	Diff.	x p.e.
Hair quantity, head						
Small	-	-	-	-	- 3.58	1.52
Large	-	-	-	-	- 8.40	2.91
Hair quantity, beard						
Small	-	-	-	-	- 1.50	0.42
Large	-	-	-	-	- 4.71	1.85
Hair quantity, body						
Small	-	-	-	-	- 2.90	0.78
Large	-	-	-	-	2.70	1.06
Skin color						
Red white	-	-	-	-	- 9.04	2.60
Pale white	-	-	-	-	6.63	1.83
Hair form						
Straight	-	-	-	-	- 4.10	1.55
Low waves	-	-	-	-	1.62	0.78
Deep waves	-	-	-	-	1.02	0.70
Curly	-	-	-	-	1.56	1.43
Hair color						
Black	-	-	-	-	- 2.49	1.52
Dark brown	-	-	-	-	4.72	1.32
Reddish brown	-	-	-	-	1.52	0.50
Light brown	-	-	-	-	- 5.51	1.68
Ash-blond	-	-	-	-	- 1.03	0.91
Golden	-	-	-	-	- 2.21	1.60
Red	-	-	-	-	3.73	2.57
Gray, white	-	-	-	-	1.27	0.77
Eye color						
Dark brown	-	-	4.19	3.13	(3.41	2.54)*
Light brown	-	-	-	-	0.68	0.53
Blue-brown	-	-	-	-	2.19	0.73
Gray-brown	-	-	- 9.88	3.49	(- 3.37	1.19)*
Green-brown	-	-	-	-	2.93	0.88
Blue	-	-	-	-	- 1.60	0.55
Blue-gray	-	-	-	-	1.49	0.67
Iris						
Homogeneous	-	-	6.03	3.02	(5.78	2.89)*
Rayed	-	-	-	-	- 0.77	0.23
Zoned	-	-	-	-	- 0.95	0.28
Speckled	-	-	-	-	- 4.46	1.37
Diffused	-	-	-	-	0.15	0.07
Eye folds						
Epicanthus	-	-	-	-	0.60	0.39
Median	-	-	-	-	0.89	0.36
External	-	-	-	-	3.55	1.67
Absent	-	-	-	-	- 5.04	1.54
Eyebrows thickness						
Submedium	-	-	-	-	0.63	0.41
Pronounced	-	-	-	-	5.22	1.50

*Independent difference corrected for state sampling.

Table VI-95 (cont'd).

	Significant and Independent of State Sampling		Crude Differences Invalidated by State Sampling		Insignificant Difference	
	Diff.	x p.e.	Diff.	x p.e.	Diff.	x p.e.
Forehead height						
Submedium	-	-	-	-	- 0.14	0.06
Medium	-	-	-	-	- 5.40	1.50
Pronounced	-	-	-	-	5.53	1.72
Forehead slope						
Absent, submedium	-	-	-	-	- 3.14	1.54
Medium	-	-	-	-	2.57	0.72
Pronounced	-	-	-	-	0.47	0.13
Nasion depression						
Submedium	-	-	7.03	3.26	(5.36	2.48)*
Medium	-	-	-	-	- 7.50	2.25
Nasal root height						
Submedium	3.00*	3.19*	-	-	-	-
Medium	-14.63*	5.08*	-	-	-	-
Pronounced	11:63*	4.20*	-	-	-	-
Nasal root breadth						
Submedium	-	-	5.16	3.22	(0.38	0.24)*
Medium	-	-	- 8.25	3.16	(1.07	0.41)*
Pronounced	-	-	-	-	3.09	1.42
Nasal bridge height						
Medium	-	-	-	-	- 8.06	2.20
Pronounced	-	-	-	-	8.39	2.29
Nasal bridge breadth						
Submedium	-	-	-	-	- 0.97	0.48
Pronounced	-	-	-	-	4.15	1.53
Nasal profile						
Concave	-	-	-	-	- 1.02	0.33
Straight	-	-	-	-	- 5.03	2.13
Convex	-	-	-	-	5.41	1.78
Concavo-convex	-	-	-	-	0.64	0.17
Nasal tip thickness						
Submedium	-	-	-	-	- 3.74	1.67
Medium	-	-	-	-	2.23	0.65
Pronounced	-	-	-	-	1.52	0.50
Nasal septum inclination						
Up	-	-	-	-	- 0.64	0.18
Down	-	-	-	-	1.08	0.31
Nasal septum deflection						
Right	-	-	-	-	- 0.99	0.31
Left	-	-	-	-	5.43	2.47
Absent	-	-	-	-	- 4.44	1.26
Lips integumental thickness						
Submedium	-	-	-	-	4.13	1.69
Medium	-	-	-	-	- 8.49	2.98
Pronounced	-	-	-	-	4.36	2.54
Lips membranous thickness						
Submedium	-	-	-	-	8.33	2.99
Medium	-	-	-12.93	3.70	(- 6.21	1.78)*
Upper, small; lower, pronounced	-	-	-	-	3.72	1.50
Pronounced	-	-	-	-	0.87	0.70
Lip seam						
Absent, submedium	-	-	-	-	- 4.48	1.70
Medium	-	-	-	-	1.14	0.32
Pronounced	-	-	-	-	3.33	1.13

*Independent difference corrected for state sampling..

Table VI-95 (cont'd).	Significant and Independent of State Sampling		Crude Differences Invalidated by State Sampling		Insignificant Difference	
	Diff.	x p.e.	Diff.	x p.e.	Diff.	x p.e.
Alveolar prognathism						
Absent	-	-	-	-	1.35	0.47
Submedium	-	-	-	-	- 4.31	1.71
Medium	-	-	-	-	2.14	1.44
Chin form						
Median	-	-	-	-	- 0.61	0.16
Bilateral	-	-	-	-	0.61	0.16
Malars prominence						
Submedium	-	-	-	-	0.59	0.34
Medium	-	-	-	-	3.57	1.04
Pronounced	-	-	-	-	- 4.16	1.28
Cheeks fullness						
Submedium	-	-	11.87	3.70	(4.23	1.32)*
Medium	-	-	-	-	-10.12	2.74
Pronounced	-	-	-	-	- 1.75	0.61
Gonial angles						
Submedium	-	-	-	-	- 3.19	1.32
Pronounced	-	-	-	-	- 2.35	0.83
Cheeks wrinkling						
Absent	-	-	-	-	- 2.84	0.76
Slight, medium	-	-	-	-	3.53	0.99
Pronounced	-	-	-	-	- 0.69	0.27
Teeth wear						
Slight, medium	-	-	-	-	- 2.43	0.85
Pronounced	-	-	-	-	3.49	1.25
Teeth lost						
None	-	-	-	-	- 9.07	2.75
Few	-	-	-	-	7.61	2.04
Many	-	-	-	-	1.45	0.45
Ear lobes						
Submedium	-	-	-	-	6.42	2.73
Medium	-	-	-	-	- 6.31	1.87
Pronounced	-	-	-	-	- 0.10	0.04
Ear lobe attachment						
Attached	-	-	-	-	1.20	0.33
Free .	-	-	-	-	- 1.16	0.32
Roll of helix						
Submedium	-	-	-	-	2.05	0.58
Medium, pronounced	-	-	-	-	- 1.96	0.56
Darwin's point						
Absent	-	-	-	-	4.38	1.18
Submedium	-	-	-	-	3.54	1.05
Pronounced	-	-	- 7.92	3.13	(- 3.37	1.33)*
Antihelix prominence						
Medium	-	-	-	-	- 6.55	2.08
Pronounced	-	-	-	-	5.81	2.20
Ear protrusion						
Submedium	-	-	-	-	- 2.49	1.26
Medium	-	-	-	-	- 4.57	1.69
Pronounced	-	-	-	-	7.06	1.97
Temporal fullness						
Submedium	-	-	-	-	- 3.93	1.38
Medium	-	-	-	-	7.30	2.20
Pronounced	-	-	-	-	- 3.37	1.52

*Independent difference corrected for state sampling.

Table VI-95 (cont'd).	Significant and Independent of State Sampling		Crude Differences Invalidated by State Sampling		Insignificant Difference	
	Diff.	x p.e.	Diff.	x p.e.	Diff.	x p.e.
Lambdoid flattening						
Absent	-	-	-13.55	3.81	(-10.20	2.86)*
Present	-	-	13.55	3.81	(10.20	2.86)*
Asymmetry						
Right	-	-	-	-	1.58	0.60
Left	-	-	-	-	1.07	0.42
None	-	-	-	-	- 2.65	0.79
Neck						
Medium in length,breadth	-	-	-	-	1.42	0.41
Long and thin	-	-	-	-	- 0.31	0.09
Short and thick	-	-	-	-	- 1.11	0.69
Shoulders slope						
Medium	-	-	10.08	3.17	(8.87	2.79)*
Pronounced	-	-	-	-	- 8.73	2.85

Table VI-96. Summary of Morphological Differentiation of Offenses from
Total Series on Basis of State Composition

Robbery

	Significant and Independent of State Sampling		Crude Differences Invalidated by State Sampling		Insignificant Differences	
	Diff.	x p.e.	Diff.	x p.e.	Diff.	x p.e.
Hair quantity, head						
Small	- 3.08*	3.11*	-	-	-	-
Large	-	-	-	-	2.67	2.19
Hair quantity, beard						
Small	- 4.91	3.25	-	-	-	-
Large	-	-	-	-	3.04	2.82
Hair quantity, body						
Small	-	-	-	-	2.10	1.33
Large	-	-	-	-	- 0.44	0.41
Skin color						
Red white	-	-	-	-	- 3.45	2.36
Pale white	-	-	4.71	3.08	(1.94	1.27)*
Hair form						
Straight	- 4.86	4.34	-	-	-	-
Low waves	3.32*	3.77*	-	-	-	-
Deep waves	-	-	-	-	1.63	2.63
Curly	-	-	-	-	0.01	0.02
Hair color						
Black	-	-	-	-	- 1.39	2.01
Dark brown	-	-	-	-	- 1.83	1.22
Reddish brown	-	-	-	-	2.52	2.00
Light brown	4.26*	3.09*	-	-	-	-
Ash-blond	-	-	-	-	- 0.85	1.81
Golden	-	-	-	-	- 1.06	1.86
Red	-	-	-	-	0.98	1.61
Gray, white	- 3.12	4.52	-	-	-	-

*Independent difference corrected for state sampling.

Table VI-96 (cont'd).	Significant and Independent of State Sampling		Crude Differences Invalidated by State Sampling		Insignificant Difference	
	Diff.	x p.e.	Diff.	x p.e.	Diff.	x p.e.
Eye color						
Dark brown	-	-	-	-	- 0.15	0.26
Light brown	-	-	2.27	4.13	(1.63	2.96)*
Blue-brown	-	-	-	-	0.32	0.25
Gray-brown	-	-	-	-	0.58	0.49
Green-brown	-	-	-	-	1.57	1.12
Blue	-	-	-	-	- 3.57	2.88
Blue-gray	-	-	-	-	- 1.02	1.09
Iris						
Homogeneous	-	-	-	-	0.10	0.12
Rayed	-	-	-	-	- 2.57	1.82
Zoned	-	-	-	-	2.30	1.58
Speckled	-	-	-	-	- 2.97	2.15
Diffused	3.14	3.53	-	-	-	-
Eye folds						
Epicanthus	-	-	-	-	- 0.51	0.78
Median	5.22*	4.92*	-	-	-	-
External	-	-	-	-	- 1.41	1.57
Absent	-	-	-	-	- 3.47	2.50
Eyebrows thickness						
Submedium	-	-	-	-	- 1.46	2.28
Pronounced	-	-	-	-	0.18	0.12
Forehead height						
Submedium	-	-	-	-	- 2.01	1.93
Medium	-	-	4.73	3.11	(3.88	2.55)*
Pronounced	-	-	-	-	- 2.73	2.02
Forehead slope						
Absent, submedium	-	-	-	-	- 0.65	0.76
Medium	-	-	-	-	2.81	1.80
Pronounced	-	-	-	-	- 2.15	1.43
Nasion depression						
Submedium	-	-	-	-	- 2.68	2.94
Medium	-	-	4.50	3.21	(1.53	1.09)*
Nasal root height						
Submedium	-	-	-	-	- 0.16	0.41
Medium	-	-	-	-	0.73	0.60
Pronounced	-	-	-	-	- 0.56	0.48
Nasal root breadth						
Submedium	-	-	-	-	0.47	0.70
Medium	-	-	-	-	0	0
Pronounced	-	-	-	-	- 0.47	0.51
Nasal bridge height						
Medium	5.18	3.36	-	-	-	-
Pronounced	- 5.34	3.47	-	-	-	-
Nasal bridge breadth						
Submedium	-	-	-	-	0.66	1.16
Pronounced	-	-	-	-	1.87	1.63
Nasal profile						
Concave	-	-	-	-	2.43	1.86
Straight	-	-	-	-	0.10	0.10
Convex	-	-	-	-	- 1.23	0.96
Concavo-convex	-	-	-	-	- 1.30	0.33
Nasal tip thickness						
Submedium	-	-	-	-	- 0.52	0.55
Medium	-	-	-	-	- 0.33	0.23
Pronounced	-	-	-	-	0.86	0.67

*Independent difference corrected for state sampling.

Table VI-96 (cont'd).

	Significant and Independent of State Sampling		Crude Differences Invalidated by State Sampling		Insignificant Difference	
	Diff.	x p.e.	Diff.	x p.e.	Diff.	x p.e.
Nasal septum inclination						
Up	-	-	-	-	2.56	1.74
Down	-	-	-	-	- 2.12	1.45
Nasal septum deflection						
Right	-	-	-	-	0.66	0.49
Left	-	-	-	-	- 2.08	2.26
Absent	-	-	-	-	1.42	0.96
Lips integumental thickness						
Submedium	-	-	-	-	- 0.26	0.26
Medium	-	-	-	-	- 0.40	0.33
Pronounced	-	-	-	-	0.66	0.90
Lips membranous thickness						
Submedium	- 3.65*	3.12*	-	-	-	-
Medium	4.53	3.08	-	-	-	-
Upper, small; lower, pronounced	-	-	-	-	- 1.18	1.14
Pronounced	-	-	-	-	1.23	2.32
Lip seam						
Absent, submedium	- 5.04	4.54	-	-	-	-
Medium	4.66*	3.13*	-	-	-	-
Pronounced	-	-	-	-	- 0.77	0.62
Alveolar prognathism						
Absent	-	-	-	-	- 0.52	0.43
Submedium	-	-	-	-	1.19	1.12
Medium	-	-	-	-	- 0.49	0.78
Facial prognathism						
Submedium	-	-	-	-	1.57	1.94
Chin form						
Median	-	-	-	-	- 0.20	0.13
Bilateral	-	-	-	-	0.20	0.13
Malars prominence						
Submedium	-	-	-	-	- 1.55	2.12
Medium	-	-	-	-	2.08	1.42
Pronounced	-	-	-	-	- 0.53	0.39
Cheeks fullness						
Submedium	-	-	-	-	- 0.71	0.53
Medium	-	-	-	-	1.80	1.15
Pronounced	-	-	-	-	- 1.09	0.90
Gonial angles						
Submedium	-	-	-	-	0.86	0.84
Pronounced	-	-	-	-	- 3.34	2.81
Cheeks wrinkling						
Absent	12.44*	7.92*	-	-	-	-
Slight, medium	- 4.88*	3.25*	-	-	-	-
Pronounced	- 7.54*	7.05*	-	-	-	-
Teeth wear						
Slight, medium	7.94*	6.67*	-	-	-	-
Pronounced	- 7.95*	6.85*	-	-	-	-
Teeth lost						
None	-	-	-	-	- 2.48	1.77
Few	6.68*	4.23*	-	-	-	-
Many	- 4.60	3.38	-	-	-	-
Bite						
Edge-to-edge	- 4.98*	3.92*	-	-	-	-
Slight over	5.91	3.65	-	-	-	-

*Independent difference corrected for state sampling.

Table VI-96 (cont'd).

	Significant and Independent of State Sampling		Crude Differences Invalidated by State Sampling		Insignificant Difference	
	Diff.	x p.e.	Diff.	x p.e.	Diff.	x p.e.
Ear lobes						
Submedium	-	-	-	-	2.20	2.24
Medium	-	-	-	-	1.64	1.16
Pronounced	-	-	- 3.83	3.19	(- 3.13	2.61)*
Ear lobe attachment						
Attached	-	-	5.27	3.42	(4.59	2.98)*
Free	-	-	- 5.23	3.40	(- 4.54	2.95)*
Roll of helix						
Submedium	-	-	-	-	- 1.86	1.25
Medium, pronounced	-	-	-	-	1.47	1.00
Darwin's point						
Absent	-	-	- 4.78	3.08	(- 3.60	2.32)*
Submedium	-	-	-	-	3.44	2.42
Pronounced	-	-	-	-	1.34	1.26
Ear protrusion						
Submedium	-	-	-	-	- 0.49	0.59
Medium	4.83*	3.10*	-	-	-	-
Pronounced	- 4.63*	3.09*	-	-	-	-
Lambdoid flattening						
Absent	-	-	-	-	- 0.45	0.30
Present	-	-	-	-	0.45	0.30
Asymmetry						
Right	-	-	-	-	- 1.46	1.32
Left	-	-	-	-	- 2.70	2.50
None	-	-	-	-	4.17	2.94
Neck						
Medium in length,breadth	-	-	-	-	1.75	1.18
Long and thin	-	-	-	-	- 2.45	1.74
Short and thick	-	-	-	-	0.70	1.04
Shoulders slope						
Medium	-	-	-	-	2.47	1.84
Pronounced	-	-	-	-	- 2.78	2.16

Table VI-97. Summary of Morphological Differentiation of Offenses from Total Series on Basis of State Composition

Burglary and Larceny

	Significant and Independent of State Sampling		Crude Differences Invalidated by State Sampling		Insignificant Difference	
	Diff.	x p.e.	Diff.	x p.e.	Diff.	x p.e.
Hair quantity, head						
Small	- 2.62*	6.24*	-	-	-	-
Large	-	-	-	-	1.09	2.14
Hair quantity, beard						
Small	3.02*	4.79*	-	-	-	-
Large	-	-	-	-	- 0.04	0.09
Hair quantity, body						
Small	7.74*	11.73*	-	-	-	-
Large	- 2.93*	6.51*	-	-	-	-

*Independent difference corrected for state sampling.

Table VI-97 (cont'd).	Significant and Independent of State Sampling		Crude Differences Invalidated by State Sampling		Insignificant Difference	
	Diff.	x p.e.	Diff.	x p.e.	Diff.	x p.e.
Hair form						
Straight	-	-	-	-	0.46	1.00
Low waves	-	-	-	-	- 0.73	1.97
Deep waves	-	-	-	-	0.25	0.96
Curly	-	-	-	-	0.05	0.26
Hair color						
Black	- 1.02*	3.64*	-	-	-	-
Dark brown	-	-	-	-	0.15	0.24
Reddish brown	-	-	-	-	0.73	1.38
Light brown	-	-	-	-	0.43	0.74
Ash-blond	0.84	4.20	-	-	-	-
Golden	1.35*	5.62*	-	-	-	-
Red	-	-	-	-	0.47	1.88
Gray, white	- 2.76*	9.20*	-	-	-	-
Eye color						
Dark brown	-	-	-	-	0.17	0.71
Light brown	0.91	4.14	-	-	-	-
Blue-brown	-	-	-	-	- 0.56	1.06
Gray-brown	-	-	-	-	- 0.86	1.72
Green-brown	-	-	-	-	0.57	0.97
Blue	-	-	-	-	- 0.84	1.62
Blue-gray	-	-	-	-	0.61	1.56
Iris						
Homogeneous	-	-	-	-	- 0.25	0.71
Rayed	-	-	-	-	- 0.26	0.44
Zoned	-	-	-	-	0.23	0.38
Speckled	-	-	-	-	0.36	0.63
Diffused	-	-	-	-	- 0.07	0.19
Eye folds						
Epicanthus	-	-	-	-	- 0.17	0.63
Median	-	-	1.32	3.00	(1.10	2.50)*
External	-	-	-	-	- 0.49	1.29
Absent	-	-	-	-	- 0.66	1.14
Eyebrows thickness						
Submedium	-	-	-	-	- 0.58	2.15
Pronounced	-	-	-	-	- 0.04	0.06
Forehead height						
Submedium	-	-	-	-	0.53	1.20
Medium	-	-	-	-	0.83	1.30
Pronounced	-	-	-	-	- 1.36	2.39
Forehead slope						
Absent, submedium	-	-	-	-	0.55	1.53
Medium	-	-	-	-	1.76	2.71
Pronounced	- 2.08*	3.30*	-	-	-	-
Nasal root height						
Submedium	-	-	-	-	- 0.18	1.12
Medium	3.05	5.98	-	-	-	-
Pronounced	- 2.85	5.82	-	-	-	-
Nasal root breadth						
Submedium	-	-	-	-	0.12	0.43
Medium	-	-	-	-	- 0.82	1.78
Pronounced	-	-	-	-	0.70	1.84
Nasal bridge height						
Medium	-	-	-	-	1.24	1.91
Pronounced	-	-	-	-	- 1.22	1.88

*Independent difference corrected for state sampling.

Table VI-97 (cont'd).	Significant and Independent of State Sampling		Crude Differences Invalidated by State Sampling		Insignificant Differences	
	Diff.	x p.e.	Diff.	x p.e.	Diff.	x p.e.
Nasal bridge breadth						
Submedium	-	-	-	-	0.69	2.88
Pronounced	-	-	-	-	- 0.09	0.19
Nasal profile						
Concave	3.57*	6.49*	-	-	-	-
Straight	-	-	-	-	- 0.11	0.26
Convex	- 3.02	5.70	-	-	-	-
Concavo-convex	-	-	-	-	- 0.79	1.20
Nasal tip thickness						
Submedium	-	-	-	-	- 0.43	1.10
Medium	-	-	-	-	1.31	2.15
Pronounced	-	-	-	-	- 0.87	1.61
Nasal septum inclination						
Up	4.78*	7.71*	-	-	-	-
Down	- 4.57*	7.49*	-	-	-	-
Nasal septum deflection						
Right	-	-	-	-	- 0.25	0.45
Left	-	-	-	-	- 1.12	2.95
Absent	-	-	-	-	1.36	2.19
Lips integumental thickness						
Submedium	-	-	-	-	0.39	0.91
Medium	-	-	-	-	1.08	2.12
Pronounced	- 1.31*	4.37*	-	-	-	-
Lips membranous thickness						
Submedium	- 2.30	4.69	-	-	-	-
Medium	-	-	-	-	0.79	1.27
Upper, small; lower, pronounced	-	-	1.46	3.32	(0.76	1.73)*
Pronounced	-	-	-	-	0.04	0.18
Lip seam						
Absent, submedium	- 2.22	4.83	-	-	-	-
Medium	-	-	-	-	1.54	2.44
Pronounced	-	-	-	-	0.68	1.28
Alveolar prognathism						
Absent	-	-	-	-	0.53	1.04
Submedium	-	-	-	-	- 1.27	2.89
Medium	-	-	-	-	0.67	2.58
Chin form						
Median	-	-	-	-	1.40	2.15
Bilateral	-	-	-	-	- 1.40	2.15
Malars prominence						
Submedium	-	-	-	-	- 0.38	1.27
Medium	2.14*	3.51*	-	-	-	-
Pronounced	-	-	- 2.17	3.81	(- 1.46	2.56)*
Cheeks fullness						
Submedium	- 2.05	3.60	-	-	-	-
Medium	2.08	3.20	-	-	-	-
Pronounced	-	-	-	-	- 0.03	0.06
Gonial angles						
Submedium	-	-	1.73	4.12	(1.10	2.62)
Pronounced	-	-	-	-	- 1.38	2.76
Cheeks wrinkling						
Absent	9.06*	13.73*	-	-	-	-
Slight, medium	- 3.07*	4.87*	-	-	-	-
Pronounced	- 5.99*	13.61*	-	-	-	-

*Independent difference corrected for state sampling.

Table VI-97 (cont'd).

	Significant and Independent of State Sampling		Crude Differences Invalidated by State Sampling		Insignificant Difference	
	Diff.	x p.e.	Diff.	x p.e.	Diff.	x p.e.
Teeth wear						
Slight, medium	4.45*	8.90*	-	-	-	-
Pronounced	- 4.85*	9.90*	-	-	-	-
Teeth caries						
Few	5.81*	9.68*	-	-	-	-
Many	- 5.58*	9.63*	-	-	-	-
Teeth lost						
None	5.41*	9.17*	-	-	-	-
Few	-	-	-	-	1.55	2.35
Many	- 6.87*	12.05*	-	-	-	-
Bite						
Under	1.45*	6.59*	-	-	-	-
Edge-to-edge	- 3.66*	6.91*	-	-	-	-
Ear lobes						
Submedium	-	-	-	-	1.10	2.62
Medium	-	-	-	-	1.41	2.39
Pronounced	- 2.16*	4.24*	-	-	-	-
Ear lobe attachment						
Attached	-	-	2.49	3.83	(1.93	2.97)*
Free	-	-	- 2.51	3.96	(- 1.93	2.97)*
Roll of helix						
Submedium	-	-	- 1.91	3.08	(- 1.78	2.87)*
Medium, pronounced	1.87*	3.02*	-	-	-	-
Darwin's point						
Absent	-	-	-	-	1.19	1.83
Submedium	-	-	-	-	- 1.76	2.98
Pronounced	-	-	-	-	0.57	1.30
Ear protrusion						
Submedium	-	-	-	-	- 0.10	0.29
Medium	-	-	-	-	0.38	0.58
Pronounced	-	-	-	-	- 0.28	0.44
Lambdoid flattening						
Absent	-	-	-	-	1.45	2.34
Present	-	-	-	-	- 1.45	2.34
Asymmetry						
Right	-	-	-	-	- 1.25	2.72
Left	- 1.43*	3.11*	-	-	-	-
None	2.66*	4.43*	-	-	-	-
Neck						
Medium in length, breadth	-	-	-	-	0.85	1.37
Long and thin	-	-	-	-	0.14	0.24
Short and thick	- 0.85*	3.04*	-	-	-	-
Shoulders slope						
Medium	-	-	-	-	- 0.58	1.02
Pronounced	-	-	-	-	0.87	1.61

*Independent difference corrected for state sampling.

Table VI-98. Summary of Morphological Differentiation of Offenses from
Total Series on Basis of State Composition

Forgery and Fraud

	Significant and Independent of State Sampling		Crude Differences Invalidated by State Sampling		Insignificant Difference	
	Diff.	x p.e.	Diff.	x p.e.	Diff.	x p.e.
Hair quantity, head					-	-
Small	3.26*	3.54*	-	-	- 1.27	1.11
Large	-	-	-	-		
Hair quantity, beard					-	-
Small	- 6.50*	4.64*	-	-	(1.12	1.12)*
Large	-	-	3.24	3.24		
Hair quantity, body					1.45	0.98
Small	-	-	-	-	. 2.83	2.80
Large	-	-	-	-		
Skin color					2.12	1.48
Pale white	-	-	-	-		
Hair form					- 0.98	0.94
Straight	-	-	-	-	1.26	1.54
Low waves	-	-	-	-	- 0.77	1.35
Deep waves	-	-	-	-	0.17	0.40
Curly						
Hair color					1.07	1.65
Black	-	-	-	-	- 1.91	1.36
Dark brown	-	-	-	-	- 1.74	1.46
Red brown	-	-	-	-	1.20	0.92
Light brown	-	-	-	-	1.18	2.68
Ash-blond	-	-	-	-	1.30	2.36
Golden	-	-	-	-	0.27	0.47
Red	-	-	-	-	- 1.36	2.09
Gray, white						
Eye color					- 0.53	1.00
Dark brown	-	-	-	-	- 1.14	2.24
Light brown	-	-	-	-	- 1.47	1.25
Blue-brown	-	-	-	-	1.04	0.94
Gray-brown	-	-	-	-	- 0.95	0.73
Green-brown	-	-	-	-	3.38	2.94
Blue	-	-	-	-	- 0.34	0.39
Blue-gray						
Iris					- 0.01	0.01
Homogeneous	-	-	-	-	- 1.97	1.50
Rayed	-	-	5.02	3.69	(2.22	1.63)*
Zoned	-	-	- 3.87	3.00	(- 2.37	1.84)*
Speckled	-	-	-	-	0.82	1.00
Diffused						
Eye folds					- 1.40	2.33
Epicanthus	-	-	-	-	- 0.44	0.45
Median	-	-	-	-	- 2.10	2.50
External	-	-	3.94	3.05	(2.33	1.81)*
Absent						
Eyebrows thickness					0.14	0.23
Submedium	-	-	-	-	- 1.81	1.31
Pronounced	-	-	-	-		
Forehead height					(- 1.88	1.92)*
Submedium	-	-	- 3.43	3.50	1.13	0.80
Medium	-	-	-	-	2.30	1.81
Pronounced	-	-	-	-		

*Independent difference corrected for state sampling.

Table VI-98 (cont'd).	Significant and Independent of State Sampling		Crude Differences Invalidated by State Sampling		Insignificant Difference	
	Diff.	x p.e.	Diff.	x p.e.	Diff.	x p.e.
Forehead slope						
Absent, submedium	-	-	-	-	- 1.93	2.41
Medium	-	-	-	-	3.91	2.68
Pronounced	-	-	-	-	- 1.98	1.41
Nasion depression						
Submedium	-	-	- 2.80	3.29	(- 0.70	0.82)*
Medium	-	-	7.59	5.75	(3.61	2.74)*
Pronounced	-	-	- 4.69	4.15	(- 2.85	2.52)*
Nasal root height						
Submedium	-	-	-	-	- 0.75	2.03
Medium	-	-	-	-	2.49	2.20
Pronounced	-	-	-	-	- 1.72	1.58
Nasal root breadth						
Submedium	-	-	-	-	0.94	1.49
Medium	-	-	-	-	1.19	1.16
Pronounced	-	-	-	-	- 2.13	2.48
Nasal bridge height						
Medium	8.14	5.65	-	-	-	-
Pronounced	- 8.03	5.58	-	-	-	-
Nasal bridge breadth						
Submedium	-	-	-	-	1.03	1.91
Pronounced	-	-	-	-	- 1.72	1 51
Nasal profile						
Concave	-	-	-	-	0.05	0.04
Straight	-	-	-	-	0.52	0.56
Convex	-	-	-	-	0.19	0.16
Concavo-convex	-	-	-	-	- 0.76	0.52
Nasal tip thickness						
Submedium	-	-	-	-	- 0.55	0.62
Medium	-	-	-	-	2.22	1.63
Pronounced	-	-	-	-	- 1.67	1.39
Nasal septum inclination						
Up	-	-	-	-	- 0.25	0.18
Down	-	-	-	-	0.48	0.35
Nasal septum deflection						
Right	-	-	- 6.11	4.89	(- 1.56	1.25)*
Left	-	-	-	-	- 1.42	1.65
Absent	-	-	7.52	5.45	(1.86	1.35)*
Lips integumental thickness						
Submedium	- 3.06*	3.19*	-	-	-	-
Medium	-	-	5.10	4.51	(3.36	2.97)*
Pronounced	-	-	-	-	- 0.28	0.41
Lips membranous thickness						
Submedium	- 4.30*	3.94*	-	-	-	-
Medium	-	-	-	-	2.31	1.67
Upper, small; lower, pronounced	-	-	3.10	3.16	(2.15	2.19)*
Pronounced	-	-	-	-	- 0.10	0.20
Lip seam						
Absent, submedium	-	-	-	-	0.94	0.90
Medium	-	-	-	-	2.38	1.71
Pronounced	-	-	-	-	- 3.32	2.86
Alveolar prognathism						
Absent	-	-	-	-	- 0.60	0.54
Submedium	-	-	-	-	0.86	0.87
Medium	-	-	-	-	- 0.47	0.80

*Independent difference corrected for state sampling.

Table VI-98 (cont'd).	Significant and Independent of State Sampling		Crude Differences Invalidated by State Sampling		Insignificant Differences	
	Diff.	x p.e.	Diff.	x p.e.	Diff.	x p.e.
Chin form						
Median	-	-	-	-	- 1.83	1.20
Bilateral	-	-	-	-	1.83	1.25
Malars prominence						
Submedium	-	-	-	-	- 1.37	2.02
Medium	-	-	-	-	- 0.48	0.35
Pronounced	-	-	-	-	1.84	1.44
Cheeks fullness						
Submedium	-	-	-	-	- 0.40	0.32
Medium	-	-	-	-	- 1.95	1.34
Pronounced	-	-	-	-	2.34	2.07
Gonial angles						
Submedium	-	-	-	-	- 1.23	1.30
Pronounced	-	-	-	-	3.21	2.89
Cheeks wrinkling						
Absent	-	-	-	-	- 2.56	1.73
Slight, medium	-	-	5.17	3.67	(3.50	2.48)*
Pronounced	-	-	-	-	- 2.61	2.61
Teeth wear						
Slight, medium	3.61*	3.20*	-	-	-	-
Pronounced	- 3.37*	3.06*	-	-	-	-
Teeth lost						
None	-	-	-	-	2.59	1.98
Few	-	-	-	-	- 3.72	2.51
Many	-	-	-	-	1.12	0.88
Bite						
Under	-	-	-	-	0.48	0.94
Ear lobes						
Submedium	-	-	- 2.93	3.18	(- 1.81	1.97)*
Medium	-	-	-	-	- 0.71	0.53
Pronounced	-	-	3.64	3.25	(2.61	2.33)*
Ear lobe attachment						
Attached	-	-	-	-	- 0.87	0.60
Free	-	-	-	-	0.91	0.63
Roll of helix						
Submedium	-	-	-	-	- 2.30	1.67
Medium, pronounced	-	-	-	-	2.18	1.58
Darwin's point						
Absent	-	-	-	-	0.10	0.07
Submedium	-	-	-	-	0.22	0.17
Pronounced	-	-	-	-	- 0.32	0.32
Antihelix prominence						
Submedium	-	-	-	-	- 1.68	2.10
Ear protrusion						
Submedium	-	-	-	-	- 1.71	2.19
Medium	-	-	-	-	3.10	2.12
Pronounced	-	-	-	-	- 1.39	0.99
Temporal fullness						
Submedium	-	-	3.87	3.42	(2.02	1.79)*
Lambdoid flattening						
Absent	-	-	-	-	0.03	0.02
Present	-	-	-	-	- 0.03	0.02
Asymmetry						
Right	-	-	-	-	- 1.56	1.49
Left	-	-	-	-	- 1.03	1.00
None	-	-	-	-	2.59	1.90

*Independent difference corrected for state sampling.

Table VI-98 (cont'd).

	Significant and Independent of State Sampling		Crude Differences Invalidated by State Sampling		Insignificant Difference	
	Diff.	x p.e.	Diff.	x p.e.	Diff.	x p.e.
Neck						
Medium in length, breadth	-	-	-	-	1.27	0.92
Long and thin	-	-	-	-	- 2.22	1.68
Short and thick	-	-	-	-	0.95	1.51
Shoulders slope						
Medium	-	-	-	-	1.51	1.21
Pronounced	-	-	-	-	- 0.84	0.69

Table VI-99. Summary of Morphological Differentiation of Offenses from Total Series on Basis of State Composition

Rape

	Significant and Independent of State Sampling		Crude Differences Invalidated by State Sampling		Insignificant Difference	
Hair quantity, head						
Small	-	-	-	-	4.15	2.82
Large	-	-	- 9.26	5.12	(- 5.18	2.86)*
Hair quantity, beard						
Small	-	-	-	-	3.72	1.65
Large	-	-	-	-	- 1.57	1.04
Hair quantity, body						
Small	- 8.89*	3.75*	-	-	-	-
Large	-	-	-	-	3.03	1.86
Skin color						
Red white	-	-	-	-	- 5.65	2.59
Pale white	-	-	-	-	6.41	2.82
Hair form						
Straight	-	-	-	-	3.99	2.40
Low waves	-	-	-	-	- 1.27	0.98
Deep waves	-	-	- 2.96	3.22	(- 2.40	2.61)*
Curly	-	-	-	-	0.35	0.51
Hair color						
Black	-	-	-	-	0.11	0.11
Dark brown	-	-	-	-	1.38	0.62
Red brown	-	-	-	-	- 1.03	0.54
Light brown	-	-	-	-	- 3.20	1.55
Ash-blond	-	-	-	-	- 0.76	1.07
Golden	-	-	-	-	- 0.40	0.46
Red	-	-	-	-	- 1.81	2.01
Gray, white	4.49*	4.36*	-	-	-	-
Eye color						
Dark brown	-	-	-	-	1.35	1.59
Light brown	-	-	-	-	- 0.48	0.59
Blue-brown	-	-	-	-	- 2.18	1.14
Gray-brown	-	-	- 7.02	3.92	(- 3.18	1.78)*
Green-brown	-	-	-	-	- 0.13	0.06
Blue	-	-	-	-	- 0.97	0.52
Blue-gray	6.41*	4.55*	-	-	-	-

*Independent difference corrected for state sampling.

Table VI-99 (cont'd).

	Significant and Independent of State Sampling		Crude Differences Invalidated by State Sampling		Insignificant Differences	
	Diff.	x p.e.	Diff.	x p.e.	Diff.	x p.e.
Sclera						
Speckled	2.96*	3.06*	-	-	-	-
Iris						
Homogeneous	-	-	-	-	- 1.05	0.83
Rayed	-	-	-	-	2.72	1.30
Zoned	-	-	-	-	5.97	2.74
Speckled	-	-	- 6.74	3.29	(- 2.46	1.20)*
Diffused	-	-	-	-	- 0.91	0.69
Eye folds						
Epicanthus	-	-	-	-	- 1.35	1.41
Median	-	-	-	-	- 3.22	2.05
External	-	-	-	-	2.22	1.66
Absent	-	-	-	-	2.35	1.15
Eyebrows thickness						
Submedium	-	-	-	-	0.20	0.21
Pronounced	-	-	-	-	- 3.35	1.53
Forehead height						
Submedium	-	-	-	-	- 1.47	0.94
Medium	-	-	-	-	- 4.52	1.99
Pronounced	-	-	-	-	5.99	2.96
Forehead slope						
Absent, submedium	-	-	-	-	1.00	0.78
Medium	-	-	-	-	- 0.98	0.42
Pronounced	-	-	-	-	- 0.01	0
Nasion depression						
Submedium	-	-	- 4.12	3.03	(- 2.36	1.74)*
Medium	-	-	-	-	3.52	1.68
Nasal root height						
Submedium	-	-	-	-	0.93	1.58
Medium	-	-	-	-	- 1.68	0.93
Pronounced	-	-	-	-	0.76	0.44
Nasal root breadth						
Submedium	-	-	4.85	4.90	(0.44	0.44)*
Medium	-	-	- 9.73	5.90	(- 2.55	1.54)*
Pronounced	-	-	4.88	3.54	(2.11	1.53)*
Nasal bridge height						
Medium	-	-	-	-	- 0.93	0.40
Pronounced	-	-	-	-	0.76	0.33
Nasal bridge breadth						
Submedium	-	-	3.67	4.27	(- 0.64	0.74)
Pronounced	-	-	-	-	5.07	2.95
Nasal profile						
Concave	- 5.94	3.03	-	-	-	-
Straight	-	-	-	-	0.96	0.64
Convex	-	-	7.22	3.78	(5.17	2.71)*
Concavo-convex	-	-	-	-	- 2.24	0.96
Nasal tip thickness						
Submedium	-	-	-	-	2.25	1.50
Medium	-	-	-	-	- 4.73	2.18
Pronounced	-	-	-	-	2.49	1.30
Nasal septum inclination						
Up	-	-	-	-	- 4.87	2.22
Down	-	-	-	-	4.29	1.97
Nasal septum deflection						
Right	6.24*	3.12*	-	-	-	-
Left	-	-	-	-	1.20	0.86
Absent	- 7.13*	3.21*	-	-	-	-

*Independent differences corrected for state sampling.

Table VI-99 (cont'd).	Significa_ and Independent of State Sampling		Crude Differences Invalidated by State Sampling		Insignificant Difference	
	Diff.	x p.e.	Diff.	x p.e.	Diff.	x p.e.
Lips integumental thickness						
Submedium	-	-	-	-	2.17	1.41
Medium	-	-	- 5.71	3.19	(- 4.50	2.51)*
Pronounced	3.54	3.25	-	-	-	-
Lips membranous thickness						
Submedium	5.39*	3.08*	-	-	-	-
Medium	- 6.67*	3.05*	-	-	-	-
Upper, small; lower, pronounced	-	-	-	-	3.29	2.11
Pronounced	-	-	-	-	- 0.33	0.42
Lip seam						
Absent, submedium	6.44	3.90	-	-	-	-
Medium	-	-	-	-	- 2.07	0.93
Pronounced	-	-	-	-	- 4.37	2.36
Alveolar prognathism						
Absent	-	-	-	-	- 0.17	0.10
Submedium	-	-	-	-	- 0.37	0.23
Medium	-	-	-	-	- 0.56	0.60
Pronounced	0.98*	3.27*	-	-	-	-
Facial prognathism						
Medium	-	-	-	-	1.74	1.81
Chin form						
Median	-	-	-	-	5.90	2.53
Bilateral	-	-	-	-	- 5.90	2.53
Malars prominence						
Submedium	-	-	-	-	- 2.11	1.94
Medium	-	-	-	-	1.12	0.52
Pronounced	-	-	-	-	0.99	0.48
Cheeks fullness						
Submedium	-	-	6.08	3.01	(2.66	1.32)*
Medium	-	-	-	-	- 1.78	0.77
Pronounced	-	-	-	-	- 4.29	2.38
Gonial angles						
Submedium	-	-	-	-	- 1.28	0.84
Pronounced	-	-	-	-	- 0.60	0.34
Cheeks wrinkling						
Absent	- 7.43	3.16	-	-	-	-
Slight, medium	-	-	-	-	0.82	0.37
Pronounced	6.61	4.18	-	-	-	-
Teeth wear						
Slight, medium	-	-	-	-	- 3.92	2.17
Pronounced	-	-	-	-	4.98	2.81
Teeth caries						
None	-	-	-	-	- 1.92	2.59
Many	-	-	-	-	4.69	2.21
Teeth lost						
None	-	-	- 7.69	3.70	(- 4.34	2.09)*
Few	-	-	-	-	- 4.76	2.03
Many	9.54*	4.70*	-	-	-	-
Bite						
Edge-to-edge	-	-	-	-	4.82	2.41
Marked over	-	-	-	-	- 2.09	0.96
Ear lobes						
Submedium	-	-	-	-	2.25	1.52
Medium	-	-	-	-	- 4.13	1.94
Pronounced	-	-	-	-	1.89	1.06

*Independent difference corrected for state sampling.

Table VI-99 (cont'd).

	Significant and Independent of State Sampling		Crude Differences Invalidated by State Sampling		Insignificant Difference	
	Diff.	x p.e.	Diff.	x p.e.	Diff.	x p.e.
Ear lobe attachment						
Attached	-	-	-	-	- 5.64	2.44
Free	-	-	-	-	5.68	2.46
Roll of helix						
Submedium	-	-	-	-	2.56	1.16
Medium, pronounced	-	-	-	-	- 2.47	1.12
Darwin's point						
Absent	-	-	-	-	- 0.45	0.19
Submedium	-	-	-	-	2.66	1.26
Pronounced	-	-	-	-	- 2.21	1.40
Antihelix prominence						
Medium	-	-	-	-	- 2.57	1.30
Pronounced	-	-	-	-	2.48	1.49
Ear protrusion						
Submedium	-	-	-	-	- 1.88	1.52
Medium	-	-	-	-	- 2.48	1.06
Pronounced	-	-	-	-	4.36	1.94
Temporal fullness						
Submedium	-	-	- 6.46	3.61	(- 1.95	1.10)*
Medium	-	-	8.93	4.25	(1.6	0.78)*
Lambdoid flattening						
Absent	-	-	-	-	- 3.45	1.55
Present	-	-	-	-	3.45	1.55
Asymmetry						
Right	6.20	3.76	-	-	-	-
Left	-	-	-	-	- 1.45	0.91
None	-	-	-	-	- 4.74	2.24
Neck						
Medium in length,breadth	-	-	-	-	4.47	2.02
Long and thin	-	-	-	-	- 3.71	1.76
Short and thick	-	-	-	-	- 0.76	0.75
Shoulder slope						
Medium	-	-	7.42	3.69	(2.61	1.30)*
Pronounced	-	-	- 7.90	4.09	(- 2.80	1.45)*

Table VI-100. Summary of Morphological Differentiation of Offenses from
Total Series on Basis of State Composition

Other Sex Offenses

	Significant and Independent of State Sampling		Crude Differences Invalidated by State Sampling		Insignificant Difference	
	Diff.	x p.e.	Diff.	x p.e.	Diff.	x p.e.
Hair quantity, head						
Small	-	-	-	-	3.49	2.06
Large	-	-	-	-	- 1.84	0.88
Hair quantity, beard						
Small	-	-	-	-	- 2.80	1.09
Large	-	-	-	-	1.11	0.60

*Independent difference corrected for state sampling.

Table VI-100 (cont'd).

	Significant and Independent of State Sampling		Crude Differences Invalidated by State Sampling		Insignificant Difference	
	Diff.	x p.e.	Diff.	x p.e.	Diff.	x p.e.
Hair quantity, body						
Small	-10.81	4.02	-	-	-	-
Large	-	-	-	-	3.01	1.63
Skin color						
Red white	-	-	-	-	- 3.06	1.22
Pale white	-	-	-	-	2.78	1.06
Hair form						
Straight	6.99*	3.59*	-	-	-	-
Low waves	- 5.82*	3.88*	-	-	-	-
Deep waves	-	-	-	-	0.02	0.02
Curly	-	-	-	-	- 1.52	1.90
Hair color						
Black	-	-	-	-	1.60	1.37
Dark brown	-	-	-	-	2.57	1.00
Red brown	-	-	-	-	2.52	1.17
Light brown	-	-	- 7.98	3.35	(- 6.68	2.84)*
Ash-blond	-	-	-	-	- 2.30	2.84
Golden	-	-	-	-	- 2.82	2.85
Red	-	-	-	-	0.11	0.11
Gray, white	6.20*	5.25*	-	-	-	-
Eye color						
Dark brown	-	-	-	-	0.69	0.71
Light brown	-	-	-	-	- 2.40	2.58
Blue-brown	-	-	-	-	- 1.64	0.76
Gray-brown	-	-	-	-	- 3.38	1.65
Green-brown	-	-	-	-	0.27	0.11
Blue	-	-	-	-	3.57	1.68
Blue-gray	-	-	-	-	2.91	1.81
Iris						
Homogeneous	-	-	-	-	2.88	2.00
Rayed	-	-	-	-	3.44	1.44
Zoned	-	-	-	-	- 4.46	1.79
Speckled	-	-	-	-	2.10	0.90
Diffused	-	-	-	-	- 3.96	2.62
Eye folds						
Epicanthus	-	-	-	-	1.60	1.44
Median	-	-	-	-	- 2.86	1.58
External	-	-	-	-	1.05	0.68
Absent	-	-	-	-	0.21	0.09
Eyebrows thickness						
Submedium	-	-	-	-	0.93	0.84
Pronounced	-	-	-	-	3.48	1.39
Forehead height						
Submedium	-	-	-	-	- 0.06	0.03
Medium	-	-	-	-	- 1.31	0.50
Pronounced	-	-	-	-	1.36	0.59
Forehead slope						
Absent, submedium	-	-	-	-	0.47	0.32
Medium	-	-	-	-	- 4.35	1.64
Pronounced	-	-	-	-	3.88	1.52
Nasal root height						
Submedium	-	-	-	-	- 0.29	0.43
Medium	-	-	- 7.71	3.71	(- 1.72	0.83)*
Pronounced	-	-	8.00	4.00	(2.32	1.16)*

*Independent difference corrected for state sampling.

Table VI-100 (cont'd).	Significant and Independent of State Sampling		Crude Differences Invalidated by State Sampling		Insignificant Difference	
	Diff.	x p.e.	Diff.	x p.e.	Diff.	x p.e.
Nasal root breadth						
Submedium	-	-	-	-	- 0.87	0.75
Medium	-	-	-	-	- 2.97	1.58
Pronounced	-	-	-	-	3.83	2.44
Nasal bridge height						
Medium	-	-	-	-	- 7.65	2.96
Pronounced	-	-	7.98	3.02	(0.67	0.25)*
Nasal bridge breadth						
Submedium	-	-	-	-	- 0.82	0.84
Pronounced	-	-	-	-	- 0.62	0.32
Nasal profile						
Concave	-	-	-	-	2.40	1.07
Straight	-	-	-	-	- 1.28	0.75
Convex	-	-	-	-	3.83	1.74
Concavo-convex	-	-	-	-	- 4.94	1.84
Nasal tip thickness						
Submedium	-	-	-	-	0.68	0.42
Medium	-	-	-	-	1.65	0.67
Pronounced	-	-	-	-	- 2.31	1.05
Nasal septum inclination						
Up	-	-	-	-	- 1.47	0.58
Down	-	-	-	-	1.25	0.50
Nasal septum deflection						
Right	-	-	10.29	4.45	(6.07	2.63)*
Left	-	-	-	-	2.59	1.62
Absent	-	-	-12.89	5.04	(- 6.84	2.67)*
Lips integumental thickness						
Submedium	-	-	-	-	- 2.12	1.20
Medium	-	-	-	-	4.43	2.15
Pronounced	-	-	-	-	- 2.30	1.84
Lips membranous thickness						
Submedium	9.31*	4.65*	-	-	-	-
Medium	-	-	-11.64	4.62	(- 7.22	2.87)*
Upper, small; lower, pronounced	-	-	-	-	- 1.27	0.71
Pronounced	-	-	-	-	0.43	0.47
Lip seam						
Absent, submedium	-	-	-	-	2.19	1.15
Medium	-	-	-	-	- 5.69	2.22
Pronounced	-	-	-	-	3.50	1.64
Alveolar prognathism						
Absent	-	-	-	-	- 5.58	2.72
Submedium	-	-	-	-	4.16	2.30
Medium	-	-	-	-	1.85	1.73
Facial prognathism						
Medium	-	-	-	-	2.27	2.06
Chin form						
Median	-	-	-	-	0.47	0.18
Bilateral	-	-	-	-	- 0.47	0.18
Malars prominence						
Submedium	-	-	-	-	- 0.36	0.29
Medium	-	-	-	-	5.24	2.10
Pronounced	-	-	-	-	- 4.88	2.08
Cheeks fullness						
Submedium	7.53*	3.25*	-	-	-	-
Medium	-	-	-	-	- 4.95	1.85
Pronounced	-	-	- 7.33	3.52	(- 4.87	2.34)*

*Independent difference corrected for state sampling.

Table VI-100 (cont'd).	Significant and Independent of State Sampling		Crude Differences Invalidated by State Sampling		Insignificant Difference	
	Diff.	x p.e.	Diff.	x p.e.	Diff.	x p.e.
Gonial angles						
Submedium	-	-	-	-	4.06	2.32
Pronounced	-	-	-	-	- 1.35	0.66
Cheeks wrinkling						
Absent	-12.26	4.54	-	-	-	-
Slight, medium	-	-	-	-	- 1.22	0.47
Pronounced	13.48	7.37	-	-	-	-
Teeth wear						
Slight, medium	-10.29	4.88	-	-	-	-
Pronounced	11.35	5.51	-	-	-	-
Teeth caries						
Few	- 9.34	3.68	-	-	-	-
Many	11.80	4.76	-	-	-	-
Teeth lost						
None	-10.14*	4.24*	-	-	-	-
Few	-	-	-	-	- 5.31	1.97
Many	15.38*	6.60*	-	-	-	-
Bite						
Edge-to-edge	7.31	3.19	-	-	-	-
Slight over	-	-	-	-	- 5.10	1.74
Ear lobes						
Submedium	-	-	-	-	- 1.15	0.68
Medium	-	-	-	-	1.54	0.63
Pronounced	-	-	-	-	- 0.38	0.18
Ear lobe attachment						
Attached	-	-	-	-	- 6.35	2.42
Free	-	-	-	-	6.39	2.44
Roll of helix						
Submedium	-	-	-	-	0.09	0.04
Medium, pronounced	-	-	-	-	0	0
Darwin's point						
Absent	-	-	-	-	2.16	0.81
Submedium	-	-	-	-	- 1.94	0.80
Pronounced	-	-	-	-	- 0.23	0.13
Ear protrusion						
Submedium	-	-	-	-	1.12	0.79
Medium	-	-	-	-	0.55	0.21
Pronounced	-	-	-	-	- 1.66	0.54
Temporal fullness						
Submedium	-	-	-	-	- 4.44	2.16
Pronounced	-	-	-	-	4.29	2.70
Lambdoid flattening						
Absent	-	-	-	-	- 1.15	0.45
Present	-	-	-	-	1.15	0.45
Asymmetry						
Right	7.26*	3.90*	-	-	-	-
Left	-	-	-	-	- 1.70	0.93
None	-	-	-	-	- 5.83	2.44
Neck						
Medium in length, breadth	-	-	-	-	0.22	0.09
Long and thin	-	-	-	-	1.33	0.55
Short and thick	-	-	-	-	- 1.55	1.34
Shoulder slope						
Medium	-	-	-	-	3.30	1.44
Pronounced	-	-	-	-	- 2.69	1.22

*Independent difference corrected for state sampling.

Table VI-101. Summary of Morphological Differentiation of Offenses from
Total Series on Basis of State Composition

Versus Public Welfare

	Significant and Independent of State Sampling		Crude Differences Invalidated by State Sampling		Insignificant Difference	
	Diff.	x p.e.	Diff.	x p.e.	Diff.	x p.e.
Hair quantity, head					-	-
Small	5.56*	4.34*	-	-	4.56	2.89
Large	-	-	-	-		
Hair quantity, beard					- 0.62	0.32
Small	-	-	-	-	1.33	0.96
Large	-	-	-	-		
Hair quantity, body					-	-
Small	- 9.65*	4.73*	-	-	3.64	2.60
Large	-	-	-	-		
Skin color						
Red white	-	-	9.32	4.90	(4.42	2.33)*
Pale white	-	-	- 6.09	3.08	(- 3.20	1.62)*
Hair form						
Straight	-	-	-	-	- 1.76	1.22
Low waves	-	-	-	-	1.78	1.58
Deep waves	-	-	-	-	- 0.46	0.58
Curly	-	-	-	-	0.15	0.25
Hair color					1.33	1.48
Black	-	-	-	-	(- 3.09	1.58)*
Dark brown	-	-	- 6.35	3.24	0.63	0.38
Red brown	-	-	-	-	0.43	0.24
Light brown	-	-	-	-	(- 1.64	2.64)*
Ash-blond	-	-	- 1.90	3.06	- 0.31	0.41
Golden	-	-	-	-	1.30	1.62
Red	-	-	-	-	-	-
Gray, white	4.43*	4.92*	-	-		
Eye color					- 0.98	1.34
Dark brown	-	-	-	-	- 1.90	2.71
Light brown	-	-	-	-	- 3.97	2.42
Blue-brown	-	-	-	-	(- 0.43	0.28)*
Gray-brown	-	-	10.25	6.66	(0.10	0.06)*
Green-brown	-	-	- 6.06	3.35	1.91	1.19
Blue	-	-	-	-	0.75	0.62
Blue-gray	-	-	-	-		
Iris					- 1.47	1.35
Homogeneous	-	-	-	-	1.10	0.61
Rayed	-	-	-	-	3.43	1.82
Zoned	-	-	-	-	- 1.49	0.84
Speckled	-	-	-	-	- 1.57	1.36
Diffused	-	-	-	-		
Eye folds					- 0.88	1.05
Epicanthus	-	-	-	-	- 3.09	2.26
Median	-	-	-	-	2.77	2.37
External	-	-	-	-	1.21	0.68
Absent	-	-	-	-		
Eyebrows thickness					1.86	2.21
Submedium	-	-	-	-	1.57	0.82
Pronounced	-	-	-	-		
Forehead height					0.20	0.15
Submedium	-	-	-	-	- 2.20	1.12
Medium	-	-	-	-	1.99	1.14
Pronounced	-	-	-	-		

*Independent difference corrected for state sampling.

Table VI-101 (cont'd).	Significant and Independent of State Sampling		Crude Differences Invalidated by State Sampling		Insignificant Difference	
	Diff.	x p.e.	Diff.	x p.e.	Diff.	x p.e.
Forehead slope						
Absent, submedium	-	-	- 3.86	3.48	(- 0.82	0.74)*
Medium	-	-	-	-	4.54	2.25
Pronounced	-	-	-	-	- 0.68	0.35
Nasion depression						
Submedium	-	-	- 5.72	4.85	(- 1.62	1.37)*
Medium	-	-	9.21	5.06	(2.89	1.59)*
Pronounced	-	-	-	-	- 3.39	2.16
Nasal root height						
Submedium	-	-	-	-	- 0.83	1.63
Medium	-	-	-	-	2.56	1.63
Pronounced	-	-	-	-	- 1.71	1.13
Nasal root breadth						
Submedium	-	-	- 3.28	3.73	(- 0.48	0.55)*
Medium	-	-	6.47	4.56	(2.06	1.45)*
Pronounced	-	-	-	-	- 3.18	2.67
Nasal bridge height						
Medium	-	-	-	-	2.17	1.08
Pronounced	-	-	-	-	- 2.23	1.12
Nasal bridge breadth						
Submedium	-	-	- 2.30	3.11	(- 0.24	0.32)*
Pronounced	-	-	-	-	- 0.29	0.19
Nasal profile						
Concave	-	-	- 6.19	3.62	(- 3.83	2.24)*
Straight	-	-	4.01	3.08	(0.59	0.45)*
Convex	-	-	-	-	3.08	1.84
Concavo-convex	-	-	-	-	- 0.91	0.45
Nasal tip thickness						
Submedium	-	-	- 8.43	6.85	(- 2.73	2.22)*
Medium	-	-	-	-	2.07	1.10
Pronounced	-	-	6.36	3.81	(4.02	2.41)*
Nasal septum inclination						
Up	-	-	- 9.55	5.03	(- 3.09	1.63)*
Down	-	-	9.60	5.05	(3.06	1.61)*
Nasal septum deflection						
Right	-	-	- 9.09	5.25	(0.57	0.33)*
Left	-	-	-	-	- 1.01	0.84
Absent	-	-	10.10	5.26	(- 2.54	1.32)*
Lips integumental thickness						
Submedium	- 4.51*	3.37*	-	-	-	-
Medium	-	-	7.60	4.87	(3.92	2.51)*
Pronounced	-	-	-	-	- 0.56	0.60
Lips membranous thickness						
Submedium	-	-	-	-	2.08	1.37
Medium	-	-	-	-	- 1.13	0.60
Upper, small; lower, pronounced	-	-	-	-	0.75	0.56
Pronounced	-	-	-	-	- 1.71	2.48
Lip seam						
Absent, submedium	-	-	8.96	6.22	(3.92	2.72)*
Medium	-	-	- 6.20	3.21	(- 1.24	0.64)*
Pronounced	-	-	-	-	- 2.76	1.72
Alveolar prognathism						
Absent	-	-	-	-	2.04	1.32
Submedium	-	-	-	-	- 1.78	1.29
Medium	-	-	-	-	0.17	0.21

*Independent difference corrected for state sampling.

Table VI-101 (cont'd).	Significant and Independent of State Sampling		Crude Differences Invalidated by State Sampling		Insignificant Difference	
	Diff.	x p.e.	Diff.	x p.e.	Diff.	x p.e.
Chin form						
Median	-	-	- 6.08	3.01	(- 2.78	1.38)*
Bilateral	-	-	6.08	3.01	(2.78	1.38)*
Malars prominence						
Submedium	-	-	-	-	- 2.52	2.68
Medium	- 6.28*	3.30*	-	-	-	-
Pronounced	6.20*	3.48*	-	-	-	-
Cheeks fullness						
Submedium	-	-	- 7.26	4.15	(0.80	0.46)*
Medium	-	-	-	-	- 4.31	2.13
Pronounced	-	-	11.57	7.42	(1.98	1.27)*
Gonial angles						
Submedium	- 6.89*	5.14*	-	-	-	-
Pronounced	-	-	6.75	4.30	(- 1.58	1.01)*
Cheeks wrinkling						
Absent	-10.58*	5.19*	-	-	-	-
Slight, medium	-	-	6.80	3.49	(1.65	0.85)*
Pronounced	8.92*	6.46*	-	-	-	-
Teeth wear						
Slight, medium	- 9.70	6.14	-	-	-	-
Pronounced	10.35	6.72	-	-	-	-
Teeth caries						
Few	- 6.60*	3.47*	-	-	-	-
Many	7.42*	4.03*	-	-	-	-
Teeth lost						
None	-	-	-	-	- 0.79	0.44
Few	- 6.28*	3.08*	-	-	-	-
Many	9.58	5.41	-	-	-	-
Bite						
Edge-to-edge	-	-	-	-	4.37	2.53
Slight over	-	-	- 6.78	3.07	(- 5.08	2.30)*
Marked over	-	-	-	-	4.33	2.28
Ear lobes						
Submedium	- 4.35*	3.40*	-	-	-	-
Medium	-	-	-	-	3.01	1.63
Pronounced	-	-	-	-	3.80	2.45
Ear lobe attachment						
Attached	- 8.12*	4.10*	-	-	-	-
Free	8.16*	4.10*	-	-	-	-
Roll of helix						
Submedium	-	-	-	-	0.68	0.36
Medium, pronounced	-	-	-	-	- 0.59	0.31
Darwin's point						
Absent	-	-	-	-	- 0.93	0.46
Submedium	-	-	-	-	- 2.04	1.11
Pronounced	-	-	-	-	2.97	2.17
Antihelix prominence						
Submedium	-	-	-	-	2.04	1.82
Pronounced	-	-	-	-	- 1.94	1.35
Ear protrusion						
Submedium	-	-	-	-	- 0.10	0.09
Medium	-	-	-	-	0.52	0.26
Pronounced	-	-	-	-	- 0.42	0.22
Temporal fullness						
Submedium	-	-	10.34	6.63	(4.45	2.85)*
Medium	-	-	- 6.94	3.83	(- 4.05	2.24)*
Pronounced	-	-	-	-	- 3.40	2.83

*Independent difference corrected for state sampling.

Table VI-101 (cont'd).	Significant and Independent of State Sampling		Crude Differences Invalidated by State Sampling		Insignificant Difference	
	Diff.	x p.e.	Diff.	x p.e.	Diff.	x p.e.
Lambdoid flattening						
Absent	-	-	11.50	5.99	(1.41	0.73)*
Present	-	-	-11.50	5.99	(- 1.41	0.73)*
Asymmetry						
Right	-	-	-	-	- 3.10	2.15
Left	-	-	-	-	3.84	2.72
None	-	-	-	-	- 0.73	0.39
Neck						
Medium in length,breadth	-	-	-	-	4.43	2.31
Long and thin	-	-	-	-	- 5.46	2.97
Short and thick	-	-	-	-	1.02	1.16
Shoulders slope						
Medium	-	-	-	-	4.21	2.42
Pronounced	-	-	-	-	- 3.98	2.38

Table VI-102. Summary of Morphological Differentiation of Offenses from
Total Series on Basis of State Composition

Arson and All Other Offenses

	Significant and Independent of State Sampling		Crude Differences Invalidated by State Sampling		Insignificant Difference	
	Diff.	x p.e.	Diff.	x p.e.	Diff.	x p.e.
Hair quantity, head						
Small	-	-	-	-	0.57	0.28
Large	-	-	-	-	- 3.84	1.51
Hair quantity, beard						
Small	-	-	-	-	- 2.24	0.71
Large	-	-	-	-	1.10	0.49
Hair quantity, body						
Small	-	-	-	-	- 0.33	0.10
Large	-	-	-	-	0.04	0.02
Skin color						
Pale white	-	-	-	-	2.93	0.92
Hair form						
Straight	-	-	-	-	- 5.74	2.47
Low waves	-	-	-	-	5.21	2.86
Deep waves	-	-	-	-	- 1.07	0.84
Curly	-	-	-	-	1.69	1.76
Hair color						
Black	-	-	-	-	3.72	2.58
Dark brown	-	-	-	-	- 1.51	0.48
Red brown	-	-	-	-	- 0.58	0.22
Light brown	-	-	-	-	- 2.46	0.86
Ash-blond	3.35*	3.38*	-	-	-	-
Golden	-	-	-	-	- 1.54	1.28
Red	-	-	-	-	- 2.89	2.29
Gray, white	-	-	-	-	1.74	1.21

*Independent difference corrected for state sampling.

Table VI-102 (cont'd).	Significant and Independent of State Sampling		Crude Differences Invalidated by State Sampling		Insignificant Difference	
	Diff.	x p.e.	Diff.	x p.e.	Diff.	x p.e.
Eye color						
Dark brown	-	-	-	-	- 0.40	0.34
Light brown	-	-	-	-	- 1.13	1.00
Blue-brown	-	-	-	-	- 0.89	0.35
Gray-brown	-	-	-	-	- 2.82	1.13
Green-brown	-	-	-	-	6.91	2.37
Blue	-	-	-	-	1.29	0.50
Blue-gray	-	-	-	-	- 2.96	1.52
Iris						
Homogeneous	-	-	-	-	1.02	0.58
Rayed	-	-	-	-	2.11	0.72
Zoned	-	-	-	-	- 3.77	1.24
Speckled	-	-	-	-	0.50	0.18
Diffused	-	-	-	-	0.14	0.08
Eye folds						
Epicanthus	4.67*	3.46*	-	-	-	-
Median	-	-	-	-	- 2.18	0.99
External	-	-	-	-	0.76	0.40
Absent	-	-	-	-	- 3.89	1.35
Eyebrows thickness						
Submedium	-	-	-	-	1.45	1.08
Pronounced	-	-	-	-	5.58	1.82
Forehead height						
Submedium	-	-	-	-	- 0.02	0.01
Medium	-	-	-	-	- 2.70	0.85
Pronounced	-	-	-	-	2.71	0.96
Forehead slope						
Absent, submedium	-	-	-	-	1.57	0.88
Medium	-	-	-	-	- 0.05	0.02
Pronounced	-	-	-	-	- 1.52	0.49
Nasion depression						
Pronounced	-	-	-	-	5.12	2.02
Nasal root height						
Submedium	-	-	-	-	- 0.64	0.78
Medium	-	-	-	-	- 3.24	1.28
Pronounced	-	-	-	-	3.89	1.59
Nasal root breadth						
Submedium	-	-	-	-	1.96	1.39
Medium	-	-	-	-	- 6.14	2.68
Pronounced	-	-	-	-	4.18	2.20
Nasal bridge height						
Medium	-	-	-	-	1.86	0.58
Pronounced	-	-	-	-	- 1.52	0.47
Nasal bridge breadth						
Submedium	-	-	-	-	1.38	1.15
Pronounced	-	-	-	-	2.60	1.09
Nasal profile						
Concave	-	-	-	-	- 1.88	0.69
Straight	-	-	-	-	- 0.60	0.29
Convex	-	-	-	-	4.40	1.65
Concavo-convex	-	-	-	-	- 1.92	0.59
Nasal tip thickness						
Submedium	-	-	-	-	- 3.19	1.62
Medium	-	-	-	-	- 3.00	0.99
Pronounced	-	-	-	-	6.20	2.32

*Independent difference corrected for state sampling.

Table VI-102 (cont'd).	Significant and Independent of State Sampling		Crude Differences Invalidated by State Sampling		Insignificant Difference	
	Diff.	x p.e.	Diff.	x p.e.	Diff.	x p.e.
Nasal septum inclination						
Up	-	-	-	-	- 4.06	1.33
Down	-	-	-	-	3.53	1.16
Nasal septum deflection						
Right	-	-	-	-	0.04	0.01
Left	-	-	-	-	2.19	1.13
Absent	-	-	-	-	- 2.23	0.72
Lips integumental thickness						
Submedium	-	-	-	-	6.33	2.96
Medium	-	-	- 9.42	3.75	(- 4.56	1.82)*
Pronounced	-	-	-	-	3.10	2.05
Lips membranous thickness						
Submedium	-	-	-	-	2.75	1.12
Medium	-	-	-	-	1.97	0.64
Upper, small; lower, pronounced	-	-	-	-	- 4.76	2.19
Pronounced	-	-	-	-	0.03	0.03
Lip seam						
Absent, submedium	-	-	-	-	- 5.74	2.48
Medium	-	-	-	-	8.40	2.71
Pronounced	-	-	-	-	- 2.67	1.04
Alveolar prognathism						
Absent	-	-	-	-	- 6.67	2.67
Submedium	8.46*	3.83*	-	-	-	-
Medium	-	-	-	-	- 3.14	2.42
Facial prognathism						
Medium	-	-	-	-	4.52	2.67
Chin form						
Median	-	-	-	-	1.39	0.43
Bilateral	-	-	-	-	- 1.39	0.43
Malars prominence						
Submedium	-	-	-	-	0.16	0.10
Medium	-	-	-	-	0	0
Pronounced	-	-	-	-	- 0.17	0.06
Cheeks fullness						
Submedium	-	-	-	-	3.07	1.08
Medium	-	-	-	-	- 2.72	0.83
Pronounced	-	-	-	-	- 0.35	0.14
Gonial angles						
Submedium	-	-	-	-	- 6.06	2.83
Cheeks wrinkling						
Absent	-	-	-	-	1.35	0.41
Slight, medium	-	-	-	-	- 2.87	0.91
Pronounced	-	-	-	-	- 1.52	0.68
Teeth wear						
Slight, medium	-	-	-	-	- 3.57	1.41
Pronounced	-	-	-	-	3.60	1.45
Teeth lost						
None	-	-	-	-	- 7.76	2.65
Few	-	-	-	-	- 1.12	0.34
Many	-	-	8.85	3.10	(8.13	2.84)*
Bite						
Under	-	-	-	-	1.51	1.31
Ear lobes						
Submedium	-	-	-	-	1.54	0.75
Medium	-	-	-	-	- 6.26	2.11
Pronounced	-	-	-	-	4.73	1.89

*Independent difference corrected for state sampling.

Table VI-102 (cont'd).	Significant and Independent of State Sampling		Crude Differences Invalidated by State Sampling		Insignificant Difference	
	Diff.	x p.e.	Diff.	x p.e.	Diff.	x p.e.
Ear lobe attachment						
Attached	-	-	-	-	0.04	0.01
Free	-	-	-	-	0	0
Roll of helix						
Submedium	-	-	-	-	3.79	1.24
Medium, pronounced	-	-	-	-	- 4.67	1.52
Darwin's point						
Absent	-	-	-	-	- 0.09	0.03
Submedium	-	-	-	-	6.20	2.09
Pronounced	-	-	-	-	- 6.12	2.76
Antihelix prominence						
Submedium	-	-	-	-	- 4.24	2.37
Pronounced	-	-	-	-	4.98	2.16
Ear protrusion						
Submedium	-	-	-	-	- 1.61	0.92
Medium	-	-	-	-	- 1.19	0.36
Pronounced	-	-	-	-	2.80	0.89
Temporal fullness						
Submedium	-	-	-	-	6.59	2.64
Medium	-	-	-	-	- 5.71	1.96
Lambdoid flattening						
Absent	-	-	-	-	- 0.37	0.12
Present	-	-	-	-	0.37	0.12
Asymmetry						
Right	-	-	-	-	0.20	0.09
Left	-	-	-	-	- 0.03	0.01
None	-	-	-	-	- 0.16	0.05
Neck						
Medium in length,breadth	-	-	-	-	5.49	1.78
Long and thin	-	-	-	-	- 4.51	1.53
Short and thick	-	-	-	-	- 0.98	0.70
Shoulders slope						
Medium	-	-	-	-	4.41	1.58
Pronounced	-	-	-	-	- 2.78	1.04

Table VI-103. Number of Significant and Insignificant Morphological Differences on Basis of State Composition by Offenses

	Total Number of Observations in Crime Group	Significant Differences Independent of State Sampling		Crude Differences Invalidated by State Sampling		Insignificant Differences	
		No.	Per Cent	No.	Per Cent	No.	Per Cent
First degree murder	164	25	15.24	18	10.98	121	73.78
Second degree murder	164	21	12.80	33	20.12	110	67.07
Assault	164	3	1.83	12	7.32	149	90.85
Robbery	164	25	15.24	8	4.88	131	79.88
Burglary and larceny	164	38	23.17	7	4.27	119	72.56
Forgery and fraud	164	8	4.88	16	9.76	140	85.37
Rape	164	16	9.76	17	10.37	131	79.88
Other sex	164	16	9.76	8	4.88	140	85.37
Vs. public welfare	164	18	10.98	34	20.73	112	68.29
Arson and all other	164	3	1.83	2	1.22	159	96.95

Table VI-104.   Differentiation by Offense Groups in Terms of Deviation of
Complete Morphological Characters from the Total Series

	Differentiated		Undifferentiated		Total
	No.	Per Cent	No.	Per Cent	No.
First degree murder	19	40.43	28	59.57	47
Second degree murder	14	29.79	33	70.21	47
Assault	1	2.13	46	97.87	47
Robbery	14	29.79	33	70.21	47
Burglary and larceny	23	48.94	24	51.06	47
Forgery and fraud	6	12.77	41	87.23	47
Rape	13	27.66	34	72.34	47
Other sex	11	23.40	36	76.60	47
Vs. public welfare	12	25.53	35	74.47	47
Arson and all other	3	6.38	44	93.62	47
Total	116	24.68	354	75.32	470

Table VI-105.   Hair Quantity by Age Grouping
                              Head

	Small		Medium		Large		Total
	No.	Per Cent	No.	Per Cent	No.	Per Cent	No.
15-19	4	.70	457	80.17	109	19.12	570
20-24	20	2.29	659	75.49	194	22.22	873
25-29	65	6.95	676	72.30	194	20.75	935
30-34	76	12.92	410	69.73	102	17.35	588
35-39	64	15.76	278	68.47	64	15.76	406
40-44	59	20.63	185	64.68	42	14.68	286
45-49	45	24.72	113	62.09	24	13.19	182
50-54	48	30.57	85	54.14	24	15.29	157
55-59	19	25.33	49	65.33	7	9.33	75
60-64	16	24.24	44	66.67	6	9.09	66
65-69	19	38.00	30	60.00	1	2.00	50
Total	435	10.39	2986	71.30	767	18.31	4188

                              Beard

	Small		Medium		Large		Total
	No.	Per Cent	No.	Per Cent	No.	Per Cent	No.
15-19	362	63.51	194	34.04	14	2.46	570
20-24	340	38.95	450	51.55	83	9.50	873
25-29	252	26.98	525	56.21	157	16.81	934
30-34	142	24.11	351	59.59	96	16.30	589
35-39	107	26.35	218	53.69	81	19.95	406
40-44	71	24.91	159	55.79	55	19.30	285
45-49	51	28.02	91	50.00	40	21.98	182
50-54	55	35.03	80	50.96	22	14.01	157
55-59	41	54.67	30	40.00	4	5.33	75
60-64	24	36.92	34	52.31	7	10.77	65
65-69	29	58.00	16	32.00	5	10.00	50
Total	1474	35.21	2148	51.31	564	13.47	4186

                              Body

	Small		Medium		Large		Total
	No.	Per Cent	No.	Per Cent	No.	Per Cent	No.
15-19	449	79.05	108	19.01	11	1.94	568
20-24	491	56.70	303	34.99	72	8.31	866
25-29	401	43.16	393	42.30	135	14.53	929
30-34	232	39.39	257	43.63	100	16.98	589
35-39	153	37.78	172	42.47	80	19.75	405
40-44	83	29.12	131	45.96	71	24.91	285
45-49	58	32.22	84	46.67	38	21.11	180
50-54	47	30.32	79	50.97	29	18.71	155
55-59	35	47.30	27	36.49	12	16.22	74
60-64	22	33.85	32	49.23	11	16.92	65
65-69	24	48.00	20	40.00	6	12.00	50
Total	1995	47.89	1606	38.55	565	13.56	4166

Table VI-106.

Skin Color by Age Grouping

	Red White		Pale White		Ruddy		Olive		Light Yellow-brown		Light Brown		Total
	No.	Per Cent	No.	Per Cent	No.	Per Cent	No.	Per Cent	No.	Per Cent	No.	Per Cent	No.
15-19	160	28.07	356	62.46	5	.88	23	4.04	1	.18	25	4.39	570
20-24	272	31.16	555	63.57	3	.34	24	2.75	0	0	19	2.18	873
25-29	288	30.74	593	63.29	8	.85	26	2.77	1	.11	21	2.24	937
30-34	177	30.00	372	63.05	10	1.69	18	3.05	0	0	13	2.20	590
35-39	128	31.53	255	62.81	2	.49	9	2.22	0	0	12	2.96	406
40-44	93	32.40	173	60.28	2	.70	14	4.88	0	0	5	1.74	287
45-49	66	36.26	100	54.94	2	1.10	5	2.75	1	.55	8	4.40	182
50-54	68	43.31	85	54.14	0	0	2	1.27	0	0	2	1.27	157
55-59	29	38.67	40	53.33	1	1.33	3	4.00	0	0	2	2.67	75
60-64	25	38.46	38	58.46	0	0	1	1.54	0	0	1	1.54	65
65-69	15	30.00	30	60.00	0	0	4	8.00	0	0	1	2.00	50
Total	1321	31.51	2597	61.95	33	.79	129	3.08	3	.07	109	2.60	4192

Table VI-107.

Hair Form by Age Grouping

	Straight		Low Waves		Deep Waves		Curly		Frizzly		Total
	No.	Per Cent	No.	Per Cent	No.	Per Cent	No.	Per Cent	No.	Per Cent	No.
15-19	483	85.03	45	7.92	22	3.87	18	3.17	0	0	568
20-24	734	84.37	79	9.08	30	3.45	27	3.10	0	0	870
25-29	784	83.76	85	9.08	49	5.24	17	1.82	1	.11	936
30-34	504	85.42	47	7.97	20	3.39	16	2.71	3	.51	590
35-39	337	83.42	38	9.41	22	5.44	7	1.73	0	0	404
40-44	245	85.37	24	8.36	14	4.88	4	1.39	0	0	287
45-49	159	88.33	10	5.56	7	3.89	4	2.22	0	0	180
50-54	72	96.00	3	4.00	0	0	0	0	0	0	75
55-59	142	90.45	10	6.37	3	1.91	2	1.27	0	0	157
60-64	61	92.42	4	6.06	0	0	1	1.51	0	0	66
65-69	47	95.92	1	2.04	0	0	1	2.04	0	0	49
Total	3568	85.32	346	8.27	167	3.99	97	2.32	4	.10	4182

Table VI-108.   Hair Color by Age Grouping

	Black		Dark Brown		Red Brown		Light Brown		Ash-blond	
	No.	Per Cent	No.	Per Cent	No.	Per Cent	No.	Per Cent	No.	Per Cent
15-19	7	1.24	166	29.43	113	20.57	194	34.40	29	5.14
20-24	19	2.19	283	32.68	200	23.10	251	28.98	26	3.00
25-29	54	5.84	312	33.73	195	21.08	258	27.89	19	2.05
30-34	34	5.78	229	38.94	110	18.71	150	25.51	8	1.36
35-39	28	6.98	154	38.40	84	20.95	94	23.44	3	.75
40-44	22	7.77	125	44.17	52	18.37	53	18.73	1	.35
45-49	14	7.73	64	35.36	39	21.55	28	15.47	2	1.10
50-54	20	12.99	56	36.36	17	11.04	19	12.34	1	.65
55-59	1	1.35	26	35.14	10	13.51	13	17.57	0	0
60-64	5	7.81	14	21.88	7	10.94	7	10.94	1	1.56
65-69	3	6.00	6	12.00	2	4.00	7	14.00	0	0
Total	207	4.99	1435	34.58	832	20.05	1074	25.88	90	2.17

	Golden		Red		Gray, White		Total	
	No.	Per Cent	No.	Per Cent	No.	Per Cent	No.	
15-19	35	6.20	15	2.66	2	.35	564	
20-24	43	4.96	40	4.62	4	.46	866	
25-29	35	3.78	45	4.86	7	.76	925	
30-34	14	2.38	26	4.42	17	2.89	588	
35-39	9	2.24	13	3.24	16	3.99	401	
40-44	4	1.41	9	3.18	17	6.01	283	
45-49	0	0	4	2.21	30	16.57	181	
50-54	0	0	4	2.60	37	24.03	154	
55-59	0	0	1	1.35	23	31.08	74	
60-64	1	1.56	2	3.13	27	42.19	64	
65-69	1	2.00	0	0	31	62.00	50	
Total	142	3.42	159	3.83	211	5.08	4150	

Table VI-109.   Eye Color by Age Grouping

	Dark Brown		Light Brown		Blue Brown		Gray Brown	
	No.	Per Cent	No.	Per Cent	No.	Per Cent	No.	Per Cent
15-19	15	2.63	13	2.28	94	16.49	80	14.03
20-24	25	2.88	33	3.80	178	20.48	141	16.22
25-29	32	3.42	44	4.70	190	20.28	156	16.65
30-34	34	5.76	18	3.05	119	20.17	108	18.30
35-39	19	4.68	5	1.23	85	20.94	88	21.67
40-44	11	3.83	5	1.74	61	21.25	45	15.68
45-49	3	1.66	5	2.76	25	13.81	47	25.97
50-54	2	1.28	5	3.20	40	25.64	30	19.23
55-59	0	0	1	1.33	26	34.67	12	16.00
60-64	2	3.03	0	0	22	33.33	13	19.70
65-69	2	4.00	1	2.00	12	24.00	10	20.00
Total	145	3.46	130	3.10	852	20.35	730	17.44

Table VI-109 (cont'd).

| | Green Brown | | Blue | | Blue Gray | | Total |
	No.	Per Cent	No.	Per Cent	No.	Per Cent	No.
15-19	190	33.33	124	21.75	54	9.47	570
20-24	253	29.11	159	18.30	80	9.21	869
25-29	249	26.57	183	19.53	83	8.86	937
30-34	152	25.76	115	19.49	44	7.46	590
35-39	99	24.38	71	17.49	39	9.61	406
40-44	80	27.87	57	19.86	28	9.76	287
45-49	51	28.18	29	16.02	21	11.60	181
50-54	34	21.79	23	14.74	22	14.10	156
55-59	14	18.67	17	22.67	5	6.67	75
60-64	7	10.61	14	21.21	8	12.12	66
65-69	4	8.00	10	20.00	11	22.00	50
Total	1133	27.06	802	19.15	395	9.43	4187

Table VI-110.   Sclera by Age Grouping

| | Clear | | Speckled | | Yellow | | Total |
	No.	Per Cent	No.	Per Cent	No.	Per Cent	No.
15-19	540	95.07	25	4.40	3	.53	568
20-24	815	94.55	43	4.99	4	.46	862
25-29	873	94.58	43	4.66	7	.76	923
30-34	554	96.01	21	3.64	2	.35	577
35-39	383	95.51	17	4.24	1	.25	401
40-44	266	95.68	10	3.60	2	.72	278
45-49	169	97.13	5	2.87	0	0	174
50-54	145	94.16	8	5.20	1	.65	154
55-59	69	93.24	5	6.76	0	0	74
60-64	59	92.19	5	7.81	0	0	64
65-69	43	89.58	5	10.42	0	0	48
Total	3916	94.98	187	4.54	20	.48	4123

Table VI-111.   Iris by Age Grouping

| | Homogeneous | | Rayed | | Zoned | | Speckled | | Diffused | | Total |
	No.	Per Cent	No.	Per Cent	No.	Per Cent	No.	Per Cent	No.	Per Cent	No.
15-19	44	7.73	147	25.83	168	29.52	162	28.47	48	8.44	569
20-24	61	7.02	224	25.78	297	34.18	204	23.48	83	9.55	869
25-29	68	7.30	278	29.86	272	29.22	231	24.81	82	8.81	931
30-34	61	10.36	147	24.96	159	26.99	164	27.84	58	9.85	589
35-39	30	7.41	106	26.17	141	34.81	104	25.68	24	5.93	405
40-44	22	7.69	78	27.27	102	35.66	63	22.03	21	7.34	286
45-49	12	6.63	51	28.18	57	31.49	42	23.20	19	10.50	181
50-54	13	8.33	42	26.92	46	29.49	41	26.28	14	8.97	156
55-59	3	4.05	19	25.68	19	25.68	28	37.84	5	6.76	74
60-64	5	7.69	21	32.31	23	35.38	15	23.07	1	1.54	65
65-69	5	10.00	15	30.00	17	34.00	13	26.00	0	0	50
Total	324	7.76	1128	27.02	1301	31.16	1067	25.56	355	8.50	4175

Table VI-112.   Eye Folds by Age Grouping

| | Epicanthus | | Median | | External | | Absent | | Total |
	No.	Per Cent	No.	Per Cent	No.	Per Cent	No.	Per Cent	No.
15-19	48	8.45	102	17.96	21	3.70	397	69.89	568
20-24	46	5.29	165	18.99	42	4.83	616	70.89	869
25-29	43	4.61	145	15.56	86	9.23	658	70.60	932
30-34	23	3.90	53	9.00	51	8.66	462	78.44	589
35-39	6	1.48	30	7.39	57	14.04	313	77.09	406
40-44	2	.70	25	8.74	37	12.94	222	77.62	286
45-49	10	5.49	8	4.40	23	12.64	141	77.47	182
50-54	0	0	7	4.49	29	18.59	120	'6.92	156
55-59	0	0	4	5.33	13	17.33	58	77.33	75
60-64	0	0	1	1.52	10	15.15	55	83.33	66
65-69	1	2.00	2	4.00	9	18.00	38	76.00	50
Total	179	4.28	542	12.97	378	9.04	3080	73.70	4179

Table VI-113.   Eyebrows Thickness by Age Grouping

| | Submedium | | Medium | | Pronounced | | Total |
	No.	Per Cent	No.	Per Cent	No.	Per Cent	No.
15-19	24	4.22	399	70.12	146	25.66	569
20-24	33	3.78	558	63.92	282	32.30	873
25-29	29	3.10	600	64.10	307	32.80	936
30-34	26	4.42	361	61.39	201	34.18	588
35-39	21	5.18	259	63.95	125	30.86	405
40-44	17	5.92	178	62.02	92	32.06	287
45-49	11	6.04	114	62.64	57	31.32	182
50-54	10	6.37	90	57.32	57	36.31	157
55-59	5	6.67	45	60.00	25	33.33	75
60-64	6	9.09	34	51.52	26	39.39	66
65-69	2	4.00	29	58.00	19	38.00	50
Total	184	4.39	2667	63.68	1337	31.92	4188

Table VI-114.   Eyebrows Concurrency by Age Grouping

| | Absent | | Submedium | | Medium | | Pronounced | | Total |
	No.	Per Cent	No.	Per Cent	No.	Per Cent	No.	Per Cent	No.
15-19	257	45.09	174	30.53	116	20.35	23	4.04	570
20-24	405	46.39	240	27.49	171	19.59	57	6.53	873
25-29	454	48.56	253	27.06	169	18.07	59	6.31	935
30-34	293	49.83	142	24.15	118	20.07	35	5.95	588
35-39	226	56.08	98	24.32	60	14.89	19	4.71	403
40-44	170	59.23	58	20.21	43	14.98	16	5.57	287
45-49	118	64.83	39	21.43	21	11.54	4	2.20	182
50-54	110	70.06	27	17.20	15	9.55	5	3.18	157
55-59	54	72.00	13	17.33	7	9.33	1	1.33	75
60-64	48	72.73	11	16.67	6	9.09	1	1.52	66
65-69	36	72.00	10	20.00	4	8.00	0	0	50
Total	2171	51.86	1065	25.44	730	17.44	220	5.26	4186

Table VI-115.   Forehead Height by Age Grouping

| | Submedium | | Medium | | Pronounced | | Total |
	No.	Per Cent	No.	Per Cent	No.	Per Cent	No.
15-19	76	13.33	378	66.32	116	20.35	570
20-24	130	14.89	572	65.52	171	19.59	873
25-29	95	10.15	608	64.96	233	24.89	936
30-34	70	11.88	377	64.01	142	24.11	589
35-39	52	12.81	244	60.10	110	27.09	406
40-44	34	11.85	168	58.54	85	29.62	287
45-49	22	12.09	103	56.59	57	31.32	182
50-54	24	15.29	88	56.05	45	28.66	157
55-59	15	20.00	41	54.67	19	25.33	75
60-64	8	12.12	35	53.03	23	34.85	66
65-69	6	12.00	27	54.00	17	34.00	50
Total	532	12.69	2641	63.02	1018	24.29	4191

Table VI-116.   Forehead Breadth by Age Grouping

| | Submedium | | Medium | | Pronounced | | Total |
	No.	Per Cent	No.	Per Cent	No.	Per Cent	No.
15-19	4	.70	384	67.37	182	31.93	570
20-24	3	.34	520	59.56	350	40.09	873
25-29	6	.64	564	60.19	367	39.17	937
30-34	7	1.19	364	61.90	217	36.90	588
35-39	4	.99	254	62.56	148	36.45	406
40-44	4	1.39	181	63.07	102	35.54	287
45-49	1	.55	112	61.54	69	37.91	182
50-54	3	1.91	101	64.33	53	33.76	157
55-59	1	1.33	39	52.00	35	46.67	75
60-64	1	1.52	45	68.18	20	30.30	66
65-69	0	0	38	76.00	12	24.00	50
Total	34	.81	2602	62.08	1555	37.10	4191

Table VI-117.   Forehead Slope by Age Grouping

| | Absent,Submedium | | Medium | | Pronounced | | Total |
	No.	Per Cent	No.	Per Cent	No.	Per Cent	No.
15-19	73	12.81	334	58.60	163	28.60	570
20-24	59	6.76	535	61.28	279	31.92	873
25-29	86	9.18	538	57.42	313	33.40	937
30-34	38	6.45	322	54.67	229	38.88	589
35-39	26	6.40	214	52.71	166	40.89	406
40-44	21	7.32	187	65.16	79	27.53	287
45-49	17	9.34	106	58.24	59	32.42	182
50-54	7	4.46	73	46.50	77	49.04	157
55-59	8	10.67	39	52.00	28	37.33	75
60-64	1	1.52	34	51.52	31	46.97	66
65-69	4	8.00	25	50.00	21	42.00	50
Total	340	8.11	2407	57.42	1445	34.47	4192

Table VI-118.   Nasal Root Height by Age Grouping

	Submedium		Medium		Pronounced		Total
	No.	Per Cent	No.	Per Cent	No.	Per Cent	No.
15-19	9	1.58	442	77.54	119	20.88	570
20-24	15	1.72	701	80.30	157	17.98	873
25-29	13	1.39	753	80.36	171	18.25	937
30-34	6	1.02	480	81.36	104	17.63	590
35-39	5	1.23	328	80.79	73	17.98	406
40-44	7	2.44	231	80.49	49	17.07	287
45-49	3	1.65	140	76.92	39	21.43	182
50-54	3	1.91	121	77.07	33	21.02	157
55-59	4	5.33	61	81.33	10	13.33	75
60-64	0	0	46	69.70	20	30.30	66
65-69	2	4.00	38	76.00	10	20.00	50
Total	67	1.60	3341	79.68	785	18.72	4193

Table VI-119.   Nasal Root Breadth by Age Grouping

	Submedium		Medium		Pronounced		Total
	No.	Per Cent	No.	Per Cent	No.	Per Cent	No.
15-19	29	5.10	487	85.59	53	9.31	569
20-24	32	3.67	774	88.66	67	7.68	873
25-29	46	4.91	802	85.59	89	9.50	937
30-34	41	6.95	495	83.90	54	9.15	590
35-39	26	6.40	350	86.21	30	7.39	406
40-44	16	5.59	236	82.52	34	11.89	286
45-49	3	1.65	152	83.52	27	14.83	182
50-54	5	3.18	130	82.80	22	14.01	157
55-59	4	5.33	64	85.33	7	9.33	75
60-64	1	1.52	59	89.39	6	9.09	66
65-69	2	4.00	41	82.00	7	14.00	50
Total	205	4.89	3590	85.66	396	9.45	4191

Table VI-120.   Nasal Bridge Height by Age Grouping

	Submedium		Medium		Pronounced		Total
	No.	Per Cent	No.	Per Cent	No.	Per Cent	No.
15-19	3	.53	367	64.39	200	35.09	570
20-24	3	.34	567	64.95	303	34.71	873
25-29	3	.32	564	60.19	370	39.49	937
30-34	2	.34	341	57.80	247	41.86	590
35-39	1	.25	222	54.68	183	45.07	406
40-44	1	.35	157	54.70	129	44.95	287
45-49	0	0	89	48.90	93	51.60	182
50-54	0	0	79	50.32	78	49.68	157
55-59	1	1.33	44	58.67	30	40.00	75
60-64	0	0	30	45.45	36	54.55	66
65-69	0	0	30	60.00	20	40.00	50
Total	14	.33	2490	59.38	1689	40.28	4193

Table VI-121.   Nasal Bridge Breadth by Age Grouping

	Submedium		Medium		Pronounced		Total
	No.	Per Cent	No.	Per Cent	No.	Per Cent	No.
15-19	20	3.51	480	84.21	70	12.28	570
20-24	24	2.75	743	85.11	106	12.14	873
25-29	33	3.53	748	79.91	155	16.56	936
30-34	31	5.26	482	81.83	76	12.90	589
35-39	19	4.69	320	79.01	66	16.30	405
40-44	11	3.85	223	77.97	52	18.18	286
45-49	3	1.65	138	75.82	41	22.53	182
50-54	6	3.82	110	70.06	41	26.11	157
55-59	2	2.67	58	77.33	15	20.00	75
60-64	0	0	49	74.24	17	25.76	66
65-69	2	4.00	33	66.00	15	30.00	50
Total	151	3.60	3384	80.78	654	15.61	4189

Table VI-122.   Nasal Profile by Age Grouping

	Concave		Straight		Convex		Concavo-convex		Total
	No.	Per Cent	No.	Per Cent	No.	Per Cent	No.	Per Cent	No.
15-19	171	30.00	57	10.00	70	12.28	272	47.72	570
20-24	232	26.70	88	10.13	129	14.84	420	48.33	869
25-29	220	23.53	109	11.65	176	18.82	430	45.99	935
30-34	121	20.51	81	13.73	131	22.20	257	43.56	590
35-39	71	17.53	44	10.86	104	25.68	186	45.93	405
40-44	53	18.53	47	16.43	73	25.52	113	39.51	286
45-49	28	15.38	16	8.79	51	28.02	87	47.80	182
50-54	15	9.62	14	8.97	64	41.03	63	40.38	156
55-59	8	10.67	6	8.00	27	36.00	34	45.33	75
60-64	7	10.61	8	12.12	27	40.91	24	36.36	66
65-69	5	10.20	5	10.20	25	51.02	14	28.57	49
Total	931	22.26	475	11.36	877	20.97	1900	45.42	4183

Table VI-123.   Nasal Tip Thickness by Age Grouping

	Submedium		Medium		Pronounced		Total
	No.	Per Cent	No.	Per Cent	No.	Per Cent	No.
15-19	55	9.65	422	74.04	93	16.32	570
20-24	82	9.40	636	72.94	154	17.66	872
25-29	89	9.52	665	71.12	181	19.36	935
30-34	76	12.88	406	68.81	108	18.30	590
35-39	45	11.11	262	64.69	98	24.20	405
40-44	36	12.59	182	63.64	68	23.78	286
45-49	13	7.18	108	59.67	60	33.15	181
50-54	13	8.33	91	58.33	52	33.33	156
55-59	7	9.33	45	60.00	23	30.67	75
60-64	2	3.03	36	54.55	28	42.42	66
65-69	3	6.12	32	65.31	14	28.57	49
Total	421	10.06	2885	68.94	879	21.00	4185

Table VI-124.   Nasal Wings by Age Grouping

| | Compressed | | Medium | | Flaring | | Total |
	No.	Per Cent	No.	Per Cent	No.	Per Cent	No.
15-19	55	9.67	448	78.73	66	11.50	569
20-24	82	9.40	650	74.54	140	16.05	872
25-29	101	10.81	671	71.84	162	17.34	934
30-34	73	12.44	380	64.74	134	22.83	587
35-39	53	13.18	260	64.68	89	22.14	402
40-44	35	12.32	175	61.62	74	26.06	284
45-49	23	12.64	97	53.30	62	34.07	182
50-54	20	12.82	77	49.36	59	37.82	156
55-59	8	10.96	41	56.15	24	32.98	73
60-64	3	4.54	39	59.09	24	36.36	66
65-69	3	6.00	30	60.00	17	34.00	50
Total	456	10.92	2868	68.70	851	20.38	4175

Table VI-125.   Nasal Septum by Age Grouping

| | Straight | | Concave | | Convex | | Total |
	No.	Per Cent	No.	Per Cent	No.	Per Cent	No.
15-19	167	29.40	198	34.86	203	35.74	568
20-24	329	37.77	327	37.54	215	24.68	871
25-29	339	36.33	339	36.33	255	27.33	933
30-34	210	35.59	242	41.02	138	23.39	590
35-39	140	34.48	175	43.10	91	22.41	406
40-44	102	35.54	122	42.51	63	21.95	287
45-49	65	35.71	84	46.15	33	18.13	182
50-54	52	33.12	70	44.59	35	22.29	157
55-59	24	32.00	30	40.00	21	28.00	75
60-64	25	37.88	29	43.94	12	18.18	66
65-69	11	22.00	22	44.00	17	34.00	50
Total	1464	34.98	1638	39.14	1083	25.88	4185

Table VI-126.   Nasal Septum Inclination by Age Grouping

| | Up | | Down | | Absent | | Total |
	No.	Per Cent	No.	Per Cent	No.	Per Cent	No.
15-19	467	81.93	99	17.37	4	.70	570
20-24	659	75.83	208	23.94	2	.23	869
25-29	674	72.47	253	27.20	3	.39	930
30-34	396	67.23	190	32.26	3	.51	589
35-39	248	61.54	152	37.72	3	.74	403
40-44	152	53.15	133	46.50	1	.35	286
45-49	97	53.30	82	45.05	3	1.65	182
50-54	70	44.59	87	55.41	0	0	157
55-59	31	41.33	44	58.67	0	0	75
60-64	25	37.88	41	62.12	0	0	66
65-69	27	54.00	23	46.00	0	0	50
Total	2846	68.14	1312	31.41	19	.45	4177

Table VI-127.   Nasal Septum Deflection by Age Grouping

| | Right | | Left | | Absent | | Total |
	No.	Per Cent	No.	Per Cent	No.	Per Cent	No.
15-19	148	26.01	49	8.61	372	65.38	569
20-24	186	21.38	72	8.28	612	70.34	870
25-29	218	23.32	99	10.59	618	66.10	935
30-34	146	24.87	58	9.88	383	65.25	587
35-39	83	20.49	35	8.64	287	70.86	405
40-44	74	25.87	28	9.79	184	64.34	286
45-49	38	20.99	12	6.63	131	72.38	181
50-54	39	24.84	18	11.46	100	63.69	157
55-59	21	28.00	10	13.33	44	58.67	75
60-64	21	31.82	7	10.61	38	57.58	66
65-69	10	20.41	10	20.41	29	59.18	49
Total	984	23.54	398	9.52	2798	66.94	4180

Table VI-128.   Lips Integumental Thickness by Age Grouping

| | Submedium | | Medium | | Pronounced | | Total |
	No.	Per Cent	No.	Per Cent	No.	Per Cent	No.
15-19	100	17.64	448	79.01	19	3.35	567
20-24	126	14.48	713	81.95	31	3.56	870
25-29	126	13.45	761	81.22	50	5.34	937
30-34	50	8.49	505	85.74	34	5.77	589
35-39	31	7.65	343	84.69	31	7.65	405
40-44	27	9.41	237	82.58	23	8.01	287
45-49	8	4.40	157	86.26	17	9.34	182
50-54	17	10.90	129	82.69	10	6.41	156
55-59	9	12.00	56	74.67	10	13.33	75
60-64	10	15.38	49	75.38	6	9.23	65
65-69	3	6.00	44	88.00	3	6.00	50
Total	507	12.12	3442	82.28	234	5.59	4183

Table VI-129.   Lips Membranous Thickness by Age Grouping

| | Submedium | | Medium | | Upper Small, Lower Pronounced | | Pronounced | | Total |
	No.	Per Cent	No.	Per Cent	No.	Per Cent	No.	Per Cent	No.
15-19	50	8.79	422	74.16	78	13.71	19	3.34	569
20-24	94	10.78	678	77.75	76	8.72	24	2.75	872
25-29	98	10.46	668	71.29	130	13.87	41	4.37	937
30-34	79	13.41	410	69.61	83	14.09	17	2.89	589
35-39	85	20.94	265	65.27	49	12.07	7	1.72	406
40-44	80	27.87	163	56.79	37	12.89	7	2.44	287
45-49	53	29.12	102	56.04	22	12.09	5	2.75	182
50-54	65	41.40	71	45.22	20	12.74	1	.64	157
55-59	34	45.33	32	42.67	9	12.00	0	0	75
60-64	32	49.23	24	36.92	9	13.85	0	0	65
65-69	28	56.00	15	30.00	7	14.00	0	0	50
Total	698	16.56	2850	68.04	520	12.41	121	2.89	4189

Table VI-130.   Lip Seam by Age Grouping

| | Absent,Submedium | | Medium | | Pronounced | | Total |
	No.	Per Cent	No.	Per Cent	No.	Per Cent	No.
15-19	48	8.45	462	81.34	58	10.21	568
.20-24	82	9.42	627	72.07	161	18.51	870
25-29	88	9.39	605	64.57	244	26.04	937
30-34	76	12.92	372	63.26	140	23.81	588
35-39	61	15.06	250	61.73	94	23.21	405
40-44	58	20.21	183	63.76	46	16.03	287
45-49	41	22.53	108	59.34	33	18.13	182
50-54	52	33.33	89	57.05	15	9.62	156
55-59	33	44.00	38	50.67	4	5.33	75
60-64	33	50.77	28	43.08	4	6.15	65
65-69	28	56.00	19	38.00	3	6.00	50
Total	600	14.34	2781	66.48	802	19.17	4183

Table VI-131.   Alveolar Prognathism by Age Grouping

| | Absent | | Submedium | | Medium | | Pronounced | | Total |
	No.	Per Cent	No.	Per Cent	No.	Per Cent	No.	Per Cent	No.
15-19	477	83.58	62	10.88	30	5.26	1	.18	570
20-24	694	79.50	131	15.01	44	5.04	4	.46	873
25-29	760	81.11	135	14.41	37	3.95	5	.53	937
30-34	489	83.02	72	12.22	23	3.90	5	.85	589
35-39	330	81.28	61	15.02	14	3.45	1	.25	406
40-44	247	86.06	31	10.81	8	2.79	1	.35	287
45-49	147	80.77	26	14.29	8	4.40	1	.55	182
50-54	133	84.71	19	12.10	5	3.18	0	0	157
55-59	70	93.33	5	6.67	0	0	0	0	75
60-64	61	92.42	3	4.55	2	3.03	0	0	66
65-69	45	90.00	2	4.00	3	6.00	0	0	50
Total	3453	82.37	547	13.05	174	4.15	18	.43	4192

Table VI-132.   Facial Prognathism by Age Grouping

| | Absent | | Submedium | | Medium | | Pronounced | | Total |
	No.	Per Cent	No.	Per Cent	No.	Per Cent	No.	Per Cent	No.
15-19	508	89.12	37	6.49	22	3.86	3	.53	570
20-24	760	87.06	66	7.56	45	5.16	2	.23	873
25-29	819	87.41	79	8.43	33	3.52	6	.64	937
30-34	508	86.25	39	6.62	39	6.52	3	.51	589
35-39	353	86.95	33	8.13	19	4.68	1	.25	406
40-44	263	91.54	17	5.92	6	2.09	1	.35	287
45-49	153	84.07	17	9.34	10	5.49	2	1.10	182
50-54	144	91.72	7	4.46	4	2.55	2	1.27	157
55-59	73	97.33	2	2.67	0	0	0	0	75
60-64	60	90.91	3	4.55	3	4.55	0	0	66
65-69	45	90.00	3	6.00	1	2.00	1	2.00	50
Total	3686	87.93	303	7.23	182	4.34	21	.50	4192

Table VI-133.   Chin Form by Age Grouping

	Median		Bilateral		Total
	No.	Per Cent	No.	Per Cent	No.
15-19	390	68.54	179	31.46	569
20-24	514	59.08	356	40.92	870
25-29	487	52.09	448	47.91	935
30-34	292	49.58	297	50.42	589
35-39	212	52.22	194	47.78	406
40-44	142	49.65	144	50.35	286
45-49	110	60.77	71	39.23	181
50-54	89	57.05	67	42.95	156
55-59	48	64.00	27	36.00	75
60-64	44	66.67	22	33.33	66
65-69	31	62.00	19	38.00	50
Total	2359	56.40	1824	43.60	4183

Table VI-134.   Malars Prominence by Age Grouping

	Submedium		Medium		Pronounced		Total
	No.	Per Cent	No.	Per Cent	No.	Per Cent	No.
15-19	45	7.92	441	77.54	82	14.44	568
20-24	56	6.44	614	70.58	200	22.99	870
25-29	44	4.70	660	70.51	232	24.79	936
30-34	33	5.59	383	64.92	174	29.49	590
35-39	19	4.59	256	63.21	130	32.10	405
40-44	8	2.80	194	67.83	84	29.37	286
45-49	7	3.85	119	65.38	56	30.77	182
50-54	11	7.05	94	60.26	51	32.69	156
55-59	4	5.33	47	62.67	24	32.00	75
60-64	7	10.51	42	63.64	17	25.76	66
65-69	3	6.00	39	78.00	8	16.00	50
Total	237	5.56	2889	69.05	1058	25.29	4184

Table VI-135.   Cheeks Fullness by Age Grouping

	Submedium		Medium		Pronounced		Total
	No.	Per Cent	No.	Per Cent	No.	Per Cent	No.
15-19	113	19.96	374	66.08	79	13.96	566
20-24	175	20.09	549	63.03	147	16.88	871
25-29	207	22.14	570	60.96	158	16.90	935
30-34	147	24.96	326	55.35	116	19.69	589
35-39	113	27.83	216	53.20	77	18.97	406
40-44	75	26.13	143	49.83	69	24.04	287
45-49	50	27.78	83	46.11	47	26.11	180
50-54	52	33.33	66	42.31	38	24.36	156
55-59	28	37.33	35	46.67	12	16.00	75
60-64	29	43.94	26	39.39	11	16.67	66
65-69	26	52.00	20	40.00	4	8.00	50
Total	1015	24.28	2408	57.59	758	18.13	4181

Table VI-136.   Gonial Angles by Age Grouping

| | Submedium | | Medium | | Pronounced | | Total |
	No.	Per Cent	No.	Per Cent	No.	Per Cent	No.
15-19	89	15.67	418	73.59	61	10.74	568
20-24	124	'14.24	636	73.02	111	12.74	871
25-29	107	11.44	662	70.80	166	17.75	935
30-34	58	9.83	405	68.64	127	21.52	590
35-39	38	9.36	280	68.96	88	21.67	406
40-44	28	9.76	197	68.64	62	21.60	287
45-49	12	6.59	124	68.13	46	25.27	182
50-54	20	12.82	100	64.10	36	23.08	156
55-59	9	12.00	53	70.67	13	17.33	75
60-64	14	21.21	39	59.09	13	19.70	66
65-69	11	22.00	31	62.00	8	16.00	50
Total	510	12.18	2945	70.35	731	17.46	4186

Table VI-137.   Cheeks Wrinkling by Age Grouping

| | Absent | | Slight, Medium | | Pronounced | | Total |
	No.	Per Cent	No.	Per Cent	No.	Per Cent	No.
15-19	485	85.69	80	14.13	1	.18	566
20-24	642	73.79	223	25.63	5	.57	870
25-29	552	59.16	351	37.62	30	3.21	933
30-34	253	43.03	286	48.63	49	8.33	588
35-39	121	29.95	220	54.46	63	15.59	404
40-44	55	19.30	143	50.17	87	30.53	285
45-49	27	14.84	66	36.26	89	48.90	182
50-54	12	7.69	66	42.31	78	50.00	156
55-59	2	2.67	18	24.00	55	73.00	75
60-64	2	3.03	13	19.70	51	77.27	66
65-69	4	8.00	8	16.00	38	76.00	50
Total	2155	51.62	1474	35.30	546	13.08	4175

Table VI-138.   Teeth Wear By Age Grouping

| | None | | Slight, Medium | | Pronounced | | Total |
	No.	Per Cent	No.	Per Cent	No.	Per Cent	No.
15-19	8	1.41	542	95.76	16	2.83	566
20-24	15	1.74	809	93.63	40	4.63	864
25-29	9	.98	820	88.94	93	10.09	922
30-34	6	1.05	471	82.63	93	16.32	570
35-39	3	.77	299	77.06	86	22.16	388
40-44	1	.36	196	71.53	77	28.10	274
45-49	0	0	103	60.23	68	39.77	171
50-54	1	.71	61	43.57	78	55.71	140
55-59	0	0	29	44.62	36	55.38	65
60-64	0	0	14	28.00	36	72.00	50
65-69	0	0	12	37.50	20	62.50	32
Total	43	1.06	3356	83.03	643	15.91	4042

Table VI-139.   Teeth Caries by Age Grouping

| | None | | Few | | Many | | Total |
	No.	Per Cent	No.	Per Cent	No.	Per Cent	No.
15-19	31	5.48	491	86.75	44	7.77	566
20-24	27	3.13	715	82.95	120	13.90	862
25-29	12	1.30	709	76.90	201	21.80	922
30-34	12	2.10	395	69.30	163	28.60	570
35-39	10	2.56	237	60.77	143	36.67	390
40-44	3	1.09	146	53.28	125	45.62	274
45-49	1	.58	84	48.84	87	50.58	172
50-54	0	0	56	39.16	87	60.84	143
55-59	0	0	31	46.97	35	53.03	66
60-64	1	1.96	10	19.61	40	78.43	51
65-69	0	0	10	30.30	23	69.70	33
Total	97	2.40	2884	71.23	1068	26.38	4049

Table VI-140.   Teeth Lost by Age Grouping

| | None | | Few | | Many | | Total |
	No.	Per Cent	No.	Per Cent	No.	Per Cent	No.
15-19	259	45.68	282	49.74	26	4.59	567
20-24	317	36.48	476	54.78	76	8.74	869
25-29	260	27.96	516	55.48	154	16.56	930
30-34	139	23.64	286	48.64	163	27.72	588
35-39	70	17.46	178	44.39	153	38.15	401
40-44	31	10.81	135	47.04	121	42.16	287
45-49	15	8.29	63	34.81	103	56.91	181
50-54	10	6.41	51	32.69	95	60.90	156
55-59	4	5.41	23	31.08	47	63.51	74
60-64	2	3.17	8	12.70	53	84.13	63
65-69	1	2.13	6	12.77	40	85.11	47
Total	1108	26.62	2024	48.62	1031	24.77	4163

Table VI-141.   Bite by Age Grouping

| | Under | | Edge-to-edge | | Slight Over | | Marked Over | | Total |
	No.	Per Cent	No.	Per Cent	No.	Per Cent	No.	Per Cent	No.
15-19	11	2.01	76	13.87	337	61.50	124	22.63	548
20-24	22	2.62	114	13.56	514	61.12	191	22.71	841
25-29	15	1.67	138	15.37	512	57.02	233	25.95	898
30-34	11	2.01	107	19.56	295	53.93	134	24.50	547
35-39	5	1.37	88	24.18	185	50.82	86	23.63	364
40-44	6	2.53	67	28.27	92	38.82	72	30.38	237
45-49	1	.70	49	34.27	67	46.85	26	18.18	143
50-54	0	0	45	40.54	41	36.94	25	22.52	111
55-59	1	1.92	28	53.85	17	32.69	6	11.54	52
60-64	0	0	17	65.38	4	15.38	5	19.23	26
65-69	0	0	7	38.89	7	38.89	4	22.22	18
Total	72	1.90	736	19.44	2071	54.72	906	23.94	3785

Table VI-142.   Ear Lobes by Age Grouping

| | Submedium | | Medium | | Pronounced | | Total |
	No.	Per Cent	No.	Per Cent	No.	Per Cent	No.
15-19	70	12.35	420	74.07	77	13.58	567
20-24	116	13.29	626	71.71	131	15.01	873
25-29	100	10.71	660	70.66	174	18.63	934
30-34	60	10.19	433	73.51	96	16.30	589
35-39	38	9.36	300	73.89	68	16.75	406
40-44	31	10.84	194	67.83	61	21.33	286
45-49	16	8.79	121	66.48	45	24.72	182
50-54	12	7.69	110	70.51	34	21.79	156
55-59	5	6.67	54	72.00	16	21.33	75
60-64	7	10.61	36	54.55	23	34.85	66
65-69	4	8.00	33	66.00	13	26.00	50
Total	459	10.97	2987	71.39	738	17.64	4184

Table VI-143.   Ear Lobe Attachment by Age Grouping

| | Attached | | Free | | Notched,Divided | | Total |
	No.	Per Cent	No.	Per Cent	No.	Per Cent	No.
15-19	232	40.92	334	58.91	1	.18	567
20-24	371	42.59	499	57.29	1	.12	871
25-29	376	40.56	550	59.33	1	.11	927
30-34	220	37.48	367	62.52	0	0	587
35-39	162	40.30	239	59.45	1	.25	402
40-44	93	32.40	194	67.60	0	0	287
45-49	56	30.77	126	69.23	0	0	182
50-54	50	31.85	106	67.52	1	.64	157
55-59	11	14.67	64	85.33	0	0	75
60-64	19	28.78	47	71.21	0	0	66
65-69	20	40.00	30	60.00	0	0	50
Total	1610	38.60	2556	61.28	5	.12	4171

Table VI-144.   Roll of Helix by Age Grouping

| | Absent | | Submedium | | Medium Pronounced | | Total |
	No.	Per Cent	No.	Per Cent	No.	Per Cent	No.
15-19	0	0	141	24.78	428	75.22	569
20-24	1	.12	245	28.23	622	71.66	868
25-29	2	.21	292	31.26	640	68.52	934
30-34	1	.17	211	35.82	377	64.01	589
35-39	0	0	153	37.68	253	62.31	406
40-44	0	0	108	37.63	179	62.37	287
45-49	0	0	68	37.78	112	62.22	180
50-54	0	0	64	40.76	93	59.24	157
55-59	0	0	26	34.67	49	65.33	75
60-64	0	0	25	38.46	40	61.54	65
65-69	0	0	13	26.00	37	74.00	50
Total	4	.10	1346	32.20	2830	67.70	4180

Table VI-145.   Darwin's Point by Age Grouping

| | Absent | | Small, Medium | | Pronounced | | Total |
	No.	Per Cent	No.	Per Cent	No.	Per Cent	No.
15-19	324	57.14	172	30.34	71	12.52	567
20-24	513	58.97	245	28.16	112	12.87	870
25-29	551	58.99	263	28.16	120	12.85	934
30-34	351	59.69	159	27.04	78	13.26	588
35-39	222	54.81	118	29.13	65	16.05	405
40-44	169	58.88	84	29.27	34	11.85	287
45-49	114	62.98	40	22.10	27	14.92	181
50-54	95	60.90	48	30.77	13	8.33	156
55-59	50	66.67	15	20.00	10	13.33	75
60-64	41	62.12	16	24.24	9	13.64	66
65-69	32	64.00	14	28.00	4	8.00	50
Total	2462	58.91	1174	28.09	543	12.99	4179

Table VI-146.   Ear Protrusion by Age Grouping

| | Submedium | | Medium | | Pronounced | | Total |
	No.	Per Cent	No.	Per Cent	No.	Per Cent	No.
15-19	48	8.48	334	59.01	184	32.51	566
20-24	59	6.76	516	59.11	298	34.14	873
25-29	60	6.41	517	55.24	359	38.35	936
30-34	35	5.94	343	58.23	211	35.82	589
35-39	31	7.64	236	58.13	139	34.24	406
40-44	27	9.41	155	54.01	105	36.58	287
45-49	11	6.04	98	53.85	73	40.11	182
50-54	17	10.83	87	55.41	53	33.76	157
55-59	7	9.33	41	54.67	27	36.00	75
60-64	9	13.64	32	48.48	25	37.88	66
65-69	5	10.00	29	58.00	16	32.00	50
Total	309	7.38	2388	57.03	1490	35.59	4187

Table VI-147.   Asymmetry by Age Grouping

| | Right | | Left | | None | | Total |
	No.	Per Cent	No.	Per Cent	No.	Per Cent	No.
15-19	60	11.70	45	8.77	408	79.53	513
20-24	86	10.25	91	10.85	662	78.90	839
25-29	119	13.06	105	11.53	687	75.41	911
30-34	88	15.25	86	14.90	403	69.84	577
35-39	52	13.37	52	13.37	285	73.26	389
40-44	45	16.24	43	15.52	189	68.23	277
45-49	35	19.66	34	19.10	109	61.24	178
50-54	27	17.31	35	22.44	94	60.26	156
55-59	17	23.29	15	20.55	41	56.16	73
60-64	16	24.62	13	20.00	36	55.38	65
65-69	6	12.00	8	16.00	36	72.00	50
Total	551	13.68	527	13.08	2950	73.24	4028

Table VI-148.   Neck by Age Grouping

	Medium in Length, Breadth No.	Per Cent	Long and Thin No.	Per Cent	Short and Thick No.	Per Cent	Total No.
15-19	400	70.18	156	22.37	14	2.46	570
20-24	595	68.31	248	28.47	28	3.22	871
25-29	629	67.49	259	27.79	44	4.72	932
30-34	396	67.35	155	26.36	37	6.29	588
35-39	264	65.51	109	27.05	30	7.44	403
40-44	203	70.98	70	24.48	13	4.54	286
45-49	121	67.22	47	26.11	12	6.67	180
50-54	92	58.97	45	28.85	19	12.18	156
55-59	51	68.00	19	25.33	5	6.67	75
60-64	37	56.06	27	40.91	2	3.03	66
65-69	36	73.47	13	26.53	0	0	49
Total	2824	67.62	1148	27.49	204	4.88	4176

Table VI-149.   Shoulders Slope by Age Grouping

	Slight No.	Per Cent	Medium No.	Per Cent	Pronounced No.	Per Cent	Total No.
15-19	8	1.41	412	72.54	148	26.06	568
20-24	13	1.49	667	76.76	189	21.75	869
25-29	23	2.46	739	79.12	172	18.42	934
30-34	8	1.36	473	80.44	107	18.20	588
35-39	11	2.72	304	75.25	89	22.03	404
40-44	4	1.40	225	78.67	57	19.93	286
45-49	7	3.87	138	76.24	36	19.89	181
50-54	7	4.46	108	68.79	42	26.75	157
55-59	3	4.00	51	68.00	21	28.00	75
60-64	3	4.54	45	68.18	18	27.27	66
65-69	1	2.00	39	78.00	10	20.00	50
Total	88	2.11	3201	76.62	889	21.28	4178

Table VI-150. Predictions on Basis of Age Grouping and Differences
from Total Series by Offenses

Hair Quantity

Head

	Predicted Per Cent	Small Diff.of Subgroup and Predicted Per Cent	x p.e.	Diff.of Subgroup and Total Per Cent ± p.e.	x p.e.
First degree murder	15.84	1.84	1.60	6.60 ± 1.15	5.74
Robbery	7.22	.04	.04	- 3.82 ± .99	3.86
Burglary and larceny	7.17	.47	1.12	- 3.44 ± .42	8.19
Forgery and fraud	10.14	4.42	4.80	3.48 ± .92	3.78
Vs. public welfare	16.21	1.30	1.02	6.43 ± 1.28	5.02

Table VI-150 (cont'd).   Beard

Small

	Predicted Per Cent	Diff.of Subgroup and Predicted Per Cent	x p.e.	Diff.of Subgroup and Total Per Cent ± p.e.	x p.e.
Robbery	34.88	- 4.54	3.01	- 4.91 ± 1.51	3.25
Burglary and larceny	38.25	1.81	2.87	4.81 ± .63	7.64
Forgery and fraud	34.14	- 6.73	4.81	- 7.84 ± 1.40	5.60

Body

Small

	Predicted Per Cent	Diff.of Subgroup and Predicted Per Cent	x p.e.	Diff.of Subgroup and Total Per Cent ± p.e.	x p.e.
First degree murder	41.05	- 9.56	5.17	-16.41 ± 1.85	8.87
Second degree murder	44.29	- 3.38	2.68	- 6.99 ± 1.26	5.55
Burglary and larceny	53.00	4.03	6.11	9.13 ± .66	13.83
Rape	41.62	- 4.31	1.82	-10.59 ± 2.37	4.47
Other sex	41.88	- 4.79	1.78	-10.81 ± 2.69	4.02
Vs. public welfare	40.00	- 3.28	1.61	-11.18 ± 2.04	5.48

Large

	Predicted Per Cent	Diff.of Subgroup and Predicted Per Cent	x p.e.	Diff.of Subgroup and Total Per Cent ± p.e.	x p.e.
Burglary and larceny	11.34	- 1.22	2.71	- 3.43 ± .45	7.62

Table VI-151.   Predictions on Basis of Age Grouping and Differences
from Total Series by Offenses

Hair Form

Straight

	Predicted Per Cent	Diff.of Subgroup and Predicted Per Cent	x p.e.	Diff.of Subgroup and Total Per Cent ± p.e.	x p.e.
Robbery	84.54	- 4.05	3.62	- 4.86 ± 1.12	4.34
Other sex	86.58	6.75	3.52	7.98 ± 1.92	4.16

Table VI-151 (cont'd).

	Predicted Per Cent	Low Waves Diff.of Subgroup and Predicted Per Cent	x p.e.	Diff.of Subgroup and Total Per Cent ± p.e.	x p.e.
Robbery	8.69	3.02	3.43	3.33 ± .88	3.78
Other sex	7.79	- 5.79	3.86	- 6.38 ± 1.50	4.25

Table VI-152.   Predictions on Basis of Age Grouping and Differences
from Total Series by Offenses

Hair Color

Black

	Predicted Per Cent	Diff.of Subgroup and Predicted Per Cent	x p.e.	Diff.of Subgroup and Total Per Cent ± p.e.	x p.e.
Burglary and larceny	4.14	- .18	.64	- 1.06 ± .28	3.79

Light Brown

	Predicted Per Cent	Diff.of Subgroup and Predicted Per Cent	x p.e.	Diff.of Subgroup and Total Per Cent ± p.e.	x p.e.
Robbery	27.66	2.95	2.06	4.75 ± 1.38	3.44

Ash-blond

	Predicted Per Cent	Diff.of Subgroup and Predicted Per Cent	x p.e.	Diff.of Subgroup and Total Per Cent ± p.e.	x p.e.
Burglary and larceny	2.70	.44	2.20	.84 ± .20	4.20
Arson and all other	1.80	4.02	4.06	3.52 ± .99	3.56

Golden

	Predicted Per Cent	Diff.of Subgroup and Predicted Per Cent	x p.e.	Diff.of Subgroup and Total Per Cent ± p.e.	x p.e.
Second degree murder	2.89	- 1.09	2.37	- 1.68 ± .46	3.55
Burglary and larceny	4.09	.75	3.12	1.36 ± .24	5.67

Gray, White

	Predicted Per Cent	Diff.of Subgroup and Predicted Per Cent	x p.e.	Diff.of Subgroup and Total Per Cent ± p.e.	x p.e.
First degree murder	10.26	.67	.83	5.87 ± .81	7.25
Second degree murder	7.49	- .44	.80	1.99 ± .55	3.62
Robbery	1.94	0	0	- 3.12 ± .69	4.52
Burglary and larceny	2.41	- .27	.90	- 2.92 ± .30	9.73
Rape	8.94	1.83	1.78	5.71 ± 1.03	5.54
Other sex	9.75	1.51	1.28	6.20 ± 1.18	5.25
Vs. public welfare	10.71	- .79	.98	4.96 ± .90	5.40

Table VI-153.   Predictions on Basis of Age Grouping and Differences
from Total Series by Offenses

Eye Color

Blue-gray

	Predicted Per Cent	Diff. of Subgroup and Predicted Per Cent	x p.e.	Diff. of Subgroup and Total Per Cent ± p.e.	x p.e.
Rape	10.09	9.08	6.44	9.41 ± 1.41	6.67

Light Brown

	Predicted Per Cent	Diff. of Subgroup and Predicted Per Cent	x p.e.	Diff. of Subgroup and Total Per Cent ± p.e.	x p.e.
Burglary and larceny	3.27	0.71	3.23	0.91 ± .22	4.14

Table VI-154.   Predictions on Basis of Age Grouping and Differences
from Total Series by Offenses

Sclera

Speckled

	Predicted Per Cent	Diff. of Subgroup and Predicted Per Cent	x p.e.	Diff. of Subgroup and Total Per Cent ± p.e.	x p.e.
Rape	4.68	3.61	3.68	3.77 ± .98	3.85

Table VI-155.   Predictions on Basis of Age Grouping and Differences
from Total Series by Offenses

Iris

Diffused

	Predicted Per Cent	Diff. of Subgroup and Predicted Per Cent	x p.e.	Diff. of Subgroup and Total Per Cent ± p.e.	x p.e.
Robbery	8.94	2.90	3.26	3.14 ± .89	3.53

Table VI-156.   Predictions on Basis of Age Grouping and Differences
from Total Series by Offenses

Eye Folds

Epicanthus

	Predicted Per Cent	Diff. of Subgroup and Predicted Per Cent	x p.e.	Diff. of Subgroup and Total Per Cent ± p.e.	x p.e.
Arson and all other	3.95	5.76	4.27	5.31 ± 1.35	3.93

Median

	Predicted Per Cent	Diff. of Subgroup and Predicted Per Cent	x p.e.	Diff. of Subgroup and Total Per Cent ± p.e.	x p.e.
Robbery	14.85	3.40	3.21	5.39 ± 1.06	5.08

Table VI-157.   Predictions on Basis of Age Grouping and Differences
from Total Series by Offenses

Forehead Slope

	Predicted Per Cent	Pronounced Diff.of Subgroup and Predicted Per Cent	x p.e.	Diff.of Subgroup and Total Per Cent ± p.e.	x p.e.
Burglary and larceny	33.19	- .97	1.54	- 2.31 ± .63	3.67

Table VI-158.   Predictions on Basis of Age Grouping and Differences
from Total Series by Offenses

Nasal Root Height

	Predicted Per Cent	Submedium Diff.of Subgroup and Predicted Per Cent	x p.p.	Diff.of Subgroup and Total Per Cent ± p.e.	x p.e.
Assault	1.64	3.36	3.57	3.39 ± .94	3.61

	Predicted Per Cent	Medium Diff.of Subgroup and Predicted Per Cent	x p.e.	Diff.of Subgroup and Total Per Cent ± p.e.	x p.e.
First degree murder	79.50	- 2.26	1.59	- 4.54 ± 1.42	3.27
Assault	79.90	-17.40	6.04	-19.38 ± 2.88	6.73
Burglary and lárceny	79.67	5.26	10.31	3.05 ± .51	5.98

	Predicted Per Cent	Pronounced Diff.of Subgroup and Predicted Per Cent	x p.e.	Diff.of Subgroup and Total Per Cent ± p.e.	x p.e.
Assault	18.46	14.04	5.07	16.00 ± 2.77	5.78
Burglary and larceny	18.80	- 5.15	10.51	- 2.95 ± .49	5.82

Table VI-159.   Predictions on Basis of Age Grouping and Differences
from Total Series by Offenses

Nasal Bridge Height

	Predicted Per Cent	Medium Diff.of Subgroup and Predicted Per Cent	x p.e.	Diff.of Subgroup and Total Per Cent ± p.e.	x p.e.
Robbery	60.92	3.57	2.32	5.18 ± 1.54	3.36
Forgery and fraud	59.48	7.97	5.54	8.14 ± 1.44	5.65

	Predicted Per Cent	Pronounced Diff.of Subgroup and Predicted Per Cent	x p.e.	Diff.of Subgroup and Total Per Cent ± p.e.	x p.e.
Second degree murder	41.55	5.62	4.57	6.81 ± 1.23	5.54
Robbery	38.74	- 3.72	2.42	- 5.34 ± 1.54	3.47
Forgery and fraud	40.19	- 7.86	5.46	- 8.03 ± 1.44	5.58

Table VI-160. Predictions on Basis of Age Grouping and Differences
from Total Series by Offenses

Nasal Bridge Breadth

Submedium

	Predicted Per Cent	Diff.of Subgroup and Predicted Per Cent	x p.e.	Diff.of Subgroup and Total Per Cent ± p.e.	x p.e.
First degree murder	3.56	- 2.92	4.36	- 2.83 ± .67	4.22

Table VI-161. Predictions on Basis of Age Grouping and Differences
from Total Series by Offenses

Nasal Profile

Concave

	Predicted Per Cent	Diff.of Subgroup and Predicted Per Cent	x p.e.	Diff.of Subgroup and Total Per Cent ± p.e.	x p.e.
First degree murder	18.99	- 3.23	2.11	- 6.51 ± 1.53	4.26
Second degree murder	20.62	- 2.66	2.53	- 4.31 ± 1.05	4.10
Burglary and larceny	24.32	1.87	3.40	3.92 ± .55	7.13
Rape	19.64	- 3.31	1.69	- 5.94 ± 1.96	3.03

Convex

	Predicted Per Cent	Diff.of Subgroup and Predicted Per Cent	x p.e.	Diff.of Subgroup and Total Per Cent ± p.e.	x p.e.
Burglary and larceny	18.21	- .39	.74	- 3.02 ± .53	5.70

Table VI-162. Predictions on Basis of Age Grouping and Differences
from Total Series by Offenses

Nasal Tip Thickness

Medium

	Predicted Per Cent	Diff.of Subgroup and Predicted Per Cent	x p.e.	Diff.of Subgroup and Total Per Cent ± p.e.	x p.e.
Second degree murder	67.58	- 2.59	2.32	- 4.13 ± 1.16	3.56

Table VI-163. Predictions on Basis of Age Grouping and Differences
from Total Series by Offenses

Nasal Septum Inclination

Up

	Predicted Per Cent	Diff.of Subgroup and Predicted Per Cent	x p.e.	Diff.of Subgroup and Total Per Cent ± p.e.	x p.e.
First degree murder	61.68	.18	.10	- 6.28 ± 1.71	3.67
Second degree murder	64.91	- 2.25	1.92	- 5.48 ± 1.17	4.68
Burglary and larceny	72.21	1.23	1.98	5.30 ± .52	8.55

Down

	Predicted Per Cent	Diff.of Subgroup and Predicted Per Cent	x p.e.	Diff.of Subgroup and Total Per Cent ± p.e.	x p.e.
Second degree murder	34.56	2.03	1.74	5.27 ± 1.17	4.50
Burglary and larceny	27.32	- .95	1.56	- 5.05 ± .61	8.28

Table VI-164.   Predictions on Basis of Age Grouping and Differences
from Total Series by Offenses

Nasal Septum Deflection

Right

	Predicted Per Cent	Diff.of Subgroup and Predicted Per Cent	x p.e.	Diff.of Subgroup and Total Per Cent ± p.e.	x p.e.
Rape	23.62	7.66	3.83	7.79 ± 2.00	3.90

Absent

	Predicted Per Cent	Diff.of Subgroup and Predicted Per Cent	x p.e.	Diff.of Subgroup and Total Per Cent ± p.e.	x p.e.
Rape	66.34	- 8.39	3.78	- 8.99 ± 2.22	4.05

Table VI-165.   Predictions on Basis of Age Grouping and Differences
from Total Series by Offenses

Lips Integumental Thickness

Submedium

	Predicted Per Cent	Diff.of Subgroup and Predicted Per Cent	x p.e.	Diff.of Subgroup and Total Per Cent ± p.e.	x p.e.
Forgery and fraud	11.98	- 4.68	4.88	- 4.82 ± .96	5.02
Vs. public welfare	10.37	- 5.29	3.95	- 7.04 ± 1.34	5.25

Pronounced

	Predicted Per Cent	Diff.of Subgroup and Predicted Per Cent	x p.e.	Diff.of Subgroup and Total Per Cent ± p.e.	x p.e.
Burglary and larceny	4.90	- .73	2.43	- 1.47 ± .30	4.90
Rape	6.30	2.88	2.54	3.54 ± 1.09	3.25

Table VI-166.   Predictions on Basis of Age Grouping and Differences
from Total Series by Offenses

Lips Membranous Thickness

Submedium

	Predicted Per Cent	Diff.of Subgroup and Predicted Per Cent	x p.e.	Diff.of Subgroup and Total Per Cent ± p.e.	x p.e.
Second degree murder	19.63	.40	.43	3.36 ± .93	3.61
Robbery	12.88	- .80	.68	- 4.59 ± 1.17	3.92
Burglary and larceny	13.17	1.20	2.45	- 2.30 ± .49	4.69
Forgery and fraud	15.92	- 4.57	4.19	- 5.32 ± 1.09	4.88
Rape	21.52	2.46	1.41	7.31 ± 1.75	4.18
Other sex	22.74	6.40	3.20	12.47 ± 2.00	6.24

Medium

	Predicted Per Cent	Diff.of Subgroup and Predicted Per Cent	x p.e.	Diff.of Subgroup and Total Per Cent ± p.e.	x p.e.
Robbery	71.86	.60	.41	4.53 ± 1.47	3.08
Rape	63.27	- 5.52	2.57	-10.28 ± 2.19	4.69

Table VI-157.   Predictions on Basis of Age Grouping and Differences
from Total Series by Offenses

Lip Seam

		Absent, Submedium			
	Predicted Per Cent	Diff.of Subgroup and Predicted Per Cent	x p.e.	Diff.of Subgroup and Total Per Cent ± p.e.	x p.e.
Robbery	11.14	- 1.70	1.53	- 5.04 ± 1.11	4.54
Burglary and larceny	11.47	.79	1.72	- 2.22 ± .46	4.83
Rape	18.29	2.53	1.59	6.44 ± 1.65	3.90

		Medium			
	Predicted Per Cent	Diff.of Subgroup and Predicted Per Cent	x p.e.	Diff.of Subgroup and Total Per Cent ± p.e.	x p.e.
Second degree murder	64.26	- 3.22	2.71	- 5.32 ± 1.19	4.47
Robbery	68.34	3.81	2.56	5.79 ± 1.49	3.89

Table VI-168.   Predictions on Basis of Age Grouping and Differences
from Total Series by Offenses

Alveolar Prognathism

		Submedium			
	Predicted Per Cent	Diff.of Subgroup and Predicted Per Cent	x p.e.	Diff.of Subgroup and Total Per Cent ± p.e.	x p.e.
Arson and all other	13.22	9.11	4.12	9.27 ± 2.21	4.20

		Pronounced			
	Predicted Per Cent	Diff.of Subgroup and Predicted Per Cent	x p.e.	Diff.of Subgroup and Total Per Cent ± p.e.	x p.e.
Rape	.48	1.04	3.47	1.09 ± .30	3.63

Table VI-169.   Predictions on Basis of Age Grouping and Differences
from Total Series by Offenses

Chin Form

		Median			
	Predicted Per Cent	Diff.of Subgroup and Predicted Per Cent	x p.e.	Diff.of Subgroup and Total Per Cent ± p.e.	x p.e.
First degree murder	55.32	9.31	5.12	7.77 ± 1.82	4.27
Second degree murder	55.62	- 4.40	3.55	- 5.64 ± 1.24	4.55

		Bilateral			
	Predicted Per Cent	Diff.of Subgroup and Predicted Per Cent	x p.e.	Diff.of Subgroup and Total Per Cent ± p.e.	x p.e.
First degree murder	44.68	- 9.31	5.12	- 7.77 ± 1.82	4.27
Second degree murder	44.38	4.40	3.55	5.54 ± 1.24	4.55

Table VI-170.   Predictions on Basis of Age Grouping and Differences
from Total Series by Offenses

Malars Prominence

	Predicted Per Cent	Submedium Diff.of Subgroup and Predicted Per Cent	x p.e.	Diff.of Subgroup and Total Per Cent ± p.e.	x p.e.
First degree murder	5.16	4.49	5.28	3.99 ± .85	4.69

	Predicted Per Cent	Medium Diff.of Subgroup and Predicted Per Cent	x p.e.	Diff.of Subgroup and Total Per Cent ± p.e.	x p.e.
Burglary and larceny	70.54	.93	1.52	2.54 ± .61	4.16
Vs. public welfare	66.53	-14.37	7.56	-16.77 ± 1.90	8.83

	Predicted Per Cent	Pronounced Diff.of Subgroup and Predicted Per Cent	x p.e.	Diff.of Subgroup and Total Per Cent ± p.e.	x p.e.
Vs. public welfare	28.05	16.65	9.35	19.29 ± 1.78	10.84

Table VI-171.   Predictions on Basis of Age Grouping and Differences
from Total Series by Offenses

Cheeks Fullness

	Predicted Per Cent	Submedium Diff.of Subgroup and Predicted Per Cent	x p.e.	Diff.of Subgroup and Total Per Cent ± p.e.	x p.e.
First degree murder	27.34	3.08	1.95	6.04 ± 1.58	3.82
Burglary and larceny	22.52	- .19	.33	- 2.05 ± .57	3.60
Other sex	26.96	9.71	4.18	12.29 ± 2.32	5.30

	Predicted Per Cent	Medium Diff.of Subgroup and Predicted Per Cent	x p.e.	Diff.of Subgroup and Total Per Cent ± p.e.	x p.e.
Burglary and larceny	60.19	- .49	.75	2.08 ± .65	3.20

Table VI-172.   Predictions on Basis of Age Grouping and Differences
from Total Series by Offenses

Gonial Angles

	Predicted Per Cent	Submedium Diff.of Subgroup and Predicted Per Cent	x p.e.	Diff.of Subgroup and Total Per Cent ± p.e.	x p.e.
Vs. public welfare	11.69	- 7.67	5.72	- 7.92 ± 1.34	5.91

Table VI-173. Predictions on Basis of Age Grouping and Differences
from Total Series by Offenses

Cheeks Wrinkling

Absent

	Predicted Per Cent	Diff.of Subgroup and Predicted Per Cent	x p.e.	Diff.of Subgroup and Total Per Cent ± p.e.	x p.e.
First degree murder	36.36	2.87	1.56	-12.36 ± 1.84	6.72
Second degree murder	44.32	- 5.95	4.72	-13.22 ± 1.26	10.49
Robbery	59.82	5.16	3.29	13.39 ± 1.57	8.53
Burglary and larceny	61.10	.37	.56	9.88 ± .66	14.97
Rape	39.76	4.40	1.87	- 7.43 ± 2.35	3.16
Other sex	38.49	.84	.31	-12.26 ± 2.70	4.54
Vs. public welfare	35.04	- 2.36	1.16	-18.91 ± 2.04	9.27

Slight, Medium

	Predicted Per Cent	Diff.of Subgroup and Predicted Per Cent	x p.e.	Diff.of Subgroup and Total Per Cent ± p.e.	x p.e.
Second degree murder	37.40	3.90	3.25	6.08 ± 1.20	5.07
Robbery	34.12	- 4.65	3.10	- 5.75 ± 1.50	3.83
Burglary and larceny	32.05	- .38	.60	- 3.55 ± .63	5.64

Pronounced

	Predicted Per Cent	Diff.of Subgroup and Predicted Per Cent	x p.e.	Diff.of Subgroup and Total Per Cent ± p.e.	x p.e.
First degree murder	24.65	.11	.09	11.57 ± 1.25	9.26
Second degree murder	18.27	2.05	2.41	7.13 ± .85	8.39
Robbery	6.06	- .50	.47	- 7.63 ± 1.07	7.13
Burglary and larceny	6.84	.02	.04	- 6.33 ± .44	14.39
Rape	21.00	- 1.20	.76	6.61 ± 1.58	4.18
Other sex	24.39	2.28	1.24	13.48 ± 1.83	7.37
Vs. public welfare	24.90	.39	.28	12.10 ± 1.38	8.77

Table VI-174. Predictions on Basis of Age Grouping and Differences
from Total Series by Offenses

Teeth Wear

Slight, Medium

	Predicted Per Cent	Diff.of Subgroup and Predicted Per Cent	x p.e.	Diff.of Subgroup and Total Per Cent ± p.e.	x p.e.
First degree murder	73.32	.82	.57	- 8.81 ± 1.44	6.12
Second degree murder	77.85	- 3.31	3.45	- 8.41 ± .96	8.76
Robbery	87.82	3.11	2.61	7.98 ± 1.19	6.71
Burglary and larceny	87.58	.06	.12	4.69 ± .50	9.38
Forgery and fraud	83.29	3.99	3.53	4.33 ± 1.13	3.83
Other sex	73.25	- .59	.28	-10.29 ± 2.11	4.88
Vs. public welfare	72.07	1.18	.75	- 9.70 ± 1.58	6.14

Table VI-174 (cont'd).

	Predicted Per Cent	Pronounced Diff.of Subgroup and Predicted Per Cent	x p.e.	Diff.of Subgroup and Total Per Cent ± p.e.	x p.e.
First degree murder	25.95	- .09	.06	9.87 ± 1.40	7.05
Second degree murder	21.23	2.38	2.53	7.62 ± .94	8.11
Robbery	10.97	- 3.13	2.70	- 8.15 ± 1.16	7.03
Burglary and larceny	11.21	- .31	.63	- 5.09 ± .49	10.39
Forgery and fraud	15.65	- 3.37	3.06	- 3.71 ± 1.10	3.37
Other sex	25.94	1.40	.68	11.35 ± 2.06	5.51
Vs. public welfare	27.16	- .82	.53	10.35 ± 1.54	6.72

Table VI-175. Predictions on Basis of Age Grouping and Differences
from Total Series by Offenses

Teeth Caries

	Predicted Per Cent	None Diff.of Subgroup and Predicted Per Cent	x p.e.	Diff.of Subgroup and Total Per Cent ± p.e.	x p.e.
Second degree murder	1.98	2.38	6.10	1.90 ± .39	4.87

	Predicted Per Cent	Few Diff.of Subgroup and Predicted Per Cent	x p.e.	Diff.of Subgroup and Total Per Cent ± p.e.	x p.e.
First degree murder	61.60	.59	.34	- 9.01 ± 1.73	5.21
Second degree murder	66.26	1.24	1.08	- 3.71 ± 1.15	3.23
Burglary and larceny	76.08	1.11	1.85	5.98 ± .60	9.97
Other sex	62.04	- .17	.07	- 9.34 ± 2.54	3.68
Vs. public welfare	60.21	- 3.65	1.92	-14.65 ± 1.90	7.71

	Predicted Per Cent	Many Diff.of Subgroup and Predicted Per Cent	x p.e.	Diff.of Subgroup and Total Per Cent ± p.e.	x p.e.
First degree murder	36.78	- 1.04	.62	9.41 ± 1.68	5.60
Burglary and larceny	21.05	- .52	.88	- 5.80 ± .59	9.83
Other sex	36.20	1.93	.78	11.80 ± 2.48	4.76
Vs. public welfare	38.12	3.68	2.00	15.47 ± 1.84	8.41

Table VI-176.   Predictions on Basis of Age Grouping and Differences
from Total Series by Offenses

Teeth Lost

	Predicted Per Cent	None Diff.of Subgroup and Predicted Per Cent	x p.e.	Diff.of Subgroup and Total Per Cent ± p.e.	x p.e.
First degree murder	19.10	- .65	.40	- 8.12 ± 1.63	4.98
Burglary and larceny	31.27	.86	1.46	5.56 ± .59	9.42
Other sex	19.94	- 3.94	1.65	-10.57 ± 2.39	4.42

Table VI-176 (cont'd).

Few

	Predicted Per Cent	Diff.of Subgroup and Predicted Per Cent	x p.e.	Diff.of Subgroup and Total Per Cent ± p.e.	x p.e.
Robbery	51.77	3.95	2.50	7.08 ± 1.58	4.48
Vs. public welfare	43.41	- 3.57	1.75	- 8.80 ± 2.04	4.31

Many

	Predicted Per Cent	Diff.of Subgroup and Predicted Per Cent	x p.e.	Diff.of Subgroup and Total Per Cent ± p.e.	x p.e.
First degree murder	36.84	- 1.24	.78	10.80 ± 1.59	6.79
Robbery	18.01	2.19	1.61	- 4.60 ± 1.36	3.38
Burglary and larceny	17.89	- .21	.37	- 7.12 ± .57	12.49
Rape	33.98	3.26	1.61	12.44 ± 2.03	6.13
Other sex	35.76	4.91	2.11	15.87 ± 2.33	6.81
Vs. public welfare	37.99	- 3.61	2.04	9.58 ± 1.77	5.41

Table VI-177.   Predictions on Basis of Age Grouping and Differences
from Total Series by Offenses

Bite

Under

	Predicted Per Cent	Diff.of Subgroup and Predicted Per Cent	x p.e.	Diff.of Subgroup and Total Per Cent ± p.e.	x p.e.
Burglary and larceny	1.99	2.31	10.50	1.46 ± .22	6.64

Edge-to-edge

	Predicted Per Cent	Diff.of Subgroup and Predicted Per Cent	x p.e.	Diff.of Subgroup and Total Per Cent ± p.e.	x p.e.
First degree murder	26.28	- .59	.37	7.02 ± 1.60	4.39
Second degree murder	23.32	2.13	2.05	6.78 ± 1.04	6.52
Robbery	17.04	- 3.83	3.02	- 5.46 ± 1.27	4.30
Burglary and larceny	17.38	- 2.38	4.49	- 3.67 ± .53	6.92
Other sex	27.01	- 1.03	.45	7.31 ± 2.29	3.19

Slight Over

	Predicted Per Cent	Diff.of Subgroup and Predicted Per Cent	x p.e.	Diff.of Subgroup and Total Per Cent ± p.e.	x p.e.
Second degree murder	51.19	- 2.28	1.73	- 5.80 ± 1.32	4.39
Robbery	56.81	3.81	2.35	5.91 ± 1.62	3.65

Table VI-178.   Predictions on Basis of Age Grouping and Differences
from Total Series by Offenses

Ear Lobes

Submedium

	Predicted Per Cent	Diff.of Subgroup and Predicted Per Cent	x p.e.	Diff.of Subgroup and Total Per Cent ± p.e.	x p.e.
Vs. public welfare	10.10	- 5.82	4.55	- 6.80 ± 1.28	5.31

Table VI-178 (cont'd).

	Predicted Per Cent	Pronounced Diff.of Subgroup and Predicted Per Cent	x p.e.	Diff.of Subgroup and Total Per Cent ± p.e.	x p.e.
First degree murder	19.62	4.50	3.21	6.52 ± 1.40	4.66
Burglary and larceny	16.52	- 1.42	2.78	- 2.50 ± .51	4.90

Table VI-179.   Predictions on Basis of Age Grouping and Differences
from Total Series by Offenses

Ear Lobe Attachment

	Predicted Per Cent	Attached Diff.of Subgroup and Predicted Per Cent	x p.e.	Diff.of Subgroup and Total Per Cent ± p.e.	x p.e.
Vs. public welfare	36.37	- 6.41	3.24	- 8.84 ± 1.98	4.46

	Predicted Per Cent	Free Diff.of Subgroup and Predicted Per Cent	x p.e.	Diff.of Subgroup and Total Per Cent ± p.e.	x p.e.
Vs. public welfare	63.50	6.54	3.29	8.88 ± 1.99	4.46

Table VI-180.   Predictions on Basis of Age Grouping and Differences
from Total Series by Offenses

Roll of Helix

	Predicted Per Cent	Medium, Pronounced Diff.of Subgroup and Predicted Per Cent	x p.e.	Diff.of Subgroup and Total Per Cent ± p.e.	x p.e.
Burglary and larceny	69.32	.46	.74	2.00 ± .62	3.23

Table VI-181.   Predictions on Basis of Age Grouping and Differences
from Total Series by Offenses

Antihelix Prominence

	Predicted Per Cent	Submedium Diff.of Subgroup and Predicted Per Cent	x p.e.	Diff.of Subgroup and Total Per Cent ± p.e.	x p.e.
First degree murder	9.04	- 4.86	4.86	- 3.94 ± 1.00	3.94

Table VI-182.   Predictions on Basis of Age Grouping and Differences
from Total Series by Offenses

Ear Protrusion

	Predicted Per Cent	Medium Diff.of Subgroup and Predicted Per Cent	x p.e.	Diff.of Subgroup and Total Per Cent ± p.e.	x p.e.
Robbery	57.44	6.57	4.21	6.94 ± 1.56	4.45

	Predicted Per Cent	Pronounced Diff.of Subgroup and Predicted Per Cent	x p.e.	Diff.of Subgroup and Total Per Cent ± p.e.	x p.e.
Robbery	35.59	- 6.60	4.40	- 6.45 ± 1.50	4.30

Table VI-183.   Predictions on Basis of Age Grouping and Differences
from Total Series by Offenses

Asymmetry

	Predicted Per Cent	Right Diff.of Subgroup and Predicted Per Cent	x p.e.	Diff.of Subgroup and Total Per Cent ± p.e.	x p.e.
Rape	14.58	5.42	3.28	6.20 ± 1.65	3.76
Other sex	15.36	5.97	3.21	7.53 ± 1.86	4.05

	Predicted Per Cent	Left Diff.of Subgroup and Predicted Per Cent	x p.e.	Diff.of Subgroup and Total Per Cent ± p.e.	x p.e.
Burglary and larceny	11.84	- .27	.59	- 1.46 ± .46	3.17

	Predicted Per Cent	None Diff.of Subgroup and Predicted Per Cent	x p.e.	Diff.of Subgroup and Total Per Cent ± p.e.	x p.e.
First degree murder	69.90	- 4.44	2.69	- 7.70 ± 1.65	4.67
Burglary and larceny	75.41	.47	.78	2.72 ± .60	4.53

Table VI-184.   Predictions on Basis of Age Grouping and Differences
from Total Series by Offenses

Neck

	Predicted Per Cent	Short and Thick Diff.of Subgroup and Predicted Per Cent	x p.e.	Diff.of Subgroup and Total Per Cent ± p.e.	x p.e.
Burglary and larceny	4.33	- .46	1.64	- .99 ± .28	3.54

Table VI-185.   Predictions on Basis of Age Grouping and Differences
from Total Series by Offenses

Shoulders Slope

	Predicted Per Cent	Slight Diff.of Subgroup and Predicted Per Cent	x p.e.	Diff.of Subgroup and Total Per Cent ± p.e.	x p.e.
First degree murder	2.51	2.96	5.02	2.87 ± .59	4.86

Table VI-186. Summary of Morphological Differentiation of Offenses from Total Series
on Basis of Age Grouping for Observations Independent of State Sampling

First Degree Murder

	Significant and Independent of Age Sampling		Crude Differences Invalidated by Age Sampling		Insignificant Difference	
	Diff.	x p.e.	Diff.	x p.e.	Diff.	x p.e.
Hair quantity, head						
Small	-	-	6.50	5.74	(1.94	1.60)
Hair quantity, body						
Small	- 9.56*	5.17*	-	-	-	-
Hair color						
Gray, white	-	-	5.87	7.25	(.67	.83)
Nasal root height						
Medium	-	-	- 2.26	1.59	-	-
Nasal bridge breadth						
Submedium	- 2.83	4.22	-	-	-	-
Nasal profile						
Concave	-	-	- 6.51	4.26	(- 3.23	2.11)
Nasal septum inclination						
Up	-	-	- 6.28	3.57	(.18	.10)
Chin form						
Median	7.77	4.27	-	-	-	-
Bilateral	- 7.77*	4.27*	-	-	-	-
Malars prominence						
Submedium	3.99	4.69	-	-	-	-
Cheeks fullness						
Submedium	-	-	6.04	3.82	(3.08	1.95)
Cheeks wrinkling						
Absent	-	-	-12.36	6.72	(2.87	1.56)
Pronounced	-	-	11.57	9.26	(.11	.09)
Teeth wear						
Slight, medium	-	-	- 8.81	6.12	(.82	.57)
Pronounced	-	-	9.87	7.05	(- .09	.06)
Teeth caries						
Few	-	-	- 9.01	5.21	(.59	.34)
Many	-	-	9.41	5.60	(- 1.04	.62)
Teeth lost						
None	-	-	- 8.12	4.98	(- .65	.40)
Many	-	-	10.80	6.79	(- 1.24	.78)
Bite						
Edge-to-edge	-	-	7.02	4.39	(- .59	.37)
Ear lobes						
Pronounced	4.50*	3.21*	-	-	-	-
Antihelix prominence						
Submedium	- 3.94	3.94	-	-	-	-
Asymmetry						
None	-	-	- 7.70	4.67	(- 4 14	2.69)
Shoulders slope						
Slight	2.87	4.86	-	-	-	-

*Independent difference corrected for age sampling.

Table VI-187. Summary of Morphological Differentiation of Offenses from Total Series on Basis of Age Grouping for Observations Independent of State Sampling

Second Degree Murder

	Significant and Independent of Age Sampling		Crude Differences Invalidated by Age Sampling		Insignificant Difference	
	Diff.	x p.e.	Diff.	x p.e.	Diff.	x p.e.
Hair quantity, body						
Small	-	-	- 6.99	5.55	(- 3.38	2.68)
Hair color						
Golden	-	-	- 1.68	3.65	(- 1.09	2.37)
Gray, white	-	-	1.99	3.62	(- .44	.80)
Nasal bridge height						
Pronounced	5.62*	4.57*	-	-	-	-
Nasal profile						
Concave	-	-	- 4.31	4.10	(- 2.66	2.53)
Nasal tip thickness						
Medium	-	-	- 4.13	3.56	(- 2.69	2.32)
Nasal septum inclination						
Up	-	-	- 5.48	4.68	(- 2.25	1.92)
Down	-	-	5.27	4.50	(2.03	1.74)
Lips membranous thickness						
Submedium	-	-	3.36	3.61	(.40	.43)
Lip seam						
Medium	-	-	- 5.32	4.47	(- 3.22	2.71)
Chin form						
Median	- 4.43*	3.57*	-	-	-	-
Bilateral	5.64	4.55	-	-	-	-
Cheeks wrinkling						
Absent	- 5.95*	4.72*	-	-	-	-
Slight, medium	3.90*	3.25*	-	-	-	-
Pronounced	-	-	7.13	8.39	(2.05	2.41)
Teeth wear						
Slight, medium	- 3.31*	3.45*	-	-	-	-
Pronounced	-	-	7.62	8.11	(2.38	2.53)
Teeth caries						
None	1.90	4.87	-	-	-	-
Few	-	-	- 3.71	3.23	(1.24	1.08)
Bite						
Edge-to-edge	-	-	6.78	6.52	(2.13	2.05)
Slight over	-	-	- 5.80	4.39	(- 2.28	1.73)

Table VI-188. Summary of Morphological Differentiation of Offenses from Total Series on Basis of Age Grouping for Observations independent of State Sampling

Assault

	Significant and Independent of Age Sampling		Crude Differences Invalidated by Age Sampling		Insignificant Difference	
	Diff.	x p.e.	Diff.	x p.e.	Diff.	x p.e.
Nasal root height						
Submedium	3.36*	3.57*	-	-	-	-
Medium	-17.40*	6.04*	-	-	-	-
Pronounced	14.04*	5.07*	-	-	-	-

*Independent difference corrected for age sampling.

Table VI-189. Summary of Morphological Differentiation of Offenses
from Total Series on Basis of Age Grouping for
Observations Independent of State Sampling

Robbery

	Significant and Independent of Age Sampling		Crude Differences Invalidated by Age Sampling		Insignificant Difference	
	Diff.	x p.e.	Diff.	x p.e.	Diff.	x p.e.
Hair quantity, head						
Small	-	-	- 3.82	3.86	(.04	.04)
Hair quantity, beard						
Small	- 4.54*	3.01*	-	-	-	-
Hair form						
Straight	- 4.05*	3.62*	-	-	-	-
Low waves	3.02*	3.43*	-	-	-	-
Hair color						
Light brown	-	-	4.75	3.44	(2.85	2.06)
Gray, white	-	-	- 3.12	4.52	(0	0)
Iris						
Diffused	2.90*	3.26*	-	-	-	-
Eye folds						
Median	3.40*	3.21*	-	-	-	-
Nasal bridge height						
Medium	-	-	5.18	3.36	(3.57	2.32)
Pronounced	-	-	- 5.34	3.47	(- 3.72	2.42)
Lips membranous thickness						
Submedium	-	-	- 4.59	3.92	(- .80	.68)
Medium	-	-	4.53	3.08	(.60	.41)
Lip seam						
Absent, submedium	-	-	- 5.04	4.54	(- 1.70	1.53)
Medium	-	-	5.79	3.89	(3.81	2.56)
Cheeks wrinkling						
Absent	5.16*	3.29*	-	-	-	-
Slight, medium	- 4.65*	3.10*	-	-	-	-
Pronounced	-	-	- 7.63	7.13	(- .50	.47)
Teeth wear						
Slight, medium	-	-	7.98	6.71	(3.11	2.61)
Pronounced	-	-	- 8.15	7.03	(- 3.13	2.70)
Teeth lost						
Few	-	-	7.08	4.48	(3.95	2.50)
Many	-	-	- 4.60	3.38	(2.19	1.61)
Bite						
Edge-to-edge	- 3.83*	3.02*	-	-	-	-
Slight over	-	-	5.91	3.65	(3.81	2.35)
Ear protrusion						
Medium	6.57*	4.21*	-	-	-	-
Pronounced	- 6.45	4.30	-	-	-	-

Table VI-190. Summary of Morphological Differentiation of Offenses
from Total Series on Basis of Age Grouping for
Observations Independent of State Sampling

Burglary and Larceny

	Significant and Independent of Age Sampling		Crude Differences Invalidated by Age Sampling		Insignificant Difference	
	Diff.	x p.e.	Diff.	x p.e.	Diff.	x p.e.
Hair quantity, head						
Small	-	-	- 3.44	8.19	(.47	1.12)
Hair quantity, beard						
Small	-	-	4.81	7.64	(1.81	2.87)

*Independent difference corrected for age sampling.

Table VI-190 (cont'd).	Significant and Independent of Age Sampling Diff.	x p.e.	Crude Differences Invalidated by Age Sampling Diff.	x p.e.	Insignificant Difference Diff.	x p.e.
Hair quantity, body						
Small	4.03*	6.11*	-	-	-	-
Large	-	-	- 3.43	7.62	(- 1.22	2.71)
Hair color						
Black	-	-	- 1.06	3.79	(- .18	.64)
Ash-blond	-	-	.84	4.20	(.44	2.20)
Golden	.75*	3.12*	-	-	-	-
Gray, white	-	-	- 2.92	9.73	(- .27	.90)
Eye color						
Light brown	.71*	3.23*	-	-	-	-
Forehead slope						
Pronounced	-	-	- 2.31	3.67	(- .97	1.54)
Nasal root height						
Medium	3.05	5.98	-	-	-	-
Pronounced	- 2.85	5.82	-	-	-	-
Nasal profile						
Concave	1.87*	3.40*	-	-	-	-
Convex	-	-	- 3.02	5.70	(- .39	.74)
Nasal septum inclination						
Up	-	-	5.30	8.55	(1.23	1.98)
Down	-	-	- 5.05	8.28	(- .95	1.56)
Lips integumental thickness						
Pronounced	-	-	- 1.47	4.90	(- .73	2.43)
Lips membranous thickness						
Submedium	-	-	- 2.30	4.69	(1.20	2.45)
Lip seam						
Absent, submedium	-	-	- 2.22	4.83	(.79	1.72)
Malars prominence						
Medium	-	-	2.54	4.16	(.93	1.52)
Cheeks fullness						
Submedium	-	-	- 2.05	3.60	(- .20	.35)
Medium	-	-	2.08	3.20	(- .49	.75)
Cheeks wrinkling						
Absent	-	-	9.88	14.97	(.37	.56)
Slight, medium	-	-	- 3.55	5.64	(- .38	.60)
Pronounced	-	-	- 6.33	14.39	(.02	.04)
Teeth wear						
Slight, medium	-	-	4.69	9.38	(.06	.12)
Pronounced	-	-	- 5.09	10.39	(- .31	.63)
Teeth caries						
Few	-	-	5.98	9.97	(1.11	1.85)
Many	-	-	- 5.80	9.83	(- .52	.88)
Teeth lost						
None	-	-	5.56	9.42	(.86	1.46)
Many	-	-	- 7.12	12.49	(- .21	.37)
Bite						
Under	1.46	6.64	-	-	-	-
Edge-to-edge	- 2.38*	4.49*	-	-	-	-
Ear lobes						
Pronounced	-	-	- 2.50	4.90	(- 1.42	2.78)
Roll of helix						
Medium, pronounced	-	-	2.00	3.23	(.46	.74)
Asymmetry						
Left	-	-	- 1.46	3.17	(- .27	.59)
None	-	-	2.72	4.53	(.47	.78)
Neck						
Short and thick	-	-	- .99	3.54	(- .46	1.64)

*Independent difference corrected for age sampling.

Table VI-191. Summary of Morphological Differentiation of Offenses from Total Series
on Basis of Age Grouping for Observations Independent of State Sampling

Forgery and Fraud

	Significant and Independent of Age Sampling		Crude Differences Invalidated by Age Sampling		Insignificant Difference	
	Diff.	x p.e.	Diff.	x p.e.	Diff.	x p.e.
Hair quantity, head						
Small	3.48	3.78	-	-	-	-
Hair quantity, beard						
Small	- 6.73*	4.81*	-	-	-	-
Nasal bridge height						
Medium	7.97*	5.54*	-	-	-	-
Pronounced	- 7.86*	5.46*	-	-	-	-
Lips integumental thickness						
Submedium	- 4.68*	4.88*	-	-	-	-
Lips membranous thickness						
Submedium	- 4.57*	4.19*	-	-	-	-
Teeth wear						
Slight, medium	3.99*	3.53*	-	-	-	-
Pronounced	- 3.37*	3.06*	-	-	-	-

Table VI-192. Summary of Morphological Differentiation of Offenses from Total Series
on Basis of Age Grouping for Observations Independent of State Sampling

Rape

	Significant and Independent of Age Sampling		Crude Differences Invalidated by Age Sampling		Insignificant Difference	
	Diff.	x p.e.	Diff.	x p.e.	Diff.	x p.e.
Hair quantity, body						
Small	-	-	-10.59	4.47	(- 4.5	1.82)
Hair color						
Gray, white	-	-	5.71	5.54	(1.83	1.78)
Eye color						
Blue-gray	9.08*	6.44*	-	-	-	-
Sclera						
Speckled	3.61*	3.68*	-	-	-	-
Nasal profile						
Concave	-	-	- 5.94	3.03	(- 3.31	1.69)
Nasal septum deflection						
Right	7.66*	3.83*	-	-	-	-
Absent	- 8.39*	3.78*	-	-	-	-
Lips integumental thickness						
Pronounced	-	-	3.54	3.25	(2.88	2.64)
Lips membranous thickness						
Submedium	-	-	7.31	4.18	(2.46	1.41)
Medium	-	-	-10.28	4.69	(- 5.62	2.57)
Lip seam						
Absent, submedium	-	-	6.44	3.90	(2.63	1.59)
Alveolar prognathism						
Pronounced	1.04*	3.47*	-	-	-	-
Cheeks wrinkling						
Absent	-	-	- 7.43	3.16	(4.40	1.87)
Pronounced	-	-	6.61	4.18	(- 1.20	.76)
Teeth lost						
Many	-	-	12.44	6.13	(3.26	1.61)
Asymmetry						
Right	5.42*	3.28*	-	-	-	-

*Independent difference corrected for age sampling.

Table VI-193. Summary of Morphological Differentiation of Offenses from Total Series on Basis of Age Grouping for Observations Independent of State Sampling

Other Sex Offenses

	Significant and Independent of Age Sampling		Crude Differences Invalidated by Age Sampling		Insignificant Difference	
	Diff.	x p.e.	Diff.	x p.e.	Diff.	x p.e.
Hair quantity, body						
Small	-	-	-10.81	4.02	(- 4.79	1.78)
Hair form						
Straight	6.75*	3.52*	-	-	-	-
Low waves	- 5.79*	3.86*	-	-	-	-
Hair color						
Gray, white	-	-	6.20	5.25	(1.51	1.28)
Lips membranous thickness						
Submedium	6.40*	3.56*	-	-	-	-
Cheeks fullness						
Submedium	9.71*	4.18*	-	-	-	-
Cheeks wrinkling						
Absent	-	-	-12.26	4.54	(.84	.31)
Pronounced	-	-	13.48	7.37	(2.28	1.24)
Teeth wear						
Slight, medium	-	-	-10.29	4.88	(- .59	.28)
Pronounced	-	-	11.35	5.51	(1.40	.68)
Teeth caries						
Few	-	-	- 9.34	3.68	(- .17	.07)
Many	-	-	11.80	4.76	(1.93	.78)
Teeth lost						
None	-	-	-10.57	4.42	(- 3.94	1.65)
Many	-	-	15.87	6.81	(4.91	2.11)
Bite						
Edge-to-edge	-	-	7.31	3.19	(- 1.03	.45)
Asymmetry						
Right	5.97*	3.21*	-	-	-	-

Table VI-194. Summary of Morphological Differentiation of Offenses from Total Series on Basis of Age Grouping for Observations Independent of State Sampling

Versus Public Welfare

	Significant and Independent of Age Sampling		Crude Differences Invalidated by Age Sampling		Insignificant Difference	
	Diff.	x p.e.	Diff.	x p.e.	Diff.	x p.e.
Hair quantity, head						
Small	-	-	6.43	5.02	(1.30	1.02)
Hair quantity, body						
Small	-	-	-11.18	5.48	(- 3.28	1.61)
Hair color						
Gray, white	-	-	4.86	5.40	(- .79	.88)
Lips integumental thickness						
Submedium	- 5.29*	3.95*	-	-	-	-
Malars prominence						
Medium	-14.37*	7.56*	-	-	-	-
Pronounced	16.65*	9.35*	-	-	-	-
Gonial angles						
Submedium	- 7.67*	5.72*	-	-	-	-

*Independent difference corrected for age sampling.

Table VI-194 (cont'd).	Significant and Independent of Age Sampling		Crude Differences Invalidated by Age Sampling		Insignificant Difference	
	Diff.	x p.e.	Diff.	x p.e.	Diff.	x p.e.
Cheeks wrinkling						
Absent	-	-	-18.91	9.27	(- 2.36	1.16)
Pronounced	-	-	12.10	8.77	(.39	.28)
Teeth wear						
Slight, medium	-	-	- 9.70	6.14	(1.18	.75)
Pronounced	-	-	10.35	6.72	(- .82	.53)
Teeth caries						
Few	-	-	-14.65	7.71	(- 3.65	1.92)
Many	-	-	15.47	8.41	(3.68	2.00)
Teeth lost						
Few	-	-	- 8.80	4.31	(- 3.57	1.75)
Many	-	-	9.58	5.41	(- 3.61	2.04)
Ear lobes						
Submedium	- 5.82*	4.55*	-	-	-	-
Ear lobe attachment						
Attached	- 6.41*	3.24*	-	-	-	-
Free	6.54*	3.29*	-	-	-	-

Table VI-195. Summary of Morphological Differentiation of Offenses from Total Series on Basis of Age Grouping for Observations Independent of State Sampling

Arson and All Other Offenses

	Significant and Independent of Age Sampling		Crude Differences Invalidated by Age Sampling		Insignificant Difference	
	Diff.	x p.e.	Diff.	x p.e.	Diff.	x p.e.
Hair color						
Ash-blond	3.52	3.56	-	-	-	-
Eye folds						
Epicanthus	5.31	3.93	-	-	-	-
Alveolar prognathism						
Submedium	9.11*	4.12*	-	-	-	-

*Independent difference corrected for age sampling.

Table VI-196. Number of Significant and Insignificant Subcategories of Morphological
Differences on Basis of Age Grouping by Offenses for Observations
Independent of State Sampling.

	Total Number of Observations in Crime Group	Significant Difference Independent of State and Age Sampling		Crude Differences Invalidated by State or Age Sampling		Insignificant Difference	
		No.	Per Cent	No.	Per Cent	No.	Per Cent
First degree murder	164	8	4.88	34	20.73	122	74.39
Second degree murder	164	7	4.27	40	24.39	117	71.34
Assault	164	3	1.83	12	7.32	149	90.85
Robbery	164	10	6.10	23	14.02	131	79.88
Burglary and larceny	164	8	4.88	37	22.56	119	72.56
Forgery and fraud	164	8	4.88	16	9.76	140	85.37
Rape	164	6	3.66	27	16.46	131	79.88
Other sex	164	5	3.05	19	11.59	140	85.37
Vs. public welfare	164	7	4.27	45	27.44	112	68.29
Arson and all other	164	3	1.83	2	1.22	159	96.95
Total	1640	65	3.96	255	15.55	1320	80.49

Table VI-197. Morphological Differentiation of Offense Groups in Terms of
Complete Morphological Characters Independent of
State Sampling and Age Correction

	Differentiated		Undifferentiated		Total
	No.	Per Cent	No.	Per Cent	No.
First degree murder	7	14.89	40	85.11	47
Second degree murder	5	10.64	42	89.36	47
Assault	1	2.13	46	97.87	47
Robbery	7	14.89	40	85.11	47
Burglary and larceny	6	12.77	41	87.23	47
Forgery and fraud	6	12.77	41	87.23	47
Rape	5	10.64	42	89.36	47
Other sex offenses	4	8.51	43	91.49	47
Versus public welfare	5	10.64	42	89.36	47
Arson and all other	3	6.38	44	93.62	47
Total	49	10.43	321	89.56	470

Table VII-1. Numbers and Percentages of Each Offense Group in Previously
Convicted Criminals and in Total Series with Mean Ages of
Total Offense Groups

	Previously Convicted		Total Series		Mean Age of Total Offense Groups
	No.	Per Cent	No.	Per Cent	
First degree murder	83	5.80	312	7.41	37.80
Second degree murder	135	9.44	619	14.70	34.05
Assault	28	1.96	80	1.90	34.00
Robbery	161	11.26	414	9.83	26.75
Burglary and larceny	655	45.80	1612	38.27	26.50
Forgery and fraud	182	12.73	467	11.09	30.25
Rape	59	4.13	197	4.68	36.10
Other sex	34	2.38	151	3.58	37.10
Vs. public welfare	55	3.85	257	6.10	38.25
Arson and all other	38	2.66	103	2.44	33.05
Total	1430		4212		

Table VII-2.   Previous Convictions, Yes

	No.	Range	Mean		S. D.		V.	
Age	1425	15- 69	30.20 ±	.19	10.65 ±	.13	35.26 ±	.44
Weight	1339	91-250	149.00 ±	.36	19.60 ±	.25	13.15 ±	.17
Height	1427	146-190	171.42 ±	.12	6.42 ±	.08	3.74 ±	.05
Biacromial diameter	1426	31- 45	38.09 ±	.04	2.28 ±	.03	5.99 ±	.08
Chest depth	1423	16- 27	21.10 ±	.03	1.64 ±	.02	7.77 ±	.10
Chest breadth	1420	20- 37	27.30 ±	.03	1.86 ±	.02	6.81 ±	.09
Sitting height	1420	66-104	90.01 ±	.06	3.57 ±	.04	3.97 ±	.05
Head length	1429	170-214	194.01 ±	.12	6.75 ±	.08	3.48 ±	.04
Head breadth	1428	129-173	152.25 ±	.10	5.34 ±	.07	3.51 ±	.04
Head height (Observer A)	1073	110-151	132.66 ±	.11	5.52 ±	.08	4.16 ±	.06
Head height (Observer B)	354	98-160	122.82 ±	.21	5.88 ±	.15	4.79 ±	.12
Head circumference	1334	514-621	564.85 ±	.30	16.20 ±	.21	2.87 ±	.04
Minimum frontal diameter	1428	93-128	111.19 ±	.09	4.84 ±	.06	4.35 ±	.06
Bizygomatic diameter	1428	120-159	138.40 ±	.10	5.30 ±	.07	3.83 ±	.05
Total face height	1429	100-154	121.90 ±	.12	6.65 ±	.08	5.46 ±	.07
Upper face height	1428	50- 94	69.30 ±	.08	4.55 ±	.06	6.57 ±	.08
Nose height	1427	40- 71	52.22 ±	.07	3.92 ±	.05	7.51 ±	.10
Nose breadth	1427	25- 48	34.76 ±	.05	2.79 ±	.04	8.03 ±	.10
Bigonial diameter	1428	82-129	107.54 ±	.10	5.60 ±	.07	5.21 ±	.07
Ear length (Observer A)	1073	44- 79	61.22 ±	.10	4.72 ±	.07	7.71 ±	.11
Ear length (Observer B)	354	40- 75	58.30 ±	.18	4.88 ±	.12	8.37 ±	.21
Ear breadth (Observer A)	1073	29- 46	37.62 ±	.06	2.76 ±	.04	7.34 ±	.11
Ear breadth (Observer B)	353	29- 46	36.60 ±	.10	2.76 ±	.07	7.54 ±	.19
Relative shoulder breadth	1425	16- 29	22.24 ±	.02	1.34 ±	.02	6.02 ±	.08
Relative sitting height	1406	46- 67	52.52 ±	.03	1.64 ±	.02	3.12 ±	.04
Cephalic index	1428	65- 94	78.57 ±	.06	3.42 ±	.04	4.35 ±	.06
Cephalo-facial index	1427	79-102	90.92 ±	.05	3.00 ±	.04	3.30 ±	.04
Length-height index								
(Observer A)	1073	55- 81	68.51 ±	.07	3.27 ±	.05	4.77 ±	.07
(Observer B)	354	52- 75	63.08 ±	.11	3.18 ±	.08	5.04 ±	.13
Breadth-height index								
(Observer A)	1072	73-102	87.32 ±	.08	3.81 ±	.06	4.36 ±	.06
(Observer B)	354	70- 96	80.39 ±	.14	3.90 ±	.10	4.85 ±	.12
Facial index	1428	70-105	88.10 ±	.07	3.99 ±	.05	4.53 ±	.06
Upper facial index	1427	37- 63	50.12 ±	.06	3.51 ±	.04	6.87 ±	.09
Nasal index	1426	48- 99	66.62 ±	.12	6.76 ±	.08	10.15 ±	.13
Ear index (Observer A)	1073	45- 80	60.78 ±	.08	4.00 ±	.06	6.58 ±	.10
Ear index (Observer B)	353	49- 80	63.18 ±	.18	5.96 ±	.13	7.85 ±	.20
Zygo-frontal index	1427	68- 99	80.38 ±	.06	3.24 ±	.04	4.03 ±	.05
Fronto-parietal index	1427	63- 89	73.12 ±	.06	3.21 ±	.04	4.39 ±	.06
Zygo-gonial index	1427	66- 92	77.71 ±	.07	3.72 ±	.05	4.79 ±	.06

Table VII-3.   Previous Convictions, No.

	No.	Range	Mean	S. D.	V.
Age	2212	15- 69	31.50 ± .17	11.70 ± .12	37.14 ± .38
Weight	2049	91-270	152.20 ± .31	21.10 ± .22	13.86 ± .15
Height	2217	146-196	172.14 ± .09	6.39 ± .06	3.71 ± .04
Biacromial diameter	2215	28- 45	38.18 ± .03	2.19 ± .02	5.74 ± .06
Chest depth	2214	16- 29	21.18 ± .02	1.70 ± .02	8.03 ± .08
Chest breadth	2211	20- 37	27.57 ± .03	1.86 ± .02	6.75 ± .07
Sitting height	2204	72-101	90.37 ± .05	3.51 ± .04	3.88 ± .04
Head length	2223	170-226	193.53 ± .09	6.42 ± .06	3.32 ± .03
Head breadth	2223	129-173	152.20 ± .08	5.37 ± .05	3.53 ± .04
Head height (Observer A)	1718	110-154	132.66 ± .09	5.52 ± .06	4.16 ± .05
Head height (Observer B)	504	104-139	122.28 ± .16	5.19 ± .11	4.24 ± .09
Head circumference	2003	502-621	564.74 ± .24	15.84 ± .17	2.80 ± .03
Minimum frontal diameter	2222	93-128	111.58 ± .07	4.84 ± .05	4.34 ± .04
Bizygomatic diameter	2225	115-159	138.75 ± .08	5.35 ± .05	3.86 ± .04
Total face height	2223	100-144	121.70 ± .09	6.40 ± .06	5.26 ± .05
Upper face height	2224	50- 94	69.25 ± .07	4.60 ± .05	6.64 ± .07
Nose height	2218	40- 71	52.50 ± .06	3.84 ± .04	7.31 ± .07
Nose breadth	2217	22- 48	34.91 ± .04	2.79 ± .03	7.99 ± .08
Bigonial diameter	2224	86-133	108.26 ± .08	5.76 ± .06	5.32 ± .05
Ear length (Observer A)	1714	44- 83	62.02 ± .08	4.88 ± .06	7.87 ± .09
Ear length (Observer B)	505	44- 75	58.30 ± .14	4.56 ± .10	7.82 ± .17
Ear breadth (Observer A)	1713	26- 49	37.77 ± .04	2.64 ± .03	6.99 ± .08
Ear breadth (Observer B)	505	29- 46	36.27 ± .08	2.76 ± .06	7.61 ± .16
Relative shoulder breadth	2207	16- 29	22.20 ± .02	1.26 ± .01	5.68 ± .06
Relative sitting height	2196	42- 61	52.48 ± .02	1.52 ± .02	2.90 ± .03
Cephalic index	2220	65- 91	78.69 ± .05	3.18 ± .03	4.04 ± .04
Cephalo-facial index	2223	82-105	91.16 ± .04	3.03 ± .03	3.32 ± .03
Length-height index					
(Observer A)	1716	58- 81	68.69 ± .05	3.21 ± .04	4.67 ± .05
(Observer B)	504	52- 78	63.05 ± .09	3.03 ± .06	4.81 ± .10
Breadth-height index					
(Observer A)	1716	73-102	87.32 ± .06	3.81 ± .04	4.36 ± .05
(Observer B)	503	70- 93	80.36 ± .10	3.48 ± .07	4.33 ± .09
Facial index	2223	74-109	87.78 ± .07	5.20 ± .05	5.92 ± .06
Upper facial index	2224	37- 66	50.00 ± .05	3.54 ± .04	7.08 ± .07
Nasal index	2216	44- 99	66.74 ± .10	6.80 ± .07	10.19 ± .10
Ear index (Observer A)	1712	45- 80	61.14 ± .07	4.52 ± .05	7.39 ± .08
Ear index (Observer B)	505	49- 76	62.58 ± .15	4.96 ± .10	7.93 ± .17
Zygo-frontal index	2222	64- 95	80.50 ± .04	3.16 ± .03	3.92 ± .04
Fronto-parietal index	2221	60- 89	73.45 ± .04	3.12 ± .03	4.25 ± .04
Zygo-gonial index	2224	57- 92	77.98 ± .05	3.69 ± .04	4.73 ± .05

Table VII-4. Differences of Means with Value in Terms of the Probable Error
of Previous Convictions Yes and No

	Differences of Means Predicted on basis of State Composition		Differences of Actual Means	
	Diff.	x p.e.	Diff. ± p.e.	x p.e.
Age	- .56	2.15	- 1.30 ± .26	5.00
Weight	- 1.53	3.19	- 3.20 ± .48	6.66
Height	- .58	3.87	- .72 ± .15	4.80
Biacromial diameter	- .08	1.60	- .09 ± .05	1.80
Chest depth	- .03	0.75	- .08 ± .04	2.00
Chest breadth	- .13	3.25	- .27 ± .04	6.75
Sitting height	- .19	2.38	- .36 ± .08	4.50
Head length	.21	1.40	.48 ± .15	3.20
Head breadth	- .07	0.54	.06 ± .13	0.46
Head height (Observer A)	- .17	1.21	0 ± .14	0
Head height (Observer B)	.20	0.77	.54 ± .26	2.08
Head circumference	- 1.10	2.89	.12 ± .38	0.32
Minimum frontal diameter	- .79	7.18	- .40 ± .11	3.64
Bizygomatic diameter	- .32	2.46	- .35 ± .13	2.69
Total face height	.22	1.47	.20 ± .15	1.33
Upper face height	.11	1.00	.05 ± .11	0.45
Nose height	- .04	0.44	- .28 ± .09	3.11
Nose breadth	- .31	5.17	- .15 ± .06	2.50
Bigonial diameter	- .46	3.54	- .72 ± .13	5.54
Ear length (Observer A)	- .67	5.15	- .80 ± .13	6.15
Ear length (Observer B)	.31	1.35	0 ± .23	0
Ear breadth (Observer A)	- .40	5.71	- .15 ± .07	2.14
Ear breadth (Observer B)	.13	1.00	.33 ± .13	2.54
Relative shoulder breadth	.11	3.67	.04 ± .03	1.33
Relative sitting height	.07	1.75	.04 ± .04	1.00
Cephalic index	- .08	1.00	- .12 ± .08	1.50
Cephalo-facial index	- .17	2.83	- .24 ± .06	4.00
Length-height index				
(Observer A)	- .19	2.11	- .18 ± .09	2.00
(Observer B)	.15	1.07	.03 ± .14	0.21
Breadth-height index				
(Observer A)	.02	0.20	0 ± .10	0
(Observer B)	- .02	0.12	.03 ± .17	0.18
Facial index	.37	3.70	.32 ± .0	3.20
Upper facial index	.22	2.75	.12 ± .08	1.50
Nasal index	- .55	3.44	- .12 ± .16	0.75
Ear index (Observer A)	.08	0.73	- .36 ± .11	3.27
Ear index (Observer B)	- .11	0.48	.60 ± .23	2.61
Zygo-frontal index	- .34	4.86	- .12 ± .07	1.71
Fronto-parietal index	- .46	6.57	- .33 ± .07	4.71
Zygo-gonial index	- .12	1.33	- .27 ± .09	3.00

Table VII-4 (cont'd.). Significant Differences of Means Independent of State Sampling

```
Weight: independent difference                              - 1.67 ( 3.48 p.e.)
Chest breadth: independent difference                      -  .14 ( 3.50 p.e.)
Ear index (Observer A): difference                         -  .36 ( 3.27 p.e.)
```

Differences Rendered Insignificant by State Sampling

```
Age: independent difference                                -  .74 ( 2.85 p.e.)
Height: independent difference                             -  .14 (  .93 p.e.)
Sitting height: independent difference                     -  .17 ( 2.12 p.e.)
Head length: independent difference                           .27 ( 1.80 p.e.)
Nose height: independent difference                        -  .24 ( 2.57 p.e.)
Bigonial diameter: independent difference                  -  .26 ( 2.00 p.e.)
Ear length (Observer A): independent difference            -  .13 ( 1.00 p.e.)
Cephalo-facial index: independent difference               -  .07 ( 1.17 p.e.)
Zygo-gonial index: independent difference                  -  .15 ( 1.67 p.e.)
```

Less Than Difference Due to State Sampling

Minimum frontal diameter
Facial index
Fronto-parietal index

Table VII-5.   Hair Form by Previous Convictions

Previous convictions	Straight No.	Per Cent	Low Waves No.	Per Cent	Deep Waves No.	Per Cent	Curly No.	Per Cent	Frizzly No.	Per Cent	Total No.
Yes	1230	86.26	104	7.29	63	4.42	28	1.96	1	.07	1426
No	1876	84.39	195	8.77	89	4.00	62	2.79	1	.04	2223
Total	3106	85.12	299	8.19	152	4.17	90	2.47	2	.06	3649

Table VII-6. Hair Form Differences between Previous Convictions Yes and No

	Difference of Per Cents Predicted on basis of State Composition		Difference of Actual Per Cents	
	Diff.	x p.e.	Diff. ± p.e.	x p.e.
Straight	1.33	1.51	1.87 ± .80	2.34
Low waves	- 1.42	2.33	- 1.48 ± .61	2.43
Deep waves	- .12	.26	- .42 ± .46	.91
Curly	.22	.65	- .83 ± .34	2.44
Frizzly	- .01	.20	- .03 ± .05	.60

No Significant Differences

Table VII-7.   Hair Color by Previous Convictions

Previous convictions	Black No.	Per Cent	Dark Brown No.	Per Cent	Reddish Brown No.	Per Cent	Light Brown No.	Per Cent	Ash-blond No.	Per Cent
Yes	78	5.51	503	35.55	315	22.26	315	22.26	38	2.69
No	100	4.54	694	31.54	443	20.14	618	28.09	48	2.18
Total	178	4.92	1194	33.11	758	20.97	933	25.81	86	2.38

Previous convictions	Golden No.	Per Cent	Red No.	Per Cent	Grey, White No.	Per Cent	Total No.
Yes	46	3.25	57	4.03	63	4.45	1415
No	78	3.54	91	4.14	128	5.82	2200
Total	124	3.43	148	4.09	191	5.28	3615

Table VII-8. Hair Color Differences between Previous Convictions Yes and No

| | Differences of Per Cents Predicted on basis of State Composition | | Difference of Actual Per Cents | |
	Diff.	x p.e.	Diff. ± p.e.	x p.e.
Black	- .15	.29	.97 ± .51	1.90
Dark brown	2.38	2.18	4.01 ± 1.09	3.68
Reddish brown	2.08	2.21	2.12 ± .94	2.26
Light brown	- 3.35	3.42	- 5.83 ± .98	5.95
Ash-blond	- .33	0.92	.51 ± .36	1.42
Golden	- .29	0.69	.29 ± .42	0.69
Red	- .80	1.78	- .11 ± .45	0.24
Gray, white	- .19	0.38	- 1.37 ± .50	2.74

No Significant Differences

Differences Rendered Insignificant by State Sampling

Dark brown: Independent difference   1.63 (1.50 p.e.)
Light brown: Independent difference   - 2.48 (2.53 p.e.)

Table VII-9.

Eye Color by Previous Convictions

| Previous convictions | Dark Brown | | Light Brown | | Blue-brown | | Gray-brown | | Green-brown | |
	No.	Per Cent	No.	Per Cent	No.	Per Cent	No.	Per Cent	No.	Per Cent
Yes	60	4.20	54	3.78	251	17.56	231	16.16	405	28.34
No	65	2.93	63	2.84	482	21.71	473	21.31	533	24.01
Total	125	3.43	117	3.21	733	20.09	704	19.29	938	25.71

| Previous convictions | Blue | | Blue-gray | | Total |
	No.	Per Cent	No.	Per Cent	No.
Yes	298	20.85	130	9.10	1429
No	431	19.41	173	7.79	2220
Total	729	19.98	303	8.30	3649

Table VII-10. Eye Color Differences between Previous Convictions Yes and No

	Differences of Per Cents Predicted on basis of State Composition		Differences of Actual Per Cents	
	Diff.	x p.e.	Diff. ± p.e.	x p.e.
Dark brown	.80	1.86	1.27 ± .43	2.95
Light brown	- .72	1.76	.94 ± .41	2.29
Blue-brown	- 2.58	2.87	- 4.15 ± .90	4.61
Gray-brown	- 4.77	5.42	- 5.15 ± .88	5.85
Green-brown	4.22	4.18	4.33 ± 1.01	4.29
Blue	.87	0.94	1.44 ± .92	1.56
Blue-grey	2.18	3.41	1.31 ± .64	2.05

No Significant Differences

Differences Rendered Insignificant by State Sampling

Blue-brown: independent difference   - 1.57 (1.74 p.e.)
Gray-brown: independent difference   - .38 (.43 p.e.)
Green-brown: independent difference   .11 (.11 p.e.)

Table VIII-1.   Subdivisions of Occupational Categories

Per Cent

Extractive

Agriculture	79.63
Mining	16.06
Animal husbandry	2.92
Fishing, forestry, milkman, nurseryman, lumberjack	1.39

Laborer

Day laborer	81.02
Textile worker	5.99
Shoe worker	2.93
Vulcanizer, polisher, chair maker, weaver, garment worker, well driller, tool dresser, tobacco worker, coach cleaner, stone cutter, blaster, auto trimmer, crane operator, furnace installer, moulder, wood turner, sawyer, pottery worker, timekeeper, oiler, steeplejack, glass worker, well digger, tile setter, marble setter, boiler firer, sand cutter, pumper	10.06

Factory

Mechanic	44.85
Machinist	15.66
Engineer	5.36
Fireman	5.79
Blacksmith	4.94
Factory worker	4.51
Metal worker	3.86
Boiler maker	3.43
Laundry worker, nickel plating, saw mill, cigar factory, motor builder, millwright, welder, marine engineer, tanner, foundery worker, tinsmith, steam shovel engineer, lineman, steam engineer, repair shop, mechanical engineer, foreman, garage worker, iron worker	11.60

Transportation

Chauffeur	35.68
Railroad man	27.86
Truckman	20.61
Teamster	6.11
Sailor	4.58
Expressman, street railway, deck hand, taxi driver, service car driver, steamboat proprietor	4.95

Skilled Trades

Painter	33.96
Carpenter	23.72
Electrician	14.56
Plumber	8.09
Builder	2.70
Brick layer, mason, interior decorator, pipe fitter, contractor, telephone linesman, cooper, upholsterer, cabinet maker, rigger, chemist, steam fitter, designer, electrical engineer, plasterer, tomb builder, radio operator, paper hanger, cement worker, auto painter, excavator	16.97

Table VIII-1 (cont'd).

		Per Cent
Trade		
	Salesman	34.05
	Sales clerk	29.74
	Merchant	7.76
	Butcher	7.76
	Stock dealer	3.88
	Storekeeper, shipper, florist, real estate agent, insurance agent, peddler, huckster, warehouse man, freight caller, window dresser, advertising man, sales manager, junkman, trader	16.81
Public Service		
	Army	40.00
	Policeman	30.00
	Postman, firefighter, fire chief, public works, inspector, detective	30.00
Semi-professional		
	Printer	39.39
	Musician	28.79
	Projectionist	6.06
	Actor	3.03
	Photographer	3.03
	Embalmer, dancer, ball player, sign writer, lithographer, vaudeville player, pugilist, pool hall operator, cartoonist, telephone operator, showman	19.70
Professional		
	Doctor	29.17
	Teacher	20.83
	Lawyer	20.83
	Minister	8.33
	Optician	8.33
	Interne, dentist, bank president	12.51
Personal Service		
	Cook	34.90
	Barber	22.35
	Baker	10.98
	Waiter	7.84
	Tailor	7.84
	Restaurant proprietor	3.92
	Nurse, attendant, hotel proprietor, cleaner, delivery boy, clothes presser, garage proprietor, soda clerk, elevator operator, messenger, porter, bartender, saloon keeper	12.17
Clerical		
	Bookkeeper	46.15
	Accountant	16.67
	Banker	8.97
	Stenographer	6.41
	Cashier	2.56
	Auditor	2.56
	Clerk	2.56
	Bank examiner, bank teller, payroll clerk, office worker, shorthand reporter	14.12

Table VIII-2.   Education by Occupation Grouping

	Illiterate		Read, Write		1-5th Grade		6th Grade	
	No.	Per Cent	No.	Per Cent	No.	Per Cent	No.	Per Cent
Extractive	247	19.09	102	7.88	433	33.46	114	8.81
Laborer	92	13.69	20	2.98	230	34.23	72	10.71
Factory	31	4.37	15	2.12	153	21.58	53	7.48
Transportation	13	4.33	12	3.99	60	20.00	30	10.00
Skilled trades	13	3.50	8	2.16	70	18.87	39	10.51
Trade	6	2.84	3	1.42	29	13.74	13	6.16
Public service	1	3.70	4	14.81	6	22.22	2	7.41
Semi-professional	2	2.90	2	2.90	1	1.45	6	8.70
Professional	0	0	0	0	0	0	0	0
Personal service	8	2.86	6	2.14	44	15.71	34	12.14
Clerical	0	0	1	0.85	2	1.71	6	5.13
Total	413	10.13	173	4.24	1028	25.22	369	9.05

	7th Grade		8th Grade		1st-2nd High		3rd-4th High	
	No.	Per Cent	No.	Per Cent	No.	Per Cent	No.	Per Cent
Extractive	103	7.96	200	15.46	72	5.56	20	1.55
Laborer	79	11.76	109	16.22	57	8.48	13	1.93
Factory	86	12.13	164	23.13	153	21.58	44	6.21
Transportation	41	13.67	72	24.00	55	18.33	12	4.00
Skilled trades	55	14.82	93	25.07	62	16.71	24	6.47
Trade	15	7.11	36	17.06	54	25.59	24	11.37
Public service	4	14.81	5	18.52	3	11.11	0	0
Semi-professional	6	8.70	15	21.74	16	23.19	9	13.04
Professional	0	0	0	0	2	7.41	1	3.70
Personal service	29	10.36	70	25.00	68	24.29	14	5.00
Clerical	5	4.27	15	12.82	35	29.91	20	17.09
Total	423	10.38	779	19.11	577	14.15	181	4.44

	College		Professional School		Total
	No.	Per Cent	No.	Per Cent	No.
Extractive	3	0.23	0	0	1294
Laborer	0	0	0	0	672
Factory	10	1.41	0	0	709
Transportation	5	1.67	0	0	300
Skilled trades	7	1.87	0	0	371
Trade	30	14.22	1	0.47	211
Public service	2	7.41	0	0	27
Semi-professional	10	14.49	2	2.90	69
Professional	20	74.07	4	14.81	27
Personal service	7	2.50	0	0	280
Clerical	33	28.21	0	0	117
Total	127	3.12	7	.17	4077

Table VIII-3. Education Differences between Occupation Subgroups and Total
Series with Value in Terms of the Probable Error

	Illiterate		Read, Write		1-5th Grade	
	Diff.	x p.e.	Diff.	x p.e.	Diff.	x p.e.
Extractive	8.96 ± .46	19.48	3.64 ± .31	11.74	8.24 ± .67	12.30
Laborer	3.56 ± .72	4.95	- 1.26 ± .48	2.62	9.01 ± 1.03	8.75
Factory	- 5.76 ± .70	8.23	- 2.12 ± .46	4.61	- 3.64 ± 1.00	3.64
Transportation	- 5.80 ± 1.13	5.13	- .25 ± .76	.33	- 5.22 ± 1.63	3.20
Skilled trades	- 6.63 ± 1.00	6.63	- 2.08 ± .67	3.10	- 6.35 ± 1.45	4.38
Trade	- 7.29 ± 1.36	5.36	- 2.82 ± .91	3.10	-11.48 ± 1.96	5.86
Public service	- 6.43 ± 3.90	1.65	10.57 ± 2.60	4.06	- 3.00 ± 5.62	.53
Semi-professional	- 7.23 ± 2.43	2.98	- 1.34 ± 1.62	.83	-23.77 ± 3.49	6.81
Professional	-10.13 ± 3.90	2.60	- 4.24 ± 2.60	1.63	-25.22 ± 5.62	4.49
Personal service	- 7.27 ± 1.17	6.21	- 2.10 ± .78	2.69	- 9.51 ± 1.69	5.63
Clerical	-10.13 ± 1.86	9.10	- 3.39 ± 1.24	2.73	-23.51 ± 2.67	8.80

	6th Grade		7th Grade		8th Grade	
	Diff.	x p.e.	Diff.	x p.e.	Diff.	x p.e.
Extractive	- .24 ± .44	.54	- 2.42 ± .47	5.15	- 3.65 ± .61	5.98
Laborer	1.66 ± .68	2.44	1.38 ± .73	1.89	- 2.89 ± .94	3.07
Factory	- 1.57 ± .63	2.49	1.75 ± .70	2.50	4.02 ± .90	4.47
Transportation	.95 ± 1.07	.89	3.29 ± 1.14	2.88	4.89 ± 1.47	3.33
Skilled trades	1.46 ± .96	1.52	4.44 ± 1.02	4.25	5.96 ± 1.32	4.52
Trade	- 2.89 ± 1.30	2.22	- 3.27 ± 1.38	2.37	- 2.05 ± 1.78	1.15
Public service	- 1.64 ± 3.71	.44	4.43 ± 3.95	1.12	- .59 ± 5.09	.12
Semi-professional	- .35 ± 2.31	.15	- 1.68 ± 2.46	.68	2.63 ± 3.16	.83
Professional	- 9.05 ± 3.71	2.44	-10.38 ± 3.95	2.63	-19.11 ± 5.09	3.75
Personal service	3.09 ± 1.12	2.76	- .02 ± 1.19	.02	5.89 ± 1.53	3.85
Clerical	- 3.92 ± 1.76	2.23	- 6.11 ± 1.88	3.25	- 6.29 ± 2.42	2.60

	1st-2nd High		3rd-4th High		College	
	Diff.	x p.e.	Diff.	x p.e.	Diff.	x p.e.
Extractive	- 8.59 ± .54	15.91	- 2.89 ± .32	9.03	- 2.89 ± .27	10.70
Laborer	- 5.67 ± .83	6.83	- 2.51 ± .49	5.12	- 3.12 ± .42	7.43
Factory	7.43 ± .80	9.29	1.77 ± .47	3.76	- 1.71 ± .40	4.28
Transportation	4.18 ± 1.31	3.19	- .44 ± .77	.57	- 1.45 ± .65	2.23
Skilled trades	2.56 ± 1.17	2.19	2.03 ± .69	2.94	- 1.25 ± .58	2.16
Trade	11.44 ± 1.58	7.24	6.93 ± .93	7.45	11.10 ± .79	14.05
Public service	- 3.04 ± 4.51	.67	- 4.44 ± 2.66	1.67	4.29 ± 2.25	1.91
Semi-professional	9.04 ± 2.81	3.22	8.60 ± 1.66	5.18	11.37 ± 1.40	8.12
Professional	- 6.74 ± 4.51	1.49	- .74 ± 2.66	.28	70.95 ± 2.25	31.53
Personal service	10.14 ± 1.36	7.46	.56 ± .80	.70	- .62 ± .67	.92
Clerical	15.76 ± 2.14	7.36	12.65 ± 1.27	9.96	25.09 ± 1.07	23.45

Table VIII-5.   Hair Color by Occupation Grouping

	Black		Dark Brown		Reddish Brown	
	No.	Per Cent	No.	Per Cent	No.	Per Cent
Extractive	70	5.46	446	34.76	237	18.47
Laborer	34	4.99	252	36.95	152	22.29
Factory	34	4.79	236	33.24	150	21.13
Transportation	14	4.67	90	30.00	74	24.67
Skilled trades	17	4.58	133	35.85	69	18.60
Trade	8	3.83	83	39.71	36	17.22
Public service	1	3.70	14	51.85	3	11.11
Semi-professional	5	7.35	22	32.35	12	17.65
Professional	2	7.41	8	29.63	6	22.22
Personal service	12	4.29	102	36.43	57	20.36
Clerical	6	5.22	35	30.43	16	13.91
Total	203	4.98	1421	34.90	812	19.94

	Light Brown		Ash-blond		Golden	
	No.	Per Cent	No.	Per Cent	No.	Per Cent
Extractive	337	26.27	36	2.81	31	2.42
Laborer	158	23.17	7	1.03	26	3.81
Factory	199	28.03	15	2.11	27	3.80
Transportation	78	26.00	0	0	13	4.33
Skilled trades	88	23.72	8	2.16	17	4.58
Trade	52	24.88	6	2.87	5	2.39
Public service	7	25.93	0	0	0	0
Semi-professional	23	33.82	1	1.47	2	2.94
Professional	7	25.93	0	0	1	3.70
Personal service	59	21.07	7	2.50	9	3.21
Clerical	38	33.04	4	3.48	6	5.22
Total	1046	25.69	84	2.06	137	3.36

	Red		Gray, White		Total	
	No.	Per Cent	No.	Per Cent	No.	
Extractive	49	3.82	77	6.00	1283	
Laborer	27	3.96	26	3.81	682	
Factory	30	4.23	19	2.68	710	
Transportation	12	4.00	19	6.33	300	
Skilled trades	13	3.50	26	7.01	371	
Trade	5	2.39	14	6.70	209	
Public service	0	0	2	7.41	27	
Semi-professional	2	2.94	1	1.47	68	
Professional	2	7.41	1	3.70	27	
Personal service	14	5.00	20	7.14	280	
Clerical	3	2.61	7	6.09	115	
Total	157	3.86	212	5.21	4072	

Table VIII-6.   Hair Color Differences between Occupation Subgroups and
                 Total Series with Value in Terms of the Probable Error

	Black		Dark Brown		Reddish-brown	
	Diff.	x p.e.	Diff.	x p.e.	Diff.	x p.e.
Laborer						
Transportation			- 4.90 ± 1.79	2.74	4.73 ± 1.50	3.15
Skilled trades	- 0.40 ± .73	0.55				
Trade			4.81 ± 2.16	2.23		
Public service			16.95 ± 6.15	2.75		
Semi-professional	2.37 ± 1.77	1.34				
Professional	2.43 ± 2.83	0.86	- 5.27 ± 6.13	0.86		
Personal service					0.42 ± .15	2.71
Clerical			- 4.47 ± 2.94	1.52	- 6.03 ± 2.48	2.43

	Light Brown		Ash-blond		Golden	
	Diff.	x p.e.	Diff.	x p.e.	Diff.	x p.e.
Laborer	- 2.52 ± 1.03	2.45				
Semi-professional	8.13 ± 3.53	2.30				
Personal service	- 4.62 ± 1.70	2.72				
Clerical	7.35 ± 2.71	2.71	1.42 ± .88	1.61	1.86 ± 1.12	1.66

	Red	
	Diff.	x p.e.
Professional	3.55 ± 2.48	1.43
Personal service	1.14 ± .75	1.52

Table VIII-8.   Eye Color by Occupation Grouping

	Dark Brown No.	Per Cent	Light Brown No.	Per Cent	Blue-brown No.	Per Cent	Gray-brown No.	Per Cent
Extractive	41	3.15	28	2.15	277	21.31	215	16.54
Laborer	35	5.12	22	3.22	148	21.64	77	11.26
Factory	21	2.94	23	3.22	134	18.77	149	20.87
Transportation	7	2.31	7	2.31	52	17.16	49	16.17
Skilled trades	9	2.41	9	2.41	78	20.91	79	21.18
Trade	7	3.30	4	1.89	44	20.75	53	25.00
Public service	0	0	2	7.41	4	14.81	3	11.11
Semi-professional	1	1.45	6	8.70	18	26.09	11	15.94
Professional	0	0	3	11.11	4	14.81	4	14.81
Personal service	12	4.26	12	4.26	50	17.73	67	23.76
Clerical	4	3.42	8	6.84	25	21.37	19	16.24
Total	137	3.33	124	3.02	834	20.30	726	17.67

	Green-brown No.	Per Cent	Blue No.	Per Cent	Blue-gray No.	Per Cent	Total No.
Extractive	336	25.85	317	24.38	86	6.62	1300
Laborer	205	29.97	103	15.06	94	13.74	684
Factory	187	26.19	135	18.91	65	9.10	714
Transportation	92	30.36	65	21.45	31	10.23	303
Skilled trades	92	24.66	69	18.50	37	9.92	373
Trade	47	22.17	44	20.75	13	6.13	212
Public service	8	29.63	6	22.22	4	14.81	27
Semi-professional	18	26.09	9	13.04	6	8.70	69
Professional	8	29.63	5	18.52	3	11.11	27
Personal service	77	27.30	41	14.54	23	8.16	282
Clerical	30	25.64	17	14.53	14	11.97	117
Total	1100	26.78	811	19.74	376	9.15	4108

Table VIII-9. Eye Color Differences between Occupation Subgroups and Total Series with Value in Terms of the Probable Error

	Dark Brown		Light Brown		Blue		Blue-grey	
	Diff.	x p.e.	Diff.	x p.e.	Diff.	x p.e.	Diff.	x p.e.
Extractive					4.64 ± .61	7.61	- 2.53 ± .45	5.62
Laborer	1.79 ± .42	4.26			- 4.68 ± .94	4.98	4.59 ± .67	6.85
Transportation					1.71 ± 1.47	1.16	1.08 ± 1.07	1.01
Trade							- 3.02 ± 1.30	2.32
Public service			4.39 ± 2.21	1.99	2.48 ± 5.17	0.48	5.66 ± 3.72	1.52
Semi-professional			5.68 ± 1.38	4.12	- 6.70 ± 3.20	2.09		
Professional							1.96 ± 3.77	0.52
Personal service	0.93 ± .70	1.33			- 5.20 ± 1.54	3.38		
Clerical			3.82 ± 1.05	3.64	- 5.21 ± 2.45	2.13	2.92 ± 1.77	1.59

Table VIII-11. Age by Occupation Grouping

	No.	Range	Mean	S. D.	V.
Extractive	1303	15-69	32.00 ± .23	12.30 ± .12	38.44 ± .36
Laborer	684	15-69	29.00 ± .30	11.55 ± .21	39.83 ± .73
Factory	713	15-69	28.90 ± .17	9.70 ± .17	33.56 ± .60
Transportation	299	15-69	29.55 ± .38	9.80 ± .27	33.16 ± .92
Skilled trades	371	15-69	31.20 ± .37	10.65 ± .26	34.14 ± .84
Trade	212	15-69	34.10 ± .57	12.25 ± .40	35.92 ± 1.18
Public service	28	15-69	34.15 ± 1.52	11.90 ± 1.07	34.85 ± 3.14
Semi-professional	68	15-69	29.80 ± .81	9.85 ± .57	33.05 ± 1.91
Professional	25	20-69	42.40 ± 1.88	13.90 ± 1.33	32.78 ± 3.13
Personal service	281	15-69	30.60 ± .44	10.95 ± .31	35.78 ± 1.02
Clerical	118	15-64	32.15 ± .68	10.95 ± .48	34.06 ± 1.50
Total	4102	15-69	30.75 ± .12	11.35 ± .08	36.91 ± .28

Table VIII-12. Weight by Occupation Grouping

	No.	Range	Mean	S. D.	V.
Extractive	1211	101-270	151.90 ± .39	19.80 ± .27	13.03 ± .18
Laborer	655	101-240	149.50 ± .50	18.80 ± .35	12.58 ± .23
Factory	672	101-260	151.10 ± .53	20.50 ± .38	13.57 ± .25
Transportation	279	101-230	153.10 ± .86	21.20 ± .61	13.85 ± .40
Skilled trades	346	101-250	150.70 ± .73	20.00 ± .51	13.27 ± .34
Trade	197	101-240	153.40 ± 1.07	22.30 ± .76	14.54 ± .49
Public service	26	111-200	153.50 ± 2.51	19.00 ± 1.78	12.37 ± 1.16
Semi-professional	62	101-220	152.30 ± 2.12	24.80 ± 1.50	16.28 ± .99
Professional	19	121-230	170.80 ± 3.93	25.40 ± 2.78	14.97 ± 1.63
Personal service	259	101-250	148.70 ± .78	18.70 ± .55	12.58 ± .37
Clerical	107	101-240	147.70 ± 1.43	22.00 ± 1.01	14.90 ± .69
Total	3833	101-270	151.20 ± .22	20.20 ± .16	13.36 ± .10

Table VIII-13. Height by Occupation Grouping

	No.	Range	Mean	S. D.	V.
Extractive	1301	146-190	172.41 ± .12	6.18 ± .08	3.58 ± .06
Laborer	683	149-190	171.33 ± .17	6.48 ± .12	3.78 ± .07
Factory	714	146-196	172.02 ± .16	6.42 ± .11	3.73 ± .07
Transportation	302	152-193	172.29 ± .25	6.42 ± .18	3.73 ± .10
Skilled trades	374	158-193	172.02 ± .21	5.97 ± .15	3.47 ± .09
Trade	210	149-190	172.20 ± .30	6.39 ± .21	3.71 ± .12
Public service	27	155-181	171.99 ± .68	5.28 ± .48	3.07 ± .28
Semi-professional	69	149-190	170.73 ± .61	7.50 ± .43	4.39 ± .25
Professional	27	155-187	171.66 ± .86	6.60 ± .61	3.84 ± .35
Personal service	281	146-196	171.03 ± .28	6.90 ± .20	4.03 ± .11
Clerical	117	149-190	170.97 ± .46	7.38 ± .33	4.32 ± .19
Total	4105	146-196	172.20 ± .07	6.48 ± .05	3.76 ± .03

Table VIII-14. Sitting Height by Occupation Grouping

	No.	Range	Mean	S. D.	V.
Extractive	1296	78-104	90.34 ± .06	3.42 ± .05	3.79 ± .05
Laborer	682	69-104	90.10 ± .09	3.51 ± .06	3.90 ± .51
Factory	711	78-101	90.37 ± .09	3.42 ± .06	3.78 ± .07
Transportation	300	72-101	90.40 ± .14	3.57 ± .10	3.95 ± .11
Skilled trades	374	81-101	90.37 ± .12	3.48 ± .09	3.85 ± .09
Trade	208	81-101	90.55 ± .16	3.36 ± .11	3.71 ± .12
Public service	26	84- 98	90.43 ± .35	2.64 ± .25	2.92 ± .27
Semi-professional	67	81- 98	90.19 ± .32	3.90 ± .23	4.32 ± .25
Professional	27	81- 98	90.79 ± .42	3.27 ± .30	3.60 ± .33
Personal service	280	78-101	90.10 ± .14	3.57 ± .10	3.96 ± .11
Clerical	114	78-101	90.04 ± .22	3.42 ± .15	3.80 ± .17
Total	4085	69-104	90.28 ± .04	3.48 ± .03	3.86 ± .03

Table VIII-15. Head Length by Occupation Grouping

	No.	Range	Mean	S. D.	V.
Extractive	1300	173-226	193.62 ± .12	6.45 ± .09	3.33 ± .04
Laborer	684	176-217	193.95 ± .17	6.69 ± .12	3.45 ± .06
Factory	716	173-214	193.92 ± .17	6.63 ± .12	3.42 ± .06
Transportation	303	176-214	194.01 ± .25	6.33 ± .17	3.26 ± .09
Skilled trades	374	176-204	193.38 ± .22	6.42 ± .16	3.32 ± .08
Trade	212	170-211	194.40 ± .30	6.48 ± .21	3.33 ± .11
Public service	27	176-205	193.56 ± .92	7.14 ± .66	3.69 ± .34
Semi-professional	69	179-220	194.10 ± .62	7.59 ± .44	3.91 ± .22
Professional	27	185-211	195.90 ± .79	6.09 ± .56	3.11 ± .29
Personal service	282	173-220	194.10 ± .26	6.54 ± .19	3.37 ± .10
Clerical	117	170-214	194.64 ± .42	6.81 ± .30	3.50 ± .15
Total	4111	170-226	193.86 ± .07	6.57 ± .05	3.39 ± .02

Table VIII-16. Head Breadth by Occupation Grouping

	No.	Range	Mean	S. D.	V.
Extractive	1302	129-173	151.84 ± .10	5.22 ± .07	3.44 ± .05
Laborer	684	129-170	151.72 ± .14	5.40 ± .10	3.56 ± .06
Factory	714	132-170	152.71 ± .13	5.22 ± .09	3.42 ± .06
Transportation	303	138-170	152.20 ± .22	5.55 ± .15	2.33 ± .06
Skilled trades	374	138-170	152.11 ± .19	5.55 ± .14	3.85 ± .09
Trade	212	138-170	153.07 ± .24	5.13 ± .17	3.35 ± .11
Public service	27	135-164	151.00 ± .83	6.42 ± .59	4.25 ± .39
Semi-professional	69	141-167	153.43 ± .44	5.40 ± .31	3.52 ± .20
Professional	27	141-164	154.21 ± .77	5.94 ± .55	3.85 ± .35
Personal service	282	135-157	151.75 ± .21	5.28 ± .15	3.48 ± .10
Clerical	117	141-173	153.70 ± .36	5.73 ± .25	3.73 ± .16
Total	4111	129-173	152.17 ± .06	5.37 ± .04	3.53 ± .03

Table VIII-17.   Head Circumference by Occupation Grouping

	No.	Range	Mean	S. D.	V.
Extractive	1188	502-621	564.74 ± .31	15.72 ± .22	2.78 ± .04
Laborer	647	502-621	560.66 ± .44	16.44 ± .31	2.93 ± .05
Factory	660	514-621	564.74 ± .42	15.96 ± .30	2.83 ± .05
Transportation	282	514-609	564.86 ± .60	14.88 ± .42	2.63 ± .07
Skilled trades	351	514-621	562.94 ± .58	16.20 ± .41	2.88 ± .07
Trade	194	526-609	565.70 ± .79	16.32 ± .56	2.88 ± .10
Public service	25	526-609	564.14 ± 2.51	18.60 ± 1.77	3.30 ± .32
Semi-professional	61	526-609	566.54 ± 1.45	16.80 ± 1.03	2.97 ± .18
Professional	25	538-609	569.90 ± 1.94	14.40 ± 1.37	2.53 ± .24
Personal service	262	514-609	562.70 ± .65	15.60 ± .46	2.77 ± .08
Clerical	107	502-621	566.18 ± 1.14	17.52 ± .81	3.09 ± .14
Total	3802	502-621	563.90 ± .18	16.08 ± .12	2.85 ± .02

Table VIII-18.   Minimum Frontal Diameter by Occupation Grouping

	No.	Range	Mean	S. D.	V.
Extractive	1301	97-128	111.18 ± .09	4.84 ± .06	4.35 ± .06
Laborer	685	93-128	111.58 ± .13	5.00 ± .09	4.48 ± .08
Factory	715	97-128	112.14 ± .12	4.72 ± .08	4.21 ± .08
Transportation	303	97-128	111.62 ± .18	4.68 ± .13	4.16 ± .11
Skilled trades	373	97-128	111.58 ± .18	5.04 ± .12	4.52 ± .11
Trade	212	97-124	111.46 ± .17	4.72 ± .15	4.23 ± .14
Public service	27	101-124	110.22 ± .57	4.36 ± .40	3.96 ± .36
Semi-professional	69	101-128	112.86 ± .53	6.52 ± .37	5.78 ± .33
Professional	26	97-124	114.66 ± .71	5.40 ± .51	4.71 ± .44
Personal service	282	97-124	111.58 ± .18	4.40 ± .12	3.94 ± .11
Clerical	117	97-128	111.82 ± .31	4.92 ± .22	4.40 ± .19
Total	4110	93-128	111.58 ± .05	4.84 ± .04	4.34 ± .03

Table VIII-19.   Bizygomatic Diameter by Occupation Grouping

	No.	Range	Mean	S. D.	V.
Extractive	1302	120-159	138.55 ± .10	5.15 ± .07	3.72 ± .05
Laborer	684	115-159	138.50 ± .14	5.40 ± .10	3.90 ± .07
Factory	716	120-159	138.90 ± .14	5.40 ± .10	3.89 ± .07
Transportation	303	125-154	138.35 ± .20	5.05 ± .14	3.65 ± .10
Skilled trades	374	125-159	138.75 ± .19	5.45 ± .13	3.93 ± .10
Trade	212	115-159	138.60 ± .26	5.55 ± .18	4.00 ± .13
Public service	27	125-149	138.50 ± .75	5.75 ± .53	4.15 ± .38
Semi-professional	69	125-154	138.45 ± .16	5.70 ± .33	4.12 ± .24
Professional	27	130-159	142.35 ± .81	6.25 ± .57	4.39 ± .40
Personal service	282	120-159	138.30 ± .21	5.25 ± .15	3.80 ± .11
Clerical	117	125-154	138.90 ± .34	5.45 ± .24	3.92 ± .17
Total	4113	115-159	138.60 ± .06	5.35 ± .04	3.86 ± .03

Table VIII-20. Cephalic Index by Occupation Grouping

	No.	Range	Mean		S. D.		V.	
Extractive	1300	62-91	78.45 ±	.06	3.18 ±	.04	4.05 ±	.05
Laborer	684	68-91	78.24 ±	.09	3.42 ±	.06	4.37 ±	.08
Factory	714	68-91	78.90 ±	.09	3.42 ±	.06	4.33 ±	.08
Transportation	302	71-94	78.63 ±	.13	3.36 ±	.09	4.27 ±	.12
Skilled trades	374	68-88	78.60 ±	.11	3.12 ±	.08	3.97 ±	.10
Trade	212	68-94	78.81 ±	.15	3.27 ±	.11	4.15 ±	.14
Public service	27	68-88	78.33 ±	.49	3.78 ±	.35	4.83 ±	.44
Semi-professional	69	68-91	80.34 ±	.38	4.71 ±	.27	5.86 ±	.37
Professional	27	74-88	79.23 ±	.44	3.39 ±	.31	4.28 ±	.39
Personal service	282	65-88	78.33 ±	.13	3.33 ±	.09	4.25 ±	.12
Clerical	117	71-88	78.84 ±	.22	3.60 ±	.16	4.57 ±	.20
Total	⁓108	62-94	78.57 ±	.04	3.36 ±	.02	4.28 ±	.03

Table VIII-21. Facial Index by Occupation Grouping

	No.	Range	Mean		S. D.		V.	
Extractive	1301	70-109	87.86 ±	.10	5.32 ±	.07	6.06 ±	.08
Laborer	684	70-101	87.62 ±	.13	5.20 ±	.09	5.93 ±	.11
Factory	715	74-105	87.62 ±	.13	5.16 ±	.09	5.89 ±	.11
Transportation	303	74-105	88.14 ±	.20	5.08 ±	.14	5.76 ±	.16
Skilled trades	374	74-105	87.78 ±	.18	5.16 ±	.13	5.88 ±	.14
Trade	212	74-105	87.86 ±	.24	5.12 ±	.17	5.83 ±	.19
Public service	27	70-101	87.06 ±	.77	6.00 ±	.55	6.89 ±	.63
Semi-professional	69	74-101	87.62 ±	.39	4.80 ±	.28	5.48 ±	.31
Professional	27	78-101	86.74 ±	.72	5.56 ±	.51	6.41 ±	.59
Personal service	282	74-105	88.06 ±	.22	5.44 ±	.15	6.18 ±	.18
Clerical	117	74-101	88.10 ±	.30	4.80 ±	.21	5.45 ±	.24
Total	4111	70-109	87.82 ±	.06	5.24 ±	.04	5.97 ±	.04

Table VIII-22. Nasal Index by Occupation Grouping

	No.	Range	Mean		S. D.		V.	
Extractive	1297	48-99	66.38 ±	.12	6.64 ±	.09	10.00 ±	.13
Laborer	684	44-91	67.10 ±	.18	7.12 ±	.13	9.57 ±	.17
Factory	715	44-87	66.90 ±	.17	6.56 ±	.12	9.81 ±	.18
Transportation	302	48-99	67.14 ±	.28	7.24 ±	.20	10.78 ±	.30
Skilled trades	372	48-99	66.62 ±	.23	6.72 ±	.17	10.09 ±	.25
Trade	212	48-87	66.22 ±	.31	6.76 ±	.22	10.21 ±	.33
Public service	27	56-83	68.46 ±	.99	7.68 ±	.70	11.22 ±	1.03
Semi-professional	69	56-83	66.38 ±	.47	5.80 ±	.33	8.74 ±	.50
Professional	27	56-91	69.22 ±	1.00	7.68 ±	.70	11.10 ±	1.02
Personal service	282	48-87	68.62 ±	.25	6.20 ±	.18	9.04 ±	.26
Clerical	116	52-87	64.54 ±	.39	6.20 ±	.27	9.61 ±	.43
Total	4103	44-99	66.62 ±	.07	6.80 ±	.05	10.21 ±	.08

Table VIII-23. Differences of Means between Occupation Subgroups and Total
Series with Value in Terms of the Probable Error

	Extractive		Laborer		Factory		Transportation	
	Diff.	x p.e.	Diff.	x p.e.	Diff.	x p.e.	Diff.	x p.e.
Age	1.25	5.95	- 1.75	6.03	- 1.85	6.38	- 1.20	2.73
Weight	0.70	1.79	- 1.70	3.21	- 0.10	0.19	1.90	2.32
Height	0.21	1.75	- 0.87	5.12	- 0.18	1.12	0.09	0.36
Sitting height	0.06	0.86	- 0.18	2.00	0.09	1.00	0.12	0.86
Head length	- 0.24	2.00	0.09	0.53	0.06	0.35	0.15	0.60
Head breadth	- 0.33	3.30	- 0.45	3.21	0.54	3.86	0.03	0.14
Head circumference	0.84	2.62	- 3.24	7.53	0.84	2.00	0.96	1.48
Minimum frontal diameter	- 0.40	4.44	0	0	0.56	4.67	0.04	0.21
Bizygomatic diameter	- 0.05	0.50	- 0.10	0.71	0.30	2.31	- 0.25	1.19
Cephalic index	- 0.12	2.00	- 0.33	3.67	0.33	4.12	0.06	0.46
Facial index	0.04	0.40	- 0.20	1.43	- 0.20	1.54	0.32	1.60
Nasal index	- 0.24	1.85	0.48	2.67	0.28	1.65	0.52	2.00

	Skilled Trades		Trade		Public Service		Semi-professional	
	Diff.	x p.e.	Diff.	x p.e.	Diff.	x p.e.	Diff.	x p.e.
Age	0.45	1.12	3.35	6.32	3.40	2.34	- 0.95	1.02
Weight	- 0.50	0.68	2.20	2.27	2.40	0.90	1.10	0.64
Height	- 0.18	0.78	0	0	- 0.21	0.25	- 1.47	2.77
Sitting height	0.09	0.75	0.27	1.69	0.15	0.33	- 0.09	0.31
Head length	- 0.48	2.09	0.54	1.80	- 0.30	0.35	0.24	0.45
Head breadth	- 0.06	0.32	0.90	3.60	- 1.17	1.67	1.26	2.86
Head circumference	- 0.96	1.66	1.80	2.31	0.24	0.11	2.64	1.90
Minimum frontal diameter	0	0	- 0.12	0.55	- 1.36	2.16	1.28	3.28
Bizygomatic diameter	0.15	0.79	0	0	- 0.10	0.14	- 0.15	0.35
Cephalic index	0.03	0.25	0.24	1.50	- 0.24	0.55	1.77	6.56
Facial index	- 0.04	0.22	0.04	0.17	- 0.76	1.12	- 0.20	0.47
Nasal index	0	0	- 0.40	1.29	1.84	2.09	- 0.24	0.44

	Professional		Personal Service		Clerical	
	Diff.	x p.e.	Diff.	x p.e.	Diff.	x p.e.
Age	11.65	7.61	- 0.15	0.33	1.40	2.00
Weight	19.60	6.26	- 2.50	2.94	- 3.50	2.65
Height	- 0.54	0.64	- 1.17	4.50	- 1.23	3.08
Sitting height	0.51	1.13	- 0.18	1.29	- 0.24	1.09
Head length	2.04	2.40	0.24	0.92	0.78	1.90
Head breadth	2.04	2.91	- 0.42	1.91	1.53	4.64
Head circumference	6.00	2.76	- 1.20	1.79	2.28	2.17
Minimum frontal diameter	3.08	4.81	0	0	0.24	0.80
Bizygomatic diameter	3.75	5.43	- 0.30	1.43	0.30	0.91
Cephalic index	0.66	1.50	- 0.24	1.85	0.27	1.29
Facial index	- 1.08	1.59	0.24	1.14	0.28	0.85
Nasal index	2.60	2.95	2.00	7.41	- 2.08	4.84

Table IX-1.   States by Body Build Grouping

	Massachusetts		Tennessee		Kentucky		Texas	
	No.	Per Cent	No.	Per Cent	No.	Per Cent	No.	Per Cent
Short-slender	14	21.98	4	6.25	13	20.31	6	9.38
Short-medium weight	28	12.90	16	7.37	59	27.19	30	13.82
Short-heavy	6	11.11	1	1.85	11	20.37	16	29.53
Medium height-slender	37	10.53	38	10.92	116	33.33	59	16.95
Medium height-medium weight	184	9.56	228	11.84	569	29.56	411	21.35
Medium height-heavy	45	6.17	72	9.88	200	27.43	180	24.69
Tall-slender	6	5.26	17	14.91	35	30.70	30	26.32
Tall-medium weight	13	4.00	36	11.07	92	28.36	102	31.37
Tall-heavy	4	2.98	9	6.72	33	24.53	47	35.07
Total	337	8.62	421	10.77	1128	28.85	881	22.53

	North Carolina		Wisconsin		Southwest		Total	
	No.	Per Cent	No.	Per Cent	No.	Per Cent	No.	
Short-slender	4	6.25	13	20.31	10	15.63	64	
Short-medium weight	20	9.22	33	15.21	31	14.28	217	
Short-heavy	9	16.67	8	14.81	3	5.56	54	
Medium height-slender	27	7.76	31	8.91	40	11.50	348	
Medium height-medium weight	221	11.48	128	6.65	184	9.56	1925	
Medium height-heavy	96	13.17	47	6.45	89	12.21	729	
Tall-slender	12	10.53	7	6.14	7	6.14	114	
Tall-medium weight	40	12.30	19	5.84	23	7.07	325	
Tall-heavy	17	12.69	13	9.70	11	8.21	134	
Total	446	11.41	299	7.65	398	10.18	3910	

Table IX-2.   State Differences between Body Build Subgroups and Total Series with Value in Terms of the Probable Error

	Massachusetts		Tennessee		Kentucky		Texas	
	Per Cent	x p.e.	Per Cent	x p.e.	Per Cent	x p.s.	Per Cent	x p.e.
Short-slender	13.26 ± 2.35	5.64	- 4.52 ± 2.59	1.74	- 8.54 ± 3.79	2.25	-13.15 ± 3.49	3.77
Short-medium weight	4.28 ± 1.24	3.45	- 3.40 ± 1.38	2.46	- 1.66 ± 2.02	.82	- 8.71 ± 1.86	4.68
Short-heavy	2.49 ± 2.56	.97	- 8.92 ± 2.83	3.15	- 8.48 ± 4.13	2.05	7.10 ± 3.90	1.87
Medium height-slender	2.01 ± .97	2.07	- .15 ± 1.07	.14	4.48 ± 1.56	2.87	- 5.58 ± 1.44	3.88
Medium height-medium weight	.94 ± .31	3.03	1.07 ± .34	3.15	.71 ± .50	1.42	- 1.18 ± .46	2.56
Medium height-heavy	- 2.45 ± .63	3.89	- .89 ± .70	1.27	- 1.42 ± 1.02	1.39	2.16 ± .94	2.30
Tall-slender	- 3.36 ± 1.75	1.92	4.14 ± 1.93	2.14	1.85 ± 2.82	.66	3.79 ± 2.60	1.46
Tall-medium weight	- 4.62 ± 1.00	4.62	.30 ± 1.11	.27	- .49 ± 1.63	.30	8.84 ± 1.50	5.89
Tall-heavy	- 5.64 ± 1.60	3.52	- 4.05 ± 1.77	2.29	- 4.22 ± 2.60	1.62	12.54 ± 2.39	5.25

	North Carolina		Wisconsin		Southwest	
	Per Cent	x p.e.	Per Cent	x p.e.	Per Cent	x p.e.
Short-slender	- 5.16 ± 2.66	1.94	12.66 ± 2.22	5.70	5.45 ± 2.53	2.15
Short-medium weight	- 2.19 ± 1.42	1.54	7.56 ± 1.18	6.41	4.10 ± 1.35	3.04
Short-heavy	5.26 ± 2.90	1.81	7.16 ± 2.42	2.96	- 4.62 ± 2.76	1.67
Medium height-slender	- 3.65 ± 1.10	3.32	1.26 ± .92	1.37	1.32 ± 1.04	1.27
Medium height-medium weight	- .07 ± .35	.20	- 1.00 ± .30	3.33	- .62 ± .33	1.88
Medium height-heavy	1.76 ± .72	2.44	- 1.20 ± .60	2.00	2.03 ± .68	2.98
Tall-slender	- .88 ± 1.98	.44	- 1.51 ± 1.65	.92	- 4.04 ± 1.88	2.15
Tall-medium weight	.89 ± 1.14	.78	- 1.81 ± .95	1.90	- 3.11 ± 1.09	2.85
Tall-heavy	1.28 ± 1.82	.70	2.05 ± 1.52	1.35	- 1.97 ± 1.73	1.14

Table IX-3.   Association of Stature Grouping with States

	Massachusetts		Tennessee		Kentucky		Texas	
	No.	Per Cent	No.	Per Cent	No.	Per Cent	No.	Per Cent
Short	48	14.33	21	6.27	83	24.78	52	15.52
Medium height	266	8.86	338	11.26	885	29.48	650	21.65
Tall	23	4.01	62	10.82	160	27.92	179	31.24
Total	337	8.62	421	10.77	1128	28.85	881	22.53

	North Carolina		Wisconsin		Southwest		Total	
	No.	Per Cent	No.	Per Cent	No.	Per Cent	No.	
Short	33	9.85	54	16.12	44	13.13	335	
Medium height	344	11.46	206	6.86	313	10.43	3002	
Tall	69	12.04	39	6.81	41	7.16	573	
Total	446	11.41	299	7.65	398	10.18	3910	

Table IX-4.   Association of Weight Grouping with States

	Massachusetts		Tennessee		Kentucky		Texas	
	No.	Per Cent	No.	Per Cent	No.	Per Cent	No.	Per Cent
Slender	57	10.84	59	11.22	164	31.18	95	18.06
Medium weight	225	9.12	280	11.35	720	29.18	543	22.01
Heavy	55	3.00	82	8.94	244	26.61	243	26.50
Total	337	8.62	421	10.77	1128	28.85	881	22.53

	North Carolina		Wisconsin		Southwest		Total	
	No.	Per Cent	No.	Per Cent	No.	Per Cent	No.	
Slender	43	8.18	51	9.70	57	10.84	526	
Medium weight	281	11.39	180	7.30	238	9.65	2467	
Heavy	122	13.30	68	7.42	103	11.23	917	
Total	446	11.41	299	7.65	398	10.18	3910	

Table IX-5.   Offenses by Body Build Grouping

	First Degree Murder		Second Degree Murder		Assault		Robbery	
	No.	Per Cent	No.	Per Cent	No.	Per Cent	No.	Per Cent
Short-slender	5	7.81	11	17.19	0	0	4	6.25
Short-medium weight	7	3.23	29	13.36	5	2.30	16	7.37
Short-heavy	2	3.70	5	9.26	2	3.70	4	7.41
Medium height-slender	24	6.90	46	13.22	7	2.01	32	9.20
Medium height-medium weight	118	6.13	280	14.54	37	1.92	201	10.44
Medium height-heavy	59	8.09	123	16.87	12	1.65	67	9.19
Tall-slender	13	11.40	22	19.30	0	0	18	15.79
Tall-medium weight	30	9.23	49	15.07	7	2.15	27	8.30
Tall-heavy	16	11.94	19	14.18	4	2.98	10	7.46
Total	274	7.01	584	14.94	74	1.89	379	9.69

	Burglary and Larceny		Forgery and Fraud		Rape		Other Sex	
	No.	Per Cent	No.	Per Cent	No.	Per Cent	No.	Per Cent
Short-slender	30	46.88	6	9.38	2	3.13	3	4.69
Short-medium weight	94	43.32	23	10.60	18	8.30	8	3.69
Short-heavy	21	38.89	7	12.96	5	9.26	4	7.41
Medium height-slender	150	43.10	35	10.06	14	4.02	15	4.31
Medium height-medium weight	790	41.04	189	9.82	90	4.68	64	3.32
Medium height-heavy	237	32.51	84	11.52	35	4.80	35	4.80
Tall-slender	33	28.95	16	14.04	2	1.75	0	0
Tall-medium weight	120	36.91	48	14.76	11	3.38	8	2.46
Tall-heavy	44	32.84	19	14.18	4	2.98	7	5.22
Total	1519	38.85	427	10.92	181	4.63	144	3.68

	Vs. Public Welfare		Arson and All Other		Total
	No.	Per Cent	No.	Per Cent	No.
Short-slender	3	4.69	0	0	64
Short-medium weight	8	3.69	9	4.15	217
Short-heavy	3	5.56	1	1.85	54
Medium height-slender	19	5.46	6	1.72	348
Medium height-medium weight	97	5.04	59	3.06	1925
Medium height-heavy	64	8.79	13	1.78	729
Tall-slender	9	7.90	1	.88	114
Tall-medium weight	22	6.77	3	.92	325
Tall-heavy	10	7.46	1	.75	134
Total	235	6.01	93	2.38	3910

Table IX-6.   Offense Differences between Body Build Subgroups and Total Series with Value in Terms of the Probable Error

	First Degree Murder Per Cent	x p.e.	Second Degree Murder Per Cent	x p.e.	Assault Per Cent	x p.e.	Robbery Per Cent	x p.e.
Short-slender	.80 ± 2.13	.38	2.25 ± 2.98	.75	- 1.89 ± 1.13	1.67	- 3.44 ± 2.48	1.39
Short-medium weight	- 3.78 ± 1.13	3.34	- 1.58 ± 1.58	1.00	.41 ± .60	.68	- 2.32 ± 1.32	1.76
Short-heavy	- 3.31 ± 2.33	1.42	- 5.68 ± 3.25	1.75	1.81 ± 1.24	1.46	- 2.28 ± 2.70	.84
Medium height-slender	- .11 ± .88	.12	- 1.72 ± 1.23	1.40	- .12 ± .46	.26	- .49 ± 1.02	.48
Medium height-medium weight	- .88 ± .28	3.14	- .40 ± .39	1.02	.03 ± .15	.20	.75 ± .32	2.34
Medium height-heavy	1.08 ± .57	1.89	1.93 ± .80	2.41	- .24 ± .31	.77	- .50 ± .67	.75
Tall-slender	4.39 ± 1.59	2.76	4.36 ± 2.22	1.96	- 1.89 ± .85	2.22	6.10 ± 1.84	3.32
Tall-medium weight	2.22 ± .92	2.41	- .13 ± 1.28	.10	.26 ± .49	.53	- 1.39 ± 1.06	1.31
Tall-heavy	4.93 ± 1.46	3.38	- .76 ± 2.04	.37	1.09 ± .78	1.40	- 2.23 ± 1.69	1.32

	Burglary and Larceny Per Cent	x p.e.	Forgery and Fraud Per Cent	x p.e.	Rape Per Cent	x p.e.	Other Sex Per Cent	x p.e.
Short-slender	8.03 ± 4.07	1.97	- 1.54 ± 2.61	.59	- 1.50 ± 1.76	.85	1.01 ± 1.57	.64
Short-medium weight	4.47 ± 2.17	2.06	- .32 ± 1.39	.23	3.67 ± .94	3.90	.01 ± .84	.01
Short-heavy	- .04 ± 4.44	.01	2.04 ± 2.85	.72	4.63 ± 1.92	2.41	3.73 ± 1.71	2.18
Medium height-slender	4.25 ± 1.68	2.53	- .86 ± 1.08	.80	.61 ± .73	.84	.63 ± .65	.97
Medium height-medium weight	2.19 ± .53	4.13	- 1.10 ± .34	3.24	- .05 ± .24	.21	- .36 ± .20	1.80
Medium height-heavy	- 6.34 ± 1.10	5.76	.60 ± .70	.86	.17 ± .47	.36	1.12 ± .42	2.67
Tall-slender	- 9.90 ± 3.04	3.26	3.12 ± 1.94	1.61	- 2.88 ± 1.31	2.20	- 3.68 ± 1.17	3.14
Tall-medium weight	- 1.94 ± 1.75	1.11	3.84 ± 1.12	3.43	- 1.25 ± .76	1.64	- 1.22 ± .67	1.82
Tall-heavy	- 6.01 ± 2.79	2.15	3.26 ± 1.79	1.82	- 1.65 ± 1.20	1.38	1.54 ± 1.08	1.42

	Vs. Public Welfare Per Cent	x p.e.	Arson and All Other Per Cent	x p.e.
Short-slender	- 1.32 ± 1.99	.66	- 2.38 ± 1.28	1.86
Short-medium weight	- 2.32 ± 1.06	2.19	1.77 ± .67	2.64
Short-heavy	- .45 ± 2.16	.21	- .53 ± 1.39	.38
Medium height-slender	- .55 ± .82	.67	.66 ± .53	1.24
Medium height-medium weight	- .97 ± .26	3.73	.68 ± .16	4.25
Medium height-heavy	2.78 ± .53	5.24	- .60 ± .34	1.76
Tall-slender	1.89 ± 1.48	1.28	1.50 ± .95	1.58
Tall-medium weight	.76 ± .85	.89	- 1.46 ± .55	2.65
Tall-heavy	1.45 ± 1.36	1.07	- 1.63 ± .87	1.87

Table IX-7.   Association of Stature Grouping with Offense

	First Degree Murder		Second Degree Murder		Assault		Robbery	
	No.	Per Cent	No.	Per Cent	No.	Per Cent	No.	Per Cent
Short	14	4.18	45	13.43	7	2.09	24	7.16
Medium height	201	6.70	449	14.96	56	1.86	300	9.99
Tall	59	10.30	90	15.71	11	1.92	55	9.60
Total	274	7.01	584	14.94	74	1.89	379	9.69

	Burglary and Larceny		Forgery and Fraud		Rape		Other Sex	
	No.	Per Cent	No.	Per Cent	No.	Per Cent	No.	Per Cent
Short	145	43.28	36	10.75	25	7.46	15	4.48
Medium height	1177	39.21	308	10.26	139	4.63	114	3.80
Tall	197	34.38	83	14.48	17	2.97	15	2.62
Total	1519	38.85	427	10.92	181	4.63	144	3.68

	Vs. Public Welfare		Arson and All Other		Total	
	No.	Per Cent	No.	Per Cent	No.	
Short	14	4.18	10	2.98	335	
Medium height	180	6.00	78	2.60	3002	
Tall	41	7.16	5	.87	573	
Total	235	6.01	93	2.38	3910	

Table IX-8.   Association of Weight Grouping with Offense

	First Degree Murder		Second Degree Murder		Assault		Robbery	
	No.	Per Cent	No.	Per Cent	No.	Per Cent	No.	Per Cent
Slender	42	7.98	79	15.02	7	1.33	54	10.27
Medium weight	155	6.28	358	14.51	49	1.99	244	9.89
Heavy	77	8.40	147	16.03	18	1.96	81	8.83
Total	274	7.01	584	14.94	74	1.89	379	9.69

	Burglary and Larceny		Forgery and Fraud		Rape		Other Sex	
	No.	Per Cent	No.	Per Cent	No.	Per Cent	No.	Per Cent
Slender	213	40.49	57	10.84	18	3.42	18	3.42
Medium weight	1004	40.70	260	10.54	119	4.82	80	3.24
Heavy	302	32.93	110	12.00	44	4.80	46	5.02
Total	1519	38.85	427	10.92	181	4.63	144	3.68

	Vs. Public Welfare		Arson and All Other		Total	
	No.	Per Cent	No.	Per Cent	No.	
Slender	31	5.89	7	1.33	526	
Medium weight	127	5.15	71	2.88	2467	
Heavy	77	8.40	15	1.64	917	
Total	235	6.01	93	2.38	3910	

Table IX-9.   Comparison of Short-Heavy and Tall-Slender Types

	Short-Heavy Per Cent	Tall-Slender Per Cent	Difference Per Cent
First degree murder	3.70	11.40	7.70
Second degree murder	9.26	19.30	10.04
Total murder	12.96	30.70	
Assault	3.70	0	3.70
Robbery	7.41	15.79	8.38
Burglary and larceny	38.89	28.95	9.94
Forgery and fraud	12.96	14.04	1.08
Rape	9.26	1.75	7.51
Other sex	7.41	0	7.41
Total sex	16.67	1.75	
Vs. public welfare	5.56	7.90	2.34
		Mean	6.46

Table IX-10.   Comparison of Short-Slender and Tall-Heavy Types

	Short-Slender Per Cent	Tall-Heavy Per Cent	Difference Per Cent
First degree murder	7.81	11.94	4.13
Second degree murder	17.19	14.18	3.01
Total murder	25.00	26.12	
Assault	0	2.98	2.98
Robbery	6.25	7.46	1.21
Burglary and larceny	46.88	32.84	14.04
Forgery and fraud	9.38	14.18	4.80
Rape	3.13	2.98	0.15
Other sex	4.69	5.22	0.53
Total sex	7.82	8.20	
Vs. public welfare	4.69	7.46	2.77
		Mean	3.74

Table IX-11. Comparison of Short-Medium Weight and Tall-Heavy Types

	Short-Medium Weight Per Cent	Tall-Heavy Per Cent	Difference Per Cent
First degree murder	3.23	11.94	8.71
Second degree murder	13.36	14.18	0.82
Total murder	16.59	26.12	
Assault	2.30	2.98	0.68
Robbery	7.37	7.46	0.09
Burglary and larceny	43.32	32.84	10.48
Forgery and fraud	10.60	14.18	3.58
Rape	8.30	2.98	5.32
Other sex	3.69	5.22	1.53
Total sex	11.99	8.20	
Vs. public welfare	3.69	7.46	3.77
		Mean	3.89

Table IX-12. Comparison of Short-Slender and Tall-Slender Types

	Short-Slender Per Cent	Tall-Slender Per Cent	Difference Per Cent
First degree murder	7.81	11.40	3.59
Second degree murder	17.19	19.30	2.11
Total murder	25.00	30.70	
Assault	0	0	0
Robbery	6.25	15.79	9.54
Burglary and larceny	46.88	28.95	17.93
Forgery and fraud	9.38	14.04	4.66
Rape	3.13	1.75	1.38
Other sex	4.69	0	4.59
Total sex	7.82	1.75	
Vs. public welfare	4.69	7.90	3.21
		Mean	5.23

Table IX-13.   Comparison of Short-Heavy and Tall-Heavy Types

	Short-Heavy Per Cent	Tall-Heavy Per Cent	Difference Per Cent
First degree murder	3.70	11.94	8.24
Second degree murder	9.26	14.18	4.92
Total murder	12.96	26.12	
Assault	3.70	2.98	0.72
Robbery	7.41	7.46	0.05
Burglary and larceny	38.89	32.84	6.05
Forgery and fraud	12.96	14.18	1.22
Rape	9.26	2.98	6.28
Other sex	7.41	5.22	2.19
Total sex	16.67	8.20	
Vs. public welfare	5.56	7.46	1.90
		Mean	3.51

Table IX-14.   Comparison of Medium Height-Medium Weight
and Tall-Medium Weight Types

	Medium Height-Medium Weight Per Cent	Tall-Medium Weight Per Cent	Difference Per Cent
First degree murder	6.13	9.23	3.10
Second degree murder	14.54	15.07	0.53
Total murder	20.67	24.30	
Assault	1.92	2.15	0.23
Robbery	10.44	8.30	2.14
Burglary and larceny	41.04	36.91	4.13
Forgery and fraud	9.82	14.76	4.94
Rape	4.68	3.38	1.30
Other sex	3.32	2.46	0.86
Total sex	8.00	5.84	
Vs. public welfare	5.04	6.77	1.73
		Mean	2.11

Table IX-15.   Previous Convictions by Body Build Grouping

	Yes		No		Total
	No.	Per Cent	No.	Per Cent	No.
Short-slender	29	48.33	31	51.67	60
Short-medium weight	94	46.54	108	53.46	202
Short-heavy	13	30.23	30	69.77	43
Medium height-slender	140	44.30	176	55.70	316
Medium height-medium weight	676	40.90	977	59.10	1653
Medium height-heavy	224	36.19	395	63.81	619
Tall-slender	39	38.24	63	61.76	102
Tall-medium weight	99	36.26	174	63.74	273
Tall-heavy	34	29.06	83	70.94	117
Total	1348	39.82	2037	60.18	3385

Table IX-16.   Marital State by Body Build Grouping

	Single		Married		Divorced		Widower		Total
	No.	Per Cent	No.	Per Cent	No.	Per Cent	No.	Per Cent	No.
Short-slender	36	57.14	24	38.10	2	3.17	1	1.59	63
Short-medium weight	111	51.39	92	42.59	8	3.70	5	2.32	216
Short-heavy	25	47.17	19	35.85	5	9.43	4	7.55	53
Medium height-slender	205	58.91	122	35.06	12	3.45	9	2.59	348
Medium height-medium weight	966	51.08	815	43.10	75	3.97	35	1.85	1891
Medium height-heavy	275	38.14	391	54.23	34	4.72	21	2.91	721
Tall-slender	58	51.79	52	46.43	1	.89	1	.89	112
Tall-medium weight	156	48.60	151	47.04	7	2.18	7	2.18	321
Tall-heavy	41	30.60	75	55.97	11	8.21	7	5.22	134
Total	1873	48.54	1741	45.11	155	4.02	90	2.33	3859

Table IX-18.   Occupation by Body Build Grouping

	Extractive		Laborer		Factory		Transportation	
	No.	Per Cent	No.	Per Cent	No.	Per Cent	No.	Per Cent
Short-slender	11	18.03	8	13.11	11	18.03	4	6.56
Short-medium weight	58	27.62	51	24.29	30	14.29	12	5.71
Short-heavy	14	26.42	8	15.09	9	16.98	6	11.32
Medium height-slender	100	29.41	63	18.53	61	17.94	26	7.65
Medium height-medium weight	598	31.88	321	17.11	339	18.07	128	6.82
Medium height-heavy	237	33.05	121	16.88	117	16.32	53	7.39
Tall-slender	38	33.93	15	13.39	24	21.43	10	8.93
Tall-medium weight	119	37.30	48	15.05	48	15.05	23	7.21
Tall-heavy	36	26.87	18	13.43	32	23.88	13	9.70
Total	1211	31.68	653	17.08	671	17.56	275	7.20

	Skilled Trade		Trade		Public Service		Semi-professional	
	No.	Per Cent	No.	Per Cent	No.	Per Cent	No.	Per Cent
Short-slender	6	9.84	5	8.20	0	0	5	8.20
Short-medium weight	16	7.62	10	4.76	1	.48	6	2.86
Short-heavy	4	7.55	3	5.66	0	0	0	0
Medium height-slender	34	10.00	16	4.71	1	.29	5	1.47
Medium height-medium weight	171	9.12	88	4.69	15	.80	21	1.12
Medium height-heavy	70	9.76	43	6.00	5	.70	15	2.09
Tall-slender	8	7.14	7	6.25	1	.89	1	.89
Tall-medium weight	26	8.15	16	5.02	0	0	5	1.57
Tall-heavy	11	8.21	6	4.48	3	2.24	3	2.24
Total	346	9.05	194	5.08	26	.68	61	1.60

	Professional		Personal Service		Clerical		Total	
	No.	Per Cent	No.	Per Cent	No.	Per Cent	No.	
Short-slender	0	0	5	8.20	6	9.84	61	
Short-medium weight	1	.48	20	9.52	5	2.38	210	
Short-heavy	2	3.77	4	7.55	3	5.66	53	
Medium height-slender	0	0	21	6.18	13	3.82	340	
Medium height-medium weight	6	.32	141	7.52	48	2.56	1876	
Medium height-heavy	8	1.12	33	4.60	15	2.09	717	
Tall-slender	0	0	4	3.57	4	3.57	112	
Tall-medium weight	0	0	24	7.52	10	3.14	319	
Tall-heavy	2	1.49	6	4.48	4	2.98	134	
Total	19	.50	258	6.75	108	2.83	3822	

Table IX-19. Occupation Differences between Body Build Subgroups and Total Series with Value in Terms of the Probable Error

	Extractive Per Cent	x p.e.	Laborer Per Cent	x p.e.	Factory Per Cent	x p.e.	Transportation Per Cent	x p.e.
Short-slender	-13.65 ± 3.99	3.42	- 3.97 ± 3.22	1.23	0.47		- 0.64	
Short-medium weight	- 4.06 ± 2.10	1.93	7.21 ± 1.70	4.24	- 3.27 ± 1.72	1.90	- 1.49 ± 1.17	1.27
Short-heavy	- 5.26 ± 4.28	1.23	- 1.99		- 0.58		4.12 ± 2.38	1.73
Medium height-slender	2.27		1.45 ± 1.32	1.10	0.38		0.45	
Medium height-medium weight	0.20		0.03		0.51		- 0.38	
Medium height-heavy	1.37		- 0.20		- 1.24		0.19	
Tall-slender	2.25		- 3.69 ± 2.36	1.56	3.87 ± 2.39	1.62	1.73 ± 1.63	1.06
Tall-medium weight	5.62 ± 1.68	3.34	- 2.03		- 2.51		0.01	
Tall-heavy	- 4.81 ± 2.66	1.81	- 3.65 ± 2.15	1.70	6.32 ± 2.18	2.90	2.50 ± 1.48	1.69

	Skilled Trade Per Cent	x p.e.	Trade Per Cent	x p.e.	Public Service Per Cent	x p.e.	Semi-professional Per Cent	x p.e.
Short-slender	0.79		3.12 ± 1.88	1.66	- 0.68		6.60 ± 1.07	6.17
Short-medium weight	- 1.43		0.32		- 0.20		0.02	
Short-heavy	- 1.50		0.58		- 0.68		- 1.60	
Medium height-slender	0.95 ± 1.00	0.95	- 0.37		- 0.39		- 0.13	
Medium height-medium weight	0.07		- 0.39		0.12		- 0.48	
Medium height-heavy	0.71		0.92		0.02		0.49	
Tall-slender	- 1.91		1.17		0.21		- 0.71	
Tall-medium weight	- 0.90		- 0.06		- 0.68		- 0.03	
Tall-heavy	- 0.84		- 0.60		1.56 ± 0.47	3.32	0.64	

	Professional Per Cent	x p.e.	Personal Service Per Cent	x p.e.	Clerical Per Cent	x p.e.
Short-slender	- 0.50		1.45 ± 2.15	0.67	7.01 ± 1.42	4.94
Short-medium weight	0.02		2.77 ± 1.13	2.45	- .45	
Short-heavy	3.27 ± 0.65	5.03	0.80		2.83 ± 1.52	1.86
Medium height-slender	- 0.50		- 0.57		0.99	
Medium height-medium weight	- 0.18		0.77		- 0.27	
Medium height-heavy	0.62		- 2.15 ± 0.57	3.77	- 0.74	
Tall-slender	- 0.50		- 3.18 ± 1.57	2.02	0.74	
Tall-medium weight	- 0.50		- 0.77		0.31	
Tall-heavy	0.99		- 2.27		0.15	

Table IX-20.   Education by Body Build Grouping

| | Illiterate | | Read,write | | 1st-5th Grade | | 6th Grade | |
	No.	Per Cent	No.	Per Cent	No.	Per Cent	No.	Per Cent
Short-slender	4	6.25	1	1.56	19	29.69	6	9.38
Short-medium weight	25	11.63	10	4.65	59	27.44	24	11.16
Short-heavy	4	7.41	2	3.70	14	25.93	8	14.81
Medium height-slender	26	7.51	8	2.31	100	28.90	31	8.96
Medium height-medium weight	205	10.73	86	4.50	488	25.54	166	8.69
Medium height-heavy	76	10.50	35	4.83	194	26.80	58	8.01
Tall-slender	14	12.28	3	2.63	26	22.81	9	7.90
Tall-medium weight	29	8.95	18	5.56	76	23.46	33	10.18
Tall-heavy	13	9.70	6	4.48	30	22.39	11	8.21
Total	396	10.19	169	4.35	1006	25.89	346	8.90

| | 7th Grade | | 8th Grade | | 1st-2nd High | | 3rd-4th High | |
	No.	Per Cent	No.	Per Cent	No.	Per Cent	No.	Per Cent
Short-slender	5	7.81	19	29.69	2	3.13	5	7.81
Short-medium weight	15	6.98	44	20.46	28	13.02	5	2.33
Short-heavy	3	5.56	10	18.52	8	14.81	1	1.85
Medium height-slender	35	10.12	60	17.34	54	15.61	23	6.65
Medium height-medium weight	225	11.77	353	18.47	264	13.82	91	4.76
Medium height-heavy	71	9.81	142	19.61	89	12.29	24	3.32
Tall-slender	12	10.53	16	14.04	19	16.67	11	9.65
Tall-medium weight	33	10.18	59	18.21	55	16.98	14	4.32
Tall-heavy	16	11.94	21	15.67	17	12.69	8	5.97
Total	415	10.68	724	18.63	536	13.79	182	4.68

| | College | | Professional School | | Total |
	No.	Per Cent	No.	Per Cent	No.
Short-slender	3	4.69	0	0	64
Short-medium weight	5	2.33	0	0	215
Short-heavy	2	3.70	2	3.70	54
Medium height-slender	9	2.60	0	0	346
Medium height-medium weight	32	1.67	1	.05	1911
Medium height-heavy	33	4.56	2	.28	724
Tall-slender	4	3.51	0	0	114
Tall-medium weight	7	2.16	0	0	324
Tall-heavy	11	8.21	1	.75	134
Total	106	2.73	6	.15	3886

Table IX-20 (cont'd). Education Differences between Body Build Subgroups and Total Series with Value in Terms of the Probable Error

	Illiterate		Read, Write		College		Professional School	
	Per Cent	x p.e.	Per Cent	x p.e.	Per Cent	x p.e.	Per Cent	x p.e.
Short-slender	- 3.94 ± 2.53	1.56	- 2.79 ± 1.71	1.63	1.96 ± 1.36	1.44	- 0.15	
Short-medium weight	1.44 ± 1.35	1.07	0.30		- 0.40		- 0.15	
Short-heavy	- 2.78		- 0.65		0.97 ± 1.48	0.56	3.55 ± 0.35	10.14
Medium height-slender	- 2.68		- 2.04		- 0.13		- 0.15	
Medium height-medium weight	0.54		0.15		- 1.06 ± 0.18	5.99	- 0.10	
Medium height-heavy	0.31		0.48		1.83 ± 0.37	4.95	0.13	
Tall-slender	2.09 ± 1.88	1.11	- 1.72		0.78		- 0.15	
Tall-medium weight	- 1.24		1.21 ± 0.74	1.64	- 0.57		- 0.15	
Tall-heavy	- 0.49		0.13		5.48 ± 0.94	5.83	0.60	

Table IX-22.   Age by Body Build Grouping

	No.	Range	Mean	S. D.	V.
Short-slender	63	15-69	31.50 ± 1.10	13.00 ± .78	41.27 ± 2.48
Short-medium weight	217	15-69	29.90 ± .54	11.70 ± .38	39.13 ± 1.27
Short-heavy	54	15-64	36.70 ± 1.18	12.85 ± .83	35.01 ± 2.27
Medium height-slender	348	15-69	30.05 ± .43	11.80 ± .30	39.27 ± 1.00
Medium height-medium weight	1922	15-69	29.25 ± .16	10.55 ± .12	36.07 ± .40
Medium height-heavy	728	15-69	33.70 ± .31	12.45 ± .22	36.94 ± .65
Tall-slender	113	15-69	29.15 ± .64	10.10 ± .45	34.65 ± 1.56
Tall-medium weight	325	15-69	29.90 ± .38	10.25 ± .27	34.28 ± .91
Tall-heavy	134	15-69	33.55 ± .66	11.25 ± .46	33.53 ± 1.38
Total	3904	15-69	30.50 ± .12	11.35 ± .09	37.21 ± .28

Table IX-23.   Height by Body Build Grouping

	No.	Range	Mean	S. D.	V.
Short-slender	64	146-163	158.01 ± .34	4.02 ± .24	2.54 ± .15
Short-medium weight	217	149-163	159.99 ± .12	2.67 ± .09	1.67 ± .05
Short-heavy	54	143-163	159.96 ± .31	3.36 ± .22	2.10 ± .14
Medium height-slender	348	164-178	169.29 ± .13	3.51 ± .09	2.07 ± .05
Medium height-medium weight	1924	164-178	171.36 ± .06	3.96 ± .04	2.31 ± .02
Medium height-heavy	728	164-178	172.95 ± .09	3.54 ± .06	2.05 ± .04
Tall-slender	114	179-190	181.38 ± .15	2.34 ± .10	1.29 ± .06
Tall-medium weight	325	179-193	181.92 ± .09	2.52 ± .07	1.38 ± .04
Tall-heavy	134	179-196	182.70 ± .20	3.36 ± .14	1.84 ± .08
Total	3908	143-196	172.02 ± .07	6.48 ± .05	3.77 ± .03

Table IX-24.   Weight by Body Build Grouping

	No.	Range	Mean	S. D.	V.
Short-slender	64	81-120	111.40 ± .53	6.30 ± .38	5.66 ± .34
Short-medium weight	217	121-150	133.40 ± .36	7.80 ± .25	5.85 ± .19
Short-heavy	54	151-230	162.90 ± 1.29	14.10 ± .92	8.66 ± .56
Medium height-slender	348	101-130	122.70 ± .19	5.30 ± .14	4.32 ± .11
Medium height-medium weight	1925	131-160	145.50 ± .12	8.00 ± .09	5.50 ± .06
Medium height-heavy	729	161-250	174.00 ± .30	12.20 ± .22	7.01 ± .12
Tall-slender	114	111-150	141.70 ± .38	6.10 ± .27	4.30 ± .19
Tall-medium weight	325	151-180	163.90 ± .30	7.90 ± .21	4.82 ± .13
Tall-heavy	134	181-270	196.90 ± .89	15.20 ± .63	7.72 ± .32
Total	3910	81-270	151.00 ± .22	20.00 ± .15	13.24 ± .10

Table IX-25   Cephalic Index by Body Build Grouping

	No.	Range	Mean	S. D.	V.
Short-slender	64	74-91	79.35 ± .26	3.06 ± .18	3.86 ± .23
Short-medium weight	217	71-91	79.08 ± .15	3.21 ± .10	4.06 ± .13
Short-heavy	54	71-88	79.29 ± .30	3.30 ± .21	4.16 ± .27
Medium height-slender	348	68-91	78.27 ± .12	3.36 ± .09	4.29 ± .11
Medium height-medium weight	1921	65-91	78.60 ± .05	3.30 ± .04	4.20 ± .05
Medium height-heavy	728	68-91	78.75 ± .08	3.21 ± .06	4.08 ± .07
Tall-slender	113	71-85	78.00 ± .19	3.06 ± .14	3.92 ± .18
Tall-medium weight	325	68-88	78.15 ± .13	3.39 ± .09	4.34 ± .12
Tall-heavy	134	65-88	77.91 ± .20	3.45 ± .14	4.43 ± .18
Total	3904	65-91	78.57 ± .04	3.30 ± .02	4.20 ± .03

Table IX-26.   Facial Index by Body Build Grouping

	No.	Range	Mean	S. D.	V.
Short-slender	64	74-101	87.86 ± .45	5.32 ± .32	6.06 ± .36
Short-medium weight	217	70-101	87.38 ± .24	5.32 ± .17	6.09 ± .20
Short-heavy	54	74-101	86.38 ± .47	5.12 ± .33	5.93 ± .38
Medium height-slender	348	74-105	88.90 ± .18	5.08 ± .13	5.71 ± .15
Medium height-medium weight	1922	70-105	87.98 ± .08	5.20 ± .06	5.91 ± .06
Medium height-heavy	729	70-109	86.70 ± .13	5.12 ± .09	5.90 ± .10
Tall-slender	114	74-105	87.74 ± .36	5.64 ± .25	6.43 ± .29
Tall-medium weight	325	74-105	88.54 ± .20	5.24 ± .14	5.92 ± .16
Tall-heavy	134	74-101	87.54 ± .28	4.72 ± .19	5.39 ± .22
Total	3907	70-109	87.82 ± .06	5.20 ± .04	5.92 ± .04

Table IX-27.   Nasal Index by Body Build Grouping

	No.	Range	Mean	S. D.	V.
Short-slender	64	48-87	65.02 ± .63	7.52 ± .45	11.57 ± .69
Short-medium weight	217	52-91	67.50 ± .32	7.04 ± .23	10.43 ± .34
Short-heavy	54	52-87	69.42 ± .64	6.96 ± .45	10.03 ± .65
Medium height-slender	348	44-87	64.70 ± .24	6.64 ± .17	10.26 ± .26
Medium height-medium weight	1918	44-99	66.58 ± .10	6.76 ± .07	10.15 ± .11
Medium height-heavy	725	44-95	68.22 ± .17	6.96 ± .12	10.20 ± .18
Tall-slender	114	48-83	65.46 ± .40	6.40 ± .29	9.78 ± .44
Tall-medium weight	325	48-83	65.74 ± .23	6.08 ± .16	9.25 ± .24
Tall-heavy	134	48-91	67.58 ± .40	6.80 ± .28	10.06 ± .41
Total	3899	44-99	66.70 ± .07	6.84 ± .05	10.26 ± .08

Table IX-28.   Hair Color by Body Build Grouping

	Black		Dark Brown		Red Brown	
	No.	Per Cent	No.	Per Cent	No.	Per Cent
Short-slender	0	0	21	33.87	14	22.58
Short-medium weight	10	4.61	79	36.41	49	22.58
Short-heavy	3	5.56	22	40.74	10	18.52
Medium height-slender	19	5.51	108	31.30	67	19.42
Medium height-medium weight	93	4.89	650	34.17	385	20.24
Medium height-heavy	35	4.85	253	35.09	142	19.70
Tall-slender	9	8.04	46	41.07	14	12.50
Tall-medium weight	16	4.92	108	33.22	68	20.92
Tall-heavy	11	8.33	44	33.33	37	28.03
Total	196	5.06	1331	34.39	786	20.31

	Light Brown		Ash-blond		Golden	
	No.	Per Cent	No.	Per Cent	No.	Per Cent
Short-slender	17	27.42	1	1.61	1	1.61
Short-medium weight	46	21.20	9	4.15	5	2.30
Short-heavy	10	18.52	0	0	2	3.70
Medium height-slender	96	27.83	12	3.48	13	3.77
Medium height-medium weight	523	27.50	40	2.10	69	3.63
Medium height-heavy	158	21.91	19	2.64	21	2.91
Tall-slender	29	25.89	4	3.57	4	3.57
Tall-medium weight	92	28.30	4	1.23	8	2.46
Tall-heavy	22	16.67	0	0	5	3.79
Total	993	25.66	89	2.30	128	3.31

	Red		Gray,White		Total	Total (without Gray, White)
	No.	Per Cent	No.	Per Cent	No.	No.
Short-slender	2	3.23	6	9.68	62	56
Short-medium weight	9	4.15	10	4.61	217	207
Short-heavy	2	3.70	5	9.26	54	49
Medium height-slender	16	4.64	14	4.06	345	331
Medium height-medium weight	63	3.31	79	4.15	1902	1823
Medium height-heavy	26	3.61	67	9.29	721	654
Tall-slender	5	4.46	1	.89	112	111
Tall-medium weight	21	6.46	8	2.46	325	317
Tall-heavy	4	3.03	9	6.82	132	123
Total	148	3.82	199	5.14	3870	3671

Table IX-29.   Hair Color Differences between Body Build Subgroups and Total Series with Value in Terms of the Probable Error

	Black		Dark Brown		Reddish Brown		Light Brown	
	Per Cent	x p.e.	Per Cent	x p.e.	Per Cent	x p.e.	Per Cent	x p.e.
Short-slender	- 5.06 ± 1.85	2.72	- 0.52		2.27		1.76 ± 3.71	0.48
Short-medium weight	- 0.45		2.02		2.27		- 4.46 ± 1.94	2.29
Short-heavy	0.50		6.33 ± 4.33	1.46	- 1.79		- 7.14 ± 3.98	1.79
Medium height-slender	0.45		- 3.09		- 0.89		2.17	
Medium height-medium weight	- 0.17		- 0.22		- 0.07		1.84	
Medium height-heavy	0.21		0.70		- 0.61		- 3.75	
Tall-slender	2.98 ± 1.38	2.16	6.66 ± 2.98	2.23	- 7.80 ± 2.53	3.08	- 0.23	
Tall-medium weight	- 0.14		- 1.17		0.61		2.64 ± 1.56	1.69
Tall-heavy	3.27 ± 1.26	2.60	- 1.06		7.73 ± 2.32	3.33	- 8.99 ± 2.52	3.56

	Ash-blond		Golden		Red		Gray, White	
	Per Cent	x p.e.	Per Cent	x p.e.	Per Cent	x p.e.	Per Cent	x p.e.
Short-slender	- 0.69		- 1.70 ± 1.52	1.12	- 0.59		4.54 ± 1.88	2.42
Short-medium weight	1.85 ± 0.67	2.76	- 1.01		- 0.33		- 0.53	
Short-heavy	- 2.30		0.39		- 0.12		4.12 ± 2.01	2.05
Medium height-slender	1.18 ± 0.52	2.27	0.45		0.82		- 1.08	
Medium height-medium weight	- 0.20		0.32		- 0.51		0.99	
Medium height-heavy	0.34		- 0.40		0.21		4.15 ± 0.50	8.30
Tall-slender	1.27 ± 0.94	1.35	0.26		0.64		- 4.25 ± 1.39	3.06
Tall-medium weight	1.07		- 0.85		2.64 ± 0.69	3.83	- 2.68 ± 0.79	3.39
Tall-heavy	- 2.30 ± 0.86	2.57	0.48		- 0.79		1.68	

Table IX-31.　　　　Eye Color by Body Build Grouping

	Dark Brown		Light Brown		Blue-brown		Gray-brown	
	No.	Per Cent	No.	Per Cent	No.	Per Cent	No.	Per Cent
Short-slender	2	3.13	4	6.25	13	20.31	11	17.19
Short-medium weight	10	4.61	12	5.53	44	20.28	26	11.98
Short-heavy	2	3.70	0	0	14	25.93	10	18.52
Medium height-slender	15	4.31	8	2.30	82	23.56	60	17.24
Medium height-medium weight	68	3.54	56	2.92	394	20.51	338	17.60
Medium height-heavy	16	2.21	13	1.79	164	22.62	130	17.93
Tall-slender	4	3.64	1	.91	19	17.27	23	20.91
Tall-medium weight	10	3.08	7	2.15	63	19.38	71	21.85
Tall-heavy	9	6.72	4	2.98	21	15.67	35	26.12
Total	136	3.49	105	2.69	814	20.88	704	18.06

	Green-brown		Blue		Blue-gray		Total
	No.	Per Cent	No.	Per Cent	No.	Per Cent	No.
Short-slender	18	28.13	11	17.19	5	7.81	64
Short-medium weight	72	33.18	32	14.75	21	9.68	217
Short-heavy	13	24.07	12	22.22	3	5.56	54
Medium height-slender	79	22.70	69	19.83	35	10.06	348
Medium height-medium weight	519	27.02	376	19.57	170	8.85	1921
Medium height-heavy	194	26.76	136	18.76	72	9.93	725
Tall-slender	31	28.18	21	19.09	11	10.00	110
Tall-medium weight	78	24.00	72	22.15	24	7.38	325
Tall-heavy	32	23.88	22	16.42	11	8.21	134
Total	1036	26.58	751	19.27	352	9.03	3898

Table IX-32. Eye Color Differences Between Body Build Subgroups and Total Series
with Value in Terms of the Probable Error

	Dark Brown		Light Brown		Blue-brown		Gray-brown	
	Per Cent	x p.e.	Per Cent	x p.e.	Per Cent	x p.e.	Per Cent	x p.e.
Short-slender	- 0.36		3.56 ± 1.35	2.62	- 0.57		- 0.87	
Short-medium weight	1.12 ± 0.82	1.37	2.84 ± 0.72	3.94	- 0.60		- 6.08 ± 1.71	3.56
Short-heavy	0.21		- 2.69		5.05 ± 3.70	1.36	- 0.45	
Medium height-slender	0.82 ± 0.63	1.30	- 0.39		2.68 ± 1.40	1.91	- 0.82	
Medium height-medium weight	0.05		0.23		- 0.37		- 0.46	
Medium height-heavy	- 1.28 ± 0.42	3.05	- 0.90		1.74		- 0.13	
Tall-slender	0.15		- 1.78 ± 1.02	1.74	- 3.61 ± 2.58	1.40	2.85 ± 2.44	1.17
Tall-medium weight	- 0.41		- 0.54		- 1.50		3.79 ± 1.38	2.75
Tall-heavy	- 3.23 ± 1.05	3.08	0.29		- 5.23 ± 2.33	2.24	8.06 ± 2.20	3.65

	Green-brown		Blue		Blue-gray	
	Per Cent	x p.e.	Per Cent	x p.e.	Per Cent	x p.e.
Short-slender	1.55		- 2.08 ± 3.30	0.63	- 1.22 ± 2.39	0.51
Short-medium weight	6.60 ± 1.96	3.37	- 4.52 ± 1.75	2.58	0.65	
Short-heavy	- 2.51 ± 4.03	0.62	2.95 ± 3.60	0.82	- 3.47 ± 2.61	1.33
Medium height-slender	3.88 ± 1.52	2.59	0.55		1.03 ± 0.98	1.02
Medium height-medium weight	0.44		0.30		- 0.15	
Medium height-heavy	0.18		- 0.51		0.90	
Tall-slender	1.60		- 0.18		0.97 ± 1.81	0.54
Tall-medium weight	- 2.58		2.88 ± 1.42	2.04	- 1.65 ± 1.02	1.62
Tall-heavy	- 2.70		- 2.85 ± 2.26	1.25	- 0.82	

Table IX-35.   Divisions of the Cephalic Index in Body Build Types

| | Dolichocephalic (x - 76) | | Mesocephalic (77 - 79) | | Brachycephalic (80 - x) | | Total |
	No.	Per Cent	No.	Per Cent	No.	Per Cent	No.
Short-slender	11	17.19	23	35.94	30	46.87	64
Short-medium weight	44	20.27	87	40.09	86	39.63	217
Short-heavy	10	18.52	21	38.89	23	42.59	54
Medium height-slender	110	31.61	110	31.61	128	36.78	348
Medium height-medium weight	505	26.28	697	36.28	719	37.42	1921
Medium height-heavy	168	23.08	280	38.46	280	38.46	728
Tall-slender	36	31.86	43	38.05	34	30.09	113
Tall-medium weight	102	31.38	116	35.69	107	32.92	325
Tall-heavy	47	35.07	43	32.09	44	32.84	134
Total	1033	26.45	1420	36.37	1451	37.16	3904

Table IX-36.   Divisions of the Facial Index in Build Types

| | Short, Broad (x - 85) | | Medium (86 - 89) | | Long, Narrow (90 - x) | | Total |
	No.	Per Cent	No.	Per Cent	No.	Per Cent	No.
Short-slender	21	32.81	18	28.13	25	39.06	64
Short-medium	78	35.94	62	28.57	77	35.48	217
Short-heavy	21	38.89	20	37.04	13	24.07	54
Medium-slender	91	26.15	104	29.88	153	43.97	348
Medium height-medium weight	600	31.22	597	31.06	725	37.72	1922
Medium height-heavy	311	42.66	209	28.67	209	28.67	729
Tall-slender	30	26.32	29	25.44	55	48.25	114
Tall-medium weight	90	27.68	102	31.37	133	40.91	325
Tall-heavy	47	35.07	39	29.10	48	35.82	134
Total	1289	32.99	1180	30.20	1438	36.81	3907

Table IX-37.   Divisions of the Nasal Index in Body Build Types

| | Narrow (x - 67) | | Medium (68 - 75) | | Broad (76 - x) | | Total |
	No.	Per Cent	No.	Per Cent	No.	Per Cent	No.
Short-slender	45	70.31	12	18.75	7	10.94	64
Short-medium weight	116	53.45	71	32.72	30	13.82	217
Short-heavy	21	38.89	25	46.30	8	14.81	54
Medium height-slender	231	66.38	97	27.87	20	5.75	348
Medium height-medium weight	1130	58.91	603	31.44	185	9.64	1918
Medium height-heavy	339	46.76	280	38.62	106	14.62	725
Tall-slender	71	62.28	37	32.46	6	5.26	114
Tall-medium weight	203	62.46	102	31.38	20	6.15	325
Tall-heavy	75	55.97	43	32.09	18	11.94	134
Total	2231	57.22	1270	32.57	398	10.21	3899

Table X-1. Empirical Sorting by Excesses in Robbery for Morphological Type

	Robbery		All Other Offense Groups		Total
	No.	Per Cent	No.	Per Cent	No.
Total	414	9.83	3798	90.17	4212
Asymmetry-none	305	10.28	2661	89.72	2966
Asymmetry-none, ear protrusion-medium	202	11.36	1577	88.64	1779
Asymmetry-none, ear protrusion-medium, ear lobe-attached	87	12.61	603	87.39	690
Asymmetry-none, ear protrusion-medium, ear lobe-attached, hair color-light brown	34	19.65	139	80.35	173
Asymmetry-none, ear protrusion-medium, ear lobe-attached, hair color-light brown, eye fold-median	8	88.89	1	11.11	9
Asymmetry-none, ear protrusion-medium, ear lobe-attached, hair color-light brown, eye fold-median, hair form-low and deep waves	1	100.00	0	0	1
Asymmetry-none, ear protrusion-medium, ear lobe-attached, hair color-light brown, eye fold-median, hair form-low and deep waves, beard quantity-large	0	0	0	0	0
Asymmetry-none, ear protrusion-medium, ear lobe-attached, hair color-light brown, eye fold-median, hair form-low and deep waves, beard quantity-large, Darwin's point-pronounced	0	0	0	0	0
Asymmetry-none, ear protrusion-medium, ear lobe-attached, hair color-light brown, eye fold-median, hair form-low and deep waves, beard quantity-large, Darwin's point-pronounced, iris-diffused	0	0	0	0	0

Table X-2   Sortings of Robbery for Combinations of Morphological Excesses

	No. of Individual Combinations	Per Cent
One Sorting Character		
Asymmetry-none	15	3.62
Ear protrusion-medium	9	2.17
Ear lobe-attached	4	0.97
Hair Color-light brown	6	1.45
Eye fold-median	2	0.48
Hair form-low waves or deep waves	1	0.24
Beard quantity-large	2	0.48
Darwin's point-pronounced	4	0.97
Iris-diffused	1	0.24
Total	44	10.62
Two Sorting Characters		
Asymmetry none:		
Ear protrusion medium	34	8.21
Ear lobe attached	14	3.38
Hair color light brown	5	1.21
Eye fold median	5	1.21
Hair form low or deep waves	4	0.97
Beard quantity large	5	1.21
Darwin's point pronounced	2	0.48
Iris diffused	2	0.48
Ear protrusion medium:		
Ear lobe attached	13	3.14
Hair color light brown	6	1.45
Hair form low or deep waves	2	0.48
Beard quantity large	2	0.48
Darwin's point pronounced	2	0.48
Iris diffused	1	0.24
Ear lobe attached:		
Hair color light brown	2	0.48
Eye fold median	2	0.48
Hair form low or deep waves	2	0.48
Darwin's point pronounced	1	0.24
Hair color light brown:		
Hair form low or deep waves	1	0.24
Beard quantity large	1	0.24
Darwin's point pronounced	1	0.24
Eye fold median:		
Hair form low or deep waves	2	0.48
Iris diffused	1	0.24
Hair form low or deep waves, iris diffused	1	0.24
Darwin's point pronounced, iris diffused	1	0.24
Total	112.	27.05

Table X-2 (cont'd).

Three Sorting Characters

	No. of Individual Combinations	Per Cent
Asymmetry none, ear protrusion medium:		
Ear lobe attached	21	5.07
Hair color light brown	21	5.07
Eye fold median	4	0.97
Hair form low or deep waves	4	0.97
Beard quantity large	13	3.14
Darwin's point pronounced	4	0.97
Iris diffused	1	0.24
Asymmetry none, ear lobe attached:		
Hair color light brown	5	1.21
Eye fold median	4	0.97
Hair form low or deep waves	3	0.72
Beard quantity large	5	1.21
Darwin's point pronounced	3	0.72
Iris diffused	1	0.24
Asymmetry none, hair color light brown:		
Eye fold median	5	1.21
Beard quantity large	1	0.24
Darwin's point pronounced	2	0.48
Asymmetry none, eye fold median, iris diffused	1	0.24
Asymmetry none, hair form low or deep waves, Darwin's point pronounced	3	0.72
Asymmetry none, beard quantity large, iris diffused	1	0.24
Asymmetry none, Darwin's point pronounced, iris diffused	2	0.48
Ear protrusion medium, ear lobe attached:		
Hair color light brown	5	1.21
Eye fold median	1	0.24
Hair form low or deep waves	1	0.24
Beard quantity large	2	0.48
Darwin's point pronounced	2	0.48
Ear protrusion medium, hair color light brown:		
Eye fold median	2	0.48
Hair form low or deep waves	1	0.24
Beard quantity large	1	0.24
Darwin's point pronounced	2	0.48
Ear protrusion medium, eye fold median:		
Beard quantity large	1	0.24
Darwin's point pronounced	1	0.24
Ear protrusion medium, hair form low or deep waves, iris diffused	1	0.24
Ear protrusion medium, Darwin's point pronounced, iris diffused	1	0.24
Ear lobe attached, hair color light brown:		
Eye fold median	1	0.24
Beard quantity large	1	0.24
Ear lobe attached, eye fold median:		
Hair form low or deep waves	2	0.48
Darwin's point pronounced	1	0.24
Hair form low or deep waves, Darwin's point pronounced, iris diffused	1	0.24
Total	131	31.64

Table X-2 (cont'd). Four Sorting Characters	No. of Individual Combinations	Per Cent
Asymmetry none, ear protrusion medium, ear lobe attached:		
Hair color light brown	15	3.62
Eye fold median	2	0.48
Hair form low or deep waves	6	1.45
Beard quantity large	4	0.97
Darwin's point pronounced	2	0.48
Iris diffused	7	1.69
Asymmetry none, ear protrusion medium, hair color light brown:		
Eye fold median	7	1.69
Hair form low or deep waves	5	1.21
Darwin's point pronounced	4	0.97
Iris diffused	2	0.48
Asymmetry none, ear protrusion medium, eye fold median:		
Hair form low or deep waves	2	0.48
Beard quantity large	2	0.48
Iris diffused	2	0.48
Asymmetry none, ear protrusion medium, hair form low or deep waves:		
Beard quantity large	2	0.48
Iris diffused	1	0.24
Asymmetry none, ear protrusion medium:		
Beard quantity large, iris diffused	1	0.24
Darwin's point pronounced, iris diffused	1	0.24
Asymmetry none, ear lobe attached:		
Hair color light brown, iris diffused	1	0.24
Eye fold median, hair form low or deep waves	1	0.24
Eye fold median, beard quantity large	1	0.24
Eye fold median, Darwin's point pronounced	1	0.24
Hair form low or deep waves, iris diffused	3	0.72
Beard quantity large, Darwin's point pronounced	1	0.24
Beard quantity large, iris diffused	1	0.24
Darwin's point pronounced, iris diffused	1	0.24
Asymmetry none, hair color light brown, eye fold median:		
Hair form low or deep waves	1	0.24
Beard quantity large	1	0.24
Iris diffused	1	0.24
Asymmetry none, hair color light brown, hair form low or deep waves, beard quantity large	1	0.24
Asymmetry none, hair form low or deep waves, beard quantity large, iris diffused	1	0.24
Ear protrusion medium, ear lobe attached:		
Eye fold median, beard quantity large	1	0.24
Hair form low or deep waves, iris diffused	1	0.24
Beard quantity large, Darwin's point pronounced	1	0.24
Ear protrusion medium, eye fold median, Darwin's point pronounced, iris diffused	1	0.24
Total	84	20.29

Table X-2 (cont'd).	No.of Individual Combinations	Per Cent

Five Sorting Characters

Asymmetry none, ear protrusion medium, ear lobe attached, hair color light brown:

Eye fold median	3	0.72
Hair form low or deep waves	6	1.45
Beard quantity large	2	0.48
Darwin's point pronounced	2	0.48

Asymmetry none, ear protrusion medium, ear lobe attached:

Eye fold median, hair form low or deep waves	3	0.72
Eye fold median, iris diffused	2	0.48
Hair form low or deep waves, beard quantity large	3	0.72
Hair form low or deep waves, iris diffused	3	0.72

Asymmetry none, ear protrusion medium:

Hair color light brown, eye fold median, beard quantity large	1	0.24
Eye fold median, beard quantity large, iris diffused	1	0.24
Beard quantity large, Darwin's point pronounced, iris diffused	1	0.24

Ear protrusion medium, ear lobe attached:

Hair color light brown, beard quantity large, iris diffused	1	0.24
Hair form low or deep waves, Darwin's point pronounced, iris diffused	1	0.24
Total	29	6.97

Six Sorting Characters

Asymmetry none, ear protrusion medium, ear lobe attached, hair color light brown:

Eye fold median, hair form low or deep waves	1	0.24
Eye fold median, beard quantity large	2	0.48
Eye fold median, Darwin's point pronounced	1	0.24
Beard quantity large, Darwin's point pronounced	1	0.24

Asymmetry none, ear protrusion medium, eye fold median:

Ear lobe attached, hair form low or deep waves, Darwin's point pronounced	1	0.24
Hair form low or deep waves, beard quantity large, iris diffused	1	0.24
Total	7	1.68

Seven Positive Characters

Asymmetry none, ear protrusion medium, ear lobe attached, hair color light brown, eye fold median, beard quantity large, Darwin's point pronounced	1	0.24
No Positive Characters	6	1.45
Grand total	414	

Table X-3.   Numbers of Possible and Actual Combinations of Nine Significant
Morphological Variations in Robbery Group

No. of Characters in Combination	Different Combinations Possible		Different Combinations Observed		Ratio of Different Combinations Observed to Different Combinations Possible
	No.	Per Cent	No.	Per Cent	
0	1	0.20	1	0.79	100.00
1	9	1.76	9	7.09	100.00
2	36	7.03	25	19.68	69.44
3	84	16.41	38	29.92	45.24
4	126	24.61	34	26.77	26.98
5	126	24.61	13	10.24	10.32
6	84	16.41	6	4.72	7.14
7	36	7.03	1	0.79	2.78
8	9	1.76	0	0	0
9	1	0.20	0	0	0
Total	512		127		24.80

Table X-4.   Actual Occurrence of Nine Significant Morphological
Variations in Robbery Group by Single Characters

	No.	Per Cent
Asymmetry - none	305	73.67
Ear protrusion - medium	264	63.77
Ear lobe - attached	178	43.00
Hair color - light brown	128	30.92
Eye fold - median	75	18.12
Hair form - low or deep waves	71	17.15
Beard quantity - large	66	15.94
Darwin's point - pronounced	53	12.80
Iris - diffused	49	11.84
Total individuals	414	
Total characters	1189	31.91
Total possible characters	3726	
Characters per individual	2.87	
Characters possible per individual	9	

Table X-5. Most Frequently Occurring Combinations of Nine Morphological
Variations in Robbery Group

	Number of Individuals	Per Cent of Series
Asymmetry none, ear protrusion medium	34	8.21
Asymmetry none, ear protrusion medium, ear lobe attached	21	5.07
Asymmetry none, ear protrusion medium, hair color light brown	21	5.07
Asymmetry none, ear protrusion medium, ear lobe attached, hair color light brown	15	3.62
Asymmetry none	15	3.62
Asymmetry none, ear lobe attached	14	3.38
Ear protrusion medium, ear lobe attached	13	3.14
Asymmetry none, ear protrusion medium, beard quantity large	13	3.14

Table X-6. Occurrence of Significant Morphological Variations in Robbery Group
with Per Cent in Each Character Group

	No.	Per Cent	Plus One Character No.	Per Cent	Plus Two Characters No.	Per Cent	Plus Three Characters No.	Per Cent	Plus Four Characters No.	Per Cent	Plus Five Characters No.	Per Cent	Plus Six Characters No.	Per Cent	Total No.
Asymmetry - none	15	4.92	71	23.28	104	34.10	80	26.23	27	8.85	7	2.30	1	.33	305
Ear protrusion - medium	9	3.41	60	22.73	89	33.71	69	26.14	29	10.98	7	2.65	1	.38	264
Ear lobe - attached	4	2.25	34	19.10	58	32.58	49	27.53	26	14.61	6	3.37	1	.56	178
Hair color - light brown	6	4.69	16	12.50	47	36.72	38	29.69	15	11.72	5	3.91	1	.78	128
Eye folds - median	2	2.67	10	13.33	23	30.67	23	30.67	10	13.33	6	8.00	1	1.33	75
Hair form - low or deep waves	1	1.41	12	16.90	16	22.54	23	32.39	16	22.54	3	4.22	0	0	71
Beard quantity - large	2	3.03	8	12.12	25	37.88	17	25.76	9	13.64	4	6.06	1	1.52	66
Darwin's point - pronounced	4	7.55	7	13.21	22	41.51	12	22.64	4	7.55	3	5.66	1	1.89	53
Iris - diffused	1	2.04	6	12.24	9	18.37	23	46.94	9	18.37	1	2.04	0	0	49

Table X-7. Occurrence and Per Cent of Significant Morphological Variations in Robbery Group

		Plus One Character		Plus Two Characters		Plus Three Characters		Plus Four Characters		Plus Five Characters		Plus Six Characters		Total	
	No.	Per Cent	No.	Per Cent	No.	Per Cent	No.	Per Cent	No.	Per Cent	No.	Per Cent	No.	Per Cent	No.	Per Cent
Asymmetry - none	15	3.62	71	17.15	104	25.12	80	19.32	27	6.52	7	1.69	1	.24	305	73.67
Ear protrusion - medium	9	2.17	60	14.49	89	21.50	69	16.67	29	7.00	7	1.69	1	.24	264	63.77
Ear lobe - attached	4	.97	34	8.21	58	14.01	49	11.84	26	6.28	6	1.45	1	.24	178	43.00
Hair color - light brown	6	1.45	16	3.86	47	11.35	38	9.18	15	3.62	5	1.21	1	.24	128	30.92
Eye folds - median	2	.48	10	2.41	23	5.56	23	5.56	10	2.41	6	1.45	1	.24	75	18.12
Hair form - low or deep waves	1	.24	12	2.90	16	3.86	23	5.56	16	3.86	3	.72	0	0	71	17.15
Beard quantity - large	2	.48	8	1.93	25	6.04	17	4.11	9	2.17	4	.97	1	.24	66	15.94
Darwin's point - pronounced	4	.97	7	1.69	22	5.31	12	2.90	4	.97	3	.72	1	.24	53	12.80
Iris - diffused	1	.24	6	1.45	9	2.17	23	5.56	9	2.17	1	.24	0	0	49	11.84

Table X-8. Combination of Four Sorting Characters in Total Series Exclusive of Robbery

Combination 1 — Asymmetry-none 2651; Ear protrusion-medium 1567; Ear lobe-attached 599; Hair color-light brown 138; 3.63

Combination 2 — Ear protrusion-medium 2136; Ear lobe-attached 832; Hair color-light brown 196; Eye fold-median 29; .76

Combination 3 — Ear lobe-attached 1444; Hair color-light brown 344; Eye fold-median 51; Hair form-low and deep waves 4; .10

	No.	Per Cent of Combination	Per Cent of Crime Group	No.	Per Cent of Combination	Per Cent of Crime Group	No.	Per Cent of Combination	Per Cent of Crime Group
First degree murder	8	5.80	2.56	2	6.90	.64	0	0	0
Second degree murder	22	15.94	3.55	6	20.68	.97	1	25.00	.16
Assault	2	1.45	2.50	0	0	0	0	0	0
Burglary and larceny	79	57.25	4.90	14	48.27	.87	1	25.00	.06
Forgery and fraud	7	5.07	1.50	2	6.90	.43	1	25.00	.21
Rape	3	2.17	1.52	1	3.45	.51	0	0	0
Other sex	4	2.90	2.65	0	0	0	0	0	0
Vs. public welfare	7	5.07	2.72	3	10.34	1.17	1	25.00	.39
Drunkenness	0			0			0		
Other	2	1.45	5.82	1	3.45	.97	0	0	0
Arson	4	2.90		0			0		
Total	138	100.00	3.28	29	99.99	.69	4	100.00	.10
Robbery	34		8.21	8		1.93	1		.24

Combination 4 — Hair color-light brown 947; Eye fold-median 123; Hair form-low and deep waves 8; Beard quantity-large 0

Combination 5 — Eye fold-median 465; Hair form-low and deep waves 66; Beard quantity-large 7; Darwin's point-pronounced 2; .05

Combination 6 — Hair form-low and deep waves 448; Beard quantity-large 68; Darwin's point-pronounced 10; Iris-diffused 2; .05

	No.	Per Cent	No.	Per Cent of Combination	Per Cent of Crime Group	No.	Per Cent of Combination	Per Cent of Crime Group
First degree murder	0	0	0	0	0	0	0	0
Second degree murder	0	0	0	0	0	1	50.00	.16
Assault	0	0	0	0	0	0	0	0
Burglary and larceny	0	0	0	0	0	1	50.00	.06
Forgery and fraud	0	0	1	50.00	.21	0	0	0

Table X-8 (cont'd).

Upper portion (trait-combination columns, lower crime-group rows)

	Group 1			Group 2			Group 3		
	No.			No.			No.		
Rape	0	0		0	0		0	0	0
Other sex	0	0		0	0		0	0	0
Vs. public welfare	0	0		1	50.00		0	0	0
Drunkenness	0	0		0		.39	0	0	0
Other	0	0		0	0		0	0	0
Arson	0	0		0	0		0	0	0
Total	0	0		2	100.00	.05	2	100.00	.05
Robbery	0	0		0			0		

Column trait definitions (with counts):

Group 2 — Darwin's point-pronounced ... Iris-diffused ... Asymmetry-none ... Ear protrusion-medium ... .21

Group 3 — Iris-diffused 486, Asymmetry-none 50, Ear protrusion-medium 28, Ear lobe-attached 16 ... .42

Far right — Iris-diffused 313, Asymmetry-none 202, Ear protrusion-medium 115, Ear lobe-attached 48 ... 1.26

Lower portion

Group 1: Beard quantity-large / Darwin's point-pronounced / Iris-diffused / Asymmetry-none

	No.	Per Cent of Combination	Per Cent of Crime Group
First degree murder	0	0	0
Second degree murder	0	0	0
Assault	0	0	0
Burglary and larceny	6	75.00	.37
Forgery and fraud	2	25.00	.43
Rape	0	0	0
Other sex	0	0	0
Vs. public welfare	0	0	0
Drunkenness	0	0	0
Other	0	0	0
Arson	0	0	0
Total	8	100.00	.19
Robbery	1		.24

Group 2: Darwin's point-pronounced (498) / Iris-diffused (61) / Asymmetry-none (13) / Ear protrusion-medium (8) — .21

	No.	Per Cent of Combination	Per Cent of Crime Group
First degree murder	0	0	0
Second degree murder	2	12.50	.32
Assault	0	0	0
Burglary and larceny	10	62.50	.62
Forgery and fraud	2	12.50	.43
Rape	1	6.25	.51
Other sex	1	6.25	.66
Vs. public welfare	0	0	0
Drunkenness	0	0	0
Other	0	0	0
Arson	0	0	0
Total	16	100.00	.38
Robbery	1		.24

Group 3: Iris-diffused (486) / Asymmetry-none (50) / Ear protrusion-medium (28) / Ear lobe-attached (16) — .42

	No.	Per Cent of Combination	Per Cent of Crime Group
First degree murder	3	6.25	.96
Second degree murder	5	10.42	.81
Assault	0	0	0
Burglary and larceny	30	62.50	1.86
Forgery and fraud	5	10.42	1.07
Rape	2	4.17	1.02
Other sex	1	2.08	.66
Vs. public welfare	2	4.17	.78
Drunkenness	0	0	0
Other	0	0	0
Arson	0	0	0
Total	48	100.01	1.14
Robbery	7		1.69

Table XI-1.   Means of Total Civil Check Sample

	No.	Range	Mean	S. D.	V.
Age	313	15- 74	34.50 ± .53	13.80 ± .37	40.00 ± 1.08
Weight	312	100-250	162.60 ± 1.06	27.80 ± .75	17.10 ± .46
Height	313	158-193	172.92 ± .23	5.97 ± .16	3.45 ± .09
Biacromial diameter	312	31- 45	38.57 ± .09	2.37 ± .06	6.14 ± .17
Chest depth	313	16- 31	21.70 ± .08	2.14 ± .06	9.86 ± .27
Chest breadth	313	23- 40	28.17 ± .09	2.37 ± .06	8.41 ± .23
Sitting height	311	78-101	90.49 ± .13	3.48 ± .09	3.85 ± .10
Head length	313	176-232	194.31 ± .25	6.66 ± .18	3.43 ± .09
Head breadth	313	141-176	152.95 ± .19	5.10 ± .14	3.33 ± .09
Head height	312	113-157	133.50 ± .23	5.94 ± .16	4.45 ± .12
Head circumference	310	514-647	570.50 ± .70	18.24 ± .49	3.20 ± .09
Minimum frontal diameter	313	97-128	111.30 ± .22	5.92 ± .16	5.32 ± .14
Bizygomatic diameter	313	110-164	139.10 ± .23	6.05 ± .16	4.35 ± .12
Total face height	313	100-144	123.10 ± .26	6.95 ± .19	5.55 ± .15
Upper face height	313	55- 84	70.10 ± .18	4.75 ± .13	6.78 ± .18
Nose height	313	44- 67	54.10 ± .16	4.09 ± .11	7.54 ± .20
Nose breadth	313	25- 42	34.76 ± .11	2.88 ± .08	8.28 ± .22
Bigonial diameter	312	90-129	107.82 ± .25	6.48 ± .17	6.01 ± .16
Ear length	310	52- 79	64.06 ± .18	4.50 ± .12	7.18 ± .19
Ear breadth	310	29- 49	38.16 ± .13	3.33 ± .09	8.73 ± .24
Relative shoulder breadth	312	18- 27	22.22 ± .05	1.34 ± .04	6.03 ± .16
Relative sitting height	311	48- 57	52.30 ± .06	1.62 ± .04	3.10 ± .08
Cephalic index	313	68- 88	78.78 ± .13	3.30 ± .09	4.19 ± .11
Cephalo-facial index	313	79-102	90.89 ± .12	3.21 ± .09	3.53 ± .10
Length-height index	312	58- 78	68.69 ± .12	3.27 ± .09	4.76 ± .13
Breadth-height index	312	76-105	87.14 ± .16	4.08 ± .11	4.58 ± .13
Facial index	313	70-105	88.58 ± .21	5.56 ± .15	6.28 ± .17
Upper facial index	313	40- 72	50.54 ± .15	4.02 ± .11	7.95 ± .21
Nasal index	313	44- 83	64.56 ± .25	6.72 ± .18	10.39 ± .28
Ear index	310	45- 72	59.42 ± .20	5.12 ± .14	8.62 ± .23
Zygo-frontal index	313	64- 95	80.06 ± .14	3.64 ± .10	4.55 ± .12
Fronto-parietal index	313	63- 83	72.73 ± .13	3.39 ± .09	4.66 ± .13
Zygo-gonial index	313	63- 95	77.74 ± .15	3.99 ± .11	5.13 ± .14

Table XI-2.   Means of Massachusetts Civil Check Sample

	No.	Range	Mean	S. D.	V.
Age	167	15- 69	30.70 ± .78	14.90 ± .55	48.53 ± 1.79
Weight	161	101-230	152.20 ± 1.24	23.30 ± .88	15.31 ± .58
Height	167	158-190	172.98 ± .34	6.51 ± .24	3.76 ± .14
Biacromial diameter	166	31- 45	38.33 ± .13	2.46 ± .09	6.42 ± .24
Chest depth	167	16- 31	21.20 ± .11	2.16 ± .08	10.19 ± .38
Chest breadth	167	23- 37	27.54 ± .12	2.28 ± .08	8.28 ± .31
Sitting height	165	78-101	90.40 ± .19	3.69 ± .14	4.08 ± .15
Head length	167	176-232	194.70 ± .37	7.08 ± .26	3.64 ± .13
Head breadth	167	141-164	151.72 ± .25	4.83 ± .18	3.18 ± .12
Head height	166	113-157	133.20 ± .34	6.48 ± .24	4.86 ± .18
Head circumference	163	526-645	566.42 ± .84	15.84 ± .59	2.90 ± .10
Minimum frontal diameter	167	97-120	108.14 ± .26	4.88 ± .18	4.51 ± .17
Bizygomatic diameter	167	110-154	137.25 ± .31	6.00 ± .22	4.37 ± .16
Total face height	167	105-144	123.50 ± .37	7.05 ± .26	5.71 ± .21
Upper face height	167	55- 84	70.30 ± .26	5.05 ± .19	7.18 ± .26
Nose height	167	44- 67	54.14 ± .24	4.52 ± .17	8.35 ± .31
Nose breadth	167	25- 42	33.56 ± .15	2.94 ± .11	8.76 ± .32
Bigonial diameter	167	90-121	104.66 ± .28	5.44 ± .20	5.20 ± .19
Ear length	164	52- 79	63.42 ± .24	4.56 ± .17	7.19 ± .27
Ear breadth	164	29- 49	36.45 ± .16	3.09 ± .12	8.48 ± .32
Relative shoulder breadth	166	18- 25	22.10 ± .07	1.32 ± .05	5.97 ± .22
Relative sitting height	165	48- 57	52.18 ± .09	1.70 ± .06	3.26 ± .12
Cephalic index	167	68- 88	78.00 ± .18	3.42 ± .13	4.39 ± .16
Cephalo-facial index	167	79-102	90.20 ± .17	3.21 ± .12	3.56 ± .13
Length-height index	166	58- 78	68.42 ± .18	3.54 ± .13	5.17 ± .19
Breadth-height index	166	76-105	87.86 ± .24	4.59 ± .17	5.22 ± .19
Facial index	167	74-105	89.90 ± .28	5.36 ± .20	5.96 ± .22
Upper facial index	167	40- 72	51.44 ± .23	4.35 ± .16	8.46 ± .31
Nasal index	167	44- 83	62.54 ± .37	7.04 ± .26	11.26 ± .42
Ear index	164	45- 72	57.22 ± .26	5.04 ± .19	8.81 ± .33
Zygo-frontal index	167	64- 95	78.74 ± .19	3.64 ± .13	4.62 ± .17
Fronto-parietal index	167	63- 83	71.20 ± .16	3.00 ± .11	4.21 ± .16
Zygo-gonial index	167	63- 89	76.63 ± .20	3.81 ± .14	4.97 ± .18

Table XI-3.   Means of Tennessee Civil Check Sample

	No.	Range	Mean	S. D.	V.
Age	146	15- 74	38.85 ± .61	11.00 ± .43	28.31 ± 1.12
Weight	145	121-250	172.00 ± 1.52	27.10 ± 1.07	15.76 ± .62
Height	146	161-193	172.80 ± .30	5.28 ± .21	3.06 ± .12
Biacromial diameter	146	31- 45	38.84 ± .13	2.23 ± .09	5.37 ± .23
Chest depth	146	18- 29	22.28 ± .11	1.96 ± .08	8.80 ± .35
Chest breadth	146	23- 40	28.92 ± .13	2.28 ± .09	7.88 ± .31
Sitting height	146	81-101	90.61 ± .18	3.24 ± .13	3.58 ± .14
Head length	146	176-211	193.83 ± .34	6.12 ± .24	3.16 ± .12
Head breadth	146	141-157	154.36 ± .28	5.01 ± .20	3.25 ± .13
Head height	146	116-148	133.80 ± .30	5.28 ± .21	3.95 ± .16
Head circumference	146	514-621	573.26 ± .94	16.92 ± .57	2.95 ± .12
Minimum frontal diameter	146	101-128	114.94 ± .27	4.84 ± .19	4.21 ± .17
Bizygomatic diameter	146	125-164	141.20 ± .29	5.15 ± .20	3.65 ± .14
Total face height	146	100-139	122.60 ± .38	6.75 ± .27	5.51 ± .22
Upper face height	146	55- 84	69.80 ± .25	4.45 ± .18	6.38 ± .25
Nose height	146	44- 67	54.02 ± .20	3.52 ± .14	6.52 ± .26
Nose breadth	146	31- 42	36.14 ± .12	2.13 ± .08	5.89 ± .23
Bigonial diameter	145	98-129	111.46 ± .32	5.58 ± .22	5.10 ± .20
Ear length	146	52- 79	64.86 ± .25	4.56 ± .18	7.03 ± .28
Ear breadth	146	32- 46	40.08 ± .14	2.43 ± .10	6.06 ± .24
Relative shoulder breadth	146	18- 27	22.36 ± .08	1.34 ± .05	5.99 ± .24
Relative sitting height	146	48- 57	52.44 ± .08	1.50 ± .06	2.86 ± .11
Cephalic index	146	71- 88	79.68 ± .16	2.94 ± .12	3.69 ± .15
Cephalo-facial index	146	82-102	91.54 ± .17	3.03 ± .12	3.31 ± .13
Length-height index	146	61- 78	68.96 ± .16	2.88 ± .11	4.18 ± .16
Breadth-height index	146	79- 99	86.81 ± .19	3.42 ± .14	3.94 ± .16
Facial index	146	70-101	87.02 ± .30	5.32 ± .21	6.11 ± .24
Upper facial index	146	40- 57	49.49 ± .18	3.30 ± .13	6.57 ± .26
Nasal index	146	56- 83	67.10 ± .30	5.36 ± .21	7.99 ± .32
Ear index	146	49- 72	61.86 ± .22	3.92 ± .16	6.34 ± .25
Zygo-frontal index	146	76- 91	81.58 ± .17	3.00 ± .12	3.68 ± .14
Fronto-parietal index	146	66- 83	74.47 ± .15	2.88 ± .11	3.87 ± .15
Zygo-gonial index	146	69- 95	79.03 ± .21	3.78 ± .15	4.78 ± .19

Table XI-4. Differences of Means with Value in Terms of the Probable Error between
Total Criminals and Total Civil Check Sample and between State Criminal
Groups and State Civil Check Samples

	Total Criminals (4212) over Total Civilians (313)		Mass. Criminals (338) over Mass. Civilians (167)		Tenn. Criminals (423) over Tenn. Civilians (146)	
	Diff.	x p.e.	Diff.	x p.e.	Diff.	x p.e.
Age	- 3.80	7.04	- 3.20	3.68	- 9.05	12.57
Weight	-11.70	10.83	- 6.30	4.38	-21.40	13.05
Height	- 1.02	4.25	- 3.21	8.02	- 0.45	1.25
Biacromial diameter	- 0.45	5.00	- 0.45	2.55	- 0.66	4.71
Chest depth	- 0.56	8.25	- 0.06	0.43	- 1.20	8.57
Chest breadth	- 0.69	7.57	- 0.87	6.21	- 1.23	8.79
Sitting height	- 0.21	1.50	- 1.35	6.14	- 0.99	4.95
Head length	- 0.42	1.52	- 2.22	5.04	- 1.83	4.58
Head breadth	- 0.81	4.05	0.06	0.18	- 2.04	6.18
Head height	- 0.84	3.50	0.18	0.45	- 0.42	1.20
Head circumference	- 6.60	9.17	- 4.92	4.73	- 4.80	4.03
Minimum frontal diameter	0.28	1.22	2.28	7.35	- 1.88	5.88
Bizygomatic diameter	- 0.50	2.08	0.05	0.14	- 2.35	7.12
Total face height	- 1.50	5.56	- 0.60	1.36	- 0.80	1.82
Upper face height	- 0.70	3.68	- 1.50	5.00	- 1.15	4.11
Nose height	- 1.84	9.20	- 2.24	8.00	- 2.04	9.27
Nose breadth	0	0	0.45	2.65	- 0.84	6.00
Bigonial diameter	- 0.04	0.15	1.40	4.00	- 3.16	8.54
Ear length	- 2.40	12.63	- 2.20	7.86	- 3.04	10.86
Ear breadth	- 0.39	2.79	0.27	1.35	- 1.56	9.18
Relative shoulder breadth	- 0.04	0	0.52	5.20	- 0.54	5.40
Relative sitting height	0.22	3.67	0.24	2.40	- 0.50	5.00
Cephalic index	- 0.21	1.52	1.02	4.64	- 0.36	1.80
Cephalo-facial index	0.21	1.75	- 0.06	0.30	- 0.57	2.85
Length-height index	- 0.09	0.69	0.93	4.23	0.57	2.85
Breadth-height index	0.18	1.06	0.06	0.23	0.78	3.54
Facial index	- 0.76	3.45	- 0.28	0.85	0.88	2.51
Upper facial index	- 0.42	2.62	- 1.08	4.15	0.09	0.43
Nasal index	1.96	7.26	2.92	6.49	1.12	2.80
Ear index	1.88	8.95	3.04	9.50	- 0.16	0.62
Zygo-frontal index	0.48	3.43	2.00	9.09	0	0
Fronto-parietal index	0.69	5.31	1.65	8.25	- 0.18	0.90
Zygo-gonial index	0	0	0.90	3.75	- 0.99	4.12

Table XI-5. Number and Significance of Deviations of Total Criminals from Total Civilians in Terms of Nature of Deviations of Criminals from Civilians in Same Two States (Massachusetts and Tennessee)

	Deviations of Total Criminals from Civilians				Total of State Criminals from State Civilians	
	Insignificant (Less than 3 p.e.)		Significant (3 p.e. and over)			
	No.	Per Cent	No.	Per Cent	No.	Per Cent
1. Insignificant and in same direction	1	3.03	1	3.03	2	6.06
2. Significant and in same direction	2	6.06	7	21.21	9	27.27
3. Insignificant and in different directions	0	0	2	6.06	2	6.06
4. Significant and in different directions	4	12.12	0	0	4	12.12
5. One insignificant, one significant in same direction	2	6.06	5	15.15	7	21.21
6. One insignificant, one significant in different directions	5	15.15	4	12.12	9	27.27
Total	14	42.42	19	57.58	33	100.00

Table XI-6. Significant Metric and Indicial Differences between Total Criminal
Series and Total Civil Check Sample with reference to State Agreement

A. Total Comparison and State Comparisons Significant and in Same Direction

    Age (- 3.80 years, 7.04 p.e.)
    Weight (-11.70* pounds, 10.83 p.e.)
    Chest breadth (- 0.69* cm., 7.67 p.e.)
    Head circumference (- 6.60 mm., 9.17 p.e.)
    Upper face height (- 0.70 mm., 3.68 p.e.)
    Nose height (- 1.84* mm., 9.20 p.e.)
    Ear length (- 2.40* mm., 12.63 p.e.)

                                                    Total
                                                      Number   7
                                                      Per Cent   21.21

B. Total and One State Comparison Significant, All Agreeing in Direction

    Height (- 1.02 cm., 4.25 p.e.), Tennessee insignificant
    Biacromial diameter (- 0.45* cm., 5.00 p.e.), Massachusetts insignificant
    Chest depth (- 0.66* cm., 8.25 p.e.), Massachusetts insignificant
    Nasal index (1.96* per cent, 7.26 p.e.), Tennessee insignificant
    Zygo-frontal index (0.48* per cent, 3.43 p.e.), Tennessee insignificant

                                                    Total
                                                      Number   5
                                                      Per Cent   15.15

C. Total Comparison Significant, State Comparisons Insignificant, All
    Agreeing in Direction

    Total face height (- 1.50 mm., 5.56 p.e.)

                                                    Total
                                                      Number   1
                                                      Per Cent   3.03

D. Total and One State Comparison Significant and in Same Direction; Other
    Opposite and Insignificant

    Head breadth (- 0.81** mm., 4.05 p.e.), Massachusetts disagreeing
    Ear index (1.88* per cent, 8.95 p.e.), Tennessee disagreeing
    Fronto-parietal index (0.69* per cent, 5.31 p.e.), Tennessee disagreeing

                                                    Total
                                                      Number   3
                                                      Per Cent   9.09

E. Total Comparison Significant and State Comparisons Insignificant, One
    Agreeing with Total in Direction

    Head height (- 0.84 mm., 3.50 p.e.), Tennessee agreeing in direction
    Facial index (- 0.76*, 3.45 p.e.), Massachusetts agreeing in direction

                                                    Total
                                                      Number   2
                                                      Per Cent   6.06

*   Independent of age effects.
** Complicated by age effects.

Table XI-6 (cont'd).

F. Total Comparison and One State Significant but in Opposite Directions,
    Other State Insignificant in Same Direction as Total

    Relative sitting height (0.22, 3.67 per cent), Massachusetts agreeing in
    direction, Tennessee agreeing in significance

	Total	
	Number	1
	Per Cent	3.03

Table XI-7. Age Distribution of Total Criminal Series
and Total Civil Check Sample

	Total Criminal		Total Civil	
	No.	Per Cent	No.	Per Cent
15-19	567	13.54	36	11.50
20-24	866	20.68	63	20.13
25-29	937	22.37	38	12.14
30-34	587	14.02	40	12.78
35-39	409	9.77	36	11.50
40-44	290	6.92	30	9.58
45-49	182	4.35	14	4.47
50-54	160	3.82	21	6.71
55-59	75	1.79	12	3.83
60-64	65	1.55	16	5.11
65-69	42	1.00	6	1.92
70-74	4	0.10	1	0.32
75-79	4	0.10		
Total	4188		313	

Table XI-8. Age Distribution of Criminals, Civilian Check Sample, and General Population by 5-Year Periods

Age	Criminals Native Whites of Native Parentage (This series) Per Cent		All Prisoners* Present (1923) Per Cent		All Prisoners** Received (1928) Per Cent		Civilians Native Whites of Native Parentage (This series) Per Cent		Population, 1930 Native Whites of Native Parentage*** (15 years and over) Per Cent		Population, 1930 Native Whites of Native Parentage*** (All ages) Per Cent	
15–19	13.54		8.4		16.2		11.50		14.8		9.8	
20–24	20.68		24.1		28.2		20.13		13.5		8.9	
25–29	22.37	36.39		34.2	18.8	30.7	12.14	24.92	11.7	22.1	7.7	14.6
30–34	14.02				11.9		12.78		10.4		6.9	
35–39	9.77	16.69	18.8		9.0	14.8	11.50	21.08	10.0	18.6	6.7	12.4
40–44	6.92				5.8		9.58		8.6		5.7	
45–49	4.35	8.17		8.7	4.1	6.5	4.47	11.18	7.6	14.1	5.0	9.3
50–54	3.82				2.4		6.71		6.5		4.3	
55–59	1.79	3.34		3.4	1.5	2.3	3.83	8.94	5.2	9.3	3.4	6.1
60–64	1.55				0.8		5.11		4.1		2.7	
65 and over	1.20		1.20		0.7		2.24		7.6		5.0	
Total number	4188		109,075		45,432		313		23,319,460		35,460,001	

* Includes all nationalities and parentages, and 4.8 per cent of females. Prisoners, 1923, p. 70, table 38.
** Includes all nationalities and parentages, males only. Prisoners, 1928, p. 24, table 16.
*** Census, 1931, table 2.

Table XI-9. Weight of Criminals over 34 Years of Age and Comparison with Civil Check Sample

	No.	Range	Mean	S. D.	V.	Diff.	
35–39	374	101–240	154.70 ± .76	21.70 ± .54	14.03 ± .35	– 7.90 ± 1.30	6.08
35–69	1104	91–270	155.20 ± .46	22.60 ± .32	14.56 ± .21	– 7.40 ± 1.15	6.44

Table XI-11.   Stature of Criminal Series Compared with Stature of
Civilian Groups of Similar Origin

	Authority	No.	Age	Stature
Criminals				
Total	This study	4202	30.70	171.90
Tennessee	This study	422	29.80	172.35
Kentucky	This study	1186	29.65	172.29
Civilians	This study			
Old Americans				
Total	Hrdlicka	727	20-	174.3
Laboratory series total	Hrdlicka	247	-	174.44
Laboratory series by age groups				
(1)	Hrdlicka	91	22-29	174.14
(2)	Hrdlicka	114	30-50	174.8
Eastern Tennessee	Hrdlicka	133	-	174.3
Virginia and neighboring states	Hrdlicka	347	-	174.2
Civil War soldiers				
Kentucky, Tennessee	Gould	12,862	31-	176.02
World War soldiers*	Davenport			
Kentucky	and Love	4033	-	173.3

*Including a small percentage of Negroes, probably not more than 2.5 per cent.

Table XI-12.   Biacromial Diameter of Criminals over 34 Years of Age
and Comparison with Civil Check Sample

	No.	Range	Mean	S. D.	V.	Diff.	x p.e.
35-39	408	28-45	38.24 ± .08	2.31 ± .05	6.04 ± .14	- 0.33 ± .12	2.75
35-69	1221	28-45	38.06 ± .04	2.31 ± .03	6.07 ± .08	- 0.51 ± .10	5.10

Table XI-13.   Chest Depth of Criminals over 34 Years of Age
and Comparison with Civil Check Sample

	No.	Range	Mean	S. D.	V.	Diff.	x p.e.
35-39	403	16-27	21.40 ± .06	1.68 ± .04	7.85 ± .19	- 0.30 ± .10	3.00
35-69	1237	16-29	21.80 ± .04	1.82 ± .02	8.35 ± .11	0.10 ± .09	1.11

Table XI-15.   Chest Breadth of Criminals over 34 Years of Age
and Comparison with Civil Check Sample

	No.	Range	Mean	S. D.	V.	Diff.	x p.e.
35-39	402	20-34	27.69 ± .06	1.86 ± .04	6.72 ± .16	- 0.48 ± .11	4.36
35-69	1235	20-34	27.69 ± .04	2.01 ± .03	7.26 ± .10	- 0.48 ± .10	4.80

Table XI-16.   Head Breadth of Criminals over 34 Years of Age and
                 Comparison with Civil Check Sample

	No.	Range	Mean	S. D.	V.	Diff.	x p.e.
35-39	408	135-170	152.80 ± .19	5.58 ± .13	3.65 ± .09	- 0.15 ± .27	0.55
35-69	1226	129-173	152.71 ± .11	5.52 ± .08	3.62 ± .05	- 0.24 ± .22	1.09

Table XI-18.   Head Circumference of Criminals over 34 Years of Age
                 and Comparison with Civil Check Sample

	No.	Range	Mean	S. D.	V.	Diff.	x p.e.
35-39	383	502-609	565.10 ± .57	16.56 ± .40	2.93 ± .07	- 5.40 ± .91	5.93
35-69	1170	502-621	564.74 ± .33	16.68 ± .23	2.95 ± .04	- 5.76 ± .78	7.38

Table XI-20.   Nose Height of Criminals over 34 Years of Age
                 and Comparison with Civil Check Sample

	No.	Range	Mean	S. D.	V.	Diff.	x p.e.
35-39	407	40-71	53.22 ± .13	3.84 ± .09	7.22 ± .17	- 0.88 ± .21	4.19
35-69	1225	40-71	53.35 ± .08	3.92 ± .05	7.35 ± .10	- 0.75 ± .18	4.17

Table XI-21.   Ear Length (Observer A) of Criminals over 34 Years of Age
                 and Comparison with Civil Check Sample

	No.	Range	Mean	S. D.	V.	Diff.	x p.e.
35-39	272	52-75	62.46 ± .19	4.60 ± .13	7.36 ± .21	- 1.60 ± .26	6.15
35-69	829	48-83	63.82 ± .11	4.84 ± .08	7.58 ± .13	- 0.24 ± .21	1.14

Table XI-22.   Ear Breadth (Observer A) of Criminals over 34 Years of Age
                 and Comparison with Civil Check Sample

	No.	Range	Mean	S. D.	V.	Diff.	x p.e.
35-39	274	29-46	37.95 ± .11	2.61 ± .08	6.88 ± .20	- 0.21 ± .17	1.24
35-69	824	26-49	38.43 ± .06	2.76 ± .05	7.18 ± .12	0.27 ± .14	1.93

Table XI-25. Facial Index of Criminal Series Compared with Facial Index
             of Civilian Groups of Similar Origin

	Authority	No.	Age	Mean
Criminals	This study	4209	30.70	87.82
Civilians	This study	313	34.50	88.58
Old Americans				
Laboratory series	Hrdlicka	247	42.5	86.03
Drafted Engineers, southern states	Hrdlicka	256	-	88.7
Drafted Engineers, other and mixed				
states	Hrdlicka	91	-	88.4
Tennessee Highlanders	Hrdlicka	132	25.1	87.75
Total	Hrdlicka	726	-	87.6

Table XI-26.   Facial Index of Criminals by Age Grouping

	No.	Range	Mean	S. D.	V.
15-19	569	74-105	87.70 ± .14	5.04 ± .10	5.75 ± .12
20-34	2400	74-109	88.14 ± .07	5.12 ± .05	5.81 ± .06
35-69	1223	70-105	87.22 ± .11	5.52 ± .08	6.33 ± .09
Total	4192	70-109	87.82 ± .06	5.28 ± .04	6.01 ± .04

Table XI-27.   Upper Facial Index of Criminals by Age Grouping

	No.	Range	Mean	S. D.	V.
15-19	569	37-63	50.21 ± .10	3.45 ± .07	6.87 ± .14
20-34	2399	37-66	50.30 ± .05	3.42 ± .03	6.80 ± .07
35-69	1223	37-66	49.76 ± .07	3.75 ± .05	7.54 ± .10
Total	4191	37-66	50.12 ± .04	3.54 ± .03	7.06 ± .05

Table XI-28.   Ear Index (Observer A) of Criminals by Age Grouping

	No.	Range	Mean	S. D.	V.
15-19	358	49-88	61.98 ± .16	4.56 ± .12	7.36 ± .19
20-34	1674	45-88	61.58 ± .07	4.48 ± .05	7.28 ± .08
35-69	821	45-88	60.42 ± .11	4.72 ± .08	7.81 ± .13
Total	2853	45-88	61.30 ± .06	4.64 ± .04	7.57 ± .07

Table XI-29.   Fronto-Parietal Index of Criminals by Age Grouping

	No.	Range	Mean	S. D.	V.
15-19	570	66-86	73.84 ± .08	2.91 ± .02	3.94 ± .08
20-34	2395	63-86	73.54 ± .04	3.12 ± .03	4.24 ± .04
35-69	1222	60-86	72.94 ± .06	3.24 ± .04	4.44 ± .06
Total	4187	60-86	73.42 ± .03	3.15 ± .02	4.29 ± .03

Table XI-30. Differences of Means with Value in Terms of the Probable Error
between Total Criminal Series and Total Civil Check Sample and
between Offense Subgroups and Total Civil Check Sample

	Total Offenses (4212)		First Degree Murder (312)		Second Degree Murder (619)	
	Diff.	x p.e.	Diff.	x p.e.	Diff.	x p.e.
Age	- 3.80	7.04	3.30	4.58	- 0.45	0.71
Weight	-11.70	10.83	- 7.10	5.00	-11.50	8.61
Height	- 1.02	4.25	0.18	0.54	- 0.78	2.69
Biacromial diameter	- 0.45	5.00	- 0.42	3.23	- 0.57	5.18
Chest depth	- 0.66	8.25	- 0.06	0.54	- 0.42	4.67
Chest breadth	- 0.69	7.67	- 0.36	3.00	- 0.54	5.40
Sitting height	- 0.21	1.50	- 0.18	1.00	- 0.30	1.88
Head length	- 0.42	1.62	0.15	0.42	- 0.21	0.70
Head breadth	- 0.81	4.05	- 0.87	3.11	- 1.08	4.50
Head height	- 0.84	3.50	- 1.20	3.64	- 1.62	5.59
Head circumference	- 6.60	9.17	- 3.84	4.36	- 5.88	7.08
Minimum frontal diameter	0.28	1.22	- 0.56	2.00	- 0.24	0.92
Bizygomatic diameter	- 0.50	2.08	- 0.25	0.81	- 0.55	2.04
Total face height	- 1.50	5.56	- 1.15	3.29	- 1.75	5.47
Upper face height	- 0.70	3.68	- 0.40	1.60	- 0.90	4.09
Nose height	- 1.84	9.20	- 1.04	4.52	- 1.76	9.26
Nose breadth	0	0	0.15	1.00	0	0
Bigonial diameter	- 0.04	0.15	1.12	3.39	0.24	0.83
Ear length	- 2.40	12.63	- 2.40	8.28	- 2.60	11.30
Ear breadth	- 0.39	2.79	0.66	3.30	- 0.48	3.00
Relative shoulder breadth	- 0.04	0.80	- 0.58	6.44	- 0.10	1.67
Relative sitting height	0.22	3.67	- 0.16	2.00	0.10	1.43
Cephalic index	- 0.21	1.62	- 0.63	3.50	- 0.48	3.00
Cephalo-facial index	0.21	1.76	0.45	2.50	0.27	1.93
Length-height index	- 0.09	0.69	- 0.54	3.00	- 0.69	4.31
Breadth-height index	0.18	1.06	0.15	0.65	- 0.39	1.95
Facial index	- 0.76	3.45	- 0.72	2.48	- 0.92	3.68
Upper facial index	- 0.42	2.62	- 0.18	0.90	- 0.51	2.83
Nasal index	1.96	7.26	1.20	3.43	1.84	5.75
Ear index	1.88	8.95	2.32	7.73	1.92	8.00
Zygo-frontal index	0.48	3.43	- 0.32	1.78	0.12	0.71
Fronto-parietal index	0.69	5.31	0.21	1.17	0.45	3.81
Zygo-gonial index	0	0	0.81	4.05	0.12	0.67

Table XI-30 (cont'd).

	Assault (80)		Robbery (414)		Burglary and Larceny (1612)	
	Diff.	x p.e.	Diff.	x p.e.	Diff.	x p.e.
Age	- 0.50	0.48	- 7.75	13.14	- 8.00	14.54
Weight	-10.90	5.40	-13.20	10.82	- 13.70	12.34
Height	- 1.26	2.33	- 0.90	2.90	- 1.32	5.28
Biacromial diameter	0.18	0.90	- 0.39	3.25	- 0.54	5.40
Chest depth	- 0.40	2.67	- 0.96	10.67	- 0.92	11.50
Chest breadth	- 0.33	1.83	- 0.78	7.09	- 0.90	9.00
Sitting height	- 0.09	0.27	0.06	0.35	- 0.33	2.36
Head length	- 0.18	0.34	- 0.05	0.18	- 0.87	3.22
Head breadth	- 1.41	2.82	- 0.48	1.85	- 1.05	5.00
Head height	- 2.28	3.35	0.21	0.68	- 0.84	3.23
Head circumference	- 9.84	6.69	- 5.52	6.27	- 8.04	10.59
Minimum frontal diameter	0.16	0.38	0.76	2.92	0.32	1.39
Bizygomatic diameter	0.10	0.21	0.15	0.52	- 0.95	3.96
Total face height	- 1.10	1.83	- 1.50	4.54	- 1.75	6.25
Upper face height	- 0.50	1.28	- 0.75	3.26	- 0.95	4.47
Nose height	- 1.36	3.89	- 2.20	11.00	- 2.36	13.88
Nose breadth	- 0.03	0.12	0.21	1.50	- 0.21	1.75
Bigonial diameter	- 0.08	0.17	0	0	- 0.55	2.07
Ear length	- 2.32	3.31	- 2.72	10.88	- 2.96	14.10
Ear breadth	- 0.75	2.42	- 0.48	3.00	- 0.66	4.71
Relative shoulder breadth	0.30	3.00	0.10	1.43	- 0.06	1.20
Relative sitting height	0.24	1.71	0.30	3.75	0.25	3.71
Cephalic index	- 0.12	0.44	- 0.12	0.67	- 0.12	0.86
Cephalo-facial index	0.39	1.39	0.27	1.69	0.09	0.59
Length-height index	- 0.78	1.90	0.21	1.17	0.09	0.69
Breadth-height index	- 1.51	2.74	0.66	2.87	0.39	2.17
Facial index	- 0.60	1.33	- 1.00	3.70	- 0.68	2.96
Upper facial index	- 0.24	0.75	- 0.57	3.00	- 0.39	2.44
Nasal index	1.64	2.48	2.84	8.11	2.24	7.72
Ear index	1.68	2.85	2.20	7.86	2.08	9.45
Zygo-frontal index	0.32	1.10	0.68	3.75	0.80	5.33
Fronto-parietal index	0.42	1.40	0.87	5.44	0.84	6.00
Zygo-gonial index	- 0.54	1.59	- 0.18	0.95	- 0.12	0.75

Table XI-30 (cont'd).

	Forgery and Fraud (467)		Rape (197)		Other Sex (151)	
	Diff.	x p.e.	Diff.	x p.e.	Diff.	x p.e.
Age	- 4.25	6.86	1.60	2.00	2.60	2.95
Weight	- 9.40	7.52	-13.40	9.05	- 9.90	5.79
Height	- 0.39	1.22	- 2.73	7.00	- 1.92	4.27
Biacromial diameter	- 0.27	2.45	- 0.48	3.43	- 0.15	1.00
Chest depth	- 0.72	7.20	- 0.32	2.67	- 0.44	3.38
Chest breadth	- 0.66	6.00	- 0.63	4.85	- 0.57	4.07
Sitting height	0.39	2.29	- 0.78	3.54	- 0.51	2.22
Head length	0.62	1.88	- 0.46	1.15	- 0.66	1.57
Head breadth	- 0.18	0.69	- 0.33	1.03	- 0.93	2.58
Head height	- 0.15	0.47	- 0.63	1.50	- 0.08	0.16
Head circumference	- 4.08	4.69	- 9.12	8.69	- 8.75	7.82
Minimum frontal diameter	0.88	3.26	0.04	0.12	- 0.44	1.26
Bizygomatic diameter	- 0.15	0.54	0.50	1.43	- 0.40	1.03
Total face height	- 0.75	2.27	- 1.15	2.80	- 0.75	1.56
Upper face height	- 0.40	1.74	- 0.40	1.33	- 0.25	0.75
Nose height	- 1.60	8.00	- 1.20	4.62	- 1.04	3.85
Nose breadth	0.06	0.43	- 0.06	0.35	0.15	0.75
Bigonial diameter	0.24	0.80	- 0.75	2.11	- 0.28	0.70
Ear length	- 1.84	7.36	- 1.76	5.03	- 1.68	4.10
Ear breadth	- 0.06	0.38	- 0.30	1.36	- 0.81	3.00
Relative shoulder breadth	- 0.02	0.33	0.34	4.25	0.14	1.56
Relative sitting height	0.32	4.00	0.62	6.20	0.22	2.00
Cephalic index	- 0.24	1.41	0.24	1.14	- 0.24	1.09
Cephalo-facial index	0.09	0.56	0.03	0.15	0.15	0.68
Length-height index	0.24	1.33	0.12	0.48	0.12	0.46
Breadth-height index	0.39	1.86	- 0.06	0.20	0	0
Facial index	- 0.48	1.85	- 0.76	2.17	- 0.44	1.13
Upper facial index	- 0.33	1.74	- 0.33	1.38	0.06	0.23
Nasal index	1.72	5.21	0.96	2.29	0.76	1.52
Ear index	2.00	7.41	1.28	3.56	0.48	1.23
Zygo-frontal index	0.60	3.53	0.32	1.52	0.16	0.73
Fronto-parietal index	0.84	5.25	0.36	1.80	0.48	2.18
Zygo-gonial index	0.06	0.32	- 0.48	2.09	0.06	0.22

Table XI-30 (cont'd).

	Vs. Public Welfare (257)		Arson and All Other (103)	
	Diff.	x p.e.	Diff.	x p.e.
Age	3.75	5.07	- 1.45	1.59
Weight	- 8.30	5.76	-14.40	9.73
Height	0	0	- 2.52	4.94
Biacromial diameter	- 0.30	2.31	- 0.30	1.76
Chest depth	- 0.18	1.50	- 0.76	5.85
Chest breadth	- 0.39	3.25	0.33	1.93
Sitting height	- 0.09	0.47	- 0.69	2.65
Head length	- 0.63	1.70	- 0.87	1.85
Head breadth	- 0.42	1.50	- 0.93	2.38
Head height	- 0.84	2.54	- 0.99	2.02
Head circumference	- 4.44	4.58	- 7.92	5.82
Minimum frontal diameter	1.28	4.27	- 0.88	2.15
Bizygomatic diameter	0.65	1.97	- 0.90	2.20
Total face height	- 1.55	3.97	- 1.30	2.55
Upper face height	- 0.95	3.15	- 0.25	0.69
Nose height	- 1.44	6.26	- 1.24	3.54
Nose breadth	0.78	4.98	0	0
Bigonial diameter	1.60	4.57	- 0.52	1.16
Ear length	- 0.16	0.53	- 2.16	5.14
Ear breadth	- 0.09	0.50	- 0.45	1.80
Relative shoulder breadth	- 0.10	1.43	0.24	3.00
Relative sitting height	0.04	0.50	0.18	1.50
Cephalic index	- 0.06	0.33	0.09	0.35
Cephalo-facial index	0.75	4.17	0	0
Length-height index	- 0.03	0.16	0.03	0.11
Breadth-height index	- 0.15	0.60	- 0.21	0.72
Facial index	- 1.72	5.55	0	0
Upper facial index	- 0.93	4.23	0.12	0.41
Nasal index	2.40	6.49	1.36	2.52
Ear index	0.44	1.42	1.54	4.10
Zygo-frontal index	0.48	2.40	- 0.12	0.41
Fronto-parietal index	1.23	6.83	0.03	0.12
Zygo-gonial index	0.39	1.86	- 0.09	0.30

Table XI-31. Number and Significance of Deviations of Criminal Offense
Groups and of Total Criminal Series from Total Civil Check
Sample in Measurements and Indices

	Significant		Insignificant	
	No.	Per Cent	No.	Per Cent
First degree murder	18	54.55	15	45.45
Second degree murder	17	51.52	16	48.48
Assault	6	18.18	27	81.82
Robbery	18	54.55	15	45.45
Burglary and larceny	21	63.54	12	36.36
Forgery and fraud	13	39.39	20	60.61
Rape	11	33.33	22	66.67
Other sex	8	24.24	25	75.76
Vs. public welfare	15	45.45	18	54.55
Arson and all other	8	24.24	25	75.76
Total series	19	57.58	14	42.42
Massachusetts	21	63.64	12	36.36
Tennessee	21	63.64	12	36.36

Table XI-32. Summary of Significant Metric and Indicial Differences between
Criminals and Civilians

Total Offenses

Age: deficiency 3.80 (7.04 p.e.)
Weight: deficiency 11.70 (10.83 p.e.)
Height: deficiency 1.02 (4.25 p.e.)
Biacromial diameter: deficiency 0.45 (5.00 p.e.)
Chest depth: deficiency 0.66 (8.25 p.e.)
Chest breadth: deficiency 0.69 (7.67 p.e.)
Head breadth: deficiency 0.81 (4.05 p.e.)
Head height: deficiency 0.84 (3.50 p.e.)
Head circumference: deficiency 6.60 (9.17 p.e.)
Total face height: deficiency 1.50 (5.56 p.e.)
Upper face height: deficiency 0.70 (3.68 p.e.)
Nose height: deficiency 1.84 (9.20 p.e.)
Ear length: deficiency 2.40 (12.63 p.e.)
Relative sitting height: excess 0.22 (3.67 p.e.)
Facial index: deficiency 0.76 (3.45 p.e.)
Nasal index: excess 1.96 (7.26 p.e.)
Ear index: excess 1.88 (8.95 p.e.)
Zygo-frontal index: excess 0.48 (3.43 p.e.)
Fronto-parietal index: excess 0.69 (5.31 p.e.)

Table XI-33. Summary of Significant Metric and Indicial Differences between
Criminals and Civilians

First Degree Murder

Age: excess 3.30 (4.58 p.e.)
Weight: deficiency 7.10 (5.00 p.e.)
Biacromial diameter: deficiency 0.42 (3.23 p.e.)
Chest breadth: deficiency 0.36 (3.00 p.e.)
Head breadth: deficiency 0.87 (3.11 p.e.)
Head height: deficiency 1.20 (3.64 p.e.)
Head circumference: deficiency 3.84 (4.36 p.e.)
Total face height: deficiency 1.15 (3.29 p.e.)
Nose height: deficiency 1.04 (4.52 p.e.)
Bigonial diameter: excess 1.12 (3.39 p.e.)
Ear length: deficiency 2.40 (8.28 p.e.)
Ear breadth: excess 0.65 (3.30 p.e.)
Relative shoulder breadth: deficiency 0.58 (6.44 p.e.)
Cephalic index: deficiency 0.63 (3.50 p.e.)
Length-height index: deficiency 0.54 (3.00 p.e.)
Nasal index: excess 1.20 (3.43 p.e.)
Ear index: excess 2.32 (7.73 p.e.)
Zygo-gonial index: excess 0.81 (4.05 p.e.)

Table XI-34. Summary of Significant Metric and Indicial Differences
between Criminals and Civilians

Second Degree Murder

Weight: deficiency 11.50 (8.61 p.e.)
Biacromial diameter: deficiency 0.57 (5.18 p.e.)
Chest depth: deficiency 0.42 (4.67 p.e.)
Chest breadth: deficiency 0.54 (5.40 p.e.)
Head breadth: deficiency 1.08 (4.50 p.e.)
Head height: deficiency 1.62 (5.59 p.e.)
Head circumference: deficiency 5.88 (7.08 p.e.)
Total face height: deficiency 1.75 (5.47 p.e.)
Upper face height: deficiency 0.90 (4.09 p.e.)
Nose height: deficiency 1.76 (9.26 p.e.)
Ear length: deficiency 2.60 (11.30 p.e.)
Ear breadth: deficiency 0.48 (3.00 p.e.)
Cephalic index: deficiency 0.48 (3.00 p.e.)
Length-height index: deficiency 0.69 (4.31 p.e.)
Facial index: deficiency 0.92 (3.68 p.e.)
Nasal index: excess 1.84 (5.75 p.e.)
Ear index: excess 1.92 (8.00 p.e.)

Table XI-35. Summary of Significant Metric and Indicial Differences
between Criminals and Civilians

Assault

Weight: deficiency 10.90 (5.40 p.e.)
Head height: deficiency 2.28 (3.35 p.e.)
Head circumference: deficiency 9.84 (6.69 p.e.)
Nose height: deficiency 1.36 (3.89 p.e.)
Ear length: deficiency 2.32 (3.31 p.e.)
Relative shoulder breadth: excess 0.30 (3.00 p.e.)

Table XI-36. Summary of Significant Metric and Indicial Differences
between Criminals and Civilians

Robbery

Age: deficiency 7.75 (13.14 p.e.)
Weight: deficiency 13.20 (10.82 p.e.)
Biacromial diameter: deficiency 0.39 (3.25 p.e.)
Chest depth: deficiency 0.96 (10.67 p.e.)
Chest breadth: deficiency 0.78 (7.09 p.e.)
Head circumference: deficiency 5.52 (6.27 p.e.)
Total face height: deficiency 1.50 (4.54 p.e.)
Upper face height: deficiency 0.75 (3.26 p.e.)
Nose height: deficiency 2.20 (11.00 p.e.)
Ear length: deficiency 2.72 (10.88 p.e.)
Ear breadth: deficiency 0.48 (3.00 p.e.)
Relative sitting height: excess 0.30 (3.75 p.e.)
Facial index: deficiency 1.00 (3.70 p.e.)
Upper facial index: deficiency 0.57 (3.00 p.e.)
Nasal index: excess 2.84 (8.11 p.e.)
Ear index: excess 2.20 (7.86 p.e.)
Zygo-frontal index: excess 0.68 (3.76 p.e.)
Fronto-parietal index: excess 0.87 (5.44 p.e.)

Table XI-37.   Summary of Significant Metric and Indicial Differences
between Criminals and Civilians

Burglary and Larceny

Age: deficiency 8.00 (14.54 p.e.)
Weight: deficiency 13.70 (12.34 p.e.)
Height: deficiency 1.32 (5.28 p.e.)
Biacromial diameter: deficiency 0.54 (5.40 p.e.)
Chest depth: deficiency 0.92 (11.50 p.e.)
Chest breadth: deficiency 0.90 (9.00 p.e.)
Head length: deficiency 0.87 (3.22 p.e.)
Head breadth: deficiency 1.05 (5.00 p.e.)
Head height: deficiency 0.84 (3.23 p.e.)
Head circumference: deficiency 8.04 (10.58 p.e.)
Bizygomatic diameter: deficiency 0.95 (3.96 p.e.)
Total face height: deficiency 1.75 (6.25 p.e.)
Upper face height: deficiency 0.85 (4.47 p.e.)
Nose height: deficiency 2.36 (13.88 p.e.)
Ear length: deficiency 2.96 (14.10 p.e.)
Ear breadth: deficiency 0.66 (4.71 p.e.)
Relative sitting height: excess 0.26 (3.71 p.e.)
Nasal index: excess 2.24 (7.72 p.e.)
Ear index: excess 2.08 (9.45 p.e.)
Zygo-frontal index: excess 0.80 (5.33 p.e.)
Fronto-parietal index: excess 0.84 (6.00 p.e.)

Table XI-38.   Summary of Significant Metric and Indicial Differences
between Criminals and Civilians

Forgery and Fraud

Age: deficiency 4.25 (6.86 p.e.)
Weight: deficiency 9.40 (7.52 p.e.)
Chest depth: deficiency 0.72 (7.20 p.e.)
Chest breadth: deficiency 0.66 (6.00 p.e.)
Head circumference: deficiency 4.08 (4.69 p.e.)
Minimum frontal diameter: excess 0.88 (3.26 p.e.)
Nose height: deficiency 1.60 (8.00 p.e.)
Ear length: deficiency 1.84 (7.36 p.e.)
Relative sitting height: excess 0.32 (4.00 p.e.)
Nasal index: excess 1.72 (5.21 p.e.)
Ear index: excess 2.00 (7.41 p.e.)
Zygo-frontal index: excess 0.60 (3.53 p.e.)
Fronto-parietal index: excess 0.84 (5.25 p.e.)

Table XI-39.   Summary of Significant Metric and Indicial Differences
between Criminals and Civilians

Rape

Weight: deficiency 13.40 (9.05 p.e.)
Height: deficiency 2.73 (7.00 p.e.)
Biacromial diameter: deficiency .48 (3.43 p.e.)
Chest breadth: deficiency 0.63 (4.85 p.e.)
Sitting height: deficiency 0.78 (3.54 p.e.)
Head circumference: deficiency 9.12 (8.69 p.e.)
Nose height: deficiency 1.20 (4.62 p.e.)
Ear length: deficiency 1.76 (5.03 p.e.)
Relative shoulder breadth: excess 0.34 (4.25 p.e.)
Relative sitting height: excess 0.62 (6.20 p.e.)
Ear index: excess 1.28 (3.56 p.e.)

Table XI-40. Summary of Significant Metric and Indicial Differences
between Criminals and Civilians

Other Sex Offenses

Weight: deficiency 9.90 (5.79 p.e.)
Height: deficiency 1.92 (4.27 p.e.)
Chest depth: deficiency 0.44 (3.38 p.e.)
Chest breadth: deficiency 0.57 (4.07 p.e.)
Head circumference: deficiency 8.76 (7.82 p.e.)
Nose height: deficiency 1.04 (3.85 p.e.)
Ear length: deficiency 1.68 (4.10 p.e.)
Ear breadth: deficiency 0.81 (3.00 p.e.)

Table XI-41. Summary of Significant Metric and Indicial Differences
between Criminals and Civilians

Versus Public Welfare

Age: excess 3.75 (5.07 p.e.)
Weight: deficiency 8.30 (5.76 p.e.)
Chest breadth: deficiency 0.39 (3.25 p.e.)
Head circumference: deficiency 4.44 (4.58 p.e.)
Minimum frontal diameter: excess 1.28 (4.27 p.e.)
Total face height: deficiency 1.55 (3.97 p.e.)
Upper face height: deficiency 0.85 (3.15 p.e.)
Nose height: deficiency 1.44 (6.26 p.e.)
Nose breadth: excess 0.78 (4.88 p.e.)
Bigonial diameter: excess 1.60 (4.57 p.e.)
Cephalo-facial index: excess 0.75 (4.17 p.e.)
Facial index: deficiency 1.72 (5.55 p.e.)
Upper facial index: deficiency 0.93 (4.23 p.e.)
Nasal index: excess 2.40 (6.49 p.e.)
Fronto-parietal index: 1.23 (6.83 p.e.)

Table XI-42. Summary of Significant Metric and Indicial Differences
between Criminals and Civilians

Arson and All Other Offenses

Weight: deficiency 14.40 (9.73 p.e.)
Height: deficiency 2.52 (4.94 p.e.)
Chest depth: deficiency .76 (5.85 p.e.)
Head circumference: deficiency 7.92 (5.82 p.e.)
Nose height: deficiency 1.24 (3.54 p.e.)
Ear length: deficiency 2.16 (5.14 p.e.)
Relative shoulder breadth: excess .24 (3.00 p.e.)
Ear index: excess 1.64 (4.10 p.e.)

Table XII-1.   Sociological Observations of Total Civil Check Sample and
Massachusetts and Tennessee Civil Check Samples

	Total Check Sample		Massachusetts Check Sample		Tennessee Check Sample	
	No.	Per Cent	No.	Per Cent	No.	Per Cent
Marital state						
Single	129	42.02	109	67.70	20	13.70
Married	177	57.65	51	31.68	126	86.30
Divorced	0	0	0	0	0	0
Widower	1	0.33	1	0.62	0	0
Total	307		161		146	
Occupation						
Extractive	3	0.99	3	1.90	0	0
Laborer	6	1.98	6	3.80	0	0
Factory	39	12.87	35	22.15	4	2.76
Transportation	16	5.28	14	8.86	2	1.38
Skilled trade	25	8.25	24	15.19	1	0.69
Trade	25	8.25	23	14.56	2	1.38
Public service	139	45.87	5	3.16	134	92.41
Semi-professional	5	1.65	5	3.16	0	0
Professional	5	1.65	5	3.16	0	0
Personal service	4	1.32	3	1.90	1	0.69
Clerical	21	6.93	21	13.29	0	0
Student	15	4.95	14	8.86	1	0.69
Total	303		158		145	
Education						
Illiterate	2	0.64	2	1.20	0	0
Read, write	3	0.96	3	1.81	0	0
1-5th grade	47	15.06	8	4.82	39	26.71
6th grade	16	5.13	1	0.60	15	10.27
7th grade	31	9.94	8	4.82	23	15.75
8th grade	77	24.68	28	16.87	49	33.56
1st-2nd high	62	19.87	52	31.32	10	6.85
3rd-4th high	42	13.46	34	20.48	8	5.48
College	28	8.97	26	15.66	2	1.37
Professional school	4	1.28	4	2.41	0	0
Total	312		166		146	

Table XII-2. Number and Significance of Deviations of Total Criminal Series from Total Civilian Series in Terms of Nature of Deviations of Criminals from Civilians in Same Two States (Massachusetts and Tennessee)

Sociological Observations*

| | Differences of Total Criminals and Civilians** | | | | Total of State Criminals from State Civilians | |
| | Insignificant (Less than 3 p.e.) | | Significant (3 p.e. and over) | | | |
	No.	Per Cent	No.	Per Cent	No.	Per Cent
1. Insignificant and in same direction	1	4.00	1	4.00	2	8.00
2. Significant and in same direction	1	4.00	3	12.00	4	16.00
3. Insignificant and in different directions	0	0	2	8.00	2	8.00
4. Significant and in different directions	1	4.00	3	12.00	4	16.00
5. One insignificant, one significant in same direction	0	0	6	24.00	6	24.00
6. One insignificant, one significant in different directions	2	8.00	5	20.00	7	28.00
Total	5	20.00	20	80.00	25	100.00

*   Each category in an observation is counted as one unit.
** Exclusive of categories occurring in the total only or in the total and one state only.

Table XII-3. Summary of Significant Sociological Differences between Total
Criminal Series and Total Civil Check Sample
with Reference to State Agreement

A. Total Comparison and State Comparisons Significant and in Same Direction

    Marital state - Divorced (4.23 per cent, 5.42 p.e.)
    Occupation - Laborer (14.74 per cent, 10.17 p.e.)
            Personal service (5.46 per cent, 5.57 p.e.)

	Total	
	Number	3
	Per Cent	12.00

B. Total and One State Comparison Significant, All Agreeing in Direction

    Marital state - Married (-12.89 per cent, 6.48 p.e.)
    Occupation - Extractive (30.64 per cent, 16.84 p.e.)
            Factory (4.53 per cent, 3.02 p.e.)
            Public service (-45.21 per cent, 59.49 p.e.)
            Student (-4.95 per cent, 20.62 p.e.)
    Education - 3rd-4th high (-9.06 per cent, 10.54 p.e.)

	Total	
	Number	6
	Per Cent	24.00

C. Total Comparison Significant, State Comparisons Insignificant, All Agreeing
in Direction

    Marital state - Widower (2.05 per cent, 3.47 p.e.)

	Total	
	Number	1
	Per Cent	4.00

D. Total and One State Comparison Significant and in Same Direction, Other State
Comparison Insignificant and in Opposite Direction

    Marital state - Single (6.51 per cent, 3.30 p.e.)
    Education - Illiterate (9.60 per cent, 8.35 p.e.)
           6th grade (3.91 per cent, 3.52 p.e.)
           College (-5.84 per cent, 8.00 p.e.)

	Total	
	Number	4
	Per Cent	16.00

E. Total Comparison Significant, State Comparisons Insignificant, One Agreeing
with Total in Direction

    Education - Read, write (3.39 per cent, 4.35 p.e.)
           1st-5th grade (10.08 per cent, 5.96 p.e.)

	Total	
	Number	2
	Per Cent	8.00

F. Total Comparison and One State Comparison Significant, but in Opposite Direction;
Other State Comparison Insignificant in Same Direction as Total

    Occupation - Trade (-3.03 per cent, 3.37 p.e.)

	Total	
	Number	1
	Per Cent	4.00

Table XII-3 (cont'd).

G. Total Comparison and One State Comparison Significant in Same Direction; Other State Comparison Significant but in Opposite Direction

Occupation - Clerical (-4.09 per cent, 5.84 p.e.)
Education - 8th grade (-5.90 per cent, 3.81 p.e.)
1st-2nd high (-5.71 per cent, 4.11 p.e.)

	Total	
	Number	3
	Per Cent	12.00

Table XII-4.   Differences between Criminals and Civilians by States
with Value in Terms of the Probable Error

Marital State

	Total Criminal over Total Civilian		Mass. Criminal over Mass. Civilian		Tenn. Criminal over Tenn. Civilian	
	Diff.	x p.e.	Diff.	x p.e.	Diff.	x p.e.
Single	6.51 ± 2.00	3.30	- 1.13 ± 3.04	0.37	37.25 ± 3.18	11.71
Married	-12.99 ± 1.99	6.48	- 3.62 ± 2.93	1.24	-43.68 ± 3.22	13.56
Divorced	4.23 ± 0.78	5.42	2.69 ± 0.86	3.13	5.00 ± 1.22	4.10
Widower	2.05 ± 0.59	3.47	2.07 ± 0.91	2.27	1.43 ± 0.66	2.17

Table XII-6.   Differences between Criminals and Civilians by States
with Value in Terms of the Probable Error

Occupation

	Total Criminal over Total Civilian		Mass. Criminal over Mass. Civilian		Tenn. Criminal over Tenn. Civilian	
	Diff.	x p.e.	Diff.	x p.e.	Diff.	x p.e.
Extractive	30.64 ± 1.82	16.84	0.63 ± 0.99	0.64	41.42 ± 3.00	13.81
Laborer	14.74 ± 1.45	10.17	10.12 ± 2.02	5.01	7.84 ± 1.52	5.16
Factory	4.53 ± 1.50	3.02	3.48 ± 2.83	1.23	17.83 ± 2.38	7.49
Transportation	2.03 ± 1.04	1.95	6.96 ± 2.25	3.09	4.99 ± 1.42	3.51
Skilled trade	0.84 ± 1.15	0.73	- 1.90 ± 2.27	0.84	5.93 ± 1.42	4.18
Trade	- 3.03 ± 0.90	3.37	- 4.43 ± 2.10	2.11	4.50 ± 1.38	3.26
Public service	-45.21 ± 0.76	59.49	- 1.58 ± 0.94	1.68	-91.67 ± 2.81	32.62
Semi-professional	0.03 ± 0.51	0.06	0.64 ± 1.22	0.52	2.21 ± 0.82	2.70
Professional	- 0.97 ± 0.34	2.85	- 2.53 ± 0.80	3.16	0.49 ± 0.38	1.29
Personal service	5.46 ± 0.98	5.57	5.70 ± 1.52	3.75	4.21 ± 1.24	3.40
Clerical	- 4.09 ± 0.70	5.84	- 8.23 ± 1.76	4.68	2.94 ± 0.94	3.13
Student	- 4.95 ± 0.24	20.62	- 8.86 ± 1.11	7.98	- 0.69 ± 0.28	2.46

Table XII-7. Occupation of Criminal Series Compared with
Civilian Groups of Similar Origin

	Criminals (This series) (4116)	Civilians (This series) (303)	General Population (10 years and over) 1930 (38,077,804)	1920 (33,064,737)
Extractive (agriculture, forestry, fishing, mining)	31.63	0.99	28.40	33.10
Laborer (not otherwise specified)	16.72	1.98		
Manufacturing and mechanical industries (factory, skilled trades)	26.49	21.12	32.10	33.00
Transportation and communication	7.31	5.28	9.40	8.70
Trade	5.22	8.25	13.40	10.80
Public service	0.66	45.87	2.20	2.20
Professional service (semi-professional and professional)	2.36	3.30	4.50	3.50
Domestic and personal service	6.78	1.32	4.70	3.60
Clerical, student	2.84	11.88	5.40	5.10

Table XII-8. Differences between Criminals and Civilians by States
with Value in Terms of the Probable Error

Education

	Total Criminal over Total Civilian Diff.	x p.e.	Mass. Criminal over Mass. Civilian Diff.	x p.e.	Tenn. Criminal over Tenn. Civilian Diff.	x p.e.
Illiterate	9.52 ± 1.16	8.21	- 0.60 ± 0.57	1.05	13.51 ± 1.94	6.96
Read, write	3.25 ± 0.78	4.17	- 1.21 ± 0.92	1.32	2.61 ± 0.89	2.93
1st-5th grade	10.18 ± 1.69	6.02	5.30 ± 1.77	2.99	- 1.59 ± 2.82	0.56
6th grade	3.89 ± 1.11	3.50	9.22 ± 1.60	5.76	- 3.16 ± 1.75	1.81
7th grade	0.49 ± 1.21	0.40	10.06 ± 2.04	4.93	-10.06 ± 1.78	5.65
8th grade	- 5.64 ± 1.55	3.64	12.59 ± 2.78	4.53	-12.47 ± 2.77	4.50
1st-2nd high	- 5.71 ± 1.39	4.11	-11.08 ± 2.73	4.06	10.69 ± 2.29	4.67
3rd-4th high	- 9.01 ± 0.86	10.48	-10.06 ± 2.21	4.55	- 2.16 ± 1.25	1.73
College	- 5.94 ± 0.73	8.00	-12.39 ± 1.67	7.42	2.66 ± 1.16	2.29
Professional	- 1.14 ± 0.19	6.00	- 1.81 ± 0.69	2.62		

Table XII-10. Morphological Observations of Total Civil Check Sample and
Massachusetts and Tennessee Civil Check Sample

	Total Check Sample		Massachusetts Check Sample		Tennessee Check Sample	
	No.	Per Cent	No.	Per Cent	No.	Per Cent
Tattooing						
None	245	93.15	113	96.58	132	90.41
Some	16	6.08	4	3.41	12	8.22
Extensive	2	0.76	0	0	2	1.37
Total	263		117		146	
Hair quantity, head						
Small	50	15.97	17	10.18	33	22.60
Medium	225	71.88	142	85.03	83	56.85
Large	38	12.14	8	4.79	30	20.55
Total	313		167		146	
Hair quantity, beard						
Small	31	9.94	8	4.79	23	15.86
Medium	209	66.99	131	78.44	78	53.79
Large	72	23.07	28	16.77	44	30.34
Total	312		167		145	
Hair quantity, body						
Small	125	40.19	60	36.36	65	44.52
Medium	142	45.66	96	58.18	46	31.51
Large	44	14.15	9	5.45	35	23.97
Total	311		165		146	
Skin color						
Red white	93	29.71	29	17.36	64	43.84
Pale white	214	68.37	134	80.24	80	54.79
Olive	6	1.92	4	2.40	2	1.37
Total	313		167		146	
Hair form						
Straight	233	75.16	117	71.34	116	79.45
Low waves	43	13.87	24	14.63	19	13.01
Deep waves	23	7.42	16	9.76	7	4.79
Curly	10	3.23	7	4.27	3	2.05
Frizzly	1	0.32	0	0	1	0.68
Total	310		164		146	
Hair color						
Black	11	3.56	3	1.81	8	5.59
Dark brown	117	37.86	65	39.16	52	36.36
Reddish brown	34	11.00	12	7.23	22	15.38
Light brown	75	24.27	46	27.71	29	20.28
Ash-blond	6	1.94	3	1.81	3	2.10
Golden	13	4.21	10	6.02	3	2.10
Red	12	3.89	4	2.41	8	5.59
Gray, white	41	13.27	23	13.86	18	12.59
Total	309		166		143	

Table XII-10 (cont'd).

	Total Check Sample		Massachusetts Check Sample		Tennessee Check Sample	
	No.	Per Cent	No.	Per Cent	No.	Per Cent
Eye color						
Dark brown	20	6.39	12	7.19	8	5.48
Light brown	13	4.15	6	3.59	7	4.79
Blue-brown	83	26.52	21	12.58	62	42.47
Gray-brown	17	5.43	6	3.59	11	7.53
Green-brown	73	23.32	48	28.74	25	17.12
Blue	90	28.75	57	34.13	33	22.60
Blue-gray	17	5.43	17	10.18	0	0
Total	313		167		146	
Sclera						
Clear	273	87.22	163	97.60	110	75.34
Speckled	32	10.22	4	2.40	28	19.18
Yellow	8	2.56	0	0	8	5.48
Total	313		167		146	
Iris						
Homogeneous	77	24.60	53	31.74	24	16.44
Rayed	100	31.95	75	44.91	25	17.12
Zoned	56	17.89	19	11.38	37	25.34
Speckled	53	16.93	12	7.19	41	28.08
Diffused	27	8.63	8	4.79	19	13.01
Total	313		167		146	
Eye folds						
Epicanthus	4	1.28	2	1.20	2	1.37
Median	39	12.50	29	17.47	10	6.85
External	20	6.41	5	3.01	15	10.27
Absent	249	79.80	130	78.31	119	81.51
Total	312		166		146	
Eyebrows thickness						
Submedium	13	4.17	7	4.19	6	4.14
Medium	230	73.72	140	83.83	90	62.07
Pronounced	69	22.12	20	11.98	49	33.79
Total	312		167		145	
Forehead height						
Submedium	13	4.15	12	7.19	1	0.68
Medium	225	71.88	138	82.63	87	59.59
Pronounced	75	23.96	17	10.18	58	39.73
Total	313		167		146	
Forehead slope						
Absent, submedium	45	14.38	14	8.38	31	21.23
Medium	215	68.69	138	82.63	77	52.74
Pronounced	53	16.93	15	8.98	38	26.03
Total	313		167		146	

Table XII-10 (cont'd).

	Total Check Sample		Massachusetts Check Sample		Tennessee Check Sample	
	No.	Per Cent	No.	Per Cent	No.	Per Cent
Nasion depression						
Submedium	18	5.77	16	9.64	2	1.37
Medium	269	86.22	141	84.94	128	87.67
Pronounced	25	8.01	9	5.42	16	10.96
Total	312		166		146	
Nasal root height						
Submedium	3	0.96	2	1.20	1	0.68
Medium	284	91.03	144	86.75	140	95.89
Pronounced	25	8.01	20	12.05	5	3.42
Total	312		166		146	
Nasal root breadth						
Submedium	6	1.92	5	3.01	1	0.68
Medium	298	95.51	153	92.17	145	99.32
Pronounced	8	2.56	8	4.82	0	0
Total	312		166		146	
Nasal bridge height						
Submedium	0	0	0	0	0	0
Medium	243	77.88	133	80.12	110	75.34
Pronounced	69	22.12	33	19.88	36	24.66
Total	312		166		146	
Nasal bridge breadth						
Submedium	2	0.64	2	1.21	0	0
Medium	285	91.64	150	90.91	135	92.47
Pronounced	24	7.72	13	7.88	11	7.53
Total	311		165		146	
Nasal profile						
Concave	57	18.51	27	16.46	30	20.83
Straight	55	17.86	38	23.17	17	11.81
Convex	92	29.87	48	29.27	44	30.56
Concavo-convex	104	33.77	51	31.10	53	36.81
Total	308		164		144	
Nasal tip thickness						
Submedium	3	0.96	3	1.80	0	0
Medium	270	86.26	142	85.03	128	87.67
Pronounced	40	12.79	22	13.17	18	12.33
Total	313		167		146	
Nasal septum inclination						
Up	174	56.49	127	77.44	47	32.64
Down	134	43.50	37	22.56	97	67.36
Total	308		164		144	

Table XII-10 (cont'd).

	Total Check Sample		Massachusetts Check Sample		Tennessee Check Sample	
	No.	Per Cent	No.	Per Cent	No.	Per Cent
Nasal septum deflection						
Right	33	11.22	23	15.54	10	6.85
Left	24	8.16	13	8.78	11	7.53
Absent	237	80.61	112	75.68	125	85.62
Total	294		148		146	
Lips integumental thickness						
Submedium	16	5.13	13	7.83	3	2.06
Medium	273	87.50	141	84.94	132	90.41
Pronounced	23	7.37	12	7.23	11	7.53
Total	312		166		146	
Lips membranous thickness						
Submedium	21	6.73	3	1.81	18	12.33
Medium	247	79.17	145	87.35	102	69.86
Upper small; lower pro-nounced	38	12.18	14	8.43	24	16.44
Pronounced	6	1.92	4	2.41	2	1.37
Total	312		166		146	
Lip seam						
Absent, submedium	26	8.36	5	3.03	21	14.38
Medium	222	71.38	137	83.03	85	58.22
Pronounced	63	20.26	23	13.94	40	27.40
Total	311		165		146	
Alveolar prognathism						
Absent	258	82.43	134	80.24	124	84.93
Submedium	19	6.07	4	2.40	15	10.27
Medium	33	10.54	27	16.17	6	4.11
Pronounced	3	0.96	2	1.20	1	0.68
Total	313		167		146	
Facial prognathism						
Absent	284	91.03	152	91.57	132	90.41
Submedium	18	5.77	10	6.02	8	5.48
Medium	9	2.88	4	2.41	5	3.42
Pronounced	1	0.32	0	0	1	0.68
Total	312		166		146	
Chin form						
Median	179	57.74	66	40.24	113	77.40
Bilateral	131	42.26	98	59.76	33	22.60
Total	310		164		146	
Malars prominence						
Submedium	8	2.56	6	3.59	2	1.37
Medium	228	72.84	151	90.42	77	52.74
Pronounced	77	24.60	10	5.99	67	45.89
Total	313		167		146	

Table XII-10 (cont'd).

	Total Check Sample		Massachusetts Check Sample		Tennessee Check Sample	
	No.	Per Cent	No.	Per Cent	No.	Per Cent
Cheeks fullness						
Submedium	13	4.15	8	4.79	5	3.42
Medium	244	77.96	149	89.22	95	65.07
Pronounced	56	17.89	10	5.99	46	31.51
Total	313		167		146	
Gonial angles						
Submedium	19	6.07	8	4.79	11	7.53
Medium	225	71.88	154	92.22	71	48.63
Pronounced	69	22.04	5	2.99	64	43.84
Total	313		167		146	
Cheeks wrinkling						
Absent	100	35.71	99	73.88	1	0.68
Slight, medium	110	39.29	32	23.88	78	53.42
Pronounced	70	25.00	3	2.24	67	45.89
Total	280		134		146	
Teeth wear						
None	2	0.68	2	1.35	0	0
Slight, medium	207	70.65	119	80.40	88	60.69
Pronounced	84	28.67	27	18.24	57	39.31
Total	293		148		145	
Teeth caries						
None	17	5.82	17	11.56	0	0
Few	140	47.95	91	61.90	49	33.79
Many	135	46.23	39	26.53	96	66.21
Total	292		147		145	
Teeth lost						
None	59	19.22	36	22.36	23	15.75
Few	137	44.63	81	50.31	56	38.36
Many	111	36.16	44	27.33	67	45.89
Total	307		161		146	
Bite						
Under	8	3.02	2	1.42	6	4.84
Edge-to-edge	49	18.49	30	21.28	19	15.32
Slight over	118	44.53	55	39.01	63	50.81
Marked over	90	33.96	54	38.30	36	29.03
Total	265		141		124	
Ear lobes						
Submedium	36	11.50	30	17.96	6	4.11
Medium	226	72.20	123	73.65	103	70.55
Pronounced	51	16.29	14	8.38	37	25.34
Total	313		167		146	

Table XII-10 (cont'd).

	Total Check Sample		Massachusetts Check Sample		Tennessee Check Sample	
	No.	Per Cent	No.	Per Cent	No.	Per Cent
Ear lobe attachment						
Attached	120	38.83	88	53.99	32	21.92
Free	189	61.17	75	46.01	114	78.08
Total	309		163		146	
Roll of helix						
Submedium	32	10.26	9	5.39	23	15.86
Medium, pronounced	280	89.74	158	94.61	122	84.14
Total	312		167		145	
Darwin's point						
Absent	215	68.69	121	72.46	94	64.38
Submedium, medium	70	22.36	42	25.15	28	19.18
Pronounced	28	8.95	4	2.40	24	16.44
Total	313		167		146	
Antihelix prominence						
Submedium	19	6.11	12	7.19	7	4.86
Medium	280	90.03	144	86.23	136	94.44
Pronounced	12	3.86	11	6.59	1	0.69
Total	311		167		144	
Ear protrusion						
Submedium	11	3.53	6	3.59	5	3.45
Medium	255	81.73	141	84.43	114	78.62
Pronounced	46	14.74	20	11.98	26	17.93
Total	312		167		145	
Temporal fullness						
Submedium	17	5.47	8	4.82	9	6.21
Medium	244	78.46	151	90.96	93	64.14
Pronounced	50	16.08	7	4.22	43	29.66
Total	311		166		145	
Lambdoid flattening						
Absent	238	77.27	101	61.58	137	95.14
Present	70	22.73	63	38.42	7	4.86
Total	308		164		144	
Asymmetry						
Right	42	14.19	20	13.07	22	15.38
Left	44	14.86	16	10.46	28	19.58
None	210	70.95	117	76.47	93	65.04
Total	296		153		143	

Table XII-10 (cont'd).

	Total Check Sample		Massachusetts Check Sample		Tennessee Check Sample	
	No.	Per Cent	No.	Per Cent	No.	Per Cent
Neck						
Medium length, breadth	247	78.91	152	91.02	95	65.07
Long and thin	29	9.27	6	3.59	23	15.75
Short and thick	37	11.82	9	5.39	28	19.18
Total	313		167		146	
Shoulder slope						
Slight	5	1.66	2	1.28	3	2.06
Medium	290	96.03	151	96.80	139	95.20
Pronounced	7	2.32	3	1.92	4	2.74
Total	302		156		146	

Table XII-11.   Number and Significance of Deviations of Total Criminal Series from Total Civilian Series in
Terms of Nature of Deviations of Criminals from Civilians in Same Two States
(Massachusetts and Tennessee)

Morphological Observations*

| | Differences of Total Criminals and Civilians** | | | | Total of State Criminals from State Civilians | |
| | Insignificant (Less than 3 p.e.) | | Significant (3 p.e. and over) | | | |
	No.	Per Cent	No.	Per Cent	No.	Per Cent
1. Insignificant and in same direction	8	5.19	5	3.25	13	8.44
2. Significant and in same direction	2	1.30	15	9.74	17	11.04
3. Insignificant and in different directions	16	10.39	3	1.95	19	12.34
4. Significant and in different directions	10	6.49	16	10.39	26	16.88
5. One insignificant, one significant in same direction	5	3.25	33	21.43	38	24.68
6. One insignificant, one significant in different directions	15	9.74	26	16.88	41	26.62
Total	56	36.36	98	63.64	154	100.00

* Exclusive of tattooing.
** Exclusive of categories occurring in the total only or in the total and one state only.

Table XII-12.   Summary of Significant Morphological Differences between
                Total Criminal Series and Total Civil Check Sample with
                Reference to State Agreement

A.   Total Comparison and State Comparisons Significant and in Same Direction

     Hair quantity, beard - Small (25.31 per cent, 13.61 p.e.)
                            Medium (-15.71 per cent, 8.02 p.e.)
     Hair form - Straight (10.19 per cent, 7.18 p.e.)
                 Low waves (-5.49 per cent, 4.95 p.e.)
     Hair color - Gray, white (-3.21 per cent, 9.12 p.e.)
     Eye color - Blue (-9.65 per cent, 6.19 p.e.)
     Iris - Homogeneous (-16.88 per cent, 15.07 p.e.)
     Cheeks fullness - Submedium (20.23 per cent, 12.41 p.e.)
     Gonial angles - Submedium (5.87 per cent, 4.66 p.e.)
     Bite - Marked over (-10.18 per cent, 5.47 p.e.)
     Roll of helix - Submedium (21.87 per cent, 12.08 p.e.)
                     Medium, pronounced (-21.96 per cent, 12.13 p.e.)
     Neck - Medium length, breadth (-11.58 per cent, 6.29 p.e.)
            Long and thin (18.54 per cent, 10.66 p.e.)

                                              Total
                                                 Number   14
                                                 Per Cent*   9.09

B.   Total and One State Comparison Significant, All Agreeing in Direction

     Hair quantity, head - Small (-4.89 per cent, 3.88 p.e.)
     Eye color - Dark brown (-3.08 per cent, 4.22 p.e.)
     Iris - Zoned (13.06 per cent, 7.26 p.e.)
            Speckled (8.78 per cent, 5.13 p.e.)
     Forehead height - Submedium (8.49 per cent, 6.63 p.e.)
     Nasion depression - Medium (-13.72 per cent, 7.88 p.e.)
                         Pronounced (10.17 per cent, 6.83 p.e.)
     Nasal root height - Medium (-9.15 per cent, 6.14 p.e.)
                         Pronounced (8.49 per cent, 5.90 p.e.)
     Nasal root breadth - Medium (-9.76 per cent, 7.23 p.e.)
     Nasal bridge breadth - Medium (-10.96 per cent, 7.16 p.e.)
     Nasal profile - Straight (-6.58 per cent, 5.18 p.e.)
                     Convex (-9.03 per cent, 5.61 p.e.)
                     Concavo-convex (11.94 per cent, 6.04 p.e.)
     Nasal tip thickness - Medium (-17.24 per cent, 9.58 p.e.)
     Nasal septum deflection - Right (12.27 per cent, 7.26 p.e.)
     Lip seam - Absent, submedium (6.12 per cent, 4.47 p.e.)
     Cheeks wrinkling - Absent (15.88 per cent, 7.64 p.e.)
                        Pronounced (-11.81 per cent, 8.20 p.e.)
     Teeth wear - Pronounced (-12.68 per cent, 8.40 p.e.)
     Teeth lost - Many (-11.36 per cent, 6.53 p.e.)
     Bite - Slight over (10.18 per cent, 4.74 p.e.)
     Darwin's point - Absent (-9.78 per cent, 5.07 p.e.)
                      Submedium, medium (5.75 per cent, 3.27 p.e.)
     Antihelix prominence - Medium (-12.59 per cent, 7.77 p.e.)
                            Pronounced (10.58 per cent, 7.84 p.e.)
     Ear protrusion - Submedium (3.96 per cent, 3.88 p.e.)
                      Medium (-24.66 per cent, 12.71 p.e.)
     Neck - Short and thick (-6.96 per cent, 7.91 p.e.)
     Shoulder slope - Medium (-19.86 per cent, 11.89 p.e.)
                      Pronounced (18.91 per cent, 11.89 p.e.)

                                              Total
                                                 Number   31
                                                 Per Cent   20.13

* Per cents calculated from total observations noted in the three cases, Massachusetts,
  Tennessee, and criminal series - 154.

Table XII-12 (cont'd).

C. Total Comparison Significant, State Comparisons Insignificant, All Agreeing in Direction

    Hair form - Deep waves (-3.44 per cent, 4.35 p.e.)
    Eye color - Gray-brown (11.95 per cent, 8.18 p.e.)
              Blue-gray (4.33 per cent, 3.77 p.e.)
    Eye fold - Epicanthus (3.12 per cent, 3.95 p.e.)
    Teeth wear - Slight, medium (12.30 per cent, 7.94 p.e.)

                                                    Total
                                                    Number   5
                                                    Per Cent   3.25

D. Total Comparison and One State Comparison Significant and in Same Direction; Other State Comparison Insignificant and in Opposite Direction from Total

    Hair quantity, beard - Large (-9.61 per cent, 7.02 p.e.)
    Skin color - Pale white (-6.25 per cent, 3.29 p.e.)
    Sclera - Yellow (-2.03 per cent, 6.34 p.e.)
    Eye fold - Absent (-6.01 per cent, 3.49 p.e.)
    Forehead slope - Absent, submedium (-6.24 per cent, 5.67 p.e.)
                Medium (-11.36 per cent, 5.86 p.e.)
                Pronounced (17.60 per cent, 9.46 p.e.)
    Nasal bridge height - Medium (-18.57 per cent, 9.52 p.e.)
                Pronounced (18.24 per cent, 9.35 p.e.)
    Nasal bridge breadth - Pronounced (8.13 per cent, 5.72 p.e.)
    Nasal tip thickness - Submedium (9.03 per cent, 7.85 p.e.)
                Pronounced (8.19 per cent, 5.18 p.e.)
    Nasal septum inclination - Up (11.65 per cent, 6.30 p.e.)
                Down (-12.08 per cent, 6.56 p.e.)
    Nasal septum deflection - Absent (-13.67 per cent, 7.23 p.e.)
    Lips integumental thickness - Submedium (6.99 per cent, 5.55 p.e.)
    Alveolar prognathism - Submedium (6.99 per cent, 5.38 p.e.)
                Medium (-6.43 per cent, 7.84 p.e.)
    Darwin's point - Pronounced (4.03 per cent, 3.08 p.e.)
    Ear protrusion - Pronounced (20.70 per cent, 11.13 p.e.)
    Temporal fullness - Submedium (12.21 per cent, 8.31 p.e.)

                                                    Total
                                                    Number   21
                                                    Per Cent   13.64

E. Total Comparison Significant, State Comparisons Insignificant, One Agreeing with Total in Direction

    Hair quantity, head - Large (6.26 per cent, 4.15 p.e.)
    Nasal bridge breadth - Submedium (2.83 per cent, 4.04 p.e.)
    Malars prominence - Submedium (3.10 per cent, 3.52 p.e.)

                                                    Total
                                                    Number   3
                                                    Per Cent   1.95

Table XII-12 (cont'd).

F. Total Comparison and One State Comparison Significant but in Opposite Directions;
    Other State Comparison Insignificant in Same Direction as Total

    Hair quantity, body - Medium (-7.11 per cent, 3.70 p.e.)
    Nasion depression - Submedium (3.45 per cent, 3.05 p.e.)
    Nasal root breadth - Submedium (2.92 per cent, 3.56 p.e.)
    Lambdoid flattening - Absent (-10.56 per cent, 5.74 p.e.)
                    Present (10.56 per cent, 5.74 p.e.)

	Total	
	Number	5
	Per Cent	3.25

G. Total Comparison and One State Comparison Significant in Same Direction;
    Other State Comparison Significant but in Opposite Direction from Total

    Hair quantity, body - Small (7.71 per cent, 3.93 p.e.)
    Hair color - Reddish brown (9.00 per cent, 5.81 p.e.)
    Sclera - Clear (7.73 per cent, 8.59 p.e.)
          Speckled (-5.70 per cent, 6.71 p.e.)
    Eyebrow thickness - Medium (-10.37 per cent, 5.49 p.e.)
                  Pronounced (10.16 per cent, 5.55 p.e.)
    Forehead height - Medium (-8.98 per cent, 4.73 p.e.)
    Lips integumental thickness - Medium (-5.26 per cent, 3.53 p.e.)
    Lips membranous thickness - Submedium (9.94 per cent, 6.90 p.e.)
                         Medium (-11.24 per cent, 6.18 p.e.)
    Cheeks fullness - Medium (-20.34 per cent, 10.70 p.e.)
    Gonial angles - Pronounced (-4.69 per cent, 3.13 p.e.)
    Teeth caries - None (-3.36 per cent, 5.17 p.e.)
             Few (23.26 per cent, 12.50 p.e.)
             Many (-19.90 per cent, 10.99 p.e.)
    Teeth lost - None (7.35 per cent, 4.20 p.e.)

	Total	
	Number	16
	Per Cent	10.39

H. Total Comparison Significant; One State Comparison Significant, Other State
    Comparison Insignificant, Both in Opposite Direction from Total

    Eye color - Blue-brown (-6.21 per cent, 3.91 p.e.)
    Temporal fullness - Medium (-5.76 per cent, 3.29 p.e.)

	Total	
	Number	2
	Per Cent	1.30

I. Total Comparison Significant, States Comparisons Significant but in Opposite
    Direction from Total

    Temporal fullness - Pronounced (-6.46 per cent, 5.43 p.e.)

	Total	
	Number	1
	Per Cent	.65

Table XII-13.   Differences between Criminals and Civilians by States
with Value in Terms of the Probable Error

Tattooing

	Total Criminal over Total Civilian		Mass. Criminal over Mass. Civilian		Tenn. Criminal over Tenn. Civilian	
	Diff.	x p.e.	Diff.	x p.e.	Diff.	x p.e.
None	- 8.24 ± 1.53	5.39	-13.79 ± 2.50	5.52	- 0.41 ± 1.93	0.21
Some	6.28 ± 1.41	4.45	11.13 ± 2.33	4.78	- 0.12 ± 1.77	0.07
Extensive	1.97 ± 0.69	2.86	2.67 ± 1.01	2.64	0.53 ± 0.85	0.62

Table XII-14.   Differences between Criminals and Civilians by States
with Value in Terms of the Probable Error

Hair Quantity

Head

	Total Criminal over Total Civilian		Mass. Criminal over Mass. Civilian		Tenn. Criminal over Tenn. Civilian	
	Diff.	x p.e.	Diff.	x p.e.	Diff.	x p.e.
Small	- 4.89 ± 1.29	3.88	- 2.17 ± 1.81	1.20	-13.36 ± 2.15	6.21
Medium	- 1.36 ± 1.79	0.76	- 0.16 ± 2.29	0.07	17.08 ± 2.98	5.73
Large	6.26 ± 1.51	4.15	2.33 ± 1.56	1.49	- 3.73 ± 2.48	1.50

Beard

	Total Criminal over Total Civilian		Mass. Criminal over Mass. Civilian		Tenn. Criminal over Tenn. Civilian	
	Diff.	x p.e.	Diff.	x p.e.	Diff.	x p.e.
Small	25.31 ± 1.86	13.61	8.86 ± 1.98	4.48	53.33 ± 3.23	16.51
Medium	-15.71 ± 1.96	8.02	-10.78 ± 2.89	3.73	-30.57 ± 3.01	10.16
Large	- 9.61 ± 1.37	7.02	1.92 ± 2.46	0.78	-22.76 ± 2.21	10.30

Body

	Total Criminal over Total Civilian		Mass. Criminal over Mass. Civilian		Tenn. Criminal over Tenn. Civilian	
	Diff.	x p.e.	Diff.	x p.e.	Diff.	x p.e.
Small	7.71 ± 1.96	3.93	-13.67 ± 2.86	4.78	20.80 ± 3.17	6.56
Medium	- 7.11 ± 1.92	3.70	12.57 ± 3.04	4.14	- 6.81 ± 2.85	2.39
Large	- 0.60 ± 1.35	0.44	1.12 ± 1.55	0.72	-13.99 ± 2.22	6.30

Table XII-15.   Differences between Criminals and Civilians by States
with Value in Terms of the Probable Error

Skin Color

	Total Criminal over Total Civilian		Mass. Criminal over Mass. Civilian		Tenn. Criminal over Tenn. Civilian	
	Diff.	x p.e.	Diff.	x p.e.	Diff.	x p.e.
Red white	1.83 ± 1.83	1.00	13.11 ± 2.81	4.56	- 7.43 ± 3.14	2.37
Pale white	- 6.25 ± 1.90	3.29	-16.34 ± 2.95	5.54	8.33 ± 3.15	2.64
Ruddy	0.71 ± 0.33	2.15	3.25 ± 0.94	3.46	0.48 ± 0.38	1.26
Olive	1.07 ± 0.65	1.65	- 0.33 ± 0.94	0.35	- 1.37 ± 0.38	3.60
Light yellow-brown	0.07 ± 0.09	0.78	0.30 ± 0.28	1.07		
Light brown	2.54 ± 0.59	4.30				
Medium red-brown	0.02 ± 0.07	0.29				

Table XII-16. Differences between Criminals and Civilians by States
with Value in Terms of the Probable Error

Hair Form

	Total Criminal over Total Civilian		Mass. Criminal over Mass. Civilian		Tenn. Criminal over Tenn. Civilian	
	Diff.	x p.e.	Diff.	x p.e.	Diff.	x p.e.
Straight	10.19 ± 1.42	7.18	9.91 ± 2.66	3.73	8.70 ± 2.25	3.87
Low waves	- 5.49 ± 1.11	4.95	- 6.59 ± 1.95	3.38	- 6.14 ± 1.90	3.41
Deep waves	- 3.44 ± 0.79	4.35	- 4.40 ± 1.52	2.72	- 1.71 ± 1.19	1.44
Curly	- 1.04 ± 0.59	1.76	1.09 ± 1.40	0.78	- 0.15 ± 0.89	0.17
Frizzly	- 0.22 ± 0.14	1.57				

Table XII-17. Differences between Criminals and Civilians by States
with Value in Terms of the Probable Error

Hair Color

	Total Criminal over Total Civilian		Mass. Criminal over Mass. Civilian		Tenn. Criminal over Tenn. Civilian	
	Diff.	x p.e.	Diff.	x p.e.	Diff.	x p.e.
Black	1.46 ± 0.85	1.72	2.38 ± 1.16	2.05	- 0.53 ± 1.45	0.37
Dark brown	- 3.34 ± 1.78	1.88	- 5.63 ± 3.06	1.84	- 8.17 ± 3.01	2.71
Reddish brown	9.00 ± 1.55	5.81	28.40 ± 2.81	10.11	- 8.87 ± 1.85	4.79
Light brown	1.49 ± 1.72	0.87	-13.34 ± 2.50	5.34	24.30 ± 3.18	7.64
Ash-blond	0.36 ± 0.59	0.61	1.18 ± 1.02	1.16	- 0.41 ± 0.86	0.48
Golden	- 0.73 ± 0.73	1.00	- 2.13 ± 1.34	1.59	1.76 ± 1.19	1.48
Red	- 0.03 ± 0.76	0.04	1.48 ± 1.16	1.28	- 1.01 ± 1.40	0.72
Gray, white	- 8.21 ± 0.90	9.12	-12.36 ± 1.47	8.41	- 7.05 ± 1.71	4.12

Table XII-18. Differences between Criminals and Civilians by States
with Value in Terms of the Probable Error

Eye Color

	Total Criminal over Total Civilian		Mass. Criminal over Mass. Civilian		Tenn. Criminal over Tenn. Civilian	
	Diff.	x p.e.	Diff.	x p.e.	Diff.	x p.e.
Dark brown	- 3.08 ± 0.73	4.22	- 1.53 ± 1.54	0.99	- 4.53 ± 0.93	4.87
Light brown	- 1.08 ± 0.71	1.52	- 2.40 ± 0.90	2.67	- 0.99 ± 1.28	0.77
Blue-brown	- 6.21 ± 1.59	3.91	5.87 ± 2.37	2.48	9.79 ± 3.24	3.02
Gray-brown	11.95 ± 1.46	8.18	3.85 ± 1.54	2.50	5.53 ± 2.08	2.66
Green-brown	3.75 ± 1.74	2.16	5.78 ± 3.00	1.93	- 1.92 ± 2.35	0.82
Blue	- 9.65 ± 1.56	6.19	-17.46 ± 2.57	6.54	- 9.77 ± 2.33	4.19
Blue-gray	4.33 ± 1.15	3.77	5.89 ± 2.23	2.64	1.90 ± 0.76	2.50

Table XII-19. Eye Color of Criminal Series Compared with Eye Color
of Civilian Groups of Similar Origin

	Authority	Number	Blue	Gray and Gray-blue	Total Light
			Per Cent	Per Cent	Per Cent
Criminals	This study	4200	19.10	9.74	28.86
Civilians	This study	313	28.75	5.43	34.18
Old Americans	Hrdlicka	1009	23.8	7.2	31.0

	Total Mixed (Blue-brown, Gray-brown, Green-brown)	Light Brown	Dark and Medium	Total Dark
	Per Cent	Per Cent	Per Cent	Per Cent
Criminals	64.76	3.07	3.31	6.38
Civilians	55.27	4.15	6.39	10.54
Old Americans	52.5	4.5	12.0	16.5

Table XII-20.   Differences between Criminals and Civilians by States
with Value in Terms of the Probable Error

Sclera

	Total Criminal over Total Civilian		Mass. Criminal over Mass. Civilian		Tenn. Criminal over Tenn. Civilian	
	Diff.	x p.e.	Diff.	x p.e.	Diff.	x p.e.
Clear	7.73 ± 0.90	8.59	-20.49 ± 2.35	8.72	16.97 ± 2.11	8.04
Speckled	- 5.70 ± 0.85	6.71	19.29 ± 2.30	8.39	-12.93 ± 1.91	6.77
Yellow	- 2.03 ± 0.32	6.34	1.20 ± 0.57	2.10	- 4.04 ± 1.00	4.04

Table XII-21.   Differences between Criminals and Civilians by States
with Value in Terms of the Probable Error

Iris

	Total Criminal over Total Civilian		Mass. Criminal over Mass. Civilian		Tenn. Criminal over Tenn. Civilian	
	Diff.	x p.e.	Diff.	x p.e.	Diff.	x p.e.
Homogeneous	-16.88 ± 1.12	15.07	-24.53 ± 2.31	10.62	- 9.33 ± 1.90	4.91
Rayed	- 4.93 ± 1.75	2.82	4.64 ± 3.20	1.45	- 8.35 ± 2.02	4.13
Zoned	13.06 ± 1.80	7.26	15.95 ± 2.65	6.02	8.55 ± 3.01	2.84
Speckled	8.78 ± 1.71	5.13	4.82 ± 1.96	2.46	10.07 ± 3.10	3.25
Diffused	- 0.03 ± 1.10	0.03	- 0.89 ± 1.28	0.70	- 0.93 ± 2.12	0.44

Table XII-22.   Differences between Criminals and Civilians by States
with Value in Terms of the Probable Error

Eye Fold

	Total Criminal over Total Civilian		Mass. Criminal over Mass. Civilian		Tenn. Criminal over Tenn. Civilian	
	Diff.	x p.e.	Diff.	x p.e.	Diff.	x p.e.
Epicanthus	3.12 ± 0.79	3.95	0.59 ± 0.80	0.74	0.76 ± 0.89	0.85
Median	0.36 ± 1.32	0.27	2.83 ± 2.53	1.12	- 0.93 ± 1.55	0.60
External	2.54 ± 1.11	2.29	16.09 ± 2.21	7.28	- 4.35 ± 1.65	2.64
Absent	- 6.01 ± 1.72	3.49	-19.50 ± 3.05	6.39	4.51 ± 2.32	1.94

Table XII-23.   Eye Folds of Criminals by Age Grouping

	Epicanthus		Median		External		Absent		Total
	No.	Per Cent	No.	Per Cent	No.	Per Cent	No.	Per Cent	No.
15-19	48	8.45	102	17.96	21	3.70	397	69.89	568
20-34	112	4.69	363	15.19	179	7.49	1736	72.64	2390
35-69	19	1.56	77	6.31	178	14.58	947	77.56	1221
Total	179	4.28	542	12.97	378	9.04	3080	73.70	4179

Table XII-24.   Differences between Criminals and Civilians by States
with Value in Terms of the Probable Error

Eyebrow Thickness

	Total Criminal over Total Civilian		Mass. Criminal over Mass. Civilian		Tenn. Criminal over Tenn. Civilian	
	Diff.	x p.e.	Diff.	x p.e.	Diff.	x p.e.
Submedium	0.20 ± 0.80	0.25	2.06 ± 1.46	1.41	- 2.96 ± 0.90	3.29
Medium	-10.37 ± 1.89	5.49	-13.89 ± 2.79	4.98	18.55 ± 2.79	6.65
Pronounced	10.16 ± 1.83	5.55	11.83 ± 2.56	4.62	-15.59 ± 2.90	5.38

Table XII-25.   Eyebrow Thickness of Criminals by Age Grouping

	Submedium		Medium		Pronounced		Total
	No.	Per Cent	No.	Per Cent	No.	Per Cent	No.
15-19	24	4.22	399	70.12	146	25.66	569
20-34	88	3.67	1519	63.37	790	32.96	2397
35-69	72	5.89	749	61.29	401	32.82	1222
Total	184	4.39	2667	63.68	1337	31.92	4188

Table XII-26.   Differences between Criminals and Civilians by States
with Value in Terms of the Probable Error

Forehead Height

	Total Crimianal over Total Civilian		Mass. Criminal over Mass. Civilian		Tenn. Criminal over Tenn. Civilian	
	Diff.	x p.e.	Diff.	x p.e.	Diff.	x p.e.
Submedium	8.49 ± 1.28	6.63	3.17 ± 1.86	1.70	4.30 ± 1.25	3.44
Medium	- 8.98 ± 1.90	4.73	-19.91 ± 2.95	6.75	20.98 ± 2.79	7.52
Pronounced	0.51 ± 1.69	0.30	16.74 ± 2.62	6.39	-25.28 ± 2.63	9.61

Table XII-27.   Differences between Criminals and Civilians by States
with Value in Terms of the Probable Error

Forehead Slope

	Total Criminal over Total Civilian		Mass. Criminal over Mass. Civilian		Tenn. Criminal over Tenn. Civilian	
	Diff.	x p.e.	Diff.	x p.e.	Diff.	x p.e.
Absent, submedium	- 6.24 ± 1.10	5.67	- 7.49 ± 1.15	6.51	2.47 ± 2.72	0.91
Medium	-11.36 ± 1.94	5.86	-13.10 ± 2.81	4.66	0.81 ± 3.22	0.25
Pronounced	17.60 ± 1.86	9.46	20.61 ± 2.68	7.69	- 3.28 ± 2.74	1.20

Table XII-28.   Differences between Criminals and Civilians by States
with Value in Terms of the Probable Error

Nasion Depression

	Total Criminal over Total Civilian		Mass. Criminal over Mass. Civilian		Tenn. Criminal over Tenn. Civilian	
	Diff.	x p.e.	Diff.	x p.e.	Diff.	x p.e.
Submedium	3.45 ± 1.13	3.05	- 5.79 ± 1.49	3.89	1.94 ± 1.07	1.81
Medium	-13.72 ± 1.74	7.88	-11.86 ± 2.69	4.41	- 3.04 ± 2.28	1.33
Pronounced	10.17 ± 1.49	6.83	17.66 ± 2.42	7.30	1.10 ± 2.08	0.53

Table XII-29.   Differences between Criminals and Civilians by States
with Value in Terms of the Probable Error

Nasal Root Height

	Total Criminal over Total Civilian		Mass. Criminal over Mass. Civilian		Tenn. Criminal over Tenn. Civilian	
	Diff.	x p.e.	Diff.	x p.e.	Diff.	x p.e.
Submedium	0.65 ± 0.49	1.33	- 0.61 ± 0.57	1.07	0.27 ± 0.60	0.45
Medium	- 9.15 ± 1.49	6.14	-19.00 ± 2.80	6.79	- 2.75 ± 1.55	1.77
Pronounced	8.49 ± 1.44	5.90	19.61 ± 2.78	7.05	2.49 ± 1.44	1.73

Table XII-30.   Nasal Root Height of Criminals by Age Grouping

	Submedium		Medium		Pronounced		Total
	No.	Per Cent	No.	Per Cent	No.	Per Cent	No.
15-19	9	1.58	442	77.54	119	20.88	570
20-34	34	1.42	1934	80.58	432	18.00	2400
35-69	24	1.96	965	78.90	234	19.13	1223
Total	67	1.60	3341	79.68	785	18.72	4193

Table XII-31.   Differences between Criminals and Civilians by States with
Value in Terms of the Probable Error

Nasal Root Breadth

	Total Criminal over Total Civilian		Mass. Criminal over Mass. Civilian		Tenn. Criminal over Tenn. Civilian	
	Diff.	x p.e.	Diff.	x p.e.	Diff.	x p.e.
Submedium	2.92 ± 0.82	3.56	- 2.42 ± 0.75	3.23	0.74 ± 0.72	1.03
Medium	- 9.76 ± 1.35	7.23	-28.56 ± 2.83	10.09	- 0.74 ± 0.72	1.03
Pronounced	6.85 ± 1.12	6.12	30.98 ± 2.80	11.06		

Table XII-32.   Nasal Root Breadth of Criminals by Age Grouping

	Submedium		Medium		Pronounced		Total
	No.	Per Cent	No.	Per Cent	No.	Per Cent	No.
15-19	29	5.10	487	85.59	53	9.31	569
20-34	119	4.96	2071	86.29	210	8.75	2400
35-69	57	4.66	1032	84.45	133	10.88	1222
Total	205	4.89	3590	85.66	396	9.45	4191

Table XII-33.   Differences between Criminals and Civilians by States
with Value in Terms of the Probable Error

Nasal Bridge Height

	Total Criminal over Total Civilian		Mass. Criminal over Mass. Civilian		Tenn. Criminal over Tenn. Civilian	
	Diff.	x p.e.	Diff.	x p.e.	Diff.	x p.e.
Submedium	0.33 ± 0.22	1.50	0.30 ± 0.28	1.07		
Medium	-18.57 ± 1.95	9.56	-33.37 ± 3.16	10.56	3.15 ± 2.69	1.17
Pronounced	18.24 ± 1.95	9.55	33.08 ± 3.16	10.47	- 3.15 ± 2.69	1.17

Table XII-34.   Nasal Bridge Height of Criminals by Age Grouping

	Submedium		Medium		Pronounced		Total
	No.	Per Cent	No.	Per Cent	No.	Per Cent	No.
15-19	3	0.53	367	64.39	200	35.09	570
20-34	8	0.33	1472	61.33	920	38.32	2400
35-69	3	0.24	651	53.23	569	46.52	1223
Total	14	0.33	2490	59.38	1689	40.28	4193

Table XII-35.   Differences between Criminals and Civilians by States
with Value in Terms of the Probable Error

Nasal Bridge Breadth

	Total Criminal over Total Civilian		Mass. Criminal over Mass. Civilian		Tenn. Criminal over Tenn. Civilian	
	Diff.	x p.e.	Diff.	x p.e.	Diff.	x p.e.
Submedium	2.83 ± 0.70	4.04	- 0.62 ± 0.57	1.09	1.42 ± 0.66	2.15
Medium	-10.96 ± 1.53	7.16	-26.41 ± 2.85	9.27	- 0.76 ± 1.77	0.43
Pronounced	8.13 ± 1.42	5.72	27.03 ± 2.83	9.55	- 0.66 ± 1.65	0.40

Table XII-36. Differences between Criminals and Civilians by States
with Value in Terms of the Probable Error

Nasal Profile

	Total Criminal over Total Civilian		Mass. Criminal over Mass. Civilian		Tenn. Criminal over Tenn. Civilian	
	Diff.	x p.e.	Diff.	x p.e.	Diff.	x p.e.
Concave	3.76 ± 1.63	2.31	10.79 ± 2.74	3.94	3.28 ± 2.75	1.19
Straight	- 6.58 ± 1.27	5.18	- 9.40 ± 2.41	3.90	- 1.17 ± 2.03	0.58
Convex	- 9.03 ± 1.61	5.61	-12.80 ± 2.60	4.92	- 8.10 ± 2.80	2.89
Concavo-convex	11.84 ± 1.96	6.04	11.42 ± 3.14	3.64	5.98 ± 3.20	1.87

Table XII-37. Differences between Criminals and Civilians by States
with Value in Terms of the Probable Error

Nasal Tip Thickness

	Total Criminal over Total Civilian		Mass. Criminal over Mass. Civilian		Tenn. Criminal over Tenn. Civilian	
	Diff.	x p.e.	Diff.	x p.e.	Diff.	x p.e.
Submedium	9.03 ± 1.15	7.85	- 0.60 ± 0.75	0.80	3.78 ± 1.07	3.53
Medium	-17.24 ± 1.80	9.58	-24.07 ± 2.96	8.13	- 1.62 ± 2.21	0.73
Pronounced	8.19 ± 1.58	5.18	24.67 ± 2.92	8.45	- 2.17 ± 2.00	1.08

Table XII-38. Differences between Criminals and Civilians by States
with Value in Terms of the Probable Error

Nasal Septum Inclination

	Total Criminal over Total Civilian		Mass. Criminal over Mass. Civilian		Tenn. Criminal over Tenn. Civilian	
	Diff.	x p.e.	Diff.	x p.e.	Diff.	x p.e.
Up	11.65 ± 1.85	6.30	- 8.44 ± 2.89	2.92	10.86 ± 3.20	3.39
Down	-12.08 ± 1.84	6.56	8.14 ± 2.89	2.82	-11.10 ± 3.20	3.47
Absent	0.43 ± 0.25	1.72	0.30 ± 0.28	1.07	0.24 ± 0.28	0.86

Table XII-39. Nasal Septum Inclination of Criminals by Age Grouping

	Up		Down		Absent		Total
	No.	Per Cent	No.	Per Cent	No.	Per Cent	No.
15-19	467	81.93	99	17.37	4	0.70	570
20-34	1729	72.40	651	27.26	8	0.34	2388
35-69	650	53.32	562	46.10	7	0.57	1219
Total	2846	68.14	1312	31.41	19	0.46	4177

Table XII-40.   Differences between Criminals and Civilians by States
with Value in Terms of the Probable Error

Nasal Septum Deflection

	Total Criminal over Total Civilian Diff.	x p.e.	Mass. Criminal over Mass. Civilian Diff.	x p.e.	Tenn. Criminal over Tenn. Civilian Diff.	x p.e.
Right	12.27 ± 1.69	7.26	17.69 ± 3.00	5.90	2.61 ± 1.84	1.42
Left	1.41 ± 1.19	1.18	- 3.69 ± 1.61	2.29	- 5.40 ± 1.19	4.54
Absent	-13.67 ± 1.89	7.23	-14.00 ± 3.16	4.43	2.80 ± 2.12	1.32

Table XII-42.   Differences between Criminals and Civilians by States
with Value in Terms of the Probable Error

Lips Integumental Thickness

	Total Criminal over Total Civilian Diff.	x p.e.	Mass. Criminal over Mass. Civilian Diff.	x p.e.	Tenn. Criminal over Tenn. Civilian Diff.	x p.e.
Submedium	6.99 ± 1.26	5.55	30.47 ± 2.87	10.62	- 0.63 ± 0.81	0.78
Medium	- 5.26 ± 1.49	3.53	-25.97 ± 3.00	8.66	6.04 ± 1.43	4.22
Pronounced	- 1.73 ± 0.92	1.88	- 4.49 ± 1.29	3.48	- 5.40 ± 1.19	4.54

Table XII-43.   Differences between Criminals and Civilians by States
with Value in Terms of the Probable Error

Lips Membranous Thickness

	Total Criminal over Total Civilian Diff.	x p.e.	Mass. Criminal over Mass. Civilian Diff.	x p.e.	Tenn. Criminal over Tenn. Civilian Diff.	x p.e.
Submedium	9.94 ± 1.44	6.90	9.87 ± 1.77	5.58	- 4.29 ± 0.61	7.03
Medium	-11.24 ± 1.82	6.18	-25.37 ± 2.92	8.69	15.01 ± 2.54	5.91
Upper submedium; lower pronounced	0.35 ± 1.30	0.27	14.32 ± 2.46	5.82	-11.00 ± 1.78	6.18
Pronounced	0.96 ± 0.65	1.48	1.18 ± 1.13	1.04	0.29 ± 0.81	0.36

Table XII-44.   Differences between Criminals and Civilians by States
with Value in Terms of the Probable Error

Lip Seam

	Total Criminal over Total Civilian Diff.	x p.e.	Mass. Criminal over Mass. Civilian Diff.	x p.e.	Tenn. Criminal over Tenn. Civilian Diff.	x p.e.
Absent, submedium	6.12 ± 1.37	4.47	5.20 ± 1.59	3.27	0.75 ± 2.31	0.32
Medium	- 5.02 ± 1.86	2.70	- 8.03 ± 2.69	2.98	5.85 ± 3.13	1.87
Pronounced	- 1.09 ± 1.55	0.70	2.83 ± 2.36	1.20	- 6.60 ± 2.70	2.44

Table XII-45.   Differences between Criminals and Civilians by States
with Value in Terms of the Probable Error

Alveolar Prognathism

	Total Criminal over Total Civilian		Mass. Criminal over Mass. Criminal		Tenn. Criminal over Tenn. Civilian	
	Diff.	x p.e.	Diff.	x p.e.	Diff.	x p.e.
Absent	- 0.03 ± 1.50	0.02	-13.38 ± 2.89	4.63	- 0.30 ± 2.35	0.13
Submedium	6.99 ± 1.30	5.38	20.97 ± 2.37	8.85	- 1.29 ± 1.88	0.69
Medium	- 6.43 ± 0.82	7.84	- 7.00 ± 2.04	3.43	1.09 ± 1.40	0.78
Pronounced	- 0.53 ± 0.27	1.96	- 0.61 ± 0.57	1.07	0.50 ± 0.66	0.76

Table XII-46.   Differences between Criminals and Civilians by States
with Value in Terms of the Probable Error

Facial Prognathism

	Total Criminal over Total Civilian		Mass. Criminal over Mass. Civilian		Tenn. Criminal over Tenn. Civilian	
	Diff.	x p.e.	Diff.	x p.e.	Diff.	x p.e.
Absent	- 2.98 ± 1.27	2.35	-18.20 ± 2.59	7.03	- 3.41 ± 2.11	1.62
Submedium	1.36 ± 1.00	1.36	5.81 ± 1.92	3.03	3.98 ± 1.80	2.21
Medium	1.47 ± 0.80	1.84	7.65 ± 1.69	4.53	- 0.35 ± 1.13	0.31
Pronounced	0.16 ± 0.27	0.59	4.73 ± 1.12	4.22	- 0.21 ± 0.46	0.46

Table XII-47.   Differences between Criminals and Civilians by States
with Value in Terms of the Probable Error

Chin Form

	Total Criminal over Total Civilian		Mass. Criminal over Mass. Civilian		Tenn. Criminal over Tenn. Civilian	
	Diff.	x p.e.	Diff.	x p.e.	Diff.	x p.e.
Median	- 0.88 ± 1.89	0.47	24.26 ± 3.19	7.60	- 6.71 ± 2.89	2.32
Bilateral	0.88 ± 1.89	0.47	- 24.26 ± 3.19	7.60	6.71 ± 2.89	2.32

Table XII-48.   Differences between Criminals and Civilians by States
with Value in Terms of the Probable Error

Malars Prominence

	Total Criminal over Total Civilian		Mass. Criminal over Mass. Civilian		Tenn. Criminal over Tenn. Civilian	
	Diff.	x p.e.	Diff.	x p.e.	Diff.	x p.e.
Submedium	3.10 ± 0.88	3.52	- 1.42 ± 1.03	1.38	1.47 ± 1.00	1.47
Medium	- 3.91 ± 1.79	2.18	-10.85 ± 2.40	4.52	23.56 ± 2.95	7.99
Pronounced	0.81 ± 1.69	0.48	12.28 ± 2.24	5.48	-25.04 ± 2.88	8.69

Table XII-49.   Differences between Criminals and Civilians by States
with Value in Terms of the Probable Error

Cheeks Fullness

	Total Criminal over Total Civilian		Mass. Criminal over Mass. Civilian		Tenn. Criminal over Tenn. Civilian	
	Diff.	x p.e.	Diff.	x p.e.	Diff.	x p.e.
Submedium	20.23 ± 1.63	12.41	13.55 ± 2.21	6.13	11.10 ± 2.08	5.34
Medium	-20.34 ± 1.90	10.70	-27.09 ± 2.90	9.34	10.88 ± 2.87	3.79
Pronounced	0.11 ± 1.49	0.07	13.54 ± 2.29	5.91	-21.99 ± 2.32	9.48

Table XII-50.   Differences between Criminals and Civilians by States
with Value in Terms of the Probable Error

Gonial Angles

	Total Criminal over Total Civilian		Mass. Criminal over Mass. Civilian		Tenn. Criminal over Tenn. Civilian	
	Diff.	x p.e.	Diff.	x p.e.	Diff.	x p.e.
Submedium	5.87 ± 1.26	4.66	10.30 ± 2.05	5.02	15.80 ± 2.55	6.20
Medium	- 1.16 ± 1.79	0.65	-15.00 ± 2.45	6.12	13.04 ± 3.19	4.09
Pronounced	- 4.69 ± 1.50	3.13	4.70 ± 1.54	3.05	-28.84 ± 2.70	10.68

Table XII-51.   Gonial Angles of Criminals by Age Grouping

	Submedium		Medium		Pronounced		Total
	No.	Per Cent	No.	Per Cent	No.	Per Cent	No.
15-19	89	15.67	418	73.59	61	10.74	568
20-34	289	12.06	1703	71.08	404	16.86	2396
35-69	132	10.80	824	67.43	266	21.77	1222
Total	510	12.18	2945	70.35	731	17.46	4186

Table XII-52.   Differences between Criminals and Civilians by States
with Value in Terms of the Probable Error

Cheeks Wrinkling

	Total Criminal over Total Civilian		Mass. Criminal over Mass. Civilian		Tenn. Criminal over Tenn. Civilian	
	Diff.	x p.e.	Diff.	x p.e.	Diff.	x p.e.
Absent	15.88 ± 2.08	7.64	5.88 ± 2.86	2.06	34.09 ± 2.83	12.05
Slight, medium	- 4.07 ± 1.99	2.04	- 5.43 ± 2.76	1.97	- 4.50 ± 3.24	1.39
Pronounced	-11.81 ± 1.44	8.20	- 0.45 ± 0.94	0.48	-29.58 ± 2.75	10.72

Table XII-53.   Cheeks Wrinkling of Criminals by Age Grouping

	Absent		Slight, Medium		Pronounced		Total
	No.	Per Cent	No.	Per Cent	No.	Per Cent	No.
15-19	485	85.69	80	14.13	1	0.18	566
20-34	1447	60.52	860	35.97	84	3.51	2391
35-69	223	18.31	534	43.84	461	37.85	1218
Total	2155	51.62	1474	35.30	546	13.08	4175

Table XII-54.   Differences between Criminals and Civilians by States
with Value in Terms of the Probable Error

Teeth Wear

	Total Criminal over Total Civilian		Mass. Criminal over Mass. Civilian		Tenn. Criminal over Tenn. Civilian	
	Diff.	x p.e.	Diff.	x p.e.	Diff.	x p.e.
None	0.38 ± 0.41	0.93	- 1.35 ± 0.44	3.07	9.38 ± 1.66	5.65
Slight, medium	12.30 ± 1.55	7.94	6.08 ± 2.43	2.50	7.95 ± 3.08	2.58
Pronounced	-12.68 ± 1.51	8.40	- 4.72 ± 2.40	1.97	-17.33 ± 2.89	6.00

Table XII-55.   Teeth Wear of Criminals by Age Grouping

	None		Slight, Medium		Pronounced		Total
	No.	Per Cent	No.	Per Cent	No.	Per Cent	No.
15-19	8	1.41	542	95.76	16	2.83	566
20-34	30	1.27	2100	89.13	226	9.59	2356
35-69	5	0.45	714	63.75	401	35.80	1120
Total	43	1.06	3356	83.03	643	15.91	4042

Table XII-56.   Differences between Criminals and Civilians by States
with Value in Terms of the Probable Error

Teeth Caries

	Total Criminal over Total Civilian		Mass. Criminal over Mass. Civilian		Tenn. Criminal over Tenn. Civilian	
	Diff.	x p.e.	Diff.	x p.e.	Diff.	x p.e.
None	- 3.36 ± 0.65	5.17	- 6.23 ± 1.75	3.56	3.70 ± 1.07	3.46
Few	23.26 ± 1.86	12.50	-13.94 ± 3.35	4.16	24.97 ± 3.25	7.65
Many	-19.90 ± 1.81	10.99	20.18 ± 3.29	6.13	-28.68 ± 3.25	8.82

Table XII-57. Differences between Criminals and Civilians by States
with Value in Terms of the Probable Error

Teeth Lost

	Total Criminal over Total Civilian		Mass. Criminal over Mass. Civilian		Tenn. Criminal over Tenn. Civilian	
	Diff.	x p.e.	Diff.	x p.e.	Diff.	x p.e.
None	7.35 ± 1.75	4.20	-11.61 ± 2.28	5.09	9.67 ± 2.72	3.56
Few	4.01 ± 2.00	2.00	12.38 ± 3.18	3.89	14.85 ± 3.24	4.58
Many	-11.36 ± 1.74	6.53	- 0.76 ± 2.87	0.26	-24.51 ± 2.89	8.48

Table XII-58.   Teeth Lost of Criminals by Age Grouping

	None		Few		Many		Total
	No.	Per Cent	No.	Per Cent	No.	Per Cent	No.
15-19	259	45.68	282	49.74	26	4.59	567
20-34	716	30.00	1278	53.54	393	16.46	2387
35-69	133	11.00	464	38.38	612	50.62	1209
Total	1108	26.58	2024	48.61	1031	24.81	41.63

Table XII-59. Differences between Criminals and Civilians by States
with Value in Terms of the Probable Error

Bite

	Total Criminal over Total Civilian		Mass. Criminal over Mass. Civilian		Tenn. Criminal over Tenn. Civilian	
	Diff.	x p.e.	Diff.	x p.e.	Diff.	x p.e.
Under	- 0.18 ± 0.72	0.25	3.34 ± 1.30	2.57	- 1.09 ± 1.38	0.79
Edge-to-edge	0.18 ± 1.68	0.11	- 8.02 ± 2.52	3.18	11.49 ± 3.00	3.83
Slight over	10.18 ± 2.15	4.74	15.41 ± 3.45	4.47	2.01 ± 3.50	0.57
Marked over	-10.18 ± 1.86	5.47	-10.75 ± 3.20	3.36	-12.41 ± 2.79	4.45

Table XII-60. Differences between Criminals and Civilians by States
with Value in Terms of the Probable Error

Ear Lobes

	Total Criminal over Total Civilian		Mass. Criminal over Mass. Civilian		Tenn. Criminal over Tenn. Civilian	
	Diff.	x p.e.	Diff.	x p.e.	Diff.	x p.e.
Submedium	- 0.42 ± 1.23	0.34	6.44 ± 2.66	2.42	- 0.80 ± 1.19	0.67
Medium	- 0.89 ± 1.78	0.50	-12.04 ± 3.04	3.96	20.21 ± 2.27	8.90
Pronounced	1.31 ± 1.50	0.87	5.61 ± 2.09	2.68	-19.42 ± 2.02	9.61

Table XII-61.   Differences between Criminals and Civilians by States
with Value in Terms of the Probable Error

Ear Lobe Attachment

	Total Criminal over Total Civilian		Mass. Criminal over Mass. Civilian		Tenn. Criminal over Tenn. Civilian	
	Diff.	x p.e.	Diff.	x p.e.	Diff.	x p.e.
Attached	- 0.03 ± 1.92	0.02	- 3.38 ± 3.22	1.05	13.39 ± 3.02	4.43
Free	- 0.01 ± 1.92	0.005	3.38 ± 3.22	1.05	-13.39 ± 3.02	4.43
Notched,divided	0.05 ± 0.07	0.71				

Table XII-62.   Differences between Criminals and Civilians by States
with Value in Terms of the Probable Error

Roll of Helix

	Total Criminal over Total Civilian		Mass. Criminal over Mass. Civilian		Tenn. Criminal over Tenn. Civilian	
	Diff.	x p.e.	Diff.	x p.e.	Diff.	x p.e.
Absent	0.10 ± 0.12	0.83			0.24 ± 0.28	0.86
Submedium	21.87 ± 1.81	12.08	23.70 ± 2.61	9.08	15.02 ± 2.89	5.20
Medium,pronounced	-21.96 ± 1.81	12.13	-23.70 ± 2.61	9.08	-15.26 ± 2.89	5.28

Table XII-63.   Roll of Helix of Criminals by Age Grouping

	Absent		Submedium		Medium,Pronounced		Total
	No.	Per Cent	No.	Per Cent	No.	Per Cent	No.
15-19	0	0	141	24.78	428	75.22	569
20-34	4	0.17	748	31.28	1639	68.55	2391
35-69	0	0	457	37.46	763	62.54	1220
Total	4	0.10	1346	32.20	2830	67.70	4180

Table XII-64.   Differences between Criminals and Civilians by States
with Value in Terms of the Probable Error

Darwin's Point

	Total Criminal over Total Civilian		Mass. Criminal over Mass. Civilian		Tenn. Criminal over Tenn. Civilian	
	Diff.	x p.e.	Diff.	x p.e.	Diff.	x p.e.
Absent	- 9.78 ± 1.93	5.07	-16.84 ± 3.12	5.40	- 7.51 ± 3.18	2.36
Submedium,medium	5.75 ± 1.76	3.27	10.41 ± 2.99	3.48	7.83 ± 2.80	2.80
Pronounced	4.03 ± 1.31	3.08	6.41 ± 1.59	4.03	- 0.33 ± 2.38	0.14

Table XII-65.   Differences between Criminals and Civilians by States
with Value in Terms of the Probable Error

Antihelix Prominence

	Total Criminal over Total Civilian		Mass. Criminal over Mass. Civilian		Tenn. Criminal over Tenn. Civilian	
	Diff.	x p.e.	Diff.	x p.e.	Diff.	x p.e.
Submedium	2.01 ± 1.07	1.88	5.84 ± 2.01	2.91	1.08 ± 1.50	0.72
Medium	-12.59 ± 1.52	7.77	-19.26 ± 2.86	6.73	- 1.09 ± 1.60	0.68
Pronounced	10.58 ± 1.35	7.84	13.41 ± 2.37	5.66	0.02 ± 0.55	0.04

Table XII-66.   Differences between Criminals and Civilians by States
with Value in Terms of the Probable Error

Ear Protrusion

	Total Criminal over Total Civilian		Mass. Criminal over Mass. Civilian		Tenn. Criminal over Tenn. Civilian	
	Diff.	x p.e.	Diff.	x p.e.	Diff.	x p.e.
Submedium	3.96 ± 1.02	3.88	6.23 ± 1.71	3.64	4.61 ± 1.63	2.83
Medium	-24.66 ± 1.94	12.71	-18.36 ± 2.87	6.40	- 0.66 ± 2.74	0.24
Pronounced	20.70 ± 1.86	11.13	12.13 ± 2.56	4.74	- 3.95 ± 2.31	1.71

Table XII-67.   Differences between Criminals and Civilians by States
with Value in Terms of the Probable Error

Temporal Fullness

	Total Criminal over Total Civilian		Mass. Criminal over Mass. Civilian		Tenn. Criminal over Tenn. Civilian	
	Diff.	x p.e.	Diff.	x p.e.	Diff.	x p.e.
Submedium	12.21 ± 1.47	8.31	- 2.71 ± 1.09	2.49	22.50 ± 2.74	8.25
Medium	- 5.76 ± 1.75	3.29	5.73 ± 1.42	4.04	0.86 ± 3.11	0.28
Pronounced	- 6.46 ± 1.19	5.43	- 3.02 ± 0.94	3.21	-23.47 ± 2.13	11.02

Table XII-68.   Differences between Criminals and Civilians by States
with Value in Terms of the Probable Error

Lambdoid Flattening

	Total Criminal over Total Civilian		Mass. Criminal over Mass. Civilian		Tenn. Criminal over Tenn. Civilian	
	Diff.	x p.e.	Diff.	x p.e.	Diff.	x p.e.
Absent	-10.56 ± 1.84	5.74	23.40 ± 2.70	8.67	- 3.95 ± 1.75	2.26
Present	10.56 ± 1.84	5.74	-23.40 ± 2.70	8.67	3.95 ± 1.75	2.26

Table XII-69.   Differences between Criminals and Civilians by States
with Value in Terms of the Probable Error

Facial Asymmetry

	Total Criminal over Total Civilian		Mass. Criminal over Mass. Civilian		Tenn. Criminal over Tenn. Civilian	
	Diff.	x p.e.	Diff.	x p.e.	Diff.	x p.e.
Right	- 0.39 ± 1.40	0.28	4.79 ± 2.44	1.96	- 5.96 ± 2.04	2.92
Left	- 1.83 ± 1.37	1.34	- 0.64 ± 1.98	0.32	1.43 ± 2.54	0.54
None	2.21 ± 1.79	1.24	- 4.15 ± 2.90	1.43	4.52 ± 3.04	1.49

Table XII-70.   Differences between Criminals and Civilians by States
with Value in Terms of the Probable Error

Neck

	Total Criminal over Total Civilian		Mass. Criminal over Mass. Civilian		Tenn. Criminal over Tenn. Civilian	
	Diff.	x p.e.	Diff.	x p.e.	Diff.	x p.e.
Medium in length, breadth	-11.58 ± 1.84	6.29	- 8.23 ± 2.25	3.66	-11.59 ± 3.21	3.61
Long and thin	18.54 ± 1.74	10.66	8.87 ± 1.88	4.72	27.65 ± 3.11	8.89
Short and thick	- 6.96 ± 0.88	7.91	- 0.54 ± 1.39	0.46	-16.06 ± 1.68	9.56

Table XII-71   Neck of Criminals by Age Grouping

	Medium in Length, Breadth		Long and Thin		Short and Thick		Total
	No.	Per Cent	No.	Per Cent	No.	Per Cent	No.
15-19	400	70.18	156	27.37	14	2.46	570
20-34	1620	67.75	662	27.69	109	4.56	2391
35-69	804	66.17	330	27.16	81	6.67	1215
Total	2824	67.52	1148	27.49	204	4.88	4176

Table XII-72.   Differences between Criminals and Civilians by States
with Value in Terms of the Probable Error

Shoulder Slope

	Total Criminal over Total Civilian		Mass. Criminal over Mass. Civilian		Tenn. Criminal over Tenn. Civilian	
	Diff.	x p.e.	Diff.	x p.e.	Diff.	x p.e.
Slight	0.94 ± 0.63	1.49	1.40 ± 0.97	1.44	0.80 ± 1.04	0.77
Medium	-19.86 ± 1.67	11.89	- 3.64 ± 1.51	2.41	-17.16 ± 2.46	6.98
Pronounced	18.91 ± 1.59	11.89	2.25 ± 1.19	1.89	16.35 ± 2.30	7.11

Table XII-73.   Shoulder Slope of Criminals by Age Grouping

	Slight		Medium		Pronounced		Total
	No.	Per Cent	No.	Per Cent	No.	Per Cent	No.
15-19	8	1.41	412	72.54	148	26.06	568
20-34	44	1.84	1879	78.59	468	19.57	2391
35-69	36	2.95	910	74.55	273	22.40	1219
Total	88	2.11	3201	76.62	889	21.28	4178

Table XII-74.   Mean Ages of Criminals by Offense Groups and of
Total Civil Check Sample by States

Criminals

First degree murder	37.80
Second degree murder	34.05
Assault	34.00
Robbery	26.75
Burglary and larceny	26.50
Forgery and fraud	30.25
Rape	36.10
Other sex	37.10
Vs. public welfare	38.25
Arson and all other	33.05
Total	30.70

Check Sample

Massachusetts	30.70
Tennessee	38.85
Total	34.50

Table XII-75. Differences between Criminals by Offense Groups and Total Civil Check Sample with Value in Terms of the Probable Error

Marital State

	Single		Married		Divorced		Widower	
	Per Cent	x p.e.	Per Cent	x p.e.	Per Cent	x p.e.	Per Cent	x p.e.
First degree murder	- 7.39 ± 2.58	2.86	- 5.55 ± 2.70	2.06	6.15 ± .94	6.54	6.79 ± 1.03	6.59
Second degree murder	- 3.75 ± 2.24	1.67	- 1.62 ± 2.34	.69	2.77 ± .63	4.40	2.60 ± .67	3.88
Assault	- 7.02 ± 4.16	1.69	- .15 ± 4.19	.04	6.25 ± .96	6.51	.92 ± .60	1.53
Robbery	18.38 ± 2.56	7.18	-23.24 ± 2.55	9.11	4.46 ± .81	5.51	.41 ± .38	1.08
Burglary and larceny	19.85 ± 2.08	9.54	-24.61 ± 2.04	12.06	3.77 ± .74	5.09	.99 ± .44	2.25
Forgery and fraud	5.60 ± 2.49	2.25	-10.90 ± 2.50	4.36	4.54 ± .82	5.54	.75 ± .44	1.70
Rape	- 8.86 ± 3.01	2.94	- 5.10 ± 3.07	1.66	8.16 ± 1.09	7.49	5.79 ± .98	5.90
Other sex	-13.35 ± 3.26	4.10	2.35 ± 3.32	.71	6.00 ± .94	6.38	5.00 ± .94	5.32
Vs. public welfare	-16.16 ± 2.74	5.90	10.88 ± 2.79	3.90	2.79 ± .64	4.36	2.46 ± .69	3.56
Arson and all other	-11.33 ± 3.78	3.00	- 7.70 ± 3.80	2.03	3.96 ± .76	5.21	- .33 ± .38	.87
Total	6.61 ± 2.00	3.30	-12.89 ± 1.99	6.48	4.23 ± .78	5.42	2.05 ± .59	3.47

Table XII-76. Differences between Criminals by Offense Groups and Total Civil Check Sample with Value in Terms of the Probable Error

Occupation

	Extractive		Laborer		Factory		Transportation	
	Per Cent	x p.e.	Per Cent	x p.e.	Per Cent	x p.e.	Per Cent	x p.e.
First degree murder	50.17 ± 2.41	20.82	9.24 ± 1.36	6.79	- 2.64 ± 1.75	1.51	2.31 ± 1.35	1.71
Second degree murder	51.31 ± 2.25	22.80	14.74 ± 1.52	9.70	- 2.71 ± 1.48	1.83	.46 ± 1.09	.42
Assault	20.81 ± 1.91	10.90	18.53 ± 2.00	9.26	- .05 ± 2.87	.02	5.22 ± 2.08	2.51
Robbery	12.46 ± 1.40	8.90	11.73 ± 1.44	8.15	15.56 ± 2.12	7.34	2.84 ± 1.30	2.18
Burglary and larceny	22.06 ± 1.67	13.21	19.36 ± 1.62	11.95	8.03 ± 1.67	4.81	2.26 ± 1.09	2.07
Forgery and fraud	24.50 ± 1.82	13.46	8.48 ± 1.28	6.62	2.60 ± 1.76	1.48	3.00 ± 1.28	2.34
Rape	35.80 ± 2.21	16.20	14.08 ± 1.63	8.64	.60 ± 2.10	.29	4.56 ± 1.59	2.87
Other sex	29.41 ± 2.09	14.07	16.94 ± 1.79	9.46	2.67 ± 2.33	1.15	- 1.23 ± 1.46	.84
Vs. public welfare	48.61 ± 2.43	20.00'	7.54 ± 1.30	5.80	1.81 ± 1.98	.91	- .12 ± 1.28	.09
Arson and all other	35.01 ± 2.30	15.22	12.02 ± 1.69	7.11	1.13 ± 2.63	.43	2.72 ± 1.84	1.48
Total	30.64 ± 1.82	16.84	14.74 ± 1.45	10.17	4.53 ± 1.50	3.02	2.03 ± 1.04	1.95

Table XII-76 (cont'd).

	Skilled Trades		Trade		Public Service		Semi-professional	
	Per Cent	x p.e.	Per Cent	x p.e.	Per Cent	x p.e.	Per Cent	x p.e.
First degree murder	- .33 ± 1.49	.22	- 3.30 ± 1.36	2.43	-45.54 ± 2.31	19.71	- 1.32 ± .55	2.40
Second degree murder	- 3.33 ± 1.12	2.97	- 3.66 ± 1.11	3.30	-44.72 ± 1.73	25.85	- 1.32 ± .41	3.22
Assault	10.98 ± 2.62	4.19	- 4.40 ± 2.23	1.97	-45.87 ± 4.12	11.13	- .91 ± 1.15	.79
Robbery	3.17 ± 1.54	2.06	- 1.14 ± 1.36	.84	-45.11 ± 2.07	21.79	- .63 ± .72	.88
Burglary and larceny	1.50 ± 1.23	1.22	- 4.39 ± .88	4.99	-45.43 ± 1.13	40.20	- .88 ± .64	1.38
Forgery and fraud	1.99 ± 1.46	1.36	- .68 ± 1.41	.48	-45.22 ± 1.95	23.19	- .31 ± .67	.46
Rape	2.63 ± 1.80	1.46	- 5.14 ± 1.50	3.43	-44.32 ± 2.81	15.77	- .10 ± .78	.13
Other sex	- .82 ± 1.84	.45	- .82 ± 1.84	.45	-44.52 ± 3.14	14.18	- .97 ± .78	1.24
Vs. public welfare	- 1.11 ± 1.54	.72	- 1.11 ± 1.54	.72	-45.47 ± 2.50	18.19	- 1.25 ± .59	2.12
Arson and all other	.75 ± 2.16	.35	- 4.25 ± 2.01	2.11	-45.87 ± 3.70	12.40	- .65 ± .94	.69
Total	.84 ± 1.15	.73	- 3.03 ± .90	3.37	-45.21 ± .76	59.49	.03 ± .51	.06

	Professional		Personal Service		Clerical		Student	
	Per Cent	x p.e.	Per Cent	x p.e.	Per Cent	x p.e.	Per Cent	x p.e.
First degree murder	- .99 ± .59	1.68	- 3.30 ± .93	3.55	- 5.94 ± 1.07	5.55	- 4.95 ± .85	5.82
Second degree murder	- 1.16 ± .44	2.64	- 1.47 ± .71	2.07	- 6.11 ± .79	7.73	- 4.95 ± .60	8.25
Assault	- 1.65 ± .97	1.70	- 6.37 ± 1.37	4.65	- 5.65 ± 2.00	2.82	- 4.95 ± 1.67	2.96
Robbery	- .63 ± .58	1.09	- 7.56 ± 1.18	6.41	- 2.11 ± 1.19	1.77	- 4.95 ± .74	6.69
Burglary and larceny	- 1.46 ± .27	5.41	- 6.79 ± 1.07	6.35	- 4.65 ± .72	6.46	- 4.95 ± .38	13.03
Forgery and fraud	- .09 ± .65	.14	- 6.52 ± 1.12	5.82	- 2.00 ± 1.37	1.46	- 4.95 ± .70	7.07
Rape	- 1.65 ± .62	2.66	- 4.38 ± 1.07	4.09	- 5.89 ± 1.30	4.53	- 4.95 ± 1.07	4.65
Other sex	- 1.73 ± 1.00	1.73	- 5.44 ± 1.17	4.65	- 2.88 ± 1.60	1.80	- 4.95 ± 1.21	4.09
Vs. public welfare	- 1.25 ± .59	2.12	- 3.04 ± .94	3.23	- 5.74 ± 1.17	4.91	- 4.95 ± .94	5.27
Arson and all other	- .35 ± 1.02	.34	- 9.68 ± 1.47	6.58	- 5.93 ± 1.77	3.35	- 4.95 ± 1.47	3.37
Total	- .97 ± .34	2.85	- 5.46 ± .98	5.57	- 4.09 ± .70	5.84	- 4.95 ± .24	20.62

Table XII-77. Differences between Criminals by Offense Groups and Total Civil Check Sample
with Value in Terms of the Probable Error

Education

	Illiterate		Read,Write		1st-5th Grade		6th Grade		7th Grade	
	Per Cent	x p.e.	Per Cent	x p.e.	Per Cent	x p.e.	Per Cent	x p.e.	Per Cent	x p.e.
First degree murder	16.57 ± 1.53	10.83	9.43 ± 1.25	7.54	16.11 ± 2.27	7.10	6.23 ± 1.48	4.21	4.42 ± 1.44	3.07
Second degree murder	19.91 ± 1.61	12.37	4.38 ± .90	4.87	19.73 ± 2.10	9.40	3.61 ± 1.23	2.94	2.34 ± 1.54	1.52
Assault	9.36 ± 1.34	6.98	.29 ± .85	.34	9.94 ± 3.18	3.13	6.12 ± 2.06	2.97	1.31 ± 2.56	.51
Robbery	3.01 ± .76	3.96	.74 ± .59	1.25	1.00 ± 1.84	.54	2.17 ± 1.23	1.76	3.44 ± 1.63	2.11
Burglary and larceny	7.68 ± 1.07	7.18	1.92 ± .66	2.91	9.96 ± 1.76	5.66	4.19 ± 1.17	3.58	2.00 ± 1.34	1.49
Forgery and fraud	3.67 ± .82	4.48	3.14 ± .82	3.83	- 1.70 ± 1.72	.99	1.98 ± 1.21	1.64	.40 ± 1.50	.27
Rape	10.58 ± 1.30	8.14	4.14 ± .97	4.27	15.04 ± 2.50	6.02	5.07 ± 1.58	3.21	- .76 ± 1.81	.42
Other sex	14.12 ± 1.49	9.48	5.75 ± 1.11	5.18	7.76 ± 2.56	3.03	- .24 ± 1.49	.16	.80 ± 2.03	.39
Vs. public welfare	6.42 ± 1.04	6.17	6.88 ± 1.12	6.14	13.18 ± 2.25	5.86	5.85 ± 1.52	3.85	1.43 ± 1.75	.82
Arson and all other	9.26 ± 1.30	7.12	3.00 ± 1.00	3.00	11.67 ± 2.96	3.94	6.75 ± 1.94	3.48	1.94 ± 2.36	.82
Total	9.52 ± 1.16	8.21	3.25 ± .78	4.17	10.18 ± 1.69	6.02	3.89 ± 1.11	3.50	.49 ± 1.21	.40

	8th Grade		1st-2nd High		3rd-4th High		College		Professional	
	Per Cent	x p.e.	Per Cent	x p.e.	Per Cent	x p.e.	Per Cent	x p.e.	Per Cent	x p.e.
First degree murder	-10.07 ± 2.14	4.71	-12.40 ± 1.86	6.67	-12.16 ± 1.42	8.56	- 8.32 ± 1.16	7.17	- .96 ± .48	2.00
Second degree murder	-12.87 ± 1.72	7.48	-11.46 ± 1.53	7.49	-12.49 ± 1.03	12.13	- 7.19 ± .94	7.65	- .03 ± .94	.03
Assault	- .93 ± 3.64	.26	- 8.62 ± 3.25	2.65	- 9.71 ± 2.69	3.61	- 7.72 ± 2.21	3.49	- 1.04 ± .42	2.48
Robbery	- 1.84 ± 2.21	.83	.81 ± 2.03	.40	- 6.16 ± 1.51	4.08	- 5.81 ± 1.17	4.97		
Burglary and larceny	- 5.54 ± 1.67	3.32	- 3.80 ± 1.55	2.45	- 8.46 ± 1.02	8.29	- 6.72 ± .75	8.96	- .85 ± .43	1.98
Forgery and fraud	- 3.78 ± 2.06	1.83	.60 ± 1.99	.30	- 6.56 ± 1.46	4.49	- 3.10 ± 1.54	2.01		
Rape	- 1.72 ± 2.62	.66	-12.73 ± 2.19	5.81	- 9.38 ± 1.83	5.13				
Other sex	- 5.22 ± 2.83	1.84	- 9.80 ± 2.44	4.02	- 8.76 ± 2.07	4.23	- 3.60 ± 1.80	2.00		
Vs. public welfare	- 7.03 ± 2.33	3.02	- 8.50 ± 2.08	4.09	- 9.15 ± 1.65	5.54	- 7.79 ± 1.29	6.04	.70 ± .92	.76
Arson and all other	- 7.85 ± 3.24	2.42	- 7.00 ± 2.97	2.36	-10.49 ± 2.40	4.37	- 7.98 ± 1.97	4.05	-1.14 ± .19	6.00
Total	- 5.64 ± 1.55	3.64	- 5.71 ± 1.39	4.11	- 9.01 ± .86	10.48	- 5.84 ± .73	8.00		

Table XII-78.   Differences between Criminals by Offense Groups and Total Civil Check Sample
with Value in Terms of the Probable Error

Hair Quantity, Head

	Small		Medium		Large	
	Per Cent	x p.e.	Per Cent	x p.e.	Per Cent	x p.e.
First degree murder	1.71 ± 2.00	0.86	- 6.29 ± 2.48	2.54	- 0.42 ± 1.88	0.22
Second degree murder	- 3.81 ± 1.60	2.38	- 2.84 ± 2.12	1.34	6.66 ± 1.72	3.87
Assault	- 8.47 ± 2.95	2.87	10.62 ± 3.70	2.87	- 2.14 ± 2.71	0.79
Robbery	- 8.71 ± 1.56	5.58	- 0.21 ± 2.25	0.09	8.93 ± 1.89	4.72
Burglary and larceny	- 8.33 ± 1.17	7.12	0.99 ± 1.83	0.54	7.35 ± 1.58	4.65
Forgery and fraud	- 1.41 ± 1.74	0.81	- 3.57 ± 2.23	1.60	4.99 ± 1.74	2.87
Rape	- 0.74 ± 2.21	0.34	3.75 ± 2.68	1.40	- 3.00 ± 1.90	1.58
Other sex	- 1.40 ± 2.41	0.58	- 3.01 ± 3.02	1.00	4.42 ± 2.27	1.95
Vs. public welfare	1.54 ± 2.09	0.74	-12.35 ± 2.65	4.66	10.82 ± 2.10	5.15
Arson and all other	- 4.32 ± 1.63	2.65	1.91 ± 3.21	0.60	2.42 ± 1.50	1.61
Total	- 4.89 ± 1.29	3.88	- 1.36 ± 1.79	0.76	6.26 ± 1.51	4.15

Table XII-79.   Differences between Criminals by Offense Groups and Total Civil Check Sample
with Value in Terms of the Probable Error

Hair Quantity, Beard

	Small		Medium		Large	
	Per Cent	x p.e.	Per Cent	x p.e.	Per Cent	x p.e.
First degree murder	13.53 ± 2.01	6.73	- 5.58 ± 2.59	2.15	- 7.96 ± 2.12	3.76
Second degree murder	28.25 ± 2.11	13.39	-13.59 ± 2.31	5.88	-14.66 ± 1.59	9.22
Assault	23.81 ± 3.00	7.94	- 9.49 ± 4.03	2.36	-14.32 ± 3.39	4.22
Robbery	20.40 ± 2.08	9.81	-13.83 ± 2.48	5.58	- 6.57 ± 2.00	3.28
Burglary and larceny	30.12 ± 1.98	15.21	-20.47 ± 2.08	9.84	- 9.65 ± 1.48	6.52
Forgery and freud	17.47 ± 1.98	8.82	-11.10 ± 2.40	4.62	- 6.37 ± 1.94	3.28
Rape	29.03 ± 2.51	11.57	-17.76 ± 3.01	5.90	-11.28 ± 2.40	4.70
Other sex	22.51 ± 2.52	8.93	-14.01 ± 3.24	4.32	- 8.50 ± 2.68	3.17
Vs. public welfare	24.69 ± 2.30	10.74	-16.41 ± 2.77	5.92	- 8.28 ± 2.23	3.71
Arson and all other	23.07 ± 2.79	8.27	-14.56 ± 3.69	3.95	- 8.51 ± 3.12	2.73
Total	25.31 ± 1.86	13.61	-15.71 ± 1.96	8.02	- 9.61 ± 1.37	7.02

Table XII-80. Differences between Criminals by Offense Groups and Total Civil Check Sample with Value in Terms of the Probable Error

Hair Quantity, Body

	Small		Medium		Large	
	Per Cent	x p.e.	Per Cent	x p.e.	Per Cent	x p.e.
First degree murder	- 8.70 ± 2.59	3.36	4.66 ± 2.70	1.73	4.03 ± 1.98	2.04
Second degree murder	0.72 ± 2.29	0.31	- 1.34 ± 2.32	0.58	0.62 ± 1.65	0.38
Assault	4.81 ± 4.16	1.16	6.91 ± 4.20	1.64	2.10 ± 2.98	0.70
Robbery	9.81 ± 2.52	3.89	- 8.77 ± 2.48	3.54	- 1.04 ± 1.73	0.60
Burglary and larceny	16.84 ± 2.07	8.14	-12.81 ± 1.98	6.47	- 4.03 ± 1.29	3.12
Forgery and fraud	9.16 ± 2.45	3.74	-11.39 ± 2.39	4.77	2.23 ± 1.77	1.26
Rape	- 2.88 ± 3.00	0.96	0.45 ± 3.06	0.15	2.43 ± 2.20	1.10
Other sex	3.10 ± 3.26	0.95	0.70 ± 3.32	0.21	2.41 ± 2.38	1.01
Vs. public welfare	- 3.47 ± 2.76	1.26	0.43 ± 2.83	0.15	3.04 ± 2.06	1.48
Arson and all other	7.38 ± 3.78	1.95	- 6.82 ± 3.80	1.80	- 0.56 ± 2.66	0.21
Total	7.71 ± 1.96	3.93	- 7.11 ± 1.92	3.70	- 0.60 ± 1.35	0.44

Table XII-81. Differences between Criminals by Offense Groups and Total Civil Check Sample with Value in Terms of the Probable Error

Skin Color

	Red White		Pale White		Ruddy		Olive	
	Per Cent	x p.e.	Per Cent	x p.e.	Per Cent	x p.e.	Per Cent	x p.e.
First degree murder	4.91 ± 2.52	1.95	- 4.91 ± 2.56	1.92	.32 ± .22	1.45	1.28 ± .43	2.98
Second degree murder	5.18 ± 2.20	2.35	-12.31 ± 2.29	5.38	1.25 ± .42	2.98	3.56 ± .71	5.01
Assault	- 7.21 ± 3.80	1.90	.38 ± 3.93	.10	.48 ± .26	1.85	3.75 ± .74	5.07
Robbery	- 1.62 ± 2.29	.71	- 1.54 ± 2.37	.65	.87 ± .35	2.49	2.91 ± .64	4.55
Burglary and larceny	1.12 ± 1.92	.58	6.58 ± 2.01	3.27	1.07 ± .39	2.74	3.23 ± .67	4.82
Forgery and fraud	1.13 ± 2.26	.50	- 4.13 ± 2.33	1.77	1.02 ± .38	2.68	3.21 ± .67	4.79
Rape	- 3.82 ± 2.76	1.38	- .16 ± 2.85	.06	1.32 ± .44	3.00	3.55 ± .72	4.93
Other sex	- 1.23 ± 3.04	.40	- 3.47 ± 3.14	1.10	.39 ± .24	1.62	1.99 ± .53	3.76
Vs. public welfare	11.15 ± 2.70	4.13	-12.34 ± 2.74	4.50	2.91 ± .65	4.48	1.95 ± .53	3.68
Arson and all other	- .58 ± 3.49	.16	3.32 ± 3.59	.92				
Total	1.83 ± 1.83	1.00	- 6.25 ± 1.90	3.29	.71 ± .33	2.15	1.07 ± .65	1.65

Table XII-81 (cont'd).

	Light Yellow-brown		Light Brown		Medium Red-brown	
	Per Cent	x p.e.	Per Cent	x p.e.	Per Cent	x p.e.
First degree murder			- 1.28 ± .61	2.10		
Second degree murder			3.25 ± .92	3.53		
Assault			1.83 ± 1.25	1.45		
Robbery		.67	- .47 ± .64	.73	.24 ± .18	1.33
Burglary and larceny	.06 ± .09		1.31 ± .71	1.84		
Forgery and fraud			- 1.28 ± .52	2.45		
Rape			- .90 ± .76	1.18		
Other sex			1.39 ± 1.02	1.36		
Vs. public welfare	.39 ± .24	1.62	- 1.53 ± .63	2.43		
Arson and all other	.97 ± .38	2.55	- .95 ± .98	.97		
Total	.07 ± .09	.78	2.54 ± .59		.02 ± .07	.29

Table XII-82.   Differences between Criminals by Offense Groups and Total Civil Check Sample with Value in Terms of the Probable Error

Hair Form

	Straight		Low Waves		Deep Waves		Curly		Frizzly	
	Per Cent	x p.e.	Per Cent	x p.e.	Per Cent	x p.e.	Per Cent	x p.e.	Per Cent	x p.e.
First degree murder	14.55 ± 2.05	7.10	- 8.73 ± 1.58	5.52	- 4.20 ± 1.21	3.47	- 1.30 ± .85	1.53	- .32 ± .22	1.45
Second degree murder	9.77 ± 1.81	5.40	- 4.96 ± 1.44	3.44	- 3.04 ± 1.05	2.90	- 1.45 ± .70	2.07	- .32 ± .15	2.13
Assault	6.09 ± 3.59	1.70	- 3.87 ± 2.85	1.36	- 2.42 ± 2.14	1.13	- .52 ± .34	.34	- .32 ± .42	.76
Robbery	5.33 ± 2.08	2.55	- 2.16 ± 1.68	1.29	- 1.81 ± 1.23	1.47	- 1.03 ± .81	1.27	- .32 ± .18	1.78
Burglary and larceny	10.65 ± 1.52	7.01	- 6.22 ± 1.17	5.32	- 3.19 ± .88	3.62	- .99 ± .63	1.57	- .26 ± .14	1.85
Forgery and fraud	9.21 ± 1.94	4.75	- 4.23 ± 1.56	2.71	- 4.21 ± 1.05	3.97	- .87 ± .80	1.09	- .11 ± .30	.37
Rape	14.18 ± 2.95	4.79	- 6.76 ± 1.94	3.48	- 6.40 ± 1.33	4.81	- .69 ± 1.04	.66	- .32 ± .27	1.18
Other sex	18.17 ± 2.63	6.91	-11.87 ± 2.01	5.90	- 3.42 ± 1.63	2.10	- 2.56 ± 1.02	2.51	- .32 ± .31	1.03
Vs. public welfare	8.43 ± 2.25	3.75	- 3.71 ± 1.86	2.00	- 3.90 ± 1.31	2.98	- .89 ± .94	.95	- .07 ± .34	.21
Arson and all other	4.45 ± 3.26	1.36	- .28 ± 2.64	.11	- 4.51 ± 1.86	2.42	- .65 ± 1.38	.47	- .32 ± .38	.84
Total	10.19 ± 1.42	7.18	- 5.49 ± 1.11	4.95	- 3.44 ± .79	4.35	- 1.04 ± .59	1.75	- .22 ± .14	1.57

Table XII-85. Differences between Criminals by Offense Groups and Total Civil Check Sample with Value in Terms of the Probable Error

Hair Color

	Black		Dark Brown		Red Brown		Light Brown	
	Per Cent	x p.e.	Per Cent	x p.e.	Per Cent	x p.e.	Per Cent	x p.e.
First degree murder	1.58 ± 1.10	1.44	- 2.17 ± 2.60	.84	8.29 ± 1.94	4.27	- .48 ± 2.31	.21
Second degree murder	3.02 ± 1.07	2.82	- .48 ± 2.27	.21	6.39 ± 1.68	3.80	1.14 ± 2.02	.56
Assault	-1.03 ± 1.52	.68	1.38 ± 4.12	.33	10.52 ± 2.87	3.67	4.02 ± 3.59	1.12
Robbery	-.07 ± .94	.07	- 5.17 ± 2.41	2.14	11.52 ± 1.92	6.00	6.24 ± 2.26	2.75
Burglary and larceny	.40 ± .90	.50	- 3.19 ± 1.98	1.61	9.73 ± 1.63	5.97	1.92 ± 1.82	1.05
Forgery and fraud	2.53 ± 1.09	2.32	- 5.25 ± 2.35	2.22	7.25 ± 1.79	4.06	2.59 ± 2.17	1.24
Rape	1.57 ± 1.23	1.28	- 1.96 ± 2.97	.66	7.97 ± 2.14	3.72	- 1.71 ± 2.61	.66
Other sex	3.05 ± 1.39	2.20	- .77 ± 3.24	.24	11.52 ± 2.37	4.86	- 6.39 ± 2.77	2.31
Vs. public welfare	2.79 ± 1.23	2.27	- 9.69 ± 2.70	3.59	9.63 ± 2.06	4.68	1.92 ± 2.48	.77
Arson and all other	5.18 ± 1.65	3.14	- 4.85 ± 3.69	1.31	8.42 ± 2.58	3.25	- .97 ± 3.27	.30
Total	1.46 ± .85	1.72	- 3.34 ± 1.78	1.88	9.00 ± 1.55	5.81	1.49 ± 1.72	.87

	Ash-blond		Golden		Red		Grey, White	
	Per Cent	x p.e.	Per Cent	x p.e.	Per Cent	x p.e.	Per Cent	x p.e.
First degree murder	- .65 ± .67	.97	- 1.96 ± .95	2.06	- 2.28 ± .88	2.59	- 2.34 ± 1.76	1.33
Second degree murder	- .46 ± .59	.78	- 2.41 ± .74	3.26	- .94 ± .83	1.13	- 6.22 ± 1.35	4.61
Assault	- .67 ± 1.13	.59	- 2.94 ± 1.58	1.86	3.70 ± 1.78	2.08	- 6.94 ± 2.74	2.53
Robbery	- .49 ± .54	.77	- 1.79 ± .88	2.03	.95 ± 1.04	.91	-11.33 ± 1.27	8.92
Burglary and larceny	1.20 ± .70	1.71	- .63 ± .88	.72	.44 ± .84	.52	-11.13 ± .81	13.74
Forgery and fraud	1.54 ± .82	1.88	.57 ± 1.03	.55	.24 ± .98	.24	- 9.57 ± 1.31	7.30
Rape	- .40 ± .81	.49	- 1.13 ± 1.17	.97	- 1.84 ± 1.08	1.70	- 2.55 ± 2.02	1.26
Other sex	- 1.94 ± .76	2.55	- 3.55 ± 1.15	3.09	.08 ± 1.30	.06	- 2.01 ± 2.21	.91
Vs. public welfare	- 1.54 ± .63	2.44	- 1.04 ± 1.09	.95	1.27 ± 1.18	1.08	+ 3.35 ± 1.84	1.82
Arson and all other	3.88 ± 1.29	3.01	- 2.27 ± 1.44	1.58	2.92 ± 1.34	2.18	- 6.47 ± 2.46	2.63
Total	.56 ± .59	.61	- .73 ± .73	1.00	- .03 ± .76	.04	- 8.21 ± .90	9.12

Table XII-84. Differences between Criminals by Offense Groups and Total Civil Check Sample with Value in Terms of the Probable Error

Eye Color

	Dark Brown		Light Brown		Blue-brown		Gray-brown	
	Per Cent	x p.e.	Per Cent	x p.e.	Per Cent	x p.e.	Per Cent	x p.e.
First degree murder	- 3.82 ± 1.12	3.41	- 1.90 ± .95	2.00	- 3.05 ± 2.33	1.31	14.51 ± 1.79	8.11
Second degree murder	- 3.31 ± .94	3.52	- 2.04 ± .77	2.65	- 2.86 ± 2.01	1.42	12.24 ± 1.50	7.65
Assault	- 1.11 ± 2.10	.53	- .40 ± 1.67	.24	- 4.02 ± 3.69	1.09	2.07 ± 1.98	1.04
Robbery	- 3.23 ± 1.05	3.08	1.19 ± 1.08	1.10	- 5.99 ± 2.13	2.76	12.53 ± 1.67	7.50
Burglary and larceny	- 2.91 ± .81	3.59	- .17 ± .82	.21	- 6.77 ± 1.69	4.01	11.09 ± 1.47	7.54
Forgery and fraud	- 3.61 ± .99	3.65	- 2.22 ± .91	2.74	- 7.68 ± 2.03	3.78	12.99 ± 1.66	7.82
Rape	- 1.73 ± 1.44	1.20	- 1.56 ± 1.15	1.36	- 8.39 ± 2.52	3.20	4.93 ± 1.50	3.08
Other sex	- 2.39 ± 1.54	1.55	- 3.48 ± 1.15	3.03	- 7.85 ± 2.87	2.74	8.57 ± 1.84	4.56
Vs. public welfare	- 4.06 ± 1.19	3.41	- 2.98 ± .94	3.17	-10.18 ± 2.35	4.33	22.20 ± 2.05	10.83
Arson and all other	- 3.48 ± 1.75	1.99	- 2.21 ± 1.43	1.54	- 7.10 ± 3.30	2.15	9.13 ± 2.04	4.48
Total	- 3.08 ± .73	4.22	- 1.08 ± .71	1.52	- 6.21 ± 1.59	3.91	11.95 ± 1.46	8.18

	Green-brown		Blue		Blue-gray	
	Per Cent	x p.e.	Per Cent	x p.e.	Per Cent	x p.e.
First degree murder	1.43 ± 2.31	.52	- 8.49 ± 2.32	3.66	1.32 ± 1.29	1.02
Second degree murder	4.07 ± 2.05	1.98	- 9.53 ± 1.95	4.94	1.54 ± 1.15	1.34
Assault	6.68 ± 3.64	1.84	-11.25 ± 3.73	3.02	5.82 ± 2.10	2.77
Robbery	5.32 ± 2.23	2.39	-13.22 ± 2.06	6.42	3.31 ± 1.32	2.51
Burglary and larceny	4.32 ± 1.85	2.34	-10.49 ± 1.56	6.32	4.94 ± 1.22	4.05
Forgery and fraud	2.80 ± 2.12	1.32	- 6.27 ± 2.12	2.96	3.99 ± 1.32	3.02
Rape	3.62 ± 2.56	1.36	-10.52 ± 2.56	3.99	13.74 ± 1.91	7.19
Other sex	4.02 ± 2.89	1.39	- 6.08 ± 2.97	2.05	7.24 ± 1.79	4.04
Vs. public welfare	- 2.31 ± 2.37	.98	- 7.74 ± 2.47	3.13	5.08 ± 1.52	3.34
Arson and all other	10.66 ± 3.36	3.17	- 8.36 ± 3.39	2.47	1.37 ± 1.79	.76
Total	3.75 ± 1.74	2.16	- 9.65 ± 1.56	6.19	4.33 ± 1.15	3.77

Table XII-85. Differences between Criminals by Offense Groups and Total Civil Check Sample with Value in Terms of the Probable Error

Sclera

	Clear		Speckled		Yellow	
	Per Cent	x p.e.	Per Cent	x p.e.	Per Cent	x p.e.
First degree murder	6.03 ± 1.50	3.77	- 4.11 ± 1.48	2.78	- 1.92 ± 0.67	2.87
Second degree murder	8.34 ± 1.21	6.89	- 6.50 ± 1.10	6.00	- 1.74 ± 0.55	3.16
Assault	6.53 ± 2.69	2.43	- 3.97 ± 2.47	1.61	- 2.56 ± 1.19	2.15
Robbery	8.34 ± 1.71	4.98	- 6.02 ± 1.58	3.81	- 2.32 ± 0.70	3.31
Burglary and larceny	7.93 ± 1.00	7.93	- 5.81 ± .94	6.18	- 2.12 ± 0.37	5.73
Forgery and fraud	9.29 ± 1.29	7.20	- 7.60 ± 1.15	6.51	- 1.69 ± 0.61	2.77
Rape	4.49 ± 1.94	2.31	- 1.93 ± 1.81	1.07	- 2.56 ± 0.77	3.32
Other sex	10.06 ± 1.98	5.08	- 7.50 ± 1.81	4.14	- 2.56 ± 0.88	2.91
Vs. public welfare	5.98 ± 1.73	3.46	- 4.22 ± 1.58	2.67	- 3.36 ± 0.76	4.42
Arson and all other	4.94 ± 2.46	2.01	- 3.36 ± 2.25	1.49	- 1.58 ± 1.12	1.41
Total	7.73 ± 0.90	8.59	- 5.70 ± 0.85	6.71	- 2.03 ± 0.32	6.34

Table XII-86. Differences between Criminals by Offense Groups and Total Civil Check Sample with Value in Terms of the Probable Error

Iris

	Homogeneous		Rayed		Zoned	
	Per Cent	x p.e.	Per Cent	x p.e.	Per Cent	x p.e.
First degree murder	-16.54 ± 2.00	8.27	- 5.82 ± 2.45	2.38	11.14 ± 2.29	4.96
Second degree murder	-17.17 ± 1.58	10.87	- 3.03 ± 2.14	1.42	6.67 ± 1.94	3.44
Assault	-10.85 ± 3.52	3.08	5.70 ± 3.90	1.46	12.11 ± 3.41	3.55
Robbery	-16.78 ± 1.81	9.27	- 7.50 ± 1.40	5.36	15.36 ± 2.23	6.89
Burglary and larceny	-17.13 ± 1.26	13.60	- 5.19 ± 1.86	2.79	13.29 ± 1.05	12.66
Forgery and fraud	-16.89 ± 1.73	9.76	- 6.90 ± 2.85	3.14	18.08 ± 2.22	8.14
Rape	-17.93 ± 2.35	7.63	- 2.21 ± 2.85	0.78	19.03 ± 2.67	7.13
Other sex	-14.00 ± 2.67	5.24	- 1.49 ± 3.10	0.48	8.60 ± 2.70	3.18
Vs. public welfare	-18.35 ± 2.10	8.74	-13.83 ± 2.61	1.47	16.49 ± 2.47	6.58
Arson and all other	-15.96 ± 3.10	5.12	- 2.82 ± 3.55	0.79	9.29 ± 3.08	3.02
Total	-16.88 ± 1.12	15.07	- 4.93 ± 1.75	2.82	13.06 ± 1.80	7.26

Table XII-86 (cont'd).

	Speckled		Diffused	
	Per Cent	x p.e.	Per Cent	x p.e.
First degree murder	11.46 ± 2.26	5.07	- 0.24 ± 1.50	0.16
Second degree murder	14.09 ± 2.06	6.84	- 0.55 ± 1.29	0.43
Assault	4.32 ± 3.23	1.34	0.12 ± 2.37	0.05
Robbery	5.81 ± 2.02	2.98	3.11 ± 1.54	2.02
Burglary and larceny	9.14 ± 1.79	5.11	- 0.10 ± 1.16	0.09
Forgery and fraud	4.91 ± 1.96	2.50	0.79 ± 1.41	0.56
Rape	2.04 ± 2.35	0.87	- 0.94 ± 1.69	0.56
Other sex	10.88 ± 2.59	4.04	- 3.99 ± 1.74	2.29
Vs. public welfare	7.29 ± 2.28	3.20	- 1.60 ± 1.53	1.05
Arson and all other	9.28 ± 3.02	3.07	0.11 ± 2.15	0.05
Total	8.78 ± 1.71	5.13	- 0.03 ± 1.10	0.03

Table XII-87. Differences between Criminals by Offense Groups and Total Civil Check Sample with Value in Terms of the Probable Error

Eye Folds

	Epicanthus		Median		External		Absent	
	Per Cent	x p.e.	Per Cent	x p.e.	Per Cent	x p.e.	Per Cent	x p.e.
First degree murder	5.13 ± 1.04	4.93	- 3.21 ± 1.58	1.91	3.21 ± 1.46	2.20	- 5.12 ± 2.26	2.26
Second degree murder	3.43 ± 0.86	3.99	- 1.30 ± 1.50	0.87	3.33 ± 1.31	2.54	- 5.45 ± 1.99	2.74
Assault	3.72 ± 1.19	3.13	1.25 ± 2.82	0.44	6.09 ± 2.24	2.72	-11.05 ± 3.53	3.13
Robbery	2.61 ± 0.83	3.14	5.75 ± 1.94	3.12	1.13 ± 1.30	0.87	- 9.48 ± 2.80	4.31
Burglary and larceny	2.95 ± 0.79	3.73	1.58 ± 4.51	0.37	2.05 ± 1.13	1.81	6.57 ± 1.92	3.56
Forgery and fraud	1.72 ± 0.74	2.32	- 0.08 ± 1.52	0.05	0.44 ± 1.23	0.36	- 2.07 ± 2.02	1.02
Rape	1.77 ± 0.85	2.08	- 2.86 ± 1.95	1.47	4.76 ± 1.59	2.92	- 3.56 ± 1.65	2.22
Other sex	4.72 ± 1.11	4.25	- 2.50 ± 2.16	1.16	3.59 ± 1.77	2.03	- 5.80 ± 2.77	2.09
Vs. public welfare	2.24 ± 0.85	2.54	2.73 ± 1.79	1.52	5.31 ± 1.61	3.30	- 4.90 ± 2.37	2.02
Arson and all other	8.43 ± 1.38	6.11	1.92 ± 2.50	0.73	3.30 ± 1.98	1.67	- 9.90 ± 3.20	3.09
Total	3.12 ± 0.79	3.95	0.36 ± 1.32	0.27	2.54 ± 1.11	2.29	- 6.01 ± 1.72	3.49

Table XII-88. Differences between Criminals by Offense Groups and Total Civil Check Sample with Value in Terms of the Probable Error

Eyebrow Thickness

	Submedium		Medium		Pronounced	
	Per Cent	x p.e.	Per Cent	x p.e.	Per Cent	x p.e.
First degree murder	.96 ± 1.13	.85	-13.14 ± 2.54	5.17	12.17 ± 2.43	5.01
Second degree murder	.85 ± .99	.86	- 9.32 ± 2.18	4.28	8.46 ± 2.09	4.05
Assault	.83 ± 1.72	.48	-15.22 ± 3.86	4.20	15.38 ± 3.67	4.19
Robbery	- 1.26 ± .92	1.37	- 9.07 ± 2.34	3.88	10.34 ± 2.27	4.56
Burglary and larceny	- .38 ± .80	.48	- 9.74 ± 1.98	4.92	10.12 ± 1.92	5.27
Forgery and fraud	.34 ± 1.00	.34	- 8.70 ± 2.28	3.82	8.35 ± 2.18	3.83
Rape	.40 ± 1.24	.32	- 7.22 ± 2.79	2.59	6.81 ± 2.55	2.57
Other sex	1.13 ± 1.59	.81	-14.78 ± 3.09	4.78	13.64 ± 2.95	4.62
Vs. public welfare	2.06 ± 1.24	1.66	-13.80 ± 2.66	5.19	11.73 ± 2.54	4.52
Arson and all other	1.55 ± 1.60	1.03	-17.41 ± 3.53	4.93	15.74 ± 3.36	4.68
Total	.20 ± .80	.25	-10.37 ± 1.99	5.49	10.16 ± 1.93	5.55

Table XII-89. Differences between Criminals by Offense Groups and Total Civil Check Sample with Value in Terms of the Probable Error

Forehead Height

	Submedium		Medium		Pronounced	
	Per Cent	x p.e.	Per Cent	x p.e.	Per Cent	x p.e.
First degree murder	8.67 ± 1.50	5.78	-11.62 ± 2.56	4.54	2.96 ± 2.35	1.26
Second degree murder	11.36 ± 1.50	7.57	-10.01 ± 2.23	4.49	- 1.34 ± 1.97	.68
Assault	8.35 ± 1.98	4.22	-14.38 ± 3.91	3.68	6.04 ± 3.67	1.65
Robbery	6.48 ± 1.36	4.76	- 4.25 ± 2.26	1.88	- 2.22 ± 2.11	1.05
Burglary and larceny	9.02 ± 1.34	6.73	- 8.15 ± 1.98	4.12	- .85 ± 1.75	.49
Forgery and fraud	5.06 ± 1.27	3.98	- 7.85 ± 2.24	3.50	2.81 ± 2.14	1.31
Rape	7.02 ± 1.55	4.53	-13.50 ± 2.90	4.66	6.50 ± 2.71	2.40
Other sex	8.43 ± 1.69	4.99	-10.29 ± 3.10	3.32	1.87 ± 2.87	.65
Vs. public welfare	8.69 ± 1.55	5.61	-11.18 ± 2.68	4.17	2.50 ± 2.46	1.02
Arson and all other	8.47 ± 1.86	4.55	-11.68 ± 3.54	3.30	3.22 ± 3.30	.98
Total	8.49 ± 1.28	6.63	- 8.98 ± 1.90	4.73	.51 ± 1.69	.30

Table XII-90.   Differences between Criminals by Offense Groups and Total Civil Check Sample with Value in Terms of the Probable Error

Forehead Slope

	Absent, Submedium		Medium		Pronounced	
	Per Cent	x p.e.	Per Cent	x p.e.	Per Cent	x p.e.
First degree murder	- 4.77 ± 1.75	2.73	-17.09 ± 2.58	6.62	21.85 ± 2.42	9.03
Second degree murder	- 5.17 ± 1.46	3.54	-18.77 ± 2.32	8.09	23.94 ± 2.19	10.93
Assault	- 9.38 ± 2.79	3.36	- 8.69 ± 3.98	2.18	18.07 ± 3.42	5.28
Robbery	- 6.89 ± 1.54	4.47	- 8.55 ± 2.43	3.52	15.45 ± 2.21	6.99
Burglary and larceny	- 5.69 ± 1.23	4.63	- 9.60 ± 2.03	4.73	15.29 ± 1.90	8.05
Forgery and fraud	- 8.17 ± 1.44	5.67	- 7.45 ± 2.35	3.17	15.62 ± 2.16	7.23
Rape	- 5.24 ± 2.02	2.59	-12.34 ± 2.95	4.18	17.59 ± 2.62	6.71
Other sex	- 5.77 ± 2.21	2.61	-15.71 ± 3.21	4.89	21.48 ± 2.85	7.54
Vs. public welfare	-10.10 ± 1.69	5.98	- 6.82 ± 2.70	2.53	16.92 ± 2.45	6.91
Arson and all other	- 4.67 ± 2.60	1.80	-11.41 ± 3.63	3.14	16.08 ± 3.12	5.15
Total	- 6.24 ± 1.10	5.67	-11.36 ± 1.94	5.86	17.60 ± 1.86	9.46

Table XII-91.   Differences between Criminals by Offense Groups and Total Civil Check Sample with Value in Terms of the Probable Error

Nasion Depression

	Submedium		Medium		Pronounced	
	Per Cent	x p.e.	Per Cent	x p.e.	Per Cent	x p.e.
First degree murder	2.56 ± 1.38	1.86	-18.27 ± 2.27	8.05	15.39 ± 1.96	7.85
Second degree murder	5.56 ± 1.37	4.06	-21.82 ± 2.10	10.39	16.10 ± 1.82	8.85
Assault	10.48 ± 2.28	4.60	-21.22 ± 3.26	6.51	10.74 ± 2.56	4.20
Robbery	0.77 ± 1.22	0.63	- 9.22 ± 1.98	4.66	8.21 ± 1.68	4.89
Burglary and larceny	5.34 ± 1.26	4.24	-14.15 ± 1.81	7.82	8.75 ± 1.50	5.83
Forgery and fraud	0.65 ± 0.19	3.42	- 6.13 ± 1.86	3.30	5.48 ± 1.55	3.54
Rape	- 0.67 ± 1.40	0.48	-10.20 ± 2.35	4.34	10.87 ± 2.01	5.41
Other sex	5.56 ± 1.77	3.14	-16.89 ± 2.64	6.40	11.32 ± 2.16	5.24
Vs. public welfare	- 2.27 ± 1.21	1.88	- 4.51 ± 2.08	2.17	6.78 ± 1.78	3.81
Arson and all other	1.03 ± 1.82	0.57	-16.32 ± 2.93	5.57	15.29 ± 2.48	6.16
Total	3.45 ± 1.13	3.05	-13.72 ± 1.74	7.88	10.17 ± 1.49	6.83

Table XII-92. Differences between Criminals by Offense Groups and Total Civil Check Sample
with Value in Terms of the Probable Error

Nasal Root Height

	Submedium		Medium		Pronounced	
	Per Cent	x p.e.	Per Cent	x p.e.	Per Cent	x p.e.
First degree murder	1.92 ± .74	2.59	-13.79 ± 1.97	7.00	11.86 ± 1.87	6.34
Second degree murder	.98 ± .59	1.66	-12.68 ± 1.77	7.16	11.70 ± 1.71	6.84
Assault	4.04 ± 1.12	3.61	-28.53 ± 3.00	9.51	24.49 ± 2.85	8.59
Robbery	.49 ± .55	.89	- 8.42 ± 1.74	4.84	7.93 ± 1.67	4.75
Burglary and larceny	.47 ± .48	.98	- 6.10 ± 1.44	4.24	5.64 ± 1.38	4.09
Forgery and fraud	- .10 ± .46	.22	- 6.66 ± 1.65	4.04	6.77 ± 1.60	4.23
Rape	1.58 ± .76	2.08	-10.83 ± 2.08	5.21	9.25 ± 1.97	4.70
Other sex	.36 ± .69	.52	-16.86 ± 2.35	7.17	16.49 ± 2.27	7.26
Vs. public welfare	- .18 ± .53	.34	- 6.59 ± 1.85	3.56	6.78 ± 1.78	3.81
Arson and all other	.01 ± .75	.01	-12.39 ± 2.50	4.96	12.38 ± 2.40	5.16
Total	.65 ± .49	1.33	- 9.15 ± 1.49	6.14	8.49 ± 1.44	5.90

Table XII-93. Differences between Criminals by Offense Groups and Total Civil Check Sample
with Value in Terms of the Probable Error

Nasal Root Breadth

	Submedium		Medium		Pronounced	
	Per Cent	x p.e.	Per Cent	x p.e.	Per Cent	x p.e.
First degree murder	.96 ± .82	1.17	- 6.09 ± 1.42	4.29	5.13 ± 1.19	4.31
Second degree murder	1.64 ± .80	2.05	- 7.16 ± 1.36	5.26	5.53 ± 1.13	4.89
Assault	8.08 ± 1.56	5.18	-20.01 ± 2.31	8.66	9.94 ± 1.77	5.62
Robbery	3.39 ± .97	3.50	- 9.76 ± 1.52	6.42	6.38 ± 1.22	5.23
Burglary and larceny	3.04 ± .86	3.54	-10.58 ± 1.42	7.45	7.55 ± 1.19	6.34
Forgery and fraud	3.86 ± .99	3.90	- 8.57 ± 1.45	5.91	4.72 ± 1.11	4.25
Rape	7.77 ± 1.33	5.84	-19.49 ± 2.00	9.74	11.72 ± 1.58	7.42
Other sex	2.05 ± 1.06	1.93	-12.73 ± 1.88	6.77	10.68 ± 1.59	6.72
Vs. public welfare	- .36 ± .75	.48	- 3.29 ± 1.35	2.44	3.67 ± 1.14	3.22
Arson and all other	4.88 ± 1.34	3.64	-15.90 ± 2.13	7.46	11.03 ± 1.72	6.41
Total	2.92 ± .82	3.56	- 9.76 ± 1.35	7.23	6.85 ± 1.12	6.12

Table XII-94. Differences between Criminals by Offense Groups and Total Civil Check Sample with Value in Terms of the Probable Error

Nasal Bridge Height

	Submedium		Medium		Pronounced	
	Per Cent	x p.e.	Per Cent	x p.e.	Per Cent	x p.e.
First degree murder	.96 ± .38	2.53	-26.92 ± 2.58	10.43	25.96 ± 2.58	10.06
Second degree murder	.16 ± .15	1.07	-25.21 ± 2.28	11.06	25.05 ± 2.28	10.99
Assault			-26.63 ± 3.78	7.04	26.63 ± 3.78	7.04
Robbery	.48 ± .26	1.85	-13.39 ± 2.31	5.80	12.90 ± 2.30	5.61
Burglary and larceny	.25 ± .19	1.32	-29.74 ± 2.08	14.30	29.49 ± 2.08	14.18
Forgery and fraud	.21 ± .16	1.31	-10.43 ± 2.21	4.72	10.21 ± 2.21	4.62
Rape	.51 ± .27	1.89	-19.50 ± 2.81	6.94	19.00 ± 2.80	6.79
Other sex			-26.22 ± 3.08	8.51	26.22 ± 3.08	8.51
Vs. public welfare	.39 ± .24	1.62	-16.40 ± 2.59	6.33	16.01 ± 2.59	6.18
Arson and all other			-16.71 ± 3.37	4.96	16.71 ± 3.37	4.96
Total	.33 ± .22	1.50	-18.57 ± 1.95	9.52	18.24 ± 1.95	9.35

Table XII-95. Differences between Criminals by Offense Groups and Total Civil Check Sample with Value in Terms of the Probable Error

Nasal Bridge Breadth

	Submedium		Medium		Pronounced	
	Per Cent	x p.e.	Per Cent	x p.e.	Per Cent	x p.e.
First degree murder	0 ± 0.43	0	- 8.04 ± 1.77	4.54	8.04 ± 1.74	4.62
Second degree murder	1.14 ± 0.55	2.07	- 7.31 ± 1.58	4.63	6.17 ± 1.51	4.09
Assault	1.86 ± 0.85	2.19	-14.14 ± 2.82	5.01	12.28 ± 2.56	4.80
Robbery	3.49 ± 0.81	4.31	-13.48 ± 1.60	7.25	10.00 ± 1.72	5.81
Burglary and larceny	3.52 ± 0.78	4.51	-11.55 ± 1.60	7.22	8.04 ± 1.46	5.51
Forgery and fraud	3.86 ± 0.83	4.65	-10.27 ± 1.73	5.94	6.41 ± 1.57	4.08
Rape	6.50 ± 1.07	6.08	-19.70 ± 2.25	8.76	13.20 ± 2.06	6.41
Other sex	2.01 ± 0.76	2.64	- 9.52 ± 2.12	4.49	7.51 ± 2.02	3.72
Vs. public welfare	0.53 ± 0.53	1.00	- 7.37 ± 1.86	3.96	7.84 ± 1.79	4.38
Arson and all other	4.21 ± 0.98	4.30	-14.94 ± 2.50	5.98	10.73 ± 2.34	4.58
Total	2.83 ± 0.70	4.04	-10.96 ± 1.53	7.16	8.13 ± 1.42	5.72

Table XII-96.   Differences between Criminals by Offense Groups and Total Civil Check Sample
with Value in Terms of the Probable Error

Nasal Profile

	Concave		Straight		Convex		Concavo-convex	
	Per Cent	x p.e.	Per Cent	x p.e.	Per Cent	x p.e.	Per Cent	x p.e.
First degree murder	- 2.75 ± 2.03	1.36	- 7.25 ± 1.88	3.86	- 7.04 ± 2.37	2.97	17.03 ± 2.66	6.40
Second degree murder	- .55 ± 1.80	.31	- 7.34 ± 1.57	4.68	- 7.38 ± 2.02	3.65	15.26 ± 2.25	6.78
Assault	2.74 ± 3.32	.82	-11.61 ± 3.06	3.79	- 3.62 ± 3.84	.94	12.48 ± 4.07	3.07
Robbery	6.19 ± 2.09	2.96	- 6.48 ± 1.76	3.68	-10.26 ± 2.16	4.75	10.54 ± 2.47	4.27
Burglary and larceny	7.68 ± 1.80	4.27	- 6.69 ± 1.36	4.92	-12.05 ± 1.65	7.30	11.05 ± 2.06	5.36
Forgery and fraud	3.81 ± 2.00	1.90	- 6.06 ± 1.71	3.54	- 8.84 ± 2.11	4.19	11.08 ± 2.41	4.60
Rape	2.18 ± 2.34	.93	- 5.62 ± 2.23	2.52	- 1.81 ± 2.79	.65	9.60 ± 2.97	3.23
Other sex	6.16 ± 2.71	2.27	- 7.86 ± 2.42	3.25	- 5.20 ± 3.02	1.72	6.90 ± 3.22	2.14
Vs. public welfare	- 2.43 ± 2.15	1.13	- 2.57 ± 2.12	1.21	- 5.95 ± 2.53	2.35	10.93 ± 2.76	3.96
Arson and all other	1.88 ± 3.00	.63	- 7.18 ± 2.81	2.56	- 4.63 ± 3.47	1.33	9.92 ± 3.68	2.70
Total	3.76 ± 1.63	2.31	- 6.58 ± 1.27	5.18	- 9.03 ± 1.61	5.61	11.84 ± 1.96	6.04

Table XII-97.   Differences between Criminals by Offense Groups and Total Civil Check Sample
with Value in Terms of the Probable Error

Nasal Tip Thickness

	Submedium		Medium		Pronounced	
	Per Cent	x p.e.	Per Cent	x p.e.	Per Cent	x p.e.
First degree murder	11.58 ± 1.35	8.58	-17.77 ± 2.26	7.86	6.18 ± 1.97	3.14
Second degree murder	13.28 ± 0.82	16.20	-21.37 ± 2.10	10.18	8.08 ± 1.80	4.49
Assault	5.29 ± 1.19	4.44	-15.01 ± 3.16	4.75	9.71 ± 3.00	3.24
Robbery	8.51 ± 1.18	7.21	-17.57 ± 2.14	8.21	9.05 ± 1.94	4.66
Burglary and larceny	8.60 ± 1.14	7.54	-15.93 ± 1.85	8.61	7.32 ± 0.46	15.91
Forgery and fraud	8.48 ± 1.17	7.25	-15.02 ± 2.06	7.29	6.52 ± 1.84	3.54
Rape	11.28 ± 1.38	8.17	-21.97 ± 2.56	8.58	10.68 ± 2.31	4.62
Other sex	9.71 ± 1.33	7.30	-15.59 ± 2.62	5.95	5.88 ± 2.37	2.48
Vs. public welfare	0.60 ± 0.63	0.95	-15.17 ± 2.30	6.60	7.55 ± 2.25	3.36
Arson and all other	5.84 ± 1.17	4.99	-20.24 ± 2.99	6.77	14.39 ± 2.83	5.08
Total	9.03 ± 1.15	7.85	-17.24 ± 1.80	9.58	8.19 ± 1.58	5.18

Table XII-98. Differences between Criminals by Offense Groups and Total Civil Check Sample with Value in Terms of the Probable Error

Nasal Septum Inclination

	Up		Down		Absent	
	Per Cent	x p.e.	Per Cent	x p.e.	Per Cent	x p.e.
First degree murder	5.37 ± 2.65	2.03	- 6.96 ± 2.64	2.54	1.60 ± .48	3.33
Second degree murder	6.17 ± 2.28	2.71	- 6.81 ± 2.28	2.99	.65 ± .31	2.10
Assault	11.01 ± 4.16	2.65	-11.00 ± 4.16	2.64		
Robbery	14.21 ± 2.42	5.87	-14.21 ± 2.42	5.87		
Burglary and larceny	16.95 ± 1.89	8.97	-17.13 ± 1.89	9.05	.19 ± .16	1.19
Forgery and fraud	11.40 ± 2.39	4.77	-11.60 ± 2.39	4.85	.22 ± .16	1.38
Rape	6.78 ± 3.02	2.24	- 7.79 ± 3.02	2.58	1.02 ± .38	2.68
Other sex	10.18 ± 3.29	3.09	-10.83 ± 3.28	3.30	.67 ± .31	2.16
Vs. public welfare	2.10 ± 2.81	.75	- 2.48 ± 2.81	.88	.39 ± .24	1.62
Arson and all other	7.59 ± 3.78	2.01	- 8.55 ± 3.77	2.27	.97 ± .38	2.55
Total	11.65 ± 1.85	6.30	-12.08 ± 1.84	6.55	.43 ± .25	1.72

Table XII-99. Differences between Criminals by Offense Groups and Total Civil Check Sample with Value in Terms of the Probable Error

Nasal Septum Deflection

	Right		Left		Absent	
	Per Cent	x p.e.	Per Cent	x p.e.	Per Cent	x p.e.
First degree murder	10.91 ± 2.05	5.32	4.34 ± 1.67	2.60	-15.23 ± 2.44	6.24
Second degree murder	16.77 ± 2.00	8.38	3.65 ± 1.47	2.48	-20.42 ± 2.25	9.08
Assault	11.28 ± 2.92	3.86	6.84 ± 2.51	2.72	-18.11 ± 3.60	5.03
Robbery	12.93 ± 2.01	6.43	- .67 ± 1.38	.48	-12.25 ± 2.27	5.40
Burglary and larceny	12.02 ± 1.75	6.87	.29 ± 1.19	.24	-12.31 ± 1.95	6.31
Forgery and fraud	6.16 ± 1.79	3.44	- .01 ± 1.37	.01	- 6.15 ± 2.11	2.92
Rape	20.06 ± 2.45	8.19	2.61 ± 1.79	1.45	-22.66 ± 2.80	8.09
Other sex	22.56 ± 2.66	8.48	4.00 ± 2.00	2.00	-26.56 ± 3.07	8.65
Vs. public welfare	3.18 ± 1.92	1.65	.40 ± 1.59	.25	- 3.57 ± 2.35	1.52
Arson and all other	12.31 ± 2.72	4.53	3.60 ± 2.22	1.62	-15.90 ± 3.28	4.85
Total	12.27 ± 1.69	7.25	1.41 ± 1.19	1.18	-13.67 ± 1.89	7.23

Table XII-100. Differences between Criminals by Offense Groups and Total Civil Check Sample with Value in Terms of the Probable Error

Lips Integumental Thickness

	Submedium		Medium		Pronounced	
	Per Cent	x p.e.	Per Cent	x p.e.	Per Cent	x p.e.
First degree murder	7.69 ± 1.54	4.99	- 8.01 ± 2.00	4.00	0.32 ± 1.42	0.22
Second degree murder	10.57 ± 1.52	6.95	- 9.99 ± 1.84	5.43	- 0.57 ± 1.19	0.48
Assault	11.12 ± 2.21	5.03	-13.75 ± 3.04	4.52	2.63 ± 2.28	1.15
Robbery	6.73 ± 1.44	4.57	- 5.66 ± 1.84	3.08	- 1.07 ± 1.27	0.84
Burglary and larceny	7.38 ± 1.32	5.59	- 4.18 ± 1.52	2.75	- 3.20 ± 0.88	3.54
Forgery and fraud	2.17 ± 0.74	2.93	- 0.16 ± 1.63	0.10	- 2.01 ± 1.18	1.70
Rape	9.16 ± 1.73	5.30	-10.97 ± 2.23	4.92	1.81 ± 1.57	1.08
Other sex	4.87 ± 1.68	2.90	- 0.83 ± 2.24	0.37	- 4.03 ± 1.60	2.52
Vs. public welfare	- 0.05 ± 1.25	0.04	- 2.34 ± 1.81	1.29	- 2.29 ± 1.38	1.66
Arson and all other	13.32 ± 2.13	6.25	-14.58 ± 2.82	5.21	1.37 ± 2.04	0.67
Total	6.99 ± 1.25	5.55	- 5.26 ± 1.49	3.53	- 1.73 ± 0.92	1.93

Table XII-101. Differences between Criminals by Offense Groups and Total Civil Check Sample with Value in Terms of the Probable Error

Lips Membranous Thickness

	Submedium		Medium		Upper small; lower pronounced		Pronounced	
	Per Cent	x p.e.	Per Cent	x p.e.	Per Cent	x p.e.	Per Cent	x p.e.
First degree murder	13.78 ± 1.85	7.45	-11.54 ± 2.39	4.83	- 3.21 ± 1.66	1.93	.96 ± .82	1.17
Second degree murder	13.30 ± 1.69	7.87	-10.03 ± 2.08	4.82	- 3.94 ± 1.38	2.86	.66 ± .71	.93
Assault	18.27 ± 2.58	7.08	-24.17 ± 3.70	6.53	4.07 ± 2.85	1.43	1.83 ± 1.26	1.45
Robbery	5.35 ± 1.50	3.57	- 6.71 ± 2.17	3.09	- .83 ± 1.62	.51	2.19 ± .98	2.49
Burglary and larceny	7.64 ± 1.40	5.45	-10.45 ± 1.90	5.50	1.81 ± 1.43	1.27	1.00 ± .68	1.47
Forgery and fraud	4.52 ± 1.43	3.23	- 8.93 ± 2.16	4.13	3.51 ± 1.71	2.05	.86 ± .75	1.13
Rape	17.25 ± 2.09	8.25	-21.52 ± 2.79	7.71	3.64 ± 2.10	1.73	.63 ± .89	.71
Other sex	22.41 ± 2.32	9.66	-22.88 ± 3.01	7.60	- .92 ± 2.16	.43	1.39 ± 1.02	1.36
Vs. public welfare	12.02 ± 1.86	6.46	-12.37 ± 2.51	4.93	1.10 ± 1.89	.58	.75 ± .71	1.06
Arson and all other	12.69 ± 2.29	5.54	- 9.27 ± 3.23	2.87	- 4.41 ± 2.40	1.84	.99 ± 1.11	.89
Total	9.94 ± 1.44	6.90	-11.24 ± 1.82	6.18	.35 ± 1.30	.27	.96 ± .55	1.48

Table XII-102. Differences between Criminals by Offense Groups and Total Civil Check Sample with Value in Terms of the Probable Error

Lip Seam

	Absent		Medium		Pronounced	
	Per Cent	x p.e.	Per Cent	x p.e.	Per Cent	x p.e.
First degree murder	8.95 ± 1.81	4.94	- 7.60 ± 2.52	3.02	- 1.35 ± 2.14	0.63
Second degree murder	8.36 ± 1.62	5.16	-10.34 ± 2.24	4.52	1.98 ± 1.92	1.03
Assault	1.64 ± 2.38	0.69	- 3.88 ± 3.85	1.01	2.24 ± 3.43	0.65
Robbery	1.08 ± 1.44	0.75	0.77 ± 2.27	0.34	1.86 ± 1.99	0.94
Burglary and larceny	3.90 ± 1.34	2.91	- 3.48 ± 1.93	1.80	- 0.41 ± 1.66	0.25
Forgery and fraud	7.06 ± 1.63	4.33	- 2.64 ± 2.25	1.17	- 4.41 ± 1.87	2.36
Rape	12.56 ± 2.08	6.04	- 7.09 ± 2.85	2.49	- 5.46 ± 2.37	2.30
Other sex	8.31 ± 1.50	5.54	-10.71 ± 3.13	3.42	2.41 ± 2.74	0.88
Vs. public welfare	15.08 ± 2.04	7.39	-11.22 ± 2.68	4.19	- 3.85 ± 2.21	1.74
Arson and all other	0.38 ± 2.13	0.18	3.38 ± 3.82	0.88	- 3.76 ± 2.83	1.33
Total	6.12 ± 1.37	4.47	- 5.02 ± 1.86	2.70	- 1.09 ± 1.55	0.70

Table XII-103. Differences between Criminals by Offense Groups and Total Civil Check Sample with Value in Terms of the Probable Error

Alveolar Prognathism

	Absent		Submedium		Medium		Pronounced	
	Per Cent	x p.e.	Per Cent	x p.e.	Per Cent	x p.e.	Per Cent	x p.e.
First degree murder	- 1.34 ± 2.08	0.64	10.28 ± 1.70	6.05	- 7.98 ± 1.34	5.96	- 0.96 ± 0.38	2.53
Second degree murder	1.55 ± 1.74	0.89	6.07 ± 1.41	4.30	- 6.82 ± 1.11	6.14	- 0.80 ± 0.31	2.58
Assault	1.32 ± 3.20	0.41	2.58 ± 2.10	1.28	- 4.29 ± 2.50	3.43	0.29 ± 0.85	0.34
Robbery	- 0.55 ± 1.94	0.28	7.18 ± 1.56	4.60	- 6.92 ± 1.26	5.49	- 0.72 ± 0.38	1.90
Burglary and larceny	0.50 ± 1.56	0.32	5.72 ± 1.30	4.40	- 5.76 ± 0.96	6.00	- 0.46 ± .32	1.44
Forgery and fraud	- 0.63 ± 1.99	0.33	7.85 ± 1.52	5.16	- 6.90 ± 1.20	5.75	- 0.32 ± 0.42	0.76
Rape	- 0.20 ± 2.34	0.08	6.62 ± 1.73	3.83	- 6.99 ± 1.55	4.24	0.56 ± 0.66	0.95
Other sex	5.61 ± 2.64	2.12	11.15 ± 1.98	5.63	- 4.58 ± 1.92	2.38	- 0.96 ± 0.53	1.81
Vs. public welfare	2.01 ± 3.28	0.61	5.21 ± 1.58	3.30	- 6.26 ± 1.52	4.12	- 0.96 ± 0.41	2.34
Arson and all other	- 6.70 ± 3.02	2.22	16.26 ± 2.31	7.04	- 9.57 ± 2.10	4.56	0.01 ± 0.75	0.02
Total	- 0.03 ± 1.50	0.02	6.99 ± 1.30	5.38	- 6.43 ± 0.82	7.84	- 0.53 ± 0.27	1.96

Table XII-104. Differences between Criminals by Offense Groups and Total Civil Check Sample with Value in Terms of the Probable Error

Facial Prognathism

	Absent		Submedium		Medium		Pronounced	
	Per Cent	x p.e.	Per Cent	x p.e.	Per Cent	x p.e.	Per Cent	x p.e.
First degree murder	- 1.00 ± 1.58	0.63	1.30 ± 1.32	0.98	0.01 ± 0.90	0.01	- 0.32 ± 0.22	1.45
Second degree murder	- 1.87 ± 1.42	1.32	1.35 ± 1.17	1.15	0.58 ± 0.84	0.91	- 0.16 ± 0.22	0.73
Assault	- 2.28 ± 2.47	0.92	1.73 ± 2.02	0.86	- 0.38 ± 1.40	0.27	0.93 ± 0.60	1.55
Robbery	- 3.35 ± 1.57	2.13	2.93 ± 1.32	2.22	0.26 ± 0.86	0.30	0.16 ± 0.32	0.50
Burglary and larceny	- 3.75 ± 1.36	2.76	1.43 ± 1.06	1.35	2.02 ± 0.87	2.32	0.30 ± 0.32	0.94
Forgery and fraud	- 1.74 ± 1.47	1.18	0.23 ± 1.16	0.20	1.52 ± 0.94	1.72	- 0.11 ± 0.25	0.44
Rape	- 2.20 ± 1.83	1.20	- 1.20 ± 1.38	0.87	3.21 ± 1.22	2.63	0.19 ± 0.38	0.50
Other sex	- 4.94 ± 2.05	2.41	0.85 ± 1.59	0.54	3.74 ± 1.32	2.83	0.34 ± 0.44	0.77
Vs. public welfare	- 3.09 ± 1.73	1.79	0.85 ± 1.36	0.52	1.40 ± 1.05	1.33	0.85 ± 0.47	1.81
Arson and all other	- 6.56 ± 2.36	2.78	5.88 ± 1.98	2.97	1.00 ± 1.34	0.75	- 0.32 ± 0.38	0.08
Total	- 2.98 ± 1.27	2.35	1.36 ± 1.00	1.36	1.47 ± 0.80	1.84	0.16 ± 0.27	0.59

Table XII-105. Differences between Criminals by Offense Groups and Total Civil Check Sample with Value in Terms of the Probable Error

Chin Form

	Median		Bilateral	
	Per Cent	x p.e.	Per Cent	x p.e.
First degree murder	6.89 ± 2.63	2.62	- 6.89 ± 2.53	2.52
Second degree murder	- 6.52 ± 2.33	2.80	6.52 ± 2.33	2.80
Assault	- 1.49 ± 4.18	0.36	1.49 ± 4.18	0.36
Robbery	- 1.08 ± 2.50	0.43	1.08 ± 2.50	0.43
Burglary and larceny	0.52 ± 2.05	0.25	- 0.52 ± 2.05	0.25
Forgery and fraud	- 2.71 ± 2.44	1.11	2.71 ± 2.44	1.11
Rape	5.02 ± 3.02	1.66	- 5.02 ± 3.02	1.56
Other sex	- 0.41 ± 3.32	0.12	0.41 ± 3.32	0.12
Vs. public welfare	- 6.96 ± 2.85	2.44	6.96 ± 2.85	2.44
Arson and all other	0.51 ± 3.78	0.14	- 0.51 ± 3.78	0.14
Total	- 0.88 ± 1.89	0.47	0.88 ± 1.89	0.47

Table XII-106. Differences between Criminals by Offense Groups and Total Civil Check Sample with Value in Terms of the Probable Error

Malars Prominence

	Submedium		Medium		Pronounced	
	Per Cent	x p.e.	Per Cent	x p.e.	Per Cent	x p.e.
First degree murder	7.09 ± 1.29	5.50	- 5.64 ± 2.47	2.28	- 1.45 ± 2.30	0.63
Second degree murder	5.87 ± 1.15	5.10	- 5.90 ± 2.16	2.73	0.04 ± 2.01	0.02
Assault	3.69 ± 1.51	2.44	- 0.34 ± 3.76	0.09	- 3.35 ± 3.60	0.93
Robbery	1.55 ± 0.92	1.68	- 1.93 ± 2.27	0.81	0.28 ± 2.18	0.13
Burglary and larceny	2.72 ± 0.89	3.06	- 1.37 ± 1.88	0.73	- 1.36 ± 1.76	0.77
Forgery and fraud	1.73 ± 0.92	1.88	- 4.39 ± 2.27	1.93	2.55 ± 2.18	1.22
Rape	0.99 ± 1.04	0.95	- 2.79 ± 2.76	1.01	1.90 ± 2.57	0.67
Other sex	2.74 ± 1.22	2.25	1.33 ± 2.95	0.45	- 4.07 ± 2.82	1.44
Vs. public welfare	0.58 ± 0.94	0.62	-20.68 ± 2.74	7.55	20.10 ± 2.71	7.42
Arson and all other	3.26 ± 1.38	2.36	- 3.91 ± 3.45	1.13	0.54 ± 3.30	0.19
Total	3.10 ± 0.88	3.52	- 3.91 ± 1.79	2.18	0.81 ± 1.69	0.48

Table XII-107. Differences between Criminals by Offense Groups and Total Civil Check Sample with Value in Terms of the Probable Error

Cheeks Fullness

	Submedium		Medium		Pronounced	
	Per Cent	x p.e.	Per Cent	x p.e.	Per Cent	x p.e.
First degree murder	26.27 ± 2.04	12.88	-23.27 ± 2.55	9.12	- 3.00 ± 2.00	1.50
Second degree murder	19.39 ± 1.75	11.08	-18.71 ± 2.22	8.43	- 0.68 ± 1.46	0.46
Assault	32.10 ± 2.61	12.30	-30.46 ± 3.80	8.02	- 1.64 ± 3.22	0.51
Robbery	19.52 ± 1.81	10.78	-18.54 ± 2.37	7.82	- 0.98 ± 1.91	0.51
Burglary and larceny	18.18 ± 1.65	11.02	-18.26 ± 2.01	9.08	0.08 ± 1.50	0.05
Forgery and fraud	19.83 ± 1.80	11.02	-22.29 ± 2.35	9.48	2.45 ± 1.94	1.26
Rape	26.31 ± 2.15	12.24	-22.12 ± 2.83	7.82	- 4.18 ± 2.27	1.94
Other sex	32.52 ± 2.37	13.72	-25.29 ± 3.08	8.21	- 7.22 ± 2.44	2.96
Vs. public welfare	12.97 ± 1.71	7.58	-24.55 ± 2.68	9.20	11.68 ± 2.40	4.87
Arson and all other	23.30 ± 2.29	10.18	-23.06 ± 3.44	6.70	- 0.24 ± 2.94	0.08
Total	20.23 ± 1.63	12.41	-20.34 ± 1.90	10.70	0.11 ± 1.49	0.07

Table XII-108. Differences between Criminals by Offense Groups and Total Civil Check Sample with Value in Terms of the Probable Error

Gonial Angles

	Submedium		Medium		Pronounced	
	Per Cent	x p.e.	Per Cent	x p.e.	Per Cent	x p.e.
First degree murder	5.15 ± 1.52	3.39	- 1.37 ± 2.44	.56	- 3.77 ± 2.16	1.74
Second degree murder	6.09 ± 1.41	4.32	- 3.16 ± 2.14	1.48	- 2.92 ± 1.88	1.55
Assault	2.68 ± 2.10	1.28	4.37 ± 3.76	1.16	- 7.04 ± 3.42	2.06
Robbery	6.73 ± 1.51	4.46	1.31 ± 2.25	.58	- 8.03 ± 1.92	4.18
Burglary and larceny	7.60 ± 1.38	5.51	- 1.53 ± .62	2.47	- 6.07 ± 1.56	3.89
Forgery and fraud	4.64 ± 1.40	3.31	- 3.14 ± 2.25	1.40	- 1.48 ± 2.00	.74
Rape	4.59 ± 1.65	2.78	.71 ± 2.75	.26	- 5.29 ± 2.46	2.15
Other sex	9.93 ± 1.95	5.09	- 3.88 ± 3.06	1.27	- 6.04 ± 2.69	2.24
Vs. public welfare	- 2.05 ± 1.27	1.61	.01 ± 2.57	0	2.06 ± 2.41	.86
Arson and all other	- .19 ± 1.83	.10	9.49 ± 3.37	2.82	- 9.30 ± 3.06	3.04
Total	5.87 ± 1.26	4.66	- 1.16 ± 1.79	.65	- 4.69 ± 1.50	3.13

Table XII-109. Differences between Criminals by Offense Groups and Total Civil Check Sample with Value in Terms of the Probable Error

Cheeks Wrinkling

	Absent		Slight, Medium		Pronounced	
	Per Cent	x p.e.	Per Cent	x p.e.	Per Cent	x p.e.
First degree murder	3.52 ± 2.69	1.31	- 3.28 ± 2.69	1.22	- 0.24 ± 2.40	0.10
Second degree murder	2.66 ± 2.35	1.13	2.01 ± 2.39	0.84	- 4.68 ± 2.01	2.33
Assault	13.04 ± 4.17	3.13	- 0.54 ± 4.18	0.13	-12.50 ± 3.56	3.51
Robbery	29.27 ± 2.60	11.26	- 9.82 ± 2.46	3.99	-19.44 ± 1.78	10.92
Burglary and larceny	25.76 ± 2.16	11.93	- 7.62 ± 2.05	3.72	-18.14 ± 1.28	14.17
Forgery and fraud	13.32 ± 2.55	5.22	1.10 ± 2.52	0.44	-14.42 ± 1.88	7.67
Rape	8.45 ± 3.07	2.75	- 3.25 ± 3.06	1.06	- 5.20 ± 2.64	1.97
Other sex	30.88 ± 3.30	9.36	- 5.29 ± 3.31	1.60	1.67 ± 2.99	0.56
Vs. public welfare	24.23 ± 2.77	8.75	2.73 ± 2.87	0.95	0.29 ± 2.54	0.11
Arson and all other	17.23 ± 3.83	4.50	- 6.94 ± 3.78	1.84	-10.29 ± 3.25	3.17
Total	15.88 ± 2.08	7.64	- 4.07 ± 1.99	2.04	-11.81 ± 1.44	8.20

Table XII-110. Differences between Criminals by Offense Groups and Total Civil Check Sample with Value in Terms of the Probable Error

Teeth Wear

	None		Slight, Medium		Pronounced	
	Per Cent	x p.e.	Per Cent	x p.e.	Per Cent	x p.e.
First degree murder	- 0.68 ± 0.32	2.12	3.49 ± 2.49	1.40	- 2.81 ± 2.48	1.13
Second degree murder	- 1.18 ± 0.58	2.03	3.89 ± 2.13	1.83	- 5.06 ± 2.09	2.42
Assault	- 0.68 ± 0.63	1.08	9.87 ± 3.84	2.57	- 9.19 ± 3.82	2.41
Robbery	0.55 ± 0.51	1.08	20.28 ± 1.96	10.35	-20.83 ± 1.91	10.91
Burglary and larceny	0.78 ± 0.49	1.59	6.99 ± 1.52	4.60	-17.77 ± 1.46	12.17
Forgery and fraud	- 0.23 ± 0.37	0.62	16.63 ± 1.99	8.36	-16.39 ± 1.97	8.32
Rape	- 0.68 ± 0.41	1.66	8.38 ± 2.78	3.01	- 7.70 ± 2.76	2.79
Other sex	- 0.68 ± 0.46	1.48	2.01 ± 3.14	0.64	- 1.33 ± 3.13	0.42
Vs. public welfare	- 0.27 ± 0.44	0.61	2.60 ± 2.63	0.99	- 2.33 ± 2.61	0.89
Arson and all other	0.35 ± 0.69	0.51	8.73 ± 3.51	2.49	- 9.08 ± 3.48	2.61
Total	0.38 ± 0.41	0.93	12.30 ± 1.55	7.94	-12.68 ± 1.51	8.40

Table XII-111. Differences between Criminals by Offense Groups and Total Civil Check Sample with Value in Terms of the Probable Error

Teeth Caries

	None		Few		Many	
	Per Cent	x p.e.	Per Cent	x p.e.	Per Cent	x p.e.
First degree murder	- 3.76 ± 1.08	3.48	14.25 ± 2.76	5.16	-10.49 ± 2.74	3.83
Second degree murder	- 1.46 ± 1.03	1.42	19.55 ± 2.35	8.32	-18.09 ± 2.28	7.93
Assault	- 3.22 ± 1.91	1.69	22.18 ± 4.31	5.15	-18.96 ± 4.27	4.44
Robbery	- 3.37 ± 0.99	3.40	24.84 ± 2.49	9.98	-21.47 ± 2.43	8.84
Burglary and larceny	- 3.54 ± 0.71	4.99	29.24 ± 1.88	15.55	-25.70 ± 1.84	13.97
Forgery and fraud	- 2.92 ± 1.00	2.92	23.54 ± 2.45	9.61	-20.62 ± 2.39	8.63
Rape	- 5.28 ± 0.21	25.14	20.50 ± 3.14	6.53	-15.21 ± 3.10	4.91
Other sex	- 5.82 ± 1.35	4.31	13.92 ± 3.47	4.01	- 8.10 ± 3.45	2.35
Vs. public welfare	- 4.18 ± 1.13	3.70	8.61 ± 2.92	2.95	- 4.43 ± 2.90	1.53
Arson and all other	- 3.76 ± 1.70	2.21	24.21 ± 3.93	6.16	-20.46 ± 3.88	5.27
Total	- 3.36 ± 0.65	5.17	23.26 ± 1.86	12.50	-19.90 ± 1.81	10.99

Table XII-112.   Differences between Criminals by Offense Groups and Total Civil Check Sample with Value in Terms of the Probable Error

Teeth Lost

	None		Few		Many	
	Per Cent	x p.e.	Per Cent	x p.e.	Per Cent	x p.e.
First degree murder	0.77 ± 2.12	0.36	1.33 ± 2.70	0.49	- 0.56 ± 2.61	0.21
Second degree murder	4.39 ± 1.96	2.24	5.04 ± 2.36	2.14	- 9.44 ± 2.16	4.37
Assault	- 1.72 ± 3.32	0.52	11.62 ± 4.23	2.75	- 9.91 ± 4.02	2.46
Robbery	4.87 ± 2.11	2.31	11.09 ± 2.54	4.37	-15.96 ± 2.26	7.06
Burglary and larceny	12.91 ± 1.93	6.69	5.56 ± 2.10	2.65	-18.48 ± 1.71	10.81
Forgery and fraud	9.94 ± 2.17	4.58	0.29 ± 2.49	0.12	-10.24 ± 2.29	4.47
Rape	- 0.34 ± 2.43	0.14	- 0.75 ± 3.07	0.24	1.08 ± 2.98	0.36
Other sex	- 3.22 ± 2.60	1.24	- 1.30 ± 3.35	0.39	4.51 ± 3.26	1.38
Vs. public welfare	6.56 ± 2.38	2.76	- 4.79 ± 2.83	1.69	- 1.78 ± 2.74	0.65
Arson and all other	- 0.41 ± 3.05	0.13	2.89 ± 3.86	0.75	- 2.50 ± 3.71	0.67
Total	9.35 ± 1.75	4.20	4.01 ± 2.00	2.00	-11.36 ± 1.74	6.53

Table XII-113.   Differences between Criminals by Offense Groups and Total Civil Check Sample with Value in Terms of the Probable Error

Bite

	Under		Edge-to-edge		Slight Over		Marked Over	
	Per Cent	x p.e.	Per Cent	x p.e.	Per Cent	x p.e.	Per Cent	x p.e.
First degree murder	- 1.04 ± .93	1.12	7.20 ± 2.47	2.92	5.67 ± 2.97	1.91	-11.83 ± 2.68	4.41
Second degree murder	- 1.57 ± .70	2.24	6.96 ± 2.13	3.27	4.38 ± 2.52	1.74	- 9.78 ± 2.25	4.35
Assault	- 1.63 ± 1.44	1.13	2.34 ± 3.52	.66	9.64 ± 4.48	2.15	-10.35 ± 4.18	2.48
Robbery	- 1.98 ± .73	2.71	- 5.28 ± 1.94	2.72	16.09 ± 2.69	5.98	- 8.83 ± 2.44	3.62
Burglary and larceny	1.28 ± .90	1.42	3.49 ± 1.64	2.13	12.84 ± 2.25	5.71	-10.63 ± 1.96	5.42
Forgery and fraud	.30 ± .94	.32	- 1.19 ± 2.03	.59	11.39 ± 2.66	4.28	-10.50 ± 2.37	4.43
Rape	- .61 ± 1.10	.55	5.00 ± 2.69	1.86	7.88 ± 3.33	2.37	-12.27 ± 3.04	4.04
Other sex	- 2.23 ± 1.09	2.14	7.49 ± 2.97	2.52	5.08 ± 3.64	1.40	-10.34 ± 3.36	3.08
Vs. public welfare	2.10 ± .88	2.39	4.55 ± 2.50	1.80	3.40 ± 3.08	1.10	- 5.85 ± 2.87	2.04
Arson and all other	1.33 ± 1.47	.90	- 1.10 ± 3.14	.35	10.91 ± 4.07	2.68	-11.13 ± 3.77	2.95
Total	- .18 ± .72	.25	.18 ± 1.68	.11	10.18 ± 2.15	4.74	-10.18 ± 1.86	5.47

Table XII-114. Differences between Criminals by Offense Groups and Total Civil Check Sample
with Value in Terms of the Probable Error

Ear Lobes

	Submedium		Medium		Pronounced	
	Per Cent	x p.e.	Per Cent	x p.e.	Per Cent	x p.e.
First degree murder	- 0.25 ± 1.71	0.15	- 7.57 ± 2.51	3.02	7.83 ± 2.16	3.62
Second degree murder	- 1.31 ± 1.44	0.91	- 0.20 ± 2.10	0.10	1.51 ± 1.77	0.85
Assault	6.00 ± 2.82	2.13	- 7.20 ± 3.84	1.88	1.21 ± 3.14	0.38
Robbery	1.78 ± 1.67	1.07	0.75 ± 2.25	0.33	- 2.52 ± 1.79	1.41
Burglary and larceny	0.56 ± 1.36	0.41	0.52 ± 1.86	0.28	- 1.19 ± 1.50	0.79
Forgery and fraud	- 3.35 ± 1.45	2.31	- 1.60 ± 2.25	0.71	4.95 ± 1.96	2.53
Rape	1.83 ± 2.01	0.91	- 5.02 ± 2.81	1.79	3.20 ± 2.33	1.37
Other sex	- 1.57 ± 2.09	0.75	0.65 ± 2.98	0.22	0.93 ± 2.48	0.38
Vs. public welfare	- 7.22 ± 2.12	3.41	2.12 ± 2.52	0.84	5.11 ± 2.21	2.31
Arson and all other	1.12 ± 2.47	0.45	7.15 ± 3.49	2.05	6.04 ± 2.93	2.06
Total	- 0.42 ± 1.23	0.34	- 0.89 ± 1.78	0.50	1.31 ± 1.50	0.87

Table XII-115. Differences between Criminals by Offense Groups and Total Civil Check Sample
with Value in Terms of the Probable Error

Ear Lobe Attachment

	Attached		Free		Notched, Divided	
	Per Cent	x p.e.	Per Cent	x p.e.	Per Cent	x p.e.
First degree murder	- 5.07 ± 2.60	1.95	5.07 ± 2.60	1.95		
Second degree murder	0.01 ± 2.28	0.004	- 0.17 ± 2.28	0.07	0.16 ± 0.15	1.07
Assault	1.17 ± 4.12	0.28	- 1.17 ± 4.12	0.28		
Robbery	5.24 ± 2.49	2.10	- 5.24 ± 2.49	2.10		
Burglary and larceny	2.46 ± 2.04	1.21	- 2.52 ± 2.04	1.21	0.06 ± 0.09	0.67
Forgery and fraud	- 0.90 ± 2.41	0.37	0.90 ± 2.41	0.37		
Rape	- 5.67 ± 2.98	1.90	5.67 ± 2.98	1.90		
Other sex	- 6.38 ± 3.22	1.98	6.38 ± 3.22	1.98		
Vs. public welfare	- 8.87 ± 2.70	3.28	8.87 ± 2.70	3.28		
Arson and all other	0.01 ± 3.74	0.002	- 0.01 ± 3.74	0.002		
Total	- 0.03 ± 1.92	0.02	- 0.01 ± 1.92	0.005	0.05 ± 0.07	0.71

Table XII-116. Differences between Criminals by Offense Groups and Total Civil Chec' Sample
with Value in Terms of the Probable Error

Roll of Helix

	Absent		Submedium		Medium, Pronounced	
	Per Cent	x p.e.	Per Cent	x p.e.	Per Cent	x p.e.
First degree murder			23.82 ± 2.24	10.63	-23.82 ± 2.24	10.63
Second degree murder			26.80 ± 2.10	12.76	-26.80 ± 2.10	12.76
Assault			23.92 ± 3.04	7.87	-23.92 ± 3.04	7.87
Robbery	.48 ± .26	1.85	20.01 ± 2.08	9.62	-20.49 ± 2.09	9.80
Burglary and larceny			19.96 ± 2.74	7.28	-19.96 ± 2.74	7.28
Forgery and fraud	.21 ± .16	1.31	19.07 ± 2.04	9.35	-19.78 ± 2.04	9.70
Rape			24.43 ± 2.44	10.01	-24.43 ± 2.44	10.01
Other sex			21.96 ± 2.54	8.65	-21.96 ± 2.54	8.65
Vs. public welfare	.97 ± .38	2.55	22.55 ± 2.29	9.85	-22.55 ± 2.29	9.85
Arson and all other			25.66 ± 2.85	9.00	-26.63 ± 2.87	9.28
Total	.10 ± .12	.83	21.87 ± 1.81	12.08	-21.96 ± 1.81	12.13

Table XII-117. Differences between Criminals by Offense Groups and Total Civil Check Sample
with Value in Terms of the Probable Error

Darwin's Point

	Absent		Small or Medium		Pronounced	
	Per Cent	x p.e.	Per Cent	x p.e.	Per Cent	x p.e.
First degree murder	-12.74 ± 2.62	4.86	9.47 ± 2.40	3.95	3.27 ± 1.66	1.97
Second degree murder	- 8.82 ± 2.26	3.90	4.99 ± 2.04	2.45	3.83 ± 1.49	2.57
Assault	- 5.40 ± 3.97	1.36	9.29 ± 3.63	2.56	- 3.89 ± 2.32	1.68
Robbery	-14.56 ± 2.47	5.90	9.19 ± 2.25	4.08	5.37 ± 1.64	3.27
Burglary and larceny	- 8.59 ± 2.02	4.25	3.99 ± 1.81	2.20	4.60 ± 1.39	3.31
Forgery and fraud	- 9.68 ± 2.37	4.08	5.97 ± 2.15	2.78	3.71 ± 1.54	2.41
Rape	-10.23 ± 2.93	3.49	8.41 ± 2.68	3.14	1.82 ± 1.81	1.01
Other sex	- 7.62 ± 3.17	2.40	3.81 ± 2.78	1.37	3.80 ± 2.03	1.87
Vs. public welfare	-10.71 ± 2.73	3.92	3.71 ± 2.43	1.53	7.00 ± 1.86	3.76
Arson and all other	- 9.87 ± 3.64	2.71	11.95 ± 3.34	3.58	- 2.09 ± 2.14	.98
Total	- 9.78 ± 1.93	5.07	5.75 ± 1.76	3.27	4.03 ± 1.31	3.08

Table XII-118. Differences between Criminals by Offense Groups and Total Civil Check Sample with Value in Terms of the Probable Error

Antihelix Prominence

	Submedium		Medium		Pronounced	
	Per Cent	x p.e.	Per Cent	x p.e.	Per Cent	x p.e.
First degree murder	- 1.93 ± 1.19	1.62	- 7.39 ± 1.86	3.97	9.32 ± 1.50	6.21
Second degree murder	3.92 ± 1.32	2.97	-13.33 ± 1.83	7.28	9.41 ± 1.41	6.67
Assault	2.75 ± 2.12	0.13	-19.14 ± 2.94	6.51	16.39 ± 2.20	7.45
Robbery	1.15 ± 1.27	0.91	-12.31 ± 1.90	6.48	11.15 ± 1.53	7.29
Burglary and larceny	2.66 ± 1.15	2.31	-13.16 ± 1.69	7.79	10.50 ± 1.38	7.61
Forgery and fraud	0.33 ± 1.21	0.27	-10.85 ± 1.84	5.90	10.52 ± 1.50	7.01
Rape	2.09 ± 1.56	1.34	-15.16 ± 2.24	6.77	13.06 ± 1.75	7.46
Other sex	1.94 ± 1.68	1.15	-12.85 ± 2.34	5.49	10.90 ± 1.75	6.23
Vs. public welfare	4.05 ± 1.54	2.63	-12.69 ± 2.16	5.88	8.64 ± 1.52	5.68
Arson and all other	- 2.23 ± 1.75	1.27	-13.33 ± 2.60	5.13	15.56 ± 2.04	7.63
Total	2.01 ± 1.07	1.88	-12.59 ± 1.62	7.77	10.58 ± 1.35	7.84

Table XII-119. Differences between Criminals by Offense Groups and Total Civil Check Sample with Value in Terms of the Probable Error

Ear Protrusion

	Submedium		Medium		Pronounced	
	Per Cent	x p.e.	Per Cent	x p.e.	Per Cent	x p.e.
First degree murder	7.08 ± 1.38	5.13	-33.18 ± 2.57	12.91	26.10 ± 2.42	10.78
Second degree murder	5.19 ± 1.19	4.36	-27.13 ± 2.25	12.06	21.93 ± 2.12	10.34
Assault	1.47 ± 1.62	.91	-29.23 ± 3.62	8.07	27.76 ± 3.41	8.14
Robbery	3.47 ± 1.15	3.02	-17.72 ± 2.27	7.81	14.25 ± 2.12	6.72
Burglary and larceny	3.86 ± 1.04	3.71	-24.28 ± 2.02	12.02	20.42 ± 1.94	10.52
Forgery and fraud	2.25 ± 1.06	2.12	-21.56 ± 2.27	9.50	19.31 ± 2.16	8.94
Rape	2.08 ± 1.25	1.66	-27.14 ± 2.78	9.76	25.06 ± 2.64	9.49
Other sex	5.08 ± 1.48	3.43	-24.11 ± 2.93	8.23	19.04 ± 2.72	7.00
Vs. public welfare	3.86 ± 1.27	3.04	-24.14 ± 2.58	9.36	20.28 ± 2.42	8.38
Arson and all other	2.35 ± 1.52	1.55	-25.85 ± 3.31	7.81	23.50 ± 3.10	7.58
Total	3.96 ± 1.02	3.88	-24.66 ± 1.94	12.71	20.70 ± 1.86	11.13

Table XII-120. Differences between Criminals by Offense Groups and Total Civil Check Sample with Value in Terms of the Probable Error

Temporal Fullness

	Submedium		Medium		Pronounced	
	Per Cent	x p.e.	Per Cent	x p.e.	Per Cent	x p.e.
First degree murder	11.89 ± 1.71	6.95	- 5.15 ± 2.31	2.24	- 6.76 ± 1.79	3.78
Second degree murder	9.90 ± 1.52	6.51	- 6.45 ± 2.04	3.16	- 3.46 ± 1.61	2.15
Assault	8.28 ± 1.32	6.27	- 1.54 ± 2.08	0.74	- 9.83 ± 1.77	5.55
Robbery	12.01 ± 1.66	7.24	- 3.46 ± 2.14	1.62	- 8.56 ± 1.59	5.39
Burglary and larceny	11.40 ± 1.48	7.70	- 5.92 ± 1.84	3.22	- 5.50 ± 1.32	4.17
Forgery and fraud	16.08 ± 1.77	9.08	- 6.69 ± 2.15	3.10	- 9.40 ± 1.52	6.18
Rape	5.75 ± 1.64	3.51	- 3.17 ± 2.48	1.28	- 8.94 ± 2.04	4.38
Other sex	7.77 ± 1.81	4.29	- 5.61 ± 2.83	1.98	- 2.17 ± 2.41	0.90
Vs. public welfare	22.55 ± 2.06	10.95	-12.70 ± 2.53	5.02	- 9.86 ± 1.82	5.42
Arson and all other	18.80 ± 2.31	8.14	-11.47 ± 3.29	3.49	- 7.34 ± 2.68	2.74
Total	12.21 ± 1.47	8.31	- 5.76 ± 1.75	3.29	- 6.46 ± 1.19	5.43

Table XII-121. Differences between Criminals by Offense Groups and Total Civil Check Sample with Value in Terms of the Probable Error

Lambdoid Flattening

	Absent		Present	
	Per Cent	x p.e.	Per Cent	x p.e.
First degree murder	-16.63 ± 2.50	6.65	16.63 ± 2.50	6.65
Second degree murder	-12.60 ± 2.16	5.83	12.60 ± 2.16	5.83
Assault	-24.11 ± 3.80	6.34	24.11 ± 3.80	6.34
Robbery	-11.01 ± 2.29	4.81	11.01 ± 2.29	4.81
Burglary and larceny	- 9.11 ± 1.92	4.74	9.11 ± 1.92	4.74
Forgery and fraud	-10.53 ± 2.25	4.68	10.53 ± 2.25	4.68
Rape	-14.01 ± 2.76	5.08	14.01 ± 2.76	5.08
Other sex	-11.71 ± 2.95	3.97	11.71 ± 2.95	3.97
Vs. public welfare	0.94 ± 2.37	0.40	- 0.94 ± 2.37	0.40
Arson and all other	-10.93 ± 3.36	3.25	10.93 ± 3.36	3.25
Total	-10.56 ± 1.84	5.74	10.56 ± 1.84	5.74

Table XII-122.   Differences between Criminals by Offense Groups and Total Civil Check Sample with Value in Terms of the Probable Error

Asymmetry

	Right		Left		None	
	Per Cent	x p.e.	Per Cent	x p.e.	Per Cent	x p.e.
First degree murder	3.57 ± 2.02	1.77	1.92 ± 2.02	.95	- 5.49 ± 2.57	2.14
Second degree murder	.07 ± 1.67	.04	1.70 ± 1.75	.97	- 1.77 ± 2.19	.81
Assault	1.19 ± 3.02	.39	- .76 ± 3.04	.25	- .44 ± 3.90	.11
Robbery	- 1.85 ± 1.75	1.06	- 4.53 ± 1.70	2.66	6.38 ± 2.25	2.84
Burglary and larceny	- 1.64 ± 1.42	1.16	- 3.29 ± 1.39	2.37	4.93 ± 1.85	2.66
Forgery and fraud	- 1.95 ± 1.71	1.14	- 2.86 ± 1.72	1.66	4.82 ± 2.24	2.14
Rape	5.81 ± 2.34	2.48	- 3.30 ± 2.16	1.53	- 2.53 ± 2.89	.88
Other sex	7.14 ± 2.52	2.83	- 3.53 ± 2.33	1.52	- 3.82 ± 3.12	1.16
Vs. public welfare	- 3.49 ± 1.94	1.90	2.01 ± 2.13	.94	1.49 ± 2.53	.55
Arson and all other	- .19 ± 2.72	.07	- 1.86 ± 2.74	.68	2.05 ± 3.53	.58
Total	- .39 ± 1.40	.28	- 1.85 ± 1.37	1.34	2.21 ± 1.79	1.24

Table XII-123.   Differences between Criminals by Offense Groups and Total Civil Check Sample with Value in Terms of the Probable Error

Neck

	Medium in Length, Breadth		Long and Thin		Short and Thick	
	Per Cent	x p.e.	Per Cent	x p.e.	Per Cent	x p.e.
First degree murder	-14.28 ± 2.43	5.88	19.99 ± 2.12	9.43	- 5.71 ± 1.54	3.71
Second degree murder	-19.01 ± 2.21	8.60	24.66 ± 2.04	12.09	- 5.65 ± 1.28	4.41
Assault	-10.16 ± 3.56	2.85	18.23 ± 2.84	6.42	- 8.07 ± 2.55	3.15
Robbery	- 9.83 ± 2.36	4.16	16.09 ± 1.95	8.21	- 6.26 ± 1.39	4.50
Burglary and larceny	-10.73 ± 1.91	.62	18.68 ± 1.79	10.44	- 7.95 ± .92	8.64
Forgery and fraud	-10.31 ± 2.21	.55	16.32 ± 1.94	8.41	- 6.01 ± 1.35	4.42
Rape	- 7.11 ± 2.62	2.71	14.83 ± 2.18	6.80	- 7.72 ± 1.75	4.41
Other sex	-11.36 ± 2.88	3.94	19.87 ± 2.43	8.18	- 8.51 ± 1.92	4.43
Vs. public welfare	- 7.15 ± 2.44	2.93	13.08 ± 2.04	6.41	- 5.94 ± 1.64	3.62
Arson and all other	- 6.09 ± 3.20	1.90	14.03 ± 2.56	5.48	- 7.94 ± 2.28	3.48
Total	-11.58 ± 1.84	6.29	18.54 ± 1.74	10.66	- 6.96 ± .98	7.91

Table XII-124. Differences between Criminals by Offense Groups and Total Civil Check Sample
with Value in Terms of the Probable Error

Shoulder Slope

	Slight		Medium		Pronounced	
	Per Cent	x p.e.	Per Cent	x p.e.	Per Cent	x p.e.
First degree murder	3.81 ± 1.01	3.77	-24.33 ± 2.01	12.10	20.51 ± 1.81	11.33
Second degree murder	1.10 ± .72	1.53	-25.85 ± 1.94	13.32	24.75 ± 1.85	13.38
Assault	- .41 ± 1.05	.39	- 4.78 ± 1.85	2.58	5.18 ± 1.54	3.36
Robbery	1.25 ± .78	1.60	-17.39 ± 1.77	9.82	16.13 ± 1.63	9.90
Burglary and larceny	.64 ± .62	1.03	-20.44 ± 1.72	11.88	19.78 ± 1.65	11.99
Forgery and fraud	.27 ± .65	.41	-18.35 ± 1.77	10.37	18.07 ± 1.68	10.76
Rape	1.42 ± .91	1.55	-12.44 ± 1.75	7.11	11.01 ± 1.54	7.15
Other sex	.33 ± .88	.38	-16.56 ± 1.97	8.41	16.22 ± 1.79	9.06
Vs. public welfare	.69 ± .80	.86	-15.55 ± 1.80	8.69	14.93 ± 1.65	9.05
Arson and all other	- .59 ± .93	.74	-15.45 ± 2.08	7.43	16.13 ± 1.88	8.58
Total	.94 ± .63	1.49	-19.86 ± 1.67	11.89	18.91 ± 1.59	11.89

Table XII-125. Number and Significance of Deviations of Criminal Offense Groups and of Total
Criminal Series from Total Civil Check Sample in Sociological Observations

	Significant		Insignificant		Total
	No.	Per Cent	No.	Per Cent	No.
First degree murder	17	65.38	9	34.62	26
Second degree murder	16	61.54	10	38.46	26
Assault	10	38.46	16	61.54	26
Robbery	12	46.15	14	53.85	26
Burglary and larceny	18	69.23	8	30.77	26
Forgery and fraud	10	38.46	16	61.54	26
Rape	15	57.69	11	42.31	26
Other sex	13	50.00	13	50.00	26
Vs. public welfare	18	69.23	8	30.77	26
Arson and all other	14	53.85	12	46.15	26
Total series	21	80.77	5	19.23	26
Massachusetts	13	50.00	13	50.00	26
Tennessee	16	61.54	10	38.46	26

Table XII-126.   Summary of Significant Sociological Differences
between Criminals and Civilians

Total Offenses

Marital State
  Single: excess 6.61* (3.30 p.e.)
  Married: deficiency 12.89* (6.48 p.e.)
  Divorced: excess 4.23** (5.42 p.e.)
  Widower: excess 2.05 (3.47 p.e.)

Occupation***
  Extractive: excess 30.64 (16.84 p.e.)
  Laborer: excess 14.74 (10.17 p.e.)
  Factory: excess 4.53 (3.02 p.e.)
  Trade: deficiency 3.03 (3.37 p.e.)
  Public service: deficiency 45.21 (59.49 p.e.)
  Personal service: excess 5.46 (5.57 p.e.)
  Clerical: deficiency 4.09 (5.84 p.e.)
  Student: deficiency 4.95 (20.62 p.e.)

Education
  Illiterate: excess 9.52 (8.21 p.e.)
  Read, write: excess 3.25 (4.17 p.e.)
  1st-5th Grade: excess 10.18 (6.02 p.e.)
  6th Grade: excess 3.89 (3.50 p.e.)
  8th Grade: deficiency 5.64 (3.64 p.e.)
  1st-2nd High: deficiency 5.71 (4.11 p.e.)
  3rd-4th High: deficiency 9.01 (10.48 p.e.)
  College: deficiency 5.84 (8.00 p.e.)

*   Partially attributable to the lower mean age of the criminals.
**   Partially due to probable suppression of divorces on the part of civilians.
*** All excesses exaggerated by the disproportionate number of public service workers
     (Nashville firemen) in the civilian check sample.

Table XII-127.   Summary of Significant Sociological Differences
between Criminals and Civilians

First Degree Murder

Marital State
  Divorced: excess 6.15 (6.54 p.e.)
  Widower: excess 6.79 (6.59 p.e.)

Occupation
  Extractive: excess 50.17* (20.82 p.e.)
  Laborer: excess 9.24* (6.79 p.e.)
  Public service: deficiency 45.54* (19.71 p.e.)
  Personal service: excess 3.30* (3.55 p.e.)
  Clerical: deficiency 5.94 (5.55 p.e.)
  Student: deficiency 4.95 (5.82 p.e.)

Education**
  Illiterate: excess 16.57 (10.83 p.e.)
  Read, write: excess 9.43 (7.54 p.e.)
  1st-5th Grade: excess 16.11 (7.10 p.e.)
  6th Grade: excess 6.23 (4.21 p.e.)
  7th Grade: deficiency 4.42 (3.07 p.e.)
  8th Grade: deficiency 10.07 (4.71 p.e.)
  1st-2nd High: deficiency 12.40 (6.67 p.e.)
  3rd-4th High: deficiency 12.16 (8.56 p.e.)
  College: deficiency 8.32 (7.17 p.e.)

* Differences exaggerated by the number of public service workers (firemen) in the check
   sample of civilians.
** All differences probably somewhat exaggerated by the overloading of this offense group
   with Kentucky mountaineers.

Table XII-128.   Summary of Significant Sociological Differences
between Criminals and Civilians

Second Degree Murder

Marital State
  Divorced: excess 2.77 (4.40 p.e.)
  Widower: excess 2.50 (3.98 p.e.)

Occupation
  Extractive: excess 51.31* (22.90 p.e.)
  Laborer: excess 14.74* (9.70 p.e.)
  Trade: deficiency 3.66 (3.30 p.e.)
  Public service: deficiency 44.72* (25.85 p.e.)
  Semi-professional: deficiency 1.32 (3.22 p.e.)
  Clerical: deficiency 6.11 (7.73 p.e.)
  Student: deficiency 4.95 (8.25 p.e.)

Education
  Illiterate: excess 19.91 (12.37 p.e.)
  Read, write: excess 4.38 (4.87 p.e.)
  1st-5th Grade: excess 19.73 (9.40 p.e.)
  8th Grade: deficiency 12.97 (7.48 p.e.)
  1st-2nd High: deficiency 11.46 (7.49 p.e.)
  3rd-4th High: deficiency 12.49 (12.13 p.e.)
  College: deficiency 7.19 (7.65 p.e.)

* Differences exaggerated by the number of public service workers (firemen) in the check
   sample of civilians.

Table XII-129.   Summary of Significant Sociological Differences
between Criminals and Civilians

Assault

Marital State
  Divorced: excess 6.25 (6.51 p.e.)

Occupation
  Extractive: excess 20.81* (10.90 p.e.)
  Laborer: excess 18.53* (9.26 p.e.)
  Skilled trades: excess 10.98* (4.19 p.e.)
  Public service: deficiency 45.87* (11.13 p.e.)
  Personal service: excess 6.37* (4.55 p.e.)

Education
  Illiterate: excess 9.36 (6.98 p.e.)
  1st-5th Grade: excess 9.94 (3.13 p.e.)
  3rd-4th High: deficiency 9.71 (3.61 p.e.)
  College: deficiency 7.72 (3.49 p.e.)

* Differences exaggerated by the number of public service workers (firemen) in the
   check sample.

Table XII-130.   Summary of Significant Sociological Differences
between Criminals and Civilians

Robbery

Marital State
  Single: excess 18.38* (7.18 p.e.)
  Married: deficiency 23.24* (9.11 p.e.)
  Divorced: excess 4.46 (5.51 p.e.)

Occupation
  Extractive: excess 12.46** (8.90 p.e.)
  Laborer: excess 11.73** (8.15 p.e.)
  Factory: excess 15.56** (7.34 p.e.)
  Public service: deficiency 45.11** (21.79 p.e.)
  Personal service: excess 7.56** (6.41 p.e.)
  Student: deficiency 4.95 (6.69 p.e.)

Education
  Illiterate: excess 3.01 (3.96 p.e.)
  3rd-4th High: deficiency 6.16·(4.08 p.e.)
  College: deficiency 5.81 (4.97 p.e.)

*   Differences partially attributable to the low mean age of this offense group.
**   Differences exaggerated by the number of public service workers (firemen) in the
     check sample of civilians.

Table XII-131.   Summary of Significant Sociological Differences
between Criminals and Civilians

Burglary and Larceny

Marital State
  Single: excess 19.85* (9.54 p.e.)
  Married: deficiency 24.61* (12.06 p.e.)
  Divorced: excess 3.77 (5.09 p.e.)

Occupation
  Extractive: excess 22.06** (13.21 p.e.)
  Laborer: excess 19.36** (11.95 p.e.)
  Factory: excess 8.03** (4.81 p.e.)
  Trade: deficiency 4.39 (4.99 p.e.)
  Public service: deficiency 45.43** (40.20 p.e.)
  Professional: deficiency 1.46 (5.41 p.e.)
  Personal service: excess 6.79** (6.35 p.e.)
  Clerical: deficiency 4.65 (6.46 p.e.)
  Student: deficiency 4.95 (13.03 p.e.)

Education
  Illiterate: excess 7.68 (7.18 p.e.)
  1st-5th Grade: excess 9.96 (5.66 p.e.)
  6th Grade: excess 4.19 (3.58 p.e.)
  8th Grade: deficiency 5.54 (3.32 p.e.)
  3rd-4th High: deficiency 8.46 (8.29 p.e.)
  College: deficiency 6.72 (8.96 p.e.)

*   Differences partially attributable to the low mean age of this offense group.
**   Differences exaggerated by the number of public service workers (firemen) in the
     check sample of civilians.

Table XII-132.   Summary of Significant Sociological Differences
between Criminals and Civilians

Forgery and Fraud

Marital State
  Married: deficiency 10.90 (4.36 p.e.)
  Divorced: excess 4.54 (5.54 p.e.)

Occupation
  Extractive: excess 24.50* (13.46 p.e.)
  Laborer: excess 8.48* (6.62 p.e.)
  Public service: deficiency 45.22* (23.19 p.e.)
  Personal service: excess 6.52* (5.82 p.e.)
  Student: deficiency 4.95 (7.07 p.e.)

Education
  Illiterate: excess 3.67 (4.48 p.e.)
  Read, write: excess 3.14 (3.83 p.e.)
  3rd-4th High: deficiency 6.56 (4.49 p.e.)

* Differences exaggerated by the number of public service workers (firemen) in the
  check sample of civilians.

Table XII-133.   Summary of Significant Sociological Differences
between Criminals and Civilians

Rape

Marital State
  Divorced: excess 8.16 (7.49 p.e.)
  Widower: excess 5.79 (5.90 p.e.)

Occupation
  Extractive: excess 35.80* (16.20 p.e.)
  Laborer: excess 14.08* (8.64 p.e.)
  Trade: deficiency 5.14 (3.43 p.e.)
  Public service: deficiency 44.32* (15.77 p.e.)
  Personal service: excess 4.38* (4.09 p.e.)
  Clerical: deficiency 5.89 (4.53 p.e.)
  Student: deficiency 4.95 (4.63 p.e.)

Education
  Illiterate: excess 10.58 (8.14 p.e.)
  Read, write: excess 4.14 (4.27 p.e.)
  1st-5th Grade: excess 15.04 (6.02 p.e.)
  6th Grade: excess 5.07 (3.21 p.e.)
  1st-2nd High: deficiency 12.73 (5.81 p.e.)
  3rd-4th High: deficiency 9.38 (5.13 p.e.)

* Differences exaggerated by the number of public service workers (firemen) in the
  check sample of civilians.

Table XII-134.   Summary of Significant Sociological Differences
between Criminals and Civilians

Other Sex Offenses

Marital State
  Single: deficiency 13.35 (4.10 p.e.)
  Divorced: excess 6.00 (6.38 p.e.)
  Widower: excess 5.00 (5.32 p.e.)

Occupation
  Extractive: excess 29.41* (14.07 p.e.)
  Laborer: excess 16.94* (9.46 p.e.)
  Public service: deficiency 44.52* (14.18 p.e.)
  Personal service: excess 5.44* (4.65 p.e.)
  Student: deficiency 4.95 (4.09 p.e.)

Education
  Illiterate: excess 14.12 (9.48 p.e.)
  Read, write: excess 5.75 (5.18 p.e.)
  1st-5th Grade: excess 7.76 (3.03 p.e.)
  1st-2nd High: deficiency 9.80 (4.02 p.e.)
  3rd-4th High: deficiency 8.76 (4.23 p.e.)

* Difrerences exaggerated by the number of public service workers (firemen) in the
  check sample of civilians.

Table XII-135.   Summary of Significant Sociological Differences
between Criminals and Civilians

Versus Public Welfare

Marital State
  Single: deficiency 16.16 (5.90 p.e.)
  Married: excess 10.88 (3.90 p.e.)
  Divorced: excess 2.79 (4.36 p.e.)
  Widower: excess 2.46 (3.56 p.e.)

Occupation
  Extractive: excess 48.61* (20.00 p.e.)
  Laborer: excess 7.54* (5.80 p.e.)
  Public service: deficiency 45.47* (18.19 p.e.)
  Personal service: excess 3.04* (3.23 p.e.)
  Clerical: deficiency 5.74 (4.91 p.e.)
  Student: deficiency 4.95 (5.27 p.e.)

Education
  Illiterate: excess 6.42 (6.17 p.e.)
  Read, write: excess 6.88 (6.14 p.e.)
  1st-5th Grade: excess 13.18 (5.86 p.e.)
  6th Grade: 5.85 (3.85 p.e.)
  8th Grade: deficiency 7.03 (3.02 p.e.)
  1st-2nd High: deficiency 8.50 (4.09 p.e.)
  3rd-4th High: deficiency 9.15 (5.54 p.e.)
  College: deficiency 7.79 (6.04 p.e.)

* Differences exaggerated by the number of public service workers (firemen) in the
  check sample of civilians.

Table XII-136.   Summary of Significant Sociological Differences
between Criminals and Civilians

Arson and All Other Offenses

Marital State
  Single: deficiency 11.33 (3.00 p.e.)
  Divorced: excess 3.96 (5.21 p.e.)

Occupation
  Extractive: excess 35.01* (15.22 p.e.)
  Laborer: excess 12.02* (7.11 p.e.)
  Public service: deficiency 45.87* (12.40 p.e.)
  Personal service: excess 9.68* (6.58 p.e.)
  Clerical: deficiency 5.93 (3.35 p.e.)
  Student: deficiency 4.95 (3.37 p.e.)

Education
  Illiterate: excess 9.26 (7.12 p.e.)
  Read, write: excess 3.00 (3.00 p.e.)
  1st-5th Grade: excess 11.67 (3.94 p.e.)
  6th Grade: excess 6.75 (3.48 p.e.)
  3rd-4th High: deficiency 10.49 (4.37 p.e.)
  College: deficiency 7.98 (4.05 p.e.)

* Differences exaggerated by the number of public service workers (firemen) in the
  check sample of civilians.

Table XII-137. Number and Significance of Deviations of Criminal Offense
Groups and of Total Criminal Series from Total Civil Check
Sample in Morphological Observations

	Significant		Insignificant		Total
	No.	Per Cent	No.	Per Cent	No.
First degree murder	75	46.30	87	53.70	162
Second degree murder	82	50.62	80	49.38	162
Assault	59	36.42	103	63.58	162
Robbery	91	56.17	71	43.83	162
Burglary and larceny	101	62.35	61	37.65	162
Forgery and fraud	83	51.23	79	48.77	162
Rape	67	41.36	95	58.64	162
Other sex	69	42.59	93	57.41	162
Vs. public welfare	72	44.44	90	55.56	162
Arson and all other	63	38.89	99	61.11	162
Total series	100	61.73	62	38.27	162
Massachusetts	96	59.26	66	40.74	162
Tennessee	71	43.83	91	56.17	162

Table XII-158.   Summary of Significant Morphological Differences
between Criminals and Civilians

Total Offenses

Hair Quantity, Head
  Small: deficiency 4.89 (3.88 p.e.)
  Large: excess 6.26 (4.15 p.e.)

Hair Quantity, Beard
  Small: excess 25.31 (13.61 p.e.)
  Medium: deficiency 15.71 (8.02 p.e.)
  Large: deficiency 9.61 (7.02 p.e.)

Hair Quantity, Body
  Small: excess 7.71 (3.93 p.e.)
  Medium: deficiency 7.11 (3.70 p.e.)

Skin Color
  Pale white: deficiency 6.25 (3.29 p.e.)
  Light brown: excess 2.54 (4.30 p.e.)

Hair Form
  Straight: excess 10.19 (7.18 p.e.)
  Low waves: deficiency 5.49 (4.95 p.e.)
  Deep waves: deficiency 3.44 (4.35 p.e.)

Hair Color
  Red brown: excess 9.00 (5.81 p.e.)
  Gray, white: deficiency 8.21 (9.12 p.e.)

Eye Color
  Dark brown: deficiency 3.08 (4.22 p.e.)
  Blue-brown: deficiency 6.21 (3.91 p.e.)
  Gray-brown: excess 11.95 (8.18 p.e.)
  Blue: deficiency 9.65 (6.19 p.e.)
  Blue-gray: excess 4.33 (3.77 p.e.)

Sclera
  Clear: excess 7.73 (8.59 p.e.)
  Speckled: deficiency 5.70 (6.71 p.e.)
  Yellow: deficiency 2.03 (6.34 p.e.)

Iris
  Homogeneous: deficiency 16.88 (15.07 p.e.)
  Zoned: excess 13.06 (7.26 p.e.)
  Speckled: excess 8.78 (5.13 p.e.)

Eye Folds
  Epicanthus: excess 3.12 (3.95 p.e.)
  Absent: deficiency 6.01 (3.49 p.e.)

Eyebrow Thickness
  Medium: deficiency 10.37 (5.49 p.e.)
  Pronounced: excess 10.16 (5.55 p.e.)

Forehead Height
  Submedium: excess 8.49 (6.63 p.e.)
  Medium: deficiency 8.98 (4.73 p.e.)

Forehead Slope
  Absent, submedium: deficiency 6.24 (5.67 p.e.)
  Medium: deficiency 11.36 (5.86 p.e.)
  Pronounced: excess 17.60 (9.46 p.e.)

Nasion Depression
  Submedium: excess 3.45 (3.05 p.e.)
  Medium: deficiency 13.72 (7.88 p.e.)
  Pronounced: excess 10.17 (6.83 p.e.)

Nasal Root Height
  Medium: deficiency 9.15 (6.14 p.e.)
  Pronounced: excess 8.49 (5.90 p.e.)

Nasal Root Breadth
  Submedium: excess 2.92 (3.56 p.e.)
  Medium: deficiency 9.76 (7.23 p.e.)
  Pronounced: excess 6.85 (6.12 p.e.)

Nasal Bridge Height
  Medium: deficiency 18.57 (9.52 p.e.)
  Pronounced: excess 18.24 (9.35 p.e.)

Nasal Bridge Breadth
  Submedium: excess 2.83 (4.04 p.e.)
  Medium: deficiency 10.96 (7.16 p.e.)
  Pronounced: excess 8.13 (5.72 p.e.)

Nasal Profile
  Straight: deficiency 6.58 (5.18 p.e.)
  Convex: deficiency 9.03 (5.61 p.e.)
  Concavo-convex: excess 11.84 (6.04 p.e.)

Nasal Tip Thickness
  Submedium: excess 9.03 (7.85 p.e.)
  Medium: deficiency 17.24 (9.58 p.e.)
  Pronounced: excess 8.19 (5.18 p.e.)

Nasal Septum Inclination
  Up: excess 11.65 (6.30 p.e.)
  Down: deficiency 12.08 (6.56 p.e.)

Nasal Septum Deflection
  Right: excess 12.27 (7.26 p.e.)
  Absent: deficiency 13.67 (7.23 p.e.

Lips Integumental Thickness
  Submedium: excess 6.99 (5.55 p.e.)
  Medium: deficiency 5.26 (3.53 p.e.)

Lips Membranous Thickness
  Submedium: excess 9.94 (6.90 p.e.)
  Medium: deficiency 11.24 (6.18 p.e.)

Lip Seam
  Absent: excess 6.12 (4.47 p.e.)
  Medium: deficiency 5.02 (2.70 p.e.)

Alveolar Prognathism
  Submedium: excess 6.99 (5.38 p.e.)

Malars Prominence
  Submedium: excess 3.10 (3.52 p.e.)

Table XII-138 (cont'd).

Cheeks Fullness
Submedium: excess 20.23 (12.41 p.e.)
Medium: deficiency 20.34 (10.70 p.e.)

Gonial Angles
Submedium: excess 5.87 (4.65 p.e.)
Pronounced: deficiency 4.69 (3.13 p.e.)

Cheeks Wrinkling
Absent: excess 15.88 (7.64 p.e.)
Pronounced: deficiency 11.81 (8.20 p.e.)

Teeth Wear
Slight, medium: excess 12.30 (7.94 p.e.)
Pronounced: deficiency 12.58 (8.40 p.e.)

Teeth Caries
None: deficiency 3.36 (5.17 p.e.)
Few: excess 23.26 (12.50 p.e.)
Many: deficiency 19.90 (10.99 p.e.)

Teeth Lost
None: excess 7.35 (4.20 p.e.)
Many: deficiency 11.36 (6.53 p.e.)

Bite
Slight over: excess 10.18 (4.74 p.e.)
Marked over: deficiency 10.18 (5.47 p.e.)

Roll of Helix
Submedium: excess 21.87 (12.08 p.e.)
Medium, pronounced: deficiency 21.96 (12.13 p.e.)

Ear Protrusion
Submedium: excess 3.96 (3.88 p.e.)
Medium: deficiency 24.66 (12.71 p.e.)
Pronounced: excess 20.70 (11.13 p.e.)

Darwin's Point
Absent: deficiency 9.78 (5.07 p.e.)
Small, medium: excess 5.75 (3.27 p.e.)
Pronounced: excess 4.03 (3.03 p.e.)

Antihelix Prominence
Medium: deficiency 12.59 (7.77 p.e.)
Pronounced: excess 10.58 (7.84 p.e.)

Temporal Fullness
Submedium: excess 12.21 (8.31 p.e.)
Medium: deficiency 5.76 (3.29 p.e.)
Pronounced: deficiency 6.46 (5.43 p.e.)

Lambdoid Flattening
Absent: deficiency 10.56 (5.74 p.e.)
Present: excess 10.56 (5.74 p.e.)

Neck
Medium in length, breadth: deficiency
11.58 (6.29 p.e.)
Long and thin: excess 18.54 (10.66 p.e.)
Short and thick: deficiency 6.96 (7.91 p.e.)

Shoulder Slope
Medium: deficiency 19.86 (11.89 p.e.)
Pronounced: excess 18.91 (11.89 p.e.)

Table XII-139.　　　　Summary of Significant Morphological Differences
between Criminals and Civilians

First Degree Murder

Hair Quantity, Beard
Small: excess 13.53 (6.73 p.e.)
Large: deficiency 7.96 (3.76 p.e.)

Hair Quantity, Body
Small: deficiency 8.70 (3.36 p.e.)

Hair Form
Straight: excess 14.55 (7.10 p.e.)
Low waves: deficiency 8.73 (5.52 p.e.)
Deep waves: deficiency 4.20 (3.47 p.e.)

Hair Color
Red brown: excess 8.29 (4.27 p.e.)

Eye Color
Dark brown: deficiency 3.82 (3.41 p.e.)
Gray brown: excess 14.51 (8.11 p.e.)
Blue: deficiency 8.49 (3.66 p.e.)

Sclera
Clear: excess 6.03 (3.77 p.e.)

Iris
Homogeneous: deficiency 16.54 (7.27 p.e.)
Zoned: excess 11.14 (4.95 p.e.)
Speckled: excess 11.46 (5.07 p.e.)

Eye Folds
Epicanthus: excess 5.13 (4.93 p.e.)

Eyebrow Thickness
Medium: deficiency 13.14 (5.17 p.e.)
Pronounced: excess 12.17 (5.01 p.e.)

Forehead Height
Submedium: excess 8.67 (5.78 p.e.)
Medium: deficiency 11.62 (4.54 p.e.)

Forehead Slope
Medium: deficiency 17.09 (6.62 p.e.)
Pronounced: excess 21.85 (9.03 p.e.)

Nasion Depression
Medium: deficiency 18.27 (8.05 p.e.)
Pronounced: excess 15.39 (7.85 p.e.)

Table XII-139 (cont'd).

Nasal Root Height
  Medium: deficiency 13.79 (7.00 p.e.)
  Pronounced: excess 11.86 (6.34 p.e.)

Nasal Root Breadth
  Medium: deficiency 6.09 (4.29 p.e.)
  Pronounced: excess 5.13 (4.31 p.e.)

Nasal Bridge Height
  Medium: deficiency 26.92 (10.43 p.e.)
  Pronounced: excess 25.96 (10.06 p.e.)

Nasal Bridge Breadth
  Medium: deficiency 8.04 (4.54 p.e.)
  Pronounced: excess 8.04 (4.62 p.e.)

Nasal Profile
  Straight: deficiency 7.25 (3.86 p.e.)
  Concavo-convex: excess 17.03 (6.40 p.e.)

Nasal Tip Thickness
  Submedium: excess 11.58 (8.58 p.e.)
  Medium: deficiency 17.77 (7.86 p.e.)
  Pronounced: excess 6.18 (3.14 p.e.)

Nasal Septum Inclination
  Absent: excess 1.50 (3.33 p.e.)

Nasal Septum Deflection
  Right: excess 10.91 (5.32 p.e.)
  Absent: deficiency 15.23 (6.24 p.e.)

Lips Integumental Thickness
  Submedium: excess 7.69 (4.99 p.e.)
  Medium: deficiency 8.01 (4.00 p.e.)

Lips Membranous Thickness
  Submedium: excess 13.78 (7.45 p.e.)
  Medium: deficiency 11.54 (4.83 p.e.)

Lip Seam
  Absent: excess 8.95 (4.94 p.e.)
  Medium: deficiency 7.60 (3.02 p.e.)

Alveolar Prognathism
  Submedium: excess 10.28 (6.05 p.e.)
  Medium: deficiency 7.98 (5.95 p.e.)

Malars Prominence
  Submedium: excess 7.09 (5.50 p.e.)

Cheeks Fullness
  Submedium: excess 26.27 (12.98 p.e.)
  Medium: deficiency 23.27 (9.12 p.e.)

Gonial Angles
  Submedium: excess 5.15 (3.39 p.e.)

Teeth Caries
  None: deficiency 3.76 (3.48 p.e.)
  Few: excess 14.25 (5.16 p.e.)
  Many: deficiency 10.49 (3.83 p.e.)

Bite
  Marked over: deficiency 11.83 (4.41 p.e.)

Ear Lobes
  Medium: deficiency 7.57 (3.02 p.e.)
  Pronounced: excess 7.83 (3.52 p.e.)

Roll of Helix
  Submedium: excess 23.82 (10.63 p.e.)
  Medium, pronounced: deficiency 23.82 (10.63 p.e.)

Darwin's Point
  Absent: deficiency 12.74 (4.86 p.e.)
  Small, medium: excess 9.47 (3.95 p.e.)

Antihelix Prominence
  Medium: deficiency 7.39 (3.97 p.e.)
  Pronounced: excess 9.32 (6.21 p.e.)

Ear Protrusion
  Submedium: excess 7.08 (5.13 p.e.)
  Medium: deficiency 33.18 (12.91 p.e.)
  Pronounced 26.10 (10.78 p.e.)

Temporal Fullness
  Submedium: excess 11.89 (6.95 p.e.)
  Pronounced: deficiency 6.76 (3.78 p.e.)

Lambdoid Flattening
  Absent: deficiency 15.63 (6.65 p.e.)
  Present: excess 15.63 (6.65 p.e.)

Neck
  Medium in length, breadth: deficiency 14.28 (5.88 p.e.)
  Long and thin: excess 19.99 (9.43 p.e.)
  Short and thick: deficiency 5.71 (3.71 p.e.)

Shoulder Slope
  Slight: excess 3.81 (3.77 p.e.)
  Medium: deficiency 24.33 (12.10 p.e.)
  Pronounced: excess 20.51 (11.33 p.e.)

Table XII-140.   Summary of Significant Morphological Differences
between Criminals and Civilians

Second Degree Murder

Hair Quantity, Head
  Large: excess 6.66 (3.87 p.e.)

Hair Quantity, Beard
  Small: excess 28.25 (13.39 p.e.)
  Medium: deficiency 13.59 (5.88 p.e.)
  Large: deficiency 14.66 (9.22 p.e.)

Skin Color
  Pale white: deficiency 12.31 (5.38 p.e.)
  Olive: excess 3.56 (5.01 p.e.)
  Light brown: excess 3.25 (3.53 p.e.)

Hair Form
  Straight: excess 9.77 (5.40 p.e.)
  Low waves: deficiency 4.96 (3.44 p.e.)

Hair Color
  Red brown: excess 6.38 (3.80 p.e.)
  Golden: deficiency 2.41 (3.26 p.e.)
  Gray, white: deficiency 6.22 (4.61 p.e.)

Eye Color
  Dark brown: deficiency 3.31 (3.52 p.e.)
  Gray brown: excess 12.24 (7.65 p.e.)
  Blue: deficiency 9.63 (4.94 p.e.)

Sclera
  Clear: excess 8.34 (6.89 p.e.)
  Speckled: deficiency 6.60 (6.00 p.e.)
  Yellow: deficiency 1.74 (3.16 p.e.)

Iris
  Homogeneous: deficiency 17.17 (10.87 p.e.)
  Zoned: excess 6.67 (3.44 p.e.)
  Speckled: excess 14.09 (6.84 p.e.)

Eye Folds
  Epicanthus: excess 3.43 (3.99 p.e.)

Eyebrow Thickness
  Medium: deficiency 9.32 (4.28 p.e.)
  Pronounced: excess 8.46 (4.05 p.e.)

Forehead Height
  Submedium: excess 11.36 (7.57 p.e.)
  Medium: deficiency 10.01 (4.49 p.e.)

Forehead Slope
  Absent, submedium: deficiency 5.17 (3.54 p.e.)
  Medium: deficiency 18.77 (8.09 p.e.)
  Pronounced: excess 23.94 (10.93 p.e.)

Nasion Depression
  Submedium: excess 5.56 (4.06 p.e.)
  Medium: deficiency 21.82 (10.39 p.e.)
  Pronounced: excess 16.10 (8.85 p.e.)

Nasal Root Height
  Medium: deficiency 12.68 (7.16 p.e.)
  Pronounced: excess 11.70 (6.84 p.e.)

Nasal Root Breadth
  Medium: deficiency 7.15 (5.26 p.e.)
  Pronounced: excess 5.53 (4.89 p.e.)

Nasal Bridge Height
  Medium: deficiency 25.21 (11.06 p.e.)
  Pronounced: excess 25.05 (10.99 p.e.)

Nasal Bridge Breadth
  Medium: deficiency 7.31 (4.63 p.e.)
  Pronounced: excess 6.17 (4.09 p.e.)

Nasal Profile
  Straight: deficiency 7.34 (4.68 p.e.)
  Convex: deficiency 7.38 (3.65 p.e.)
  Concavo-convex: excess 15.26 (6.78 p.e.)

Nasal Tip Thickness
  Submedium: excess 13.28 (16.20 p.e.)
  Medium: deficiency 21.37 (10.18 p.e.)
  Pronounced: excess 8.08 (4.49 p.e.)

Nasal Septum Deflection
  Right: excess 16.77 (8.38 p.e.)
  Absent: deficiency 20.42 (9.08 p.e.)

Lips Integumental Thickness
  Submedium: excess 10.57 (6.95 p.e.)
  Medium: deficiency 9.99 (5.43 p.e.)

Lips Membranous Thickness
  Submedium: excess 13.30 (7.87 p.e.)
  Medium: deficiency 10.03 (4.82 p.e.)

Lip Seam
  Absent: excess 8.36 (5.16 p.e.)
  Medium: deficiency 10.34 (4.62 p.e.)

Alveolar Prognathism
  Submedium: excess 6.07 (4.30 p.e.)
  Medium: deficiency 6.82 (6.14 p.e.)

Malars Prominence
  Submedium: excess 5.87 (5.10 p.e.)

Cheeks Fullness
  Submedium: excess 19.39 (11.08 p.e.)
  Medium: deficiency 18.71 (8.43 p.e.)

Gonial Angles
  Submedium: excess 6.09 (4.32 p.e.)

Teeth Caries
  Few: excess 19.55 (8.32 p.e.)
  Many: deficiency 18.09 (7.93 p.e.)

Table XII-140 (cont'd).

Teeth Lost
  Many: deficiency 9.44 (4.37 p.e.)

Bite
  Edge-to-edge: excess 6.96 (3.27 p.e.)
  Marked over: deficiency 9.78 (4.35 p.e.)

Roll of Helix
  Submedium: excess 26.80 (12.76 p.e.)
  Medium,pronounced: deficiency 26.80 (12.76 p.e.)

Ear Protrusion
  Submedium: excess 5.19 (4.36 p.e.)
  Medium: deficiency 27.13 (12.06 p.e.)
  Pronounced: excess 21.93 (10.34 p.e.)

Darwin's Point
  Absent: deficiency 8.82 (3.90 p.e.)

Antihelix Prominence
  Medium: deficiency 13.33 (7.28 p.e.)
  Pronounced: excess 9.41 (6.67 p.e.)

Temporal Fullness
  Submedium: excess 9.90 (6.51 p.e.)
  Medium: deficiency 6.45 (3.16 p.e.)

Lambdoid Flattening
  Absent: deficiency 12.60 (5.83 p.e.)
  Present: excess 12.60 (5.83 p.e.)

Neck
  Medium in length,breadth: deficiency 19.01
  (8.50 p.e.)
  Long and thin: excess 24.66 (12.09 p.e.)
  Short and thick: deficiency 5.65 (4.41 p.e.)

Shoulder Slope
  Medium: deficiency 25.85 (13.32 p.e.)
  Pronounced: excess 24.75 (13.38 p.e.)

Table XII-141.   Summary of Significant Morphological Differences
between Criminals and Civilians

Assault

Hair Quantity, Beard
  Small: excess 23.81 (7.94 p.e.)
  Large: deficiency 14.32 (4.22 p.e.)

Skin Color
  Olive: excess 3.75 (5.07 p.e.)

Hair Color
  Red brown: excess 10.52 (3.67 p.e.)

Eye Color
  Blue: deficiency 11.25 (3.02 p.e.)

Iris
  Homogeneous: deficiency 10.85 (3.08 p.e.)
  Zoned: excess 12.11 (3.55 p.e.)

Eye Folds
  Epicanthus: excess 3.72 (3.13 p.e.)
  Absent: deficiency 11.05 (3.13 p.e.)

Eyebrow Thickness
  Medium: deficiency 16.22 (4.20 p.e.)
  Pronounced: excess 15.38 (4.19 p.e.)

Forehead Height
  Submedium: excess 8.35 (4.22 p.e.)
  Medium: deficiency 14.38 (3.68 p.e.)

Forehead Slope
  Absent,submedium:deficiency 9.38 (3.36 p.e.)
  Pronounced: excess 18.07 (5.28 p.e.)

Nasion Depression
  Submedium: excess 10.48 (4.50 p.e.)
  Medium: deficiency 21.22 (6.51 p.e.)
  Pronounced: excess 10.74 (4.20 p.e.)

Nasal Root Height
  Submedium: excess 4.04 (3.61 p.e.)
  Medium: deficiency 28.53 (9.51 p.e.)
  Pronounced: excess 24.49 (8.59 p.e.)

Nasal Root Breadth
  Submedium: excess 8.08 (5.18 p.e.)
  Medium: deficiency 20.01 (8.66 p.e.)
  Pronounced: excess 9.94 (5.62 p.e.)

Nasal Bridge Height
  Medium: deficiency 26.53 (7.04 p.e.)
  Pronounced: excess 26.53 (7.04 p.e.)

Nasal Bridge Breadth
  Medium: deficiency 14.14 (5.01 p.e.)
  Pronounced: excess 12.28 (4.80 p.e.)

Nasal Profile
  Straight: deficiency 11.61 (3.79 p.e.)
  Concavo-convex: excess 12.48 (3.07 p.e.)

Nasal Tip Thickness
  Submedium: excess 5.29 (4.44 p.e.)
  Medium: deficiency 15.01 (4.75 p.e.)
  Pronounced: excess 9.71 (3.24 p.e.)

Nasal Septum Deflection
  Right: excess 11.28 (3.86 p.e.)
  Absent: deficiency 18.11 (5.03 p.e.)

Lips Integumental Thickness
  Submedium: excess 11.12 (5.03 p.e.)
  Medium: deficiency 13.75 (4.52 p.e.)

Table XII-141 (cont'd).

Lips Membranous Thickness
  Submedium: excess 18.27 (7.08 p.e.)
  Medium: deficiency 24.17 (6.53 p.e.)

Alveolar Prognathism
  Medium: deficiency 4.29 (3.43 p.e.)

Cheeks Fullness
  Submedium: excess 32.10 (12.30 p.e.)
  Medium: deficiency 30.45 (8.02 p.e.)

Cheeks Wrinkling
  Absent: excess 13.04 (3.13 p.e.)
  Pronounced: deficiency 12.50 (3.51 p.e.)

Teeth Caries
  Few: excess 22.18 (5.15 p.e.)
  Many: deficiency 18.96 (4.44 p.e.)

Roll of Helix
  Submedium: excess 23.92 (7.87 p.e.)
  Medium,pronounced:deficiency 23.92 (7.87 p.e.)

Ear Protrusion
  Medium: deficiency 29.23 (8.07 p.e.)
  Pronounced: excess 27.76 (8.14 p.e.)

Antihelix Prominence
  Medium: deficiency 19.14 (6.51 p.e.)
  Pronounced: excess 16.39 (7.45 p.e.)

Temporal Fullness
  Submedium: excess 8.28 (6.27 p.e.)
  Pronounced: deficiency 9.83 (5.55 p.e.)

Lambdoid Flattening
  Absent: deficiency 24.11 (6.34 p.e.)
  Present: excess 24.11 (6.34 p.e.)

Neck
  Long and thin: excess 18.23 (6.42 p.e.)
  Short and thick: deficiency 8.07 (3.15 p.e.)

Shoulder Slope
  Pronounced: excess 5.18 (3.36 p.e.)

Table XII-142.   Summary of Significant Morphological Differences
                          between Criminals and Civilians

                                  Robbery

Hair Quantity, Head
  Small: deficiency 8.71 (5.58 p.e.)
  Large: excess 8.93 (4.72 p.e.)

Hair Quantity, Beard
  Small: excess 20.40 (9.81 p.e.)
  Medium: deficiency 13.83 (5.58 p.e.)
  Large: deficiency 6.57 (3.28 p.e.)

Hair Quantity, Body
  Small: excess 9.81 (3.89 p.e.)
  Medium: deficiency 8.77 (3.54 p.e.)

Skin Color
  Olive: excess 2.91 (4.55 p.e.)

Hair Color
  Red brown: excess 11.52 (6.00 p.e.)
  Gray, white: deficiency 11.33 (8.92 p.e.)

Eye Color
  Dark brown: deficiency 3.23 (3.08 p.e.)
  Gray brown: excess 12.53 (7.50 p.e.)
  Blue: deficiency 13.22 (6.42 p.e.)

Sclera
  Clear: excess 8.34 (4.88 p.e.)
  Speckled: deficiency 6.02 (3.81 p.e.)
  Yellow: deficiency 2.32 (3.31 p.e.)

Iris
  Homogeneous: deficiency 16.78 (9.27 p.e.)
  Rayed: deficiency 7.50 (5.36 p.e.)
  Zoned: excess 15.36 (6.89 p.e.)

Eye Folds
  Epicanthus: excess 2.61 (3.14 p.e.)
  Median: excess 5.75 (3.12 p.e.)
  Absent: deficiency 9.48 (4.31 p.e.)

Eyebrow Thickness
  Medium: deficiency 9.07 (3.88 p.e.)
  Pronounced: excess 10.34 (4.56 p.e.)

Forehead Height
  Submedium: excess 6.48 (4.76 p.e.)

Forehead Slope
  Absent,submedium: deficiency 6.89 (4.47 p.e.)
  Medium: deficiency 8.55 (3.52 p.e.)
  Pronounced: excess 15.45 (6.99 p.e.)

Nasion Depression
  Medium: deficiency 9.22 (4.66 p.e.)
  Pronounced: excess 8.21 (4.89 p.e.)

Nasal Root Height
  Medium: deficiency 8.42 (4.84 p.e.)
  Pronounced: excess 7.93 (4.75 p.e.)

Nasal Root Breadth
  Submedium: excess 3.39 (3.50 p.e.)
  Medium: deficiency 9.76 (6.42 p.e.)
  Pronounced: excess 6.38 (5.23 p.e.)

Nasal Bridge Height
  Medium: deficiency 13.39 (5.80 p.e.)
  Pronounced: excess 12.90 (5.51 p.e.)

Table XII-142 (cont'd).

Nasal Bridge Breadth
  Submedium: excess 3.49 (4.31 p.e.)
  Medium: deficiency 13.48 (7.25 p.e.)
  Pronounced: excess 10.00 (5.81 p.e.)

Nasal Profile
  Straight: deficiency 6.48 (3.68 p.e.)
  Convex: deficiency 10.26 (4.75 p.e.)
  Concavo-convex: excess 10.54 (4.27 p.e.)

Nasal Tip Thickness
  Submedium: excess 8.51 (7.21 p.e.)
  Medium: deficiency 17.57 (8.21 p.e.)
  Pronounced: excess 9.05 (4.66 p.e.)

Nasal Septum Inclination
  Up: excess 14.21 (5.87 p.e.)
  Down: deficiency 14.21 (5.87 p.e.)

Nasal Septum Deflection
  Right: excess 12.93 (6.43 p.e.)
  Absent: deficiency 12.25 (5.40 p.e.)

Lips Integumental Thickness
  Submedium: excess 6.73 (4.67 p.e.)
  Medium: deficiency 5.56 (3.08 p.e.)

Lips Membranous Thickness
  Submedium: excess 5.35 (3.57 p.e.)
  Medium: deficiency 6.71 (3.09 p.e.)

Alveolar Prognathism
  Submedium: excess 7.18 (4.60 p.e.)
  Medium: deficiency 6.92 (5.49 p.e.)

Cheeks Fullness
  Submedium: excess 19.52 (10.78 p.e.)
  Medium: deficiency 18.54 (7.82 p.e.)

Gonial Angles
  Submedium: excess 6.73 (4.46 p.e.)
  Pronounced: deficiency 8.03 (4.18 p.e.)

Cheeks Wrinkling
  Absent: excess 29.27 (11.26 p.e.)
  Slight,medium: deficiency 9.82 (3.99 p.e.)
  Pronounced: deficiency 19.44 (10.92 p.e.)

Teeth Wear
  Slight, medium: excess 20.28 (10.35 p.e.)
  Pronounced: deficiency 20.83 (10.91 p.e.)

Teeth Caries
  None: deficiency 3.37 (3.40 p.e.)
  Few: excess 24.84 (9.98 p.e.)
  Many: deficiency 21.47 (8.84 p.e.)

Teeth Lost
  Few: excess 11.09 (4.37 p.e.)
  Many: deficiency 15.95 (7.06 p.e.)

Bite
  Slight over: excess 16.09 (5.98 p.e.)
  Marked over: deficiency 8.83 (3.62 p.e.)

Roll of Helix
  Submedium: excess 20.01 (9.62 p.e.)
  Medium,pronounced: deficiency 20.49 (9.80 p.e.)

Ear Protrusion
  Submedium: excess 3.47 (3.02 p.e.)
  Medium: deficiency 17.72 (7.81 p.e.)
  Pronounced: excess 14.25 (6.72 p.e.)

Darwin's Point
  Absent: deficiency 14.56 (5.90 p.e.)
  Small, medium: excess 9.19 (4.08 p.e.)
  Pronounced: excess 5.37 (3.27 p.e.)

Antihelix Prominence
  Medium: deficiency 12.31 (6.48 p.e.)
  Pronounced: excess 11.15 (7.29 p.e.)

Temporal Fullness
  Submedium: excess 12.01 (7.24 p.e.)
  Pronounced: deficiency 8.56 (5.38 p.e.)

Lambdoid Flattening
  Absent: deficiency 11.01 (4.81 p.e.)
  Present: excess 11.01 (4.81 p.e.)

Neck
  Medium in length, breadth: deficiency 9.83
  (4.16 p.e.)
  Long and thin: excess 16.09 (8.21 p.e.)
  Short and thick: deficiency 6.26 (4.50 p.e.)

Shoulder Slope
  Medium: deficiency 17.39 (9.82 p.e.)
  Pronounced: excess 16.13 (9.90 p.e.)

Table XII-143.   Summary of Significant Morphological Differences
between Criminals and Civilians

Burglary and Larceny

Hair Quantity, Head
  Small: deficiency 8.33 (7.12 p.e.)
  Large: excess 7.35 (4.65 p.e.)

Hair Quantity, Beard
  Small: excess 30.12 (15.21 p.e.)
  Medium: deficiency 20.47 (9.84 p.e.)
  Large: deficiency 9.65 (6.52 p.e.)

Hair Quantity, Body
  Small: excess 16.84 (8.14 p.e.)
  Medium: deficiency 12.81 (6.47 p.e.)
  Large: deficiency 4.03 (3.12 p.e.)

Skin Color
  Pale white: deficiency 6.58 (3.27 p.e.)
  Olive: excess 3.23 (4.82 p.e.)

Hair Form
  Straight: excess 10.65 (7.01 p.e.)
  Low waves: deficiency 6.22 (5.32 p.e.)
  Deep waves: deficiency 3.19 (3.62 p.e.)

Hair Color
  Red brown: excess 9.73 (5.97 p.e.)
  Gray, white: deficiency 11.13 (13.74 p.e.)

Eye Color
  Dark brown: deficiency 2.91 (3.59 p.e.)
  Blue brown: deficiency 6.77 (4.01 p.e.)
  Gray brown: excess 11.09 (7.54 p.e.)
  Blue: deficiency 10.49 (6.32 p.e.)
  Blue gray: excess 4.94 (4.05 p.e.)

Sclera
  Clear: excess 7.93 (7.93 p.e.)
  Speckled: deficiency 5.81 (6.18 p.e.)
  Yellow: deficiency 2.12 (5.73 p.e.)

Iris
  Homogeneous: deficiency 17.13 (13.60 p.e.)
  Zoned: excess 13.29 (12.66 p.e.)
  Speckled: excess 9.14 (5.11 p.e.)

Eye Folds
  Epicanthus: excess 2.95 (3.73 p.e.)
  Absent: deficiency 6.67 (3.66 p.e.)

Eyebrow Thickness
  Medium: deficiency 9.74 (4.92 p.e.)
  Pronounced: excess 10.12 (5.27 p.e.)

Forehead Height
  Submedium: excess 9.02 (6.73 p.e.)
  Medium: deficiency 8.15 (4.12 p.e.)

Forehead Slope
  Absent,submedium:deficiency 5.69 (4.63 p.e.)
  Medium: deficiency 9.60 (4.73 p.e.)
  Pronounced: excess 15.29 (8.05 p.e.)

Nasion Depression
  Submedium: excess 5.34 (4.24 p.e.)
  Medium: deficiency 14.15 (7.82 p.e.)
  Pronounced: excess 8.75 (5.83 p.e.)

Nasal Root Height
  Medium: deficiency 6.10 (4.24 p.e.)
  Pronounced: excess 5.64 (4.09 p.e.)

Nasal Root Breadth
  Submedium: excess 3.04 (3.54 p.e.)
  Medium: deficiency 10.58 (7.45 p.e.)
  Pronounced: excess 7.55 (6.34 p.e.)

Nasal Bridge Height
  Medium: deficiency 29.74 (14.30 p.e.)
  Pronounced: excess 29.49 (14.18 p.e.)

Nasal Bridge Breadth
  Submedium: excess 3.52 (4.51 p.e.)
  Medium: deficiency 11.55 (7.22 p.e.)
  Pronounced: excess 8.04 (5.51 p.e.)

Nasal Profile
  Concave: excess 7.68 (4.27 p.e.)
  Straight: deficiency 6.69 (4.92 p.e.)
  Convex: deficiency 12.05 (7.30 p.e.)
  Concavo-convex: excess 11.05 (5.36 p.e.)

Nasal Tip Thickness
  Submedium: excess 8.60 (7.54 p.e.)
  Medium: deficiency 15.93 (8.61 p.e.)
  Pronounced: excess 7.32 (15.91 p.e.)

Nasal Septum Inclination
  Up: excess 16.95 (8.97 p.e.)
  Down: deficiency 17.13 (9.06 p.e.)

Nasal Septum Deflection
  Right: excess 12.02 (6.87 p.e.)
  Absent: deficiency 12.31 (6.31 p.e.)

Lips Integumental Thickness
  Submedium: excess 7.38 (5.59 p.e.)
  Pronounced: deficiency 3.20 (3.64 p.e.)

Lips Membranous Thickness
  Submedium: excess 7.64 (5.46 p.e.)
  Medium: deficiency 10.45 (5.50 p.e.)

Alveolar Prognathism
  Submedium: excess 5.72 (4.40 p.e.)
  Medium: deficiency 5.76 (6.00 p.e.)

Malars Prominence
  Submedium: excess 2.72 (3.06 p.e.)

Cheeks Fullness
  Submedium: excess 18.18 (11.02 p.e.)
  Medium: deficiency 18.26 (9.08 p.e.)

Table XII-143 (cont'd)

Gonial Angles
  Submedium: excess 7.60 (5.51 p.e.)
  Pronounced: deficiency 6.07 (3.89 p.e.)

Cheeks Wrinkling
  Absent: excess 25.76 (11.93 p.e.)
  Slight,medium: deficiency 7.62 (3.72 p.e.)
  Pronounced: deficiency 18.14 (14.17 p.e.)

Teeth Wear
  Slight, medium: excess 6.99 (4.60 p.e.)
  Pronounced: deficiency 17.77 (12.17 p.e.)

Teeth Caries
  None: deficiency 3.54 (4.99 p.e.)
  Few: excess 29.24 (15.55 p.e.)
  Many: deficiency 25.70 (13.97 p.e.)

Teeth Lost
  None: excess 12.91 (6.69 p.e.)
  Many: deficiency 18.48 (10.81 p.e.)

Bite
  Slight over: excess 12.84 (5.71 p.e.)
  Marked over: deficiency 10.63 (5.42 p.e.)

Roll of Helix
  Submedium: excess 19.96 (7.28 p.e.)
  Medium, pronounced: deficiency 19.96 (7.28 p.e.)

Ear Protrusion
  Submedium: excess 3.86 (3.71 p.e.)
  Medium: deficiency 24.28 (12.02 p.e.)
  Pronounced: excess 20.42 (10.52 p.e.)

Darwin's Point
  Absent: deficiency 8.59 (4.25 p.e.)
  Pronounced: excess 4.60 (3.31 p.e.)

Antihelix Prominence
  Medium: deficiency 13.16 (7.79 p.e.)
  Pronounced: excess 10.50 (7.61 p.e.)

Temporal Fullness
  Submedium: excess 11.40 (7.70 p.e.)
  Medium: deficiency 5.92 (3.22 p.e.)
  Pronounced: deficiency 5.50 (4.17 p.e.)

Lambdoid Flattening
  Absent: deficiency 9.11 (4.74 p.e.)
  Present: excess 9.11 (4.74 p.e.)

Neck
  Medium in length, breadth: deficiency 10.73
  (5.62 p.e.)
  Long and thin: excess 18.68 (10.44 p.e.)
  Short and thick: deficiency 7.95 (8.64 p.e.)

Shoulder Slope
  Medium: deficiency 20.44 (11.68 p.e.)
  Pronounced: excess 19.78 (11.99 p.e.)

Table XII-144.   Summary of Significant Morphological Differences
                        between Criminals and Civilians

Forgery and Fraud

Hair Quantity, Beard
  Small: excess 17.47 (8.82 p.e.)
  Medium: deficiency 11.10 (4.62 p.e.)
  Large: deficiency 6.37 (3.28 p.e.)

Hair Quantity, Body
  Small: excess 9.16 (3.74 p.e.)
  Medium: deficiency 11.39 (4.77 p.e.)

Skin Color
  Olive: excess 3.21 (4.79 p.e.)

Hair Form
  Straight: excess 9.21 (4.75 p.e.)
  Deep waves: deficiency 4.21 (3.97 p.e.)

Hair Color
  Red brown: excess 7.26 (4.06 p.e.)
  Gray, white: deficiency 9.57 (7.30 p.e.)

Eye Color
  Dark brown: deficiency 3.61 (3.65 p.e.)
  Blue-brown: deficiency 7.68 (3.78 p.e.)
  Gray-brown: excess 12.99 (7.82 p.e.)
  Blue-gray: excess 3.99 (3.02 p.e.)

Sclera
  Clear: excess 9.29 (7.20 p.e.)
  Speckled: deficiency 7.60 (6.61 p.e.)

Iris
  Homogeneous: deficiency 16.89 (9.76 p.e.)
  Rayed: deficiency 6.90 (3.14 p.e.)
  Zoned: excess 18.08 (8.14 p.e.)

Eyebrow Thickness
  Medium: deficiency 8.70 (3.82 p.e.)
  Pronounced: excess 8.35 (3.83 p.e.)

Table XII-144 (cont'd)

Forehead Height
  Submedium: excess 5.06 (3.98 p.e.)
  Medium: deficiency 7.85 (3.50 p.e.)

Forehead Slope
  Absent,submedium: deficiency 8.17 (5.67 p.e.)
  Medium: deficiency 7.45 (3.17 p.e.)
  Pronounced: excess 15.62 (7.23 p.e.)

Nasion Depression
  Submedium: excess .65 (3.42 p.e.)
  Medium: deficiency 6.13 (3.30 p.e.)
  Pronounced: excess 5.48 (3.54 p.e.)

Nasal Root Height
  Medium: deficiency 6.66 (4.04 p.e.)
  Pronounced: excess 5.77 (4.23 p.e.)

Nasal Root Breadth
  Submedium: excess 3.86 (3.90 p.e.)
  Medium: deficiency 8.57 (5.91 p.e.)
  Pronounced: excess 4.72 (4.25 p.e.)

Nasal Bridge Height
  Medium: deficiency 10.43 (4.72 p.e.)
  Pronounced: excess 10.21 (4.62 p.e.)

Nasal Bridge Breadth
  Submedium: excess 3.86 (4.65 p.e.)
  Medium: deficiency 10.27 (5.94 p.e.)
  Pronounced: excess 6.41 (4.08 p.e.)

Nasal Profile
  Straight: deficiency 6.06 (3.54 p.e.)
  Convex: deficiency 8.84 (4.19 p.e.)
  Concavo-convex: excess 11.08 (4.60 p.e.)

Nasal Tip Thickness
  Submedium: excess 8.48 (7.25 p.e.)
  Medium: deficiency 15.02 (7.29 p.e.)
  Pronounced: excess 6.52 (3.54 p.e.)

Nasal Septum Inclination
  Up: excess 11.40 (4.77 p.e.)
  Down: deficiency 11.60 (4.85 p.e.)

Nasal Septum Deflection
  Right: excess 6.16 (3.44 p.e.)

Lips Membranous Thickness
  Submedium: excess 4.62 (3.23 p.e.)
  Medium: deficiency 8.93 (4.13 p.e.)

Lip Seam
  Absent: excess 7.06 (4.33 p.e.)

Alveolar Prognathism
  Submedium: excess 7.85 (5.16 p.e.)
  Medium: deficiency 6.90 (5.75 p.e.)

Cheeks Fullness
  Submedium: excess 19.83 (11.02 p.e.)
  Medium: deficiency 22.29 (9.48 p.e.)

Goniel Angles
  Submedium: excess 4.64 (3.31 p.e.)

Cheeks Wrinkling
  Absent: excess 13.32 (5.22 p.e.)
  Pronounced: deficiency 14.42 (7.67 p.e.)

Teeth Wear
  Slight, medium: excess 16.63 (8.36 p.e.)
  Pronounced: deficiency 16.39 (8.32 p.e.)

Teeth Caries
  Few: excess 23.54 (9.61 p.e.)
  Many: deficiency 20.62 (8.63 p.e.)

Teeth Lost
  None: excess 9.94 (4.58 p.e.)
  Many: deficiency 10.24 (4.47 p.e.)

Bite
  Slight over: excess 11.39 (4.28 p.e.)
  Marked over: deficiency 10.50 (4.43 p.e.)

Roll of Helix
  Submedium: excess 19.07 (9.35 p.e.)
  Medium,pronounced:deficiency 19.78 (9.70 p.e.)

Ear Protrusion
  Medium: deficiency 21.56 (9.50 p.e.)
  Pronounced: excess 19.31 (8.94 p.e.)

Darwin's Point
  Absent: deficiency 9.68 (4.08 p.e.)

Antihelix Prominence
  Medium: deficiency 10.85 (5.90 p.e.)
  Pronounced: excess 10.52 (7.01 p.e.)

Temporal Fullness
  Submedium: excess 16.08 (9.08 p.e.)
  Medium: deficiency 6.69 (3.10 p.e.)
  Pronounced: deficiency 9.40 (6.18 p.e.)

Lambdoid Flattening
  Absent: deficiency 10.53 (4.68 p.e.)
  Present: excess 10.53 (4.68 p.e.)

Neck
  Medium in length,breadth: deficiency 10.31
  (4.66 p.e.)
  Long and thin: excess 16.32 (8.41 p.e.)
  Short and thick: deficiency 6.01 (4.42 p.e.)

Shoulder Slope
  Medium: deficiency 18.35 (10.37 p.e.)
  Pronounced: excess 18.07 (10.76 p.e.)

Table XII-145. Summary of Significant Morphological Differences
between Criminals and Civilians

Rape

Hair Quantity, Beard
  Small: excess 29.03 (11.57 p.e.)
  Medium: deficiency 17.76 (5.90 p.e.)
  Large: deficiency 11.28 (4.70 p.e.)

Skin Color
  Olive: excess 3.55 (4.93 p.e.)

Hair Form
  Straight: excess 14.18 (4.79 p.e.)
  Low waves: deficiency 6.76 (3.48 p.e.)
  Deep waves: deficiency 6.40 (4.81 p.e.)

Hair Color
  Red brown: excess 7.97 (3.72 p.e.)

Eye Color
  Blue-brown: deficiency 8.39 (3.20 p.e.)
  Gray-brown: excess 4.93 (3.08 p.e.)
  Blue: deficiency 10.62 (3.99 p.e.)
  Blue-gray: excess 13.74 (7.19 p.e.)

Sclera
  Yellow: deficiency 2.56 (3.32 p.e.)

Iris
  Homogeneous: deficiency 17.93 (2.35 p.e.)
  Zoned: excess 19.03 (7.13 p.e.)

Forehead Height
  Submedium: excess 7.02 (4.53 p.e.)
  Medium: deficiency 13.50 (4.65 p.e.)

Forehead Slope
  Medium: deficiency 12.34 (4.18 p.e.)
  Pronounced: excess 17.59 (6.71 p.e.)

Nasion Depression
  Medium: deficiency 10.20 (4.34 p.e.)
  Pronounced: excess 10.87 (5.41 p.e.)

Nasal Root Height
  Medium: deficiency 10.83 (5.21 p.e.)
  Pronounced: excess 9.25 (4.70 p.e.)

Nasal Root Breadth
  Submedium: excess 7.77 (5.84 p.e.)
  Medium: deficiency 19.49 (9.74 p.e.)
  Pronounced: excess 11.72 (7.42 p.e.)

Nasal Bridge Height
  Medium: deficiency 19.50 (6.94 p.e.)
  Pronounced: excess 19.00 (6.79 p.e.)

Nasal Bridge Breadth
  Submedium: excess 6.50 (6.08 p.e.)
  Medium: deficiency 19.70 (8.76 p.e.)
  Pronounced: excess 13.20 (6.41 p.e.)

Nasal Profile
  Concavo-convex: excess 9.60 (3.23 p.e.)

Nasal Tip Thickness
  Submedium: excess 11.28 (8.17 p.e.)
  Medium: deficiency 21.97 (8.58 p.e.)
  Pronounced: excess 10.68 (4.62 p.e.)

Nasal Septum Deflection
  Right: excess 20.06 (8.19 p.e.)
  Absent: deficiency 22.66 (8.09 p.e.)

Lips Integumental Thickness
  Submedium: excess 9.16 (5.30 p.e.)
  Medium: deficiency 10.97 (4.92 p.e.)

Lips Membranous Thickness
  Submedium: excess 17.25 (8.25 p.e.)
  Medium: deficiency 21.52 (7.71 p.e.)

Lip Seam
  Absent: excess 12.56 (6.04 p.e.)

Alveolar Prognathism
  Submedium: excess 6.62 (3.83 p.e.)
  Medium: deficiency 6.99 (4.24 p.e.)

Cheeks Fullness
  Submedium: excess 26.31 (12.24 p.e.)
  Medium: deficiency 22.12 (7.82 p.e.)

Teeth Wear
  Slight, medium: excess 8.38 (3.01 p.e.)

Teeth Caries
  None: deficiency 5.28 (25.14 p.e.)
  Few: excess 20.50 (6.53 p.e.)
  Many: deficiency 15.21 (4.91 p.e.)

Bite
  Marked over: deficiency 12.27 (4.04 p.e.)

Roll of Helix
  Submedium: excess 24.43 (10.01 p.e.)
  Medium, pronounced: deficiency 24.43 (10.01 p.e.)

Ear Protrusion
  Medium: deficiency 27.14 (9.76 p.e.)
  Pronounced: excess 25.06 (9.49 p.e.)

Darwin's Point
  Absent: deficiency 10.23 (3.49 p.e.)
  Small, medium: excess 8.41 (3.14 p.e.)

Antihelix Prominence
  Medium: deficiency 15.16 (6.77 p.e.)
  Pronounced: excess 13.06 (7.46 p.e.)

Table XII-145 (cont'd).

Temporal Fullness
  Submedium: excess 5.75 (3.51 p.e.)
  Pronounced: deficiency 8.94 (4.38 p.e.)

Lambdoid Flattening
  Absent: deficiency 14.01 (5.08 p.e.)
  Present: excess 14.01 (5.08 p.e.)

Neck
  Long and thin: excess 14.83 (6.80 p.e.)
  Short and thick: deficiency 7.72 (4.41 p.e.)

Shoulder Slope
  Medium: deficiency 12.44 (7.11 p.e.)
  Pronounced: excess 11.01 (7.15 p.e.)

Table XII-146.   Summary of Significant Morphological Differences
between Criminals and Civilians

Other Sex Offenses

Hair Quantity, Beard
  Small: excess 22.51 (8.93 p.e.)
  Medium: deficiency 14.01 (4.32 p.e.)
  Large: deficiency 8.50 (3.17 p.e.)

Skin Color
  Ruddy: excess 1.32 (3.00 p.e.)
  Olive: excess 1.99 (3.76 p.e.)

Hair Form
  Straight: excess 18.17 (6.91 p.e.)
  Low waves: deficiency 11.87 (5.90 p.e.)

Hair Color
  Red brown: excess 11.52 (4.86 p.e.)
  Golden: deficiency 3.55 (3.09 p.e.)

Eye Color
  Light brown: deficiency 3.48 (3.03 p.e.)
  Gray-brown: excess 8.57 (4.66 p.e.)
  Blue-gray: excess 7.24 (4.04 p.e.)

Sclera
  Clear: excess 10.06 (5.08 p.e.)
  Speckled: deficiency 7.50 (4.14 p.e.)

Iris
  Homogeneous: deficiency 14.00 (5.24 p.e.)
  Zoned: excess 8.60 (3.18 p.e.)
  Speckled: excess 10.88 (4.04 p.e.)

Eye Folds
  Epicanthus: excess 4.72 (4.25 p.e.)

Eyebrow Thickness
  Medium: deficiency 14.78 (4.78 p.e.)
  Pronounced: excess 13.64 (4.62 p.e.)

Forehead Height
  Submedium: excess 8.43 (4.99 p.e.)
  Medium: deficiency 10.29 (3.32 p.e.)

Forehead Slope
  Medium: deficiency 15.71 (4.89 p.e.)
  Pronounced: excess 21.48 (7.54 p.e.)

Nasion Depression
  Submedium: excess 5.56 (3.14 p.e.)
  Medium: deficiency 16.89 (6.40 p.e.)
  Pronounced: excess 11.32 (5.24 p.e.)

Nasal Root Height
  Medium: deficiency 16.86 (7.17 p.e.)
  Pronounced: excess 16.49 (7.26 p.e.)

Nasal Root Breadth
  Medium: deficiency 12.73 (6.77 p.e.)
  Pronounced: excess 10.68 (6.72 p.e.)

Nasal Bridge Height
  Medium: deficiency 26.22 (8.51 p.e.)
  Pronounced: excess 26.22 (8.51 p.e.)

Nasal Bridge Breadth
  Medium: deficiency 9.52 (4.49 p.e.)
  Pronounced: excess 7.51 (3.72 p.e.)

Nasal Profile
  Straight: deficiency 7.86 (3.25 p.e.)

Nasal Tip Thickness
  Submedium: excess 9.71 (7.30 p.e.)
  Medium: deficiency 15.59 (5.95 p.e.)

Nasal Septum Inclination
  Up: excess 10.18 (3.09 p.e.)
  Down: deficiency 10.83 (3.30 p.e.)

Nasal Septum Deflection
  Right: excess 22.56 (8.48 p.e.)
  Absent: deficiency 26.56 (8.65 p.e.)

Lips Membranous Thickness
  Submedium: excess 22.41 (9.66 p.e.)
  Medium: deficiency 22.88 (7.60 p.e.)

Lip Seam
  Absent: excess 8.31 (5.54 p.e.)
  Medium: deficiency 10.71 (3.42 p.e.)

Alveolar Prognathism
  Submedium: excess 11.15 (5.63 p.e.)

Cheeks Fullness
  Submedium: excess 32.52 (13.72 p.e.)
  Medium: deficiency 25.29 (8.21 p.e.)

Gonial Angles
  Submedium: excess 9.93 (5.09 p.e.)

Cheeks Wrinkling
  Absent: excess 30.88 (9.36 p.e.)

Teeth Caries
  None: deficiency 5.82 (4.31 p.e.)
  Few: excess 13.92 (4.01 p.e.)

Bite
  Marked over: deficiency 10.34 (3.08 p.e.)

Roll of Helix
  Submedium: excess 21.96 (8.65 p.e.)
  Medium,pronounced:deficiency 21.96 (8.65 p.e.)

Ear Protrusion
  Submedium: excess 5.08 (3.43 p.e.)
  Medium: deficiency 24.11 (8.23 p.e.)
  Pronounced: excess 19.04 (7.00 p.e.)

Table XII-146 (cont'd).

Antihelix Prominence
Medium: deficiency 12.85 (5.49 p.e.)
Pronounced: excess 10.90 (6.23 p.e.)

Temporal Fullness
Submedium: excess 7.77 (4.29 p.e.)

Lambdoid Flattening
Absent: deficiency 11.71 (3.97 p.e.)
Present: excess 11.71 (3.97 p.e.)

Neck
Medium in length, breadth: deficiency 11.36 (3.94 p.e.)
Long and thin: excess 19.87 (8.18 p.e.)
Short and thick: deficiency 8.51 (4.43 p.e.)

Shoulder Slope
Medium: deficiency 16.56 (8.41 p.e.)
Pronounced: excess 16.22 (9.06 p.e.)

Table XII-147. Summary of Significant Morphological Differences between Criminals and Civilians

Versus Public Welfare

Hair Quantity, Head
Medium: deficiency 12.35 (4.66 p.e.)
Large: excess 10.82 (5.15 p.e.)

Hair Quantity, Beard
Small: excess 24.69 (10.74 p.e.)
Medium: deficiency 16.41 (5.92 p.e.)
Large: deficiency 8.28 (3.71 p.e.)

Skin Color
Red white: excess 11.15 (4.13 p.e.)
Pale white: deficiency 12.34 (4.50 p.e.)
Olive: excess 1.95 (3.68 p.e.)

Hair Form
Straight: excess 8.43 (3.75 p.e.)

Hair Color
Dark brown: deficiency 9.69 (3.59 p.e.)
Red brown: excess 9.63 (4.68 p.e.)

Eye Color
Dark brown: deficiency 4.06 (3.41 p.e.)
Light brown: deficiency 2.98 (3.17 p.e.)
Blue-brown: deficiency 10.18 (4.33 p.e.)
Gray-brown: excess 22.20 (10.83 p.e.)
Blue: deficiency 7.74 (3.13 p.e.)
Blue-gray: excess 5.08 (3.34 p.e.)

Sclera
Clear: excess 5.98 (3.46 p.e.)
Yellow: deficiency 3.36 (4.42 p.e.)

Iris
Homogeneous: deficiency 18.35 (8.74 p.e.)
Zoned: excess 16.49 (6.68 p.e.)
Speckled: excess 7.29 (3.20 p.e.)

Eye Folds
External: excess 5.31 (3.30 p.e.)

Eyebrow Thickness
Medium: deficiency 13.80 (5.19 p.e.)
Pronounced: excess 11.73 (4.62 p.e.)

Forehead Height
Submedium: excess 8.69 (5.61 p.e.)
Medium: deficiency 11.18 (4.17 p.e.)

Forehead Slope
Absent,submedium: deficiency 10.10 (5.98 p.e.)
Pronounced: excess 16.92 (6.91 p.e.)

Nasion Depression
Pronounced: excess 6.78 (3.81 p.e.)

Nasal Root Height
Medium: deficiency 6.59 (3.56 p.e.)
Pronounced: excess 6.78 (3.81 p.e.)

Nasal Root Breadth
Pronounced: excess 3.67 (3.22 p.e.)

Nasal Bridge Height
Medium: deficiency 16.40 (6.33 p.e.)
Pronounced: excess 16.01 (6.18 p.e.)

Nasal Bridge Breadth
Medium: deficiency 7.37 (3.96 p.e.)
Pronounced: excess 7.84 (4.38 p.e.)

Nasal Profile
Concavo-convex: excess 10.93 (3.96 p.e.)

Nasal Tip Thickness
Medium: deficiency 15.17 (6.60 p.e.)
Pronounced: excess 7.55 (3.36 p.e.)

Lips Membranous Thickness
Submedium: excess 12.02 (6.46 p.e.)
Medium: deficiency 12.37 (4.93 p.e.)

Lip Seam
Absent: excess 15.08 (7.39 p.e.).
Medium: deficiency 11.22 (4.19 p.e.)

Alveolar Prognathism
Submedium: excess 5.21 (3.30 p.e.)
Medium: deficiency 6.26 (4.12 p.e.)

Table XII-147 (cont'd).

Malars Prominence
Medium: deficiency 20.68 (7.55 p.e.)
Pronounced: 20.10 (7.42 p.e.)

Cheeks Fullness
Submedium: excess 12.97 (7.58 p.e.)
Medium: deficiency 24.65 (9.20 p.e.)
Pronounced: excess 11.68 (4.87 p.e.)

Cheeks Wrinkling
Absent: excess 24.23 (8.75 p.e.)

Teeth Caries
None: deficiency 4.18 (3.70 p.e.)

Ear Lobes
Submedium: deficiency 7.22 (3.41 p.e.)

Ear Lobe Attachment
Attached: deficiency 8.87 (3.28 p.e.)
Free: excess 8.87 (3.28 p.e.)

Roll of Helix
Submedium: excess 22.55 (9.85 p.e.)
Medium,pronounced:deficiency 22.55 (9.85 p.e.)

Ear Protrusion
Submedium: excess 3.86 (3.04 p.e.)
Medium: deficiency 24.14 (9.36 p.e.)
Pronounced: excess 20.28 (8.38 p.e.)

Darwin's Point
Absent: deficiency 10.71 (3.92 p.e.)
Pronounced: excess 7.00 (3.76 p.e.)

Antihelix Prominence
Medium: deficiency 12.69 (5.88 p.e.)
Pronounced: excess 8.64 (5.68 p.e.)

Temporal Fullness
Submedium: excess 22.55 (10.95 p.e.)
Medium: deficiency 12.70 (5.02 p.e.)
Pronounced: deficiency 9.86 (5.42 p.e.)

Neck
Long and thin: excess 13.08 (6.41 p.e.)
Short and thick: deficiency 5.94 (3.62 p.e.)

Shoulder Slope
Medium: deficiency 15.65 (8.69 p.e.)
Pronounced: excess 14.93 (9.05 p.e.)

Table XII-148.   Summary of Significant Morphological Differences
between Criminals and Civilians

Arson and All Other Offenses

Hair Quantity, Beard
Small: excess 23.07 (8.27 p.e.)
Medium: deficiency 14.56 (3.95 p.e.)

Skin Color
Ruddy: excess 2.91 (4.48 p.e.)

Hair Color
Black: excess 5.18 (3.14 p.e.)
Red brown: excess 8.42 (3.26 p.e.)
Ash blond: excess 3.88 (3.01 p.e.)

Eye Color
Gray-brown: excess 9.13 (4.48 p.e.)
Green-brown: excess 10.66 (3.17 p.e.)

Iris
Homogeneous: deficiency 15.86 (5.12 p.e.)
Zoned: excess 9.29 (3.02 p.e.)
Speckled: excess 9.28 (3.07 p.e.)

Eye Folds
Epicanthus: excess 8.43 (6.11 p.e.)
Absent: deficiency 9.90 (3.09 p.e.)

Eyebrow Thickness
Medium: deficiency 17.41 (4.93 p.e.)
Pronounced: excess 15.74 (4.68 p.e.)

Forehead Height
Submedium: excess 8.47 (4.55 p.e.)
Medium: deficiency 11.68 (3.30 p.e.)

Forehead Slope
Medium: deficiency 11.41 (3.14 p.e.)
Pronounced: excess 16.08 (5.15 p.e.)

Nasion Depression
Medium: deficiency 16.32 (5.57 p.e.)
Pronounced: excess 15.29 (6.16 p.e.)

Nasal Root Height
Medium: deficiency 12.39 (4.96 p.e.)
Pronounced: excess 12.38 (5.16 p.e.)

Nasal Root Breadth
Submedium: excess 4.88 (3.64 p.e.)
Medium: deficiency 15.90 (7.46 p.e.)
Pronounced: excess 11.03 (6.41 p.e.)

Nasal Bridge Height
Medium: deficiency 16.71 (4.96 p.e.)
Pronounced: excess 16.71 (4.96 p.e.)

Nasal Bridge Breadth
Submedium: excess 4.21 (4.30 p.e.)
Medium: deficiency 14.94 (5.98 p.e.)
Pronounced: excess 10.73 (4.58 p.e.)

Table XII-148 (cont'd)

Nasal Tip Thickness
  Submedium: excess 5.84 (4.99 p.e.)
  Medium: deficiency 20.24 (6.77 p.e.)
  Pronounced: excess 14.39 (5.08 p.e.)

Nasal Septum Deflection
  Right: excess 12.31 (4.53 p.e.)
  Absent: deficiency 15.90 (4.85 p.e.)

Lips Integumental Thickness
  Submedium: excess 13.32 (6.25 p.e.)
  Medium: deficiency 14.68 (5.21 p.e.)

Lips Membranous Thickness
  Submedium: excess 12.69 (5.54 p.e.)

Alveolar Prognathism
  Submedium: excess 15.26 (7.04 p.e.)
  Medium: deficiency 9.57 (4.56 p.e.)

Cheeks Fullness
  Submedium: excess 23.30 (10.18 p.e.)
  Medium: deficiency 23.06 (6.70 p.e.)

Gonial Angles
  Pronounced: deficiency 9.30 (3.04 p.e.)

Cheeks Wrinkling
  Absent: excess 17.23 (4.50 p.e.)
  Pronounced: deficiency 10.29 (3.17 p.e.)

Teeth Caries
  Few: excess 24.21 (6.16 p.e.)
  Many: deficiency 20.46 (5.27 p.e.)

Roll of Helix
  Submedium: excess 25.66 (9.00 p.e.)
  Medium,pronounced:deficiency 26.63 (9.28 p.e.)

Ear Protrusion
  Medium: deficiency 25.85 (7.81 p.e.)
  Pronounced: excess 23.50 (7.58 p.e.)

Darwin's Point
  Small, medium: excess 11.95 (3.58 p.e.)

Antihelix Prominence
  Medium: deficiency 13.33 (5.13 p.e.)
  Pronounced: excess 15.56 (7.63 p.e.)

Temporal Fullness
  Submedium: excess 18.80 (8.14 p.e.)
  Medium: deficiency 11.47 (3.49 p.e.)

Lambdoid Flattening
  Absent: deficiency 10.93 (3.25 p.e.)
  Present: excess 10.93 (3.25 p.e.)

Neck
  Long and thin: excess 14.03 (5.48 p.e.)
  Short and thick: deficiency 7.94 (3.48 p.e.)

Shoulder Slope
  Medium: deficiency 15.45 (7.43 p.e.)
  Pronounced: excess 16.13 (8.58 p.e.)

INDEX

INDEX

INDEX

INDEX

INDEX

INDEX

INDEX

INDEX

INDEX

INDEX

INDEX